DATE DUE

MY 26 '95			
DE 22 '95			
MAR 0 8 1996			
MY 1 0 99			
MY 15 00			

DEMCO 38-296

Management Control Systems

Management Control Systems

Robert N. Anthony
Ross Graham Walker Professor Emeritus of Management Control
Graduate School of Business Administration
Harvard University

John Dearden
Herman C. Krannert Professor Emeritus of Business Administration
Graduate School of Business Administration
Harvard University

Vijay Govindarajan
Professor of Strategy and Control
The Amos Tuck School of Business Administration
Dartmouth College

Seventh Edition

IRWIN

Homewood, IL 60430
Boston, MA 02116

Case material of the Harvard Graduate School of Business Administration
is made possible by the cooperation of business firms, who may wish to
remain anonymous by having names, quantities, and other identifying
details disguised while basic relationships are maintained. Cases are
prepared as the basis for class discussion rather than to illustrate
either effective or ineffective handling of administrative situations.

Sponsoring editor: Ron M. Regis
Project editor: Paula Buschman
Production manager: Diane Palmer
Cover designer: Ivy Snider
Compositor: BookMasters, Inc.
Typeface: 10/12 Times Roman
Printer: R. R. Donnelley & Sons Company

Library of Congress Cataloging-in-Publication Data

Anthony, Robert Newton, 1916–
     Management control systems / Robert N. Anthony, John Dearden,
Vijay Govindarajan.—7th ed.
        p.   cm.
     Includes indexes.
     ISBN 0-256-10472-7   ISBN 0-256-10824-2 (Int'l. ed.)
     1. Industrial management.   2. Industrial management—Case studies.
3. Cost control.   4. Cost control—Case studies.   I. Dearden, John.
II. Govindarajan, Vijay.   III. Title.
HD31.A589   1991
658.15—dc20   91–14467

Printed in the United States of America
2 3 4 5 6 7 8 9 0 DOC 8 7 6 5 4 3 2

To Our Wives: Katherine, Helen-Marie, and Kirthi
BOB, JOHN, and VG

With Special Appreciation to My Parents
for Reasons They Know Well
VG

About the Authors

Robert N. Anthony is the Ross Graham Walker Professor Emeritus of Management Control, at Harvard Business School. Harvard has been his home base, except between 1940–46 when he was in the Navy Supply Corps, and between 1965–68 when he was Assistant Secretary of Defense, Controller.

Professor Anthony is the author or co-author of 27 books; they have been translated into 13 languages.

Professor Anthony has been a director of Carborundum Company and Warnaco, Inc., both Fortune 500 companies; and for 25 years has been a trustee of Colby College, including five years as chairman of the board. He has been a consultant to many companies and government agencies, including General Motors Corporation, American Telephone & Telegraph Company, the General Accounting Office, and the Cost Accounting Standards Board. He has also participated in short educational programs in North America, South America, Europe, Australia, and Asia.

Among Professor Anthony's awards are honorary MA and LHD degrees from Colby College, election to the Accounting Hall of Fame, the Distinguished Accounting Educator Award from the American Accounting Association, the Accounting Educator of the Year Award from Beta Alpha Psi, the Meritorious Service Award from the Executive Office of the President, and the Distinguished Public Service Medal of the Department of Defense.

John Dearden is the Herman C. Krannert Professor Emeritus of Business Administration, at Harvard Business School. Professor Dearden has taught at Harvard since 1959. Prior to joining the Harvard faculty, he spent 10 years on the finance staff at Ford Motor Company. Professor Dearden is the author or co-author of 12 books and some 40 articles.

Professor Dearden received his AB as well as an honorary Doctor of Commercial Science from American International College. He received his MBA from the Wharton School, where he was awarded the 50th anniversary gold medal for outstanding contribution to business education.

Vijay Govindarajan is a Professor of Strategy and Control at the Amos Tuck School of Business Administration, at Dartmouth College. Prior to joining the faculty at Tuck, Professor Govindarajan was on the faculties of the Ohio State University, Harvard Business School, and the Indian Institute of Management, at Ahmedabad, India. He was voted the "Outstanding Teacher of the Year" by MBA students and was nominated for the Pacesetter's "Outstanding Faculty Award" during several academic years.

Professor Govindarajan is the co-author of the book *Strategic Cost Analysis.* He is the author of more than 30 articles, which have been published in major academic as well as in practitioner-oriented journals, such as *The Accounting Review, Accounting Organizations and Society, Decision Sciences, Management Accounting, Academy of Management Journal, Accounting Horizons, Academy of Management Review,* and *Sloan Management Review.*

Professor Govindarajan has served as a consultant to several organizations, including Abbott Laboratories, Champion International, Digital Equipment Corporation, GTE, B.F. Goodrich, IBM, Price Waterhouse, and Weyerhaeuser. He is a Visiting Professor at the International University of Japan (Urasa, Japan).

Professor Govindarajan received his MBA, with distinction, and his doctorate from Harvard Business School. Prior to this, he received his chartered accountancy degree in India, where he was awarded the President's Gold Medal for obtaining the first rank.

Preface

This book provides concepts, text, and cases for a course in Management Control Systems. It is designed to allow the students to gain knowledge, insights, and analytical skills that are related to how a firm's managers go about designing, implementing, and using planning and control systems to accomplish a firm's strategies. It does not deal extensively with such topics as cost accounting and budgeting procedures, which are discussed in separate accounting courses. The book gives roughly equal emphasis to (1) the techniques of the management control process (e.g., transfer pricing, budget preparation, management compensation) and (2) the behavioral considerations involved in the use of these techniques (e.g., motivation, goal congruence, relative roles of superiors and subordinates).

CHANGES TO TEXT MATERIAL

This seventh edition represents a *major* revision. While retaining the strengths of the sixth edition, we have made significant changes in both text and case material that we hope will increase their usefulness. In undertaking this revision, we surveyed users of the sixth edition; and over 80 users responded to the survey. This revision has benefited from their constructive comments and suggestions. Some of the major changes in the seventh edition are highlighted below:

- *New author team:* Robert N. Anthony and John Dearden, both of the Harvard Business School, continue as authors. Vijay Govindarajan, who teaches a highly successful second-year elective on management control systems at The Amos Tuck School of Business Administration, Dartmouth College, joins this edition as a new author. The three authors have been teaching and doing research in management control systems throughout their academic careers. They have written or supervised the preparation of more than 200 case studies of domestic, foreign, and multinational companies, and they have written 40 books. They have served as consultants to over 100 companies on control systems problems. The materials in this book, therefore, are derived not from theoretical modeling or laboratory inquiries and simulations of management science but from real-world experience.

- *Improvements in pedagogy:* Several improvements have been made to assist student learning. These include: chapter introductions presenting a synopsis of the major topics to be covered, more diagrams and exhibits, real-world examples, consistent terminology (e.g., the use of the word *business unit,* as compared to *division,* throughout the book), chapter summaries, and an up-to-date reference list in each chapter.
- *Changes in sequence:* The book is now reorganized into three main parts. Chapter 1 introduces the overall conceptual framework for the book. Part I (Chapters 2 to 7) describes the environment in which management control takes place (responsibility centers, profit centers, transfer pricing, and investment centers). Part II (Chapters 8 to 12) describes the sequential steps in the typical management control process (programming, budget preparation, operations, analysis of operations, and incentive compensation). Part III (Chapters 13 to 17) describes variations in management control systems (controls for differentiated strategies, service organizations, multinational organizations, and project control).
- *New topics:* New techniques (e.g., flexible manufacturing systems, just-in-time, total quality management, computer integrated manufacturing, and decision support systems) are described and their practical applications for management control are analyzed (Chapter 10). New theoretical concepts, such as activity-based costing (Chapter 8) and agency theory (Chapter 12), are incorporated. Two new chapters (Chapters 7 and 13) relate management control to various types of organizational strategies. The discussion of service organizations has been doubled, with a whole new chapter on financial service organizations (Chapter 15). There is expanded coverage on unique management control issues in multinational organizations (Chapter 16). Almost all chapters have been entirely rewritten, to increase logical sequencing and clarity and to reflect the current perspectives on the subject matter.

We are confident that you will find the text material in this seventh edition well organized, concisely written, laden with current examples, and consistent with the current theory and practice of management control.

CHANGES IN CASES

A key strength of this book is its collection of cases, which emphasize actual practice. The cases come from Harvard Business School, The Tuck School at Dartmouth, and from a number of other schools, both in the United States and abroad. The cases not only require the student to analyze situations but also give a feel for what actually happens in companies, a feeling that cannot be conveyed adequately in the text. In this sense, the cases can be viewed as extended examples of practice.

The cases are not necessarily intended to illustrate either correct or incorrect handling of management problems. As in most cases of this type, there are no right answers. The educational value of the cases comes from the practice the student receives in analyzing management control problems and in discussing and defending his or her analysis before the class.

In the development of this edition, we have retained those cases that our users have found most helpful in accomplishing the objectives of their course. Of the 85 cases in this edition, 46 cases are retained from the sixth edition; some of the cases deleted from the sixth edition are reproduced in the *Teacher's Guide*. We have 39 new cases in this edition. We are confident that instructors will find this case collection does an excellent job of meeting classroom needs for several reasons:

- The collection offers a rich diversity of domestic, foreign, and international companies.
- The cases expose students to varied contexts: small organizations, large organizations, manufacturing organizations, service organizations, and non-profit organizations.
- The collection presents contemporary, interesting situations, which students will recognize, enjoy, and learn from.
- Videotapes accompany several of the cases. In these tapes, the chief executives describe their approach to managing the firms. Students find the videotapes beneficial in understanding the implications of top management style on the control process.
- We have given significant attention to case length. A major effort has been made to ensure that a majority of the cases are short. We still include a few medium-to-long cases, "two-day" cases, and "two-part" cases. The instructor's needs in this regard are further supplemented by information in the *Teacher's Guide*.
- The case collection is flexible in terms of course sequencing, and the cases are comfortably teachable.

TARGET AUDIENCE

This book is intended for each of the following uses:

- A one-semester or one-quarter course for *graduate* students who have had a course in management accounting and who wish to study management control in greater depth.
- A one-semester or one-quarter course for *undergraduate* juniors or seniors who have already had one or two courses in management accounting.
- *Executive development* programs.

- A *handbook* for general managers, management consultants, computer-based systems designers, and controllers—those people who are involved in, or who are affected by, the management control process.

ACKNOWLEDGMENTS

We have benefited from the help of many people in the evolution of this book over seven editions. Students, adopters, colleagues, and reviewers have generously supplied insightful comments, helpful suggestions, and contributions, all of which have progressively enhanced this book.

The course from which the material in this book was drawn was originally developed at the Harvard Business School by the late Ross G. Walker. We wish to acknowledge his pioneering work in the development of both the concepts underlying the course and the methods of teaching these concepts. We thank the following members and former members of the Harvard Business School faculty who have contributed much to the development of this book:

Francis J. Aguilar, Robert H. Caplan, Charles J. Christenson, Robin Cooper, Russell H. Hassler, Regina E. Herzlinger, Julie H. Hertenstein, Robert A. Howell, Gerard G. Johnson, Robert Kaplan, Warren F. McFarlan, Kenneth Merchant, Krishna G. Palepu, John K. Shank, Robert Simons, Richard F. Vancil, and John R. Yeager. In addition, we wish to acknowledge the assistance provided us by Robert H. Deming, James S. Hekiman, John Mauriel, Chei-Min Paik, and Jack L. Treynor.

A special debt of gratitude is due to Anil K. Gupta, University of Maryland, for many discussions that were useful in the development of Chapter 7, Strategies, and of Chapter 13, Controls for Differentiated Strategies; to Nathan Pearson, Diane Butterfield, and Herbert Wells, for contributions to the new Chapter 15, Financial Service Organizations; to Professor Patricia Douglas, University of Montana, for insights into the nonprofit section of Chapter 14; and to Professor William Rotch, Darden Graduate School of the University of Virginia, for contributions throughout the text and for judgments about cases.

Joseph Fisher, The Amos Tuck School of Business Administration, Dartmouth College, contributed the material on "Agency Theory" included in Chapter 12, Management Compensation. Anant K. Sundaram, The Amos Tuck School of Business Administration, Dartmouth College, contributed the material on "Exchange Rates and Performance Evaluation" included in Chapter 16, Multinational Organizations. Our sincere thanks to Joe Fisher and Anant Sundaram for their fine contributions.

The selection of cases is always vital to a successful Management Control Systems course. In this text, our appreciation goes to the supervisors and authors who are responsible for case development. Each has been recognized in the citation to the cases. We are particularly indebted to the companies whose cooperation made the cases possible.

We wish to thank the following scholars who reviewed the manuscript and made many useful suggestions: Joe Fisher, John K. Shank, and Anant K. Sundaram, The Amos Tuck School of Business Administration, Dartmouth College; Joe San Miguel, of the Naval Post Graduate School. We especially appreciate the users who responded to our survey.

One of us used the manuscript of the seventh edition with Tuck MBA students during the 1990 fall term. They contributed several ideas and constructive suggestions for revising the chapters.

Although he has decided not to continue as a co-author, Norton Bedford has made many useful suggestions, which we appreciate.

Mary Munter, The Amos Tuck School of Business Administration, Dartmouth College, was an excellent source in the organization, presentation, and editing of the manuscript.

Kirthi Govindarajan carefully read the typed manuscript pages, galley proofs, and page proofs and carried out this assignment with extraordinary efficiency and good humor. Kirthi deserves a special thanks not only for her skillful editorial help but also for being a constant source of encouragement for VG at times when the work on the book seemed most difficult.

The organization and development of the vast amounts of material necessary to complete this project was no small task. A special note of thanks to Ms. Susan Schwarz, secretary to Professor Govindarajan; to Eileen Hankins and Jane Barrett, secretaries to Professor Dearden; and to Judith Grady, secretary to Professor Anthony, who professionally managed thousands of pages of original text and revisions with secretarial and computer skills that were invaluable. We also thank Ron Regis, Paula Buschman, and Jimmy Bartlett at our publisher, Richard D. Irwin, Inc., for their help and commitment to our project.

We hope that you will share our enthusiasm both for the rich subject of management control and for the learning approach that we have taken. As always, we value your recommendations and thoughts about the book. Your comments regarding coverage and content will be most welcome, as will your calling our attention to specific errors. Please contact: Vijay Govindarajan, Professor of Strategy and Control, The Amos Tuck School of Business Administration, Dartmouth College, Hanover, NH 03755; phone (603) 646–2156; fax (603) 646–1308.

Robert N. Anthony
John Dearden
Vijay Govindarajan

Contents

An Overview

Chapter 1

The Nature of Management Control Systems

The first section of this introductory chapter describes the meaning of three words in the title of this book: control, management, and systems. The second section distinguishes the management control function, which is our focus, from two other planning and control functions: strategic planning and task control. The third section describes aspects of the environment in which management control takes place. The final section is an overview of the management control process.

BASIC CONCEPTS

Control

When the brake pedal is pressed, an automobile slows or stops. When the accelerator is pressed, the automobile goes faster. When the steering wheel is rotated, the automobile changes its direction. With these devices, the driver *controls* the speed and direction of the vehicle. If any of these devices were inoperative, the automobile would not do what the driver wanted it to do and it would be out of control. An organization must also be controlled—that is, there must be devices that ensure that it goes where its leaders want it to go. Control in an organization is, however, much more complicated than the control of an automobile. We shall lead into a discussion of control in organizations by describing the control process in simpler situations.

Elements of a control system.   Any control system has at least four elements:

1. A *detector* or *sensor,* which is a measuring device that identifies what is actually happening in the situation being controlled.
2. An *assessor,* which is a device for determining the significance of what is happening. Usually, significance is assessed by comparing the information on what is *actually happening* with some standard or expectation of what *should be happening.*
3. An *effector,* which is a device that alters behavior if the assessor indicates the need for doing so. This device is often called "feedback."
4. A *communications network,* which transmits information between the detector and the assessor and between the assessor and the effector.

These basic elements of a control system are diagrammed in Exhibit 1–1. We shall illustrate these with three examples: the thermostat, the regulation of body temperature, and the automobile driver.[1]

Thermostat.   The thermostat is a device for controlling the temperature of a room. Its elements are: (1) a detector, which is a thermometer that measures the current temperature of the room; (2) an assessor, which compares the cur-

EXHIBIT 1–1   The Control Process

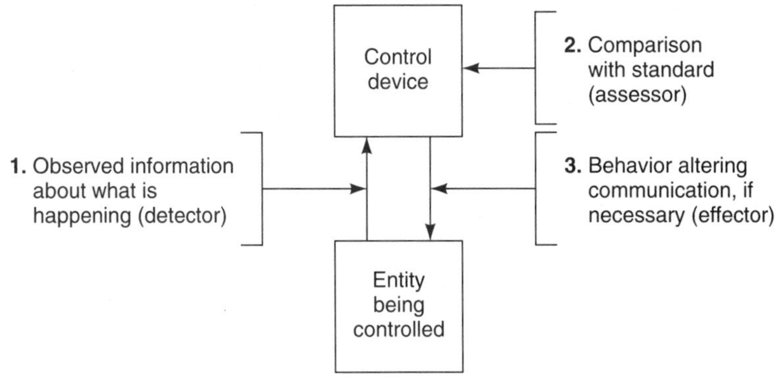

---

[1] These examples of control systems are arranged in order of increasing complexity. Systems theorists point out that the universe consists of a hierarchy of systems, in which each higher level system is more complicated than systems at lower levels. One list of such a hierarchy is: atoms, molecules, crystals, viruses, cells, organs, organisms (e.g., human beings), groups (e.g., teams), organizations, societies, and supranational organizations. See James G. Miller, "Living Systems: Basic Concepts," *Behavior* 10, no. 4 (1965), pp. 192–236. For additional information on systems theory, see Norbert Wiener, *Cybernetics: Or Control and Communication in the Animal and Machine* (New York: John Wiley & Sons, 1948); and W. Ross Ashby, *Design for a Brain,* 2nd ed. (New York: John Wiley & Sons, 1960).

rent temperature with a preset standard of what the temperature should be; (3) an effector, which causes a furnace or other heating device to send heat to the room if the actual temperature is lower than the standard (or which causes an air conditioner to turn on if the temperature is higher than standard), and which causes these appliances to turn off when the temperature reaches the standard level; and (4) a communications network, which transmits information from the thermometer to the assessor and from the assessor to the appliance.

Body temperature.   Most mammals are born with a built-in standard of desirable body temperature. In humans, it is 98.6°F. The control of body temperature is achieved as follows: (1) detectors are sensory nerves that are scattered throughout the body; (2) the assessor is the hypothalamus center in the brain, which compares information received from the detectors with the standard of 98.6°F; (3) effectors are muscles and organs for reducing the temperature if it is higher than the standard (panting, sweating, opening of skin pores), or of increasing the temperature if it is below the standard (closing skin pores, shivering); and (4) the communication system of nerves.[2] This control process is called "homeostasis," which means self-regulating. If the system is functioning properly, it automatically corrects for deviations from the desired state without conscious effort by the human being.

Two important differences make understanding the body temperature control system more difficult than understanding the thermostat. First, the body temperature system is more complicated: sensors are scattered throughout the body, and the actions directed by the hypothalamus involve a variety of muscles and organs. Second, although we know *what* the hypothalamus does, scientists don't really understand *how* this is done.

Automobile driver.   Assume an automobile driver is on a highway where the speed limit is 65 mph. The driver's control system acts as follows: (1) actual speed is detected by the eye that observes the speedometer (or perhaps the sense of speed is detected by a general perception of movement); (2) the brain assesses this speed in comparison with the driver's desired speed; (3) if the brain judges the speed is too fast, it directs the foot to ease up on the accelerator; and (4) as in the case of body temperature, the detected speed and the action are conveyed by nerves.

This control system has an additional complication over the body temperature system: we cannot state with confidence what, if any, action the brain will direct if the actual speed exceeds 65 mph. Some people obey the speed limit and, therefore, will ease up on the accelerator; others obey the speed limit at certain times, but not at other times. In this system, control is not automatic; as a minimum, we must also know something about the personality of the driver to predict the actual speed of the automobile.

---

[2] S. A. Richards. *Temperature Regulation* (London: Wykeman Publications, Ltd., 1973).

Management

An organization consists of a group of people who work together. The organization has *goals*— that is, it wants to accomplish certain results.[3] In a business organization, earning a satisfactory profit usually is an important goal. The leaders of the organizations are its management. There is a hierarchy of managers, with the chief executive officer (CEO) at the top, and business unit, departmental, section and other managers below the CEO. Depending on the size and complexity of the organization, there may be several layers in the hierarchy. Except for the chief executive officer, each manager is both a superior and a subordinate. Each supervises people in his or her own organization unit and is a subordinate of the manager to whom he or she reports. These relationships usually are shown on an organization chart.

The chief executive officer (or, in some organizations, a team of senior managers) decides on *strategies* that are expected to attain the organization's goals. If the company is organized into business units (divisions), business unit managers formulate strategies for their units, subject to the approval of the CEO. The management control process is the process that managers use to assure that the members of the organization implement these strategies.

Managers, when they are acting as managers, do not themselves do the work of the organization; they see to it that the work gets done by others. The production manager does not ordinarily operate machines; the sales manager does not ordinarily call on customers. (When they do operate machines or call on customers, they are not acting as managers.) Many professionals who work in organizations—lawyers, physicians, engineers, teachers—perform important functions, but are not managers; they do the work personally, rather than seeing to it that the work gets done by others.[4]

Contrast with simpler control processes.   The control process that managers use has the same elements as those in the control systems described above: detectors, assessors, effectors, and a communications system. Detectors report what is actually happening throughout the organization; assessors compare this information with the desired state, which is the implementation of strategies; effectors take corrective action if there is a significant difference between the actual state and the desired state; and there is a communications system that tells members of the organization what they are supposed to do. There are, however, significant differences between the management control

---

[3] Literally, the organization is inanimate and cannot have goals. The goals are the goals of the leader or leaders of the organization.

[4] Some people who are called managers have no subordinates. A 1989 survey by The Conference Board found that of 47,000 managers surveyed 14 percent did not manage anyone. Usually this happens when the personnel in a department are replaced by a computer. (*Across the Board*, October 1989, p. 7.)

process and the processes described in the earlier examples. The more important of these are as follows:

1. Unlike the thermostat or body temperature systems, *the standard is not preset.* Rather, it is a result of a conscious planning process. In this process, management decides what the organization should be doing, and part of the control process is a comparison of actual accomplishments with these plans. Thus, the control process in an organization involves planning. In many situations, planning and control can be viewed as two separate activities. By contrast, management control involves both planning and control.

2. Like control of an automobile, but unlike the thermostat and body temperature systems, *management control is not automatic.* Some of the detectors (i.e., the instruments for detecting what is happening in the organization) are mechanical, but important information is often detected through the manager's own eyes, ears, and other senses. Although there are routine ways of comparing certain reports of what is actually happening against some standard of what should be happening, managers themselves must judge whether the difference between actual and standard performance is significant enough to warrant action, and, if it is, what action to take. Actions taken to alter the organization's behavior involve human beings; in order to effect change, a manager must interact with another person.

3. Unlike the automobile that involves a single individual (or in some cases the driver and a kibitzer), *management control requires coordination among individuals.* An organization consists of many separate parts, and management control must ensure that the work of these parts is in harmony with one another. This need does not exist at all in the case of the thermostat, and it exists only to a limited extent in the case of the various organs that control body temperature.

4. *The connection between the observed need for action and the behavior that is required to obtain the desired action is by no means clear-cut.* In the assessor function, a manager may decide that "costs are too high"; but there is no easy or automatic action, or series of actions, that is guaranteed to bring costs down to what the standard says they should be. The term *black box* is used to describe an operation whose exact nature cannot be observed. A management control system is a black box. We cannot know what action a given manager will take when a significant difference between actual and expected performance is assessed, nor what (if any) action others will take in response to the manager's signal. A thermostat is not a black box; we know exactly when it will signal that an action should be taken and what that action will be. In the automobile driver example, the assessor phase also involves judgment, but the effector phase is mechanical.

5. Control in an organization does not come about solely, or even primarily, as a consequence of actions that are taken by an external regulating device like the thermostat. *Much control is self control;* that is, people act in the way they do, not primarily because they are given specific instructions by their superior but, rather, because their own judgment tells them what action is appropriate. Automobile drivers who obey the 65 mph speed limit do so, not because the sign commands them to do so but, rather, because they have consciously decided that it is in their best interest to obey the law.

Activities in management control. From the above, it should be apparent that management control involves a variety of activities, some of which are not present in the simpler control situations described earlier. These include: (1) *planning* what the organization should do, (2) *coordinating* the activities of the several parts of the organization, (3) *communicating* information, (4) *evaluating* information, (5) *deciding* what, if any, action should be taken, and (6) *influencing* people to change their behavior.

Management control does not necessarily mean that actions should correspond to a plan, such as a budget. The stated plans were based on circumstances that, at the time when they were formulated, were believed to exist, both inside and outside the organization. If the circumstances are now believed to be different from those assumed in the plan, the planned actions may no longer be appropriate. A thermostat responds to the actual temperature in a room. Management control, by contrast, should anticipate what conditions are going to be in the future.

The purpose of management control is to ensure that strategies are carried out so that the organization's goals are attained. If a manager discovers a better way of operating—one that is more likely to achieve the organization's goals than the actions stated in the plan—then the management control system should not prohibit him or her from operating in that fashion. (In certain circumstances, the manager may be required to obtain approval for such a departure.) Conforming to a budget is not necessarily good, and departure from a budget is not necessarily bad.

Systems

A system is a prescribed way of carrying out an activity or set of activities; usually the activities are repeated. The thermostat and the body temperature systems described above are examples. A software program that controls the thousands or millions of steps that the computer takes in carrying out an operation is another example; the computer does precisely what the software instructs it to do. Most systems are less precise than computer programs; their instructions do not cover all eventualities, and the user of the system must make judgments when these eventualities occur. Nevertheless, a system is characterized by a more or less rhythmic, recurring, coordinated series of steps that are intended to accomplish a specified purpose.

Many management actions are unsystematic. A situation is encountered that the rules of the system do not deal with, and the manager uses his or her best judgment in acting. Many interactions between managers or between a manager and a subordinate are of this character. The appropriate response is determined by the manager's skill in dealing with people, not by a rule specified by the system (although the system may suggest the general nature of the appropriate response). Indeed, if the system provided the correct action for all situations, there would be no need for human managers. This is almost the case with an automated factory; managers are needed only in the event of a system failure.

In this book, we focus primarily on the systematic aspects of the management control function. We can describe in considerable depth the nature of the various steps in the system, the information that is collected and used in each step, and the principles that govern systems operations; but we cannot, except in general terms, describe appropriate behaviors for the unsystematic aspects of management control. These depend on the skills and personalities of the parties involved, their relationships with one another, the environment existing when a particular problem arises, and many other factors. Thus, this book deals primarily with the *formal* part of the management control process. However, the way the formal control systems are designed affects the informal processes that go on in the organization.

Our emphasis on formal systems may place too much stress on the importance of these systems. You should keep in mind the fact that control consists of a number of interrelated activities. Exhibit 1–2 makes this point. Control involves both formal financial control systems and formal nonfinancial control systems, but it also involves informal processes, and it is influenced by the company's structure and the capabilities of its people.

BOUNDARIES OF MANAGEMENT CONTROL

Management control is one of several types of planning and control activities that occur in an organization. In this section, we define management control and two other types of planning and control: strategic planning and task control. Our purpose is to draw boundaries that distinguish management control from the other types. Making these distinctions helps to explain what management control is all about; this is done by contrasting management control with the other activities. Serious mistakes can be made if principles and generalizations that are applicable to one activity are used in another type for which they are not applicable.

As will be seen, management control fits between the other two activities in several respects. Strategic planning occurs at top-management levels, task control occurs at the lowest levels in the organization, and management control is in between. Strategic planning is the least systematic, task control is the most systematic, and management control is in between. Strategic planning focuses on the long run, task control focuses on short-run operating activities, and management control is in between. Strategic planning uses rough approximations of the future, task control uses accurate current data, and management control is in between. Each activity involves both planning and control; but the

EXHIBIT 1–2   The Total Management Control Process

The circle represents the set of formal and informal mechanisms that help to implement strategies:

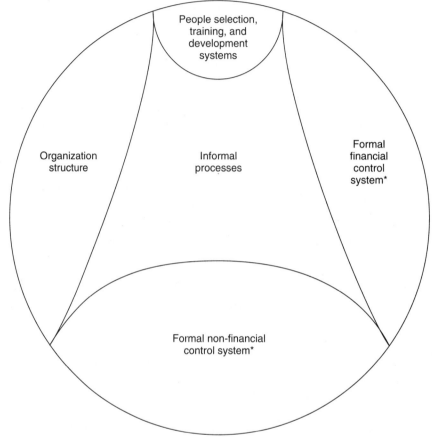

* The book discusses the topics marked with asterisks.

planning process is much more important in strategic planning, the control process is much more important in task control, and planning and control are of approximately equal importance in management control.

The relationships of these activities to one another are indicated in Exhibit 1–3.

Management Control

Management control is the process by which managers influence other members of the organization to implement the organization's strategies.

EXHIBIT 1–3 General Relationships among Planning and Control Functions

Activity	Nature of end product
Strategic planning →	Goals, strategies, and policies
Management control →	Implemenation of strategies
Task control →	Efficient and effective performance of individual tasks

Nature of decisions. Management control decisions are made within the guidance established by strategic planning. Without such guidance, the manager of a business unit might be inclined to accept any investment opportunity that is likely to improve the performance of the unit. Senior management, however, may have a strategy that involves using available funds in another business unit in which the profit opportunities are even greater. Within the framework of these strategies and overall organization policies, the manager of a business unit has considerable latitude in deciding on the actions that are best for the unit.

Management control takes place within a functioning organization whose current activities are limited by the nature and amount of available resources. An apparel manufacturer has physical resources for producing and distributing apparel, and it has human resources who are skilled in the design of apparel, in its production, and in its marketing. Although the design of the apparel will change, although some production methods may change, and although better ways of doing things may be discovered, many activities will continue without change from one year to the next. Considerable lead time is required to increase or change the physical resources and to hire or retrain human resources to meet changing needs.

Valid generalizations can be made about the best way of arriving at some of these decisions. These include generalizations about preparing a budget and about reviewing a proposed budget for consistency with strategies and for the appropriateness of proposed amounts of certain expense items. For certain budget items, however, there are no rules for determining the optimum amounts. These are called *discretionary* items. The amounts are determined by judgment, rather than by techniques that can be used to arrive at the optimum amounts. Optimum amounts often can be determined for direct labor costs and direct material costs; most overhead and support costs are discretionary.

Systematic and rhythmic.   In the management control process, decisions are made according to procedures and timetables that are repeated year after year. As will be described in Part II, the first step in the sequence is formulating a strategic plan or program; next, one year of this program (the ''budget year'') is translated into a budget; next, operations take place, usually more or less guided by this budget and by prescribed policies and procedures; and finally, actual results are compared with this budget and evaluated, and corrective action is taken if necessary. These steps are labelled programming, budget preparation, execution, and evaluation. The activities of each of these steps can be described, and for many of them written instructions are worthwhile.

A management control system is a *total system*. The plans developed in the management control process encompass the whole organization, and one important aspect is that plans for each part of the organization must be so coordinated with one another that the various parts are in balance. Manufacturing and distribution capacity must be balanced with sales programs, for example.

The system is built around a *financial core*—that is, the management control system focuses on the monetary ''bottom line'', which is net income, return on equity, or some similar financial amount. This is because the system is partly a coordinating device, and money is the only common denominator that can be used to measure, summarize, aggregate, and compare heterogeneous quantitative measures (e.g., hours of labor, pounds of material, units of product). The system is by no means entirely financial, however; it includes such nonmonetary information as quantities of material, pounds of waste, hours of labor, defect rates, customer complaints, market share, and many others.

Although the budget usually contains numbers only for the current year, it does not follow that managers should be interested primarily in short-range performance. The budget includes amounts for research and development, training, advertising, and other expenses that are incurred currently but benefit future periods.

Behavioral considerations.   Although systematic, the management control process is by no means mechanical. The process involves interactions among individuals, and there is no mechanical way of describing these interactions.

Managers have personal goals, and the central control problem is to induce them to act so that, when they seek their personal goals, they are also helping to achieve organizational goals; this is called *goal congruence*. This term means that the goals of individual members of an organization should be, so far as feasible, consistent with the goals of the organization itself. For reasons that will be explained in Chapter 2, perfect goal congruence cannot be achieved. Nevertheless, the system should go as far in this direction as is feasible. In promoting goal congruence, the development of optimum compensation plans and other incentives is an important consideration.

Strategic Planning

> *Strategic planning is the process of deciding on the goals of the organization and the strategies for attaining these goals.*[5]

Goals are timeless; they exist until they are changed, and they are changed only rarely. In many businesses, earning a satisfactory profit (or more specifically, a satisfactory return on investment), is an important goal; in others, attaining a large market share is a goal. Nonprofit organizations also have goals. In some organizations the goals are reduced to writing; but in many, they are no more than a general understanding. In the strategic planning process, the goals of the organization are usually taken as a given; but, occasionally, strategic thinking focuses on the goals themselves.

An organization may select any of innumerable ways of seeking to attain its goals. If, for example, the goal is profitability, an organization may select one or more industries, geographical territories, product lines, and niches within product lines; whether to both produce and market the product lines or to focus on marketing goods produced by other manufacturers; the relative emphasis between advertising and sales promotion in marketing; the emphasis to be given to research/development and the areas on which research and development efforts are to focus, and on and on. The strategies followed in various organizations differ from one another in many ways.

Strategies are big plans, important plans. They state in a general way the direction in which senior management wants the organization to be heading. They are *timeless*—that is, they exist until they are changed. A decision by an automobile manufacturer to produce and sell an electric automobile is a strategic decision; decisions to change the weight, horsepower, appearance, or accessories of vehicles already in the line are operating decisions (although the line between these two types of decisions is fuzzy).

At any given time, an organization operates according to the set of strategies that it has previously adopted. The strategic planning process involves reexamining some of these strategies, perhaps changing them or perhaps adopting new strategies. Rarely, if ever, does this examination involve all the organization's strategies. The task of doing so would be much too complicated. Thus, although the process is often called *strategy formulation*, it is more accurately described as *strategy revision*.

The need for reconsidering strategies typically arises either in response to a perceived threat or to take advantage of a perceived opportunity. Examples of

---

[5] In this book we use the word *goals* for the broad overall aims of the organization, and *objectives* for the more specific statements of planned accomplishments in one year or other specified time period. Some people use these two words interchangeably, and others reverse the meanings given above. The words *target* and *aim* are also used as synonyms for either word. If these differences in intended meaning are not made clear, the consequence is confusion.

threats are market inroads by competitors, a shift in consumer tastes, or new government regulations. Examples of opportunities are technological innovations, new perceptions of customer behavior, or development of new applications for existing products. A new chief executive officer usually has somewhat different perceptions of either threats or opportunities than his predecessor and, for this reason, changes in strategies often occur when a new chief executive officer takes over.[6]

Ideas to meet threats or for new opportunities may originate from anywhere within the organization and at any time. There is a widely held impression that ideas originate entirely within the research and development organization or within the headquarters staff; although many ideas do come from these departments, they are by no means the exclusive source. Anyone can have a "bright idea" that, after analysis and discussion, becomes a new strategy. Because there is no way of knowing who will come up with a worthwhile idea, complete responsibility for strategy development should not be assigned to a particular person or organization unit. Also, it is important that there be a means of calling worthwhile ideas to the attention of senior management.

Distinctions between strategic planning and management control.

From the standpoint of systems design, the most important distinction between strategic planning and management control is that strategic planning is essentially unsystematic. Whenever a threat is perceived or when a new idea surfaces, strategic planning takes place. Since threats or opportunities are not discovered systematically or at regular intervals, strategic decisions are unsystematic (i.e., they can arise at any time, not according to a set timetable). To quote an IBM executive: "Strategic decisions are made [at IBM] all year around, night and day, not constrained by the plan time . . . people make a (strategic) decision whenever it is time to make a decision."[7]

The nature of the analysis made of a proposed strategy varies with the type of strategy; there is no single model that applies to all strategic analyses. The analysis involves much judgment, and the numbers used in the analysis are usually rough estimates. By contrast, the management control process take place according to a more-or-less fixed timetable, and the steps occur one after the other. Consulting firms have developed what they call "systems" for analyzing an organization's strategies; but these systems are used when the firm happens to be called in, and they are applied to the situation as it exists at that time; they are not systems in the sense of a recurring set of steps followed one after the other every three years or five years, or at some other regular interval.

---

[6] An example of a new CEO revising the company's strategy is contained in "Operation Turn-around: How Westinghouse's New CEO Plans to Fire Up an Old-line Company," *Business Week*, December 5, 1983, pp. 124–33.

[7] Richard F. Vancil, "IBM Corporation: Background Note," Harvard Business School, No. 180–034, 1982, p. 7.

Another important distinction is that strategic planning almost always involves only part of the organization; it may result in a change in one or a few existing strategies, but many other strategies are unaffected by it. The management control process necessarily involves the whole organization; an important aspect of the process is ensuring that the various parts are coordinated with one another.

Analysis of a proposed strategy usually involves relatively few people—the sponsor of the idea, headquarters staff, and senior management, possibly assisted by a consultant. (In exceptional cases, a serious crisis may lead to a strategy that has repercussions throughout the organization.) By contrast, the management control process involves managers and their staff at all levels in the organization. Because relatively few people are involved in strategic planning, communication among them is relatively simple. In the management control process, many more people are involved and communication, therefore, is much more complicated. Managers interact with one another, and behavioral considerations are therefore crucial; they are relatively less important (but by no means absent) in the strategic planning process.

Task Control

> *Task control is the process of assuring that specified tasks are carried out effectively and efficiently.*

Task control is transaction-oriented—that is, it involves the control of individual tasks. Rules to be followed in carrying out these tasks are prescribed as part of the management control process; unless there are unforeseen circumstances, control of many types of tasks consists of seeing to it that the rules are followed. Indeed, for some tasks, control can be achieved without the presence of human beings. Numerically controlled machine tools, process control computers, and robots are task control devices. Human beings are used in these tasks only if they are less expensive than computers or other control devices. Human beings are likely to be less expensive if the occurrence of unusual events is such that programming a computer with rules for dealing with these events is not worthwhile.

The above description is not applicable to some types of tasks, in particular the tasks performed by professionals—engineers, researchers, lawyers, physicians, teachers. These tasks are not routine; they are not carried out by following a set of rules. Nevertheless, they are repetitive, and there are general guidelines that are useful in performing the tasks.

Many task control activities are *scientific* in that the relationship between cause and effect, the action required to bring an out-of-control condition back to the desired state, or the optimum decision, are known within acceptable limits. Rules for economic order quantity determine the amount and timing of purchase orders; principles of probability determine when a process is out of control. The techniques developed in management science and operations research focus principally on task control. The analogy with the thermostat is valid for task control.

Systems exist for various types of tasks, and each is structured to meet the requirements of a specific type of task. There are procurement systems, scheduling systems, order-entry systems, logistics systems, quality control systems, cash management systems, and many others. Most of the information in an organization is task control information. The number of items ordered by customers, the pounds of material and units of components used in the manufacture of products, the number of hours employees work, and the amount of cash disbursed are examples of task control information.

Task control systems can be extremely complicated. An entire steel mill can be controlled by electronic devices. The Material Requirements Planning II system that is used to control manufacturing operations in many companies requires the use of large computers. The switching gear mechanisms used to connect the two parties in a telephone conversation cost billions of dollars. Systems for program trading and other types of decisions made by traders in the stock market involve complicated decision rules and minute-by-minute information about the prices of hundreds of stocks.

As the preceding examples suggest, certain activities that once were performed by managers are now automated and, hence, become task control activities. The shift from management control to task control frees some of the manager's time for truly management activities (and in some cases it eliminates management positions).

Distinctions between task control and management control. From the viewpoint of systems development, the most important distinction between task control and management control is that many task control systems are *scientific,* whereas management control can never be reduced to a science. By definition, management control involves the behavior of managers, and these behaviors cannot be expressed by equations. Serious errors are made when principles developed by management scientists for task control situations are applied to management control situations. In management control, managers interact with other managers; in task control, either human beings are not involved at all (as is the case with some automated production processes), or the interaction is between a manager and a nonmanager.

The management control system is basically similar throughout the organization; such similarity is essential so the revenues and expenses of the organization can be aggregated into the summaries that managers need. By contrast, each types of task requires a different task control system. A production control system is quite different from a program trading system.

In management control, the focus is on organization units; in task control, the focus is on specific tasks performed by these organization units (e.g., manufacturing Job No. 59268, or ordering 100 units of Part No. 3642).

Management control relates to broad types of activities, and managers decide what is to be done within the general constraints of the strategies. Task control relates to specified tasks, and for most of these tasks little or no judgment is required as to what is to be done.

Exhibit 1–4 illustrates differences among these three activities by giving examples of each.

EXHIBIT 1–4   Examples of Decisions

Strategic Planning	Management Control	Task Control
Acquire an unrelated business	New product or brand within product line	Order entry
Add product line	Expand a plant	Production scheduling
Add direct-mail selling	Advertising budget	Book TV commercials
Change debt/equity ratio	Issue new debt	Cash management
Adopt affirmative action policy	Implement minority recruitment program	Personnel record-keeping
Inventory speculation policy	Decide inventory levels	Reorder an item
Magnitude and direction of research	Control of research organization	Individual research project

Relation to Management Accounting

The broad field of accounting is divided into two main parts: financial accounting and management accounting. Financial accounting deals with financial reports prepared for shareholders, investment analysts, and other outside parties; it is governed by generally accepted accounting principles established by the Financial Accounting Standards Board. Management accounting deals with information prepared for management and others within the organization; its principles are not governed by an established rule-making body—rather, the principles are those that provide useful information to these internal parties.

Management accounting has three subdivisions: full cost accounting, differential accounting, and management control. Full cost accounting measures the full cost of products, processes, and other cost objects; it is useful principally as an aid in product pricing and measuring product profitability, and also for inventory valuation and for the analysis of certain long-run situations. Differential accounting estimates what costs would be under alternative courses of action. Management control (also called "responsibility accounting") is the subject matter of this text.

These three types of management accounting are governed by different principles. However, they do not require three separate accounting systems. Much information can be collected in a single system and adapted for use for one of the three purposes outlined above.

Relation to Planning and Control

Some authors classify management activities as either "planning" or "control," and they discuss each class separately. We believe that such a classification is misleading. Most people in an organization engage in planning, from the salesperson who decides on which customer to call on next to the chief executive officer who is thinking about acquisition of a new subsidiary. But the planning done by the salesperson is so different in its purpose and nature from that done by the CEO that few generalizations can be made that apply to both, and those generalizations are so vague and broad that they are of little help in solving practical problems. Similarly, everyone in an organization is affected by control, and most managers exercise control; but, as suggested in the distinctions made above, the nature of control is quite different in the three types of activities: strategic planning, management control, and task control. For this reason, we do not consider planning and control as separate activities but, rather, as subsets of the three main processes.

Internal Auditing

The topic of internal auditing does not fit neatly into the above structure. It is an important function in any sizable organization, and texts (or sections of auditing texts) discuss it in depth. We mention the topic here because some people confuse this activity with management control. Management control is an activity that is carried out primarily by managers. Internal audit is a staff activity intended to ensure that information is reported accurately in accordance with prescribed rules, that fraud and misappropriation of assets is kept to a minimum, and, in some cases, to suggest ways of improving the organization's efficiency and effectiveness.

OVERVIEW OF THE TEXT

To understand a system, one needs to know about the environment in which it occurs. Part 1 describes this environment. The later parts describe the management control process.

The Environment (Part 1)

The management control process takes place in an organization. In Chapter 2 we describe some of the characteristics of organizations that affect the process, focusing principally on the behavior of members of an organization. An organization has goals, and a function of the management control system is to induce members of the organization to help achieve these goals. Chapters 3, 4, and 5 describe types of organization units and techniques that are important in the control of the several types of organization units.

Chapter 3 introduces the idea of responsibility centers. A *responsibility center* is an organization unit headed by a responsible manager. Each responsibility center has inputs and outputs. Inputs are the resources that the responsibility center uses in doing whatever it does. Outputs are the results of its work. Technically, these outputs are *products*, but they are not necessarily products that are sold to outside customers. Services rendered by one responsibility center to another responsibility center also are products. Responsibility centers can be classified according to the degree to which their inputs and outputs are measured in monetary terms.

Expense centers and revenue centers are described in Chapter 3. In an *expense center*, inputs are measured as monetary costs; but outputs either are not measured at all or, if measured, the measurement is a quantitative, nonmonetary amount. In an expense center the manager is responsible primarily for expense control. There are two types of expense centers. In a *standard cost center*, actual costs can be compared with standard costs to obtain a measure of how efficiently the center operated.[8] In a *discretionary expense center*, there is no way of arriving at sound standard costs, and expenses vary at the discretion of the manager and of his or her superiors. The efficiency of a discretionary expense center cannot be measured (although the efficiency of some activities within the expense center may be measurable).

In a *revenue center*, revenues are measured in monetary terms, but expenses are not matched with these revenues. Branch sales offices often are revenue centers. A comparison of budgeted with actual revenues indicates the effectiveness of the revenue center.[9]

In a *profit center*, both revenues and the expenses associated with earning those revenues are measured, the difference between them being profit. Actual profit compared with budgeted profit is a measure of the manager's efficiency and effectiveness. Profit centers are discussed in Chapter 4.

If a profit center provides outputs to other responsibility centers, or if it receives inputs from other responsibility centers, prices must be established for these outputs and inputs. These prices are called *transfer prices* to distinguish them from the market prices charged to outside customers. Developing transfers prices in a way that facilitates management control is discussed in Chapter 5.

---

[8] As will be described in more detail in Chapter 3, *efficiency* measures the relationship between inputs and outputs. The most efficient responsibility center is the one that produces a given quantity of output at the lowest amount of inputs, or the one that produces the most outputs from a given quantity of inputs.

[9] As will be described in more detail in Chapter 3, *effectiveness* is a measurement of how well the responsibility center contributed to the organization's objectives.

In an *investment center,* both the profit and the investment (i.e., the assets or capital) used in a responsibility center are measured. The return on investment is the broadest measure of the manager's efficiency and effectiveness. Investment centers are discussed in Chapter 6.

Management control involves the implementation of strategies. As background, therefore, generic types of organization strategies are described in Chapter 7.

The Management Control Process (Part 2)

Much of the management control process involves informal communications and interactions between managers and other managers and between managers and workers. Informal communications occur by means of memoranda, meetings, conversations, and even by such signals as facial expressions. These informal activities take place within a formal planning and control system. Such a formal system includes the following activities: (1) programming, (2) budget preparation, (3) execution, and (4) evaluation. As shown in Exhibit 1–5, each activity leads to the next. They recur in a regular cycle, and collectively they constitute a "closed loop." These four types of activities are described briefly here and are discussed in more depth in the chapters indicated.

Programming (Chapter 8).   Programming is the process of deciding on the major programs that the organization will undertake to implement its strategies and the approximate amount of resources that will be devoted to each. The output of the programming process results in a document called the *strategic plan* (some companies refer to this document as the *long-range plan*). The information about a program covers a period of several future years, usually three or five years. In a profit-oriented company, each principal product or product line is a program. In a nonprofit organization, the principal types of service that the organization renders are programs. There are also research and development programs and programs for support and overhead activities.

Programming is the first step in the management control cycle. In a company that operates on a calendar year basis, it takes place in the spring or summer of the year that precedes the budget year. At that time, program decisions are made, taking account of any changes in strategies that have occurred since the last program was developed. The monetary consequences and other information about the anticipated effect of these decisions over the planning period is set forth in the strategic plan.

Budget preparation (Chapter 9).   An operating budget is the organization's financial plan for a specified period, usually one year. The approved program is the starting point in preparing the budget. The budget represents a "fine

EXHIBIT 1–5   Phases of Management Control

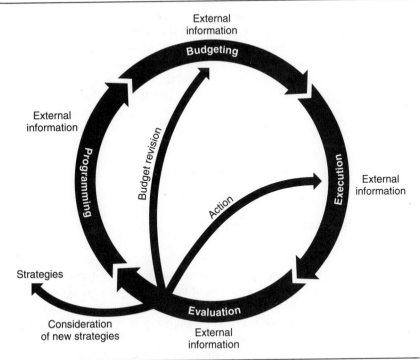

tuning'' of the program, using the most current information. In the budget, the program is realigned to correspond to responsibility centers, rather than individual programs—that is, the budget shows the expenses that can be incurred by each manager who is responsible for a program or a part of a program. The process of preparing the budget is essentially one of negotiation between the manager of a responsibility center and his or her superior. The end product of these negotiations is an agreed-upon statement of the expenses that are expected to be incurred during the year (if the responsibility center is an expense center), or the profit or return on investment (if the responsibility center is a profit center or an investment center).

Execution and evaluation. (Chapters 10, 11, and 12).   During the year, managers execute the program or part of a program for which they are responsible. Reports of what has happened are prepared and circulated. Ideally, these reports are so structured that they provide information about both programs and responsibility centers. Reports on responsibility centers show both budgeted and actual information, both monetary and nonmonetary information, and both internal and external information. These reports keep managers at higher levels informed about what is going on and also help to ensure that the work of the various responsibility centers is coordinated.

Reports also are used as a basis for control. Basically, the process of evaluation is a comparison of actual amounts with the amounts that should have been expected under the circumstances. Unless circumstances have changed from those assumed in the budget process, the comparison is between budgeted and actual amounts. If circumstances have changed, the changes are taken into account in the analysis. The analysis leads to praise or constructive criticism of responsibility center managers. Under some circumstances, it leads to revisions of the budget.

Chapter 12 describes the considerations involved in designing management incentive compensation plans.

Variations in Management Control (Part 3)

The chapters in Part 2 describe the typical management control process. In Part 3, we describe variations from the typical pattern. The essentials are similar, but the environment results in significant differences in the details. These variations are: controls for different strategies (Chapter 13), service organizations (Chapter 14), financial services organizations (Chapter 15), and multinational organizations (Chapter 16).

The final chapter describes management control of projects, which is somewhat different from management control of ongoing operations that has been the focus so far.

SUMMARY

Management control is the process by which managers influence other members of the organization to implement the organization's strategies. It differs from the two other planning and control processes—strategic planning and task control—in important respects. Mistakes may be made if generalizations that are applicable to one process are applied to another.

SUGGESTED ADDITIONAL READINGS

Anthony, Robert N. *The Management Control Function.* Boston: Harvard Business School Press, 1989.

Camillus, John. *Strategic Planning and Management Control.* Lexington, Mass: D. C. Heath, 1986.

Emmanuel, Clive R., and David Otley. *Accounting for Management Control.* Woking-
ham, Berkshire, England: Van Nostrand Reinhold (UK), 1985.

Galbraith, J. R., and R. K. Kazanjian. *Strategy Implementation: The Role of Structure
and Process.* 2nd ed. St. Paul, Minn.: West Publishing, 1986.

Govindarajan, Vijay. "A Contingency Approach to Strategy Implementation at the
Business Unit Level: Integrating Administrative Mechanisms with Strategy." *Academy of Management Journal* 31, no. 4 (1988), pp. 828–53.

Lorange, Peter; M. F. S. Morton; and S. Ghosal. *Strategic Control Systems.* St. Paul,
Minn.: West Publishing, 1986.

Maciariello, Joseph. *Management Control Systems.* Englewood Cliffs, N.J.: Prentice
Hall, 1984.

Merchant, Kenneth A. *Control in Business Organizations.* Marshfield, Mass.: Pitman,
1985.

McIntosh, Norman. *The Social Software of Accounting and Control Systems.* New York:
John Wiley & Sons, 1985.

Steiner, George A. *Strategic Planning.* New York: Free Press, 1979.

Wiener, Norbert. *Cybernetics: Or Control and Communication in the Animal and Machine.* New York: John Wiley & Sons, 1948.

Case 1–1

General Electric Company*

In 1981, General Electric Company was the world's largest diversified industrial corporation. This note is intended to provide a description of some of the systems and procedures designed and used by GE's top managers as they collectively addressed themselves to the ongoing task of conducting the affairs of the company. Following the brief historical section below, this note is divided into three main sections: Organization Structure, Planning Systems, and Operating Systems.

History and Managerial Philosophy

General Electric traced its origins to the establishment of the Edison General Electric Company in 1878. Its original business strategy was developed around the exploitation of the commercial opportunity presented by the harnessing of electricity, the invention of electric lighting, and the electric motor. This led the company into the design, manufacture, and marketing of electric motors and related industrial, farm, and home machinery and appliances, as well as lighting and electricity-generating equipment. As electricity became a ubiquitous part of 20th-century life, the scope of GE's involvement expanded in many directions to include synthetic materials, electronics, nuclear energy, broadcasting, natural resources, and consumer credit.

Already a large company before World War II, GE grew rapidly during the war and continued to grow steadily thereafter. Over the four decades, GE's revenues increased fiftyfold—a compound annual growth rate of 10.5 percent per year. The rate of inflation varied during these years, but in constant dollars the growth in sales was 5.7 percent per year.

In 1980, GE's revenues were nearly $25 billion, its net earnings exceeded $1.5 billion, and it ranked ninth on *Fortune*'s roster of U.S. industrial corporations.

During this period of growth and diversification, GE's management systems were also evolving. The material below is excerpted from "Strategic Management for the '80s," an internal document prepared by GE in 1977 to explain to all GE managers the rationale for creating the new position of Sector executive.

> Adapting the company's management system and structure to internal or external challenges has been a continuous process throughout General Electric's 100 year history. As the company has grown, the complexities brought about by increasing size and diversity have consistently challenged generations of managers to develop new approaches, systems and organization structures to more effectively meet our goals.
>
> **Decentralization in the '50s.** In the 1950s, the company was decentralized to allow for greater organizational flexibility, management opportunity and entrepreneurship. The company was well positioned for explosive growth during the favorable economic climate of the 1960s.
>
> **Growth in the '60s.** Overall company growth was quite dramatic in the 1960s. However, we encountered a phenomenon affecting most large companies at that time called "profitless growth," which means tremendous growth in sales without commensurate growth in earnings. Further, heavy investment in areas which were not

* This case was abridged with permission from Harvard Business School Case 181–111, written under the direction of Professor Richard F. Vancil.
Copyright © by the President and Fellows of Harvard College.

yielding profitable growth put us close to our debt/ capital limit for an Aaa company. Greater investment selectivity was required along with a system to assist management in allocating financial resources according to the varying potentials and paces of GE's many businesses.

Strategic Planning for the '70s. As a result, an organization and system change was made based on strategic planning concepts, to focus our resources on the strategic requirements of our diverse businesses. Organizationally, we overlaid on our hierarchical structure of Groups, Divisions, and Departments a structure for planning through the identification of unique, stand-alone businesses called Strategic Business Units. In addition, a planning process was designed to surface strategic plans, required of each SBU, for critical review and resource allocation at Corporate level. The profitless growth pattern was reversed, but just as important, SBU management developed a style of management that stresses strategic positioning of businesses and selective allocation of key resources for competitive advantage.

Strategic Management for the '80s. Judging from the expected challenges of the 1980s, it is timely to move from strategic planning as a process designed for one level—the SBU—to "strategic management" as a management style for all levels of GE managers. The strategic management concept combines planning and management responsibilities at every level where value may be added for the effective implementation of strategic objectives. This value added not only involves the integration of lower-level objectives and strategies, but also requires each level to develop plans for strengthening key internal resources and establishing business development programs unique to the scope of that business level. In short, planning and managing is done at the SBU level for worldwide businesses, at Sector level for multinational industries and at Corporate level for global/multi-industry strategies.

Commenting on these changes in 1981, one GE executive said:

> We don't change our basic structure very often, but when we do, it's a reflection of a basic change in our managerial philosophy. We came out of World War II a finely honed, central-

ized, functionally organized company. When we decentralized in the early fifties, we did so with a vengeance, almost to the point of acting like a holding company. Setting up the SBUs in 1970 was a recognition that we had gone too far, and that the strategic direction of the company should be directed from the top to some extent. The Sector executives in 1977 helped to move the pendulum a little further in that direction.

Organization Structure

There were five echelons of general managers in the organizational hierarchy: the Chief Executive Office (CEO), Sector executives (6), Group executives (12), Division general managers (54), and Department general managers (181).

Line Management

Exhibit 1 uses the Consumer Product and Services Sector in 1978 to illustrate how the executives at these five levels related to each other for operating management and for strategic management. It shows how the company's operating facilites—production plants, laboratories, warehouses, sales offices, and so forth—which would have required several pages to list, were grouped by product categories or markets under the responsibility of department managers. These, in turn, where the scale of the operations warranted it, were grouped under division general managers. In some instances, several divisions were brought together under a group executive. These operating level designations expressed the management skills and resources required to manage each business or functional component successfully.

Some of these components had the word *business* in their designation. This was the key to their relationship with the strategic planning process, for each such component was the top management level of an SBU. These were viewed as the basic business entities of General Electric. They were set up to assure organization integrity while permitting the SBU general manager to carry out a business strategy effectively and competitively. As such, the SBUs could have stood

EXHIBIT 1   Partial Representation of Organization Structure

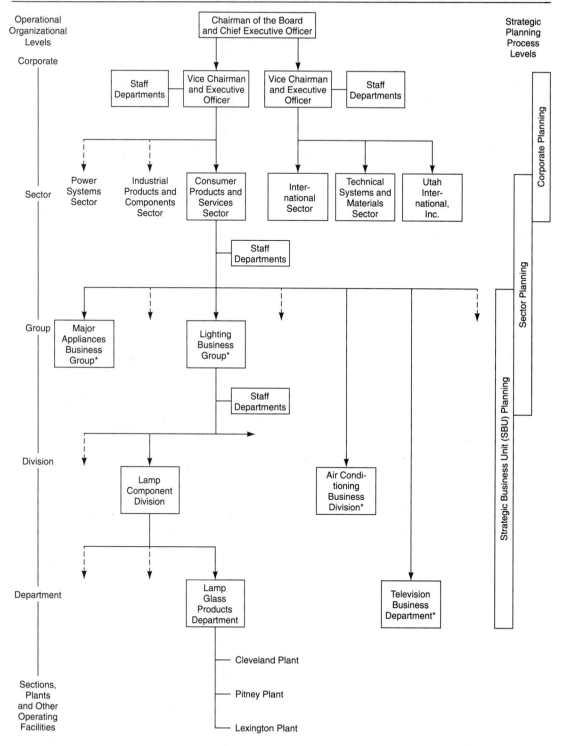

Operational Organizational Levels

Corporate

Sector

Group

Division

Department

Sections, Plants and Other Operating Facilities

Chairman of the Board and Chief Executive Officer

Staff Departments

Vice Chairman and Executive Officer

Vice Chairman and Executive Officer

Staff Departments

Power Systems Sector

Industrial Products and Components Sector

Consumer Products and Services Sector

International Sector

Technical Systems and Materials Sector

Utah International, Inc.

Staff Departments

Major Appliances Business Group*

Lighting Business Group*

Staff Departments

Lamp Component Division

Air Conditioning Business Division*

Lamp Glass Products Department

Television Business Department*

Cleveland Plant

Pitney Plant

Lexington Plant

Strategic Planning Process Levels

Corporate Planning

Sector Planning

Strategic Business Unit (SBU) Planning

*49 SBUs

alone as viable and completely successful independent companies, each within its own defined market or market segment. Depending on the size of its business, an SBU might be located at one of several levels in the hierarchy of the operating structure: a group (as in the case of the Lighting Business Group); a division (as in the case of the Air Conditioning Business Division); a department (as in the case of the Television Business Department, which in 1981 was promoted to Division status); or it could even be an unconsolidated subsidiary (such as GE Credit Corporation). In total, General Electric had 49 SBUs in 1978 (and 39 in 1981).

The general manager of an SBU was responsible for the planning and operation of his or her business. This involved managing various functions, product areas, and business segments. It was the manager's job to review and approve (within delegated limits) lower-level echelon decisions on investment, organization, manpower, and compensation. The SBU manager was also responsible for developing the SBU's strategic plan, and reviewing and integrating operating, functional, and business segment plans. The formal assignment of authority to managers at the various operational levels (see the left scale in Exhibit 1) did not differ between SBUs and non-SBUs except for the additional responsibilities of the SBU manager in the strategic planning and reporting process.

Above the SBUs were the Sectors. These were macro-business/industry areas made up of businesses with common strategic challenges defined by critical market, customer, product, or technology characteristics. Each sector was headed by an executive vice president and sector executive who was assisted by a small staff of functional specialists and strategic planners. As the chief operating executive for the sector, the sector executive managed all SBU managers, reviewed and approved SBU strategies, plans, budgets, investment requests, and key changes in organization and manpower. He was also responsible for the sector's strategic plan. Assisted by his staff, the sector executive was not to replace or replicate

the strategic planning and management functions of the units at lower levels, but rather to complement them and "add value" to the management process by identifying and acting upon strategic issues of a sector-wide nature.

One sector executive made the following comment about how this newest echelon of GE management was working out:

> We have made progress in establishing ourselves at the sector management level as it was intended—to provide added value. The job has been made easier because General Electric is well organized and has the management systems and tools already in place. In fact, many of us believe General Electric has one of the best systems going. If one thinks of this organization structure and these management processes as a giant plumbing system, our job at the sector management level is to plug into the system and serve as a high-pressure pump, and thus generate a more dynamic business operation.

In addition to the operational and strategic management functions, the sector executive also assumed responsibility as the company spokesman for his industry area. The International Sector, in addition to managing affiliates in specific countries, was responsible for integrating resources and capabilities in support of the international strategies of the other sectors.

Functional Staff Departments

Seven major staff organizations were located at GE headquarters in Fairfield, Connecticut. Several of these units had counterparts at lower levels in the line-management hierarchy. For example, each general manager at the department level and higher was supported by a manager of Finance and, in most cases, a manager of Relations, and each SBU manager had a manager for Strategic Planning and other staff officers as necessary to operate in a competitive environment. The existence of other staff offices depended on the nature of the operating unit and the need for staff support at that echelon.

Resource Planning. The role of staff units, in addition to providing functional support to their line manager, was to contribute to strategic planning by identifying resource issues that might have an impact on the operating unit's ability to meet its business objectives. This task was called *resource planning,* and was expected to "add value" in several ways, three examples of which are discussed below.

By reviewing the functional activities of the operating components at their level and below, a staff unit might identify the opportunity to create a new capability with sufficient critical mass to serve the operating units better. (Setting up a research lab at the group level might be feasible even though no single component could afford such a lab.) A second type of staff initiative might identify an existing resource that could gain further economies of scale if it were utilized by other operating components. (A college recruiting program in one division might screen candidates for another division.) Finally, higher-level staff groups had a special responsibility for anticipating future needs for resources, and might identify such needs before the operating components did. (The pervasive effect of electronic microprocessors on many of GE's products was first surfaced in this manner.)

Executive Manpower Staff. The Executive Manpower Staff was created and centralized because the company had in its managers a rich resource which had to be developed for all its businesses. There was also the need to be able to move people from one part of the organization to another as they developed and grew.

The Executive Manpower Staff had extensive information on the company's managers. It organized the annual manpower review known as Session C that reached down to the lower levels of the organization. All exempt employees were involved. Each filled out a form on his or her background, self-assessment, and plans. The individual's boss then provided an evaluation and assessment. (This was not a performance appraisal, as those were carried out separately.) There was then a feedback session with the subordinate. The boss followed the same procedure with his superior and, in addition, discussed his own people

with him. As the process moved on up the pyramid, the focus narrowed to the half-dozen direct reports, but perhaps two dozen individuals farther down the ladder might be discussed. Session C culminated in a review with the executive officers of the manpower resources at the division and SBU management levels.

The Executive Manpower Staff kept on file the annual manpower review reports on all managers from level 15 (section managers) to level 27 (sector executives), a total of about 5,000 managers and individual contributors. It also kept track of 13s and 14s that were rated as promotable and they, too, were in the inventory. This information was filed in computerized form for easy access and retrieval.

It was also the responsibility of the Executive Manpower Staff to prepare slates of candidates for all management positions at the department level and above. Sector executives were usually involved in these decisions, working with a consultant assigned to them from the staff in identifying candidates. Sector executives often had the consultant participate in all types of management activities in the sector which allowed him or her to learn firsthand about people. Then the executive and the consultant would talk about individuals and their relative performance. Because of the strategic management orientation of SBU and sector management, the manpower management process was made easier. Once the strategy had been established, it was easier to assess managers in terms of their capacity to contribute to its accomplishment.

Commenting on the management of executive manpower, one staff consultant stressed the importance of the role played by the sector executive:

> Finding the right people for key management jobs is only part of the task; motivating them is also important. The sector executive that I'm assigned to works hard at motivating his managers, and cannot just appeal to the pocketbook. At this level, compensation, although important, is not the primary motivator. This might seem surprising since the amounts are sizable. They range from between $70,000 and $90,000 in base pay plus

about 20 percent to 60 percent in incentive compensation at the department level (level 18 or 19), up to a maximum in 1980 of $1 million in salary and incentive compensation for the chairman of the board. Such levels of compensation are important to preserve our quality pool of managerial talent, but other factors provide the key to good motivation. The sector executive with whom I work participates actively with his staff and with me in reviewing performance screens proposed by all his direct reports and all corporate officers in his SBUs. He also knows how to give people responsibility. He encourages risk taking. But he also gives his managers support when they need it. He uses his staff very well. As a result, the good people under him tend to derive a sense of competence.

Top-Management Boards

Each manager in GE had a line or staff role, as defined by the organization structure, and also a role as a member of one or more boards or communities. This section focuses on the four boards at the top levels of GE, but committees were widely used at all levels in the company.

Corporate Executive Office. The CEO was the top line management unit in GE and was not viewed as a committee. The CEO had multiple responsibilities for overall company policy, planning, and operations, and provided direction and leadership across a broad range of complex internal and external challenges. Specifically, the CEO was responsible for the corporate plan, determined corporate objectives and strategies, and reviewed and approved sector strategies, objectives, and budgets. Staff assistance was provided to the chief executive officer (CXO) in his policy making, strategic, and operational roles by a Corporate Policy Board, which he chaired. The vice chairmen managed sector executives and were aided in their sector strategy and investment review roles by a Corporate Operations Board.

Corporate Policy Board. The CPB was the highest internal forum for reviewing company policies and strategies. In a sense, the CPB could be viewed as a CXO staff meeting, providing him the opportunity to hear an open discussion of issues and using his key staff officers as a sounding board. Sector strategies (I) and budgets (II) were presented to the CPB by the sector executive and his staff.

Corporate Operations Board. The COB was co-chaired by the vice chairmen and consisted of selected corporate staff officers. COB meetings for investment reviews and critical-issue resolution were designed to review several sector(s) requests per session.

Sector Executive Board. Each sector executive chaired an SEB that assisted him in reviewing SBU strategies, budgets, and investment requests. SEB members, in addition to key sector staff managers, included two or more members from either corporate or other sector staffs. These outside SEB members were selected by the sector executive with the approval of his vice chairman and the concurrence of the candidate's immediate superior.

Corporate Executive Council. The CEC was composed of the CPB and sector executives and provided a forum for operating and staff executives to meet, review, and discuss corporate and sector operating and planning issues. The CEC meetings were viewed as necessary for high-level operations reviews, and as a valuable opportunity for interchange between the CXO and his operating executives.

One implication of GE's use of several top management committees was that careful advance scheduling for executive time commitments was required.

Planning Systems

General Electric's planning system used the organizational structure in two ways. Operational planning and reporting was carried out routinely, as appropriate, at each organizational level within GE. Strategic planning and related evaluations and reviews, however, were carried out only at the designated strategic levels: corporate, sector, SBU, and, in some instances, business segments. While written plans were prepared at each level, the emphasis was more on dialogue between levels. The plans differed in style and content, reflecting the varied nature of the environment faced by each unique business and the particular approach of its manager. The common threads in strategic plans at each level (see the right scale in Exhibit 1) were that: (1) they performed rigorous environmental analyses and position assessments, identifying major discontinuities; (2) they summarized the objectives and strategies of the components under them; and (3) they specifically addressed priorities and major programs for business development and resource development. Each strategic planning level, thus, was expected to "add value" to General Electric through its participation in the planning process.

To make the planning system work efficiently and effectively across the broad spectrum of organizational units that made up the entire company, GE followed a formal strategic planning cycle. The cycle was divided into three parts: Communication/Direction, Review/Evaluation, and Allocation/Approval. These occurred sequentially as the year progressed, and each is discussed in turn below.

Communication/Direction

For several years prior to the 1981 planning cycle, the GE corporate plan for the coming year was approved at the close of each year. The distribution of this document was restricted to corporate and sector executives and their key staff officers—a group of about 50 individuals. As a part of that document, corporate planning challenges for the subsequent year were passed down to the sector executives who, in turn, provided sector planning challenges to the SBUs. These challenges identified topics which were relevant to most SBUs (e.g., productivity), and which the CEO wished to receive special attention in the forthcoming strategic planning cycle. Early in the year, formal meetings were held with all corporate officers and general managers together (Belleair, General Managers Conference) to review these challenges, along with pertinent background studies, and to consider their implications for strategies and directions.

For 1981, the corporate initiation of the planning cycle was handled somewhat differently. The 1981 corporate plan was distributed to approximately 200 people, including SBU managers and their key staff officers. The challenges approach was expanded to encompass business issues as well as functional issues. For example, the plan defined several Arenas that required coordinated strategic efforts by several SBUs. Energy was an *arena* where the CEO saw an opportunity for concerted action by several operating units, and the 1981 plan identified each unit and the role that it should play. As one corporate staff executive explained the rationale for this approach, "It's an attempt to deal with one of our most difficult problems—getting the units in our decentralized structure to work together. Opportunities don't always align themselves with our organization structure. Arenas are intended to bridge the gap between organizational components and to get the components to focus on opportunities that transcend their normal scope."

Review/Evaluation

In June, each SBU submitted its strategic plan to sector and corporate headquarters. The bulk of this document was externally focused, analyzing competitors, assessing market opportunities, and defining major strategic thrusts in terms of new product developments and possible acquisitions. An appendix to the document was the Long Range Forecast, which presented financial information for the prior five years, the current year, and a forecast of the next five years. The data for the first forecast year was, in effect, the SBU's preliminary proposal for its operating budget and its capital expenditures budget.

Since the establishment of SBUs in 1970, the corporate review and evaluation of strategic plans was accomplished in part through a "portfolio analysis," with each SBU being viewed as a separate business vying for a share of the company's resources with which to pursue growth in its defined market(s). Generally, the sum of the profits proposed by the SBUs was less than the corporate expectation, and the capital requirements were more than corporate believed prudent. The task for corporate management was to close these "gaps." The growth potential of the market and the SBU's current competitive position in that market were considered along with its business strategy, and decisions were then made as to how much of the gaps to assign to each SBU, based on the corporate view of the appropriate overall portfolio of GE's businesses. For example, some SBUs were squeezed for maximum contribution, thus being guided into a harvest strategy, while others were permitted to incur discretionary operating expenses that would result in future growth. This process of assigning the responsibility for the company's profit and capital expenditure requirements was labeled the "resource allocation process."

With the establishment of the Sector management level in 1977, the review of SBUs' strategies was delegated to the sector executives, along with the responsibility for allocating resources among their SBUs. This, however, still produced gaps when the sector proposals reached the CEO. The corporate officers performed the same SBU-level portfolio analysis as before, but aggregated the SBU adjustments and assigned the gaps to each sector, rather than to the individual SBUs. It was then up to the sector executive to decide how to allocate resources among his SBUs. He was free to do it according to criteria different from those utilized at the corporate level, the only requirement being that the sector deliver its budgeted results at the end of the year.

Allocation/Approval

Resource allocation at GE not only involved two levels of management above the SBUs, it also involved iterative negotiations among all three strategic levels that began in the summer and might continue into the early fall. The initial discussions resulted in tentative allocations of net income requirements and capital budgets from corporate to sectors, and from sector to SBUs. The SBU managers then reviewed their situations

and could reclamor their case if they felt a serious strategic error was about to be made. Sometimes the sector executive could accommodate the request within his own allocations; other times he might raise the issue at the corporate level. According to one GE executive, "The SBUs don't always win, of course, but it's surprising how often they do."

In the latter part of the year, SBU budgets were presented to sector and corporate levels. They would then be analyzed, discussed, modified, and approved in a series of additional meetings. With the issuance of the corporate plan for the next year, the cycle would start again.

Operating Systems

Once the strategic plans and operating budgets had been agreed upon, as described above, the day-by-day execution of operating activities was the responsibility of the general managers of the operating components (left scale in Exhibit 1). The top management of GE still believed strongly in the concept of decentralization as the best way to run current operations in its diverse set of businesses. Three formal management systems were used to constrain the operating autonomy of GE's managers, as described below under the headings of Reservations of Authority, Monitoring Financial Performance, and Appraising and Rewarding Managerial Performance.

Reservations of Authority

General Electric had a formal set of corporate policies designed primarily to insure (1) that its managers conformed to corporate standards of conduct in dealing with individuals, organizations, and agencies outside the company, and (2) internal administrative consistency. In the spring of 1981, GE was just completing a review and revision of its formal policies, reducing the total number to about 15 and covering topics such as "Compliance with the Anti-Trust Laws" and "Reimbursing Employees for Business Expenses." The typical policy statement required only two or three pages, but some policies were supplemented by detailed compliance procedures.

One policy that affected every operating general manager covered investments in plant and facilities. The capital budgets that were approved in the planning process had been based on detailed schedules listing each major investment; but the approval of the capital budget represented a strategic commitment to the business, rather than specific approval of the details of each project. Securing authority to expend the funds required that the sponsoring manager prepare an Appropriation Request (A/R) on a prescribed set of forms. Approval authority for A/Rs was limited to $500,000 for a department manager, $1 million for a division manager, $2 million for a group executive, $6 million for a sector executive, and $20 million for the CEO, with larger amounts reserved for the board of directors. The approver of an A/R was to ascertain that the strategic purpose was still valid and then, taking a project perspective, determine that the proposed investment was optimally designed for its intended purpose.

Monitoring Financial Performance

The current operating performance of GE managers at every level was monitored monthly by a comprehensive integrated set of financial reports. The amount of detailed information available at each level was sufficient to permit the manager at that level to review the performance of the operations beneath him or her, and the information was progressively summarized as it moved to higher levels in the management hierarchy.

Profit responsibility in GE was decentralized down to the department level. Each department general manager was responsible for meeting his or her budgeted net income (defined below), and the total of the net income for all the departments in GE was equal to the corporate net income, with only minor adjustments. For a typical department engaged in the manufacture and sale of a line of products, the major categories of expenses in its operating statement are shown in Table A.

Each expense category could, of course, be broken down in great detail. Three categories, known collectively as "base costs," require brief explanations. Readiness-to-serve costs were the fixed expenses of the operating components, reflecting its current capacity. These included depreciation and other manufacturing costs, and sales and administrative overhead. Program expenses were discretionary expenditures intended to increase future profits through specific programs for developing new products, entering new markets, or improving productivity. Assessments from corporate headquarters were an allocation of corporate overhead based on the department's cost of operations as a proportion of such costs in all departments; the assessment worked out to roughly 1 percent of sales. The amount of assessments from group and division echelons varied, depending on the extent to which they provided common services, such as a common sales force or computer services, to several departments beneath them; such assessments were usually based on usage of the services rather than a proration.

Department general managers were also responsible for the return on investment of their operating unit, and especially for managing the

TABLE A

Net sales billed	xxx
Less: Materials in cost of goods sold	(xxx)
Contributed value from operations	xxx
Less: Direct labor	(xxx)
Other variable costs	(xxx)
LIFO revaluation provision	(xx)
Contribution margin	xxx
Less: Readiness to serve costs	(xxx)
Program expenses	(xx)
Assessments from corporate, sector, group, and division	(xx)
Operating profit	xx
Less: Interest expense/income	(x)
Income taxes	(xx)
Net Income	xx

investment in working capital. At the beginning of 1980, a base amount of working capital was established for each department based on its average working capital in 1978. Increases in working capital above that base were funds provided by corporate, and the department was charged interest at the prime rate; decreasing working capital below that amount permitted the department manager to earn interest income at the same rate.

The operating components in GE were relatively free standing, and net income was defined as shown in Table A to encourage each general manager to accept responsibility for his or her "piece of the bottom line." Given an approved budget, department general managers had substantial latitude concerning how they achieved their targeted results. Higher-level managers were interested in more than the bottom line, however. They paid particular attention to program expenses, for example, to insure that the net income budget had not been achieved by cutting program expenses, thus, in effect, "eating our seed corn."

Many other aspects of departmental operations were monitored at higher levels, as illustrated by the monthly Review and Estimate of Operations report. This single piece of paper contained a variety of required data, ratios, and analyses, but also provided space for key measurements which the general manager of the component felt were relevant for his or her operation, such as the sales break-even point or the capacity utilization rate. In the comments section on the reverse of the form, the managers could provide a brief overview and identify particular problems that were receiving current attention. This report was sent up the operating hierarchy until it reached the SBU level. At that point, the same form was used to prepare a consolidated report for the SBU, and those forms were sent up to the sector executive and the CXO.

Appraising and Rewarding Managerial Performance

Closely related to, but distinguishable from, monitoring performance of each business was the process of evaluating the performance of GE's managers. Because of the diverse nature of the businesses in each sector, the details of this process varied. In general terms, however, each manager developed a set of financial and nonfinancial objectives on which he felt he should be evaluated. These goals, as described below, were called his *performance screen*. He would then review these with his superior, who might suggest revisions and changes. In reaching agreement, they would attach relative weights to each measure.

Financial objectives included several measurements of budgeted performance, such as sales, net income, ROI, cash flow, operating margin, and so on. The weight assigned to each of these elements would vary depending upon the portfolio category of the manager's SBU. Nonfinancial objectives were actions that would provide future benefits to GE, and included items such as "increase market share by——," "maintain cost leadership," "develop a total quality program for the business, encompassing all functions," and so on. Individual weights were assigned to each such element. For an "invest/grow" SBU, the weights on future benefits were usually greater than the weights on current performance; for a "harvest/divest" SBU, the weights on current performance might be several times the weights on future benefits.

Once a year, and more often when appropriate, the performance screens were reviewed by each manager and his boss in order to assess performance. The performance screens, together with Session C manpower reviews and the multiple contacts that took place during the conduct of day-to-day business, provided GE management with a comprehensive evaluation of managerial performance.

The performance evaluation process provided one of several criteria used by management to rank managers for yearly salary reviews and the award of incentive compensation. Salaries were kept competitive with the pertinent markets for managerial talent. Given the size of the organization, however, there was a formal salary scale which limited the discretion that a given organizational unit manager had in assigning salary levels. Yet, at each step in the scale, there was a range within which discretionary increases were permitted.

Incentive compensation was organized in three tiers. There was a pool of incentive compensation funds for managers from levels 15 to 18, another for nonofficers in levels 19 and above, and a third pool for corporate officers. The amount in each pool was determined each year by the Manpower Development and Compensation Committee, based on recommendations coming from the SBUs, and reviewed at sector and corporate level, as well as on general business performance as compared with the market and the economy. Once the pools were determined, sector and SBU management had substantial discretion in assigning amounts to individual managers.

For corporate officers, recommendations for both salary increases and incentive compensation were reviewed by the Executive Compensation staff under the vice president for executive manpower, which then made recommendations to the chairman and to the Executive Compensation Committee of the board of directors, where the final determination was made.

QUESTIONS

1. Describe and evaluate the elements of General Electric's planning and control systems that are designed to facilitate the simultaneous implementation of the variety of strategies being pursued by this widely diversified corporation.
2. What is your assessment of Reginald Jones's tenure (who was the CEO during the 1970s) as the CEO of General Electric?
3. What problems caused General Electric to change its planning and control approach in early 1970 and again in 1977?
4. What should Welch (who succeeded Reginald Jones) try to accomplish during his first six months in office as the CEO?

Case 1–2

Stewart Box Company*

Stewart Box company was a well-established manufacturer of paperboard cartons and boxes, which were sold primarily as packages for consumer products. The cartons were manufactured in the company's carton factory. The raw material for the carton factory was paperboard, which was manufactured in the company's paperboard mill adjacent to the carton factory. The plant complex also included a 60,000-square foot warehouse where finished orders were stored pending delivery. The company had approximately 425 employees in 1979. Robert Stewart, the president, was also a large stockholder.

The company marketed its products within a radius of about 500 miles from its factory, which was located in a fairly small town. It had seven sales engineers, who were compensated on the basis of a nominal salary, plus commission. In the marketing organization were six other persons, including three who prepared price quotations for prospective customers, according to specifications obtained from the customers. The company had an excellent reputation for product quality and customer service.

The paperboard and carton industry was characterized by strong competition because of the potential overcapacity that existed in most plants. Because of this overcapacity, competition for large orders was particularly keen, and price cutting was common. Stewart met this competition by designing special boxes to customer specifications, by actively catering to its customers' wishes, and by strict adherence to promised delivery dates.

The production process required that the paperboard mill operate continuously on three shifts for maximum efficiency, but the carton factory operated an average of only one and one-half shifts per day.

A partial organization chart is shown as Exhibit 1. The paperboard mill and the carton factory were profit centers. In the carton factory were 10 production departments, each consisting of a printing press or a group of similar presses and associated equipment and each headed by a foreman. There were five service departments, which performed functions such as ink manufacture, quality control, and warehouse storage; each was headed by a supervisor. Each of these 15 departments was an expense center. The 10 production departments were production cost centers, and the five service departments were service cost centers.

Accounting System

The company had a job cost accounting system, using standard costs. The board mill was a single cost center, operating a single paperboard manufacturing machine. A rate per machine-hour was established annually, which combined direct labor and manufacturing overhead costs. Manufactured paperboard was charged to the carton factory at a transfer price that included standard cost plus a standard return on the assets employed in the board mill. The profit component of this charge was subtracted from the inventory amounts as shown on the financial statements

* This case was prepared by R. N. Anthony, Harvard Business School.
Copyright © by the President and Fellows of Harvard College.

EXHIBIT 1 Organization Chart

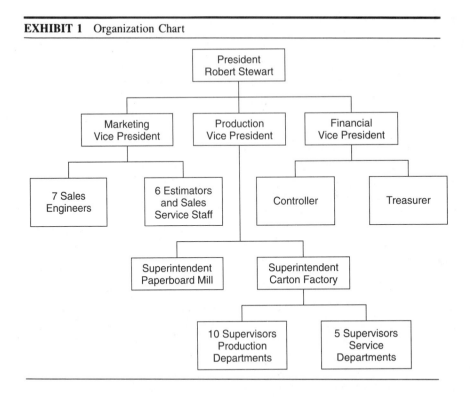

(because generally accepted accounting principles do not permit a profit allowance to be included in inventory).

In the carton factory, each order was a job. The job was costed at the standard cost of the materials used on the job, a standard rate per press hour for the time that the job used on presses, and a standard rate per direct labor-hour for other operations. These rates included both labor and factory overhead costs and were estimated annually. The system also collected actual labor and overhead costs for each responsibility center.

Programming

The company had a five-year plan, which it revised annually. The management team (president, vice presidents, and superintendents) spent a total of about two days each summer discussing and agreeing on this revision. In 1979, for example,

the sales estimates for 1980–84 indicated that the capacity of the warehouse would become inadequate by 1981. This led to an investigation of alternative warehousing arrangements, and a decision to build a larger warehouse and to tear down the existing one. The capital required for this warehouse was significant, and it was decided to borrow part of the cost and to finance the remainder from funds generated by operations.

As an aid in deciding on proposed capital acquisitions, the company calculated the net present value and a profitability index whenever the available information was sufficiently reliable to warrant a formal analysis. About 85 percent of the proposals in terms of numbers, but less than 50 percent in terms of dollar magnitude, were in this category. Exhibit 2 is an example of the numerical part of such an analysis. (The accompanying explanation is omitted.) It is for the replacement of a printing press which was so old and worn that maintenance and operating costs were high. The decision was made to acquire this press in 1979, and the $20,000 cost was included in the capital budget for 1980.

Over a period of about five years the company conducted a review of each facet of its operations. For production operations, it usually hired a consulting firm expert in carton manufacturing methods to conduct this review. For marketing and general administrative functions, it used the management services division of the firm of certified public accountants that audited its financial statements.

Budget Preparation

The controller was responsible for the mechanics of the annual budgeting process. He saw to it that the sales staff prepared sales estimates. These were discussed at length in a meeting attended by Mr. Stewart, the marketing vice president, and the controller. After final sales estimates were agreed upon, the controller communicated these estimates to heads of responsibility centers as a basis for their budget preparation.

Some budget items were stated as a fixed amount per month, others were stated as variable amounts per unit of output, and still others were stated as a fixed amount per month plus a variable amount per unit of output. For the production departments, output was measured in terms of machine-hours or direct labor-hours; and for the service departments, it was measured in terms of an appropriate measure of activity, such as pounds of ink manufactured.

Each responsibility center head discussed his proposed budget first with the controller (who had had long experience in the industry and hence could point out discrepancies or soft spots), and, in the case of the carton factory, with its superintendent. Mr. Stewart then discussed the proposed budgets for the board mill and the carton factory with the superintendents of these

---

EXHIBIT 2   Analysis of Proposed Printing Press

	Tax Calculation	Present Value Calculation
Annual cash inflows:		
Saving in maintenance costs		$ 2,000
Saving in direct labor costs		6,200
Saving in power		1,000
Saving in supplies		500
Annual pretax cash inflow	$9,700	9,700
Less: Depreciation* $20,000 ÷ 10	2,000	
Additional taxable income	7,700	
Additional income tax 50% × $7,700		3,800
Annual aftertax cash inflow		5,900
Present value of cash inflows ($A_{10/10} = 6.145$)		22,400
Investment in press installed		20,000
Net present value		$ 2,400
Profitability index $22,400/$20,000		1.12

*For simplicity in this illustration, straight-line depreciation is used. The company actually used sum-of-the-years'-digits depreciation for income tax purposes.

profit centers. He discussed the marketing budget with the marketing vice president. From these discussions, an approved budget emerged. It consisted of a master budget showing planned revenues and expenses at the estimated sales volume, a variable budget for each responsibility center showing the fixed amount per month and the variable rate per unit of output for each significant item of expense, a purchasing budget, and a cash budget. Standard unit costs and overhead rates were revised if necessary, so that they were consistent with the approved budget.

Product Pricing

Pricing was a crucial element in the company's marketing tactics. Prices were prepared by the company's estimators for each bid or order, on the basis of sales specifications and the appropriate standard cost elements as shown in tables the company had developed for this purpose. To the calculated amount of total factory costs, there were added allowances for selling and administrative expenses, sales commissions, cash discounts, and a profit margin. These allowances were expressed as percentages, and were based on the budget. A sample price estimate is reproduced as Exhibit 3.[1] The price calculated in the estimate was often adjusted for quotation purposes. It might be lowered to meet competitive conditions, or it might be increased because the design work on the order was judged to be particularly good, or for other reasons. In Exhibit 3, the calculated selling price came to $28.14 per thousand boxes, but the actual quotation was increased to $30.60.

Estimators of several companies met regularly under the auspices of a trade association to price sample boxes according to their own formulas. Based on these meetings, Mr. Stewart concluded that, while most of his competitors were shaving

---

[1] Many of the abbreviations and terms in this form are peculiar to the company. The purpose of Exhibit 3 is only to illustrate the form used in preparing a price estimate. An understanding of its details in not necessary for this purpose.

prices below formula, Stewart's quoted prices were higher than the calculated estimate about 65 percent of the time and lower 15 percent of the time. "It all depends on the competition, and on your assessment of the whole situation," he once said.

On some occasions, the company departed from its normal pricing practices. This usually happened when orders for cartons were not in sufficient volume to keep the board mill working at capacity. On these occasions the company took orders for paperboard at prices below full cost, in order to keep the board mill busy. Such contribution pricing was not used often, however.

Reports

Each month an income statement was prepared (Exhibit 4). It was constructed to focus on the performance of the two profit centers. Also, a spending report was prepared for each of the 15 expense centers in the carton factory. An example is given in Exhibit 5.

In addition, Mr. Stewart received a variety of other reports on a regular basis. The *internally generated* reports were as follows:

1. Balance sheet, monthly.
2. Selling, general and administrative statement, monthly.
3. Overdue accounts receivable, monthly.
4. Overdue shipments, monthly.
5. Inventory size, monthly.
6. Raw materials shrinkage report, monthly.
7. Cash and securities listing, monthly.
8. Actual sales, weekly, with a monthly comparison of actual and budgeted sales.
9. Carton factory production, monthly. This included operating hours statistics and efficiency percentages.
10. Outstanding orders (backlog) weekly.
11. Machine production report, daily.
12. Quality control report, monthly.

Mr. Stewart examined the reports illustrated in Exhibits 4 and 5 carefully. If there were impor-

EXHIBIT 3 Price Estimate

Preparatory Cost	Production per Hours	Rate	Unit	Material Cost		Mfg. Cost	
Original Plates	F. or E.						
Electros 9¾ x 9¼		18.94	28	530	32		
Wood				15	99		
Rule				34	09		
Composing							
Die Making	③	4.85	41.8			202	73
Make-Ready—Ptg.	2 x	12.80	30.0			384	00
Make-Ready—C. & C.	11.55	11.25	15.8			177	75
Total Preparatory Cost				580	40	764	48
Quantity Cost							
Board 65,005 (3¾)	171.00+25			5557	93		
Board				25	00		
Ink				111	00		
Ink				328	95		
Cases Corrugated	700	.30	1429	428	70		
Cellulose Material							
Board, Storage, & Handling		1.87				60	78
Cutting Stock							
Printing		22.7	66				
Cut and Crease						813	09
Stripping	.933-4	.178+	120			391	60
Cellulose							
Auto Gluing		.562 .466+	11.24			477	24
Hand Gluing							
Wrapping or Packing		6.503				92	93
Inspection							
Total Quantity Cost				6451	58	1835	64
Total Preparatory Cost				580	40	764	48
Total Cost to Make				7031	98	2600	12
Selling & Commercial		45+8	(% + $)			1178	05
Material Forward						7031	98
Shipping 56 +		7.25+	260,287			220	54
Freight and Cartage		.40				241	15
Total Cost						11271	84
Profit		20%				2254	37
Total Selling Price						13526	21
Finished Stock Price							
Commission & Discount		4%				541	05
Total Selling Price						14067	26
Selling Price per M—Calculated						28	14
Selling Price per M—Quoted						30	60

EXHIBIT 4

STEWART BOX COMPANY
Income Statement
($000 omitted)

	December 1979		12 Months 1979	
	Actual	*Variance**	*Actual*	*Variance**
Board Mill:				
External sales	$ 52	$ 12	$ 344	$ 38
Transfers to carton factory	168	16	1,970	130
Total revenues	220	28	2,314	168
Cost of goods sold	169	(16)	1,831	(154)
Gross margin	51	12	483	14
Volume variance		15		34
Other variances		(13)		(14)
Selling and administrative expenses	30	(4)	374	(6)
Board mill profit	21	10	109	28
Carton Factory:				
Sales	666	22	7,968	248
Standard cost of goods sold	492	(18)	5,664	(130)
Gross margin	174	4	2,304	118
Manufacturing variances		16		40
Selling expenses	50	(5)	552	(12)
Administrative expenses	12	1	143	7
Carton factory profit	112	16	1,609	153
Company:				
Total factory and mill profits	133	26	1,718	181
Corporate expenses	52	2	457	18
Nonoperating income (loss)	(4)		(12)	2
Income before income tax	77	28	1,249	201
Income tax	38	(13)	617	(96)
Net income	$ 39	$ 15	$ 632	$ 105

* ( ) = unfavorable.

tant departures from plan, he discussed them with the manager responsible. Other reports were prepared primarily for the use of some other executive, and Mr. Stewart received only an information copy. He might or might not glance at these reports in a given month, but he was certain to do so if he suspected that trouble might be brewing in the area covered by the report.

Mr. Stewart also paid close attention to several *external* reports he received regularly from the industry trade association. They showed current economic trends, the probable effects of these trends on different segments of the paperboard carton industry, and sales orders, actual sales, production volume, and other related statistics for all members of the association.

EXHIBIT 5   Spending Report, Department 14 (two-color Meihle printing presses)

	December 1979		12 Months 1979	
	Actual	*Variance**	*Actual*	*Variance**
Labor—pressmen	$ 5,885	$(107)	$ 81,057	$ (647)
Labor—helpers	2,074	(46)	28,978	(235)
Press supplies	373	120	3,279	146
Repairs	1,472	(604)	8,562	120
Power	484	66	6,369	322
Other controllable overhead	242	52	3,444	461
Total controllable costs	10,530	(519)	131,689	167
Departmental fixed cost	2,426	—	29,112	—
Allocated costs	3,352	—	40,224	—
Total costs	$16,308	—	$201,025	—
Volume variance		(340)		1,012
Total variance		($859)		$ 1,179

* ( ) = unfavorable.

QUESTIONS

1. The following questions relate to Exhibit 4 and the December 1979 amounts:
   a. A transfer price was used in connection with *two* items. What are these two items?
   b. Assuming that inventory levels did not vary in December, what was the actual cost of goods manufactured in the carton factory?
   c. Why is the assumption in question *b* necessary to answer that question?
   d. What is the budgeted amount of corporate expenses?
   e. In December, was activity in the board mill above or below the standard volume?
2. The following questions relate to Exhibit 5 and the December amounts:
   a. What was the actual cost of labor—pressmen?
   b. What was the budgeted amount of total controllable cost?
   c. What amount of total controllable cost was applied to products?
   d. Why do no amounts appear in the spending variance column for departmental fixed costs and allocated costs?
3. As his assistant, write a memorandum calling Mr. Stewart's attention to matters you think he should note when he reads Exhibit 4.
4. Do the same with Exhibit 5.
5. What do you regard as the particularly strong points of the system described in this case? What are its weak points? Can you suggest ways of overcoming these weaknesses?

Part I

The Management Control Environment

In Chapter 1, management control was described as the process by which managers influence other members of the organization to implement the organization's strategies. This process relates to two somewhat different types of activities: (1) ongoing operations and (2) projects. The discussion of management control of projects (e.g., research and development projects, construction projects, production of motion pictures) is deferred to Chapter 17. In Part I and in Part II, we limit the discussion to the management control of ongoing operations.

We start with a discussion of the behavioral characteristics of individuals who work in organizations (Chapter 2). The next four chapters discuss responsibility centers, which are organization units that are central to the management control process. A responsibility center is any organization unit headed by a manager who is responsible for its activities.

Characteristics of a responsibility center that are relevant to management control are discussed in Chapter 3. All responsibility centers produce outputs (i.e., they do something), and all have inputs (i.e., they use resources). They can be classified on the basis of the measurement of inputs and outputs into one of four types: revenue centers, expense centers, profit centers, and investment centers.

In a *revenue center,* outputs are measured in monetary terms, but inputs are not measured in monetary terms. These responsibility centers usually are part of the marketing organization. They are discussed in Chapter 3.

In an *expense center,* the management control system measures inputs in monetary terms (i.e., as costs), but it does not measure outputs in monetary terms. Various types of expense centers are also discussed in Chapter 3.

In a *profit center,* the management control system measures both inputs and outputs in monetary terms; that is, inputs are measured as expenses and outputs as revenues. Profit is the difference between expenses and revenues. Profit centers are discussed in Chapter 4. Many profit centers transfer products (either goods or services) to other profit centers within the company. The price used in measuring the amount of products transferred is called a *transfer price*. Chapter 5 discusses transfer pricing.

In an *investment center*, the control system measures not only the inputs and outputs in monetary terms but also measures the investment that is employed in the responsibility center. Investment centers are discussed in Chapter 6. Chapter 6 also discusses some of the organizational considerations that are involved in deciding whether a responsibility center should, or should not, be treated as an investment center.

Chapter 7 describes the types of strategies that an organization may decide to adopt.

Chapter 2

Behavior in Organizations

The function of every organization is to attain its goals. In this chapter we first describe the typical goals in organizations, both profit-oriented and nonprofit. We then explain the concept of goal congruence, which is central to an understanding of control in organizations. Control is affected by informal factors, some of which are external to the organization and some are internal; these are described. Control is also attained by two types of formal devices. One consists of "rules," broadly defined; the other is a systematic way of planning and controlling. The next part of the chapter describes different types of organization structures that can be used to implement strategies. A discussion of the types of organization structures is essential, since the design of management control systems should fit the organization structure used. Finally, we describe the function of the controller in the management control process.

GOALS

Although we often refer to the goals of a corporation, a corporation as such does not have goals. The corporation is an artificial being with no mind or decision-making ability of its own. The goals are arrived at by the chief executive officer (CEO) of the corporation, with the advice of other members of senior management, and usually ratified by the board of directors. In many well-known corporations the goals originally set by the founder persist for generations.[1] In the formal management control system in a business, profit-

---

[1] For example, Henry Ford, Ford Motor Company: Alfred P. Sloan, General Motors; Thomas Watson, IBM; and George Eastman, Eastman Kodak.

ability usually is the most important goal, so we discuss it first. Profitability is by no means the only goal, however; we describe other goals in a following section.

Profitability

A principal goal of a business corporation is profitability. Specifically, this means earning a satisfactory profit at an acceptable level of risk. In the broadest and conceptually soundest sense, profitability is expressed by an equation that is the product of two ratios:

$$\frac{\text{Revenues} - \text{Expenses}}{\text{Revenues}} \times \frac{\text{Revenues}}{\text{Investment}} = \text{Return on investment}$$

An example is:

$$\frac{\$10,000 - \$9,500}{\$10,000} \times \frac{\$10,000}{\$4,000} = 12.5\%$$

The first ratio in this equation is the profit margin percentage:

$$(\$10,000 - \$9,500)/\$10,000 = 5\%$$

The second ratio is the investment turnover: $(10,000/\$4,000) = 2.5$ times.

The product of these two ratios yields the return on investment: $5\% \times 2.5$ times $= 12.5\%$. It can be found directly by dividing profit (i.e., revenue minus expenses) by investment; but this does not draw attention to the two principal components: profit percentage and investment turnover.

In the most basic form of this equation, "investment" is the shareholders' investment, which consists of funds from issuance of stock plus retained earnings. One of management's responsibilities is to arrive at the right balance between the two main sources of financing: debt and equity. The shareholders' investment (i.e., equity) is the amount of financing that was not obtained by debt—that is, by borrowing. However, for many purposes the source of financing is not relevant, and "investment" then is the total of debt capital and equity capital.

"Profitability" refers to profits in the long run, rather than in the current year or the current quarter; many current expenditures for advertising, research and development, and other items reduce current profits but add to long-run profits.

Some CEOs focus on only part of the equation. Jack Welch, CEO of General Electric Company, explicitly focused on revenue; he stated that General Electric should not be in any business in which its sales revenues were not the first or second largest of any company in that business. This does not imply that he neglected the other components of the equation; rather, the implication is that if the company is dominant in an industry, the other elements in the equation can be satisfactorily controlled.

Some other CEOs focus on revenues because they think size itself is a goal; this could lead to problems. If expenses are not satisfactorily low, the profit margin will not produce a satisfactory return on the shareholders' investment. Even if the profit margin is satisfactory, the organization will not earn a satisfactory return if the amount of investment is too high.

Some CEOs focus on profit, either as a money amount or as a percentage. This overlooks the fact that, if additional profits are obtained by a greater than proportional increase in investment, each dollar of investment has earned less than before.

"Maximizing shareholder value".   In the 1980s, the term *shareholder value* appeared frequently in the literature; it was said that the appropriate goal of a business corporation is to maximize shareholder value. Although the meaning of this term is not always clear from the context, presumably it refers to the market price of the corporation's stock. We believe that "satisfactory profit," rather than "maximizing shareholder value," is a better way of stating a corporation's goal. Put succinctly, a company could not maximize profits if it wanted to, and it would not want to if it could.[2] In 1957, Herbert Simon coined the term *satisficing* to describe the appropriate goal, a concept that was an important basis for his award of the Nobel prize for economics.[3] *Satisficing* is a better term than *maximizing* for three principal reasons.

First, "maximizing" implies that there is a way of finding the maximum amount that a company can earn. This is not the case. In deciding on one course of action rather than another, management does believe (with some qualifications) that the selected alternative will add more to profitability than the rejected alternatives. Management rarely discovers, however, all the alternatives that could have been considered and the effect on profitability of each. Profit maximization requires that marginal costs and a demand curve be calculated, and managers usually do not know what these are, especially the demand curve.[4] If maximization were the goal, managers would spend every working hour (and many sleepless nights) thinking about other alternatives for increasing profitability; life is too short to warrant such an effort.

Second, although optimizing shareholder value may be one goal, it is by no means the only goal in most organizations. Most managers want to behave ethically, and most feel an obligation to other stakeholders in the organization. We shall expand on this point in the next section.

---

[2] See Robert N. Anthony, "The Trouble with Profit Maximization," *Harvard Business Review,* November/December 1960, pp. 126–34.

[3] Although later than his original paper on this topic, a convenient source for reading about his analysis is Herbert A. Simon, *The New Science of Management Decision* (Englewood Cliffs, N.J.: Prentice Hall, 1977).

[4] Moreover, as Saari has demonstrated, economic models based on profit maximization behave erratically, with slight changes in their assumptions, so they have limited value in solving practical problems. Donald G. Saari, "Erratic Behavior of Economic Models," *Working Paper No. 225,* The Industrial Institute for Economic and Social Research, Stockholm, 1990.

Third, shareholder value is usually equated with the market value of the company's stock; but market value is not an accurate measure of what the shareholders' investment is actually worth, except at the moment at which the shares are quoted. Today's stock price results from the judgment of the *average* investor; but the average investor tends to think primarily about the company's prospects in the short run, whereas shareholders should want management to make decisions that benefit the corporation in the long run, even at the expense of short-run profitability. Moreover, the average investor is not privy to much of the information that management has as to the company's long-run prospects.

Of course, by rejecting the maximization concept, we do not mean to question the validity of certain obvious principles. A course of action that decreases expenses without affecting other elements in the equation is sound. So is a course of action that increases expenses with a greater than proportional increase in revenues (such as increased advertising expense in some cases). So is a course of action that increases profit without an increase in shareholder investment, or is one that increases profit with a less than proportional increase in shareholder investment (such as an investment in a cost-saving machine). These principles assume, in all cases, that the course of action is ethical and consistent with the corporation's other goals.

Risk.   An organization's pursuit of profitability is limited by management's willingness to take risks. The acceptable degree of risk taking varies with the personalities of individual managers. Nevertheless, there is an upper limit. In some organizations, there is an explicit statement to the effect that management's primary responsibility is to preserve the company's assets, and that the goal of profitability is subordinate to this. The calamitous bankruptcy of hundreds of savings and loan associations in the 1980s is traceable in large part to managements that made what appeared to be highly profitable loans without giving adequate recognition to their riskiness.

Other Goals

A survey by Posner and Schmidt of 900 American executives ranked their goals in the following order of importance: organizational effectiveness, high productivity, good organizational leadership, high morale, good organizational reputation, high organizational efficiency, *profit maximization,* organizational growth, organizational stability, value to local community, and service to the public.[5] Even with due allowance for the subjectivity of such a survey, the fact

---

[5] B. Z. Posner and W. H. Schmidt, "Values and the American Manager: An Update," *California Management Review,* Spring 1986, pp. 202–16.

that profit maximization was listed 7th of the 11 goals casts doubt on the validity of the profit maximization assumption. The same survey asked executives to rank the importance of various "stakeholders" in the corporation. Customers were ranked No. 1, followed by "myself," subordinates, employees as a whole, bosses, coworkers and colleagues, managers, technical and white-collar employees, founders of the company, craftsmen and skilled workers, *public stockholders,* and elected public officials and government bureaucrats. Again, with due allowance for subjectivity, the fact that public stockholders were ranked 11th out of 12 stakeholders casts doubt on the assumption that corporations operate solely, or even primarily, for the benefit of their shareholders.

Other studies show that (with some well-publicized exceptions) managements will not condone unethical behavior; that they forbid the payment of bribes, even though this would increase profitability; and that they support participation in community activities and contributions to educational and charitable organizations, even though these activities reduce profits.

Statement of Goals

Many businesses state their financial goals explicitly: a specified return on investment, a specified earnings per share. The following is an unusually specific example:

> **Example.**   Richard C. Ashley, President of Allied Chemical Company, says he has a personal "contract" with Edward L. Hennessey, Jr., CEO of Allied Corporation, to achieve three objectives by 1986: shift the current product mix away from a heavy emphasis on capital-intensive cyclical commodity chemicals, so that at least 25 percent of his pretax income comes from specialty chemicals; top the industry average for that year in both profit growth and market share; and make at least one significant acquisition.
>
> He has specific benchmarks to meet within that five-year span. . . . Specific bonuses have been attached to the achievement of each step, as well as to meeting the overall goal at the end of five years. "Hennessey sets very demanding but obtainable objectives, and he's there to help you reach them," says Ashley. "I'm much clearer about where the chemical company is going."[6]

The more typical set of financial goals is not time-specific—that is, the goals remain unchanged for relatively long periods. Often the change occurs when a new chief executive officer takes over. The nonfinancial goals typically are not stated in writing or, if stated, are in general terms.

---

[6] *Business Week,* January 11, 1982, pp. 126–27.

Nonprofit Organizations

By definition, nonprofit organizations do not have profitability as a goal. Their principal goal is to provide services: education and new knowledge for a college or university; treatment of patients for a hospital; and law enforcement, fire protection, roads, recreation, and other services for a municipality. Measuring the quality and quantity of these services is difficult, and this is why measuring the attainment of goals in a nonprofit organization is much less precise than similar measurements in a business.

Nonprofit organizations do have a *financial* goal, which corresponds to, but is different from, the goal of profitability in a business. Over a period, these organizations should do a little better than breaking even—that is, in an average year their revenues should be a little more than their expenses. They need to more than break even in order to (1) provide a cushion against unforeseen events (i.e., "rainy days") and (2) have a source of funds for such assets as additional working capital and certain fixed assets that cannot be financed by borrowing. If a nonprofit organization has a large profit, it is not providing the amount of services that those who contributed funds expect of it. If it has a succession of losses, it will go bankrupt, just like a business.

GOAL CONGRUENCE AND MOTIVATION

Senior management wants the organization to attain the organization's goals. However, the members of the organization have their personal goals, and these are not entirely consistent with the goals of the organization. The actions of individual members of the organization are directed toward achieving their personal goals. The central purpose of a management control system, therefore, is to assure, so far as is feasible, that *actions that it leads people to take in accordance with their perceived self-interest are also in the best interest of the organization.* This is the principle of *goal congruence.*

Perfect congruence between individual goals and organizational goals does not exist. One obvious reason is that individual participants usually want as much compensation as they can get; whereas, from the organization's viewpoint, there is an upper limit to salaries, beyond which profits would be adversely and unnecessarily affected. As a minimum, however, the management control system should not encourage individuals to act against the best interests of the organization. For example, if the system signals that the emphasis should be only on reducing costs, and if a manager responds by reducing costs at the expense of adequate quality or by reducing costs that he or she controls by causing a more than offsetting increase in costs in other parts of the organization, then the manager has been motivated, but in the wrong direction.

Two questions, therefore, are important in evaluating any management control practice:

1. What action does it motivate people to take in their perceived self-interest?
2. Is this action in the best interest of the organization?

Personal Needs

Personal goals can be expressed as needs. People join, and stay with, an organization because they believe that the organization will satisfy some of their needs. These needs can be so arranged in a hierarchy that, for most people, needs at the lowest level must be satisfied before needs at higher levels affect behavior.[7] At the lowest level are basic physical needs, such as the need for food and shelter. At the highest level is a feeling for power and achievement. Some of these needs are *material:* They can be satisfied by money earned on the job. Other needs are *psychological:* People need to have their abilities and achievements recognized, they need social acceptance as members of a group, they need to feel a sense of personal worth, they need to feel secure, they need the freedom to exercise discretion.

These personal needs may be either extrinsic or intrinsic. *Extrinsic needs* are satisfied by the actions of others. Examples are money received from the organization and praise received from a superior. *Intrinsic needs* are satisfied by the attitudes people have about themselves. Examples are a feeling of achievement, of competence, or of a clear conscience.

The relative importance of these needs varies with different persons, and their relative importance to a given individual varies at different times. For some people, earning a great deal of money is a dominant need; for others, monetary considerations are much less important. Some people attach much importance to the achievement need, and they tend to be the leaders of the organization.[8] The relative importance that individuals attach to their own needs is heavily influenced by the attitudes of their colleagues and of their superiors. A management control system should provide for the harmonization of personal goals with organization goals.[9]

Expectancy theory. Many psychologists discuss motivation in terms of an expectancy theory model. This theory states that the motivation to engage in a

---

[7] See Abraham H. Maslow, *Motivation and Personality* (New York: Harper & Row, 1970).

[8] McClelland argues that there is a relationship between the strength of the achievement motivation of the leaders of an organization and the success of that organization, and that a similar relationship helps to explain why certain countries have a rapid economic growth at certain times while others do not. See David McClelland, *The Achieving Society* (New York: Irvington Publishers, 1961); and David C. McClelland and David G. Winter, *Motivating Economic Achievement* (New York: Free Press, 1969).

[9] This paragraph implies, correctly, that people are selfish. "Selfish" should not be taken to mean the narrow sense of "greedy," however. Most people are motivated by the need for self-esteem, and this leads them to altruistic actions—that is, to actions that are, in fact, unselfish.

given behavior is determined by (1) a person's belief or "expectancy" about what outcomes are likely to result from that behavior and (2) the attractiveness that the person attaches to those outcomes, in terms of their ability to satisfy his or her need. For example, a person who has a high need for achievement and who is not a good player of card games probably will not join a bridge club whose members are skilled card players. However, another person, no better at playing bridge than the first, might be motivated to join the bridge club because of having a high need for social contacts. The first person has a low expectancy that playing bridge with the club's members will satisfy the need for achievement, while the second person feels there is a good chance that affiliating with the group will help satisfy the social need.

Incentives

The solution to the management problem of motivating people to behave in a way that furthers the goals of the organization relies on the relationship of organization incentives to personal expectations. Individuals are influenced both by positive and negative incentives. A positive incentive, or "reward," is an outcome that results in increased satisfaction of individual needs. A negative incentive, or "punishment," is an outcome that results in a decrease in the satisfaction of personal needs. Reward incentives are inducements to satisfy those needs that individuals cannot obtain without joining the organization. Organizations provide rewards to participants who perform in agreed-upon ways. Research on incentives tends to support the following:

1. Individuals tend to be more strongly motivated by the potential of earning rewards than by the fear of punishment, which suggests that management control systems should be reward-oriented.
2. A personal reward is situational. Monetary compensation is an important means of satisfying certain needs; but beyond a satisfaction level, the amount of compensation is not necessarily as important as nonmonetary rewards.
3. If senior management signals by its actions that it regards the management control system as important, operating managers will also so regard it. If senior management pays little attention to the system, operating managers are likely to pay little attention.
4. Individuals are highly motivated when they receive reports (feedback) about their performance. Without such feedback, people are unlikely to obtain a feeling of achievement or self-realization or to sense corrective actions that are needed to satisfy their needs.
5. The effectiveness of incentives diminishes rapidly as time elapses between an action and the reward for it. At lower levels in the organization, the

optimal frequency of feedback between the action and the feedback may be only hours; for senior management, it may be months.

6. Motivation is weakest when the person perceives an incentive as being either unattainable or too easily attainable. Motivation is strong when the objective can be obtained with some effort and when the individual regards its attainment as important in relation to personal needs.

7. The incentive provided by a budget or other statement of objective is strongest when managers participate actively with their superiors in the process of arriving at the budgeted amounts. Objectives, goals, or standards are likely to provide strong incentives only if the manager perceives them as fair and feels committed to attaining them. The commitment is strongest when it is a matter of public record—that is, when the manager has explicitly agreed that the budgeted amounts are attainable.

INFORMAL FACTORS THAT INFLUENCE CONTROL

The system of programs, budgets, and reports is a *formal* control system. Before discussing the formal system, we shall describe certain *informal* forces that affect the degree to which goal congruence is achieved in a given organization. Some are external to the organization; most are internal.

External Factors

External factors are norms of desirable behavior that exist in the society of which the organization is a part. They are often referred to as the "work ethic." They are manifest in employees' loyalty to the organization, their diligence, their spirit, and their pride in doing a good job (as contrasted with merely putting in time.) Some of these attitudes are local; they are specific to the city or region in which the organization does its work. In encouraging companies to locate in their city or state, chambers of commerce or other promotional organizations often claim that their locality has a loyal, diligent work force. Others are industry-specific; the railroad industry has norms that differ from those in the airline industry. Still others are national; some countries have a reputation for excellent work ethics. Currently, for example, Japan, Korea, Hong Kong, and other East Asian countries have a high reputation on this dimension.

> **Example.**　Many large Japanese companies go to great lengths to instill loyalty. They have company "pep" songs. They support baseball teams that compete regionally and nationally. The teams are accompanied by cheer leaders (with cheers specific to the company) and marching bands. These activities are similar to those that instill loyalty in students at an American college or university. Employees dress in the company uniform.

Internal Factors

Culture. The most important internal factor is the organizations' culture, or climate. Organization culture refers to the set of common beliefs, attitudes, relationships, and assumptions that are explicitly or implicitly accepted and used throughout the organizations.[10] Similarly, as defined by Kenneth R. Andrews, the term *climate* is used to designate the quality of the internal environment that conditions, in turn, the quality of cooperation, the development of individuals, the extent of members' dedication or commitment to organizational purpose, and the efficiency with which that purpose is translated into results. Climate is the atmosphere in which individuals help, judge, reward, constrain, and find out about each other. It influences morale—the attitude of the individual toward his or her work and his or her environment.[11]

The best-seller *In Search of Excellence* is primarily an attempt to describe the culture in several companies that were judged to be well managed. The failure of that book to provide an accurate analysis (as evidenced by the fact that several of these companies ran into serious trouble shortly after the book was published) illustrates the difficulty of explaining the influence of culture in a given situation.[12]

Cultural norms are extremely important. They explain why each of two organizations may have an excellent formal management control system, but why one has much better actual control than the other. An organization's culture is rarely stated in writing, and attempts to do so almost always result in platitudes.

Example. In the 1980s, a young, rapidly growing microcomputer manufacturing company attempted to prepare a statement of its "corporate culture." One paragraph in the statement read, "Management by personal communication is part of our way of life. We encourage open, direct, person-to-person communication as part of our daily routine." Notwithstanding the "open communication" buzzword, the statement itself was developed by senior management in strict secrecy, and it was not communicated to the organization until after it had been adopted. Management's deeds were the exact opposite of its words.[13]

A company's culture exists unchanged for many years. Certain practices are "rituals"; they are carried on almost automatically because "this is the way

---

[10] For a discussion of the concept of corporate culture, see T. E. Deal and A. A. Kennedy, "Culture: A New Look through Old Lenses." *Journal of Applied Behavioral Science* (1983), pp. 498–506.

[11] Kenneth R. Andrews, *The Concept of Corporate Strategy* (Homewood, Ill.: Dow Jones-Irwin, 1980).

[12] Thomas J. Peters and Robert Waterman, *In Search of Excellence* (New York: Harper & Row, 1982). An excellent analysis is Daniel Carroll, "A Disappointing Search for Excellence," *Harvard Business Review* (November–December 1983), pp. 78–88.

[13] Reported by Peter C. Reynolds in "Corporate Culture on the Rocks," *Across the Board*, October 1986, p. 53.

things are done here.'' Others are ''taboos''; ''we just don't do that here,'' although no one remembers why. Culture is influenced strongly by the personality and policies of the chief executive officer (and by those of lower-level managers with respect to the part of the organization that they manage). If the organization is unionized, the rules and norms accepted by the union has an important influence on the organization's culture. Attempts to change practices meet resistance; and, the larger and more mature the organization, the greater the resistance is.[14]

Management behavior.   The internal factor that probably has the strongest impact on management control is the attitude of a manager's superior toward control. Usually, the attitude of subordinates reflects in a general way their perception of the attitude of their superiors, modified, of course, by the subordinate's own attitude. The attitude ultimately stems from the attitude of the chief executive officer. This is another way of saying ''an institution is the lengthened shadow of a man.''[15]

Managers come in all shapes and sizes. Some are charismatic and outgoing; others are less ebullient. Some spend much time looking and talking to people (called ''management by walking around''); others rely more heavily on written reports. We know of no way of generalizing about the ''ideal'' manager. The student may form conclusions about the differences between effective and ineffective managers from the cases in this book.

> **Example.**   When he [Reginald Jones] was tapped to run General Electric, it was a large, multi-industry company that performed fairly well in a number of mature markets. The company, however, was experiencing a bit of midlife crisis: a price-fixing scandal that sent several executives to jail, coupled with GE's sound defeat in, and subsequent retreat from, the mainframe computer business. Jones provided the salve for those wounds. He instituted formal strategy planning and built up one of the first strategic planning units of a major corporation. Jones was psychologically suited for such an operation: dignified, refined, very bright, able to delegate enormous amounts of authority. GE moved into new areas, but carefully, after much thought, and efficiently. Business was good.
>
> When he retired, Jones and the GE board had the wisdom to select not a man just like him but one as different as night from day: Jack Welch. Welch nearly eliminated the planning group, shifting planning to line managers. He cut the work force by 20 percent, closed dozens of plants. Not surprisingly, Welch became as well known for his extroverted personality as the introverted Jones had been for his. ''He demands action immediately,'' said one top GE executive.[16]

---

[14] Perhaps stimulated by the contrast between Japanese and American workers with respect to their willingness to accept change, there has been much research on this topic. See, for example, Richard E. Walton, ''Planned Changes to Improve Organization Effectiveness,'' *Technology in Society* II no.4 (1980), pp. 391–412.

[15] Ralph Waldo Emerson, *Self Reliance* (1841).

[16] Robert E. Lamb, ''CEOs for This Season,'' *Across the Board*, April 1987.

The informal organization. The lines on an organization chart depict the formal organization—that is, the formal authority and responsibility relationships of the several managers. The organization chart may show, for example, that the production manager of Division A reports only to the general manager. Actually the production manager communicates with several other people in the organization: other managers, support units, and staff people at headquarters—and simply friends and acquaintances. In extreme situations, the production manager may pay inadequate attention to messages received from the general manager. This tends to happen when the production manager is evaluated more on production efficiency than on overall performance. The relationships that constitute the informal organization are important in understanding the realities of the management control process.

Perception and communication. In working toward the goals of the organization, operating managers must know what these goals are and what actions they are supposed to take in order to achieve them. They receive information through various channels about what they are supposed to do. In part this information is conveyed by budgets and other formal documents; in part it is conveyed by conversations and other informal means. This information often is not a clear and unambiguous message about what senior management wants done. An organization is complicated, and the actions that should be taken by one part of it to accomplish the overall goals cannot be stated with absolute clarity, even under the best of circumstances.

Moreover, the messages received through various information channels may conflict with one another, or managers may interpret them in different ways. For example, the budget mechanism may convey the impression that managers are supposed to make this year's profits as high as possible, whereas senior management actually doesn't want operating managers to skimp on maintenance or employee training; such actions, although increasing current profits, would reduce future profitability. As pointed out in Chapter 1, operating managers' perceptions of what they are supposed to do are vastly less clear cut than the message that the furnace receives from the thermostat.

Many erroneous perceptions arise from *functional fixation*—that is, the tendency of people to interpret the meaning of words and phrases according to accustomed definitions, even though these definitions have become obsolete or are not applicable to the current situation. Managers, because of their background in another company or from what they have learned in school, may assume that a term has a different meaning from that intended. Greater emphasis in management control reports on a standard terminology is one way of reducing the impact of functional fixation.

Cooperation and conflict. The lines connecting the boxes on an organization chart imply that the way organizational goals are attained is that senior management makes a decision and communicates that decision down through the organizational hierarchy to managers at lower levels of the organization, who then implement it. This ignores the personal goals of individuals, and it is not the way an organization actually functions.

In fact, each operating manager reacts to instructions from senior management in accordance with how those instructions affect his or her personal needs. Also, usually more than one manager is involved in carrying out senior management plans, so the interactions among managers also affect how well the plans are implemented. For example, the manager of the maintenance department may be assigned responsibility for ensuring that the maintenance needs of the production departments are satisfied, but the needs of one department may be slighted if there is friction between the maintenance manager and the manager of that department. More important, many actions that a manager may want to take in order to achieve personal goals may have an adverse effect on other managers and on overall profitability. For example, managers may argue about which of them is to obtain the use of limited production capacity or other scarce resources, or about potential customers that several managers want to solicit, unless the management control system provides instructions in advance. For these and many other reasons, conflicts exist within organizations, and management control systems should help to minimize them.[17]

An organization attempts to maintain an appropriate balance between the forces that create conflict and those that create cooperation. Some conflict is desirable. Conflict results in part from the competition among participants for promotion or other forms of need satisfaction; such competition is, within limits, healthy. A certain amount of cooperation is also obviously essential; but, if undue emphasis is placed on developing cooperative attitudes, the most able participants will be denied the opportunity of using their talents fully. The management control system must help to maintain the appropriate balance between conflict and cooperation within the organization.

THE FORMAL CONTROL SYSTEM

The informal factors discussed above have a great influence on the effectiveness of management control in an organization. The other influence is, of course, the formal systems. These systems can be classified into two types: (1) the management control system, which is our main emphasis in this book and, therefore, not discussed further at this point; and (2) rules, which are described briefly below.

---

[17] For an explanation of the role of organization culture on cooperation and conflict see J. Van Maanen and S. R. Barley, "Occupational Communities: Culture and Control in Organizations," in *Research in Organizational Behavior*, vol. 6, ed. B. M. Staw and L. L. Cummings (Greenwich, Conn.: JAI Press, 1984).

Rules

We use the word *rules* as shorthand to stand for all types of formal instructions and controls. They include standing instructions, practices, job descriptions, standard operating procedures, manuals, and codes of ethics. They also include physical controls of all types. Unlike the directives or guidance implicit in budget amounts, which change from month to month, these rules are in force indefinitely—that is, they exist until they are modified. Typically, rules are changed infrequently. They relate to matters that range from the most trivial (e.g., paper clips will be issued only on the basis of a signed requisition) to the most important (e.g., capital expenditures of over $5 million must be approved by the board of directors).[18]

Types of rules. Some rules are guides—that is, organization members are permitted, and indeed expected, to depart from them, either under specified circumstances or if in the person's judgment a departure is in the best interests of the organization. To illustrate, there may be a rule stating the criteria for extending credit to customers, but the credit manager may OK credit to a customer who currently does not meet these criteria if the customer has been especially valuable and may become so again. Departures from the rules may or may not require the approval of higher authority.

Some rules should never be broken. A rule that prohibits payment of bribes and a rule that an airline pilot should never take off without permission of the air traffic controller are examples. Some rules are prohibitions against unethical, illegal, or other undesirable actions. Others are positive requirements that certain actions be taken (e.g., fire drills at prescribed intervals). The distinction between prohibitions and positive requirements may not be apparent, and managers should be made aware of the distinction.

Some of the specific types of rules are listed below.

Physical controls. Security guards, locked storerooms, vaults, computer passwords, television surveillance, and other physical controls are part of the control structure. Most of them are associated with task control, rather than with management control.

Manuals. Much judgment is required in deciding which rules should be written and put in a manual; which should be guidelines, rather than fixed rules; what discretion should be allowed; and a variety of other matters. The literature does not contain anything but obvious guidance on these matters. Bureaucratic organizations have more detailed manuals than other organizations; large organizations have more than small ones; centralized organizations have more than decentralized ones; and organizations with geographically dispersed units performing similar functions (such as fast-food restaurant chains) have more rules than single-site organizations.

---

[18] For a thorough treatment of this topic, see Kenneth A. Merchant, *Control in Business Organizations* (Marshfield, Mass.: Pitman, 1985).

With the passage of time, some rules become outdated. Manuals and other sets of rules, therefore, need to be reexamined periodically to ensure that they are consistent with the desires of the current senior management. In the pressure of day-to-day activities, the need for reexamination often is overlooked; if so, the manuals are likely to contain rules for situations that no longer exist, or for practices that are obsolete. If these rules are permitted to remain, managers are likely to have an unfavorable impression of the whole manual.

System safeguards. Various safeguards are built into the information processing system to ensure that the information flowing through the system is accurate and to prevent (or at least minimize) fraud and defalcation. They include cross-checks of totals with details, required signatures or other evidence that a transaction has been authorized, separation of duties, frequent counts of cash and other portable assets, and a number of other rules that are described in texts on auditing. They also include checks of the system that are made by the internal auditors and the external auditors.

Task control systems. In Chapter 1 we defined task control as the process of assuring that specific tasks are carried out efficiently and effectively. Many of these tasks are controlled by rules. There are rules for procurement, production scheduling, inventory control, quality control, payroll, cost accounting, cash management, accounts receivable, accounts payable, and many others. Task control systems are outside the scope of this book.

If a task is automated, the automated system itself provides the control. Human beings are involved only if the system malfunctions or if a situation arises that cannot be handled electronically. These systems are rapidly eliminating the need for most human control in many, often complex, operations.

> **Example.** An entire steel mill may be controlled by electronic devices. Each piece of equipment is controlled by a computer that instructs the equipment to carry out prescribed tasks. The computer senses the environment (e.g., it finds out the temperature of a steel ingot). If the environment is not at the desired state, the computer initiates action to bring it to this state. If the variation cannot be corrected by that computer, the need for corrective action is referred to a computer that controls all the computers in one section of the mill. If necessary, this computer refers the problem to a coordinating computer for the mill as a whole.[19]

Formal Control Process

Exhibit 2–1 is a sketch of the formal management control process. Its foundation is the organization's goals and its strategies for attaining these goals. A strategic plan is prepared in order to implement these strategies; all available

---

[19] For this and other striking examples, see F. Warren McFarlan and William J. Bruns, Jr., "Information Technology Puts Power in Control Systems," *Harvard Business Review,* September–October 1987, pp. 89–94.

EXHIBIT 2–1 The Formal Control Process

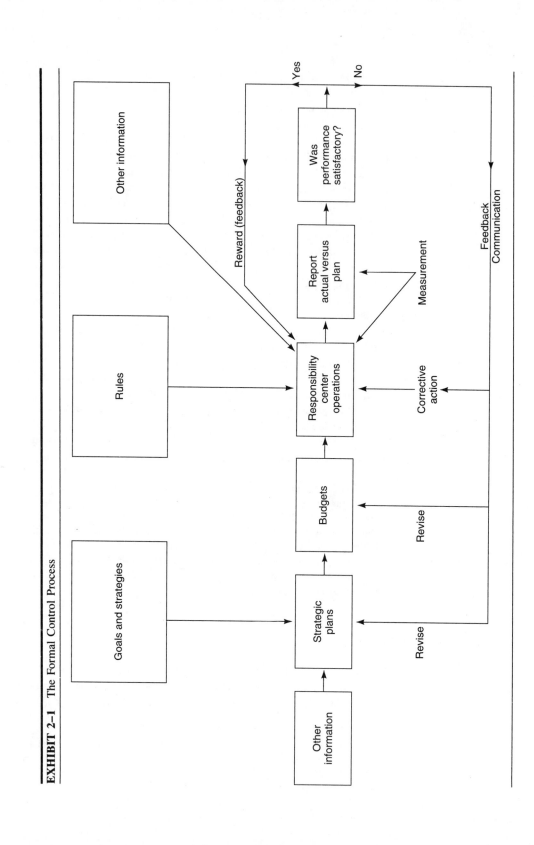

information is used in making this plan. The strategic plan is converted to an annual budget that focuses on the planned revenues and expenses for individual responsibility centers. Responsibility centers also are guided by a large number of rules. They operate, and the results of their operation are measured and reported. Actual results are compared with the plan, to answer the question "was performance satisfactory?" If it was satisfactory, there is feedback to the responsibility center in the form of praise or other reward. If performance was not satisfactory, there is feedback leading to corrective action in the responsibility center and possible revision of the plan. (Like most such diagrams, this sketch is valid only as a generalization. As we shall show in later chapters, the process in practice is less straightforward than this sketch indicates.)

Exhibit 2–2 relates the process to the chapters in which each step is discussed.

TYPES OF ORGANIZATIONS

The firm's strategy has an important influence on the type of organization structure that the firm adopts.[20] The type of organization structure, in turn, has an influence on the design of management control systems. Although organizations come in all sizes and shapes, their structures can be grouped into three general categories: (1) a functional structure, in which each manager is responsible for a specified function, such as production or marketing; (2) a business unit structure, in which each business unit manager is responsible for most of the activities of a business unit, which is a semi-independent part of the company; and (3) a matrix structure, in which functional units have dual responsibilities. Abbreviated organization charts for each type are shown in Exhibit 2–3. The discussion here is limited to functional and business unit organizations; matrix organizations are discussed in Chapter 17.

Business units have functional structures within them—that is, a business unit has a production function and a marketing function—so the contrast between the two types of organizations can be stated more explicitly as between companies that are organized into business units and those that are not.

Functional Organizations

The rationale for the functional form of organization is the same as that developed by Frederick Taylor and others for specialization of labor in large-scale production. It involves the notion of a specialized manager who brings specialized knowledge to bear on decisions related to the function. This contrasts

---

[20] Alfred D. Chandler, Jr., *Strategy and Structure* (Cambridge, Mass,: MIT Press, 1962).

EXHIBIT 2–2   Management Control System

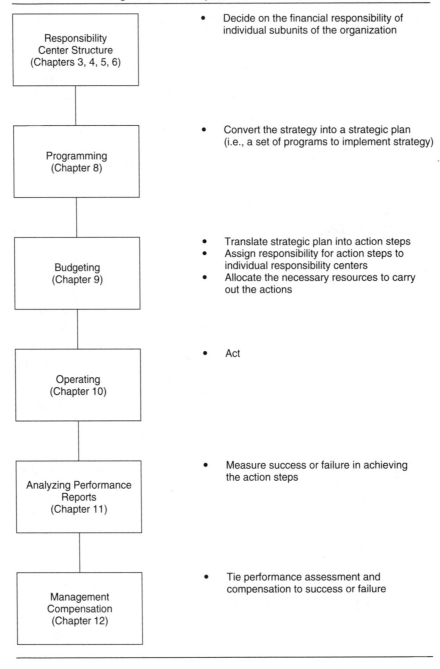

EXHIBIT 2–3 Types of Organization

Functional Organization

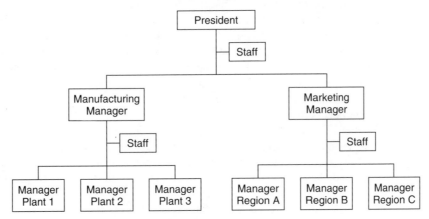

Business Unit Organization

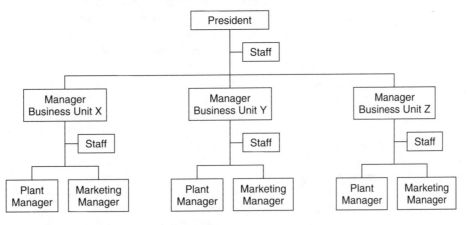

Matrix Organization

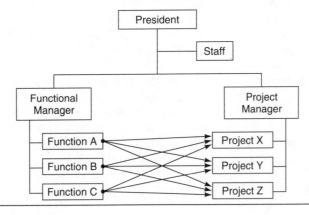

with the general-purpose manager, who cannot possibly have as much knowledge about a given function as a specialist in that function. A skilled marketing manager should make better marketing decisions and a skilled production manager should make better production decisions than the decisions made by a manager who is responsible for both marketing and production. Moreover, the skilled specialist should be able to supervise workers in the same function better than the generalist; similarly, skilled higher-level managers should be able to provide better supervision of lower-level managers in the same or similar function.

In terms of the need satisfaction discussed earlier in this chapter, a functional organization tends to bring together people with similar skills and interests, and these groups are more congenial and more likely to recognize an individual's special skills, thus gratifying the need for esteem.

A disadvantage of the functional organization is that there is no unambiguous way of determining the effectiveness of the separate functional managers because each function contributes jointly to the final output of the organization. When there is a marketing manager and a production manager, there is no way of measuring what fraction of the profit was contributed by each. Similarly, at lower levels in the organization, there is no way of determining how much of the profit was earned by each production department, by the product engineering department, and by the sales office, respectively.

Another disadvantage of the functional organization is that there is no good way of planning the work of the separate functions at lower levels in the organization. In a functional organization, plans for the organization as a whole must be made at the very top because these plans necessarily involve coordination of all the functions that contribute to the final output. Plans for the marketing department must take into account the ability of the production department to produce goods with the specifications and in the quantities that it judges customers will buy, and plans of the production department must take into account the ability of the marketing department to sell goods with the specifications and in the quantities that it is prepared to produce.

Similarly, if the organization consists of managers in one function who report to higher-level managers of the same function, who, in turn, report to still higher-level managers of that function, then a dispute between different functional managers can be resolved only at the very top of the organization, even though it originates with managers at a low level. The marketing department may want to satisfy a customer's need for a certain quantity of product even if it involves overtime work by the manufacturing department; but the manufacturing department may be unwilling to incur the additional costs associated with overtime. Such a dispute can theoretically be resolved only at headquarters, even though it may involve only a branch sales office and one small department of a manufacturing plant. Taking the issue up through several levels in the organization and then communicating the decision down to the level where the dispute originated can be time consuming and frustrating. (As a practical matter, the parties involved may settle such disputes informally, even though this involves crossing organizational lines of authority, but there is no guarantee that this will happen.)

Business Unit Organizations

The business unit form of organization is designed to solve these problems. A business unit (also called a "division") is responsible for all the functions involved in producing and marketing a specified product line. Business unit managers act almost as if their units were separate companies. They are responsible for planning and coordinating the work of the separate functions, and they resolve disputes that arise between these functions. They ensure that the plans of the marketing department are consistent with production capabilities. Their performance is measured by the profitability of the business unit, and this is a satisfactory measure because profit incorporates the activities of both marketing and production.

Business unit managers do not have complete authority. Headquarters reserves the right to make certain decisions. As a minimum, headquarters is responsible for obtaining funds for the company as a whole, and it allocates funds to business units according to its judgment on where the available funds can be put to the best use. Headquarters also approves the business unit budgets, judges the performance of business unit managers, sets their compensation, and, if the situation warrants, removes them. Headquarters establishes the "charter" of each business unit—that is, the product lines it is permitted to make and sell or the geographical territory in which it can operate, or both, and, occasionally, the customers that it may sell to.

Headquarters also establishes companywide policies. Depending on the wishes of the chief executive officer, these may be few and general, or they may be set forth in several thick volumes of manuals. Headquarters staff offices may assist the business units in production and marketing activities and in specialized areas, such as accounting, legal, public relations, controller, treasury functions, and training. These headquarters functions are valuable. If this were not the case, the business units would be better off being separate companies.

An advantage of the business unit form of organization is that it provides a training ground in general management. The business unit manager should also have the entrepreneurial spirit that characterizes the CEO of an independent company.

Another advantage is that the business unit, being closer to the market for its products than the headquarters organization, may make sounder decisions than headquarters can make and can react to new threats or opportunities more quickly.

Offsetting these advantages is the possibility that each business unit staff may duplicate some work that in a functional organization is done at headquarters. The business unit manager is presumably a generalist, but his or her subordinates are functional specialists, and they must deal with many of the same problems that specialists in other business units and at headquarters address. The layers of business unit staff may be more expensive than the value gained by divisionalization. Moreover, skilled specialists in certain functions are in short supply, and business units may be unable to attract qualified persons.

Also, the disputes between functional specialists in a functional organization may be replaced by disputes between business units in a business unit organization. These may involve one business unit infringing on the charter of another unit. There may also be disputes between business unit staffs and headquarters staffs.

Although the possibility of holding several managers responsible for pieces of the company's overall profit performance is attractive, these disadvantages may outweigh the benefits of business unit structure. Business units are profit centers or investment centers, and further discussion of the merits and disadvantages of business unit structure in various circumstances is deferred to Chapters 4 and 6, which deal with these responsibility centers.

Implications for Systems Design

If ease of control were the only criterion, companies would be organized into business units whenever it were feasible to do so, because in a business unit organization each unit manager is held responsible for the profitability of the unit's product line and he or she presumably plans, coordinates, and controls the elements that affect its profitability. Control is not the only criterion, however. A functional organization may be more efficient because larger functional units give economies of scale. A business unit organization requires a somewhat broader type of manager than the specialist who manages a function; competent general managers may be difficult to find.

Because of the apparently clear-cut nature of the assignment of profit responsibility in a business unit organization, designers of management control systems sometimes recommend such an organization without giving appropriate weight to the other considerations involved in organization design.[21] Finally, the systems designer must fit the system to the organization, not the other way around. In other words, although the control implications of various organization structures should be discussed with senior management, once management has decided that a given structure is best, all things considered, then the system designer must take that structure as given. Enthusiasts for some control technique may overlook this essential point.

---

[21] For an excellent discussion of the complex factors that must be considered in making a basic change in organization structure, see Alfred D. Chandler, Jr., *Strategy and Structure* (Cambridge, Mass.: MIT Press, 1962).

The point also is important in other contexts. For example, many advertising agencies follow the practice of shifting account supervisors from one account to another at fairly frequent intervals and so bring a fresh point of view to the various advertising programs. This practice increases the difficulty of measuring the performance of an account supervisor, because the fruits of an advertising campaign may require a long time to ripen. Nevertheless, the systems designer should not insist that the rotation policy be abandoned simply because to do so would make performance measurement easier.

FUNCTIONS OF THE CONTROLLER

We shall refer to the person who is responsible for designing and operating the management control system as the *controller*. Actually, in many organizations, the title of this person is chief financial officer, and, in a few, chief information officer.[22]

Controller Responsibilities

Conceptually, the controller should be responsible for the design and operation of all systems for processing recurring, quantitative information that relates to resources, personnel, materials, services, and money. In most companies, the controller is directly responsible for the design and operation of programming, budgeting, and accounting systems. Collectively, these are called "financial systems," because most of the information flowing through them is stated in monetary terms. The functional manager has primary responsibility for nonfinancial systems that relate to a certain function, such as the personnel records of the human resources department or the materials control and production scheduling systems in a factory. The controller's responsibility for such systems is to ensure that systems throughout the organization are efficient and compatible with one another, that one system provides information for another, that unnecessary duplication is eliminated, and that common terminology is used in all systems.

---

[22] The chief financial officer typically is responsible both for the controllership function (as described here) and also for the treasury function. The title came into common use in the 1970s. At that time, the Controllers Institute became the Financial Executives Institute. The controller and the treasurer report to the chief financial officer. Because we do not discuss the treasurer's function, we use the narrower term, *controller*.

The spelling "comptroller" is also used. This spelling originated with an error made in the 18th century in translating from French to English, but the erroneous spelling has become embedded in dozens of federal and state statutes and in the bylaws of many companies and still persists. "Comptroller" is pronounced the same as "controller"; not *compt'*roller.

In addition to the design and operation of various types of information and control systems, the controller usually performs the following functions:

- Prepares financial statements and financial reports (including tax returns) to shareholders and other external parties.
- Prepares and analyzes reports on financial performance and assists managers by interpreting these reports, by analyzing program and budget proposals, and by consolidating the plans of various segments into an overall annual budget.[23]
- Supervises internal audit and accounting control procedures to ensure the validity of information, establishes adequate safeguards against theft and defalcation, and performs operational audits.
- Develops personnel in the controller organization and participates in the education of management personnel in matters relating to the controller function.

Relation to line organization. The controllership function is a staff function. Although the controller usually is responsible for the *design and operation* of systems in which control information is collected and reported, the *use* of this information in actual control is the responsibility of line management. In addition to responsibility for processing information, the controller also may be responsible for developing and analyzing control measurements, and for making recommendations for action to management. Moreover, the controller may police adherence to limitations on spending laid down by the chief executive, control the integrity of the accounting system, and be responsible for safeguarding assets from theft and fraud.

The controller does not make or enforce management decisions, however. The responsibility for control runs from the chief executive officer down through the line organization, which uses information provided by the controller; the controller is a staff officer.

The controller does make some decisions. In general, these are decisions that implement policies decided on by line management. For example, a member of the controller organization often decides on the propriety of expenses listed on a travel voucher; line managers usually prefer not to get involved in discussions of whether the traveler spent too much on meals, or whether the airplane trip should have been made in tourist class rather than first class.

The controller plays an important role in the preparation of strategic plans and budgets. Also, the controller organization typically analyzes performance

---

[23] A survey of chief financial officers of multinational corporations sponsored by KPMG Peat Marwick and Business International found that they have an increasing influence over operations and work more closely with the chief executive officer. KPMG Peat Marwick Main & Co., *The Changing Role of the Modern CFO* (New York, 1989).

reports, assures that they are accurate, and calls the line manager's attention to items that may indicate the need for action. In these activities, the controller acts almost like a line manager. The difference is that the controller's decision can be overruled by the line manager to whom the subordinate manager is responsible.

The Business Unit Controller

Many companies are organized into business units, each headed by a manager who has considerable autonomy, and each with a controller. Business unit controllers inevitably have a divided loyalty. On the one hand, they owe some allegiance to the corporate controller, who is presumably responsible for the overall operation of the control system. On the other hand, they owe allegiance to their business unit managers, since controllers are responsible for furnishing staff assistance to their managers. The two possible types of relationships are diagramed in Exhibit 2–4. In some companies, the business unit controller reports to the business unit manager, and has what is called a "dotted line" relationship with the corporate controller. This means that the corporate controller is responsible for specifying the ground rules within which the control system must operate, and he or she participates in decisions relating to hiring, training, transferring, compensation, promotion, and firing business unit controllers; nevertheless, the business unit manager is the controller's immediate boss. General Electric Company uses this approach, as described by the following comment by Bernard R. Doyle, manager of Corporate accounting:

> Our controllership structure is based on a strong functional reporting line. The business unit controllers report directly to the general managers of their business units, but they have a functional or "dotted line" responsibility to the chief financial officer of the company. The glue that holds it together is that the people in those business unit functional jobs can be appointed only from a slate of candidates the corporate chief financial officer first approves, and he has the unqualified right to remove these people. But, as importantly, these people are the chief financial officers of their business units. They are team players.[24]

In other companies, business unit controllers report directly to the corporate controller—that is, the corporate controller is their boss, as indicated by a "solid line" on the organization chart. ITT uses this approach.[25]

---

[24] Jonathan B. Schiff, "Interview with Bernard Doyle of General Electric," *Controllers Quarterly,* 1990.

[25] Vijay Sathe, *Controllership in Divisionalized Firms: Structure, Evaluation, and Development* (New York: American Management Association, 1978), pp. 20–21.

EXHIBIT 2–4 Alternative Controllership Organizations

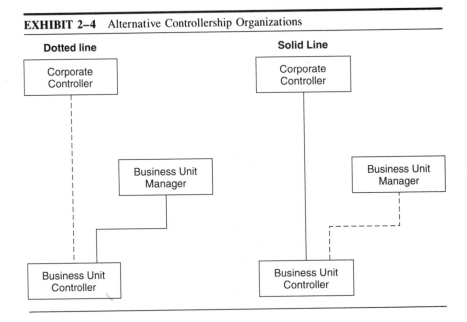

There are problems with each of these relationships. If the business unit controller works primarily for the business unit manager, there is the possibility that he or she will not reveal "fat" in the proposed budget nor provide completely objective reports on performance. On the other hand, if the business unit controller works primarily for the corporate controller, the business unit manager may treat him or her as a "spy from the front office," rather than as a trusted aide.

In companies in which the business unit controller's primary loyalty is to the business unit manager, it is expected that business unit controllers will not condone or participate in the transmission of misleading information or the concealment of unfavorable information; their overall ethical responsibilities should not countenance such practices.

Example. In a talk to new business unit controllers, the chief executive officer of a large multinational company said: "As controller, you report to the business unit manager. The business unit manager has complete responsibility for the unit. However, in rare cases something may happen that means your loyalty to the unit manager is finished and your loyalty to [the company] takes over. I want a clear line of command, but everything has its limits; and, in that case, you cannot excuse yourself. I want your loyalty in general to be to the business unit manager; but, if he has five girl friends and drinks too much, you must tell us at headquarters. This is your higher priority of loyalty."

SUMMARY

Every organization has one or more goals. In a profit-oriented business, profitability is an important goal. The goals of nonprofit organizations are to provide services; their financial goal is to do a little more than break even.

Senior management wants the organization to attain these goals. Members of the organization have personal goals, which are expressed as needs, and these are not in all respects consistent with the organization's goals. The central purpose of the management control system is to assure, so far as is feasible, that actions it leads people to take in their perceived self-interest are also in the best interest of the organization. To do this, the system provides rewards for performance consistent with the organization's goals and penalties for unsatisfactory performance.

Informal factors have an important influence on control. The most important of these is an organization's culture or climate. There is an informal organization alongside the formal organization. An individual's perception and communication of information may be imperfect. Management must ensure a proper balance between the need for cooperation and the need for competition, both of which are desirable within limits. Management behavior has an important influence on control.

In addition to the management control system, there are rules, guidelines, and procedures that also are of assistance in the control process.

Companies can choose from three basic organization structures: functional, business unit, and matrix. The specific choice of organizational form has an influence on the design of the management control system.

The controller is responsible for the design and operation of the control system; but, as a staff officer, he or she does not make management decisions. In companies organized into business units, the proper relationship between the business unit controller and the corporate controller is debatable.

SUGGESTED ADDITIONAL READINGS

Atkinson, John W. *Personality, Motivation, and Action*. New York: Praeger Publishers, 1983.

Barnard, Chester I. *The Functions of the Executive*. Cambridge, Mass.: Harvard University Press, 1938.

Bruns, William J., Jr., and Don T. DeCoster. *Accounting and Its Behavioral Implications*. New York: McGraw-Hill, 1969.

Chamberlain, Neil W. *The Firm: Micro-Economic Planning and Action.* New York: McGraw-Hill, 1962.

Chandler, Alfred D., Jr. *The Dynamics of Industrial Capitalism.* Cambridge, Mass.: Harvard University Press: 1990.

————. *The Visible Hand.* Cambridge, Mass.: Harvard University Press, 1978.

Cyert, Richard M., and James G. March. *A Behavioral Theory of the Firm.* Englewood Cliffs, N.J.: Prentice Hall, 1963.

Dalton, Gene W., and Paul R. Lawrence, eds. *Motivation and Control in Organizations.* Homewood, Ill.: Richard D. Irwin, 1971.

Deal, T. E., and A. A. Kennedy. *Corporate Cultures: The Rites and Rituals of Corporate Life.* Reading, Mass.: Addison-Wesley Publishing, 1982.

Govindarajan, Vijay, and Joseph G. San Miguel. "Contingent Relationship between the Controller and Internal Audit Functions in Large Organizations." *Accounting, Organizations and Society* IX, no. 2, 1984, pp. 179–88.

Keating, Patrick J. and Stephen P. Jablonsky. *Changing Roles of Financial Management.* New York: Financial Executives Research Foundation, 1990.

Kotter, John P. *The General Managers.* New York: Free Press, 1982.

Lawrence, Paul R., and Jay W. Lorsch. *Organization and Environment.* Homewood, Ill.: Richard D. Irwin, 1969.

March, James G., and Herbert A. Simon. *Organizations.* New York: John Wiley & Sons, 1958.

Merchant, Kenneth A. *Control in Business Organizations.* Marshfield, Mass.: Pitman, 1985.

Miner, John B. *Theories of Organization Behavior.* Hinsdale, Ill.: Dryden Press, 1980.

Mintzberg, H. *The Nature of Managerial Work.* New York: Harper & Row, 1973.

Reitz, H. J. *Behavior in Organizations.* 3rd ed. Homewood, Ill.: Richard D. Irwin, 1987.

Sathe, Vijay. *Controller Involvement in Management.* Englewood Cliffs, N.J.: Prentice Hall, 1982.

Schlesinger, L. A.; R. G. Eccles; and J. J. Gabarro. *Managing Behavior in Organizations.* New York: McGraw-Hill, 1983.

Simon, Herbert A. *The New Science of Management Decision.* Rev. ed. Englewood Cliffs, N.J.: Prentice Hall, 1977.

Staw, Barry M. *Psychological Foundations of Organization Behavior.* Glenview, Ill.: Scott, Foresman, 1983.

Staw, Barry M., and L. L. Cummings, eds. *Work in Organizations.* Greenwich, Conn.: JAI Press, 1990.

Treynor, John L. "The Financial Objective in the Widely Held Corporation." *Financial Analysts Journal,* March–April 1981, pp. 68–71.

Vancil, Richard. *Decentralization: Managerial Ambiguity by Design.* Homewood, Ill.: Dow Jones-Irwin, 1979.

Case 2-1

Rendell Company*

Fred Bevins, controller of the Rendell Company, was concerned about the organizational status of his divisional controllers. In 1985 and for many years previously, the divisional controllers reported to the general managers of their divisions. Although Mr. Bevins knew this to be the general practice in many other divisionally organized companies, he was not entirely satisfied with it. His interest in making a change was stimulated by a description of organizational responsibilities given him by the controller of the Martex Corporation.

The Rendell Company had seven operating divisions; the smallest had $50 million in annual sales and the largest over $500 million. Each division was responsible for both the manufacturing and the marketing of a distinct product line. Some parts and components were transferred between divisions, but the volume of such interdivisional business was not large.

The company had been in business and profitable for over 50 years. In the late 1970s, although it continued to make profits, its rate of growth slowed considerably. James Hodgkin, later the president, was hired in 1980 by the directors because of their concern about this situation. His first position was controller. He became executive vice president in 1983 and president in 1984. Mr. Bevins joined the company as assistant controller in 1981, when he was 33 years old. He became controller in 1983.

In 1980, the corporate control organization was primarily responsible for (1) financial accounting, (2) internal auditing, and (3) analysis of capital budgeting requests. A budgetary control system was in existence, but the reports prepared under this system were submitted to the top management group directly by the operating divisions, with little analysis by the corporate control organization.

Mr. Hodgkin, as controller, thought it essential that the corporate control organization play a more active role in the process of establishing budgets and analyzing performance. He personally took an active role in reviewing budgets and studying divisional performance reports and hired several young analysts to assist him. Mr. Bevins continued to move in the same direction after his promotion to controller. By 1985, the corporate organization was beginning to be well enough staffed so that it could, and did, give careful attention to the information submitted by the divisions.

Divisional controllers reported directly to the divisional general managers, but the corporate controller always was consulted prior to the appointment of a new division controller, and he also was consulted in connection with salary increases for divisional controllers. The corporate controller specified the accounting system to which the divisions were expected to conform and the general procedures they were to follow in connection with budgeting and reporting performance. It was clearly understood, however, that budgets and performance reports coming from a division were the responsibility of that division's

* This case was prepared by R. N. Anthony, Harvard Business School.
Copyright © by the President and Fellows of Harvard College.
Harvard Business School case 109-033.

general manager, with the divisional controller acting as his staff assistant in the preparation of these documents. For example, the divisional general manager personally discussed his budget with top management prior to its approval, and, although the divisional controller usually was present at these meetings to give information on technical points, his role was strictly that of a staff man.

Most of the divisional controllers had worked for Rendell for 10 years or more. Usually, they worked up through various positions in the controller organization, either at headquarters, in their division, or both. Two of the divisional controllers were in their early 30s, however, and had only a few years' experience in the headquarters controller organization before being made, first, divisional assistant controller and then divisional controller.

Mr. Bevins foresaw increasing difficulties with this relationship as the corporation introduced more modern control techniques. For one thing, he thought the existing relationship between himself and the divisional controllers was not so close that he could urge the development and use of new techniques as rapidly as he wished. More important, he thought that he was not getting adequate information about what was actually happening in the divisions. The divisional controller's primary loyalty was to his division manager, and it was unreasonable to expect that he would give Mr. Bevins frank, unbiased reports. For example, Mr. Bevins was quite sure that some fat was hidden in the divisional expense budgets, and that the divisional controllers had a pretty good idea where it was. In short, he thought he would get a much better idea of what was going on in the divisions if reports on divisional activities came directly from controllers working for him, rather than for the divisional manager.

Mr. Bevins was therefore especially interested in the controller organization at the Martex Company as he learned about it from E. F. Ingraham, the Martex controller, when he visited that company.

Until his visit to Martex, Mr. Bevins had not discussed the organization problem with anyone. Shortly thereafter, he gave William Harrigan, his assistant controller, a memorandum describing his visit (see the appendix) and asked for Mr. Harrigan's reaction. Mr. Harrigan had been with Rendell for 25 years and had been a divisional controller before going to headquarters in 1982. Mr. Bevins respected his knowledge of the company and his opinion on organizational matters. Mr. Harrigan was accustomed to speaking frankly with Mr. Bevins. The gist of his comments follows:

I don't think the Martex plan would work with us; in fact, I am not even sure it works at Martex in the way suggested by the job descriptions and organizations charts.

Before coming to headquarters, I had five years' experience as a divisional controller. When I took the job, I was told by the corporate controller and by my general manager that my function was to help the general manager every way I could. This is the way I operated. My people got together a lot of the information that was helpful in preparing the divisional budget, but the final product represented the thinking and decisions of my general manager, and he was the person who sold it to top management. I always went with him to the budget meetings, and he often asked me to explain some of the figures. When the monthly reports were prepared, I usually went over them, looking for danger signals, and then took them in to the general manager. He might agree with me, or he might spot other things that needed looking into. In either case, he usually was the one to put the heat on the operating organization, not me.

We did have some problems. The worst, and this happened several times a year, was when someone from the corporate controller's office would telephone and ask questions such as, "Do you think your division could get along all right if we cut $X out of the advertising budget?" Or, "Do you really believe that the cost savings estimate on this equipment is realistic?" Usually, I was in complete agreement with the data in question and defended them as best I could. Once in a while, however, I might privately disagree with the "official" figures, but I tried not to say so.

Questions of this sort really should be asked of the general manager, not of me. I realize that the head office people probably didn't think the question was important enough to warrant bothering the general manager, and in many cases they were right. The line is a fine one.

The business of the division controller's being an "unbiased source of information" sounds fine when you word it that way, but another way to say it is that he is a front office spy, and that doesn't sound so good. It would indeed make our life easier if we could count on the divisional controllers to give us the real lowdown on what is going on. But if this is to be their position, then we can't expect that the general manager will continue to treat his controller as a trusted assistant. Either the general manager will find somebody else to take over this work unofficially, or it won't get done.

I think we are better off the way we are. Sure, the budgets will have some fat in them, and not all the bad situations will be highlighted in the operating reports, and this makes our job more difficult. But I'd rather have this than the alternative. If we used the Martex method (or, rather, what they claim is their method), we can be sure that the divisional controller will no longer be a member of the management team. They'll isolate him as much as they can, and the control function in the division will suffer.

QUESTIONS

1. What is the organizational philosophy of Martex with respect to the controller function? What do you think of it? Should Rendell adopt this philosophy?
2. To whom should the divisional controllers report in the Rendell Company? Why?
3. What should be the relationship between the corporate controller and the divisional controllers? What steps would you take to establish this relationship on a sound footing?
4. Would you recommend any major changes in the basic responsibilities of either the corporate controller or the divisional controller?

Appendix
Notes on Martex Controller Organization

Mr. Ingraham, the corporate controller, reports directly to the president and has reporting to him all division controllers and other accounting, data processing, and analysis groups. The Martex Company's descriptions of responsibility and organization charts are included herein (Exhibits 1, 2, 3, and 4) and indicate the structure and function of the organization.

EXHIBIT 1 Positon Description from the Martex Management Guidebook

Controller

The trend of modern business management is to change the basic concept of the controller's position from that of an administrative function concerned largely with accounting detail to that of an important position in management as it relates to the control of costs and the profitable operation of the business as a whole.

The more our business becomes diversified with operations scattered throughout the United States, the greater is the need for an officer to whom the president delegates authority with respect to those factors affecting costs and profits in the same manner as he may delegate authority to others in strong staff positions.

In our vertical type of organization there is a great need for an appointed officer whose responsibility it is to establish budgetary standards of operations and objective percent of profit on sales targets for each of the operating divisions and domestic subsidiaries. He shall also establish budgetary standards of operation for staff functions in line with divisional and overall company profit objectives. When the standard of operations or profit target is not attained, the controller has the right and the responsibility within his delegated authority to question the failure and recommend changes to accomplish the desired result.

The controller shall work with the various divisions of the company through divisional controllers assigned to each major operating division and staff function. It is not intended that the controller take the initiative away from the division managers, since the responsibility for efficient operations and profits is assumed by the managers. However, the controller and his staff should have the right and the responsibility to expect certain operating results from the division head; and when a difference of opinion occurs as to the reasonableness of the demand for results, the matter should then be referred by either party to the president.

Along with the foregoing, the following responsibilities are an essential part of the position and apply to the corporation and its subsidiaries:

1. The installation and supervision of all accounting records.
2. The preparation, supervision, and interpretation of all divisional and product profit and loss statements, operating statements, and cost reports, including reports of costs of production, research, distribution, and administration.
3. The supervision of taking and costing of all physical inventories.
4. The preparation and interpretation of all operating statistics and reports, including interpretation of charts and graphs, for use by management committees and the board of directors.
5. The preparation, as budget director, in conjunction with staff officers and heads of divisions and subsidiaries, of an annual budget covering all operations for submission to the president prior to the beginning of the fiscal year.
6. The initiation, preparation, and issuance of standard practice regulations and the coordination of systems, including clerical and office methods relating to all operating accounting procedures.
7. Membership of the controller or his designated representative in all division and subsidiary management committees.

He shall be responsible for the selection, training, development and promotion of qualified personnel for his organization and their compensation within established company policy. He shall submit to the president an organization plan for accomplishing desired objectives.

The controller may delegate to members of his organization certain of his responsibilities, but in so doing he does not relinquish his overall responsibility or accountability for results.

Treasurer and Assistant Treasurers

Subject to the rules and regulations of the Finance Committee, the treasurer is the chief financial officer and generally his functions include control of corporate funds and attending to the financial affairs of the corporation

---

EXHIBIT 1   (*continued*)

---

and its domestic and foreign subsidiaries wherever located. More specifically the duties and responsibilities are as follows:

Banking: He shall have custody of and be responsible for all money and securities and shall deposit in the name of the corporation in such depositories as are approved by the president all funds coming into his possession for the company account.

Credits and collections: He shall have supervision over all cashiers, cash receipts, and collection records and accounts receivable ledgers. He shall initiate and approve all credit policies and procedures.

Disbursements: He shall authorize disbursements of any kind by signature on checks. This includes direct supervision over accounts payable and payroll departments and indirect supervision over all receiving departments for the purpose of checking on the accuracy of invoices presented for payment. He shall maintain adequate records of authorized appropriations and also determine that all financial transactions covered by minutes of management and executive committees and the board of directors are properly executed and recorded.

General financial reports: He shall prepare and supervise all general accounting records. He shall prepare and interpret all general financial statements, including the preparation of the quarterly and annual reports for mailing to stockholders. This also includes the preparation and approval of the regulations on standard practices required to assure compliance with orders or regulations issued by duly constituted governmental agencies and stock exchanges.

He shall supervise the continuous audit (including internal controls) of all accounts and records and shall supervise the audit and procedures of Certified Public Accountants.

Taxes: He shall supervise the preparation and filing of all tax returns and shall have supervision of all matters relating to taxes and shall refer to the general counsel all such matters requiring interpretation of tax laws and regulations.

Insurance property records: He shall supervise the purchase and placing of insurance of any kind including the insurance required in connection with employee benefits. He shall be responsible for recommending adequate coverage for all ascertainable risks and shall maintain such records as to avoid any possibility that various hazards are not being properly insured. He shall maintain adequate property records and valuations for insurance and other purposes and, if necessary, employ appraisal experts to assist in determining such valuations and records.

Loans: He shall approve all loans and advances made to employees within limits prescribed by the Executive Committee.

Investments: As funds are available beyond normal requirements, he shall recommend suitable investments to the Finance Committee. He shall have custody of securities so acquired and shall use the safekeeping facilities of the banks for that purpose. As securities are added or removed from such vaults or facilities, he shall be accompanied by an authorized officer of the corporation.

Office management: He will be responsible for the coordination of all office management functions throughout the company and its domestic subsidiaries.

Financial planning: He shall initiate and prepare current and long-range cash forecasts, particularly as such forecasts are needed for financing programs to meet anticipated cash requirements for future growth and expansion. He shall arrange to meet sinking fund requirements for all outstanding debenture bonds and preferred stock and shall anticipate such requirements whenever possible.

He shall have such other powers and shall perform such other duties as may be assigned to him by the board of directors and the president.

The treasurer shall be responsible for the selection, training, development, and promotion of qualified personnel for his organization and their compensation within established company policy. It is expected that since he will have to delegate many of the duties and responsibilities enumerated above, he shall confer with and submit to the president an organization plan and chart.

EXHIBIT 1 *(concluded)*

The treasurer may delegate to members of his organization certain of his responsibilities together with appropriate authority for fulfillment; however, in so doing he does not relinquish his overall responsibility or accountability for results.

The treasurer is a member of the Finance, Retirement, and Inventory Review Committees.

The controller's organization is charged with the responsibility of establishing cost and profit standards in the corporation and of taking appropriate action to see that these standards are attained. It reviews all research projects and assigns names and numbers to them in order to coordinate research activities in the various divisions and their central research. The organization also handles all matters involving cost and profit estimates.

The present size of divisional controllers' staffs ranges from 3 to 22. Division controllers are not involved in preparing division profit and loss statements; these are prepared by a separate group for all divisions and the corporation.

Line-Staff Relationships

A division manager has no staff of his own, not even a personal assistant. He receives staff assistance from two sources.

First, he has some people assigned to him from the general staff—typically, a controller, an engineer, and a purchasing agent.

All division management and all the corporate staff are located in the corporate headquarters building. However, the "assigned staff" are located physically with their staff colleagues; for example, a divisional controller and his assistants are located in the controller's section of the building, not near his divisional manager's office.

Second, the division can call on the central staff to the extent that the manager wishes. The divisions are charged for these services on the basis of service rendered. The cental staff units are listed in the General Staff Services box of Exhibit 2.

Division Manager-Controller Relationships

The success of the Martex controller organization and its relations with divisional managers appears to be largely the result of managers and controllers having grown up with the arrangement and accepting it long before they arrived at their managerial positions.

Some additional factors that appear to contribute to their successful relationship are the following:

1. A uniform and centralized accounting system.
2. Predetermined financial objectives for each division.
   a. Growth in dollar sales.
   b. A specified rate of profit as a percent of sales.
3. Profit sharing by managers and controllers.

Accounting System

The controller's division has complete control of the accounting system. It determines how and what accounts will be kept. The controller's division has developed an accounting system that is the same for all divisions. Mr. Ingraham pointed out that no division had a system perfectly tailored to its needs, but he believes that the disadvantages to the divisions were more than offset by having a system uniform over all divisions and understood by all concerned. Mr. Ingraham indicated it was likely that, if Martex divisions were free to establish their own accounting systems, every division would have a different one within two years, and interpretation by corporate management would be difficult, if possible at all.

EXHIBIT 2   Organization Chart, Division A, January 1, 1985

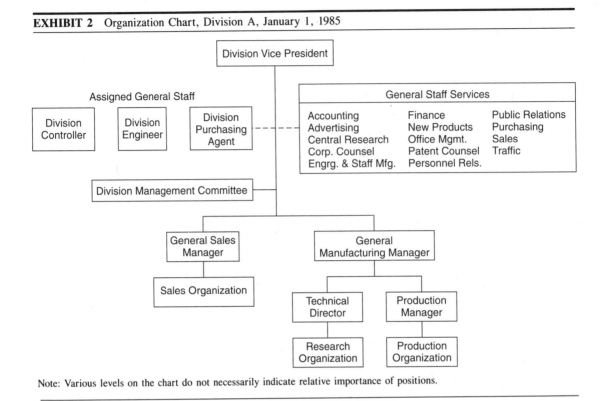

Note: Various levels on the chart do not necessarily indicate relative importance of positions.

The accounting system appears to provide a common basis for all divisional financial reports and analyses, and it aids in maintaining the bond of confidence between division managers and controllers.

Division Objectives

The corporation has established two financial objectives for each division. These are (a) growth in dollar sales, (b) a specified rate of profit as a percent of sales.

These objectives are determined in advance by recommendations of the controller's division with the advice and counsel of divisional managers. The objectives are long range in nature; the target profit rate has been changed only three times since 1965.

The particular percentage of sales selected as the target profit rate is based on several factors, among which are (1) the patentability of products, (2) a desired rate of return on investment, (3) the industry's margin of profit, and (4) the industry's rate of return on investment. These factors and others determine the profit rate finally selected.

Within limits, attainment of these financial objectives represents the primary task required of division general managers by corporate management.

Profit Sharing

Divisional managers receive about 75 percent of their total compensation from profit sharing and stock options. Divisional controllers receive

EXHIBIT 3 Organization Chart of Controller's Division, January 1, 1985

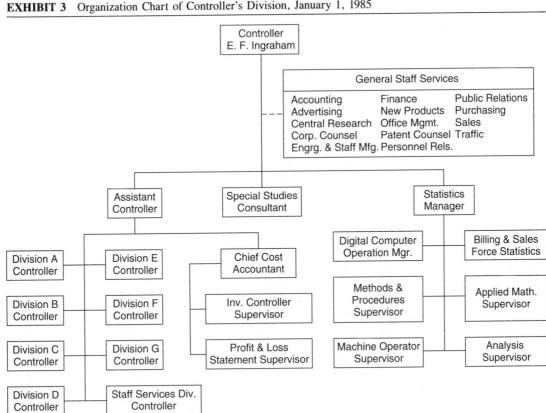

about 25 percent of their compensation from profit sharing—half from a share in divisional profits and the other half from corporate profits.

Division Managers' View of the System

Mr. Ingraham indicated that divisional managers like to have divisional controllers report to the corporate controller because (1) it gives them an unbiased partner armed with relevant information, (2) the controller is in a better position to do the analysis needed for decision making, and (3) when cost reports are issued there is little or no argument about them among affected parties.

EXHIBIT 4 Organization Chart of Treasurer's Division, January 1, 1985

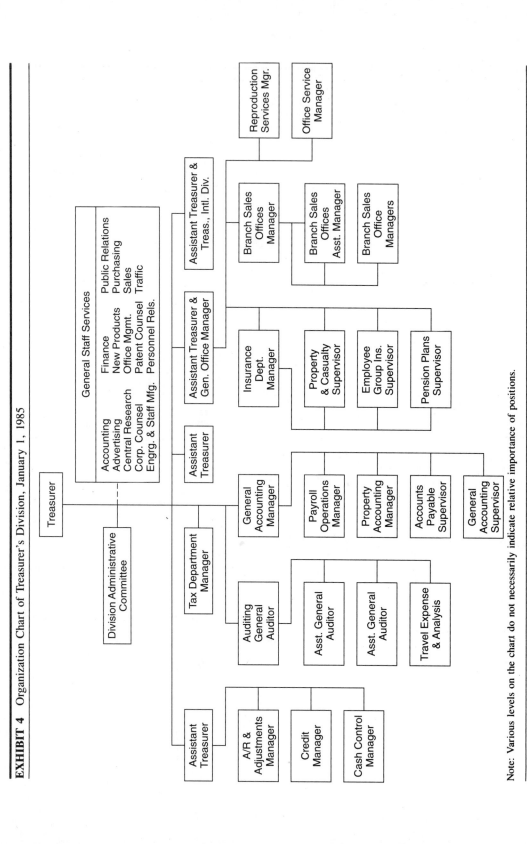

Note: Various levels on the chart do not necessarily indicate relative importance of positions.

Case 2-2

Cummins Engine Company*

In November 1974, Jim Henderson, 40, executive vice president and chief operating officer of Cummins Engine Company, faced a difficult inventory situation. Although marketing was projecting continued high demand for the company's product—diesel engines—into the foreseeable future, Henderson's other sources, and his analysis of industry and economic trends, gave him little cause for optimism. Anticipating a sharp downturn in early 1975, he viewed the company's rising inventory levels, now approaching 80 days' supply, with growing concern. In addition, there was a major discrepancy between the materials management records and the financial accounting records on inventory levels. No one knew where the missing inventory was physically located. As the discrepancy approached the inventory levels of a typical Cummins engine plant, it became dubbed "the phantom plant."

The ballooning inventories and the phantom plant were particularly alarming because recent new plant start-ups and acquisitions had already caused the debt-to-capital ratio to climb to nearly 50 percent, well above the historical Cummins average of about 35 percent. The added strain from inventories on working capital threatened to push the ratio above 50 percent for the first time in the company's history, and bankers were beginning to express concern about the company's leverage. Continued growth in sales would be difficult to sustain if inventories were not brought back in line.

Company History

Cummins Engine Company, incorporated in 1919, had its headquarters in Columbus, Indiana. From modest beginnings as a machining shop, the company had become a major industrial firm by 1974, with some 20,000 employees worldwide, net sales of $802 million, and after-tax profit of $24 million. The company's growth occurred in roughly three major phases: survival (1919–1933), take-off (1934–1945), and post-war boom (1946–1969).

The company was founded by Clessie Cummins, with the financial backing of William G. Irwin, banker and industrialist. Cummins was Mr. Irwin's chauffeur and had earlier started building engines in the family garage. Operations began in a single 15,000-square-foot factory with less than 20 employees. From the start there were many technical difficulties, but Clessie Cummins was not easily discouraged. With his persistence and the continued financial support of Mr. Irwin, the company was able to sustain losses during its first 17 years while it learned how to make a successful truck diesel engine.

Several key developments marked the take-off period (1934–1945). In 1934, Mr. Irwin's nephew, J. Irwin Miller, recently graduated from Yale and Oxford, joined the company as general manager. Miller assumed full leadershp of the company almost immediately and steered it through much of its period of rapid growth. Another key development was the establishment of a

* This case was abridged with permission from Harvard Business School Case 182–264, written under the direction of Professor Richard F. Vancil.
Copyright © by the President and Fellows of Harvard College.

strong network of independent regional distribution and service centers to attend to the ongoing needs of customers. This network became the cornerstone of Cummins's competitive success in the following years.

The company became profitable for the first time in 1936. In 1937, Irwin Miller suggested that Cummins's workers organize to improve cooperation between management and labor, and in 1938 they chose to do so. The Cummins labor force opted for an independent local union, rather than joining the United Auto Workers which had sought to organize them. This critical event set the stage for several decades of constructive relations between labor and management, in spite of occasional layoffs during slack periods.

In 1940, Mr. Irwin publicly stated that Cummins did not wish to grow, but rather would avoid the problems of a big engine works with peaks of production and periods of shutdown. At the time, the company employed between 700 and 800 people. The entry of the United States into the Second World War put an end to this slow-growth strategy. By 1945, the company had more than 1,700 employees. In 1947, Cummins Engine Company became publicly owned. Clessie Cummins sold most of his common shares and the Irwins made some of their holdings available to the public. Even then, the Irwin family continued to own about 75 percent of the company's common stock.

After the war, the company continued to experience remarkable sales growth, mainly from the production of diesel truck engines. The expansion was spurred by the conversion of an increasing number of truck fleets from gasoline to diesel engines—what came to be called the "dieselization of the U.S. trucking fleet." At the same time, opportunities opened up in overseas markets as a result of the use of many diesel trucks abroad during the war. Many of these vehicles remained overseas and required servicing and parts. Thus the Cummins dealer network was expanded. In 1956, an engine assembly plant was established in Scotland, the first of what was later to become

a sizable group of plants, both wholly owned and joint ventures, in various parts of the world.

Cummins maintained its competitive posture during the postwar boom period by undertaking extensive cost-saving and efficiency campaigns and by continuing to emphasize engineering and design improvements based on engine performance feedback from users through the dealer and service network.

Evolution of Cummins's Leadership

The dominant figures in the early years were Clessie Cummins and Mr. Irwin. From his arrival on the scene in 1934, however, Irwin Miller was the central figure in the company. Miller grew up a small-town boy. He had contracted polio as a child, but recovered fully, growing to an imposing six feet, two inches tall. His education in the liberal arts and his family background made him a man of broad-ranging interests. He was a lover of the arts and an accomplished musician. Miller was active in community and national political affairs, and was also a philanthropist and civic leader. Under his guidance, Cummins set aside 5 percent of its earnings for charitable causes.

Although Miller joined the company as a member of the Irwin family, he clearly intended to run the business. Despite his liberal arts background, he became well versed in the technical side of the business. Miller emphasized the importance of hiring competent people, and of community involvement. He set a strong ethical tone for the organization, and focused his attention on rooting out any "bureaucratic" behavior. Miller commanded the respect of all in the company. A hallmark of his leadership style was the ability to ask the tough but important questions.

As a strong, visionary leader, Miller found he worked best with a strong operating head, and he discovered an ideal one in Don Tull. When Tull became foreman in 1935, he began a lengthy management career that took him to the company's presidency in 1960. Tull was a contrast to Miller in many ways. With only a high school education, Tull was a self-taught businessman.

Through years of intimate exposure, he became familiar with all the details of the company's operations. He also excelled in customer relations. The truck fleet owners and the people in the distributor network trusted Tull, and he represented them well in the company. Tull managed by staying on top of everything personally. He knew most employees by name, having interviewed almost everyone hired in the '40s and '50s. He was close to the union and well known in Columbus and the surrounding communities. Where Miller was eclectic and visionary, Tull was practical and focused on the immediate. While Miller planned for the future, Tull managed in the present.

Together, Miller and Tull had a profound influence on the Cummins organization during a period spanning 30 years, from the late '30s to the late '60s. During this time the company was closely directed from the top. Emphasis was placed on finding managers who were strong individual performers and who stayed on top of all the details of their parts of the business. Because the company was largely under one roof, costly and cumbersome management systems were not required. Tull himself was constantly present on the plant floor, checking the work flow, quality control, employee morale, inventory levels, and shipment schedules. Since the company emphasized extraordinary service to its customers—particularly the original equipment manufacturers (OEMs)—which was an important competitive edge over other suppliers, a good manager in top management's eyes was one who could always find a way to expedite a special customer request.

During the periodic business cycle downturns which hit the truck manufacturing industry and its component suppliers especially hard, Tull did not hesitate to batten down the hatches. He would let part of the work force go, cut off all capital spending, and cancel orders to suppliers. Tull and the controller could be found on such occasions out on the receiving dock turning away deliveries. If a purchasing agent was reluctant to cancel an order for fear of jeopardizing relations with a supplier, Tull would do so himself.

In the mid-'60s, as the company grew and the facilities expanded, Miller realized the need to build a management team. He began to turn top management responsibilities over to younger, more professionally trained managers. Henry Schacht was appointed vice president for finance, and Jim Henderson vice president for personnel and management development. Both had MBAs from the Harvard Business School. When Tull stepped up as chairman of the Executive Committee in 1969, Schacht became president and Henderson executive vice president for operations. Both were then 35 years old.

Schacht grew up in Pennsylvania and studied at Yale before going to Harvard. He was viewed within the organization as bright, self-confident, and able to grasp things quickly. His role soon emerged as that of planner, risk assessor, external deal maker, and company spokesman. He became heavily involved with OEMs and customers in the trucking industry. Prior to his assumption of the presidency, Schacht had held no line position within the Columbus operations.

By way of contrast, Henderson was a local Indiana boy who went to Princeton and joined the Navy before going for his MBA at Harvard. He was seen in the organization as equally bright and quick on his feet, but more people-oriented than Schacht. Henderson believed in organizational development, and was interested in fostering the growth of the company's human resources. As such, he tended to give his subordinates greater responsibility and accept the risk that some failures would occur in the process of enhancing their growth. Henderson's role emerged as head of operations for the engine business. He tended to spend a lot of time and attention on details, frequently visiting the shop floor. He would talk at length with workers on such visits. One notable feature of Henderson's job was that the two executives who had preceded him in it had been less than successful.

Schacht and Henderson were only two of a large number of young managers whom Miller attracted into the company in the '60s from various

EXHIBIT 1 Personal Data on Key Managers (as of December 31, 1974)

Name	Title and Position	Age	Education	Years with Company — Total	Years with Company — Current Job	Career Path in Company
J. Irwin Miller	Chairman of the Board of Directors	65	BA, Yale MA, Oxford	40	23	President, Executive VP, VP, and General Manager
Richard B. Stoner	Vice Chairman of the Board of Directors	54	BS, Indiana Univ. JD, Harvard	27	5	Executive VP and Corporate General Manager, Executive VP Operations, VP Operations, VP Manufacturing, VP Personnel, Other Administrative and Executive positions
E. Don Tull	Board Member and Chairman of the Executive Committee	68	AMP, Harvard LLD, Franklin	38	15	President, Executive VP, VP Personnel, Works Manager
Henry B. Schacht	President and Chief Executive Officer	40	BA, Yale MBA, Harvard	10	5	Group VP International and Subsidiaries, VP and Manager Central Area (International), VP Finance
James A. Henderson,	Executive VP for Operations and Chief Operating Officer	40	AB, Princeton MBA, Harvard	10	4	VP Operations, VP Personnel, VP Management Development, Assistant to the Chairman
John T. Hackett	Executive VP for Finance and Chief Financial Officer	42	BS, Indiana Univ. MBA, Indiana Univ. PhD, Ohio State	9	4	VP Finance, Director Long-Range Planning
C. R. Boll	Executive Vice President	54	BS(EE), Purdue	28	7	Executive VP Corporate Marketing, Executive VP International, Executive VP Marketing, VP Sales, General Sales Manager, Manager Engine Sales, Asst. Regional Manager, Sales Engineer
W. D. Schwab	Vice President Research and Engineering	54	BS(ME), Rose PolyTech	27	2	VP Product Development, Executive Direct Product Development, Administrator Research Laboratory, Technical Specialist, Design Engineer
T. W. Head	Vice President Management Systems	48	BS(ME), Purdue	10	2	VP Program Management, VP Research and Engineering, VP En-

Name	Position	Education	Age			Prior Positions
						...gineering, Executive Director Engineering, Director Product Improvement, Project Manager
P. W. Schutz	Vice President North American Automotive	BS(ME), Illinois Institute of Technology	44	9	3	VP Market Development, Executive Director Product Development, Director Technical Planning, Technical Advisor, Engineering Department
L. P. Brewer	Vice President U.S. Manufacturing	BS (Ind. Eng.), Iowa State; MBA (Business) Univ. of Detroit	43	4	3	VP Columbus Manufacturing
H. E. O'Shaughnessey	VP Parts, Advertising, and Promotion	BA (Ec.), Wittenberg; JD, Indiana Univ.	54	8	3	VP Parts, Sales—Special Products, VP Advertising and Field Sales
M. C. Dietrich	Executive VP and General Manager Industrial Group	BA (Ec.), Yale; MBA, Harvard	52	12	3	VP Marketing, VP International Marketing, VP Corporate Development and Planning, VP Special Sales
T. A. Lyon	Vice President International	BS(EE), Univ. of Arkansas; MBA, Chicago	47	10	1	VP and Managing Director UK/Europe, VP International Manufacturing, VP UK Manufacturing, Controller
W. P. Snyder	Vice President Columbus	AB (Soc.), Notre Dame	39	18	2	Plant Manager Columbus Engine Plant, VP and General Manager Atlas, Director of Production Control, Director of Customer Services, Assistant to the President, Manager Material Planning and Scheduling

business schools and from other companies. Schacht and Henderson continued this policy of bringing trained managers into entry-level jobs, but the bulk of the senior operating management and staff positions were filled by older managers with proven track records. Exhibit 1 provides summary background information on 14 key managers in the company.

Evolution of Cummins's Strategy

The thrust of Cummins's early business strategy focused on the technical development of a working diesel engine and the discovery of the most promising market for its application—trucking. In a second stage the company added a marketing dimension. It built a dealer and service network through which it could communicate with engine users. This allowed Cummins to make engineering and design decisions that were responsive to user needs, and to pursue a "pull" marketing strategy with the OEMs. Later, the company entered the international diesel engine market. It then diversified into allied industries. Anticipating a slackening in growth of engine sales to about 6 percent a year, the company undertook diversification into carefully selected high-growth, unrelated businesses in the late '60s.

The bulk of Cummins's sales and earnings remained in the engine business, however. The key to the company's success lay in its ability to design a technically superior engine, with high performance and reliability, coupled with an aggressive, user-oriented parts distribution and service network, which created among truck buyers a demand for trucks with Cummins engines.

As the '70s rolled along, Cummins found that it had greatly underestimated the rate of growth of the North American diesel engine market, which continued to surge ahead at close to 15 percent per year. The company was overextended financially as it struggled to keep up with demand. It had to retrench from its diversification into unrelated businesses by selling all of them, in order to finance the continued growth of its engine manufacturing capacity and reduce the danger of a major loss in market share. Organiza-

tionally, the company was bursting at its seams. Plant capacity in Columbus was woefully inadequate to meet the rising demands of the engine business. Exhibit 2 shows the dramatic increase in sales, earnings, engine shipments, and physical plant capacity through 1974.

The facilities expansion was first undertaken on a crash basis in Columbus in 1970. Ground was broken for a second major manufacturing plant, and a separate parts distribution center was established. This was done under heavy time pressure and involved difficult coordination tasks. Disruptions occurred as heavy machinery was moved and the production of particular engine or component series was transferred from one plant to another at short notice. The rationalization and development of formal management and control systems to support a multiplant operating mode had to wait until later. For example, inventory control for all three plants in Columbus continued to be carried out at the main engine plant.

It soon became clear that these facilities would prove inadequate. Instead of tapering off, truck demand hit record highs in 1973 and 1974—well above any trend line on the most optimistic predictions. Plans were therefore set in motion to expand production facilities once again. A plant in Charleston, South Carolina, was bought in 1972 and another in Jamestown, New York, in 1974. A separate facility to handle engines for the industrial markets was purchased in Seymour, Indiana.

Cummins entered 1974 pushing against the limits of its plant capacity. It was also straining under the growing difficulty its suppliers were having in delivering orders on time and in the amounts needed. As a result, the prospect of a significant drop in market share again developed. Managers were pushing their people and machines to their limits and making heroic efforts to break production bottlenecks.

Corporate Culture

In spite of its dramatic growth, in many ways Cummins Engine Company still was a small-town company. It remained the largest employer in Columbus, and its history of close relations with

EXHIBIT 2 Selected Historical Data

	1960	1969	1973	1974
Financial operating data:				
Sales (millions)	$136	$392	$637	$802
Net earnings (millions)	6	18	26	24
Percent of sales	4.4%	4.6%	4.1%	3.0%
Per share data:				
Earnings		$2.87	$3.87	$3.31
Dividends		0.71	0.95	0.98
Percent return on equity		14.7%	13.9%	10.8%
Physical facilities:				
Columbus:				
Plants/other	2/–	5/5		7/6
Square footage (000)	1,496	2,224		3,340
Other U.S.:				
No. plants/other		3/–		6/2
Square footage (000)		683		3,160
Overseas:				
No. plants/other	1/–	3/1		5/1
Square footage (000)	145	650		1,477
Market share data				
Cummins share of truck market:				
Diesel trucks	61.1%	43.5%	37.9%	40.1%
All heavy duty trucks	27.4%	30.9%	30.3%	32.2%
Number of engines shipped	20,000	89,000	115,000	126,000

Source: Annual reports and company records.

an independent local union fostered a sense of special concern for local issues. There was a long tradition of keeping people on the payroll unless unusually difficult times came along. Many employees belonged to families with members who worked or had worked for the company. Most of the middle-aged and older employees and managers had grown up with the business. They had come on board in the '30s, '40s, and '50s when the organization was still small and relatively simple.

Cummins employees had experienced years of successful growth under the leadership of Miller and Tull. It was an informal management style, where close supervision and attention to detail went hand in hand with the expectation that each manager and employee would show initiative in responding adequately to changing condi-

tions, particularly with regard to customers' late requests. For years, employees had been rewarded for expediting a critical piece of work without upsetting the smooth operation of the plant. Over time, ad hoc relationships and arrangements became customary practice. These informal networks of communication extended to customers and suppliers as well. Many of these relationshps were often personal, with particular individuals becoming indispensable members of a chain without whom it was hard to get things done. A permanent sense of crisis management pervaded the operating side of the engine business much of the time. Several managers had attempted to introduce systems to provide a more orderly approach to production management. These efforts, however, never had the support of top management.

Organization

Managers found it difficult to discuss the company's organization in concrete terms. There was no ready made chart to which one could turn. Rather, managers spoke of Leo Brewer's division or Marion Dietrich's group, personalizing the organization, yet acknowledging its divisions. Alternatively, they referred to specific plants or office locations. The organizational structure was fluid, with new arrangements coming about frequently.

It was with the emergence of the international markets and the early diversification moves of the '60s that Miller and Tull first clearly parceled out functional responsibility. With the appearance of Jim Henderson as the operating manager for the engine business after 1969, certain pieces of the organization began to drift under his influence, but the process was gradual. Research and engineering as well as marketing were still formally reporting directly to the president. By 1974, Henderson's formal authority over all aspects of the engine business was clearly recognized. The corporate controller did not report to him, however.

Operating Interdependence

The manufacture of components and assembly of engines took place in a web of interrelationships among many plants and distribution facilities throughout the world. Between and among plants flowed large quantities of bulky semiprocessed and finished goods. Exhibit 3 attempts to represent some of the complexity involved.

In order to comprehend the magnitude of the coordination problem, consider that, on a typical day in 1974, 600 engines were completed at six different engine assembly plants, each typically comprising 600 to 700 distinct parts. Each of these was either manufactured at one of 11 machining plants or purchased from a supplier. To make matters more complicated, Cummins built eight different types of engines and encouraged users to request special design or assembly features.

Management Processes

Perhaps the most salient management process in 1974 was still the traditional exercise of the art of expediting. Since the mid-'60s, top management had been pushing to professionalize management and build a more rational and systematic set of organizational systems. The reality of 1974, however, was that demand was growing so fast that only the expert old hands who knew how to coax the last ounce of productivity out of the operating system could keep the production schedule from slipping. Given these circumstances, the principal feedback to top management on organizational performance came from the line organization. This was in the form of weekly and sometimes daily verbal or telex reports on the engine build rate and the engine ship rate, and reports from marketing on demand projections for the coming months.

On the other side of the house, the financial staff captured the overall results of operations in terms of their impact on the company's financial position. This information was also made available to top management on a regular basis, but was not reported to all operating managers because it could not be adequately broken down according to their areas of responsibility. This dual flow of information sometimes provided contradictory data to top management, causing considerable consternation and a call for more consistent and reliable reports.

At the lower levels of the organization, the systems analysts and the data processing people were also dissatisfied. As the relationships among multiple organizational units became increasingly complex, they felt a need for more elaborate, accurate, and timely exchanges of relevant information. But they were hard pressed to come up with an adequate design that could handle the various pieces under different people's control. Several task forces had been established for improving information generating, reporting, forecasting, and plan integration. However, they frequently found that the assumptions upon which they were working had become outdated by the

EXHIBIT 3   Partial Representation of Parts and Components Flow among Plants and Distribution Centers in 1974

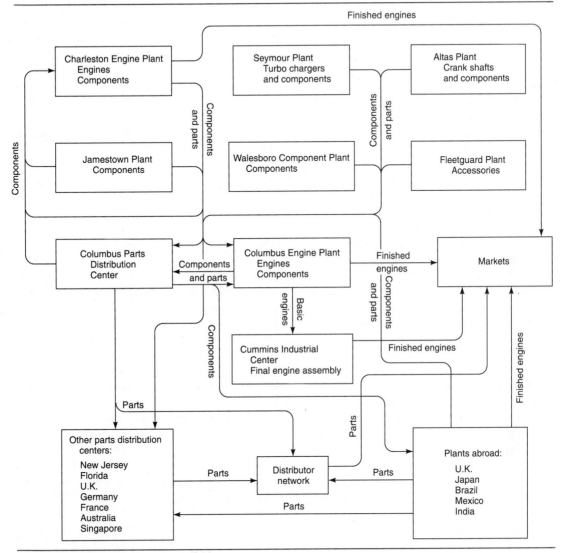

Source: Information supplied by company officials.

time they were ready to present their recommendations. Also, upper-level managers were frequently tied up in crisis management and were unavailable to participate.

In short, as the complexity of interrelationships among operating units increased as a result of continued rapid growth, the traditional coordination processes absorbed more and more time, leaving operating managers with little or no time to search for improved modes of coordination.

The Situation in the Fall of 1974

The October Meeting

Jim Henderson reviewed the inventory situation at the monthly sales and production planning meeting with his division managers and staff officers in October 1974. Sales forecasts for the next six months from the marketing departments were bullish. OEMs in the truck manufacturing industry continued to report record order levels with up to 11-month backlogs. These projections indicated that the build rates should be kept as high as possible.

Henderson took a more cautious view, based on personal contacts with industry executives and analyses of broader industry and economic trends. He reminded his colleagues that Cummins was in a strongly cyclical business. In the past, purchases of new trucks had dropped considerably during periods of recession, sometimes with reductions of up to 20 percent in sales. On such occasions, the company had had to run a very tight ship. Order backlogs were meaningless, as orders could be canceled. Henderson also had a nagging feeling that much of the current backlog of orders facing the truck manufacturers reflected unusually heavy buying before new, controversial, and costly regulations concerning truck braking systems, which had recently been passed by Congress, went into effect in mid-1975.

With inventories exceeding projections, efforts were started at several levels of management to determine the causes. Pat Snyder, vice president for the U.S. Automotive Group, informed the group that the inventory problem was in part due to a build-up of work in process, because delays in the arrival of components made it difficult to complete engines. Growing numbers of "90 percent finished" engines were sitting around waiting for parts. Suppliers were stretched, and lead times for deliveries were getting very long. The purchasing people had been doing a

great job selling suppliers on the advantages of giving Cummins preferential treatment as a stable and reliable customer, but difficulties were inevitable because of the surging demand for machined parts throughout the industry. "But if we can agree on a forecast for the next six months," Snyder assured the group, "our production people will move mountains to meet it. In the past year we have surprised even ourselves in exceeding what everyone thought was the limit of our production capacity at the Columbus engine plant."

The controller was less exuberant. He knew that the current severe inflation accounted for some of the rise in inventory value and that this aspect of the problem would continue to put pressure on working capital even if measures to reduce physical inventories were successful. (Cummins's materials costs rose 26 percent in 1974.) It also bothered him that the materials management record-keeping system and the corporate accounting system had never been adequately integrated. His financial records suggested that the inventory problem was more severe than the production people realized. In his judgment, the company lacked sufficient control over its inventory to cope adequately with a sharp downturn in sales.

The October meeting closed with an agreement to trim back the sales forecast slightly, recognizing that the market might be softening. It was also agreed that the production control and materials management people in each plant would initiate steps to bring inventory levels back down from about 75 days' supply to a more manageable 60 days'.

The November Meeting

At the November 1974 meeting, marketing reported continued high levels of demand for the foreseeable future. Henderson, however, could see definite black clouds gathering on the horizon. Production managers indicated that engine shipments in October had dipped by about 5 percent under the build rate for the month (indicating engines awaiting parts), but the inventories would soon be brought into line because of the projected strength in the market forecast for the upcoming six months. The Cummins controller, however, reported a further sharp rise in inventory levels, now approaching 80 days' supply.

After deciding to keep material ordering rates well below sales forecasts, Henderson felt it would be a good idea if weekly meetings were also held to monitor inventory trends. He hoped that the increased visibility this would give to the inventory problem would lead plant management to take a serious look at what it could do to tighten things up.

Weekly Inventory Meetings

Henderson began to meet weekly with his group heads, their plant managers, and the controller to monitor the inventory situation. The Columbus plant managers usually brought their materials people to these meetings. A pattern soon emerged. The more they talked about lowering inventories, the higher they went. The initial downward shifts in production schedules due to the trimming back of sales forecasts took three weeks to be reflected in revised detailed part specifications, on which the purchasing department based its orders. These, in turn, were followed by lead times of from six to eight weeks (six months for international suppliers). Furthermore, the purchasing agents in contact with suppliers were very reluctant to cut back or reschedule orders, because demand for parts and components throughout the industry remained at record highs. Poor relations with suppliers would mean the sure loss of their goodwill, which was critical to maintain to secure deliver-

ies. With the lower build rate out of synchronization with the arrival of supplies, inventories continued to edge up.

There was also disagreement between the materials management records and the financial records as to the rate of growth in inventories. According to the accounting records, engine inventories in Columbus alone were reaching $100 million, whereas the sum of the dollar values of the inventory records at the various Columbus plants was only $88 million. No one knew for sure where the remaining $12 million worth of inventory was physically located. It became a grim joke at the meetings to refer to this missing inventory as "the phantom plant." At one point, Henderson quipped that he would have to stop calling the weekly meetings, because every time they met the inventories went up, and nobody knew where. Finally Henderson said he was appointing the controller as plant manager for the phantom plant.

It soon became clear to Henderson that the production and materials control departments were so caught up in translating production schedules into specific detailed part breakdowns for use by the purchasing department that little if any time was spent on the physical control of materials after their arrival at the plant. What control there was, was done from the office with computer printouts. At the time, Cummins had over 75,000 active part numbers. There was no prioritization of parts according to cost and volume that would allow particular attention to be paid to the small number of parts that accounted for the bulk of inventory value. The goals for inventory turns that existed at plant levels were not meaningful, and no plans existed to meet them.

QUESTIONS

1. How could a problem like this occur in a company that had been run for more than five years by a pair of young professional managers?
2. What should Jim Henderson do in November 1974?

Case 2–3

International Telephone and Telegraph Company*

In early 1968, Herbert C. Knortz, comptroller of the International Telephone and Telegraph Corporation, appointed an ad hoc committee to develop a procedure for critically examining the effectiveness with which various functions within the comptroller's area of responsibility were being carried out. Four months of full-time effort by the five-member committee led to the development of a "Comptrollership Rating Manual" for the formal review of comptrollership activities at ITT.

The underlying goal of the manual was "to assist in the establishment within each operating unit of the ITT system a professional comptrollership function which could be objectively rated best in the industry." This case describes the comptrollership evaluation procedure in 1977 which evolved from that earlier effort.

In 1977, ITT employed approximately 400,000 people worldwide and about 23,000 of these were engaged in comptrollership activities. The organization of the 325 people in the comptroller's headquarters staff is shown in Exhibit 1. The scope of the comptrollership function at the 240 field units reporting to ITT headquarters varied greatly depending upon the diversity of the unit's operations, the duration of time that the unit had been in the ITT system, and the relative size of the unit. A list of the comptrollership activities performed at these units together with the approximate distribution of employees across activities for all units combined is shown in Exhibit 2.

Reporting System for Unit Comptrollers

The performance of the comptrollership function at each unit within the ITT system was monitored and reviewed by 10 directors of financial control (DFCs). Seven were located in ITT's world headquarters in New York and the remaining three were based in ITT's European headquarters in Brussels. Each DFC was responsible for between 20 and 30 field units.

For each of the 240 units within the ITT system, an effectiveness score was computed for each of 30 areas of comptrollership responsibility. A listing of the specific areas evaluated is shown in Exhibit 3. For each of these areas, the unit comptroller answered between 30 to 60 yes–no type questions directed at how well activities in the particular area were being performed. For the 30 areas combined, the unit comptroller answered 1,600 questions. This self-evaluation accounted for 75 percent of the scores assigned to the unit. The other 25 percent was determined by answers to five questions for each of the 30 areas by the director of financial control responsible for monitoring the activities of the unit. Thus, the DFC answered 150 questions for each of the 20 to 30 field units under his jurisdiction.

To illustrate the computational procedure, consider questionnaire no. 28, "Unit Comptroller's Interface with Unit Management and Director of Financial Controls" (use Exhibit 3). The specific questions answered by the unit comptroller and the DFC in order to determine the effectiveness

* This case was prepared by Vijay Sathe, Harvard Business School.
Copyright © by the President and Fellows of Harvard College.
Harvard Business School case 478–022.

EXHIBIT 1 Comptroller's Organization at Headquarters

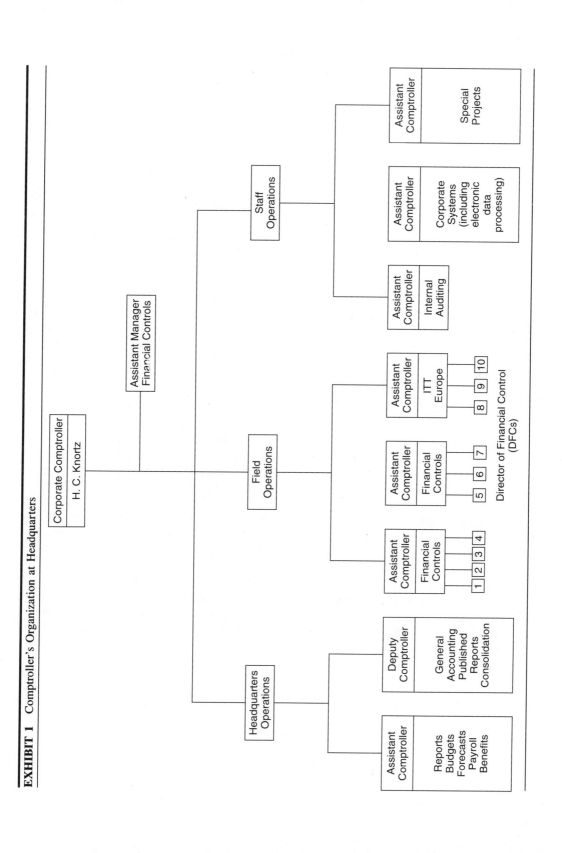

EXHIBIT 2 Comptrollership Activities in Field Units

Comptrollership Activity	Percent of Unit Comptroller's Staff Performing the Activity*
General accounting	45%
Cost accounting	20
Budgets and forecasts	4
Internal Audit	2
Data processing	13
Systems and procedures	6
Treasury	5
Other	5
Total	100%

*The breakdown shown is an approximate percentage based on numbers for all field units combined.

with which this function was being performed for a given field unit are shown in Exhibit 4. A hypothetical example showing how a numerical score was determined for a unit on questionnaire no. 28 is included as Exhibit 5. A perfect evaluation (score of 100) was possible only if the unit comptroller could answer yes to every question and the DFC gave a score of 5 for each of the five items.

The ratings achieved for each of the 30 areas evaluated for comptrollership effectiveness formed the basis for establishing a rerating timetable and for initiating action programs. The ratings were interpreted as follows.

It was the DFC's responsibility to initiate the required action programs and provide each unit comptroller under his jurisdiction with the appropriate questionnaire in accordance with the rerating timetable. The color codes were used in constructing a "comptrollership grid" to provide a convenient overview of how effectively the 240 units within the ITT system were performing in the 30 specific areas of comptrollership responsibility. A schematic of the grid is shown in Exhibit 6. The various units of the ITT system were grouped by area and product line and a glance across the grid revealed the performance of any unit in any specific area of controllership responsibility.

It should be noted that the grid revealed how well a particular comptrollership *activity* was being performed in a given unit and did not necessarily refer to the performance of the unit's *comptroller.* For example, it was not unusual for a unit newly acquired by ITT to have an initial yellow or red rating in several areas. This did not automatically imply that the unit's comptroller was ineffective, because it could take one or two years to get the unit's comptrollership function "up to speed" in some instances. Indeed, one measure of the unit comptroller's effectiveness was the time it took him to do so, given the unit's "situation complexity." Examples of high situation complexity included a bad business environment, inadequate staff, multiplant operations, high-technology business, or the requirement of dealing in government contracts or foreign currency transactions. For units that had been in the ITT system for some time, unit comptrollers were evaluated using regular ITT personnel evaluation forms, but the unit's comptrollership effectiveness did account for 10 to 15 percent of the individual's total rating.

EXHIBIT 3   List of Specific Comptrollership Areas Evaluated

Questionnaire No.	*Comptrollership Area*
1	Intercompany accounting
2	Fixed asset accounting
3	Budgets and forecasts
4	Personnel expense reporting
5	Cost accounting
6	Cost reduction programs
7	Headquarters reporting requirements
8	Capital expenditures
9	Payables
10	Management development and other personnel practices
11	Credit and collections
12	Receivables and billing
13	Inventory controls
14	Cash management and controls
15	Scrap accounting and controls
16	Payroll
17	Tax accounting
18	Responsibility accounting and flexible budgeting
19	Accounting for engineering costs and expenses
20	Contract accounting
21	Debt management and foreign exchange
22	Insurance administration
23	Comptroller's monthly operating and financial review
24	Auditing
25	Product/business planning
26	Financial analyses and managerial reports
27	Systems and data processing
28	Unit comptroller's interface with unit management and director of financial controls
29	Accounting and control of marketing and A&G expenses
30	Installation cost accounting

EXHIBIT 4

ITT COMPTROLLERSHIP RATING MANUAL	SUBJECT: UNIT COMPTROLLER'S INTERFACE WITH UNIT MGMT. & DIRECTOR OF FINANCIAL CONTROLS	QUESTIONNAIRE NO. 28
		PAGE NO. 1 OF 4
	AFFECTS: ALL COMPANIES	EFFECTIVE DATE September 23, 1968

	Yes	No
1. Does your unit General Manager hold regular weekly staff meetings?	___	___
2. Do you participate regularly in those staff meetings?	___	___
3. Do you participate with the unit General Manager in periodic reviews held with group management?	___	___
4. Do you regularly review "The Comptroller's Monthly Letter" with the General Manager prior to release?	___	___
5. Does the General manager routinely brief you on "The Manager's Monthly Letter"?	___	___
6. Are you or a member of your staff presently assigned to a unit level "task force" or special project by the General Manager?	___	___
7. Are all projections of financial data, applicable to your unit, coordinated by the Comptroller's Department?	___	___
8. Are all publications pertinent to the actual results of your unit's operations coordinated by the Comptroller's Department?	___	___
9. Prior to publication, do you discuss all Comptroller's Department reports and correspondence on matters sensitive to your unit with the unit General Manager?	___	___
10. Have you formally reviewed with the General Manager and/or all other department heads within the past 12 months, the format, content, timeliness, and degree of detail included in all recurring internal financial reports?	___	___
11. Does your current internal financial reporting system provide each department head and the unit General Manager with the current and projected financial status of his areas of responsibility?	___	___
12. Are you responsive to requests for special reports from the General Manager and other department heads?	___	___
13. Do you regularly participate in the satff meetings of other departments?	___	___
14. Do you regularly discuss the financial results of each department with the responsible department head?	___	___
15. Do you keep the unit General Manager apprised of the volume and content of the Comptroller's Headquarters reporting requirements?	___	___

EXHIBIT 4 *(continued)*

INTERNATIONAL TELEPHONE AND TELEGRAPH CORPORATION	
SUBJECT:	QUESTIONNAIRE NO. 28
UNIT COMPTROLLER'S INTERFACE WITH UNIT MANAGEMENT AND DIRECTOR OF FINANCIAL CONTROLS	PAGE NO. 2 OF 4

	Yes	*No*
16. Have you developed an internal distribution of Headquarters reports that are of special interest to local management?	____	____
17. Do you regularly make presentations to the General Manager and his staff concerning the in-depth financial status of your unit?	____	____
18. Do you use appropriate visual aids in these presentations?	____	____
19. Do you encourage the active participation of nonfinancial management in these presentations?	____	____
20. Do you use trade publications or other media pertinent to your unit's product lines and specific industry, to develop your knowledge of your unit's position in its particular area of endeavor?	____	____
21. Did your department within the last year participate in a formal review of your unit's market position?	____	____
22. Has your department within the last year participated in a formal review of proposed new products?	____	____
23. Do you advise your Director of Financial Controls of major problems in your unit when they occur rather than wait for "The Comptroller's Monthly Letter"?	____	____
24. In the past six months, have you notified your Director of Financial Controls of all significant revisions to forecasts prior to their being released by the unit?	____	____
25. During the past six months, have your monthly Comptroller's letters been sufficiently comprehensive and informative so as to keep the requests for clarification from the Director to an acceptable minimum?	____	____
26. Do you supply your Director with extracts from memos issued by the members of unit management which will have an impact on unit profitability?	____	____
27. Do you keep your Director advised of all significant unit projects in which your department is involved?	____	____
28. Do you periodically review the reports issued to your Director with him to determine their continuing significance?	____	____
29. Do you periodically review your internal reporting requirements with your Director?	____	____

EXHIBIT 4 (*continued*)

INTERNATIONAL TELEPHONE AND TELEGRAPH CORPORATION	
SUBJECT:	QUESTIONNAIRE NO. 28
UNIT COMPTROLLER'S INTERFACE WITH UNIT MANAGEMENT AND DIRECTOR OF FINANCIAL CONTROLS	PAGE NO. 3 OF 4

		Yes	*No*
30.	Do you keep your Director advised of your manpower requirements?	___	___
31.	Do you discuss your future manpower needs with your Director prior to incorporating them into a final budget?	___	___
32.	Do you discuss open positions with your Director in order to determine required specifications for candidates?	___	___
33.	Do you advise your Director of openings when they occur to obtain his assistance in finding suitable candidates?	___	___
34.	Do you request your Director to interview job candidates for supervisory level positions in your department?	___	___

Unit _____

Comptroller's signature _____

EXHIBIT 4 (*concluded*)

INTERNATIONAL TELEPHONE AND TELEGRAPH CORPORATION

SUBJECT:	QUESTIONNAIRE NO. 28
UNIT COMPTROLLER'S INTERFACE WITH UNIT MANAGEMENT AND DIRECTOR OF FINANCIAL CONTROLS	PAGE NO. 4 OF 4

****

TO BE RATED BY THE DIRECTOR OF FINANCIAL CONTROLS:

To assess the qualitative performance of the function being rated by this questionnaire, the Director of Financial Controls is requested to score the unit Comptrollership function to the following:

	Score		
	0	2	5

1. Rapport with General Manager.

2. Effectiveness in dealings with General Manager.

3. Rapport and effectiveness in dealings with other members of unit management.

4. Rapport with Director.

5. Keeping Director advised of all significant problems.

EXHIBIT 5 Illustration of the Procedure Used to Compute a Unit's Rating

QUESTIONNAIRE NO. 28

UNIT NUMBER _____

PART I—Responses from unit comptrollers

Number of "no" responses or responses rejected by directors of financial controls	Total applicable questions in questionnaire*	Score
(A)	(B)	$\dfrac{B - A}{B} \times 75 =$
4	34	66

PART II—Responses from directors of financial controls

	Question	Point value assigned†
1.	_____	5
2.	_____	5
3.	_____	5
4.	_____	2
5.	_____	2

Total 19

Total rating (Part I and Part II) 85

Comments (use additional pages if required):

Signed _____
Director of Financial Controls

Notes:
* If certain questions are not applicable to the unit, they can be deleted with the DFC's concurrence.

† 0 = Not acceptable, 2 = Minimum acceptable, 5 = Satisfactory

EXHIBIT 6 Schematic of "Comptrollership Grid"

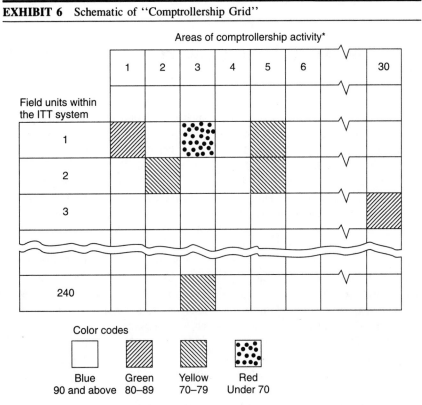

Areas of comptrollership activity*

Field units within the ITT system

Color codes

Blue	Green	Yellow	Red
90 and above	80–89	70–79	Under 70

*See Exhibit 3 for a list of the areas.

QUESTIONS

1. List the strong and weak points of this rating system.
2. What types of companies should use such a system? What types should not?

Case 2–4

National Tractor and Equipment Company*

National Tractor and Equipment Company, Inc., was a manufacturer of a number of products, including a wide line of farm tractors. Tractors were divided into several fairly well-defined types, according to their capacity, and National manufactured tractors of each type. This case deals with one of these types, here referred to as a type X.

Fixed costs represented a relatively large share of total costs at National, and, therefore, achieving a strong sales position was an important means of reducing unit costs and improving profits. Consequently, a major objective of the company was to be the sales leader in each of the several types. If National was not the leader during a particular year, its goal was to surpass whoever was the leader. If National was the leader, its goal was to maintain the size of its lead.

The company had experienced a rather erratic showing in sales of the type X tractors over the previous several years. Though National had been the sales leader in four of the previous six years (1970–75) its lead in 1973 and 1974 had been slim, and in 1975 its chief competitor took over first place. Meanwhile, profits of this division of its business had fluctuated widely. Accordingly, early in 1976, the controller's department made a sales analysis of the type X tractor division.

William Lawrence, who was given the job of making the analysis decided to use the approach the controller had used for other analyses. Usually these analyses started with a comparison of actual costs or actual profit with some benchmark, such as the budget or the figures for some prior year when performance was satisfactory. The analyst then sought to isolate and quantify the various causes of the difference between actual and the standard applied in that particular case.

In the case of tractors, since management's objective was to surpass the sales leader, unit sales of the leading competitor—here called "competitor A"—seemed to be the most logical standard. Competitor A had sold 13,449 type X tractors in 1975, compared with 10,356 for National—a deficiency of 3,093. (A copy of Mr. Lawrence's analysis as presented to management appears as an appendix to this case.)

Mr. Lawrence began his analysis by looking at the profits and return on assets of the type X tractor division (see Appendix Exhibit 1). Both had improved significantly over the 1973 and 1974 levels. However, in 1975 National dropped from the first-place sales position it had held during 1973 and 1974 and this was of grave concern to management. Furthermore, its market share had decreased from 25.0 percent to 23.5 percent (see Appendix Exhibit 2). Both of its major competitors had increased their market shares, and competitor A had outsold National for the first time in five years.

Mr. Lawrence next prepared the sales portion of the table that appears as Exhibit 3 in the appendix. This exhibit compares sales of type X tractors by National and competitor A for the preceding three years, 1973–1975. The major task, then—and this was the crux of the analy-

* This case was prepared by J. S. Hekimian under the supervision of R. N. Anthony, Harvard Business School. Copyright © by the President and Fellows of Harvard College. Harvard Business School case 161–010.

sis—was to identify and analyze those factors that accounted for the volume difference in each of the three years.

After he had completed this initial analysis, Mr. Lawrence, representing the controller's department, met with representatives of the sales department and the product development department. Together, they discussed the various factors that might have accounted for the volume differences in each of the three years under review. Using their collective judgments and estimates, they broke down the volume difference into as many specific factors as they could agree on. All the remaining factors, they decided, must have accounted for the remaining difference, although they could not agree on the proportions; so they gave the total under other factors.

The first matter that Mr. Lawrence called to the attention of this group was that a major fire in one of competitor A's plants in the latter part of 1974 had severely limited production. He had compiled monthly production estimates for competitor A for 1974 and two prior years. He then had gathered estimates of industry sales during those years and developed certain relationships that seemed to him to hold among estimated monthly sales, actual monthly sales, and actual monthly production for 1972 and 1973 by competitor A. When he applied these relationships to 1974, it seemed evident to him that competitor A had produced significantly fewer type X tractors than it normally would have during the months when its plant was shut down.

Mr. Lawrence then had looked at sales patterns during 1972 and 1973 so that he could make an estimate of how much this lost production had resulted in a shifting of demand from 1974 to 1975; he tried to estimate how many competitor A customers for type X tractors delayed purchase of a new type X tractor from 1974 to 1975 because of the fire. In addition to research with the data available in his office, Mr. Lawrence traveled around the country and talked to distributors and dealers. He became convinced that a large number of potential purchasers of tractors annually

had deferred their purchases of new type X tractors. Some of competitor A's dealers had had no type X tractors in stock in the latter part of 1974 because of the fire, and others had had only a limited supply.

On the basis of Mr. Lawrence's analysis and the collective judgments of the other members, the group agreed that the fire caused a shift of 1,500 of competitor A's tractor sales from 1974 to 1975. This shift was recorded as a minus factor in 1975 and a plus factor in 1974.

Sales of type X tractors to government agencies was another factor studied by this group. Since government sales figures were published, the group ascertained that National outsold competitor A by 138 units. Government sales depended almost entirely on price; therefore, this was the type of business a tractor manufacturer could "buy" depending on how badly he wanted it.

Mr. Lawrence had done a considerable amount of research into the advantage that competitor A enjoyed because of its larger owner body.[1] National's owner body had always been smaller than competitor A's, but National had made sizable gains since 1967. There was a tendency for the owner of a tractor to buy the same make when he purchased a new tractor; thus, competitor A enjoyed an advantage. Mr. Lawrence wanted to know *how much* this advantage was. An annual survey made by the trade association of the industry indicated the behavior of a representative sample of buyers of new type X tractors. This survey indicated that owners of competitor A's tractors were more loyal than were National tractor owners (see Table 1). Using these survey results, Mr. Lawrence was able to calculate the advantage to competitor A of its larger owner body. Although only the calculations for 1975 are shown, he applied the same methodology to 1973 and 1974. Members of the group were impressed with this analysis and agreed to accept Mr.

---

[1] Owner body is the number of tractors in the hands of owners.

Lawrence's figures—a net advantage of 700 units for competitor A in 1975.

The next factor he analyzed was product differences. National did not have so varied a product line as did competitor A. Because of this, National dealers were at a competitive disadvantage for certain models of type X tractors. The group was able to agree on the approximate extent of this disadvantage.

The last main heading for variances listed in Exhibit 3 was other factors, which the group thought accounted for the remaining difference between National's sales and competitor A's sales. Mr. Lawrence had prepared a thorough analysis of these factors, too. For example, he had heard that competitor A built a more efficient and more durable type X tractor. He tried to quantify the effect of these variables by use of the data shown in Tables 3 and 4. He also requisitioned five National type X tractors and five competitor A type X tractors, and arranged to have these tractors tested at National's experimental farm to determine their operating characteristics, including power, performance, durability, reliability, and economy. Mr. Lawrence himself actually drove some of these tractors. He also inspected each tractor and its performance at the end of the testing period.

The group could not agree, however, on the quantitative effect on sales volume of these factors or of the remaining factors listed under other. Therefore, they were represented by one figure. The total variance of all the factors affecting market penetration, of course, equaled the difference in sales between National and competitor A.

QUESTIONS

1. Are analyses of this type within the proper scope of a controller's function?
2. Can you suggest a better way of making the analysis?
3. What action, if any, should be taken on the basis of this study?

Appendix
An Analysis of Type X Tractors*

Profits, Assets, and After-Tax Returns

Exhibit 1 depicts National's profits, assets, and return on assets for the years 1970–75. Profits have ranged from a high of $2.7 million in 1972 to a loss of $200,000 in 1974 and a profit of $2.5 million in 1975. Return on assets employed in 1975 was 20.5 percent after taxes.

Market Penetration versus Competition

Exhibit 2 shows National's penetration of the domestic market for type X tractors for 1970–75, compared with its two major competitors.

---

* Prepared by the controller's department.

EXHIBIT 1   Profits, Assets, and After-tax Returns

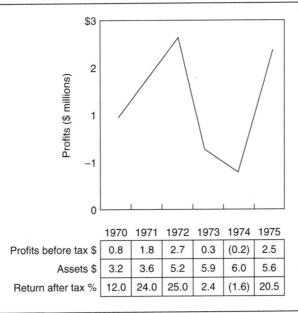

	1970	1971	1972	1973	1974	1975
Profits before tax $	0.8	1.8	2.7	0.3	(0.2)	2.5
Assets $	3.2	3.6	5.2	5.9	6.0	5.6
Return after tax %	12.0	24.0	25.0	2.4	(1.6)	20.5

National's penetration rose from 24.3 percent in 1970 to a peak of 35.5 percent in 1971. In 1975, National's penetration was 23.5 percent. Competitor A's penetration, which was 27.9 percent in 1970, fell to a low of 21.8 percent in 1971 and then increased to 30.5 percent in 1975. In four out of the last six years, National outsold competitor A in the type X tractor market. Competitor B's penetration moved from 27.4 percent in 1970 to 23.0 percent in 1971 but declined to 9.9 percent in 1973, rising to 21.2 percent in 1975.

Exhibit 3 sets forth those factors that accounted for differences in market penetration between National and competitor A—its chief competitor in the type X tractor market. The upper portion of the table compares National's and competitor A's sales during the years 1973–75. The lower portion of the table shows the various factors that account for the differences between National's and competitor A's share of the market in each of

these years. National's volume was 10,611 units in 1973, compared to competitor A's 10,246. In 1975, National's volume was 10,356 units, representing a market penetration of 23.5 percent, compared with A's volume of 13,449 units and 30.5 percent of the market. In 1975, National was outsold by 3,093 units.

Turning to the specific factors that account for this volume difference, we have estimated that the effect of a major fire at one of competitor A's plants in the last half of 1974, which halted production for nearly five months, resulted in a deferral of demand for 1,500 of its type X tractors from 1974 to 1975. This estimate is based on our knowledge of competitor A's output in 1974, compared with other years, and represents our best estimate on what sales might have been without the fire. In 1975, these 1,500 units represented 3.4 percent of market penetration. In 1975, National sold 138 more units to government agencies, equivalent to 0.3 percent of

EXHIBIT 2   Market Penetration versus Competition

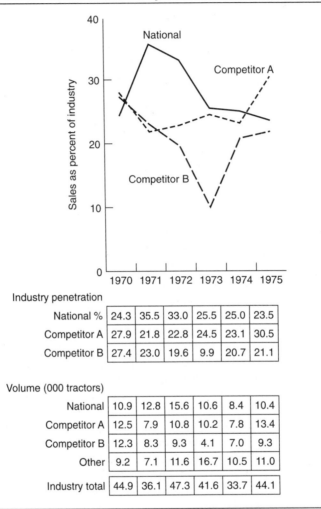

Industry penetration						
National %	24.3	35.5	33.0	25.5	25.0	23.5
Competitor A	27.9	21.8	22.8	24.5	23.1	30.5
Competitor B	27.4	23.0	19.6	9.9	20.7	21.1

Volume (000 tractors)						
National	10.9	12.8	15.6	10.6	8.4	10.4
Competitor A	12.5	7.9	10.8	10.2	7.8	13.4
Competitor B	12.3	8.3	9.3	4.1	7.0	9.3
Other	9.2	7.1	11.6	16.7	10.5	11.0
Industry total	44.9	36.1	47.3	41.6	33.7	44.1

market penetration. We shall examine the effect on our market penetration of differences in the size of our respective owner bodies in subsequent tables.

The product differences result from gaps in our product line that prevent National from entering certain segments of the type X tractor market, thereby providing competitor A with a clear prod-uct advantage. For example, competitor A offers a larger variety of attachments and related equipment, which increase the number of different jobs its tractor can perform. We have estimated, for each year, the net market advantage accruing to competitor A because of its broader product line.

Other factors, whose effects cannot be measured quantitatively, are summarized at the bot-

EXHIBIT 3 Sales of Type X Tractors and Factors Affecting Market Penetration (National versus Competitor A, 1973 to 1975)

	Jan.–Dec. 1973		Jan.–Dec. 1974		Jan.–Dec. 1975	
	Units	Percent of Market*	Units	Percent of Market*	Units	Percent of Market*
Sales:						
National	10,611	25.5%	8,431	25.0%	10,356	23.5%
Competitor A	10,246	24.5	7,828	23.1	13,449	30.5
National over/(under) A	365	1.0%	603	1.9%	(3,093)	(7.0%)
Factors affecting market penetration:						
Effect of major fire at one of competitor A's plants	—	—	1,500	4.5	(1,500)	(3.4)
Sales to government agencies	(3)	—	321	1.0	138	0.3
Competitor A's advantage in size of owner body	(850)	(2.0)	(660)	(1.9)	(700)	(1.6)
Product differences	(269)	(0.6)	(1,071)	(3.2)	(1,986)	(4.5)
Other factors:						
Customer attitudes toward National						
Operating cost						
Durability and quality						
National's price position	1,487	3.6	513	1.5	955	2.2
National's distribution system						
Sales administration						
Other factors						
Total variance	365	1.0%	603	1.9%	(3,093)	(7.0%)

* These percentages were calculated from the rounded numbers given on the preceding page; if calculated from the exact number of units, they would be somewhat different.

tom of the table, including customer attitudes toward National with respect to operating cost, durability, quality, and similar factors. In 1975, these other factors, in total, represented a net advantage to National of 955 units, or 2.2 percent of market penetration.

Basis for Estimated Advantage to Competitor A of Owner Body

Exhibit 4 shows the estimated number of National and competitor A type X tractors in operation for the years 1967–75.

In 1967, it is estimated that competitor A had approximately 88,000 type X tractors in operation, while National had approximately 27,000 units in use. By 1975, National units in operation had more than quadrupled to a level of approximately 127,000 units. Competitor A units, on the other hand, had increased by almost 100 percent to a level of 158,000 units. During this period, National units as a percent of competitor A increased from 31 percent in 1967 to 80 percent in 1975. At the same time, our variance, in terms of units, decreased from 60,700 in 1967 to 31,200 in 1975.

EXHIBIT 4   Units in Operation

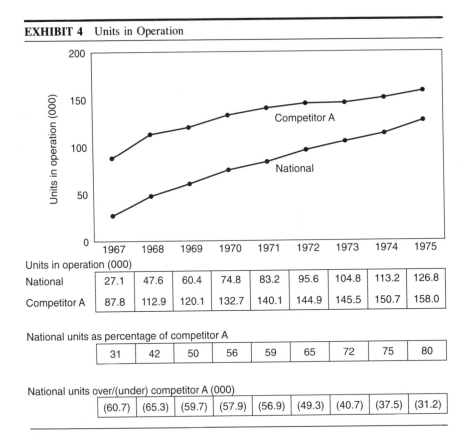

Units in operation (000)

	1967	1968	1969	1970	1971	1972	1973	1974	1975
National	27.1	47.6	60.4	74.8	83.2	95.6	104.8	113.2	126.8
Competitor A	87.8	112.9	120.1	132.7	140.1	144.9	145.5	150.7	158.0

National units as percentage of competitor A

31	42	50	56	59	65	72	75	80

National units over/(under) competitor A (000)

(60.7)	(65.3)	(59.7)	(57.9)	(56.9)	(49.3)	(40.7)	(37.5)	(31.2)

Because of the importance of owner loyalty, competitor A's advantage in owner body represents an automatic advantage in market penetration, as indicated in the succeeding pages.

1975 Type X Replacement Patterns

Table 1 indicates the relative loyalty in 1975 of National and competitor A type X tractor owners. In this sample, 48 percent of the National owners who replaced a tractor bought a new National, 27 percent bought an A model, and 25 percent bought some other type X tractor. In contrast, 73 percent of A owners bought a new A, 14 percent bought some type X tractor other than National, and 13 percent of A owners purchased a National tractor when they reentered the market.

Effect on Differences in Owner Body on 1975 Tractor Purchases

In Table 2, we have calculated the effect of owner bodies on type X tractor purchases in 1975. We have used actual figures for the size of National and competitor A owner bodies but have assumed that all other factors, including owner loyalty rates, are equal. In this calculation, we have applied National loyalty to both National and competitor A owner bodies. Based on these premises, one would expect National to have a deficiency in market penetration relative to competitor A of 1.6 percent solely as a result of the differences in the size of the two owner bodies, with National market penetration at 27.9 percent and competitor A penetration at 29.5 percent.

Type X Tractor Warranty Expense[1]

Some indication of National's type X tractor quality and durability problem is found in the level of our warranty expense as shown in Table 3. From 1970 to 1973, our warranty expense on the average type X tractor increased from $21.48 to $55.06, an increase of $33.58 per unit. Since 1973 warranty costs have declined to $31.38, a

reduction of $23.68. Expense on all components, with the exception of the hydraulic system, has increased over 1970 levels. It seems clear that warranty costs of over $31 per unit are too high and represent an unsatisfactory level of quality as far as the user is concerned.

National N–50 Type X Tractor—Warranty and Design[2] Cost

Table 4 indicates changes in warranty expense and design costs per unit on the N–50 tractor in the 1973, 1974, and 1975 models. In total, during this period, warranty expense has been reduced approximately $33, while design costs have increased $36. Engine warranty expense on this model had declined $40 per unit, while design costs have increased $24. In the case of the transmission, warranty expense has increased $3.30 per unit, despite an increase of $1.77 per unit in design costs.

TABLE 1*

	Make Purchased			
Make Replaced	National	A	Other	Total
National	48%	27%	25%	100%
Competitor A	13	73	14	100
Other	17	20	63	100

* Source: Replacement analysis published annually by trade association.

TABLE 2

	Make Replaced (thousands of units)			
Make Replaced	National	A	Other	Total Purchased
National	5.0	2.8	2.6	10.4
Competitor A	3.6	6.4	3.4	13.4
Other	3.7	3.8	12.8	20.3
Total	12.3	13.0	18.8	44.1
Penetration	27.9%	29.5%	42.6%	100.0%

National (under) competitor A:
　Percentage points　(1.6)
　Units　　　　　　　(0.7)

[1] Warranty expense is the amount spent by National for replacements and repairs to tractors in use for which it had accepted responsibility. The company kept detailed records of such costs, broken down not only in the main classifications indicated in Table 4 but also for individual parts within each classification.

[2] Design cost refers to the costs of the tractor itself. These costs are a function of the way in which the tractor is designed. For example, the total standard cost of the 1973 model was $9.78 more than the total standard cost of the 1972 model; the designers had devised a more expensive tractor in 1973. In making the comparisons, wage rates and material costs are held constant.

TABLE 3

| | Model Year | | | | | | 1975 (Over)/Under 1970 | |
	1970	1971	1972	1973	1974	1975	Per Unit	Percent
Engine	$11.30	$ 7.56	$28.05	$28.40	$22.58	$12.76	$(1.46)	(13%)
Transmission	3.70	3.09	3.90	6.60	6.00	7.19	(3.49)	(94)
Hydraulic system	.80	.46	.74	5.21	1.35	.57	.23	29
Electrical	.65	1.14	1.93	3.88	4.40	3.27	(2.62)	(403)
Other	5.03	4.20	5.20	10.97	8.90	7.59	(2.56)	(51)
Total	21.48	16.45	39.82	55.06	43.23	31.38	(9.90)	(46%)

TABLE 4   Changes by Year

| | 1973 (Over)/Under 1972 | | 1974 (Over)/Under 1973 | | 1975 (Over)/Under 1974 | | 1975 (Over)/Under 1972 | |
	Warranty	Design	Warranty	Design	Warranty	Design	Warranty	Design
Engine	$ 9.80	$(3.74)	$24.00	$(12.99)	$ 6.48	$ (7.62)	40.28	$(24.35)
Transmission	(2.69)	(1.31)	0.59	—	(1.20)	(0.46)	(3.30)	(1.77)
Hydraulic system	(4.48)	(8.90)	3.87	0.94	0.77	(2.97)	0.16	(10.93)
Electrical	(1.93)	—	(.53)	(1.09)	1.13	0.32	(1.33)	(0.77)
Other	(5.70)	4.17	2.00	(.50)	1.33	(1.73)	(2.37)	1.94
Total	(5.00)	(9.78)	29.93	(13.64)	8.51	(12.46)	33.44	(35.88)

Case 2–5

Eli Lilly and Company*

One of the most important problems I faced when I was named to this job was the lack of a well-designed succession plan to insure continual financial management of the company. For a variety of reasons, there was a missing generation of financial managers. So, while the company was growing, financial management was relatively inexperienced and not well rounded.

The Management Appraisal and Profile System has been particularly helpful to me. It has helped me sort through my financial directors and look again at our talent here when I arrived. It's also specified for me some of the performance dimensions which separate an effective financial manager from one who is simply a good financial analyst or accountant.

The issue is that the process which is implicit in the Appraisal and Profile System requires an enormous amount of time and effort. Even though only managers above salary class M are subject to the process, and not all of the hundred or so of those managers who report to me have been profiled, the time the process has consumed is far from trivial. I would really like to have the profile process applied to all 325 people who report directly to me, but I don't believe that it would be easy to show that the benefits would make the cost of doing so worthwhile.

The other question with which we have to grapple is the appropriate frequency of appraisal and profiling in activities like financial management and accounting. The written guidelines provided by the Personnel Resources Planning Group say that each member of management should have the opportunity for appraisal and profiling at least once a year, but we're falling well short of that. I wonder how the process will work if we repeat it on a two- or three-year cycle, as it now looks like we will.

Jim Cornelius, vice president of finance and chief financial officer of Eli Lilly and Company, was speaking about the management appraisal system used at the company since 1983. Replacing less-formal and unsystematic appraisal and personnel development systems, the new system achieved great specificity in appraisal, development, and possible behavioral changes for all managers. It also increased the time required for personnel appraisal and highlighted a number of problems in measuring the performance of professional financial managers.

Eli Lilly and Company

Eli Lilly and Company was one of the oldest pharmaceutical companies in the United States. It characterized itself as "a research-based corporation that develops, manufactures, and markets human medicines as well as electronic medical instruments, agricultural products, and cosmetics." Its revenues in 1985 were $3.3 billion, about triple the amount in 1975, and net income was $517.6 million. Its headquarters were in Indianapolis; it had manufacturing operations in North America, Latin America, Europe, Asia, and Africa; and its products were marketed in more than 150 countries. In 1985, it had more than 28,000 employees, more than 10 percent of whom were directly engaged in research and development activities.

---

* This case was adapted by permission from cases 187-064 and 187–168 developed by William J. Bruns, Jr., Harvard Business School.
Copyright by the President and Fellows of Harvard College.

Emphasizing recognition of the importance of personnel resources, a company publication summarized:

> Lilly traditionally has operated under a promotion-from-within policy. This policy—coupled with company growth—has meant advancement at all levels and has made possible the selection of highly competent persons for positions of responsibility and leadership throughout the organization. Personnel policies are designed and carried out so individuals can move through their initial assignment area into other areas as rapidly as their abilities, drive, and performance merit.

Development of the Management Appraisal and Profile System

The task of making judgments about managers' performance had become more complicated and had evolved significantly as the company grew in size, scope, and international commitment. The processes employed in earlier years were based on the personnel philosophies of careful selection, commitment, and continuous employment with the company. Although appraisals had always been done for the purpose of setting salary levels, they were often somewhat informal. There was little to help people plan their careers on a year-to-year basis, or to help supervisors plot individual development, decide on the relative importance of technical versus managerial skills, or evaluate individual contributions and leadership skills. As a result, managers and supervisory employees often did not know which aspects of their performance to stress.

By the mid-1970s, the personnel resources staff began to think about improving the process by more explicitly identifying performance dimensions and making appraisal processes more uniform. International operations managers were the first to see the advantage of using uniform dimensions from country to country. The Management Appraisal and Profile System (MAPS) evolved to its current form by late 1983, when it was introduced at corporate headquarters in Indianapolis.

The primary objectives of the personnel resources staff were to reduce confusion and inconsistency about managerial roles, performance, and compensation actions; to increase feedback to managers regarding areas for improvement and their personal development; and to avoid costly selection and management development mistakes. Explicit attention was given to the publication and discussion of these objectives, and to their consistent use across organizational boundaries and levels. The personnel resources staff paid particular attention to resolving the dilemma of appraising people who performed well technically but who had not yet developed the necessary leadership qualities to achieve their projected potential in the company.

The Management Appraisal and Profile System

The principal elements of the MAPS were as follows:

- *Dimensions of management performance* were specified in the system (these are the 11 boxes shown in Exhibit 1).
- An *appraisal group* was selected to include two levels of immediate supervision, a personnel manager/director, and other individuals who had worked closely with the individual being appraised.
- A *Management Appraisal and Profile meeting* was held, during which the profile panel rated the manager on each dimension on a four-point scale.
- An *overall management effectiveness rating* was determined.
- A *development and follow-up plan* was prepared.
- A *feedback discussion* was held with the manager, during which development objectives, which were mutually agreed upon, and employee comments were recorded.

The MAPS process was initiated by personnel staff; a staff member acted as scribe for each profile panel. The scribe identified the need for a profile, helped select the panel members by referring to supervisors and the individual, and invited participation one or two months before the meeting. The makeup of a panel could vary, but in most cases it was likely to include the immediate supervisor and one level above, the prior supervisor, intracompany clients from outside the manager's area of activity, and one representative from personnel. The objective was to choose a panel of people who could give the most relevant feedback to the employee.

Prior to the first meeting of the panel, members were contacted and were encouraged to write on a previously distributed worksheet their views of the dimensions which would be evaluated and summarized by the panel. The objective of this step was to get relevant input from a variety of people. When a profile had been prepared previously on an individual, its observations might be provided to panel members. Most panel members would have served on other panels and, therefore, would be familiar with the performance dimensions. Information was distributed to provide definitions of dimensions and possible ratings.

The panel had to reach a consensus. Meetings generally lasted about one and one-half hours, but not more than three hours. The scribe prepared notes and summaries of statements, which were reviewed by all panel members and the supervisor, who then reviewed these with the employee. The employee had an opportunity to agree or disagree with the results of the process and the development plan, and then signed the plan, which became part of the personnel record. Personnel was charged with responsibility for following up on this development plan, which was the output of the process.

The forms that the profile panel completed are shown in Exhibit 1. Each dimension was rated by the panel according to the following instructions:

In considering each dimension, the following scale should be used. It is expected that most individuals will exhibit a range of skill levels dependent upon their particular abilities and background. Thus, raters should use as much of the scale as appropriate. Only a highly exceptional person would be rated as Good or Top in every dimension.

Top signifies competence significantly beyond job requirements relating to a particular dimension. Exceptional achievement is demonstrated in key areas of responsibility. Performance is generally excellent in quality and quantity.

Good signifies competence that meets and sometimes exceeds job requirements relating to a particular dimension. Performance is above average in quality and quantity.

Satisfactory competence indicates that all job requirements are met with regard to that dimension. Major responsibilities are carried out in an acceptable manner. Continued development effort will ensure meeting future requirements.

Needs Improvement describes an individual's lack of skill or knowledge to meet significant requirements in a particular dimension. Development action steps should be designed to enable the individual to attain the necessary skills or knowledge.

In evaluating performance against appraisal dimensions, a STAR—an acronym standing for Situation, Task, Action, and Result—system was used. The panel, recalling its contact with the individual, described STARs, which provided the basis for evaluating the degree to which the individual had achieved a high or low performance against a particular appraisal dimension. In almost all profiles, in spite of the 13 or more performance dimensions and multiple STARs, one theme would develop as the panel proceeded with its work. The theme tended to concur with the strengths and the weaknesses with which an individual was associated. Coaching was then planned and developed around the result of the appraisal discussion.

The panel then prepared a summary of overall management effectiveness, based on a five-point scale described as follows:

There are five zones to define overall management effectiveness. There is no set formula that establishes the placement of an individual in a given zone. Most people will have a variety of ratings on the skill dimensions and varying performance levels. Overall Management Effectiveness is determined on an individual basis, giving consideration to performance, skills, and potential. Obviously, an individual's placement in a zone will change over time. The following are guidelines that should be used to determine the Overall Management Effectiveness zone:

Achiever. Performance consistently exceeds job requirements. Has potential for a higher level of responsibility.

OR

Performance consistently exceeds job requirements. Potential for higher level of responsibility is questionable.

Contributor. Performance consistently meets job requirements and occasionally exceeds them. Potential for a higher level of responsibility is questionable.

Learner. Performance exceeded job requirements in previous position. Potential for a higher level of responsibility is being assessed.

Maintainer. Performance meets job requirements. Potential for a higher level of responsibility is limited.

Marginal performer. Performance does not meet job requirements. Improvement in performance must be shown or demotion or termination is probable.

The final stage of the panel's work was the creation of a development plan, which summarized key areas for improvement, action to be taken, proposed timing, and follow up. This summary was reviewed with the employee. A copy of this summary, as well as the Management Appraisal and Profile form, were distributed to the employee's supervisor, the personnel director, and the person responsible for personnel resource planning. The personnel director was responsible for reviewing the development plan, following up on the plan to see that it was being implemented, and for recording the development of actions taken.

Management Views on the Appraisal and Profile System

Jim Cornelius spoke about his feeling that the profile system was exceptionally important:

One of my major tasks has been reestablishing the depth of talent of the financial organization on a worldwide basis so it can function more efficiently with or without my direct supervision. I've been trying to centralize many of the treasury functions, particularly those that relate to international operations. At the same time, I've been trying to improve the "back-office accounting/administrative" functions and consolidate them here in Indianapolis.

To do this, I have to sort through the senior financial management group to be sure that I have the right people in the right places. The Management Appraisal and Profiling System has been particularly helpful to me. Also, it has probably helped us in a dozen instances where current performance didn't match up with job requirements.

I suppose I would have had to work on talent and succession issues, anyway, but the appraisals and profiles helped a great deal. In particular, they helped us in dealing with those who were no longer performing adequately. They also helped to identify people who might be ready for and also appropriate for early promotions. And finally, they helped me decide when we had to go outside the company for experienced talent in areas like auditing and strategic planning. Although our focus here at Lilly is on internal personnel development, we occasionally go outside to hire. In the long run, the appraisal and profile process will help us maintain a better long-term focus on future talent.

One of the things I like about the system is that it provides a "crisper" process and an ongoing "code" for communication with my management. They will now be reviewed periodically and systematically through the remainder of their careers. To me, the main purpose in this process is behavioral change. It provides a way of focusing people's attention on areas where they need to change if they are to develop and achieve their full potential. The purpose is to encourage everybody to work at 100 percent of their abilities. Quite often, before we had this system, there was an assumption that some people simply didn't have the necessary talents; I think the system has also shown us that talent can be developed. If we work together more productively over time through the profile and appraisal system, we will have accomplished a major breakthrough in the personnel management process within the financial organization.

As chief financial officer, I would normally receive copies of the profiles of all management people in my division. From these, we have identified 5 to 10 possible successors to myself and prepared a list of people who are tracking toward the other key positions of controller, treasurer, strategic planner, and so on. The profile process is enormously helpful in this, because it summarizes past assignments and accomplishments. At the same time, it shows where people need to grow and what they have to do to broaden their management skills. It reveals the people who communicate well, and it creates an environment that signals when learning or new experiences are necessary.

The profiling system quite frequently encourages people to stretch beyond the point they have previously achieved. We hired a specialist from the outside who was profiled as a clear achiever in that role. However, when we transferred him, he was only rated a learner. As a result of this rating through the profiling process, we signaled him that he should ask for more help on occasion and that he needed to develop his communication abilities further. The profiling forced feedback to him and as a result of this he now has five or six areas to improve in order to regain the Achiever status. The system got his attention and I'm fairly confident that he can make the change.

Mike Hunt, vice president and treasurer reporting directly to Cornelius, also spoke about the Appraisal and Profile system:

In the financial group, our use of the profile has had substantial effect. In the old days, people were evaluated to a very large extent on their technical/accounting competence. Involvement in the business was not rewarded. But, as we have grown to a large highly diversified corporation, a proactive financial organization is also very important. Profiling has helped us manage the change. It allows us to focus on leadership and the ability to effectively work in our environment. The system has some real teeth in it, too. It is tied directly to the administration of salary, performance awards, and stock options. Because so much information is explicitly summarized, we can better differentiate people in terms of current performance, potential, and compensation. The information from the profiling system helps us identify candidates for promotion and

determine what we need to do to prepare them for added responsibility.

Dick Warne, vice president and controller reporting to Cornelius, compared the profiling system to other management appraisal systems that had been used at Lilly:

There is simply no question that the present appraisal and profiling system is much better than anything we used before. Prior systems lacked specificity and were not reviewed with the manager being appraised. They tended to be sporadic, narrowly based, and subjective.

However, we still have some sorting out to do for the system to achieve its maximum benefit. While the dimensions provide insight into specific activities relevant to management, it makes the process complex and time consuming; and sometimes the dimensions don't reflect the nature of staff work, since it tends to have a higher advisory and quantitative, as opposed to supervisory and directive, content.

The rating *grid* for performance and potential is another area for gaining greater understanding. Since we are dealing with management succession, it would seem that potential is as important, or more important, than performance, but the process and dimensions appear to emphasize the latter; and, as we go further down in the organization, I'm concerned that the system tends to value performance more than potential.

Another issue with the rating grid is the use of the specific words: *Achiever, Learner, Contributor, Maintainer, Marginal performer.* These words evoke emotional reactions from appraisees when they are given feedback on the appraisal system—everyone wants to be an Achiever. People who are told they are Maintainers feel they are being perceived negatively when, actually, they are doing a good job. The labels can become a hindrance in the appraisal process. I don't know, maybe a numerical rating system would serve us better. The Pharmaceutical Division used numbers in its appraisal of salesmen; maybe we should also, to avoid "word" labels with their emotional content.

A final point of concern on the ratings is one common to many grading systems, and that is the tendency to appraise everyone as a medium performer—in this system, a Contributor, I wonder if we aren't tending to rank Maintainers as low contributors. More importantly, I'm concerned that we may be rating high potential people as high contributors who might, with encouragement and coaching, be Achievers. We don't have enough Achievers to replace present senior management. We need, therefore, to identify deeper into the organization, or face the reality of outside hiring, which then has to be reconciled with our promotion-from-within philosophy.

But don't get me wrong. There's no question that the present system is working. It's much better than what we've done previously and is providing excellent input into our management succession planning.

Finally, Fred Ruebeck, controller of the Pharmaceutical Division, talked about specific profiles and his opinion of the Appraisal and Profile System:

One case I remember was a person who was labeled a Maintainer. The profiling system gave him a clear opportunity to see where he stood and to think about changing his performance. The individual had been with the company for most of his career and was a credit manager in my division. He was thoroughly professional and he performed the credit managing function very well. However, the Maintainer category reflected his limited desire and potential to perform in other financial jobs.

The system does not reward people who do just one thing well. Therefore, when an individual is not adding value to the job and is labeled a Maintainer, he may conclude, as this individual did, "the company is changing and it's tougher on people than it used to be." But when I compare that manager (who retired) to his replacement, I see that the present manager has broader capability and is willing to learn at the same time.

A second case that I recall was a person about 35 years of age. He had unrealistically favorable perceptions of himself and, after profiling, it took him a year to accept the results. He did many things well and was a good supervisor. He probably could have come around, since a large part of his problem, I think, stemmed directly from his self-concept. He couldn't accept the need for upward communication and lacked flexibility.

When he was told that an evaluation panel would be selected, he suggested two persons to be on it

and asked that two others not be selected. He had no objection to the process, and he respected the system. But when the profile led to a less-favorable evaluation than he felt was justified, he said, "This has ruined my career. I want to be a director by age 40; I'll leave." He left Lilly to join a smaller competitor.

A third case which I think illustrates that the system is working involves a very young manager. He has moved up quickly and his brash style has caused problems with some people. He's had a great deal of sponsorship from top management. When I provided feedback from the profiling process which labeled him as a Contributor, he didn't like the message. Nevertheless, he is dealing with the feedback, and I think he is likely to grow from it. By giving hard appraisals and basing compensation on those appraisals, the profile is an effective multidimensional motivation process.

Because the Management Appraisal and Profile system uses common dimensions for all managers, I think it tends to encourage line behavior in the staff functions. To succeed in a staff function, a person has to be able to make presentations, to convince others, both higher and lower, about ideas and things that need to be done. The dimensions used in the profile reward breadth of management, talent, experience, and performance.

Jim Cornelius summed up his questions about the Management Appraisal and Profile System:

I'm trying to build a first-class financial managers' organization here at Eli Lilly. There's been about a 100 percent growth in my function's headcount since 1982 while the rest of the company has been consolidating in terms of size. My real questions concern how I can best use the profiling process. Should I apply it to more people, even though this will take more time? Or should I just focus on top managers and my "fast trackers" by initiating profiles on them more frequently? I'm still grappling with the system's costs and benefits to me as chief financial officer. What do you think?

Appraisal of David Campbell

The Appraisal and Profile Panel reviewing David Campbell's performance as controller for manufacturing had completed their late morning discussion. Campbell's supervisor, Eric Neilsen, executive director of manufacturing, had suggested breaking for lunch before they assigned an Overall Management Effectiveness rating and created an employee development plan. Other panel members, from manufacturing, product development, systems, and control, agreed that a break would help them digest all of the views they had heard.

Campbell had worked for Eli Lilly for over 20 years and had been in his present function for about 10 years. Each panel member was chosen because of his or her familiarity with a different area of Campbell's work. For the most part, they had agreed with each other's assessments of Campbell's job performance, interpersonal characteristics, and leadership abilities. Martin Rand, director of personnel, acting as scribe, had summarized the panel's comments about Campbell in

each of the categories on the Management Appraisal and Profile form (Exhibit 1); as the panel gathered their information and opinions together, he quickly read the summaries to focus everyone's thinking.

After lunch, the six panel members reconvened in the conference room. Now, standing before them, Neilsen reminded them that they had to agree on the ratings (Needs Improvement, Satisfactory, Good, Top) for each category on the profile form, as well as the Overall Management Effectiveness rating (Achiever, Contributor, Learner, Maintainer, Marginal performer). Neilsen was concerned with how best to serve the needs of Campbell, the manufacturing group, and the financial organization within Eli Lilly. As he prepared to open the discussion of performance ratings and development plans, he wondered what he should recommend.

EXHIBIT 1   Management Appraisal and Profile Form

Name (Last) CAMPBELL	(First) DAVID	(MI)	Job Title: Controller—Manufacturing			
Department Number/Location:	Social Security Number; Identification Number:		Date of Last Appraisal:		Current Date: 2 23 85	
			MO DAY YR		MO DAY YR	

Appraisal Group: Executive Dir.—Manufacturing ___Yrs.___Mo.	V.P. Manufacturing (Product Development)
Supervisor Director of Personnel Supervised Employee	Participant V.P. Systems
Scribe	Participant V.P. Manufacturing
Personnel	Participant V.P. Controller

Management Process—Analyzes situations, decides on a course of action, plans, implements, and follows up on results.

David has been a good participant in the manufacturing management process, especially on the development side. He has shown that he is very effective in taking direction and in implementation. His focus, however, is narrow (accounting versus the broader management/business issues). He should strive to push out, to challenge and improve on a broad front. He needs to initiate actions in order to improve his management process.

Rating S

Problem Solving—Identifies problems, evaluates relevant facts, generates ideas/alternatives, and reaches sound conclusions.

David has approached problem solving more often than not from a rather narrow financial (accounting) perspective. While his strength has not been in problem identification, he has been most effective in implementing agreed-upon solutions. David should concentrate on approaching broader business issues (e.g., the opportunity that the idle plant provided for "pushing out").

Rating G

Leadership—Influences others to reach decisions, plan a course of action, and work toward common goals and objectives.

David has shown that he is a strong influence on others, choosing to accommodate versus challenge. An example of this can be seen in the manner in which he is handling the subordinate personnel issue—an issue that has not as yet been clearly defined, but which clearly needs to be dealt with. He needs to be a more active participant in many of the meetings he attends (staff/F.P.P., etc.). David is very good in one-on-one situations, and has demonstrated that he is very responsive to the issues of his user areas.

Rating S

Communication Skills—Understands what is meant by others and clearly expresses one's own message.
(*Note*: Consider how communications are handled upward, laterally, and downward—orally and in writing.)

David is a good listener. He has demonstrated this through follow-up to issues brought forth in the various meetings he attends. He is very good in one-on-one situations, but his reserved style limits his impact (low-key approach with a presentation style that, while factual and concise, is lacking in enthusiasm).

Rating S

Rating key: N I = N e e d s   I m p r o v e m e n t ;   S = S a t i s f a c t o r y ;   G = G o o d ;   T = T o p .

EXHIBIT 1 *(continued)*

Interpersonal Skills—Interacts and collaborates with a variety of people, especially in difficult and sensitive situations.

David needs to be a more active participant in group settings, but he is very effective in one-on-one situations geared to implementation. He possesses a very warm, but quiet-/passive, approach. He comes across to all people as definitely interested in their issues, and as most sincere.

Rating S

Effort—Initiates action(s), meets tight deadlines, and maintains a positive outlook despite obstacles.

Meets deadlines in most cases. He possesses a positive attitude. David cannot be faulted in his effort; rather, he could help himself by channeling his involvement into broader business issues and initiating issues (as described elsewhere in this write-up). David clearly puts a lot of effort into all that is asked of him.

Rating T

Developing People—Selects, appraises, trains, and coaches employees; sets standards of performance, and develops employees to assume greater responsibility.

David has been involved with a couple of the younger people where he has worked through people issues (the MBA in finance and the BS in accounting). He is not known for setting tough standards, but rather uses a lenient style in motivation. Executive Director needed to encourage David to push an employee, to give her guidance as a young professional. Once done, it was very effective. David uses a "father"-type leadership style.

Rating G

Job Content Knowledge—Demonstrates knowledge of requirements, methods, techniques, and business fundamentals involved in doing the job, and applies this to increase productivity.

David possesses an outstanding knowledge in the controller function within manufacturing. He knows the history and the accounting to a point where he can effectively respond to all inquiries. He could improve in the area of Job Content Knowledge by expanding beyond the accounting issue to focus also on the broader business issues facing the component (idle plant/Capital Appropriations/M.R.P.).

Rating G

Resource Utilization—Identifies, locates, and mobilizes internal and external resources necessary for the completion of job objectives.

Working within the production/development areas, David does a very effective job of utilizing the resources available. Again, there is the continuation of the theme of broadening his involvement beyond the accounting function. He needs to develop a broader involvement with pharmaceuticals and the planning group, C.M.C.S., etc. Some of the problems in B.H.I. might have been better dealt with had David acted in a more proactive manner.

Rating S/G

Creativity/Innovation—Generates worthwhile new ideas or techniques, builds on the ideas of others, and helps others apply their ideas.

David does not merchandise creativity but is very responsive to the issues raised by his user areas. He has had a tendency to be somewhat inflexible on occasion.

Rating S

Presence—Instills confidence and does not add to the stress on others when under pressure.

David is seen as maybe too tactful. While this style does not necessarily create stress, it can reduce his influence when coupled with his tendency to be somewhat passive.

Rating S

Rating key: N I = N e e d s   I m p r o v e m e n t;   S = S a t i s f a c t o r y;   G = G o o d;   T = T o p.

EXHIBIT 1   *(continued)*

Commitment—Understands and accepts corporate goals and values; makes sacrifices, when necessary, to accomplish them.
David will give of himself in any way possible to accomplish objectives. He accepts and fairly represents our corporate goals and values. <div align="right">Rating T</div>

Constructive Confrontation—Expresses ideas that differ with supervision, peers, and subordinates without being offensive and shares negative information when necessary.
David needs to develop a stronger stand with subordinates [specific situation deleted]. David seems to seek out agreement, rather than to confront issues immediately or directly. <div align="right">Rating S</div>

Other dimension—   <div align="right">Rating___</div>

Other dimension—   <div align="right">Rating___</div>

Rating key: N I = N e e d s I m p r o v e m e n t ;   S = S a t i s f a c t o r y ;   G = G o o d ;   T = T o p .

Summary of Management Effectiveness— **(Describe the individual's major job accomplishments and summarize his or her skill level in the above dimensions.)**

	Marginal performer	Maintainer	Learner	Contributor	Achiever
OVERALL MANAGEMENT EFFECTIVENESS— According to the Managerial Grid definitions, which zone best describes the appraised individual?					

EXHIBIT 1 *(continued)*

I. Development Plan

Development Objectives	Action Steps to Accomplish Development Objectives	Timing

II. Follow-up on the Development Plan

Date	Personnel Director Responsible for Follow Up	Action Taken

EXHIBIT 1   *(concluded)*

Management Appraisal and Profile Discussion

Summary of Management Effectiveness:

Development Objectives:

Overall Management Effectiveness: _____

Comments: _____

_____

_____

I acknowledge this appraisal was reviewed with me on _____.

Date

_____

Employee Signature

_____

Supervisor

_____

Personnel

_____

Next Level Supervision

QUESTIONS

1. What are the strengths and weaknesses of the Management Appraisal and Profile System (MAPS) developed and used by Eli Lilly and Company?
2. How would you answer the questions raised by Jim Cornelius at the end of the Eli Lilly and Company case?
3. Using the information in Exhibit 1:
   a. prepare a summary of management effectiveness for David Campbell.
   b. Rate Campbell's overall management effectiveness.
   c. Prepare a development plan for David Campbell.
4. What are your personal reactions to the MAPS system? Would you like to work in an organization that uses this or a similar process for evaluation?

Chapter 3

Responsibility Centers: Revenue and Expense Centers

Management control focuses on the behavior of managers in responsibility centers. This is the first of four chapters dealing with responsibility centers. We describe the nature of responsibility centers in general and the criteria of efficiency and effectiveness that are relevant in measuring the performance of responsibility center managers. We then discuss revenue centers and expense centers, which are two types of responsibility centers. There are two general types of expense centers: engineered expense centers and discretionary expense centers. Discretionary expense centers can be further classified as administrative and support centers, research and development (R&D) centers, and marketing centers; each is discussed.

RESPONSIBILITY CENTERS

We use the term *responsibility center* to denote any organization unit that is headed by a responsible manager. In a sense, a company is a collection of responsibility centers, each of which is represented by a box on the organization chart. These responsibility centers form a hierarchy. At the lowest level in the organization are responsibility centers for sections, work shifts, or other small organization units. At a higher level are departments or business units (divisions) that consist of several of these smaller units plus overall departmental or business unit staff and management people; these larger units are also responsibility centers. And from the standpoint of senior management and the board of directors, the whole company is a responsibility center, although the term is usually used to refer to units *within* the company.

EXHIBIT 3–1 Responsibility Center

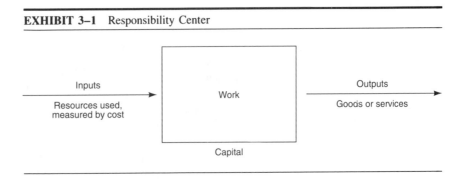

Nature of Responsibility Centers

A responsibility center exists to accomplish one or more purposes; these purposes are its *objectives*. The organization has goals, and senior management has decided on a set of strategies to accomplish these goals. The objectives of responsibility centers are to do their part in implementing these strategies. Because the organization is the sum of all the responsibility centers within it, if the strategies are sound, and if each responsibility center meets its objectives, the whole organization will achieve its goals.

Exhibit 3–1 is a schematic diagram that shows the essence of any responsibility center. A responsibility center uses inputs, which are physical quantities of material, hours of various types of labor, and a variety of services. It works with these resources, and it usually requires working capital (e.g., inventory, receivables), equipment, and other assets to do this work. As a result of this work, the responsibility center produces outputs, which are classified either as goods, if they are tangible, or as services, if they are intangible. Every responsibility center has outputs—that is, it does something. In a production plant, the outputs are goods. In staff units, such as human resources, transportation, engineering, accounting, and administration, the outputs are services. For many responsibility centers, especially staff units, outputs are difficult to measure; nevertheless, they exist. Presumably, these outputs are consistent with the responsibility center's objectives, but this is not necessarily so. For example, a manufacturing center may produce more goods than the marketing department can sell, or it may provide goods of inferior quality. These are outputs, even though they are not consistent with the company's overall strategies. Whatever a responsibility center produces, whether good or bad, desired or unwanted, constitutes its outputs.

The goods and services produced by a responsibility center may be furnished either to another responsibility center or to the outside world. In the first case, they are inputs to the other responsibility center; in the latter case, they are outputs of the whole organization. Revenues are the amounts earned from selling these outputs.

Relation between Inputs and Outputs

Management is responsible for obtaining the optimum relationship between inputs and outputs. In some situations, the relationship is causal and direct. In a production department, the inputs of raw material resources become a physical part of the finished goods output, and control focuses on producing the outputs at the time needed, in the desired quantities, according to the correct specifications and with minimum inputs.

In many situations, however, inputs are not directly related to outputs. Advertising expense is an input that is expected to increase sales revenue; but revenue is affected by many factors other than advertising, so the relationship between an additional dollar of advertising and the resulting revenue rarely is known. Management's decision on the amount to spend for advertising is based on judgments. For research and development, the relationship between inputs and outputs is even more tenuous; the value of today's R&D effort may not be known for several years in the future, and the optimum amount that a given company should spend for R&D is unknowable.

Measurement of Inputs and Outputs

The amount of labor, material, and services used in a responsibility center are physical quantities: hours of labor, quarts of oil, reams of paper, and kilowatt-hours of electricity. In a management control system it is necessary to translate these amounts into monetary terms. Money provides a common denominator that permits the amounts of individual resources to be combined. The monetary amount is ordinarily obtained by multiplying the physical quantity by a price per unit of quantity (e.g., hours of labor times a rate per hour). This amount is called "cost." Thus, the inputs of a responsibility center are ordinarily expressed as costs. *Cost* is a monetary measure of the amount of resources used by a responsibility center.

Note that inputs are resources *used* by the responsibility center. The patients in a hospital or the students in a school are *not* inputs. Rather, inputs are the resources that are used in accomplishing the objectives of *treating* the patients or *educating* the students.

Although the cost of inputs almost always can be measured, outputs are much more difficult to measure. In a profit-oriented organization, revenue is an important measure of output of the whole organization, but such a measure is rarely a complete expression of outputs; it does not encompass everything that the organization does. For example, this year's revenue does not measure the value of R&D work, employee training, or advertising and sales promotion carried out this year; these inputs produce outputs that will benefit future years. In many responsibility centers, outputs cannot be measured satisfactorily. How can one measure the value of the work done by a public relations department, a quality control department, or a legal staff? In many nonprofit organizations, no good quantitative measure of output exists. A school can easily measure the number of students graduated, but it cannot measure how much education each of them acquired. Many organizations do not attempt to measure the outputs of such responsibility centers. Others use an approximation, or *surrogate,* of the output of some of them, recognizing its limitations.

Efficiency and Effectiveness

The concepts stated above can be used to explain the meaning of *efficiency* and *effectiveness,* which are the two criteria for judging the performance of a responsibility center. The terms are almost always used in a comparative, rather than in an absolute sense—that is, we do not ordinarily say that Responsibility Center A is 80 percent efficient but, rather, that it is more (or less) efficient than Responsibility Center B, or more (or less) efficient currently than it was in the past, or more (or less) efficient compared to its budget.

Efficiency is the ratio of outputs to inputs, or the amount of output per unit of input. Responsibility Center A is more efficient than Responsibility Center B either (1) if it uses less resources than Responsibility Center B, but has the same output, or (2) if it uses the same amount of resources as Responsibility Center B and has a greater output than Responsibility Center B. Note that the first type of measure does not require that output be quantified; it is only necessary to judge that the outputs of the two units are approximately the same. If management is satisfied that Responsibility Centers A and B are both doing a satisfactory job, and if it is a job of comparable magnitude, then the unit with the lower inputs (i.e., the lower costs) is the more efficient. The second type of measure does require some quantitative measure of output; it is, therefore, a more difficult type of measurement in many situations.

In many responsibility centers, a measure of efficiency can be developed that relates actual costs to some standard—that is, to a number that expresses what costs should be incurred for the amount of measured output. Such a measure can be a useful indication of efficiency; but it is never a perfect measure for at least two reasons: (1) recorded costs are not a precisely accurate measure of resources consumed and (2) standards are, at best, only approximate measures of what resource consumption ideally should have been in the circumstances prevailing.

Effectiveness is the relationship between a responsibility center's outputs and its objectives. The more these outputs contribute to the objectives, the more effective the unit is. Since both objectives and outputs are often difficult to quantify, measures of effectiveness are difficult to come by. Effectiveness, therefore, is often expressed in nonquantitative, judgmental terms, such as "College A is doing a first-rate job, but College B has slipped somewhat in recent years."

An organization unit should be *both* efficient and effective; it is not a case of choosing one or the other. Efficient responsibility centers are those that do whatever they do with the lowest consumption of resources; but if what they do (i.e., their output) is an inadequate contribution to the accomplishment of the organization's goals, they are ineffective. If a credit department handles the paperwork connected with delinquent accounts at a low cost per unit, it is efficient; but if it is unsuccessful in making collections, or, if in the process of collecting accounts it needlessly antagonizes customers, it is ineffective.

In summary, a responsibility center is efficient if it does things right, and it is effective if it does the right things.

The role of profits.   One important objective in a profit-oriented organization is to earn profits, and the amount of profits, therefore, is an important measure of effectiveness. Since profit is the difference between revenue, which is a measure of output, and expense, which is a measure of input, profit also is a measure of efficiency. Thus, profit measures both effectiveness and efficiency. When such an overall measure exists, it is unnecessary to determine the relative importance of effectiveness versus efficiency. When such an overall measure does not exist, it is feasible and useful to classify performance measures as relating either to effectiveness or to efficiency. In these situations, there is the problem of balancing the two types of measurements. For example, how do we compare the profligate perfectionist with the frugal manager who obtains less than the optimum output?

There are four types of responsibility centers, classified according to the nature of the monetary inputs or outputs, or both, that are measured: revenue centers, expense centers, profit centers, and investment centers. Their characteristics are shown in Exhibit 3–2. In revenue centers, only outputs are measured in monetary terms; in expense centers, only inputs are measured; in profit centers, both revenues and expenses are measured; and in investment centers, the relationship between profits and investment is measured.

The planning and control systems for responsibility centers will be different depending on whether they are revenue centers, expense centers, profit centers, or investment centers. We discuss the appropriate planning and control techniques for revenue centers and expense centers in the next part of this chapter. Profit centers are discussed in Chapter 4 and investment centers in Chapter 6.

REVENUE CENTERS

In a revenue center, outputs are measured in monetary terms; but no formal attempt is made to relate inputs (i.e., expenses or costs) to outputs. (If expenses were matched with revenues, the unit would be a profit center.) Revenue centers are, therefore, marketing organizations that do not have profit responsibility. Actual sales or orders booked are measured against budgets or quotas.

Each revenue center is also an expense center. The primary measurement, however, is revenue. Revenue centers are not charged for the cost of the goods

EXHIBIT 3–2 Types of Responsibility Centers

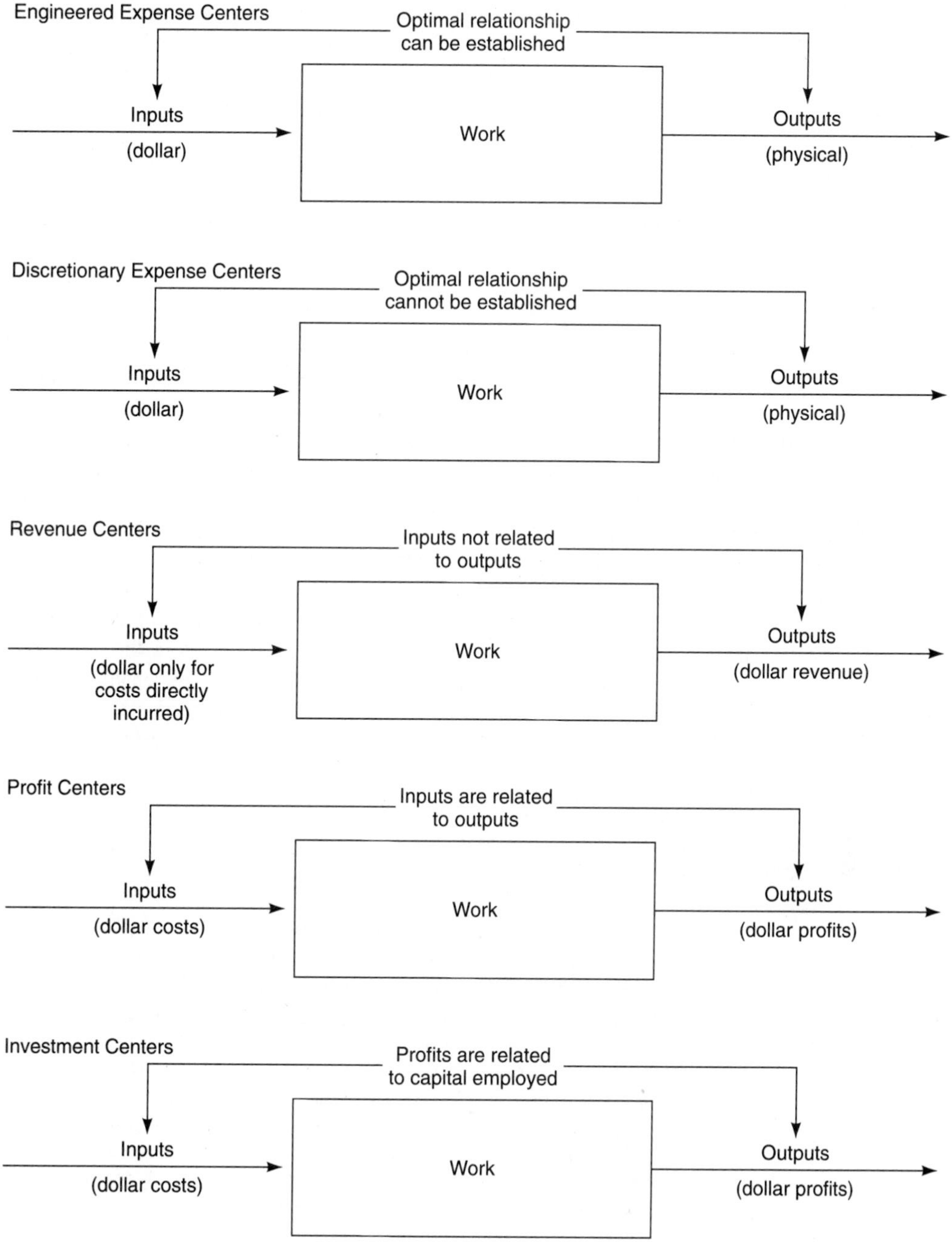

Engineered Expense Centers

Optimal relationship
can be established

Inputs
(dollar)

Work

Outputs
(physical)

Discretionary Expense Centers

Optimal relationship
cannot be established

Inputs
(dollar)

Work

Outputs
(physical)

Revenue Centers

Inputs not related
to outputs

Inputs
(dollar only for
costs directly
incurred)

Work

Outputs
(dollar revenue)

Profit Centers

Inputs are related
to outputs

Inputs
(dollar costs)

Work

Outputs
(dollar profits)

Investment Centers

Profits are related
to capital employed

Inputs
(dollar costs)

Work

Outputs
(dollar profits)

that they market. Consequently, they are not profit centers, because this important expense item is omitted.

The manager of a revenue center does not have knowledge that is needed to make the cost/revenue trade-off required for optimum marketing decisions. Therefore, responsibility for this type of decision cannot be delegated to a revenue center manager. For instance, revenue centers typically do not have authority to set selling prices.

In this book, we do not discuss revenue centers as such. We shall discuss the management of revenue as part of our discussion of profit centers. The control of expenses in these units is discussed in the next section.

EXPENSE CENTERS

Expense centers are responsibility centers for which inputs, or expenses, are measured in monetary terms, but in which outputs are not measured in monetary terms.[1] There are two general types: engineered expense centers and discretionary expense centers. They correspond to two types of costs. *Engineered costs* are elements of cost for which the "right" or "proper" amount of costs that should be incurred can be estimated with a reasonable degree of reliability. Costs incurred in a factory for direct labor, direct material, components, supplies, and utilities are examples. *Discretionary costs* (also called "managed" costs) are those for which no such engineered estimate is feasible; the amount of costs incurred depends on management's judgment about the amount that is appropriate under the circumstances. Expense centers in which all, or most, costs are engineered costs are engineered expense centers; expense centers in which most costs are discretionary are discretionary expense centers. Each is described below.

Engineered Expense Centers

Engineered expense centers (also called "standard cost centers") are usually found in manufacturing operations that employ some form of standard cost system. Warehousing, distribution, trucking, and similar units in the marketing organization also may be engineered expense centers, and so may certain responsibility centers within administrative and support departments. Examples

---

[1] Many expense centers are also cost centers, as this term is used in cost accounting. The distinction is that an expense center is a responsibility center—that is, it has a manager; whereas some cost centers do not have identifiable managers. For example, in a factory, there is usually an "occupancy" cost center, which collects the costs associated with the building, such as heat, air conditioning, light, insurance, and building maintenance. No one manager is responsible for these costs, so this cost center is not an expense center. Similarly, each of the printing presses in a print shop may be cost centers, but only the whole department is an expense center.

are accounts receivable, accounts payable, and payroll sections in the controller department; personnel records and the cafeteria in the human resources department; shareholder records in the corporate secretary department; and the company motor pool. Such units perform repetitive tasks for which standard costs can be developed. (Note that the departments of which these sections are a part are discretionary expense centers.)

In an engineered expense center, the output multiplied by the standard cost of each unit produced represents what the finished product ''should'' have cost. When this cost is compared to actual costs, the difference between the two represents the efficiency of the organizational unit being measured.

Engineered expense centers have the following characteristics:

1. Their inputs can be measured in monetary terms.
2. Their outputs can be measured in physical terms.
3. The optimal dollar amount of inputs required to produce one unit of output can be established.

We emphasize that, in engineered expense centers, there are other important tasks not measured by costs alone. The effectiveness of these aspects of performance should be controlled. For example, expense center supervisors are responsible for the quality of the products and for the volume of production, in addition to their responsibility for cost efficiency. It is necessary, therefore, to prescribe the type and amount of production and to set specific quality standards; otherwise, manufacturing costs could be minimized at the expense of quality. Moreover, these managers may be responsible for activities that are not related to current production, such as training, and judgments about their performance should include an appraisal of how well they carry out these responsibilities.

There are few, if any, responsibility centers in which all items of cost are engineered. Even in highly automated production departments, the amount of indirect labor and of various services used can vary with management's discretion. Thus, the term *engineered expense center* refers to responsibility centers in which engineered costs predominate, but it does not imply that valid engineering estimates can be made for each and every cost item.

Because standard cost systems are described in detail in cost accounting texts, we do not discuss them further here.

Discretionary Expense Centers

The output of discretionary expense centers cannot be measured in monetary terms. They include administrative and support units (e.g., accounting, legal, industrial relations, public relations, human resources); research and development organizations; and most marketing activities.

The term ''discretionary'' does *not* mean that management's judgments are capricious or haphazard. Management has decided on certain policies that should govern the operation of the company: whether to match, exceed, or spend less than the marketing efforts of its competitors; the level of service that the company provides to its customers, the appropriate amount of spending for R&D, financial planning, public relations and many other activities. One company may have a small headquarters staff; another company of similar size and in the same industry may have a staff that is 10 times its size. The managements of both companies are convinced that they made the correct decision on staff size; but there is no objective way of judging which decision was actually better (or whether they were equally good, and the differences reflect other differences about the way the companies operated.) Managers are hired and paid to make such decisions.

Management's view about the proper level of discretionary costs is subject to change. Dramatic changes may occur when a new management takes over.

Examples.   1. Shortly after he became CEO of General Electric Company in 1981, John F. Welch, Jr., cut the corporate staff to 1,000 from 1,700.[2]

2. When Lee Iacocca became CEO of Chrysler in 1980, he almost immediately cut the white-collar ranks by 7,000 people, and a few months later laid off 8,500 more. These two moves cut $500 million in annual costs.[3]

After such a drastic change, the level of discretionary expenses generally has a similar pattern from one year to the next.

There are three points in the control of discretionary expense centers.

First, the management control system helps only in expense control. The budget for this type of expense center represents only the planned inputs to the expense center.

Second, the difference between budgeted and actual expense is *not* a measure of efficiency. It is simply the difference between the budgeted input and the actual input. It in no way measures the value of the output. If actual expenses do not exceed the budget amount, the manager has "lived within the budget"; however, because by definition the budget does not purport to measure the optimum amount of spending, we cannot say that living within the budget is efficient performance.

Third, the financial control system measures neither the efficiency nor the effectiveness of these responsibility centers. It is necessary, therefore, that nonfinancial measures and judgments be employed in evaluating their performance.

In the next section, we discuss the management control systems for discretionary expense centers in general. We then discuss the special considerations involved in designing systems for the three of the most common types of discretionary expense centers: administrative and support centers, R&D centers, and marketing centers.

---

[2] L. J. Davis, "They Call Him Neutron," *Business Month,* March 1988, p. 27.

[3] From Lee Iacocca, *Iacocca: An Autobiography* (New York: Bantam, 1984), p. 199.

General Control Characteristics

Budget preparation. The decision that management must make about a discretionary expense budget is different from the decision that it must make about the budget for an engineered expense center. For the latter, management must decide whether the proposed operating budget represents the cost of performing a task efficiently for the coming period. Management is not so much concerned with the magnitude of the task, because this is largely determined by the actions of other responsibility centers, such as the marketing department's ability to generate sales. In formulating the budget for a discretionary expense center, however, management's principal task is to decide on the magnitude of the job that should be done.

In preparing a proposed budget, the responsibility center manager should include all relevant data but should exclude irrelevant data that might obscure the important information that the superior needs as a basis for a decision. Some budget proposals include a breakdown of the number of people by classification, the expense by each account, and a history of these costs for several years, all in great detail; but there may be little or no information about the tasks that are planned to be accomplished. If the proposal is of this nature, management must either rubber-stamp the budget, try to question individual expense items, or make arbitrary reductions. Questioning individual items is unlikely to be fruitful, for, if a proposal has been prepared carefully, a reasonable rationale can be given for any individual expense (whether or not it is really justifiable). If management reduces a budget arbitrarily, it can expect to receive a budget proposal the following year that contains sufficient "water" that a reduction creates no hardship. The following questions should be asked about a discretionary expense budget proposal:

1. What are the precise decisions that management should make?
2. Does the proposal include all the available information pertinent to making these decisions?
3. Does the proposal include irrelevant information which, at best, will tend to obscure the real issues?

These tasks can be divided generally into two types—continuing and special. *Continuing* tasks are those that continue from year to year—for example, financial statement preparation by the controller's office. *Special* tasks are "one-shot" projects—for example, developing and installing a profit budgeting system in a newly acquired division.

The starting point in preparing the budget is the current level of spending. The budgetee adjusts these amounts for anticipated inflation, for the cost implications of changes in the job to be done, and in some cases for anticipated productivity improvements. In some companies the preparation of the budget is preceded by a *zero base review,* as described in Chapter 8. Occasionally, a company may sharply prune its discretionary costs; but this usually happens as the result of a special campaign, rather than as the result of the normal budget preparation process. In recent years, many companies have reduced substantially the size of their administrative and support organizations.[4]

Some companies include a section in the budget explaining the activities that would be curtailed or canceled if the budget were reduced 5 or 10 percent, and another section explaining the activities that would be increased or started if the budget were increased 5 or 10 percent. This technique is called *sensitivity analysis.* Senior management can use this information to form judgments regarding the appropriate level of spending in a discretionary expense center. Most companies, however, do not require a sensitivity analysis; they prefer that departmental managers concentrate their efforts on preparing the best possible budget for the activities that they believe should be undertaken.

Some companies use data for competitors or data from trade and industry associations. For instance, information on R&D spending as a percent of sales for several competitors in the industry may be used as one input in deciding the budget for the R&D department. Because industry and competitor comparisons have obvious limitations, they should be supplemented with other information.

The technique called *management by objectives* is often used in preparing the budget for a discretionary expense center. Management by objectives is a formal process in which a budgetee proposes to accomplish specific tasks and states a means for measuring whether these tasks have been accomplished.

Cost variability. In discretionary expense centers, costs tend to vary with volume from one year to the next, but they tend *not* to vary with short-run fluctuations in volume within a given year. By contrast, costs in engineered expense centers are expected to vary with short-run changes in volume. The reason for the difference is that, in preparing budgets for discretionary expense centers, managements tend to approve a change in their size that corresponds to changes in budgeted sales volume—that is, additional personnel are budgeted when volume is expected to increase, and layoffs or attrition are planned when volume is expected to decrease. In part, this reflects the fact that volume changes do have an impact throughout the company, even though their actual impact cannot be measured; in part, this results from a management judgment that the company can afford to spend more in prosperous times than in other times. Since personnel costs and personnel-related costs are by far the largest expense item in most discretionary expense centers, the annual budgets for these centers tend to be a constant percentage of budgeted sales volume.

Based on the approved budget, managers of discretionary expense centers hire additional personnel or plan attrition. Having done so, it is uneconomical for them to adjust the work force for short-run fluctuations that occur within the year. Hiring and training personnel for additional short-run needs is expensive, and temporary layoffs hurt morale. Thus, although costs of discretionary

---

[4] According to the chairman of the board's report at the 1990 shareholder meeting, International Business Machines Corporation took two levels of staff out of its organization structure and eliminated more than 50,000 staff positions during the preceding four years.

expense centers are sometimes classified as fixed, they are in fact fixed only within a year; they tend to change with changes in volume from one year to the next.

Type of financial control.   The financial control exercised in a discretionary expense center is quite different from the financial control exercised through an operating expense budget in an engineered expense center. The latter attempts to minimize operating costs by setting a standard and reporting actual costs against this standard. Costs are minimized by motivating line managers to attain maximum efficiency and by giving higher management a means of evaluating the efficiency of departmental management. The main purpose of a discretionary expense budget, on the other hand, is to allow the superior to control costs by *participating in the planning*. Costs are controlled primarily by deciding what tasks should be undertaken and what level of effort is appropriate for each. Thus, in a discretionary expense center, financial control is primarily exercised at the planning stage *before* the amounts are incurred.

Some authorities state that a tight budget is a good budget, because a tight budget will result in more pressure to reduce costs than one that is easily attainable. While this philosophy may have merit for a standard cost budget, it is of questionable validity for a discretionary expense budget. The head of a discretionary expense center can easily cut costs by reducing the magnitude of the job that is done. However, when this happens, the individual responsible for spending the money is making the decision about the job to be done. Such decisions should properly be made by higher management.

The general rule, then, is that discretionary expense budgets should reflect as closely as possible the *actual costs* of doing the tasks that should be done. A deviation from this rule should be backed by adequate reasons, and this condition should be known to the superior when the budget is presented for approval.

Measurement of performance.   In discretionary expense centers, the financial performance report is used to ensure that the budget commitment will not be exceeded without the superior's knowledge. It is not a means for evaluating the efficiency of the manager. This is in contrast to the report in an engineered expense center, which helps higher management to evaluate the manager's efficiency. If these two types of responsibility centers are not carefully distinguished, management may treat the performance report for a discretionary expense center as if it were an indication of efficiency. If this is done, the people responsible for spending may be motivated to spend less than budgeted. This pressure toward lower costs may possibly result in the task being done for less money; but it is more likely that the lower spending will be accomplished by less output. In any event, there is little point in trying to increase efficiency by such indirect methods as rewarding executives who spend less than budget.

Control over spending can be exercised by requiring that the superior's approval be obtained before the budget is overrun. Sometimes, a certain percentage of overrun (say, 5 percent) is permitted without additional approval. If the budget really sets forth the best estimate of actual costs, there is a 50 percent probability that it will be overrun, and this is the reason that some latitude is often permitted.

The preceding paragraphs relate to *financial* control. Total control over discretionary expense centers is achieved primarily by the use of nonfinancial performance measures. For instance, the quality of service provided by many discretionary expense centers can be judged based on the opinions of its users.

ADMINISTRATIVE AND SUPPORT CENTERS

Administrative centers include senior corporate management, business unit management, and managers who are responsible for staff units. Support centers are units that provide services to other responsibility centers.

Control Problems

The control of administrative expense is especially difficult because of (1) the near impossibility of measuring output and (2) the frequent lack of congruence between the goals of the staff department and the goals of the company.

Difficulty in measuring output. Some staff activities, such as payroll accounting, are so routinized that they are engineered expense centers. For others, however, the principal output is advice and service; and there are no valid means of measuring the value, or even the amount, of this output. If output cannot be measured, it is not possible to set cost standards and measure financial performance against these standards. A budget variance, therefore, cannot be interpreted as representing either efficient or inefficient performance. For instance, if the finance staff were given a budget allowance to "develop a profit budgeting system," a comparison of actual cost to budgeted cost would in no way tell management how effectively or efficiently the job had been done. The job of development and installation might have been poor, regardless of the amount spent.

Lack of goal congruence. In most administrative staff offices, managers want to have as excellent a department as they possible can. Superficially, it may appear that an excellent department is best for the company. Actually, a great deal depends on how one defines an "excellent department." For example:

• It is to the benefit of the controller to be able to answer immediately any question involving accounting data that he or she is asked by management. The cost of a system to do this, however, might far exceed the benefits it provides.

- It is to the benefit of the legal staff never to have the slightest flaws in any contract that it approves. It can be very costly to review all proposed contracts so intensively that one will be completely sure that nothing will happen that might be construed as a mistake by the legal staff. The potential loss may be much less than the cost of ensuring perfection.

What these points boil down to is that, at best, the staff office may want to develop the "ideal" system, program, or function. However, the ideal can be too costly in terms of additional profits that it generates. At worst, there can be a tendency to "empire build" or to "safeguard one's position," without regard for its value to the company.

The severity of these two problems—the difficulty of measuring output and the lack of goal congruence—is fairly directly related to the size and prosperity of the company. In small and medium-sized businesses, senior management is in close personal contact with staff units and can determine from personal observation what they are doing and whether a unit is worth its cost. Also, in a business with low earnings, discretionary expenses are often kept under tight control. In a large business, senior management cannot possibly know about, much less evaluate, all the staff activities; also, in a profitable company, there is a temptation to approve staff requests for constantly increasing budgets.

The severity of these two problems is also related directly to the organizational level of the staff activity. For example, at the plant level, the administrative staff tends to be carefully controlled by the plant manager who has personal knowledge of what is happening. Furthermore, there is less discretion in the tasks to be performed. At the business unit level, the staff has more discretion in the tasks that it performs than at the plant level; at the corporate level, there is even more discretion. In general, the type of staff activity that is performed at the plant and business unit level is closely related to organizational objectives. Discretionary expense centers at the corporate level are the most difficult to judge in relation to objectives.

Support centers often charge other responsibility centers for the services that they provide. For example, the management information services department may charge others for computer services. These responsibility centers are profit centers, as discussed in Chapter 4.

Budget Preparation

The proposed budget for an administrative or support center usually consists of a list of expense items, with the proposed budget compared with the current year's actual. In some companies, the presentation is more elaborate, consisting of some or all of the following components:

- A section covering the basic costs of the center. This includes the costs of "being in business" plus the costs of all activities that *must* be undertaken and for which no general management decisions are required.

- A section covering the discretionary activities of the center. This includes a description of the objectives and the estimated costs of each such activity. The purpose of this section is to provide information to allow management to make cost-effective decisions. For example, management may decide that some of the activities are not worth the cost. Senior management, therefore, is able to decide the magnitude of the tasks to be done.
- A section fully explaining all proposed increases in budget other than those related to inflation.
- A section explaining the activities that would be curtailed or canceled if the budget was reduced 5 percent and 10 percent.
- A section explaining the activities that would be increased or started if the budget was increased 5 percent and 10 percent.

Clearly, all of these sections are worthwhile only where the budget is large and where management wishes to decide on the extent of the activities of the center. For other centers, the amount of detail depends on the importance of the expenses and the desires of management. The important point, however, is that, *if* management is expected to decide the level of administrative activity, the presentation should be aimed at providing the information needed for an intelligent decision. Although the last two items are not prepared in most budget analyses, they can be important. In effect, they indicate to management the costs of the marginal activities.

Management Considerations

Even under the best circumstances, the management control system is of limited help in determining the optimum level of expenses. Consequently, the decisions on how much to spend must be based largely on management judgment. These decisions become more difficult as staff offices become more numerous and specialized. It is not unusual to have a dozen staff groups in corporate headquarters. They include, among others, legal, treasury, controller, systems and operations research, industrial relations, community relations, government relations, human resources, and planning staffs. The president often has neither the time nor the specialized knowledge to exercise more than cursory control over these activities. Consequently, many large companies have an administrative vice president, to whom all or most of these groups report. This ensures adequate attention by an executive with the time and expertise required to plan and exercise the necessary control over these staff activities.

RESEARCH AND DEVELOPMENT CENTERS

Control Problems

The control of R&D expense is difficult for the following reasons.

1. Results are difficult to measure quantitatively. As contrasted with administrative activities, R&D usually has at least a semitangible output in patents, new products, or new processes. Nevertheless, the relationship of these outputs to inputs is difficult to measure and appraise. A complete "product" of an R&D group may require several years of effort; consequently, inputs as stated in an annual budget may be unrelated to outputs. Even if an output can be identified, a reliable estimate of its value often cannot be made. Even if the value of the output can be calculated, it is usually not possible for management to evaluate the efficiency of the R&D effort because of its technical nature. A brilliant effort may come up against an insuperable obstacle, whereas a mediocre effort may, by luck, result in a bonanza.

2. The goal congruence problem in R&D centers is similar to that in administrative centers. The research manager typically wants to build the best research organization that money can buy, even though this is more expensive than the company can afford. A further problem is that research people often may not have sufficient knowledge of (or interest in) the business to determine the optimum direction of the research efforts.

3. Research and development can seldom be controlled effectively on an annual basis. A research project may take years to reach fruition, and the organization must be built up slowly over a long time period. The principal cost is for the work force. Obtaining highly skilled scientific talent is often difficult, and a person working on a given project often cannot be easily replaced, because only that person has knowledge of the project. Consequently, short-term fluctuations in the work force are inefficient. It is not reasonable, therefore, to reduce R&D costs in years when profits are low and increase them in years when profits are high. R&D should be looked at as a long-term investment, not as an activity that varies with short-run corporate profitability.

The R&D Continuum

Activities conducted by R&D organizations lie along a continuum. At one extreme is basic research, and at the other extreme is product development and testing. Basic research has two characteristics. First, it is unplanned; management at most can specify the general area that is to be explored. Second, there is often a very long time lag before basic research will result in successful new product introductions.[5] Financial control systems have, therefore, little value in managing basic research activities.

In some companies, basic research is included as a lump sum in the research program and budget. In others, no specific allowance is made for basic research as such; but there is an understanding that scientists and engineers can devote part of their time (perhaps 20 percent, or one day a week) to explora-

---

[5] In the biotechnology field it took nearly 26 years from the time Watson and Crick defined the structure of the DNA molecule until the first introduction of a product (from 1958 to 1984). It took nearly 24 years from basic research to the successful introduction of a copy machine by Xerox Corporation (from 1936 to 1960).

tions in whatever direction they find most interesting, subject only to informal agreement with their supervisor.[6]

For product development and testing projects, on the other hand, the time and financial requirements can be estimated, not as accurately as production activities, but with sufficient accuracy that budgets can be prepared and a comparison of actual and budget has some validity.

As a project moves along the continuum from basic research, to applied research, to development and testing, to production engineering, the amount spent per year tends to increase drastically. Thus, if a project ultimately will turn out to be unprofitable, as is the case with many projects (90 percent by some estimates), it is important that it be terminated as soon as possible. The decision to terminate a project is difficult; the project sponsors are likely to report its likelihood of success in the most favorable light. In some cases, failure is not discernible until after the product reaches the market.

Example. After 10 years of research and development and many tens of millions of dollars of expense, Polaroid Corporation introduced its instant movie camera, Polavision, with great fanfare at its shareholder meeting in 1977. At that time Dr. Edwin Land, chairman, said, "A new art has been born." Mark Olshaker, author of a 1978 book on Polaroid, wrote, "For the foreseeable future Polavision will be more convenient and economical to use than video tape."[7] But home video cameras quickly came to dominate the market, and by 1981 Polavision was gone; it never made a profit.

R&D Program

There is no scientific way of determining the optimum size of the R&D budget. In many companies, the amount is specified as a percentage of average revenues; "average," rather than revenue for a specific year, is used because the size of the R&D organization should not fluctuate with short-term swings in revenues. In particular, except in drastic circumstances, there should not be layoffs in the organization because of a temporary downturn in profitability. Such layoffs would curtail certain projects, some of which may result in profitable products.

The percentage is arrived at partly by comparisons with what competitors are spending (the amounts must be disclosed in published annual reports), partly by what the company is accustomed to spending, and partly by other factors. For example, senior management may authorize a large and rapid increase in the budget if it thinks there has been a significant breakthrough.

---

[6] The discovery of "warm" superconductivity in 1986 was one of the most important breakthroughs of the decade. It was made by two scientists at the IBM research laboratory in Zurich, who were working "on their own time." IBM senior management in Armonk, New York, did not even know that such research was underway.

[7] *The Instant Image* (New York: Stein and Day), p. 248.

The R&D program consists of a number of projects plus, in some companies, a blanket allowance for unplanned work, as mentioned earlier. This program is reviewed annually by senior management, often by a research committee consisting of the chief executive officer, the research director, and the production and marketing managers who will use the output of successful research projects. This committee makes broad decisions about the magnitude of projects: new projects, projects in which work is to be expanded, projects in which work is to be cut back, and projects that are to be discontinued. These decisions, of course, are highly subjective. They are made within the ceiling established by the overall policy on the total research spending. Thus, the research program is determined not by adding the total amount of approved projects but, rather, by dividing the "research pie" into what seems to be the most worthwhile slices.

Annual Budgets

If a company has decided on a long-range R&D program and has implemented this program with a system of project approval, the preparation of the annual R&D budget is a fairly simple matter. The annual budget is the calendarization of the expected expenses for the budget period. If the annual budget is in line with the strategic plan and the approved projects (as it should be), the budget approval is routine, and its main function is to assist in cash and personnel planning. Preparation of the budget gives management an opportunity for another look at the R&D program. Management can ask: "In view of what we now know, is this the best way to use our resources next year?" Also, the annual budget ensures that actual costs will not exceed budget without management knowing about it. Significant variances from budget should be approved by management before they are incurred.

Measurement of Performance

Each month or each quarter, actual expenses are compared to budgeted expenses for all responsibility centers and also for projects. These are summarized progressively for managers at higher levels. The purpose of these reports is to assist the managers of responsibility centers to plan their expenses and to assure their superiors that expenses are within approved plans.

In many companies, two types of financial reports are provided to management. The first type compares the latest forecast of total cost with the approved amount for each active project. This is prepared periodically and given to the executive or group of executives that controls research spending. The main purpose of this report is to help determine whether changes should be made in approved projects. The second type is a report of actual expenses compared with the budget and prepared by responsibility centers. Its main purpose is to help research executives in expense planning and to make sure expense commitments are being met. Neither report of financial information tells management about the effectiveness of the research effort. Progress reports are the formal source for this information. Management makes judgments about effectiveness, partly on the basis of these progress reports but primarily on the basis of face-to-face discussions.

MARKETING CENTERS

In many companies, the activities that are grouped under the heading of marketing consist of two quite different types, and the control that is appropriate for one type is quite different from the control that is appropriate for the other. One set of activities relates to filling orders, and they are called "order-filling" or "logistics" activities. The other type relates to efforts to obtain orders. These are the true marketing activities, and are sometimes labeled as such. Alternatively, they may be called "order-getting" activities. Order-filling activities take place *after* an order has been received, and order-getting activities take place *before* an order has been received. In both types of activities, administrative functions have the same characteristics as those discussed in a previous section.

Logistics Activities

Logistics activities are those involved in getting the goods from the company to its customers and collecting the amounts due from customers. They include transportation to distribution centers, warehousing, shipping and delivery expense, salesmen's commissions, billing and the related credit function, and collection of accounts receivables. The responsibility centers that perform these functions are fundamentally similar to expense centers in manufacturing plants. Many are engineered expense centers that can be controlled through standard costs and budgets that are adjusted to reflect the costs at different levels of volume (i.e., flexible budgets).

Marketing Activities

Marketing activities are those directed at obtaining orders. They include test marketing; establishing, training, and supervising the sales force; advertising; and sales promotion. These activities have important characteristics that affect the management control problem.

The output of a marketing organization can be measured; however, it is difficult to evaluate the effectiveness of the marketing effort because the environment in which it operates cannot be controlled. For example, economic conditions or competitive actions, over which the marketing department has no control, may be different from that expected when sales budgets were established.

Meeting the budgetary commitment for selling expense is normally a minor part of the evaluation of marketing performance. If a marketing group sells twice as much as its quota, it is unlikely that management will worry if it exceeded its budgeted cost by 10 percent. The impact of sales volume on profits is so great that it tends to overshadow the cost performance. Few companies evaluate a marketing organization primarily on its ability to meet its cost targets. The sales target is the critical factor in evaluation.

The control techniques that are applicable to logistics activities are generally not applicable to order-getting activities. Failure to appreciate this fact can lead to wrong decisions. For example, a reasonably good correlation is often found between volume of sales and the level of sales promotion and advertising expense. This may be taken to mean that sales expenses are variable with sales volume. Such a conclusion is fallacious. Budgets that are flexible with changes in sales volume cannot be used to control selling expenses that are incurred *before* the time of sale. Advertising or sales promotion expense budgets should not be adjusted with short-run changes in sales volume. As indicated above, many companies budget marketing expenses as a percentage of budgeted sales, on the theory that, the higher the sales volumes, the more the company can afford to spend on advertising.

A marketing organization has three types of activities and, consequently, three types of activity measures. First, there is the amount of revenue that the activity generates. This is usually measured by comparing actual revenue with budgeted revenues and comparing physical quantities sold with budgeted units. Second, there is the order-filling or logistics activity. Many of these costs are engineered expenses. Third, there are order-getting costs. Order-getting costs *are* discretionary; no one knows what the optimum amounts are. Consequently, the measurement of efficiency and effectiveness for these costs is highly subjective.

SUMMARY

A responsibility center is an organization unit that is headed by a responsible manager. In this chapter we have described revenue centers and expense centers. Their performance is judged by the criteria of efficiency and effectiveness. In revenue centers, revenues are measured and controlled separately from expenses. There are two broad types of expense centers: engineered and discretionary. In engineered expense centers, the "right" amount of costs that should be incurred for a given level of output can be estimated. In discretionary expense centers, on the other hand, budgets describe the amounts that can be spent; but these are not necessarily the optimum amounts, so financial controls do not measure either efficiency or effectiveness. The principal types of discretionary expense centers are administrative and support centers, R&D centers, and marketing centers. Control is most difficult in R&D units, next most difficult in true marketing units (as contrasted with logistic units), and less difficult, but nevertheless more difficult than manufacturing, in administrative and support units.

SUGGESTED ADDITIONAL READINGS

Bonoma, Thomas V. *Managing Marketing: Text, Cases, and Readings.* New York: Free Press, 1984.

Horngren, Charles T., and George Foster. *Cost Accounting: A Managerial Emphasis.* Englewood Cliffs, N.J.: Prentice Hall, 1991.

Koning, John W. *The Manager Looks at Research Scientists,* Madison, Wis.: Science Tech Publishers, 1988.

Kotler, Philip. *Marketing Management: Analysis, Planning, and Control.* Englewood Cliffs N.J.: Prentice Hall, 1984.

National Association of Accountants. *Statements on Management Accounting.* Statement 4B, "Allocation of Service and Administrative Costs"; Statement 4F, "Allocation of Information Systems Costs"; Statement 4I, "Cost Management for Freight Transportation"; and Statement 4K, "Cost Management for Warehousing." Englewood Cliffs, N.J.: Prentice Hall, 1990.

Shillinglaw, Gordon, and Philip E. Meyer. *Accounting: A Management Approach.* 7th ed. Homewood, Ill.: Richard D. Irwin, 1983.

Vancil, Richard F. "What Kind of Management Control Do You Need?" *Harvard Business Review,* March–April 1973, pp. 75–86.

Case 3-1

New Jersey Insurance Company*

On July 16, 1987, John W. Montgomery, a member of the budget committee of the New Jersey Insurance Company, was reading over the current budget report for the law division in preparation for a conference scheduled for the next day with the head of that division. He held such conferences quarterly with each division head. Mr. Montgomery's practice was to think out in advance the questions he wished to ask and the points he thought he should make about each division's performance.

The law division of the New Jersey Insurance Company (NJIC) was responsible for all legal matters relating to the company's operations. Among other things, it advised company management on current and prospective developments in tax and other legislation and on recent court decisions affecting the company. It represented the company in litigation, counseled the departments concerned on the legal implications of policies, such as employee benefit plans, and it examined all major contracts to which the company was a party. It also rendered various legal services with respect to the company's proposed and existing investments.

As shown in Exhibit 1, the head of the law division, William Somersby, reported directly to top management. This relationship ensured that Mr. Somersby would be free to comment on the legal implications of management decisions, much the same as would an outside counsel. The law division was divided into five sections. This case is concerned with only two of these sec-

tions, the individual loan section and the corporate loan section. It does not attempt to describe completely the work of these two sections or the professional service rendered by the lawyers.

Individual Loan Section

The individual loan section was responsible for the legal processing of loans made to individuals and secured by mortgages on real property. The loan instruments were submitted by independent companies situated throughout the country. The company made no loans directly to individual borrowers, although at one time it had made direct loans in the New Jersey area. Most common among the loans submitted by the independent companies were FHA, VA, and conventional loans on homes, ranging in amounts from $160,000 to $400,000. These loans usually were made directly by banks or similar financial institutions organized for the purpose. They would batch together a number of loans and sell them to NJIC in a package. The insurance company purchased many thousands of such loans each year.

The investment division of the company was responsible for establishing the terms of these loans, including their amount, interest rate, and maturity. An independent company would submit to the investment division an offer to sell a mortgage loan. It was the function of this division to determine whether or not the property to be mortgaged and the mortgagor were acceptable to NJIC for a mortgage loan. After the proposed loan was

* This case was prepared by J. S. Hekimian under the supervision of Robert N. Anthony, Harvard Business School.
Copyright © by the President and Fellows of Harvard College.
Harvard Business School case 106–049.

EXHIBIT 1 Partial Organization Chart

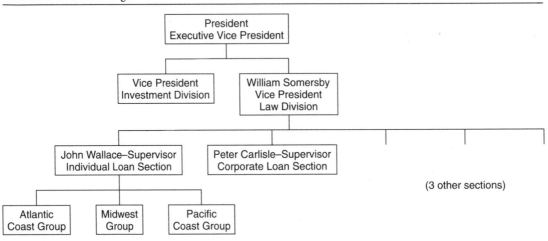

```
                    ┌───────────────────────┐
                    │      President         │
                    │Executive Vice President│
                    └───────────────────────┘
              ┌──────────────┴──────────────┐
    ┌──────────────────┐          ┌──────────────────┐
    │  Vice President   │          │ William Somersby │
    │Investment Division│          │  Vice President  │
    └──────────────────┘          │   Law Division   │
                                  └──────────────────┘
         ┌──────────────────┬──────────────┬────────┬────────┐
┌────────────────────┐  ┌────────────────────┐
│John Wallace–Supervisor│ │Peter Carlisle–Supervisor│
│Individual Loan Section │ │ Corporate Loan Section  │
└────────────────────┘  └────────────────────┘
                                                    (3 other sections)
    ┌──────────┬──────────────┐
┌──────────┐ ┌──────────┐ ┌──────────┐
│ Atlantic │ │ Midwest  │ │ Pacific  │
│Coast Group│ │  Group   │ │Coast Group│
└──────────┘ └──────────┘ └──────────┘
```

approved and its terms worked out, the investment division would forward to the law division the note, mortgage, and related papers which it received from the seller.

The major function of the individual loan section was to perform the legal work necessary on all new loans purchased and on all existing loans. Among other things, it had to check all the loan instruments to make sure they did, in fact, protect the interests of NJIC as required by law and by the investment division. Organizationally, the section was divided into three groups, each headed by an attorney and each responsible for a geographical section of the country—Atlantic Coast, Midwest, and Pacific Coast. In addition to the three attorneys who headed regional groups, there were two other attorneys—one who helped out in busy spots and took over a group in case of sickness or vacation, and another who was in a training status.

Other than these five attorneys and a supporting secretarial staff, the section was comprised of 26 so-called mortgage examiners. These were persons who had had no formal legal training, but who had been carefully selected and company trained to check over and approve certain of the loan transactions that came into the section. Because of the repetitive nature of the routine loan transactions, management believed that properly selected and trained laymen could, under the supervision of lawyers, perform this task, which at one time had been performed only by lawyers. Problem cases were referred by the mortgage examiners to the attorneys. John Wallace, head of the individual loan section, estimated that it took about three months initially to train a person to do this type of work. It then took about a year and a half of on-the-job training and experience before the examiner achieved a satisfactory rate of output, and two to three years before the average examiner reached optimum performance.

Since the work performed by the mortgage examiners was repetitive, management felt that it could exercise considerable control over a substantial part of this section. Based on a time study, a work standard of 12 loan transactions per examiner per day had been established some years previously, and this standard later was raised to 15. Records were maintained within the section of the number of loan transactions received each day, the number processed by each examiner, and the backlog.

In evaluating the work of individual examiners, some judgment had to be exercised in applying this standard. For example, in the Atlantic Coast group, an examiner sometimes received a batch of loan transactions in which the mortgaged properties were in a single, large housing subdivision. The legal issues in these transactions tended to be the same. In other parts of the country, however, loans tended to come from scattered localities and, thus, would be quite different from one another in many respects. A supervisor, therefore, in applying the standard would have to be familiar with the type of work an examiner was doing.

Budget Process

Although considerable control could be achieved over the output of individual examiners, control over the entire section was a more difficult problem. Each September, the budget committee of the company issued a memorandum to all division heads, asking them to prepare a budget for the operation of their division during the following year.

The basic intent of the budget process was to get division heads to plan and report in advance the scope of their operations for the following year. Usually, the budgets were prepared by anticipating first the changes in activity levels from the current year and then the cost implications of these changes. Management checked each individual budget for reasonableness, and also checked the total expected cost and revenue to ensure that the overall anticipated profit was satisfactory. The budget was viewed as a device for informing management of the plans a division head had for the coming year so that management could appraise these plans in relation to what other divisional heads had planned and in relation to company policy. The budget was also considered to be a measure of a division head's ability to plan the division's operations and then to operate in accordance with that plan.

On receipt of the budget committee's memorandum in September, division heads began forecasting operations within their divisions for the following year. First, each section head made plans for the section. For example, the individual loan section obtained an estimate of the amount of money that the investment division would have available for individual loans in the following year. Based partially on this estimate and partially on its estimated needs for other activities, the individual loan section developed a budget. This estimate, along with the estimated budgets for the other sections of the law division, was reviewed by Mr. Somersby. The law division then sent its budget to the budget committee for review. Usually, the law division's figures were accepted. Each quarter during the year, actual performance to date was compared with budgeted performance. Heads of divisions were required to explain large deviations from projected estimates.

Although management within the law division could, in theory, vary the size of the staff in the individual loan section, in fact, there was great reluctance to increase or decrease the work force unless a definite trend in volume was apparent. One reason for this was company policy. The company felt a great responsibility toward its employees, and as a matter of policy would lay off or discharge employees only for serious offenses. This same policy made management reluctant to hire new employees unless there was assurance that the need for them was permanent. Therefore, the law division tended to maintain a staff sufficient to handle a minimum work load, and it supplemented this with overtime.

Another reason for the tendency to maintain a level work force of mortgage examiners was the cost of selecting and training them. Management went to great pains to select outstanding clerks for these jobs. This was followed by a thorough course of study and on-the-job training. Because of this large investment, management wanted to be sure that anyone trained for this job would be needed permanently in the section.

Management within the individual loan section, in attempting to achieve control over the section as a whole and yet in keeping with company policy, had devised several controls. Occasionally, when the work load lessened, supervisors would call the investment division to see if they could get some work that, although perhaps not quite ready to be sent over as a complete batch, could, nevertheless, be sent in parts. Also, since in periods when loan applications were low foreclosures tended to increase, the mortgage examiners were trained to handle some aspects of foreclosures, and this provided a degree of dovetailing in the work flow. Other than these measures, however, the division preferred to rely on overtime work. The use of outside law firms was out of the question for this type of work because of the far greater cost, even in comparison with overtime wages.

Corporate Loan Section

The corporate loan section was a much different kind of operation. A corporate loan, generally for a much larger amount than an individual loan, was one made directly by NJIC to a borrower, such as an industrial or commercial enterprise or a public utility. The loan might be either secured or unsecured. An important advantage to the borrower of this type of loan, compared with a loan evidenced by a bond issue sold to the general public, was that the borrower was not required to furnish a formal prospectus or to file a registration statement with the SEC.

In this type of loan, financial determinations, such as the amount of the loan, interest rate, timing of repayments, restrictive covenants, and so forth were made by the investment division, as was the case with individual loans, but by a different section in that division. Because of the size and complexity of corporate loans, the corporate loan section worked closely with the investment division people, who made these financial determinations. This involved sitting in on the negotiations and rendering advice on all the terms of the transaction. It was the responsibility of the corporate loan section to ensure that the final loan instruments protected the interests of NJIC in the manner intended by the financial people.

On this type of loan, for various reasons, the corporate loan section almost without exception retained well-known outside counsel. One important reason was that an opinion from such an independent law firm contributed to the marketability of the investment in the event of a sale at a later date. Further, in many of these transactions, a number of other investors were involved, and NJIC's law division could not appropriately represent these other investors. If NJIC was the leading investor, it did, however, select the outside counsel to be retained. In addition, it was not possible, without greatly increasing the size of the present staff, for company attorneys to handle all the legal work connected with this type of loan, especially at the time of peak loads. Under this system, any one lawyer had a large number of loan negotiations in process at all times with various outside counsel, and this was beneficial both to the individual and to the company in providing lawyers with a broad base of experience in a variety of situations. The background and experience of company attorneys assured the company of consistency of policy in the negotiation of direct placements.

A substantial part of the work in corporate loans consisted of drafting legal documents. The extent to which company attorneys relied on outside counsel to perform parts of this work depended on the complexity of the transaction (company attorneys tended to do more of the work on more complex transactions) and on how busy company attorneys were. In general, company attorneys handled as a minimum enough of the work to be thoroughly familiar with all aspects of the transaction. In many cases, they prepared the first drafts of all legal papers. But in the event that first drafts were left to outside counsel, company attorneys reviewed the work and redrafted it as necessary.

Borrowers were required to pay all expenses incurred in employing outside counsel. However, NJIC made clear to both prospective borrowers and to outside counsel that the counsel were representing NJIC and that their loyalty belonged to

NJIC, much the same as for a company attorney. Even though the borrower paid the fee for outside counsel, the head of the corporate loan section, Peter Carlisle, checked closely on the fees charged by outside counsel. Over the years, a thorough tabulation of fees charged for different types of legal work throughout the country had been built up. Mr. Carlisle, simply by referring to this tabulation, could readily determine whether a particular fee was apparently out of line. If there was any substantial deviation, he looked into the case more closely to determine if there was some reasonable explanation; if not, he discussed the matter with the outside counsel and adjusted the fee. Over the years, NJIC had established excellent working relationships with many law firms throughout the country.

The control procedure in this section was substantially different from that in the individual loan section. At the initiation of each transaction, Mr. Carlisle was consulted by the attorney to whom it was referred. Reassignments to equalize the work load of the various attorneys were made as necessary: A degree of control also was achieved through weekly staff conferences with Mr. Carlisle. At this conference, lawyers raised individual problems they had encountered. In addition to keeping Mr. Carlisle informed in detail on what was going on, the conference provided an opportunity for each staff member to draw on the experience of other lawyers, and it served as a vehicle for developing a consistent policy on various matters. Also, the discussion of current negotiations made it more likely that in case of illness another lawyer would be prepared to take over the work.

Another control device was the current work assignment report, which each attorney in the section submitted to Mr. Carlisle. Because corporate loan transactions took varying amounts of time to complete, ranging from several weeks to many months, it was found that daily and, in some cases, weekly reports were not feasible. Accordingly, each attorney submitted a report when his work situation suggested to him that a

new one was desirable. Each report covered all the time elapsed since the preceding report.

At the top of this report the lawyer briefly indicated his current work status, such as "fully occupied" or "available." Although a detailed format was not prescribed, in general the report described briefly how the lawyer's present jobs were going, what kinds of problems were involved, and what he had completed since his previous report. These reports, in addition to supplementing Mr. Carlisle's knowledge of what was being done in this section, helped tell who was available for more work.

The amount of time a lawyer had to spend on a particular job was not predictable. Major variables were the number and complexity of restrictive covenants in an unsecured note, for example, and the terms and provisions of the security instruments in a secured transaction. The number and complexity of the various covenants in these security instruments did not necessarily vary with the size of the loan, but depended, rather, on the nature, size, and credit standing of the corporate borrower. Many times, a relatively small loan was more complicated than a larger one.

Also, even though the details of a loan had been worked out initially to the satisfaction of the borrower and NJIC, and, even though the loan had been in effect for a considerable time, borrowers frequently came back to NJIC to ask for waivers or modifications—that is, they requested changes in the restrictive covenants, the terms, or other conditions or agreements. Such events increased the difficulty of planning in advance how a lawyer was to spend his time.

Unusually heavy work loads in the section were met not only by overtime but also by increasing to the extent feasible the amount of work given to outside counsel. Within limitations, the lawyer responsible for a particular job generally decided how much work would be assigned to outside counsel.

Although the corporate loan section followed the same budget procedure as the individual loan section, one of the variable factors—that is, the

EXHIBIT 2   Budget Report, Law Division—First Six Months, 1987

Sections	Budget	Actual	Over Budget	Under Budget
Individual loans	$1,698,893	$1,753,154	$54,261	
Corporate loans	1,641,302	1,598,073		$43,229
(Three other sections omitted)	—	—	—	—
Total	$5,082,448	$5,107,822	$25,374	
Number of full-time employees	166	160		6

extent to which work was delegated to outside counsel—did not affect the budget, since the borrower paid for these services.

Budget Reports

Mr. Montgomery was thoroughly familiar with the background information given above as he began his review of the law division's budget performance for the first half of 1987. The report he had before him consisted of a summary page for the law division (Exhibit 2) and a page for each of the five sections, two of which are shown in Exhibits 3 and 4. The budget figures on the report were one half the budget for the year.

QUESTIONS

1. In what ways does Mr. Somersby control the operations of the sections of his division? In what ways does top management control the operation of the law division?
2. What possibilities for improving control, if any, do you think should be explored?
3. As Mr. Montgomery, what comments would you make and what questions would you ask Mr. Somersby about the performance of the two sections of the law division for the first six months of 1987?

EXHIBIT 3   Budget Report, Individual Loan Section—First Six Months, 1987

Costs	Budget	Actual	Over Budget	Under Budget
Employee costs:				
Salaries, full time	$ 924,092	$ 932,201	$ 8,109	
Salaries, part time	—	—	—	
Salaries, overtime	4,500	33,610	29,110	
Borrowed labor	—	5,905	5,905	
Employee lunches	17,055	19,180	2,125	
Insurance retirement, SS, etc.	206,024	208,051	2,027	
Total	1,151,671	1,198,947	47,276	
Direct service costs:				
Photography	9,205	10,667	1,462	
Tracing	370	690	320	
Mimeograph	407	587	180	
Reproduction	237	515	278	
Total	10,219	12,459	2,240	
Other costs:				
Rent	100,230	100,230		
Office supplies	2,267	3,067	800	
Equipment depreciation and maintenance	11,940	11,940		
Printed forms	3,842	5,367	1,525	
Travel	2,835	3,155	320	
Telephone	7,577	8,690	1,113	
Postage	3,057	3,227	170	
Prorated company services	36,810	37,405	595	
Professional dues	50	100	50	
Miscellaneous	395	567	172	
Total	169,003	173,748	4,745	
Grand total	$1,330,893	$1,385,154	$54,261	
Number of full-time employees	46	46		

EXHIBIT 4   Budget Report, Corporate Loan Section—First Six Months, 1987

Costs	Budget	Actual	Over Budget	Under Budget
Employee costs:				
Salaries, full time	$ 838,720	$ 807,488		$31,232
Salaries, part time	3,000	—		3,000
Salaries, overtime	3,000	—		3,000
Borrowed labor				
Employee lunches	10,325	9,355		970
Insurance retirement, SS, etc.	219,681	211,872		7,809
Total	1,074,726	1,028,715		46,011
Direct service costs:				
Photography	3,637	3,353		284
Tracing	730	265		465
Mimeograph	—	67	67	
Reproduction	—	35	35	
Total	4,367	3,720		647
Other costs:				
Rent	61,953	61,953		
Office supplies	1,850	2,955	1,105	
Equipment depreciation and maintenance	7,740	7,740		
Printed forms	445	915	470	
Travel	1,930	1,880		50
Telephone	2,275	2,835	560	
Postage	420	390		30
Prorated company services	20,213	18,357		1,856
Professional dues	200	200		
Miscellaneous	183	413	230	
Total	$ 97,209	$ 97,638	$ 429	
Grand total	$1,176,302	$1,130,073		$46,229
Number of full-time employees	26	24		2

Case 3–2
Reed Paint Company*

In August 1982, C. H. Macrae was elected president of the Reed Paint Company to fill the vacancy created by the retirement from active business life of the former chief executive. Mr. Macrae had been with the company for 15 years, and for the preceding 6 years he had been vice president in charge of manufacturing. Shortly after taking over his new position, Mr. Macrae held a series of conferences with the controller in which the general subject under discussion was budgetary control technique. The new president thought that the existing method of planning and checking on selling costs was particularly unsatisfactory, and he requested the controller to devise a system which would provide better control over these costs.

The Reed Paint Company manufactured a complete line of paints which it sold through branch offices to wholesalers, retailers, builders, and industrial users. Most of the products carried the Reed brand name, which was nationally advertised. The company was one of the largest in the industry.

Under the procedure then being used, selling expenses were budgeted on a "fixed" or "appropriation" basis. Each October the accounting department sent to branch managers and to other executives in charge of selling departments a detailed record of the actual expenses of their departments for the preceding year and for the current year to date. Guided by this record, by estimates of the succeeding year's sales and by his own judgment, each department head drew up and submitted an estimate of the expenses of his department for the succeeding year, detailed as to main items of expense. The estimates made by the branch managers were sent to the sales manager, who was in charge of all branch sales. He determined whether or not they were reasonable and cleared up any questionable items by correspondence. Upon approval by the sales manager, the estimates of branch expenses were submitted to the manager of distribution, Mr. Campbell, who was in charge of all selling, promotional, and warehousing activities.

The manager of distribution discussed these figures and the expense estimates furnished by the other department heads with the executives concerned; and, after differences were reconciled, he combined the estimates of all the selling departments into a selling expense budget. This budget was submitted to the budget committee for final approval. For control purposes, the annual budget was divided into 12 equal amounts, and actual expenses were compared each month with the budgeted figures. Exhibit 1 shows the form in which these monthly comparisons were made.

Mr. Macrae believed that there were two important weaknesses in this method of setting the selling expense budget.

1. It was impossible for anyone to ascertain with any feeling of certainty the reasonableness of the estimates made by the various department heads. Clearly, the expenses of the preceding year did not constitute adequate standards against which these expense estimates could

* This case was prepared by R. G. Walker.
Copyright © by the President and Fellows of Harvard University.
Harvard Business School case 147–002.

EXHIBIT 1

Branch Sales and Expense Performance
Branch A Manager: H. C. Obermeyer
Date: October 1982

	This Month				Year to Date
	Budget†	Actual	Over* Under	Percent of Sales	Over* Under
Net sales	$1,900,000	$1,600,000			
Executive salaries	$ 20,000	$ 20,000	—	1.25%	—
Office salaries	11,500	11,340	$ 160	0.71	$12,030
Salespeople's compensation	114,000	96,000	18,000	6.00	28,020*
Traveling expense	34,200	31,270	2,930	1.95	10,120*
Stationery, office supplies, and expense	10,420	8,900	1,520	0.56	3,600
Postage	2,300	2,620	320*	0.16	210
Light and heat	1,340	870	470	0.05	1,280
Subscriptions and dues	1,500	1,120	380	0.07	260
Donations	1,250	—	1,250	0.00	1,300
Advertising expense (local)	19,000	18,000	1,000	1.12	12,000*
Social security taxes	2,910	2,050	860	0.13	270*
Rental	9,750	9,750	—	0.61	—
Depreciation	7,620	7,620	—	0.48	—
Other branch expense	25,510	24,260	1,250	1.52	2,470*
Total	$261,300	$233,800	$27,500	14.61	$34,200*

† $\frac{1}{12}$ of annual budget.

be judged, since selling conditions were never the same in two different years. One obvious cause of variation in selling expenses was the variation in the "job to be done," as defined in the sales budget.

2. Selling conditions often changed substantially after the budget was adopted, but there was no provision for making the proper corresponding changes in the selling expense budget. Neither was there a logical basis for relating selling expenses to the actual sales volume obtained or to any other measure of sales effort. The chief executive believed that it was reasonable to expect that sales expenses would increase, though not proportionately, if actual sales volume were greater than the forecasted volume;

but that with the existing method of control it was impossible to determine how large the increase in expenses should be.

As a means of overcoming these weaknesses the president suggested the possibility of setting selling cost budget standards on a fixed and variable basis, a method similar to the techniques used in the control of manufacturing expenses. The controller agreed that this manner of approach seemed to offer the most feasible solution to the problem, and he therefore undertook with the cooperation of the sales department a study of selling expenses for the purpose of devising a method of setting reasonable standards. Over a period of several years, the accounting department had made many analyses of selling costs, the results of which had been used in determining the proper bases for allocating costs to products, customers, functions, and territories and in assisting in the solution of certain special problems, such as the problem of determining how large an individual order had to be in order to be profitable to the company. Many of the data which had been accumulated for these purposes were helpful in the controller's current study.

The controller was convinced that the fixed portion of selling expenses—in other words, the portion which was independent of any fluctuation in volume—could be established by determining the amount of expenses which had to be incurred at the minimum sales volume at which the company was likely to operate. He therefore asked Mr. Campbell, the manager of distribution, to suggest a minimum volume figure and the amount of expenses which would have to be incurred at this volume level. A staff assistant was assigned the task of studying the past sales records of the company over several business cycles, the long-term outlook for sales and sales trends in other companies in the industry. From the report prepared by his assistant Mr. Campbell concluded that sales volume would not drop below 45 percent of the current capacity of the factory.

Mr. Campbell then attempted to determine the selling expenses which would be incurred at the minimum volume. With the help of his staff assistant, he worked out a hypothetical selling organization which in his opinion would be required to sell merchandise equivalent to 45 percent of factory capacity, complete as to the number of persons needed to staff each branch office and the other selling departments, including the advertising, merchandise, and sales administration departments. Using current salary and commission figures, the assistant calculated the amount of money which would be required to pay salaries for such an organization. The manager of distribution also estimated the other expenses, such as advertising, branch office upkeep, supplies, and travel which he thought would be incurred by each branch and staff department at the minimum sales volume.

The controller decided that the variable portion of the selling expense standard should be expressed as a certain amount per sales dollar. He realized that the use of the sales dollar as a measuring stick had certain disadvantages in that it would not reflect such important influences on costs as the size of the order, the selling difficulty of certain territories, changes in buyer psychology, and the like. The sales dollar, however, was the measuring stick most convenient to use, the only figure readily available from the records then being kept, and also a figure which all the individuals concerned thoroughly understood. The controller believed that a budget which varied with sales would certainly be better than a budget which did not vary at all. He planned to devise a more accurate measure of causes of variation in selling expenses after he had had an opportunity to study the nature of these factors over a longer period.

As a basis for setting the initial variable expense standards, the controller prepared a series of charts on which the actual annual expenditures for the principal groups of expense items for several preceding years were correlated with sales volume for the year. Using these charts, which showed to what extent the principal expense items had fluctuated with sales volume in the past, and modifying them in accordance with his own judgment, the controller determined a rate of variation for the variable portion of each item of selling expense. The controller thought that, after the new system had been tested in practice, it would be possible to refine these rates, perhaps by the use of a technique analogous to the time-study technique which was employed to determine certain expense standards in the factory.

At this point the controller had both a rate of variation and one point (i.e., at 45 percent of capacity) on the selling expense curve for each expense item. He was therefore able to construct a formula for each item by extending a line through the known point at the slope represented by the rate of variation. He determined the height of this

EXHIBIT 2   Budget for "Other Branch Expense," Branch A

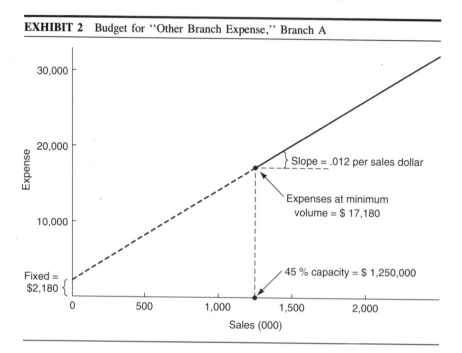

line at zero volume and called this amount the fixed portion of the selling expense formula. The diagram in Exhibit 2 illustrates the procedure, although the actual computations were mathematical rather than graphic.

The selling expense budget for 1982 was determined by adding to the new standards for the various fixed components the indicated flexible allowances for the 1982 estimated sales volume. This budget was submitted to the budget committee, which studied the fixed amounts and the variable rates underlying the final figures, making only minor changes before passing final approval.

The controller planned to issue each month reports showing for each department actual ex-penses compared with budgeted expenses. The variable portion of the budgeted allowances would be adjusted to correspond to the actual volume of sales obtained during the month. Exhibit 3 shows the budget report which he planned to send to branch managers.

One sales executive privately belittled the controller's proposal. "Anyone in the selling game," he asserted, "knows that sometimes customers fall all over each other in their hurry to buy, and other times, no matter what we do, they won't even nibble. It's a waste of time to make fancy formulas for selling cost budgets under conditions like that."

EXHIBIT 3 Budget Report

Branch Sales and Expense Performance
Branch A Manager: H. C. Obermeyer
Date: October 1, 1982

	Budget†	Actual	Over* Under	Percent of Sales	Year to Date Over* Under
Net sales	$1,900,000	$1,600,000			
Executive salaries	$ 20,000	$ 20,000	—	1.25	—
Office salaries	11,320	11,340	$ 20*	0.71	$ 8,200
Salespeople's compensation	96,000	96,000	—	6.00	—
Traveling expense	33,120	31,270	1,850	1.95	9,460*
Stationary, office supplies, and expense	9,600	8,900	700	0.56	4,800
Postage	2,082	2,620	538*	0.16	620*
Light and heat	1,340	870	470	0.05	1,620*
Subscriptions and dues	1,450	1,120	330	0.07	530
Donations	1,150	—	1,150	0.00	1,300
Advertising expense (local)	17,500	18,000	500*	1.12	15,000*
Social security taxes	2,542	2,050	492	0.13	100
Rental	9,750	9,750	—	0.61	—
Depreciation	7,620	7,620	—	0.48	—
Other branch expense	21,380	24,260	2,880*	1.52	5,260*
	$234,854	$233,800	$1,054	14.61	$17,030*

† $\frac{1}{12}$ of annual budget, with variable cost adjusted to the actual volume of sales.

QUESTIONS

1. From the information given in Exhibits 2 and 3, determine, insofar as you can, whether each item of expense is (a) nonvariable, (b) partly variable with sales volume, (c) variable with sales volume, or (d) variable with some other factor.
2. Should the proposed sales expense budget be adopted?
3. If a variable budget is used, should dollar sales be used as the measure of variation?

Case 3-3*

Westport Electric Corporation

On a day in the late autumn of 1987, Peter Ensign, the controller of Westport Electric; Michael Kelly, the manager of the budgeting department (reporting to Ensign); and James King, the supervisor of the administrative staff budget section (reporting to Kelly) were discussing a problem raised by King. In reviewing the proposed 1988 budgets of the various administrative staff offices, King was disturbed by the increases in expenditures that were being proposed. He believed that, in particular, the proposed increases in two offices were not justified. King's main concern, however, was with the entire process of reviewing and approving the administrative staff budgets. The purpose of the meeting was to discuss what should be done about the two budgets in question and to consider what revisions should be made in the approval procedure of administrative staff budgets.

Organization of Westport

Westport Electric is one of the giant U.S. corporations that manufactures and sells electric and electronic products. Sales in 1983 were in excess of $9 billion, and profits after taxes were over $750 million. The operating activities of the corporation are divided into four groups, each headed by a group vice president. These groups are: the Electrical Generating and Transmission Group, the Home Appliance Group, the Military and Space Group, and the Electronics Group. Each of these groups is comprised of a number of relatively independent divisions, each headed by a divisional manager. The division is the basic operating unit of the corporation and each is a profit center. The divisional manager is responsible for earning an adequate profit on his investment. There are 25 divisions in the corporation.

At the corporate level there is a research and development staff and six administrative staff offices, each headed by a vice president, as follows: finance, industrial relations, legal, marketing, manufacturing, and public relations. The responsibilities of the administrative staff offices, although they vary depending upon their nature, can be divided into the following categories.

1. *Top management advice.* Each of the staff offices is responsible for providing advice to the top management of the corporation in the area of its specialty. Also, all of the staff vice presidents are members of the Policy Committee, the top decision-making body of the corporation.

2. *Advice to operating divisions and other staff offices.* Each staff office gives advice to operating divisions and, in some instances, to other staff offices. (An example of the latter is the advice the legal staff might give to the finance staff with respect to a contract.) In theory, at least, the operating divisions can accept or reject the advice, as they see fit. In most cases, there is no formal requirement that the operating divisions even seek advice from the central staff. In fact, however, the advice of the staff office usually carries considerable weight and divisional managers rarely ignore it.

3. *Coordination among the divisions.* The staff offices have the responsibility for coordinating their areas of activities among the divisions. The extent of this coordination varies considerably, depending upon the nature of the activity. For example the finance staff has the greatest

---

*This case was prepared by John Dearden, Harvard Business School.

EXHIBIT 1   Organization Chart—January 1, 1988

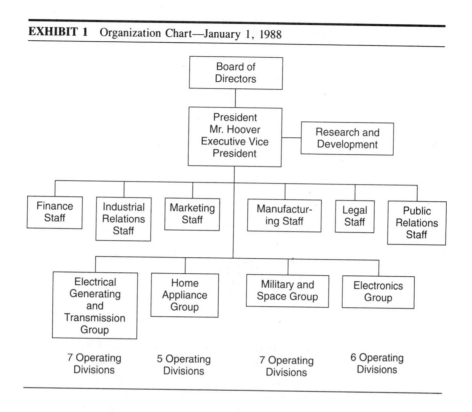

amount of this coordination to do, because it is necessary to establish and maintain a consistent accounting and budgetary control system. On the other hand, the legal and public relations staffs have no direct representation in the activities of the division.

Exhibit 1 is an organizational chart of the Westport Electric Corporation.

The Budgeting Organization

Exhibit 2 provides a partial organization chart of the finance staff. As you can see from the chart, Ensign, the controller, reports to the finance vice president. Reporting to him is Kelly, who is in charge of the budgeting department. Reporting to Kelly is King, who is in charge of the administrative staff budget section.

Approval Procedure
Information submitted.   In the early autumn

of each year, the budgeting department issues instructions and timetables for the preparation, submission, and approval of the budgets for the coming year. Since we are concerned in this case with the administrative staff budgets, we will limit our description to the nature of the information submitted by each administrative staff office.

Each staff office completes the following schedule.

Budget by expense classification.   This schedule shows the proposed budget, last year's budget, and the current year's expected actual costs, by expense classification (professional salaries, clerical salaries, supplies, consulting services, utilities, and so forth). The purpose of this schedule is to compare the new budget with the current year's budget and the current year's expected actual costs by expense categories.

Budget by activity.   This schedule shows the same information as the previous schedule except

EXHIBIT 2 Finance Staff—January 1988

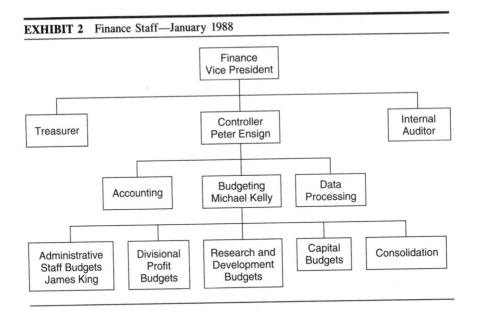

that the information is classified by organizational component. The purpose of this schedule is to show which activities are being increased, which decreased, and which new activities are being proposed.

Explanation of changes. This schedule is really a letter that accompanies the budget proposal and explains the reasons for the proposed budget. Explanations are divided into the following categories: economic changes (i.e., changes in the general level of wages and materials); increases or decreases in existing activities; new activities added and old activities dropped.

These reports are submitted by each administrative staff office to the budgeting department two weeks before the office is to present its proposed budget.

Presentation of Budget Proposal

Each administrative staff office budget was approved by the president and the executive vice president in a budget review meeting. The finance vice president sat in on all the budget presentations but had no official power to approve or disapprove.

On the day scheduled for presentation, the vice president of the administrative staff office whose budget was to be approved would make a presentation to the president and executive vice president. The presentation would be based on the budget schedules previously submitted, but the explanations justifying the proposals might go into much greater detail. For example, last year the marketing vice president used three-dimensional color slides to describe a new activity that he was proposing to organize.

Attending these meetings were the president, the executive vice president, the administrative staff office vice president and his principal executives, the financial vice president, the controller, the budgeting manager, and the particular budget supervisor involved.

Typically, a budget meeting would proceed as follows: The presentation would be made by the administrative staff vice president. During the presentation, questions would be raised by the president and the executive vice president. These would be answered by the administrative staff vice president or one of his executives. At the one end of the presentation, the president and executive vice president would decide whether to approve the budget or whether to curtail some of the proposed activities. Before the final decision, the finance vice president would be asked to comment. In almost every case, he would agree with the decision of the president and executive vice president.

Once approved, the budget became authorization to undertake the budgeted activity for the coming year.

Function of the Budgeting Department

The functions of the budgeting department with respect to administrative staff budgets has been to prescribe the schedules to be submitted and timetable for their submission and to "keep the presentations honest." In fulfilling the last function, the budgeting department analyzed the proposed budgets and made sure that the facts were correctly stated. For instance, they checked to make sure that the increases due to economic changes were accurate; or, if some present activity were to be dropped, they made sure that the cost of this activity was shown as a reduction, so that the cost savings could not be used to hide an increase in another activity. The details of the presentation were worked out beforehand between James King and the administrative assistant to the administrative staff vice president involved. When the presentation was made, the budgeting department would be asked to concur with the financial information being presented. The budgeting department, however, took no position on the appropriateness of the proposed budget or the efficiency of the activity. It was this situation that bothered James King.

Budget Evaluation

This was James King's second year as supervisor of the administrative staff budget section. Prior to that, he had been the budget manager in the Electric Stove Division. At the divisional level, the budget analysts exercised considerable influence over the level of efficiency represented in the operating budgets. For example, in the Electric Stove Division, the divisional controller attended every divisional budget meeting and argued long and hard for rejecting any budget that he believed was not sufficiently "tight." Because he had had a considerable amount of experience in the operations of that division, he was usually successful. King found it hard to reconcile the attitude of the finance vice president (who never seemed to raise any objections to the proposed budgets) with his former boss, the controller of the Electric Stove Division. Consequently, he asked to meet with Ensign and Kelly to see if something could not be done to improve the evaluation techniques for administrative staff budgets. Below is an edited version of the meeting between Ensign, Kelly, and King on this problem.

King: All we do about these budgets is to make sure that the accounting figures are correct. We don't do anything about the efficiency represented by the figures and I know for a fact that it is lousy in at least two cases and I have my suspicion about some of the others.

Kelly: Tell Peter about Legal.

King: Earlier this year, you remember, we hired a consultant to work with our Data Processing Group. We gave the contract to the legal staff to look over and it took them three months before they approved it. They had all kinds of nitpicking changes that didn't amount to a hill of beans, but which took up everybody's time.

Shortly after the contract was approved, I had a college friend of mine visiting who's a lawyer in one of the biggest New York firms. We discussed the matter and he looked over the original contract and the revised one and was astounded at the time that it had taken to get it approved. He said that a simple contract like that would be handled in a day or two by an outside lawyer. Since then, I find that everyone in the organization seems to feel the same way about Legal. They take forever to do a five-minute job and they never stick their necks out in the slightest.

To add insult to injury, this year the legal staff is asking for a 30 percent increase in their budget to take care of the added cost resulting from the expansion of their work load. The trouble is that, unless we do something, they will get this increase.

Ensign: If everyone feels that the Legal staff is so inefficient, why should Mr. Hoover [the president] approve their budget?

King: I think that Mr. Hoover has neither the time nor the knowledge to evaluate the Legal staff. Any time Mr. Hoover asks for anything from them, he gets superdeluxe treatment. Since none of us are lawyers we have a hard time proving inefficiency, but we know it is there.

Ensign: What is the other budget that you think is out of line?

King: Industrial relations—especially management training: We are spending more money on senseless training than you can shake a stick at. It's not only costing us money but it is wasting management's time. For instance, last month we all had to take a course in quality control. It was the most simple-minded course I have ever seen. They gave us a test at the end to see how much progress we have made. I gave a copy of the test to my secretary and she got a 100 percent, without taking the course, or really even knowing what quality control is. Out in the division, the training was even worse. At one time they had a slide film that was supposed to teach us economics in three lessons! The film consisted of "Doc Dollar" explaining to "Jim Foreman" about money markets, capitalism, and so forth. We all felt that it was an insult to our intelligence. In their new budget, industrial relations is proposing to increase training by nearly 50 percent and, because the general profit picture is so good, it will probably be approved.

Ensign: If the training program is so bad, why don't we hear more complaints?

King: I will have to admit that I feel more strongly than most of the other people. A lot of managers and supervisors just go along with these programs because to be against management training is like being against motherhood. Also, the personnel evaluation forms that industrial relations prescribes have a section on the performance of the individual in these courses. I guess people are afraid to rebel against them because it might hurt their chances of promotion. The point is, at best, they are not worth the money that they cost. No one seems to get much out of them as far as I can see, so we certainly don't want to *increase* the training budget.

The conversation continued for some time. Although he did not express it in exactly these terms, King's other concern was a lack of goal congruence between the activities of the administrative staff office and the earnings for the corporation. It seemed to him that each administrative staff officer, at best wanted to have the "best" operation in the country and, at worst, was simply interested in building an empire. Even the best operation, however, might cost much more than it was worth in terms of increasing profits. He was also concerned about the ability of the president and the executive vice president to evaluate the efficiency and the effectiveness of the staff offices, or even to decide whether additional activities were really worthwhile. King, therefore, believed it was necessary for someone to evaluate the budget proposals critically, as they did at the divisional level.

The meeting closed with Ensign asking Kelly and King to prepare a proposal that would solve the issue raised in the meeting.

QUESTION

What should Westport Electric do about the evaluation problem raised in the case?

Case 3–4*

Worldwide Motor Company

Worldwide Motor Company manufactured automobiles and trucks throughout the world. Its annual sales totaled more than $40 billion with net profits of over $5 billion. This case is concerned with the budgeting and cost control system of the Chicago Engine Plant of the Engine Division, which is part of the North American Automotive Operation (NAAO) of Worldwide Motor Company.

The Chicago Engine Plant

The Chicago Engine Plant produced two basic engines, a 4.9 liter and a 5.0 liter model, each with a number of modifications. In total, the plant produced approximately 800,000 engines annually and supplied components to other engine plants equivalent to an additional 100,000 engines.

The cost of production of the Chicago Engine Plant was in the range of $800 million annually, of which about $600 million was direct material, $50 million direct labor, and $150 million manufacturing overhead. About one third of the overhead was considered to be variable. Most of the direct material was purchased from other divisions of the NAAO. There were 3,000 hourly workers employed during the typical working day.

Thirty-one manufacturing departments reported to the three area superintendents, approximately 10 departments to each. Each department was responsible for the manufacture of an engine component (e.g., intake manifold, cylinder head,

crankshaft, piston, cylinder block) or for the subassembly or assembly of these components. In addition, there were 27 support departments (e.g., quality control, industrial relations, materials management, productivity, controller.)

The Plant Ledger

All expenses incurred by the engine plant were recorded in the plant ledger. The plant maintained a general ledger, of which the plant ledger was a subsidiary. (The relationship between the general ledger and the plant ledger is described later in the case.) The information for all cost control reports was generated from information recorded in the plant ledger.

The chart of accounts was divided between direct labor and overhead. The overhead accounts were divided into 10 series, and each account series was divided into a number of subaccounts. For example, indirect labor, 1 of the 10 series, included 27 subaccounts, of which the following are examples:

121H Clerical and Office
　　　Nonsupervisory—Hourly
121S Clerical and Office
　　　Nonsupervisory—Salaried
151H Machine Set-up
171H Inspection Hourly

In total there were over 200 subaccounts. These accounts were further subdivided by departments—that is, records were kept on the expenses incurred by each department. Since there

---

* This case was prepared by John Dearden, Harvard Business School.
Copyright © by the President and Fellows of Harvard College.
Harvard Business School Case 190–069.

were 58 departments, the plant ledger included about 12,000 individual accounts. The controller explained that this was a companywide chart of accounts and that some of the accounts were not used in Chicago; a relatively small number of accounts represented a large volume of the activity. He further explained that, with modern data processing, it cost no more to make 10 entries to 10 different accounts than 10 entries to a single account. He also pointed out that, if more details on a given account series were needed, it would be necessary to go back to the original documents unless that detail was already segregated in the plant ledger.

Budgeting Process

The budgeting process for 1990 began on July 1, 1989, when the NAAO staff issued Financial Planning Volume (FPV) for 1990. The FPV was described as a conservative estimate of 1990 unit sales by type of vehicle.

Adjusting the 1989 Budget

The divisional staff translated the FPV into requirements for engines and components and assigned these requirements to each of the engine plants in the division. Thus, the Chicago Engine Plant received a 1990 FPV expressed in numbers and types of engines and components. The total engine and component volumes were then translated into specific volumes for each manufacturing department.

Each department started with the 1989 budget.[1] This budget was adjusted by individual account for the following changes expected in 1990:

1. The 1989 budget was adjusted to reflect the volume and mix of products forecast by the 1990 FPV.

2. The budget obtained after step 1 was adjusted to reflect the expected 1990 economic levels (e.g., wages and salary levels, fringe benefits, and so forth).[2]

3. The budget obtained after step 2 was further adjusted for changes in the product design between the 1989 models and the 1990 models. For example, some 1990 engines may have had design changes, and adjustment was made for the expected cost of these changes.

4. Finally, the 1989 budget was adjusted for expected changes in certain noncontrollable fixed and nonvariable expenses.

These adjustments resulted in a 1990 budget that was comparable to the 1989 budget in all respects except the level of efficiency.

The Improvement Factor

An annual improvement factor represented the implementation of one of Worldwide Motors' basic strategies: to maintain a competitive cost advantage. This was based on the conviction that the only way a cost advantage could be maintained was by continual improvement in the level of manufacturing costs.

During August of each year, the Engine Division presented a business plan to the president of NAAO. As part of this plan, the divisional manager proposed an "improvement factor" for the coming year. The proposed improvement factor was either accepted or adjusted through negotiations. The approved improvement factor was expressed as a percentage of the total budgeted direct labor and manufacturing overhead expense. For 1990, the improvement factor for the Engine Division was 5 percent.

The divisional manager then assigned an improvement factor to each plant. The plant improvement factor usually was higher than the

---

[1] Note that in this system the basis for the new budget was the old budget. This contrasts with some systems that start with the current years actual costs.

[2] Note that cost changes for direct material was not a factor, because the budgets covered only direct labor and manufacturing overhead. Direct material budgeting was handled at the divisional office.

divisional improvement factor. In 1990, the Chicago Engine Plant's improvement factor was 6 percent.

The final task in budget preparation was to assign the improvement factor to individual departments. This was done in different ways by the various plants of Worldwide Motors. At the Chicago Engine Plant, this was done as follows:

1. The improvement factor was translated into a dollar amount. For example, if the total 1990 budgeted direct labor and overhead costs had been $200 million before adjustment, the total cost reductions required to meet the objective would be $12 million ($200 million × 0.06).
2. The actual direct labor and overhead costs of all departments were calculated for the past 14 months.
3. The $12 million was prorated proportionately to departments on the basis of the cumulative department costs calculated in way 2.
4. The plant manager adjusted these amounts for any perceived inequities.
5. The 1990 departmental budgets were adjusted for the amounts assigned in item 4 above.
6. Managers were required to identify specific ways in which they could save 150 percent of their individual improvement factor. The additional planned savings were to provide a margin not only because all of the planned savings may not be realized but also because other expense items might exceed budget expense.

Once the budget was completed, it was reviewed by the divisional staff and approved. Since the divisional staff had been working with the plant, particularly on the adjustments to the 1989 budget, the approval was largely a formality as long as the improvement factor was met.

Flexible Budget

At this point the approved budget had been assigned to all of the accounts in the plant ledger.

The individual accounts were designated as either fixed or variable. An authorization rate was calculated for each variable overhead account as follows: The amount budgeted for each account was divided by the total budgeted direct labor dollars at the FPV for each department. This was the budget authorization rate for each variable overhead account for any time period. For example, indirect labor was a variable cost. If budgeted indirect labor cost in a certain department was $60,000, and if the standard direct labor dollars at the Financial Planning Volume in that department was $120,000, the authorization rate for indirect labor was $0.500 (= 60,000/120,000) per dollar of standard direct labor cost.

The purpose of the authorization rate was to make the budget "flexible"—that is, the budgeted overhead could be adjusted to the actual volume of operations. The higher the production level, the higher the budget authorization and vice versa.

Reporting System

Daily Reports

Reports were prepared showing actual cost, budgeted cost, and variances for direct labor, variable indirect labor, supplies, expense tools, maintenance material, and scrap. These were utilities, the costs considered to be variable.

At the end of each day, the manager of each department keyed into a computer the actual units produced in that day. The computer translated the production volume into budget standard direct labor dollars. The computer then calculated the authorized amount for each variable account by multiplying these dollar amounts by the authorization rate calculated in the approved budget. (Note that the only input to this entire process was recording the number of units produced. All other figures were already in computer memory.)

Actual costs were recorded in the accounts as incurred. Actual direct labor and indirect labor hours were recorded each day for payroll purposes. These hours were multiplied by the actual wage rates and debited to the appropriate accounts. Supplies, expense tools, and maintenance material were recorded as they were withdrawn from the appropriate inventories. Scrap was recorded on the basis of "scrap tickets" that were prepared each time a part was scrapped.

Daily reports were compiled showing the actual costs compared to the budgeted cost adjusted to the actual volume of operations. These were available on the computer as soon as the plant opened in the following morning. The reports were summarized by account series, but the department manager could obtain details by interrogating the computer. Hard copies of the reports, summarizing cost performance by account series, were also prepared each day.

The daily reports were read principally by the department manager and, to some extent, by the superintendents. The plant manager received copies of the daily reports but did not usually raise any questions about them. The plant manager found that the trend of daily performances was useful mainly in evaluating the effectiveness of corrective action where performance had been off-standard.

Weekly Reports

The daily budget performance reports were restricted to direct labor and the variable overhead costs, as described earlier. The weekly reports, however, included *all* manufacturing costs. Exhibit 1 is an example of this type of report.

The weekly direct labor and manufacturing overhead report was the principal means by which the plant manager exercised day-to-day control over manufacturing costs. Each week the plant manager met with line and staff managers to review the cost performance of the past week. The performance report for each department was displayed and discussed. The appropriate managers explained why variances had occurred, what had been done to correct unfavorable variances, and what further action was being taken.

The plant controller described these meetings as follows:

The purpose of these meetings is not to castigate managers who are not meeting budget but to help them identify the problem and to suggest corrective courses of action. The meetings take the team approach to solving problems.

Monthly Reports

The monthly reports had the same format as the weekly reports. They reported, however, only total plant performance. These reports went to divisional headquarters and included explanations of significant variances. Periodically, the plant managers met with the divisional manager and his or her staff to discuss these reports.

The division incorporated the monthly plant reports into a consolidated divisional report that was sent to NAAO headquarters.

Profitability was calculated monthly. The plant manager was not held responsible for profits, however, because he or she had little influence over raw material costs and no influence over selling prices. All engines and components were transferred (sold) to other divisions of the company, and transfer prices were negotiated by the divisional staff. Outside purchases were negotiated by a central purchasing department at NAAO headquarters.

Variances

Because the Chicago Engine Plant used a standard cost system, the usual variances were calculated and added to or subtracted from the cost of sales. A brief description of these variances follows:

Purchased Material

Price variance. The cost of material purchases was debited to the raw material inventory at standard cost. The differences between standard cost and the actual cost was debited or credited to the material price variance account.

Usage variance. There was no usage variance for most raw material. The cost of spoiled material was considered an overhead cost. During the production process, defective items were placed

EXHIBIT 1   Direct Labor and Manufacturing Overhead

	Actual	Budget	Actual (over) Amount	Under Budget Percent
			Current Month*	
1. Direct labor				
2. Fringe benefits				
3. Total direct labor				
4. Hourly indirect labor				
5. Fringe benefits				
6. Total hourly indirect labor				
7. Salary				
8. Fringe benefits				
9. Total salary				
10. Supplies excl. fuel				
11. Fuel				
12. Expense tools				
13. Utilities				
14. Maintenance material				
15. Losses and defects				
16. Sundry charges				
17. Fixed charge				
18. Overtime premium hourly				
19. Overtime premium salary				
20. Overtime premium total				
21. Total overhead				
22. Total DL and overhead				

* The same information was also reported for the year to date.

in a scrap bin and a scrap report was prepared. This report identified the original cost of the item plus the labor and overhead incurred up to the point in the manufacturing process where the defect was discovered. This amount was debited to one of the "losses and defects" accounts.

A usage variance did occur for a few items, however. For example, oil pans were stamped out of coils of steel. There was a standard number of pans per coil. The actual number of oil pans produced from a coil could vary because of variations in the thickness of the steel. The cost of these variances was debited or credited to the material usage variance account.

Labor and Overhead Variances

The plant ledger was part of the work-in-process inventory account. All charges to the plant ledger increased the work-in-process inventory and all credits for completed engines decreased it. The plant ledger was debited with the *actual* costs of manufacture and credited with the *standard* cost of the units produced. The difference between these two amounts was the manufacturing expense variance. This included two elements: an efficiency variance, calculated for the monthly performance reports, and a volume variance. The volume variance was the difference between the actual production volume and the budgeted production volume, both expressed in units, multiplied by the standard fixed cost per unit. The plant manager was responsible for the efficiency variance but not for the volume variance.

Each month all of the variances were removed from the work-in-process inventory and debited or credited to variance accounts. Thus, work-in-process was valued at standard cost for balance sheet purposes.

Direct labor rate and efficiency variance. The direct labor variance was not normally divided between rate and efficiency variances, as described in many cost accounting texts. The reason was that labor rates were kept up to date; consequently, any rate variance was caused by people working out of their labor rate classification. Since this was also the responsibility of the department manager, there was little point in segregating it from the efficiency variance. If the rate variance was significant, it could be easily calculated. In these instances, it was usually shown as an *explanation* of variance. Exhibit 2 diagrams the flow of information through the plant ledger.

Financial Statements

Plant financial statements were prepared monthly and submitted to divisional headquarters. These were combined with divisional accounts and other plant statements. A consolidated divisional balance sheet and income statement was prepared and submitted to NAAO headquarters.

QUESTIONS

1. Do you believe that daily expense reports are useful? Why or why not? Would you modify them in any way?
2. Explain why such an extensive plant ledger (12,000 accounts) is necessary at the Chicago Engine Plant? In what ways would you change it?
3. Do you think the management of the Chicago Engine Plant should spend the best part of a day every week reviewing cost performances? When you consider the number of plants, plus divisional and headquarters monthly reviews, a large amount of time is spent on these reviews. What do they accomplish? Would you change these reviews in any way?
4. How do you evaluate the imposition of an "improvement factor" each year? Can you think of any dysfunctional effects of this procedure? Should the Chicago Engine Plant have a higher improvement factor than the Engine Division? How, if at all, would you change any part of the procedure for implementing the improvement factor?
5. Purchased materials account for 75 percent of the Chicago Engine Plant's manufacturing cost and over 50 percent of manufacturing cost company-wide. What type of system would you employ to control these costs?

EXHIBIT 2   Flow of Manufacturing Costs through the Accounting System

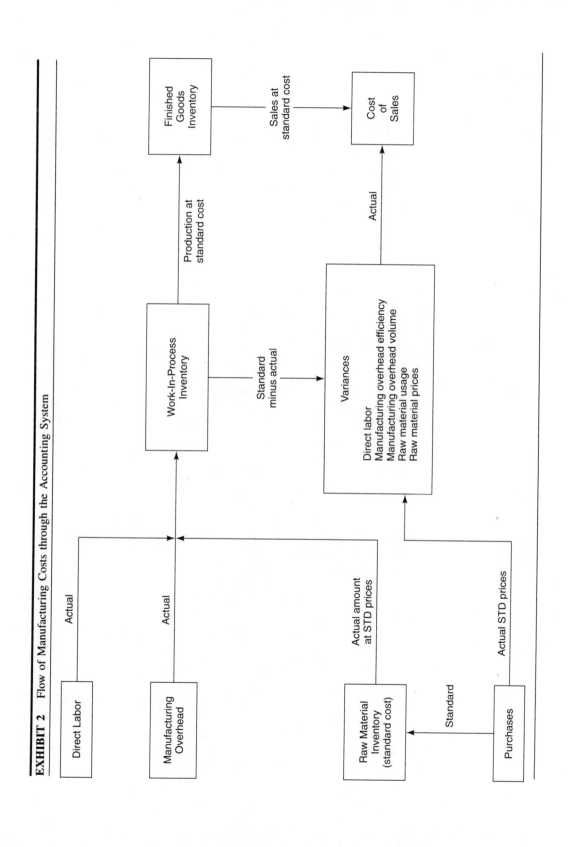

Chapter 4

Profit Centers

When financial performance in a responsibility center is measured in terms of profit, which is the difference between the revenues and expenses, the responsibility center is called a "profit center." Profit as a measure of performance is especially useful, since it enables senior management to use one comprehensive measure instead of several measures that often point to different directions. In this chapter, we discuss considerations involved in deciding whether profit centers should be created. The first part of the discussion focuses on constituting business units (divisions) as profit centers. We then discuss other types of profit centers. Finally, we discuss alternative ways of measuring the profitability of a profit center.

BUSINESS UNITS

A functional organization is one in which each of the principal functions of manufacturing and marketing is performed by separate organization units. When such an organization is converted to one in which each major organization unit is responsible for both the manufacturing and the marketing of a product or a family of products, the process is termed *divisionalization*. In general, a company creates business units because it has decided to delegate more authority to operating managers. Some generalizations to keep in mind about organizations are:

- All companies are organized functionally at some level.
- The difference between a functional organization and a business unit organization is a continuum. Between the extremes of the entirely functional structure and the entirely business unit structure are all types of combinations of functional and business unit structures.
- Complete authority for generating profits is never delegated to a segment of the business. The degree of delegation differs among businesses.

172

Conditions for Delegating Profit Responsibility

Many management decisions involve proposals to increase expenses in the expectation of a greater increase in sales revenue; such decisions are said to involve expense/revenue trade-offs. Additional advertising expense is an example. Another example is increased quality control expense, which can result in more satisfied customers and, hence, increased revenue. Before such a trade-off decision can be delegated safely to a lower-level manager, two conditions should exist.

1. The manager should have the *relevant information* in making cost/revenue trade-offs.
2. There should be some way to measure how effectively the manager is making such trade-offs.

These two conditions limit the delegation of profit responsibility. A major consideration in identifying profit centers is to determine the lowest point in an organization where these two conditions prevail. All responsibility centers fit on a continuum ranging between those that clearly should be profit centers to those that clearly should not. Management must decide where the advantages of giving profit responsibility offset the disadvantages. As with all management control system design choices, there is no clear line of demarcation.

The Movement toward Profit Centers

Although E. I. du Pont de Nemours & Company and General Motors Corporation divisionalized in the early 1920s,[1] most companies in the United States remained functionally organized until after the end of World War II. Since that time many major U.S. corporations have divisionalized and have decentralized profit responsibility at the business unit level. Alfred P. Sloan (General Motors) and Ralph J. Cordiner (General Electric) have documented the philosophy of divisionalization and profit decentralization.[2]

A study by Richard F. Vancil shows the extent that manufacturing companies used the profit center concept in the 1970s.[3] Questionnaires were sent to 684 manufacturing companies whose financial officers were members of the Financial Executives Institute. Forty-six percent of these firms responded. Only 17 firms reported that they did not have two or more profit centers. Vancil states:

---

[1] See Alfred D. Chandler, Jr., *Strategy and Structure* (Cambridge, Mass.: MIT Press, 1962), chaps. 2 and 3.

[2] Alfred P. Sloan, Jr., *My Years with General Motors* (Garden City, N.Y.: Doubleday, 1964); Ralph J. Cordiner, *New Frontiers for Professional Managers* (New York: McGraw-Hill, 1956).

[3] Richard F. Vancil, *Decentralization: Management Ambiguity by Design* (Homewood, Ill.: Dow Jones-Irwin, 1979), pp. 25, 144–45.

If decentralization was a managerial invention in 1920, it was an articulated philosophy by 1950, a reorganization trend by 1960, and a universal practice by 1970. Today, the issue for a manufacturing corporation of any size is not whether it should decentralize, but how much. . . .

Vancil cautions, however, that:

It would be an overstatement to conclude that 95 percent of U.S. manufacturing firms have profit centers because many people who received the questionnaire may have failed to return it *because* they had no profit centers.

Similar data were obtained by James S. Reece and William A. Cool in a survey of the Fortune 1,000 industrial companies in 1977.[4] Of the 620 companies responding, 96 percent had profit centers.

Business Units as Profit Centers: Advantages[5]

Making business units into profit centers may have the following advantages:

- The *speed* of operating decisions may be increased because many decisions do not have to be referred to corporate headquarters.
- The *quality* of many decisions may be improved because they can be made by the business unit managers closest to the point of decision.
- Headquarters management may be *relieved of day-to-day decisions* and can, therefore, concentrate on broader issues.
- *Profit consciousness* may be enhanced. Business unit managers, who are responsible for profits, will be looking constantly for ways to improve them. For example, a manager who is responsible only for marketing activities will be motivated to make sales promotion expenditures that maximize sales, whereas a manager who is responsible for profits will be motivated to make sales promotion expenditures that maximize profits.
- *Measurement of performance is broadened.* Profitability is a more comprehensive measure of performance than the measurement of either revenues or expenses separately. It measures the effects of management actions that affect *both* revenues and expenses.
- Business unit managers, with fewer corporate restraints, should be freer to use their *imagination and initiative*.
- A business unit provides an excellent *training ground* for general management. Because a business unit is similar to an independent company, the business unit manager is trained in managing all of the functional areas. At

---

[4] James S. Reece and William A. Cool, "Measuring Investment Center Performance," *Harvard Business Review,* May–June 1978, pp. 28–49.

[5] These advantages accrue to profit centers in general. They are discussed in the context of business units in this section.

the same time, it provides an excellent means for evaluating a business unit manager's potential for higher management jobs.

- If a company has a strategy of diversification, business unit structure facilitates use of different talents and expertise in different types of businesses. For example, people who are best trained in managing a certain type of business can be assigned to work exclusively in that business if it is a separate business unit.
- Divisionalization provides top management with information on the *profitability of components* of the company.
- Business units are subject to pressures to improve their competitive performance.

Difficulties with Divisionalization

However, divisionalization may cause difficulties:

- To the extent that decisions are decentralized, top management may *lose some control*. Relying on control reports is not as effective as an intimate, personal knowledge of an operation. With divisionalization, top management must change its approach to control. Instead of personal direction, senior management must rely to a considerable extent on management control reports.
- Competent *business unit managers* may not be available in a functional organization, because there may not have been sufficient opportunities for them to develop general management competence.
- Organization units that were once cooperating as functional units may now compete with one another. An increase in one business unit manager's profits may decrease that of another's. This decrease in cooperation may manifest itself in manager's unwillingness to refer sales leads to another business unit, even though that unit is better qualified to follow up on the lead, to production decisions that have undesirable cost consequences on other units, or to the hoarding of personnel or equipment, which, from the overall company standpoint, would be better off assigned to, or used in, another unit.
- *Friction* can increase. There may be arguments over the appropriate transfer price, the assignment of common costs, and the credit for revenues that were generated jointly by the efforts of two or more business units.
- There may be too much emphasis on *short-run profitability* at the expense of long-run profitablity. In the desire to report high current profits, the business unit manager may skimp on R&D, training programs, or maintenance. This tendency is especially prevalent when the turnover of business unit managers is relatively high. In these circumstances, managers may have good reason to believe that their actions may not come home to roost until after they have moved to other jobs.
- There is no completely satisfactory system for ensuring that each business unit, by optimizing its own profits, will *optimize company profits.*

- If headquarters management is more capable or has better information than the average business unit manager, the *quality* of some of the decisions may be reduced.
- Divisionalization may cause *additional costs* because it may require additional management and staff personnel and additional recordkeeping.

Constraints on Business Unit Authority

A business unit manager must be able to exercise a significant amount of influence over the factors that affect the profitability of the unit. To realize fully the advantages listed above, the business unit manager would have to be as autonomous as the president of an independent company. As a practical matter, however, such autonomy is not feasible. If a company were divided into completely independent units, the organization would be giving up the advantages of size and synergism. Also, senior management would be abdicating its responsibility if it delegated to business unit management all the authority that the board of directors gives to the chief executive. Consequently, business unit structures represent trade-offs between business unit autonomy and corporate constraints. The effectiveness of a business unit organization is largely dependent on how well these trade-offs are made.

Constraints from other business units.   One of the main problems associated with divisionalization occurs when business units must deal with one another. It is useful to think of managing a profit center in terms of control over three types of decisions: (1) the product decision (what goods or services to make and sell); (2) the procurement or sourcing decision (how to obtain or manufacture the goods or services); and (3) the marketing decision (how, where, and for how much are these goods or services to be sold). If a business unit manager controls all three of these activities, there is usually no difficulty in assigning profit responsibility and measuring performance. In general, the greater the degree of integration within a company, the more difficult it becomes to assign responsibility to a single profit center for all three activities in a given product line—that is, if, for example, the production, procurement, and marketing decisions for a single product line are split among two or more business units, it may be difficult to separate the contribution of each business unit to the overall success of the product line.

Constraints from corporate management.   The constraints imposed by corporate management can be grouped into three types: (1) those resulting from strategic considerations, especially financing decisions; (2) those resulting because uniformity is required; and (3) those resulting from the economies of centralization.

Most companies retain certain decisions, such as the acquiring of capital, at the corporate level, at least for domestic activities. Consequently, one of the major constraints on business units results from corporate control over new investments. Business units must compete with one another for a share of the available funds. Thus, a business unit could find its expansion plans thwarted because another unit has convinced senior management that it has a more attractive program. In addition to financial constraints, corporate management exercises other strategic constraints. For example, restrictions on markets and products are often imposed. Each business unit has a "charter" that specifies the marketing and/or production activities that it is permitted to undertake, and it must refrain from operating beyond its charter, even though it sees profit opportunities in doing so. Also, the maintenance of the proper corporate image may require constraints on the quality and engineering of products or on the development of public relations activities.

Companies impose some constraints on business units because of the necessity for uniformity. One constraint is that business units must conform to corporate accounting and management control systems. This constraint is especially troublesome for units that have been acquired from another company and that have been accustomed to using different systems.

Examples. Schering-Plough Corporation completed in 1989 a seven-year effort to install a companywide accounting and control system. The long elapsed time was caused principally by difficulties in persuading the business units to adopt the corporate-specified system. By contrast, General Electric Corporation requires only a relatively few numbers to be submitted to headquarters with corporate-specified definitions. At one time, Nestlé Company permitted business units to report to headquarters in either English, French, German, or Spanish; at that time, most senior managers at headquarters were multilingual.

Some companies require large amounts of planning and reporting information from each profit center. Corporate headquarters may also require uniform pay and other personnel policies, ethical policies, policies on selection of vendors, policies regarding computers and communication equipment, and even the design of the business unit's letterheads.

Certain services are centralized at corporate headquarters because a central organization can provide a particular service to all business units (e.g., data processing, legal, public relations, training) more economically or because a central service is required (e.g., internal auditing). To some extent, all staff offices provide service to business units and the business units are generally required to use some staff services.

In general, these corporate constraints do not cause severe problems in decentralization so long as they are dealt with explicitly. Business unit management should understand the necessity for most of them and should accept them with good grace. The major problems seem to revolve around the optional service activities. Often business units believe (sometimes rightly) that they can obtain a particular service less expensively from an outside source.

Vancil's study (described earlier) has a thorough discussion of these restrictions on autonomy. Vancil reports that the median profit center manager in his survey believed the profit center relied on other units for about one quarter to one third of its resources and that the manager had authority to make decisions for about three quarters of the profit center's costs.

OTHER PROFIT CENTERS

There are, in addition to business units, other profit centers. Some examples are described below.

Functional Units

A multibusiness company is divided into business units that are treated as far as practical as independent profit-generating units. Within these business units, subunits may be functionally organized. In such business units, as well as in companies that are functionally organized, it is sometimes desirable that one or more of the functional units be treated as profit centers. These include marketing, manufacturing, and service units. The important point to remember is that no principle states that certain types of units are inherently profit centers and other types are not. The decision on whether a unit should be a profit center is a management option, based on whether the responsibility center manager has enough *influence* (even if not total control) over the activities that affect the "bottom line."

Marketing.   A marketing activity can be made into a profit center by charging the cost of the products sold to the marketing manager. A transfer price provides the marketing manager with the relevant information to make the optimum revenue/cost trade-offs. Since managers are measured on profitability, there is a check on how well these decisions are being made. Also, since the managers are being evaluated on profitability, they will be motivated to maximize profits. The marketing manager should be charged with a transfer price based on *standard* cost, not the actual cost of products sold. This separates manufacturing cost performance from the marketing performance. The former is affected by changes in the levels of efficiency that are outside of the control of the marketing manager.

When should a marketing activity be given profit responsibility? The answer is: When the marketing manager is in the best position to make the principal cost/revenue trade-offs. This often occurs where different conditions exist in different geographical areas—for example, a *foreign marketing activity*. In such an activity, it may be difficult to control centrally such decisions as: How to market a product? How much to spend on sales promotion, when to spend it, and on which media? How to train salesmen or dealers? Where and when to establish new dealers?[6]

Manufacturing. The manufacturing activity is usually an expense center, and the management of such activities is judged based on performance against standard costs and overhead budgets. Problems can occur because standard cost performance does not measure how well all of the responsibilities of the manufacturing manager are being performed. Examples:

- Quality control may be inadequate; products of inferior quality may be shipped to obtain standard cost credit.
- Manufacturing managers may be reluctant to interrupt production schedules in order to produce a rush order to accommodate a customer.
- When a manager is measured against standards, there may be no incentive to manufacture products that are difficult to produce.
- There may be little incentive to improve standards.

As a consequence, where the performance of the manufacturing activities is measured against standard costs, it is necessary that quality control, production scheduling, make-or-buy decisions, and the setting of standards be controlled separately.

An overall measure of the manufacturing organization is obtained if the organization is made into a profit center. One way to do this is to give the organization credit for the selling price of the products minus the estimated marketing expenses. Such an arrangement is far from perfect, partly because many factors influencing the volume of sales are outside the control of the manufacturing manager. However, it seems to work better in some cases than the alternative of holding the manufacturing operation responsible only for costs.

Some authors maintain that manufacturing units should not be made into profit centers unless they sell a large fraction of their output to outside customers; they regard such units as *pseudo* profit centers on the grounds that the revenues assigned to them for sales to other units within the company are artificial. Many companies create profit centers for such units. They believe that, if properly designed, the system can create almost the same motivation that exists in sales to outside customers.

Service and support units. Maintenance units, data processing units, transportation units, engineering units, consulting units, customer service units, and similar support units of an organization can be made into profit centers. These may be headquarters units that service divisions, or they may be similar units

---

[6] In a 1989 survey of members of the Controllers Council of the National Association of Accountants, 70 percent of the respondents treated marketing activities as revenue centers, rather than profit centers. (Montvale, N.J.: National Association of Accountants, *Controllers Update*, February 1990, p. 1.)

EXHIBIT 4-1   Prevalence of Charging for Administrative Services (percent of firms which charge for administrative services and percent employing the major types of cost assignment methods)

		Percent by Method		
Administrative Service Category	Percent of Firms Which Charge*	Usage (actual or estimated)	Prorated	Other
1. Finance and accounting	73%	35%	54%	11%
2. Legal	70	35	55	10
3. Electronic data processing	87	63	29	8
4. General marketing services	73	35	56	9
5. Advertising	72	50	41	9
6. Market research services	70	36	54	10
7. Public relations	63	24	62	14
8. Industrial relations	70	32	56	12
9. Personnel	70	35	53	12
10. Real estate	62	37	53	10
11. Operations research department	60	47	42	11
12. Purchasing department	51	40	51	9
13. Top corporate management overhead	63	13	72	15
14. Corporate planning department	61	20	66	14

* The total for the denominator includes only respondents who answered "yes" or "no" and excludes missing values and respondents who answered "not applicable."

Source: Richard F. Vancil, *Decentralization: Management Ambiguity by Design* (Homewood, Ill.: Dow Jones-Irwin, 1979), p. 251.

within business units. They charge customers for services rendered, and their financial objective is to generate enough business so that their revenues equal expenses. The prevalence of such practices, as reported in the Vancil study, is shown in Exhibit 4-1. (The firms that charge "based on usage" probably treat these units as profit centers.) Usually, the units receiving the services have the alternative of procuring them from an outside vendor if a vendor can offer services of equal quality at a lower price.

Managers of such service units are motivated to control costs; otherwise, customers will go elsewhere. Managers of the receiving units are motivated to make decisions about whether a request for service is worth the cost. For example, if transportation is furnished without cost from a central pool, those that use the pool need not consider whether a specific request for a vehicle is worth the cost.

Other Organizations

A company having branch operations that are responsible for marketing the company's products in a particular geographical area is often a natural for a profit center type of organization. Even though the branch managers have no manufacturing or procurement responsibilities, profitability is often the best single measure of their performance. Furthermore, the profit measurement is frequently an excellent motivating device. Thus, the individual stores of most retail chains, the individual restaurants in fast-food chains, the individual hotels in hotel chains, and the branches of many commercial banks are profit centers.

MEASURING PROFITABILITY

There are two types of profitability measurements in a profit center, just as there are for the organization as a whole. There is, first, a measure of *management performance*, in which the focus is on how well the manager is doing. This measure is used for planning, coordinating, and controlling the day-to-day activities of the profit center and as a device for providing the proper motivation to the manager. Second, there is a measure of *economic performance*, in which the focus is on how well the profit center is doing as an economic entity. The messages given by these two measures may be quite different. For example, the management performance report of a branch store may show that the profit center manager may be doing an excellent job, under the circumstances; but the economic performance report may indicate that, because of economic and competitive conditions in its area, the store is a losing proposition and should be closed.

The necessary information for both purposes usually can be obtained from a single underlying set of data. Since the management report is used frequently, but the economic report is prepared only on those occasions when economic decisions must be made, considerations relating to management performance measurement have first priority in systems design—that is, the system is designed to measure management performance routinely, and economic information is derived from them.

Types of Profitability Measures

To evaluate the economic performance of the profit center itself, it is necessary to use net income after allocating all costs (including a fair share of the corporate overhead) to the profit center. However, in evaluating the performance of the profit center manager, any of five different measures of profitability could be used: (1) contribution margin, (2) direct business unit profit, (3) controllable business unit profit, (4) income before income taxes, or (5) net income. The nature of these measures is indicated by Exhibit 4–2. Their relative popularity, as reported in the Reece/Cool survey is summarized in Exhibit 4–3.[7] Each is discussed below.

---

[7] James S. Reece and William R. Cool, "Measuring Investment Center Performance," *Harvard Business Review*, May–June 1978, p. 36.

EXHIBIT 4–2   Income Statement

			Measure
Revenue		$1,000	
Cost of sales		600	
Gross margin		400	
Variable expenses		180	
Contribution margin		220	←①
Other business unit expenses	$60		
Charges from other business units	30	90	
Direct business unit profit		130	←②
Controllable corporate allocations		10	
Controllable business unit profit		120	←③
Other corporate allocations		20	
Income before taxes		100	←④
Taxes		50	
Net income		$ 50	←⑤

---

1. Contribution margin.   The principal argument for measuring the profit center manager's performance on the basis of contribution margin is that the fixed expenses are noncontrollable by the manager, and that the manager, therefore, should focus attention on maximizing the spread between revenue amd variable expenses. The problem with this method is that some fixed expenses are entirely controllable, and that almost all fixed expenses are partially controllable. As discussed in Chapter 3, many items of expenses are discretionary; they can be changed at the discretion of the profit center manager. Presumably, senior management wants the profit center to be concerned about keeping these discretionary expenses in line with amounts agreed on in the budget formulation process. A focus on the contribution margin tends to direct attention away from this responsibility. Further, even if an expense, such as administrative salaries, cannot be changed in the short-run, the profit center manager can certainly control the efficiency and productivity of the employees.

2. Direct business unit profit.   This measure shows the amount that the business unit contributes to the general overhead and profit of the corporation. It incorporates all expenses incurred in or directly traced to the business units, regardless of whether these items are entirely controllable by the business unit manager. With the use of this measure, corporate expenses are not allocated to business units.

The principal weakness of this measure is that it does not recognize the motivational benefit of charging headquarters costs.

3. Controllable business unit profit.   Headquarters expenses can be divided into two categories: controllable and noncontrollable. The former in-

---

EXHIBIT 4–3   Methods of Measuring Profit

Survey question:

Is profit center or investment center "profit" calculated in a manner consistent with the way net income is calculated for your shareholder reports?

	Number	*Percentage*
Yes	239	40%
No	351	59
No answer	4	1
Total	594	100%

If your answer was no, in which of the following ways does the profit center's calculation differ from net income calculation? (Check as many as apply.)

	*Number**	*Percentage of 351 Companies**
No taxes are assessed to profit centers	249	71%
No depreciation charge is deducated	11	3
The depreciation calculation differs	25	7
No corporate administrative expenses are allocated to the center	173	49
No interest charges on corporate debt are allocated to the center	225	64
Profit center reports use direct (variable) costing, rather than full (absorption) costing	19	5
Other differences exist	51	15

*Includes multiple responses.

Source: James S. Reece and William R. Cool, "Measuring Investment Center Performance," *Harvard Business Review,* May–June 1978.

cludes headquarters expenses that are controllable, at least to a degree, by the business unit manager (e.g., management information service). Consequently, if these costs are included in the measurement system, the profit will be after the deduction of all expenses that may be *influenced* by the business unit manager.[8] Controllable business unit profits, however, cannot be compared directly with published data, or with trade association data that report the profits of other companies in the industry, because it excludes noncontrollable headquarters expenses.

   4. Income before taxes.   In this measure, all corporate overhead is allocated to business units. The basis of allocation reflects the relative amount of

---

   [8] This "influenceability" criterion is discussed in John Dearden, "Measuring Profit Center Performance," *Harvard Business Review,* September–October 1987, pp. 84–88. This criterion implies that business unit managers should be held responsible for costs that they can influence, even if they do not have total control over the costs.

expense that is incurred for each unit or, alternatively, the amount of benefit received by each unit.

There are two arguments against such allocations. First, the costs incurred by corporate staff departments, such as finance, accounting, and human resource management, are not controllable by profit center managers. Therefore, they should not be held accountable for what they do not control. Second, it may be difficult to find acceptable bases of allocating the corporate staff services that would properly reflect the relative amount of corporate costs caused by each profit center.

There are, however, arguments for allocating corporate overhead to profit centers in their performance reports:

- Corporate service units have a tendency to "empire build" to increase their power base and to make their units as excellent as it is possible to have, without regard for their value to the company. If such costs are allocated to profit centers, there is a greater possibility that the profit center managers will raise questions about the amount of corporate overhead; this helps to keep the head office spending in check. For instance, companies have been known to sell a corporate aircraft because of complaints about its costs from profit center managers.
- Profit centers' performance would be more realistic and comparable to competitors because the competitors would pay for similar services.
- The profit center manager is given the message that the profit center has not earned a profit unless it recovers all costs, including a share of allocated corporate overhead. Thus, profit center managers would be motivated to make optimum long-term marketing decisions (pricing, product mix, and so on), because they must keep in mind that they must recover their share of the corporate overhead. This is desirable, since the company will not otherwise be viable in the long run.

If corporate overheads are allocated to profit centers, budgeted costs, not the actual costs, should be allocated. That is to say, the profit center's performance report will show an identical amount in the "budget" and "actual" columns for such corporate overhead. This ensures that the profit center managers will not complain either about the arbitrariness of allocations or the lack of control over allocated costs since, in their performance reports, no variances would be shown for allocated overheads. The variances would appear in the reports of the responsibility center that incurred the costs.

5. Net income.   Not many companies measure performance of domestic business units at the bottom line, the amount of net income after income tax. There are two principal reasons for this: *(a)* In many situations, the income after tax is a constant percentage of the pretax income, so there is no advantage in incorporating income taxes; and *(b)* decisions that have an impact on income taxes are made at headquarters, and it is believed that business unit profitability should not affect, or be affected by, these decisions.

In some companies, however, the effective income tax rate *does* vary among business units. For example, foreign subsidiaries or business units with foreign operations may have different effective income tax rates. In other situations, business units may influence income taxes by their decisions on acquiring or disposing of equipment, installment credit policies, and other ways in which taxable income differs from income as measured by generally accepted accounting principles. In these situations, it may be desirable to allocate income tax expenses, not only to measure the economic profitability of the business unit but also to motivate the business unit manager to minimize taxes.

Bases of comparison. The performance of a profit center is appraised by comparing actual results for one or more of these measures with budgeted amounts. In addition, data on competitors and industry data provide a good cross check on the appropriateness of the budget. Data for individual companies are available in annual and quarterly reports and in Form 10K (Form 10K data are published by the Securities and Exchange Commission for about 11,000 companies). Data for industries are published in Dun & Bradstreet, Inc., Key Business Ratios; Standard & Poor's Compustat Services, Inc.; Robert Morris Associates Annual Statement Studies; and annual surveys published in *Fortune, Business Week,* and *Forbes.* Trade associations publish data for the companies in their industries.

Common revenues. Although, in most circumstances, the measurement of the revenues earned by a profit center is straightforward, there are some situations in which two or more profit centers participated in the sales effort that resulted in a sale; ideally, each should be given appropriate credit for its part in the transaction. For example, the principal contact between the company and a certain customer may be a salesperson from Business Unit A, but the customer may sometimes place orders with the Business Unit A salesperson for products carried by Business Unit B. Although the Unit A salesperson should be motivated to seek such orders, he or she is unlikely to do so if all the revenue resulting from them is credited to Unit B. Similarly, a customer of a bank may carry an account in Branch C, which is credited with the revenue generated by this account; but the customer may prefer to do some banking business with Branch D, because it is more conveniently located or for other reasons. Branch D is unlikely to be eager to provide services to such a customer if all the revenue is credited to Branch C.

Many companies have not given much attention to the solution of these common revenue problems. They take the position that the identification of precise responsibility for revenue generation is too complicated to be practical, and that sales personnel must recognize they are working not only for their own profit center but also for the overall good of the company. Some companies attempt to untangle the responsibility for common sales. They may, for example, credit the business unit that takes an order for a product handled by another unit (Business Unit A in the above example) with the equivalent of a brokerage commission or a finder's fee. In the case of a bank, the branch performing a service may be given explicit credit for that service, even though the customer's account is kept in another branch.

Management considerations.   Each of the types of profitability measures described in Exhibit 4–2 is used by some companies. Most companies in the United States include some, if not all, of the costs discussed earlier, whether or not they can be influenced by the business unit manager. For example, a large proportion of United States multinational corporations measure the performance of managers of foreign subsidiaries in dollars. Performance, thus, is affected by fluctuations in the value of the dollar relative to the home currency. There are few instances where individual managers can exercise any influence over the value of the dollar.

Most of the confusion in measuring the performance of profit center managers is the result of *not* separating the measurement of the manager from the economic measurement of the business unit. If we consider the measurement of the manager alone, the solution becomes evident: Managers should be measured against those items that they can *influence*. In the typical company, this would probably be all expenses incurred directly for the business unit. The managers would be measured on an after-tax basis only if they can influence the amount of tax that they pay. Items that they clearly cannot influence, such as currency fluctuation, should be eliminated.

Following the guide of including only those items that the manager can influence does not solve all the problems. Degrees of influence are many. There will always be items over which a manager may exercise some influence but little real control. This is why variance analysis is always important in judging management performance. Even with the best variance analysis system, however, judgment will always be necessary in evaluating managerial performance. If all items over which the manager has no influence are eliminated (or are reported in such a way that variances do not develop), however, it will make the exercise of this judgment more reliable.

SUMMARY

A profit center is an organization unit in which both revenues and expenses are measured in monetary terms. Most business units responsible for both producing and marketing a product line are profit centers. Setting up these units as profit centers pushes decision making to lower levels where relevant information in making expense/revenue trade-offs exists, which can speed up decision making, improve the quality of decisions, focus attention on profitability, provide a broader measure of management performance, and have other advantages. Nevertheless, there are certain limitations in the use of profit centers. Production, marketing, and administrative and support responsibility centers within a business unit and at headquarters may be profit centers if management decides that the benefits of doing so exceed the extra bookkeeping costs and possible other drawbacks.

SUGGESTED ADDITIONAL READINGS

Dearden, John. "Measuring Profit Center Managers." *Harvard Business Review,* September–October 1987, pp. 84–88.

Govindarajan, Vijay. "Decentralization, Strategy, and Effectiveness of Strategic Business Units in Multi-Business Organizations." *Academy of Management Review* XI, no. 4 (1986), 844–56.

Leibenstein, H. *Inside the Firm: The Inefficiencies of Hierarchy.* Cambridge, Mass.: Harvard University Press, 1987.

Solomons, David. *Divisional Performance: Measurement and Control.* Homewood, Ill.: Richard D. Irwin, 1965.

Vancil, Richard F. *Decentralization: Management Ambiguity by Design.* Homewood, Ill.: Dow Jones-Irwin, 1979.

Walsh, Francis J. *Measuring Business-Unit Performance.* Research Bulletin no. 206, New York: The Conference Board, Inc., 1987.

Case 4-1

North Country Auto, Inc.*

George G. Liddy, part owner of North Country Auto, Inc., was feeling pretty good about the new control systems recently put in place for his five department managers (new and used car sales, service, body, and parts departments.) Exhibit 1 describes each department. Mr. Liddy strongly believed in the concept of evaluating each department individually as a profit center. But he also recognized the challenge of getting his managers to "buy in" to the system by working together for the good of the dealership.

Background

North Country Auto, Inc., is a franchised dealer and factory-authorized service center for Ford, Saab, and Volkswagen. Multiple franchises were becoming more and more common in the 1980s. But the value of multiple franchises does not come without its costs. Each of the three manufacturers used a different computerized system for tracking inventory and placing new orders. They also required their dealerships to maintain an adequate service facility with a crew of trained technicians, which in turn necessitated carrying an inventory of parts to be used in repairs. Exhibit 2 gives balance sheet data with a break-out of investment for each product line. North Country also operated a body shop and in mid-1989 opened a "while you wait" oil change service for any make of vehicle.

The dealership was situated in an Upstate New York town with a population of about 20,000. It served two nearby towns of about 4,000 as well as rural areas covering a 20-mile radius. North Country began operation in 1968 and in 1983 moved one mile down the road to its current six-acre lot/25,000-square-foot facility. It was owned as a corporation by George Liddy and Andrew Jones, who were both equally active in day-to-day operations. Mr. Liddy purchased an interest in the dealership from a previous partner in 1988. Mr. Jones had been part owner since the start of the business. Whereas Mr. Liddy focused his energies on new and used car sales, Mr. Jones concentrated on managing the parts, service, and body shop departments—commonly referred to as the "back end" of a dealership.

The owners were determined to maintain a profitable back end as a hedge against depressed sales and lower margins in vehicles sales. In an industry characterized by aggressive discounting fueled by a combination of high inventories, a more educated consumer, and a proliferation of new entrants, alternative sources of cash flow were crucial. Industry analysts were estimating that fewer than 50 percent of the dealers in the United States would make a profit on new car sales in 1989. Overall net profit margins were expected to fall below 1 percent of sales (*The Wall Street Journal*, December 11, 1989).

George Liddy's Challenge

Before George Liddy bought into the dealership, all the departments operated as part of one business. Department managers were paid salaries and a year-end bonus determined at the owners' discretion based on overall results for the year and a subjective appraisal of each manager.

---

* This case was prepared and is copyrighted by Joseph Fisher.

George Liddy believed this system did not provide proper motivation for the managers. He believed in decentralized profit centers and performance-based compensation as superior methods of control. He knew that the success of the profit center control system was dependent upon the support of his managers. They must understand the rationale for allocating costs to their departments and believe that they have reasonable control over profitability. The managers' bonuses

---

EXHIBIT 1 The Departmental Structure

New Car Sales and Used Car Sales

The new and used car departments each had a sales manager. They shared six salespersons. In addition, this department contained an office manager and clerks. The managers were paid a flat salary, plus a fixed sum per new or used vehicle sold, and a percentage of their department's gross profit (calculated as sales minus cost of vehicles sold). When the owners and the managers agreed on annual unit volume and margin goals, the dollar weights were set to make each portion approximately one third of the manager's expected total compensation. The owners claimed that this type of dual incentive bonus structure allowed the managers flexibility in targeting margins and volume To quote George Liddy: "If the margins are low, the sales manager can try to make it up in volume." The sales force was paid strictly a commission on gross profit. Many dealerships in the area were changing sales compensation to a flat salary, plus a partial commission on gross profits generated.

The new car sales manager was responsible for recommending to Liddy new model orders and inventory mix among the three product lines. He also had the authority to approve selling prices and trade-in allowances on customer transactions. Typically, the new car manager was allowed to transfer the trade-in at blue book. However, if the car was obviously of below-average quality, the used car department may be asked for their estimate of value. The used car manager was responsible for controlling the mix of used car inventory through buying and selling used vehicles at wholesale auto auctions.

Service

The service department occupied over half of the building's usable square footage and was the most labor intensive operation. Service comprised 11 bays with hydraulic lifts, one of which was used for the oil change operation. The department employed a manager, 10 technicians, 3 semiskilled mechanics, 2 counter clerks, and 3 office clerks. The manager was paid a flat salary, plus a bonus on the department's gross profit on labor-hours billed (computed as labor-dollars billed minus total wages of billable technicians and mechanics). The bonus portion was planned to be approximately 50 percent of his salary. The technicians, mechanics, and clerks were all paid a flat salary, regardless of actual hours billed. The technicians required specialty training to perform factory-authorized work on each of the specific lines. Sending a technician to school cost about $4,000 over a two-year period. The owners estimated that a new hire could cost as much as $10,000 in nonbillable overruns on warranty jobs where reimbursement was emitted to standard allowable labor-hours. Of the 10 techs, 4 were certified for Ford, 3 for Saab, and 3 for Volkswagen. George Liddy and Andrew Jones contemplated reducing the cost of idle time by cross-training but were averse to risks of turnover among highly skilled labor. Retraining costs could triple when one person quits.

The primary sources of service department revenue were warranty maintenance and repair work, nonwarranty maintenance and repair work, used car reconditioning, and the oil change operation. Warranty work was reimbursed by the factories at their prescribed labor rates, which were typically as much as 20 percent lower than the rates charged directly for nonwarranty work. Lower margins on warranty work were a potential problem for the dealership if they dissuaded the service manager from delivering prompt service to recent buyers. During times of near-capacity utilization, the manager would be motivated to schedule higher-margin nonwarranty jobs in the place of warranty work.

EXHIBIT 1 *(concluded)*

Parts

The parts department consisted of a manager, three stock keepers, and two clerks. The parts manager was paid a flat salary, plus a bonus on department gross profits (computed as total parts sold less cost of parts). The parts manager was responsible for tracking parts inventory for the three lines and minimizing both carrying costs and "obsolescence." The owners defined obsolescence as a part in stock which was not sold in over a year. Mr. Liddy estimated that as many as 25 percent of the parts on hand fall into this category. Days-supply of parts (inventory turnover) averaged 100 days for the industry. The manager had to be an expert on the return policies, stock requirements, and secondary market of three distinct and unrelated lines of merchandise. It was the parts manager's job to use factory return credits most effectively and identify outside wholesale opportunities so as to minimize large write-downs. Local wholesalers would pay as much as 80 percent of dealer cost for old parts.

Demand for parts was almost completely derived from other departments. Dollar sales volume in parts broke down as follows: 50 percent through service, 30 percent through the body shop, 10 percent wholesale, and 10 percent over-the-counter retail. Similar to service, parts needed in warranty work were reimbursed at rates as much as 20 percent less than prices charged for nonwarranty work.

Body Shop

The body shop consisted of a manager, three technicians, and a clerk. The manager, like the others, was paid a flat salary, plus a bonus on departmental profitability. To keep the shop in business in the long run, they would need to invest an additional $50,000 in new spray painting equipment. As it was, the body shop was showing a loss after allocation of fixed overhead. Gross margins as high as 60 percent could be attained, but rework and hidden damage beyond estimates tended to drive them down to closer to 40 percent.

Oil Change Operation

The dealership's oil change business operated under the nationally franchised "Qwik Change" logo, using one bay in the service department and one of the semiskilled mechanics. Volume averaged 68 changes per week. This was not evaluated as an independent profit center but as a means to fill unused capacity in the service department. The oil change franchise paid for all of the equipment, reducing the dealership's out-of-pocket investment to $500. After direct labor, direct parts, and the franchise fee, the dealership made about $10.00 on each oil change priced at $21.95. The owners were willing to devote an extra bay to this operation if volume warranted.

in 1989 were calculated on the basis of departmental *gross* profits. Expenses below the gross profit line were not considered in the bonus calculation. They were only told in a statement outlining their responsibilities to exercise "judicious control over discretionary expenses." Implementing a more comprehensive control system tied to actual departmental net profits would require that Liddy break down costs traditionally regarded as general overhead into separate activities associated with specific departments. His strategy with the managers involved a gradual phasing in over

the next few years of an "almost" full cost allocation system, where each department manager would eventually have responsibility for all controllable costs incurred in the department. Fixed expenses, such as interest expense, would be allocated by Liddy for his own decisions but would not be used in the managers' bonus calculations.

The gradual changeover would allow Liddy, who was new to the dealership, time to become more knowledgeable of the intricacies of North Country Auto's accounting records. He did not want to lose credibility because of perceived arbi-

EXHIBIT 2

Balance Sheet
October 31, 1989
(in thousands)

Assets		Liabilities and Equity	
Cash	$ 32	Accounts payable	$ 73
Accounts receivable	228	Notes payable—vehicles	1,294
Saab inventory	253	Long-term debt	344
VW inventory	243		
Ford inventory	773		
		Total liabilities	1,711
Used cars	231		
Saab parts	75		
VW parts	75		
Ford parts	226		
Body shop materials	6	Stockholders' Equity	
Other current assets	89	Common stock	$ 400
		Retained earnings	205
Property & equipment*(net)			
($377M gross)	85		
Total assets	$2,316	Total liabilities and equity	$2,316

* North Country leases both the land and building.

trary cost allocations. Exhibit 3 gives a breakdown of departmental profitability on an "almost" full-cost basis using the casewriter's allocation of fixed costs. Exhibit 4 gives additional information on the financial statements.

In addition to finding a way to effectively track departmental performance, George Liddy had to devise a sensible system for transfer pricing. Though Mr. Liddy believed that each department at North Country could theoretically operate as an independent business, he acknowledged that a complex interrelationship existed among the profit centers in the course of normal business transactions. A recent new vehicle purchase illustrates the problems that could arise:

1. A selling price of $14,150 was financed by cash down of $2,000, a trade-in allowance of $4,800, and a bank loan of $7,350. The dealer's cost was $11,420, which included factory price plus sales commission.

2. The trade-in had a wholesale guidebook value of $3,500. The guidebook, published monthly, was, at best, a near estimate of liquidation value. Actual values varied daily with the supply-demand balance at auto auctions. These variances could be as much as 25 percent of the book value.

3. The used car sales manager believed that she could sell the trade-in quickly at $5,000 and earn a good margin, so she chose to carry it in inventory instead of wholesaling it for a value estimated to be $3,500. The new car manager, in turn, used the $3,500 value in calculating his actual profit on the new car sale. In performing the routine maintenance check, the service department reported that the front

EXHIBIT 3

October 31, 1989 (10 months)
(dollar figures in thousands)

	New	Used	Service	Body	Parts
Sales	$6,558	$1,557	$ 672	$186	$ 1,417
Gross profit	502	189	379	100	362
Number of units					
(no. of vehicles, repairs, or parts)	474	390	9,765	406	40,139
Direct selling (commission and delivery)	$141	$45	n/a	n/a	n/a
Indirect labor	145	64	237	64	156
Department advertising	108	40	19	2	3
Policy work—parts and					
service (give-aways and rework)	29	12	14	12	1
Supplies and utilities	22	18	19	28	12
Depreciation	3	1	15	5	2
Rent	89	22	67	13	9
Profit before common expenses	($35)	($13)	$8	($24)	$178
Other expenses:					
Interest (on new inventory)	187				
Other interest	58				
Owners' salary	70				
Insurance	50				
Operating profit	($250)				
Extraordinary income	$179				
Net operating profit	($71)				

NOTE: n/a means not available.

wheels would need new brake pads and rotors and that the rear door lock assembly was jammed. The retail estimates for repair would be $300 for the brakes ($125 in parts, $175 in labor) and $75 to fix the lock assembly ($30 in parts, $45 in labor). Cleaning and touch-up would cost $75. The service department also recommended that a full tune-up be performed for a retail price of $255 ($80 in parts, $175 in labor).

4. The repair and tune-up work was completed and capitalized at retail cost into used car inventory at $705. These mechanical repairs would not necessarily increase wholesale value if the car were subsequently sold at the auction. The transfer price for internal work was recently changed from cost to full retail

equivalent. The retail markup for labor was 3.5 times the direct hourly rate and about 1.4 times for parts.

5. George Liddy was concerned that the retail transfer price of the repairs in conjunction with his plan to eventually allocate full costs to each department (as illustrated in Exhibit 3) might encourage the used car sales manager to avoid the possibility of losses in her department by wholesaling trade-in cars that could be resold at a profit for the dealership. This might also hurt the dealership by making its "deals" less attractive for new car customers.

Knowing how important it was to maintain credibility with each department, Liddy tried to anticipate the reaction of each manager in the

EXHIBIT 4 Notes to Financial Statements (in 000s)

1. New car sales and gross margins break down as:

	Sales	*Gross Profit*	*No. of Units*
Ford	$3,114	$193	243
Saab	1,502	90	73
VW	1,794	117	158
Financing fees*	148	102	n/a
Total	$6,558	$502	474

2. Used car sales and margins break down as:

	Sales	*Gross Profit*	*No. of Units*
Retail	$1,045	$212	177
Wholesale	423	(59)	213
Financing fees*	89	36	n/a
Total	$1,557	$189	390

3. Notes payable for vehicles is a revolving line of credit secured by new car inventory. Payments to the bank are due upon sale of each vehicle financed in inventory. This liability has been reduced over the past 10 months by approximately $1.5 million.

4. Indirect labor consists of department managers, clerks, bookkeepers, and other employees performing tasks directly related to the activities in a specific department. It does not include sales commissions or billable employees in the back-end.

5. Departmental advertising is assigned to departments based on actual ads placed.

6. Policy work consists of dealer concessions made to customers arising from disputes over dealer-installed options on new vehicles, warranty coverage, or cost of repairs. These costs are allocated to the departments in which they occur.

7. Depreciation is allocated by historical cost of leasehold improvements or equipment in each department.

8. Rent is allocated by square footage used by each department, adjusted for the value of the space.

9. Interest expense is treated as a common expense for the purpose of keeping investing and financing costs separate.

10. Insurance consists of both umbrella liability and property damage for the dealership as a whole. Because of the multiple types of coverages included and the bundled pricing, it is not feasible to break out coverage costs by department.

11. Extraordinary income represent the forgiving of $179,000 of debt due to a previous owner. The obligation was eliminated as a condition in the buy-sell agreement that stipulated the terms of the change in stock ownership from all previous owner to George Liddy.

12. Approximately 75 percent of the fixed costs in the used car department related closely to retail vehicle sales and approximately 25 percent to wholesale sales.

13. Using Exhibit 3, North Country determined the following allocations:
New: $835/vehicle = 396,000/474 vehicles
Used: $665/vehicle = $157,000 × 0.75/177 vehicles
Parts: $32 = $183,000/40,139 parts = 4.55/part × 7 parts (2 brake kits, 1 lock assembly, 4 tune-up parts)
Service: $114 = $371,000/9,795 orders × 3 orders (lock, brakes, tune-up)

* Finance fees consists of income that the dealer earns on dealer-sourced auto loans. It also includes the dealer's commission on service contracts and extended warranties sold through the dealership.

context of this series of transactions. The new car sales manager would understand that the allowance above book value on the trade-in could not be accounted for as profit. There would be a conflict, however, over where to allocate losses on erroneous wholesale valuations. If the trade-in were liquidated at the auction for only $3,000, the new car sales manager would be adamant about requiring the used manager to absorb the $500 loss, using the argument that the used department should be accountable for its valuation errors. The used car sales manager would reject the notion of her department subsidizing the profitability of new car sales. Mr. Liddy was still looking for a way to equitably distribute this type of loss.

The retail transfer price for parts and labor used in the repairs would draw additional resistance from the used car sales manager. With excess capacity in service, she would grow increasingly discontent over the idea of the service department shifting part of its underutilized labor costs to new and used gross margins. She also would become more conservative in evaluating the retail/wholesale decision on trade-ins. In an interview with the casewriter, she indicated that, when she was unsure of the actual retail value, she would be more likely to wholesale rather than take a risk of a zero or negative margin at retail. Higher reconditioning and lower gross margins meant less tolerance for error in estimating resale value.

The new car sales manager expressed a similar attitude towards being charged full retail price by parts and service on dealer-installed options on new cars. The incentive to either add options to new cars in the showroom or sell them as extras during delivery was virtually eliminated by the prospect of zero or negative incremental margins for the new car department.

George Liddy also questioned the behavioral impact of capitalizing the repairs into inventory instead of recognizing them as periodic expenses. It was possible that, when a used car was slow to sell, the sales manager might be more reluctant to accept her mistake and wholesale the car because of the higher loss that would result. Liddy knew that used car retail and wholesale values tended to drop with each new monthly publication of the guidebook. He also realized that used car inventory tied up cash and that a key measure of departmental success was maintaining an adequate level of inventory turnover. (Average inventory turnover in the industry was about 75 days for new cars and 45 days for used).

The service and parts managers (now profit centers) had welcomed the change from wholesale transfer rates to full retail. There was, however, some contention over how the markup on parts should be distributed between the two departments. The dealership's current policy is to allocate all parts income to the parts department—regardless of its actual *source*. The possibility of growing tension between parts and service concerned the owners. The service department relies heavily on the parts department to provide quick delivery of parts used on repair orders. Intentional delays in delivery would consume billable labor-hours and drive up service department overhead.

QUESTIONS

1. Using the data in the transaction and Exhibit 3, compute the profitability of this one transaction to the new, used, parts, and service departments. Assume a sales commission of $250 for the trade-in on a selling price of $5,000.

2. Evaluate North Country's accounting system. Specifically, how should the transfer pricing system operate for each department (market price, full retail, full cost, variable cost)?
3. If it were found one week later that the trade-in could be wholesaled for only $3,000, which manager should take the loss?
4. North Country incurred a year-to-date loss of about $59,000 *before* allocation of fixed costs on the wholesaling of used cars, which is theoretically supposed to be a break-even operation. Where do you think the problem lies?
5. What advice do you have for the owners?

Case 4–2
Polysar Limited*

As soon as Pierre Choquette received the September report of operations for NASA Rubber (Exhibits 1 and 2), he called Alf Devereux, controller, and Ron Britton, sales manager, into his office to discuss the year-to-date results. Next week, he would make his presentation to the board of directors and the results for his division for the first nine months of the year were not as good as expected. Pierre knew that the NASA management team had performed well. Sales volume was up and feedstock costs were down, resulting in a gross margin that was better than budget. Why did the bottom line look so bad?

As the three men worked through the numbers, their discussion kept coming back to the fixed costs of the butyl rubber plant. Fixed costs were high. The plant had yet to reach capacity. The European division had taken less output than projected.

Still, Choquette felt that these factors were outside his control. His division had performed well—it just didn't show in the profit results.

Choquette knew that Henderson, his counterpart in Europe, did not face these problems. The European rubber profits would be compared to those of NASA. How would the board react to the numbers he had to work with? He would need to educate them in his presentation, especially concerning the volume variance. He knew that many of the board members would not understand what that number represented or that it was due in part to the actions of Henderson's group.

Pierre Choquette, Alf Devereux, and Ron Britton decided to meet the next day to work on a strategy for the board presentation.

Polysar Limited

In 1986, Polysar Limited was Canada's largest chemical company, with $1.8 billion in annual sales. Based in Sarnia, Ontario, Polysar was the world's largest producer of synthetic rubber and latex and a major producer of basic petrochemicals and fuel products.

Polysar was established in 1942 to meet wartime needs for a synthetic substitute for natural rubber. The supply of natural rubber to the Allied forces had been interrupted by the declaration of war against the United States by Japan in December 1941. During 1942 and 1943, 10 synthetic rubber plants were built by the governments of the United States and Canada, including the Polysar plant in Sarnia.

After the war, the supply of natural rubber was again secure and the nine U.S. plants were sold to private industry or closed. Polysar remained in operation as a Crown Corporation, wholly owned by the government of Canada. In 1972, by an act of Parliament, the Canada Development Corporation (CDC) was created as a government-owned venture capital company to encourage Canadian business development; at that time, the equity shares of Polysar were transferred to the Canada Development Corporation. In 1986, Polysar remained wholly owned by the CDC; however, in a

* This case was prepared by Robert L. Simons, Harvard Business School.
Copyright © by the President and Fellows of Harvard College.
Harvard Business School case 187–098.

EXHIBIT 1   Regular Butyl Rubber Statistics and Analyses

	9 Months Ended September 30, 1986		
Volume Tonnes	*Actual* (000s)	*Budget* (000s)	*Deviation* (000s)
Sales	35.8	33.0	2.8
Production	47.5	55.0	− 7.5
Transfers:			
To EROW	12.2	19.5	− 7.3
From EROW	2.1	1.0	1.1
Production costs	($000s)	($000s)	($000s)
Fixed cost—Direct	−21,466	−21,900	434
Allocated cash	− 7,036	− 7,125	89
Allocated noncash	−15,625	−15,600	− 25
Fixed cost to production	−44,127	−44,625	498
Transfers to/from FG inventory	1,120	2,450	−1,330
Transfers to Erow	8,540	13,650	−5,110
Transfers from EROW	−1,302	− 620	− 682
Fixed cost of sales	−35,769	−29,145	−6,624

Note: As indicated previously, financial data have been disguised and do not represent the true financial results of the company.

government sponsored move to privatization, the majority of the shares of the CDC were sold to the Canadian public in the period 1982 to 1985.

Through acquisition and internal growth, Polysar had grown considerably from its original single plant. Polysar now employed 6,650 people, including 3,100 in Canada, 1,050 in the United States, and 2,500 in Europe and elsewhere. The company operated 20 manufacturing plants in Canada, United States, Belgium, France, The Netherlands, and West Germany.

Structure

The operations of the company were structured into three groups: basic petrochemicals, rubber, and diversified products (Exhibit 3).

Basic Petrochemicals

Firman Bentley, 51, was group vice president of Basic Petrochemicals. This business unit pro-
duced primary petrochemicals, such as ethylene, as well as intermediate products, such as propylene, butadiene, and styrene monomers. Group sales in 1985 were approximately $800 million, of which $500 million was sold to outside customers and the remainder was sold as intermediate feedstock to Polysar's downstream operations.

Rubber

The Rubber Group was headed by Charles Ambridge, 61, group vice president. Polysar held 9 percent of the world synthetic rubber market (excluding Communist bloc countries). As the largest group in the company, Rubber Group produced 46 percent of Polysar sales. Major competitors included Goodyear, Bayer, Exxon, and Du Pont.

Rubber products, such as butyl and halobutyl, were sold primarily to manufacturers of automobile tires (six of the world's largest tire

EXHIBIT 2   Regular Butyl Rubber Statement of Net Contribution

	9 Months Ended September 30, 1986		
	Actual ($000s)	Budget ($000s)	Deviation ($000s)
Sales revenue—Third party	$ 65,872	$ 61,050	$ 4,822
Diversified products group	160	210	− 50
Total	66,032	61,260	4,772
Delivery cost	− 2,793	− 2,600	− 193
Net sales revenue	63,239	58,660	4,579
Variable costs:			
Standard	−22,589	−21,450	−1,139
Cost adjustments	54	—	54
Efficiency variance	241	—	241
Total	−22,294	−21,450	− 844
Gross margin—$	40,945	37,210	3,735
Fixed costs:			
Standard	−25,060	−23,100	−1,960
Cost adjustments	168	80	88
Spending variance	498	—	498
Volume variance	−11,375	− 6,125	−5,250
Total	−35,769	−29,145	−6,624
Gross profit—$	5,176	8,065	−2,889
% of NSR	8.2%	13.7%	− 5.5%
Period costs:			
Administration, selling, distribution	− 4,163	− 4,000	− 163
Technical service	− 222	− 210	− 12
Other income expense	208	50	158
Total	− 4,177	− 4,160	− 17
Business contribution	999	3,905	−2,906
Interest on working capital	− 1,875	− 1,900	25
Net contribution	− 876	2,005	−2,881

Note: As indicated previously, financial data have been disguised and do not represent the true financial results of the company.

companies[1] accounted for 70 percent of the world butyl and halobutyl demand); other uses included

belting, footwear, adhesives, hose, seals, plastics modification, and chewing gum.

The rubber group was split into two operating divisions that were managed as profit centers: NASA (North and South America) and EROW (Europe and rest of world). In addition to the two

[1] Michelin, Goodyear, Bridgestone, Firestone, Pirelli, and Dunlop.

EXHIBIT 3 Partial Organization Chart

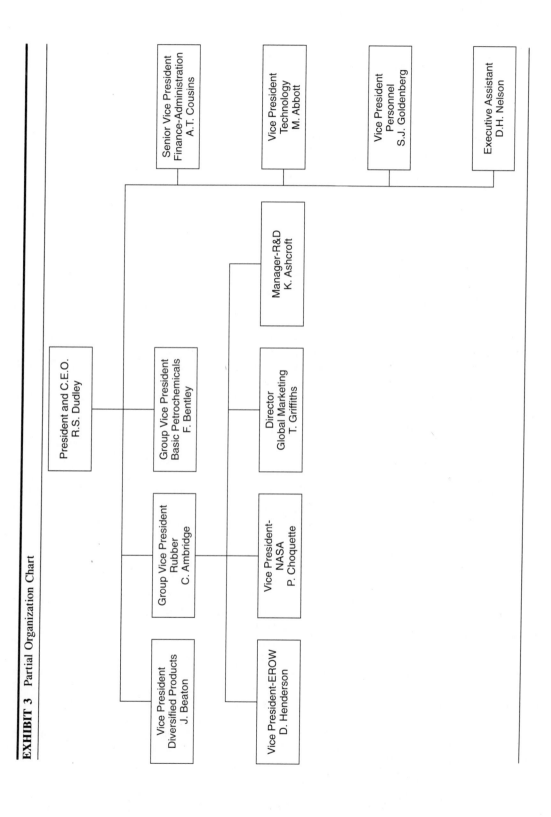

EXHIBIT 4   Rubber Production Process

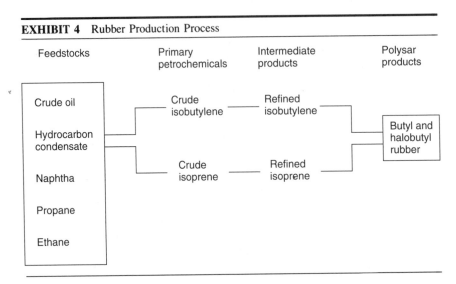

operating profit centers, the rubber group included a global marketing department and a research division. The costs of these departments were not charged to the two operating profit centers but, instead, were charged against group profits.

Diversified Products

John Beaton, 48, was vice president of diversified products, a group that consisted of the latex, plastics, and specialty products divisions. This group was composed of high-technology product categories that were expected to double sales within five years. In 1985, the group provided 27 percent of Polysar's sales revenue.

Bentley, Ambridge, and Beaton reported to Robert Dudley, 60, president and chief executive officer.

Rubber Group

A key component of Polysar's strategy was to be a leader in high-margin specialty rubbers. The leading products in this category were the butyl and halobutyl rubbers. Attributes of butyl rubber include low permeability to gas and moisture, resistance to steam and weathering, high energy absorption, and chemical resistance. Butyl rubber

was traditionally used in inner tubes and general-purpose applications. Halobutyl rubber, a modified derivative, possesses the same attributes as regular butyl, with additional properties that allow bonding to other materials. Thus, halobutyls were used extensively as liners and sidewalls in tubeless tires.

Butyl and halobutyl rubber were manufactured from feedstocks, such as crude oil, naphtha, butane, propane, and ethane (Exhibit 4). Polysar manufactured butyl rubbers at two locations: NASA division's Sarnia plant and EROW division's Antwerp plant.

NASA Butyl Plant

The original Sarnia plant, built in 1942, manufactured regular butyl until 1972. At that time, market studies predicted rapid growth in the demand for high-quality radial tires manufactured with halobutyl. Demand for regular butyl was predicted to remain steady, since poor road conditions in many countries of the world necessitated the use of tires with inner tubes. In 1972, the Sarnia plant was converted to allow production of halobutyls as well as regular butyl.

By the 1980s, demand for halobutyl had increased to the point that Polysar forecast capacity constraints. During 1983 and 1984, the company built a second plant at Sarnia, known as Sarnia 2, to produce regular butyl. The original plant, Sarnia 1, was then dedicated solely to the production of halobutyl.

Sarnia 2, with a capital cost of $550 million, began full operations late in 1984. Its annual nameplate (i.e., design) production capacity for regular butyl was 95,000 tonnes. During 1985, the plant produced 65,000 tonnes.

EROW Butyl Plant

The EROW division's butyl plant was located in Antwerp, Belgium. Built in 1964 as a regular butyl unit, the plant was modified in 1979–80 to allow it to produce halobutyl as well as regular butyl.

The annual nameplate production capacity of the Antwerp plant was 90,000 tonnes. In 1985, as in previous years, the plant operated near or at its nameplate capacity. The Antwerp plant was operated to meet fully the halobutyl demand of EROW customers; the remainder of capacity was used to produce regular butyl.

In 1981, the plant's output was 75 percent regular butyl and 25 percent halobutyl; by 1985, halobutyl represented 50 percent of the plant's production. Since regular butyl demand outpaced the plant's remaining capacity, EROW took its regular butyl shortfall from the Sarnia 2 plant; in 1985, 21,000 tonnes of regular butyl were shipped from NASA to EROW.

Product Scheduling

Although NASA served customers in North and South America and EROW serviced customers in Europe and the rest of the world, regular butyl could be shipped from either the Sarnia 2 or Antwerp plant. NASA shipped approximately one third of its regular butyl output to EROW. Also, customers located in distant locations could receive shipments from either plant due to certain cost or logistical advantages. For example,

Antwerp sometimes shipped to Brazil and Sarnia sometimes shipped to the Far East.

A global marketing department worked with regional directors of marketing and regional product managers to coordinate product flows. Three sets of factors influenced these analyses. First, certain customers demanded products from a specific plant, due to slight product differences resulting from the type of feedstock used and the plant configuration. Second, costs varied between Sarnia and Antwerp, due to differences in variable costs (primarily feedstock and energy), shipping, and currency rates. Finally, inventory levels, production interruptions, and planned shutdowns were considered.

In September and October of each year, NASA and EROW divisions prepared production estimates for the upcoming year. These estimates were based on estimated sales volumes and plant loadings (i.e., capacity utilization). Since the Antwerp plant operated at capacity, the planning exercise was largely for the benefit of the managers of the Sarnia 2 plant, who needed to know how much regular butyl Antwerp would need from the Sarnia 2 plant.

Product Costing and Transfer Prices

Butyl rubbers were costed using standard rates for variable and fixed costs.

Variable costs included feedstocks, chemicals, and energy. Standard variable cost per tonnes of butyl was calculated by multiplying a standard utilization factor (i.e., the standard quantity of inputs used) by a standard price established for each unit of input. Since feedstock prices varied with worldwide market conditions, and represented the largest component of costs, it was impossible to establish standard input prices that remained valid for extended periods. Therefore, the company reset feedstock standard costs each month to a price that reflected market prices. Chemical and energy standard costs were established annually. A purchase price variance (were input prices above or below standard prices?) and

EXHIBIT 5 Controller's Guide

Polysar	NUMBER: 03:02	
	PAGE 1 of 14 PAGES.	
Subject Accounting for Inventories	NEW: X	REPLACES
	ISSUE DATE: Jan. 1/81	
ISSUED BY: Director Accounting	Authorized By: Corporate Controller	

Purpose

To set out criteria and guidelines for the application of the company's accounting policy for inventories:

> "Inventories are valued at the lower of FIFO (first-in, first-out) cost and net realizable value except for raw materials and supplies which are valued at the lower of FIFO cost and replacement cost."

Specific exclusion

This release does not apply to SWAP transactions.

Definitions

By-products—one or more products of relatively small per unit market value that emerge from the production process of a product or products of greater value.

Cost system—a system to facilitate the classification, recording, analysis and interpretation of data pertaining to the production and distribution of products and services.

Demonstrated capacity is the actual annualized production of a plant which was required to run full out within the last fiscal year for a sufficiently long period to assess production capability after adjusting for abnormally low or high unscheduled shutdowns, scheduled shutdowns, and unusual or annualized items which impacted either favorably or unfavorably on the period's production. The resulting adjusted historical base should be further modified for changes planned to be implemented within the current fiscal year.

  a. Where a plant has been required to run full out within the last fiscal year, production data may be used for a past period after adjusting for changes (debottleneckings/inefficiencies) since that time affecting production.

  b. Where a plant has never been required to run full out, demonstrated capacity could be reasonably considered as "name plate" capacity after adjusting for

  (1.) Known invalid assumptions in arriving at "name plate."
  (2.) Changes to original design affecting "name plate."
  (3.) A reasonable negative allowance for error.

an efficiency variance (did production require more or less inputs than standard?) were calculated for variable costs each accounting period.

Fixed costs comprised three categories of cost. Direct costs included direct labor, maintenance, chemicals required to keep the plant bubbling, and fixed utilities. Allocated cash costs included plant management, purchasing department costs, engineering, planning, and accounting. Allocated noncash costs represented primarily depreciation.

Fixed costs were allocated to production based on a plant's "demonstrated capacity" using the following formula:

$$\frac{\text{Standard fixed}}{\text{cost per tonne}} = \frac{\text{Estimated annual total fixed costs}}{\text{Annual demonstrated plant capacity}}$$

To apply the formula, production estimates were established each fall for the upcoming year. Then, the amount of total fixed costs applicable to this level of production was estimated. The amount of total fixed cost to be allocated to each tonne of output was calculated by dividing total fixed cost by the plant's demonstrated capacity. Exhibit 5 reproduces a section of the controller's guide that defines demonstrated capacity.

Each accounting period, two variances were calculated for fixed costs. The first was a spending variance calculated as the simple difference between actual total fixed costs and estimated total fixed costs. The second variance was a volume variance calculated using the formula:

$$\text{Volume variance} = \frac{\text{Standard fixed}}{\text{cost per tonne}} \times \text{Actual tonnes} - \text{Demonstrated capacity}$$

Product transfers between divisions for performance accounting purposes were made at standard full cost, representing, for each tonne, the sum of standard variable cost and standard fixed cost.

Compensation

Employees at Polysar had in the past been paid by fixed salary, with little use of bonuses except at the executive level of the company. In 1984, a bonus system was instituted throughout the company to link pay with performance and strengthen the profit center orientation.

Nonmanagement Employees

The bonus system varied by employee group but was developed with the intention of paying salaries that were approximately 5 percent less than those paid by a reference group of 25 major Canadian manufacturing companies. To augment salaries, annual bonuses were awarded, in amounts up to 12 percent of salary, based on corporate and divisional performance. Hourly workers could receive annual bonuses in similar proportions based on performance.

All bonuses were based on achieving or exceeding budgeted profit targets. For salaried workers, for example, meeting the 1985 corporate profit objective would result in a 5 percent bonus; an additional $25 million in profits would provide an additional 4 percent bonus. Meeting and exceeding division profit targets could provide an additional 3 percent bonus.

Using periodic accounting information, divisional vice presidents met in quarterly communication meetings with salaried and wage employees to discuss divisional and corporate performance levels.

Management

For managers, the percent of remuneration received through annual bonuses was greater than 12 percent and increased with responsibility levels.

The bonuses of top division management in 1985 were calculated by a formula that awarded 50 percent of bonus potential to meeting or exceeding divisional profit targets and 50 percent to meeting or exceeding corporate profit targets.

Interviews with Rubber Group Vice Presidents[2]

Pierre Choquette

Pierre Choquette, 43, was vice president[3] of the NASA Rubber Division. A professional engineer, Choquette had begun his career with Polysar in plant management. Over the years, he had assumed responsibilities for product management in the United States, managed a small subsidiary, managed a European plant, and directed European sales.

This business is managed on price and margin. Quality, service, and technology are also important, but it is difficult to differentiate ourselves from other competitors on these dimensions.

When the price of oil took off, this affected our feedstock prices drastically, and Polysar's worldwide business suffered. Now that prices are back down, we are trying to regroup our efforts and bring the business back to long term health. Polysar will break even in 1985 and show a normal profit again in 1986. Of course, the Rubber Division will, as in the past, be the major producer of profit for the company.

As you know, this is a continuous process industry. The plant is computerized so that we need the same number of people and incur most of the same overhead costs whether the plant is running fast or slow.

The regular butyl plant, Sarnia 2, is running at less than capacity. Although the plant should be able to produce 95,000 tonnes, its demonstrated capacity is 85,000. Last year, we produced 65,000.

This leaves us sitting with a lot of unabsorbed fixed costs, especially when you consider depreciation charges.

Still, NASA Rubber has been growing nicely. I think this is in part due to our strong commitment to run the Divisions as profit centers. We have been pushing hard to build both volume and efficiency and I am pleased that our programs and incentives are paying off.

Our transfers to EROW are still a problem. Since the transfers are at standard cost and are not recorded as revenue, these transfers do nothing for our profit. Also, if they cut back on orders, our profit is hurt through the volume variance. Few of our senior managers truly understand the volume variance and why profit results are so different in the two regions. The accounting is not a problem, but having to continuously explain it to very senior-level managers is. It always comes down to the huge asset that we carry whether the plant is at capacity or not.

We run our businesses on return on net assets, which looks ridiculous for NASA. I worry that, if I am not around to explain it, people will form the wrong conclusion about the health of the business. Also, you sometimes wonder if people ascribe results to factors that are outside your control.

Doug Henderson

Doug Henderson, 46, vice president of EROW Rubber Division, was also a professional engineer. His career included management responsibilities in plant operations, market research, venture analysis and corporate planning, running a small regional business in Canada, and director of European sales.

The Antwerp plant produces about 45,000 tonnes of halobutyl and 45,000 tonnes of regular butyl each year. In addition, we import approximately 15,000 to 20,000 tonnes of regular butyl from Sarnia each year (Exhibit 6).

We inform Sarnia each fall of our estimated regular butyl needs. These estimates are based on our predictions of butyl and halobutyl sales and how hard we can load our plant. The overall sales estimates are usually within 10 percent, say plus or minus 8,000 tonnes, unless an unexpected crisis occurs.

---

[2] Pierre Choquette was interviewed at Harvard Business School in 1985; Doug Henderson was interviewed at Harvard in 1986. Both men were attending the 13-week Advanced Management Program that was developed to strengthen the management skills of individuals with potential to become chief executive officers of their companies. In addition to Choquette and Henderson, Polysar had sent Firman Bentley to the program in 1984.

[3] Due to its relatively large size, Rubber Group was the only group with regional vice presidents. Regional responsibilities of the Basic Petrochemicals Group and the Diversified Products Group were managed by lower-ranking general managers.

EXHIBIT 6 Schedule of Regular Butyl Shipments from NASA to EROW

	Actual Tonnes	Budget Tonnes
1985	21,710	23,500
1984	12,831	13,700
1983	1,432	4,000
1982	792	600
1981	1,069	700

The EROW business has been extremely successful since I arrived here in 1982. We have increased our share in the high growth halobutyl market; the plant is running well; and we have kept the operation simple and compact.

Looking at our Statement of Net Contribution (Exhibit 7), our margins are better than NASA's. For one thing, there is a great surplus of feedstock in Europe and we benefit from lower prices. Also, market dynamics are substantially different.

We pay a lot of attention to plant capacity. For example, we budgeted to produce 250 tonnes per day this year and we have got it up to 275. We are also working hard to reduce our "off-spec" material as a way of pushing up our yield. If we can produce more, it's free—other than variable cost, it goes right to the bottom line.

Given these factors, Pierre loves it when I tell him jokingly that our success at EROW is attributable to superb management.

QUESTIONS

1. Prepare a presentation for the Polysar board of directors to review the performance of the NASA Rubber Division. Pay particular attention to questions that may be raised concerning the accuracy and meaning of the volume variance.
2. What is the best sales and production strategy for EROW Division? NASA Division? Rubber Group in total?
3. What changes, if any, would you recommend be made in the management accounting performance system to improve the reporting and evaluation of Rubber Group performance?

EXHIBIT 7 Regular Butyl Rubber Condensed Statement of New Contribution

	9 Months Ended September 30, 1986
Sales volume—tonnes	47,850
	($000s)
Sales revenue	94,504
Delivery cost	4,584
Net sales revenue	89,920
Variable cost:	
Standard	−28,662
Purchase price variance	203
Inventory revaluation	− 46
Efficiency variance	32
Total	−28,473
Gross margin—$	61,447
Fixed cost to production:	
Depreciation	− 4,900
Other	−16,390
	−21,290
Transfers to/from F. G. inventory	− 775
Transfers to/from NASA	− 7,238
	−29,303
Gross profit—$	32,144
Period costs	− 7,560
Business contribution	24,584
Interest on W/C	− 1,923
Net contribution	22,661

Notes: 1. Fixed costs are allocated between regular butyl production (above) and halobutyl production (reported separately).
2. Financial data have been disguised and do not represent the true financial results of the company.

Case 4-3
Thunderbolt Manufacturing Company*

Early in 1976, Mr. Ray Alexander, recently elected president of the Thunderbolt Manufacturing Company, was reflecting on the progress the company had made since 1968. That was the year in which his predecessor, Mr. Earl Goodwin, became president. Annual sales had increased from about $90 million to nearly $240 million during this period and profits had risen from $3 million to about $12 million.

In Mr. Alexander's view, however, current operation practices were not satisfactory in several areas. For example, there were many disagreements between the plant managers and those in charge of marketing. There also were disagreements between plant managers and corporate management. The disputes centered upon transfer prices, out-of-stock position, and production mix. Many of the problems seemed to arise from the fact that performance was measured by profit and loss statements for three plants in the manufacturing group (excluding the OEM plant at Ironville) and for the marketing group.

Profit centers had been introduced in 1968. Thunderbolt had only two plants at that time, and each had its own product lines. Even though they both sold through a common sales force, it was relatively easy to think of each plant manager as the president of his own small company.

But circumstances had changed. Now there were four plants, and product lines were no longer associated with particular plants. Also the company now had six profit centers, instead of just two.

It seemed to Mr. Alexander that, under the present organization, the managers of the various profit centers had relatively little control over the factors that influenced the profitability of their operations. He wondered whether conditions had changed enough since 1968 to call for reconsideration of the use of profit centers. Consequently, he called in an acquaintance, Mr. James Smith. Mr. Smith was a management consultant, recognized as an authority on organization and management control.

Mr. Smith began his assignment by familiarizing himself with the company in general terms—its environment, its history, and its present organization. His notes from this familiarization phase are given in the appendix.

As his second major step, Mr. Smith interviewed several members of Thunderbolt management to obtain their views on the company's use of profit centers. He started his interviewing with Mr. Charles Campbell, vice president and treasurer (see organization chart, Exhibit 1).

Campbell: We've discovered that there are a number of problems with making profit centers work well, now that our company is quite a bit different from the way it used to be. In fact, it makes you wonder sometimes if the whole thing is still worthwhile, and if it might not be better to drop the profit center idea completely.

Smith: Mr. Campbell, can you tell me about some of the problems you have encountered?

Campbell: Yes. One of them is caused by the fact that measurement of performance tends to be

---

* This case was prepared by R. H. Caplan.
Copyright © by the President and Fellows of Harvard University.
Harvard Business School case 113–036.

EXHIBIT 1 Organization Chart

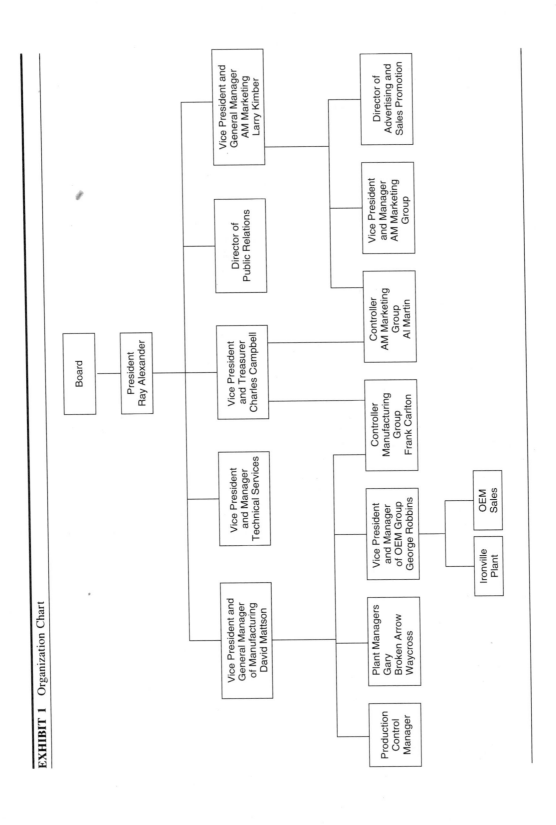

unfair. A plant manager really has little control over some of the major factors that influence his profitability. Product mix, production volume, transfer price, all things he does not control, can make a plant manager show a low profit. Thus, a poor plant P&L may not necessarily mean poor performance. Of course, we try to recognize all this, because we compare actual profits to budget. But somehow, performance measurement always seems to get back to the profit figure alone. Even though a plant manager may be doing a tremendous job, he'll get discouraged if his profit is low for period after period. He figures that no matter how hard he tries he just can't improve profits. Worse yet is the opposite case, where a manager is not doing a good job but has a high profit figure. Whenever we try to question this guy on some of his variances from budgeted figures, the first thing he'll say is: "Yeah, but look at the profits I brought in." And it becomes somewhat difficult to motivate him to improve his performance because he is unwilling to give up this crutch.

Another problem we've found is that some managers tend to spend too much time worrying about the wrong things. For example, they'll often argue about the product mix assigned to them by the production scheduling group, or they'll grumble about transfer prices not being fair, or they'll complain that their assigned production volume is too low.

Of course, it is good to have some tension in an organization; it motivates people to produce. But it has to be aimed in the proper direction—that is, it should make managers worry about matters that they have some control over, not about things they can't change. Also, while it is good to have some tension, there should not be too much tension. If there is, then people become frustrated and their output suffers. Now, in our case, we sometimes get the feeling that we have too much tension, and tension aimed in the wrong direction. And that both are the result of profit centers.

There is another disadvantage to profit centers. As you know, we have a considerable number of product transfers between profit centers. But in order to figure out how the company as a whole is doing, we have to eliminate profits on these transfers from corporate financial statements. And this makes an awful lot of extra work for the accounting department. So, if we did away with profit centers, we probably would save a nice bundle of cash.

Smith: Mr. Campbell, so far you've told me about the disadvantages of profit centers. Can you tell me about some advantages that apply to them?

Campbell: You're right, I have. I didn't mean to paint such a bleak picture. If there were only disadvantages, we would have done away with profit centers some time ago.

Earlier I mentioned two advantages that existed in 1968, when profit centers were installed. [See the appendix for a more complete discussion of these points.] One was that managers received valuable training for top management jobs; the other was that they tended to become more profit conscious. These advantages still hold today.

There is another advantage, related to this greater profit consciousness. As we see it, the alternative to using profit centers is expense centers controlled by budgets. But holding a manager responsible only for variances from expense budgets is nit-picking; such an approach doesn't look at the major economic factors that make or break a business. Thus, despite all the problems I mentioned earlier, I feel that control by means of expense centers would not be as effective as with profit centers.

And then, I think we also should consider how the managers feel about profit centers before making a decision to drop them. Now that our managers are used to being measured on the basis of their profit contribution, they might not want to change to something else, despite the fact that this measurement by profits may not be fair to them. I think that they get quite a bit of satisfaction out of being held responsible for running their own show.

Mr. Smith next interviewed Mr. Frank Carlton, manufacturing group controller. As his title indicates, Mr. Carlton was mainly responsible for control functions within the manufacturing group. He reported directly to Mr. David Mattson, vice president and general manager of manufacturing. Because of his position, Carlton was described by other members of Thunderbolt management as being "able to present the plant managers' side of the situation." Since some of his comments were similar to those made by Mr. Campbell, only selected remarks representing additional points are reported here.

Carlton: . . . And since there is no real market price for transfers between the plants and marketing, transfer prices are fictitious. Therefore, management is just playing games, and the managers know this. . . .

If you are going to judge a man on the profits of his group, he's going to try to maximize these profits, even if this may not be in the best interest of the whole company. Let me give you a few examples of this here at Thunderbolt. Sometimes a plant manager will make production runs that are longer than scheduled, because this reduces his set-up costs. Now, you can't really blame him for doing this, because it increases his profits. But it also increases the finished goods inventory. And by deviating from his production schedule in order to have longer production runs, he may even increase the out-of-stock position of other items, a situation clearly not in the best interest of the company.

Another example: when it comes to new products, the marketing people like to include just about everything. As long as they can get even a small contribution from an item, they're willing to add it to their line, regardless of the volume they can get, because it will increase their profit figure. On the other hand, the people in manufacturing lean in the opposite direction. Since there are start-up and capital costs associated with a new product, they need a certain volume before they reach the break-even point. The net result is that marketing tends to overestimate demand for new products, just to increase the chance that these will be added to the line. On the other hand, manufacturing tends to overestimate their costs, just to make sure that marginal products are not authorized by headquarters for production.

Actually, there's another reason why the people in manufacturing tend to overestimate their costs. Cost estimates are used in setting the initial transfer prices, and, of course, the higher the

transfer prices, the better their chance of showing a profit of any items added. . . . It is obvious, of course, that this, too, can lead to decisions that are contrary to the best interests of the company.

Another problem we have encountered with profit centers is that feelings between manufacturing and marketing run pretty high sometimes. Arguments may result over transfer prices, out-of-stock position, or whatever. And the result is that these two groups then become antagonistic, don't communicate well, and withhold information from each other. . . .

Despite all I've said against profit centers, I'm still not sure that we should do away with them. We haven't really got anything that is *better* for management control purposes than our present profit center P&L reports.

And then, there's the fact that our managers don't want to do away with the profit center approach, despite all their complaints. And they feel quite strongly about this. In fact, one of our managers told me that he would quit if we eliminated profit centers at the plant level. And he may very well mean it. You know, there's quite a bit of prestige in being responsible for the whole operation. . . . If we replace profit centers with expense centers, we're reducing our plant managers to mere supervisors, mere foremen.

Mr. Smith also asked Mr. Al Martin, marketing group controller, for his views on profit centers. Mr. Martin was responsible for control functions within the AM marketing group. He reported to Mr. Larry Kimber, vice president and general manager of AM marketing. (See the appendix for explanation of the term AM.)

Martin: When you measure a manager's performance by profits, he's going to try to maximize this measure. And that may not always be the best thing for the company. Let me give you an example. You're aware that marketing is permitted to obtain products either from our plants or from the outside. But when they do buy outside, it usually turns out that they are not making a good decision from the company's standpoint. Of course, they're only looking at their own profits, so they don't recognize this. Now, even though my associates and I report to Mr. Kimber, we are also members of the treasurer's staff. Consequently, we have some information on our manufacturing costs, too, and we can usually figure out which way such a decision should go. And we've had to intervene time after time in situations like this, trying to convince marketing to buy from our plants.

Now you may say that we could easily eliminate this problem by setting transfer prices in such a way that we would have "goal congruence," or whatever you call this animal. But before you do, let me tell you that it is impossible to set goal congruent prices on over 3,000 different items when manufacturing costs, and even selling prices, are constantly changing. About the only way we can eliminate this problem is by eliminating profit centers.

. . . And there's another reason why I don't think that profit centers are a good idea here at Thunderbolt. Marketing people are sales-oriented, and they perform best if they are measured in terms of sales. If you hold them responsible for profits, and costs, and inventories, and warehousing and this and that, you're just confusing them and taking their attention away from the only thing that really means something to them, namely sales.

Mr. Smith concluded his interviewing with Mr. Ray Alexander, president of Thunderbolt.

Smith: Mr. Alexander, would you tell me how you judge the performance of a plant manager?

Alexander: Yes. Since we use flexible budgeting, I know what each manager's costs should have been for the period in question, given a particular volume of activity. Then, all I need to do is look at his variances by individual expense classifications to tell how well he has done his job.

Smith: I gather, then, you don't just look at his profit figure on the P&L report and see how that compares with the budgeted profit?

Alexander: No, I don't. I feel it is more meaningful to look at the variances. Besides, if a manager's costs are in line with his particular volume, then his budgeted profit will result automatically.

Smith: Mr. Alexander, if you did in fact discontinue the profit center approach, what would you

substitute in order to meet the company's needs for management control?

Alexander: I think we would use expense centers. Each plant, for example, would become an expense center, and that would be about the only change here. We would still use a flexible budget, and we would measure performance by variances from the budget. As before, we would expect each plant manager to keep his out-of-stock position down. Also, we'd still judge him on intangibles, such as his labor relations and his community relations.

For the marketing group, we would use sales quotas instead of profit budgets. Sales is a more direct and more meaningful measure for marketing-oriented people. To control their selling expenses, we would use a flexible expense budget and measure their variances from that. Also, we would hold them responsible for keeping finished goods inventories at budgeted levels, similar to the way we do it now. . . .

You see, what we would like to do is to hold each manager responsible only for items he can control. Of course, we probably will never be able to achieve this goal completely; however, I think that this system would be better in this respect than what we have now. . . .

Of course, we'd probably have to pay a price for changing to expense centers. For example, we might lose some profit consciousness at the plant manager level. . . .

However, I feel that there are two offsetting factors here. First, our plant managers would receive corporate financial statements on a monthly basis. Right now, they see these only once a year. For that reason, these corporate statements aren't too meaningful to them; that is, they can't trace the effect of their decisions on the corporate picture. But now, if they become familiar with and use the corporate statements, they will be able to see better the implications of their decisions on the company. And I feel that this will motivate them to act in the best interest of the company.

Second, we are now in the process of installing an advanced computer system, and we expect this to give us at headquarters more and better information for decision making. Without such information available at headquarters, it is probably best to place a good bit of decision making authority in the hands of those managers who are close to the day-to-day operations. However, with the right information available at headquarters, I don't see any good reasons why decisions can't be made there. And if they're made there, they are more likely to be in the best interest of the company, and so we get around the problem of profit consciousness at lower management levels.

QUESTIONS

1. Thunderbolt currently has six pools of functional resources: four plants and two sales forces. Accepting that (and ignoring the personalities and competencies of existing incumbents, for which we have no data) design an alternative responsibility structure for this company. For each of six functional managers, plus any intervening superiors between them and the president, specify the manager's responsibility for revenues, costs and assets.

    In order to guide your thinking, four alternative structures are provided below:
    a. The existing organization structure.
    b. A functional organization (i.e., a vice president for manufacturing and a vice president for sales).
    c. A two-divisional organization (i.e., one divisional general manager for OEM and another for after market).
    d. A divisional organization based on products (e.g., one division each for ignition parts, carburetors, and electric motors).
2. Precisely how does the acquisition of a computer make centralization of profit responsibility more practicable?

Appendix

Mr. Smith's Notes on the Thunderbolt Manufacturing Company

Nature of the business. Thunderbolt Manufacturing Company is in the automotive parts business and is a major supplier of ignition parts for both passenger cars and commercial vehicles. Other major product lines are carburetors and electic motors. Total company sales were about $240 million in 1975. Of this, about 70 percent was accounted for by ignition parts.

There are nine major classifications of ignition parts: coils, distributors, condensers, spark plugs, points, relays, switches, connectors, and fuses. Within each classification, there may be many different types of items. (For example, spark plugs are made with five different heat ranges, six different reaches, regular and extended tip, three different thread sizes, and four different types of alloys.) Thunderbolt manufactures over 3,000 different ignition items.

Markets and customers. The company sells its products both to automobile manufacturers (commonly referred to as original equipment manufacturer or OEM) and to the replacement market (called the "aftermarket" or "AM").

The OEM market. This market accounts for about one third of the total ignition parts volume. Sales are made to automobile companies.

In this business, three major factors determine whether a parts manufacturer will be successful in establishing and continuing a relationship with an OEM. The most important factor is service, and there are two aspects to this: (1) The ability to design ignition parts that meet OEM specifications and to come up with innovations beneficial to the OEM; and (2) the ability to meet OEM delivery requirements, even though these may change drastically from original estimates.

Close behind service as an important factor is price. Very small differences in unit selling prices of parts can mean the difference between winning or losing a bid.

The third factor is quality. Parts suppliers are expected to meet or exceed OEM quality specifications consistently.

The aftermarket. This market accounts for the other two thirds of Thunderbolt's ignition parts volume. Whereas in OEM sales a relatively small number of sales engineers handle sales to only a few automobile companies, in the aftermarket a national sales force covers a large number of accounts. A Thunderbolt salesman may sell to a wholesaler, who in turn sells a jobber; from there the product moves to a retailer, who then sells it to the ultimate customer, the car owner.

As in the OEM business, service, price, and quality are essential for success in the aftermar-

ket. Here, however, price is less important than either serivce or quality.

Competition. The automobile parts business is keenly competitive. There are other manufacturers who have product lines similar to those of Thunderbolt. In addition, there is a further pressure in the OEM market. The automobile companies have value analysis staffs that review a supplier's cost structure and manufacturing methods and, because of their huge purchasing power, they often specify what they think the costs—and prices—should be.

Pricing practices. Thunderbolt's OEM bid prices are calculated by the price estimating group, which is located at headquarters. For a particular item, this group obtains the estimated full manufacturing cost from the plant (or plants), making it. The group also gets an estimate from the salespeople of what the product can be sold for. If this sales price estimate in view of estimated costs meets certain profit criteria (such as a 10 percent profit on sales), the estimate then becomes the bid price. If the estimate does not meet the profit criteria, the pricing decision is then usually made by Mr. David Mattson, vice president and general manager of manufacturing.

Because of competitive pressures and the negotiating power of the OEM, the profit criteria usually are not met and, thus, top management quite frequently gets into OEM pricing decisions. Also, management may be especially interested in getting an item used in a particular automobile model, in the hope that "a foot in the door" will lead to increased sales later. As a result of these factors, profit margins are generally quite low in this area.

Another factor that complicates OEM pricing decisions is that there is a one to two year lag between the time a bid is submitted and the time the product is delivered. (As an example, in July 1976, Thunderbolt was quoting on parts for the 1978 model.) Even though there is a clause in each purchase contract that permits a renegotiation of the price if there have been increases in material or labor costs, the seller is not always successful in obtaining an increase in bid prices. Thus, it is desirable to take any foreseeable changes in costs into account at the time the bid price is determined.

In the aftermarket, parts suppliers also have limited freedom in setting prices. This is because the OEM service divisions set the retail prices that are charged by automobile dealers for replacement parts that the OEM supplies them, and these prices, in turn, largely determine the retail prices that can be charged for similar parts by the independent dealers. With dealer prices fixed, the prices that a parts manufacturer is able to obtain are also relatively fixed, because all distributors involved in handling AM products receive standard markups. About the only area where some pricing flexibility exists is in special designs, such as "hot" coils or special-purpose spark plugs. Even here, however, flexibility is limited by competitive pressures.

With this lack of flexibility in pricing, parts manufacturers' profit margins for a particular product are highly dependent on the level of manufacturing costs. On the average, the profit margins for AM products are considerably larger than those in the OEM area. This difference in profit margins, however, may be partly due to the method of allocating costs. For example, whenever Thunderbolt manufactures a product for an OEM, the cost of tooling is charged completely to that part of the OEM business. Consequently, if no new tooling is required to produce the same item for the aftermarket, no tooling costs are charged.

Organization. In 1968 Thunderbolt had only two plants, one in Ironville, Ohio, the other in Gary, Indiana. The Ironville plant manufactured coils, condensers, and spark plugs, while the Gary plant concentrated on distributors, points, and relays. (Switches, connectors, and fuses were not produced by Thunderbolt at that time.) A single sales force dealt with both the OEM market and the aftermarket and handled the products of both plants.

Each plant was made a profit center in 1968. The marketing group, however, was not made a profit center at that time. Thus, revenues on the plant P&L statements were shown at the dollar value of sales to the outside, rather than at some (lower) transfer price.

This organization by profit centers was initiated by Mr. Earl Goodwin, who joined Thunderbolt in 1968 as president. He had come from an automobile manufacturing company where profit centers had been used for some time with great success.

According to Mr. Charles Campbell, vice president and treasurer, there were essentially three reasons for introducing profit centers:

1. At the time Earl Goodwin joined Thunderbolt, its competitive position and profits had been dropping and there was considerable pressure for improvement. From his experience, Mr. Goodwin felt that holding operating managers responsible for profits, instead of just for costs, and giving them corresponding authority would improve the situation by inducing in them a strong profit consciousness.

2. There was need for an effective means of developing managers. Under the old approach, plant managers and their immediate subordinates were only supervisors—they just didn't have the opportunity to participate in decisions outside of their own limited areas of responsibility. Thunderbolt needed good managers. Mr. Goodwin believed that by holding them responsible for profits and, thus, forcing them to deal with all phases of the business, they would receive the training they needed.

3. Mr. Goodwin had brought with him a number of top-flight managers from his previous employer. Some of these men came to the head office, others went to the plants. They were familiar with profit centers, and Mr. Goodwin thought this would be of great help in introducing such centers at Thunderbolt.

Changes since 1968. Since profit centers were introduced in 1968, quite a number of changes have taken place at Thunderbolt. Late in 1975, Mr. Earl Goodwin became chairman of the board and Mr. Ray Alexander was elected president. Mr. Alexander's background has been in finance.

The company has grown considerably, not only in terms of sales and profits, but also physically and organizationally. There are now four plants: one in Broken Arrow, Oklahoma, and one in Waycross, Georgia, in addition to the two original plants in Ironville, Ohio, and Gary, Indiana.

There has been a trend to specialization by market among the plants. In 1968, the plants were specialized by product line, emphasizing neither the OEM nor the AM business. Now, however, the Ironville plant produces almost 80 percent of its volume for the OEM market. The other three plants do about 90 percent of their business in the AM area. Consequently, the plants are not limited to the manufacture of certain product lines. Each plant now handles a wide mix of items—considerably wider than the original plants did in 1968.

Profit centers. Currently there are six profit centers. All manufacturing under Mr. David Mattson (vice president and general manager of manufacturing) is treated as a profit center. Each of the three plants reporting to Mr. Mattson (those at Gary, Broken Arrow, and Waycross) is also a profit center. These plants do not have responsibility for outside sales of their products, as they did in 1968.

The OEM group, under Mr. George Robbins (vice president and general manager of the group) is a profit center. Mr. Robbins reports to Mr. Mattson. The Ironville plant, which produces mainly for the OEM market, is part of this profit center. So also are the OEM sales engineers, who sell only to the automobile manufacturers. The responsibility of this profit center for sales extends to all products purchased by the automobile companies whether manufactured at Ironville or at the other plants. The responsibility of the center for manufacturing, however, includes only production at the Ironville plant.

The sixth profit center is AM marketing, with responsiblity for all sales in the aftermarket regardless of which plant manufactured the products or whether they were acquired from outside suppliers. This center is headed by Mr. Larry Kimber.

Transfer pricing. Because all four plants manufacture products for both the OEM and the replacement markets, and because AM marketing is a separate profit center, transfers of finished goods between profit centers are necessary. In addition, there are transfers between profit centers of materials in various stages of completion. For example, partly finished distributors are sometimes transferred from the Ironville plant (mainly OEM production) to the Gary plant (mainly AM production) for special processing and then back to Ironville for sale by OEM sales engineers. Or, parts manufactured by one plant may be shipped to another for completion and eventual sale by AM marketing.

Transfers of finished and unfinished parts are made at transfer prices based on standard costs, because market prices are not readily available. Standard costs are set by headquarters. In setting the prices for transfers of finished goods from the plants to AM marketing, the aim is to allocate the total margin equitably among the involved profit centers on the basis of their costs. (Total margin is the difference between the selling price to wholesalers and the standard cost.)

For ignition parts, transfer prices are determined for the nine product lines rather than for individual items. According to Mr. Campbell, it would be impractical to have a transfer price for each of the 3,000 different items. A percentage markup over standard costs is used for each product line. This markup is set by headquarters in such a way that the producing plant and the AM marketing group receive approximately equal profits after all expenses directly associated with the product are included.

Thus, in theory, only nine transfer markups are needed. In practice, however, it has been necessary to make adjustments to these markups for a few items. After agreeing in general with a particular product line markup, the AM marketing group has found instances in which some items could be purchased for less on the outside than from the plants. For these items, a below-standard markup is used, so the outside market price is equaled.

Similarly, for parts transferred between plants, the total margin is allocated between the affected plants. Here, also, a markup over standard costs is used. According to a member of management, this practice has been satisfactory mainly because the volume of parts so transferred is less than 5 percent of the company's total production.

Budgets. Measurement of performance at Thunderbolt is based on actual profit. Preparation of profit budgets for the coming fiscal year is initiated in July and the "big push" occurs during September, when the budgets are consolidated. Budgets are broken down by months.

Individual plant schedules are used by the plants as a basis for developing their own budgets. For the volume of production scheduled, both revenues (based on transfer prices) and costs are developed. After corporate management has reviewed the completed budgets and agreement has been reached, they become the official budgets for the next year. The budgets for the OEM group and the AM marketing group are prepared in a way very similar to the plant budgets.

In order to control the inventories and fixed assets that are related to a profit center, capital appropriations and monthly inventory budgets are determined at the same time as the profit budgets. These budgets are also developed by the "bottom-up" approach, by which the individual profit centers first arrive at tentative figures, which are then reviewed by top management, revised as necessary, and agreed to.

Responsibilities of managers. Each manager of a profit center is responsible for achieving his budgeted profit. His performance is not judged on the basis of his profits relative to the investment required to achieve these profits.

Plant managers, also are responsible for the out-of-stock position of their plants. An out-of-stock position of 2 percent is the allowed limit for the plant managers.

The basic reason for this is that marketing makes the estimates that determine the inventory levels and is charged with selling the products.

As part of its responsibility for the warehousing of the finished goods inventory, the marketing group is charged with warehousing expenses. One reason for this is to discourage marketing from exceeding budgeted inventory levels. Because competition is on the basis of delivery (among other factors), marketing has a tendency to stockpile inventory so that products will be available for immediate delivery. Finished goods inventories account for almost one third of total current assets, and for almost 20 percent of total assets.

Degree of latitude. Even though managers are held responsible for the profits of their groups, they do not have complete control over all the factors that influence profitability. Plant managers, for example, do not have direct control over their production volume; they are told by the production scheduling group at headquarters what and how much to produce. They cannot refuse to produce an item, nor may they sell to the outside directly. Product mix can have a large impact on a plant's profitability, because there is a large variation in margins for different products.

Plant managers do have control over their manufacturing costs, and they have some control over such factors as quality of product and service.

The AM marketing group also does not have complete control over the important factors that influence its profitability. Although it does have considerably more latitude than the plants in determining sales volume, sales volume which is affected by the out-of-stock position at the warehouses, is mainly under the control of the plant managers.[2]

As far as margins are concerned, AM marketing has little control. As pointed out earlier, selling prices for parts are essentially predetermined by the OEM service divisions. Similarly, product costs for AM marketing are relatively fixed. These are determined by transfer prices, which, although reviewed at least once a year, are changed only when conditions change.

AM marketing does have control over its selling and administrative expenses.[3] The AM marketing group can influence its profits by purchasing products outside of the company, either when the prices charged by the plants are too high or when the plants cannot meet delivery requirements.

OEM sales volume is determined largely by automobile manufacturers and by the vagaries of the automobile market.

With respect to margins, the degree of latitude of the OEM group is about the same as for the other three plants. Where negotiated transfer prices determine revenues in their case, negotiated product prices fix revenues for the OEM group; and because of the great purchasing power of the automobile manufacturers, pricing flexibility is limited. Similarly, since manufacturing methods are essentially the same for the Ironville plant as for the other three, flexibility with respect to costs is about the same. However, if the need arises, the OEM group may purchase products from the outside, which is a freedom the other plants do not have.

---

[2] A member of top management estimated that about one half of the back-ordered AM business is lost. He was unable to provide a similar estimate for the OEM business, here the buyer/seller relationship is of longer term than in the AM business.

[3] S&A expenses for the AM marketing group amount to about 15 percent of net sales, while cost of goods sold is over 60 percent. (The remaining 25 percent is made up of such items as R&D expense, interest expense, taxes, and profits.)

Case 4-4
VDW, AG*

In October 1980, Rolf Ernst, financial director of VDW, AG, was considering what, if any, changes should be made to that part of the accounting system used to measure the financial performance of the company's sales subsidiaries. The system had operated without significant changes for many years; however, the events of 1980 brought out in a rather dramatic fashion some of the problems with measuring the profitability of the sales subsidiaries. The immediate impetus for considering a change was a letter describing the 1980 situation of VDW, Suisse, from Hans Weber, the financial director of that sales subsidiary (Exhibit 1).

The Organization

VDW was a multinational manufacturer of passenger automobiles, with 1980 revenues in excess of DM (deutsche marks) 15 billion. Headquarters were located in Germany and manufacturing and sales were conducted throughout Europe and parts of Africa.

Operations

Operations were divided into three functional areas: product development, manufacturing, and marketing.

Product development. This area was responsible for the styling and engineering of all new product lines and the improvement of all existing product lines. Both the marketing and manufacturing operations had product-planning personnel assigned to them. These people reported directly to the director of product development.

Manufacturing. Its operations were divided into three groups: stampings, engine and power train, and assembly. There were several plants in each group.

Manufacturing operations were located in three countries: Germany, France, and Italy. All three countries had stamping plants, engine and power train plants, and assembly plants. For the most part, the stamping plants located in a country provided stamped parts for the assembly plants within the same country; however, all stamping plants provided some parts for assembly plants in the other two countries. For the most part, the engine and power train plants were rationalized to obtain the maximum economies of scale. Consequently, all engine and power train plants produced parts for all assembly plants. Some assembly plants assembled only one product line, some assembled several. Some product lines were assembled exclusively in one assembly plant. Other product lines were assembled at two assembly plants.

The total manufacturing capacity by country was Germany 50 percent, France 30 percent, and Italy 20 percent.

Marketing. Operations were composed of 24 sales subsidiaries, one for each country within which the company sold vehicles. Most of these subsidiaries were in Europe; some were located in Africa. All sales subsidiaries sold the full range of product lines.

* This case was prepared by John Dearden, Harvard Business School.
Copyright © by the President and Fellows of Harvard College.
Harvard Business School case 181–125.

Accounting and Control

VDW employed a dual accounting system. One was an accounting system for fiscal and tax purposes. The other was a system for management control.

An accounting system was maintained in each country for fiscal and tax purposes. Under this system, each country was a profit center, and products were bought and sold among units of the company at transfer prices. Transfer prices were negotiated by the finance directors of the units involved. The objective of these negotiations was to develop prices that distributed the profits or losses among the participating units as fairly as possible, so as to avoid conflict with fiscal authorities. The fiscal accounting system was *not* used to measure the financial performance of either the operations within a country or the financial performance of the managers of those operations.

For control purposes, senior management of VDW looked only at companywide revenues, costs, and profits. Each quarter, total company profits were assigned first to product lines and then reassigned to market areas. *All* costs and revenues were assigned to some product and to some market area. Thus, the sum of the profits before taxes of all product lines equalled the sum of the profits of all market areas, which, in turn, equaled the total company pretax profit shown on the external financial statement. The performance of managers in manufacturing and product development was measured on the basis of cost targets and a number of nonfinancial objectives; for example, quality, meeting time commitments, and so forth. Since the issue in this case concerns the measurement of market area financial performance, the specific methods for measuring product development or manufacturing performance are not described.

Measuring Market Performance

Market area profitability analysis was based on two underlying principles.

1. Only companywide revenues, costs, and returns were considered. All accounting transactions involving transfer prices for the sales and purchases of vehicles and components were eliminated.
2. *All* companywide costs, revenues, and assets were assigned to some market area.

Revenues

Revenues were the actual revenues received in each market area converted to deutsche marks.

Variable Costs

Variable manufacturing costs included direct material, direct labor, and variable overhead. The latter included the variable portion of indirect labor, utilities, supplies, maintenance, and fringe benefits. The variable costs of the components produced by the engine and power train plants, the stamping plants, and the assembly plants were calculated each quarter for each product line and for each model within the product line. Each marketing area was charged with the specific variable cost for each product and model sold. If products were produced at different assembly plants, the variable costs incurred by the assembly plant that produced the specific vehicle were charged to the marketing area receiving the vehicle. Then companywide manufacturing costs were calculated for each type of vehicle.

Fixed Costs

Manufacturing. An average unit-fixed manufacturing cost was calculated for each component based on the relative standard direct labor content. Then a total unit-fixed manufacturing cost was assigned to each product line and model, representing the sum of the unit-fixed manufacturing costs for all manufactured components included in the vehicle, plus the unit-fixed cost of assembly.

Special tools, launching costs, and product development. Amortization of special tools, launching costs, and product development was assigned directly to product line and model where possible. Common costs were assigned to applicable product lines on the basis of relative unit sales volume. Unit costs were calculated by dividing the total costs by the unit sales volume for each product line and for each model within a product line.

Marketing. Marketing costs were assigned directly to sales subsidiaries where this was possible. Common marketing costs were allocated to market area on the basis of the relative volume of sales revenues.

Administration. Administration costs were assigned directly to market area where possible. Common administrative costs were allocated to market area on the basis of relative volume of sales revenues.

Summary. A unit-fixed manufacturing cost, special tool cost, launching cost, and product development cost were calculated for each model. These unit costs were multiplied by the number of the appropriate models sold by each sales subsidiary. In addition to the above, each sales district was assigned unique marketing and administrative costs, plus a share of the common costs based on the relative sales revenue in each market area.

Assets were also assigned to product and marketing areas so that a ''return on assets'' could be calculated.

An Example of Profitability Analysis

Exhibit 2 provides a hypothetical and somewhat simplified picture of how the profitability of the sales subsidiaries was calculated. This example assumes that there are two product lines and two models within each product line. Product line 1 has model A and model B. Product line 2 has model C and model D. There are four sales subsidiaries: W, X, Y, and Z.

Measuring the Performance of Sales Subsidiary Managers

Responsibilities of Sales Subsidiary Managers

Pricing. Vehicle price recommendations were submitted to the headquarters marketing staff for review. Differences of opinion between the sub-

sidiary manager and the staff were negotiated; disputes that could not be resolved readily were reviewed with the top operating management for decision.

Sales volume and mix. The subsidiary manager was entirely responsible for all of sales within the country, although headquarters staff units often provided guidance. The subsidiary manager was responsible for dealer recruitment, development, and control. He or she was also responsible for all local advertising and sales promotion, including special incentives. In short, all sales activities within the country were the direct responsibility of the subsidiary manager.

Costs. The subsidiary manager was responsible for all costs incurred within the country. This included all subsidiary administration and selling costs, as well as all warranty costs incurred by the dealers.

Bases for Measuring Actual Performance

How well sales subsidiary managers met their responsibilities was measured in financial and nonfinancial terms.

Financial. Financial performance was evaluated by comparing actual perfomance with the profit budget prepared by the subsidiary manager and approved by headquarters management. In order to arrive at the numbers for the profit budget, each year each subsidiary manager prepared: (1) a revenue budget based on budgeted prices, unit volumes, and accessory installations; (2) a cost budget based on the expected expenditures incurred directly by the subsidiary. These budgets, calculated in deutsche marks, were submitted to headquarters for review and approval. Budgets were approved after negotiating changes, where such changes were deemed appropriate by the top operating management.

Subsequently, each subsidiary manager was provided with the following costs based on company-wide budgets:

Unit-variable cost by model.
Unit-fixed manufacturing cost by model.
Unit-special tool amortization, launching costs, and product development costs by model.

Total allocated sales costs.
Total allocated administrative costs.
Total allocated assets.

On the basis of these numbers, the managers prepared a profit budget for the subsidiary, stressing profits and returns on sales and assets.

Each quarter the actual costs and revenues were calculated, and the costs and revenues for the remainder of the year were projected. Thus, each quarter there was an updated estimate of the profitablity for the year. This estimate was compared to the original budget, and variances analyzed and explained. Each subsequent quarter was composed more of actual costs and revenues and less of projections. The final quarter compared the actual costs and revenues for the year with the original budget. Note that each quarter all items of costs and revenues were completely recalculated to reflect the latest amounts for the year.

Nonfinancial measures.   The performance of subsidiary managers was also evaluated on the basis of three nonfinancial measures:

1. Market penetration.
2. Percentage recovery of price-level and exchange-rate changes. This was the relationship between sales-price increases and price-level increases, plus changes in the exchange rate of the local currency relative to the deutsche mark.
3. Mix and option rates. This measured the improvement in the profits per car.

Events in 1980

In 1980, two events occurred that were not anticipated in the 1980 budget. First, the sale of vehicles fell significantly below budget as a result of the recession in Europe. Second, fixed manufacturing costs and launching costs seriously exceeded budget. As a result, beginning in the first quarter of 1980, major changes were made to all of the budgeted allocations. These shifts reduced the profitability of all marketing areas, with many areas even showing losses.

One of the subsidiaries that was most severely affected was VDW, Suisse (Switzerland). This situation led to a daylong discussion in April between Hans Weber, the financial director of VDW, Suisse, and Rolf Ernst, the finance director of VDW, AG. The principal topic discussed in the meeting was the drop in profits and returns by VDW, Suisse, in spite of improvements in sales, volume and mix, and locally incurred costs. At the end of the discussion, Rolf Ernst asked Hans Weber to prepare a letter describing his objections to the accounting system and his reasons for these objections. This letter is reproduced as Exhibit 1.

On receipt of Weber's letter, Ernst assigned members of his staff to review two of the issues raised by Weber. Memoranda covering these issues are reproduced in Exhibits 3 and 4.

EXHIBIT 1   VDW

Subject: Profit decline in VDW, Suisse

August 21, 1980

Dear Mr. Ernst:

Our discussion of July 17 isolated three reasons for the decline in profitability of VDW, Suisse, from a budgeted 1980 profit of DM 13.9 million to a loss of DM 2.1 million. These were:

1. The variable costs increased because the sourcing of some models was changed from an assembly plant in Germany to an assembly plant in Italy. Not only are the variable costs considerably higher in Italy, but the plant utilization is much lower. This also increased fixed costs.
2. The worldwide sales of vehicles was 25 percent less than was anticipated in the budget. Because the vehicle sales of VDW, Suisse, was higher than budget, the subsidiary was assigned a much higher amount of allocated fixed costs.
3. Actual fixed costs were and are expected to be considerably higher than budget. In particular, development and launching costs of Model X, which had just been introduced, were considerably in excess of budget. This model is selling well in Switzerland and, consequently, VDW, Suisse, was assigned a relatively large proportion of these costs.

PROBLEMS

This situation distorts managerial performance and misrepresents the contribution made by this subsidiary, particularly in period-to-period comparisons.

Managerial Performance

So far in 1980, VDW, Suisse has equaled or exceeded its budgeted goals on the items that it controls. Sales volume is somewhat above budgeted levels, the product mix and option rates are at budget, price recovery is only slightly below budget, and local selling and administrative costs are approximately at budget. (The only costs above budget are warranty expenses. This resulted from unanticipated quality problems with model X.) Yet the profit performance of VDW, Suisse, is DM 16.0 million worse than budget. The entire decline has been caused by factors completely beyond the control of management.

In our discussion, you assured me that management was measured on performance factors other than profit. This, however, creates a dilemma for management. Nonfinancial goals can often be met by taking action that may be contrary to the overall interests of the company. For example, we could increase the sale of Model X by offering special incentives, minimizing option installation, and increasing sales and promotional effort. In fact, we really should do this because it is our best defense against the threat of increasing Japanese imports. Yet if we were to do this, we would lower all the nonfinancial ratios except market penetration. Also, we would exceed our budgeted marketing costs. Not only would we change all of our ratios, but our profits would actually decrease! This occurs because the fixed cost per unit on Model X is so high that, if we lowered our price, we would sustain a loss on each unit sold. Yet, it would seem to me that any increase in volume would be desirable this year in view of the current amount of excess manufacturing capacity.

Subsidiary Performance

As indicated, this year VDW, Suisse, will show a loss, down from a DM 12.6 million profit in 1979. This would seem to indicate that we are experiencing a profit slump. Yet, this is completely untrue. We are having our best year yet. The reason for the profit decrease is entirely due to causes outside of Switzerland, in particular the lower sales volumes in the rest of Europe. Does top management understand this? I find this situation very difficult to explain to our operating managers.

EXHIBIT 1   *(concluded)*

We agree that the problem is not an easy one and is largely compounded by lower overall business activity at source locations. It would seem to us, however, that because of these major fluctuations in accounted profit results, we need to review alternatives that more appropriately identify the true worth of profit center contributions. We realize, in the end analysis, that all fixed costs must be recovered, and satisfactory returns earned on all assets. For the present, however, it would appear that incremental profits are the appropriate basis for making decisions. The presentation of data based on the present fully accounted conventions is totally accepted, and we recognize that it is not practical to calculate incremental profits for every market every month. Your present measurement, however, does not properly identify our true contribution and my operating management is very heavily criticized for actions that we believe were in the best interests of the company. We realize that the problem is not new, but because of the magnitude of the aberration we suggest a coordinated corporate review be made on how best to reflect data to management.

Best regards,

Hans Weber

Hans Weber
Director of Finance

EXHIBIT 2   Example of Profitability Calculation

Product Line Statistics—First Quarter, 1981

	Product Line 1		Product Line 2	
	Model A	*Model B*	*Model C*	*Model D*
Unit volume	1,000	2,000	3,000	4,000
Price per unit	DM10,000	DM12,000	DM20,000	DM25,000
Cost per unit				
Variable cost:				
Italy	—	6,000[a]	9,000	13,000[b]
Germany	4,000	5,000[c]	—	11,000[d]
Fixed mfg. costs	2,000	3,000	4,000	5,000
Other fixed costs[e]	1,000	1,000	1,500	2,000

a. Vehicles delivered to subsidiaries W and X.
b. Vehicles delivered to subsidiaries W and Y.
c. Vehicles delivered to subsidiaries Y and Z.
d. Vehicles delivered to subsidiaries X and Z.
e. Other fixed costs include special tools, launching, and product development.

Subsidiary Statistics—First Quarter, 1981

	Unit Sales Volumes				
Model	*Subsidiary W*	*Subsidiary X*	*Subsidiary Y*	*Subsidiary Z*	*Total*
A	250	200	300	250	1,000
B	1,000	500	300	200	2,000
C	1,000	500	500	1,000	3,000
D	1,000	1,000	1,500	500	4,000
Total	3,250	2,200	2,600	1,950	10,000

Marketing and Administrative Costs (DM 000)

	Sub. W	*Sub. X*	*Sub. Y*	*Sub. Z*	*Total*
Marketing:					
Unique	3,000	5,500	5,000	4,000	17,500
Common	—	—	—	—	15,000
Administration:					
Unique	100	300	600	500	1,500
Common	—	—	—	—	16,000

EXHIBIT 2 *(concluded)*

Market Area Profitability—First Quarter 1981 (DM 000)

	Sub. W	Sub. X	Sub. Y	Sub. Z	Total
Revenues:					
Model A	2,500	2,000	3,000	2,500	10,000
Model B	12,000	6,000	3,600	2,400	24,000
Model C	20,000	10,000	10,000	20,000	60,000
Model D	25,000	25,000	37,500	12,500	100,000
Total	59,500	43,000	54,100	37,400	194,000
Variable costs:					
Model A	1,000	800	1,200	1,000	4,000
Model B[a]	6,000	3,000	1,500	1,000	11,500
Model C	4,000	2,000	2,000	4,000	12,000
Model D[a]	13,000	11,000	19,500	5,500	49,000
Total	24,000	16,800	24,200	11,500	76,500
Contribution	35,500	26,200	29,900	25,900	117,500
Fixed costs:[b]					
Model A	750	600	900	750	3,000
Model B	4,000	2,000	1,200	800	8,000
Model C	5,500	2,750	2,750	5,500	16,500
Model D	7,000	7,000	10,550	3,500	28,000
Total	17,250	12,350	15,350	10,550	55,500
	18,250	13,850	14,550	15,350	62,000
Mkt. & adm[c]	12,586	12,682	14,249	10,483	50,000
Net profit	5,664	1,168	301	4,867	12,000

[a] Calculation of variable costs for models B and D:

		Sub. W	Sub. X	Sub. Y	Sub. Z	Total
Model B:						
Volume		1,000	500	300	200	
Unit variable cost		6,000	6,000	5,000	5,000	
Total variable cost (DM 000)		6,000	3,000	1,500	1,000	11,500
Model D:						
Volume		1,000	1,000	1,500	500	
Unit variable cost		13,000	11,000	13,000	11,000	
Total variable cost (DM 000)		13,000	11,000	19,500	5,500	49,000

[b] Includes manufacturing fixed costs, special tool amortization, launching costs, and product development costs.
[c] Allocation of marketing and administrative costs. (See table below.)

Allocation of Marketing and Administrative Costs (DM 000)

	Sub. W	Sub. X	Sub. Y	Sub. Z	Total
Unique costs	3,100	5,800	5,600	4,500	19,000
Common costs*	9,486	6,882	8,649	5,983	31,000
Total	12,586	12,682	14,249	10,483	50,000

* Common costs were allocated on the basis of the subsidiaries' sales volume.

EXHIBIT 3   Market Profitability Review—Fixed Market Concept

Market profitability is presently projected using the latest economic profits* less an allocation of fixed costs based on ratios calculated using the latest volume and cost estimates. Only fixed costs directly related to a market are allocated specifically. These represent about 20 percent of total fixed costs. The use of estimated actual volume to allocate fixed costs is termed the "variable market concept." Alternative methods would be where allocations are based on budgeted ratios that remain fixed throughout the year, and the "unit fixed cost concept," in which the budgeted amount of fixed costs is allocated regardless of volume or cost level changes.

The basic advantage of the fixed market concept is that performance in one market is not affected by sales performance in another market. *The major disadvantage is that movements from budget are amplified—because volume changes are translated directly into economic profits.* This can lead to substantial distortion in year-to-year comparisons within markets and intrayear distortions among markets as returns in individual years differ from a fully accounted approach.

The variable market concept tends to have the opposite advantages and disadvantages of the fixed-market concept. It results in the performance of one market affecting others, but year-to-year comparisons at equal volume are not distorted.

The unit-cost concept would avoid the problems of the above but could result in major differences between total corporate profits and operational profits, if volume was substantially off budget. Such a large consolidation item would be unacceptable.

The use of a fixed or variable market allocation basis for fixed costs becomes a trade-off between the incentive advantages to managing directors under the fixed concept and the more representative trend profits that occur with the variable concept. A potential plan to reduce the financial disadvantages of the present methodology would be to change the primary measurement to a variable system, while maintaining the fixed system for performance measurement of general managers. Finance staff recommends implementation of the latter change for the 1981 budget, with all historical years restated. This could lead to situations where management presentations would show performance different from how the managing directors would be measured. If sales group prefers, performance measurement also can use the variable concept.

September 19, 1980.

* Editor's note: Economic profit is revenue minus variable costs.

EXHIBIT 4   Market Profitability Review—Average Sourcing

At present, the product profit system details the cost of each vehicle in each market. The revenue and cost assumptions are provided by the relevant sales and manufacturing areas and reflect the actual vehicle sourcing pattern. As a result, the costs of identical vehicles assembled in different plants will vary because of differences in labor and material costs, in freight patterns, in plant capacity utilization, and in other factors. This system provides an accurate estimate of the actual cost incurred in producing a specific vehicle in a specific plant, and offers the following advantages:

1. It provides an excellent base for financial analysis—all costs and revenues can be tracked from sales/manufacturing input.
2. It highlights problems—a comparison of variable cost data between sources can lead to the identification of cost-saving opportunities.
3. Proposals for product or capacity changes must be based on actual costs to evaluate the correct corporate profit effect.

An alternative to use of specific sourcing would be to provide cost data on an "average-source basis." The major advantage of such a policy would be to eliminate potential profit distortions that result from sourcing decisions that are not within the control of managing directors. Although this change has advantages for financial incentives, this value appears to be outweighed by the following weaknesses:

1. Elimination of sourcing variances from market profits would require average-source material, labor, overhead, and freight costs. This would require the development of theoretical costs. The development of these data would necessarily lead to cost increases.
2. The product system is fully computerized and does not have the capacity to derive average source costs without a major change to existing computer systems.
3. The use of average-source costs would mask specific pricing problems, such as tax and duty in Scandinavian markets. In these markets, the tax and duty implications are a function of the transfer price charged by the national company owning the final assembly source. It is essential that specific tax and duty levels are reflected in pricing decisions to ensure full recovery of costs.
4. Even if average sourcing were used, intermarket comparisons would still include substantial factors outside the direct control of managing directors, such as exchange rates. Use of average sourcing could lessen attention to real issues, such as source/sales exchange rate changes that require positive action.

Continued use of specific sourcing is recommended.

September 30, 1980

QUESTION

Assume that you were employed as a consultant to VDW. What changes would you recommend that VDW make in their system of measuring and controlling the sales subsidiaries?

Chapter 5

Transfer Pricing

Today's organizational thinking is oriented toward decentralization. One of the principal challenges in operating a decentralized profit center system is to devise a satisfactory method of accounting for the transfer of goods and services from one profit center to another, in those companies having significant amounts of these transactions. In this chapter we discuss various approaches to arriving at transfer prices for transactions between profit centers and the system of negotiation and arbitration that is essential when transfer prices are used. We also discuss the pricing of services that corporate staff units furnish to profit centers. We discuss international transfer pricing in Chapter 16.

OBJECTIVES OF TRANSFER PRICES

If two or more profit centers are jointly responsible for product development, manufacturing, and marketing, each should share in the revenue that is generated when the product is finally sold. The transfer price is the mechanism for distributing this revenue. The transfer price is not primarily an accounting tool. Rather, it is a behavioral tool that motivates managers to take the right decisions. In particular, the transfer price should be designed in such a way that it accomplishes the following objectives:

- It should provide each segment with the relevant information required to determine the optimum trade-off between *company* costs and revenues.
- It should induce *goal congruent* decisions—that is, the system should be so designed that decisions that improve business unit (divisional) profits will also improve company profits.
- It should help determine the economic performance of the individual profit centers as accurately as possible.
- The system should be simple to understand and easy to administer.

A survey by Richard Vancil[1] of 291 divisionalized manufacturing companies found that about 85 percent of the profit centers transfer goods, and that transfers of services and joint use of common facilities existed in 55 percent and 71 percent of companies, respectively.

TRANSFER PRICING METHODS

Some writers use "transfer price" to refer to the amount used in accounting for *any* transfer of goods and services between responsibility centers. We use a somewhat narrower definition and limit the term *transfer price* to the value placed on a transfer of goods or services in transactions in which at least one of the two parties involved is a *profit center.* Such a price normally includes a profit element, because an independent company would not normally transfer goods or services to another independent company at cost or less. We, therefore, exclude the mechanics for the allocation of costs in a cost accounting system; such costs do not include a profit element. The term *price,* as used here, has the same meaning as it has when it is used in connection with transactions between independent companies.

Fundamental Principle

The fundamental principle is that the *transfer price should be similar to the price that would be charged if the product were sold to outside customers or purchased from outside vendors.* Application of this principle is complicated by the fact that there is much disagreement in the literature as to how outside selling prices should be established. The classical economics literature states that selling prices should be equal to marginal costs, and some authors advocate a transfer price based on marginal cost.[2] This is unrealistic. Few companies follow such a policy in arriving at either selling prices or transfer prices.[3]

---

[1] Richard F. Vancil, *Decentralization: Management Ambiguity by Design* (Homewood, Ill.: Dow Jones-Irwin, 1979), p. 169.

[2] The most widely quoted article is Jack Hirshleifer, "On the Economics of Transfer Pricing," *Journal of Business,* July 1956, pp. 172–84.

[3] A study by two of the authors of methods of arriving at market prices, with respondents from 501 of the Fortune 1,000 companies, reported that only 17 percent followed such a policy. (V. Govindarajan and Robert N. Anthony, "How Firms Use Cost Data in Pricing Decisions," *Management Accounting,* July 1983, pp. 30–34.) Vancil's study of transfer pricing (see Exhibit 5–1) reported that less than 5 percent used variable costs as a basis for pricing.

Authors sometimes ignore the results of research in their enthusiasm for the classical economics approach. For example, Benke and Edwards interviewed 19 companies and found that *none* of them based transfer prices on variable costs or opportunity costs. They nevertheless recommended a general rule that was based entirely on variable costs and opportunity costs. (Ralph L. Benke,

Modern economics literature recognizes this fact; but there are few discussions of how to price individual jobs in a job order company (such as a printing shop), or how to price take-or-pay contracts, or how to negotiate reduction from normal prices when a reduction is in the best interest of both parties. Thus, the transfer pricing literature is actually about pricing in general, modified slightly to take into account factors that are unique to internal transactions.

When profit centers of a company buy from and sell to one another, two decisions must be made periodically for each product that is being produced by one business unit and sold to another:

1. Should the company produce the product inside the company or purchase it from an outside vendor? This is the *sourcing decision*.
2. If produced inside, at what price should the product be transferred between profit centers? This is the *transfer price decision*.

Transfer price systems can range from the very simple to the extremely complex, depending on the nature of the business. We start with the ideal situation and then describe increasingly complex situations.

The Ideal Situation

A transfer price will induce goal congruence if all the conditions listed below exist. Rarely, if ever, will all these conditions exist in practice. The list, therefore, does not set forth criteria that must be met to have a transfer price. Rather, it suggests a way of looking at a situation to see what changes should be made to improve the operation of the transfer price mechanism.

Competent people.   Ideally, managers should be interested in the long-run as well as the short-run performances of their responsibility centers. Staff people involved in negotiation and arbitration of transfer prices also must be competent.

Good atmosphere.   Managers must regard profitability as measured in their income statement as an important goal and as a significant consideration in the judgment of their performance. They should perceive that the transfer prices are just.

A market price.   The ideal transfer price is based on a well-established, normal market price for the identical product being transferred—that is, a market price reflecting the same conditions (quantity, deliver time, and the like) as the product to which the transfer price applies. The market price may be adjusted downward to reflect savings by the selling unit from dealing inside the company. For example, there would be no bad debt expense and smaller advertising and selling costs. Although less than ideal, a market price for a similar, but not identical, product is better than no market price at all.

Jr., and James Don Edwards, *Transfer Pricing: Techniques and Uses,* National Association of Accountants, 1980.)

Freedom to source. Alternatives should exist, and managers should choose the alternative that is in their own best interests. In particular, the buying manager should be free to buy from the outside, and the selling manager should be free to sell outside.

In this instance, the only transfer price policy necessary is to give the managers of each profit center the right to deal with either insiders or outsiders, at their discretion. The market, thus, establishes the transfer price. The decision to deal inside or outside also is made by the marketplace. If buyers cannot get a satisfactory price from the inside source, they are free to buy from the outside.

If the selling profit center can sell all of its products, either to insiders or to outsiders, and as long as the buying center can obtain all of its requirements from either outsiders or insiders, this method is optimum. The market price represents the opportunity cost to the seller of selling the product inside. This is so because, if the product were not sold inside, it would be sold outside. From a company point of view, therefore, the relevant cost of the product is the market price, because that is the amount of cash that has been forgone by selling inside. The transfer price, therefore, represents the opportunity cost to the company.

Full flow of information. Managers must know about the available alternatives and the relevant costs and revenues of each.

Negotiation. There must be a smoothly working mechanism for negotiating "contracts" between business units.

Constraints on Sourcing

If all of the above conditions are present, a transfer price system based on market prices would fulfill all of the objectives stated in the previous section and yet need no central administration. We will now consider situations where one or more of these conditions are not present.

Ideally, the buying manager should be given freedom to make sourcing decisions, if the profit center is to operate in an entrepreneurial manner. Similarly, the selling manager should be free to sell its products in the most advantageous market. However, in real life, freedom to source either might not be feasible or, even if it is feasible, might be constrained by corporate policy. We now consider the situations where profit center managers may not have the freedom to make sourcing decisions and the implications of constraints on sourcing on the appropriate transfer pricing policies.

Limited markets. In many companies, markets for the buying or selling profit centers may be limited. There are several reasons for this.

First, the existence of internal capacity might limit the development of external sales. If most of the large companies in an industry are highly integrated, as in the pulp and paper industry, there tends to be little independent production capacity for the intermediate products. Thus, these producers can handle only a limited amount of demand from other producers. When internal capacity becomes tight, the market is quickly flooded with demands for the intermediate products. Even though outside capacity exists, it may not be available to the integrated company unless this capacity is used on a regular basis. If the integrated company does not purchase a product on a regular basis, it might have trouble obtaining it from the outside when the capacity is limited.

Second, if a company is the sole producer of a differentiated product, no outside capacity exists.

Third, if a company has made significant investment in facilities, it is unlikely to use outside sources even though outside capacity exists, unless the outside selling price approaches the company's variable cost, which is not usual. For practical purposes, the products produced are captive. Integrated oil companies are good examples of this practice. The producing unit would be required to send the crude oil to the refining unit, even though the former could potentially sell the crude oil in the open market.

Even in the case of limited markets, the transfer price that best satisfies the requirements of a profit center system is, nevertheless, the *competitive* price. Competitive prices will measure the contribution of each profit center to the total company profits. In the case of an integrated oil company, use of the crude oil market prices is the most effective way of evaluating the extracting and refining units as if they were stand-alone businesses. If internal capacity were not available, the company would buy outside at the competitive price. The difference between the competitive price and the inside cost is the money saved by making instead of buying. Moreover, a competitive price measures how well a profit center may be performing against competition.

The problem is: How does a company find out what the competitive price is, if it does not buy or sell the product in an outside market? Here are some ways.

1. If *published market prices* are available, they can be used to establish transfer prices. However, these should be prices actually paid in the marketplace, and the conditions that exist in the outside market should be consistent with those existing within the company. For example, market prices that are applicable to relatively small purchases (e.g., a "spot" market) would not be valid for measuring for what is essentially a long-term commitment.

2. Market prices may be set by *bids*. This generally can be done only if the low bidder has a reasonable chance of obtaining the business. One company accomplishes this by buying about one half of a particular group of products outside the company and one half inside the company. The company puts *all* of the products out to bid, but selects one half to stay inside. The company obtains valid bids, because low bidders can expect to get some of the business. By contrast, if a company requests bids solely to obtain a competitive price and does not award contracts to the low bidder, it will soon find that either no one bids or that the bids are of questionable value.

3. If the *production profit center* sells similar products in *outside markets*, it is often possible to replicate a competitive price on the basis of the outside price. For example, if a manufacturing profit center normally earns a 10 percent profit over standard cost on the products that it sells to outside markets, it can replicate a competitive price by adding 10 percent to the standard cost of its proprietary products.

4. If the *buying profit center* purchases similar products from the *outside* market, it may be possible to replicate competitive prices for its proprietary products. This can be done by calculating the cost of the difference in design and other conditions of sale between the competitive products and the proprietary products.

Excess or shortage of industry capacity.

Suppose the selling profit center cannot sell to the outside market all it can produce—that is, it has excess capacity. The company may not optimize profits if the buying profit center purchased from outside vendors while capacity is available on the inside.

Conversely, suppose the buying profit center cannot obtain all the product it requires from the outside, while the selling profit center is selling to the outside. This situation occurs when there is a shortage of capacity in the industry. In this case, the output of the buying profit center is constrained and, again, company profits may not be optimum.

If the amount of intracompany transfers is small or if the situation is temporary, many companies let buyers and sellers work out their own relationships without central intervention. Even if the amount of intracompany transfers is significant, some companies still do not intervene, on the theory that the benefits of keeping the profit centers independent offsets the loss from suboptimizing company profits.

Some companies allow either the buying or the selling profit center to appeal a sourcing decision to a central person or a committee. For example, a selling profit center could appeal a buying profit center's decision to buy a product from outside when capacity was available inside. In the same way, a buying profit center could appeal a selling profit center's decision to sell outside. The person or group (hereafter called an "arbitration committee") would, then, make the sourcing decision on the basis of the company's best interests. In every case, the transfer price would be the *competitive price*. In other words, the profit center is appealing only the sourcing decision. It must accept the product at the competitive price.

A word of caution is in order at this point. In some companies, given the option, buying profit centers prefer to deal with an outside source. One reason is service: outside sources are perceived to provide better service. Another reason may be the internal rivalry that sometimes exists in divisionalized companies. For whatever reason, management should be aware of the strong political overtones that sometimes occur in transfer price negotiations. There is no guarantee that a profit center will voluntarily buy from the inside source when excess capacity exists.

To conclude, even if there are constraints on sourcing, the market price is the best transfer price. *If the market price exists (or can be approximated as discussed earlier), use it.* However, if there are no ways of approximating valid competitive prices, the other option is to develop *cost-based* transfer prices. These are discussed in the next section.

Cost-Based Transfer Prices

If competitive prices are not available, transfer prices may be set on the basis of cost plus a profit, even though such transfer prices may be complex to calculate and the results less satisfactory than a market-based price. Two decisions must be made in a cost-based transfer price system: (1) How to define cost? (2) How to calculate the profit markup?

The cost basis.   The usual basis is standard cost. Actual costs should not be used, because production inefficiencies will then be passed on to the buying profit center. If standard costs are used, there is a need to provide an incentive to set tight standards and to improve standards.

Some companies have tried using "efficient producer" costs, but someone has to decide what these costs are, which is difficult.

Under both cost-plus pricing and market-based pricing, companies typically eliminate advertising, financing, or other expenses that the seller does not incur on internal transactions. (This is similar to the practice when two outside companies are arriving at a price. The buyer ordinarily will not pay for cost components that do not apply to the contract.)

The profit markup.   In calculating the profit markup, there also are two decisions: (1) On what is the profit markup to be based? (2) What is the level of profit allowed?

The simplest and most widely used base is a *percentage of costs.* If this is done, however, no account is taken of capital required. A conceptually better base is a percentage of *investment,* but there may be a major practical problem in calculating the investment applicable to a given product. If the historical cost of the fixed assets is used, new facilities designed to reduce prices could actually increase costs because old assets are undervalued.

The second problem with the profit allowance is the amount of the profit. Senior management's perception of the financial performance of a profit center will be affected by the profit it shows. Consequently, to the extent possible, the profit allowance should be the best approximation of the rate of return that would be earned if the business unit were an independent company, selling to outside customers. The conceptual solution is to base the profit allowance on the investment required to meet the volume needed by the buying profit centers. This investment would be calculated at a "standard" level, with fixed assets and inventories at current replacement costs. This solution is rarely found in practice, however.

Upstream Fixed Costs and Profits

Transfer pricing can create a significant problem in integrated companies. The profit center that finally sells to the outside customer may not even be aware of the amount of upstream fixed costs and profit included in its internal purchase price. Even if the final profit center were aware of the costs and profit, it might be reluctant to reduce its own profit to optimize company profit. Methods that companies use to mitigate this problem are described below.

Agreement among business units. A company could establish a formal mechanism whereby representatives from the buying and selling units meet periodically to decide on outside selling prices and on the distribution of the profit for products having significant amounts of upstream fixed costs and profit. This mechanism is workable only if the review process is limited to decisions that involve a significant amount of business to at least one of the profit centers; otherwise, the value of these negotiations may not be worth the effort.

Two-step pricing. Another way to handle this problem is to establish a transfer price that includes two charges. First, a charge is made for each unit sold that is equal to the standard variable cost of production. Second, a periodic (usually monthly) charge is made that is equal to the fixed costs associated with the facilities reserved for the buying unit. One or both of these components should include a profit margin. For example, assume the following conditions:

Business Unit X (manufacturer)

	Product A
Expected monthly sales to Business Unit Y	5,000 units
Variable cost per unit	$ 5
Monthly fixed costs assigned to product	20,000
Investment in working capital and facilities	1,200,000
Competitive return on investment per year	10%

One way to transfer product A to Business Unit Y is at a price per unit, calculated as follows:

	Transfer Price for Product A
Variable cost per unit	$ 5
Plus fixed cost per unit	4
Plus profit per unit[*]	2
Transfer price per unit	$11

[*] 10% of monthly investment per unit $= \dfrac{(\$1{,}200{,}000/12) \times 0.10}{5{,}000}$

In this method, the transfer price of $11 per unit is a variable cost so far as Unit Y is concerned. However, the company's variable cost for product A is $5 per unit. Thus, Unit Y does not have the right information to make appropriate short-term marketing decisions. For example, if Unit Y knew the company's variable costs, it could safely take business at less than its normal price under certain conditions.

The two-step pricing method corrects this problem by transferring variable cost on a per unit basis and fixed cost and profit on a lump sum basis. Under this method, the transfer price for product A would be $5 for each unit that Unit Y purchases plus $20,000 per month for fixed cost, plus $10,000 per month for profit:

$$\frac{\$1,200,000}{12} \times 0.10$$

If transfers of product A in a certain month are at the expected amount of 5,000 units, then, under the two-step method, Unit Y will pay the variable cost of $25,000 (5,000 units × $5 per unit) plus $30,000 for fixed costs and profit, a total of $55,000. This is the same amount as the amount it would pay Unit X if the transfer price were $11 per unit (5,000 × $11 = $55,000). If transfers in another month were less than 5,000 units, say 4,000 units, Unit Y would pay $50,000 [(4,000 × 5) + $30,000] under the two-step method, compared with the $44,000 it would pay if the transfer price were $11 per unit (4,000 × $11 = $44,000). The difference is its penalty for not using a portion of Unit X's capacity that it has reserved. Conversely, Unit Y would pay less under the two-step method if the transfer were more than 5,000 units in a given month; this represents the savings that Unit X would have because it could produce the additional units without incurring additional fixed costs.

Note that under the two-step pricing, the company's variable cost for product A is identical to Unit Y's variable cost for this product, and Unit Y will make the correct short-term marketing decisions. Unit Y also has information on upstream fixed costs and profit relating to product A, and it can use these data for long-term decisions.

The fixed-cost calculation in the two-step pricing method is based on the capacity that is reserved for the production of product A that is sold to Unit Y. The investment represented by this capacity is allocated to product A. The return turn on investment that Unit X earns on competitive (and, if possible, comparable) products is calculated and multiplied by the investment assigned to the product.

In the example, we calculated the profit allowance as a fixed monthly amount. It would be appropriate under some circumstances to divide the investment into variable (e.g., receivables and inventory) and fixed (physical assets) components. Then, a profit allowance based on a return on the variable assets would be added to the standard variable cost for each unit sold.

Following are some points to consider about this method of pricing.

• The monthly charge for fixed costs and profit should be negotiated periodically and would depend on the capacity reserved for the buying unit.

- Some questions may be raised about the accuracy of the cost and investment allocation. In most situations, there is no great difficulty in assigning costs and assets to individual products. In any event, approximate accuracy is adequate. The principal problem is usually not the allocation technique; rather, it is the decision about how much capacity is to be reserved for the various products. Moreover, if capacity is reserved for a group of products sold to the same business unit, there is no need to allocate fixed costs and investments to individual products in the group.
- Under this pricing system, the manufacturing unit's profit performance is not affected by the sales volume of the final unit, which solves the problem that arises when other business units' marketing efforts affect the profit performance of a purely manufacturing unit.
- There could be a conflict between the interests of the manufacturing unit and the interests of the company. If capacity is limited, the manufacturing unit could increase its profit by using the capacity to produce parts for outside sale, if it is advantageous to do so. (This weakness is mitigated by stipulating that the selling units have first claim on the capacity they have contracted for.)
- This method is similar to the "take or pay" pricing that is frequently used in public utilities, pipelines, coal mining companies, and other long-term contracts. These companies are able to solve the above problems in an acceptable fashion.

Profit sharing.   If the two-step pricing system just described is not appropriate, a profit-sharing system might be used to ensure congruence of business unit interest with company interest. This system operates somewhat as follows.

1. The product is transferred to the marketing unit at standard variable cost.
2. After the product is sold, the business units share the contribution earned, which is the selling price minus the variable manufacturing and marketing costs.

This method of pricing may be appropriate if the demand for the manufactured product is not steady enough to warrant the permanent assignment of facilities, as in the two-step method. In general, this method accomplishes the purpose of making the marketing unit's interest congruent with the company's.

There are several practical problems in implementing such a profit-sharing system. First, there can be arguments over the way contribution is divided between the two profit centers. Senior management might have to intervene to settle these disputes, which is costly, time consuming, and works against a basic reason for decentralization, namely, autonomy of business unit managers. Second, arbitrarily dividing up the profits between centers does not give valid information on the profitability of each segment of the organization. Third, since the contribution is not allocated until after the sale has been made, the manufacturing unit's contribution depends on the marketing unit's ability to sell and on the actual selling price. Manufacturing units may perceive this situation to be unfair.

Two sets of prices.   A few companies use two sets of transfer prices. The manufacturing unit's revenue is credited at the outside sales price, minus a percentage to cover marketing costs, and the buying unit is charged the variable standard costs (or, sometimes, the total standard cost). The difference is charged to a headquarters account and eliminated when the business unit statements are consolidated. This transfer pricing method is sometimes used when there are frequent conflicts between the buying and selling units that cannot be resolved by one of the other methods. Both the buying and selling units benefit under this method.

There are several disadvantages to the system of having two sets of transfer prices, however. The sum of the business unit profits is greater than overall company profits. Senior management must be aware of this situation in approving budgets for the business units and in subsequent evaluation of performance against these budgets. Also, this system creates an illusive feeling that business units are making money while, in fact, the overall company might be losing after taking account of the debits to headquarters. Further, this system might motivate business units to concentrate more on internal transfers (where they are assured of a good markup), at the expense of outside sales. Finally, there is additional bookkeeping involved in first debiting the headquarters account every time a transfer is made and then eliminating this account when business unit statements are consolidated.

The fact that the conflicts between the business units would be lessened under this system could be viewed as a weakness. Sometimes, it is better for headquarters to be aware of the conflicts arising out of transfer prices because such conflicts may signal problems in either the organizational structure or in other management systems. Under the two-sets-of-prices method, these conflicts are smoothed over, thereby not calling senior management attention to these problems.

Business Practice

Exhibit 5–1 summarizes the results of a survey made in 1978 by Richard F. Vancil of the transfer pricing practices of 239 divisionalized manufacturing companies.

In a survey of Fortune 150 companies in 1984, Price Waterhouse found that 84 percent of the companies used market prices, and 44 percent of the companies used cost-plus pricing (some companies used more than one transfer price method).[4]

---

[4] Robert C. Eccles, *The Transfer Price Problem* (Lexington, Mass.: Lexington Books, 1985), pp. 40–43.

EXHIBIT 5–1   Transfer Pricing Policies for Goods

| | Respondents Specifying the Method Used | | | |
Method Used	Number	Number Total	Percentage	Percentage Total
Variable cost:				
Variable standard	7	11	2.9%	4.6%
Variable actual	4		1.7	
Full cost:				
Full standard	30	61	12.5	25.5
Full actual	31		13.0	
Cost plus or negotiated:				
Profit on sales	7		2.9	
Profit on investment	7	93	2.9	38.9
Negotiation	53		22.2	
Full cost + markup	26		10.9	
Market price:				
Competitor's price	28		11.7	
Market price—list	41	74	17.2	31.0
Market price—bid	5		2.1	
Total	239*	239*	100.0	100.0

* Of the 249 companies reporting that they transfer goods between profit centers, 239 specified the transfer pricing policies.

Source: Richard F. Vancil, *Decentralization: Management Ambiguity by Design* (Homewood, Ill.: Dow Jones-Irwin, 1979), p. 180.

TRANSFER PRICING IN COST-TYPE CONTRACTS

A business unit that is working on a cost-type contract may purchase material or parts from another unit of the company. The question then arises about whether the cost of the purchased goods allowed under the contract is the selling unit's cost or a transfer price that includes a profit margin. It is to the company's benefit to use the transfer price, because the price to the customer is based on the costs of the final unit.

Federal regulations state that transfers from other business units, subsidiaries, or affiliates will be at cost, excluding profit, except under the following conditions:[5]

1. The transfer price is based on an established catalog or market price of commercial items sold in substantial quantities to the general public.
2. It is the result of adequate price competition and is the price at which an award was made to an affiliated organization after obtaining quotations on

---

[5] Federal Acquisition Regulations.

an equal basis from such organizations and from one or more outside sources that normally produce the item or its equivalent in significant quantities.

3. The price must not be in excess of the selling unit's current price to its most favored customer.

4. The transfer price must be adjusted, when appropriate, to reflect the quantities being procured and may be adjusted for the actual costs of any modifications required by the contract.

Cost Accounting Standard 414 requires a capital charge on the use of fixed assets as an element of cost. Consequently, even where the transfer is at cost, an element of profit is included.

Even where all of the requirements above are met, contracting officers may determine that a particular transfer price is unreasonable. If they so determine, however, they must support this position with appropriate facts.

PRICING CORPORATE SERVICES

In this section we describe some of the problems associated with charging business units for services furnished by corporate staff units. We exclude the cost of central service staff units that business units have no control over (e.g., central accounting, public relations, administration). As described in Chapter 4, if these costs are charged at all, they are allocated, and the allocations do not include a profit component. The allocations are not transfer prices. There remain two types of transfers:

1. For central services that the receiving unit must accept, but for which the amount of the service is at least partially controllable by the unit.

2. For central services over which the business unit has the discretion of using or not using.

Control over Amount of Service

Business units may be required to use company staffs for services, such as management information systems and research and development. In these situations, the business unit manager cannot control the *efficiency* with which these activities are performed; however, the business unit manager can control the *amount* of the service that it receives. There are three schools of thought about such services.

One school holds that a business unit should pay the *standard variable costs* of the discretionary services. If it pays less than this, it will be motivated to use more of the service than is economically justified. For example, if business unit managers were not required to pay at least the variable cost of reports prepared for them by the MIS department, they might request reports or special computer runs that were of little value to them. On the other hand, if business unit managers were required to pay more than the variable cost, they might not elect to use certain services that senior management thought was worthwhile from the company's viewpoint. This possibility is most likely when senior management is introducing a new service, such as a new project analysis program. The low price is analogous to the introductory price that companies sometimes use for new products.

A second school advocates a price equal to the standard variable cost plus a fair share of the standard fixed costs—that is, *the full cost* (but not more than the market price). It is argued that, if the business units do not believe the services are worth at least this amount, then there is something wrong with either the quality or the efficiency of the service unit. Full cost represents the company's long-run costs, and this is the amount that should be paid.

A third school advocates a price that is equivalent to the *market price,* or to standard full cost plus a profit margin. The market price would be used if available (e.g., the costs charged by a computer service bureau); if not, the price would be full cost plus a return on investment. The rationale for this position is that the capital employed by the service unit should earn a return just as much as the capital employed by manufacturing units. Also, the business units would incur the investment if they provided their own service.

Optional Use of Services

In some cases, management may decide that business units have the option of using, or not using, central service units. Business units may procure the service from outside, develop their own capability, or simply not use the service at all. This type of arrangement is most often found for such activities as information processing or internal consulting groups. These service centers are independent; they must stand on their own feet. If the services are not used by the business units, the scope of their activity will be contracted or they may even be eliminated entirely. In effect, management is delegating the responsibility for supporting these particular central services to the users.

In this situation, business unit managers control both the *amount and the efficiency* of the central services. Under these conditions, these central groups are profit centers. Their transfer prices should be based on the same considerations as those governing other transfer prices.

Simplicity of the Price Mechanism

The prices charged for corporate services will not accomplish their intended result unless the methods of calculating them are so sufficiently straightforward that business unit managers understand them. Computer experts are accustomed to dealing with complex equations, and the computer itself provides information on the use made of it on a second-by-second basis and at low cost. There is sometimes a tendency, therefore, to charge computer users on the basis of rules that are so complicated that the user cannot understand what the effect on costs would be if he or she decided to use the computer for a given application, or, alternatively, to discontinue a current application. Such rules are counterproductive.

ADMINISTRATION OF TRANSFER PRICES

We have so far discussed how to formulate a sound transfer pricing policy. In this section, we discuss how the selected policy should be implemented; specifically, the degree of negotiation allowed in setting the transfer prices, methods of resolving transfer pricing conflicts, and classification of products according to the appropriate method.

Negotiation

In most companies, business units negotiate transfer prices with each other—that is, transfer prices are not set by a central staff group. Perhaps the most important reason for this is the belief that one of the primary functions of line management is to establish selling prices and to arrive at satisfactory purchase prices. If control of pricing is left to the headquarters staff, line management's ability to affect profitability is reduced. Also, many transfer prices require a degree of subjective judgment. Consequently, a negotiated transfer price often is the result of compromises made by both buyer and seller. If headquarters establishes transfer prices, business unit managers can argue that their low profits are due to the arbitrariness of the transfer prices. Another reason for having the business units negotiate their prices is that they usually have the best information on markets and costs and, consequently, are best able to arrive at reasonable prices.

Example

Business Unit A has an opportunity to supply a large quantity of a certain product to an outside company at a price of $100 per unit. The raw material for this product would be supplied by Business Unit B. Unit B's normal transfer price for this material is $35 per unit, of which $10 is variable cost. Unit A's processing cost (excluding raw material) plus normal profit is $85, of which $50 is variable cost. Unit A's total cost plus normal profit, therefore, is $120; at this amount, the selling price of $100 is unattractive. Rejecting the contract would be dysfunctional for the company as a whole, because both business units have available capacity. The two units, therefore, would negotiate a lower price for the raw material, so both units would make a contribution to their profit.

If, instead of two business units within a single company, one company had an offer to sell raw material to another company that had a similar sales prospect, the two companies should negotiate in the same fashion. The fact that a transfer price was involved in the first example does not affect how reasonable managers should behave.[6]

Business units must know the ground rules within which these transfer price negotiations are to be conducted. In a few companies, headquarters inform business units that they are free to deal with each other or with outsiders as they see fit, subject only to the qualification that, if there is a tie, the business must be kept inside. If this is done and there are outside sources and outside markets, no further administrative procedures are required. The price is set in the outside marketplace and, if business units cannot agree on a price, they simply buy from or sell to outsiders. In many companies, however, business units are required to deal with one another; and, if they do not have the threat of doing business with competitors as a bargaining point in the negotiation process, headquarters staff must develop a set of rules that govern both pricing and sourcing of intracompany products.

Because line managers do not spend an undue amount of time on transfer price negotiations, these rules should be specific enough that skill in negotiations is not a significant factor in the determination of the transfer price. Without such rules, the most stubborn manager will negotiate the most favorable prices.

Arbitration and Conflict Resolution

No matter how specific the pricing rules are, there may be instances in which business units will not be able to agree on a price. For this reason, some procedure should be in place for arbitrating transfer price disputes. There can be widely different degrees of formality in transfer price arbitration. At one extreme, the responsibility for arbitrating disputes is assigned to a single executive—for example, the financial vice president or the executive vice president, who talks to business unit managers involved and then announces the price orally. The other extreme is to set up a committee. Usually such a committee will have three responsibilities; (1) to settle transfer price disputes; (2) to review sourcing changes; and (3) to change the transfer price rules where appropriate. The degree of formality employed depends on the extent and type of potential transfer price disputes. In any case, transfer price arbitration should be the responsibility of a high-level headquarters executive or group, since arbitration decisions can have an important effect on business unit profits.

---

[6] David Solomons, in *Divisional Performance: Measurement and Control* (Homewood, Ill.: Richard D. Irwin, 1968, chapter VI), discusses a similar example. He concludes that the transfer pricing system would be dysfunctional, because Division A would reject a contract that was in the best interest of the company. He does not mention the possibility of negotiation, and his conclusion is, therefore, incorrect.

Arbitration can be conducted in a number of ways. With a formal system, both parties submit a written case to the arbitrator. The arbitrator reviews both positions and decides on the price. In establishing a price, the assistance of other staff offices may be obtained. For example, the purchasing department might review the validity of a proposed competitive price quotation, or the industrial engineering department might review the appropriateness of a disputed standard labor cost. As indicated above, in less formal systems, the presentations may be largely oral.

It is important that relatively few disputes be submitted to arbitration. If a large number of disputes are arbitrated, this indicates that the rules are not specific enough, the rules are difficult to apply, or the business unit organization is illogical. In short, this is a symptom that something is wrong. Not only is arbitration time consuming to both line managers and headquarters executives but also arbitrated prices often satisfy neither the buyer nor the seller. In some companies, such an onus is involved in submitting a price dispute to arbitration that very few are ever submitted. If, as a consequence, legitimate grievances do not surface, the results are undesirable. Preventing disputes from being submitted to arbitration will tend to hide the fact that there are problems with the transfer price system.

Irrespective of the degree of formality of the arbitration, the type of conflict resolution process that is used will also influence the effectiveness of a transfer pricing system. Lawrence and Lorsch pointed out four ways to resolve conflicts: forcing, smoothing, bargaining, and problem solving.[7] The conflict resolution mechanisms range from conflict avoidance through forcing and smoothing to conflict resolution through bargaining and problem solving.

Product Classification

The extent and formality of the sourcing and transfer pricing rules will depend to a great extent on the amount of intracompany transfers and the availability of markets and market prices. The greater the amount of intracompany transfers, and the less the availability of market prices, the more formal and specific the rules must be. If market prices are readily available, sourcing can be controlled by having headquarters review make-or-buy decisions that exceed a specified amount.

Some companies divide products into two main classes:

Class I includes all products for which senior management wishes to control the sourcing. These would normally be the large-volume products, products where no outside source exists, and products where for quality or secrecy reasons senior management wishes to maintain control over manufacturing.

Class II are all other products. In general, these are products that can be produced outside the company without any significant disruption to present operations. These are products of relatively small volume, produced with general-purpose equipment. Class II products are transferred at market prices.

---

[7] Paul R. Lawrence, and Jay W. Lorsch, *Organization and Environment* (Homewood, Ill.: Richard D. Irwin, 1967), pp. 73–78.

The sourcing of Class I products can be changed only with permission of central management. The sourcing of Class II products is determined by the business units involved. Both the buying and selling units are free to deal either inside or outside the company.

Under this arrangement, management can concentrate on the sourcing and pricing of a relatively small number of high-volume products. Rules for transfer prices would be established, using the different methods described in the preceding section as appropriate.

SUMMARY

The delegation of significant amounts of authority is dependent upon the ability to delegate responsibility for profits. Profit responsibility cannot be safely delegated unless two conditions exist:

1. The delegatee has all of the relevant information to make optimum profit decisions.
2. The delegatee's performance is measured on how well he or she has made cost/revenue trade-offs.

Where segments of a company share responsibility for product development, manufacturing, and marketing, a transfer price system is required if these segments are to be delegated profit responsibility. This transfer price system must result in the two conditions described above. In complex organizations it can be a difficult problem to devise a transfer price system that assures the necessary knowledge and motivation for optimum decision making.

There are probably few instances in complex organizations where there is a completely satisfactory transfer price system. As with many management control design choices, it is necessary to choose the best of perhaps several less than perfect courses of action. The important thing is to be aware of the areas of imperfections and to be sure that administrative procedures are employed to avoid suboptimum decisions.

Appendix

Some Theoretical Considerations

There is a considerable body of literature on theoretical transfer pricing models. Few, if any, of these models are used in actual business situations, however, and, for reasons explained below, it is unlikely that they ever will be widely used. Consequently, we have not referred to these models in the body of this chapter. Although they are not directly applicable to real business situations, they are useful in conceptualizing transfer price systems. The purpose of this appendix is to give a brief description of some of these models. Transfer pricing models may be divided into three types: (1) models based on classical economic theory, (2) models based on linear programming, and (3) models based on the Shapley value.

Economic Models

The classic economic model was first described by Jack Hirschleifer in the 1956 article referred to in footnote 2. Professor Hirschleifer developed a series of marginal revenue, marginal cost, and demand curves for the transfer of an intermediate product from one business unit to another. He used these curves to establish transfer prices, under various sets of economic assumptions, that would optimize the total profit of the two business units. Using the transfer prices thus developed, the two units would produce the maximum total profit by optimizing their unit profits.

A difficulty with the Hirschleifer model is that it can be used only when a specified set of conditions exist: It must be possible to estimate the demand curve for the intermediate product; the assumed conditions must remain stable; there can be no alternative uses for the facilities used to make the intermediate product; and the model is applicable only to the situation in which the selling unit makes a single intermediate product, which it transfers to a single buying unit, which uses that intermediate product in a single final product. Such conditions exist rarely, if at all, in the real world.

This model (and also the other models) assumes that transfer prices will be imposed by the central staff, and it denies the importance of negotiation among business units. Business unit managers usually have better information than is available to the central staff. Indeed, if the central staff could determine the optimum production pattern, the question arises on why this pattern is not imposed directly, rather than attempting to arrive at it indirectly via the transfer price mechanism.

Linear Programming Model

The linear programming model is based on an opportunity cost approach. This model also incorporates capacity constraints. The model calculates an optimum companywide production pattern; and, using this pattern, it calculates a set of values that impute the profit contributions of each of the scarce resources. These are termed *shadow prices,* and one process of calculating them is called "obtaining the dual solution" to the linear program. If the variable costs of the intermediate products are added to their shadow prices, a set of transfer prices results that should motivate business units to produce according to the optimum production pattern for the entire company. This is so because, if these transfer prices are used, each business unit will optimize its profits only by producing in accordance with the patterns developed through the linear program.

If reliable shadow prices could be calculated, this model would be useful in arriving at transfer prices. However, to make the model manageable, even on a computer, many simplifying assumptions must be incorporated in it. It is assumed that the demand curve is known, that it is static, that the cost function is linear, and that alternative uses of production facilities and their profitability can be estimated in advance. As is the case with the economic model, these conditions rarely exist in the real world.

Shapley Value

The theoretical literature has a few articles advocating the use of a number termed the *Shapley value* as the transfer price.[8] The Shapley value was developed in 1953 by L. S. Shapley as a method of dividing the profits of a coalition of companies or individuals among its individual members in proportion to the contribution that each of them made. This is a problem that arises in the theory of games, and the Shapley value generally is considered to provide an equitable solution to that problem.

Whether the same technique is applicable to the transfer price problem is a highly debatable issue. Although the method has been described in the literature for a number of years, few practical applications have been reported. In part, the reason for its lack of acceptance is that the computation is lengthy unless there are only a few products involved in the transfer. In part, the reason is that many of those who have studied the Shapley method do not believe that its underlying assumptions are valid for the transfer pricing problem.

SUGGESTED ADDITIONAL READINGS

Cassel, Herbert S., and Vincent F. McCormack. "The Transfer Price Dilemma—And a Dual Price Solution." *Journal of Accounting,* September 1987.

Eccles, Robert G. *The Transfer Price Problem.* Lexington, Mass.: Lexington Books, 1985.

Govindarajan, Vijay. "Effective Management of Interrelationships across Business Units." Working paper, the Amos Tuck School of Business Administration, Dartmouth College, 1990.

Govindarajan, Vijay, and Robert N. Anthony. "How Firms Use Cost Data in Pricing Decisions." *Management Accounting,* July 1983, pp. 30–34.

Govindarajan, Vijay, and Bala Ramamurthy. "Transfer Pricing Policies in Indian Companies: A Survey." *The Chartered Accountant,* November 1983, pp. 296–301.

Gupta, Anil K., and Vijay Govindarajan. "Resource Sharing among SBUs: Strategic Antecedents and Administrative Implications." *Academy of Management Journal* 29, 4 (1986), pp. 695–714.

Kovac, Edward J., and Henry P. Troy. "Getting Transfer Prices Right: What Bellcore Did." *Harvard Business Review,* September–October 1989, pp. 148–54.

Madison, Roland L. "Responsibility Accounting and Transfer Pricing: Approach with Caution." *Management Accounting,* January 1979.

Mailahdt, Peter. "An Alternative to Transfer Pricing." *Business Horizons,* October 1975.

Shillinglaw, Gordon. *Managerial Cost Accounting.* 5th ed. Homewood, Ill.: Richard D. Irwin, 1982, chap. 26.

Solomons, David. *Divisional Performance: Measurement and Control.* Homewood, Ill.: Richard D. Irwin, 1968, chap. VI.

Watson, David J. H., and John L. Baumier. "Transfer Pricing: A Behavioral Context." *Accounting Review,* July 1985, pp. 466–74.

---

[8] For a description and bibliography, see Daniel L. Jensen, "A Class of Mutually Satisfactory Allocations," *The Accounting Review,* October 1977, pp. 842–56.

Case 5-1

Transfer Pricing Problems*

1. Division A of Lambda Company manufactures Product X, which is sold to Division B as a component of Product Y. Product Y is sold to Division C, which uses it as a component in Product Z. Product Z is sold to customers outside of the company. The intracompany pricing rule is that products are transferred between divisions at standard cost plus a 10 percent return on inventories and fixed assets. From the information provided below, calculate the transfer price for Products X and Y and the standard cost of Product Z.

Standard Cost per Unit	Product X	Product Y	Product Z
Material purchased outside	$2.00	$3.00	$1.00
Direct labor	1.00	1.00	2.00
Variable overhead	1.00	1.00	2.00
Fixed overhead per unit	3.00	4.00	1.00
Standard volume	10,000	10,000	10,000
Inventories (average)	$70,000	$15,000	$30,000
Fixed assets (net)	30,000	45,000	16,000

2. Assume the same facts as stated in Problem **1,** except that the transfer price rule is as follows: Goods are transferred among divisions at the standard variable cost per unit transferred plus a monthly charge. This charge is equal to the fixed costs assigned to the product plus a 10 percent return on the average inventories and fixed assets assignable to the product. Calculate the transfer price for Products X and Y and calculate the unit standard cost for Products Y and Z.

3. The present selling price of Product Z is $28.00. Listed below is a series of possible price reductions by competition and the probable impact of these reductions on the volume of sales if Division C does not also reduce its price.

Possible competitive price	$27.00	$26.00	$25.00	$23.00	$22.00
Sales volume if price of Product Z is maintained at $28.00	9,000	7,000	5,000	2,000	0
Sales volume if price of Product Z is reduced to competitive levels	10,000	10,000	10,000	10,000	10,000

Required

(a) With transfer prices calculated in Problem **1,** is Division C better advised to maintain its price at $28.00 or to follow competition in each of the instances above?

(b) With the transfer prices calculated in Problem **2,** is Division C better advised to maintain its present price of $28.00 or to follow competition in each of the instances above?

---

* This case was prepared by John Dearden, Harvard Business School.

(c) Which decisions are to the best economic interests of the company, other things being equal?

(d) Using the transfer prices calculated in problem **1**, is the manager of Division C making a decision contrary to the overall interests of the company? If so, what is the opportunity loss to the company in each of the competitive pricing actions described above?

4. Division C is interested in increasing the sales of Product Z. A survey is made and sales increases resulting from increases in television advertising are estimated. The results of this survey are provided below. (Note that this particular type of advertising can be purchased only in units of $100,000).

(in thousands)					
Advertising expenditures	$100	$200	$300	$400	$500
Additional volume resulting from additional advertising	10	19	27	34	40

Required

(a) As manager of Division C, how much television advertising would you use if you purchased Product Y at the transfer price calculated in Problem **1**?

(b) How much television advertising would you use if you purchased Product Y for the transfer price calculated in Problem **2**?

(c) Which is correct from the overall company viewpoint?

(d) How much would the company lose in sub-optimum profits from using the first transfer price?

5. Two of the divisions of the Chambers Corporation are the Intermediate Division and the Final Division. The Intermediate Division produces three products; A, B, and C. Normally these products are sold both to outside customers and to the Final Division. The Final Division uses Products A, B, and C in manufacturing Products X,

Y, and Z, respectively. In recent weeks, the supply of Products A, B, and C has tightened to such an extent that the Final Division has been operating considerably below capacity, because of the lack of these products. Consequently, the Intermediate Division has been told to sell all its products to the Final Division. The financial facts about these products are as follows:

Intermediate Division

	Product A	Product B	Product C
Transfer price	$ 10.00	$ 10.00	$ 15.00
Variable manufacturing cost	3.00	6.00	5.00
Contribution per unit..	$ 7.00	$ 4.00	$ 10.00
Fixed costs (total)	$50,000	$100,000	$75,000

The Intermediate Division has a monthly capacity of 50,000 units. The processing constraints are such that capacity production can be obtained only by producing at least 10,000 units of each product. The remaining capacity can be used to produce 20,000 units of any combination of the three products. The Intermediate Division cannot exceed the capacity of 50,000 units.

Final Division

	Product X	Product Y	Product Z
Selling price	$28.00	$30.00	$30.00
Variable cost:			
Inside purchases	10.00	10.00	15.00
Other variable costs	5.00	5.00	8.00
Total variable cost	$15.00	$15.00	$23.00
Contribution per unit	$13.00	$15.00	$7.00
Fixed costs (total)	$100,000	$100,000	$200,000

The Final Division has sufficient capacity to produce about 40 percent more than it is now producing, because the availability of Products A, B, and C is limiting production. Also, the Final Division can sell all the products that it can produce at the prices indicated above.

Required

(a) If you were the manager of the Intermediate Division, what products would you sell to the Final Division? What is the amount of profit that you would earn on these sales?

(b) If you were the manager of the Final Division, what products would you order from the Intermediate Division, assuming that the Intermediate Division must sell all its production to you? What profits would you earn?

(c) What production pattern optimizes total company profit? How does this affect the profits of the Intermediate Division? If you were the executive vice president of Chambers and prescribed this optimum pattern, what, if anything, would you do about the distribution of profits between the two divisions?

6. How, if at all, would your answers to Problem **5** change if there were no outside markets for Products A, B, or C?

7. The Chambers Company has determined that capacity can be increased in excess of 50,000 units, but these increases require an out-of-pocket cost penalty. These penalties are as follows:

Volume in Excess of Present Capacity (unit)	Cost Penalty		
	Product A	Product B	Product C
1,000	$10,000	$12,000	$10,000
2,000	25,000	24,000	20,000
3,000	50,000	50,000	35,000
4,000	80,000	80,000	50,000

Each of these increases is independent—that is, increases in the production of Product A do not affect the costs of increasing the production of Product B. Changes can be made only in quantities of 100 units, with a maximum increase of 4,000 units for each product. All other conditions are as stated in Problem **5.**

Required

(a) What would be the Intermediate Division's production pattern, assuming that it can charge all penalty costs to the Final Division?

(b) The Final Division's optimum production pattern, assuming that it is required to accept the penalty costs?

(c) The optimum Company production pattern?

8. How would your answer to Problem **7** differ if the Intermediate Division had no outside markets for Products A, B, and C?

9.[1] Division A of Kappa Company is the only source of supply for an intermediate product that is converted by Division B into a salable final product. A substantial part of A's costs are fixed. For any output up to 1,000 units a day, its total costs are $500 a day. Total costs increase by $100 a day for every additional thousand units made. Division A judges that its own results will be optimized if it sets its price at $0.40 a unit, and it acts accordingly.

Division B incurs additional costs in converting the intermediate product supplied by A into a finished product. These costs are $1,250 for any output up to 1,000 units, and $250 per thousand for outputs in excess of 1,000. On the revenue side, B can increase its revenue only by spending more on sales promotion and by reducing selling prices. Its sales forecast would look like the table on page 251.

Looking at the situation from B's point of view, we can compare its costs and revenues at various levels of output while considering both its

---

[1] Reproduced with permission from David Solomons, *Divisional Performance: Measurement and Control* (Homewood, Ill.: Richard D. Irwin, 1965).

Sales Forecast

Sales (units)	Revenue Net of Selling Costs $ (per thousand units)
1,000	1,750
2,000	1,325
3,000	1,100
4,000	925
5,000	800
6,000	666

own processing costs and what it is charged by A for the intermediates that A will supply. The relevant information is set out in Exhibit 1.

The exhibit makes it clear that the most profitable policy for Division B, in the circumstances, is to set its output at either 2,000 or 3,000 units a day and to accept a profit of $350 a day. If its output is more than 3,000 or less than 2,000 it will make even less profit.

With Division B taking 3,000 units a day from it, Division A's revenue, at $0.40 a unit, is $1,200, and its total costs are $700. Therefore, A's separate profit is $500 a day. Adding this to B's profit of $350 a day, we get an aggregate profit for the corporation of $850 a day.

Assume now that the company abandons its divisionalized structure and, instead of having two profit centers, A and B, it combines them into a single profit center, with responsibility for both production of the intermediate and processing it to completion. Let us further suppose that, apart from this change of structure, all the other conditions previously present continue to apply. Then the market conditions that formerly faced Division B now confront the single profit center. Its costs are equal to the combined costs of A and B, eliminating, of course, the charge previously made by A to B for the supply of intermediates. The schedule of costs and revenues for the single profit center will then appear as shown in Exhibit 2.

Exhibit 2 shows that the single profit center will operate more profitably than the two divisions together formerly did. By making and selling 4,000 units a day, it can earn a profit of $900 or $50 a day in excess of the best result achieved by the combined activities of Divisions A and B.

The company is seen to have been paying a price for the luxury of divisionalization. By suboptimizing (i.e., by seeking maximum profits for themselves as separate entities), the divisions have caused the corporation to less than optimize its profits as a whole. The reason was, of course, that Division B reacted to the transfer price of $0.40 a unit by restricting both its demand for the intermediate and its own output of the finished

EXHIBIT 1

Division B's Output (units) (1)	B's Own Processing Costs (2) $	A's Charge to B for Intermediates @ $0.40 a Unit (3) $	B's Total Costs (4) = (2) + (3) $	B's Revenue (net of selling costs) per 1,000 Units (5) $	B's Total Revenue (6) = (1) × (5) $	B's Profit (loss) (7) = (6) − (4) $
1,000	1,250	400	1,650	1,750	1,750	100
2,000	1,500	800	2,300	1,325	2,650	350
3,000	1,750	1,200	2,950	1,100	3,300	350
4,000	2,000	1,600	3,600	925	3,700	100
5,000	2,250	2,000	4,250	800	4,000	(250)
6,000	2,500	2,400	4,900	666	4,000	(900)

EXHIBIT 2

Output (units) (1)	Cost of Producing Intermediates (2) $	Cost of Processing to Completion (3) $	Total Cost (4) = (2) + (3) $	Total Revenue* (5) $	Profit (6) = (5) − (4) $
1,000	500	1,250	1,750	1,750	—
2,000	600	1,500	2,100	2,650	550
3,000	700	1,750	2,450	3,300	850
4,000	800	2,000	2,800	3,700	900
5,000	900	2,250	3,150	4,000	850
6,000	1,000	2,500	3,500	4,000	500

* Taken from column (6) of Exhibit 1.

product. By making for itself the best of a bad job, it created an unsatisfactory situation for the company. But who can blame it? Assuming that the instructions to its general manager were to maximize the division's separate profit, the manager did just that, given the conditions confronting him or her. The responsibility for the final result really lay with Division A. Yet it is not fair to blame that division, either, for it, too, was only carrying out instructions in seeking to maximize its own profit; and a transfer price of $0.40, while it leads to a less than optimal result for the corporation, does maximize's A's own profit.

One further feature of this illustration is worth noting. So far as its own profit was concerned, it was a matter of indifference to Division B whether it sold 2,000 or 3,000 units. We assumed that it decided to sell 3,000. If it had chosen to sell only 2,000, its own profit would have been unaffected, while A's profit would have been diminished by $300. In a situation like this, negotiations about the price between A and B would probably have prevented this further damage to the corporation resulting from suboptimization. But it is unlikely that the divisions, left to themselves, would arrive at an optimal solution from the corporate point of view.

Required

1. What is the lowest price that Division A should be willing to accept from Division B for 4,000 units?
2. What is the highest price at which Division B should be willing to buy 4,000 units from Division A?
3. If Division A does sell 4,000 units to Division B, what should the transfer price be?
4. Under what circumstances, if any, would the transfer price system be dysfunctional?

Case 5–2

Birch Paper Company*

"If I were to price these boxes any lower than $480 a thousand," said James Brunner, manager of Birch Paper Company's Thompson Division, "I'd be countermanding my order of last month for our salesmen to stop shaving their bids and to bid full-cost quotations. I've been trying for weeks to improve the quality of our business, and, if I turn around now and accept this job at $430 or $450 or something less than $480, I'll be tearing down this program I've been working so hard to build up. The division can't very well show a profit by putting in bids that don't even cover a fair share of overhead costs, let alone give us a profit."

Birch Paper Company was a medium-sized, partly integrated paper company, producing white and kraft papers and paperboard. A portion of its paperboard output was converted into corrugated boxes by the Thompson Division, which also printed and colored the outside surface of the boxes. Including Thompson, the company had four producing divisions and a timberland division, which supplied part of the company's pulp requirements.

For several years, each division had been judged independently on the basis of its profit and return on investment. Top management had been working to gain effective results from a policy of decentralizing responsibility and authority for all decisions except those relating to overall company policy. The company's top officials believed that in the past few years the concept of decentralization had been successfully applied and that the company's profits and competitive position had definitely improved.

The Northern Division had designed a special display box for one of its papers in conjunction with the Thompson Division, which was equipped to make the box. Thompson's staff for package design and development spent several months perfecting the design, production methods, and materials to be used. Because of the unusual color and shape, these were far from standard. According to an agreement between the two divisions, the Thompson Division was reimbursed by the Northern Division for the cost of its design and development work.

When all the specifications were prepared, the Northern Division asked for bids on the box from the Thompson Division and from two outside companies. Each division manager was normally free to buy from whatever supplier he wished; and, even on sales within the company, divisions were expected to meet the going market price if they wanted the business.

During this period, the profit margins of such converters as the Thompson Division were being squeezed. Thompson, as did many other similar converters, bought its paperboard, and its function was to print, cut, and shape it into boxes. Though it bought most of its materials from other Birch divisions, most of Thompson's sales were made to outside customers. If Thompson got the order from Northern, it probably would buy its linerboard and corrugating medium from the Southern Division of Birch. The walls of a

* This case was prepared by William Rotch under the supervision of Neil Harlan, Harvard Business School.
Copyright © by the President and Fellows of Harvard College.
Harvard Business School case 158–001.

corrugated box consist of outside and inside sheets of linerboard sandwiching the fluted corrugating medium. About 70 percent of Thompson's out-of-pocket cost of $400 for the order represented the cost of linerboard and corrugating medium. Though Southern had been running below capacity and had excess inventory, it quoted the market price, which had not noticeably weakened as a result of the oversupply. Its out-of-pocket costs on both liner and corrugating medium were about 60 percent of the selling price.

The Northern Division received bids on the boxes of $480 a thousand from the Thompson Division, $430 a thousand from West Paper Company, and $432 a thousand from Eire Papers, Ltd. Eire Papers offered to buy from Birch the outside linerboard with the special printing already on it, but would supply its own inside liner and corrugating medium. The outside liner would be supplied by the Southern Division at a price equivalent of $90 a thousand boxes, and it would be printed for $30 a thousand by the Thompson Division. Of the $30, about $25 would be out-of-pocket costs.

Since this situation appeared to be a little unusual, William Kenton, manager of the Northern Division, discussed the wide discrepancy of bids with Birch's commercial vice president. He told the vice president: "We sell in a very competitive market, where higher costs cannot be passed on. How can we be expected to show a decent profit and return on investment if we have to buy our supplies at more than 10 percent over the going market?"

Knowing that Mr. Brunner had on occasion in the past few months been unable to operate the Thompson Division at capacity, it seemed odd to the vice president that Mr. Brunner would add the full 20 percent overhead and profit charge to his out-of-pocket costs. When asked about this, Mr. Brunner's answer was the statement that appears at the beginning of the case. He went on to say that having done the developmental work on the box, and having received no profit on that, he felt entitled to a good markup on the production of the box itself.

The vice president explored further the cost structures of the various divisions. He remembered a comment that the controller had made at a meeting the week before to the effect that costs which were variable for one division could be largely fixed for the company as a whole. He knew that in the absence of specific orders from top management Mr. Kenton would accept the lowest bid, which was that of the West Paper Company for $430. However, it would be possible for top management to order the acceptance of another bid if the situation warranted such action. And though the volume represented by the transactions in question was less than 5 percent of the volume of any of the divisions involved, other transactions could conceivably raise similar problems later.

QUESTIONS

1. Which bid should Northern Division accept that is in the best interests of Birch Paper Company?
2. Should Mr. Kenton accept this bid? Why or why not?
3. Should the vice president of Birch Paper Company take any action?
4. In the controversy described, how, if at all, is the transfer price system dysfunctional? Does this problem call for some change, or changes, in the transfer pricing policy of the overall firm? If so, what *specific* changes do you suggest?

Case 5–3

General Appliance Corporation*

Organization

The General Appliance Corporation was an integrated manufacturer of all types of home appliances. As shown in Exhibit 1, the company had a decentralized, divisional organization consisting of four product divisions, four manufacturing divisions, and six staff offices. Each division and staff office was headed by a vice president. The staff offices had functional authority over their counterparts in the divisions, but they had no direct line authority over the divisional general managers. The company's organization manual stated: "All divisional personnel are responsible to the division manager. Except in functional areas specifically delegated, staff personnel have no line authority in a division."

The product divisions designed, engineered, assembled, and sold various home appliances. They manufactured very few component parts; rather, they assembled the appliances from parts purchased either from the manufacturing divisions or from outside vendors. The manufacturing divisions made approximately 75 percent of their sales to the product divisions. Parts made by the manufacturing divisions were generally designed by the product divisions; the manufacturing divisions merely produced the parts to specifications provided to them. Although all the manufacturing divisions had engineering departments, these departments did only about 20 percent of the total company engineering.

Transfer Prices

The divisions were expected to deal with one another as though they were independent companies. Parts were to be transferred at prices arrived at by negotiation between the divisions. These prices generally were based on the actual prices paid to outside suppliers for the same or comparable parts. These outside prices were adjusted to reflect differences in design of the outside part from that of the inside part. Also, if the outside price was based on purchases made at an earlier date, it was adjusted for changes in the general price level since that date. In general, the divisions established prices by negotiation among themselves; but if the divisions could not agree on a price, they could submit the dispute to the finance staff for arbitration.

Source Determination

Although the divisions were instructed to deal with one another as independent companies, in practice this was not always feasible, because a product division did not have the power to decide whether to buy from within the company or from outside. Once a manufacturing division began to produce a part, the only way the product division buying this part could change to an outside supplier was to obtain permission of the manufacturing division or, in case of disagreement, appeal to

* This case was prepared by John Dearden and R. N. Anthony, Harvard Business School. Copyright © by the President and Fellows of Harvard College. Harvard Business School case 160–003.

EXHIBIT 1   Organization Chart

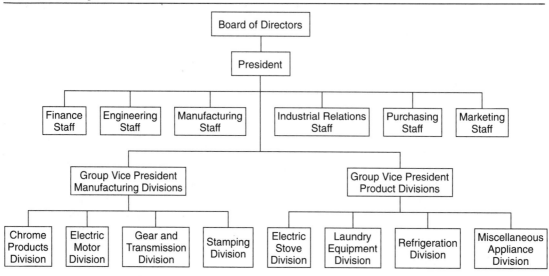

the purchasing staff. The purchasing staff had the authority to settle disputes between the product and manufacturing divisions with respect to whether a manufacturing division should continue to produce a part or whether the product division could buy outside. In nearly every case of dispute, the purchasing staff had decided that the part would continue to be manufactured within the company. When the manufacturing divisions were instructed to continue producing a part, they had to hold the price of the part at the level at which the product division could purchase it from the outside vendor.

In the case of new parts, a product division had the authority to decide on the source of supply. Even for new parts, however, a manufacturing division could appeal to the purchasing staff to reverse the decision if a product division planned to purchase a part from an outside vendor.

Stove Top Problem

The Chrome Products Division sold to the Electric Stove Division a chrome-plated unit that

fitted on top of the stove; the unit had to be resistant to corrosion and stain from spilled food. It was also essential that the unit remain bright and new-looking. The Chrome Products Division had been producing this unit since January 1, 1986; prior to that time, it had been produced by an outside vendor.

The unit in question was produced from a steel stamping. Until June 1987, the stamping was processed as follows:

Operations	Processes
1	Machine buffing
2	Nickel plating
3	Machine buffing
4	Chrome plating
5	Machine buffing

About the middle of 1986, the president of General Appliance Corporation became concerned over complaints from customers and dealers about the quality of the company's products.

A customer survey appeared to indicate quite definitely that in the previous year the company's reputation as a producer of quality products had deteriorated. Although this deterioration was believed to have been caused principally by the poor performance of a new electric motor, which was soon corrected, the president had come to the conclusion that the overall quality of the company's products had been decreasing for the past several years. Furthermore, he believed that it was essential for the company to reestablish itself as a leader in the production of quality products. Accordingly, early in 1987 he called in the manufacturing vice president (i.e., the director of the manufacturing staff office) and told him that for the next six months his most important job was to bring the quality of all products up to a satisfactory level.

In the course of carrying out this assignment, the manufacturing vice president decided that the appearance of the chrome-plated stove top was unsatisfactory. Until now, the bases for rejection or acceptance of this part by the quality control section of the Chrome Products Division were a corrosion test and an appearance test; appearance was largely subjective and, in the final analysis, dependent on the judgment of the quality control person. In order to make the test more objective, three tops were selected and set up as standards for the minimum acceptable quality. Because better than average units were selected, rejects increased to over 80 percent. Personnel from the Chrome Products Division and the manufacturing staff jointly studied the manufacturing process to find a way of making the stove tops conform to the new quality standards. They added copper plating and buffing operations at the beginning of the process, and a hand-buffing operation at the end of the manufacturing cycle. The total cost of these added operations was 80 cents a unit. As soon as the new operations were put into effect in June 1987, the rejection rate for poor quality declined to less than 1 percent.

In July 1987, the Chrome Products Division proposed to increase the price of the stove top by 90 cents; 80 cents represented the cost of the added operations, and 10 cents was the profit markup on the added costs. The current price, before the proposed increase, was $10 a unit. This price had been developed as shown below.

Development of Price

Price charged by an outside producer (12/31/85)	$ 9.00
Design changes since 12/31/85	0.50
Changes in raw materials and labor prices since 12/31/85	0.50
Price as of 6/30/87	$10.00

The Electric Stove Division objected to the proposed price increase, and after three weeks of fruitless negotiations it was decided that the dispute should be submitted to the finance staff for arbitration. The positions of the parties to the dispute are summarized in the following sections.

Chrome Products Division

In a letter to the vice president for finance, the general manager of the Chrome Products Division stated that he believed he was entitled to the increased price because:

1. He had been required by the manufacturing staff to add operations at a cost of 80 cents a unit.
2. These operations resulted in improved quality that could benefit only the Electric Stove Division.
3. The present price of $10.00 was based on old quality standards. Had the outside supplier been required to meet these new standards, the price would have been 90 cents higher.

Electric Stove Division

The general manager of the Electric Stove Division, in appealing the price increase, based his position on the following arguments.

1. There had been no change in engineering specifications. The only change that had

taken place was in what was purported to be "acceptable appearance." This was a subjective matter that could not be measured with any degree of precision. Further, both the particular case and the possible effects of establishing a precedent were objectionable. "If we were to pay for any change in quality standards, not accompanied by a change in engineering specification, we would be opening up a Pandora's box. Every division would request higher prices based on giving us better quality based on some subjective standard. Every request by this division to a manufacturing division to improve quality would be accompanied by a price increase, even though we were requesting only that the quality be brought up to competitive levels."

2. The Electric Stove Division had not requested that quality be improved. In fact, the division had not even been consulted on the change. Thus, the division should not be responsible for paying for a so-called improvement that it neither requested nor approved.

3. Whether there was any improvement in quality from the customer's viewpoint was doubtful, although to the highly trained eye of the quality control personnel there may have been an improvement. The customer would not notice a significant difference between the appearance of the part before and after the change in quality standards.

4. Even if there were an improvement in quality perceptible to the consumer, it was not worth 90 cents. By adding 90 cents to the cost of the stove, features could be added that would be far more marketable than the quality improvement.

5. Any improvement in quality only brought the part up to the quality level that the former outside producer had provided. The cost of the improved quality, therefore, was included in the $10.00 price.

Finance Staff Review

The finance staff reviewed the dispute. In the course of this review, the engineering department of the manufacturing staff was asked to review the added operations and comment on the acceptability of the proposed cost increases. The quality control department of the manufacturing staff was asked to verify whether quality was actually better as the result of the added operations and whether the new units were of higher quality than the units purchased from the outside vendor 18 months ago. The engineering department stated that the proposed costs were reasonable and represented efficient processing. The quality control department slated that the quality was improved and that the new parts were of superior quality to the parts previously purchased from outside sources.

Thermostatic Control Problem

One of the plants of the Electric Motor Division produced thermostatic control units. The Laundry Equipment Division bought all its requirements for thermostatic control units (about 100,000 a year) from the Electric Motor Division. The Refrigeration Division used a similar unit, and until 1985 it had purchased all its requirements (20,000 a year) from an outside supplier, the Monson Controls Corporation. In 1985, at the request of the Electric Motor Division, the Refrigeration Division purchased 25 percent of its requirements from the Electric Motor Division. In 1986, this percentage was increased to 50 percent, and in 1987 to 75 percent. In July 1987, the Refrigeration Division informed the Monson Controls Corporation that beginning January 1, 1988, it would buy all its thermostatic control units from the Electric Motor Division. The Refrigeration Division made these source changes as a result of Electric Motor Division requests, which were, it said, "in the best interests of the company." The units made outside and inside were comparable in quality, and the price paid to the Electric Motor Division was the same as the price paid to the Monson Controls Corporation. The Laundry Division also paid this same price to the Electric Motor Division.

In 1984, the demand for this kind of thermostatic control unit was high in relation to the industry's production capacity. Between 1985 and 1987, several appliance companies, including the General Appliance Corporation, built or expanded their own facilities to produce this unit, so that by the middle of 1987 the production capacity of the independent companies considerably exceeded the demand. One of the results of this situation was a declining price level. Prices of the Monson Controls Corporation had been as follows:

1984	$3.00
1985	2.70
1986	2.50
1987 (January–June)	2.40

As a result of these price reductions, which the Electric Motor Division had met, the profits of the Electric Motor Division on this product had dropped from a before-tax profit of 15 percent on its investment in 1984 to nearly zero in 1987.

In August 1987, after being told it could no longer supply the Refrigeration Division, the Monson Controls Corporation reduced its price to the Refrigeration Division by 25 cents, retroactive to July 1. The price reduction was not reflected immediately in the intracompany price, because the three divisions involved had agreed to use $2.40 for the entire year.

In October 1987, the Electric Motor Division and the Refrigeration Division were negotiating 1988 prices. The Refrigeration Division proposed a price of $2.15, the price paid to the Monson Controls Corporation. The Electric Motor Division, however, refused to reduce its prices below $2.40 to either the Refrigeration Division or the Laundry Equipment Division. After several weeks of negotiations, the disagreement was submitted to the finance staff for settlement.

Electric Motor Division

The Electric Motor Division based its refusal to accept the last price reduction of the Monson Controls Corporation on the premise that it was made as a last, desperate effort to continue supplying General Appliance Corporation with this part. (Monson Controls Corporation continued to supply General Appliance Corporation with other products, although this control unit had been a major item.) As support for this premise, the Electric Motor Division indicated that at the lower price it would lose money. Since it was as efficient as the Monson Controls Corporation, it concluded that Monson must also be losing money. The price was, therefore, a distress price and not a valid basis for determining an internal price. To support its case further, the Electric Motor Division pointed out the downward trend in the price of this part as evidence of distress pricing practices growing out of the excess capacity in the industry.

The general manager of Electric Motor Division stated that it was going to take all his ability and ingenuity to make a profit even at the $2.40 price. At $2.15, he could never be in a profit position; and if forced to accept a price of $2.15, he would immediately make plans to close the plant and let outside suppliers furnish all the thermostatic control units.

Laundry Equipment Division

The Laundry Equipment Division based its case for a $2.15 price on the intracompany pricing rules that required products to be transferred between divisions at competitive prices. The general manager pointed out that his annual volume was 100,000 units a year, compared to a total of only 20,000 for the Refrigeration Division. He believed that with his higher volume he could probably obtain an even more favorable price if he were to procure his requirements from outside the corporation.

Refrigeration Division

The Refrigeration Division based its case on the fact that the division not only could, but did, buy the thermostatic control unit from a reliable outside supplier for $2.15. The division was sure that the Monson Controls Corporation had capacity to produce all its requirements and would be happy to do so for $2.15 a unit. Since patronage had been transferred to the Electric Motor Division only as a favor and to benefit the company as a whole, the Refrigeration Division believed it was unjust to make it pay a higher price than it would have paid if the division had not allowed the business to be taken inside the company.

As further evidence to support its case, the Refrigeration Division pointed to an agreement made with the Electric Motor Division at the time it had agreed to purchase all its requirements of the thermostatic control unit from that division. This agreement read, in part: "In the event of a major pricing disparity, it is agreed that further model requirements will be competitively sourced [i.e., sourced to the lowest bidder]."

The Refrigeration Division stated that in light of the major pricing disparity it should be allowed to request quotations from outside suppliers and place the business outside should such a supplier bid lower than the Electric Motor Division.

Finance Staff Review

In the course of arbitrating this transfer price dispute, the finance staff asked the purchasing staff to review the outside market situation for the thermostatic control unit. The purchasing staff replied that there was excess capacity and that, as a result of this, prices were very soft. Eventually, the prices would rise either when the demand for comparable units increased or when some of the suppliers went out of business. The purchasing staff had no doubt that the Refrigeration Division could purchase all its requirements for the next year or two for $2.15 a unit, or even less. The purchasing staff believed, however, that, if all the corporation's requirements for this

unit were placed with outside suppliers, the price would rise to at least $2.40 because this action would dry up the excess capacity.

Transmission Problem

The Laundry Equipment Division began production of automatic washers shortly after the end of World War II. Initially, it had purchased its transmissions from two sources—the Gear and Transmission Division and the Thorndike Machining Corporation. The transmission had been developed and engineered by the Thorndike Machining Corporation. In consideration of an agreement to buy one half of its transmissions from the Thorndike Machining Corporation, the General Appliance Corporation had been licensed to produce the transmission. The agreement ran from 1977 to 1987; at the expiration of the 10 years, General Appliance would have the right to use the design without restrictions.

In early 1985, nearly two years before the end of the agreement, the management of the General Appliance Corporation decided that it would not extend the agreement when it expired, but that it would expand the facilities of the Gear and Transmission Division enough to produce all the company's requirements. Accordingly, in March 1985, the Thorndike Machining Corporation was notified that beginning January 1, 1987, the General Appliance Corporation would manufacture all its own transmissions and, consequently, would not renew the current agreement.

This notification came as a surprise to the Thorndike Machining Corporation; furthermore, its implications were very unpleasant, because the General Appliance Corporation took a major share of the output of an entire plant, and there was little likelihood that the lost business could be replaced. The Thorndike Machining Corporation consequently faced the prospect of an idle plant and a permanent reduction in the level of profits.

In April 1985, the president of the Thorndike Machining Corporation wrote to the president of the General Appliance Corporation, asking that the decision not to extend the current agreement be reconsidered. He submitted a proposed schedule of price reductions that would be made if the current agreement was extended. He stated that these reductions would be possible because *(a)* Thorndike would be better off to obtain a lower price than to abandon the special-purpose machinery used for transmissions and *(b)* it expected increases in productivity. These proposed reductions were as follows:

Present price	$14.00
Price effective 7/1/85	13.50
Price effective 7/1/86	13.00
Price effective 7/1/87	12.50
Price effective 7/1/88	12.00

The letter further stated that the corporation had developed a low-cost transmission suitable for economy washers; this transmission was designed to cost $2 less than the present models and could be made available by January 1, 1988.

On receiving a copy of the letter, the general manager of the Laundry Equipment Division reopened the issue of continuing to buy from the Thorndike Machining Corporation. He had been interested in adding to the line a low-cost automatic washer, and the possibility of a $10 transmission appealed to him. The general manager of the Gear and Transmission Division, however, was interested in expanding his production of transmissions; and to satisfy the Laundry Equipment Division he offered to develop a unit that would be comparable in price and performance to the proposed Thorndike Machining Corporation's economy unit. The offer was set forth in a letter signed by the general manager of the Gear and Transmission Division, dated April 22, 1985. The general manager of the Laundry Equipment Division accepted this offer, and no further question was raised about continuing to buy from the Thorndike Machining Corporation.

During the next two months, the engineering departments of the Gear and Transmission and the Laundry Equipment division jointly determined the exact performance features needed for the economy transmission; some of these features were different from those of the proposed Thorndike transmission. In June 1985, the general manager of the Gear and Transmission Division wrote a letter to the general manager of the Laundry Equipment Division, outlining the agreed-on engineering features and including the following price proposal.

Proposed selling price of Thorndike model			$10.00
Probable cost (assuming 11% profit)			9.00
Add:			
Cost of added design features		$ 0.85	
Increased cost of material and labor since date of quotation		0.75	1.60
Total cost			10.60
Profit			1.06
Adjusted price of G & T Unit			$11.66

The letter went on to say: "Because a price of $11.66 will not give us our objective profit, we proposed to sell you this unit for $12. We believe that this a fair and equitable price, and decidedly to your benefit."

This letter was never acknowledged by the Laundry and Equipment Division.

In October 1985, the Gear and Transmission Division submitted a project proposal to the top management of the corporation, requesting money to build facilities to produce the new economy transmission. The project proposal included a profit projection based on a $12 price. The Laundry Equipment Division was quoted in the project proposal as agreeing to the price.

There was no objection to this statement from the Laundry Equipment Division personnel who were asked to comment on the proposed project. The project was approved, and the Gear and Transmission Division proceeded to buy and install the equipment to produce the new transmission.

In the latter part of 1985, the Gear and Transmission Division opened negotiations with the Laundry Equipment Division on the price of the new transmission, proposing $12 plus some minor adjustments for changes in cost levels since the previous year. The Laundry Equipment Division refused to accept the proposed price and countered with an offer of $11.21, developed as shown below.

Development of $11.21 Price

Proposed selling price of Thorndike model		$10.00
Adjustments:		
Cost of added design features	$ 0.85	
Cost of eliminated design features	(0.50)	
Increased cost of material and labor since date of quotation	0.75	
Net cost change	1.10	
Profit on added cost	0.11	
Total price increase		1.21
Proposed price		$11.21

The Gear and Transmission Division refused even to consider this proposal, and after several days of acrimonious debate both divisions decided to submit the dispute to the finance staff for arbitration.

Laundry Equipment Division

The Laundry Equipment Division based its case on the following argument:

1. The division could have purchased a transmission, comparable in performance char-

acteristics to the Gear and Transmission Division's unit, from the Thorndike Machining Corporation for $11.21.
2. The Gear and Transmission Division had agreed to this price in consideration of being allowed to produce all the transmissions.
3. The intracompany pricing policy was that the supplying divisions should sell at competitive prices.

The general manager of the Laundry Equipment Division stated that it would be unfair to penalize him for keeping the transmission business inside the corporation as a benefit to the Gear and Transmission Division, particularly in the light of the promise made by the general manager of the Gear and Transmission Division.

The general manager also stated that he had not protested the price proposal included in the May 1985 letter, because he believed that it was then too early to open negotiations. His cost analysis had not evaluated the proposal, but he assumed that the Gear and Transmission Division was approximately correct in its evaluation of the cost differences from the Thorndike unit. His position was that the difference of 34 cents between the adjusted Thorndike price and the quoted Gear and Transmission price was not worth negotiating until nearer the production date. The Laundry Equipment Division had naturally assumed that the Gear and Transmission Division would live up to its agreement and, therefore, regarded the request for $12 as just a negotiating gimmick.

Gear and Transmission Division

The Gear and Transmission Division based its case on two arguments:

1. The $10 quotation of the Thorndike Machining Corporation was invalid because it represented a final desperate effort to keep a share of the transmission business. A price of this nature should not form a long-term intracompany pricing base. If the Thorndike Machining Corporation had received the business, it would have eventually raised its price.

2. The Laundry Equipment Division did not object to the Gear and Transmission Division's price proposal until after the facilities to build the transmission were already in place. The $12 price was used in the calculations that showed the profitability of the project, and on which the project approval was based. If the Laundry Equipment Division wished to object, it should have done so when the project was presented to top management. Because facilities were purchased on the assumption of a $12 price, the Laundry Equipment Division should not be allowed to object after the money had been spent.

Finance Staff Review

A review by the finance staff disclosed the following:

1. If the Thorndike Machining quotation of $10 were adjusted for the cost effect of changes in performance characteristics and the increase in general cost levels since the original quotation, the price would be $11.25, or approximately the same as that proposed by the Laundry Equipment Division. The price of $11.66 developed by the Gear and Transmission Division was in error because it failed to allow for a design elimination that would reduce the cost of the Thorndike unit by 50 cents.

2. At $12, the Gear and Transmission Division could expect to earn an aftertax profit of 15 percent on its investment; this was equal to its profit objective. At the $11.25 price, the division would earn about 6 percent after taxes.

3. The purchasing staff stated that in its opinion the transmission could be obtained from the Thorndike Machining Corporation at the quoted price level for the foreseeable future.

QUESTIONS

1. Be prepared in each of the disputes to play all three of the following roles: general manager of the supplying division, general manager of the buying division, member of the financial staff responsible for arbitrating the dispute. In the case of the general managers, you should not simply repeat the arguments presented in the case; you should also be prepared to give ground where your position is weak, to introduce new (but realistic) arguments to buttress your case, and to deal rationally with your adversary's arguments.

2. What, if any, changes in the company's transfer price policies and procedures would you recommend?

Case 5–4

Strider Chemical Company*

On December 9, 1986, the president of the Strider Chemical Company, which had sales of around $175 million, announced that on January 1, 1987, the company would be reorganized into separate divisions. Until that time, the company had been organized on a functional basis, with the manufacturing, sales, finance, and research departments each under one person's responsibility. Six divisions were to be set up—four by product group and two by geographical area. Each division was to have its own production, sales, and accounting staff, and a general manager who would be responsible for its operation. The division's operating performance was to be judged by the profit it produced in relation to the investment assigned to it. It was anticipated that the procedure for computing the investment base and the return thereon would have to be carefully worked out if the resultant ratio was to be acceptable to the new division managers as a reasonable measure of their performance.

One of the biggest obstacles to the establishment of the desired monthly profit and loss statement for each division was the pricing of products for transfer from one to another of the various divisions. At the time the divisions were established, the company's president issued a policy statement upon which a pricing procedure was to be based. The president's statement follows.

Statement of Policy

The *maximum*, and usual, price for transfers between profit units is that price which enables the producing unit to earn a return on the investment required, consistent with what it can earn doing business with the *average* of its customers for the product group concerned.

Established prices will be reviewed each six months or when a general change in market prices occurs.

Discussion

Pricing policy between operating units is particularly important, because to the extent that the price is wrong, the return on one segment of the business is understated, and the return on another is overstated. This not only gives a false measure of how well individuals are performing, but also may make for bad decisions on the business as a whole, which will affect everyone.

Certain elements of expense that may not be found in intracompany relations are:

1. Deductions for cash discounts, freight, royalties, sales taxes, customer allowances, etc.
2. Usual selling expenses and, in many cases, order and billing services.
3. Certain customer services by the research laboratories, such as sales service where this applies.

The producing division that acts as a supplier will establish a price by discounting its *regular*

---

* This case was prepared by R. N. Anthony, Harvard Business School.
Copyright © by the President and Fellows of Harvard College.
Harvard Business School case 166–016.

price structure for the elements listed above which apply.

In case the buying division disagrees with the price as computed above, it will explain the basis of its disagreement to the president, who will decide what is to be done.

We are hopeful that this policy will work out equitably, giving each division a fair basis for the business they do. If, in practice, it is found that the policy is not working properly, is complicated in its application or calculation, or is working a hardship, the policy will have to be changed.

Williams Division

The largest of the newly formed divisions, the Williams Division, was strongly affected by the problem of transfer prices, since about 23 percent of its sales would be to other divisions.

With only three weeks before the separation into divisions, it was important that a schedule of prices be quickly established for the transfer of products between divisions. The Williams Division's task was complicated by its large number of products. There were several hundred different compounds and materials for which a price had to be fixed. It was, therefore, partly for the sake of expediency that the Williams Division chose to set the prices on the basis of direct manufacturing cost. The figures used in this method were more readily available than those used in setting a price based on the current market price.

A week after the president's policy statement on transfer pricing had been distributed, the Williams Division issued an interpretation of the policy which stated its proposed method for setting prices for the sale of products by the Williams Division to other divisions. The key paragraphs from this statement were as follows:

The Williams Division will charge the same price to another division as it charges to the average of its existing customers, less an allowance for those expenses incurred with average customers but not

with interdivisional customers. These noncomparable expenses to be deducted include Sales Deductions and a part of Selling Expenses. The prices will be calculated in terms of a markup or multiplier factor on Direct Manufacturing Cost. A markup will be recalculated each six months, based on the prior twelve months' experience with regular customers.

The markup for the first six months of 1987 will be 1.41 times Direct Manufacturing Cost as shown in Exhibit 1 which uses actual data for the 12-month period ended October 31, 1986.

By the end of March 1987, the president had received a number of letters from division managers, raising questions about transfer prices. Three of these are summarized as follows:

1. The Williams division questioned the price which the Johnson Division had established for compound A, a raw material for the Williams Division. The Johnson Division had initially calculated a markup of 1.33, computed in the same way the Williams Division computed its markup of 1.41. At a markup of 1.33, however, the Johnson Division would show a net loss, since the division had not operated at a profit in the preceding 12 months. It therefore raised its markup to 1.41, the same as that used by the Williams Division. At this markup, it would show about the same profit as that of the Williams Division. The Williams Division argued that this markup violated company policy.

2. The International Division questioned the transfer price of several products it purchased from the Williams Division for sale abroad. It said that at these prices the International Division could not meet competitive prices in European markets and still make a profit.

3. The Western Division purchased chemical B from the Williams Division for resale to its own customers. It submitted data to show that at the computed transfer price the Western Division would be better off to manufacture chemical B in one of its own plants. Rather than do this, it proposed that the transfer price be cut by 15 percent, which

would still leave a margin over direct manufacturing cost for the Williams Division.

As of the end of March, the president had not acted on any of these letters, other than to reply that existing relationships between divisions should be continued until further notice, and that after the questions had been decided, adjustments in transfer prices would be made retroactive to January 1.

In view of the numerous questions that had already arisen about the markup, the president was considering the possibility of transferring all products at cost, without any markup.

EXHIBIT 1   Markup Calculation

		Dollars	*Percent*
Gross sales to outside customers		$5,126,328	
Less: Amounts not applicable to internal sales:			
a. Freight, royalties, sales taxes	$ 58,625		
b. Selling expenses	260,123		
Total deductions		318,748	
Adjusted sales		4,807,580	100%
Direct manufacturing cost		3,404,923	71
Margin		1,402,657	29%
Computation: 100 ÷ 71 = 1.41 times			

QUESTION

What change, if any, should be made in the transfer price practices of Strider Chemical Company?

Case 5-5

Warren Corporation*

Warren Corporation was a large conglomerate. A significant portion of its business was in electronics. In this area, there were 15 profit centers, and most of these profit centers dealt with one another. More than 50 percent of the sales in some of these profit centers were to other Warren units. The central finance staff had developed a manual that prescribed company policy with respect to intracompany relationships, particularly how transfer prices were to be established. This manual was changed when decisions of the Price Arbitration Committee made it evident that it was incomplete or that policy had changed. In some respects, these revisions were like the codification of common law, in that decisions of the Price Arbitration Committee were incorporated into the transfer pricing rules in the same way that court decisions affect legal principles.

The Price Arbitration Committee (called hereafter PAC), had been set up to arbitrate intracompany pricing disputes. It consisted of three staff vice presidents—finance, manufacturing, and purchasing. The secretary of this committee was the manager of the price analysis department of the finance staff. This department was responsible for providing staff service to the PAC.

This case presents three disputes that were submitted to the PAC by divisional managers of the Warren Corporation.

Product Development

Division X produced a low-volume, high-grade line of electronic products. Its engineering group had spent $300,000 developing a new type of unit to be attached to one of its major products. When the development was completed, a marketing survey showed that the number of units that was likely to be sold would not warrant the expenditure required for the tooling and facilities to produce the new unit. The total number of units likely to be sold by Division X was only 2,500 annually. Consequently, the project was shelved.

Division Y sold an electronic product, with a much higher sales volume, that could use the new unit. Six months after the project was shelved, at a companywide meeting of certain research personnel, a research manager of Division Y learned of this new unit and requested a copy of the blueprints. This was provided to him.

Within the next nine months, Division Y decided to produce the new unit and proceeded to purchase the necessary tools and facilities. About three months later (a year and a half after Division X had shelved the project) the general manager of Division X heard that Division Y was going to produce the unit that had been developed by his division. He immediately called in his controller and told him to send Division Y a bill for $300,000. He was particularly interested in receiving payment because the Division X's profits were less than budget. Since the costs of development had been written off in the previous year, the $300,000 would be a direct increase in profitability.

Division Y refused to pay and Division X brought the matter to the PAC. *The Intracompany*

* This case was prepared by John Dearden, Harvard Business School.
Copyright © by the President and Fellows of Harvard College.
Harvard Business School case 171-509.

Pricing Manual said nothing about the transfer of research and development costs.

Division X based its case on a statement in the manual that said: "In general, divisions will deal with each other in the same way that they deal with outside companies." Division X's position was that, if it was independent, it could have sold the blueprints for at least $300,000 to an outside company. (Company rules forbade the sale of research findings to outside companies, however.)

The position of Division Y was that the product was marginal. If Division Y had to pay $300,000 for the blueprints, it would not have gone ahead with the project.

Split Sourcing

Division A bought a complex electronic component. Of the total quantity, 50 percent was purchased with an outside source, and 50 percent was purchased from Division B. The outside source had developed the component and had licensed Division B to produce it in consideration of a five-year contract to provide half of Warren's requirements. The contract with the outside source established an initial price, with provision for annual negotiations. These negotiations were to determine the amount that the price would be reduced as manufacturing efficiency increased. Division A requested detailed information from Division B on the manufacturing processes to be able to negotiate with the outside source more effectively. If the engineers of Division A knew precisely in what ways and the extent to which Division B was increasing its efficiency, they could pinpoint the amount of the price reduction that should be obtained. Division B refused to provide this information. Division A submitted the dispute to the PAC.

The Intracompany Pricing Manual stated that split-sourced products should be transferred within the company at the same price as that charged by the outside source. Nothing else was said about split-source pricing.

Division B based its refusal on the statement that "Divisions deal with each other in the same way that they deal with outside companies." Under no conditions, it stated, would it provide customers with details of its production process. Furthermore, Division B pointed out that it would be "cutting their own throats." The greater the price reduction that Division A negotiated, the lower would be the profits of Division B.

Division A based its case on company welfare. Company profits would be maximized if Division B cooperated with Division A.

Reserved Capacity

Division S was essentially a marketing division. It purchased most of its products from Division M. The transfer price agreement was that products were transferred at the standard variable cost per unit, plus a monthly charge equal to the fixed costs assigned to the products produced for Division S, including a 10 percent return on the investment associated with these products. By agreement, half of the capacity of Plant M–1 was reserved for Division S. The other half of the capacity of that plant was used by Division M to produce products that were sold to outside customers. Plant M–1 could produce either Division S products or Division M products on all of its facilities.

During the current year the demand for Division S products declined, while the demand for Division M products increased. As a result, about 75 percent of the capacity for Plant M–1 was used to produce products for Division M and only 25 percent was used for products of Division S. Division S objected to paying for 50 percent of the capacity of Plant M–1. Division M refused to reduce the price and the case was submitted to the PAC.

The Intracompany Pricing Manual stated that products of the type produced by Division M for

Division S should be priced at "the standard variable cost per unit plus a monthly charge equal to the fixed costs and 10 percent of the book value of the assets assigned to the capacity reserved for the products of the buying division."

Division M argued that it had reserved 50 percent of the capacity of Plant M–1 for Division S. Division S, however, was not using this capacity currently. Because the demand was sufficiently strong for Division M products, Division M utilized this excess capacity. It would be foolish to leave it idle. If, however, Division S had needed the capacity, Division M would have been able and willing to provide it.

Division S felt that, to pay Division M for capacity that Division M was using, was unfair to Division S. Division S felt that it should pay just for the capacity that it was using, or, at a maximum, for the capacity it used plus the cost of any idle capacity up to a total of 50 percent of Plant M–1's capacity.

QUESTIONS

1. How would you settle each of these disputes?
2. In each case, how, if at all, would you change the manual?

Case 5–6

Medoc Company*

The Milling Division of the Medoc Company milled flour and manufactured a variety of consumer products from it. Its output was distributed as follows:

1. Approximately 70 percent (by weight) was transferred to the Consumer Products Division and marketed by this division through retail stores. The Consumer Products Division was responsible for these items from the time of packaging; that is, it handled warehousing, shipping, billing, and collections as well as advertising and other sales promotion efforts.
2. Approximately 20 percent was sold by the Milling Division as flour to large industrial users.
3. Approximately 10 percent was flour transferred to the Consumer Products Division and sold by that division to industrial users, but in different industries than those serviced directly by the Milling Division.

Counting each size and pack as one unit, there were several hundred products in the line marketed by the Consumer Products Division. The gross margin percentage on these products was considerably higher than that on flour sold to industrial users.

Wheat was purchased by the grain department, which was separate from the Milling Division. The price of wheat fluctuated widely and frequently. Other ingredients and supplies were purchased by the Milling Division.

The Milling Division and Consumer Products Division were two of 15 investment centers in the Medoc Company.

Products were transferred from the Milling Division to the Consumer Products Division at a unit price that corresponded to actual cost. There was a variation among products, but on the average, this cost included elements in the following approximate proportions:

Flour	30%
Other ingredients and packaging material	25
Labor and variable overhead	20
Nonvariable overhead	25
Total	100%

Also, 75 percent of the Milling Division's investment was charged to the Consumer Products Division in computing the latter's return on investment. This investment consisted of property, plant, equipment, and inventory, all of which was "owned and operated" by the Milling Division.

This transfer price resulted in friction between the Milling Division and the Consumer Products Division, primarily for three reasons.

1. As in many process industries, unit costs were significantly lower when the plant operated at capacity. Indeed, the principal reason for accepting the low-margin industrial business was to permit capacity operations. There was general agreement that acceptance of such business at a low margin, or even at something less than full-cost, was preferable to operating at less than ca-

* This case was prepared by R. N. Anthony, Harvard Business School.
Copyright © by the President and Fellows of Harvard College.
Harvard Business School case 171–284.

pacity. In recent years, the Milling Division had operated at at least 98 percent of capacity.

The Milling Division alleged that the Consumer Products Division was not aggressive enough in seeking this capacity-filling volume. The Milling Division believed that the Consumer Products Division could increase the volume of consumer sales by increasing its marketing efforts and by offering more attractive special deals, and that it could do more to obtain industrial business at a price which, although not profitable, nevertheless would result in a smaller loss than what the Milling Division incurred from sales made to the industry it served. This additional volume would benefit the company, even though it reduced the average profit margin of the Consumer Products Division. The Consumer Products Division admitted that there was some validity in this argument, but pointed out that it had little incentive to seek such business when it was charged full cost for every unit it sold.

2. The Consumer Products Division complained that, although it was charged for 75 percent of the investment in the Milling Division, it did not participate in any of the decisions regarding the acquisition of new equipment, inventory levels, etc. It admitted, however, that the people in the Milling Division were technically more competent to make these decisions.

3. The Consumer Products Division complained that, since products were charged to it at actual cost, it must automatically pay for production inefficiencies that were the responsibility of the Milling Division.

A careful study had been made of the possibility of relating the transfer price either to a market price or to the price charged by the Milling Division to its industrial customers. Because of differences in product composition, however, this possibility had been definitely ruled out.

The Consumer Products Division currently earned about 20 percent pretax return on investment, and the Milling Division earned about 6 percent.

Top management of the Medoc Company was convinced that, some way or other, the profit performance of the Milling Division and the Consumer Products Division should be measured separately; that is, it ruled out the simple solution of combining the two divisions for profit-reporting purposes.

One proposal for solving the problem was that the transfer price should consist of two elements: *(a)* a standard monthly charge representing the Consumer Products Division's fair share of the nonvariable overhead, plus *(b)* a per-unit charge equivalent to the actual material, labor, and variable overhead costs applied to each unit billed. Investment would no longer be allocated to the Consumer Products Division. Instead, a standard profit would be included in computing the fixed monthly charge.

The monthly nonvariable overhead charge would be set annually. It would consist of two parts:

1. A fraction of the budgeted nonvariable overhead cost of the Milling Division, corresponding to the fraction of products that was estimated would be transferred to the Consumer Products Division (about 80 percent). This amount would be changed only if there were changes in wage rates or other significant noncontrollable items during the year.
2. A return of 10 percent on the same fraction of the Milling Division's investment. This was higher than the return that the Milling Division earned on sales to industrial users. The selection of 10 percent was arbitrary because there was no way of determining a "true" return on products sold by the Consumer Products Division.

QUESTIONS

1. Is the general approach to transfer pricing proposed here—namely, a non-variable dollar amount per month, plus a variable amount per unit—better than the present method in this situation? Why?
2. Suggest improvements in the details of the proposed method.

Chapter 6

Investment Centers

In a profit center, the focus is on profit as measured by the difference between revenues and expenses. In an investment center, this profit is compared with the assets employed in earning it. Many people consider an investment center as a special type of profit center and use the term *profit center* for both. Our reason for treating them separately is primarily pedagogical—that is, there are so many problems involved in measuring the assets employed in a profit center that the topic warrants a separate chapter.

In this chapter we first discuss each of the principal types of assets that may be employed in an investment center. The sum of these assets is termed the *investment base*. We then discuss the two methods of relating profit to the investment base: (1) the percentage return on investment (ROI) and (2) residual income, and then we describe the advantages and qualifications relating to the use of each in performance measurement. Finally, we discuss the somewhat different problem of measuring the economic value of an investment center.

STRUCTURE OF THE ANALYSIS

The purposes of measuring assets employed are analogous to those discussed for profit centers in Chapter 4, namely:

- To provide information that is useful in making decisions about assets employed and to motivate managers to make sound decisions—that is, decisions in the best interests of the company.
- To measure the performance of the business unit (division) as an economic entity.

In examining the several alternative treatments of assets and in comparing ROI and residual income—the two ways of relating profit to assets employed—we are primarily interested in how well the alternatives serve these two purposes.

It should be recognized at the outset that a focus on profits without consideration of the assets employed to generate those profits is an inadequate basis for control. Except in certain types of service organizations, in which the amount of capital is insignificant, an important objective of a profit-oriented company is to earn a satisfactory return on the capital that the company uses. A profit of $1 million in a company that has $10 million of capital does not represent as good a performance as a profit of $1 million in a company that has only $5 million of capital.

Unless the amount of assets employed is taken into account, it is difficult for senior management to compare the profit performance of one business unit with that of other units or of similar outside companies. Comparisons of absolute differences in profits are not meaningful if business units use different amounts of resources; clearly, the greater the resources used, the greater should be the profits. Such comparisons are used both to judge how well business unit managers are performing and also as a basis for deciding how resources should be allocated.

In general, business unit managers have two performance objectives. First, they should generate adequate profits from the resources at their disposal (subject, of course, to legal and ethical considerations). Second, they should invest in additional resources only when such an investment will produce an adequate return. Conversely, they should disinvest if the expected annual profits of any resource, discounted at the company's required earnings rate, is less than the cash that could be realized from its sale. The purpose of relating profits and investments is to motivate business unit managers to accomplish these objectives. As we shall see, however, there are significant practical difficulties involved in creating a system that focuses on both profits and assets employed.

Exhibit 6–1 is a hypothetical, simplified set of business unit financial statements that will be used throughout this analysis. (In the interest of simplicity, income taxes have been omitted from this exhibit and generally will be omitted in the discussion in this chapter. Inclusion of income taxes would change the magnitudes in the calculations that follow, but it would not change the conclusions.) The exhibit shows the two ways of relating profits to assets employed; namely, return on investment and residual income.

Return on investment is a *ratio*. The numerator is income, as reported on the income statement. The denominator is assets employed. In Exhibit 6–1, the denominator is taken as the corporation's equity in the business unit. This amount corresponds to the sum of noncurrent liabilities plus shareholders' equity in the balance sheet of a separate company. It is mathematically equivalent to total assets less current liabilities, and also to noncurrent assets plus working capital. (This statement can be easily checked against the numbers in Exhibit 6–1.)

Residual income (RI) is a dollar amount, rather than a ratio. It is found by subtracting a capital charge from the reported income. This capital charge is

---

EXHIBIT 6–1 Business Unit Financial Statements

Balance Sheet
(000s omitted)

Current assets:		Current liabilities:	
Cash	$ 50	Accounts payable	$ 90
Receivables	150	Other current	110
Inventory	200		
Total current assets	400	Total current liabilities	200
Fixed assets:			
Cost	$ 600	Corporate equity	500
Depreciation	−300		
Book value	300		
Total assets	700	Total equities	700

Income Statement

Revenue		$1,000
Expenses, except depreciation	$850	
Depreciation	50	900
Income before taxes		100
Capital charge ($500 × 10%)		50
Residual income		50

Return on investment $\dfrac{\$100}{\$500} = 20\%$

---

found by multiplying the amount of assets employed by a rate, which in Exhibit 6–1 is 10 percent. We shall discuss the derivation of this rate in a later section.

In the study of James S. Reece and William R. Cool[1] 620 companies out of the Fortune 1,000 companies answered a questionnaire. Of those responding, 96 percent or 594 companies had either profit centers or investment centers. Profit centers were used by 185 (23 percent) and investment centers by 459 (77 percent). Of the companies using investment centers, 65 percent evaluated them on the basis of ROI alone and 28 percent used both ROI and RI. Only 2 percent used RI alone.

For reasons to be explained later, residual income is conceptually superior to return on investment; and, therefore, we shall generally use residual income in our examples. Nevertheless, it is clear from the survey that return on investment is more widely used in business than is residual income.

---

[1] James S. Reece and William R. Cool, "Measuring Investment Center Performance," *Harvard Business Review,* May–June 1978, pp. 28–49.

MEASUREMENT OF ASSETS EMPLOYED

In deciding on the investment base to be used for evaluating managers of investment centers, the general questions are: (1) What practices will induce business unit managers to use their assets most efficiently and to acquire the proper amount and kind of new assets? Presumably, when their profits are related to assets employed, business unit managers will try to improve their performance as measured in this way, and senior management wants the actions that they take toward this end to be actions that are in the best interest of the whole corporation. (2) What practices best measure the performance of the entity as an economic entity?

Cash

Most companies control cash centrally, because central control permits the use of a smaller cash balance than would be the case if each business unit held cash balances sufficient to provide the necessary buffer for the unevenness of cash inflows and cash outflows. Business unit cash balances may well be only the "float" between daily receipts and daily disbursements. Consequently, the actual cash balances at the business unit level tend to be much smaller than would be required if the business unit were an independent company. Many companies, therefore, calculate the cash to be included in the investment base by means of a formula. For example, General Motors is reported to use 4.5 percent of annual sales; Du Pont is reported to use two months' costs of sales minus depreciation. The formula is designed to approximate the amount of cash the business unit would have if it were an independent company.

A reason for including cash at a higher amount than the nominal balance normally carried by business units, is that the higher amount is necessary to permit comparability among units or with outside companies. If only the actual cash were shown, the return shown by internal units would be abnormally high and might be misleading to senior management.

Some companies omit cash from the investment base on the theory that the investment base consists of working capital plus fixed assets. These companies reason that the amount of cash approximates the current liabilities; if this is so, the sum of the accounts receivable and the inventories will approximate the amount of working capital.

Receivables

Business unit managers are able to influence the level of receivables, not only indirectly by their ability to generate sales but also directly by establishing credit terms, by approving individual credit accounts and credit limits, and by their vigor in collecting overdue amounts. In the interest of simplicity, receivables often are included at the actual end-of-period balances, although the average of intraperiod balances is conceptually a better measure of the amount that should be related to profits.

Whether the accounts receivable should be included at selling prices or at cost of goods sold is also debatable. One could argue that the business unit's real investment in accounts receivable is only the cost of goods sold and that a satisfactory return on this investment is probably enough. On the other hand, it is possible to argue that the business unit has the opportunity to reinvest the money collected from accounts receivable; therefore, accounts receivable should be included at selling prices. The usual practice is to include receivables at the selling price—that is, the book amount.

If the business unit does not control credits and collections, receivables may be calculated on a formula basis. This formula should be consistent with the normal payment period—for example, 30 days' sales where payment is normally made 30 days after the shipment of goods.

Inventories

Inventories are ordinarily treated in a manner similar to receivables—that is, they are often recorded at end-of-period amounts even though intraperiod averages would be conceptually preferable. If the company uses LIFO (last in, first out) for financial accounting purposes, a different valuation method is ordinarily used for business unit profit reporting, because, in periods of inflation, the LIFO inventory balances tend to be unrealistically low. In these circumstances, inventories should be valued at standard or average costs, and these same costs should be used to measure cost of sales on the business unit income statement.

In work-in-process inventory is financed by *advance payments* or by *progress payments* from the customer, as is typically the case with goods that require a long manufacturing period, these payments are either subtracted from the gross inventory amounts or reported as liabilities.

Some companies subtract *accounts payable* from inventory on the grounds that the amount of accounts payable represents financing of part of the inventory by vendors, at zero cost to the business unit; the corporate capital required for inventories is only the difference between the gross inventory amount and accounts payable. If the business unit can influence the payment period allowed by vendors, the inclusion of accounts payable in the calculation encourages the manager to seek the most favorable terms. In times of high interest rates or credit stringency, managers might be encouraged to consider the possibility of foregoing the cash discount in order, in effect, to have additional financing provided by vendors. On the other hand, delaying payments unduly to reduce net current assets may not be in the company's best interest, since this may hurt its credit rating.

Working Capital in General

As can be seen from the above, there is considerable variation in how working capital items are treated. At one extreme, companies include all current assets in the investment base, with no offset for any current liabilities. This is sound from a motivational standpoint if the business units have no influence over accounts payable or other current liabilities. It overstates the amount of corporate capital required to finance the business unit, however, because the current liabilities are a source of capital, often at zero interest cost. At the other extreme, all current liabilities may be deducted from current assets, as was done in calculating the investment base in Exhibit 6–1. This provides a good measure of the capital provided by the corporation, on which it expects the business unit to earn a return. However, it may imply that business unit managers are responsible for certain current liabilities over which they have no control.

Property, Plant, and Equipment

In financial accounting, fixed assets are initially recorded at their acquisition cost, and this cost is written off over the asset's useful life by the depreciation mechanism. Most companies use a similar approach in measuring profitability of the business unit's asset base. This causes some serious problems in using the system for its intended purposes. In this part of the chapter, we shall examine these problems.

Acquisition of new equipment.   Suppose a business unit has an opportunity to acquire a new machine at a cost of $100,000. This machine is estimated to produce cash savings of $27,000 a year for five years. If the company has a required return of 10 percent, such an investment is attractive, as shown by the calculations in section A of Exhibit 6–2. The proposed investment has a net present value of $2,400, and, therefore, should be undertaken. However, if the machine is acquired, and if the business unit measures its asset base as shown in Exhibit 6–1, the reported residual income of the unit in the first year will decrease, rather than increase. The income statement without the machine and the income statement if the machine is acquired are shown in section B of Exhibit 6–2. Note that, with the acquisition of the machine, income before taxes has increased, but this increase is more than offset by the increase in the capital charge. Thus, the residual income calculation signals that profitability has decreased, whereas the economic facts are that profitability has increased. Under these circumstances, the business unit manager may be reluctant to purchase this machine.

In Exhibit 6–2, depreciation was calculated on the straight-line basis. If it had been calculated on an accelerated basis, which is not uncommon, the discrepancy between the economic facts and the reported results would have been even greater.

EXHIBIT 6–2 Incorrect Motivation for Asset Acquisition ($000)

A. Economic calculation

Investment in machine	$100
Life, 5 years	
Cash inflow, $27,000 per year	
Present value of cash inflow ($27,000 × 3.791*)	102.4
Net present value	2.4
Decision: acquire the machine	

B. As reflected on business unit income statement

	As in Exhibit 6–1		First Year with Machine	
Revenue		$1,000		$1,000
Expenses, except depreciation	$850		$823	
Depreciation	50	900	70	893
Income before taxes		100		107
Less capital charge at 10%[†]		50		60
Residual income		50		47

Note: Income taxes are not shown separately for simplicity. Assume they are included in the calculation of the cash flow and expense.

* 3.791 is the present value of $1 per year for five years at 10 percent.

[†] Interest on the new machine is calculated at its beginning book value, which for the first year is $100 × 10% = 10. We have used the beginning-of-the-year book value for simplicity. Many companies use the average book value $\left(\frac{100 + 80}{2} = 90\right)$. The results will be similar.

In later years, the amount of residual income will increase, as the book value of the machine declines, as shown in Exhibit 6–3; it goes from −$3,000 in year 1 to + $5,000 in year 5. The increases in residual income each year do not represent real economic changes. They appear to show constantly improving profitability; whereas, the facts are that there has been no real change in profitability after the time the machine was acquired. Generalizing from this example, it is evident that business units that have old, almost fully depreciated assets will tend to report larger residual income than units that have newer assets.

If profitability is measured by return on investment, the same inconsistency exists, as shown in the last column of Exhibit 6–3. Although we know from the present value calculation that the true return is about 11 percent, the business unit financial statement reports that it is less than 10 percent in the first year, and that it increases from year to year. Furthermore, the average of the five annual percentages shown is 16 percent, which far exceeds what we know to be the true annual return.

EXHIBIT 6–3   Effect of Acquisition on Reported Annual Profits ($000)

Year	Book Value at Beginning of Year (a)	Income* (b)	Capital Charge† (c)	Residual Income (b − c)	ROI (b ÷ c)
1	100	7	10	−3	7%
2	80	7	8	−1	9
3	60	7	6	1	12
4	40	7	4	3	18
5	20	7	2	5	35

Note: True return = approximately 11 percent.
* 27,000 cash inflow − $20,000 depreciation = $7,000.
† 10 percent of beginning book value.

It is evident that, if depreciable assets are included in the investment base at net book value, business unit profitability is misstated, and business unit managers may not be motivated to make correct acquisition decisions.

Gross book value.   The fluctuations in residual income and return on investment from year to year in Exhibit 6–3 can be avoided by including depreciable assets in the investment base at gross book value, rather than net book value. Some companies do this. If this were done, the investment each year would be the $100,000 original cost, and the additional income would be $7,000 ($27,000 cash inflow − $20,000 depreciation). The residual income, however, would be decreased by $3,000 ($7,000 − $10,000 interest), and return on investment would be 7 percent ($7,000 ÷ $100,000). Both of these numbers indicate that the business unit's profitability has decreased, which, in fact, is not the case. Return on investment calculated on gross book value always understates the true return.

Equipment replacement.   If a new machine is being considered as a replacement for an existing machine that has some undepreciated book value, we know that the undepreciated book value is irrelevant in the economic analysis of the proposed purchase (except indirectly as it may affect income taxes). Nevertheless, in the calculation of business unit profitability, the removal of the book value of the old machine can have a substantial effect. Gross book value will increase only by the difference between the cost of the new machine and the cost of the old. Net book value will increase only by the difference between the net book value after year 1 of the new machine and the net book value of the old machine. In either case, the relevant amount of additional investment is understated, and the residual income is correspondingly overstated. Managers, therefore, are encouraged to replace old equipment with new equipment, even in situations in which such replacement is not economically justified. Furthermore, business units that are able to make the most replacements will show the greatest improvement in profitability.

EXHIBIT 6–4   Profitability Using Annuity Depreciation—Smoothing Residual
Income ($000)

Year	Beginning Book Value	Cash Inflow	Residual Income*	Capital Charge[†]	Depreciation[‡]
1	$100.0	$ 27.0	$0.6	$10.0	$ 16.4
2	83.6	27.0	0.6	8.4	18.0
3	65.6	27.0	0.6	6.6	19.8
4	45.8	27.0	0.6	4.6	21.8
5	24.0	27.0	0.6	2.4	24.0
Total		$135.0	$3.0	$32.0	$100.0

* Annuity depreciation makes the residual income the same each year by changing the amount of depreciation charged. Consequently, we must estimate the total residual income earned over the five years. A 10 percent return on $100,000 would require five annual cash inflows of $26,378. The actual cash inflows are $27,000. Therefore, the residual income (the amount in excess of $26,378) is $622 per year.

[†] This is 10 percent of the balance at the beginning of the year.

[‡] Depreciation is the amount required to make the residual income (profits after the capital charge and depreciation) equal $622 per year (rounded here to $600). This is calculated as follows:

$$\$27.0 - \text{Capital charge} - \text{Depreciation} = \$0.6$$

therefore,

$$\text{Depreciation} = \$26.4 - \text{Capital charge}$$

Disposition of assets.   If assets are included in the investment base at their original cost, then the business unit manager is motivated to get rid of them, even if they have some usefulness, because the business unit's investment base is reduced by the full cost of the asset.

Annuity depreciation.   If, instead of straight-line depreciation, depreciation is calculated by the annuity basis, the business unit profitability calculation will show the correct residual income and return on investment, as demonstrated in Exhibits 6–4 and 6–5. This is because the annuity depreciation method actually matches the recovery of investment that is implicit in the present value calculation. Annuity depreciation is the opposite of accelerated depreciation, in that the annual amount of depreciation is low in the early years when the investment values are high and increases each year as the investments decrease; the rate of return remains constant.

Exhibits 6–4 and 6–5 show the calculations when the cash inflows are level in each year. Equations are available that derive the depreciation for other cash flow patterns, such as a decreasing cash flow as repair costs increase, or an increasing cash flow as a new product gains market acceptance.[2]

---

[2] For a complete analysis of this and other problems of accounting for depreciable assets, see John Dearden, "Problem in Decentralized Profit Responsibility," *Harvard Business Review*, May–June 1960, pp. 78–89.

EXHIBIT 6–5   Profitability Using Annuity Depreciation—Smoothing Return on Investment ($000)

Year	Beginning Book Balance	Cash Inflow	Net Profit*	Depreciation[†]	Return on Beginning Investment
1	$100.0	$ 27.0	$11.0	$ 16.0	11%
2	84.0	27.0	9.2	17.8	11
3	66.2	27.0	7.3	19.7	11
4	46.5	27.0	5.1	21.9	11
5	24.6	27.0	2.4	24.6	10[‡]
Total		$135.0	$35.0	$100.0	10%

* A return on $27,000 a year for five years on an investment of $100,000 provides a return of approximately 11 percent on the beginning of the year investment. Consequently, in order to have a constant 11 percent return each year, the net profit must equal 11 percent of the beginning of the year investment.
[†] Depreciation is the difference between the cash flow and the net profit.
[‡] The difference results because the return is not exactly 11 percent.

Very few managers accept the idea of a depreciation allowance that increases as the asset ages, however. They visualize accounting depreciation as representing physical deterioration or loss in economic value. Therefore, they believe that accelerated or straight-line depreciation is a valid representation of what is taking place, whereas annuity depreciation is not. Consequently, it is difficult to convince management to use the annuity method for business unit profit measurement.

Annuity depreciation also presents some practical problems. For example, the depreciation schedule in Exhibits 6–4 and 6–5 was developed based on an estimated cash flow pattern. If the actual cash flow pattern differs from that assumed, even though the total cash flow might result in the same rate of return, some years would show higher than expected profits and others would show lower. Should the depreciation schedule be changed each year to conform to the actual pattern of cash flow? This probably is not practical. Annuity depreciation would not be desirable for income tax purposes, of course; and although, as a "systematic and rational" method, it clearly is acceptable for financial accounting purposes, companies do not use it in their financial reporting. Indeed, surveys of company practice in measuring their business unit profitability show practically no use of the annuity method.[3]

Other valuation methods.   A few companies depart from the use of either gross book value or net book value in calculating the investment base. Some use net book value but set a lower limit, usually 50 percent, as the amount of original cost that can be written off; this lessens the distortions that occur in

---

[3] For example, Reece and Cool, "Measuring Investment Center Performance."

business units with relatively old assets. A difficulty with this method is that a business unit with fixed assets that have a net book value of less than 50 percent of gross book value can decrease its investment base by scrapping perfectly good assets. Other companies depart entirely from the accounting records and use an approximation of the current value of the asset. They arrive at this amount by a periodic appraisal of assets (say, every five years or when a new business unit manager takes over), or by adjusting original cost by an index of changes in equipment prices, or by using insurance values.

A major problem with using nonaccounting values is that they tend to be subjective, as contrasted with accounting values, which appear to be objective and generally not subject to argument. Consequently, accounting data have an aura of reality for operating management. Although the intensity of this sentiment will vary with different managers, the further one departs from accounting numbers in measuring financial performance, the more likely that business unit managers will regard the system as playing a game of numbers; senior management will regard it likewise.

A related problem with using nonaccounting amounts in internal systems is that business unit profitability will be inconsistent with the corporate profitability as reported to the shareholders. Although the management control system need not necessarily be consistent with the external financial reporting, as a practical matter some managers regard net income, as reported on the financial statements, as constituting the "name of the game." Consequently, they do not favor an internal system that uses a different method of "keeping score," regardless of its theoretical merits. Another problem with the economic value approach is deciding how the economic values are to be determined. Conceptually, the economic value of a group of assets is equal to the present value of the cash flows that these assets will generate in the future. As a practical matter, this amount cannot be determined. Although published indexes of replacement costs of plant and equipment can be used, most price indexes are not entirely relevant, because they make no allowance for the impact of changes in technology.

In any case, the inclusion of the investment base of fixed assets at other than the amounts derived from the accounting records appears to be used so rarely that it is of little more than academic interest.[4]

Leased Assets

Suppose the business unit whose financial statements are shown in Exhibit 6–1 sold its fixed assets for their book value of $300,000, returned the proceeds of the sale to corporate headquarters, and then leased back the assets at a rental

---

[4] In a 1984 survey of 101 firms from the Fortune 1,000 list, only 1 respondent reported using replacement cost of fixed assets. (Francis J. Walsh, Jr., *Measuring Business Performance*, The Conference Board Research Bulletin no. 153, p. 8.) In a followup 1987 study by The Conference Board, this question was not even asked.

EXHIBIT 6–6   Effect of Leasing Assets—Income Statement ($000)

	As in Exhibit 6–1		If Assets Are Leased	
Revenue		$1,000		$1,000
Expenses other than below	$850		$850	
Depreciation	50	900		
Rental expense			60	910
Income before taxes		100		90
Capital charge $500 \times 10\%$		50		
$200 \times 10\%$				20
Residual income		50		70

rate of $60,000 per year. As shown in Exhibit 6–6, the business unit's income before taxes would be reduced, because the new rental expense would be higher than the depreciation charge that has been eliminated. Nevertheless, residual income would be increased because the higher cost would be more than offset by the decrease in the capital charge. Because of this tendency, business unit managers are induced to lease assets, rather than own them, under any circumstances in which the interest charge that is built into the rental cost is less than the capital charge that is applied to the business unit's investment base. (Here, as elsewhere, this generalization is an oversimplification, because in the real world the impact of income taxes must also be taken into account.)

Many leases are financing arrangements—that is, they provide an alternative way of obtaining the use of assets that otherwise would be acquired by funds obtained from debt and equity financing. Financial leases (i.e., long-term leases equivalent to the present value of the cost of the asset) are similar to debt and are so reported on the balance sheet.[5] Financing decisions are usually made by corporate headquarters. For these reasons, restrictions are usually placed on the business unit manager's freedom to lease assets.

Idle Assets

If a business unit has idle assets that can be used by other units, the business unit may be permitted to exclude them from the investment base if it classifies them as available. The purpose of this permission is to encourage business unit managers to release underutilized assets to units that may have better use for

---

[5] This is required by *FASB Statement of Financial Accounting Standards No. 13.*

them. However, if the fixed assets cannot be used by other units, permitting the business unit manager to remove them from the investment base could result in dysfunctional actions. For example, it could encourage the business unit manager to idle partially utilized assets that are not earning a return equal to the business unit's profit objective. If there is no alternative use for the equipment, *any* contribution from this equipment will improve company profits.

Noncurrent Liabilities

Ordinarily, a business unit receives its permanent capital from the corporate pool of funds. The corporation obtained these funds from debt securities, from equity investors, and from retained earnings. To the business unit, the total amount of these funds is relevant; but the sources from which they were obtained are irrelevant. In unusual situations, however, a business unit's financing may be peculiar to its own situation. For example, a business unit that builds or operates residential housing or office buildings uses a much larger proportion of debt capital than is the case with typical manufacturing and marketing units. Since this capital is obtained through mortgage loans on the business unit's assets, it may be appropriate to account for the borrowed funds separately and to compute a residual income based on the assets that were obtained from general corporate sources, rather than on total assets.

The Capital Charge

The rate used to calculate the capital charge is set by corporate headquarters. It should be higher than the corporation's rate for debt financing because the funds involved are a mixture of debt and higher cost equity. Usually, the rate is set somewhat below the company's estimated cost of capital (assuming that a company can calculate its cost of capital) so the residual income of an average business unit will be above zero.

Although conceptually a good argument can be made for using different rates for business units with different risk characteristics, in practice this is rarely done—that is, the same rate is used for all units. Some companies use a lower rate for working capital than for fixed assets. This may represent a judgment that working capital is less risky than fixed assets because the funds are committed for a shorter time period. In other cases, the lower rate is a way of compensating for the fact that the company included inventory and receivables in the investment base at their gross amount (i.e., without a deduction for accounts payable); the lower rate is an implicit recognition of the fact that funds obtained from accounts payable have zero interest.

EXHIBIT 6–7   Valuation of Plant and Equipment

	Percent of Respondents Using Method	
	*Vancil Survey**	*Reece and Cool Survey[†]*
Gross book value (original cost)	15%	14%
Net book value (cost less accumulated depreciation)	85	85
Replacement cost	—	2
Total	100%	101%[‡]

* Richard F. Vancil, *Decentralization: Management Ambiguity by Design* (Homewood, Ill.: Dow Jones-Irwin, 1979), p. 351.
† James S. Reece and William R. Cool, "Measuring Investment Center Performance," *Harvard Business Review*, May–June 1978, p. 42.
‡ Includes multiple responses.

Surveys of Practice

Two studies of industry practices in calculating the investment base in investment centers are summarized in Exhibits 6–7, 6–8, and 6–9. The great majority of companies include fixed assets in their investment base at their net book value. They do this because this is the amount at which the assets are carried in the financial account and, therefore, represents, according to the accounts, the amount of capital that the corporation has employed in the division. Managements recognize the fact that this method gives misleading signals; but they believe it is the responsibility of users of the business unit profit reports to make allowances for these errors in interpreting the reports, and that alternative methods of calculating the investment base are so subjective that they are not to be trusted. They reject the annuity depreciation approach on the grounds that it is inconsistent with the way in which depreciation is calculated for financial statement purposes.

RESIDUAL INCOME VERSUS ROI

Most companies employing investment centers evaluate business units on the basis of the return on investment percentage. They do this because the meaning of ROI is well understood, and because ROI data are available for other companies or industries that can be used as a basis of comparison. The dollar amount of residual income does not provide such a basis for comparison. Nevertheless, the residual income approach has some inherent advantages over ROI.

EXHIBIT 6–8   Assets Included in Investment Base

	Percent of Respondents Including the Asset in the Investment Base	
	Vancil Survey* *239* *Respondents*	*Reece and Cool Survey†* *459* *Respondents*
Current assets:		
Cash	64%	63%
External receivables	98	94
Intracompany receivables	46	
Inventories	98	95
Other current assets	78	76
Fixed assets:		
Used solely by the profit center:		
Land and buildings	96	94
Equipment	98	83
Used by two or more profit centers:		
Land and buildings	56	45
Equipment	46	41
Assets of headquarters, central research, or similar units	25	16
Other assets:		
Investments	49	n/a
Goodwill	40	n/a
Capitalized rent charges	92	n/a

n/a means not available.
* Richard F. Vancil, *Decentralization: Management Ambiguity by Design* (Homewood, Ill.: Dow Jones-Irwin, 1979), p. 349.
† James S. Reece and William R. Cool, "Measuring Investment Center Performance," *Harvard Business Review,* May–June 1978, p. 36.

Its most important advantage is that, with residual income, all business units have the same profit objective for comparable investments, while the ROI approach provides a different incentive for investments. An ROI objective may be a constant objective set by senior management that is meant to represent the long-run potential of the business unit, or it may be an annual objective derived, for example, from the profit budget. If a business unit is expected to meet a constant ROI objective, a business unit manager will not be likely to propose a capital investment unless the unit is expected to earn a return at least as high as this objective. Thus, a business unit with an objective of 20 percent ROI would not invest at less than this rate, while a unit with an objective of 5 percent ROI would benefit from anything over this rate. Since the profit objectives of some business units are higher than the company's overall rate of re-

EXHIBIT 6–9 Liabilities Deducted in Measuring Investment Base

	Percent of Respondents Deducting the Liability from the Investment Base	
	Vancil Survey*	*Reece and Cool Survey[†]*
Current external payables	49%	51%
Current intracompany payables	29	30
Other current liabilities	42	45
Deferred taxes	19	n/a
Other noncurrent liabilities	77	20

n/a means not available.
* Richard F. Vancil, *Decentralization: Management Ambiguity by Design* (Homewood, Ill.: Dow Jones-Irwin, 1979), p. 351.
[†] James S. Reece and William R. Cool, "Measuring Investment Center Performance," *Harvard Business Review,* May–June 1978, p. 40.

turn for capital expenditures, and the profit objectives of other units are lower, this situation can cause seriously dysfunctional capital investment actions. (Senior management attempts to correct for this behavior in the capital budgeting process.) For similar reasons, inventories in one business unit will have a different implicit carrying charge from identical types of inventories in another unit that has a different profit objective.

A second advantage of residual income is that different interest rates may be used for different types of assets. For example, a relatively low rate can be used for inventories, while a higher rate can be used for investments in fixed assets. Furthermore, different rates can be used for different types of fixed assets to take into account different degrees of risk. In short, the measurement system can be made consistent with the decision rules that affect the acquisition of the assets. It follows that the same type of asset can be required to earn the same return throughout the company, regardless of the profitability of the particular business unit. Thus, business units should act consistently in decisions involving investments in new assets.

Differences between ROI and residual income are shown in Exhibit 6–10. Assume that the company's required rate of return for investing in fixed assets is 10 percent after taxes, and that the companywide cost of money tied up in inventories and receivables is 4 percent after taxes. The top section of Exhibit 6–10 shows the ROI calculation. Columns 1 through 5 show the amount of investment in assets that has been budgeted by each business unit for the coming year. Column 6 is the amount of budgeted profit. Column 7 is the budgeted profit divided by the budgeted investment. Column 7 shows, therefore, the ROI objectives for the coming year for each of the business units.

In only one business unit (C) is the ROI objective consistent with the companywide cutoff rate, and in no unit is the objective consistent with the com-

EXHIBIT 6–10 Difference between ROI and RI ($000)

ROI Method

Business Unit	*(1)* Cash	*(2)* Receivables	*(3)* Inventories	*(4)* Fixed Assets	*(5)* Total Investment	*(6)* Budgeted Profit	*(7)* ROI Objective
A	$10	$20	$30	$60	$120	$24.0	20%
B	20	20	30	50	120	14.4	12
C	15	40	40	10	105	10.5	10
D	5	10	20	40	75	3.8	5
E	10	5	10	10	35	(1.8)	(5)

Residual Income Method

Business Unit	*(1)* Profit Potential	Current Assets *(2)* Amount	*(3)* Rate	*(4)* Required Earnings	Fixed Assets *(5)* Amount	*(6)* Rate	*(7)* Required Earnings	Budgeted Residual Income *(1) − [(4) + (7)]*
A	24.0	$60	4%	$2.4	$60	10%	$6.0	$15.6
B	14.4	70	4	2.8	50	10	5.0	6.6
C	10.5	95	4	3.8	10	10	1.0	5.7
D	3.8	35	4	1.4	40	10	4.0	(1.6)
E	(1.8)	25	4	1.0	10	10	1.0	(3.8)

panywide 4 percent cost of carrying current assets. Business Unit A would decrease its chances of meeting its profit objective, if it did not earn at least 20 percent on added investments in either current or fixed assets, whereas Units D and E would benefit from investments with a much lower return.

The residual income method corrects these inconsistencies in the following manner: The investments, multiplied by the appropriate rates (representing the companywide rules), are subtracted from the budgeted profit. The resulting amount is the budgeted residual income. Periodically, the actual residual income is calculated by subtracting from the actual profits the actual investment multiplied by the appropriate rates. The lower section of Exhibit 6–10 shows how the budgeted residual income would be calculated. For example, if Business Unit A earned $28,000 and employed average current assets of $65,000 and average fixed assets of $65,000, its actual residual income would be calculated as follows:

$$RI = 28,000 - 0.04(65,000) - 0.10(65,000)$$
$$= 28,000 - 2,600 - 6,500$$
$$= 18,900$$

This is $3,300 = ($18,900 − $15,600) better than its objective.

Note that if any business unit earns more than 10 percent on added fixed assets, it will increase its residual income. (In the case of C and D, the additional profit will decrease the amount of negative residual income, which amounts to the same thing.) A similar result occurs for current assets. Inventory decision rules will be based on a cost of 4 percent for financial carrying charges. (There will be, of course, additional costs for physically storing the inventory.) In this way, the financial decision rules of the business units will be consistent with those of the company.

The residual income method solves the problem of differing profit objectives for the same asset in different business units and the same profit objective for different assets in the same unit. Residual income makes it possible to incorporate in the measurement system the same decision rules that are used in the planning process. The more sophisticated the planning process, the more complex can be the residual income calculation. For example, assume the capital investment decision rules called for a 10 percent return on general-purpose assets and 15 percent return on special-purpose assets. Business unit fixed assets could be classified accordingly, and different rates applied when measuring performance. Managers may be reluctant to make new nonprofitable investments that improve working conditions, reduce pollution, or meet other social goals. Investments of this type would be much more acceptable to business unit managers if they are expected to earn a reduced return on them.

It should be noted many companies use a capital charge that is less than the required earnings rate—that is, the capital charge is frequently closer to the company's borrowing rate than to its cost of capital. To the extent that this inconsistency exists, residual income will not achieve perfectly the results described above.

ALTERNATIVE APPROACHES TO EVALUATING MANAGERS

The residual income method does not solve all the problems of measuring profitability in an investment center. In particular, it does not solve the problem of accounting for fixed assets discussed above unless annuity depreciation is also used, and this is rarely done in practice. If gross book value is used, a business unit can increase its residual income by taking action contrary to the interest of the company, as shown in Exhibit 6–2. If net book value is used, residual income will increase simply from the passage of time. Furthermore, residual income will be temporarily depressed by new investments because of the high net book value in the early years. Residual income does solve the problem created by differing profit potentials. All business units, regardless of profitability, will be motivated to increase investments if the rate of return from a potential investment exceeds the required rate prescribed by the measurement system.

Moreover, some assets may be undervalued when they are capitalized, and others when they are expensed, rather than capitalized. Although the purchase cost of fixed assets is ordinarily capitalized, a substantial amount of investment in start-up costs, new product development, dealer organization, and so forth may be written off as expenses and, therefore, not appear in the investment base. This situation applies especially in marketing units. In these units the accounted investment may be limited to inventories, receivables, and office furniture and equipment. In a purely marketing unit, the understatement of true investment is usually clear; consequently, residual income is often ignored. However, when a group of units with varying degrees of marketing responsibility are ranked, the unit with the relatively larger marketing operations will tend to have the highest residual income.

In view of all these problems, some companies have decided to exclude fixed assets from the investment base. These companies make an interest charge for controllable assets only, and they control fixed assets by separate devices. Controllable assets are, essentially, receivables and inventory. Business unit management can make day-to-day decisions that affect the level of these assets. If these decisions are wrong, serious consequences can occur—quickly. For example, if inventories are too high, unnecessary capital is tied up in them and the risk of obsolescence is increased; whereas, if inventories are too low, production interruptions or lost customer business can result from the stockouts. To focus attention on these important controllable items, some companies include a capital charge for them as an element of cost in the business unit income statement. This acts both to motivate business unit management properly and also to measure the real cost of resources committed to these items.

Investments in fixed assets are controlled by the capital budgeting process before the fact and by postcompletion audits to determine whether the anticipated cash flows, in fact, materialized. This is far from being completely satisfactory because actual savings or revenues from a fixed asset acquisition may not be identifiable. For example, if a new machine or a new production line produces a variety of products, the cost accounting system usually will not identify the savings attributable to each.

The argument for evaluating profits and capital investments separately is that this often is consistent with what senior management wants the business unit manager to accomplish; namely, to obtain the maximum long-run cash flow from the capital investments the business unit manager controls, and to add capital investments only when they will provide a net return in excess of the company's cost of providing that investment. Investment decisions are controlled at the point where these decisions are made. Consequently, the capital investment analysis procedure is of primary importance in investment control. Once the investment has been made, it is largely a sunk cost and should not influence future decisions. Nevertheless, management wants to know when capital investment decisions have been made incorrectly, not only because some action may be appropriate with respect to the person responsible for the mistakes but also because safeguards to prevent a recurrence may be appropriate.

Management control systems designers disagree about whether it is better to use a single measure—residual income or ROI—or whether it is better to evaluate profit performance and capital investment performance separately. Most seem to feel that it is important to have a single overall measurement of financial performance. For example, if the actual profit was better than the budgeted profit but the capital investment performance was worse, how does management judge overall financial performance? Residual income or ROI weighs the impact of the poorer investment performance against the improved profit performance and provides this single measure. Another reason for using a single measure is that it may motivate managers to be more careful about adding capital investments that may not be profitable. A third reason is that only major capital expenditures can be examined carefully by corporate headquarters. Many minor acquisitions (e.g., routine replacements) are for practical purposes almost solely decided by the business unit manager and, in total, these can be significant. (One possible approach is to include minor acquisitions, such as routine replacements, as part of controllable assets while calculating residual income. Only major capital expenditures will be controlled separately.)

In view of the disadvantages of ROI, it seems surprising that it is so widely used in the United States. Reece and Cool conclude that the disadvantages of ROI are exaggerated, and that designers of control systems are aware of the conceptual flaws of the ROI approach; but they do not believe that these flaws are serious. We are unable to determine the extent of this dysfunctional conduct, however, because few managers are likely to admit its existence and many are unaware of it when it *does* exist. The likelihood of dysfunctional conduct seems related to the importance attached to meeting the ROI objective. Some companies calculate ROI but place primary importance on some other financial objective for evaluating performance (e.g., meeting the budgeted profit goal). Other companies, however, *do* place primary emphasis on meeting the ROI objective and this latter group is in greater danger of inducing dysfunctional actions on the part of business unit managers.[6]

EVALUATING ECONOMIC PERFORMANCE

The discussion to this point has focused on measuring the performance of business unit managers. As pointed out in Chapter 4, reports are also made on economic performance of business units. The two types of report are quite different. Management reports are prepared monthly or quarterly, whereas economic performance reports are prepared at irregular intervals, usually once

---

[6] For a more complete discussion of the above, see John Dearden, "Measuring Profit Center Managers," *Harvard Business Review,* September–October 1987, pp. 84–88.

every several years. For reasons given earlier, management reports tend to use historical information on actual cost incurred, whereas economic reports use quite different information. In this section, we discuss the purpose and nature of the economic information.

Economic reports are a diagnostic instrument; they indicate whether the current strategy of the business unit is satisfactory, or whether a decision should be made to do something about the business unit: expand it, shrink it, change its direction, sell it. The economic analysis of an individual business unit may reveal that current plans for new products, new plant and equipment, or other new strategies, when considered as a whole, will not produce a satisfactory future profit, even though each separate decision seemed sound at the time it was made.

Economic reports are also made as a basis for arriving at the value of the company as a whole. Such a value is called the "breakup value"—that is, the estimated amount that shareholders would receive if individual business units were sold separately. (Consulting firms often use the term *shareholder value*.) The breakup value is useful to an outside organization that is considering making a takeover bid for the company, and, of course, it is equally useful to company management in appraising the attractiveness of such a bid. Such a report indicates the relative attractiveness of the several business units, and it may suggest that senior management is misallocating its scarce time—that is, spending an undue amount of time on business units that are unlikely to contribute much to the company's total profitability. If there is a gap between current profitability and shareholder value, there is an indication that changes may need to be made. (Alternatively, current profitability may be depressed by costs that will enhance future profitability, such as new product development and advertising, as mentioned in an earlier section.)

The most important difference between the two types of reports is that economic reports focus on what profitability is expected to be in the future, rather than what profitability is or has been. The book value of assets and depreciation based on historical cost of these assets is used in performance reports, despite their known limitations, but this information is irrelevant in reports that estimate the future; in these reports, the emphasis is on replacement costs. (Nevertheless, some analysts use historical depreciation, adjusted for inflation, on the grounds that estimating replacements is highly difficult.)

Conceptually, the value of a business unit is the present value of its future earnings stream. This is found by estimating cash flows for each future year and discounting each of these annual flows at a required earnings rate. The analysis may cover 5, or perhaps 10, future years. Assets on hand at the end of the period covered are assumed to have a certain value, and this *terminal value* is discounted and added to the value of the annual cash flows. Although these estimates are necessarily rough, they provide a quite different way of looking at the business units from that conveyed in the performance reports.

SUMMARY

An important goal of a business organization is to optimize return on stockholder equity, (i.e., the net present value of future cash flows). It is not practical to use such a measure to evaluate the performance of business unit managers on a monthly or quarterly basis. Accounting rate of return is the best surrogate measure of business unit managers' performance. Residual income is superior to return on investment in evaluating business unit managers. While setting the annual profit objectives, in addition to the usual income statement items, there should be an implicit interest charge against the projected balance of controllable working capital items, principally receivables and inventories. There is considerable debate about the right approach to management control over fixed assets. Reporting on the economic performance of an investment center is quite different from reporting on management performance.

SUGGESTED ADDITIONAL READINGS

Dearden, John. "Measuring Profit Center Managers." *Harvard Business Review,* September–October 1987, pp. 84–88.

Henrici, Stanley. "The Perversity, Peril, and Pathos of ROI." *Financial Analyst Journal,* September–October 1983, pp. 79–80.

Reece, James S. and William R. Cool. "Measuring Investment Center Performance." *Harvard Business Review,* May–June 1978, pp. 28–49.

Solomons, David. *Divisional Performance: Measurement and Control.* Homewood, Ill.: Richard D. Irwin, 1965.

Walsh, Francis J. *Measuring Business-Unit Performance.* Research Bulletin no. 206. New York: The Conference Board, 1987.

Wanner, David L. and Richard W. Leer. "Managing for Shareholder Value—From Top to Bottom." *Harvard Business Review,* November–December 1989, pp. 52–60.

Case 6–1

Investment Center Problems*

1. The ABC Company has three divisions— A, B, and C. Division A is exclusively a marketing division, Division B is exclusively a manufacturing division, and Division C is both a manufacturing and marketing division. Exhibit 1 shows financial facts for each of these divisions.

Required

Assume that the ABC Company depreciates fixed assets on a straight-line basis over 10 years. To maintain its markets and productive facilities, it has to invest $100,000 per year in market development in Division A and $50,000 per year in Division C. This is written off as an expense. It also has to replace 10 percent of its productive facilities each year. Under these equilibrium conditions, what are the annual rates of return earned by each of the divisions?

EXHIBIT 1   Information about Divisions

	Division A	Division B	Division C
Current assets	$100,000	$ 100,000	$100,000
Fixed assets	—	1,000,000	500,000
Total assets	$100,000	$1,100,000	$600,000
Profits before depreciation and market development costs	$200,000	$ 200,000	$200,000

2. The D Division of the DEF Corporation has budgeted aftertax profits of $1 million for 1987. It has budgeted assets as of January 1, 1987 of $10 million, consisting of $4 million in current assets and $6 million in fixed assets. Fixed assets are included in the asset base at gross book value. The net book value of these fixed assets is $3 million. All fixed assets are depreciated over a 10-year period on a straight-line basis.

The manager of the D Division has submitted a capital investment project to replace a major group of machines. The financial details of this project are as follows:

New equipment:	
Estimated cost	$2,000,000
Estimated aftertax annual	
savings*	300,000
Estimated life	10 years
Old equipment to be replaced:	
Original cost	$1,500,000
Original estimate of life	10 years
Present age	7 years
Present book value	
($1,500,000 − $1,050,000).	$450,000
Salvage value	0

* These are cash inflows, disregarding depreciation and capital gains or losses (except for their tax impact).

---

* This case was prepared by John Dearden, Harvard business School.
Note: In solving these problems, ignore income taxes. Most of the problems state that savings or earnings are "after taxes." Assume that the amount of income taxes will not be affected by alternative accounting treatment.

Required

The capital investment project was approved and the new machinery was installed on January 1, 1987. Calculate the rate of return that is earned on the new investment, using the divisional accounting rules, and calculate the revised 1987 and 1988 budgeted rate of return:

(a) Assuming that the investment and savings are exactly as stated in the project.

(b) Assuming that the investment is overrun by $500,000 and the annual savings are only $200,000.

Notes

A. In answering Problem **2,** ignore the time value of money in your calculations. Use composite straight-line depreciation over the 10-year period. The essential differences between "composite" and "unit" depreciation are these: (1) Under "unit" depreciation, each asset is accounted for as an individual entity. One result of this is that assets disposed of for more (or less) than their net book value give rise to an accounting gain (or loss), which is included in the profit calculation. (2) Under "group" or "composite" depreciation, a pool of assets is accounted for by applying an annual depreciation rate to the gross book value (i.e., original cost) of the entire pool. When an individual asset is retired, the gross book value of the pool of assets is reduced by the original cost of the asset, and the accumulated depreciation account for the pool is reduced by the difference between the asset's original cost and scrap value, if any (i.e., a retired asset is assumed to be fully depreciated). Thus, any gains or losses from the disposal of assets are "buried" in the accumulated depreciation account and do not flow through the income statement.

B. Assume everything is as stated in Problem **2** — *except* that the company used *unit* depreciation. Answer the questions in Problem **2** for the years 1987 and 1988.

3. Assume that everything is as stated in Problem **2** — except that the fixed assets are included in the divisional assets base at their net book value at the end of the year. Answer the questions in Problem **2** for 1987 and 1988.

A. Do Problem **3** using *unit* depreciation.

B. Do Problem **3** using *composite* depreciation.

C. Do Problem **3** on the basis that DEF Corporation depreciates the pool of assets on the basis of the sum-of-the-years'-digits method, using composite depreciation. Calculate the rate of return on the new investment for 1987 and 1988 using the divisional accounting rules, assuming that:

(1) The investment and savings were exactly as stated in the project proposal.

(2) The investment was overrun by $500,000 and the annual savings were only $200,000.

Incorporate the following numbers to do your calculations:

$$
\begin{aligned}
&\text{Sum of digits } 1\text{--}10 = 55\\
&\$2,000 \times 10/55 = \$364\\
&\$2,000 \times 9/55 = \$327\\
&\$2,500 \times 10/55 = \$455\\
&\$2,500 \times 9/55 = \$409\\
&\$1,500 \times 3/55 = \$82\\
&\$1,500 \times 2/55 = \$55
\end{aligned}
$$

4. The G Division of the GHI Corporation proposes the following investment in a new product line:

Investment in fixed assets	$100,000
Annual profits before depreciation but after taxes (i.e., annual cash flow)	25,000
Life	5 years

The GHI Corporation used the time-adjusted rate of return, with a cutoff rate of 8 percent in evaluating its capital investment proposals. A $25,000 cash inflow for five years on an investment of $100,000 has a time-adjusted return of 8 percent. Consequently, the proposed investment is acceptable under the company's criterion. Assume that the project is approved and that the investment and profit were the same as estimated. Assets are included in the divisional investment base at the average of the beginning of the year's net book value.

Required

(a) Calculate the rate of return that is earned by the G Division on the new investment for each year and the average rate for the five years, using straight-line depreciation.
(b) Calculate the rate of return that is earned by the G Division on the new investment for each year, and the average for the five years using the sum-of-the-years'-digits depreciation.

5. A proposed investment of $100,000 in fixed assets is expected to yield aftertax cash flows of $16,275 a year for 10 years. Calculate a depreciation schedule, based on annuity-type depreciation, that provides an equal rate of return each year on the investment at the beginning of the year, assuming that the investment and earnings are the same as estimated.

6. The JKL Company used the residual income method for measuring divisional profit performance. The company charges each division a 5 percent return on its average current assets and a 10 percent return on its average fixed assets. Listed below are some financial statistics for three divisions of the JKL Company.

	Division		
	J	K	L
Budget data ($000s):			
1987 budgeted profit	$ 90	$ 55	$ 50
1987 budgeted current assets	100	200	300
1987 budgeted fixed assets	400	400	500

	Division		
	J	K	L
Actual data ($000s):			
1987 profits	80	60	50
1987 current assets	90	190	350
1987 fixed assets	400	450	550

Required

(a) Calculate the ROI objective and actual ROI for each division for 1987.
(b) Calculate the RI objective for each division for 1987.
(c) Calculate the actual RI for each division for 1987 and calculate the extent that it is above or below objective.

7. Refer to the budgeted profits and assets of the three divisions of the JKL Company provided in Problem **6.** Listed below are four management actions, together with the financial impact of these actions. For each of these situations, calculate the impact on the budgeted ROI and RI for each division. (Another way of looking at this problem is to calculate the extent to which these actions help or hurt the divisional managers in attaining their profit goals.)

Situation 1. An investment in fixed assets is made. This action increases the average fixed assets by $100,000 and profits by $10,000.

Situation 2. An investment in fixed assets is made. This action increases the average assets by $100,000 and profits by $7,000.

Situation 3. A program to reduce inventories is instituted. As a result inventories are reduced by $50,000. Increased costs and reduced sales resulting from the lower inventory levels reduce profits by $5,000.

Situation 4. A plant is closed down and sold. Fixed assets are reduced by $75,000 and profits (from reduced sales) are decreased by $7,500.

Case 6-2

Enager Industries, Inc.*

I don't get it. I've got a nifty new product proposal that can't help but make money, and top management turns thumbs down. No matter how we price this new item, we expect to make $130,000 on it pretax. That would contribute over ten cents per share to our earnings after taxes, which is more than the nine cent earnings-per-share increase in 1968 that the president made such a big thing about in the shareholders' annual report. It just doesn't make sense for the president to be touting e.p.s. while his subordinates are rejecting profitable projects like this one.

The frustrated speaker was Sarah McNeil, product development manager of the Consumer Products Division of Enager Industries, Inc. Enager was a relatively young company, which had grown rapidly to its 1968 sales level of over $74 million. (See Exhibits 1 and 2 for financial data for 1967 and 1968.)

Enager had three divisions—Consumer Products, Industrial Products, and Professional Services—each of which accounted for about one third of Enager's total sales. Consumer Products, the oldest of the three divisions, designed, manufactured, and marketed a line of houseware items, primarily for use in the kitchen. The Industrial Products Division built one-of-a-kind machine tools to customer specifications (i.e., it was a large "job shop"), with the typical job taking several months to complete. The Professional Services Division, the newest of the three, had been added to Enager by acquiring a large firm that provided land planning, landscape architecture, structural architecture, and consulting engi-

neering services. This division has grown rapidly, in part because of its capability to perform "environmental impact" studies, as required by law on many new land development projects.

Because of the differing nature of their activities, each division was treated as an essentially independent company. There were only a few corporate-level managers and staff people, whose job was to coordinate the activities of the three divisions. One aspect of this coordination was that all new project proposals requiring investment in excess of $500,000 had to be reviewed by the corporate vice president of finance, Henry Hubbard. It was Hubbard who had recently rejected McNeil's new product proposal, the essentials of which are shown in Exhibit 3.

Performance Evaluation

Prior to 1967, each division had been treated as a profit center, with annual division profit budgets negotiated between the president and the respective division general managers. In 1966 Enager's president, Carl Randall, had become concerned about high interest rates and their impact on the company's profitability. At the urging of Henry Hubbard, Randall had decided to begin treating each division as an investment center, so as to be able to relate each division's profit to the assets the division used to generate its profits.

Starting in 1967, each division was measured as based on its return on assets, which was defined to be the division's net income divided by its total assets. Net income for a division was cal-

---

* This case was prepared by James S. Reece, University of Michigan. Copyrighted by the University of Michigan.

EXHIBIT 1

Income Statements
For 1967 and 1968
($000s, except earnings per share figures)

| | Year Ended December 31 | |
	1967	1968
Sales	$70,731	$74,225
Cost of goods sold	54,109	56,257
Gross margin	16,622	17,968
Other expenses:		
Development	4,032	4,008
Selling and general	6,507	6,846
Interest	594	976
Total	11,133	11,830
Income before taxes	5,489	6,138
Income tax expense	2,854	3,192
Net income	$ 2,635	$ 2,946
Earnings per share (500,000 and 550,000 shares outstanding in 1967 and 1968, respectively)	$5.27	$5.36

culated by taking the division's "direct income before taxes," then subtracting the division's share of corporate administrative expenses (allocated on the basis of divisional revenues) and its share of income tax expense (the tax rate applied to the division's "direct income before taxes" after subtraction of the allocated corporate administrative expenses). Although Hubbard realized there were other ways to define a division's income, he and the president preferred this method since "it made the sum of the [divisional] parts equal to the [corporate] whole."

Similarly, Enager's total assets were subdivided among three divisions. Since each division operated in physically separate facilities, it was easy to attribute most assets, including receivables, to specific divisions. The corporate-office assets, including the centrally controlled cash account, were allocated to the divisions on the basis of divisional revenues. All fixed assets were recorded at their balance sheet values—that is, original

cost less accumulated straight-line depreciation. Thus, the sum of the divisional assets was equal to the amount shown on the corporate balance sheet ($75,419,000 as of December 31, 1968).

In 1966, Enager had as its return on year-end assets (net income divided by total assets) a rate of 3.8 percent. According to Hubbard, this corresponded to a "gross return" of 9.3 percent; he defined gross return as equal to earnings *before* interest and taxes ("EBIT") divided by assets. Hubbard felt that a company like Enager should have a gross (EBIT) return on assets of at least 12 percent, especially given the interest rates the corporation had had to pay on its recent borrowings. He, therefore, instructed each division manager that the division was to try to earn a gross return of 12 percent in 1967 and 1968. In order to help pull the return up to this level, Hubbard decided that new investment proposals would have to show a return of at least 15 percent in order to be approved.

EXHIBIT 2

Balance Sheets
For 1967 and 1968
(thousands of dollars)

	As of December 31	
	1967	1968
Assets		
Cash and temporary investments	$ 1,404	$ 1,469
Accounts receivable	13,688	15,607
Inventories	22,162	25,467
Total current assets	37,254	42,543
Plant and equipment:		
Original cost	37,326	45,736
Accumulated depreciation	12,691	15,979
Net	24,635	29,757
Investments and other assets	2,143	3,119
Total assets	$64,032	$75,419
Liabilities and Owners' Equity		
Accounts payable	$ 9,720	$12,286
Taxes payable	1,210	1,045
Current portion of long-term debt	—	1,634
Total current liabilities	10,930	14,965
Deferred income taxes	559	985
Long-term debt	12,622	15,448
Total liabilities	24,111	31,398
Common stock	17,368	19,512
Retained earnings	22,553	24,509
Total owners' equity	39,921	44,021
Total liabilities and owners' equity	$64,032	$75,419

1967–68 Results

Hubbard and Randall were moderately pleased with 1967 results. The year was a particularly difficult one for some of Enager's competitors, yet Enager had managed to increase its return on assets from 3.8 percent to 4.1 percent, and its gross return from 9.3 percent to 9.5 percent.

At the end of 1967, the president put pressure on the general manager of the Industrial Products Division to improve its return on investment, suggesting that this division was not "carrying its share of the load." The division manager had bristled at this comment, saying the division could get a higher return "if we had a lot of old

EXHIBIT 3 Financial Data from New Product Proposal

1. Projected asset investment:*

Cash	$ 50,000
Accounts receivable	150,000
Inventories	300,000
Plant and equipment[†]	500,000
Total	$1,000,000

2. Cost data:

Variable cost per unit	$ 3
Differential fixed costs (per year)[‡]	$ 170,000

3. Price/market estimates (per year):

Unit Price	Unit Sales	Break-Even Volume
$6	100,000 units	56,667 units
7	75,000	42,500
8	60,000	34,000

* Assumes 100,000 units sales.
† Annual capacity of 120,000 units.
‡ Includes straight-line depreciation on new plant and equipment.

EXHIBIT 4 Calculation of Gross Return on Assets, 1968

Division	Sales	EBIT	Assets				Gross ROA
			Specific		Alloc.	Total	
			W/C	Fxd.			
Consumer	24.8	3.6	20.3	11.5	1.6	33.4	10.8
Industrial	24.7	2.4	14.8	18.2	1.5	34.5	7.0
Professional Services	24.7	1.1	6.0	—	1.5	7.5	14.7
Total	74.2	7.1	41.1	29.7	4.6	75.4	9.4

machines the way Consumer Products does.'' The president had responded that he did not understand the relevance of the division manager's remark, adding, ''I don't see why the return on an old asset should be higher than that on a new asset, just because the old one cost less.''

The 1968 results both disappointed and puzzled Carl Randall. Return on assets fell from 4.1 percent to 3.9 percent, and gross return dropped from 9.5 percent to 9.4 percent. At the same time, return on sales (net income divided by sales) rose from 3.7 percent to 4.0 percent, and return on owners' equity also increased, from 6.6 percent to 6.7 percent. The Professional Services Division easily exceeded the 12 percent gross return target; Consumer Products' gross return on assets was 10.8 percent; but Industrial Products' return was only 7.0 percent (see Exhibit 4). These results prompted Randall to say the following to Hubbard:

You know, Henry, I've been a marketer most of my career; but, until recently, I thought I understood the notion of return on investment. Now I see in 1968 our profit margin was up and our earnings per share were up; yet two of your return on investment figures were down; return on invested capital held constant, and return on owners' equity went up. I just don't understand these discrepancies.

Moreover, there seems to be a lot more tension among our managers the last two years. The general manager of Professional Services seems to be doing a good job, and she's happy as a lark about the praise I've given her. But the general manager of Industrial Products looks daggers at me every time we meet. And last week, when I was eating lunch with the division manager at Consumer Products, the product development manager came over to our table and really burned my ears over a new product proposal of hers you rejected the other day.

I'm wondering if I should follow up on the idea that Karen Kraus in Personnel brought back from the two-day organization development workshop she attended over at the university. She thinks we ought to have a one-day off-site ''retreat'' of all the corporate and divisional managers to talk over this entire return on investment matter.

QUESTIONS

1. Why was McNeil's new product proposal rejected? Should it have been? Explain.
2. Evaluate the manner in which Randall and Hubbard have implemented their investment center concept. What pitfalls did they apparently not anticipate?
3. What, if anything, should Randall do now about his investment center approach?

Case 6-3

Quality Metal Service Center*

In early March 1982, the casewriter met with Edward Brown, president and chief executive officer of Quality Metal Service Center (Quality). Excerpts of their conversation are given below:

BROWN: It has been quite a while since we took a hard look at our planning and control systems. Since you have a special interest in this area, I thought you might want to spend some time examining our systems.

CASEWRITER: Do you perceive any weaknesses in your current systems?

BROWN: I'm not sure. Though I am satisfied with our past performance, I believe that we are capable of achieving even higher levels of sales and profits. Considering the market expansion and the state of competition, I feel we might have missed out on some growth opportunities. I don't know if our controls have inhibited managers from pursuing our goals of aggressive growth and above-average return on assets, as compared to the industry, but you might keep that in mind while evaluating our systems.

The Metal Distribution Industry

Service centers bought metals from many of the mills including USS, Bethlehem, Alcoa, Reynolds, and such smaller firms as Crucible, Northwestern, and Youngstown. These suppliers sold their products in large lots, thereby optimizing the efficiencies associated with large production runs. Service centers sold their products to metal users in smaller lots and on a short lead-time basis.

The metal distribution industry was generally regarded as a mature, highly competitive, and fragmented industry. The percentage of industrial steel products shipped through service centers had increased dramatically during 1974–82. In 1982, about 22 million tons were shipped through service centers, accounting for approximately 33 percent of all steel shipments in the United States, up from 18 percent in 1974. Some industry experts believed that the service center share could climb as high as 40 percent by 1990. There were a number of key trends in the metal industry that were enhancing service centers' growth potential.

Steel Mills' Retrenchment

In their efforts to become more competitive through increased productivity, most of the major domestic metals producers had been scaling back product lines by dropping low-volume specialty products. Further, they had cut back on service to customers by reducing sales force size and technical support. Full-line service centers, recognizing that many customers preferred to deal with only a few primary suppliers, had profited from this trend by maintaining wide product lines and increasing customer service.

Just-in-Time Inventory Management

Given the high cost of ownership and maintenance of inventory, most metal users were attempting to reduce their costs by lowering their levels of raw materials inventories ("just-in-time" inventory management). This resulted in smaller order quantities and more frequent deliveries. Metal service centers had a natural advantage over the mills here, because inventory was the service center's stock in trade.

---

* This case was prepared and is copyrighted by Vijay Govindarajan.

While the service center's price was always higher than buying from the mills, customers were increasingly willing to pay the extra charge. They recognized that the savings they generated from lower inventories and handling costs, plus reduced scrap and risk of obsolescence, would lower the total cost of getting the metal into their production system.

Productivity Improvement and Quality Enhancement

Quality and productivity had become overriding issues with metal users. They had implemented major quality and productivity improvement programs aimed at increasing both the reputation of their products and the overall profitability of operations. In their attempt to focus on quality, end users were reducing the number of suppliers with whom they did business and were concentrating their purchases with those that were best able to meet their specific quality, availability, and service requirements. End users found that closer relationships with fewer suppliers resulted in better quality conformance and stronger ties between supplier and customer as each sought to maximize the long-term benefits of the relationship.

Quality Metal's Strategy

Quality Metal had been established a century ago as a local metals distributor. Since then, it had grown into a firm with national distribution, and its sales in 1981 were well over $300 million. Quality's business strategy provided the framework for the development of specific goals and objectives. According to Mr. Brown, three fundamental objectives guided Quality.

Objective 1: To Focus Sales Efforts on Targeted Markets of Specialty Metal Users.

During the 1970s, Quality recognized that it could compete much more effectively in specialty product lines of its own selection than in the broader commodity carbon steel markets where price was the primary determining factor. Consequently, Quality decided to diminish its participation in commodity product lines and redeploy those resources into higher-technology metals, such as carbon alloy bars, stainless steel, aluminum, nickel alloys, titanium, copper, and brass, which offered higher returns and had less-effective competition. More than 60 percent of its revenues were derived from higher-technology metals in 1982, compared with 29 percent in 1972.

Quality had made a long-term commitment to high-technology metal users. The company's recent introduction of titanium, a natural adjunct to the existing product line, was indicative of the company's strategy of bringing new products to the market to meet the needs of existing customers. Previously, titanium was not readily available on the distributor market. Quality planned to continue to diversify into complementary higher-technology products as new customer requirements arose.

Objective 2: To Identify Those Industries and Geographic Markets Where These Metals Were Consumed.

To identify more accurately the major industries and geographies for these products, Quality developed the industry's first metal usage database in the early 1980s. Mr. Brown believed that this database, which was continually refined and updated, was the most accurate in the country. Its use enabled Quality to profile product consumption by industry and by geography. It also enabled the company to analyze total market demand on a nationwide basis and to project potential sales on a market by market basis. As a result, Quality had a competitive edge in determining where customers were located and what products they were buying. It used this information in selecting locations for opening new service centers.

Objective 3: To Develop Techniques and Marketing Programs That Would Increase Market Share.

To build market share, Quality offered programs that assisted its customers in implementing just-in-time inventory management systems coordinated with their materials requirement planning programs. The company worked with customer representatives in purchasing, manufacturing, and quality assurance to determine their precise requirements for product specifications, quantities, and delivery schedules.

Similarly, Quality emphasized value-added business by offering a wide range of processing services for its customers, such as saw cutting to specific sizes, flame cutting into both pattern and nonpattern shapes, flattening, surface grinding, shearing, bending, edge conditioning, polishing, and thermal treatment. Because of Quality's volume, the sophisticated equipment required for these production steps was operated at a lower cost per unit than most customer-owned equipment.

Organizational Structure

Since the Great Depression, Quality had experienced rapid sales growth and geographical expansion. In 1982, Quality operated in 27 locations, situated in markets representing about 75 percent of metal consumption in the United States. Consistent with this growth was the necessity to decentralize line functions. The firm currently had four regions, each of which had about 6 districts for a total of 23 districts. There were staff departments in finance, marketing, operations, and human resources. A partial organizational structure is given in Exhibit 1.

Typically, a district manager had under him a warehouse superintendent, a sales manager, a credit manager, a purchasing manager, and an administration manager (Exhibit 1). The decision-making authorities of these managers are described below:

The Warehouse Superintendent oversees transportation, loading and unloading, storage, and preproduction processing.

The Sales Manager coordinates a staff that includes "inside" salespersons who establish contacts and take orders over the phone, and an "outside" team who make direct customer contacts and close large deals. Sales price and discount terms are gen-

erally established by the District Manager; freight adjustments are also made at the district level.

The Credit Manager assesses the risk of new customer accounts, approves customer credit periods within a range established by corporate headquarters, and enforces customer collections.

The Purchasing Manager acquires inventory from the regional warehouse, other districts, and outside companies. Districts have freedom to purchase from outside suppliers. However, senior management has established Economic Order Quantity guidelines for the purchase of inventory, and metals are stocked in a district warehouse only if local demand is sufficient to justify it. Within this overall constraint, the Purchasing Manager has authority to choose suppliers and negotiate credit terms, although payments to suppliers are handled centrally at the home office.

Capital expenditures in excess of $5,000 and all capital leasing decisions require corporate approval.

Responsibility Allocation and Performance Measurement

District managers were responsible for attaining predetermined return on asset (ROA) levels, which were agreed to at the beginning of the year. The following items were included in the asset base for ROA calculations.

1. Land, warehouse buildings, and equipment were included in the asset base at gross book value.

2. Leased buildings and equipment (except for leased trucks) were included in the asset base at the capitalized lease value. (Leased trucks were not capitalized; rather, lease expenses on trucks were reported as an operating expense.)

3. Averge inventory, in units, was calculated. The replacement costs, based on current mill price schedules, was determined for these units and included in the asset base.

4. Average accounts receivable balance for the period was included in the asset base. (Cash was excluded from district's assets; the amounts were trivial.)

5. As a general rule, accounts payable was not deducted from the asset base. However, an adjustment was made if the negotiated credit period

EXHIBIT 1 Partial Organizational Chart

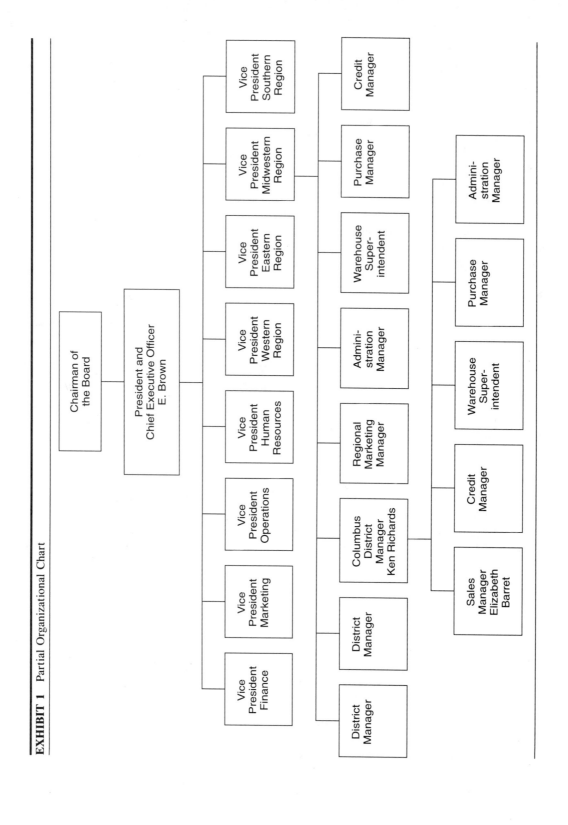

EXHIBIT 2 Incentive Calculation Procedure

Step 1: Measure actual asset base, and compare it with targeted asset base.
If actual assets exceed targeted assets, multiply excess by the targeted ROA for the district, and charge this amount to profits.

$$\text{Assets overemployed} \times \text{District ROA target} = \text{Charge to Profits}$$

If actual assets are less than targeted assets, multiply difference by the district's ROA target, and credit this to profits.

$$\text{Assets underemployed} \times \text{District ROA target} = \text{Credit to Profits}$$

Step 2: Adjusted profits are compared with 90% of the original profit objective.

$$\text{Adjusted profits} - (90\% \text{ of objective}) = \text{Incentive profits}$$

Step 3: $\dfrac{\text{Incentive Profit}}{90\% \text{ of objective}} = \text{Payout rate}$

Step 4: Payout rate $\times$ Manager's base salary = Bonus payable

Step 5: Bonuses are awarded on the basis of incentive profits. If incentive profits are less than zero, no bonus is awarded. The bonus increases in proportion to incentive profit, with a maximum bonus of 75 percent of manager's base salary.

---

was greater than the company standard of 30 days. If this occurred, "deferred inventory," a contra-asset account, was deducted from the amount of the inventory value, for the period in excess of the 30-day standard. This is equivalent to a reduction of inventory asset corresponding to the excess credit period. For example, if a district negotiated a credit period of 50 days, then the inventory expenditure will be removed from the asset base for 20 days. However, a penalty was not assessed if the negotiated credit period was less than the 30-day company standard.

Income before taxes, for each district, was calculated in accordance with generally accepted accounting principles, except for cost of sales, which was calculated based on current inventory replacement values. Expenses were separated into controllable and noncontrollable categories. Controllable expenses included such items as warehouse labor and sales commissions; rent, utilities, and property taxes are examples of noncontrollable expenses.

No corporate overhead expenses were allocated to the districts. A few years earlier, the company had considered a proposal to allocate corporate overheads to the districts. However, the proposal had been rejected on the grounds that the "allocation bases" were arbitrary and that such expenses could not be controlled at the district level.

Performance Evaluation and Incentives

ROA was the sole performance criterion for evaluation of district managers. The incentive bonus for district managers was based on a formula that rigidly tied the bonus to meeting and exceeding 90 percent of their ROA targets. Exhibit 2 contains the detailed procedure used to calculate the incentive bonus. The calculations determine an applicable payout rate, which was then multiplied by the district manager's base salary to yield the amount of the bonus award. Thus, the size of the bonus depended on (1) the amount of the manager's base salary and (2) how far 90 percent of the ROA target was exceeded; there was a maximum bonus amount.

The bonus of a district manager was also affected by his or her region's performance. In

1982, 75 percent of a district manager's bonus was based on district performance, and 25 percent was based on his or her region's performance. The bonus of the district manager's staff was based solely on the performance of that district.

Meeting with the Columbus District Manager

A few days after speaking with Mr. Brown, the casewriter visited Ken Richards, the district manager for the Columbus Service Center. Mr. Brown recommended him as one of the company's brightest and most successful district managers. The district had been highly successful in recent years, consistently earning well above 30 percent ROA (pretax).

For 1982, Ken Richards's targeted figure for operating profit was $3.8 million; targeted assets were set at $10 million. He felt that an ROA of 38 percent was reachable, considering historical performance and market opportunities.

As of March 1982, Ken was reviewing a capital investment proposal (for the purchase of new processing equipment) which he received from his sales manager (Exhibits 3 and 4). Before submitting the proposal to corporate headquarters for approval Ken wanted to make sure that the new investment would have a favorable effect on his incentive bonus for 1982. Using 1982 profit and asset targets as the benchmark, he compared his incentive bonus for 1982 with and without the new investment. These calculations are shown in Exhibit 5.

EXHIBIT 3   Memorandum

To: Kenneth Richards, District Manager

From: Elizabeth Barret, Sales Manager

Subject: Purchase of Processing Equipment

This district, at present, sells no inventory which has been altered through pre-production processing. Such alterations can be made at other districts with processing capabilities, but many customers in this area complain that, because of transportation time, the lead times are too great to satisfy their needs in acquiring such inventory.

Market research has established that a reasonable demand for processed inventory exists within this district. Therefore, our district should consider obtaining the processing equipment necessary to satisfy this demand.

The economics of this project is summarized in the attached sheet [Exhibit 4]. Let me provide some information as background for these calculations.

We can acquire the equipment for $600,000. Since its expected life is 10 years (negligible salvage value), Quality would benefit from a 10% Investment Tax Credit, making the net investment equal to $540,000.

Sales projections were made by the district's sales department, and costs were based upon the experiences of districts with processing capabilities. Growth in sales and costs include a 7% inflation factor and projected increases in production.

Annual cash flows are calculated by adjusting Earnings after Taxes to account for depreciation, which is expensed by the Sum-of-the-Years'-digit method, and growth in Working Capital investment, which is calculated using our standard 20% of sales on incremental growth. The resultant end-of-year cash flows, discounted at the cost of capital of 15% (which is the rate head office requires on projects in similar risk class such as this one), yield a positive net present value of $286,000. The payback period for this project is 4.5 years which is well within the company's criteria of 10 years.

This investment is worth your careful consideration, Ken. This district has the opportunity to expand into a new market, and to benefit from favorable earnings and positive sales growth.

I hope you will submit this proposal to the home office for consideration. Please let me know if you have any questions.

Sd/-
Elizabeth Barret

EXHIBIT 4 Columbus District Processing Equipment Proposal

	1982	1983	1984	1985	1986	1987	1988	1989	1990	1991
I. Cash flows (000s)										
Sales (1)	$ 600	1,375	1,510	1,665	1,830	2,010	2,215	2,435	2,680	2,945
Cost of sales	$(560)	(1,145)	(1,236)	(1,355)	(1,490)	(1,660)	(1,845)	(2,051)	(2,290)	(2,545)
Earnings before taxes	40	230	274	310	340	350	370	384	390	400
Tax at 50%	$ (20)	(115)	(137)	(155)	(170)	(175)	(185)	(192)	(195)	(200)
Earnings after taxes	20	115	137	155	170	175	185	192	195	200
Depreciation	110	100	85	75	65	55	45	35	20	10
Investment in working capital (2)	$(120)	(155)	(25)	(35)	(30)	(35)	(45)	(40)	(50)	535
Cash flow	$ 10	60	197	195	205	195	185	187	165	745
(1) Revenue for 1982 reflects 3-month start-up period										
(2) Investment in working capital										
20% of sales	$ 120	275	300	335	365	400	445	485	535	590
Old level	0	120	275	300	335	365	400	445	485	535
Increase in working capital	$(120)	(155)	(25)	(35)	(30)	(35)	(45)	(40)	(50)	(55)
Recovery of working capital										590
Net incremental investment in working capital	$(120)	(155)	(25)	(35)	(30)	(35)	(45)	(40)	(50)	535

II. Project evaluation

A. Payback period: 4.5 years

B. Internal rate of return: 21.8%

C. Net present value (at 15% cost of capital): $286,000

EXHIBIT 5   Incentive Bonus for Columbus District Manager for 1982

A. *Incentive Bonus for 1982 without the New Project*

	Target for 1982	Projected Actual for 1982*
Profit	$ 3,800,000	$ 3,800,000
Asset	$10,000,000	$10,000,000

$$Incentive\ profit = Actual\ profit - (90\%\ of\ targeted\ profit)$$
$$= \$3,800,000 - \$3,420,000 = \$380,000$$

$$Pay\ out\ rate = \frac{Incentive\ profit}{90\%\ of\ targeted\ profit}$$

$$= \frac{\$380,000}{\$3,420,000} = 11.1\%$$

Therefore, incentive bonus without the new project = 11.1% of base salary.

* Assumes that actual results exactly meet the targets in 1982.

B. *Incentive Bonus for 1982 with the New Project*

	Target for 1982	Projected Actual for 1982*
Profit	$ 3,800,000	$ 3,840,000
Asset	$10,000,000	$10,720,000

Step 1:   Actual assets − Target assets = Asset overemployed
$$\$10,720,000 - \$10,000,000 = \$720,000$$

Step 2:   Asset overemployed × District ROA target = Charge to profits
$$\$720,000 \times 0.38 = \$273,600$$

Actual profits − Charge to profits = Adjusted profits
$$\$3,840,000 - \$273,600 = \$3,566,400$$

Step 3:   Adjusted profits − 90% of targeted profit = Incentive profit
$$\$3,566,400 - \$3,420,000 = \$146,400$$

Step 4: $\dfrac{Incentive\ Profit}{90\%\ of\ targeted\ profit} = $ Payout rate

$$\frac{\$\ 146,400}{\$3,420,000} = 4.28\%$$

Therefore, incentive bonus with the new project = 4.28% of base salary.

* Reflects marginal effects of project implementation *only* —that is, an addition of earnings before taxes of $40,000 and an addition to assets of $720,000 (equipment $600,000 plus working capital $120,000). Otherwise, assumes that other district operations meet targets exactly in 1982.

QUESTIONS

1. Is the capital investment proposal described in Exhibit 3 an attractive one for Quality Metal Service Center?

2. Should Ken Richards, the Columbus district manager, send that proposal to home office for approval?

3. Comment on the general usefulness of ROA as the basis of evaluating district managers' performance. Could this performance measure be made more effective?

4. In deciding the investment base for evaluating managers of investment centers, the general question is: What practices will motivate the district managers to use their assets most efficiently and to acquire the proper amount and kind of new assets? Presumably, when his return on assets is being measured, the district manager will try to increase his ROA, and we desire that the action he takes towards this end be actions that are in the best interest of the whole corporation. Given this general line of reasoning, evaluate the way Quality computes the "investment base" for its districts. For each asset category, discuss whether the basis of measurement used by the company is the best for the purpose of measuring district's return on assets. What are the likely motivational problems that could arise in such a system? What can you recommend to overcome such dysfunctional effects?

5. While computing district profits for performance evaluation purposes, should there be a charge for income taxes? Should corporate overheads be allocated to districts? Should profits be computed on the basis of historical costs or on the basis of replacement costs? Evaluate these issues from the standpoint of their motivational impact on the district managers.

6. Evaluate Quality's incentive compensation system. Does the present system motivate district managers to make decisions which are consistent with the strategy of the firm? If not, make specific recommendations to improve the system.

Case 6–4
Diversified Products Corporation*

The Diversified Products Corporation manufactured consumer and industrial products in more than a dozen divisions. Plants were located throughout the country, one or more to a division, and company headquarters was in a large eastern city. Each division was run by a division manager and had its own balance sheet and income statement. The company made extensive use of long- and short-run planning programs, which included budgets for sales, costs, expenditures, and rate of return on investment. Monthly reports on operating results were sent in by each division and were received by headquarters executives.

The Able Division of the Diversified Products Corporation manufactured and assembled large industrial pumps, most of which sold for more than $10,000. A great variety of models were made to order from the standard parts that the division either bought or manufactured for stock. In addition, components were individually designed and fabricated when pumps were made for special applications. A variety of metalworking machines were used, some large and heavy, and a few designed especially for the division's kind of business.

The division operated three plants, two of which were much smaller than the third and were located in distant parts of the country. Headquarters offices were located in the main plant, where more than 1,000 people were employed. They performed design and manufacturing operations as well as the usual staff and clerical work. Marketing activities were carried out by sales engineers in the field, who worked closely with customers on design and installation. Reporting to Mr. Allen, the division manager, were men in charge of design, sales, manufacturing, purchasing, and budgets.

The division's product line had been broken down into five product groups, so that the profitability of each could be studied separately. Evaluation was based on the margin above factory cost as a percentage of sales. No attempt had been made to allocate investment to the product lines. The budget director said this not only would be difficult in view of the common facilities but also such a mathematical computation would not provide any new information, since the products had approximately the same turnover of assets. Furthermore, he said it was difficult enough to allocate common factory costs between products, and even margin on sales was a disputable figure. "If we were larger," he said, "and had separate facilities for each product line, we might be able to do it. But it wouldn't mean much in this division right now."

Only half a dozen men ever looked at the division's rate of return, for other measures were used in the division's internal control system. The division manager used shipments per week and certain cost areas, such as overtime payments, to check on divisional operations.

The Division Manager's Control of Assets

During 1987, the total assets of the Able Division were turned over approximately 1.7 times, and late that year they were made up as follows.

* This case was written by Professor William Rotch, University of Virginia, published by Intercollegiate Case Clearing House (ICH4C53R), Soldiers Field, Boston, and reproduced here with the permission of the author. Copyright © by University of Virginia.

Cash	12%
Accounts receivable	21
Inventory:	
Raw material	7
About 3% metal stock	
About 4% purchased parts	
Work-in-process	11
About 7% manufactured parts	
About 4% floor stocks	
Finished goods	2
Machinery (original cost)	29
Land and buildings (original cost)	18
Total	100%

Cash (12 percent of total assets)

The Able Division, like all divisions in the Diversified Products Corporation, maintained a petty cash account in a local bank to which company headquarters transferred funds as they were needed. This local working account was used primarily for making up the plant payroll and for payment of other local bills. Payment of suppliers' invoices as well as collection of accounts receivable was handled by headquarters for Able as well as for most of the other divisions.

The division's cash account at headquarters was shown on the division's balance sheet as cash and marketable securities. The amount shown as cash had been established by agreement between top management and the division manager, and it was considered by both to be about the minimum amount necessary to operate the division. The excess above this amount was shown on the division's balance sheet as marketable securities, and earned interest from headquarters at the rate of 6 percent a year. It was this account which varied with receipts and disbursements, leaving the cash account fixed as long as there was a balance in the securities account. It was possible for the securities account to be wiped out and for cash to decline below the minimum agreed on; but if this continued for more than a month or two, corrective action was taken. For Able Division, the minimum level was equal to about one month's sales, and in recent years cash had seldom gone below this amount.

Whether or not the company as a whole actually owned cash and marketable securities equal to the sum of all the respective divisions' cash and security accounts was strictly a headquarters matter. It probably was not necessary to hold this amount of cash and securities, since the division accounts had to cover division peak needs and, from headquarters' point of view, not all the peak needs necessarily occurred at the same time.

The size of a division's combined cash and marketable securities accounts was directly affected by all phases of the division's operation that used or produced cash. It also was affected in three other ways. One was the automatic deduction of 48 percent of income for tax purposes. Another was the payment of "dividends" by the division to headquarters. All earnings that the division manager did not wish to keep for future use were transferred to the corporation's cash account by payment of a dividend. Since a division was expected to retain a sufficient balance to provide for capital expenditures, dividends were paid generally only by the profitable divisions that were not expanding rapidly.

The third action affecting the cash account occurred if cash declined below the minimum, or if extensive capital expenditures had been approved. A division might then "borrow" from headquarters, paying interest as if it were a separate company. At the end of 1987, the Able Division had no loan and had been able to operate since about 1980 without borrowing from headquarters. Borrowing was not, in fact, currently being considered by the Able Division.

Except for its part in the establishment of a minimum cash level, top management was not involved in the determination of the division's investment in cash and marketable securities. Mr. Allen could control the level of this investment by deciding how much was to be paid in dividends. Since only a 6 percent return was received on the marketable securities and since the division earned more than that on its total investment, it was to its advantage to pay out as much as possible in dividends. When asked how he determined the size of the dividends, Mr. Allen said that he simply kept what he thought he would need to cover peak demands, capital expenditures, and contingencies. Improving the division's rate of return may have been part of the decision, but he did not mention it.

Accounts Receivable (21 percent of total assets)

All accounts receivable for the Able Division were collected at company headquarters. Though, in theory, Mr. Allen was allowed to set his own terms for divisional sales, in practice it would have been difficult to change the company's usual terms. Since Able Division sold to important customers of other divisions, any change from the net-30-day terms would disturb a large segment of the corporation's business. Furthermore, industry practice was well established, and the division would hardly try to change it.

The possibility of cash sales in situations in which credit was poor was virtually nonexistent. Credit was investigated for all customers by the headquarters credit department, and no sales were made without a prior credit check. For the Able Division, this policy presented no problem, for it sold primarily to well-established customers.

Inventory, Raw Material Metal Stock (about 3 percent of total investment)

In late 1987, inventory as a whole made up 20 percent of Able Division's total assets. A subdivision of the various kinds of inventory showed that raw material accounted for 7 percent; work-in-process, 11 percent; and finished goods and miscellaneous supplies, 2 percent. Since the Able Division produced to order, finished goods inventory was normally small, leaving raw material and work-in-process as the most significant classes of inventory.

The raw material inventory could be further subdivided to separate the raw material inventory from a variety of purchased parts. The strictly raw material inventory was composed primarily of metals and shapes, such as steel sheets or copper tubes. Most of the steel was bought according to a schedule arranged with the steel companies several months ahead of the delivery date. About a month before the steel company was to ship the order, Able Division would send the rolling instructions by shapes and weights. If the weight on any particular shape was below a minimum set by the steel company, Able Division would pay an extra charge for processing. Although this method of purchasing accounted for the bulk of steel purchases, smaller amounts were also bought as needed from warehouse stocks and specialty producers.

Copper was bought by headquarters and processed by the company's own mill. The divisions could buy the quantities they needed, but the price paid depended on corporate buying practices and processing costs. The price paid by Able Division had generally been competitive with outside sources, though it often lagged behind the market both in increases and in reductions in price.

The amounts of copper and steel bought were usually determined by the purchasing agent without recourse to any formal calculations of an economic ordering quantity. The reason for this was that, since such a large number of uncertain factors continually had to be estimated, a formal computation would not improve the process of determining how much to buy. Purchases depended on the amounts on hand, expected consumption, and current delivery time and price expectations. If delivery was fast, smaller amounts were usually bought. If a price increase was anticipated, somewhat larger orders often were placed at the current price. Larger amounts of steel were bought, for example, just before an anticipated steel strike, when steel negotiations were expected to result in a price increase, and perhaps also in a delay in deliveries.

The level of investment in raw material varied with the rates of purchase and use. Mr. Allen could control this class of asset within a fairly wide range, and there were no top-management directives governing the size of his raw material inventory.

Inventory, Purchased Parts, and Manufactured Parts (about 11 percent of total assets— 4 percent from raw material, 7 percent from work-in-process)

The Able Division purchased and manufactured parts for stock to be used later in the assembly of pumps. The method used to determine the purchase quantity was the same as that used to determine the length of production run on parts made for work-in-process stocks. The number of parts bought or manufactured was based on a series of calculations of an economical ordering quantity (EOQ).

Inventory, Floor Stocks (about 4 percent of total investment)

Floor stock inventory consisted of parts and components being worked on and assembled. Items became part of the floor stock inventory when they were requisitioned from the storage areas, or when delivered directly to the production floor. Pumps were worked on individually, so that lot size was not a factor to be considered. Mr. Allen could do little to control the level of floor stock inventory, except to see that there was no excess of parts piled around the production area.

Inventory, Finished Goods (2 percent of total investment)

As a rule, pumps were made to order and for immediate shipment. Finished goods inventory consisted of those few pumps on which shipment was delayed. Control of this investment was a matter of keeping it low by shipping the pumps as fast as possible.

Land, Buildings, and Machinery (47 pecent of total investment)

Since the Able Division's fixed assets, stated at gross cost, comprised 47 percent of total assets

at the end of 1987, the control of this particular group of assets was extremely important. Changes in the level of these investments depended on retirements and additions, the additions being entirely covered by the capital budgeting program.

Diversified Products Corporation's capital budgeting procedures were described in a planning manual. The planning sequence was as follows:

1. Headquarters forecasts economic conditions. (March)
2. The divisions plan long-term objectives. (June)
3. Supporting programs are submitted. (September) These are plans for specific actions, such as sales plans, advertising programs, and cost-reduction programs, and include the facilities program which is the capital expenditure request. The planning manual states under the heading, ''General Approach in the Development of a Coordinated Supporting Program,'' this advice:

Formulation and evaluation of a supporting program for each product line can generally be improved if projects are classified by purpose. The key objective of all planning is return on assets, a function of margin and turnover. These ratios are, in turn, determined by the three factors in the business equation—volume, costs, and assets. All projects, therefore, should be directed primarily at one of the following:

To increase volume.

To reduce costs and expenses.

To minimize assets.

4. Annual objective is submitted. (November 11, by 8 A.M.) The annual objective states projected sales, costs, expenses, profits, and cash expenditures and receipts, and show pro forma balance sheets and income statements.

Mr. Allen was ''responsible for the division's assets and for provision for the growth and expansion of the division.'' Growth referred to the internal refinements of product design and production methods as well as to the cost-reduction programs. Expansion involved a 5- or 10-year program, including about 2 years for construction.

In the actual capital expenditure request there were four kinds of facilities proposals.

1. Cost-reduction projects, which were self-liquidating investments. Reduction in labor costs was usually the largest source of the savings, which were stated in terms of the liquidation period and the rate of return.

2. Necessity projects. These included replacement of worn-out machinery, technical changes to meet competition, and facilties for the safety and comfort of the workers.

3. Product-improvement projects.

4. Expansion projects.

Justification of the cost-reduction proposals was based on a comparison of the estimated rate of return (estimated return before taxes divided by gross investment) with the 20 percent standard, as specified by headquarters. If the project was considered desirable and yet showed a return of less than 20 percent, it had to be justified on other grounds and was included in the necessities category. Cost-reduction proposals made up about 60 percent of the 1988 capital expenditure budget, and in earlier years these proposals had accounted for at least 50 percent. Very little of Able Division's 1988 capital budget had been allocated specifically for product improvement and none for expansion, so that most of the remaining 40 percent was to be used for necessity projects. Thus, a little over half of Able Division's capital expenditure was justified primarily on the estimated rate of return on the investment. The remainder, having advantages that could not be stated in terms of the rate of return, was justified on other grounds.

Mr. Allen was free to include what he wanted in his capital budget request, and for the three years that he had been division manager his requests had always been granted. However, no large expansion projects had been included in the capital budget requests of the last three years. Most of the capital expenditures had been for cost-reduction projects, and the remainder were for necessities. Annual additions had approximately equaled annual retirements.

Since Mr. Allen could authorize expenditures of up to $100,000 per project for purposes approved by the board, there was, in fact, some flexibility in his choice of projects after the budget had been approved by higher management. Not only could he schedule the order of expenditure but, in some circumstances, he could substitute unforeseen projects of a similar nature. If top management approved $50,000 for miscellaneous cost-reduction projects, Mr. Allen could spend this on the projects he considered most important, whether or not they were specifically described in his original budget request.

For the corporation as a whole, about one quarter of the capital expenditure was for projects of under $100,000, which could be authorized for expenditure by the division managers. This portion was considered by top management to be about right; if, however, it rose much above this fraction, the $100,000 dividing line would probably be lowered.

QUESTIONS

1. Evaluate the company's methods of establishing the working capital portion (i.e., current assets and liabilities) and fixed asset portion of the investment base. For each element of the investment base, ask:

   a. What is the nature of the responsibility of divisional management?

   b. What is the extent of control in discharging this responsibility?

   c. How is the company's practice for incorporating this element into the ROI yardstick most likely to influence the actions of divisional management?

    d. Are such actions in the best interest of the entire company?

2. When considering the company's treatment of cash, you may find it useful to try diagramming the procedures using T-accounts at the divisional and corporate levels.

Case 6–5

Cheetah Division*

The Cheetah Division of the Multi-National Motors Corporation designed and sold Cheetah automobiles and parts to dealers throughout the United States and Europe. The division was responsible for designing, engineering, and marketing its products; but the Assembly Division manufactured Cheetah products.

Each division of Multi-National Motors was responsible for earning a return on its investment. Investment in Multi-National was calculated as follows:

Cash: 10 percent of the costs of sales.

Receivables } Average end-of-month
Inventories } actual balances.

Fixed assets: Average actual gross book value at end of the month.

Profits were calculated in accordance with the company's accounting system. Because of its relatively low asset base (few fixed assets) and its high profit potential, the Cheetah Division had a profit objective of 40 percent return on investment before income taxes.

Inventory Control Problem

In addition to marketing automobiles, the Cheetah Division was responsible for supplying repair and replacement parts and accessories to its dealers throughout the country. This required an extensive warehouse system since parts were supplied for automobiles as much as 15 years old. The system handled over 20,000 different parts, with annual sales in excess of $100 million.

In 1983, the corporation established an operations research group, with responsibility for reviewing inventory control procedures throughout the company. In carrying out this assignment, members of this group visited the Cheetah Division.

An important inventory control problem was one involving buying current model parts at the end of the model year. At the end of each model year, any parts to be discontinued with the new model became past model service parts. A past model service part was usually much more expensive to produce (and consequently buy) than a current model part because of setup time and the short length of the run. For example, at the end of the 1983 model year, front fenders were to be changed. During regular production, fenders were run continuously over an automated line. There was no setup cost, and production was very efficient. Consequently, the manufacturing cost of a 1983 fender was low during the 1983 model year. Once the part had been discontinued, however, the costs of production became quite high. It was necessary to pull the dies out of storage, clean them, place them in presses, try them out (usually involving spoiling a certain amount of material), and then run off the required number of parts without any automation. Thus, the cost of a past model service part was typically several times higher than what it was as a current model part.

Because of this cost differential, it was usual to order at the end of a model year a relatively large

* This case was prepared by John Dearden, Harvard Business School.
Copyright © by the President and Fellows of Harvard College.
Harvard Business School case 113–068.

supply of those parts that were to be discontinued. A formula had been developed that provided the economic order quantity. This formula determined the point where the added cost of carrying the inventory was equal to the cost savings from buying at current model prices. The formula was quite complex and need not be described here. An important feature of the formula, however, was that the cost of carrying inventory included a return on the capital tied up in the inventory. The operation research group reviewed the formula and agreed that it was a reasonable method for calculating the economic order quantity. The group, however, was surprised to find that the Cheetah Division used a 40 percent capital cost for carrying inventory. Other divisions used between 15 and 25 percent in their inventory decision formulas. Currently, the corporation had over $500 million invested in government securities that were earning only 7 percent before taxes.

The operations research group raised two questions concerning the economic order quantity formula.

1. They questioned whether 40 percent was too high a percentage for the capital charge of carrying inventories. Their estimate was that it should be no more than 20 percent.

2. They questioned the fact that the Cheetah Division used the purchase price (charged by the Assembly Division) to calculate the investment in the inventory. The company's out-of-pocket cost of most parts was between 50 percent and 60 percent of the purchase price.

The controller of the Cheetah Division met with the operations research group and told them bluntly that she had no intention of changing the formula. This formula optimized her rate of return, she believed. If she followed the group's suggestions she would be lowering the rate of return that her division earned. She stated that if it was really to the benefit of the company for her to use a 20 percent cost of investment on 60 percent of her purchase price, she would be glad to comply provided that the Cheetah Division were

given the benefit of the increased profit that the company would earn. Otherwise, she would continue to do as she was instructed—and that was to maximize the division's return on investment.

The Parts Warehouse Problem

In 1986, the Cheetah Division was in the process of building two new parts warehouses on the West Coast. At that time, the Sparrow Division of Multi-National requested that Cheetah provide some space in those warehouses for Sparrow parts. Sparrow was a much smaller division than Cheetah and could not justify economically a new warehouse. However, the location on the West Coast of two new supply points would improve the effectiveness of Sparrow's distribution system. Sparrow asked for space equal to about 10 percent of the total.

After the warehouses had been completed and both the Cheetah and Sparrow parts systems were placed in operation, the question of charging for the service came up. Cheetah proposed that Sparrow pay a proportionate share of the cost of running the warehouses plus a return on their proportionate share of the investment. The calculation was made as follows:

10% of cost of operating warehouses	$ 200,000
10% of the investment in warehouses;	
$2,000,000	
40% of $2,000,000	800,000
Total annual charges	$1,000,000

The Sparrow Division was astounded with the charge, which was several times higher than the going rate for available leased warehouse space. Sparrow agreed with the $200,000 but disagreed violently with paying $800,000 for the return on investment. The Cheetah Division pointed out that it had invested $2,000,000 at the request of Sparrow and that it had to earn $800,000 before taxes on this investment in order to meet its profit objective. The Sparrow Division said that it could lease space anywhere on the West Coast for a fraction of Cheetah's charge and that was what it proposed to do. Sparrow stated that Cheetah may have a 40 percent return but Sparrow was lucky to break even without the exorbitant rental.

QUESTION

How should each of these problems be resolved?

Case 6-6

Marden Company*

A typical division of Marden Company had financial statements as shown in Exhibit 1. Accounts receivable were billed by the division, but customers make payment to bank accounts (i.e., lockboxes) maintained in the name of Marden Company and located throughout the country. The debt item on the balance sheet is a proportionate part of the corporate 9 percent bond issue. Interest on this debt was not charged to the division.

EXHIBIT 1 Typical Division Financial Statements

Balance Sheet
End of Year (condensed; $000)

Assets		Equities	
Cash	$ 100	Accounts payable	$ 400
Accounts receivable	800		
Inventory	900		
Total current assets	1,800	Total current liabilities	400
Plant and equipment, cost	1,000	Debt	700
Depreciation (straight line)	400	Equity	1,300
Plant and equipment, net	600		2,000
Total assets	$2,400	Total equities	$2,400

Divisional Income Statement

Sales	$4,000
Costs, other than those listed below	3,200
Depreciation	100
Allocated share of corporate expenses	100
Income before income tax	600

QUESTION

Recommend the best way of measuring the performance of the division manager. If you need additional information, make the assumption you believe to be most reasonable.

---

* This case was prepared by Robert N. Anthony.
Copyright © by Osceola Institute.

Case 6-7

Lemfert Company*

Lemfert Company was a large manufacturing company organized into divisions, each with responsibility for earning a satisfactory return on its investment. Division managers had considerable autonomy in carrying out this responsibility. Some divisions fabricated parts; others—here called "end-item divisions"—assembled these parts, together with purchased parts, into finished products and marketed the finished products. Transfer prices were used in connection with the transfer of parts among the various fabricating divisions and from the fabricating divisions to the end-item divisions. Wherever possible, these transfer prices were the lowest prices charged by outside manufacturers for the same or comparable items, with appropriate adjustments for inbound freight, volume, and similar factors.

Parts that were not similar to those manufactured by outside companies were called "type K items." In most fabricating divisions, these items constituted only 5 to 10 percent of total volume. In Division F, however, approximately 75 percent of total volume was accounted for by type K items. Division F manufactured 10 such items for various end-item divisions; they were less than 5 percent of the total cost of any one of these end-item divisions. The procedure for arriving at the transfer price for type K items is described below.

First, a tentative transfer price was calculated by the value analysis staff of the corporate purchasing department and was submitted to the two divisions involved for their consideration. This price was supposed to be based on the estimated costs of an efficient producer plus a profit margin. An "efficient producer" was considered to be one conducting its purchasing and using modern equipment in a manner that could reasonably be expected of the company's principal competitors.

The material cost portion of the total cost was based on current competitive price levels. Direct labor cost was supposed to reflect efficient processing on modern equipment. Overhead cost represented an amount that could be expected of an efficient producer using modern equipment. Depreciation expense, expenditures on special tooling, and a standard allowance for administrative expense were included in the overhead figure.

The profit margin was equal to the divisional profit objective applied to the cost of the assets employed to produce the product in question. Assets employed was the sum of the following items.

Cash and receivables—18 percent of the total manufacturing cost.

Inventories—the value of the optimum inventory size required at standard volume.

Fixed assets—the depreciated book value (but not less than one-half original cost) of assets used to fabricate the part, including a fair share of buildings and other general assets, but excluding standby and obsolete facilities.

The percentage used for cash and receivables was based on studies of the cash and receivables balances of the principal outside manufacturers of parts similar to those manufactured in the fabri-

* This case was prepared by R. N. Anthony, Harvard Business School.
Copyright © by the President and Fellows of Harvard College.
Harvard Business School case 113–116.

cating divisions. The standard volume was an estimate of the volume that the plants should *normally* be expected to produce, which was not necessarily the same as current volume or projected volume for the next year.

For an average division, the budgeted profit objective was 20 percent of assets employed; but there were variations among divisions. The divisional budget profit objective multiplied by the assets employed, as calculated above, gave the profit margin for the item. This profit was added to the cost to arrive at the suggested transfer price, which then was submitted to the two divisions. If either the buying or the selling division believed that the price thus determined was unfair, it first attempted to negotiate a mutually satisfactory price. If the parties were unable to agree, they submitted the dispute to the controller for arbitration. Either party might appeal the results of this arbitration to the executive vice president.

QUESTIONS

1. Are these the best transfer price practices for the Lemfert Company? If not, how should they be revised?
2. For what types of companies would the revised policy not be best? Why?
3. Do you think the attempt to measure profitability in Division F is worthwhile? If not, how would you measure performance in this division?

Case 6–8
Schoppert Company*

Mr. P. A. Franken, controller of Schoppert, was considering the appropriateness of available means for appraising the annual operating results for each of the company's product lines. Schoppert Gereedschapfabrieken, N.V., located near Leiden in the Netherlands, manufactured a variety of hand tools, such as wrenches, screwdrivers, chisels, and so forth. The company produced several hundred different products, but from the point of view of sales and production these could be grouped into five quite different product lines or groups.

Mr. Franken was interested in applying the concept of return on investment to the evaluation of the company's individual product line. He stated his reasons for this as follows:

> When a company sells a number of different product groups there is a danger that the relative position of each product group in the total is judged by the profit made on the turnover of each separate group. There is a tendency to judge the yield of each group by comparing these percentages. In doing so, one forgets that the first purpose of a business is to make a profit on its employed capital, and that making a profit on the turnover is only a means to that purpose. As some of our product groups for a given turnover need a much higher employed capital than others, I think it is necessary to take these differences into account, by showing the profit in each product group as a percentage of the employed capital.

Product-Line Profit

The company regularly prepared product-line income statements based on what was known as a cost price calculation. The profit for each product line was obtained by deducting product costs from turn-over (sales) for the product line. There were four elements of cost in the product-line income statements, as follows:

1. Variable cost. These included raw materials, direct labor, paint, solder, and the like. These were standard costs, which were based on time studies, product specifications, and so forth, and could be traced directly to individual products. They tended to vary more or less proportionately with volume of production. These variable costs accounted for about 74 percent of total costs at normal volume levels.

2. Direct fixed costs. These included costs of operating and maintaining factory buildings (allocated on a square meter basis), costs of maintenance of machinery, machine depreciation, interest, cleaning, and so forth. All of these except the building costs could be readily traced to small groups of products. They were allocated to individual products on the basis of machine hours. These costs accounted for about 12 percent of total costs at normal volume levels.

3. Plant costs. These included such things as maintenance, operation, and depreciation of forklift trucks, salaries and wages of supervisory and clerical staffs, and maintenance of office buildings. These costs were allocated to product lines on a value-added basis—that is, the total of the costs included in groups 1 and 2 above, less the costs of raw material. At usual operating levels they amounted to about 8 percent of total costs.

4. Head office expenses. These included wages and salaries of head office personnel and of man-

---

agement, maintenance and depreciation of head office buildings and equipment, and laboratory expense. They were allocated to products on the basis of the ratio of these costs to the total of costs in groups 1, 2, and 3, including raw material. They usually amounted to about 6 percent of all other costs.

These cost calculations provided a basis for overall evaluation of product lines and for selling price calculations. For control purposes, the company had a system of manufacturing expense budgets and standards for the variable and traceable costs in each department.

Product-Line Investment

Evaluation and appraisal of the results of each of the product lines was traditionally made by comparing this profit with sales. Mr. Franken, for reasons given earlier, felt that this product-line profit should be compared with the investment necessary to support production and sale of the product line.

To do this, it was necessary to determine what the investment in each product line actually was. Mr. Franken made an analysis of product-line investments, which he regarded only as a preliminary step. His procedures are described below and the results, for the five product groups, are shown in Exhibit 1.

Current Assets

In the case of current assets, it was possible to trace the investment in stocks (inventories) directly to the product group. Accounts receivable could also be traced to the product groups that gave rise to them. Mr. Franken deducted accounts payable (also traceable to product lines) from accounts receivable in determining product-line investments.

Mr. Franken felt that it was not possible to relate cash to individual product groups: that the amount of cash required by any particular product group could not be determined accurately. Consequently, he excluded cash from his calculations of product-line investments.

Fixed Assets

In dealing with fixed assets Mr. Franken used replacement value less accumulated depreciation rather than net book value based on historical cost. He felt that the use of historical cost would make it impossible to compare departments with each other, if some utilized older machinery purchased when price levels were lower while others worked with machinery that had a much higher cost as a result of price inflation.

Mr. Franken initially used insured values as an estimate of replacement value, but he expected to develop a system of price indexes that would permit a more precise determination of replacement

---

EXHIBIT 1   Analysis of Product-Line Profits*

	Product Line					
	A	*B*	*C*	*D*	*E*	*Total*
Investment	fl. 56.0	fl.11.8	fl. 1.6	fl. 1.0	fl. 0.6	fl. 71.0
Sales	118.0	18.5	3.3	1.2	1.0	142.0
Profits	4.5	.6	.4	.2	.2	5.5
Profit as percent of investment	8.0%	5.1%	25.0%	20.0%	33.3%	7.7%
Profits as percent of sales	3.8%	3.2%	12.1%	16.7%	20.0%	3.9%

*Monetary amounts are in millions of Dutch guilders.

value. From insured value an allowance of 40 percent (of insured value) was deducted to give an approximation of replacement value less accumulated depreciation. In the case of depreciation, as in the case of replacement value, Mr. Franken looked forward to the development of more refined procedures for determining the amounts involved.

Most buildings, machinery, and equipment could be traced directly to individual product groups. In a great many cases, the machinery used by Schoppert was quite highly specialized and was used only for manufacturing certain specific products.

In the case of buildings and other facilities utilized by more than one product group, and in the case of such things as the company's head office and its research laboratory, the problem was considerably more complex. Mr. Franken simply allocated these costs to product lines on the basis of the costs that were traceable to the product lines.

The value of current assets (less accounts payable) and of machinery and equipment traced directly to product lines amounted to about 90 percent of total assets (not including cash and less accounts payable and depreciation). Thus, the allocated portion of product-line investment represented about 10 percent of the total.

QUESTIONS

1. What were Mr. Franken's objectives in designing the new product-line income statements?
2. Are the statements likely to meet these objectives in their present form, or would you suggest some improvements?

Chapter 7

Strategies

Management control systems are tools to implement strategies. Strategies differ in different types of organizations, and controls should be tailored to the requirements of specific strategies. Different strategies require different task priorities; different key success factors; and different skills, perspectives, and behaviors. Thus, a continuing concern in the design of control systems should be whether the behavior induced by the system is the one desired by the strategy.

In this chapter we discuss strategies at two levels in an organization: the corporate level and the business unit level. In Chapter 13, we discuss how to vary the form and structure of control systems in accordance with variations in corporate and business unit strategies.

TWO LEVELS OF STRATEGY

Since about 1960, a dramatic increase in attention has been paid to strategy formulation concepts among academics and practitioners. Several influential books and articles in the major academic journals have contributed to this. Since 1970, two journals (*Strategic Management Journal* and *Journal of Business Strategy*) devoted to strategic management issues and concerns have been started. The major management journals (*Harvard Business Review, Sloan Management Review, California Management Review*) have for many years published articles on strategy. In 1979, *Business Week* claimed that strategic planning is the concept that has become the major thrust and emphasis in the management of corporations.[1]

Although there are minor differences in the definitions, there is general agreement that "strategies" describe the general directions in which an orga-

---

[1] "Publishers' Memo," *Business Week*, January 9, 1979, p. 5.

nization plans to go to attain its goals. They are big plans, important plans.[2] Every well-managed organization has strategies, although they may not be stated explicitly. Strategies can be described at two levels: (1) strategies for the organization as a whole and (2) strategies for business units within the organization.

About 85 percent of Fortune 500 industrial firms in the United States are diversified into more than one business and consequently undertake strategy formulation at two levels—corporate and business unit levels.

Level 1: Corporate Strategy

At the corporate level, the key strategic questions are:

1. In what set of businesses—industries or subindustries—should the firm be?
2. What should be the missions of the business units?

Answers to these questions result in the deletion, retention, and addition of businesses to the firm's portfolio as well as the help to the corporate office in deciding how many resources should be allocated to each.

Level 2: Business Unit Strategy

At the business unit level, the key strategic questions are:

1. For each chosen business, what should be its mission (a question that is relevant for both corporate and business unit levels)?
2. How should the business unit compete to accomplish its mission?

For diversified firms, the corporate level is distinct from the business unit level. For these firms, the corporate strategy deals with deciding the appropriate portfolio of businesses, and the business unit strategy deals with the specific product market strategy for each business. For single business firms, there is, of course, no business unit strategy. The CEO of a single business firm deals with the same strategic issues as the general manager of a business unit in a diversified firm.

Although strategic choices are different at different hierarchical levels, there is a clear need for consistency in strategies across organizational levels. Corporate strategy provides the organizing concept that guides the activities of the separate business units within the diversified firm. Exhibit 7–1 summarizes the strategy concerns at the two organizational levels and the generic strategic

---

[2] Writings on military strategy go back thousands of years. The military distinguishes between *strategy,* which refers to operations in a particular theater, and *grand strategy,* which relates to worldwide geopolitical goals. As used here, strategy corresponds to grand strategy as used in the military.

EXHIBIT 7–1   Two Levels of Strategy

Strategy Level	Key Strategic Issues	Generic Strategic Options	Primary Organizational Levels Involved
Corporate level	Are we in the right mix of businesses? What set of businesses—industries or subindustries—should we be in?	Single business. Related diversification. Unrelated diversification.	Corporate office.
Business unit level	What should be the mission of the business unit?	Build. Hold. Harvest. Divest.	Corporate office and business unit general manager.
	How should the business unit compete to realize its mission?	Low cost. Differentiation.	Business unit general manager.

options at each level. The remainder of this chapter will elaborate on the ideas summarized in Exhibit 7–1. Given the systems orientation of this book, we will not attempt an exhaustive analysis of the appropriate content of strategies. We rather provide enough appreciation for the strategy development process so the reader is able to identify the strategies at various organizational levels as part of an evaluation of the firm's management control system.

CORPORATE-LEVEL STRATEGY

Corporate strategy is about being in the right set of businesses. Thus, corporate strategy is concerned more with the question of *where* to compete than with *how* to compete in a particular business; the latter is the territory of business unit strategy. At the corporate level, the issues are: (1) the definition of businesses in which the firm will participate (and, by omission, those in which it will not participate) and (2) the deployment of resources among those businesses. The net result of corporatewide strategic analysis are decisions involving businesses to delete, businesses to retain, and businesses to add to the firm's portfolio.

Companies can be classified into one of three categories. A "single business" firm operates in one line of business. Apple Computers, which is in the personal computing business, is an example. A "related diversified" firm operates in several businesses, which are broadly related to one another. Procter & Gamble, with business units in detergents, diapers, and other branded consumer products, is an example. In related diversified firms, the units share common skills and resources; the business units of Procter & Gamble share a common sales force and common distribution channels. An "unrelated diversi-

EXHIBIT 7–2 Corporate-Level Strategies: Graphical Representation of Generic Corporate Strategies

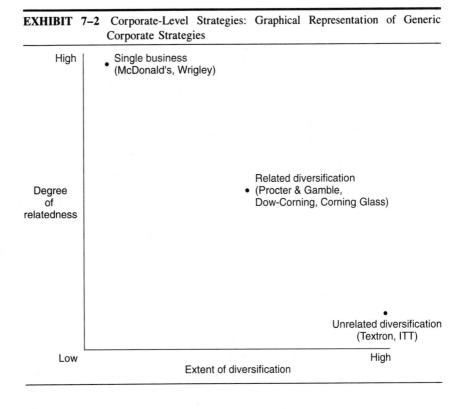

fied'' firm operates in businesses that are unrelated to one another. International Telephone and Telegraph (ITT), which has business units as diverse as telecommunications, insurance, and hotels, is an example.

At the corporate level, one of the most significant dimensions along which strategic contexts differ is the *extent and type* of diversification undertaken by different firms, as depicted in Exhibit 7–2.

Single Business Firms

One axis in Exhibit 7–2—extent of diversification—relates to the number of industries (or businesses) in which the company operates. At one extreme, the company may be totally committed to one industry. We refer to such a firm as a single business corporation. In addition to Apple Computers, other firms that pursue a single business strategy include Maytag (major household appliances), Wrigley (chewing gum), Perdue Farms (poultry), and Stihl (chain saws). A single business firm also pursues a corporate strategy by choosing to concentrate on one business, rather than spreading itself over many.

Unrelated Diversified Firms

At the other extreme, there are firms, such as Textron, that participate in a number of different industries. For instance, Textron operates in businesses as diverse as writing instruments, helicopters, chain saws, aircraft engine components, forklifts, machine tools, specialty fasteners, and gas turbine engines.

The other axis in Exhibit 7–2—degree of relatedness—refers to the nature of linkages across the multiple business units. Here we refer to "operating synergies" across businesses—such as common technology, common manufacturing, common marketing, or common distribution across several business units. In the case of Textron, except for financial transactions, its business units have little in common. Textron headquarters functions like a holding company, lending money to business units that are expected to have high financial returns. We refer to such firms as "unrelated diversified firms" or "conglomerates." Other examples of conglomerates are ITT, FMC, Litton, Gulf & Western, and LTV. Conglomerates diversify their activities primarily through acquisition.

Related Diversified Firms

Another group consists of firms that participate in a number of industries; but their businesses are connected to each other either by common customers, common distribution channels, common technology, or some other common factor. We refer to these firms as "related diversified firms."

The key characteristic of related diversified firms is that they possess *core competencies* that benefit many of their business units.[3] They accomplish diversification by relating new businesses to old. These firms set out to exploit operating synergies across businesses. Dow Corning is a diversified firm but usually enters those new products/markets that use its core competence in silicon chemistry. Similarly, Corning Glass has a diversified set of businesses (cookware, optical wave guides) but most of their products derive from glass technology. Other examples of related diversified firms include Procter & Gamble, Philip Morris, Du Pont, Texas Instruments, Emerson Electric, and American Telephone & Telegraph. Related diversified firms typically grow through internal research and development.

Implications of Different Corporate Strategies on Control Systems Design

Corporate strategy is a continuum, with "single business" strategy at one end and "unrelated diversification" at the other end. Many companies do not fit neatly into one of the three classes. However, most companies can be classified

---

[3] C. K. Prahalad and G. Hamel, "The Core Competence of the Corporation," *Harvard Business Review,* May–June 1990, pp.79–91.

along this continuum. A firm's location on this continuum depends on the extent and type of its diversification. Exhibit 7–3 summarizes the key characteristics of the generic corporate strategies.

Control system designers need not concern themselves with when and how a firm should choose one of the three corporate strategies. Choosing the right strategy is the task of senior management. Systems designers fit the controls to that strategy.

The planning and control requirements of companies pursuing different corporate-level diversification strategies (i.e., extent and type of diversification) are quite different. The key issue for control systems designers, therefore, is: How should the structure and form of control differ across an Apple Computers Corporation (a single business firm), a Procter & Gamble (a related diversified firm), or an ITT (an unrelated diversified firm)? In Chapters 8 through 12, we discuss the steps in the management control process. In Chapter 13, we discuss how these control systems should be designed so they implement a given firm's strategies.

BUSINESS UNIT STRATEGY: MISSION AND COMPETITIVE ADVANTAGE

Diversified firms do not compete with one another in the same industry. Rather, their individual business units compete with other business units. The corporate office of a diversified firm does not produce profit by itself. Revenues are generated and costs are incurred in the business units. Business unit strategies deal with how to create and maintain competitive advantage in each of the businesses in which a company participates. The strategy of a business unit depends upon two interrelated aspects: (1) its mission ("what are its overall objectives"?) and (2) its competitive advantage ("how should the business unit compete in its industry to accomplish its mission?").

Possible missions and approaches that senior management can use in deciding on the appropriate mission for each of its business units are described in this section. The choice of competitive advantage for accomplishing the mission is discussed in the next section.

Business Unit Mission

The CEO of a single business firm is directly involved in decisions regarding how to compete in that business. In contrast, at the headquarters level in a diversified company, a comparable level of detail regarding the product market strategies of its various businesses is not possible. Rather, the CEO's primary task in a diversified firm becomes portfolio management—that is, what businesses to be in, how to deploy resources between them, and how to integrate the multiple businesses into a total corporate picture. One important advantage that a diversified firm has over a single business firm is that it can use the cash

EXHIBIT 7–3 Corporate-Level Strategies: Summary of Three Generic Strategies

Type of corporate strategy	Single business firm	Related diversified firm	Unrelated diversified firm
Pictorial representation of strategy			
Identifying features	Competes in only one product market	Sharing of core competencies across businesses	Totally autonomous businesses in very different markets
Examples	Apple Computers McDonald's Corporation Perdue Farms Iowa Beef Wrigley Stihl Crown, Cork & Seal Maytag Texas Air	Procter & Gamble Emerson Electric Corning Glass Johnson & Johnson Philip Morris Dow-Corning Du Pont General Foods Gillette Texas Instruments AT&T	ITT Textron Gulf & Western Fuqua LTV FMC Litton Rockwell Colt Industries

generated from some business units to finance growth in other business units. A single business firm has to rely on the profits generated by that business (and on external capital markets) to finance additional resource needs, whereas the diversified firm can internalize the traditional capital market function of allocating resources to different businesses.

Portfolio planning models. Several portfolio planning models have been developed to help corporate-level managers of diversified firms allocate resources among varied businesses.[4] Since these models relate to the identification of the missions of individual business units, we discuss them in this section. Both the corporate office and the business unit general manager are involved in defining the mission of the business unit.

While differences exist, the focus of all portfolio planning models is similar: combine measures of the attractiveness of market opportunities available to a business unit with measures of the unit's competitive ability to exploit these opportunities so the CEO can make a reasoned judgment regarding investments in that business unit relative to other units. More specifically, the central themes of these models are:

1. Two broad sets of factors—factors *external* to the firm and factors *internal* to the firm—determine, respectively, the attractiveness of market opportunities available to individual business units and their competitive ability to exploit these opportunities.
2. Within the firm, competitive ability is likely to vary from one business unit to another.
3. The relevant industry's attractiveness is also likely to vary from one business unit to another.
4. Thus, the mission (in terms of growth and profitability) varies from one business unit to another.
5. Collectively, the missions assigned to the different business units should help the firm achieve its overall goals.
6. Resource allocation among business units should be based on their respective missions.

Of the many portfolio analysis approaches, three of the most widely used are: Boston Consulting Group's two-by-two growth-share matrix (Exhibit 7–4), General Electric Company/McKinsey & Company's three-by-three industry attractiveness–business strength matrix (Exhibit 7–5), and Arthur D. Little, Inc.'s, life cycle approach (Exhibit 7–6). While these models differ in the methodologies they use to develop the most appropriate missions for the various

---

[4] In a survey of Fortune 1,000 companies, Haspeslagh reported that 75 percent of the companies practice portfolio planning. P. Haspeslagh, "Portfolio Planning: Uses and Limits," *Harvard Business Review*, January–February 1982, pp. 58–73.

EXHIBIT 7–4   Business Unit Mission: The BCG Portfolio Model

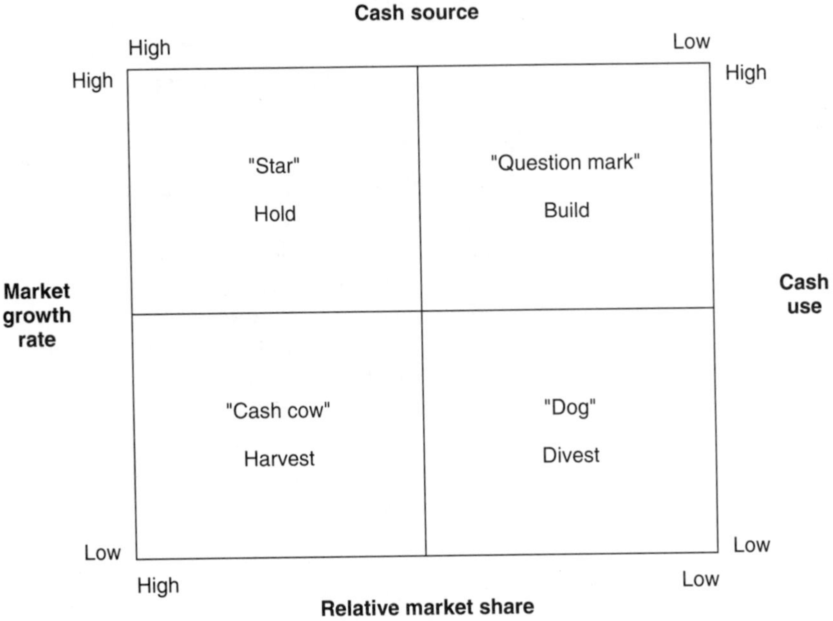

Cash source

	High		Low	
High		"Star" Hold	"Question mark" Build	High
Market growth rate				**Cash use**
		"Cash cow" Harvest	"Dog" Divest	
Low				Low
	High		Low	

Relative market share

Sources: R. A. Kerin, V. Mahajan, and P. R. Varadarajan, *Strategic Market Planning* (Boston, Mass.: Allyn & Bacon, 1990).

B. D. Henderson, *Corporate Strategy* (Cambridge, Mass.: Abt Books, 1979).

---

business units, they have the same set of missions that one has to choose from: *build, hold, harvest,* and *divest.*

According to the Boston Consulting Group (BCG) model, every business unit can be placed in one of four categories—**question mark, star, cash cow, and dog**—that represent the four cells of a 2x2 matrix, which measures industry growth rate on one axis and relative market share on the other (Exhibit 7–4). BCG views industry growth rate as an indicator of relative industry attractiveness and relative market share as an indicator of the relative competitive position of a business unit within a given industry. Because market growth for the whole industry is largely uncontrollable, portfolio analysis reduces to determining a market share strategy for each business unit.

BCG singled out market share as the primary strategy variable, because of the importance it placed on the notion of "experience curve." According to BCG, cost per unit (adjusted for inflation and for changes in the cost of purchased items) decreases predictably with the number of units produced (cumulative experience). Since the market share leader will have the greatest accumulated production experience, such a firm should have the lowest costs and highest profits in the industry. BCG used the following line of thinking to argue that the route to higher profitability is via building market share:

Higher market share	→	Higher accumulated experience	→	Lower unit cost	→	Higher profitability

The association between market share and profitability has also been empirically supported by the Profit Impact of Market Strategy (PIMS) data base.[5] If applied with caution, the experience curve is a powerful analytical tool; however, it has limitations, some of which are as follows.

1. The concept applies to undifferentiated products where the primary basis of competition is on price. For these products, becoming the low cost player is critical. However, market share and low cost are not the only routes to success. There are low market share firms (such as Mercedes-Benz in automobiles) that earn high profits by emphasizing product uniqueness rather than low cost.[6]

2. An aggressive pursuit of reducing cost via accumulated production of standardized items can lead to loss of flexibility in the marketplace. The classic example of this problem is when, during the 1920s, Henry Ford standardized the car ("I will give you any color provided it is black") and aggressively reduced costs. Ford lost its leadership in the auto industry when General Motors sold the consumers on product variety ("A car for every purse and every purpose"), so much so that, in 1927, Ford discontinued the Model T and suffered a 12-month shutdown for retooling.[7]

3. Commitment to the experience curve concept can be a severe disadvantage if new technologies emerge in the industry. Timex's low cost position in the watch industry, built over several years, was erased overnight when Texas Instruments entered the market with digital watches.

4. Experience is not the only cost driver. There are other drivers that regulate cost behavior: scale, scope, technology, and complexity, just to name a few.[8] A firm needs to consider carefully the relevant cost drivers at work to achieve the low cost position.

BCG used the following logic to make strategic prescriptions for each of the four cells in Exhibit 7–4:

1. Profit margins and cash generation increase with relative market share, due to experience effects.
2. Market growth requires cash for working capital and perhaps for additional plant. Actual cash requirement is, therefore, a function of market growth rate and market share strategy.

---

[5] Robert D. Buzzell, Bradley T. Gale, and Ralph G. M. Sultan, "Market Share—A Key to Profitability," *Harvard Business Review* 53 (January–February 1975), pp. 97–106.

[6] Richard G. Hammermesh, et al., "Strategies for Low Market Share Companies," *Harvard Business Review,* May–June 1978, pp. 95–102.

[7] William J. Abernathy and Kenneth Wayne, "Limits of the Learning Curve," *Harvard Business Review,* September–October 1974, pp. 109–19.

[8] For a discussion on multiple cost drivers, refer to J. K. Shank and V. Govindarajan, *Strategic Cost Analysis* (Homewood, Ill.: Richard D. Irwin, 1989), chap. 3.

3. Some business units will be self-sufficient in cash, some will need more cash than they can generate, while some other units will generate more cash than they can use.

4. The corporation's overall cash flow must be balanced. Therefore, the role of the corporate office is to select a portfolio of business units from the standpoint of balancing the firm's total cash needs and its cash-generating ability plus outside financing.

Business units that fall in the **question mark** quadrant are typically assigned the mission: "build" market share. The logic behind this recommendation is related to the beneficial effects of the experience curve. BCG argues that, by building market share early in the growth phase of an industry, the business unit will have the greatest accumulated experience and consequently the lowest costs in the industry. These units are cash guzzlers, since major expenditures are needed in the areas of product development, market development, and capacity expansion. These expenditures are aimed at establishing market leadership in the short term, which will depress short-term profits. However, the increased market share is intended to result in long-term profitability. Some businesses in the question mark quadrant might also be divested if their cash needs to build competitive position are extremely high. For instance, in the early 70s, RCA decided to divest its computer division, because of the enormous cash outflows that would be required to build market share in such a capital-intensive and highly competitive industry.

Business units that fall in the **star** quadrant are typically assigned the mission: "hold" market share. These units already have a high market share in their industry, and the objective is to invest cash to maintain that competitive position. These units generate significant amounts of cash (because of their market leadership), but they also need significant infusions of cash to maintain their competitive strength in a growing market. On balance, therefore, these units are self-sufficient and do not require resources from other parts of the organization.

Business units that fall in the **cash cow** quadrant are the primary sources of cash for the firm. Since these units have high relative market share, they probably have the lowest unit costs and consequently the highest profits. On the other hand, since these units operate in low-growth or declining industries, they do not need much cash for reinvestment. Therefore, on a net basis, these units generate significant amounts of positive cash flows. Such units are typically assigned the mission: "harvest" for short-term profits and cash flows.

Businesses in the **dog** quadrant have weak competitive position in unattractive industries. They usually are divested unless there is a good possibility of turning them around.

The role of the corporate office is to identify enough cash cows with positive cash flows and redeploy those resources to build market share in question marks (presumably, the star business units would be self-sufficient in cash).

The General Electric Company/McKinsey & Company grid (Exhibit 7–5) and the Arthur D. Little, grid (Exhibit 7–6) are similar to the BCG grid in helping corporations assign missions across business units. However, their methodology differs from the BCG approach in the following respects:

1. BCG uses industry growth rate as a proxy for industry attractiveness. In the General Electric grid, industry attractiveness is computed based on weighted judgments about such factors as market size, market growth, cyclicality, entry barriers, technological obsolescence, and the like. The Arthur D. Little grid uses the product life cycle concept to operationalize industry attractiveness.

2. BCG uses relative market share as a proxy for the business unit's current competitive position. The General Electric and Arthur D. Little grids, on the other hand, use multiple factors (e.g., market share, distribution strengths, engineering strengths, and so on) to assess the competitive position of the business unit.

Four missions. The portfolio models discussed earlier essentially deal with the choice among the following four missions:

Build. This mission implies an objective of increased market share, even at the expense of short-term earnings and cash flow (examples: Apple Computer's Macintosh, Monsanto's biotechnology, Corning Glass's optical wave guides, Black and Decker's hand-held electric tool).

Hold. This strategic mission is geared to the protection of the business unit's market share and competitive position (example: IBM's mainframe computers).

Harvest. This mission implies an objective of maximizing short-term earnings and cash flow, even at the expense of market share (examples: American Brands' tobacco products, General Electric's and Sylvania's light bulbs, Apple Computer's Apple II).

Divest. This mission indicates a decision to withdraw from the business either through a process of slow liquidation or outright sale.

While portfolio analysis techniques can aid in the formulation of missions, these techniques should not be used in a mechanistic manner. The portfolio matrices are not exact tools. A business unit's position on a portfolio grid should not be the sole basis for deciding its mission. These matrices need to be supplemented with managerial initiative, imagination, and creativity.

Control system designers need to know *what* the mission of a particular business unit is, but *not* necessarily *why* the firm has chosen that particular mission. Since this book focuses on designing control systems for ongoing businesses, it deals with the implementation of build, hold, harvest—but not divest—missions. These missions constitute a continuum, with "pure build" at one end and "pure harvest" at the other end. A business unit could be anywhere on this continuum, depending upon the trade-off it is supposed to make between building market share and maximizing short-term profits.

EXHIBIT 7–5 Business Unit Mission: The General Electric Portfolio Planning Model

The Portfolio Matrix

		Strong	Average	Weak
Industry attractiveness	High	Winners	Winners	Question marks
	Average	Winners	Average businesses	Losers
	Low	Profit producers	Losers	Losers

Business strength

Recommended Business Strategies

		Strong	Average	Weak
Industry attractiveness	High	Invest/Grow strongly (build)	Invest/Grow selectively (build)	Dominate/ Delay/ Divest
	Average	Invest/Grow selectively (build)	Earn/ Protect (hold)	Harvest/ Divest
	Low	Earn/ Protect (hold)	Harvest/ Divest	Harvest/ Divest

Business strength

Source: R. A. Kerin, V. Mahajan, and P. R. Varadarajan, *Strategic Market Planning* (Boston: Allyn & Bacon, 1990).

EXHIBIT 7–6 Business Unit Mission: The Arthur D. Little Portfolio Planning Model

Stage of Industry Maturity

	Embryonic	Growth	Mature	Aging
Dominant	Build	Build	Hold	Harvest
Strong	Build	Build	Hold	Harvest
Tenable	Build	Build	Hold/Harvest	Divest
Weak	Build	Harvest/Divest	Harvest/Divest	Divest

Competitive Position

Source: R. A. Kerin, V. Mahajan, and P. R. Varadarajan, *Strategic Market Planning* (Boston: Allyn & Bacon, 1990).

Business Unit Competitive Advantage

Every business unit should develop a competitive advantage in order to accomplish its mission. Three interrelated questions have to be considered in developing the business unit's competitive advantage:[9] First, what is the competitive structure of the industry in which the business unit participates? Second, how should the business unit exploit the industry's competitive structure? Third, what will be the basis of the business unit's competitive advantage?

Five force analysis.   In answering the first two questions, Porter states that the structure of an industry should be analyzed in terms of the *collective strength* of five competitive forces (see Exhibit 7–7):

1. *The intensity of rivalry among existing competitors.*   Factors affecting direct rivalry are: industry growth, product differentiability, number and diversity of competitors, level of fixed costs, intermittent overcapacity, and exit barriers.
2. *The bargaining power of buyers.*   Factors affecting buyer power are: number of buyers, buyer's switching costs, buyer's ability to integrate backward, impact of the business unit's product on buyer's total costs, impact of the business unit's product on buyer's quality/performance, and significance of the business unit's volume to buyers.
3. *The bargaining power of suppliers.*   Factors affecting supplier power are: number of suppliers, supplier's ability to integrate forward, presence of substitute inputs, and importance of the business unit's volume to suppliers.
4. *Threat from substitutes.*   Factors affecting substitute threat are: relative price/performance of substitutes, buyer's switching costs, buyer's propensity to substitute.
5. *The threat of new entry.*   Factors affecting entry barriers are: capital requirements, access to distribution channels, economies of scale, product differentiation, expected retaliation from existing firms, and government policy.

We make a few observations with regard to the five force analysis:

1. The more powerful the five forces are, the less profitable an industry is likely to be. In industries where average profitability is high (such as soft drinks and pharmaceuticals), the five forces are weak (example: in the soft drinks industry, entry barriers are high). In industries where the average profitability is low (such as steel and coal), the five forces are strong (example: in the steel industry, threat from substitutes is high).

2. Depending upon the relative strength of the five forces, the key strategic issues facing the business unit will differ from one industry to another.

---

[9] For a comprehensive examination of the methodology used to develop a sustainable competitive advantage, see Michael E. Porter, *Competitive Advantage* (New York: Free Press, 1985).

EXHIBIT 7-7 Business Unit Competitive Advantage: Analyzing the Structure of Industries

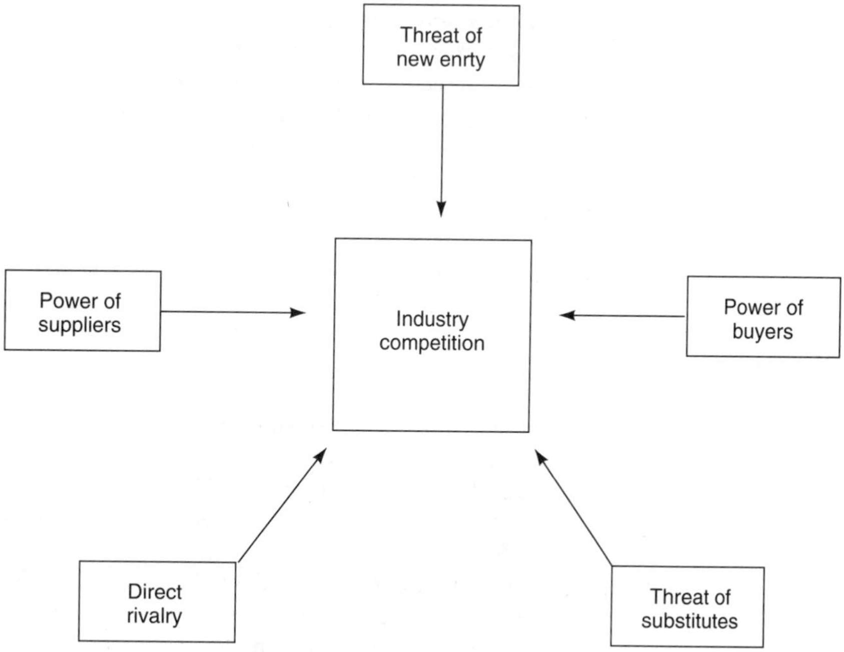

Source: M. E. Porter, *Competitive Strategy* (New York: Free Press, 1980), p. 4.

---

3. Understanding the nature of each force helps the firm to formulate effective strategies. Supplier selection (a strategic issue) is aided by the analysis of the relative power of several supplier groups; the business unit should link with the supplier group for which it has the best competitive advantage. Similarly, analyzing the relative bargaining power of several buyer groups will facilitate selection of target buyers.

Generic competitive advantages. The five force analysis is the starting point for developing a competitive advantage, since it helps to identify the opportunities and threats in the external environment. With this understanding, the business unit has two generic ways in which it can respond to the opportunities in the external environment and develop a sustainable competitive advantage:

Low cost. The primary focus of this strategy is to achieve low cost relative to competitors. Cost leadership can be achieved through such approaches as economies of scale in production, experience curve effects, tight cost control, and cost minimization (in such areas as research and development, service, sales force, or advertising). Examples of firms following this strategy in the early 1990s include: Texas Instruments in consumer electronics, Emerson

Electric in electric motors, Hyundai in automobiles, Briggs and Stratton in gasoline engines, Black and Decker in machine tools, Commodore in business machines, K mart in retailing, and BIC in pens.

Differentiation. The primary focus of this strategy is to differentiate the product offering of the business unit, creating something that is perceived by customers as being unique. Approaches to product differentiation include: brand loyalty (Coca Cola and Pepsi Cola in soft drinks), superior customer service (IBM in computers), dealer network (Caterpillar Tractors in construction equipment), product design and product features (Hewlett-Packard in electronics), and technology. Other examples of firms following a differentiation strategy include: Mercedes in automobiles, Stouffer's in frozen foods, Neiman-Marcus in retailing, Cross in pens, and Rolex in wristwatches.

SUMMARY

Diversified firms undertake strategy formulation at two levels—corporate and business unit. At the corporate level, the key strategic question is: What set of businesses should the firm be in? The "generic" options for corporate-level strategic question are: (1) a single business firm, (2) a related diversified firm, and (3) an unrelated diversified firm. At the business unit level, the key strategic questions are: (1) What should be the business unit's mission? (The "generic" business unit missions are build, hold, and harvest.) (2) How should the business unit compete to accomplish its mission? (The "generic" competitive advantages are low cost and differentiation.) In Chapter 13, we discuss the planning and control requirements of different corporate and business unit strategies.

SUGGESTED ADDITIONAL READINGS

Abell, Derick F., and John S. Hammond. *Strategic Market Planning.* Englewood Cliffs, N.J.: Prentice Hall, 1979. Chapters 3, 4, 5 contain a good summary of portfolio planning models.

Andrews, Kenneth R., *The Concept of Corporate Strategy.* Homewood, Ill.: Richard D. Irwin, 1980.

Bower, Joseph L.; Christopher A. Bartlett; Roland C. Christensen; Andrall E. Pearson; and Kenneth R. Andrews. *Business Policy: Text and Cases.* Homewood, Ill.: Richard D. Irwin, 1990.

Chandler, Alfred A. *Strategy and Structure: Chapters in the History of American Industrial Enterprise.* Cambridge, Mass.: MIT Press, 1962.

Donaldson, Gordon. *Managing Corporate Wealth.* New York: Praeger, 1984.

Govindarajan, Vijay, and Anil K. Gupta. "Linking Control Systems to Business Unit Strategy: Impact on Performance." *Accounting Organizations and Society,* (1985), pp. 51–66.

Govindarajan, Vijay, and John K. Shank. "Cash Sufficiency: The Missing Link in Strategic Planning." *The Journal of Business Strategy,* Summer 1986, pp. 88–95.

————. "Independence between and Performance Implications of Low Cost and Differentiation Strategies." Working paper, Amos Tuck School of Business Administration, Dartmouth College, 1990.

Govindarajan, Vijay, and D. Sharma. "Generic Competitive Strategies: An Empirical Analysis." *Proceedings of the National Decision Science Institute,* 1986.

Gupta, A. K., and Vijay Govindarajan. "Business Unit Strategy, Managerial Characteristics, and Business Unit Effectiveness at Strategy Implementation." *Academy of Management Journal* 27, no. 1 (1984), pp. 25–41.

Hax, A. C., and N. S. Majluf. *The Strategy Concept & Process.* Englewood Cliffs, N.J.: Prentice Hall, 1991.

Henderson, Bruce D. *Henderson on Corporate Strategy.* Cambridge, Mass.: Abt Books, 1979. A source book on the Boston Consulting Group's portfolio planning model.

Kerin, Roger A.; Vijay Mahajan; and P. Rajan Varadarajan. *Contemporary Perspectives on Strategic Market Planning.* Boston: Allyn & Bacon, 1990.

Oster, Sharon M. *Modern Competitive Analysis.* Oxford University Press, 1990.

Porter, Michael E. *Competitive Strategy.* New York: Free Press, 1980.

————. *Competitive Advantage.* New York: Free Press, 1985.

————. *Competitive Advantage of Nations.* New York: Free Press, 1990.

Quinn, James B. *Strategies for Change: Logical Incrementalism.* Homewood, Ill: Richard D. Irwin, 1980.

Quinn, J. B., and H. Mintzberg. *Strategy Process.* Englewood Cliffs, N.J.: Prentice Hall, 1991.

Rothschild, W. E. *Putting It All Together: A Guide to Strategic Thinking.* New York: AMACOM, 1976. Describes General Electric's portfolio planning model.

Case 7-1

South American Coffee Company*

South American Coffee Company sold its own brands of coffee throughout the Midwest. Stock of the company, which was founded in 1903, was closely held by members of the family of the founder. The president and secretary-treasurer were members of the stock-owning family; other management personnel had no stock interest.

Sales policies and direction of the company were handled from the home office in Cincinnati, and all salespersons reported to the sales manager through two assistants. The sales manager and the president assumed responsibility for advertising and promotion work. Roasting, grinding, and packaging of coffee was under the direction of the vice president of manufacturing, whose office was in Cincinnati.

The company operated three roasting plants in the Midwest. Each plant had profit and loss responsibility, and the plant manager was paid a bonus on the basis of a percent of his plant's gross margin. Monthly gross margin statements were prepared for each plant by the home office (see Exhibit 1). Exhibit 2 shows gross margin for the entire company. Each month the plant manager was given a production schedule for the current month and a tentative schedule for the next succeeding month. Deliveries were made as directed by the home office.

All financial statements were prepared in the home office and billing, credit, and collection were done there. Each plant had a small accounting office at which all manufacturing costs were recorded. Plant payrolls were prepared at the plant. Green coffee costs were supplied each plant on a lot basis, as described below.

The procurement of green coffee for the roasting operations was handled by a separate purchasing unit of the company, which reported to the secretary-treasurer in Cincinnati. Because of the specialized problems and the need for constant contact with coffee brokers, the unit was located in the section of New York City where the green coffee business was concentrated. The purchasing unit operated on an autonomous basis, keeping all records and handling all financial transactions pertaining to purchasing, sales to outsiders, and transfer to three company-operated roasting plants.

The primary function of the purchasing unit was to have available for the roasting plants the variety of green coffees necessary to produce the blends that were to be roasted, packed, and sold to customers. This necessitated dealing in 40 types and grades of coffee, which came from tropical countries all over the world.

Based on estimated sales budgets, purchase commitments were made that would provide for delivery in from 3 to 15 months from the date that contracts for purchase were made. While it was possible to purchase from local brokers for immediate delivery, such purchases usually were more costly than purchases made for delivery in the country of origin and, hence, these "spot" purchases were kept to a minimum. A most important factor was the market "know-how" of the purchasing agent, who must judge whether the market trend was apt to be up or down and make commitments accordingly.

The result was that the green coffee purchasing unit was buying a range of coffees for advance

* This case was prepared by R. H. Hassler, Harvard University.
Copyright © by The President and Fellows of Harvard College.

EXHIBIT 1

Operating Statement
Plant No. 1
April

Net sales (shipments at billing prices)		$744,620
Less: Cost of sales:		
Green coffee—at contract cost		373,660
Roasting and grinding:		
Labor	$38,220	
Fuel	24,780	
Manufacturing expenses	33,620	96,620
Packaging:		
Container	84,620	
Packing carton	9,140	
Labor	12,260	
Manufacturing expenses	25,440	131,460
Total manufacturing cost		601,740
Gross margin on sales		$142,880

EXHIBIT 2

Income Statement
April

	Plants*			Green Coffee	Total
	1	2	3		
Net sales	$744,620			$123,740	$2,856,400
Cost of sales:					
Green coffee	373,680			111,270	1,421,680
Roasting and grinding	96,620				299,440
Packaging	131,460				600,410
Purchasing department					78,400
	601,740				2,399,930
Gross margin	$142,880			$ 12,470	$ 456,470

* Detailed amounts for Plants 2 and 3 omitted here; total amounts include all three plants plus green coffee.

delivery at various dates. At the time of actual delivery, the sales of the company's coffees might not be going as anticipated when the purchase commitment was made. The difference between actual deliveries and current requirements was handled through "spot" sales or purchase transactions in green coffee with outside brokers or other coffee roasters.

As an example, the commitments of the company for Santos No. 4 (a grade of Brazilian coffee) might call for deliveries in May of 20,000 bags. These deliveries would be made under 50 contracts executed at varying prices from 3 to 12 months before the month of delivery. An unseasonal hot spell at the end of April had brought a slump in coffee sales, and it was found that the company plants required only 16,000 bags in May. The green coffee purchasing unit, therefore, had to decide whether to store the surplus in outside storage facilities (which would increase the cost) or to sell it on the open market. This example was typical of the normal operation.

Generally speaking, the large volume of the company permitted it to buy favorably and to realize a normal brokerage and trading profit when selling in smaller lots to small roasting companies. Hence, the usual policy was to make purchase commitments on a basis of maximum requirements; the usual result was that there was a surplus to be sold on a "spot" basis.

In accounting for coffee purchases, a separate cost record was maintained for each purchase contract. This record was charged with payments for coffee purchased, with shipping charges, import expenses, and similar items, with the result that net cost per bag was developed for each purchase. Thus, the 50 deliveries of Santos 4 coffee cited in the example would come into inventory at 50 separate costs. The established policy was to treat each contract on an individual basis. When green coffee was shipped to a plant, a charge was made for the cost represented by the contracts which covered that particular shipment of coffee, with no element of profit or loss. When green coffee was sold to outsiders, the sales were likewise costed on a specific contract basis with a resulting profit or loss on these transactions.

The operating cost of running the purchasing unit was transferred in total to the central office, where it was recorded as an element in the general cost of coffee sales.

For the past several years there had been some dissatisfaction on the part of plant managers with the method of computing gross margin subject to bonuses. This had finally led to a request from the president to the controller to study the whole method of reporting on results of plant operations and the purchasing operation.

QUESTIONS

1. Evaluate South American Coffee Company's (SACC's) current control system over manufacturing, marketing, and purchasing departments. Are these controls good ones?
2. Explain in detail, using specific examples, why you think the current system is or is not effective, in each department.
3. How would you change the controls over each of the three departments? (*Hint:* Be sure to consider SACC's competitive strategy when making suggestions.)

Case 7–2

PC&D, Inc.*

When we promoted you to the presidency five years ago, we expected that there would be changes, but we never expected you to diminish the importance of the old line businesses to the extent that you have. I think you have erred in doing so. . . .

The new entrepreneurial subs are certainly dynamic and have brought positive press to the company. But, by investing all new resources in them, you are jeopardizing the health of the company as a whole. . . .

My division's reputation has been built over the past 50 years on the superior quality of its products and sales force. But, as the leadership of our products begins to erode, my salesmen are beginning to leave. Without resources, I cannot stop this trend, and, as much as it saddens me to say so, I am losing my own motivation to stay with the company.

These were some excerpts from a letter that the senior vice president and head of the Machinery Division, George McElroy, 58, sent to John Martell, president of PC&D, Inc., in February 1976. McElroy was highly respected in both the company and the industry, a member of the board of directors, and a senior officer of the company for 20 years. Therefore, Martell knew that it was important to respond and to resolve the issues with McElroy successfully. At the same time Martell had no intention of giving up his own prerogatives to direct the company.

History of PC&D, Inc.

Payson & Clark Company

Payson & Clark, the forerunner of PC&D, was founded during the merger movement around the turn of the century. With the growth of industry across the country at the time, the demand for heavy machinery also grew rapidly. The new company benefited from economies of scale, both in production and distribution, and so it prospered.

By 1965 Payson & Clark Company, was an old, stable company still producing machinery. With revenues of $300 million and net after-tax profits of $6 million, it was still the largest firm in the industry. The company offered the most complete line of heavy industrial equipment in the industry, with its different configurations of standard and custom models filling a large, encyclopedic sales manual.

Although Payson & Clark was the leader in quality and breadth of its product line, it was not the leader in innovations. Rather, it left expensive R&D to others, copying products after they were widely accepted. It could afford to follow others primarily because the industry itself was slow-moving. In 1965 the business was essentially the same as when the company was founded.

In 1965 the company was still structured as it had been in the 1920s, with a standard functional organization and highly centralized chain of command. Its top executives were old-time managers, the average age being 55. Many had spent their entire careers with the firm and could remember the days when old Mr. Payson had kept tight reins on the company in the 1930s and 1940s. Harold C. Payson IV, age 53 in 1965, was president of the company from the late 1940s and the president and chairman since 1955. Although the company

---

* This case is an abridged version of Harvard Business School case 380–072, prepared by Richard Hammermesh. Copyright © by the President and Fellows of Harvard College.

was publicly held, the Payson family still owned a considerable amount of its stock.

In the early 1960s, Mr. Payson began to consider succession. One way in which Mr. Payson sought to implement this suggestion was to use some of the excess capital thrown off by the machinery business to enter into joint ventures with young, new companies developing high-technology innovative products. Several such investments were made in the early 1960s, including one with the Datronics Company in 1962.

Datronics Company

In 1965, the Datronics Company was 10 years old with revenues of $50 million. The company had started as an engineering firm subsisting on government research grants and contracts. As a by-product of the government projects, the company also developed several types of sophisticated electronic equipment with wide industrial applications. The company concentrated its efforts on R&D, however, subcontracted production, and bought marketing services for its commercial products. The lack of control over marketing and production and the lost profits passed to the marketers and subcontractors displeased the company's young president, John Martell. In his opinion, the company's growth was limited until the right product emerged to justify becoming a full manufacturing and marketing company.

Following Payson & Clark's investment in 1962, Datronic's engineers developed an existing new product toward the end of 1964 that promised to sell extremely well due to its increased capacity and lower cost. Martell saw the promise of the new product as the waited-for opportunity to expand the company. It was clear, however, that a major influx of capital was needed to bring the product to the market, build a sales force, and begin volume production. Therefore, Martell began a search for external capital that included a presentation to the joint venture partner, Payson & Clark, which already owned 20 percent of Datronics' stock.

Meanwhile, Mr. Payson had been following the activities at Datronics closely and was quite aware of the growth potential of the company before Martell's visit. Further, Mr. Payson recognized that Datronics, once its manufacturing operations started, would have a continual need for new capital. If Payson & Clark invested once, it would not be long until another request for resources came from Datronics. With these factors in mind, Mr. Payson decided that the most beneficial arrangement for both parties would be for his company to acquire Datronics. Martell agreed to this offer and negotiations for a friendly take-over were consummated. Payson & Clark acquired Datronics for $42 million in November 1965, with Martell himself receiving $8.4 million in cash, notes, and securities. The acquisition provided an opportunity for Payson & Clark to update its image. Patterning itself after other successful growth companies of the time, it changed its name to PC&D, Inc., to denote the beginning of a new era in the company.

PC&D, 1965–1970

After the acquisition, Mr. Payson restructured the company with the help of consultants, setting up a divisional organization. The old Payson & Clark Company now became the Machinery Division headed by George McElroy, formerly vice president of manufacturing. The Datronics Company became the Electronics Division headed by Martell.

Electronics Division

At the time of the acquisition, the Datronics Company consisted of several scientific labs, some test equipment, 10 professional engineers, an administrative staff, and Martell. An electrical engineer by training, Martell was a man in his mid-30s. He was energetic and a risk taker by nature, and even as a child in Iowa could not imagine working for someone else all his life. After college at MIT, he worked for eight years at a large scientific equipment company in the Boston area. Initially, he was hired for the research group, but he was more attracted to the company's management positions. He transferred first to the corporate planning office and then became a division plant manager. With his technical competence and management experience, it was not surprising that he was approached by several of the more innovative of the company's research engineers to invest in and head up a new, independent R&D company. Martell bought in for 25 percent of the founding stock and thus began the Datronics Company.

During his term as president of Datronics, Martell was highly regarded by the small group of employees. Although he had a respectable command of the technology, he left the research to the engineers, devoting his time to developing sources of challenging and lucrative contracts.

After the acquisition by the Payson & Clark Company, Martell retained full control of the operations of his old organization, which became the Electronics Division. He hired an experienced industrial marketer from a large technical firm to set up the marketing operations and a friend from his old employer to head up the production operations. As expected, the demand for the division's new product was very high. Five years later, in 1970, the division was a successful growing enterprise, having expanded into other electronics fields. It had 700 employees, marketing offices established or opening throughout the United States, Europe, and Japan, plants at three different sites, and revenues of over $160 million. The business press reported these activities very favorably, giving much credit to Martell's leadership.

Machinery Division

Meanwhile, the Machinery Division continued to be the stalwart of the industry it had always been, retaining its structure and activities of the earlier time. George McElroy, division manager and senior vice president, was considered the division's mainstay. He had joined the company in the early 1950s and was primarily responsible for the plastics innovations of that time. Advisor and confidant of Mr. Payson, McElroy was thought by his subordinates to be next in line for the presidency.

Mr. Payson limited his involvement in the company's internal affairs to reviewing budgets and year-end results, while spending most of his time with community activities and lobbying in Washington. He felt justified in this hands-off policy, because of the quality of both his division vice presidents, McElroy and Martell. PC&D's performance further supported Mr. Payson's approach. Revenues climbed to $530 million, and profits after tax to $14 million by 1970. The solid 26 multiple of its stock price reflected the confidence in PC&D's prospects (see Exhibit 1).

The compensation schemes reflected the extent to which Mr. Payson allowed the division managers to be autonomous. McElroy's compensation was 90 percent salary, with a 10 percent bonus based on ROI. Martell received two thirds of his pay as a bonus based on growth in revenues. Compensation policies within each division were entirely at the discretion of either Martell or McElroy. In general, Martell made much greater use of incentive compensation than McElroy.

Change at PC&D, 1970

Toward the end of 1970, Mr. Payson decided that it was time to limit his involvement to that of chairman of the board and to name a new president of PC&D. He supported the appointment of McElroy as the next president. McElroy was the next senior officer in the company and, after years of working with Mr. Payson, held many of the same views on the traditional values of PC&D. Mr. Payson agreed with the school of thought, however, that chief executives should not choose their own successors. He, therefore, established a search committee, consisting of three outside members of the board of directors and a thorough job was done. The result was the nomination of Martell. Although his relative youth was a surprise to some, the search committee's report explained the thinking behind the choice: "During the past five years PC&D has experienced an exciting and profitable period of growth and diversification. But it is essential that the company not become complacent. One of our major criteria in choosing a new president was to

EXHIBIT 1 PC&D, Inc., Income Statement and Balance Sheet, 1966–1970 ($ millions, except per share data)

	1966	1967	1968	1969	1970
Sales:					
Machinery	$315.1	$327.5	$340.2	$354.1	$368.2
Electronics	66.1	84.7	106.7	132.3	161.4
Total sales	381.2	412.2	446.9	486.4	529.6
COGS:*					
Machinery	251.7	264.3	271.8	284.7	297.9
Electronics	49.6	63.0	79.6	96.8	118.5
Total COGS	301.3	327.3	351.4	381.5	416.4
Gross margin	79.9	84.9	95.5	104.9	113.2
Expenses:					
Marketing G&A expense	46.1	48.3	50.3	51.6	53.1
Product development—machinery	4.9	4.6	4.7	4.1	4.5
R&D—electronics	4.2	5.3	10.3	17.8	27.3
Total expense	55.2	58.2	65.3	73.5	84.9
Profit before interest and tax	24.7	26.7	30.2	31.4	28.3
Interest	3.0	3.0	0.2	0.2	0.2
Profit before tax	21.7	23.7	30.0	31.2	28.1
Income tax	10.8	11.8	15.0	15.6	14.0
Net profit	10.9	11.9	15.0	15.6	14.1
Earnings per share	$3.63	$3.97	$5.00	$5.20	$4.70
Average stock price	$94	$111	$145	$146	$103
Total assets	286	320	345	385	427
Total current assets	187	214	231	260	292
Total current liabilities	122	130	135	145	165
Total long-term debt	16	30	35	49	57

* COGS means cost of goods sold.

find a person with the energy and vision to continue PC&D's growth and expansion.'' The board unanimously approved the selection of Martell as president and CEO.

Martell began his new position with the board's mandate in mind. He planned to continue the diversification of PC&D into high-growth industries. He expected to follow both an acquisition mode and a startup mode, using the excess funds from the Machinery Division and PC&D's rising stock to finance the growth. For startups, Martell planned to use joint ventures supporting newer companies, much as the old Payson & Clark Company had supported his venture in its early days.

Martell brought to his position a very definite management style. He was a strong believer in the benefits deriving from an opportunistic, entrepreneurial spirit, and he wanted to inject PC&D with this kind of energy. He was concerned, however, that the people with this kind of spirit would not be attracted to work with PC&D because of the stigma, real or imagined, of working for a large company. Martell commented:

It was my experience that there are two worlds of people, some of whom are very secure and comfortable and satisfied in their career pursuits in large institutionalized companies, and others of whom are, I think, wild ducks, and who are interested in perhaps greater challenges that small companies present in terms of the necessity to succeed or die.

Martell himself credited the success of the Electronics Division to Mr. Payson's willingness to turn the reins completely over to him. The secret, Martell thought, was in spotting the right person with both ability and integrity. Corporate headquarters' role should be to provide resources in terms of both money and expertise as needed, to set timetables, to provide measurement points and incentive, and then to keep its hands off.

Although the board's directives were clear to Martell, the specifics for implementation were not. Not only were the larger questions of which way to diversify or how to encourage innovation unanswered, but questions of how to plan and who to involve were also left unclear. Martell was not given the luxury of time to resolve these issues. Within the first week in his new position, three professionals from the Electronics Division called on Martell. Bert Rogers and Elaine Patterson were the key engineers from the research department and Thomas Grennan was head of marketing, western region. They had been working on some ideas for a new product (not competing with any of PC&D's existing lines), and they were ready to leave the company to start their own business to develop and market it. Indeed, they had already had a prospectus prepared for their new venture with the hope that either Martell, personally, or PC&D might be able to provide some venture capital. The president particularly liked these three and admired their willingness to take such personal risks with a product as yet unresearched as to market or design. With his energy and can-do aggressive style, Grennan reminded Martell of himself just a few years ago when he left to start the Datronics Company.

Martell liked the product and saw the idea as a possible route for continuing PC&D's diversification and growth, but there was a problem. It was clear from the presentation of the three, that much of their motivation came from the desire to start their own company and, through their equity interest, reap the high rewards of their efforts if successful. Martell did not fault this motivation, for it had been his route as well. He could not expect PC&D's managers to take large personal risks if there was no potential for a large payoff. Further, a fair offer to the group, if in salary, required more than PC&D could afford or could justify to the older divisions. Martell told Rogers, Patterson, and Grennan that he was very interested and asked if he could review the prospectus overnight and get back to them the next day. That night he devised a plan with a major feature called the Entrepreneurial Subsidiary. Martell presented this proposal to Grennan, Rogers, and Patterson the next day. They readily accepted it, and thus a pattern began for most PC&D's diversification over the next five years.

The Entrepreneurial Subsidiary

Martell's plan, of which he was particularly proud, worked as follows. When a proposal for a new product area was made to the PC&D corporate office, a new subsidiary would be incorporated—the entrepreneurial subsidiary. The initiators of the idea would leave their old division or company and become officers and employees of the new subsidiary. In the above example, the new subsidiary would be the Pro Instrument Corporation with Grennan as president and Rogers and Patterson as vice presidents.

The new subsidiary would issue stock in its name, $1 par value, 80 percent of which would be bought by PC&D and 20 percent by the entrepreneurs involved—engineers and other key officers. This initial capitalization, plus sizable direct loans from PC&D, provided the funds for the research and development of the new product up to its commercialization. In the case of Pro Instruments, Patterson and Rogers hired 10 other researchers, while Grennan hired a market researcher and a finance-accounting person. These 15 people invested $50,000 together and PC&D invested another $200,000.

Two kinds of agreements were signed between the two parties. The first was a research contract between the parent company and the subsidiary, setting time schedules for the research, defining requirements for a commercializable product, outlining budgets, and otherwise stipulating obligations on both sides. In general, the subsidiary was responsible for the R&D and production and testing of a set number of prototypes of a new product, while the parent company would market and produce the product on an international scale. Pro Instruments' agreement stipulated two phases, one lasting 18 months to produce a prototype and another lasting 6 months to test the product in the field and produce a marketing plan. Detailed budget and personnel needs were outlined, providing for a $900,000 working capital loan from PC&D during the first phase and $425,000 during the second.

Although PC&D had proprietary rights on the product and all revenues received from marketing it, the agreement often included an incentive kicker for the key engineers in the form of additional stock to be issued if the finished product produced certain specified amounts of revenue by given dates. This was the case for Pro Instruments: 5,000 shares in year 1, to be issued if net profits were over $250,000; 20,000 shares in year 2 if profits were over $1 million; and 10,000 in year 3 if profits were over $3 million.

The second agreement specified the financial obligations and terms for merger. Once the terms of the research contract were met, PC&D, with board approval, had the option for a stated time period (usually four years) to merge the subsidiary through a one-for-one exchange of PC&D stock for the stock of the subsidiary, which would then be dissolved. To protect the interests of entrepreneurs, PC&D was required to vote on merger of the subsidiary within 60 days if it met certain criteria. For Pro Instruments, the criteria were (1) the product earned cumulative profits of

$500,000 and (2) if the earnings of PC&D and the subsidiary were consolidated, dilution of PC&D's earnings-per-share would not have occurred over three consecutive quarters. If PC&D did not choose to merge during the 60 days, then the subsidiary had a right to buy out PC&D's interest.

Since PC&D's stock was selling for $103 in 1970 and subsidiary stock was bought for $1/share, the exchange of stock represented a tremendous potential return. Depending on the value of PC&D's stock at the time of merger, the net worth of the entrepreneurs who originally invested in the subsidiary multiplied overnight. Indeed, as subsidiaries were merged in ensuing years, typical gains ranged from 100 to 200 times the original investments in the entrepreneurial subsidiary. For example, PC&D exercised its option to merge Pro Instruments when its product was brought to market in 1972. Grennan, who had bought 6,000 shares of Pro Instruments stock, found his 6,000 shares of PC&D valued at $936,000 (PC&D common selling for $156 on the New York Stock Exchange at the time). By the end of 1974, Pro Instruments' new product had earned $50 million in revenue and $4.8 million in profits, thus qualifying the original entrepreneurs for stock bonuses. Grennan received another 4,200 shares valued at $684,600. Thus, in four years, he had earned about $1.6 million on a $6,000 investment.

By setting up entrepreneurial subsidiaries, like Pro Instruments, Martell had several expectations. In the process of setting up a subsidiary with the dynamics of a small, independent group, Martell hoped to create the loyalty, cohesion, and informal structure conducive to successful R&D efforts. The subsidiary would have a separate location and its own officers who decided structure and operating policies. Further, it provided the opportunity to buy into and reap the benefits of ownership in the equity of a company.

PC&D, 1970–1975

During the first five years of Martell's presidency, PC&D's growth was quite impressive.

EXHIBIT 2   PC&D, Inc., Income Statements and Balance Sheets, 1971–1975 ($ millions, except per share data)

	1971	1972	1973	1974	1975
Sales:					
Machinery	$382.9	$397.8	$412.5	$426.9	$440.6
Electronics*	193.6	235.6	300.1	397.4	561.4
Total sales	576.5	633.4	712.6	824.3	1,002.0
COGS:[†]					
Machinery	311.3	322.6	338.2	350.9	359.1
Electronics	145.2	174.3	216.1	282.2	421.1
Total COGS	456.5	496.9	554.3	633.1	780.2
Gross margin	120.0	136.5	158.3	191.2	221.8
Expenses:					
Marketing G&A expense	54.7	56.3	59.1	63.3	67.7
Development—machinery	5.0	5.1	5.2	5.2	5.3
R&D—electronics	28.4	29.5	30.7	31.9	33.5
Total	88.1	90.9	95.0	100.4	106.5
Profit and taxes:					
Before interest	31.9	45.6	63.3	90.8	115.3
Interest	0.2	3.0	3.0	7.0	11.0
Profit before tax	31.7	42.6	60.3	83.8	104.3
Income tax	15.8	21.3	30.1	41.9	52.1
Net profit	15.9	21.3	30.2	41.9	52.2
EPS	$5.30	$6.45[‡]	$8.39	$10.47	$13.05
Avgerage stock price	$106	$156	$158	$163	$238
Total assets	468	505	586	706	882
Total current assets	327	359	427	500	617
Total current liabilities	192	205	229	250	315
Total long-term debt	55	58	84	138	193

*Sales figures for Electronics included both sales by the original division plus sales of new subsidiaries after they are merged. Thus, in 1975, the $561.4 million in sales for Electronics included $179.2 from products developed in subs. Profit before interest and taxes from new products was $22.1 million.

[†] COGS means cost of goods sold.

[‡] Number of shares increased in 1972 by 0.3 million from the merger of Pro Instruments. They increased in 1973 by 0.3 million from merger of Sub #2, and again by 0.4 million in 1974 from the merger of Subs #3 and #4. Thus, in 1974, there was a total of 4 million shares outstanding. In late 1973, there was a secondary offering of 1 million shares.

With revenues topping the billion dollar mark in 1975, growth had averaged about 15 percent in revenues and 35 percent in profits after tax during the five years (see Exhibit 2 for financials). Such growth had been achieved, to a large extent, from new products developed in entrepreneurial subsidiaries. In 1975, sales of $179.2 million and profit before taxes and interest of $22.1 million came from these new products.[1] All together, 11 entrepreneurial subsidiaries had been organized during the 1970–1975 time frame. Of these, four had

[1] Of PC&D's total assets in 1975, approximately 40 percent were devoted to the Machinery Division, 35 percent to the traditional Electronics Division, and 25 percent to the entrepreneurial subsidiaries.

successfully developed products and had been merged into PC&D—one in 1972, one in 1973, and two in 1974. The other seven were younger and their work was still in process; to date, none had failed.

Most subsidiaries grew out of needs of the Electronics Division or Pro Instruments. Competitors in the electronics equipment industry were beginning to integrate backward, thus lowering costs by producing their own semiconductors. The need to remain cost competitive caused PC&D to establish entrepreneurial subsidiaries to develop specialized components, including semiconductors, assuming that these could be used both by PC&D and sold in outside markets. In the process of selling semiconductors to outside customers, ideas for new products using PC&D components were stimulated, and new subsidiaries were formed to develop these equipment products. The cost of merging the two types of subsidiaries—components or equipment—however, differed. Equipment subsidiaries were cheaper, because they could share the already existent sales force of the Electronics Division; many parts could be standard ones already utilized in other products; and the processes were similar to other Electronics products. But with semiconductors, new plant, new sales channels, new manufacturing processes, and new skills at all levels had to be built. Although Martell thought the move into semiconductors promised a large cash flow in the future in a booming industry, some in the company were concerned that the cash drain was not the best use of scarce cash resources.

When Martell first became president, he made few changes in PC&D's organization structure. McElroy continued as vice president of the Machinery Division and retained control over that division's structure and policies. Martell himself retained his responsibilities as manager of the Electronics Division. This he did reluctantly and with all intentions of finding a new executive for the job: however, the unexpected nature of his promotion left Martell without a ready candidate.

As the subsidiaries were merged, beginning with Pro Instruments in 1972, questions of organization began to rise. In typical fashion, Martell wanted to pass involvement in these decisions down to the appropriate managers. There was also no question that Pro Instrument's president, Grennan, had proven himself with the new subsidiary. Therefore, in 1972, Martell appointed Grennan to division vice president, Electronics, based on Grennan's superlative performance. Further, because the products were complementary, all of the subsidiaries merged during this period were placed in the Electronics Division. Moreover, in recognition of the increased number of products, Grennan reorganized the Electronics Division. He appointed his Pro Instruments colleague, Bert Rogers, to be director of research, which was organized by product area. Manufacturing, also organized by product, reflected the development by subsidiary as well. Marketing, on the other hand, was organized by region as it had been previously. Until they were merged, however, subsidiary presidents reported directly to Martell for resolution of problems that arose (see Exhibit 3 for a 1975 organization chart).

By 1975, the Electronics Division's enlarged marketing and production departments employed 4,000 people, with production plants in three different locations. Electronics then had sales of $561.4 million, compared to Machinery's $440.6 million.

Although successful development projects from subsidiaries had been largely responsible for the sales growth at PC&D, this result had not come without costs. First, the subsidiaries required funds—$60 million by the end of 1975. Some of these funds came from retained earnings, but much was new money raised in the form of long-term debt. Further, stock issued to capitalize subsidiaries and pay bonuses to entrepreneurs had a diluting effect on PC&D's shares. If all subsidiaries were merged and successful, the number of new shares could be significant. Although raising such a sizable amount of new funds was not particularly difficult for a company as large as

EXHIBIT 3   Organization Chart

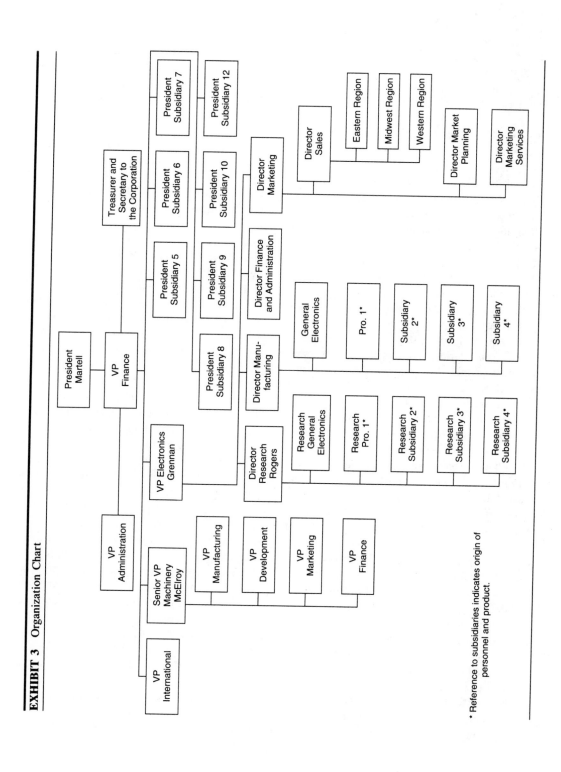

* Reference to subsidiaries indicates origin of personnel and product.

PC&D, the needs arising from the subsidiaries left little new money for the core businesses of PC&D. The Machinery Division, for example, had not had its development budget increased at all during the five years ending 1975.

Further Concerns

Despite PC&D's successes, Martell was not without worries—several problems had appeared in both the Electronics and Machinery Divisions. In Electronics, personnel and products originating in subsidiaries now equaled or surpassed those from the original division. It had been part of the strategy of the entrepreneurial subsidiaries to use them as devices to attract talent from other firms. A key researcher hired from outside was encouraged to hire, in turn, the best of his or her former colleagues. Thus, the loyalty and friendships between key entrepreneurs and their staffs were often strong and long-standing. As the entrepreneurial subsidiaries were merged, their personnel tended to retain this loyalty to the president or key officers of the old subsidiary, rather than transferring it to PC&D. Thus, several warring spheres of influence were developing in the division, particularly in the research department and between research and other departments. Martell was concerned that such influences and warring would lead to poor decisions and much wasted energy in this division.

Turnover in Electronics was also increasing. This was of particular concern to Martell, for it was those talented engineers that the entrepreneurial subsidiaries were meant to attract who were beginning to leave. For example, Elaine Patterson, formerly of Pro Instruments, left during 1975 to start her own company, taking 20 research engineers with her. The source of the turnover was unclear, but possible factors included distaste for the kind of warring atmosphere mentioned above and the inability to be a part of a large corporate R&D department with its demand for budgets and reports.

For many employees, however, the sudden absence of monetary incentives changed the climate drastically. This lack of incentive, coupled with the discovery that the most challenging projects were taken on by newly formed subsidiaries, which favored hiring outside expertise, caused dissatisfaction. For Martell, such turnover was of greatest concern in the long run, for the inability to create a strong central R&D department in Electronics created a continuing need for more entrepreneurial subsidiaries. These subsidiaries were still too new an idea for Martell to want to risk his entire future R&D program on their successes. Further, most of the new products were in highly competitive areas. Without continuing upgrades, these products would soon become obsolete. A strong central R&D department was needed for follow-up development of products started by subsidiaries.

Finally, Martell was concerned by indications of serious operating problems in the Electronics Division. This was particularly disturbing, since Martell had placed complete faith in Grennan's managerial ability. The most recent cost report, for example, indicated that the division's marketing, G&A, and engineering expenses were way out of line. Further, the marketing and production departments reported problems in several products originating in the subsidiaries. One product, with expected obsolescence of four years, now showed a six-year break-even just to cover the engineering and production costs. Another product, completing its first year on the market, had been forecasted by the subsidiary to achieve $20 million in sales in its first two years. During the first six months, however, losses had been incurred because of customer returns. A report on the causes of the returns showed a predominance of product failures. The chances for break-even on this product looked bleak. While none of these problems had affected operating results to date, Martell was especially concerned that these operating problems would have a negative impact on 1976 first-quarter earnings.

Martell had not confronted Grennan with these operating problems. He wanted to see how the division itself was attacking these issues through its long-range plan. Martell had requested Grennan to prepare a long-range plan (five years) as well as the usual one-year operating plan. The product of this effort had just arrived (February 1976) and Martell had not had a chance to study it. Its 100-page bulk loomed on Martell's desk. Quick perusal had indicated four pages of prose scattered through the plan, and dozens of charts, graphs, and tables of numbers, every one of which manifested an upward trend.

In an attempt to get employee feedback on all of these problems, Martell contracted an outside consulting firm to carry out confidential interviews with personnel in the Electronics Division. The interviews found middle managers quite concerned over the confusion in the division which was causing a loss of morale there. The consultant's report cited concrete problems, including lost equipment, missed billings, and confusion in the plant. Typical comments from lower-level personnel included the following:

Either upper management is not being informed of problems or they don't know how to solve them.

Morale is very poor, job security is nil.

There is little emphasis on production efficiencies.

Scrap is unaccounted for.

Market forecasts are grossly inaccurate.

Production schedules have a definite saw-tooth pattern. There is very little good planning.

There are no systematic controls.

These were not the sort of comments Martell expected from the division responsible for the major portion of PC&D's future growth. His concern was not so much the problems themselves but what was being done about them. His preferred policy was to stay out of day-to-day operating problems. He wondered how long it was prudent to allow such problems to continue without some intervention on his part.

Meanwhile, the Machinery Division had its own problems. The last major construction of new plant had been in the early 1950s. Since that time, McElroy had upgraded production methods,

which succeeded in checking rising costs. Since 1965, however, resources for such improvements had not been increased, and, with inflation in the 1970s, less and less could be done on a marginal basis. McElroy believed that capacity was sufficient for the short term, but that it was impossible to remain state of the art.[2] Indeed, the Machinery Division's products were beginning to fall behind the new developments of competitors, and the costs of Machinery's products were beginning to inch up. As the production line aged, quality control reported an increasing percentage of defective goods. In contrast to the situation in Machinery, the rather extensive investment in new plant for the production of semiconductors did not sit too well with McElroy, who was concerned with the lack of flexibility that could result from backward integrating. He thought component needs should be farmed out to the cheapest bidder from the numerous small component firms. Martell was concerned with how long he could keep McElroy satisfied without a major investment in Machinery and how long he could count on the cash flow from Machinery for other users.

Turnover, a problem never before experienced in the Machinery Division, had also appeared. Here, however, it was the salespeople who were leaving. Martell worried about this trend, for the sales force was the division's strength. According to the head of marketing, the salespeople considered themselves the best in the industry, and they did not wish to sell products that were not the best. They saw Machinery's products as no longer the best in quality nor state of the art. Further, they did not wish to work for a company where they felt unimportant. Whether true or not, the sales force appeared less aggressive than it had in previous times.

---

[2] McElroy suspected that the Machinery Division would require an investment of $100–$125 million over two or three years to revitalize the product line and plant and equipment. McElroy believed that in the long term the return on this investment would match the division's historic ROI.

Martell was not overly surprised, therefore, when he received McElroy's letter, nor was he certain that some of McElroy's anger concerning the Electronics Division was not justified. Martell know he had to do something about McElroy, as well as Grennan and the Electronics Division. He also had to decide whether entrepreneurial subsidiaries should continue to be part of PC&D's research and development strategy. Finally, all of Martell's decisions concerning the divisions and subsidiaries needed to be consistent with a strategy that would continue PC&D's growth.

QUESTIONS

1. Identify and evaluate the strategy of and controls over the Electronics Division and Machinery Division during 1965–70.
2. Evaluate the concept of the Entrepreneurial Subsidiary.
3. Identify and evaluate the strategy of and controls over the Electronics Division, Machinery Division, and Entrepreneurial Subsidiary since 1970.

Case 7-3

Corning Glass Works*

In August 1978, Tom MacAvoy, president and chief operating officer of Corning Glass Works, reflected on the decision-making process at Corning:

> Resource allocation decisions seem to be the biggest bones of contention. Corning's operating management is decentralized, but capital funds and engineers from our central pool are divided up through a resource allocation process, which attempts to rank the various development projects proposed by the divisions according to their potential value to the corporation as a whole. With the international scope of our business and our complex reporting relationships, resource allocation decisions are conceptually difficult and potentially divisive. Managing the process becomes a challenge in itself. The basic problem is how to get mature people through the posturing to the real issue of achievement.

Background

Corning Glass Works was recognized as a leading producer of products made from specialty glasses and related inorganic materials. Corning also produced a limited line of medical instruments, electronic devices, and special refractory materials. The company's reputation, growth, and profitability were based on technological innovation and manufacturing capabilities. It had a remarkable history of inventing products using glass and related materials with superior technical qualities, such as heat resistance, chemical stability, mechanical strength, or light transparency.

Many of these products were invented to order at the request of original equipment manufacturers (OEMs). The development process usually began in the Technical Staffs Division—a staff research and development unit under the purview of Dr. William H. Armistead, vice chairman of the board and chief technical officer. Once the basic technology was developed, the Manufacturing and Engineering Division (M&E)—a central pool of Corning's top engineers—took primary responsibility for applying the technology to specific products and manufacturing processes. M&E engineers worked closely with the line organization units responsible for producing and marketing the new product. Ideally, this development sequence resulted in the introduction of a new product with high growth potential and a strong market position protected by patents, manufacturing expertise, and heavy capital investment in the production process.

Corning's ability to apply its technological superiority in glass to the development of useful products was reflected in its long record of growth and profitability. However, the company's dependence on cyclical OEM customers and the sporadic nature of research breakthroughs had caused its financial performance to vary. Corning's vulnerability to economic downturns became a serious problem in 1975, when the recession made it necessary for the company to lay off about 10 percent of all salaried employees—including a similar proportion of its 600 executive-payroll employees—as part of a

* This case was abridged with permission from Harvard Business School case 179-074, written under the direction of Professor Richard F. Vancil.
Copyright © by the President and Fellows of Harvard College.

general reduction in work force. This was the most severe cutback of executive and salaried personnel in the company's history, and it was an extremely painful step for Corning.

In spite of its size and international scope, the company resembled a small-town firm in many ways. The chairman, Amory Houghton, Jr., and vice chairman, James R. Houghton, were fifth-generation descendants of Corning's founders. The Houghton family still controlled over 30 percent of the voting common stock, and the small upstate New York town of Corning served as headquarters for the firm, where all but one of its division managements were located. People from the several divisions saw each other frequently on Corning's premises, on the streets of Corning, and on social occasions. Business matters were discussed face to face. Personal relationships were informal; even top officers were addressed on a first-name basis. In a sense, the corporation operated like a family. Employment security was always an implicit assumption for managers who made a career commitment to the company. In the words of one manager, the 1975 layoffs left an "invisible scar" on the company psyche. Avoiding a repetition of this experience was still an important factor in management thinking in 1978.

Corning's Management Structure

Corning's line management organization was influenced by its historical development as a multinational corporation. In the early phases of its expansion into foreign markets, Corning relied on exports. Products were developed and manufactured in the United States and sold in other countries through overseas sales offices. As the international market became more important, the company set up an international division and began to acquire and build foreign manufacturing facilities. In 1975, Corning initiated a major restructuring of its organization under the rubric of internationalization. The objectives of restructuring were to eliminate the sharp split between domestic and foreign operations (the two sides sometimes competed for the same business), and to enable a rationalization of production and marketing decisions on a worldwide basis. This restructuring was carried out at the same time as the major layoff in 1975.

Corning's 1978 organizational structure is illustrated in Exhibit 1. Line management of the company's business units was based on a matrix concept of shared responsibility. One side of the matrix consisted of the company's worldwide product divisions. Management responsibilities along this dimension included strategy formulation, technological development, and resource allocation. The time horizon for typical decisions was intermediate to long term. The other dimension of the matrix was based on geographic markets. Area managers were responsible for Corning's assets in each geographic region, for day-to-day operations, and for relations with host countries. The North American area for each of the product divisions was under the direct control of the worldwide product division managers. Decision making in the areas focused on shorter-term management problems. In practice, of course, the two dimensions of responsibility often overlapped. Major investments, acquisitions, or marketing decisions required the cooperation of both product division managers and area managers. Corning's chairman, Amory Houghton, stressed that "part of a manager's job is to live with ambiguity. We look to Corning's managers not only to watch over and direct their specific areas of responsibility but also not to become so driven by strict organizational lines that they are unable to share with each other and the chairman the total responsibility for the corporation, with its close, intertwining relationships."

The company's organization was also complicated by what MacAvoy called "an ongoing ambiguity in the company's top management structure." MacAvoy had responsibility for assets and day-to-day operations in North America. He also had worldwide business responsibility for the seven product line divisions and for budgeting

EXHIBIT 1 Organization Chart

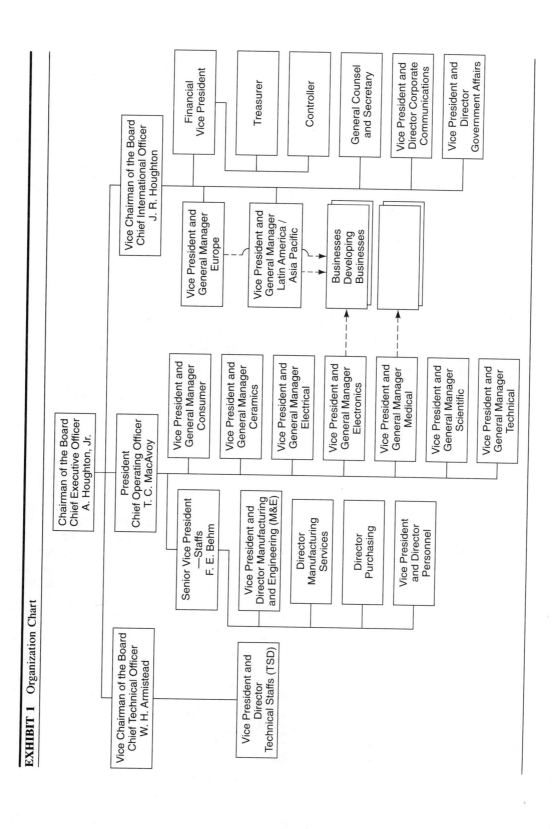

and resource allocation. James Houghton, vice chairman and chief international officer, was responsible for assets and operations outside North America. Thus, while MacAvoy had clear responsibility for domestic business, he and Houghton shared responsibility for the company's international development.

The line organization was supported by two centralized staff development units: the Technical Staffs Division (basic and applied R&D and product development) and the Manufacturing and Engineering Division (product and process engineering). The development process was coordinated by two committees: the Business Development Committee and the Resource Allocation Committee. The Business Development Committee's role was to help identify opportunities for new products or new markets that were well suited to Corning's technological capabilities and to make sure these opportunities were fully explored by the appropriate organizational units. The Resource Allocation Committee (which one officer called ''an exclusive club for accountants'') was responsible for recommending priorities and funding levels for development projects. These two committees were originally formed as a single unit. However, it was found that the critical stance of committee members with control responsibilities tended to stifle the initiative, creativity, enthusiasm, and effectiveness of members whose primary goals were to stimulate and exploit new technologies and market opportunities.

Strategic Planning and Resource Allocation

Corning's strategic planning process was based on a business unit classification, which roughly followed the operating organization structure. The company was divided into 7 product line divisions, 20 business groups, 60 businesses, and 130 geographic subdivisions of business. Each unit prepared two basic documents: Business Strategies and Resource Requests. Business Strategies (see Exhibit 2) included a narrative explanation of the proposed strategy; a planning matrix which positioned the business according to the maturity of the market and the business's competitive strength; and a long-range forecast of financial performance indicators such as sales, profit margins, turnover, and return on assets. Resource Requests for capital funds and M&E engineers were prepared for each capital project. The Business Strategies and Resource Requests were reviewed and prioritized by both geographic area and worldwide business managers for submission to corporate management.

At the corporate level, the review process was coordinated by the Resource Allocation Committee, headed by Forrest Behm. The committee's job was to recommend priorities for capital funding and assignment of M&E engineers to MacAvoy and J. Houghton. The committee was composed of the financial vice president, the controller, the director of strategic planning, the director of M&E, and the director of the Technical Staffs Division.

The company's strategic planner, who reported to the financial vice president, described his role as ''keeping the process on a strategic level so we don't get lost in the numbers.'' One way this was accomplished was to rank each business according to its strategic role and importance. The categories used to determine rank were: super-thrust, thrust, emphasis, reposition, sustain, and selective. These rankings were used as one criterion for setting resource allocation priorities. The optical waveguides business, for example, was a super-thrust business. Optical waveguides are thin glass fibers used in medical instruments, telecommunications, and computers. One of Corning's most dynamic new technologies, this business opened a pilot facility in 1977 and doubled its capacity twice that year to meet rising demand. ''It's a resource hog,'' said MacAvoy. ''It chews up engineering talent, especially our key process engineers. But you can't allocate resources to a business like that on the basis of internal rate-of-return calculations. It's a major strategic decision—either we're in the business or not—and we're in it. The main question we ask is whether

EXHIBIT 2 Division Business Strategy Summary

Division
Business _____

Worldwide, *or*
Geographic Area,
or Subsidiary _____

Date Prepared
or Modified _____

Stage of Market Life Cycle

Financial Data

Competitive Strength		Embryonic	Growth	Mature	Aging
Strong					
Favor-able					
Equal					
Weak					

	1977 *Actual*	1978 *Forecast*	1982 *Estimate*
Sales $000	_____	_____	_____
O.E. $000	_____	_____	_____
D.O.M. $000	_____	_____	_____
D.O.M. %	_____	_____	_____
Sales/net assets	_____	_____	_____
ROA %	_____	_____	_____

Strategy Summary

Measurement and Goal

Major Resources Required/Working Capital Changes

Competitive Position

Threats/Risks/Opportunities

Significant Changes from 1977 Strategy

they can use more engineers or capital funds than they've requested.''

The Manufacturing and Engineering Division played a pivotal role in reviewing the Resource Requests. Dave Leibson, director of M&E, said:

> In the early phases of developing the resource allocation process, the emphasis was on capital funds. Estimates of the number of M&E engineers required were included in the project description, but these were usually inaccurate. Even the capital estimates were wrong, since they were prepared without engineering input, and the total number of engineers estimated as required in the approved projects didn't jibe with the schedules or availability of M&E engineers. But my guys are the scarce resource. In 1976, we had good solid projects that would have required 50 percent more engineers than were available. In 1977, this figure was 75 percent, and this year the requests were double what we could assign. So now, the Resource Requests are submitted to us, and we recommend our own priorities based on engineering practicality, ROI [return on investment], ROE [return on engineering dollars], and strategic category. In fact, the engineering ranking is becoming dominant. Our fixed commitments, prior year projects, and contract obligations are so large that the new project options are pretty narrow.

The role of the controller was to manage the process from a budgeting standpoint. Decisions made about strategies and resources during the resource allocation process provided the basis for the annual capital and operating budgets used for management control. The controller's office reviewed the plans and requests to see that proposed expenditures were properly classified under corporate guidelines and to supervise the consolidation of the plans at the corporate level. The analytical emphasis was on making sure that everyone involved understood the budgetary and financial implications of the resource allocation options.

Based on the analyses of its various members, the Resource Allocation Committee listed the proposed projects by priority and recommended a total capital funding level and engineering head-count ceiling for the coming year to Tom MacAvoy and Jamie Houghton. This recommendation was also sent to division managers for their review and comment. The resource allocation process culminated in a three-day resource allocation meeting attended by division and area managers, staff officers, and the two top managers. Staff recommendations were discussed, and managers whose projects were not slated for funding were given a chance to present their cases to the group. The final decisions about total resource and project allocations were made by MacAvoy and J. Houghton at the end of the meeting.

Performance Measurements and Rewards

Management control at Corning was based on the annual operating budget.

Performance was measured by using profit centers for all line organization units down to the plant level. Profit itself was measured in terms of gross margin, operating margin, and contributed margin, as shown in the abbreviated format below:

Sales revenue	xxx
Manufacturing cost	xxx
Gross margin	xx
Selling and administrative expenses	xx
Operating margin	xx
Corporate expenses (assigned)	xx
Contributed margin	xx

At the divisional level, performance was measured primarily on the basis of variance from the budgeted divisional operating margin (DOM). Other profit measures were budgeted and reported, as were standard financial ratios such as return on assets (ROA), but most attention focused on the DOM.

This emphasis was reflected in Corning's executive compensation system. Top management traditionally relied on operating margin as the key performance variable when reviewing salary increases for all of its managers—including division managers—although the review was broad enough to encompass other areas of performance as well. In calculating bonuses for managers below the officer level, the formula gave half weight to operating margin variance and half weight to Individual Performance Factors (IPF)—a series of personal objectives much like a Management by Objectives system. For many managers, however, the most important IPF was to meet the DOM budget.

The overall emphasis on operating margin was modified in several ways. Annual bonuses for corporate officers, including division managers, were based on corporate profits only. Payments were made from a pool of funds equal to 5 percent of corporate additional profits, defined as net income in excess of 8 percent of capital invested. Except in particularly bad years (such as 1975), the pool usually exceeded the sum of individual bonus entitlements.

Corning's compensation system also included an Employee Equity Participation Program. This program had three parts: an equity purchase plan, a stock option plan, and an incentive stock plan. The equity purchase plan permitted about 1,100 of Corning's managers and professionals to buy Corning stock at book value up to an annual ceiling of 10–20 percent of the buyer's salary, depending on position level. The buyer was prohibited from reselling the shares to anyone other than Corning, but could resell them to the corporation, at book value at the time of resale, upon retirement or termination of employment.

The stock option plan granted participants the option to buy shares of Corning common stock for up to 10 years at the market price on the day the option was granted. Over the last four years, each officer received options to buy an average of 2,500 shares under this plan. However, the depressed price of Corning's stock in recent years had significantly reduced the value of these options as a form of compensation.

The incentive stock plan, originally established in 1974, was designed to give Corning's top 30 officers a significant equity position in the company through grants of stock. About 36,000 shares had been distributed in the three years since the plan was approved, at prices ranging from $31 to $71 per share. Under this original plan, each participant received an ownership amount of stock in proportion to the level of the participant's position. Individual performance was not a factor. Stock ownership was vested in the employee over a four-year period.

Top Management Goals

In spite of its technological capabilities and financial strength, Corning's top managers were not satisfied with the company's performance.

As part of the drive to close the profit gap, Corning instituted a revised incentive stock plan in April 1978. The principal new element in this plan was that stock awards were to be paid only to the extent that certain predetermined, long-term, individually tailored performance goals (among them a 15 percent ROI) were met by 1982. The plan included the company's top 50 to 60 key profit center and new business managers. It was expected to be worth from $60,000 to $200,000 in the 1978 value of the stock to each participant, depending on base salary and achievements.

MacAvoy saw the resource allocation process as a key tool for improving performance over the long run:

> One reason we instituted this process was to improve the way we were using our critical resources, which are capital funds and engineers from M&E. In the past, there wasn't much of a process for allocating engineers. The M&E people worked out their own priorities and schedules with each division. The resource allocation process has been difficult for them. They can still effectively veto a project on technical grounds, but they no longer decide what to work on by themselves. Until we developed the resource allocation process, we never had a good handle on what they were doing!
>
> The process is also useful as a way of getting people to think about strategy in concrete terms.

Traditionally, the budget has been taken as the serious performance measurement tool. The division manager usually filters out the more outrageous stuff in the strategic plans he gets from his business, but he's not as rigorous as with the budget. I'm trying to get the same kind of hard-nosed thinking about strategy. The overriding question at the big resource allocation meeting, which included the division managers, was not just "how are we going to allocate resources?" but "how are we going to get to 15 percent ROI by 1982?" The incentive stock plan gives us a reason to think about that, and the resource allocation process ties that thinking into here-and-now decisions.

I think perhaps the most important reason for having the big meeting at the end of the process is to gain commitment. The compensation system won't do it alone. It's a matter of managerial team-building. I want the division managers to see the process from the corporate point of view as well as their own. That's the only way they'll really internalize these goals we're setting. No more "we/they." When good projects get turned down, it's important for the manager involved to accept the decision as best for the corporation, rather than simply as a rejection of an idea he believes in and has worked hard on. You can't just say it—he's got to see all the projects he's competing with and understand how tight the resource constraints are in relation. And he's got to feel the process is fair. You give him the chance to make his pitch to justify the project not only to me but to his peers as well. And if the project gets cut, well, at least he went down fighting.

But the way you handle the meeting is critical. Last year we listed all the projects by priority and opened it up for discussion. We went way down below the cutoff points we'd set for capital funding and head count. It took a long time for people to realize how narrow our options were. And having to reject so many projects after they were discussed in the meeting caused a lot of pain. This year Jamie and I reviewed the staff recommendations in detail first, closed down some options, and held some one-on-one meetings with managers whose projects were cut or rejected. We made some compromises, but when people went into the meeting they knew what to expect. Things went much more smoothly than last year.

Two Proposals from Electronics

MacAvoy continued:

The Lee Wilson incident is a good example of how it worked this year—not earthshaking, but interesting. Lee Wilson is the head of the Electronics Division, which he manages on a worldwide basis. He had two proposed projects, each requiring about six engineers. He did a good deal of politicking before the resource allocation meeting. I first heard about the projects in the Business Development Committee (which I chair) and we were very enthusiastic. But the electronic components part of Lee's division, where the project came from, is a "sustain" business, so the projects didn't rank very high on the Resource Allocation Committee's list of priorities. As a side issue, it's interesting to note that Alain Thiney, who originated the projects, is the only key guy at his level who's not an American. When the division was internationalized he was brought from France to the United States as head of Wilson's product and planning unit. He's first rate—he knows the technology, he's creative, aggressive—just what we want. Anyway, I got together with Wilson before the meeting and conditioned him that he would get only six engineers in total for the two projects. So even though he made an impassioned plea for those two projects at the resource allocation meeting, he was prepared to lose. He could see how tight the engineering constraint was. The other managers also got on him about what a resource hog optical waveguides is, which is one of his businesses. And it helped that fewer people were making special appeals this year.

Commenting on the decision, Lee Wilson, vice president and general manager of the Electronics Division, said:

The rejection of those projects may not have been an earthshaking issue to the company, but I assure you it was earthshaking to me. In the resource allocation meeting, the question put to me was: "If you get half the engineers you need, couldn't you stretch the projects out over time and do them both?" The answer is that neither one can be delayed since both are related to the economic cycle. The coppertone resistor project is designed to develop a proprietary process to lower the cost of precision resistors so we can build volume profitably with IBM. It's a highly competitive business; cost reduction and volume are the keys to profit. But the time to go for volume is now, when demand is growing. If we wait, we may get hit with an economic downturn, which will make it all the harder. The same applies to the resistor network project. There we're entering an existing market, which is very tough to do in this business if demand is soft, so we've got to move.

The problem with the decision to give us only six engineers is not that there is no money to go outside but that we need trained people with some stake in the project, some continuity of involvement. I want M&E to feel some responsibility for the project. I need their competence over the long run. But with M&E, you've got to get them to buy in early, to get them on the board. Actually, I'm pleased that at least we got the six engineers from M&E. The plan now is to divide them up between the two projects and use them to supervise outside engineers or the division's own people who can do the work. The six are enough so that M&E will own the projects.

One problem, of course, is that this way the money may have to come out of operating expenses. The operating budget gets put together based on what happens at the resource allocation meeting. We may raise the question about who pays for the outside consulting engineers. If Electronics pays, it comes out of our divisional operating margin. If M&E pays, it will get charged back to us, but as a corporate expense below the DOM line.

As for the Electronics Division's strategic role, Wilson said:

I'm not sure whether we're a "sustain" or "emphasis" business—I think "emphasis" better describes it. I think it should be remembered that in the book the chairman put together this year [an overview of Corning's management philosophy, mission, organization, and key objectives], he identified electronic components, ophthalmic, and ceramics as three profitable businesses that should be supported to make sure they stay profitable. We have a reputation for good estimates of what a project is going to cost and for getting results.

That's why we're usually successful in getting resources. Tom MacAvoy used to be the Electronics Division manager and he knows this. He's very open about the way he manages the managers of this company. The strategy is clearly understood, and he runs a simple, open process.

Interviewed about the two projects, Jim Riesbeck, assistant controller, commented first on the accounting issue raised by Wilson, and then on the resource allocation process as a whole:

No, they can't charge the outside engineers to M&E. M&E pays only for *major* cost reduction projects—the coppertone project doesn't qualify. And for new products like the resistor network, the engineering expense comes out of the division's operating margin. Lee Wilson will have to pay for the engineers he hires out of his operating budget.

But the real issue isn't who pays—it's what gets done. Look, the idea behind the resource allocation process was to limit the capital dollars spent on development to projects with real payoff—the ones that represent the future of the company. Electronics is a good business, but with only $90 million a year in sales and a mature product, it isn't Corning's future. We don't want to spend all the cash we can find, and we don't want to get caught in another 1975 situation again. One of the big issues for this company is how to deal with this drive to expand head count, not only in M&E but operating people as well. It's a result of the push for better return; people respond by proposing all kinds of new projects. There's been a steady increase in head count—especially staff—since 1975, but there hasn't been an equivalent increase in performance. We ought to have learned after 1975 not to hire unless we're sure we've got a permanent job. The resource allocation process is supposed to help us limit the rate of growth of these development projects to what's profitable and manageable in the long run. But I'm not exactly thrilled with the result—the process is too mushy. Take these two projects from Electronics. They asked for 12 engineers from the M&E pool. That's their opening bid—it's almost certainly more than they needed. They got six, which is probably less than they wanted, although they did pretty well, considering their position. But look what they're going to do!

EXHIBIT 3   Chronology for Resistor Network Project

Prepared by A. Thiney for Resource Allocation Committee, 7/1/78

2/14/77   CMC review of Electronics business strategy
   —Outlined product development strategy
   —Proposed resistor network project

3/10/77   CMC approved "aggressively going after resistor network opportunity."
   (T. C. MacAvoy memo)

5/23/77   1977 three-year plan strategy summary
   —Key decision: business plan to enter network market in United States and
    Europe by 12/77. A. Thiney

6/15/77   Reorganized division product development
   —Product extensions: Raleigh and Bradford
   —Product renewals: Thiney (plus TSD and M&E)

1/16/78   Division completed major market study to confirm and segment network
   market.

2/22/78   Division reviewed project proposal and pro-forma A/R, made final decision
   to proceed.

3/17/78   Presented network project to BDC.

3/20/78   "BDC considers networks to be a good project deserving of corporate support." (W. T. B. memo)

3/29/78   Technical request accepted by TSD.
   —Dr. E. Griest appointed project leader at TSD

4/3/78   T. Mercer appointed project manager in Electronics Division.

4/20/78   1978 three-year plan.

5/12/78   Reviewed again with BDC in division BDC review.

CMC—Corporate Management Committee (A. Houghton, Jr., J. Houghton, T. Mac-
   Avoy, W. Armistead)
TSD—Technical Staffs Division
M&E—Manufacturing and Engineering Division
BDC—Business Development Committee

They bootstrap the project with outside engineers, charge it to operating expense, and go ahead as they planned. So how have we allocated any resources? How have we limited the dollars spent for development? What has the process really accomplished?

One big problem is the one-shot nature of the process—there's only one major resource allocation meeting per year, and that's where all the decisions are supposed to be made. This just invites people to ask for everything they think they might get around to. Pretending we know how these projects are going to progress and what we'll be doing 18 months out is ridiculous. Halfway through the year you find that only 30 percent of the budget has been spent, even though people were screaming about how tight the allocations were. People come in high to be safe and to establish a negotiating position. When they see how tight the constraints are, they come in even higher. We wind up having to raise the capital budget authorization from $120 million to $134 million, and we still don't really know where we are.

I'd like to see two things. First, there should be top level determination of firm limits on capital resources and M&E head count. The limits should be based on our long-run sustainable growth, and they shouldn't be subject to a lot of horse trading at the resource allocation meeting. Second, there should be more frequent allocation and reviews, say, every quarter. We should allocate the resources on the basis of rough estimates, and then track the capital funds and M&E man-years actually used. Based on the progress of the development portfolio, the allocation could be adjusted to give more to the projects that move and less to those with problems. That way, your decision making is based on more recent estimates of cost, schedule, and market potential. And if managers know they can come in with new proposals whenever they are ready, they feel less pressure to play games with the process.

Alain Thiney, product and planning manager for the Electronics Division, was the originator and prime mover of the two projects:

Frankly, I was pretty frustrated. I go through all these meetings—here, look, we even put together a chronology on the resistor networks project [Exhibit 3]—and we made good presentations. A big part of my job is communicating with top management. They have to judge so many proposals; I want my projects to be clearly understood and easy to remember. So I put a lot of time into the presentations. And the response was, "These are good projects." Corporate management was very enthusiastic. But then I get to the resource allocation meeting—when dollars get involved—and the whole thing is called into question. I think they're saying yes to a lot of projects that add up to more than they can spend. The lack of coordination causes wasted time and expense. You spend time and money, maybe hire some staff, and then. . . .

QUESTIONS

1. Be prepared to explain your understanding of the relationship between Corning's strategy, the design of its organization, and the role of the Houghton family in the management of the firm.
2. What is your appraisal of the effectiveness of Corning's resource allocation process? How is that process helped or hindered by the design of (1) the divisional performance measurement system and (2) the incentive compensation system?
3. Regarding Wilson's two projects, was anything decided? Why is Thiney frustrated? Would the resource allocation process be improved if Riesbeck's two proposals were adopted?

Note: Perhaps the most critical aspect of implementing any strategy is "resource allocation." Typically, resource allocation decisions must be made by senior management. Yet, their knowledge about the actual project or business unit which is asking for these resources tends to be very meager—certainly much less than that of those lower-level project or business managers who actually wrote the investment proposals. This is especially true in large, diversified corporations. The purpose of this case is to look at and understand how corporate executives make such resource allocation decisions in the face of enormous ambiguity. Also, the case allows you to look at what the implications of such a resource allocation process are for a typical middle-level manager.

Case 7-4

General Motors Corporation*

In an article in the *NACA Bulletin,* January 1, 1927, Albert Bradley described the pricing policy of General Motors Corporation. At that time, Mr. Bradley was general assistant treasurer; subsequently, he became vice president, executive vice president, and chairman of the board. The following description consists principally of excerpts from Mr. Bradley's article.

General Policy

Return on investment is the basis of the General Motors policy in regard to the pricing of product. The fundamental consideration is the average return over a protracted period of time, not the specific rate of return over any particular year or short period of time. The long-term rate of return on investment represents the official viewpoint as to the highest average rate of return that can be expected consistent with a healthy growth of the business, and may be referred to as the economic return attainable. The adjudged necessary rate of return on capital will vary as between separate lines of industry as a result of differences in their economic situations; and within each industry there will be important differences in return on capital, resulting primarily from the relatively greater efficiency of certain producers.

The fundamental policy in regard to pricing product and expansion of the business also necessitates an official viewpoint as to the normal average rate of plant operation. This relationship between assumed normal average rate of operation and practical annual capacity is known as standard volume.

The fundamental price policy is completely expressed in the conception of standard volume and economic return attainable. For example, if it is the accepted policy that standard volume represents 80 percent of practical annual capacity, and that an average of 20 percent per annum must be earned on the operating capital, it becomes possible to determine the standard price of a product—that is, that price which with plants operating at 80 percent of capacity will produce an annual return of 20 percent of the investment.

Standard Volume

Costs of production and distribution per unit of product vary with fluctuation in volume, because of the fixed or nonvariable nature of some of the expense items. Productive materials and productive labor may be considered costs which are 100 percent variable, since within reasonable limits the aggregate varies directly with volume, and the cost per unit of product, therefore, remains uniform.

Among the items classified as manufacturing expense or burden there exist varying degrees of fluctuation with volume, owing to their greater or lesser degree of variability. Among the absolutely fixed items are such expenses as depreciation and taxes, which may be referred to as 100 percent fixed since within the limits of plant capacity the aggregate will not change, but the amount per-

* This case was prepared R. N. Anthony, Harvard Business School.
Copyright © by the President and Fellows of Harvard College.
Harvard Business School case 160–005.

unit of product will vary in inverse ratio to the input.

Another group of items may be classified as 100 percent variable, such as inspection and material handling; the amount per unit of product is unaffected by volume. Between the classes of 100 percent fixed and 100 percent variable is a large group of expense items that are partially variable, such as light, heat, power, and salaries.

In General Motors Corporation, standard burden rates are developed for each burden center, so that there will be included in costs a reasonable average allowance for manufacturing expense. In order to establish this rate, it is first necessary to obtain an expression of the estimated normal average rate of plant operation.

Rate of plant operation is affected by such factors as general business conditions, extent of seasonal fluctuation in sales likely within years of large volume, policy with respect to seasonal accumulation of finished and/or semifinished product for the purpose of leveling the production curve, necessity or desirability of maintaining excess plant capacity for emergency use, and many others. Each of these factors should be carefully considered by a manufacturer in the determination of size of a new plant to be constructed, and before making additions to existing plants, in order that there may be a logical relationship between assumed normal average rate of plant operation and practical annual capacity. The percentage accepted by General Motors Corporation as its policy in regard to the relationship between assumed normal rate of plant operation and practical annual capacity is referred to as standard volume.

Having determined the degree of variability of manufacturing expense, the established total expense at the standard volume rate of operations can be estimated. A *standard burden rate* is then developed, which represents the proper absorption of burden in costs at standard volume. In periods of low volume, the unabsorbed manufacturing expense is charged directly against profits as unabsorbed burden, while, in periods of high volume, the overabsorbed manufacturing expense is credited to profits, as overabsorbed burden.

Return on Investment

Factory costs and commercial expenses for the most part represent outlays by the manufacturer during the accounting period. An exception is depreciation of capital assets, which have a greater length of life than the accounting period. To allow for this element of cost, there is included an allowance for depreciation in the burden rates used in compiling costs. Before an enterprise can be considered successful and worthy of continuation or expansion, however, still another element of cost must be reckoned with. This is the cost of capital, including an allowance for profit.

Thus, the calculation of standard prices of products necessitates the establishment of standards of capital requirement as well as expense factors, representative of the normal average operating condition. The standard for capital employed in fixed assets is expressed as a percentage of factory cost, and the standards for working capital are expressed in part as a percentage of sales, and in part as a percentage of factory cost.

The calculation of the standard allowance for fixed investment is illustrated by the example in Exhibit 1.

The amount tied up in working capital items should be directly proportional to the volume of business. For example, raw materials on hand should be in direct proportion to the manufacturing requirements—so many days' supply of this material, so many days' supply of that material, and so on—depending on the condition and location of sources of supply, transportation conditions, etc. Work-in-process should be in direct proportion to the requirements of finished production, since it is dependent on the length of time required for the material to pass from the raw to the finished state, and the amount of labor and other charges to be absorbed in the process. Finished product should be in direct proportion to sales requirements. Accounts receivable should be

EXHIBIT 1   Allowance for Fixed Investment

Investment in plant and other fixed assets	$15,000,000
Practical annual capacity	50,000 units
Standard volume, percent of practical annual capacity	80%
Standard volume equivalent (50,000 × 80%)	40,000 units
Factory cost per unit at standard volume	$1,000
Annual factory cost of production at standard volume (40,000 × $1,000)	$40,000,000
Standard factor for fixed investment (ratio of investment to annual factory cost of production; $15,000,000 ÷ $40,000,000)	0.375

in direct proportion to sales, being dependent on terms of payment and efficiency of collections.

The Standard Price

These elements are combined to construct the standard price as shown in Exhibit 2. Note that the economic return attainable (20 percent in the illustration) and the standard volume (80 percent in the illustration) are long-run figures and are rarely changed;[1] the other elements of the price are based on current estimates.

Differences among Products

Responsibility for investment must be considered in calculating the standard price of each product as well as in calculating the overall price for all products, since products with identical accounting costs may be responsible for investments that vary greatly. In Exhibit 2, a uniform standard selling price of $1,250 was determined. Let us now suppose that this organization makes and

sells two products, A and B, with equal manufacturing costs of $1,000 per unit and equal working capital requirements, and that 20,000 units of each product are produced. However, an analysis of fixed investment indicates that $10 million is applicable to product A, while only $5 million of fixed investment is applicable to product B. Each product must earn 20 percent on its investment in order to satisfy the standard condition. Exhibit 3 illustrates the determination of the standard price for product A and product B.

From this analysis of investment, it becomes apparent that product A, which has the heavier fixed investment, should sell for $1,278, while product B should sell for only $1,222, in order to produce a return of 20 percent on the investment. Were both products sold for the composite average standard price of $1,250, then product A would not be bearing its share of the investment burden, while product B would be correspondingly overpriced.

Differences in working capital requirements as between different products may also be important due to differences in manufacturing methods, sales terms, merchandising policies, etc. The inventory turnover rate of one line of products sold by a division of General Motors Corporation may

---

[1] A Brookings Institution survey reported that the principal pricing goal of General Motors Corporation in the 1950s was 20 percent of investment after taxes. See Robert F. Lanzillotti, "Pricing Objectives in Large Companies," *American Economic Review,* December 1958.

EXHIBIT 2 Illustration of Method of Determination of Standard Price

	In Relation to	Turnover per Year	Ratio to Sales Annual Basis	Ratio to Factory Cost Annual Basis
Cash	Sales	20 times	0.050	—
Drafts and accounts receivable	Sales	10 times	0.100	—
Raw material and work-in-process	Factory cost	6 times	—	$0.16\frac{2}{3}$
Finished product	Factory cost	12 times	—	$0.08\frac{1}{3}$
Gross working capital			0.150	0.250
Fixed investment				0.375
Total investment				0.625
Economic return attainable, 20%			—	—
Multiplying the investment ratio by this, the necessary net profit margin is arrived at			0.030	0.125
Standard allowance for commercial expenses, 7%			0.070	—
Gross margin over factory cost			0.100	0.125
			$\underline{a}$	$\underline{b}$

$$\text{Selling price, as a ratio to factory cost} = \frac{1 + b}{1 - a} = \frac{1 + 0.125}{1 - 0.100} = 1.250$$

If standard cost = $1,000

Then standard price = $1,000 × 1.250 = $1,250

be 6 times a year, while inventory applicable to another line of products is turned over 30 times a year. In the second case, the inventory investment required per dollar cost of sales is only one fifth of that required in the case of the product with the slower turnover. Just as there are differences in capital requirements as between different classes of product, so may the standard requirements for the same class of product require modification from time to time due to permanent changes in manufacturing processes, in location of sources of supply, more efficient scheduling and handling of materials, etc.

The importance of this improvement to the buyer of General Motors products may be appreciated from the following example. The total inventory investment for the 12 months ended September 30, 1926, would have averaged $182,490,000 if the turnover rate of 1923 (the best performance prior to 1925) had not been bettered, or an excess of $74,367,000 over the actual average investment. In other words, General Motors would have been compelled to charge $14,873,000 more for its product during this 12-month period than was actually charged if prices had been established to yield, say, 20 percent on the operating capital required.

Conclusion

The analysis as to the degree of variability of manufacturing and commercial expenses with increases or decreases in volume of output, and the establishment of "standards" for the various investment items, makes it possible not only to de-

EXHIBIT 3 Variances in Standard Price, Due to Variances in Rate of Capital Turnover

	Product A		Product B		Total Product (A plus B)	
	Ratio to Sales Annual Basis	Ratio to Factory Cost Annual Basis	Ratio to Sales Annual Basis	Ratio to Factory Cost Annual Basis	Ratio to Sales Annual Basis	Ratio to Factory Cost Annual Basis
Gross working capital	0.150	0.250	0.150	0.250	0.150	0.250
Fixed investment	—	0.500	—	0.250	—	0.375
Total investment	0.150	0.750	0.150	0.500	0.150	0.625
Economic return attainable, 20%	—	—	—	—	—	—
Multiplying the investment ratio by this, the necessary net profit margin is arrived at	0.030	0.150	0.030	0.100	0.030	0.125
Standard allowance for commercial expenses, 7%	0.070	—	0.070	—	0.070	—
Gross margin over factory cost	0.100 _a_	0.150 _b_	0.100 _a_	0.100 _b_	0.100 _a_	0.125 _b_
Selling price, as a ratio to Factory cost $= \dfrac{1+b}{1-a}$	$\dfrac{1.0 + 0.150}{1.0 - 0.100} = 1.278$		$\dfrac{1.0 + 0.100}{1.0 - 0.100} = 1.222$		$\dfrac{1.0 + 0.125}{1.0 - 0.100} = 1.250$	
If standard cost equals	$1,000		$1,000		$1,000	
Then standard price equals	$1,278		$1,222		$1,250	

velop "Standard Prices," but also to forecast, with much greater accuracy than otherwise would be possible, the capital requirements, profits, and return on capital at the different rates of operation, which may result from seasonal conditions or from changes in the general business situation. Moreover, whenever it is necessary to calculate in advance the final effect on net profits of proposed increases or deceases in price, with their resulting changes in volume of output, consideration of the real economics of the situation is facilitated by the availability of reliable basic data.

It should be emphasized that the basic pricing policy stated in terms of the economic return attainable is a policy, and it does not absolutely dictate the specific price. At times, the actual price may be above, and at other times below, the standard price. The standard price calculation affords a means not only of interpreting actual or proposed prices in relation to the established policy, but at the same time affords a practical demonstration as to whether the policy itself is sound. If the prevailing price of product is found to be at variance with the standard price other than to the extent due to temporary causes, it follows that prices should be adjusted; or else, in the event of conditions being such that prices cannot be brought into line with the standard price, the conclusion is necessarily drawn that the terms of the expressed policy must be modified.[2]

---

[2] This paragraph is taken from an article by Donaldson Brown, then vice president, finance, General Motors Corporation, in *Management and Administration*, March 1924.

QUESTIONS

1. An article in *The Wall Street Journal*, December 10, 1957, gave estimates of cost figures in "an imaginary car-making division in the Ford–Chevrolet–Plymouth field." Most of the data given below are derived from that article. Using these data, compute the standard price. Working capital ratios are not given; assume that they are the same as those in Exhibit 2.

Investment in plant and other fixed assets	$600,000,000
Required return on investment	30% before income taxes
Practical annual capacity	1,250,000
Standard volume—assume	80%
Factory cost per unit:	
Outside purchases of parts	$ 500*
Parts manufactured inside	$ 600*
Assembly labor	75
Burden	125
Total	$ $1,300

* Each of these items includes $50 of labor costs.

"Commercial cost," corresponding to the 7 percent in Exhibit 2, is added as a dollar amount, and includes the following:

Inbound and outbound freight	$ 85
Tooling and engineering	50
Sales and advertising	50
Administrative and miscellaneous	50
Warranty (repairs within guarantee)	15
Total	$250

Therefore, the 7 percent commercial allowance in Exhibit 2 should be eliminated, and in its place $250 should be added to the price as computed from the formula.

2. What would happen to profits and return on investment before taxes in a year in which volume was only 60 percent of capacity? What would happen in a year in which volume was 100 percent of capacity? Assume that nonvariable costs included in the $1,550 unit cost above are $350 million (i.e., variable costs are $1,550 − $350 = $1,200). In both situations, assume that cars were sold at the standard price established in Question 1, since the standard price is not changed to reflect annual changes in volume.

3. In the 1975 model year, General Motors gave cash rebates of as high as $300 per car off the list price. In 1972 and 1973 prices had been restricted by price control legislation, which required that selling prices could be increased only if costs had increased. Selling prices thereafter were not controlled, although there was always the possibility that price controls could be reimposed. In 1975, demand for automobiles was sharply lower than in 1974, partly because of a general recession and partly because of concerns about high gasoline prices. Does the cash rebate indicate that General Motors adopted a new pricing policy in 1975, or is it consistent with the policy described in the case?

4. Was this policy good for General Motors? Was it good for America?

Part II

The Management Control Process

The management control process is primarily behavioral. It involves interactions among and between managers and their subordinates. Managers differ in their technical ability, their leadership style, their interpersonal skills, their experience, their approach to decision making, their attitude toward the entity, their liking for or dislike of numbers, and in other ways. Because of these differences, the details of the management control process vary among companies and among the responsibility centers within a company.

Nevertheless, the formal management control system is basically the same throughout an organization; the differences relate principally to how the system is used. For example, managers differ in their attitude toward the relative importance of cooperation and competition. As explained in Chapter 2, a certain amount of each is essential.

The chapters in Part II discuss steps in the management control process in the sequence in which they occur in practice: Chapter 8 describes programming and program analysis; Chapter 9, budget preparation; Chapter 10, management control of operations; Chapter 11, analyzing performance reports and evaluating managerial performance; Chapter 12 discusses management compensation as it relates to the management control process.

Chapter 8

Programming and Program Analysis

This is the first of five chapters that describe the management control process. Chapter 8 describes programming, which is the first activity, sequentially, in the process. The first part of Chapter 8 describes the nature of programming. The second part discusses techniques for analyzing and deciding on proposed new programs. The third part describes techniques that are useful in analyzing ongoing programs. The final part describes the several steps in the programming process.

The discussion implicitly assumes a moderately large organization, typically consisting of a headquarters and several decentralized business units (divisions). In such an organization, programming takes place both at headquarters and in the business units. If the organization is small, and especially if it does not have business units, the process involves only senior executives and a planning staff. In a very small organization, the process may involve only the chief executive officer, perhaps assisted by the controller.

NATURE OF PROGRAMMING

Most competent managers spend considerable time thinking about the future. The result may be an informal understanding of the future direction the entity is going to take, or it may be a formal statement of plans. The formal statement of plans is here called a "strategic plan," and the process of preparing and revising this statement is called "programming"; it is also called "long-range planning." *Programming is the process of deciding on the programs that the organization will undertake and the approximate amount of resources that will be allocated to each program over the next several years.*

Relation to Strategic Planning

In Chapter 1, we drew a line between two management processes, strategic planning and management control. Because "strategic" is used in the definition of both terms, there is a possibility for confusion. The distinction is that strategic planning is the process of *formulating* strategies, whereas the programming is the process of deciding how to *implement* strategies. The program that describes how strategies are to be implemented is here called a "strategic plan."

In the strategic planning process, as we have defined it, management decides on the goals of the organization and the main strategies for achieving these goals. Conceptually, the programming process takes these goals and strategies as given and seeks to develop programs that will implement the strategies effectively. The decision by an industrial goods manufacturer to diversify into consumer goods is a strategic decision. Having made this basic decision, a number of programming decisions then must be made: whether to implement the strategy by acquisition or by building a new organization, what product lines to emphasize, whether to make or to buy, what marketing channels to use, and so on.

In practice, there is a considerable amount of overlap between strategic planning and programming. Studies made during the programming process may indicate the desirability of changing goals or strategies. Conversely, strategic planning usually includes a preliminary consideration of the programs that will be adopted as means of achieving goals.

An important reason for making a separation in practice between programming and strategic planning is that the programming process tends to become institutionalized, and this tends to put a damper on purely creative activities. Segregating strategic planning as a separate activity, either organizationally or at least in the thinking of top management, can provide an offset to this tendency. Strategic planning should be an activity in which creative, innovative thinking is strongly encouraged.

Programming is systematic; there is an annual programming process, with prescribed procedures and a timetable. Strategic planning is unsystematic. Strategies are reexamined in response to a perceived opportunity or threat. A possible strategic initiative may surface at any time and by anyone in the organization. If initially judged to be worth pursuing, it is analyzed immediately, without waiting to be fitted into a programming timetable.

Example   IBM had two planning processes: strategic planning and period planning. The strategic planning process was not calendar-driven; strategic decisions were made all year round, night and day, not according to a timetable. The period planning process complemented strategic planning and was characterized by its regular, calendar-driven sequence of events. The time horizons of period plans were fixed by corporate management at two years for the operating plan and five years for the strategic plan. The strategic plan dealt with where the businesses were going, and it identified programs based on product, technology, and market trends. The strategic plan also formed the basis for the operating plan, which dealt with the specific application of resources and made a commitment to results for the next fiscal year.

The relationship between strategic planning and period planning at IBM can be summed as follows: Strategic decisions were made whenever it was time to make such decisions, not according to a timetable; strategic decisions were made visible in an integrated way in the strategic plan.[1]

In many companies, goals and strategies are not stated explicitly or communicated clearly to the managers who need to use them as a framework within which program decisions are made. Thus, in a formal programming process an important first step often is to write descriptions of these goals and strategies. This may be a difficult task, for, although top management presumably has an intuitive feel for what they are, the goals and strategies may not have been verbalized with the specificity that is necessary if they are to be used in making program decisions.

Evolution of Programming

Fifty years ago the programming process in most organizations was unsystematic. Management did give some thought to long-range planning, but not in a systematic and coordinated way. (There were exceptions, not often recognized in the programming literature. Utilities projected their plant requirements for 20 years or more; forest product companies made plans over the 40-year cycle of timber growth; any company that built a new plant gave some thought to the likelihood of making profitable use of the new capacity over many future years.)

A few companies started formal programming systems in the late 1950s. Most of the first efforts were failures. They were minor adaptations of existing budget preparation systems; the required data were much more detailed than was appropriate; most of the work was done by staffs, rather than by line management; and participants spent more time filling in forms than thinking deeply about alternatives and selecting the best ones. Lessons were quickly learned, however: the objectives should be to make difficult choices among alternative programs, not to extrapolate numbers in budgetary detail; much time should be spent on analysis and informal discussion, and relatively less time on paperwork; the focus should be on the program itself, rather than on the responsibility center's responsibility for carrying it out.

Currently, many organizations appreciate the advantages of making a plan for the next three to five years. The practice of stating this plan in a formal

---

[1] "IBM Corporation: Background Note," in R. F. Vancil, *Implementing Strategy*, Division of Research, Harvard Business School, 1982, pp. 37–50.

program document, or model, is widely, but by no means universally, accepted. The amount of detail is usually much less than the programs used in the 1950s.

Benefits and Limitations of Programming

A strategic plan provides the framework within which the operating budget is developed. An operating budget involves resource commitments for the next year; it is essential that such resource commitments are made with a clear idea of where the organization is heading over the next several years. Thus, an important benefit of preparing a strategic plan is that it facilitates the formulation of an effective operating budget.

The strategic plan shows the financial and other implications, for the next several years, of programming decisions. As will be described, program decisions are made one at a time, and the strategic plan brings them all together. Preparing the strategic plan may reveal that individual decisions do not add up to a satisfactory whole. Planned new investments may require more funds in certain years than the company can obtain in those years; planned changes in direct programs may require changes in the size of support programs (e.g., research and development, general and administrative) that were not taken into account when these changes were considered one at a time. The profits anticipated from individual programs may not add up to a satisfactory profit for the whole organization.

On the other hand, programming is time consuming and expensive. The most significant expense is the time devoted to it by management, and it also requires a special staff and considerable paperwork. A formal programming process is not worthwhile in some organizations; the formal planning process in these organizations starts with the preparation of the annual budget, and the decisions that govern the budget are made informally. A formal program is desirable in organizations that have the following characteristics:

1. Its top management is convinced that programming is important. Otherwise, programming is likely to be a staff exercise that has little impact on actual decision making.

2. It is relatively large and complex. In small, simple organizations, an informal understanding of the organization's future directions is adequate for making decisions about resource allocations, which is a principal purpose of preparing a strategic plan.

3. Considerable uncertainty about the future exists, but the organization has the flexibility to adjust to changed circumstances. In a relatively stable organization, a strategic plan is unnecessary; the future is sufficiently like the past, so the strategic plan would be only an exercise in extrapolation. (If a stable organization foresees the possible need for a change in direction, such as a decline in its markets or drastic changes in the cost of materials, it prepares a contingency plan showing the actions to be taken to meet these new conditions.) If the future is so uncertain that reasonably reliable estimates cannot be made, preparation of a formal strategic plan is a waste of time.

In summary, a formal programming process is not needed in small, relatively stable organizations, and it is not worthwhile in organizations that cannot make reliable estimates about the future or in organizations whose senior management prefers not to manage in this fashion.

Program Structure and Content

In most industrial organizations, programs are products or product families plus research and development, general and administrative activities, planned acquisitions, or other important activities that do not fit into existing product lines. In IBM, for example, mainframe computers, desktop computers, and computer networks are programs, although responsibility for each may not be associated with a single organization unit. By contrast, General Electric structures its programs by profit centers—that is, business units; each business unit is responsible for a specified product line.

In service organizations, including government and other nonprofit organizations, programs tend to correspond to the types of services rendered by the entity. The federal government, for example, divides its activities into 10 main programs. Program 3, national resources and environment, is further divided into water resources, conservation and land management, recreational resources, pollution control and abatement, and others; these programs cut across organizational lines. In a multi-unit service organization, such as a hotel chain, each unit or each geographical region may constitute a program.

The typical strategic plan covers a period of five future years. Five years is a long enough period to estimate the consequences of program decisions made currently. The consequences of a decision to develop and market a new product or to acquire a major new capital asset may not be fully felt within a short period. The horizon beyond five years may be so murky that attempts to make a program for a longer period are not worthwhile. Some public utilities prepare formal strategic plans that extend as much as 20 years. Many organizations prepare very rough plans that extend beyond five years. By contrast, in some organizations the strategic plan covers only the next three years.

The dollar amounts for each program show the approximate magnitude of its revenues, expenses, and capital expenditures. Because of the relatively long time horizon, only rough estimates are feasible. Such estimates are satisfactory as a basis for indicating the organization's general direction. If the strategic plan is structured by business units, the "charter," which specifies the boundaries within which the business unit is expected to operate, is also stated.

Organizational Relationships

The programming process involves senior management and the managers of business units or other principal responsibility centers, assisted by their staffs. A primary purpose is to improve the communication between corporate and business unit executives by providing a sequence of scheduled activities through which they can arrive at a mutually agreeable set of objectives and plans. Managers of individual departments usually do not participate in the programming process.

In some organizations, the strategic plan is prepared by the controller organization; in others, there is a separate planning staff. Programming requires analytical skills and a broad outlook that may not exist in the controller organization; the controller organization may be skilled in the detailed analytical techniques that are required in fine-tuning the annual budget and analyzing variances between actual and budgeted amounts.

Even if there is a separate planning staff, the work of disseminating guidelines and assembling the proposed numbers, as described in a later section, is usually done by the controller organization. The numbers in the strategic plan, the annual budget, and the accounting system must be consistent with one another, and the best way of assuring this consistency is to assign responsibility for all three to the same staff. Moreover, in some companies, the numbers for all three systems are included in a single computer model.

Headquarters staff members facilitate the programming process, but they should not intervene in it too strongly. The role of staff members is best conceived of as that of a catalyst; they ensure that the process is properly carried out, but they do not make the program decisions. In particular, if business unit managers perceive that the headquarters staff is overly influential in the decision-making process, these managers will be reluctant to have the frank discussions with staff that are essential in developing sound plans. (Business unit managers, of course, have their own staffs who presumably are loyal to them.)

Top management style. Programming is a management process, and the way in which it is conducted in a given company is heavily dependent on the style of the chief executive officer. Some chief executives prefer to make decisions without the benefit of a formal programming apparatus. If the controller of such a company attempts to introduce a formal system, he or she is likely to be unsuccessful. No system will function effectively unless the chief executive actually uses it; and, if other managers perceive that the system is not a vital part of the management process, they will give only lip service to it.

In some companies, the chief executive wants some overall programming apparatus for the reasons given earlier but, by temperament, has an aversion to paperwork. In such companies, the system can contain all the elements that will be described in a later section, but with a minimum amount of detail in the written documents and relatively greater emphasis on informal discussion. In other companies, senior management prefers extensive analysis and documentation of plans, and in these companies the formal part of the system is relatively elaborate.

In designing the system, it is important that the style of senior management be correctly diagnosed and that the system be appropriate for that style. This is a difficult task, for formal programming has become somewhat of a fad, and some managers think they may be viewed as being old-fashioned if they do not embrace all its trappings. Thus, they may instruct the staff to install an elaborate system, or permit one to be installed, even though they later are uncomfortable in using it.

ANALYSIS OF PROPOSED NEW PROGRAMS

Ideas for new programs can originate anywhere in the organization: with the chief executive, with a headquarters planning staff, or in various parts of the operating organization. Some units are a more likely source than others, for fairly obvious reasons. The R&D organization is expected to generate ideas for new products or processes, the marketing organization for marketing innovations, and the production engineering organization for new equipment and manufacturing methods. Proposals for programs are essentially either *reactive* or *proactive*—that is, they arise either as the reaction to a perceived threat to the company, such as rumors of the introduction of a new product by a competitor, or they represent an initiative designed to capitalize on a newly perceived opportunity.

Because a company's success depends in part on its ability to find and implement new programs, and because ideas for these can come from a wide variety of sources, it is important that the atmosphere be such that these ideas come to light and that they receive appropriate management attention. A highly structured, formal system may create the wrong atmosphere for this purpose, and therefore, it is important that the system be flexible enough and receptive enough so that good new ideas do not get killed off before they come to the attention of the proper decision maker.

It is also important that, wherever possible, the adoption of a new program be viewed not as a single all-or-nothing decision but, rather, as a series of decisions, each one involving a relatively small step in testing and developing the proposed program, with full implementation and its consequent significant investment being decided upon if, but only if, the tests indicate that the proposal has a good chance of success. Most new programs are not like the Edsel automobile, which involved the commitment of several hundred million dollars in a single decision; rather, they involve many successive decisions: agreement that the initial idea for a product is worth pursuing, then examining its technical feasibility in a laboratory, then examining production problems and cost characteristics in a pilot plant, then testing consumer acceptance in test markets, and only then making a major commitment to full production and marketing. The system must provide for these successive steps, and for a thorough evaluation of the results of each step as a basis for making the decision on the next step.

Capital Investment Analysis

Most proposals require significant amounts of new capital. Techniques for analyzing such proposals are described in many texts and are not repeated here. In general, the techniques attempt either to find *(a)* the net present value of the project—that is, the excess of the present value of the estimated cash inflows over the amount of investment required, with present value being determined by discounting the flows at a rate that the company believes to be a satisfactory return on investment; or *(b)* the internal rate of return implicit in the relationship between inflows and outflows. An important point is that these techniques, in fact, are used in only about half the situations in which, conceptually, they are applicable.[2] There are at least four reasons for not using present value techniques in analyzing all proposals.

1. The proposal may be so obviously attractive that a calculation of its net present value is unnecessary. A newly developed machine that reduces costs so substantially that it will pay for itself in a year is an example.
2. The estimates involved in the proposal are so uncertain that making present value calculations is believed to be not worth the effort—one can't draw a reliable conclusion from unreliable data. This situation is common when the results are heavily dependent on estimates of sales volume of new products for which no good market data exist. (In these situations, the ''payback period'' criterion is used frequently.)
3. The rationale for the proposal is something other than increased profitability. The present value approach assumes that the ''objective function'' is to increase profits in some sense; but many proposed investments are justified on the grounds that they improve employee morale, improve the company's image, or are needed for safety reasons.
4. There is no feasible alternative to adoption of the proposal. An investment that is required to comply with antipollution legislation is an example.

The management control system should provide an orderly way of reaching a decision on proposals that cannot be analyzed by quantitative techniques; these proposals may account for as much as half the funds that the company commits

---

[2] See the following surveys for information on the prevalence of various techniques in practice: Thomas Klammer, Bruce Koch, and Neil Wilmer, *Capital Budgeting Practice: A Survey of Corporate Use,* 1990, University of North Texas (forthcoming);   Lawrence J. Gitman and Vincent A. Mercurio, ''Cost of Capital Techniques Used by Major U.S. Firms,'' *Financial Management,* Winter 1982, pp. 21–29;   Suk H. Kim, Trevor Crick, and Seung H. Kim, ''Do Executives Practice What Academics Preach?'' *Management Accounting,* November 1986, pp. 49–52.

to capital projects. In particular, the fact that these nonquantifiable proposals exist means that systems that attempt to rank projects in order of profitability are unlikely to be practical; many projects do not fit into a mechanical ranking scheme.

We describe briefly some considerations that are useful in implementing capital expenditure evaluation systems.

Rules.

Companies usually publish rules and procedures for the submission of capital expenditure proposals.[3] These rules specify the approval requirements for proposals of various magnitudes—that is, proposed expenditures of relatively small amounts may be approved by the plant manager, subject to a total specified amount in one year, and larger proposals go successively to business unit managers, to the chief executive officer, and, in case of very important proposals, to the board of directors.

The rules also contain guidelines for preparing proposals and general criteria for approving proposals. For example small cost-saving proposals may require a maximum payback period of two (sometimes three) years. For larger proposals, there is usually a minimum required earnings rate, to be used either in net present value or discounted cash flow analysis. The required earnings rate may be the same for all proposals, or there may be different rates for projects with different risk characteristics; also, proposals for additional working capital may use a lower rate than proposals for fixed assets.

Avoiding manipulation.

Sponsors know that a project with a net present value of less than zero is not likely to be approved. They, nevertheless, may have a "gut feel" that a certain proposal should be undertaken. In some cases, a proposal may be made attractive by so adjusting the original estimates that the project does meet the numerical criteria—perhaps by making more optimistic estimates of sales revenues, perhaps by reducing allowances for contingencies in some of the cost elements. One of the most difficult tasks of the project analysis is to detect such manipulations. The reputation of project sponsors can provide a safeguard—that is, more reliance is placed on numbers from a sponsor who has an excellent track record of past performance. In any event, although all proposals that come up for approval are likely to satisfy the formal criteria, not all of them are truly attractive.

Models.

In addition to the basic capital budgeting model, there are specialized techniques, such as risk analysis, sensitivity analysis, game theory, option pricing models, contingent claims analysis, and decision tree analysis. Some of them have been oversold, but others are of practical value. The planning staff should be acquainted with them and require their use in situations in which the necessary data are available.

---

[3] For an example, see International Federation of Accountants, *Statements on International Management Accounting*, no. 3, "The Capital Expenditure Decision," 1989.

Benefit/Cost Analysis

To use the capital budgeting techniques, the analyst must make monetary estimates of both the outlays and the savings or additional profits involved in the proposed investment. The techniques then make it possible to judge whether the benefits exceed the outlays (i.e., the cost of the project). In many situations, reliable estimates of both these sets of factors are not possible. In such situations, the analyst may use a less-rigorous but nevertheless valuable technique called ''benefit/cost analysis.''

If the benefits from the proposed project are either the savings resulting from the introduction of more efficient equipment or the additional profit resulting from new products or from increased volume of existing products, then these benefits can be expressed as monetary amounts. For some proposed projects, however, the benefits are more nebulous; the projects are proposed to improve working conditions, to create a more favorable ''image'' of the company in the eyes of the public, to increase product quality, to decrease pollution of the environment, for other reasons whose magnitude cannot be expressed as dollar amounts. In other proposals, the dollar magnitude of some of the benefits can be estimated, but there are other benefits whose magnitude cannot be measured. Therefore, in estimating the total benefits, both the measured and the unmeasured elements must be taken into account.

Benefit/cost analysis incorporates these unmeasured factors. In its most general form, the analyst merely attempts to identify the unmeasured benefits and to judge, subjectively, whether the benefits probably exceed the cost, all things considered. In more sophisticated versions, point values and weights are assigned to the unmeasured benefits, and these are aggregated and compared with the costs.

In most capital budgeting problems, the cost component is much easier to estimate than the ''benefit'' component. Benefit/cost techniques provide a way of getting some handle on the merits of the project, even when monetary estimates of benefits cannot be made. In all cases, of course, the project should not be approved unless the benefits, however estimated, are expected to exceed the costs.

Organization for Analysis

A team may be formed to evaluate extremely large and important proposals, and the process may require a year or more. Even for smaller proposals, there is usually considerable discussion between the person who is sponsoring the proposal and the headquarters staff. As many as a dozen functional and line executives may be required to sign off on an important proposal before it is submitted to the chief executive officer. The proposals may be returned by the CEO for further analysis several times before the final decision is made to go ahead or reject the project. And, as noted earlier, the decision to proceed may require that a succession of development and testing hurdles be crossed before full implementation.

Recent work in the rapidly developing field of *expert systems* has found ways of using computer software in the analysis of proposed programs. Software has been developed that permits each participant in the group that is considering a proposal to vote on, and to explicitly rank, each of the criteria used to judge the project. The computer tabulates the results, uncovers inconsistencies or misunderstandings, and raises questions about them. A succession of such votes can lead to a conclusion that expresses the consensus of the group, much as what an expert group chairman attempts to do judgmentally.[4]

As contrasted with the programming process for ongoing activities, there can be no set timetable for analyzing investment proposals. Analysis is started as soon after receipt of the proposal as people are available. Approved projects are collected during the year for inclusion in the capital budget. There is a deadline in the sense that the capital budget for next year has a deadline (usually just prior to the beginning of the budget year). If a proposal doesn't make that deadline, its formal approval may wait until next year, unless there are unusual circumstances. The capital budget contains the authorized capital expenditures for the budget year, and, if additional amounts are approved, cash plans must be revised; there may be problems in financing the additional amount.

ANALYSIS OF ONGOING PROGRAMS

In addition to developing new programs, many companies have systematic ways of analyzing ongoing programs. Two such analyses are described in this section: value-chain analysis and zero-base review.

Value-Chain Analysis

The term *value chain* means all the activities that add value, starting with product design, continuing with the procurement of resources, then with the steps in the production process, and concluding with the movement of the product from the factory to the customer.[5] From time to time, a company analyzes various links in this value chain, seeking to improve their efficiency. The overall objective is to move materials from vendors, through production, and to the customer at the lowest cost and in the shortest time.

Efficiency of the design portion of the value chain might be increased by reducing the number of separate parts and increasing their ease of manufacture.

---

[4] "Peer Review: Software for Hard Choices," *Science,* 19 October 1990, pp. 367–68.

[5] For a discussion, see John K. Shank and Vijay Govindarajan, *Strategic Cost Analysis,* especially chapter 3.

Efficiency of the "inward" portion (i.e., the portion that precedes production) might be improved by reducing the number of vendors; by having a computer system place orders automatically; by limiting deliveries to "just-in-time" amounts, which reduces inventories; and by holding vendors responsible for quality, which reduces or eliminates inspection costs.

Efficiency of the production portion might be improved by increased automation and increased use of robots; by rearranging machines into "cells," each of which performs a series of related production steps; and by better production control systems.

Efficiency of the "outward" portion (i.e., the portion from the factory door to receipt by the customer) might be improved by having customers place orders electronically (which is now common in hospital supply companies and in certain types of retailing); by changing the location of warehouses; by changing channels of distribution and placing more, or less, emphasis on distributors and wholesalers; by improving the efficiency of warehouse operations; or by changing the mix between company-operated trucks and transportation furnished by outside agencies.

These changes usually involve trade-offs. For example, direct orders from customer computers may speed delivery and reduce paperwork but lead to an increase in order-filling costs, because of the smaller quantities ordered. Thus, it is important that all related parts of the value chain be analyzed together; otherwise, improvements in one link may be offset by additional costs in another.

Example Mr. John Young of Hewlett-Packard Corporation uses a logic similar to the value-chain analysis, which he terms *break-even time*: "When the product is in engineering, you have negative cash flow. When it gets into manufacturing, you spend a certain amount of money or time, depending on whether the product you design fits your manufacturing process or calls for lots of new things; thus, you have more negative cash flow. Finally you start selling products and a positive cash flow begins. The more you sell with bigger margins the more rapidly you build up a positive cash flow. The time it takes for all the cash flow to come back to you is the break-even time. We want to cut that time in half."[6]

Zero-Base Review

Most service and support departments in a factory and most marketing, R&D, and administrative departments are discretionary expense centers. By definition, there is no way of knowing what the optimum expense of a discretionary expense center is. Therefore, in the programming process, and also in the subsequent budget preparation process, the tendency is to take the current level

---

[6] *Across the Board*, January/February 1990, p. 38.

of expenses in a discretionary expense center as a starting point, adjusting it upward for inflation, and adjusting it further for anticipated changes in the workload.

Because managers of these centers typically want to provide more services, they tend to request additional resources in the programming and budgeting processes; and, if they make a sufficiently strong case, these requests will be granted. This tendency is expressed in Parkinson's Second Law: Overhead costs tend to increase, period. There is ample evidence that not all this upward creep in costs is necessary. When a company faces a crisis or when a new management takes over, overhead costs are sometimes drastically reduced, without any adverse consequences.

During the regular programming and budget preparation processes, there is not sufficient time to analyze the expenses of discretionary expense centers in depth. An alternative approach is to make a thorough analysis of each discretionary expense center on a schedule that will cover all of them over a period of five years or so. The analysis provides a new base. There is a likelihood that expenses will creep up gradually over the next five years, and this is tolerated. At the end of five years, another new base is established.

Such an analysis is called a "zero-base review."[7] In contrast with the usual budget review, which takes the current level of spending as the starting point, this more intensive review attempts to build up, *de novo*, the resources that actually are needed by the activity. Basic questions are raised, such as: (1) Should the function be performed at all? (2) What should the quality level be? Are we doing too much? (3) Should it be performed in this way? (4) How much should it cost?

As a part of this approach, it is desirable to compare costs and, if feasible, the output measures for similar operations. Comparisons may identify activities that appear to be out of line and, thus, lead to a more thorough examination of these activities. Such comparisons can be useful, even though there are problems in achieving comparability, finding a "correct" relationship between the cost and output in a discretionary cost situation, and danger in taking an outside average as a standard. They often lead to the following interesting question: If other organizations get the job done for $X, why can't we?

A zero-base review is time consuming, and it is also likely to be a traumatic experience for the managers whose operations are being reviewed. This is one reason why such reviews are scheduled once every four or five years, rather than annually. This review establishes a new base for the budget, and the annual budget review attempts to keep costs reasonably in line with this base for the intervening period until the next review is made.

---

[7] A zero-base review is to be distinguished from a zero-base budget (ZBB). Zero-base budgeting has been advocated in the literature, was tried in some government agencies and companies in the 1970s, and now has been abandoned. The procedure took more time than was available during the budget preparation process.

Zero-base review is difficult. Managers under scrutiny will not only do their best to justify their current level of spending but they may also do their best to thwart the entire effort. They consider the annual budget review as a necessary evil, but the zero-base review as something to be put off indefinitely in favor of "more pressing business." If all else fails, they sometimes create enough doubts that the findings are inconclusive, and the status quo prevails.

The U.S. General Accounting Office makes zero-base reviews of federal agencies on a regular basis; it calls them "general management reviews." As an indication of their magnitude, the following information is taken from a GAO internal planning document:

> The elapsed time, start to finish, should be estimated to be 12 months: 2 months for planning, scoping, and assembling the team; 6 months for collecting information; 3 months for developing the report; and 1 month for briefing the agency.
>
> One review should involve approximately 2,200 staff days. The team should consist of not more than 10 persons, headed by an associate director.

Companies rarely spend as much time or resources as the above on a single zero-base review. This is because the activity being reviewed is much smaller than the activities typically reviewed by the General Accounting Office.

THE PROGRAMMING PROCESS

In a company that operates on a calendar-year basis, the programming process starts in the spring and is completed in the fall, just prior to the preparation of the annual budget. The process involves the following steps:

1. Updating the strategic plan from last year.
2. Deciding on assumptions and guidelines.
3. First iteration of the new strategic plan.
4. Analysis.
5. Second iteration of the new strategic plan.
6. Review and approval.

Updating the Strategic Plan

During the past year, decisions were made that changed the program; management makes decisions whenever there is a need to do so, not in response to a set timetable. These decisions were to undertake new programs or to restructure ongoing programs, as described in preceding sections. Conceptually, the implications of each decision over the next five years should be incorporated in the strategic plan as soon as the decision is made. Otherwise, the formal plan no longer represents the path that the company plans to follow. In particular, the plan may not be a valid base for testing proposed strategies and programs, which is one of its principal values. As a practical matter, however, very few organizations continuously update their strategic plans. Updating involves more paperwork and computer time than management believes is worthwhile.

The first step in the annual programming process, therefore, is to update the strategic plan that was agreed to last year. Actual experience for the first few months of the current year is already reflected in the accounting reports, and these are extrapolated for the current best estimate of the year as a whole. If the computer program is sufficiently flexible, it can extend the impact of current forces to the "out years"—that is, the years beyond the current year; if not, rough estimates are made manually. The implications of new program decisions on revenues, expenses, capital expenditures, and cash flow are incorporated. This update is usually made by the programming staff. Management may be involved if there are uncertainties or ambiguities in the program decisions that must be resolved.

Deciding on Assumptions and Guidelines

The updated strategic plan incorporates many assumptions. These include such broad assumptions as the growth in gross national product, cyclical movements, the rate of general inflation, labor rates, prices of important raw materials, interest rates, selling prices, market conditions, including the actions of competitors, and the impact of government legislation in each of the countries in which the company operates. These assumptions are reexamined, and, if necessary, they are changed to incorporate the latest information.

The updated strategic plan contains the implications on revenues, expenses, and cash flows of the existing operating facilities and changes in these facilities from opening new plants, expanding existing plants, closing plants, and relocating facilities. It reflects the business unit "charters"—that is, the product lines that each business unit is permitted to manufacture or to sell, or both; this is intended to clarify the activities in which a business unit can engage. It shows the amount of new capital likely to be available from retained earnings and new financing. These conditions are examined to ensure that they are currently valid, and the amounts are extended for another year.

The resulting update is not done in great detail. A rough approximation is adequate as a basis for senior management decisions about objectives that are to be attained in the program years and about the key guidelines that are to be observed in planning how to attain these objectives. The objectives usually are stated separately for each product line and are expressed as sales revenue, or as a profit percentage or a return on capital employed. The principal guidelines are assumptions on wage and salary increases (including new benefits programs that may affect compensation), new or discontinued product lines, and selling prices. For overhead units, personnel ceilings may be specified. At this stage, they represent senior management's tentative views. In the next stage, business unit managers have an opportunity to present their views.

Management meetings.   Many companies hold an annual meeting of corporate and business unit managers (often called a ''summit conference'') to discuss the proposed objectives and guidelines. Such a meeting typically lasts several days and is held away from company facilities to minimize distractions. In addition to the formal agenda, such a meeting provides an opportunity for managers throughout the corporation to get to know one another.

First Iteration of the Strategic Plan

Based on the assumptions, objectives, and guidelines, the business units and other operating units prepare their ''first cut'' of the strategic plan. It may include different operating plans than those included in the current plan, such as a change in marketing tactics; these are supported by reasons. Much of the analytical work is done by the business unit staffs, but the final judgments are made by business unit managers. Depending on the personal relationships, business unit personnel may seek the advice of the headquarters staff in the development of these plans. Members of the headquarters staff often visit the business units during this process, for the purpose of clarifying the guidelines, assumptions, and instructions and, in general, to assist in the planning process.

The completed strategic plan consists of income statements; of inventory, accounts receivable, and other key balance sheet items; of number of employees; of quantitative information about sales and production; of expenditures for plant and other capital acquisitions; of any other unusual cash flows; and of a narrative explanation and justification. (The business units need not submit complete balance sheets and cash flow statements; these statements for the whole corporation can be derived from details given in the plan.) The numbers are in considerable detail (although in much less detail than in the annual budget) for the next year and the following year, with only summary information for the later years. Some companies require numbers only for the first year, the second or third year, and the fifth year.

Analysis

When the business unit plans are received at headquarters, they are aggregated into an overall corporate strategic plan, and this plan is analyzed in depth. The analysis is done both by the planning staff and by the marketing, production, and other functional executives at headquarters. Business Unit X plans a new marketing tactic; is it likely that the resulting sales will be as large as the plan indicates? Business Unit Y plans an increase in general and administrative personnel; are the additional people really needed? Business Unit Z assumes a large increase in productivity; is the supporting justification realistic? Research and development promises important new products; are the business units prepared to manufacture and sell these products? Some business unit managers tend to build *slack* into their estimates, so their objectives are more easily accomplished; can some of this slack be detected and eliminated?

Some of these questions are resolved by discussions between the headquarters staff and their counterparts in the business units. Others are reported to corporate management, and they are the basis for discussions between corporate managers and business unit managers. This discussion is the heart of the formal programming process. It usually requires several hours and often goes on for a day or more in each business unit.

In many cases, the sum of the business unit plans reveals a *planning gap*—that is, the sum of the individual plans does not add up to attainment of the corporate objectives. There are only three ways to close a planning gap: (1) find opportunities for improvements in the business unit plans, (2) make acquisitions, or (3) revise the corporate objectives. Senior management usually focuses on the first.

Comparisons with past performance, with the performance of other companies, or with standard costs for certain types of activities may indicate opportunities for improvement. Headquarters people discuss these possibilities with business unit personnel. Their aim is to close the planning gap.

The headquarters people also examine the business unit plans for consistency. If one business unit manufactures for another unit, are the planned shipments from the manufacturing unit equal to the planned sales of the sales unit? In particular, are planned shipments to overseas subsidiaries consistent with the planned sales volume of these subsidiaries?

From the planning numbers, the headquarters staff can develop planned cash requirements for the whole organization. These may indicate the need for additional financing or, alternatively, the possibility of increasing dividends.[8]

Second Iteration of the Strategic Plan

Analysis of the first submission may lead only to a revision of the plans of certain business units, but it may also lead to a change in the assumptions and guidelines that affect all business units. For example, the aggregation of all plans may indicate that the cash drain from increasing inventories and capital expenditures is more than the company can safely tolerate; if so, there may be a requirement for postponement of expenditures throughout the organization. These decisions lead to a revision of the plan. Technically, the revision is much simpler to prepare than the original submission, because it requires changes in only a few numbers; but organizationally, it is the most painful part of the process, because difficult decisions must be made.

---

[8] For a discussion of this point, see V. Govindarajan and John K. Shank, "Cash Sufficiency: The Missing Link in Strategy Planning," *Journal of Business Strategy*, Summer 1986, pp. 88–95.

Some companies do not require a formal revision from the business units. The changes are negotiated informally, and the results are entered into the plan at headquarters.

Final Review and Approval

The revised plan usually is discussed at length in a meeting of senior corporate officials. It also may be presented at a meeting of the board of directors. Final approval comes from the chief executive officer. The approval should come prior to the beginning of the budget preparation process, because the strategic plan is an important input to that process.

Analytical Techniques

Several analytical techniques can aid the programming process. This section describes the following analytical tools: computer models, activity-based costing, variable cost analysis, and productivity gains.

Computer models.   The strategic plan is assembled in a computer. Until the late 1970s, the computer models were not much more than financial income statements, with a few rules that related changes in one variable to others.[9] The development of Lotus 1-2-3, Excel, and similar spreadsheets made it easy to relate changes in a large number of variables to one another. Currently, several computer programs are specifically designed for the programming process (and the related budgeting and performance reporting processes). Advances in telecommunication facilitates the transmission of data from business units to headquarters. The widespread use of personal computers connected to corporate networks permits many persons to participate in the process. A few companies develop their own model, but most adapt a program that is sold by one of several software companies.

Companies are experimenting with two approaches to an overall corporate model: the optimization approach and the heuristic approach.

In the **optimization approach**, the objective is to make a single model that encompasses all variables and that explains the profitability of the company under a given set of assumptions. This approach requires the use of *linear pro-*

---

[9] A 1974 study of members of the Financial Executives Institute reported that only about 20 percent of the respondents had a corporate model, and these were relatively simple. Jeffrey W. Traenkle et al., *The Use of Financial Models in Business* (New York: Financial Executives Research Foundation, 1975).

gramming, which is a device for finding the optimum combination of variables when there are constraints (such as production capacity limitations) on the amount of resources available. Estimating the behavior of variables and of the interaction among them is complicated, and, to date, few companies have been able to make estimates that are reliable enough to produce a model in which managers have confidence. Nevertheless, many companies are working to develop such a model.

The **heuristic approach** is less ambitious and, therefore, more practical. Instead of attempting to model all variables in the company at once, the mathematical expressions are developed only for certain segments of the company for which reliable estimates can be made. These are termed *blocks*. The results of the analysis of these blocks are then fitted into a conventional income statement and balance sheet. These financial statements constitute the overall model. In the Sun Oil Company model, for example, one block estimates the investment required for new service stations to achieve a specified market share for the program years. Another block estimates the amount of crude oil and other raw materials that will be produced in each year, based on the number of wells available and the estimated output of each. The outputs of each of these blocks are combined with those of other blocks to provide an estimate of net income and of balance sheet amounts.

The task of developing a computer model in a large, diversified company is sizable. Three years is usually considered to be a reasonable time to get a complete system up and running, with improvements being made constantly thereafter. And, unfortunately, there are reports of organizations that spent millions of dollars with no results.

Activity-based costing. Increased mechanization and automation in factories has led to important changes in systems for collecting and using cost information. Fifty years ago, most companies allocated overhead costs to products by means of a plantwide overhead rate based on direct labor-hours or dollars. Today, an increasing number of companies collect costs for material-related costs (e.g., transportation, storage) separately from other manufacturing costs; and they collect manufacturing costs for individual departments, individual machines, or individual "cells," which consist of groups of machines that perform a series of related operations on a product. In these cost centers, direct labor costs are combined with other cost elements, giving what is called the "conversion cost";—that is, the cost of converting raw materials and parts into finished products. The basis of allocating conversion costs to products is usually a machine-hour rate or a unit of product rate, which is different for each cost center. The newer systems also assign R&D, general and administrative, and marketing costs to products. In the recent literature, the word *activity* is often used instead of *cost center* and *cost driver* instead of *basis of allocation*; and the cost system is called an "activity-based cost system.''[10] Exhibit 8–1 indicates differences between traditional and activity-based cost systems.

The basis of allocation, or cost driver, for each of the cost centers reflects the *cause* of cost incurrence—that is, the element that explains why the amount of cost incurred in the cost center, or activity, varies. For example, in procurement, the cost driver may be the number of orders placed; for internal transportation, the number of parts moved; for product design, the number of different parts in the product; for production control, the number of setups. Note that ''cause'' here means the factor causing the costs in the individual cost center, in contrast with the traditional system, in which the cause of cost is taken to be the volume of products as a whole.

Collecting this information on a routine basis may not be worthwhile. Nevertheless, activity-based costing may provide insights useful in program analysis. For example, it may show that complex products with many separate parts have higher design and production costs than simpler products; that products with low volume have higher unit costs than high-volume products; that products with many setups or many engineering change orders have higher unit costs than other products; and that products with a short life cycle have higher unit costs than other products. Information on the magnitude of these differences may lead to changes in product pricing policies, make-or-buy policies, policies on adding products, and to an emphasis on simplicity in product design.[11]

Variable costs. The costs that should be considered as being variable for programming purposes are different from those that are variable for the purpose of making short-run decisions, such as whether to accept an order at less than the normal price, or whether to produce additional volume with overtime or with a second shift. Cost accounting systems used in day-to-day operations classify costs as variable or fixed, with these short-run problems in mind. In such systems, relatively few costs are variable. They include direct material, direct labor, and a few overhead items, but they acknowledge that the size of

---

[10] Shank points out that many of the essentials go back to J. M. Clark's 1923 book, *Studies in the Economics of Overhead Costs*. John K. Shank, ''Strategic Cost Management: New Wine, or Just New Bottles,'' *Journal of Management Accounting Research*, Fall 1989, p. 48.

In a 1989 survey of 298 plant managers, 16 percent reported that they used or were considering activity-based costing systems. (Keith Smith and Charlene Sullivan, *Survey of Cost Management Systems in Manufacturing*. W. Lafayette, Ind.: Krannert School of Management, Purdue University 1990.)

In a 1990 survey with 666 respondents from manufacturing companies, 11 percent reported they were using activity-based costing. Fifty seven percent of these did not use outside assistance in developing the system. In the median company, the cost of implementing the system was less than $50,000. (National Association of Accountants, *Cost Management Update*, January 1991.)

[11] For examples of these findings, see Robert S. Kaplan, ed., *Measures of Manufacturing Excellence* (Boston: Harvard Business School Press, 1990).

EXHIBIT 8–1 Contrast in Product Costing

A. Traditional Costing

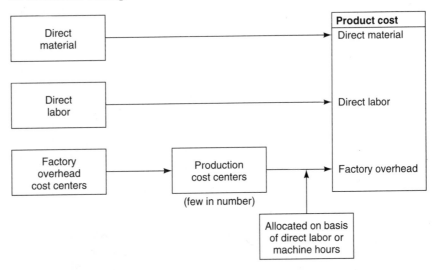

B. Activity-Based Costing

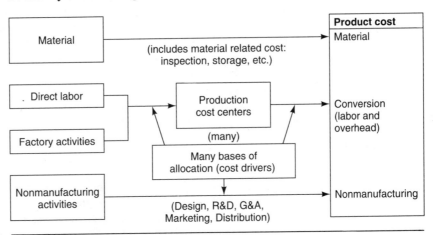

most factory support departments and almost all general and administrative departments will not change with short-run changes in production volume.

For programming purposes, many more cost categories are variable. Support and staff departments are unlikely to change in size, with temporary changes in volume; and salaried people typically are not laid off in a month of low activity and then rehired when volume resumes. Nevertheless, these costs most certainly change with changes in volume from one year to the next. The programming process permits additions to these costs when volume is expected to increase over the next several years and requires reductions when volume is expected to decrease.

> **Example**   In the law suit that decided the amount of lost profit that Polaroid Corporation would have incurred over the 10-year period in which Eastman Kodak Corporation infringed its patents, the Polaroid expert claimed that variable nonmanufacturing costs were 14 percent of sales revenue. This estimate was based on how costs varied *within* a year. Actually, the Kodak expert showed that, during this 10-year period, in which sales volume changed by substantial amounts from one year to the next (up in some years, down in others), Polaroid's nonmanufacturing costs were never less than 29 percent of revenue and averaged 34 percent of revenue. The average difference of 20 percentage points (i.e., between the Kodak number of 34 percent and the Polaroid number of 14 percent) resulted in a difference in the estimate of these costs that totalled hundreds of millions of dollars over the 10-year period. The court essentially accepted the Kodak percentage.[12]

Productivity gains.   Productivity is supposed to increase regularly in most companies. Much of the millions of dollars that a sizable company spends annually on equipment is intended to reduce costs. The amount of productivity saving is difficult to measure, however. Aerospace companies routinely use learning curves[13] to measure productivity gains; but few other companies know what the productivity improvement percentage was historically, let alone what it is likely to be in the planning years. If equipment acquisitions were justified on the grounds that they would reduce costs, it is conceptually possible to reduce the relevant program cost items as of the date the equipment goes on line; however, this is rarely done in practice. Some companies have a programming guideline that requires an across-the-board percentage cut in direct labor and other costs for which productivity savings are likely, even though they cannot demonstrate that the specific percentage is the correct one.

SUMMARY

A program, or strategic plan, shows the financial and other implications, over the next several years, of implementing the company's strategies.

In the period since the current strategic plan was prepared, the organization has made capital investment decisions. The process of approving proposed cap-

---

[12] *Polaroid Corporation* v. *Eastman Kodak Company*, U.S. District Court, District of Massachusetts, 1989. C.A. 76–1634–MA.

[13] A learning curve measures the decrease in unit costs, with cumulative increases in production volume. An 80 percent curve shows that, when cumulative production volume doubles, cumulative unit costs will be 80 percent of what they were at the beginning of the doubling period. For example, if cumulative unit costs were $100 at a cumulative volume of 1,000 units, cumulative unit costs will be $80 at a cumulative volume of 2,000 units. A curve called an "experience curve" has the same characteristics.

ital investments does not follow a set timetable; the decisions are made as soon as the need for them is identified. Also, zero-base reviews of certain responsibility centers are made. These may result in changes in the cost characteristics of these responsibility centers. The implications of these decisions and reviews are incorporated in the strategic plan. Assumptions and guidelines about external forces, such as inflation, and internal policies, such as product pricing, are also incorporated.

Based on this information, the business units and support units prepare proposed strategic plans, and these are discussed in depth with senior management. If the resulting plan does not indicate that profitability will be adequate, there is a planning gap, which is dealt with by a second iteration of the strategic plan.

Activity-based costing is a technique for analyzing costs that are relevant in the programming process. The variable costs that are relevant in the programming process are a higher percentage of revenue than the variable costs that are relevant in short-range operating decisions.

Appendix

Merck's Research Planning Model*

Research is the life blood of the pharmaceutical industry; but research by its nature is risky, because management must invest without knowing if that investment is ever going to yield a new drug. Exacerbating this is the trend of increasing R&D costs, which means companies are putting more of their shareholders' money at risk to find that next new drug. To discover one drug, companies must evaluate thousands of compounds, and, even after identifying that one promising drug, there is still only a one in eight chance that it will complete the seven-year development phase and be approved for sale. Of those drugs that are eventually commercialized, only 3 in 10 ever recover their full cost of discovery and development. A recent study estimated that the cost to discover and develop a new chemical entity was approximately $230 million, including the cost of failures and the time value of money. Consequently, management must actively monitor its research investments to increase the likelihood of returning the company's cost of capital.

To facilitate the R&D management process at Merck & Co., Inc., a comprehensive quantitative planning model, which combines discounted cash flow analysis with probabilistic risk analysis, was developed. This model incorporates monetary and nonmon-

---

* This appendix was written by Judy C. Lewent, Vice President, Finance and Chief Financial Officer of Merck & Co., Inc.

etary factors affecting an R&D project, and then it applies state-of-the-art financial evaluation techniques to quantify the expected returns and to measure the risks associated with a project or a portfolio of projects.

The Merck model covers a 20-year time horizon and includes drivers of commercial performance, such as unit volume forecasts, pricing projections, manufacturing costs, manufacturing capital, and exchange and inflation rate projections. To capture the variability and uncertainty that is inherent in projecting these variables, the model uses inputs in the form of frequency distributions, rather than just single point estimates.

As an example of how the inputs are derived, the sales forecast for a product is made by the product manager who takes into consideration the factors which affect the product's performance over the forecast period. These factors include such things as patent life, other competitive products, size of market, and therapeutic profile. For each year, the product manager provides estimates of the optimistic, most likely, and pessimistic forecast levels. These forecasts are then submitted to senior marketing management for approval.

In addition to the financial variables, the model also requires assumptions for key nonmonetary variables, such as dosage, launch date, and, most important, the probability of technical success.

The Merck model runs several hundred iterations for each product development candidate, and then statistically describes several critical output variables, including annual nominal and constant dollar sales projections, cash flows, return on investment, and net present value (NPV). Frequency distributions for key variables are created in order to quantify riskiness in terms of dispersion of results, as well as the expected value of the project.

An example of a frequency table for one of the output statistics, net present value, is shown in Exhibit I. In this case, the project has a 30 percent chance that the NPV will exceed the cost of capital. By selecting points along the x- and y-axis, the probability of a certain NPV being achieved can be determined.

EXHIBIT 1 Probability of Exceeding Cost of Capital

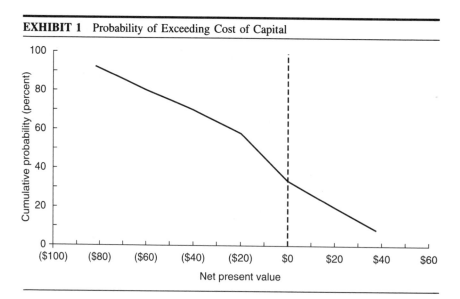

Periodically, forecasts from the Merck model are compared with the actual results for that same period. This process helps test the accuracy and reliability of the model's projections, and highlights areas where assumptions in future forecasts may need to be more closely examined. It also helps to identify areas for future methodological improvements.

This model is used extensively within Merck in three ways: to evaluate business opportunities; to help manage R&D; and to assist in long-range planning. Concerning business opportunities, the model is used in evaluating proposed product licensing candidates, capital expenditures, existing businesses, and acquisition candidates. Regarding management of R&D, it is employed in: making the go/no go investment decisions for product development candidates at various stages of the development process; quantifying the value of back-up compounds; optimizing the portfolio of development projects undertaken; and providing a measure for judging productivity of the R&D organization. Last, the Merck model is used to extend the time horizon of the company's five-year long range operating plan to 10- and 15-year projections. Such projections can be used to identify strategic issues that face the company, as well as to assess the impact of proposed business alliances on the company's longer-term growth prospects.

SUGGESTED ADDITIONAL READINGS

Cooper, Robin. "The Rise of Activity-Based Costing." *Journal of Cost Management*, Summer 1988, Fall 1988, Winter 1989, Spring 1989.

Donaldson, Gordon. *Managing Corporate Wealth*. New York: Praeger, 1984.

Govindarajan, Vijay, and John K. Shank. *Strategic Cost Analysis*. Homewood, Ill.: Richard D. Irwin, 1989.

Haka, S. F.; L. A. Gordan; and G. E. Pinches. "Sophisticated Capital Budgeting Selection Techniques and Firm Performance." *The Accounting Review* LX4 (October 1985), pp. 651–69.

Hertenstein, Julie H. "Introductory Note on Capital Budgeting Practices." Boston: Harvard Business School, No. 9–188–059, 1988.

Hrebiniak, Larry G., and William F. Joyce. *Implementing Strategy*. New York: Macmillan, 1984.

Lin, W. Thomas, and Paul R. Watkins. *The Use of Mathematical Models*. Montvale, N.J.: National Association of Accountants, 1986.

Lorange, Peter. *Corporate Planning: An Executive Viewpoint*. Englewood Cliffs, N.J.: Prentice Hall, 1980.

Magee, John F.; William C. Copacino; and Donald B. Rosenfield. *Modern Logistics Management*. 2nd ed. New York: John Wiley and Sons, 1985.

Mowitz, Robert. *The Design of Public Decision Systems*. Baltimore: University Park Press, 1980.

Pearce, John A. II. "The Tenuous Link between Formal Strategic Planning and Financial Performance." *Academy of Management Review* 12, no. 4 (1987), pp. 658–75. (Reviews many recent articles.)

Porter, Michael E. *Competitive Advantage*. New York: Free Press, 1985.

Raiffa, Howard. *Decision Analysis: Introductory Lectures on Choices under Uncertainty*. Reading, Mass.: Addison-Wesley, 1968.

Schlaifer, Robert O. *Strategic Planning*. New York: Free Press, 1979.

Shank, John K., and V. Govindarajan. "The Perils of Cost Allocation Based on Production Volumes." *Accounting Horizons* 2, no. 4, (December 1988) pp. 5–16.

Case 8–1

Copley Manufacturing Company*

Copley Manufacturing Company had begun formal corporatewide planning in 1981. Its planning system was modified in 1982 and modified again in 1983. Company executives reviewed the experiences of these three years to see what lessons could be learned that would lead to an improved planning system.

Copley had grown fairly steadily in size and profitability since its founding in 1919; its growth was particularly rapid in the late 1960s and the 1970s. For most of its history, it was primarily a manufacturer of a wide line of cutting tools and related parts and supplies, and the Cutting Tool Division in 1983 was the largest division. In 1983, there were eight other operating divisions, each making and selling a line of industrial products. Some of these divisions were the outgrowth of acquisitions; others had their origin in products developed by the corporate research department. Divisions had considerable autonomy. Sales volume in 1983 was $700 million, net income was $42 million, and there were 17,000 employees.

Introduction to Formal Planning

The formal planning effort at the corporate level was an outgrowth of work initiated by Russell A. Wilde, in mid-1977. Mr. Wilde had been head of the Precipitator Division's commercial development department and, as such, had been deeply involved in the division's efforts beginning early in 1977 to "plan ahead." Mr. Wilde's effort at the corporate level actually began as a search for companies to acquire, since Copley's top management saw the key question to be: "How should we diversify?" Within six months, Mr. Wilde was arguing that the crucial questions to be asked really were: "What are our objectives?" and "What is our potential?"

One result of the dialogue that followed was a request by Stanley Burton, president of Copley, for the divisions to look 10 years ahead and to predict sales, profit, cash flow, and return on investment. Mr. Wilde composed the actual questions asked of the divisions and co-ordinated collection of the data. The resulting consolidated growth projection was not ideal in the eyes of top management, but no imminent crisis was seen.

The 10-year look indicated that many of Copley's markets were mature, that its profits were indeed sensitive to cyclical swings, and that a large cash flow could be expected in the coming years. Before the end of 1978, Charles N. Sagan was appointed director of corporate development, reporting to Mr. Burton. Mr. Sagan was to be mainly concerned with growth through acquisition and merger.

Late in 1980, Mr. Sagan began reporting to Mr. Albert, executive vice president. The two easily agreed that regular formal planning should become part of management's way of life at Copley. They were encouraged to work toward this end when Samuel K. Savage, chairman of the board, suggested that Copley should do some five-year sales forecasting.

* This case was prepared by Robert N. Anthony, Harvard Business School.
Copyright © by the President and Fellows of Harvard College.
Harvard Business School case 176–189.

The 1981 Effort

A corporate planning committee was set up in February 1981 by Mr. Albert to guide the move toward a regular formal planning process. The planning committee comprised the vice president for research, the controller, the corporate economist, Mr. Albert, and Mr. Sagan. The latter was named chief coordinator of the committee.

The planning committee met almost weekly for the next few months and attacked two major questions.

1. By what process should formalized planning be ingrained into life at Copley?
2. What are appropriate corporate goals for Copley?

A year later, in early 1982, no answer had yet been given to the second question, but decisions were made concerning the first.

A March 21, 1981, memorandum from Mr. Albert to division general managers cited a need for regular formal planning and outlined a plan and schedule for starting such an effort. The basic idea was to survey divisional planning history and attitudes and, after discussions, to issue guidelines for the preparation of divisional "provisional plans."

Visits by Corporate Groups

The concept of formal planning activities was introduced by the organization through a series of visits to the divisions by corporate groups beginning June 6. The composition of the groups varied somewhat but always included Mr. Albert and Mr. Sagan. In these introductory meetings, Mr. Albert explained the importance of the planning effort, and Mr. Sagan explained the details. Divisions were asked to produce a five-year plan by October 1, 1981. It was left to the divisions to decide exactly who would do what in the process and in what format the final plans would be presented. Corporate staff groups were also instructed to submit plans.

The controller described the financial data to be submitted in the five-year plan in a memorandum dated July 19, 1981, as follows:

Sales—Please state past and future sales at 1981 prices and also in actual dollars, in total, by major product group, and by market group (e.g., domestic customers, export customers, intercompany).

Profit before Taxes—Analyze projected dollars profit in terms of variance from projected 1981 dollars profit. The four significant areas of variance should be:

Price Realization—The change in profit due to prices being higher or lower than 1981.

Volume and Product Mix—The change in profit contribution due to changes in physical volume and product mix. This is calculated by applying 1981 contribution ratios to the change in physical volume, by product line.

Cost Variances—Changes in unit variable costs or aggregate fixed costs should be stated. These aggregated changes should be separated into *price* (wage and material rates) variances and *efficiency* (all other) variances.

Profit after Taxes—Translate pretax to after-tax profit dollars for future years at the 1981 tax rate. Show income taxes and investment credit separately.

Cash Flow—The following should be drawn by years in total and by product line where a determination can be made. *Full* product line data is not required, but some indication of cash flow, say inventories and capital expenditures, by product line will be helpful.

    Profit after taxes.
    Depreciation.
    Accounts receivable.
    Inventories.
    Capital expenditures.
    Other working capital items:
        Cash (working balance only).
        Prepaid expense.
        Accounts payable and accruals.
        Etc.
    All other.
        Total Cash Flow

Planning Review Meetings

Meetings to review divisional plans were held in November and December. As was expected, the format of the divisional plans and presentations varied widely. Attendance at the planning reviews varied, also. The planning committee always attended, as did the head of the division being reviewed. In addition, members of the executive committee attended on occasion. Divisions were free to bring whomever they wished to their planning review. Representatives of other divisions than the one being reviewed on a given day were not invited to attend.

Planning Response Meetings

A second series of meetings was started December 28, 1981. In these meetings, the planning committee commented on the divisional presentation to the division general managers. The divisions had been expecting some reaction by corporate management ever since the planning reviews, and these planning responses were designed to meet this expectation. Typical of these meetings was that of the Cutting Tool Division, whose general manager, Mr. Tyler, had recently become a member of the planning committee. The Cutting Tool Division discussion lasted three hours, with Mr. Tyler and the rest of the committee openly evaluating the Cutting Tool Division's plans and its planning review.

Mr. Albert sent a memorandum to the general manager of each division after its "planning response" meeting. Each memorandum summarized the major points agreed upon in the meeting, thanked the participants for their effort in 1981, and expressed the desire for continued progress in making planning a way of life for the Copley manager.

The results of the first planning cycle were judged as mixed by Mr. Sagan and by members of top management. It was generally felt that the divisions had made a good beginning, but that they had only begun to dent the planning task. Divisional plans were seen generally to be optimistic extrapolations of past operating trends. Some members of management criticized the effort as having been a numbers game. Others countered that these results were a necessary first step. Most agreed that the plans had been helpful in providing information that would aid top management in understanding better the various business activities of the corporation.

1982 Organizational Changes

In 1982, a number of organizational changes affected planning in major ways. Chief among these was the elevation of Mr. Albert to president in March. The corporate planning function moved up with Mr. Albert, continuing to report directly to him.

Several other important organizational changes followed shortly after. Two corporate staff functions were created, one for marketing and the other for research/development. Operating responsibility was further delegated: the International Division was to report to the new executive vice president, John A. Tyler, the former general manager of the Cutting Tool Division. The Cutting Tool Division was divided along product lines to become two separate divisions.

Two group vice presidents were named, each responsible for three divisions, with the remaining four divisions reporting directly to Mr. Tyler.

Beginning of the 1982 Planning Activities

In contrast with the "numbers" orientation of the 1981 planning efforts, Mr. Sagan recommended an increased emphasis on strategic concepts in 1982. After some discussion, the planning committee decided to separate the formal planning cycle into three phases. The first phase, to be held in the spring, was termed the *Strategy Development* phase. The second, or *Quantitative*, phase would summarize, during the fall, the financial and manpower implications of the strategies selected in the first phase. The final, or *Action*, phase would aim to translate the results of planning into specific programs for action.

In mid-March, the new president, Mr. Albert, sent a letter to each division manager outlining the planning cycle for 1982 and the objectives for the planning efforts that had been agreed to by the planning committee.

The division's strategic plans were presented to corporate management by each division in a review meeting and subsequently evaluated in a response meeting. Unlike 1981, when they were held a month apart, these meetings in 1982 followed each other on the same day.

Further Developments in 1982

Several developments were to impede progress of the planning efforts in 1982. As already mentioned, there was a new president, who introduced seven persons into new corporate executive positions. These changes in top management were temporarily disruptive to the planning effort.

Also, considerable management effort was required in assimilating a recently acquired large company and in working out the split-up of the old Cutting Tool Division into the two new divisions.

In 1981, the company had reported its highest sales and earnings ever. The annual report stated that prospects were for a strong 1982. But the machine tool industry was to suffer from depressed market conditions. Sales were down 1.6 percent from 1981; earnings per share declined 35.8 percent. Efforts to counter the unfavorable business conditions became a dominant preoccupation for key line executives.

On July 11, after completion of the strategy development phase of the planning cycle, the planning committee met to consider the planning efforts for the remainder of 1982. In view of the developments noted above, it decided against proceeding with the quantitative phase originally scheduled for the fall. It did, however, recommend that staff departments begin the planning process by analyzing past results and identifying resources, strengths, weaknesses, major problems, and major opportunities of their divisions. Mr. Albert approved the recommendations. The Corporate Goals Committee also lessened its efforts to prepare a statement of corporate goals.

In view of the disruption of formal planning at Copley, top management made special efforts to declare that long-range planning was there to stay. In a letter to division managers dated October 24, Mr. Albert explained the decision to curtail formal planning and emphasized that nothing would be allowed to stand in the way of doing the complete planning job in 1983. He reaffirmed his intention to emphasize planning at Copley in his president's statement in the 1982 annual report: "Long-range planning will become a way of life at our Company. By this medium we will set specific goals, allocate resources of talent and money, and measure our progress. There will be increased emphasis on the delegation of responsibility and in the measurement of performance against predetermined goals."

Situation in 1983

The Copley Company recovered financially in 1983 with a 6.2 percent improvement in net sales and a 58 cent gain in earnings per share.

The corporate goals committee held several informal dinner meetings during the first half of 1982 to discuss a framework developed by Mr. Sagan for arriving at corporate goals. Although a definite statement of corporate goals was not drawn up, the members generally felt that much progress had been made and that it had been a useful and educational experience for all who had participated. The committee as originally constituted was inactive in late 1982 and early 1983, but Mr. Sagan continued to work independently with Mr. Albert on that task. In line with these activities, Mr. Albert was quoted in the business press as stating corporate expectations to include a minimum annual profit growth of 10 percent and a return on equity of 12.5 percent.

In 1983, the planning process in large part came to be influenced and administered by Mr. Tyler, executive vice president. Mr. Tyler, who had moved up from head of the Cutting Tool Division when Mr. Albert assumed the presidency of Copley, enjoyed the reputation among his colleagues as a hard-driving, no-nonsense line manager who had little patience for elaborate staff support.

In Mr. Tyler's opinion, division managers had been planning in previous years largely to satisfy the requirements set by the planning staff and had failed to become committed to the plans. He saw voluminous documentation required in 1982 to present a divisional strategy and financial plan as one reason for this failure to identify with the planning output. Thus, in 1983, division managers were asked to present each product group strategy in a statement of two pages or less and the related financial five-year plan on only one page.

The divisional strategy statements were to cover information on such items as industry trends, market size, competition, and major opportunities or threats, as well as a description of the proposed strategic response. For the financial plan, divisions were required to submit figures for only the first, second, and fifth years of the five-year plan. The purpose of this abbreviation was to reduce the time spent on the numbers, thereby allowing divisional management more time for strategic considerations.

The management review process was also altered. Divisional presentations before the planning committee was replaced by two other meetings. The first of these was a one-hour "premeeting" attended by Mr. Albert, Mr. Tyler, the division general manager, and the responsible group vice president. In this premeeting, Albert and Tyler explained Copley's strategy and acquisition policy and reviewed the findings and conclusions of the Product Line Study. During the remainder of the hour, the division manager had to explain and to defend the division's strategy for the coming year. At the end of the one-hour meeting the president gave his decision on the division's plans. This review was immediately followed by a three-hour meeting in which the division manager and his staff presented their plans for the first time to the remaining members of the Executive Committee and to selected members of the corporate staff.

Mr. Sagan, director of corporate development, became visibly disturbed by the recent turn of events in planning. He felt himself increasingly limited to corporate merger and acquisition stud-ies. He was fearful that the company would revert to a short-term orientation if it continued along the present path. In voicing these objectives to Mr. Albert, he realized that the formal planning system that he had worked so hard to develop was at stake. As a result of these discussions, he felt that he still had the full confidence and support of the chief executive. At the same time, Mr. Albert publicly acknowledged the benefits of getting increased line involvement in planning.

Recent Developments

In an interview in late 1984, Mr. Tyler described recent developments:

> As was John Albert's desire, we believe planning is now a way of life at Copley. There just does not appear to be as much need today for a structured management of the process with a planning department per se at the corporate level. This is not to say that all line managers develop plans and strategies to the same degree of effectiveness. But the actual responsibility for planning has been placed directly on the line—that is, the executive vice president, the group vice presidents, and, in turn, their various division managers.
>
> For various reasons, Charlie Sagan left the company earlier this year. Fred Fisher has been appointed director of corporate development, but his job description was rewritten to put the emphasis on the planning and execution of growth through acquisition.
>
> The planning process in 1983 followed pretty well the steps we had laid out.
>
> In January 1984, we changed the format for the divisional planning presentations. My letter of January 30 [Exhibit 1] describes our current system of informing all key managers within the company of each division's long-range plans and broad strategies.
>
> This technique of communicating divisional plans was preceded in December of 1983 by a two-day conference in Bermuda, with essentially the same group in attendance. At that conference, we reviewed all of the divisional plans up until that point and announced the broad corporate goals and strategies.

EXHIBIT 1 Letter Announcing a Series of Executive Meetings (excerpts)

January 30, 1984

It is always difficult to draw lines across an organization, but those to whom this letter is addressed are either managing profit centers or are directing broad staff functions vital to Copley's operations and to its future growth.

We believe it is important to provide the means for keeping each person in this group better informed of the plans and progress of each division and each staff function as well as the total corporate programs.

The method selected to provide better communications will be tested over the next 12 months and will involve a series of 9 meetings; the time and place of each are listed on the attached schedule. Each meeting will start at 1:30 P.M. on the first Monday of the month. They will end at 5:00 P.M. A different division will host each meeting on a rotating basis.

An agenda is planned as follows. From 1:30 to 2:00 P.M. five or six prepared talks of five minutes' duration will be given on subjects of current and general interest selected by the chairman in consultation with others. The following half hour (2:00–2:30) will be devoted to announcements from both the floor and the chairman.

At 2:30, the division manager serving as host will take charge of the meeting. He will have a total of two and one half hours, during which he is asked to present his long-range plans, allow time for questions and comments, and complete a plant tour of some portion of his facilities.

The group of key executives in attendance does not make up a decision-making committee or a review board in the general sense. They are, however, encouraged to ask questions for interpretation and better understanding. The long-range plans presented by the division manager will previously have been approved by the president, executive and group vice presidents. The division managers are asked to present their plans in simply written reports using an expanded outline technique. Copies will be reproduced by the division manager following the meeting on a request basis.

This test period will last through February 1985 meeting. If it is felt these meetings cannot be made to serve their original intention, they will be discontinued.

/s/John A. Tyler
Executive Vice President

In the same interview Mr. Tyler furnished a copy of a recent talk in which he stated his personal belief about management.

I believe that corporate planning is *the* major responsibility of top management. It involves the direction of the whole company (not the parts) in deciding specifically what businesses the company wants to be in, in determining what rate of growth is desirable, in determining what method of growth is intended (research, acquisition, merger). I am a believer in decentralization; in delegating a great deal of authority; giving people their head; permitting some experiments and some mistakes; but sink or swim is the theory.

I do not believe in too many specialized staff functions to clutter up an organization. I avoid "assistant to's" and "administrative assistants" except for short-term projects or as training spots in someone's career.

I believe a good manager by definition must put out the daily fires, improve the current quarter's earnings, and at the same time be a long-range planner. If a manager cannot do both, I do not believe the solution lies in shoring him up via a corporate planning department. I *do* believe it lies in using the talent of both line and specific staff personnel who surround him.

I believe in using the talents already present in marketing, finance, research, and manufacturing—and the head of each of these areas must be a planner himself or *he* will fail. I am opposed to separating the division managers from the top management by allowing any staff group to represent or speak for them—or to take their cues from them.

I believe that America's greatest companies succeeded because one man or group of individuals with strong convictions made things happen. They had vision and used intuition in varying degrees but they did their own planning and monitoring of results. I may be overgeneralizing, but normally a company has its best all-around talent in top line positions. They are there because they have a good balance of talents and experience. For that reason, their judgment should have the greatest influence in strategy formation as well as final decision making. By this, I do not mean to imply that line personnel think more strategically than staff personnel. The opposite may, in fact, be true. There are often individuals way down the organization in both line and staff who are thinking persons.

Finally, I strongly believe there is a great tendency in American business to overmanage, overplan, overstaff, and overorganize, which is contributing in a major way to our declining ability to compete in world markets. Our fixed costs in staff and management are often a larger factor than factory labor in making us noncompetitive.

QUESTIONS

1. How do you appraise for formal planning efforts at the Copley Company?
2. What do you predict will occur with respect to formal planning at Copley?
3. How would *you* handle formal planning at Copley?

Case 8–2

The Quaker Oats Company*

Harry T. Ambrose had recently been appointed The Quaker Oats Company's director—long-range planning. An MBA with nine years of managerial experience (but no previous exposure to the management of formal planning systems), in early 1971 Mr. Ambrose had the task of guiding the company through what was essentially the initiation of formal, long-range planning.

The Company

During the five-year period ended June 1970, Quaker Oats' per share earnings grew at an average annual rate of 11 percent. That performance was in striking contrast to the company's record in the five previous years, when earnings were almost on a plateau, and represented one of the best records achieved in the packaged food industry in the second half of the 1960s. Exhibit 1 presents a five-year review of Quaker Oats' financial performance.

A highly successful product development program was the principal contributor to the improved earnings record of the company. Out of fiscal 1970's revenues of $598 million, the company spent $7.4 million on research and development, 21 percent higher than in fiscal 1969 and almost twice the amount spent five years earlier. Management felt that those expenditures were fully justified by the success achieved in the introduction of such new products as Aunt Jemima Complete Pancake Mix, Aunt Jemima Frozen French Toast, Quaker Instant Oats, King Vitamin (a nutritional cereal for children), and Ken-L Ration Burgers.

Also contributing to the company's improved earnings record was management's decision to minimize commodity operations and emphasize consumer-product areas in order to take greater advantage of the company's marketing capabilities. The decision to reduce commodity operations resulted in the divestiture of a line of country elevators in 1967 and a sizable feed operation early in 1969 and the acquisition of Fisher-Price toys, a manufacturer of toys for preschool children, later that year. In addition, Quaker made several acquisitions outside the United States, including pet food companies in England and Canada and a leading manufacturer of chocolate in Mexico.

In recognition of the change in the company's product line and the broadening scope of its operations, Robert D. Stuart, Jr., the president and chief architect of Quaker Oats' growth since 1962, announced in September 1970 a reorganization of the company's management structure. In the current management structure the following officers reported to the president and chief executive officer:

1. Group vice president, administration, who was responsible for corporate staff activities.
2. Group vice president, corporate development, who was responsible for research and development, for corporate planning, and for certain divisions formed to market new products.
3. Executive vice president, international.
4. Executive vice president, operations, who was responsible for manufacturing, engineering, purchasing, distribution, and employee relations.

---

* This case was prepared by R. F. Vancil, Harvard Business School.
Copyright © by the President and Fellows of Harvard College.

EXHIBIT 1

THE QUAKER OATS COMPANY AND SUBSIDIARIES
Statement of Consolidated Income and Reinvested Earnings

Year Ended June 30

	1970	1969	1968	1967	1966
			($000)		
Revenues:					
Net Sales	$597,652	$553,879	$547,194	$555,133	$498,358
Other income—net	2,745	2,738	956	881	432
	$600,397	$556,617	$548,150	$556,014	$498,790
Cost and expenses:					
Cost of goods sold	399,426	375,661	382,419	403,010	358,178
Selling, general and administrative expenses	142,572	129,675	122,693	115,132	103,750
Interest expense	4,433	2,083	2,315	2,417	1,950
	546,431	507,419	507,427	520,559	463,878
Income before federal and foreign income taxes	53,966	49,198	40,723	35,455	34,912
Federal and foreign income taxes	25,823	23,492	19,400	16,673	17,340
Income before extraordinary items	28,143	25,706	21,323	18,782	17,572
Extraordinary (charges) credits (net of income taxes)	—	(1,092)	—	898	—
Net income	28,143	24,614	21,323	19,680	17,572
Reinvested earnings					
Dividends: Preferred stock	490	495	507	528	568
Common stock	11,737	10,704	9,710	8,868	8,864
Earnings reinvested during the year	15,916	13,415	11,106	10,284	8,140
Balance at beginning of year	139,567	129,996	118,890	108,606	100,466
Transfer to common stock re stock split	(3,731)	—	—	—	—
Excess of cost over par value of treasury preferred stock retired (95,489 shares)	—	(3,844)	—	—	—
Balance at end of year	$151,752	$139,567	$129,996	$118,890	$108,606
Per common share:*					
Income before extraordinary items	$ 2.21	$ 2.04	$ 1.72	$ 1.51	$ 1.41
Extraordinary (charges) credits	—	(0.09)	—	(0.07)	—
Net income	$ 2.21	$ 1.95	$ 1.72	$ 1.58	$ 1.41
Dividends declared	$ 0.94	$ 0.87	$ 0.80	$ 0.73	$ 0.73

* Adjusted for stock splits.

EXHIBIT 2 Executive Reporting Relationships

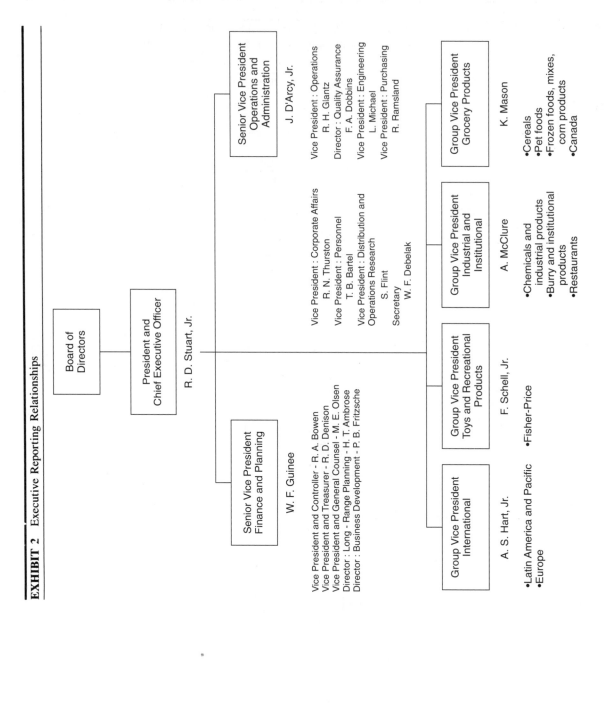

Board of
Directors

President and
Chief Executive Officer

R. D. Stuart, Jr.

Senior Vice President
Finance and Planning

W. F. Guinee

Vice President and Controller - R. A. Bowen
Vice President and Treasurer - R. D. Denison
Vice President and General Counsel - M. E. Olsen
Director : Long - Range Planning - H. T. Ambrose
Director : Business Development - P. B. Fritzsche

Senior Vice President
Operations and
Administration

J. D'Arcy, Jr.

Vice President : Operations
R. H. Glantz
Director : Quality Assurance
F. A. Dobbins
Vice President : Engineering
L. Michael
Vice President : Purchasing
R. Ramsland

Vice President : Corporate Affairs
R. N. Thurston
Vice President : Personnel
T. B. Bartel
Vice President : Distribution and
Operations Research
S. Flint
Secretary
W. F. Debelak

Group Vice President
International

A. S. Hart, Jr.

• Latin America and Pacific
• Europe

Group Vice President
Toys and Recreational
Products

F. Schell, Jr.

• Fisher-Price

Group Vice President
Industrial and
Institutional

A. McClure

• Chemicals and
  industrial products
• Burry and institutional
  products
• Restaurants

Group Vice President
Grocery Products

K. Mason

• Cereals
• Pet foods
• Frozen foods, mixes,
  corn products
• Canada

5. Group vice president, grocery products, who was responsible for marketing activities.

The reorganization decentralized all operations into four major profit centers called "groups": grocery products (United States and Canada), international grocery products, industrial and institutional products, and toys and recreational products. Mr. Stuart stated that the toy and recreational group would be expanded considerably by means of internal growth and acquisitions. The decentralized corporate structure was expected to facilitate the implementation of top management's plans to continue to expand and diversify the enterprise. Exhibit 2 presents Quaker Oats' management structure after the 1970 reorganization.

Planning History

Quaker began long-range planning in fiscal 1965. The plans created that year, and annually thereafter, were primarily numbers-oriented estimates of income and requirements of capital. Emphasis was placed on the first year of the annual, three-year plans; the last two years were more or less extrapolations of the first year. Concentration was on existing businesses, which were treated in great financial detail.

Initially, responsibility for supervision of both long- and short-range plans reposed with a director of corporate planning. However, the corporate planner's heavy involvement in acquisition studies and negotiations coupled with his limited staff capability forced him to rely upon the controller's office for staff support in supervising, reviewing, and consolidating the company's plans. By mid-1968, responsibility for short-range planning (annual two-year plans) had been shifted to the corporate controller's office, which created a department entitled profit planning and analysis (PP&A) to handle the task. Responsibilities for long-range planning and acquisitions were split. When the director of long-range planning left the company in early 1969, the long-range planning position was left vacant.

Robert A. Bowen, vice president and controller since the mid-1960s, stated that while he had been in a position to influence the company's planning he had endeavored to gain a more explicit grasp of what made the business tick. He had collected, through the planning process, detailed quantitative indicators of product group performance over the previous three to four years. The *back data,* as he termed this information, included historical comparisons of product expenses and asset utilization. In addition, Mr. Bowen had accumulated comparative information on 10 of Quaker Oats' chief competitors. He had distributed relevant portions of the back data to Quaker's managers annually as a part of the planning process. Mr. Bowen intended to continue this practice, which he believed aided operating managers in formulating realistic operating plans.

However, in 1969, overall responsibility for Quaker's long-range planning processes was assumed by W. Fenton Guinee. Previously the vice president–marketing services, Mr. Guinee had recently been appointed to the position group vice president–corporate development. (In September 1970, his title was again changed to senior vice president–finance and planning.) After, in his words, "taking awhile to figure out what long-range planning was . . . through reading and discussion with the president and business school contacts," Mr. Guinee decided that Quaker needed more strategic thinking and fewer numbers in its plans. He characterized the company as evolving from a rather homogeneous business to a montage of partial profit centers and functional organizations in substantially different businesses and having different needs. Mr. Guinee thought that the information flows represented by plans should be altered to fit the changing management structure. In particular, plans should reflect the rationale behind operating management's decisions and performance.

Harry Ambrose's job

Following extensive discussions with the president, in September 1970 Mr. Guinee appointed Harry T. Ambrose to the position of director–

long-range planning. Mr. Ambrose was to aid Mr. Guinee in designing and overseeing a formal planning system that recognized the changing management needs of the company. Mr. Ambrose was instructed to work closely with the head of the profit planning and analysis department in coordinating a formal planning system, which accounted for both short-term and long-term planning needs.

To guide Mr. Ambrose in his work, Mr. Guinee gave him copies of memorandums exchanged by Messrs. Stuart and Guinee, which laid out their expectations regarding the formal planning system. Following is a summary of their position:

A. The purpose of long-range planning was to be:
  1. Develop agreement among divisional, group, and corporate management on written goals and strategies based on projections of long-term needs.
  2. Identify future resource needs of skills, personnel, organization, finances, and new businesses to allow for their development in an orderly manner.

B. No substantive changes in the concept, content, and administration of the two-year planning effort were to be contemplated.

C. The long-range plan was to cover five fiscal years beginning after the current fiscal year. (Quaker's fiscal year ran from July 1 to June 30.) The content of the long-range plan was to include:
  1. Description of current state of the business and of each of its major functional areas.
  2. Assumptions about future economy, social and political environment, technological developments, and competition.
  3. Recommended objectives.
  4. Recommended strategies.
  5. Identification of risks.

  The plans were to include statements describing a selected strategy supported by numbers defining the magnitude of growth, investments, and risks. The alternative strategies considered were to be described, along with the reason for the one recommended. Compared with the two-year plan, in the five-year plan relatively greater emphasis was to be placed on the written statements and recommendations with numbers being used to provide reasonably quantified approximations of the direction chosen, rather than as an instrument for controlling or for measuring managerial performance.

D. Responsibility for development of divisional plans was to rest with divisional vice presidents and/or general managers; for group plans, with group vice presidents; and for corporate plans, with the planning committee (identified as the president plus the two senior vice presidents).

E. Divisional management was to be responsible for securing approval of their plans from group management, who in turn was to be responsible for securing approval of group plans from the planning committee. The latter was to review group plans in detail, to direct appropriate modifications and the development of a consolidated corporate plan for presentation to the executive committee of the board of directors.

F. Responsibility for the format and administration of both two-year and long-range plans was to be that of the senior vice president–finance and planning. Responsibilities of individual departments in finance and planning were to be as indicated in Exhibit 3.

G. For the first annual planning process, both the two-year and long-range planning efforts were to proceed concurrently, commencing in January 1971 and concluding in June of that year. Timing of future planning was to be reviewed after the completion of 1971's planning.

H. Review of the five-year plans was to be focused upon the quality of current and previous analyses and conclusions, rather than the accuracy of numerical projections. Whereas

EXHIBIT 3 Delineation of Responsibilities in Planning

	Two-Year		Five-Year	
	*Profit Planning and Analysis**	*Long-range Planning*	*Profit Planning and Analysis**	*Long-range Planning*
Develop manual	Primary	Collaborative	Collaborative	Primary
Develop financial format	Primary	None	Primary	Collaborative
Develop format for statement and recommendations	Primary	None	Collaborative	Primary
Provide financial back data	Primary	None	Primary	None
Coordinate planning	Primary	None	None	Primary
Consolidate into corporate figures	Primary	None	Primary	None
Critque plans	Primary	Collaborative	Collaborative	Primary
Identify deviations from plan	Primary	None	None	Primary

*Under direction of vice president–controller.

responsibility for achievement of two-year plan goals was to rest primarily with the person responsible for operating a particular area, responsibility for the strategies selected in the five-year plan was to be shared between the person recommending the plan and the person approving it.

Remarks by Fenton Guinee

What we are trying to accomplish with our planning system must be considered in light of the corporate situation. Our determination to achieve profitable diversification as a basis for future growth has spurred some notable changes in the way the company is managed.

Operational responsibilities were restructured last September so that many of our managers now have overall responsibility for all four functions (marketing, finance, production, and personnel) instead of only one. We have found that this is a very difficult reorientation for some managers to make.

Even if we had not reorganized in 1970, we probably would reintroduce long-range planning now. Quaker needs to be looking beyond its immediate future and next year's profits to the issues which will determine its long-term viability.

But, also, we expect the introduction of a planning system at a time when the managers' tasks are changing to help them to define their new tasks. Sure the work load is going to be enormous, but we are forcing them to look beyond their own previous functional expertises immediately. Therefore, they are going to develop as general managers much quicker.

Harry's task is to work out a working balance between the amount and quality of effort managers put into short-term versus long-term planning. Right now we don't know what this balance should be. We do know, however, that each type of planning is important in its own right.

Short-term planning is well established at Quaker. We have fine budgeting and control systems. The managers use them and seem to believe in them. But the quality of the decisions made through these systems may begin to deteriorate if the decision makers lose pace with corporate objectives and strategies. Long-range planning should function to maintain this pace through the introduction of new information, analysis, and properly disseminated decisions.

Harry Ambrose's Comments

I suppose that I was selected for this job because my background was in line management [not staff] and because I am on good terms with most of the division managers. I was formerly director of materials purchasing under the old functional corporate setup, and I got to know most of the present division managers pretty well because my job took me all over the company.

Mr. Stuart and Mr. Guinee have pretty well thought out what they want planning to do and how Quaker ought to go about doing it. Nevertheless, there always remain a number of practical problems to be ironed out. This much I know from my own experience as a manager and from my investigations into how other companies plan.

I don't expect that we are going to leap right into an ideal planning system immediately. With the uncertainty arising from the new corporate structure and the two-year planning going on at the same time as long-range planning, I expect that long-range planning is not going to get as much attention as I would like.

Therefore, I think that I should try to achieve some limited objectives in planning this year. First, I would like to establish in the managers' minds that long-range planning is here to stay and is an important part of their jobs. Second, I would like to educate them in the rationale of long-range planning. In particular, I need to break them away from thinking that long-range planning is the extrapolation of short-term quantitative relationships. Quaker's managers must come to realize that different kinds of factors are at work in the long term and that because many of these factors are very intangible their handling requires the use of a disciplined, logical, technique.

There are a lot of factors which will determine the ultimate success or failure of the planning program. Certainly one of these factors will be the kind and quality of cooperation that I get from PP&A. It appears to me that the delineation of responsibilities in planning between PP&A and the long-range planning department was based primarily upon existing staff capabilities. In essence, any of the planning which dealt with financial statements was assigned to PP&A. Financial analysis is their specialty and they have a staff of about 12 skilled people. The long-range planning department consists of myself plus an assistant and a secretary.

Fortunately I have a good working relationship with the head of PP&A. We have managed to resolve amicably differences of opinion relating to the format and content of the long-range plans. In general, he tends to see more of a need in the plans for detailed, precise information than I do. For example, one of our arguments revolved around whether to round all financial data in the plans off to the nearest thousand dollars or the nearest million dollars. I finally managed to persuade him that the larger figure was adequate to indicate the direction and magnitude of financial results—which was all that was necessary for the long-range plans.

The head of PP&A also would like to see (as would I) the long-range plans precede the short-range plans so that the former could be used to provide direction for the latter. However, we differ on the question of how tight the linkage between long-range plans and short-range plans should be. His opinion (which is shared by Mr. Guinee) is that the forecast performance in the first two years of the five-year plan should be required to match precisely the forecast performance in the short-range plan. I believe that he feels that this requirement is necessary to gain commitment to, and inject reality in, the long-range plans. I feel that it would be more useful at this time to concentrate more upon developing the managers' ability to create alternative strategies than to tie them to a rigid planning program.

QUESTIONS

1. Evaluate Quaker Oats' planning system.
2. Do the various aspects of Quaker Oats' planning and control system tie together?
3. What advice would you give to Harry Ambrose concerning activities that will achieve his objectives?

Case 8–3

Ajax Manufacturing Company*

The simplified case consists of unit cost calculations for three different products under each of three different cost accounting systems: "traditional" volume-based, "modern" volume-based, and transaction-based. The company and situation described here are highly simplified to keep the case short. The situation is not hypothetical, however. Much more extensive examples of essentially this same problem are quite common in the managerial accounting literature today. We will call the company "Ajax Manufacturing, Inc." Ajax manufactures three different products for an industrial market. This constitutes a "full line" in the simplified context. The cost accounting system used by Ajax will be termed a *traditional* one in the sense it is very much like the system that literally thousands of firms across North America and Europe have used for many years and still use today.

Sales prices and sales volume data for the three products are shown in Exhibit 1. along with basic production and standard cost statistics. Target sales prices reflect the prices needed to achieve the planned 35 percent gross margin, given the product costs generated by the accounting system (Standard cost + 0.65 = Target price). The product costs are calculated as follows:

1. Charge each product for standard raw material cost (the sum of purchased components × standard price)
2. Charge each product for standard direct labor cost (standard labor hours per unit × standard charge per hour)

3. Assign overhead costs to units based on a *two-staged* allocation formula. First *(stage 1)*, assign the costs of overhead departments to production departments based on some "relevant" measure of activity (square feet of floor space for janitorial cost, machine value for insurance cost, employee head count for personnel cost, etc.). Then, after all costs have been assigned to production departments, *stage 2* is to assign costs to units of product based on some measure of "thruput" or output volume in the production department. The most frequently used measure of production volume in multiproduct plants has traditionally been labor dollars (or labor hours).

In our example, since there is only one production department ("machines"), the first stage allocation is trivial. Since there is only one production department, allocating 100 percent of indirect overhead to it *must be* totally correct! Yet, even when the *stage 1* allocations are perfectly accurate, meaningful product costing is not assured. The false belief that "reasonableness" of the allocations at *stage 1* produces "reasonable" end-unit costs is part of the problem with volume-based costing.

Assuming setup labor is included, the total overhead to be assigned to the production in the machines department is:

Allocated overhead:		
Set-up	$ 3,000	
Receiving	300,000	
Engineering	500,000	
Packing	200,000	$1,003,000

* This case was prepared and is copyrighted by Vijay Govindarajan and John K. Shank.

Directly assignable
overhead:
Machines cost
(10,000 hours
× $70/hour) $ 700,000
Total overhead $1,703,000

In a traditional costing system such as this, overhead is assigned to products based on direct labor dollars. Using this information, Ajax calculates the unit cost of products A, B, and C as follows:

As shown here, product A is achieving its planned margin. Product B is achieving only 31 percent gross margin, because this product has come under heavy price pressure from foreign competitors. Ajax knows its factory is as modern and efficient as any in the world and, thus, is convinced that the foreign firms are "dumping" product B in the U.S. market. Ajax has dropped its price somewhat in response to the foreign firms, but it is very reluctant to cut further, because of the low achieved gross margin. Its sales volume for product B has fallen substantially, although B is still the highest-volume product.

		"Traditional" Approach		
		A	B	C
Raw material		$ 20.00	$30.00	$10.00
Direct labor		10.00	6.67	5.00
Overhead (labor $ basis):		75.70	50.49	37.85
Setup	$ 3,000			
Machines	700,000			
Receiving	300,000			
Engineering	500,000			
Packing	200,000			
Total	$1,703,000			
[Overhead	$1,703,000			
rate =	$ 225,000 = 757%]			
Total		$105.70	$87.16	$52.85

Product profitability data can be summarized as follows:

Fortunately for Ajax, it has been partially able to offset the declining profits from B by signifi-

	A	B	C
Standard cost	$105.70	$87.16	52.85
Target selling price	$162.61	$134.09	$ 81.31
Planned gross margin %	35%	35%	35%
Actual selling price	$162.61	$125.96	$105.70
Actual gross margin %	35%	31%	50%

EXHIBIT 1 Basic Product Information

	Three Products		
	A	*B*	*C*
Production	10,000 units in 1 run	15,000 units in 3 runs	5,000 units in 10 runs
Shipments	10,000 units in 1 shipment	15,000 units in 5 shipments	5,000 units in 20 shipments
Selling prices:			
Target	$162.61	$134.09	$81.31
Actual	$162.61	$125.96	$105.70

	Manufacturing Cost			
Raw material	5 components @ $4 ea. = $20	6 components @ $5 ea. = $30	10 components @ $1 ea. = $10	
Labor usage: (labor = $20/hr: including fringe benefits)				*Total*
Setup labor	10 hrs. per production run	10 hrs. per production run	11 hrs. per production run	150 hours
Run labor	$\frac{1}{2}$ hr. per part	$\frac{1}{3}$ hr. per part	$\frac{1}{4}$ hr. per part	11,250 hrs.
Machines usage: (Machine cost = $70/hr)	$\frac{1}{4}$ hr. per part	$\frac{1}{3}$ hr. per part	$\frac{1}{2}$ hr. per part	10,000 hrs.

There is only one production department—"machines"—and it takes a little more than one labor hour for each machine hour (11,250/10,000) at the current product mix.

*Other Overhead**	
Receiving department	$300,000
Engineering department	500,000
Packing department	200,000

* Again, the categories of manufacturing overhead have been greatly simplified for purposes of this case.

cantly raising the price of C. Ajax was pleasantly surprised when customers readily accepted the price increases for C. Also, even with the higher prices, competition has not challenged Ajax very much for the volume with product C. The result seems to be a very profitable low volume niche, which competitors don't invade. Management presumes that product C must have some unique characteristics, which are very attractive for the customer but which are not apparent to Ajax. Because of the market dominance it has achieved with C, Ajax hopes to still earn its target overall gross margin of 35 percent. But actual results seem to lag the projected results consistently. Management attributes the decline to "inexplicable" overhead "creep," which it believes results from a lack of "discipline" among cost center managers.

Concern with costs and prices for its volume leader, product B, has led Ajax to experiment with some "modern" refinements to its cost accounting system. In fact, a new approach to product costing has been developed by the controller, even though top management has not yet seen his calculations. Still using only the information in Exhibit 1, he has incorporated three refinements to the "traditional" system. His "modern" touches are:

1. Break out setup labor from the overhead pool and charge it to each product based on setup time per production run divided by the number of units in a production run. For example, for product A, one setup costs $200 (10 hours x $20/hr.) and one run is 10,000 units. Setup cost is thus 0.02 per unit ($200/10,000). This refinement goes beyond averaging setup cost across the products to specifically identify it with the individual products. This refinement can be very important when products differ in setup time, or number of production setups, or in length of production runs (or all three).

2. Break out the overhead that is more related to material cost (receiving or inbound inspection, for example) and charge it to products based on material cost, rather than labor cost. Under this refinement, there is a pool of material handling overhead separate from the pool of production overhead. Material handling overhead is charged to products based on raw material dollars, rather than direct labor dollars. This refinement can be very important when products differ in raw material content.

3. Substitute machine hours for labor dollars (or labor hours) as the measure of production volume. As factories have become much less labor-paced and much more machines-paced in recent years, the notion of labor content as the best measure of "thruput" has lost its salience. When one worker tends several machines, which perform different functions, run at different speeds, and differ markedly in cost and complexity, labor cost loses its meaning as a central element in product costing. The overhead rate of 757 percent (Overhead + Direct labor) for Ajax is a clear signal that labor is no longer a dominant cost component.

In fact, for this case, direct labor cost is only 8 percent of total cost, a far cry from the factory of our history or from textbook lore. When direct labor cost finally dropped to 3 percent of total cost in Hewlett-Packard, management relegated it to just another component of overhead in a two-component cost system—material cost and overhead.

For Ajax, where the machines are ostensibly identical and machines-specific cost is three times as high as direct labor cost, machine hours consumed can well be viewed as a *better* measure of thruput and, thus, as a *superior* basis for assigning indirect overhead.

Using these three refinements, the controller has calculated new product costs, using standard raw material cost, standard direct labor cost, standard product-specific setup cost, material handling overhead charged in proportion to material cost, and production overhead charged in proportion to machine hours consumed. With these refinements, product costs of A, B, and C are shown on the next page.

The controller is just about ready to present his "modern" cost accounting system ideas to top management. He feels sure that this information will further strengthen management's resolve not to cut prices on product B any further. The new system shows that margins on B are even lower than management currently believes. The controller sees this as further evidence that foreign firms must be dumping product B to Ajax customers. Part of his hesitation in releasing the new cost data had been based on his concern about how management would view the news that C is not really as profitable as they had thought (even though A is much more profitable). This concern had lessened greatly when he heard the sales manager say recently that Ajax was experimenting with even further 15 percent price increases for product C in some regions. Amazingly, salesmen had found customers still willing to order

	"Modern Approach		
	A	B	C
Raw material	$20.00	$30.00	$10.00
Material overhead:			
(Material $ basis)			
(300K/700K = 43%)	8.60	12.90	4.30
Setup labor	0.02	0.04	0.44
Direct labor	10.00	6.67	5.00
Other overhead (machine hours basis)	35.00	46.67	70.00

Machines	$ 700,000
Engineering	500,000
Packing	200,000
Total	$1,400,000

$$[\text{Overhead rate} = \frac{\$1,400,000}{10,000} = \$140/\text{hr.}]$$

	A	B	C
Total	$73.62	$96.28	$89.74

normal quantities. "C certainly is a real winner," the controller thought to himself.

We will leave our narrative account of Ajax Manufacturing at this point to turn to a description of a much different system for allocating indirect costs—transactions-based overhead allocation. If only Ajax were aware of this system, it would see how painfully inaccurate its cost system is, even with the refinements the controller is about to propose. One purpose of the case is to consider how the transactions-based view of costs might lead to a dramatically different assessment of the managerial options being considered.

"Transaction Costing"

In spite of the very good logic embodied in the controller's three refinements, the results still *fundamentally* misallocate overhead to products. Fundamentally, each component of overhead is caused by some activity. Each product should be charged for a share of that component based on the proportion of that activity which the product causes. Production scheduling cost, for example, is generated by the number of production runs to be scheduled. This cost should be allocated to products based on the number of production runs each product generates. Allocation based on labor hours or machine hours of production yields a fundamentally inaccurate picture. Products that generate a large number of relatively short production runs will *always* carry a less than proportionate share of the cost under *any* volume-based allocation scheme. Scheduling cost is not volume dependent in the short run. Even in the long run it is not dependent on production *volume*. In the long run it is dependent on how many runs must be scheduled, not how many units we produce. Whether machine hours or labor hours are the better measure of output, *whichever* measure of output volume is used understates the extent to which the product with many short runs causes scheduling cost. The basic idea is that transaction volume (number of production runs) is a better proxy for long-run variable cost than is output volume.

This concept is not particularly subtle or counter intuitive. In fact, it is very much in line with our common sense. But, transaction costing would involve much more work, and, in earlier days, this extra work was not viewed as worth the extra effort. In those earlier days, factories tended to produce fewer different products, and cost was labor dominated (high labor cost relative to overhead), and products tended to differ less in the amount of support services they consumed. Thus, the more time-consuming transaction basis for overhead allocation was not likely to produce product cost results much different from a simple volume-driven basis tied to labor cost. Over time, the circumstances under which the more complicated transaction approach would produce comparable results have eroded. But eroding along with these circumstances was our awareness that volume-based costing is only useful when the simplifications on which it is based are reasonable.

Helping to reestablish that awareness is one purpose of this case. There is no question that a transactions-based overhead allocation system adopts a long-run focus on cost behavior, rather than short-run. That is, transaction costing does not imply that overhead can be saved in the short run if the transactions which cause it are stopped. There is almost always a lag between changes in the volume of transactions and changes in the level of cost. For example, salaried production schedulers are not fired immediately if the number of production runs declines. Yet, over the longer run, scheduling cost is surely tied to one fundamental activity, one transaction—the number of production runs to schedule. A similar logic applies to each component of production overhead, such as shipping orders for shipping cost or receiving orders for receiving cost.

The transaction approach also disavows the notion that all overhead allocation is arbitrary, anyway, and thus is not worth trying to do "better." It presumes that meaningful allocation of fixed costs *is* possible and worth doing. In fact, the gradual rise to prominence over the past 30 years of the concept—that full cost is less useful than variable cost, and the concept that full costing is only an exercise in applied arbitrariness—also helps to explain why transaction-based allocation of fixed overhead has not received more serious attention in recent years.

In 1988, labor was not only a dramatically less important cost component all over the developed world, it was also viewed less and less as a cost to be varied when production volume varies. "Labor" is now part of the "team" in a large and growing number of companies, which means that labor is a fixed cost, as well as a minor cost component. But business after business is choking on overhead. Indirect cost is now the dominant part of cost, and businesses are desperately seeking ways to understand why its growth so undermines their efforts to generate adequate profits. In the modern "flexible factory," only raw material cost is volume-dependent and directly relatable to individual products. A meaningful assessment of indirect cost in 1988 *must* involve assigning overhead in proportion to the transactions that generate it in the long run.

For Ajax, Exhibit 2 summarizes the distribution of cost-causing activities or transactions for each of the three indirect overhead departments:

Receiving orders for the receiving department.

Packing orders for the packing department.

Work orders for the engineering department.

This framework obviously simplifies a very complex phenomenon—determining what activities ultimately cause cost in any given department. Receiving cost, for example, is partly caused by bulk of receipts, partly by weight of receipts, and partly by fragility of receipts, as well as by number of shipments received. For purposes of this example, however, the concept is demonstrated, even though it is not fully amplified. The basic idea is that receiving cost is caused by receiving workload, rather than by production volume, and receiving workload for products may differ markedly from production volume.

EXHIBIT 2   Overhead Transactions Workload

	Products		
	A	*B*	*C*
Receiving orders: Receive each component once per run (a "just-in-time" inventory policy)	5 (4%)	18 (15%)	100 (81%)
Packing orders: One packing order per shipment	1 (4%)	5 (19%)	20 (77%)
Engineering Workload: Distribution of workload in the engineering department is based on subjective assessment of long-run trends in number of engineering work orders for each product	25% [The standard, smooth running product]	35%	40% [The complex, special problems product]

QUESTIONS

1. Using the information given in Exhibit 2, calculate transaction-based indirect overhead cost (receiving, engineering, and packing) per unit for each of the three products. Use this new information to recalculate overall cost per unit for products A, B, and C.

2. How can Ajax use the transaction costing data to improve programming decisions. Specifically consider:
   —Product pricing.
   —Product emphasis.
   —Most likely cause of the decline, over time, in control over overhead spending as the product mix has shifted away from product B and toward product C.

Case 8–4

AmElectric*

AmElectric is a large, diversified, multinational manufacturer with headquarters in New York City. The corporation consisted of several groups; within each group, a number of business units; and within most divisions, a number of plants. One division, the Operations Division, specialized in the manufacture of extremely large and complicated equipment; a single order often required several years to design, manufacture, install, and test. In recent years, AmElectric received relatively few orders for original equipment; most were for replacement parts. Some of these replacements were identical with the component being replaced; many were upgrades that provided improved capability. In recent years, AmElectric faced strong competitive pressure, much of it from foreign sources.

Headquarters of the Operations Division was located some distance from corporate headquarters; it was responsible for managing several plants and 5,000 employees. Jeremy Thatcher, the division manager, made a practice of keeping a close contact with plants through frequent phone calls and regular visits every few weeks. Quality assurance managers and managers of product design in the plants also reported directly to division headquarters engineering. The plant controllers reported directly to the plant managers but had strong "dotted-line" relationships with the division headquarters controller.

Plant A in the Operations Division manufactured components; some of these required a year or more to manufacture. In 1988, it had 600 production employees and 250 management and professional employees. Plant B assembled replacement components for this equipment. It had 486 production employees and 226 management and professional employees. Both plants were built in 1971.

The Annual Capital Investment Process

The capital investment process at AmElectric can be considered in three phases: budgeting, appropriating, and monitoring. Planning for capital investment began in July, as production forecasts and budgets got under way.

Budgeting for Capital Investment

In August, a technical manager from each plant area submitted proposals of his or her projects to the manager of advance manufacturing technology; documentation included return on investment (ROI), timing, and so on. The technology manager and the manager of accounting services met with the plant staff and selected the projects to promote. Then they presented their proposals to the plant manager and prepared a description of the projects, set priorities, and determined how the funds would be spent annually for the next three years.

Projects were first evaluated according to their support of strategic objectives and then by the net present value, rate of return, and risk category. In terms of strategic objective, there was a fairly even division among equipment replacement, cost reduction, and product improvement; few projects are based on volume increase.

* Adapted and reprinted by permission of Harvard Business School Press. This case was drawn from Chapter 8, prepared by Shiela Puffer and Vitale Ozira, of *Behind the Factory Walls: Decision Making in Soviet and U.S. Enterprises*, eds. Paul R. Lawrence and Charalambos A. Vlachoutsicos. Boston: 1990, pp. 85–91 and 184–95. Copyright © 1990 by the President and Fellows of Harvard College.

There were four risk categories. Category A, the lowest risk, was for investments in existing product or technology, existing facility, and existing market. Risk increased when any or all of these factors were new. Therefore, category D, the fourth and highest level of risk, was assigned to projects that involved a new product or technology, a new facility, and a new market.

Whether a project was considered *annual* or *major* depended on a combination of its cost and its risk category. A project was classified as major when the investment exceeded $5 million in risk category A, $2 million in category B, $1 million in category C, and all projects in category D; all other investments were classified as annual projects. Authorized approval levels were based on these classifications.

In September, the plant manager submitted Plant B's plan to Jeremy Thatcher, divisional general manager; Thatcher set priorities among plants. In November, the revised plans moved on to the Capital Review Committee of the business unit, which consisted of a technical representative from each division. The committee met for two or three days to review all divisions; each was allotted 30–40 minutes to present its major projects. Each plant sent a technical expert as its spokesperson to explain the technical justification for the investment. Plant managers did not attend but were aware of the issues and the money involved and trusted their subordinates to represent their interests.

The Capital Review Committee reviewed all projects over $100,000, devoting approximately five minutes to a discussion of each project. Members completed a rating form to evaluate projects according to six criteria and then voted on which projects to fund; their recommendations were sent to the business unit headquarters. Major projects also had to be approved at the group and corporate levels.

One plant engineer said that there was no personal favoritism in the capital investment allocation process because the Capital Review Committee was composed of peers of the technical specialist representing the plant. He noted that it would be simpler, though not as fair, if the plant manager "fought all the battles," adding that:

> The plan is the plant's capital plan, and it is up to the plant to prepare it and justify it. The plan is not dictated from above. Sometimes hourly workers and lower-level salaried staff become frustrated that the plant does not promote their projects, but the plant technical manager explains the criteria to them and emphasizes that they should submit to the capital review committee only those projects that they are confident will be accepted.

The engineer did not recall any projects being rejected and said that the committee trusts the plant's judgment.

Approving Capital Appropriations

Even after a project was approved for the annual capital budget, it nevertheless was reviewed again as a separate capital appropriation request. Preparing such a request often took months. Those responsible tried hard to get it right the first time, because there was seldom a second chance to plead their case. Plant engineers researched and wrote the specifications with the help of purchasing and other staff. Detailed descriptions were provided on the following items: benefits, personnel effects, market and economic risks, level of utilization at which the project breaks even, technology and implementation risks, alternatives, key milestone schedule, and breakdown of specific items and costs. Plant personnel informed Jeremy Thatcher early in the process with the hope that he would approve it without revisions. Within the plant, the signature route for appropriation requests moved from department head to controller, marketing, human resources, engineering, and the plant manager.

It usually took about three weeks for an appropriation to be reviewed at divisional headquarters. Then it was submitted to the Capital Review Committee at the business unit level, which met monthly. The plant usually sent the appropriation request a week before the meeting. If the request involved a lot of money or was urgent, the plant manager would call the secretary of the committee to make sure everything was in order and to answer questions prior to the meeting.

Jeb Boxer, head of technical services at divisional headquarters, coordinated the plants' capital appropriation plans and discussed them with Jeremy Thatcher. (Officially, Boxer reported to the division materials manager, but for capital appropriation matters he reported directly to Thatcher.) Boxer also worked with the plants' technical specialists who wrote the appropriations requests. Some plant managers thought that it was unnecessary to go through Boxer, because they had already told Jeremy Thatcher about an appropriation during one of his plant visits. However, Thatcher had instructed Boxer not to let himself be bypassed even though he was hierarchically lower than the plant managers. Thatcher relied on Boxer to see that the appropriation requests were prepared properly and to ensure that all appropriate organizational members were involved. This had been a problem, because people in different parts of the organization did not always talk to one another. Boxer was able informally to give Thatcher "the inside scoop" on which of the plants' capital appropriation justifications were "shaky." Boxer also was responsible for coordinating refinements of proposals by going back to the plants and sometimes revising the appropriations line by line with them. Jeb Boxer explained his relationship with the plant management:

> I'm straight with the plants. I tell them, "Don't lie to me, because I'm going to be the biggest help you've got." We have a relationship where they trust me, and I give them a hard time, but I go to bat for what I think is right. So I think I have a reputation that I make them happy if I feel comfortable about the approach they've taken. It usually does work out.

Boxer's self-assessment of his role was confirmed by Jeremy Thatcher: "Jeb's a super-straight guy. He's the keeper of the books, and he ensures the quality of the documentation to support our capital projects."

Some of the plant management staff were frustrated with the present situation because the plant manager did not have authority to make capital appropriation decisions. They believed that the staff assistants to Jeremy Thatcher at divisional headquarters had the real authority and that Thatcher was too busy to do more than rubber-stamp the appropriations. They maintained that the plant manager was more experienced and competent to make such decisions than Thatcher's assistants, but they nevertheless cultivated good relations with the assistants in recognition of their authority. They also primed Jeremy Thatcher approximately six weeks in advance of submitting an appropriation request to smooth the way during the limited time they ultimately get with him when seeking his formal approval.

To alleviate the problem of accountability for appropriation requests, Jeremy Thatcher authorized Jeb Boxer to monitor a signature sheet on which individuals acknowledge exactly what they are responsible for. The eight signers were: the divisional headquarters managers of marketing, engineering, technical services, and information systems; the plant department head, human resources manager, and controller; and, finally, the plant manager. For example, the plant controller signed the following statement:

> All financial data is correct, including cost justification and NPV [net present value] and ROR [rate of return]. All required financial forms have been attached and are correct. Source of funds is correctly identified.

On a separate summary sheet of the appropriation request, additional approval signatures were recorded: divisional controller, divisional general manager, business unit general manager, group executive vice president, and corporate president (as required by the size and risk of the investment).

In the past, plant managers had been authorized to approve capital appropriations within limits set by the approved capital budget plan. When business conditions worsened, approval levels were "bumped up the organization." A plant engineer noted that, although this process kept good control of expenditures, the negative side is that it took months to get an appropriation approved. Staff at divisional headquarters were currently trying to streamline the complex approval process.

Monitoring Capital Investments

Throughout the year, actual capital spendings were tracked against the plan by routine accounting procedures; managers devoted their time only to variances. The budget could be modified if business conditions change—that is, it might be cut if a downturn developed, or projects might be substituted in midyear. For example, a project could be stopped, despite the availability of capital funds, if the expense budget contained no money to install the equipment; there was a policy against letting equipment sit idle. Hedge buying (buying tooling in anticipation of a project being funded) was also prohibited.

In the midyear review, plants could be asked to prepare contingency plans—that is, to prioritize their projects in case available funds increased or diminished. Overall, about 80 percent of the projects in the capital budget were eventually implemented. The others were not pursued by the plants, either because they were not viable, because conditions changed, or because the plant submitted substitute projects.

If a project was originally proposed as a cost improvement but did not meet the criteria, it could be reclassified as a replacement project and funding sought on that basis. Cost reduction was a current priority, however. Plant B generated more cost reduction proposals in 1988 than it had in the previous 10 years.

Throughout the year, the division asked for "make good" reports giving updates on how well the projects were doing. Only about 50 percent of the projects met all expectations, primarily because of the difficulty of achieving the forecast cost savings. It was difficult to squeeze out cost savings in direct labor, because hourly workers already had been cut to a minimum. Cost savings, therefore, had to be obtained from reductions in overhead and professional staff.

Another type of problem arose when money was unspent at the end of the year—for example, because a piece of equipment had not been delivered from the manufacturer as scheduled. In this situation, the plants had to find ways to reallocate the money to other projects, because the money could not be rolled over into the next year. Recently, division headquarters instituted a rule that a certain percentage of the annual budget had to be spent or allocated each quarter. Jeb Boxer, coordinator of capital appropriations at divisional headquarters, said that the plants were overly optimistic about their ability to spend capital funds, and they seldom spent all of them. Plants lost credibility, however, if they asked for new funds after failing to spend the previous year's allocation.

Plants could also ask for extra funds for an unforseen "hot" or high-need project. If the project fitted corporate's strategic thrust, a plant could bypass the formal procedure and get quick approval from the corporate executive vice president by preparing a simple justification. Plant B acquired robots in this way when productivity improvement was a key corporate strategy.

There were monthly reports and midyear reviews of capital expenditures. They helped everyone keep an overview of the situation and address problems in a timely manner.

Transfer Safety Plan

The Original Budget Decision

In May 1987, the AmElectric management committee announced its decision to shut down a Northeast plant and transfer a main-product manufacturing line to plant B. The decision was based on recommendations of a five-member team that for a year had studied ways to rationalize the plants and reduce surplus capacity. Jeremy Thatcher, the divisional general manager to whom the team reported, had instructed its members to take a no-frills approach and budget the move only for transportation and installation of existing equipment. Equipment upgrading was to be funded by the receiving plant and would have to be justified on an item-by-item basis. Because of the issue's sensitivity, the study team was kept small and secret. According to the Plant B staff, the team lacked sufficient knowledge of detail and did not budget enough capital for the transfer. However, Thatcher noted that he himself had pruned the team's capital budget by one third before presenting it for corporate approval.

To facilitate that approval, Thatcher spent three days at corporate headquarters explaining the plan to management committee members and key corporate staff. At its decisive meeting, the management committee approved the transfer plan but cut the capital portion of the budget by another one third; then it added several million dollars for expenses, such as equipment transfer, employee benefits, and capital write-down. Jeremy Thatcher recalled his thoughts at that meeting:

> I was not sure we could do it all for the budgeted amount, and I probably should have said so. But I thought there might be a way to make it as a pure transfer plan excluding process and technological improvements. This project was the most important strategic program we had. Our whole business survival depended on it. We were going to lose money and just bleed to death if we didn't do it. So at that point I accepted the budget cut. I just wanted to get out of the room and get on with the job.

The Decision to Request an Additional $3 Million

In the fall of 1987, midway thought the transfer, Plant B staff proposed a change in the plan: upgrade certain equipment, buy some new ma-chines, and transfer other equipment not designated initially. These changes would cost $3 million extra. A few of the items were approved as productivity improvements, but some equipment upgrades could not be justified in this way.

In March 1988, Thatcher, Jeb Boxer, and Vic Hoffman, the division controller, visited Plant B to see if the proposed equipment was really necessary. They agreed that it was, and they sought a way to obtain the money. Thatcher knew that, if he exceeded the budget by $3 million with a string of disparate appropriation requests, his career would be in jeopardy:

> I could have been in real hot water. When I accepted the budget cut, I owned the problem and was responsible for it. That's where the ownership thing comes in. It wasn't the plant's fault. They could have said to me, "Look what you did, boss." It was up to me to fix it. I thought, "We're about to go off the cliff. What are we going to do?"

While his staff worked on a solution, Thatcher asked the plant to keep a separate set of records on the project. This showed the overall project had a reasonable chance of beating its budget. Ultimately, Thatcher and his staff decided to adopt the plant controller's suggestion that the additional items be repackaged under the label of a safety plan. Analyses had shown the Northeast plant's facilities did not meet current safety standards, and each new expenditure could be justified on the ground it would improve plant safety. For example, for the test facility, Plant B wanted an explosion-proof concrete bunker, which would double the original approved cost of facility. A major test failure could result in extensive damage and personal injury. One manager at Plant B admitted that the chances of that happening were one in a million, but he pointed out that plant staff insisted on safety precautions before accepting responsibility for any equipment.

Thus, safety and environmental issues were the common thread linking the capital equipment requests that "just so happened" to result in the technological upgrades that the Plant B staff wanted. "Everything is true. It was just so cleverly packaged," confided a manager in the plant. "And we thought, who would have the audacity not to approve these things? And we went all the way up and got approval."

In May 1988, Thatcher presented the plan to the Strategic Capital Review Committee (SCRC). Committee members were sympathetic but approved the plant reluctantly; in their opinion, the safety features should have been included in the original plan.

While admitting that the safety plan was "one of the more unnerving things that happened to me in the past couple of years," Jeremy Thatcher staunchly defended it: "We haven't wasted a nickel. We'll end up with the world's best assembly shop. The problem was it didn't fit the original plan." He added that in the end he "didn't get his wrists slapped," because the expense side of the transfer came in considerably under budget; hence, the total cost of the transfer would not exceed the allocated $47 million, although the capital cost was higher than originally budgeted and accounting rules would not permit mixing capital items and expense items.

Flexible Machining System (FMS)

Phase 1

Plant A's flexible machining system was a multimillion-dollar project to be implemented in several stages. FMS was the largest capital investment program undertaken at Plant A since the plant was built. Its strategic thrust was threefold: (1) to improve competitive advantage by reducing costs, (2) to add flexibility in meeting customer needs with engineering changes to upgrade products, and (3) to reduce lead time. FMS would be not only a metal removal system but also a software system. The system was expected to enable new styles to be introduced quickly and phased out promptly when demand was met and other styles were required.

The project was the brainchild of the plant's manager of manufacturing planning, Juan Carerra. It was "his baby," and he pushed it all the way to the top of the corporation, striking up a friendship with AmElectric's chairman, with whom he could converse in Spanish. Carerra even gained the chairman's informal support of the project during one of the chairman's plant visits.

In January 1985, Juan Carerra began holding weekly brainstorming sessions with 25 plant engineers and, in his words, "planting seeds at divisional headquarters for FMS projects." The weekly meetings were "participative to the extreme" and became unwieldy. At that point, the group was trimmed to include just 10 engineers, who met on a monthly basis. Finally, a five-member FMS review team was formed: Juan Carerra; Tom Aster, Carerra's subordinate manager of advanced manufacturing technology (later to be named FMS project head); the manager of shop operations; his subordinate, the area manager for machining (where the equipment was to be installed); and the manager of quality assurance. The review team was responsible for providing justification for FMS, allocating staff resources to the project, and planning for implementation. The shop operations staff contributed data on what the costs and lead times had to be to make FMS worthwhile.

In late 1985, Jeb Boxer, the divisional technical services manager, reviewed the situation with Jeremy Thatcher and suggested that Carerra and the plant facilities manager submit an appropriation even though they did not know exactly what equipment they wanted. FMS technology was changing rapidly, and Plant A had been hesitant because its personnel lacked sufficient expertise to evaluate the options properly. However, the plant had not spent all of its appropriation for the year, and Boxer saw FMS as an opportunity to allocate some of the remaining funds. He warned the plant that it might not get its requested funds the following year if it had funds remaining in the current budget. Carerra's team decided to write an appropriation for phase 1 of the FMS project, consisting of some large machine tools. This was consistent with the corporate policy of phasing large projects and calculating benefits at each stage. In phase 1 of FMS, the plant could already claim cost savings from the machine tools.

Phase 2

By the second quarter of 1986, Plant A engineers had homed in on what products would work and what additional machine tools would be needed for FMS. Late in 1986, Plant A began preparations for phase 2. The FMS team met with the divisional managers of marketing, engineering, and manufacturing and got them to commit to the changes in production volumes that could be expected based on proposed cost reductions. In September 1986, Plant A prepared a $4.9 million appropriation request for phase 2. However, as Jeb Boxer said, the figure looked "too fishy"; it barely fell under the $5 million threshold for major projects that require approval by the board of directors. Boxer believed that political problems with corporate would ensue when it became apparent that the entire project (phases 1 and 2) would actually cost more than $5 million.

Boxer presented Jeremy Thatcher with two options: "Should we throw in a few more bucks to make it $5.1 million so it doesn't appear as though we're trying to skirt the fact that it's a major? Or would we cancel the first appropriation [for phase 1] and wrap the whole thing up into one?" The first option was unattractive, because "there's so much more pain involved that you don't want to do a major unless you really have to." The second option's drawback was that it violated the chairman's preference for phasing large projects.

Thatcher conferred with his superiors in the business unit and Boxer contacted the secretary of the Strategic Capital Review Committee for advice. The SCRC suggested that the appropria-

tion be written as phase 2 for $4.9 million as originally proposed. Remarked Boxer: "It was a revelation to me that the board of directors didn't want to spend time on it. They don't want to be messing around with things unless they are well over $5 million or risky."

So Thatcher agreed to keep the appropriation under $5 million but was "up front with the review board" about the scope of the project and its total cost. With the groundwork carefully laid, the project was approved by both the Capital Review Committee and the executive vice president without requiring approval by the board of directors. Not only did the project as a whole show a very good rate of return but phase 1 would realize savings on its own.

During the summer and fall of 1987, a team of engineers from Plant A toured machine-tool manufacturers in Europe and Japan to study the technology. Tom Aster, the FMS project head, had 13 professionals in his group work on the project's design phase and write bid specifications for equipment. By the end of June 1988, all equipment purchases were to be finalized; but some ordering delays occurred because Juan Carerra was out of the country. Nobody wanted to order the equipment in his absence.

Another major problem was the selection of software to run FMS. The AmElectric in-house software developers, a separate business unit, had a history of not always delivering on their promises, and Jeremy Thatcher expressed initial concern about the capacity and commitment of that group. He resolved the matter with the head of the unit and Plant A signed an agreement with the in-house group. The 200 pages of specifications were revised six times, and negotiations went back and forth between Tom Aster's staff and the software group. Aster would have preferred to contract with an outside firm, but he admitted that those arrangements also can cause problems.

The goal to have FMS fully operational by the end of 1989 was viewed as unrealistic by some plant management staff. Nevertheless, pilot operation was scheduled for early 1989. According to the manager of shop operations, "The rest of the world is moving in the direction of FMS. The sooner we get it up and running the more competitive we'll be in the world market. It will impact new products and should lower our costs."

QUESTIONS

1. Some people thought that the procedure for approving capital projects was too cumbersome. Should it be simplified? If so, how?
2. The "repackaging" mentioned near the end of the case seems to some people to be a subterfuge. Was this the best way to handle the problem? If not, what should have been done?
3. Can you suggest rules that would help to ensure that revisions of approved projects are properly authorized?
4. Would the process be improved if certain behaviors were changed? If so, how could this be accomplished?
5. There seems to be an overlap between the budget preparation process and the project authorization. Should the two processes be consistent? If so, how can this be done?

Chapter 9

Budget Preparation

This and the next two chapters focus on management control of operations in the current year. Chapter 9 describes the process of budget preparation that takes place *before* the year begins, Chapter 10 describes the control of operating activities *during* their occurrence, and Chapter 11 describes the appraisal of operations *after* their occurrence.

Chapter 9 starts by describing the purposes of a budget and distinguishing a budget from a program and from a forecast. The next section describes several types of budgets and lists some of the details given in a typical operating budget. The following section describes the steps in the process of preparing an operating budget. Finally, there is a discussion of the behavioral implications of the budget preparation process.

NATURE OF A BUDGET

Budgets are an important tool for effective short-term planning and control in organizations. A budget is a financial plan, usually covering the period of one year. An operating budget states the revenues and expenses planned for that year. It has these characteristics:

- It approximates the profit potential available to the business unit (division).
- It is stated in monetary terms, although the monetary amounts may be backed up by nonmonetary amounts (e.g., units sold or produced).
- It generally covers a period of one year.[1]
- It contains an element of management commitment, in that managers agree to accept the responsibility for attaining the budgeted objectives.

---

[1] In businesses that are strongly influenced by seasonal factors, there may be two budgets per year—for example, apparel companies typically have a fall budget and a spring budget.

- The budget proposal is reviewed and approved by an authority higher than the budgetee.
- Once approved, the budget can be changed only under specified conditions.
- Periodically, actual financial performance is compared to budget and variances are analyzed and explained.

The process of preparing a budget should be distinguished from (a) programming and (b) forecasting.

Relation to Programming

Programming, as we discussed in Chapter 8, is the process of deciding on the nature and size of the several programs that are to be undertaken in implementing an organization's strategies. Both programming and budget preparation involve planning, but the types of planning activities are different in the two processes. The budgeting process focuses on a single year, whereas programming focuses on activities that extend over a period of several years. Programming precedes budgeting and provides the framework within which the annual budget is developed. A budget is, in a sense, a one-year slice of the organization's program, although, for reasons discussed later in this chapter, this is not a complete description of a budget; the budgeting process involves more than simply carving out such a slice.

Another difference between a program and a budget is that the former is essentially structured by product lines or other programs, while the latter is structured by responsibility centers. This rearrangement of the program—so it corresponds to the responsibility centers charged with executing it—is necessary, because the budget will be used to influence a manager's performance before the fact and to appraise performance after the fact.

Contrast with Forecasting

A budget differs in several respects from a forecast. A *budget* is a management plan, with the implicit assumption that positive steps will be taken by the budgetee—the manager who prepares the budget—to make actual events correspond to the plan; whereas a *forecast* is merely a prediction of what will most likely happen, carrying no implication that the forecaster will attempt to so shape events that the forecast will be realized. As contrasted with a budget, a forecast has the following characteristics:

- It may or may not be stated in monetary terms.
- It can be for any time period.
- The forecaster does not accept responsibility for meeting the forecast results.
- Forecasts are not usually approved by higher authority.

- A forecast is updated as soon as new information indicates there is a change in conditions.
- Variances from forecast are not analyzed formally or periodically. (The forecaster does some analysis, but this is to improve the ability to forecast.)

An example of a financial forecast is one that is made by the treasurer's office to help in cash planning. Such a forecast includes estimates of revenues, expenses, and other items that affect cash flows. The treasurer, however, has no responsibility for making the actual sales, expenses, or other items conform to the forecast. The cash forecast is not cleared with top management; it may change weekly or even daily, without approval from higher authority; and usually the variances between actual and forecast are not systematically analyzed.

From management's point of view, a financial forecast is exclusively a planning tool, whereas a budget is both a planning tool and a control tool. All budgets include elements of forecasting, in that budgetees cannot be held responsible for certain events that affect their ability to meet budgeted objectives. If, however, a budgetee can change a so-called budget each quarter without formal approval (or, if the formal approval is perfunctory), such a budget is essentially a forecast, rather than a true budget. It cannot be used for evaluation and control, since, by the end of the year, actual results will always equal the revised budget.

Uses of a Budget

Preparation of an operating budget has four principal purposes: (1) to fine tune the strategic plan; (2) to help coordinate the activities of the several parts of the organization; (3) to assign responsibility to managers, to authorize the amounts they are permitted to spend, and to inform them of the performance that is expected of them; and (4) to obtain a commitment that is a basis for evaluating a manager's actual performance.

Fine tuning the strategic plan.   As discussed in Chapter 8, the program has the following characteristics: it is prepared early in the year, it is developed on the basis of the best information available at that time, its preparation involves relatively few managers, and it is stated in fairly broad terms. The budget, which is completed just prior to the beginning of the budget year, provides an opportunity to use the latest available information and is based on the judgement of managers at all levels throughout the organization. The "first cut" at the budget may reveal that the overall performance of the organization, or of a business unit within the organization, would not be satisfactory. If so, budget preparation is an opportunity to make decisions that will improve performance before a commitment is made to a specific way of operating during the year.

Coordination.   Every responsibility center manager in the organization participates in the preparation of the budget. When the pieces are assembled into an overall plan by the staff, inconsistencies may be detected. The most common is the possibility that the plans of the production organization are not consistent with the planned sales volume, in total, or in certain product lines. Within the production organization, plans for shipments of finished products may be inconsistent with the plans of plants or departments within plants to provide components for these products. As another example, line organizations may be assuming a higher level of service from support organizations than those organizations plan to give. During the budget preparation process, these inconsistencies are identified and resolved.

Assign responsibility. The approved budget should make clear what each manager is responsible for. The budget also authorizes responsibility center managers to spend specified amounts of money for certain designated purposes without seeking the approval of higher authority.

Basis for performance evaluation. The budget represents a commitment by the budgetee to his or her superior. It, therefore, represents a benchmark against which actual performance can be judged. The commitment is subject to change if the assumptions on which it is based change, but it nevertheless is an excellent starting point for performance appraisal. Responsibility is assigned for each responsibility center in the organization: At the top level, the budget summary assigns responsibility to individual profit centers; within profit centers, the budget assigns responsibility to functional areas (such as marketing); and within functional areas, the budget assigns responsibility to individual responsibility centers (such as regional sales offices in the marketing organization).

Content of an Operating Budget

Exhibit 9–1 shows the content of a typical operating budget and contrasts the operating budget with other types of planning documents: the strategic plan (which was described in Chapter 8); and the capital budget, the cash budget, and the budgeted balance sheet (which will be described in a later subsection). The amounts are the planned dollar amounts for the year,[2] together with quantitative amounts, such as head counts (i.e., number of employees) and sales in units.

---

[2] In a thought-provoking study, Ijiri suggests that the amounts be stated as rates per period, rather than as dollar amounts. He calls this approach "momentum accounting." Yuji Ijiri, *Momentum Accounting and Triple-Entry Bookkeeping: Exploring the Dynamic Structure of Accounting Measurements* (Sarasota, Fla.: American Accounting Association, 1989).

EXHIBIT 9–1   Types of Plans and Their Contents

Strategic Plan	Operating Budget	Capital Budget
Revenue and expense for each major program	For organization as a whole and for each business unit	Each major capital project listed separately
Not necessarily by responsibility centers	Classified by responsibility centers	
Not as much detail as operating budget	Typically includes: revenues production cost and cost of sales marketing expense logistics expense (sometimes) general and administrative research and development income taxes (sometimes) net income	
More expenses are variable	Expenses may be: flexible discretionary committed	
For several years	For one year divided into months or quarters	
Total reconciles to operating budget	Total reconciles to strategic plan (unless revised)	For total project expenditures by quarters

Cash Forecast
Budgeted Balance Sheet

Operating Budget Categories

The summary page of a typical operating budget for a business unit contains the categories listed in Exhibit 9–1; there is a detailed listing of expense items within each of the expense categories. In a relatively small organization, especially one that has no business units, the whole budget may fit on one page. In larger organizations, other pages contain the details for individual business units, plus research and developmemt and general and administrative expenses. The revenue item is listed first, both because it is the first item on an income statement and also because the amount of budgeted revenues influences the amount of many of the other items.

Revenue budgets.   A revenue budget consists of unit sales projection multiplied by expected selling prices. Of all of the elements of a profit budget, the revenue budget is the most critical, but it is also the element that is subject to the greatest uncertainty. The degree of uncertainty differs among companies, and within the same company the degree of uncertainty is different at different times. Companies with large back orders or companies whose sales volume is constrained by production capacity will have less uncertainty in sales projections than companies whose sales volume is subject to the uncertainties of the marketplace. The revenue budget usually is based on forecasts of some conditions for which the sales manager cannot he held responsible. For example, the state of the economy must be anticipated in preparing a revenue budget, but the marketing manager obviously has no control over it. Nevertheless, the marketing manager does have a considerable degree of control over sales volume. Effective advertising, good service, good quality, and well-trained salespeople influence the sales volume, and the manager does control these factors.

Budgeted production cost and cost of sales. Although textbook illustrations typically show that direct material cost and direct labor cost are developed from the product volumes contained in the sales budget, this often is not feasible in practice because these details depend on the actual mix of products that are to be manufactured. Instead, the standard material and labor costs of the planned volume level of a *standard mix of products* are shown in the budget. Production managers make plans for obtaining quantities of material and labor, and they may prepare procurement budgets for long-lead-time items. They also develop production schedules to ensure that resources needed to produce the budgeted quantities will be available.

The budgeted cost developed by the production managers may not be for the same quantities of products as those shown in the sales budget; the difference represents additions to or subtractions from finished goods inventory. Nevertheless, the cost of sales reported in the summary budget is the standard cost of the products budgeted to be sold. Similarly, the budgeted cost of sales in wholesale and retail establishments is not necessarily the cost of the goods that will be purchased in the budget year. Control over the amounts that may be purchased is obtained by detailed *open to buy* authorizations made during the year, rather than by the amounts shown in the budget. As is the case with manufacturing companies, the difference represents additions to or decreases in inventory.

Marketing expenses. Marketing expenses are expenses incurred to obtain sales. A considerable fraction of the amounts included in the budget may have been committed before the year begins. If the budget contemplates a selling organization of a specified number of sales offices with specified personnel, then plans for opening or closing offices and for hiring and training new personnel (or for laying off personnel) must be well underway before the year begins. Advertising must be prepared months in advance of its release, and contracts with media also are placed months in advance. As a practical matter, therefore, commitments for many marketing expenses are agreed to, and implementation is started, well before the beginning of the year.

Logistics expenses. Logistics expenses are those incurred to fill orders (in contrast with marketing expenses, which are incurred to obtain orders). They include order entry, transportation from the factory to the customer, warehousing and order picking, and collection of accounts receivable. Conceptually, they behave more like production costs than marketing costs—that is, many of them are engineered costs. Nevertheless, many companies include them in the marketing budget, because they tend to be the responsibility of the marketing organization.

General and administrative expenses. These are G&A expenses of staff units, both at headquarters and at business units. Overall, they are discretionary expenses, although some parts (such as bookkeeping costs in the accounting department) are engineered expenses. In budget preparation, much attention is given to these categories; being discretionary, the appropriate amount to authorize is subject to much debate.

Research and development expenses. Either of two approaches, or a combination of both, may be used in developing the R&D budget. In one approach, the focus is on the total amount. This may be the current level of spending, adjusted for inflation; or it may be a larger amount if an increase in sales revenue is planned in the belief that the company can afford to spend more in good times; or it may be a larger amount if there is a good chance of developing a significantly new product or process. The other approach is to obtain the total by aggregating the planned spending on each approved project, plus an allowance for work that is likely to be undertaken even though it is not currently identified. Many companies decide to spend a specified percentage of sales revenue on R&D, but this percentage is based on a long-run average— that is, R&D spending is not geared to short-run changes in sales volume. To permit it to do so could have undesirable effects on the R&D organization; hiring and organizing researchers is a difficult task, and, if spending fluctuates in the short run, inefficiencies are likely.

Income taxes. Although the bottom line is income after income taxes, some companies do not take income taxes into account in preparing the budgets for business units. This is because income tax policies are determined at corporate headquarters.

Types of Expenses

The expense items in the budget can be classified as either (a) flexible, (b) discretionary, or (c) committed.

Flexible expenses. Flexible expenses are expenses that are expected to fluctuate with changes in either sales revenue or production volume—that is, they have a variable component. (We use "flexible," rather than "variable," because they do not vary proportionately with changes in volume.) Most of them are *engineered* costs. (Some companies permit certain discretionary items, such as sales promotion, to vary with volume.) The budgeted amount of a flexible expense item is stated in the familiar equation TC = FC + (UVC × X)—that is total cost (or expense) equals fixed cost, plus the variable cost per unit times the number of units. For engineered expenses, the amounts are taken from the standard cost system, and the standard costs are usually brought up to date as part of the budget preparation process. These equations are not shown separately on the operating budget, rather, they appear on a separate flexible budget. The amount shown on the operating budget is the total cost at the budgeted volume. The flexible budget provides a means of separating the spending variance, which normally is the responsibility of the production manager, from the volume variance, which is normally the responsibility of someone else.

Discretionary expenses.   As described in Chapter 3, there is no way of determining the optimum amount of certain expenses. These include the expenses of most G&A units, certain overhead items of production units, true marketing activities (as distinguished from logistics expenses), and R&D expenses. The budget set forth the amount on which the budgetee and his or her superior have agreed. The budgetee understands that expenses exceeding this amount (in some cases by any amount; in other cases, by a defined percentage) require prior approval of higher authority.

Committed expenses.   These are expenses that cannot be changed by the responsibility center manager during the budget year, or expenses that can be changed only in extraordinary circumstances. Depreciation is the most obvious example; the amount is fixed by the amount of depreciable assets in place during the year, and can be changed only by the disposal or addition of assets. Commitments under long-term leases and for certain types of "take or pay" contracts are other examples. These amounts are not useful for management control purposes; they are included in the budget to show the overall profitability of business units and to indicate to responsibility center managers the size of the resources that they use. In judging actual performance, the "actual" amount is set equal to the budgeted amount, so no variance develops.

OTHER BUDGETS

Although our attention is focused primarily on the preparation of the operating budget, the complete budget also consists of a capital budget, a budgeted balance sheet, and a budgeted cash flow statement. Some companies also prepare a statement of nonfinancial objectives.

Capital Budget

The capital budget states the approved capital projects, plus a lump-sum amount for small projects that do not require high level approval. It usually is prepared separately from the operating budget and by different people. During the year, proposals for capital expenditures are considered at various levels within the organization, and some are finally approved. This is part of the programming process.

At budget time, the approved projects are assembled into an overall package and examined in total. It may turn out that this total exceeds the amount that the company is willing to spend on capital projects; if so, some are deleted, others are reduced in size, and others are deferred. For the projects that remain, an estimate of the cash that will be paid out each quarter is prepared. This is necessary to prepare the cash flow statement.

Budgeted Balance Sheet

The budgeted balance sheet shows the balance sheet implications of decisions included in the operating budget and the capital budget. Overall, it is not a management control device, but some parts of it are useful for control. Operating managers who can influence the level of inventories, accounts receivable, or accounts payable often are held responsible for the level of these items.

Budgeted Cash Flow Statement

The budgeted cash flow statement shows how much of the cash needs during the year will be supplied by retained earnings and how much, if any, must be obtained by borrowing or other outside sources. It is, of course, important for financial planning. As its title indicates, the cash flow statement shows the inflows and outflows of cash during the year, usually by quarters. In addition, the treasurer needs an estimate of cash requirements for monthly, or even shorter intervals, as a basis for planning lines of credit and short-term borrowing.

Nonfinancial Objectives

The financial objectives that managers are responsible for attaining during the budget year are set forth in the budgets described above. Implicit in the budget amounts are also certain specific objectives: open new sales offices, introduce a new product line, retrain employees, install a new computer system, and so on. Some companies make these objectives explicit. The process of doing so is called "management by objectives" in the literature. The objectives of each responsibility center are set forth in quantitative terms wherever possible, and, as is the case with the budget amounts, are accepted by the responsible manager. If nonfinancial objectives can be stated in concrete terms, they may serve a useful purpose in motivating managers and in appraising their performance.

Unfortunately, some management by objectives (MBO) systems are separated from the budget preparation process. In part, this is because MBO was initially advocated by authors of personnel texts and articles, whereas the financial budget is the province of management accounting authors. MBO and budgeting should be two parts of the same planning process.

Companies that do not have an MBO system believe that the effort is not worthwhile. For many responsibility centers, the objectives are implicit in the budget. For others, especially staff and support units, the objectives are versions of "keep on doing what we are now doing as best as we can." In part, the decision to adopt an MBO system depends on senior management's attitude toward the delegation of authority. Many senior managers believe that the way in which a responsibility center accomplishes its financial objectives is up to its manager. That is to say, they hold the manager responsible for the "ends" (i.e., the bottom line) but leave the "means" (i.e., the decision and actions that lead to the bottom line) up to the manager.

THE BUDGET PREPARATION PROCESS

Organization

The budget department. The information flow of a budgetary control system is usually administered by the budget department, which normally (but not always) reports to the corporate controller. It performs the following functions:

- It publishes procedures and forms for the preparation of the budget.
- It coordinates and publishes each year the basic corporatewide assumptions that are to be the basis for the budgets (e.g., assumptions about the economy).
- It makes sure that information is properly communicated between interrelated organization units (e.g., sales and production).
- It provides assistance to budgetees in the preparation of their budgets.
- It analyzes proposed budgets and makes recommendations, first to the budgetee and subsequently to senior management.
- It analyzes reported performance against budget, interprets the results, and prepares summary reports for senior management.
- It administers the process of making budget revisions during the year.
- It coordinates the work of budget departments in lower echelons (e.g., business unit budget departments).

The budget committee.   The budget committee consists of members of senior management, such as chief executive officer, chief operating officer, and the financial vice president. In some companies, the chief executive officer decides without the committee. Regardless of its composition, the budget committee performs a vital role. This committee reviews and either approves or adjusts each of the budgets. In a large diversified company, the budget committee might meet only with the senior operating executives to review the budgets for a business unit or group of business units. In some companies, however, each business unit manager meets with the budget committee and presents his or her budget proposals. Usually, the budget committee must approve any budget revisions made during the year.

Issuance of Guidelines

If a company has a programming process, the first year of the strategic plan, which is usually approved in the summer, is the beginning of the budget preparation process. If the company has no strategic plan, management needs to think about the future in the manner suggested in Chapter 8 as a basis for budget preparation.

Unlike budget preparation, development of the strategic plan does not involve lower-level responsibility center managers. Thus, whether or not there is a strategic plan, the first step in the budget preparation process is to develop guidelines that govern the preparation of the budget, for dissemination to all managers. These guidelines are those that are implicit in the strategic plan, modified by developments that have occurred since its approval, especially the company's performance for the year to date and its current outlook. Some of these guidelines are to be followed by all responsibility centers; examples are assumed inflation, in general, and for specific items, such as: wages; corporate policies on how many persons can be promoted; compensation at each wage and salary level, including employee benefits; and a possible hiring freeze. Others are specific to certain responsibility centers.

These guidelines are developed by the budget staff and approved by senior management. In some cases they may be discussed with lower-level managers before being approved. A timetable for the steps in the budget preparation process also is developed. This material then is disseminated throughout the organization.

Initial Budget Proposal

Based on the guidelines, responsibility center managers, assisted by their staffs, develop a budget request. Because most responsibility centers will start the budget year with the same facilities, personnel, and other resources that they have currently, this budget is based on the existing levels, which are then modified in accordance with the guidelines.[3] Changes from the current level of performance can be classified as (*a*) changes in external forces and (*b*) changes in internal policies and practices. They include, but are not limited to, the following:

Changes in external forces.   These include:

- Changes in the general level of economic activity as it affects the volume of sales—for example, expected growth in the demand for a product line.
- Expected changes in the price of purchased materials and services.
- Expected changes in labor rates.
- Expected changes in the cost of discretionary activities (e.g., marketing, R&D, and administration).
- Changes in selling prices. These often are equal to the sum of the changes in the related costs, which assumes that changes in costs should be recovered in selling prices because similar changes will be experienced by competitors.

Changes in internal policies and practices.   These include:

- Changes in production costs, reflecting new equipment and methods.
- Changes in discretionary costs, based on anticipated changes in workload.
- Changes in market share and product mix.

Some companies require that specific changes from the current level of spending be classified according to such causes as the above. Although this involves extra work, it provides a useful tool for analyzing the validity of proposed changes.

Negotiation

The budgetee discusses the proposed budget with his or her superior. This is the heart of the process. The superior attempts to judge the validity of each of the adjustments. Ordinarily, a governing consideration is that performance in the budget year should be an improvement over performance in the current year. The superior recognizes that he or she will become the budgetee at the next level of the budget process and, therefore, must be prepared to defend the budget that is finally agreed to.

Slack.   Many budgetees tend to budget revenues somewhat lower, and expenses somewhat higher, than their best estimates of these amounts. The result-

---

[3] In the 1970s, there was a proposal for "zero-base budgeting," which involved analyzing each responsibility center's expenses from scratch. Some economists also criticize starting with the current spending levels; they disparage this as "incremental budgeting." Experience has shown that starting from zero is not practical in the time available for budget formulation, nor is it necessary in view of the ongoing nature of most activities. "Zero-base Review," discussed in Chapter 8, is another matter entirely.

ing budget, therefore, is an easier target for them to achieve. The difference between the budget amount and the best estimate is called "slack." Superiors who examine the budget attempt to discover and eliminate slack, but this is a difficult task. Beginning about 1970, some Soviet industries attempted to offset this tendency by developing bonus formulas that attempted to counteract slack. In these formulas, the bonus was proportionally greater for a manager whose actual performance exceeded the budget by a small amount than for a manager who exceeded the budget by a large amount. Although these formulas have been discussed in the literature, they have had practically no acceptance in practice, either in the Soviet Union or elsewhere.[4]

Review and Approval

The proposed budgets go up through successive levels in the organization. When they reach the top of a business unit, the pieces are put together and the total is examined. In part, the examination studies consistency—for example, is the production budget consistent with planned sales volume? Are service and support centers planning for the services that are being requested of them? In part, the examination asks whether the budget will produce a satisfactory profit. If not, it often is sent back for reworking. The same type of analysis takes place at corporate headquarters.

Final approval is recommended by the budget committee to the chief executive officer. The CEO also submits the approved budget to the board of directors for ratification. This happens in December, just prior to the beginning of the budget year.

Budget Revisions

One of the principal considerations in budget administration is the procedure for revising a budget after it has been approved. Clearly, if it can be revised at will by the budgetee, there would be no point in reviewing and approving the budget in the first instance. On the other hand, if the budget assumptions turn out to be so unrealistic that the comparisons of actual against budget are meaningless, budget revisions may be desirable.

There are two general types of procedures for budget revisions:

1. Procedures that provide for a systematic (say, quarterly) updating of the budgets.
2. Procedures that allow revisions under special circumstances.

---

[4] For a description of the formulas, see Gary J. Mann, "Reducing Budget Slack," *Journal of Accountancy,* August 1988, pp. 118–22.

Systematic updating obviously requires extra work. Nevertheless, large Japanese companies believe this is worthwhile. They prepare a budget for the whole year, but only the first six months of this budget is formally approved by senior management. The budget for the second six months is revised and approved shortly before the period begins.[5]

If budget revisions are limited only to unusual circumstances, such revision should be adequately reviewed. In general, permission to make revisions should be difficult to obtain. Budget revisions should be limited to those circumstances where the approved budget is so unrealistic that it no longer provides a useful control device. That is to say, budget revisions must be justified on the basis of significantly changed conditions from those existing when the original budget was approved.

An important consideration is that managers should not be required to adhere to plans that subsequent events prove to be suboptimum. This can be a serious problem in budgeting. Because of the time required for budget preparation and review, budgets may provide for actions that are planned months ahead of the time they take place. It is important that management actions be based on the latest information available. Consequently, managers should be encouraged to change their actions to reflect the latest information. Performance would continue to be measured against the original budget, but explanations for reasonable variances would be acceptable.

BEHAVIORAL ASPECTS

One of the purposes of a management control system is to encourage the manager to be effective and efficient in attaining the goals of the organization. Some motivational considerations in the preparation of operating budgets are mentioned below.[6]

Participation in the Budgetary Process

Budget processes are either "top down" or "bottom up." With top down budgeting, senior management sets the budget for the lower levels. With bottom up budgeting, lower-level managers participate in setting the budget targets. The top down approach rarely works, however. It leads to a lack of commitment on the part of budgetees who are responsible for achieving the budgeted targets; this endangers the plan's success. Bottom up budgeting is most likely to generate commitment to meeting the budgeted goals; however, unless carefully

---

[5] John F. Rechfeld, "What Working for a Japanese Company Taught Me," *Harvard Business Review,* November-December 1990, pp. 168–69.

[6] For a description of the behavioral problems associated with budget systems, see G. H. Hofstede, *The Game of Budget Control* (New York: Barnes & Noble, 1968).

controlled, it may result in goals that are too easy or in goals that may not match the company's overall goals.

Actually, an effective budget preparation process blends the two approaches (as described in the preceding sections). Budgetees prepare the first draft of the budget for their area of responsibility, which is "bottom up"; but they do so within guidelines established at higher levels, which is "top down." Senior managers review and critique these proposed budgets. A hardheaded approval process helps to ensure that budgetees do not "play games" with the budgeting system. The review process, nevertheless, should be perceived as being fair; if a superior changes the budgeted amounts, he or she should try to convince the budgetee that such a change is reasonable.

Research has shown that budget participation (i.e., a process in which the budgetee is both *involved* in and has *influence* over the setting of budget amounts) has positive effects on managerial motivation, for two reasons:

1. There is likely to be greater acceptance of budget goals if they are perceived as being under personal control, rather than being imposed externally. This leads to higher personal commitment to achieve the goals.

2. Participative budgeting results in effective information exchanges. The approved budget amounts benefit from the expertise and personal knowledge of the budgetees, who are closest to the product market environment. Further, budgetees have a clearer understanding of their jobs through interactions with superiors during the review and approval phase.

Participative budgeting is especially beneficial for responsibility centers operating in uncertain environments since managers in charge of such responsibility centers are likely to have the best information regarding the variables that affect their revenues and expenses.[7]

Degree of Budget Goal Difficulty

The ideal budget is one that is challenging but attainable. In operational terms, this may be interpreted as meaning that a manager who performs reasonably well has at least a 50 percent chance of achieving the budget amount. We shall refer to such a budget as "achievable." Merchant and Manzoni, in a field study of business unit managers, concluded that business unit budget achievability in practice is usually considerably higher than 50 percent.[8] There are several reasons why senior management approves achievable budgets for business units:

---

[7] Empirical support for this conclusion is reported in V. Govindarajan "Impact of Participation in the Budgetary Process on Managerial Attitudes and Performance: Universalistic and Contingency Perspectives," *Decision Sciences* 17, no. 4 (Fall 1986), pp. 459–516.

[8] K. A. Merchant and J. Manzoni, "The Achievability of Budget Targets in Profit Centers: A Field Study," *The Accounting Review* LXIV, no. 3 (July 1989), pp. 539–58.

- If the budgeted goal is too difficult, managers are motivated to take short-term actions that may not be in the long-term interests of the company. Attainable profit targets is one way to minimize these dysfunctional actions.
- Achievable budget targets reduce the motivation for managers to engage in data manipulation (e.g., inadequate provision for warranty claims, bad debts, inventory obsolescence, and the like) to meet the budget.
- If business unit profit budgets represent achievable targets, senior management can, in turn, promise a profit target to security analysts, shareholders, and other external constituencies with a reasonable expectation of being correct.
- A profit budget that is very difficult to attain usually implies an overly optimistic sales target. This may lead to an over commitment of resources to gear up for the higher sales activity. It is administratively and politically awkward to downsize operations, if the actual sales levels do not reach the optimistic targets.
- When business unit managers are able to meet and exceed their targets, there is a "winning" atmosphere and positive attitudes within the company.

One limitation of an achievable target is the possibility that business unit managers will not put forth satisfactory effort once the budget is met. This limitation can be overcome by providing bonus payments for actual performance that exceeds the budget.

If a business unit manager achieves more than the budgeted profit, senior management should not automatically include the excess in the profit budget for the following year. If this happens, business unit managers may not perform up to their maximum capability in order to avoid showing too large a favorable variance.

Senior Management Involvement

Senior management involvement is necessary for any budget system to be effective in motivating budgetees. Management must participate in the review and approval of the budgets, and the approval should not be a rubber stamp. Without their active participation in the approval process, there will be a great temptation for the budgetee to "play games" with the system—that is, some managers will submit easily attained budgets or budgets that contain excessive allowances for possible contingencies.

Management also must follow up on budget results. If there is no top management feedback, with respect to budget results, the budget system will not be effective in motivating the budgetee.

The Budget Department

The budget department has a particularly difficult behavioral problem. It must analyze the budgets in detail, and it must be certain that budgets are prepared properly and that the information is accurate. To accomplish these tasks, the budget department sometimes must act in ways that line managers perceive as being threatening or even hostile. For example, the budget department tries to ensure that the budget does not contain excessive allowances (or "water"). In other cases, the explanation of budget variances provided by the budgetee may hide or minimize a potentially serious situation; and when the budget department discloses the facts, the line manager is placed in an uncomfortable position. The budget department must walk a fine line between helping the line manager and insuring the integrity of the system.

To perform its function effectively, the members of the budget department must have a reputation for impartiality and fairness. If they do not have this reputation, it becomes difficult, if not impossible, for them to perform the tasks necessary to maintain an effective budgetary control system. The members of the budget department should, of course, also have the personal skills required to deal effectively with people.

QUANTITATIVE TECHNIQUES

There have been numerous articles on the use of mathematical techniques in the budget preparation process. Although mathematical techniques and computers improve the budgetary process, they do not solve the critical problems of budgetary control. The critical problems in budgeting tend to be in the behavioral area.

Simulation

Simulation is a method that constructs a model of a real situation, and then manipulates this model in such a way as to draw some conclusions about the real situation. The preparation and review of a budget is a simulation process. If the computer is used to make simulations, senior management can ask what the effect of different types of changes would be and receive almost instantaneous answers. This gives senior management a chance to participate more fully in the budgetary process.

Several computer software packages are available. Some are specific to certain industries, others are general-purpose. Most require adaptation to the company's own way of doing things; and this process may require a year, or several years, of intensive effort on the part of company employees or consultants. In some cases, the resulting program has proved to be more complicated than managers will tolerate. If the needs of managers, both budgetees and senior management, are properly taken into account, however, the resulting program can have great benefits.

Probability Estimates

Each number in a budget is a point estimate—that is, it is the single "most likely" amount. For example, sales estimates are stated in terms of the specific number of units of each type of product to be sold. Point estimates are necessary for control purposes. For planning purposes, however, a range of probable outcomes may be more helpful. After a budget has been tentatively approved, it may be possible with a computer model to substitute a probability distribution for each major point estimate. The model then is run a number of times, and a probability distribution of the expected profits can be calculated and used for planning purposes.

Some have proposed that budgets be prepared initially using probability distributions instead of point estimates—that is, the budget committee would approve a number of probability distributions, rather than specific amounts. Subsequent variance analysis would be based on these probability distributions. The work involved in making these estimates is considerable, however. Also, if the procedure is to ask for three numbers—pessimistic, most likely, and optimistic—the result is likely to be a normal curve, with an expected value equal to the most likely number. This is no better than estimating the most likely number in the first instance, except that theoretically a measure of dispersion is reported. In any event, probabilistic budgets are rarely found in practice.

Contingency Budgets

Some companies routinely prepare contingency budgets that identify management actions to be taken if there is a significant decrease in the sales volume from what was anticipated at the time of developing the budget (e.g., a contingency budget might determine actions to be taken based on a decrease of 20 percent from the best estimate of sales volume). The contingency budget provides a way of quickly adjusting to changed conditions if the situation arises. That is to say, the response time for management action in cases of unexpected happenings is considerably reduced. If sales volume declines by 20 percent, business unit managers can determine for themselves, according to the predetermined contingency budget, actions to be taken.

Examples A large diversified firm required contingency budgets from its business units. The budget for business units closed with a series of comparative financial statements, which depicted the estimated item-by-item effect if sales fell to 60 percent or 80 percent of forecast or increased to 120 percent of forecast. For each of these levels of possible sales, costs were divided into three categories: fixed costs, unavoidable variable costs, and management discretionary costs. Business unit managers described the specific actions they would take to control employment, total assets, and capital expenditures in case of a reduction in sales, and when these actions would be put into effect.[9]

Emerson Electric executives budget for bad news by writing three different plans for varying contingencies.[10]

SUMMARY

A budget is related to a one-year slice of the strategic plan. It is prepared in more detail than the plan, and its preparation involves managers at all levels in the organization. An operating budget shows the details of revenues and expenses for the budget year, for each responsibility center, and for the organization as a whole. It is so structured that amounts are identified with specific responsibility centers. The process starts with the dissemination of guidelines approved by senior management. Based on these guidelines, each responsibility center manager prepares a proposed budget. This is reviewed with his or her superior, and an agreed position is negotiated. When these individual pieces reach the top of the business unit, or of the whole organization, they are reviewed for consistency and whether they result in a satisfactory profit. The whole process is primarily behavioral. Responsibility center managers must participate in the process, but they do so within constraints decided on by senior management.

SUGGESTED ADDITIONAL READINGS

Brownell, P. "Participation in the Budgeting Process: When It Works and When It Doesn't." *Journal of Accounting Literature,* no. 1 (1982), pp. 124–53,

——·"A Field Study Examination of Budgetary Participation and Locus of Control." *The Accounting Review* LVII, no. 4 (October 1982), pp. 766–77.

Bruns, W. J., and J. H. Waterhouse. "Budgetary Control and Organization Structure." *The Journal of Accounting Research* 13 (Autumn 1975), pp. 177–203.

Camillus, John. *Strategic Planning and Management.* Lexington, Mass.: Lexington Books, 1986, chap. 10 and 12.

Chow, C. W.; J. C. Cooper; and W. S. Waller. "Participative Budgeting: Effects of a Truth-Inducing Pay Scheme and Information Asymmetry on Slack and Performance." *The Accounting Review* LXIII, no. 1 (January 1988), pp. 111–22.

Collins, F.; P. Munter; and D. W. Finn. "The Budgeting Games People Play." *The Accounting Review* LXII, no. 1 (January 1987), pp. 29–49.

---

[9] Galvor Company, Case 11–3.

[10] Thomas A. Stewart, "Why Budgets Are Bad for Business," *Fortune,* June 4, 1990, pp, 179–87.

Govindarajan, Vijay. "Impact of Participation in the Budgetary Process on Managerial Attitudes and Performance: Universalistic and Contingency Perspectives." *Decision Sciences* 17, no. 4 (Fall 1986), pp. 496–516.

Hirst, Mark K. "The Effects of Setting Budget Goals and Task Uncertainty on Performance: A Theoretical Analysis." *The Accounting Review,* October 1987, pp. 774–84.

Hopwood, Anthony. *Accounting and Human Behavior.* London, England: Accountancy Age Books, 1974, chap. 4.

Kenis, I. "Effects of Budgetary Goal Characteristics on Managerial Attitudes and Performance." *The Accounting Review,* October 1979, pp. 707–21.

Onsi, Mohamed. "Factor Analysis of Behavioral Variables Affecting Budgeting Slack." *The Accounting Review* 52 (July 1977), pp. 535–48.

Penne, Mark. "Accounting Systems, Participation in Budgeting, and Performance Evaluation." *The Accounting Review* 65, no. 2 (April 1990), pp. 303–14.

Rockness, H. O. "Expectancy Theory in a Budgetary Setting: An Experimental Examination." *The Accounting Review,* October 1977, pp. 893–903.

Case 9–1

National Motors, Inc.*

William Franklin, controller of the Panther Automobile Division of National Motors, a manufacturer of numerous products including a wide line of automobiles and trucks, was faced with a difficult decision in 1983. The manufacturing office had submitted a supplemental budget in which it had requested additional funds for increased administrative costs in its operations control department. The controller's office had written a memorandum in reply, explaining why it thought this request was not justified, and the manufacturing office had now answered this memorandum.

Mr. Franklin now had three possible courses of action: (1) to concur with the manufacturing offices' position, in which case the request would undoubtedly receive the necessary approval of the general manager; (2) to continue his opposition, in which case his views and those of the manufacturing office would be placed before the general manager, who would decide the issue; and (3) to reply with a further analysis in the hope that the manufacturing office would become convinced of the soundness of his position.

During the last quarter of 1982, the Panther Automobile Division had absorbed the manufacturing activities of the Starling Automobile Division. Responsibility for product planning and marketing of Starling cars, however, remained with the Starling Division.

A major reason for the consolidation of manufacturing activities was to reduce operating costs. There had been an anticipated annual saving in the operations control department, for example, of $368,000 from a reduction in the number of salaried personnel by 24. There also had been an expected saving from computerization of parts control in that department.

Prior to the consolidation, the Starling Division had a computer system of parts control in its operations control department. The Panther Division, on the other hand, had been using a manual system in its corresponding department.

In December 1982, a study was made to determine which system would serve the division best. On the basis of an estimated reduction of 23 salaried people and of $276,000 in salary and other costs in the operations control department, because of computerization, the decision was made to completely computerize the Panther Division's system of parts control. The results of this study were concurred by the manufacturing office of the Panther Division.

Strong budgetary control was exercised throughout the National Motors organization. In the fall of each year, every department manager developed his or her proposed budget for the next year. Each proposed budget then entered an extensive process of analysis, revision, consolidation, review, and approval by higher levels of management, first within a division and then at the corporate level. At each management level, budgets for subordinate units were consolidated prior to submission to the next higher management level. Controllers at the divisional and corporate levels participated actively in this process.

* This case was prepared by J. Hekimian under the supervision of R. N. Anthony, Harvard Business School.
Copyright © by the President and Fellows of Harvard College.
Harvard Business School case 161–004.

Once formal approval had been given a budget, it became a firm commitment for the responsible manager. He or she could not exceed this budget except by submitting and obtaining approval of a supplemental budget. A supplemental budget was prepared and processed in essentially the same way as the original budget. Policy prescribed that a supplemental budget be justified on the basis of changes in conditions after the original budget was approved.

The 1983 budgets had been approved prior to the consolidation of the Panther and Starling Divisions, so there was a separate budget for each division and, consequently, for the operations control departments of the two divisions. The approved budgets for 1983 for these two operations control departments are summarized below, together with the estimated savings resulting from consolidation and control computerization.

Exhibit 1 shows the Starling Division's personnel ceiling commitment as of December 31, 1982, the expected saving in numbers resulting from the consolidation, and the proposed ceiling for 1983. Since the manufacturing office believed that the new consolidated system of parts control in the operations control department was going to be about the same as the Starling Division's computerized system, the standards that it used to develop the proposed personnel requirements were based on the Starling Division's work load and authorized personnel levels for 1982.

Specifications Control Section (25 People)

The work load determinant used in this activity was the number of specifications requests to be processed. In the previous year, 20 employees had been approved in the Starling Division's specifications control section: 5 were clerical and

	Panther Division		Starling Division		Total	
	Number	Dollars (000s)	Number	Dollars (000s)	Number	Dollars (000s)
Budget before consolidation	76	$1,444	55*	$1,336	131	$2,780
Savings from consolidation					(24)	(368)
Savings from computerization†					(23)	(276)
Total					84	$2,136

* After the transfer of five specifications follow-up personnel out of the specifications control section.
† Based on the study completed in December 1982, concurred by the manufacturing office.

Manufacturing Office's Proposed Supplemental Budget

In April 1983, the manufacturing office proposed in a supplemental budget that the Panther operations control department, now servicing both Starling and Panther automobiles, be allotted for 1983 a personnel ceiling of 109 people to handle the combined work load. Its proposal and reasoning are summarized in Exhibit 1 and in the following paragraphs.

supervisory, 10 processed specifications requests, and 5 were involved in specifications follow-up. The specifications control procedure currently used in the Panther Division operations was generally the same as that used by Starling. But in the future, the specifications follow-up procedure would no longer be done in this section or, for that matter, in the operations control department.

In 1982, the 10 analysts in the Starling specifications control section had processed 2,964 specifications requests, or an average of 296 specifications each.

In the Panther Division, 3,680 specifications requests had been processed during 1982. The manufacturing office believed that a comparison of both Starling and Panther data, as shown in Exhibit 2, indicated that there was a definite relationship between the number of specifications requests processed and the number of unique, new model parts.

On the basis of the above calculations, the manufacturing office estimated the total number of specifications requests for 1983 for both Panther and Starling automobiles, and the personnel required to handle this work load as in Exhibit 3.

Design Parts Section (67 People)

The number of unique parts to be processed was used as the general work load determinant in

this section. In 1982, for 6,584 parts there were 27 specifications coordinators in the Starling Division budget for an average of 242 parts per coordinator. According to Exhibit 4, which was drawn up in the manufacturing office, 58 specifications coordinators would be required to handle the combined work load in 1983 plus 9 supervisors and clerical workers.

Planning and Control Section (15 People)

The requirements for this section were determined by the manufacturing office as shown in Exhibit 5, based on an overall work load indicator of number of parts to be handled.

Manager's Office (2 People)

A personnel ceiling of two was requested: the manager and his secretary.

EXHIBIT 1 Personnel Ceilings for Operations Control Department in 1983 (proposed by manufacturing office)

Positions	Starling Commitment 12/31/82	Starling Savings	Proposed Levels		
			Starling	Panther	Totals
Manager and secretary	2	2	—	2	2
Specifications control	20	12	8	17	25
Design parts control	31	12	19	48	67
Planning and control	7	3	4	11	15
Total	60	29	31	78	109

EXHIBIT 2 Relationship of Number of Parts to Specification Requests

Division	Number of Unique Parts	Number of Specifications Requests	Specifications Requests per Unique Part
Panther	8,810	3,680	0.42
Starling	6,584	2,964	0.45
Total	15,394	6,644	0.43

EXHIBIT 3 Estimates of Personnel Requirements for Specifications Control Section, 1983

A. Specifications requests and equivalent personnel:

Division	Estimated Number of Unique Parts*	×	Specifications Requests per Unique Part	÷	Actual Output per Worker	=	Equivalent Personnel
Panther	11,600		0.42		296		16.5
Starling	4,800		0.45		296		7.3
Total	16,400						23.8

B. Salaried personnel requirements:

Division	Equivalent Personnel	Less Planned Efficiency (approx: 10%)[†]	Less Planned Overtime (approx: 5%)	Salaried Ceiling Required
Panther	16.5	1.7	0.9	14
Starling	7.3	0.8	0.4	6
Total	23.8	2.5	1.3	20

C. Other personnel requirements:

Position	Panther	Starling	Total
Section supervisor and secretary	2	—	2
Unit supervisor	1	1	2
Clerk-typist	—	1	1
Total fixed	3	2	5[‡]
Total salaried and other			25

* The Panther Division had added a new car to its line, and the Starling Division had dropped one.
† "Planned efficiency" reduces the calculated personnel requirements to a level approximately consistent with the lowest work load level anticipated during the coming year. In order to handle periodic work load increases during a year, the department is forced to improve its efficiency and, if necessary, to utilize overtime or temporary clerical help from outside agencies.
‡ Same as Starling commitment of December 31, 1982.

Estimated Dollar Requirements

The manufacturing office estimated that a total of $2,916,000 would be needed to operate the consolidated operations control department for 1983. This figure was broken down as follows:

Personnel.	$2,320,000
Material and supplies.	90,000
Computer services.	490,000
Miscellaneous.	16,000
Total.	$2,916,000

Personnel expenses. This estimate was based on the figure for actual salaries plus approved fringe benefits, in accordance with the level of requested salaried personnel ceilings.

Materials and supplies. This expense was about $20,000 higher than the 1982 Starling actual. According to the manufacturing office, the job to be accomplished now was about two-and-one-half times the job accomplished by the Starling Division in 1982, but the expense was only 30 percent greater. This was a result of efficiencies in programming and reporting, which, in

EXHIBIT 4   Estimates of Personnel Requirements for Design Parts Section, 1983

A. Specifications coordinators requested:

Division	1983 Parts Count	Estimated Output per Worker	Equivalent Personnel Required	Less Planned Efficiency (approx: 10%)	Less Planned Overtime (approx: 5%)	Ceiling Required
Panther	11,600	242	48.0	4.7	2.3	41
Starling	4,800	242	19.8	1.9	.9	17
Total	16,400		67.8	6.6	3.2	58

B. Supervisory and clerical workers requested:

Position	Panther	Starling	Total
Section supervisor and secretary	2	—	2
Unit supervisors	2	1	3
Clerk-typists	3	1	4
Total	7	2	9
Unit supervisors to coordinators	1:20	1:17	1:19
Clerk-typists to coordinators	1:13	1:17	1:15
Total for the section			67

turn, would result in savings in materials and supplies.

Computer services. Starling had spent $380,000 in 1982 to accomplish a job that was about 40 percent as great as the combined Starling–Panther job. Included in the proposed amount was $68,000 for start-up cost associated with the conversion of the manual Panther system to a computerized system. Therefore, the real cost was $422,000, or only about 10 percent more than the 1982 Starling actual. The manufacturing office was proposing to do a job 150 percent greater than done at Starling for only 10 percent more money. This was said to be the result of efficiencies in programming and reporting.

Analysis by the Controller's Office

The controller's office did not concur with the manufacturing office's proposal. It summarized both the 1983 Panther Division's budget and the Starling Division's budget as approved prior to the consolidation, and compared these figures with those proposed by the manufacturing office. This summary is shown in Exhibit 6 and is explained in the following paragraphs.

Although the proposed combined Panther and Starling budgets for 1983 showed a decrease of 22 salaried personnel, there was an increase in cost of $136,000.

The manufacturing office had referred to a saving of 24 people and $368,000 in the Starling Division. This reduction, according to the controller, was the result of (*a*) a reduction in the 1983 parts count and (*b*) a reduction of supervisory and clerical personnel. This saving of 24 people, therefore, had nothing to do with computerization and would have occurred under either a computerized or a manual system.

Although the main reason for computerizing the Panther Division's system of parts control had

EXHIBIT 5 Estimate of Personnel Requirements for Planning and Control Section, 1983

Position	Starling Personnel	Number of Unique Parts for Starling, 1982	Parts per Person
Programming computer	3	6,584	2,195
Programming timing and coordination	2	6,584	3,292

	Number of Unique Parts, 1983		Estimated Output per Person	Equivalent Personnel		Personnel Ceiling Requested		
	Panther	Starling		Panther	Starling	Panther	Starling	Total
Program timing and coordination	11,600	4,800	3.292	3.5	1.5	4	2	6
Programming	11,600	4,800	2.195	5.3	2.2	5	2	7
Total				8.8	3.7	9	4	13
Section supervisor and secretary								2
Total for the section								15

EXHIBIT 6 Budget Comparison for Salaried Personnel Prepared by Controller

Budget Status	Panther Division		Starling Division		Total	
	Number	Dollars (000s)	Number	Dollars (000s)	Number	Dollars (000s)
Budget before consolidation	76	$1,444	55*	1,336	131	$2,780
Proposed	78	1,948	31	968	109	2,916
Net change	(2)	(504)	24	368	22	(136)
Explanatation of changes:						
Savings from computerization of Panther system	23 [†]	276 [†]	—	—	23	276
Savings from consolidation	—	—	24	368	24	368
Proposed increase to Panther budget	(25)	(780)	—	—	(25)	(780)
Net change	(2)	$ (504)	24	$ 368	22	$ (136)

( ) = Adverse effect on profit.
* Reflects the transfer of five specifications follow-up personnel out of the specifications control system.
[†] Based on study of December 1982, concurred in by manufacturing office.

EXHIBIT 7   Controller's Revised Budget Comparison for Salaried Personnel, 1983

System	Panther Division		Starling Division		Total	
	Number	Dollars (000s)	Number	Dollars (000s)	Number	Dollars (000s)
Combined manual systems	76	$1,444	35	$812	111	$2,256
Proposed computerized systems	78	1,948	31	960	109	2,916
Difference between cost of computerized system and manual system	(2)	(504)	4	(156)	2	(660)

EXHIBIT 8   Controller's Proposed Budget, 1983

Salaried Personnel	Panther	Starling	Total
Number	53	31	84
Budget dollars (000s)	$1,168	$968	$2,136

been financial savings, the controller calculated what the combined budget would have been if, in fact, the Starling Division's system had been changed to a manual one comparable to the one in use by the Panther Division prior to the consolidation. The budget requirement for the Panther Division, of course, would not change. However, 35 people and $812,000 would be required for the Starling Division, on the basis of Panther Division's standards as developed in the manufacturing office's analysis. Thus, a comparison between the manual system and the computerized system was as shown in Exhibit 7.

According to Exhibit 7, the effect of the computerization and the consolidation on the 1983 Panther budget, which was based on a manual system, was to increase the 1983 salaried personnel level by two people and to increase costs by $504,000. The controller was at a loss to know why these increases should result from computerization. Moreover, the manufacturing office had committed itself to a saving of 23 people and $276,000 in the Panther Division, whereas the

current proposal was 25 people and $780,000 *over* the levels committed.

The controller believed that budget figures under a *combined computerized system,* instead, should be as shown in Exhibit 8.

In this calculation, the Panther Division's number of salaried personnel was based on the precomputerization figure (76) minus the saving agreed to by the manufacturing office as a result of computerization (23). The Panther Division's budget dollars were based on the same sort of analysis—$1,444,000 minus $276,000. Starling Division's figures were those used in Exhibit 7, based on a reduced parts count, supervisory savings, and the functional transfer of personnel. The budget figures for the new division should be 84 people and $2,136,000.

On the basis of its analysis, the controller's office recommended that the manufacturing office at least not increase its 1983 costs for the operations control department over the level that would have occurred under a combined manual system. This meant a dollar budget of $2,256,000. Per-

EXHIBIT 9   Detail of Controller's Recommended Budget, 1983

Proposals	Panther		Starling		Total	
	Number	Dollars (000s)	Number	Dollars (000s)	Number	Dollars (000s)
Manufacturing office's request	78	$1,948	31	$968	109	$2,916
Controller's recommended reductions:						
Salary mix	—	170	—	—	—	170
Overtime	—	54	—	42	—	96
Required personnel (to meet financial objective)	25	394	—	—	25	394
Total recommended reductions	25	618	—	42	25	660
Total recommended level	53	1,330	31	926	84	2,256

EXHIBIT 10   Revised Estimates of Number of Unique Parts

Division	1983 Original Budget Estimates	Current Known Conditions
Panther	10,200	11,600
Starling	—	4,800
Total	10,200	16,400

sonnel reductions would be required to contain costs within recommended levels; these were set forth in Exhibit 9.

Protest from the Manufacturing Office

The manufacturing office did not accept the controller's recommendation of a reduction of 25 salaried people and $660,000, though it agreed that, generally speaking, a computerized operations control system should not be any more costly than the previously used manual system.

Work-Load Content and Volume Adjustments

One of the arguments of the manufacturing office was that its proposed Starling–Panther budget included additional people to handle actual work-load volume increases over the estimated levels used in developing the 1983 Panther budget for a manual system. The parts counts estimates used in developing the 1983 annual budget and the proposed consolidated computerized budget were as shown in Exhibit 10.

According to the manufacturing office, in addition to increased work as a result of the added work load of the Starling Division, there had been an increase of 1,400 parts in the Panther Division as a result of understated original estimates. This increased parts count would have resulted in a requirement for at least 10 more people under the manual system, at a cost of about $180,000, plus an estimated $8,000 for operating expenses.

EXHIBIT 11   Budget Increase Due to Salary Mix

Salary Base	Proposed Ceiling	×	Average Annual Salary	=	Total Annual Salaries
At approved budget rates	109		$14,088		$1,535,592
At proposed budget rates	109		15,768		1,718,712
Total					($ 183,120)

Unavoidable Increases in Salary Mix

As a result of Starling–Panther consolidation and the consequent personnel changes, the average salary per employee retained in the operations control department had increased significantly. This resulted from the retention of employees on the basis of seniority. The approved budget provided for an average salary of $14,088. The Starling–Panther budget, proposed by the manufacturing office for 1983 based on actual salaries, provided for an average annual salary in excess of $15,600. Therefore, if average salaries had remained unchanged after the consolidation, the manufacturing office's budget proposal would have been $183,120 less, as shown in Exhibit 11.

Association with Integrated Data Processing Plan

By implementing the computerized operations control system, the manufacturing office contended that it had taken an inevitable step included in the company's integrated data processing plan, which provided for eventual establishment of a completely computerized master parts control system. This step would make it possible to reduce significantly the original expense estimates associated with setting up this master system.

The original proposal, submitted prior to the consolidation of the two divisions, contained cost estimates of $189,774 during 1983 and $209,344

EXHIBIT 12   Effective Cost Decrease Due to Mechanization

Revised Cost Factors	1983	1984 Going Level
Original cost estimates	$189,774	$209,344
Cost of consolidation and revised assumptions based on manual system	33,970	109,138
Total cost estimates to include effect of consolidation based on a manual system	233,744	318,482
Reduction in cost estimates to give effect to consolidation	17,400	122,020
Savings directly associated with a computerized versus manual system	203,344	196,462

each year thereafter for providing a master parts control system to preproduction control. According to the manufacturing office, these cost estimates would have been increased to $223,744 and $318,482, respectively, as a result of the consolidation if a manual system were used. As a direct benefit of implementing a computerized operations control system, however, the manufacturing office believed that it could show a saving of about $206,000 during 1983 and $196,000 for each year thereafter. See Exhibit 12.

Nonrecurring Cost Penalties

The manufacturing office's proposed budget included a nonrecurring cost penalty of $224,610, resulting from the change in organization and procedure. This was comprised of $144,610 in salaries and wages and $80,000 in computer expense. If work volume remained at the same levels in future years, the manufacturing office felt that its budget could be revised as shown in Exhibit 13.

Functional Improvements and Advantages

The manufacturing office contended, furthermore, that a computerized operations control system offered certain other advantages over a manual system.

1. It provided a single and better integrated program progress report that reflected the status of engineering, manufacturing, and purchasing actions against schedules on a more timely basis than did a manual system.

2. It provided a master file that, once stored in the computer, could be used to produce other useful information.

3. It was compatible with the objective to mechanize the issuance of specifications and would result in a more efficient method of handling this activity. The manufacturing office said that it could not put a dollar value on these advantages, but that it was reasonable to expect them to yield cost savings.

Summary

A cost comparison for a manual versus a computerized operations control system, based on the above adjustments, was as shown in Exhibit 14.

The manufacturing office concluded its arguments by pointing out that the computerized system cost only $82,000 a year more than a manual system, as shown in the preceding table, rather than $660,000 more, as stated by the controller.

EXHIBIT 13 Future Savings of Nonrecurring Costs

Budget Items	1983	Future Years	Reductions
Average personnel ceiling	117	109	9
Personnel costs	$2,317,752	$2,173,142	$144,610
Computer expense	490,000	410,000	80,000
Other operating costs	108,272	108,272	—
Total	$2,916,024	$2,691,414	224,610

EXHIBIT 14 Manufacturing Office's Summary of Adjusted Cost Estimates

| | 1983 Cost Comparison (000s) | |
Costs	Manual System	Computerized System
Unadjusted costs:		
Panther Division	$1,414	$1,948
Starling Division	812	968
	2,256*	2,916†
Increases:		
Parts count	(188)	—
Average salaries	(184)	—
Implementation of computerized operations control system in accordance with company's integrated data processing plan	(224)	(18)
Total adjusted costs	2,852	2,934

* Estimated by controller's office.
† Proposed by manufacturing office.

QUESTIONS

1. The following table summarizes the dispute:

	People	Money (000s)
Manufacturing position	109	$2,916
Controller's position	84	2,256
Total	25	$ 660

    Of the disputed difference, how many people and how much money is attributable to alleged workload increase? To salary mix change? To unanticipated one-time computerization implementation costs?

2. There are three alternatives opened to Mr. Franklin (as per the case). As Mr. Franklin, which alternative would you choose? As general manager of the Panther Division, which alternative would you want Mr. Franklin to choose?

Note: The basic question here is, What should the controller do next? The contest is one of a "tight" control system, where budgets have teeth in them and cost control is not just a nice phrase—it is a way of life.

You should first try to reconcile the difference that is floating around (25 people and $660,000). What factors account for the difference, in managerial terms, and what is the dollar impact of each factor you identify? Push this idea far enough so you get a handle on the real "agendas" here.

Based on this analysis, what seems to be a "reasonable" budget allowance for the operations control department for 1983? Why is the number you propose for dollars and people the most "reasonable" one?

Once you have developed a viewpoint on what constitutes a "reasonable" solution, how do you propose that the controller respond to the manufacturing office?

Finally, take a few steps backward from the problems and ask yourself what approach to management is at work here and what you see as the strengths and weaknesses of this approach.

This is an involved case, and you will find it difficult to make much progress without doing some analysis of the conflicting presentations. The core issue is: How much power should the divisional controller have?

Case 9–2

Empire Glass Company (A)*

Organization

Empire Glass Company was a diversified company organized into several major product divisions, one of which was the Glass Products Division. This division was responsible for manufacturing and selling glass food and beverage bottles. Each division was headed by a divisional vice president, who reported directly to the company's executive vice president, Landon McGregor.

Mr. McGregor's corporate staff included three men in the financial area—the controller, the chief accountant, and the treasurer. The controller's department consisted of only two men—Mr. Walker and the assistant controller, Allen Newell. The market research and labor relations departments also reported in a staff capacity to Mr. McGregor.

All the product divisions were organized along similar lines. Reporting to each product division vice president were several staff members in the customer service and product research areas. Reporting in a line capacity to each individual vice president were also a general manager of manufacturing and a general manager of marketing. The general manager of manufacturing was responsible for all the division's manufacturing activities. Similarly, the general manager of marketing was responsible for all the division's marketing activities. Both of these executives were assisted by a small staff of specialists. There are also a controller and supporting staff in each division. Exhibit 1 presents an organization chart of the Glass Product Division's top management group. All the corporate and divisional management group were located in British City, Canada. Exhibit 2 shows the typical organization structure of a plant within the Glass Products Division.

Products and Technology

The Glass Products Division operated a number of plants in Canada producing glass food and beverage bottles. Of these products, food jars constituted the largest group, including jars for products like tomato catsup, mayonnaise, jams and jellies, honey, and soluble coffee. Milk bottles and beer and soft drink bottles were also produced in large quantities. A great variety of shapes and sizes of containers for wines, liquors, drugs, cosmetics, and chemicals were produced in smaller quantities.

Most of the thousands of different products, varying in size, shape, color, and decoration were produced to order. According to British City executives, during 1963 the typical lead time between the customer's order and shipment from the plant was between two and three weeks.

The principal raw materials for container glass were sand, soda ash, and lime. The first step in the manufacturing process was to melt batches of these materials in furnaces of "tanks." The molten mass was then passed into automatic or semiautomatic machines, which filled molds with the molten glass and blew the glass into the desired shape. The ware then went through an automatic

---

* This case was prepared by David Hawkins, Harvard Business School.
Copyright © by the President and Fellows of Harvard College.
Harvard Business School case 109–043.

EXHIBIT 1   Glass Products Division Top Management and Staff

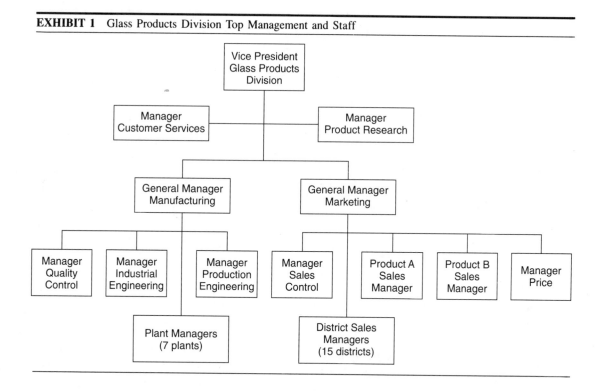

annealing oven, or lehr, where it was cooled slowly under carefully controlled conditions. If the glass was to be coated on the exterior to increase its resistance to abrasion and scratches, this coating—often a silicone film—was applied at the lehr. Any decorating (such as a trademark or other design) was then added, the product inspected again, and the finished goods packed in corrugated containers (or wooden cases for some bottles).

Quality inspection was critical in the manufacturing process. If the melt in the furnace was not completely free from bubbles and stones (unmelted ingredients or pieces of refinery material), or if the fabricating machinery was slightly out of adjustment, or molds were worn, the rejection rate was very high. Although a number of machines were used in the inspection process, including electric eyes, much of the inspection was still visual.

Although glassmaking was one of the oldest arts, and bottles and jars had been machine molded at relatively high speed for over half a century, the Glass Products Division had spent substantial sums each year to modernize its equipment. These improvements had greatly increased the speed of operations and had substantially reduced the visual inspection and manual holding of glassware.

Most of the jobs were relatively unskilled, highly repetitive, and gave the worker little control over work methods or pace. The moldmakers who made and repaired the molds, the machine repairmen, and those who made the equipment setup changes between different products were considered to be the highest classes of skilled workers. Wages were relatively high in the glass industry. Production employees belonged to two national unions, and for many years bargaining had been conducted on a national basis. Output

EXHIBIT 2   Typical Plant Organization—Glass Products Division

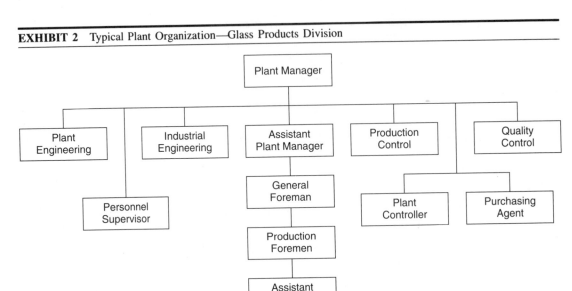

standards were established for all jobs, but no bonus was paid to hourly plant workers for exceeding standard.

Marketing

Over the years, the sales of the Glass Products Division had grown at a slightly faster rate than had the total market for glass containers. Until the late 1950s, the division had charged a premium for most of its products, primarily because they were of better quality than competitive products. In recent years, however, the quality of the competitive products had improved to the point where they now matched the division's quality level. In the meantime, the division's competitors had retained their former price structure. Consequently, the Glass Products Division had been forced to lower its prices to meet its competitors' lower market prices. According to one division executive:

> Currently, price competition is not severe, particularly among the two or three larger companies that dominate the glass bottle industry. Most of our

competition is with respect to product quality and customer service. . . . In fact, our biggest competitive threat is from containers other than glass.

Each of the division's various plants shipped their products throughout Canada to some extent, although transportation costs limited each plant's market primarily to its immediate vicinity. While some of customers were large and bought in huge quantities, many were relatively small.

Budgetary Control System

In the fall of 1963, James Walker, Empire Glass Company controller, described the company's budgetary control system to a casewriter. Mr. Walker had been controller for some 15 years. Excerpts from that interview are reproduced below.

Mr. Walker's Interview

To understand the role of the budgetary control system, you must first understand our management philosophy. Fundamentally, we have a divisional organization based on broad product categories.

These divisional activities are coordinated by the company's executive vice president, while the head office group provides a policy and review function for him. Within the broad policy limits, we operate on a decentralized basis; each of the decentralized divisions performs the full management job that normally would be inherent in any independent company. The only exceptions to this philosophy are the head office group's sole responsibilities for sources of funds and labor relations with those bargaining units that cross division lines.

Given this form of organization, the budget is the principal management tool used by head office to direct the efforts of the various segments of the company toward a common goal. Certainly, in our case, the budget is much more than a narrow statistical accounting device.

Sales Budget

As early as May 15 of the year preceding the budget year, top management of the company asks the various product division vice presidents to submit preliminary reports stating what they think their division's capital requirements and outlook in terms of sales and income will be during the next budget year. In addition, corporate top management also wants an expression of the division vice president's general feelings toward the trends in these particular items over the two years following the upcoming budget year. At this stage, head office is not interested in too much detail. Since all divisions plan their capital requirements five years in advance and had made predictions of the forthcoming budget year's market when the budget estimates were prepared last year, these rough estimates of next year's conditions and requirements are far from wild guesses.

After the opinions of the divisional vice presidents are in, the market research staff goes to work. They develop a formal statement of the marketing climate in detail for the forthcoming budget year and in general terms for the subsequent two years. Once these general factors have been assessed, a sales forecast is constructed for the company and for each division. Consideration is given to the relationship of the general economic climate to our customers' needs and Empire's share of each market. Explicitly stated are basic assumptions as to price, weather conditions, introduction of new products, gains or losses in particular accounts, forward buying, new manufacturing plants, industry growth trends, packaging trends, inventory carryovers, and the development of alternative packages to or from glass. This review of all the relevant factors is followed for each of our product lines, regardless of its size and importance. The completed forecasts of the market research staff are then forwarded to the appropriate divisions for review, criticism, and adjustments.

The primary goal of the head office group in developing these sales forecasts is to assure uniformity among the divisions with respect to the basic assumptions on business conditions, pricing, and the treatment of possible emergencies. Also, we provide a yardstick so as to assure us that the company's overall sales forecast will be reasonable and obtainable.

The product division top management then asks each district manager what he expects to do in the way of sales during the budget year. Head office and the divisional staffs will give the district sales managers as much guidance as they request, but it is the sole responsibility of each district sales manager to come up with his particular forecast.

After the district sales managers' forecasts are received by the divisional top management, the forecasts are consolidated and reviewed by the division's general manager of marketing. Let me emphasize, however, that nothing is changed in the district sales manager's budget unless the district manager agrees. Then, once the budget is approved, nobody is relieved of his responsibility without top management approval. Also, no arbitrary changes are made in the approved budgets without the concurrence of all the people responsible for the budget.

Next, we go through the same process at the division and headquarters levels. We continue to repeat the process until everyone agrees that the sales budgets are sound. Then, each level of management takes responsibility for its particular portion of the budget. These sales budgets then become fixed objectives.

I would say we have four general objectives in mind in reviewing the sales forecast:
1. A review of the division's competitive position, including plans for improving that position.

2. An evaluation of its efforts to gain either a larger share of the market or offset competitors' activities.
3. A consideration of the need to expand facilities to improve the division's products or introduce new products.
4. A review and development of plans to improve product quality, delivery methods, and service.

Manufacturing Budgets

Once the vice presidents, executive vice president, and company president have given final approval to the sales budgets, we make a sales budget for each plant by breaking down the division sales budgets according to the plants from which the finished goods will be shipped. These plant sales budgets are then further broken down on a monthly basis by price, volume, and end use. With this information available, the plants then budget their gross profit, fixed expenses, and income before taxes. Gross profit is the difference between gross sales, less discounts, and variable manufacturing costs—such as direct labor, direct material, and variable manufacturing overheads. Income is the difference between the gross profit and the fixed costs.

The plant manager's primary responsibility extends to profits. The budgeted plant profit is the difference between the fixed sales dollar budget and the sum of the budgeted variable costs at standard and the fixed overhead budget. It is the plant manager's responsibility to meet this budget profit figure, even if actual dollar sales drop below the budgeted level.

Given his sales budget, it is up to the plant manager to determine the fixed overhead and variable costs—at standard—that he will need to incur so as to meet the demands of the sales budget. In my opinion, requiring the plant managers to make their own plans is one of the most valuable things associated with the budget system. Each plant manager divides the preparation of the overall plant budget among his plant's various departments. First, the departments spell out the program in terms of physical requirements, such as tons of raw material, and then the plans are priced at standard cost.

The plant industrial engineering department is assigned responsibility for developing engineered cost standards and reduced costs. Consequently, the phase of budget preparation covered by the industrial engineers includes budget standards of performance for each operation, cost center, and department within the plant. This phase of the budget also includes budgeted cost reductions, budgeted unfavorable variances from standards, and certain budgeted programmed fixed costs in the manufacturing area, such as service labor. The industrial engineer prepares this phase of the budget in conjunction with departmental line supervision.

Before each plant sends its budget into British City, a group of us from head office goes out to visit each plant. For example, in the case of the Glass Products Division, Allen Newell, assistant controller, and I, along with representatives of the Glass Products Division manufacturing staffs, visit each of the division's plants. Let me stress this point: We do not go on these trips to pass judgment on the plant's proposed budget. Rather, we go with two purposes in mind. First, we wish to acquaint ourselves with the thinking behind the figures that each plant manager will send in to British City. This is helpful, because, when we come to review these budgets with the top management—that is, management above our level—we will have to answer questions about the budgets, and we will know the answers. Second, the review is a way of giving guidance to the plant managers in determining whether or not they are in line with what the company needs to make in the way of profits.

Of course, when we make our field reviews we do not know what each of the other plants is doing. Therefore, we explain to the plant managers that, while their budgets may look good now, when we put all the plans together in a consolidated budget the plant managers may have to make some changes because the projected profit is not high enough. When this happens, we must tell the plant managers that it is not their programs that are unsound. The problem is that the company cannot afford the programs. I think it is very important that each plant manager has a chance to tell his story. Also, it gives them the feeling that we at headquarters are not living in an ivory tower.

These plant visits are spread over a three-week period, and we spend an average of half a day at each plant. The plant manager is free to bring to these meetings any of his supervisors he wishes. We ask him not to bring in anybody below the supervisory level. Then, of course, you get into organized labor. During the half day we spend at each plant we discuss the budget primarily. However, if I have time I like to wander through the plant and see how things are going. Also, I go over in great detail the property replacement and maintenance budget with the plant manager.

About September 1, the plant budgets come into British City, and the accounting department consolidates them. Then, the product division vice presidents review their respective divisional budgets to see if the division budget is reasonable in terms of what the vice president thinks the corporate management wants. If he is not satisfied with the consolidated plant budgets, he will ask the various plants within the division to trim their budget figures.

When the division vice presidents and the executive vice president are happy, they will send their budgets to the company president. He may accept the division budgets at this point. If he doesn't, he will specify the areas to be reexamined by division and, if necessary, by plant management. The final budget is approved at our December board of directors' meeting.

Comparison of Actual and Standard Performance

At the end of the sixth business day after the close of the month, each plant wires to the head office certain operating variances, which we put together on what we call the "variance analysis sheet." Within a half-hour after the last plant report comes through, variance analysis sheets for the divisions and plants are compiled. On the morning of the seventh business day after the end of the month, these reports are usually on the desks of the interested top management. The variance analysis sheet highlights the variances in what we consider to be critical areas. Receiving this report as soon as we do helps us at head office to take timely action. Let me emphasize, however, we do not accept the excuse that the plant manager has to go to the end of the month to know what happened during the month. He has to be on top of these particular items daily.

When the actual results come into the head office, we go over them on the basis of exception—that is, we only look at those figures that are in

excess of the budgeted amounts. We believe this has a good effect on morale. The plant managers don't have to explain everything they do. They have to explain only where they go off base. In particular, we pay close attention to the net sales, gross margin, and the plant's ability to meet its standard manufacturing cost. Incidentally, when analyzing the gross sales, we look closely at the price and mix changes.

All this information is summarized on a form known as Profit Planning and Control Report No. 1 (see Exhibit 3). This document is backed up by a number of supporting documents (see Exhibit 4). The plant PPCR No. 1 and the month-end trial balance showing both actual and budget figures are received in British City at the close of the eighth business day after the end of the month. These two very important reports, along with the supporting reports (PPCR No. 2, PPCR No. 11) are then consolidated by the accounting department on PPCR-type forms to show the results of operations by division and company. The consolidated reports are distributed the next day.

In connection with the fixed-cost items, we want to know whether or not the plants carried out the programs they said they would carry out. If they have not, we want to know why they have not. Here, we are looking for sound reasons. Also, we want to know if they have carried out their projected programs at the cost they said they would.

In addition to these reports, at the beginning of each month the plant managers prepare current estimates for the upcoming month and quarter on forms similar to the variance analysis sheets. Since our budget is based on known programs, the value of this current estimate is that it gets the plant people to look at their programs. Hopefully, they will realize that they cannot run their plants on a day-to-day basis.

If we see a sore spot coming up, or if the plant manager draws our attention to a potential trouble area, we may ask the daily reports concerning this item be sent to the particular division top management involved. In addition, the division top management may send a division staff specialist—say, a quality control expert if it is a quality problem—to the plant concerned. The division staff members can make recommendations, but it is up to the plant manager to accept or reject these recommen-

EXHIBIT 3 Profit-Planning and Control Report

MONTH					YEAR TO DATE		
Income Gain (+) or Loss (-) From		Actual	Ref.		Actual	Income Gain (+) or Loss (-) From	
Prev. Year	Budget					Budget	Prev. Year
			1	Gross Sales to Customers			
			2	Discounts & Allowances			
			3	Net Sales to Customers			
%	%	///////	4	% Gain (+)/Loss (-)	///////	%	%
				DOLLAR VOLUME GAIN (+)/ LOSS (-) DUE TO:			
		///////	5	Sales Price	///////		
		///////	6	Sales Volume	///////		
			6(a)	Trade Mix	///////		
			7	Variable Cost of Sales			
			8	Profit Margin			
				PROFIT MARGIN GAIN (+)/ LOSS (-) DUE TO:			
		///////	9	Profit Volume Ratio (P/V) *	///////		
		///////	10	Dollar Volume	///////		
%	%	%	11	Profit Volume Ratio (P/V) *		%	%	%
	Income Addition (+)				Income Addition (+)		
			12	Total Fixed Manufacturing Cost			
			13	Fixed Manufacturing Cost-Transfers			
			14	Plant Income (Standard)			
%	%	%	15	% of Net Sales	%	%	%
	Income Addition (+) Income Reduction (-)				Income Addition (+) Income Reduction (-)		
%	%	%	16	% Performance	%	%	%
			17	Manufacturing Efficiency			
	Income Addition (+)				Income Addition (+)		
			18	Methods Improvements			
			19	Other Revisions of Standards			
			20	Material Price Changes			
			21	Division Special Projects			
			22	Company Special Projects			
			23	New Plant Expense			
			24	Other Plant Expenses			
			25	Income on Seconds			
			26				
			27				
			28	Plant Income (Actual)			
%	%	///////	29	% Gain (+)/Loss (-)	///////	%	%
%	%	%	30	% of Net Sales	%	%	%
			36A				
	Increase (+) or Decrease (-)			EMPLOYED CAPITAL		Increase (+) or Decrease (-)	
			37	Total Employed Capital			
%	%	%	38	% Return	%	%	%
			39	Turnover Rate			

_____ Plant   _____ Division   _____ 19____ Month

EXHIBIT 4   Brief Description of PPCR No. 2—PPCR No.11

Individual plant reports

Report	Description
PPCR No. 2	Manufacturing expense: Plant materials, labor, and variable overhead consumed. Detail of actual figures compared with budget and previous year's figures for year to date and current month.
PPCR No. 3	Plant expense: Plant fixed expenses incurred. Details of actual figures compared with budget and previous year's figures for year to date and current month.
PPCR No. 4	Analysis of sales and income: Plant operating gains and losses due to changes in sales revenue, profit margins, and other sources of income. Details of actual figures compared with budget and previous year's figures for year to date and current month.
PPCR No. 5	Plant control statement: Analysis of plant raw material gains and losses, spoilage costs, and cost reductions programs. Actual figures compared with budget figures for current month and year to date.
PPCR No. 6	Comparison of sales by principal and product groups: Plant sales dollars, profit margin, and P/V ratios broken down by end product use (i.e., soft drinks, beer). Compares actual figures for year to date and current month.

Division summary reports

Report	Description
PPCR No. 7	Comparative plant performance, sales, and income: Gross sales and income figures by plants. Actual figures compared with budget figures for year to date and current month.
PPCR No. 8	Comparative plant performance, total plant expenses: Profit margin, total fixed costs, manufacturing efficiency, other plant expenses and P/V ratios by plants. Actual figures compared with budgeted and previous year's figures for current month and year to date.
PPCR No. 9	Manufacturing efficiency: Analysis of gains and losses by plant in areas of materials, spoilage, supplies, and labor. Current month and year to date actuals reported in total dollars and as a percentage of budget.
PPCR No. 10	Inventory: Comparison of actual and budget inventory figures by major inventory accounts and plants.
PPCR No. 11	Status of capital expenditures: Analysis of the status of capital expenditures by plants, months, and relative to budget.

dations. Of course, it is well known throughout the company that we expect the plant managers to accept gracefully the help of the head office and division staffs.

Sales-Manufacturing Relations

If a sales decline occurs during the early part of the year, and if the plant managers can convince us that the change is permanent, we may revise the plant budgets to reflect these new circumstances. However, if toward the end of the year the actual sales volume suddenly drops below the predicted sales volume, we don't have much time to change the budget plans. What we do is ask the plant managers to go back over their budgets with their staffs and see where reduction of expense programs will do the least harm. Specifically, we ask them to consider what they may be able to eliminate this year or delay until next year.

I believe it was Confucius who said: "We make plans so we have plans to discard." Nevertheless, I think it is wise to make plans, even if you have to discard them. Having plans makes it a lot easier to figure out what to do when sales fall off from the budget level. The understanding of operations that comes from preparing the budget removes a lot of the potential chaos and confusion that might arise if we were under pressure to meet a stated profit goal and sales declined quickly and unexpectedly at year end, just as they did last year. In these circumstances, we don't try to ram anything down the plant managers' throats. We ask them to tell us where they can reasonably expect to cut costs below the budgeted level.

Whenever a problem arises at a plant between sales and production, the local people are supposed to solve the problem themselves. For example, a customer's purchasing agent may insist he wants an immediate delivery, and this delivery will disrupt the production department's plans. The production group can make recommendations as to alternative ways to take care of the problem, but it's the sales manager's responsibility to get the product to the customer. The salesmen are supposed to know their customers well enough to judge whether or not the customer really needs the product. If the sales manager says the customer needs the product, that ends the matter. As far as we are concerned, the customer's wants are primary; our company is a case where sales wags the rest of the dog.

Of course, if the change in the sales program involves a major plant expense which is out of line with the budget, then the matter is passed up to division for decision.

As I said earlier, the sales department has the sole responsibility for the product price, sales mix, and delivery schedules. They do not have direct responsibility for plant operations or profit. That's the plant management's responsibility. However, it is understood that sales group will cooperate with the plant people wherever possible.

Motivation

There are various ways in which we motivate the plant managers to meet their profit goals. First of all, we only promote capable people. Also, a monetary incentive program has been established that stimulates their efforts to achieve their profit goals. In addition, each month we put together a bar chart which shows, by division and plant, the ranking of the various manufacturing units with respect to manufacturing efficiency.[1] We feel that plant managers are 100 percent responsible for variable manufacturing costs. I believe this is true, since all manufacturing standards have to be approved by plant managers. Most of the plant managers give wide publicity to these bar charts. The efficiency bar chart and efficiency measure itself is perhaps a little unfair in some respects when you are comparing one plant with another. Different kinds of products are run through different plants. These require different setups, etc., which have an important impact on a position of the plant. However, in general, the efficiency rating is a good indication of the quality of the plant manager and his supervisory staff.

Also, a number of plants run competitions within the plants, which reward department heads, or foremen, based on their relative standing with respect to a certain cost item. The plant managers, their staffs, and employees have great pride in their plants.

The number one item now stressed at the plant level is *quality*. The market situation is such that in order to make sales you have to meet the market price and exceed the market quality. By quality, I mean not only the physical characteristics of the product but also such things as delivery schedules. As I read the company employee publications, their message is that if the company is to be profitable it must produce high-quality items at a reasonable cost. This is necessary so that the plants can meet their obligation to produce the maximum profits for the company in the prevailing circumstances.

The Future

An essential part of the budgetary control system is planning. We have developed a philosophy that we must begin our plans where the work is done— in the line organization and out in the field. Perhaps, in the future, we can avoid or cut back some

---

[1] Manufacturing efficiency =
$$\frac{\text{Total actual variable manufacturing costs}}{\text{Total standard variable manufacturing costs}} \times 100\%$$

of the budget preparation steps and start putting together our sales budget later than May 15. However, I doubt if we will change the basic philosophy.

Frankly, I doubt if the line operators would want any major change in the system; they are very jealous of the management prerogatives the system gives to them.

It is very important that we manage the budget. We have to be continually on guard against it managing us. Sometimes, the plants lose sight of this

fact. We have to be made conscious daily of the necessity of having the sales volume to make a profit. And when sales fall off and their plant programs are reduced, they do not always appear to see the justification for these budget cuts. Although I do suspect that they see more of the justification for these cuts than they will admit. It is this human side of the budget to which we have to pay more attention in the future.

QUESTIONS

1. Trace through the profit budgeting process at Empire, starting on May 15 and ending in December with the approval by the board of directors. Be prepared to describe the sorts of activities at each step of the process and the rationale for them.
2. Should the plant managers be held responsible for profits?

Case 9-3

Midwest Ice Cream Company (A)*

Frank Roberts, marketing vice president of Midwest Ice Cream Company, was pleased when he saw the final earnings statement for the company for 1983. He knew that it had been a good year for Midwest, but he hadn't expected a large favorable operating income variance. Only the year before, the company had installed a new financial planning and control system; 1983 was the first year for which figures comparing budgeted and actual results were available.

Midwest's Planning and Control System

The following description of the financial planning and control system installed at Midwest in 1983 is taken from an internal company operating manual.

The Planning Function

The starting point in making a profit plan is separating costs into fixed and variable categories. Some costs are purely variable and, as such, will require an additional amount with each increase in volume levels. The manager has little control over this type of cost, other than to avoid waste. The accountant can easily determine the variable manufacturing cost per unit for any given product or package by using current prices and yield records. Variable marketing cost per unit is based on the allowable rate; for example, $0.06 per gallon for advertising. Costs that are not purely variable are classified as fixed, but they, too, will vary if significant changes in volume occur. There will be varying degrees of sensitivity to volume changes among these costs, ranging from a point just short of purely variable to an extremely fixed type of expense that has no relationship to volume.

The reason for differentiating between fixed and variable so emphatically is because a variable cost requires no decision on when to add or take off a unit of cost; it is dictated by volume. Fixed costs, on the other hand, require a management judgment on decisions to increase or decrease the cost. Sugar is an example of purely variable cost. Each change in volume will automatically bring a change in the sugar cost; only the yield can be controlled. Route salesmen's salaries would be an example of a fixed cost that is fairly sensitive to volume, but not purely variable. As volume changes, pressure will be felt to increase or decrease this expense, but management must make the decision; the change in cost level is not automatic. Depreciation charges for plant would be an example of a relatively extreme fixed cost, in that large increases in volume can usually be realized before this type of cost is pressured to change. In both cases, the fixed cost requires a decision from management to increase or decrease the cost. It is this dilemma that management is constantly facing: to withstand the pressure to increase or be ready to decrease when the situation demands it.

The first step in planning is to develop a unit standard cost for each element of variable cost by product and package size. Examples of four different products and packages are shown in Exhibit 1. As already pointed out, the accountant can do this by using current prices and yield records for material costs and current allowance rates for marketing costs. Advertising is the only cost element not fitting the explanation of a variable cost given in the

* This case was prepared by W. J. Reueverdink under the supervision of J. K. Shank, Harvard Business School. Copyright © by the President and Fellows of Harvard College. Harvard Business School case 175–070.

preceding paragraph. Advertising costs are set by management decision, rather than being an "automatic" cost item like sugar or packaging. In this sense, advertising is just like route salesmen's expense. For our company, however, management has decided that the allowance for advertising expense is equal to $0.06 per gallon for the actual number of gallons sold. This management decision, therefore, has transformed advertising into an expense that is treated as variable for profit planning.

After the total unit variable cost has been developed, this amount is subtracted from the selling price to arrive at a marginal contribution per unit, by product and package type. At any level of volume, it is easy to determine the contribution that should be generated to cover the fixed costs and provide profits. This will be illustrated in Exhibit 4.

Step 2 is perhaps the most critical of all the phases in making a profit plan, because all plans are built around the anticipated level of sales activity. Much thought should be given in forecasting a realistic sales level and product mix. Consideration should be given to the number of days in a given period, as well as to the number of Fridays and Mondays, as these are two of the heaviest days and will make a difference in the sales forecast.

Other factors that should be considered are (1) general economic condition of the marketing area (2) weather, (3) anticipated promotions, and (4) competition.

Step 3 involves the setting of fixed-cost budgets based on management's judgment as to the need in light of the sales forecast. It is here that good planning makes for a profitable operation. The number of routes needed for both winter and summer volume is planned. The level of manufacturing payroll is set,[1] insurance and taxes are budgeted, and so on. After step 4 has been performed, it may be necessary to return to step 3 and make adjustments to some of the costs that are discretionary in nature.

Step 4 is the profit plan itself. By combining our marginal contribution developed in step 1 with our

sales forecast, we arrive at a total marginal contribution by month. Subtracting the fixed cost budgeted in Step 3, we have an operating profit by months. As mentioned above, if this profit figure is not sufficient, then a new evaluation should be made of the fixed costs developed in step 3.

The following four tables (Exhibits 1–4) illustrate each of the four planning steps for a hypothetical ice cream plant. (The numbers in the tables are not intended to be realistic.)

The Control Function

To illustrate the control system, we will take the month of January and assume the level of sales activity for the month to be 520,000 gallons, as shown in Exhibit 5. Looking back to our sales forecast (step 2) we see that 495,000 gallons had been forecasted. When we apply our marginal contribution per unit for each product and package, we find that the 520,000 gallons have produced $6,125 less standard contribution than the 495,000 gallons would have produced at the forecasted mix. So, even though there has been a nice increase in sales volume, the mix has been unfavorable. The $6,125 represents the difference between standard profit contribution at forecasted volume and standard profit contribution at actual volume. It is thus due to differences in volume and to differences in average mix. The impact of each of these two factors is shown on the bottom of Exhibit 5.

Exhibit 6 shows a typical departmental budget sheet comparing actual with budget. A sheet is issued for each department so the person responsible for a particular area of the business can see the items that are in line and those that need his attention. In our example, there is an unfavorable operating variance of about $22,700. You should note that the budget for variable cost items has been adjusted to reflect actual volume, thereby eliminating wide cost variances due strictly to the difference between planned and actual volume.

Since the level of fixed costs is independent of volume anyway, it is not necessary to adjust the budget for these items for volume differences. The original budget for fixed-cost items is still appropriate. The totals for each department are carried forward to an earnings statement, Exhibit 7. We have assumed all other departments' actual and budget

---

[1] Because this system is based on a one-year time frame, manufacturing labor is considered to be a fixed cost. The level of the manufacturing work force is not really variable until a time frame longer than one year is adopted.

are in line, so the only operating variances is the one for manufacturing. This variance added to the sales volume and mix variance of $6,125 results in an overall variance from the original plan of $28,825, as shown at the bottom of Exhibit 7.

The illustration here has been on a monthly basis, but there is no need to wait until the end of the month to see what is happening. Each week, sales can be multiplied by the contribution margins to see how much standard contribution has been generated. This can be compared to one fourth of the monthly forecasted contribution to see if volume and mix are in line with forecast. Neither is it necessary to wait until the end of the month to see if

---

EXHIBIT 1   Step 1: Establish Standards for Selling Price, Variable Expenses, and Marginal Contribution per Gallon (vanilla ice cream)

| | Regular | | | Premium |
| | | | | |
Item	*One-1 gallon Paper Container*	*One-1 gallon Plastic Container*	*Two-1 gallon Paper Container*	*One-1 gallon Plastic Container*
Dairy ingredients	$0.53	$0.53	$0.53	$0.79
Sugar	0.15	0.15	0.15	0.15
Flavor	0.10	0.10	0.105	0.12
Production	0.10	0.16	0.125	0.16
Warehouse	0.06	0.08	0.07	0.08
Transportation	0.02	0.025	0.02	0.025
Total manufacturing	0.96	1.045	1.00	1.325
Advertising	0.06	0.06	0.06	0.06
Delivery	0.04	0.04	0.04	0.04
Total Marketing	0.10	0.10	0.10	0.10
Total variable costs	1.06	1.145	1.10	1.425
Selling price	1.50	1.70	1.45	2.40
Marginal contribution/gallon before packaging	0.44	0.555	0.35	0.975
Packaging	0.10	0.25	0.085	0.25
Marginal contribution/gallon	0.34	0.305	0.265	0.725

EXHIBIT 2   Step 2: Vanilla Ice Cream Sales Forecast in Gallons

	January	*February*		*December*	*Total*
One gallon—paper	100,000	100,000	. . . . . .	100,000	1,200,000
One gallon—plastic	50,000	50,000	. . . . . .	50,000	600,000
Two gallon—paper	225,000	225,000	. . . . . .	225,000	2,700,000
One gallon—premium	120,000	120,000	. . . . . .	120,000	1,440,000
Total	495,000	495,000	. . . . . .	495,000	5,940,000

EXHIBIT 3 Step 3: Budget Fixed Expenses

	January	February		December	Total
Manufacturing expense:					
Labor	$ 7,333	$ 7,333	. . . .	$ 7,333	$ 88,000
Equipment repair	3,333	3,333	. . . .	3,333	40,000
Depreciation	6,667	6,667	. . . .	6,667	80,000
Taxes	3,333	3,333	. . . .	3,333	40,000
Total	20,667	20,667	. . . .	20,667	248,000
Delivery expense:					
Salaries—General	10,000	10,000	. . . .	10,000	120,000
Salaries—Drivers	10,667	10,667	. . . .	10,667	128,000
Helpers	10,667	10,667	. . . .	10,667	128,000
Suppliers	667	667	. . . .	667	8,000
Total	32,000	32,000	. . . .	32,000	384,000
Administrative expense:					
Salaries	5,167	5,167	. . . .	5,167	62,000
Insurance	1,667	1,667	. . . .	1,667	20,000
Taxes	1,667	1,667	. . . .	1,667	20,000
Depreciation	833	833	. . . .	833	10,000
Total	9,333	9,333	. . . .	9,333	112,000
Selling expense:					
Repairs	2,667	2,667	. . . .	2,667	32,000
Gasoline	5,000	5,000	. . . .	5,000	60,000
Salaries	5,000	5,000	. . . .	5,000	60,000
Total	$12,667	$12,667	. . . .	$12,667	$152,000

expenses are in line. Weekly reports of such items as production or sugar can be made, comparing budget with actual. By combining the variances as shown on weekly reports, and adjusting the forecasted profit figure, an approximate profit figure can be had long before the books are closed and monthly statements issued. More important, action can be taken to correct an undesirable situation much sooner.

EXHIBIT 4   Step 4: The Profit Plan

	Marginal Contribution (see step 1)	Gallons Sold per month	Contribution			
			January	February	December	Total
One gallon—paper	0.34	100,000	$ 34,000	$ 34,000	$ 34,000	$ 408,000
One gallon—plastic	0.305	50,000	15,250	15,250	15,250	83,000
Two gallon—paper	0.265	225,000	59,625	59,625	59,625	715,500
One gallon—premium	0.725	120,000	87,000	87,000	87,000	1,044,000
Total contribution			195,875	195,875	195,875	2,350,500
Fixed costs (see step 3):						
Manuacting costs			20,667	20,667	20,667	248,000
Delivery expense			32,000	32,000	32,000	384,000
Administrative expense			9,333	9,333	9,333	112,000
Selling expense			12,667	12,667	12,667	152,000
Total fixed			74,667	74,667	74,667	896,000
Operating profit			121,208	121,208	121,208	1,454,500
Income tax			60,604	60,604	60,604	727,250
Net profit			$ 60,604	$ 60,604	$ 60,604	$ 727,250

EXHIBIT 5   Contribution Analysis (January)

	Actual Gallon Sales	Standard Contribution per Gallon	Total Standard Contribution
One gallon—paper	90,000	0.340	$ 30,600
One gallon—plastic	95,000	0.305	28,975
Two gallon—paper	245,000	0.265	64,925
One gallon—premium	90,000	0.725	65,250
Total	520,000		189,750

Forecast (step 2):
  495,000 gallons

Forecasted marginal contribution (at 495,000 gallons)			195,875
Over (under) forecast			$(6,125)

	Planned	Actual	Variance due to volume:		
Gallons	495,000	520,000	25,000 gallons × $0.3957	=	9.892F
Contribution	$195,875	$189,750	Variance due to mix:		
Avg. per gallon	$0.3957	$0.3649	$0.0308 × 520,000 gallons	=	16,017U
Difference	$0.0308		Total variance	=	6,125U

F = favorable; U = unfavorable.

EXHIBIT 6 Manufacturing Cost of Goods Sold (January)

	Month		Year to Date	
	Actual	*Budget*	*Actual*	*Budget*
Dairy ingredients	$312,744	$299,000		
Sugar	82,304	78,000		
Flavorings	56,290	55,025		
Warehouse	38,770	37,350		
Production	70,300	69,225		
Transportation	11,514	11,325		
Subtotal, variable	571,922	549,925		
Labor	7,300	7,329		
Equipment repair	4,065	3,333		
Depreciation	6,667	6,667		
Taxes	3,333	3,333		
Subtotal, fixed	21,365	20,662		
Total	$593,287	$570,587		

EXHIBIT 7   Earnings Statement (January)

	Month		Year to Date	
	Actual	*Budget*	*Actual*	*Budget*
Total ice cream sales	$867,750	$867,750		
Mfg. cost of goods sold	$593,287	$570,592		
Delivery expense	52,804	52,800		
Advertising expense	31,200	31,200		
Packaging expense	76,075	76,075		
Selling expense	12,667	12,667		
Administrative expense	9,334	9,333		
Total expense	$775,367	$752,667		
Profit or loss	$ 92,383	$115,083		
Provision for income taxes	46,192	—		
Net profit or (loss)	46,191	—		

Actual profit before taxes		92,383		(1)		
Original profit forecast (step 4)		121,208		(2)		
Revised profit forecast based on actual volume		115,083		(3)		
		(2)	–	(3)		
Variance due to volume and mix (unfavorable)	=	121,208	–	115,083	=	6,125U
		(3)	–	(1)		
Variance due to operations (unfavorable)	=	115,083	–	92,383	=	22,700U
		(2)		(1)		
Total variance	=	(121,208	–	92,383)	=	28,825U

QUESTIONS

1. Explain in as much detail as possible where *all* the numbers for Exhibits 1—4 would come from. (You will need to use your imagination; the case does not describe all details of the profit planning process.)
2. Explain the difference between a month's planned profit as shown in Exhibit 4 and a month's budgeted profit as shown in Exhibit 7. Why would Midwest want to have *two* target profit amounts for a given month? (*Hint:* Study the variance calculations at the bottom of Exhibit 7.)
3. Evaluate Midwest's planning and control processes.

Case 9–4

Codman & Shurtleff, Inc.*

"This revision combines our results from January to April with the preliminary estimates supplied by each department for the remainder of the year. Of course, there are still a lot of unknown factors to weigh in, but this will give you some idea of our preliminary updated forecast."

As the board members reviewed the document provided to them by Gus Fleites, vice president of information and control at Codman & Shurtleff, Roy Black, president, addressed the six men sitting at the conference table. "This revised forecast leaves us with a big stretch. We are almost $2 million short of our profit objective for the year. As we discussed last week, we are estimating sales to be $1.1 million above original forecast. This is due in part to the early introduction of the new chest drainage unit. However, three major factors that we didn't foresee last September will affect our profit plan estimates for the remainder of the year.

"First, there's the currency issue—our hedging has partially protected us, but the continued rapid deterioration of the dollar has pushed our costs up on European specialty instruments. Although this has improved Codman's competitive market position in Europe, those profits accrue to the European company and are not reflected in this forecast. Second, we have an unfavorable mix variance. And finally, we will have to absorb inventory variances due to higher than anticipated start-up costs of our recently combined manufacturing operations."

"When do we have to take the figures to corporate?" asked Chuck Dunn, vice president of business development.

"Wednesday, May 14, which is next week," replied Black, "so we have to settle this by Monday. That gives us only tomorrow and the weekend to wrap up the June budget revision. I know that each of you has worked on these estimates, but I think that the next look will be critical to achieving our profit objective."

"Bob, do you have anything you can give us?"

Bob Dick, vice president of marketing, shook his head. "I've been working with my people looking at price and mix. At the moment, we can't realistically get more price. Most of the mix variance for the balance of the year will be due to increased sales of products that we are handling under the new distribution agreement. The mix for the remainder of the year may change, but with 2,700 active products in the catalog, I don't want to move too far from our original projections. My expenses are cut right to the bone. Further cuts will mean letting staff go."

Black nodded his head in agreement. "Chuck, you and I should meet to review our research and development priorities. I know that Herb Stolzer will want to spend time reviewing the status of our programs. I think we should be sure that we have cut back to reflect our spending to date. I wouldn't be surprised if we could find another $400,000 without jeopardizing our long-term programs."

* This case was prepared by Robert L. Simons, Harvard Business School.
Copyright © by the President and Fellows of Harvard College.
Harvard Business School case 187–087.

"Well, it seems our work is cut out for us. The rest of you keep working on this. Excluding R&D, we need at least another $500,000 before we start drawing down our contingency fund. Let's meet here tomorrow at two o'clock and see where we stand."

Codman & Shurtleff, Inc.

Codman & Shurtleff, Inc., a subsidiary of Johnson & Johnson, was established in 1838 in Boston by Thomas Codman to design and fashion surgical instruments. The company developed surgical instrument kits for use in army field hospitals during the Civil War and issued its first catalog in 1860. After the turn of the century, Codman & Shurtleff specialized in working with orthopedic surgeons and with pioneers in the field of neurosurgery.

In 1986, Codman & Shurtleff supplied hospitals and surgeons worldwide with over 2,700 products for surgery, including instruments, equipment, implants, surgical disposables, fiber-optic light sources and cables, surgical head lamps, surgical microscopes, coagulators, and electronic pain control simulators and electrodes. These products involved advanced technologies from the fields of metallurgy, electronics, and optics.

Codman & Shurtleff operated three manufacturing locations in Randolph, New Bedford, and Southbridge, Massachusetts, and a distribution facility in Avon, Massachusetts. The company employed 800 people in the United States.

In 1964, Codman & Shurtleff was acquired by Johnson & Johnson, Inc., as an addition to its professional products business. Johnson & Johnson operated manufacturing subsidiaries in 46 countries, sold its products in most countries of the world, and employed 75,000 people worldwide. Its 1985 sales were $6.4 billion, with before tax profits of $900 million.

Roy Black had been president of Codman & Shurtleff since 1983. In his 25 years with Johnson & Johnson, Black had spent 18 years with Codman, primarily in the marketing department.

He also had worked at Johnson & Johnson's Ethicon and Surgikos subsidiaries. He described his job:

> This is a tough business to manage because it is so complex. We rely heavily on the neurosurgeons for ideas in product generation and for the testing and ultimate acceptance of our products. We have to stay in close contact with the leading neurosurgeons around the world. For example, last week I returned from a tour of the Pacific rim. During the trip, I visited eight Johnson & Johnson/Codman affiliates and 25 neurosurgeons.
>
> At the same time, we are forced to push technological innovation to reduce costs. This is a matter of survival. In the past, we concentrated on producing superior quality goods, and the market was willing to pay whatever it took to get the best. But the environment has changed; the shift has been massive. We are trying to adapt to a situation where doctors and hospitals are under severe pressure to be more efficient and cost-effective.
>
> We compete in 12 major product groups. Since our markets are so competitive, the business is very price-sensitive. The only way we can support our price is to offer unique products with cost-in-use benefits to the professional user.
>
> Since the introduction of DRG costing[1] by hospitals in 1983, industry volume has been off approximately 20 percent. We have condensed 14 locations to 4 and have reduced staff levels by over 20 percent. There have also been some cuts in R&D, although our goal is to maintain research spending at near double the historical Codman level.

Chuck Dunn had moved three years earlier from Johnson & Johnson Products to join Codman as vice president for information and

---

[1] On October 1, 1983, Medicare reimbursement to hospitals changed from a cost-plus system to a fixed-rate system as called for in the 1983 Social Security refinancing legislation. The new system was called "prospective payment," because rates were set in advance of treatment according to which of 467 "diagnostic-related groups" (or DRGs) a patient was deemed to fall into. This change in reimbursement philosophy made cost control much more important for the nation's 5,800 acute-care hospitals, which received an average of 36 percent of their revenues from Medicare and Medicaid.

control. During his 24 years with Johnson & Johnson, he had worked with four different marketing divisions as well as the corporate office. He recalled the process of establishing a new mission statement at Codman:

> When I arrived here, Codman was in the process of defining a more clearly focused mission. Our mission was product-oriented, but Johnson & Johnson was oriented by medical specialty. On a matrix, this resulted in missed product opportunities as well as turf problems with other Johnson & Johnson companies.
>
> It took several years of hard work to arrive at a new worldwide mission statement oriented to medical specialty, but this process was very useful in obtaining group consensus. Our worldwide mission is now defined in terms of a primary focus in the neurospinal surgery business. This turns out to be a large market and allows better positioning of our products.
>
> In addition to clarifying our planning, we use the mission statement as a screening device. We look carefully at any new R&D project to see if it fits our mission. The same is true for acquisitions.

Reporting Relationships at Johnson & Johnson

In 1985, Johnson & Johnson comprised 155 autonomous subsidiaries operating in three health care markets: consumer products, pharmaceutical products, and professional products.

Johnson & Johnson was managed on a decentralized basis, as described in the following excerpt from the 1985 annual report:

> The company is organized on the principles of decentralized management and conducts its business through operating subsidiaries, which are themselves, for the most part, integral, autonomous operations. Direct responsibility for each company lies with its operating management, headed by the president, general manager or managing director who reports directly or through a company group chairman to a member of the executive committee. In line with this policy of decentralization, each internal subsidiary is, with some exceptions, managed by citizens of the country where it is located.

Roy Black at Codman & Shurtleff reported directly to Herbert Stolzer at Johnson & Johnson headquarters in New Brunswick, New Jersey. Mr. Stolzer, 59, was a member of the executive committee of Johnson & Johnson, with responsibility for 16 operating companies in addition to Codman & Shurtleff (see Exhibit 1). Stolzer had worked for Johnson & Johnson for 35 years and had engineering, manufacturing, and senior management experience in Johnson & Johnson Products and at the corporate office.

The senior policy- and decision-making group at Johnson & Johnson was the executive committee, comprising the chairman, president, chief financial officer, vice president of administration, and eight executive committee members with responsibilities for company sectors. The 155 business units of the company were organized in sectors based primarily on products (e.g., consumer, pharmaceutical, professional) and secondarily on geographic markets.

5- and 10-Year Plans at Johnson & Johnson

Each operating company within Johnson & Johnson was responsible for preparing its own plans and strategies. David Clare, president of Johnson & Johnson, believed that this was one of the key elements in their success. "Our success is due to three basic tenets: a basic belief in decentralized management, a sense of responsibility to our key constituents, and a desire to manage for the long term. We have no corporate strategic planning function nor one strategic plan. Our strategic plan is the sum of the strategic plans of each of our 155 business units."

Each operating company prepared annually a 5- and 10-year plan. Financial estimates in these plans were limited to only four numbers: estimated unit sales volume, estimated sales revenue, estimated net income, and estimated return on investment. Accompanying these financial estimates was a narrative description of how these targets would be achieved.

To ensure that managers were committed to the plan that they developed, Johnson & Johnson

EXHIBIT 1 Johnson & Johnson: Partial Organization Chart

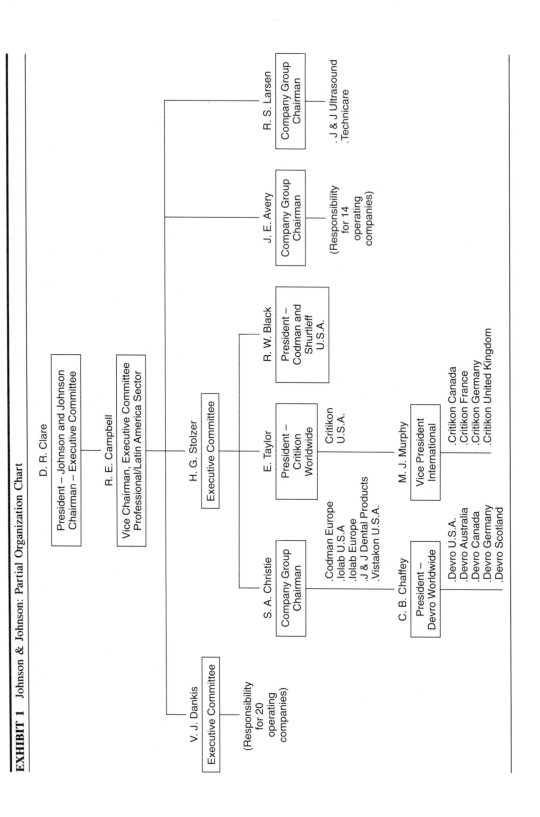

required that the planning horizon focus on two years only and remain fixed over a five-year period. Thus, in 1983 a budget and second-year forecast was developed for 1984 and 1985 and a strategic plan was developed for the years 1990 and 1995. In each of the years 1984 through 1987, the 5- and 10-year plan was redrawn in respect of only years 1990 and 1995. Only in year 1988 would the strategic planning horizon shift five years forward to cover years 1995 and 2000. These two years will then remain the focus of subsequent 5- and 10-year plans for the succeeding four years, and so on.

At Codman & Shurtleff, work on the annual 5- and 10-year plan commenced each January and took approximately six months to complete. Based on the mission statement, a business plan was developed for each significant segment of the business. In addition, the anticipated activities of competitors were discussed. For each competitor, the marketing plan included an estimated pro forma income statement (volume, sales, profit) as well as a one page narrative description of their strategy.

Based on the tentative marketing plan, draft plans were prepared by the other departments, including research and development, production, finance, and personnel. The tentative plan was assembled in a binder with sections describing mission, strategies, opportunities and threats, environment, and financial forecasts. This plan was debated, adjusted, and approved over the course of several meetings in May by the Codman board of directors (see Exhibit 2), comprising the president and seven key subordinates.

In June, Herb Stolzer travelled to Boston to preside over the annual review of the 5- and 10-year plan. Codman executives considered this a key meeting that could last up to three days. During the meeting Stolzer reviewed the plan, aired his concerns, and challenged the Codman board on assumptions, strategies, and forecasts. A recurring question during the session was, "If your new projection for 1990 is below what you predicted last year, how do you intend to make up the shortfall?"

After this meeting, Roy Black summarized the plan that had been approved by Stolzer in a two-page memorandum that he sent directly to Jim Burke, chairman and chief executive officer of Johnson & Johnson.

Based on the two-page "Burke letters," the 5- and 10-year plans for all operating companies were presented by Executive Committee members and debated and approved at the September meeting of the Executive Committee in New Brunswick. Company presidents, including Roy Black, were often invited to prepare formal presentations. The discussion in these meetings was described by those in attendance as, "very frank," "extremely challenging," and "grilling."

Financial Planning at Johnson & Johnson

Financial planning at Johnson & Johnson focused on profit plans (i.e., budgets) for the upcoming operating year and a second-year forecast. Profit plans were detailed financial documents prepared down to the expense center level for each operating company. The second-year forecast was in a similar format but contained less detail than the profit plans for the upcoming year.

Revenues and expenses were budgeted by month. Selected balance sheet items (e.g., accounts receivable and inventory) were also budgeted to reflect year-end targets.

Profit plan targets were developed on a bottom up basis by each operating company by reference to two documents: (1) the approved 5- and 10-year plan and (2) the second-year forecast prepared the previous year. ChuckDunn described the profit planning process at Codman & Shurtleff:

> We wrote the initial draft of our 1987 profit plan in the summer of 1986 based on the revision of our 5- and 10-year plan. By August, the profit plan started to crystallize; we had brought in the support areas, such as accounting, quality assurance, R&D, and engineering, to ensure that they "bought in" to the new 1987 profit and marketing plans.
>
> The first year of the strategic plan is used as a basis for the departments to prepare their own one-year plans for both capital and expense items. The

EXHIBIT 2 Codman & Shurtleff, Inc.:: Partial Organiztion Chart

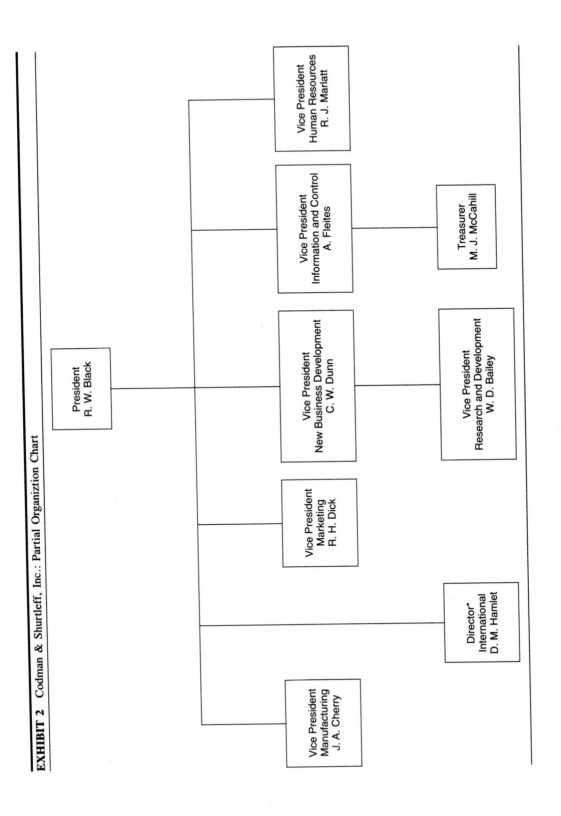

production budget is based on standard costs and nonstandard costs, such as development programs and plant consolidations. As for the R&D budget, the project list is always too long, so we are forced to rank the projects. For each project, we look at returns, costs, time expended, sales projections, expected profit, and gross profit percentages, as well as support to be supplied to the plants.

The individual budgets are then consolidated by the information and control department. We look very carefully at how this profit plan compares with our previous forecasts. For example, the first consolidation of the 1986 profit plan revealed a $2.4 million profit shortfall against the second-year forecast that was developed in 1984 and updated in June 1985. To reconcile this, it was necessary to put on special budget presentations by each department to remove all slack and ensure that our earlier target could be met if possible. The commitment to this process is very strong.

We are paying more and more attention to our second-year forecast, since it forces us to reexamine strategic plans. The second-year forecast is also used as a benchmark for next year's profit plan and, as such, it will be used in a hindsight way to evaluate the forecasting ability and performance of managers.

The procedure for approving the annual profit plan and second-year forecast followed closely the procedures described above for the review of the 5- and 10-year plans. During the early fall, Herbert Stolzer reviewed the proposed budget with Roy Black and the Codman & Shurtleff board of directors. Changes in profit commitments from previous forecasts and the overall profitability and tactics of the company were discussed in detail.

After all anticipated revenues and expenses were budgeted, a separate contingency expense line item was added to the budget; the amount of the contingency changed from year to year and was negotiated between Stolzer and Black based on the perceived uncertainty in achieving budget targets. In 1986, the Codman & Shurtleff contingency was set at $1.1 million.

Stolzer presented the profit plan for approval at the November meeting of the Johnson & Johnson executive committee.

Budget Revisions and Reviews

During the year, performance was monitored closely. Each week, sales revenue performance figures were sent to Herb Stolzer. In addition, Roy Black sent a monthly management report to Stolzer that included income statement highlights and a summary of key balance sheet figures and ratios. All information was provided with reference to (1) position last month, (2) position this month, (3) budgeted position. All variances that Black considered significant were explained in a narrative summary.

The accuracy of profit plan projections was also monitored during the year and formally revised on three occasions. The first of these occasions occurred at the March meeting of the executive committee. Going around the table, each executive committee member was asked to update the committee on his or her most recent estimates of sales and profits for each operating company for the current year. Herb Stolzer relied on Roy Black to provide this information for Stolzer's review prior to the March meeting.

The "June Revision" referred to the revised profit plan for the current year that was presented to the executive committee in June. The preparation of this revised profit plan required managers at Codman & Shurtleff and all other Johnson & Johnson companies to rebudget in May for the remainder of the fiscal year. This revision involved rechecking all budget estimates starting with the lowest-level expense center, as well as revising the second-year forecast when necessary. .

The third review of profit plan projections was the "November update," which was presented to the executive committee at the November meeting concurrently with their consideration of the profit plan and second-year forecast for the upcoming budget year. The November update focused on results for the 10 months just completed and the revised projections for the remaining 2 months. At

Codman & Shurtleff, preparation of the November update involved performance estimates from all departments but was not conducted to the same level of detail as the June revision.

Corporate View of the Planning and Control Process

David Clare, president of Johnson & Johnson:

The sales and profit forecasts are always optimistic in the 5- and 10-year plans, but this is OK. We want people to stretch their imagination and think expansively. In these plans we don't anticipate failure; they are a device to open up thinking. There is no penalty for inaccuracies.

The profit plan and second-year forecast are used to run the business and evaluate managers on planning, forecasts, and achievements.

We ask our managers to always include in their plans an account of how and why their estimates have changed over time. That is why we use the 5- and 10-year planning concept rather than a moving planning horizon. This allows us to revise our thinking over time and allows for retrospective learning.

If a manager insists on a course of action and we (the executive committee) have misgivings, 9 times out of 10 we will let him go ahead. If we say, "No," and the answer should have been, "Yes," we say, "Don't blame us, it was your job to sell us on the idea and you didn't do that."

Johnson & Johnson is extremely decentralized, but that does not mean that managers are free from challenge as to what they are doing. In the final analysis, managing conflict is what management is all about. Healthy conflict is about *what* is right, not *who* is right.

Our company philosophy is to manage for the long term. We do not use short-term bonus plans. Salary and bonus reviews are entirely subjective and qualitative and are intended to reward effort and give special recognition to those who have performed uniquely. The executive committee reviews salary recommendations for all managers above a certain salary level, but company presidents, such as Roy Black, have full discretion on how they remunerate their employees.

Herbert Stolzer, executive committee member:

The planning and control systems used in Johnson & Johnson provide real benefits. These systems allow us to find problems and run the business. This is true not only for us at corporate but also at the operating companies, where they are a tremendous tool. Once a year, managers are forced to review their businesses in depth for costs, trends, manufacturing efficiency, marketing plans, and their competitive situation. Programs and action plans result.

You have to force busy people to do this. Otherwise, they will be caught up in day-to-day activities—account visits, riding with salesmen, standing on the manufacturing floor.

Our long-term plans are not meant to be a financial forecast; rather, they are meant to be an objective way of setting aspirations. We never make those numbers—who can forecast sales 5 or 10 years out with unforeseen markets, products, and competitors? Even the accuracy of our two-year forecast is bad. The inaccuracy is an indication of how fast our markets are changing. Our businesses are so diverse, with so many competitors, that it is difficult to forecast out two years.

I visit at least twice a year with each operating company board. We usually spend the better part of a week going over results, planning issues, strategic plans, and short- and long-term problems. The Executive Committee, to the best of my knowledge, never issues quantitative performance targets before the bottom up process begins.

At the executive committee meetings, a lot of argument takes place around strategic planning issues: How fast can we get a business up to higher returns? Are the returns in some business too high? Are we moving too fast? However, the outcome is never to go back to the operating company and say we need 8 percent, rather than 6 percent. The challenge has already taken place between the executive committee member and the company board. If the executive committee member is satisfied with the answers provided by the board, that's the end of it.

It happens very rarely that the consolidated profit plan is unacceptable. Occasionally, we might say, "We really could use some more money." However, in the second review, this may not turn up any extra. If so, that's OK.

Our systems are not used to punish. They are used to try and find and correct problems. Bonuses are not tied to achieving budget targets. They are subjectively determined, although we use whatever objective indicators are available—for example, sales and new product introductions for a marketing vice president.

The key to our whole system is the operating company presidents. We are so decentralized that they define their own destiny. A successful company president needs to be able to stand up to pressure from above. He needs to have the courage to say, "I have spent hours and hours on that forecast and, for the long-term health of the company, we have to spend that budget."

Clark Johnson, corporate controller:

At the executive committee review meetings, we always review the past five years before starting on the forecast. We look at volume growth rates—sales growth adjusted for inflation—and discuss problems. Then, we compare growth rate against GNP growth. We keep currency translation out of it. We evaluate foreign subsidiaries in their own currency and compare growth against country-specific GNP. We are looking for market share by country. On almost any topic, we start with forecast versus past track record.

The committee never dictates or changes proposals—only challenges ideas. If it becomes clear to the individual presenting that the forecast is not good enough, only that person decides whether a revision is necessary. These discussions can be very frank and sometimes acrimonious. The result of the review may be agreement to present a revision at the next meeting, specific action items to be addressed, or personal feedback to David Clare.

This process cascades down the organization. Executive committee members review and challenge the proposals of company presidents. Company presidents review and challenge the proposals of their vice presidents.

Thursday, May 8, 1986—8 P.M.

Following the Codman & Shurtleff board meeting to discuss the June budget revision on the afternoon of Thursday, May 8 (described at the

beginning of the case), Roy Black, Chuck Dunn, Bob Dick, and Gus Fleites worked into the evening going over the list of active R&D projects. Their review focused on R&D projects that had been included in the original 1986 profit plan. They searched for projects that could be eliminated, due to changed market conditions or deferred to 1987, because of unplanned slowdowns. After discussing the progress and priority of each major project, Roy Black asked Chuck Dunn to have his staff work the next morning to go over the 40 active projects in detail and look for any savings that could be reflected in the June revision of the budget.

Friday, May 9, 1986—7:45 A.M.

In addition to Chuck Dunn, four people were seated around the table in the small conference room. Bob Sullivan and Gino Lombardo were program managers who reported to Bill Bailey, vice president of research. John Smith was manager, technical development, of the research facility in Southbridge that specialized in microscopes, fiberoptics, and light scopes. Gordon Thompson was the research accountant representing the finance department.

After coffee was delivered, Chuck closed the door and turned to the others.

Here's the situation. We are approximately two million short of the June Revision pretax profit target. As you know, our sales volume this year has been good—better than budget, in fact—but a few recent unpredictable events, including unfavorable product mix, and that large variance in the cost of specialty European products, are hurting our profit projection.

This morning, I want the four of you to look at our marginal spending projections to see where we stand. For example, we know that R&D underspent $200,000 in the first quarter. Therefore, I think we should take it as a starting point that R&D has $200,000 to give up from its '86 budget. I know that you can argue that this is just a timing difference; but you know as well as I do that, given the record of the R&D department, this money will probably not be spent this year.

It's time to get the hopes and dreams out of the R&D list. If we roll up our sleeves, we can probably find $400,000 without sacrificing either our 1986 objectives or our long-term growth.

We worked late last night looking at the project list and I think it can be done. I have to meet again today at 2:00 with the board and I want to be able to tell them that we can do it. That leaves it up to you to sift through these projects and find that money. We're looking for projects that have stalled and can be put on hold, and some belt-tightening on ongoing work.

After Chuck Dunn had left the group to its work, Gordon led the group through the list of projects. For each project, the group discussed spending to date, problems with the project, and spending needed for the remainder of the year. For each project, Gordon asked if anything could be cut and occasionally asked for points of clarification. On a separate sheet of paper, he kept track of the cuts to which the R&D managers had agreed. He turned to Project 23.

How about 23? You were planning on a pilot run of 100 prototypes this year. Should that still be included in the schedule?

Yes, the project is on track and looks promising. I suppose we could cut the run to 50 without sacrificing our objective. Would anyone have a problem with that?

It's a bad idea. That item has a very high material component and we have a devil of a time getting it at a reasonable price, even for a run of 100. If we cut the volume any more, the unit material cost will double.

OK, we'll stick with 100. How about the salesmen's samples? Is there anything there?

If we reduced the number of samples by a third, we could save $20,000. I suppose I could live with that, but I don't know how that will impact the marketing plan. Let me call Bob Dick and see what he thinks.

Gordon kept a running total of the expense reductions as the morning progressed. Dunn stopped in approximately once an hour to ask how the work was coming.

Friday, May 9—2 P.M.

Roy Black opened the meeting: "Gus, do you have the revised profit plan with the changes we've made? What does it look like?"

As Gus Fleites distributed copies of the budget document to the Codman & Shurtleff board, Chuck Dunn interjected, "Roy, at the moment, we have found $300,000 in R&D. That reflects adjusting our priority list for the rest of the year and cutting the fat out of ongoing projects. As for the last $100,000, we are still working on recasting the numbers to reflect what I call our 'project experience factor.' In other words, I think we can find that $100,000 by recognizing that our projects always take longer than originally planned. My people say that we've cut right to the bone on ongoing programs. The next round of cuts will have to be programs themselves, and we know we don't want to do that."

"We've discussed this before," responded Black, "and I think we all agree on the answer. In the past, we have authorized more projects than we can handle and have drawn the work out over too long a time. The way to go is fewer projects, sooner. It's the only thing that makes sense. Our mission is more focused now and should result in fewer projects. It's unfortunate that Bill Bailey is unavailable this week, but we are going to have to go ahead and make those decisions."

As Fleites briefed the board on the revised profit plan, Roy Black turned to Bob Dick to discuss inventory carrying costs. "Bob, don't you think that our inventory level is too high on some of our low turnover products? Wouldn't we be better to cut our inventory position and take a higher back order level? With 2,700 products, does it make sense to carry such a large inventory?"

Bob Dick nodded his head in agreement. "You're right, of course, our stocking charges are substantial and we could recover part of our shortfall if we could cut those expenses. But our first concern has to be our level of service to customers."

"Agreed. But perhaps there is room here to provide fast turnaround on a core of critical products and risk back orders on the high-specialty items. The 80/20 rule applies to most of our business. For example, say we offered top service for all our disposables and implants and flagged set-up products for new hospital construction in our catalog as '90-day delivery' or 'made to order.' We could then concentrate on the fastest possible turnaround for products where that is important and a slower delivery for products that are usually ordered well in advance in any case."

"I think that may be a good tactic. It won't help us for the June revision, but I'll have our market research people look at it and report back next month."

"Good," responded Black, "that just leaves our operating expenses. We need some donations from each of you. What I am suggesting is that each of you go back to your departments and think in terms of giving up 2 percent of your operating expenses. If everyone gives up 2 percent, this will give us $500,000. In my opinion, we have to bring the shortfall down to $900,000 before we can draw down part of our contingency fund. We're a long way from the end of the year and it's too early to start drawing down a major portion of the contingency."

Black turned to Bob Marlatt, vice president of human resources. "Bob, where do we stand on headcount projections?"

"The early retirement program is set to clear our corporate compensation department next month. That should yield 14 headcount reductions. Otherwise, no changes have been made in our projections through the end of the year. I think that we could all benefit from thinking about opportunities to reduce staff and pay overtime on an as-needed basis to compensate."

Black summed up the discussion:

Well, I think we all know what is needed. Chuck, keep working on that last $100,000. All of you should think in terms of giving up 2 percent on operating expenses and reducing noncritical headcount. That means that you will have to rank your activities and see what you can lose at the bottom end. Bob, I think that we should go back and look at our marketing plan again to see if we can make any changes to boost revenues.

We need to take a revised budget to Stolzer that is short by no more than $250,000. If necessary, I think we can live with drawing down the contingency to make up the difference.

So, your work is cut out for you. See you back here on Monday. Have a nice weekend! (laughter all around)

After the meeting, Roy Black reflected on what had transpired and his role as an operating manager in Johnson & Johnson:

These meetings are very important. We should always be thinking about such issues, but it is tough when you are constantly fighting fires. The Johnson & Johnson system forces us to stop and really look at where we have been and where we are going.

We know where the problems are. We face them every day. But these meetings force us to think about how we should respond and to look at both the upside and downside of changes in the business. They really get our creative juices flowing.

Some of our managers complain. They say that we are planning and budgeting all the time and that every little change means that they have to go back and rebudget the year and the second-year forecasts. There is also some concern that the financial focus may make us less innovative. But we try to manage this business for the long term. We avoid at all costs actions that will hurt us long term. I believe that Herb Stolzer is in complete agreement on that issue.

It is important to understand what decentralized management is all about. It is unequivocal accountability for what you do. And the Johnson & Johnson system provides that very well.

QUESTIONS

1. Evaluate the planning and control system in use at Johnson & Johnson. What are its strengths and weaknesses?

2. Over the last several years, *Fortune* magazine has polled the CEOs of the 250 largest U.S. companies to gather data on the management quality of major U.S. corporations. CEOs responding to the survey have repeatedly ranked Johnson & Johnson as one of the most innovative and well-managed firms in its industry. What role, if any, do you believe that J&J's management planning and control systems play in achieving (or hindering) innovation?

3. From information provided in the case, suggest how you would design a reward/incentive system for Roy Black and the Codman & Shurtleff board to capture maximum benefit from planning and control procedures. How would you deal with relating pay to performance in rapidly changing environments?

4. Roy Black states that decentralized management is "unequivocal accountability for what you do" (last paragraph). Do you agree with his statement?

Chapter 10

Management Control of Operations

This chapter describes the management control process during the period in which operations take place. The first part mentions management activities that directly or indirectly influence control and describes several types of information used in these activities. The second part describes certain relatively new techniques that are useful in the management control of operations—just-in-time, total quality control, computer integrated manufacturing, and decision support systems—and suggests how they influence the management control process.

INFORMATION USED IN CONTROL OF OPERATIONS

As pointed out in Chapter 2, managers, when they are acting as managers, do not personally do the work. Their function is to ensure that the work gets done efficiently and effectively. Managers literally do not "control costs." What managers do—or at least what they attempt to do—is to influence the actions of the people who are responsible for incurring the costs.

Thus, the management control of operations involves working through others. The manager selects the work force, makes sure they are adequately trained, decides where they fit best in the organization, provides advice and suggestions, solves problems, ensures that the environment in the work place is satisfactory, disciplines, resolves disputes within the responsibility center, approves proposed actions that employees are not authorized to take on their own authority, interacts with other managers to obtain their cooperation and to resolve problems when their activities impede the work of the responsibility center, and above all, seeks to create a climate that induces employees to work efficiently and effectively.

To carry on these activities, managers need information. In the following paragraphs we describe the nature of the several types of information that are useful in the control of operations. *Information* is used here in the broad sense of anything that reduces the user's uncertainty.

Informal Information

Much of the information that managers use is informal—that is, the manager receives it through observation, face-to-face conversations, telephone conversations, and meetings, as contrasted with information obtained from formal reports. Recently, the term *management by walking around* has come to signify the importance of this information. Because it is informal, this information is difficult to describe and categorize. We shall say simply that most managers find informal information more important than any formal report. (A manager who relies principally on the formal reports is the exception.)

Task Control Information

Most of the formal information that flows through an organization in its day-to-day operations is task control information. A production control system provides information that schedules the flow of material, labor, and other resources, so the correct end products in the correct quantities emerge at the end of the process. Systems also control procurement, payroll, storage, and other activities. Management control information is primarily a summary of this task control information. Because of the increasing speed of computers and their low cost per transaction, the principal problem of obtaining useful management information has become one of deciding what small fraction of the available information is worthwhile for the use of managers. Texts on cost accounting and on production and operations management are the best sources for the details of task control systems.

Budget Reports

The approved budget is the principal financial device for controlling the activities of responsibility centers, and a report that compares actual revenues and expenses with budgeted amounts is the principal financial report. Although an important guide to the responsibility center manager, the budget is only a guide. If the manager discovers a better way of achieving objectives, or if conditions change from those assumed in the budget, the manager should depart from the budget. Nevertheless, there is a presumption that the manager will operate in accordance with the budget unless there is good reason to do otherwise. (Certain departures, such as spending significantly more than the budget amount, require the approval of the manager's superior.) The manager's job is to achieve objectives; conformance with the budget is not desirable if the plan assumed in the budget turns out not to be the best way of achieving objectives. Adherence to the budget is not necessarily good, and departure from it is not necessarily bad.

Budget signals. Operating managers should understand which budget amounts are expected amounts, which are ceilings, and which are floors. Some items are ceilings (e.g., entertainment expense, dues and subscriptions, advertising); they signal that the manager is expected to spend *no more than* the budget amount without obtaining specific approval. Others are floors (e.g., training); they signal that the manager should spend *at least* the budget amount. Still others are general guides in the sense that spending is expected to be approximately, but not exactly, the amount stated. These distinctions may not be explicitly stated in the budget; nevertheless, managers should be aware of them. For items that are guides, managers should be aware of the permissible variation from the amount stated.

Moreover, achieving the bottom line is usually considered to be more important than performance with respect to individual revenue and expense items on the income statement. Except for the floor amounts, the spending that exceeds the budget amount for one item is not criticized if there is an offsetting underspending for other items.

Internal audit. Although the budget is important, if too much emphasis is placed on it, there is a danger that managers will manipulate the numbers to report the attainment of the budgeted profitability in the current period. One device for doing this is to record as revenue in the current period goods that have not actually been shipped to customers in that period. Conversely, if performance greatly exceeds the budget, a manager may not report certain revenue transactions in the belief that reporting a high profit may lead to an increase in the budget amount in the following year.[1]

One function of the internal audit organization is to detect such behaviors, and one function of the audit committee of the board of directors is to ensure that appropriate action is taken on internal audit reports. (This is, of course, in addition to the audit functions of ensuring that the controls are adequate to minimize theft and defalcation and of detecting such actions that do occur.) This is a difficult task and it is a sensitive one, because the improper actions often involve high-level managers.

---

[1] For a description of several actual instances, see *Dun's Business Month*, January 1983, pp. 44–47. Texts on internal auditing report other examples.

Nonfinancial Information

The budget and financial reports on performance provide ways of aggregating the overall effect of operating activities on profits. It translates individual indications of performance into money amounts that can be added and subtracted. Financial performance is the end result of managerial decisions and actions. Effective management control systems should not only be concerned with the ends but also with the process and means. Just as financial information provides knowledge of the ends, nonfinancial information provides insights relating to the means. Some nonfinancial information is reported routinely as a supplement to the financial amounts (e.g., sales volume in units, as well as in dollars). Others are reported because the information may require prompt action. These are termed *key variables* (also *strategic factors, key success factors, key result factors,* or *pulse points*).

Nature of key variables.
Key variables are variables that need to be watched especially closely, because they indicate factors that determine the success of the business, and an unfavorable change in any of them indicates the need for prompt action. In any business unit, there are relatively few of them; six is a good rule of thumb. They are best uncovered by discussions with persons who have acquired a deep understanding of the activities of the business unit through long experience with it. These persons know intuitively the important things to watch—and these are the key variables.

Managers have "pet" key variables that they have developed based on years of experience. In some cases, they are not able to explain why they believe these variables to be important; but if the key variable does the job of signaling the need for prompt management action, the management control system should accept it as satisfactory and use it to implement activities at all levels—from strategic planning to policies, programs, and business unit control.

A key variable has the following characteristics:

- It is *important* in explaining the success or failure of the business unit.
- It is *volatile* and can change quickly, often for reasons not controllable by the manager.
- A change is *unpredictable*.
- It is significant enough that *prompt action* is required when a change occurs.
- The variable can be *measured*, either directly or via a surrogate. For example, customers' *satisfaction* cannot be measured directly; but its surrogate, *number of sales returns*, can be a key variable.

In most business units, some aspect of sales volume is a key variable. Ideally, this is sales orders booked, because unexpected changes in this variable can have future repercussions throughout the business. Because bookings precede sales revenue, this is a better indicator than sales revenue itself; a decrease is a warning that adjustments may need to be made in marketing activities, in the hope of increasing sales or production activities or both, to change operating levels. There are many variations in this general idea. For example, in magazine publishing, the percentage of expiring subscriptions that become renewals is a key variable; a decrease indicates something wrong with promotional efforts or in the contents of the magazine itself. In a restaurant, it is the number of meals served, adjusted for the day of the week, season of the year, the weather, and possibly other factors.

Possible key variables. Following is a listing of variables that may be key variables. We emphasize that the number of key variables that are selected for a given business unit is much less than the number of items on this list.

The following key variables provide insights relating to decisions and actions in marketing:

- *Bookings,* as mentioned above.
- *Back orders,* an indication of an imbalance between sales and production, and of customer dissatisfaction.
- *Market share.* Unless the market share is watched closely, a deterioration in the unit's competitive position can be obscured by reported increases in sales volume that result from overall industry growth. (However, current data may not be available.)
- *Key account orders.* In business units that sell to retailers, the orders received from certain important accounts—large department stores, discount chains, supermarkets, mail-order houses—may provide an early indication of the success of the entire marketing strategy.

The following key variables can be used to monitor decisions and actions in production:

- *Capacity utilization.* Capacity utilization rates are especially key in businesses where fixed costs are high (e.g., paper, steel, aluminum manufacture). Similarly, in a professional organization, the percentage of the total available professional hours that is billed to clients, *sold time,* is a measure of fixed-resource utilization. In a hotel, *occupancy rate,* the percentage of rooms occupied each day, is the capacity utilization measure.
- *Quality.*
- *On-time delivery.*
- *Flexibility.*
- *Inventory turnover.*

Exhibit 10–1 lists key variables in certain industries, as an indication of the diversity found in practice.

Exception variables. In addition to the key variables that are reported routinely, certain items need to be reported when their behavior goes outside acceptable limits. They are similar to the warning lights on an airplane instrument panel, which go on when there is trouble, in contrast with the

EXHIBIT 10–1   Key Variables Used in Certain Industries

Industry	*Key Variable*
Accounting firm	Billed hours/available hours
Airline	Paid seats/capacity seats
	Fuel cost/miles flown
College	Acceptances/offers made
Counselling center	Number of appointments
	Number of cancellations
Dairy farming	Pounds of milk/number of cows
Electrical utility	KWH sold
Health clinic	Customer contacts per day
Hospital	Beds occupied/available beds
Hotel	Beds occupied/available beds
Leasing company	Number of transactions
Magazine	Renewals/subscription expired
Professional organization	Meeting attendance/total members
Railroad	Carloadings
Restaurant	Labor cost/revenue
	Raw food cost/revenue
Retail store	Gross margin by departments
Telephone company	Access minutes of use

Sources: Henry Wichmann, Jr., et al., "Key Variables as a Management Tool," *CMA Magazine*, March 1990, p. 23; The Conference Board, *Research Bulletin No. 206;* and personal experience.

instruments that are read constantly. Some cost elements in a factory, such as direct material and direct labor costs and certain elements of overhead costs, are examples. Normally, exception variables can be expected to behave as planned, and they need to be subject to management scrutiny only when they do not perform as expected. The management control system should be designed to identify and call attention to exception variables only when there is a significant deviation from the plan—*the exception principle*. If there were a scientific way of determining when a variation between budgeted and actual costs is significant, variances would provide such a signal automatically. Unfortunately, this is not the case; in the absence of such a measure, rules of thumb and management judgment identify these deviations, or *red flags*. By contrast, the current behavior of key variables is always reported and is carefully scrutinized by management.

Information Relationships

Exhibit 10–2 is a way of illustrating the relationships among reports and other information at various levels in an organization. Starting at the bottom, information about actual performance (i.e., task control information) is reported

EXHIBIT 10–2   The Performance Loops

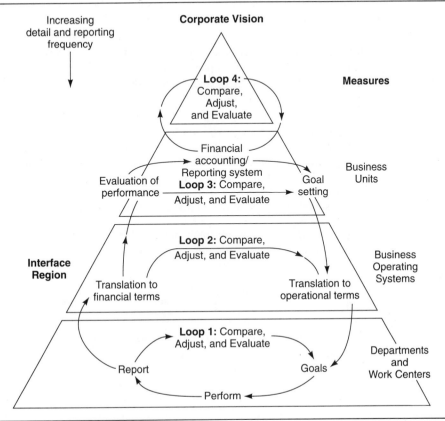

Source: C. J. McNair, Richard L. Lynch, and Kelvin F. Cross, "Do Financial and Nonfinancial Performance Measures Have to Agree?" *Management Accounting*, November 1990, p. 31.

and compared with objectives (here called "goals") that have been stated in operational, often nonfinancial terms. Summaries of these reports, translated to financial terms, is reported at the next higher level, and the process of evaluation is carried out at that level. At the business unit level, the same processes take place, using information that is even more summarized. Finally, at the apex of the diagram, overall performance is examined, and this may lead to a change in plans and, occasionally, to a change in goals.

RECENT DEVELOPMENTS

Beginning about 1980, the literature reported significant new developments in management control techniques. (Their actual use in leading companies probably began earlier.) In part, these were consequences of the development of vastly increased computer power. In part, they were a reaction in the United States to the realization that many companies in Japan, Germany, Sweden, and other European countries were manufacturing products at higher quality and lower cost than their American counterparts. A flood of books and articles have described the practices in these countries and the consequent changes in American production.[2] Companies that had access to companies in these countries studied their practices and adopted their production standards as benchmarks that they sought to match.

> **Example.** In the early 1980s, a team from Ford Motor Company studied Mazda, a Japanese auto maker in which Ford had a 25 percent interest. It concluded that Mazda could land a car in the United States (including shipping costs) at a cost that was $2,600 lower than the cost of a similar Ford. The study team analyzed each direct production and overhead activity. It concluded, for example, that Mazda produced almost three times as many cars per accounting employee as did Ford.[3]

Some of these practices and their implications for management control are described in the following sections.

JUST-IN-TIME

The equation for deciding on the economic order quantity, or the economic purchase quantity is:

$$EOQ = \sqrt{\frac{2 \times S \times R}{C \times K}}$$

This shows the optimum relationship between setup costs per setup or per purchase order (S), and the cost of carrying one unit in inventory (K), for a given annual number of units (R), and a given production cost per unit (C). In certain industries, application of what is called the "just-in-time" approach (also, "JIT") has resulted in significant decreases in setup costs or procurement costs and in a recognition that carrying costs per unit are often understated. These developments result in a decrease in the optimum lot size. At the extreme, the optimum lot size is one—that is, there is zero inventory, and goods are produced or ordered only when they are needed. Hence the name, *Just-in-Time*. This extreme case is not common, but the term is a catchy way of stating the direction in which lot size should be headed.

---

[2] Early articles were Robert H. Hayes and W. J. Abernathy, "Managing Our Way to Economic Decline," *Harvard Business Review*, July–August 1980; and Robert H. Hayes, "Why Japanese Factories Work," *Harvard Business Review*, July–August 1981.

[3] Patrick J. Keating and Stephen F. Jablonsky *Changing Roles of Financial Management* (Morristown, N.J.: Financial Executives Research Foundation, 1990), pp. 77–78.

Cycle Time Analysis

A tool in the analysis of inventory requirements is the equation for *cycle time:*

Cycle time = Processing time + Storage time + Movement time + Inspection time

Only the first element, processing time, adds value to the product. The other three elements do nothing to make the product more valuable. The analysis, therefore, attempts to identify all activities that do not directly add value to the product and to eliminate these activities, or at least reduce their cost. For example, the transportation of in-process work from one work station to another does not add value, so an effort is made to rearrange the location of work stations to minimize transportation costs.

Just-in-Time Techniques

Reducing buffer inventory.   The purpose of just-in-time is to ensure that every work station produces and delivers to the next work station the right items in the right quantity at the right time. If this purpose were achieved, there would be no need for buffer inventory. Buffer inventory exists partly because work stations break down and partly because they produce defective products. When these events happen, production in following work stations ceases unless there is an inventory that they can draw on. Indeed, it is said that the existence of buffer inventory causes work stations to be less concerned about producing good products than they should be. The amount of buffer inventory is reduced if steps are taken to minimize machine breakdown and improve quality.

Buffer inventory also results from bottlenecks. The thruput on a production process is no greater than the output of the slowest work station. If the output of one work station slows down, inventory tends to build up in earlier work stations unless steps are taken to stop their work temporarily, which is often expensive. This problem can be mitigated by balancing the output of the several work stations and thus eliminating bottlenecks, and by taking immediate action to stop production when a breakdown or other factor causes a bottleneck. Some companies install lights above each worker that can be lit when a worker cannot keep up the pace without making errors or when quality problems are detected. Some Japanese companies have designed systems where a yellow light signals that a worker has fallen behind and where a red light signals that some fundamental quality problem has surfaced and that the production line should be stopped; this results in immediate corrective action.

Decrease set-up costs.   With numerically controlled machine tools, setup involves simply inserting a new computer program into a machine. Thus, after the computer program has been created, the cost of setting up for the next and all succeeding lots is trivial. The existence of a computer program to control machines decreases the cost of providing replacement parts for discontinued models of appliances, automobiles, aircraft, and various other types of machines. Traditionally, when a model was discontinued, a sizable production run of each part that became obsolete was made (in some cases, enough to meet the total anticipated replacement demand for the obsolete part), and these parts were held in inventory awaiting orders for replacement. With numerically controlled machine tools, the need for this inventory is greatly reduced; orders for obsolete parts can be filled simply by inserting the proper computer program into the machine. For expensive parts with low replacement demand (which are found on ships, aircraft, heavy construction equipment, and weapons), some manufacturers now carry no replacement inventory at all.

Instead of regarding a setup as one operation, setup time also may be reduced by dividing the total time to set up into two categories: (1) that portion of the setup that must be done while the machine is stopped and (2) that portion that can be done while the machine is operating. The portion in the second category can be avoided by attending to those setup tasks that can be accomplished while the machine is running.

With smaller lot sizes, the scrap and rework costs resulting from a defect in a single production run is minimized. With lower inventory, storage space is decreased.

Decrease procurement costs.   Traditionally, procurement involved issuing requests for bids from many vendors, analyzing bids, placing an order with the best vendor, and receiving and inspecting the incoming goods. Some companies now reduce the cost of each of these components by establishing relationships with one to two vendors for each item. Instead of requesting bids for each order, they place orders with no more paperwork than notification of how many items are needed on a certain date (or, in some cases, on a certain hour each day). Instead of inspecting the incoming goods, they expect the vendor to inspect them and assure that all items are of acceptable quality.

Relation with customers.   The other side of this coin is the practice of establishing relationships with customers for automatic ordering. Some manufacturers have systems in which their salespersons automatically place orders from retailers or other customers, on the basis of preset formulas that determine reorder times and quantities; this reduces the customers' ordering costs (and also cements a relationship between the customers and the manufacturer.) Others provide retailers with bar-coded shelf slips for each item; the route sales-person uses a hand-held scanner to identify the item and enters an order when the supply falls below a preset level. Hospital supply houses provide computer programs to hospitals, which permit them to place orders without human intervention. These systems also provide rapid, accurate information to managers.

Example.   Using hand-held scanners, 10,000 Frito-Lay salespeople collect information on 100 Frito product lines in 400,000 stores, and summaries appear on PC computer screens available to all executives in easy-to-read charts. Not only is the information provided more rapidly but also the scanner eliminates a day of paperwork from each salesperson's weekly schedule, according to Michael H. Jordan, president of Frito's parent. He reports: "Two years ago if I asked how we did in Kansas City on July 4th weekend, I'd get five partial responses three weeks later. Now I get it the next day."[4]

Exhibit 10–3 shows the results of installing just-in-time systems in four of the early companies that did so. In every category, the improvements are striking.

Implications for Management Control

With some just-in-time systems, work-in-process inventory becomes so insignificant that it can be disregarded. The only inventories are for raw materials and finished goods; and issuances from raw materials inventory are charged directly to finished goods inventory. In effect, a job-cost system is transformed into a process-cost system with only one cost center; this results in a considerable reduction in recordkeeping. Recordkeeping is further reduced by the elimination of the tedious task of calculating "equivalent production," which is necessary to find work-in-process inventory amounts when the inventory in a cost center consists of partially completed products. Products are carried in inventory at standard costs, without tracing actual costs to individual products or batches of a product.

A just-in-time system focuses management attention on *time* in addition to the traditional focus on *cost*. A reduction in cycle time can lead to a reduction in cost. One of the effective ways to monitor progress on just-in-time is to compute the following ratio:

$$\frac{\text{Processing time}}{\text{Cycle time}}$$

Ideally, this ratio should be equal to 1. However, this goal cannot be achieved overnight. The just-in-time system is not a turnkey installation; rather, it is an evolutionary system that seeks to improve the manufacturing process continually. The firm can establish targets for this ratio and monitor progress against the targets. Best results can be obtained by emphasizing continuous improvements in this ratio toward the ideal number of 1.

Example. Wang Laboratories adopted the just-in-time philosophy in its manufacturing operations. To support its efforts on just-in-time, Wang designed a performance measurement system to track ongoing performance in four areas: quality, delivery,

---

[4] *Business Week*, July 2, 1990, p. 55.

EXHIBIT 10–3 Results of JIT for Four American Companies during 1982–84

Company (Division)	Labor Productivity Improvement	Setup Time Improvement	Inventory Reductions	Quality Improvements	Space Savings	Production Lead Times
Deere & Co.	Subassembly: 19–35% Welding: 7–38% Manufacturing: 10–20% Materials handling: 40%	Presses: 38–80% Shears: 45% Grinders: 44% Average: 45%	Raw steel: 40% Crank shafts: from 30 days to 3 days Average: 31%	Implemented: process control charting in 40% of operations	Significant	Significant
Black & Decker (consumer power tools)	Assembly: from 24 operators to 6 operators	Punching press: from 1 hr. to 1 min. Drastic in many areas	Turns: from 16 to 30	Reduced complaints in packaging: 98%	Significant	Products made in weekly lots: from 50% to 95%
Hewlett-Packard (consumer systems division)	Standard hours: from 87 hours to 39 hours	Not available	PC assembly inventory: from $675,000 to $190,000	Solder defects: from 5,000 defective parts per million (PPM) to 100 PPM Scrap: from $80,000 per month to $5,000	PC assembly: from 8,500 sq.ft. to 5,750 sq.ft.	PC assembly: from 15 days to 1.5 days
FMC	Direct labor productivity: 13%	Defense equipment group: 60–75% Automotive/ electrical: 80%	Turns: from 1.9 to 4.0	Customer service: from 88% to 98% Cost of quality: from 3.5% of sales to 2.1%	Automotive/ electrical: 25% Eliminated stockroom	Automotive/ electrical: from 1 month to 1 week

Source: Kiyoshi Suzaki, "Comparative Study of JIT/TQC Activities in Japanese and Western Companies," First World Congress of Production and Inventory Control, Vienna, Austria, 1985, pp. 63–66.

process time, and waste. Some illustrative measures in these four categories are given below:[5]

1. Quality (in all areas of the company, not just in manufacturing):
   a. Percent "plug and play" achieved in final assembly.
   b. Parts per thousand (or other denominator) accepted in purchased parts.
   c. Percentage of targets met in research and development.
2. Delivery:
   a. Percentage of end products delivered in a particular time frame as compared to the master production schedule.
   b. Percentage of all component parts delivered to an assembly line at the appropriate time.
   c. Percentage of engineering change orders completed on time.
   d. Percentage of customer orders delivered on time.
3. Process time:
   a. Manufacturing cycle time.
   b. Set up time in a work cell.
   c. Time to design a new product.
   d. Time to bring out a new product concept to the marketplace.
4. Waste:
   a. Yield losses in manufacturing.
   b. Rejected materials in purchasing.
   c. Inventory costs.
   d. Total costs associated with engineering changes.

TOTAL QUALITY CONTROL

The Japanese have led the way in greater attention to product quality. Efforts that they initiated and that have been adopted by many American companies are usually described under the rubric *total quality control*.

Consequences of Poor Quality

Product quality can mean either of two things: design quality or conformance quality. Design quality refers to the inherent value to the customer; Rolex watches have a higher quality than Timex watches. Conformance quality refers to adherence to specifications; if a product meets specifications, it is a quality product. Nonconformance means poor quality; it is measured by the proportion of defective products. The discussion here is limited to conformance quality.

According to total quality control, "zero defects" and "doing it right the first time" should be the firm's quality goals, because anything short of that will result in cost penalties. The earlier a defect is detected, the lower the cost penalty.

---

[5] Source: J. R. Dixon, A. J. Nanni, and T. E. Vollmann, *Breaking the Barriers: Measuring Performance for World Class Operations* (Homewood, Ill.: Dow-Jones Irwin, 1990).

Example. Richard W. Anderson, general manager of the Computer Systems Division of Hewlett-Packard, illustrates the damage a 2-cent resistor can do: "If you catch the resistor before it is used and throw it away, you lose 2 cents. If you don't find it until it has been soldered into a computer component, it may cost $10 to repair the part. If you don't catch the component until it is in a computer user's hands, the repair will cost hundreds of dollars. Indeed, if a $5,000 computer has to be repaired in the field, the expenses may exceed the manufacturing costs."[6]

In addition to these measurable quality costs, a defective product hurts the company's reputation significantly.

Total Quality Control Approach

The total quality control approach is summarized below under three headings: responsibility for quality, product design, and relation with suppliers.

Responsibility for quality. The traditional view was that quality problems start on the factory floor, that workers were primarily responsible for poor quality, and that the best way to control quality, therefore, was to "inspect quality into the product." This required a large quality control department. It also set up an adversarial relationship between manufacturing personnel, whose objective was to maximize output, and the quality control staff.

The total quality control view is that responsibility for quality should be shared by everyone in the organization; in fact, most of the quality problems arise before the product even reaches the factory floor. Edward Deming, after whom Japan's Deming Prize for quality is named, states that the production process can be separated into two parts: (1) the system, which is under the control of management; and (2) the workers, who are under their own control. He found that 85 percent of quality problems can be attributed to faulty systems and only 15 percent to the workers.[7] The system could be faulty for several reasons: designing a product that is difficult to manufacture, procuring inferior raw materials, providing inadequate equipment maintenance, permitting poor working conditions, and applying excessive pressure to maximize output. Since the system is designed by management, quality is primarily a management responsibility, he wrote.

Under total quality control, the philosophy is to "*build* quality into the product," rather than "*inspect* quality into the product." Errors in design, raw material procurement, and so on should be detected at the source. Workers should be held responsible for their own work and should not pass a defective unit on to the next work station; thus, the workers are their own inspectors. Instead of

---

[6] Quoted in Jeremy Main, "The Battle for Quality Begins," *Fortune,* December 29, 1980.

[7] E. W. Deming, *Quality, Productivity, and Competitive Position* (Cambridge, Mass.: MIT Center for Advanced Engineering Study, 1982).

inspecting product quality at the end of production, the quality control staff should monitor the production process and enable workers to "make the product right the first time."

Product design. Studies have shown that many quality problems originate with the design of the product. Some designers pay inadequate attention to the "manufacturability" of the product. Others include parts that are unique to the product, whereas parts that are common to several products would be satisfactory and are available at lower cost; or they design more separate parts than are necessary, which gives inadequate recognition to the cost involved in setting up machines for each part. Under total quality control, there has been an effort to have the designers work closely with production engineers who are familiar with the manufacturing problems.

Designing for manufacturability is one aspect of design. The other aspect of design is designing for marketability—that is, the quality of a product should be what the customer wants, not more. Some designers tend to "gold plate" an item—that is, they include features or specifications that do not lead to additional sales in the marketplace. This suggests the need for close cooperation between designers and marketing people.

Relation with suppliers. Total quality control involves a change in the traditional relationship with suppliers, as mentioned in the preceding section. Instead of awarding contracts to several suppliers, based primarily on which one bid the lowest price, there are only one or two suppliers for a given item; they are selected on the basis of quality and on-time delivery as well as on price, and long-term relationships are established with them. For example, the average General Motors Corporation assembly plant had 425 suppliers in 1989, compared with 800 in 1986.[8]

Implications for Management Control

Financial measures. Traditionally, conformance quality was measured by the cost of products scrapped or reworked. In the new approach, all the costs of doing things wrong are estimated and aggregated. The total cost of quality is a financial measure of conformance quality and is the sum of four elements:[9]

- *Prevention costs:* Costs incurred to make the product right the first time. It includes quality engineering, receiving inspection, preventive maintenance, the estimated fraction of manufacturing engineering and design engineering spent on prevention of defects, and quality training.

---

[8] General Motors 1989 annual report, p. 16.

[9] Based on the list used by Texas Instruments, as described in Harvard Business School case 9–189–029.

- *Appraisal costs:* Costs incurred to measure the level of quality in the manufacturing system. It includes the technical services laboratory, design analysis, and actual inspection costs.
- *Internal failure costs:* Costs incurred on products that are scrapped and on costs of reworking products.
- *External failure costs:* Costs associated with delivering a defective product to the customer. It includes cost of returns, marketing expenses dealing with returns, repair costs including travel time, and, in some cases, legal fees. (Conceptually, this cost should include the lost profit on sales that would have been made to dissatisfied customers, but this cost may be too difficult to estimate as a practical matter.)

Few companies collect these costs monthly; reports are usually prepared semiannually or annually. They highlight both the total cost associated with quality and areas on which special attention should be focused.

In some American companies, the total cost of bad quality represents as much as 25 percent of total cost, as contrasted with Japanese companies, where bad quality represents only 2.5 percent to 4 percent.[10] The opportunities for cost savings, therefore, are significant.

Classifying quality costs into the categories listed above provides an incentive for managers to spend money on prevention. This can result in more than offsetting savings in internal and external failure costs. One authority claims that, as a rough rule of thumb, for every dollar the firm spends on prevention the firm can eventually save $10 in appraisal and failure costs.[11]

The traditional reporting system can be a barrier to total quality control initiatives. Additional costs incurred in prevention reduce current profitability on a manager's performance report, but the resulting benefits in reducing failures may not be related to them; or, the benefits may not show up as reduced failure costs until later periods.

Total cost of quality measurement and reporting can yield several benefits.

- It is an attention-directing tool, especially when the firm conducts such an analysis for the first time. If the cost of poor quality is found to be a high percentage of total costs, senior management is likely to more easily adopt total quality control.
- Based on such reports, the company can develop specific programs to improve quality (and lower total costs) by understanding the interactive effects between prevention and failure costs.
- By preparing such a report once a year, the firm can keep the pressure on managers and workers to continue to work towards quality goals.

---

[10] H. P. Roth and W. J. Morse, "Let's Help Measure and Report Quality Costs," *Management Accounting*, August 1983, p. 51.

[11] P. B. Crosby, *Quality Is Free* (New York: McGraw-Hill, 1979).

Nonfinancial measures. In addition, companies collect nonfinancial information about quality, including the number of defective units delivered by each
supplier, number and frequency of late deliveries, number of parts in a product, percentage of common versus unique parts in a product, percentage yields,
first-pass yields (i.e., percentage of units finished without rework), scrap, rework, machine breakdowns, number and frequency of times that production
and delivery schedules were not met, number of employee suggestions, number
of customer complaints, level of customer satisfaction (obtained by questionnaire surveys), warranty claims, field service expenses, number and frequency
of product returns, and so on.

There are two major advantages with these nonfinancial measures: *(i)* most
of them can be reported almost on a daily basis and *(ii)* corrective actions can
be taken almost immediately. Thus, reporting performance on nonfinancial
measures is essential to provide continuous feedback to managers and workers
in their pursuit for better quality. In summary, total cost of quality reports give
the "big picture," and the individual nonfinancial measures provide details on
where troubles may be occurring.

Example. Don Davis, Jr., president of Allen-Bradley Company, wrote: "At Allen-
Bradley's Control-Communication Group, we produce solid state devices, such as
industrial computers. Their integrity depends on printed circuit boards. We developed
a quality-information system (QIS) that automates and organizes quality information.
It's an on-line, real-time data collection and measuring system. It's also a huge data
base of component, process, and workmanship information, which is generated by
incoming inspection, on-line testing, and field repair centers. QIS can tell us which
component from which vendor was placed on which board in which location. QIS
helps identify problems, redesign the product, and beat down the reject rates on a
part-by-part, component-by-component basis. It also helps us select vendors more
carefully and choose them on the basis of the best quality instead of the best price."[12]

COMPUTER INTEGRATED MANUFACTURING

In petroleum refineries, chemical processing and similar processing plants, materials and energy enter at the beginning and at various stages of the process,
and finished products emerge at the end, all without any hands-on labor. Human beings maintain the equipment, check the quality of the process, shut it
down if it gets out of control, and bring it back into control; that is all. Recent
developments have led to production control systems in other industries that
are close to those found in process manufacturing. These developments include
numerically controlled machine tools, robots, and computers that integrate the

---

[12] Don Davis, Jr. "Zero-Defects: Cornerstone for Computer Implementation," Working Paper
Series 90–3–3, Krannert School of Management, Purdue University, West Lafayette, Indiana,
March 1990.

work of other computers. These have resulted in decreases in the amount of hands-on labor, improvements in quality, reductions in paperwork, elimination of duplicate recordkeeping and of the annoying inconsistencies of data among the formerly separate systems, decreases in inventory, decreases in thruput time, and consequent decreases in production costs.

Complicated, expensive computer systems are now used to link together various stages of production. These go by such names (and acronyms) as Manufacturing Resource Planning II (MRP II),[13] synchronous manufacturing, Flexible Manufacturing System (FMS), Manufacturing Accounting and Production Information Control System (MAPICS II), Manufacturing Resource Planning and Execution System (MRPX), and Computer Aided Manufacturing–International (CAMI). These systems have the common characteristics that they incorporate into a single system, all, or at least several, of the formerly separate systems for product design, order processing, accounts receivable, payroll, accounts payable, inventory control, bills of materials, capacity planning, product scheduling, and product cost accounting. Such a system has the following components:

- *Computer-aided design (CAD):* use of computers to design new products, replacing the drafting that was traditionally done by hand, and improving the quality of the design effort. The completed designs are converted automatically to detailed instructions for the robots and the computers that control machine tools.
- *Computer-aided manufacturing (CAM):* use of computers to control machine tools and the flow of materials.
- *Numerically controlled machines:* machine tools that are programmed to perform a variety of functions (bore, drill, turn, and the like) on parts with different sizes and shapes.
- *Robots* (Also called "steel-collar workers"): programmable machines with "arms" and "legs" (and, in a few cases, "eyes") that perform a variety of repetitive tasks, such as welding, assembly, and painting.
- *Automated material handling systems:* storage and retrieval systems that locate materials, pick them, and move them from storage bins to the factory floor for processing and to shipping docks for delivery to customers. Also, automated guided vehicles that move materials automatically from one work station to the next.
- *Flexible manufacturing systems:* computer-controlled work stations. Often, the machines used for producing one product or product line are grouped together in a single location, or "cell."[14] They record financial and cost

---

[13] The "II" is used because this system has superseded an earlier system with the same initials; that system is now called MRP I.

[14] The General Motors Windsor Trim Plant is divided into nine "focused factories," one for each of the plant's nine product lines. Previously, the plant had been divided into four main areas: receiving, cutting, sewing, and shipping. Each focused factory has all these functions in one con-

accounting transactions, and they also incorporate the following types of transactions, which were previously handled separately.[15]

1. *Logistical:* order, execute, and confirm material movements.
2. *Balancing:* match supply of material, labor, and machines with demand.
3. *Quality:* validate that production is in conformance with specifications.
4. *Change:* update manufacturing information, engineering change orders, schedules, routings, standards, specifications, and bills of material.

Computer software can be purchased as a starting point in installing such a system, but it must be adapted to the company's specific requirements. This is an extremely complicated task, often requiring several years.

Example The General Motors C4 program is a computer-aided engineering, design, and manufacturing system to shorten vehicle production lead times and reduce production costs. In this system a new vehicle concept will become a computer image early in the design phase. The resulting data base will then be used to design the vehicle's individual parts and create the tooling that will eventually make those parts. As of 1990, General Motors had been working on this system for several years, but according to its 1990 annual report (page 13) it did not plan to implement the system until 1993, three or four years more.

These systems work especially well in companies that produce for inventory and in companies that process batches of raw materials (such as meat products). They are useful in some job shops (i.e., shops that produce to customers' orders); however, in some job shops each job is sufficiently different that the

---

EXHIBIT 10–4 Performance of FMS: Comparison between American and Japanese Machine Tool Companies

	American Companies	Japanese Companies
System development time	2.5–3.0 years	1.25–1.75 years
Number of different parts made	10	93
Average volume per part	1,727	258
Number of parts produced daily	88	120
Number of new parts introduced each year	1	22
Number of systems running untended	0	18
Ratio of actual cutting time to total available	52%	84%
Average cutting time per day	8.3 hours	20.2 hours

Source: R. Jaikumar, "Postindustrial Manufacturing," *Harvard Business Review,* November–December 1986, p. 70.

---

tiguous location. (Anthony A. Atkinson, "GM's Innovation for Performance," *CMA Magazine* [Canada], June 1990, pp. 10–13.)

[15] Jeffrey G. Miller and Thomas E. Vollman, "The Hidden Factory," *Harvard Business Review,* September–October 1985, pp. 143–46.

application of an integrated system is not worthwhile. Because of the cost involved in development and installation, an integrated system is not worthwhile in small companies. Less-expensive software that incorporates only some of the functions listed above is the solution in these companies. (As costs of all computer-related systems continue to decrease, they will become useful in an increasing number of companies.)

The initial introduction of these systems has been criticized as not taking full advantage of the Japanese approach.

> **Example.** With few exceptions, the flexible manufacturing systems (FMS) in the United States show an astonishing lack of flexibility. Compared with Japanese systems, those in U.S. plants produce an order-of-magnitude less variety of parts. Further, they cannot run untended for a whole shift, are not integrated with the rest of their factories, and are less reliable.
>
> The average number of parts made by an FMS in the United States was 10; in Japan the average was 93, almost 10 times greater. The U.S. companies used FMSs the wrong way for high-volume production of a few parts, rather than for high-variety production of many parts at a low cost per unit.[16]

Additional comparisons from the Jaikumar article are given in Exhibit 10–4.

Implications for Management Control

Increase in task control. Fully developed systems convert certain production activities that once required management control into task control. Managers no longer supervise employees; they are required only to handle unusual situations.

Better information. The systems provide information more accurately, more consistently, with more detail, and at much less cost than the systems they supersede. They provide better information about how costs actually behave. One of the problems is that they can provide so much information that systems designers have a difficult task in deciding on the relatively small fraction of the information reported to managers. The general solution is to provide a relatively small quantity of information routinely and permit the manager to access a large data base for other information he or she may wish.

> **Example.** In a manufacturing plant with about 2,000 people, data processing produced 41 reports each month, with 321 copies and 140,000 pages distributed to 63 persons. Interviews with managers showed that 32 of the reports were not used. Their

---

[16] Ramchandran Jaikumar, "Postindustrial Manufacturing," *Harvard Business Review,* November–December 1986, pp. 69–76.

elimination, and reducing the distribution of other reports, resulted in the removal of 300 filing cabinets from the shop floor and other savings amounting to $100,000 a year.[17]

More prompt information. Information is available shortly after the event occurs, in some cases practically instantaneously, with summary information available daily on the following morning, instead of several days after the end of the month.

Work teams. Some of these systems are built around work teams that are responsible for all the operations, or for some related operations, in the production of products. If work at a certain work station has broken down, workers at other work stations are expected to help solve the problem. Under the traditional system, a worker's performance was judged by his or her individual output; at the extreme, pay was based on the number of pieces produced. Under the newer systems, performance focuses on the performance of the whole team. Moreover, performance is not based on quantity alone; quality is also important. Rewards, therefore, tend to become group rewards, rather than individual rewards.

Business unit controllers. In Chapter 2, we described two extreme views of the role of the business unit controller: in some companies the business unit controller is primarily responsible to the business unit manager; in others, the business unit controller is primarily responsible to the corporate controller. One consequence of the team approach is that the former view is increasingly favored—that is, the business unit controller is primarily responsible for assisting the business unit manager in planning and controlling the unit's operations.

DECISION SUPPORT SYSTEMS

We use the term *decision support systems* to apply broadly to systems that aid decision making by providing the answers to a series of "what-if" questions. In this sense, they include expert systems, natural language systems, artificial intelligence systems, and knowledge-based systems, although technically there are some differences among these systems.

Nature of Decision Support Systems

A decision support system incorporates decision rules that presumably show how an expert in the area would solve a problem, given a certain set of facts; these are "if-then" rules. The decision maker answers a series of questions

---

[17] Donald A. J. Byrum, "The Right Way to Control Period Expense," *Management Accounting*, September 1990, p. 56.

EXHIBIT 10–5   Example of Decision Support Rules[*]

IF the part-group for the ordered part = 44
    AND the ordered part has been received
    AND the ordered part was ordered LESS THAN 2 weeks ago
    AND the ordered part HAS BEEN placed in inventory
THEN display on computer screen "inventory status is OK."

IF the part-group number for the ordered part = 44
    AND the ordered part has been received
    AND the ordered part was ordered MORE THAN 2 weeks ago
    AND the ordered part HAS NOT BEEN placed in inventory
THEN display on computer screen "inventory status is NOT OK.
    Call receiving room at extension 29."

IF the part-group number for the ordered part = 44
    AND the ordered part has NOT been received
    AND the ordered part was ordered MORE THAN 2 weeks ago
THEN display on computer screen "Follow up. Phone supplier."

[*] Adapted from Richard W. Kaiser, "Knowledge-Based Systems," *Journal of Accountancy,* January 1990, p. 114.

---

that provide the relevant information. These questions are asked in plain English—no knowledge of computer programming is required—which is why they are called "natural language" programs. The computer then suggests a course of action. They are called decision "support" systems, because they help the decision maker to arrive at a decision; but the decision maker is free to reject the computer's recommendation, or to modify it. This is not the case with computer programs that govern the actions of machines, that record and summarize accounting transactions, or that calculate ratios or other numbers from these summaries.

    Example.   A certain system aids the person responsible for order expediting. It contains hundreds of rules, three of which are shown in Exhibit 10–5. In this case, the "part" in question is one of those that are supposed to be delivered and entered in inventory within two weeks from the date the order was placed; all such parts are classified in Group 44. A frequently updated data base provides automatic answers to the "if" questions. If the part was ordered more than two weeks ago and has not been added to inventory, a potential problem exists. If the part has been received but not added to inventory, the user is told to follow up with the receiving department. If the part has not been received, the user is told to follow up with the vendor.

    Development of a sound set of decision rules is a time-consuming task. A moderately complicated set of rules may require the efforts of a sizable team for many months and involve interviews with experts, which takes more of their time than they are happy to give. Conflicting opinions from individual experts must be resolved. The initial output is a prototype, which is then tested in practice. This test may show that some of the rules are not sensible, and more months are then required to correct them. The effort is worthwhile only when the system will be used frequently by a number of people. Nevertheless, when a sound set of rules is established, the quality of decisions can be improved and there can be significant savings in the time required to make them.

In the late 1980s, the basic idea of decision support systems was improved by designing systems that modify the decision rules themselves, based on experience in using them.

Example.   Sears Mortgage Corporation is one of the 20 largest mortgage originators in the United States. Prior to the development of what it calls a "neural network system," the average underwriter could make a good loan decision in about 45 minutes. The system requires an input of 30 facts taken from the mortgage application. In one second, the neural network then makes a decision for about 65 percent of the loan applications that are routine and refers the other to an underwriter. Underwriters then spend their time on the 35 percent of borderline applications.

Initially, the rules were developed by testing 5,000 previously approved or rejected loan applications. The weight given to each of the 30 variables was modified by trial and error until the program produced results that matched those of the actual decisions. Subsequently, the computer will modify the weights given to the variables according to its actual experience in applying the rules. For example, although "frequency of move" is a criterion, the initial program did not allow for the fact that military personnel moved frequently, and the program penalized their applications unfairly. The computer discovered and allowed for this factor.[18]

Implications for Management Control

Decision support systems may reduce the need for managers—that is, they may convert management control activities into task control activities. They may also permit managers to spend a larger fraction of their time on other problems.

Decision support systems are a two-edged sword insofar as their users are concerned. On the one hand, they can increase the quality of decisions and reduce (or, in some cases, eliminate) the time required to make them. On the other hand, they permit many types of decisions to be made by the computer or by lower-level personnel and, thus, reduce the level of expertise required and, in some cases, eliminate jobs entirely.

---

[18] Condensed from J. Clarke Smith, executive vice president and chief financial officer of Sears Mortgage Corporation, "A Neural Network—Could It Work for You?" *Financial Executive*, May/June 1990, pp. 26–30.

PROBLEMS IN TERMINOLOGY

The terms *just-in-time, total quality control, zero defects,* and *zero setup times* used in the above sections can be misleading if taken literally. Rarely is it feasible to have zero work-in-process inventory, to control all aspects of quality, to have no defects at all, or to reduce setup times to zero. These terms were developed by consultants as attractive labels for the new techniques they were selling; and they are used by managers to suggest a goal, a direction in which to aim, even though this goal is not achievable. Zero inventory is attainable only in a completely automated process. In most real-world situations, materials do not always arrive just when they are needed, machines do break down, and human beings do make mistakes; inventory buffers are needed to provide for these eventualities. The number of defects can be reduced by better machine maintenance or by having standby machines available when one breaks down; but maintaining a machine so it never has a breakdown, or having standby machines that are idle most of the time, is usually too expensive. Similarly, better training of employees and other actions described above have costs. Also, insisting that suppliers furnish perfect materials means that inspection previously done by the company must now be done by the supplier, which involves a shift in costs. Moreover, some improvements are difficult to categorize.

> **Example.**   Several companies have improved their procedures for deciding whether to grant credit to customers. One company (or its consultant) may label the new system "just-in-time," because it reduces the interval between the credit application and the decision. Another may label it "total quality control," because it reduces clerical errors. A third may label it "decision support system," because it contains what-if rules that aid the decision maker.

In brief, a new system should not be accepted just because it has an impressive label, nor should it be rejected because its label promises more than it actually can achieve. Regardless of the label, it should be accepted if it improves the efficiency and effectiveness of operations.

SUMMARY

During the operating phase of management control, managers interact with other people. They use information from various sources. Perhaps the most important information is informal, obtained by "walking around." Formal sources include summaries of task control reports, financial information in budgets and reports comparing actual performance with budget, and nonfinancial information, especially reports on key results areas.

Recent developments have influenced the management control process. They include just-in-time systems, total quality control, computer integrated manufacturing, and decision support systems.

SUGGESTED ADDITIONAL READINGS

American Institute of Certified Public Accountants. *Introduction to Natural Language Processing*. New York: AICPA, 1988.

Crosby, Phillip B. *Quality is Free*. New York: McGraw-Hill, 1979.

Deming, W. Edwards. *Quality, Productivity, and Competitive Position*. Cambridge, Mass.: MIT Center for Advanced Engineering Study, 1982.

Dixon, J. R.; A. J. Nanni; and T. E. Vollmann. *The New Performance Challenge: Measuring Operations for World-Class Competition*. Homewood, Ill.: Dow Jones-Irwin, 1990.

Feigenbaum, A. V. *Total Quality Control: Engineering and Management*. New York: McGraw-Hill, 1983.

Garvin, David A. *Managing Quality: The Strategic and Competitive Edge*. New York: Free Press, 1988.

Hall, Robert W. *Zero Inventories*. Homewood, Ill.: Dow Jones-Irwin, 1983.

————— . *Attaining Manufacturing Excellence: Just-in-Time, Total Quality Control, Total People Involvement*. Homewood, Ill.: Dow Jones-Irwin, 1987.

Howell, Robert A., and Stephen R. Soucy. "Operating Controls in the New Manufacturing Environment." *Management Accounting*, October 1987, pp. 25–31.

Jaikumar, Ramchandran. "Postindustrial Manufacturing." *Harvard Business Review*, November–December 1986, pp. 69–76.

Juran, J. M., and F. M. Gryna, Jr. *Quality Planning and Analysis*. New York: McGraw-Hill, 1970.

Kaplan, Robert S. "Management Accounting for Advanced Technological Environments." *Science*, 25, August 1989, pp. 819–23.

————— . *Measures for Manufacturing Excellence*. Boston, Mass.: Harvard Business School, 1990.

Keating, Patrick J., and Stephen F. Jablonsky. *Changing Roles of Financial Management*. Morristown, N.J.: Financial Executives Research Foundation, 1990.

Lee, John Y. *Managerial Accounting Changes for the 1990s*. Reading, Mass.: Addison-Wesley, 1987.

Monden, Y. *Toyota Production System: Practical Approach to Production Management*. Atlanta, Ga.: Industrial Engineering and Management Press, 1983.

Roth, Harold P., and Wayne J. Morse. "Let's Help Measure and Report Quality Costs." *Management Accounting*, August 1983, pp. 50–53.

Schonberger, R. J. *World Class Manufacturing: The Lessons of Simplicity Applied*. New York: Free Press, 1986.

Turney, Peter B. B., ed. *Performance Excellence in Manufacturing and Service Organizations*. Sarasota, Fla.: American Accounting Association, 1990.

Case 10–1

Iron River Paper Mill*

Mike Lawson:

While our cost accounting reports don't show it, I would not be surprised if quality costs us about $40 million a year, or about 20 percent of sales.

Lawson, quality assurance department, Iron River Mill, arrived at this estimate of the cost of quality after studying the writings of Deming, Crosby, and Juran and attending a seminar on quality costing presented by Philip Crosby Associates. Lawson elaborated:

Crosby believes that the average U.S. manufacturing company spends about 20 percent of total sales on quality. According to Crosby, the cost of quality consists of two elements: the Price of Conformance (POC) and the Price of Non-Conformance (PONC). POC refers to what it costs to do things right the first time, while PONC refers to what it costs when you do things wrong. Typically, companies spend far more on non-conformance than on conformance. My experience at the Crosby seminar leads me to believe that we could maintain or even increase the overall quality of our product while spending a lot less money on quality, by worrying more about conformance, instead of spending so much time and money correcting non-conformance. But I can't prove this because we have not yet spent the time necessary to identify all the quality costs in this plant.

In June of 1988, management at the Iron River, Michigan, Paper Mill of Chippewa Paper Company, with the assistance of consultants provided by the corporate office, set out to do a cost of quality analysis (COQA) at the mill.

The Business Setting—"Groundwood Magazine Paper"

The Iron River mill, along with mills in Wisconsin and Maine, was part of the Magazine Papers Division of Chippewa. These mills made papers that were typically used for printing magazines (e.g., *Time* or *Newsweek*) and retail catalogs (e.g., the Sears and J. C. Penney catalogs).

Chippewa's magazine paper was used by publishers of magazines and catalogs because it met three important criteria: low cost, light weight, and good print quality. Paper comprised approximately 50 percent of the total cost of producing a magazine or catalog. As a result, it was important to the magazine publishers to keep the cost of paper as low as possible.

Customers

Iron River's customers fell into two classes, printers and publishers. Printers bought paper for publishers who had not specified the source of the paper to be used (although they probably did specify the weight and type of paper). Often, however, the publisher (especially large-volume publishers) bought the paper to be used and had it shipped directly to the printer.

Most customers, whether printer or publisher, bought paper from multiple sources. This is because most customers had very strict printing

* This case was prepared and copyrighted by Scott Keating and John K. Shank, The Amos Tuck School of Business Administration, Dartmouth College.

deadlines, and multiple sourcing was a form of guarantee that paper will be available when it is needed. In addition, printers wanted to have paper from several sources on hand in case the paper from one of the sources developed printing problems on the printing presses (a common occurrence). In many ways this customer-supplier relationship was still the old-style adversarial game.

Two types of printing processes dominate magazine and catalog printing in 1988—offset printing and rotogravure printing. In offset printing, the image to be printed is etched onto a metal plate, which is wrapped around a steel cylinder (a roll). The ink is picked up on the plate and then transferred from the plate to the "blanket" (another roller). The ink is then transferred from the blanket onto the paper. In rotogravure printing, the ink is transferred directly from an etched impression cylinder onto the paper. Rotogravure printing produces a higher-quality print image but is much more expensive than offset. Rotogravure printing requires very long print runs to amortize the extra costs of the etched rolls. The magazine industry uses mostly offset printers. Although these printers generally prefer coated paper, some magazines, especially magazines for European distribution, now use a super-calendered uncoated sheet. The market for such paper in the United States is about 4 million tons per year.

Paper prices can vary widely. For example, prices for Iron River's paper rose on average by about 20 percent from May of 1987 (a low point in the business cycle) to May of 1988 (a high point). Some individual prices rose more than 50 percent.

For the most part, makers of magazine papers view it as a commodity. They believe that customers choose suppliers largely on the basis of price. Others believe that even though it is a large-volume business, it is nevertheless possible to compete on other bases than price (e.g., quality, flexibility, or service).

Regardless of their overall view, all magazine papers manufacturers recognize that there are important quality and service elements to the business.

Quality

In this business, quality had two elements: runability and printability. *Runability* describes the degree to which paper will run through a printing press without problems. Problems, when they occur, usually result in breaks or bursts in the roll of paper as it goes through the printing press. When the roll, or "web," breaks, the printer must shut down the press for about 30 minutes to clear out the torn paper, and refeed the roll through the press. Each web break represents printer downtime, which is very expensive. "Zero defects" is not achieved by any paper manufacturer and "web breaks" is a constant problem for printers. Three breaks for every 100 rolls used is a typical industry standard.

Printability, discussed above, describes the degree to which a sheet of paper will provide a good-quality printed page. Printability is typically measured by such specifications as gloss, smoothness, opacity, brightness, and porosity. It is a much more subjective measure than runability.

It was a widely held view in the industry that runability plays a very large role in the selection of a paper by a customer. If a paper runs well on the press, a printer will do almost anything to get it to print well. But if it does not run well—that is, it has a lot of breaks—a printer will reject it no matter how good the print quality.

Service

For the most part, "service" represented the ability of a supplier to provide timely delivery of paper. Most customers had very strict deadlines to meet. For example, *Time* magazine did not believe it could afford to have its weekly issue arrive on the newsstands even half a day late. As a result, customers put considerable value on a manufacturer's ability to provide on-time delivery of paper to the printer.

Similarly, customers also valued supplier loyalty, even though they wanted loyalty from *several* suppliers. The paper industry was marked by periods of paper shortages. Just as customers could not afford to have paper arrive late, they could not afford to have no paper arrive at all because of a shortage. Customers put considerable value on those suppliers who will guarantee paper availability even in periods of short paper supply.

Iron River Mill

The paper mill in Iron River, Michigan, was built in 1906 and was originally the Iron River Pulp and Paper Company. The mill was acquired by the Iroquois Paper Company in 1946. Iroquois was acquired by Chippewa in 1980.

The mill had a capacity of 800 tons per day and employed 632 people (511 hourly workers and 121 salaried). In 1987, sales volume at the mill exceeded 290,000 tons, with a total sales value of $220 million.

The mill had three paper machines. Machines #1 and #2 date to 1906, when the mill was first built (although they have been rebuilt on numerous occasions over the past 80 years), and make uncoated paper. Machine #3 was completed in 1982 and makes coated paper.

The mill was organized into 22 departments, each of which reports to one of 12 managers who, in turn, report to the mill manager. Of the 22 departments, 10 are directly involved in the paper-making process; the remaining 12 are support departments (e.g., accounting, engineering, maintenance, and so on).

The mill was a typical paper mill. Timber was purchased, debarked, and cut into small (approximately 1–2 inches) chips. The chips were converted into pulp using a thermo-mechanical process. After various chemicals were added, the pulp went to one of the three paper machines, where it was converted into paper and, on #3 machine, then coated. After the paper machine,

the paper went through various finishing processes (e.g., calendering) before it was cut into rolls of specific width to meet customers orders.

Exhibit 1 provides a schematic of the papermaking process at Iron River.

Quality and Cost Accounting at the Mill

Ken Gibson, the mill manager at Iron River, described the mill's quality position:

> I don't think our quality, or the cost of it, is very much different from the rest of the industry. About four years ago, the mill was the leader in the industry in terms of quality. Since then, our position has slipped a little, not because our quality has declined but because our competitors' quality has increased while ours has not.

Ward Dana, supervisor of the cost accounting department, commented on cost accounting at the mill:

> Our cost accounting system is very conventional. While we have identified some costs at the mill as quality costs, we certainly do not track quality costs in the depth advocated by the quality gurus like Crosby.
>
> The mill does not have any quality cost reports per se. Quality costs are not routinely tracked and documented. Further, the cost accounting system at the mill does not provide for easy cost of quality analysis. COQ analysis must be done independently of the cost accounting system.

Some of the larger quality costs identified by the mill's cost accounting system include: paper shrinkage (i.e., the difference between the amount of paper made and the amount actually shipped to customers), defective materials, quality-related machine downtime, quality-related capital investments, and the quality assurance department. Dana estimated that the spending in these areas amounted to approximately $20–25 million per year.

Neal Evers, comptroller of the mill, commented on the mill's quality costs:

> I think there are a lot of quality costs out there which we are missing. For example, 60 percent of

Exhibit 1   Iron River Paper-Making Process Flow

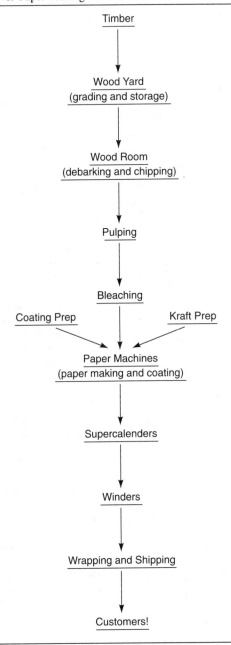

the daily production meetings, attended by our top 15 or so managers, are consumed by quality-related issues. That's equivalent to about one man-day of top management time every day. I'm sure there are other quality costs like that one that are hard to see, unless you are really looking for them.

A New Approach to Costing Quality

Neal Evers described how the recent quality costing initiative came about:

Mike Lawson had been arguing for a while that our cost accounting system was not identifying all of the quality costs. Mike believed, from what he had learned at the Crosby quality program, that we might change the way we run the mill if we knew what quality costs we were really incurring. The problem was that we did not have the time to go through the exercise of more accurately measuring quality costs. So when the head office offered us consultants to do the work, we jumped at the opportunity.

Ward Dana described the process which the consultants followed in measuring the quality costs at the mill:

The consultants weren't experts in the paper industry, so they spent some time understanding how paper was made and how the mill operated. They interviewed the head of the departments at the mill, first to understand the role which that department played in making the paper, and second, to get an idea of how each department contributed to the quality of our product.

Once they had identified the elements of the total quality cost of the mill, they had to figure out how much each of those elements cost. Each of our departments is followed by a cost analyst in the cost accounting department. The consultants met with the analysts to try to put a dollar figure on each of the quality costs which they had identified. After we agreed on what to include in quality costs, we put a value on it.

This was no easy task. For example, the consultants had reasoned that the cost of the softwood debarker operator in the woodroom is a quality cost since the operator's major responsibility was to look for logs which were not perfectly debarked.

They not only wanted to include the wages and benefits of the operators but also the cost of the equipment which is used to accept or reject a log after debarking. To get an accurate estimate of the cost, we had to include not only the cost of the equipment but also a portion of the cost of the building (based on the amount of floor space taken up by the equipment), electricity consumed, and a portion of insurance and other expenses. Our cost accounting system is not designed to provide that information, so it took some time getting it.

Sometimes we had to make estimates. For example, some of the maintenance department's time is devoted to routine maintenance of facilities which is unrelated to quality, while other time is clearly quality-related. While we used as much data as we could in accurately apportioning the cost of the department to quality, we invariably had to estimate some of it. Nevertheless, I am confident that the numbers are reasonable, given the purpose of the exercise.

In addition to the departments at the mill, the consultants examined the quality costs incurred at the division headquarters. For example, there is a technical service department which deals with customer complaints. They had to figure out how much of that department's time was spent responding to complaints about Iron River paper.

Neal Evers described the interaction between the consultants and the mill staff during the process of identifying and quantifying quality costs:

We didn't always agree with the costs which the consultants were calling quality costs. For example, they wanted to include all four of the sets of centrifugal cleaners in the pulp mill as quality cost. It is true that these Bauer cleaners are designed to remove impurities from the pulp, and that, if the wood supplied included no impurities, then there would be no need for the cleaners. But, no one in their right mind would build a mill without at least one series of cleaners. We resolved the problem by classifying one set of the cleaners as an inspection cost and the other three as internal failure cost.

Dana described a similar incident:

We also had a lively debate over the maintenance department. Originally, the consultants felt that all of the maintenance department was a quality cost since you have to maintain your equipment in order to make a good quality product. But that isn't the only reason for maintenance. Maintenance also contributes to productivity and efficiency. The consultants ultimately agreed, and we included only those maintenance costs which were directly related to quality.

The study revealed that the total cost of quality at the mill was approximately $43 million. Of that amount, $7.6 million were conformance costs (i.e., prevention and inspection) and $35.3 million were nonconformance costs (i.e., internal and external failure). Exhibits 2 and 3 provide a breakdown, by department, of these costs.

Neal Evers reflected upon the results of the study:

For the most part, the study confirmed what we had been thinking. Forty-three million dollars is a lot to be spending on quality, especially when most of that spending is on bad-quality paper.

One of the concerns I have, however, is how useful these numbers are. They would be good if we were building a new mill, because we would have total flexibility in deciding how to do things. But it isn't clear to me how to use them if what we are trying to do is to run an existing mill more effectively.

Nevertheless, the study does provide some valuable insights. For example, more than 80 percent of our quality costs are related to off-quality paper. If we could reduce the amount of off-quality paper we are producing, by concentrating on up-front prevention and inspection, we might be able to significantly reduce the amount of off-quality paper we make. Currently, we don't look at the detail behind shrinkage to know where the specific problems are.

We have already had some success, however. Not too long ago, we discovered that the kraft pulp we were using contained a lot of "sieve cells," and that these cells were causing holes in our paper. We were able to reduce the sieve cell content in the pulp, thereby reducing the amount of defective paper. Conservative estimates suggested that we save $500,000 a year as a result of this.

Another area where we've made changes is in process control. There is a real advantage to knowing when you *are about to make* bad paper, versus knowing when you *are making,* or *have just made,* bad paper. By installing on-line sensors, such as color monitors and moisture content monitors at the wet end of the machine, rather than the dry end, we've substantially reduced our quality costs. But there is clearly room for more improvement.

Arnie Pogue, quality assurance manager, commented on potential improvements:

We have a lot of on-line measurement equipment, but we could still use more. For example, we currently measure the acidity in the headbox by taking periodic samples. A lot of time can elapse before we know that the acidity has changed, and acidity changes can result in bad paper. If we had an on-line sensor, we could react a lot sooner to correct the problem, and, as a result, reduce our "broke" [bad paper].

One of the larger costs identified in the study was the external failure cost. On this, Ken Gibson, the mill manager commented:

A lot of people might not agree with the $9 million identified as a cost of sending defective paper to customers, but I suspect it is pretty accurate. In the early 70s, I was at the Searsport [Maine] mill, which was regarded as the best quality producer of magazine papers. When the market for paper went bad, every mill except Searsport had to shut down for some time because there was not enough demand. Searsport operated at 100 percent capacity throughout, largely, I believe, because of the higher quality of their paper. Clearly, quality can really affect your customer goodwill.

A comment from the head buyer of one of Iron River's largest customers confirms Gibson's position. When he heard that the mill was doing a quality cost study, the buyer said, "That's the biggest waste of time and money I've ever heard of. Who cares what it cost to make bad paper? The point is really to make sure you spend the money to make good paper, because without quality you won't have any customers, and without customers, you won't have any sales."

EXHIBIT 2 Results of Cost of Quality Analysis

Mill Department	Prevention	Inspection	Internal Failure	External Failure	Total COQ	Total Dept.	COQ as percent of Dept.
Wood yard	0	4,930	0	0	4,930	626,123	0.8%
Wood room	0	269,000	594,174	0	863,174	2,589,374	33.3
TMP	0	424,537	419,757	0	844,294	13,088,991	6.5
Bleach plant	0	63,500	0	0	63,500	976,906	6.5
Kraft prep.	0	17,200	0	0	17,200	1,740,904	1.0
Coating prep.	0	206,650	0	0	206,650	1,640,908	12.6
Paper machines	151,460	481,481	1,674,290	0	2,307,231	23,722,355	9.7
Supercalenders and winders	408,600	35,784	294,785	0	739,169	8,691,187	8.5
Salvage winders	0	0	521,804	0	521,804	521,804	100.0
Finishing and shipping	0	134,508	0	0	134,508	2,573,343	5.2
Production control	0	0	0	0	0	363,096	0.0
Utilities	32,772	0	0	0	32,772	13,294,592	0.2
Accounting	0	118,311	0	0	118,311	473,246	25.0
Data processing	0	48,789	0	0	48,789	227,675	21.4
Technical	477,001	2,031,386	0	0	2,508,387	2,508,387	100.0
Quality control	0	99,362	0	0	99,362	99,362	100.0
Engineering	122,855	0	0	0	122,855	491,442	25.0
Human resources	41,379	0	0	0	41,379	897,535	4.6
—Lost work time	251,356	0	0	0	251,356		
General mill	0	0	90,000	0	90,000	4,091,906	2.2
Mill management	132,715	0	0	0	132,715	530,860	25.0
Materials	126,913	0	0	0	126,913	797,268	15.9
Process control	60,000	0	0	0	60,000	60,000	100.0
Accounting for broke	0	0	16,077,423	0	16,077,423		
Downtime	1,632,168	0	4,954,504	0	6,586,672		
Returns and claims	0	0	0	1,276,900	1,276,900		
Goodwill/lost sales	0	0	0	9,000,000	9,000,000		
Raw Materials:							
Pulpwood						8,528,078	
Kraft pulp						42,239,000	
Chemicals and other						27,112,000	
Total mill cost	3,437,219	3,935,438	24,626,737	10,276,900	42,276,294	157,886,342	26.8%
Division expenses:							
Timberlands	236,430	1,305	0	0	237,735	358,228	66.4
Customer technical services	0	0	0	250,000	250,000		
Marketing and sales	0	0	0	150,000	150,000		
Total division expenses	236,430	1,305	0	400,000	637,735		
Total cost of quality	3,673,649	3,936,743	24,626,737	10,676,900	42,914,029		

EXHIBIT 3 COQ Analysis Methodology

General Procedure

When any work station or machine was identified as a cost of quality, the COQ figure was obtained by including the direct and indirect costs, including depreciation, insurance, and taxes.

Examples are:

Cost	Type	Amount	Rationale
Wood room:			
Debarker operator	Inspection	159,000	Operator's role is to inspect for proper debarking.
Debarker rework	Internal failure	110,880	Every rejected log must be sent through debarker again.
Chip screens	Inspection	110,000	Checks for proper chip size.
Chip rework	Internal failure	25,848	Oversized chips must be rechipped.
Chip reject	Internal failure	458,246	Undersized chips are rejected. Cost includes cost of rejected chips.
		863,174	
Paper machines:			
Pulp rejection	Internal failure	126,198	Pulp rejected for improper consistency.
Monitoring equipment	Inspection	481,481	Consistency monitor, scanner, hole detector.
Wet end monitoring	Prevention	151,460	Make good paper the first time.
Rejection equipment	Internal failure	1,548,092	Cleaners, save all system, rereelers, broke chest, and broke pulper.
		2,307,231	
Accounting:			
Cost reporting	Inspection	118,311	Based on portion of department's time spent on quality analysis.
Data processing	Inspection	48,789	Based on portion of department's time (personnel and computer time) spent on quality reporting.
Technical:			
Process engineers	Prevention	477,001	Responsible for maintaining paper quality.
Technical staff	Inspection	2,031,386	Performs lab tests on in-process and finished paper.
Quality control	Inspection	99,362	Liaison between customers and mill for quality problems.
Engineering	Prevention	122,855	Portion of department's time spent on preparing and reviewing quality improvement projects.
Human Resources:			
Training	Prevention	292,735	Portion of training time devoted to quality training. Includes cost of personnel (salaried and hourly) hours spent in quality training.

Goodwill/Lost Sales Cost ($9 million)

An explanation of the calculation of this large, important, and very "soft" number is as follows:

1. We compared the product mix in May '87 (a bad time in the industry) to May '88 (a good time). We asked the question: "What if in May '87 we could have had a product mix like that of May '88? How much different would our profit have been?"

EXHIBIT 3 *(continued)*

---

2. To do the analysis, we looked at the profit margins of the different paper grades.

	May '87	
Margin	*Percent of Maximum Margin*	*Percent of Total Paper Production*
$195	100%	1%
167	86	3
110	56	66
95	49	6
35	18	24
		100%

	May '88	
Margin	*Percent of Maximum Margin*	*Percent of Total Paper Production*
$237	100%	1%
176	74	4
164	69	93
136	57	2
		100%

3. We then said: "What if in May '87 our production was distributed among the different profit margins like May '88?"

Percent of Maximum Margin (May '88 distribution)	*Percent of Total Production (May '88 distribution)*	*Margin (using May '87 margins)*
100%	1%	$195
74	4	144 (74% of $195)
69	93	135
57	2	111
	100%	

Weighted Average

1%	×	$195	=	$ 1.95
4%	×	144	=	5.79
93%	×	135	=	125.49
2%	×	111	=	2.24
				$135.47

EXHIBIT 3 *(concluded)*

4. What would be the profit impact?

Actual avg. margin May '87	=	93.66	
Theoretical	=	135.47	
Difference		$41.81	per ton
Production		5,945	tons
Total difference		$248,560	per month
or		$2,982,725	per year for PMs 1 and 2

5. Similar analysis for PM #3 yields:

Actual margin	=	$61.00	
Theoretical	=	$87.80	
Difference		$26.84	per ton
Production		17,195	tons
Total difference		461,513	per month
or		$5,538,166	per year

6. Combined total is $3.0 million + $5.5 million, rounded to $9.0 million for the report.

Another of Chippewa's large customers commented on the potential advantage of good quality paper:

Chippewa might not see the benefits of quality immediately, but there would certainly be benefits. For example, if Chippewa were considering building a new mill, and if they were showing a consistent record of good quality paper, then we might consider committing to buy a certain portion of the new mill's output. That sort of commitment would be good enough to take to the bank.

Neal Evers continued:

One of the more intangible benefits of a study like this is that it changes the way we think about quality. The resource allocation process at Chippewa provides a good example of this. One of the classes of applications for capital spending [ARA] is a quality improvement ARA. About one third of the total number of ARAs which we process every year are quality improvement ARAs. Interestingly, a "hurdle rate" is not applied to this type of project. If we are going to start following the cost of quality, then maybe we should start doing investment

return analysis on quality-improvement projects. On the other hand, perhaps we should adopt the policy of "quality at any cost," and therefore maintain the status quo.

But the big question is, Where do we go from here? The usefulness of a study like this is that it identifies the problem areas so that we know where to get maximum return for our efforts.

Ken Gibson also commented on the practical applications of the study:

The big point of this study for me is that we have to build quality in our paper in the first place instead of inspecting it after it has been made. To do that, however, you have to give considerable responsibility to the people lower down in the mill who can actually control the quality of the paper as it is being made. Interestingly, we've been recently working on a participative management program at Chippewa, and it makes the exact same point: Give the decision-making power to the people who can most effectively use it to impact the mill's performance.

But we're not ready to do that yet for two reasons. First, many of our workers are not sufficiently trained yet to be able to make effective decisions. Second, our managers are not yet ready to give up some of the decision-making power which has traditionally been theirs. So we have to put some of the possible projects which come out of this study on hold until we get people prepared, and that's going to take time.

A lot of people think that our problem is that we do not understand the paper-making process suffi-ciently to be able to build in consistently better quality. I disagree. We already know much more about the process than we make use of. True, we still have a lot to learn, but we could make a lot of progress just by using more effectively what we already know. Maybe generating accounting reports that explicitly show quality costs is a good way to help keep our attention focussed on this issue.

QUESTIONS

1. Be prepared to describe the methodology used by Iron River mill to quantify cost of quality.
2. How can senior management use Exhibits 2 and 3 to make better decisions?
3. How can senior management use Exhibits 2 and 3 to develop an evaluation system to track performance on quality?
4. "COQ analysis is likely to become an important on-going management control tool in more and more American companies in future years." Comment critically.
5. "COQ analysis is much more a strategic positioning tool than a management control tool." Comment critically.
6. "COQ analysis is quantification futilely searching for a rationale." Comment critically.

Case 10–2
Motorola Inc.*

The controller of Motorola's newly formed Application Specific Integrated Circuit (ASIC) Division sensed that he and his staff could play a significant part in determining the success of what promised to be an important new business. Not only was his division competing in a new and dynamic market with unique requirements but it also was radically changing the way in which it delivered its product. These circumstances led the controller to reassess the most basic issues involved in designing a management accounting system: What should be measured? How should it be measured? Who should measure it? and, For whom should it be measured?

The Company

Founded in 1928, Motorola soon became widely known for its radios and other consumer electrical and electronic products. By the 1960s, it sold semiconductor products, communications equipment, and components to consumers, industrial companies, and the military throughout the world.

Headquartered in Schaumburg, Illinois, in 1984, Motorola achieved over $5.5 billion in sales, employed over 99,000 people, and spent $411 million in research and development. It was one of the few American companies that marketed a wide range of electronic products, from highly sophisticated integrated circuits to consumer electronic products.

Organization

The company was organized along product and technology lines. Each business unit was structured as a sector, group, or division, depending on size.

The Semiconductor Products Sector (SPS) was headquartered in Phoenix, Arizona; sales in 1984 were over $2.2 billion, which was 39 percent of Motorola's net sales. The sector sold its products worldwide to original equipment manufacturers through its own sales force. Semiconductor products are subject to rapid changes in technology. Accordingly, SPS maintained an extensive research and development program in advanced semiconductor technology.

Formation of the ASIC Division

In the early 1980s, the Semiconductor Products Sector produced a large line of both discrete semiconductor components and integrated circuits. Integrated circuits (ICs) can be thought of (at least functionally) as miniature circuit boards. For example, the designer of a video cassette recorder could replace a $12'' \times 12''$ circuit board and all its individual components with a single $1'' \times 1''$ integrated circuit on a silicon chip, saving space and reducing power consumption. By 1985, worldwide sales of integrated circuits reached $20.2 billion.

Among integrated circuit manufacturers, Motorola was widely known for its design and process expertise, and it became a leader in the increasingly popular semicustom integrated circuits.

Semicustom integrated circuits are designed using predetermined functional blocks. In the early 1980s, Motorola produced a version of semi-

* This case was prepared and copyrighted by Joseph Fisher and Steve Knight, The Amos Tuck School of Business Administration, Dartmouth College.

custom ICs called "gate arrays". Each "gate" on a gate array was a transistor that performed a single operation. These were interconnected to produce the desired set of functions. One chip could contain a thousand or more gates. Each was designed to meet the requirements of a specific customer. Gate array customizations were relatively cheap and quick to manufacture, and they were designed by computer-aided design systems. By 1984, the market for gate arrays had grown to $455 million. Sales in 1985 were expected to be $740 million, and the market was estimated to reach $1.4 billion in sales annually by 1990. The high-performance gate array market totaled $90 million in 1984. Forecasts stated that the market should grow to $600 million by 1990.

Motorola manufactured high-performance gate arrays using two different semiconductor technologies: (1) bipolar and (2) complementary metal-oxide semiconductor (CMOS). Bipolar technology provides increased speeds at which the circuit could perform but at the cost of increased power consumption (and increased difficulty in meeting cooling requirements) when compared to CMOS technology. For this reason, the demand for CMOS gate arrays was expected to grow more rapidly than that for bipolar gate arrays. In 1984, CMOS captured 40 percent of the market. This was expected to increase to 70 percent.

Bipolar gate arrays were produced in Phoenix by the Logic Division of the SPS. Under the Logic Division, Motorola's bipolar gate array business grew rapidly. Motorola achieved a dominant share of this market and became the acknowledged technological leader.

CMOS gate arrays were produced in Austin, Texas, by the Microprocessor Products Group. Since Motorola focused on maintaining its position in the microprocessor market, the CMOS gate arrays did not receive adequate attention in this group. As a result, Motorola had only a small share of the CMOS gate array market and faced stiff competition from such companies as LSI, Hitachi, Toshiba, Fujitsu, and NEC.

To exploit fully the growing demand for semi-custom integrated circuits, Motorola organized the Application Specific Integrated Circuit (ASIC) Division as part of the Semiconductor Products Sector in 1984. In 1985, the ASIC Division occupied Motorola's Chandler facility, the newest of the company's five Phoenix-area locations. Typically, Motorola worked closely with a customer to design the semicustom integrated circuit. However, several designs were considered standard designs and were kept in stock.

Organization of ASIC Division

The division was organized along functional lines (see Exhibit 1).

Product Engineering Department

Product engineering interacted with the customer and assumed the role of a troubleshooter in dealing with customer complaints. It was responsible for the technical aspects of ongoing product manufacturing. Engineers were assigned to one or more products and served the customers for these products. If a customer had a complaint about an integrated circuit, product engineering responded to the request. Therefore, product engineering was the technical interface between the company and customer for existing products.

Product engineers designed the manufacturing process for existing products, and they typically were responsible for customer-driven capital expenditures. If a customer wanted or required an additional manufacturing process that required a capital expenditure, the process engineering department made a feasibility study. This study divided costs between nonrecurring engineering expenses (NRE) and the per unit cost of production after the initial NRE. In addition, an estimate of revenues was made to estimate product profitability. This report was examined by the marketing department to ensure that the assumptions and estimates made by the product engineers were reasonable.

Part of the start-up cost of a new product was the nonrecurring engineering cost (NRE). This cost included design and software development

EXHIBIT 1   Organization of ASIC Division

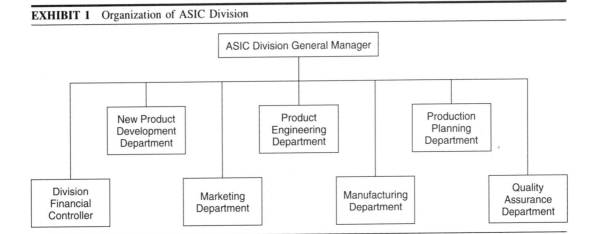

cost but typically did not include investment in process technologies, unless a very specialized piece of equipment was a unique requirement of the product's manufacture. The NRE was billed to the customer in two stages: 30 percent upon agreement of the development contract and 70 percent upon the shipment of the first prototype units.

Production Planning Department

The production planning and customer service department scheduled orders from the customer. This department told manufacturing when to start production and when the product run should be finished. Since Motorola did not have a computerized production planning system, this work was done with only standard microcomputer software, such as spreadsheets. Orders had to be tracked manually through the factory floor. When the product was shipped, the department billed the client and reported this information to the financial controller.

Marketing Department

The marketing department was responsible for identifying initial prospects and making sales to them. In addition, the department had certain responsibilities for product pricing and accurate forecasting of market demands.

Once a prospect was identified, the marketing department acted as a liaison to ensure that the requirements of the product were accurately communicated from the prospect to the new products development group. The new products development group then estimated a manufacturing cost, and the marketing department calculated a price, using as target margin of around 60 percent above manufacturing cost. This price was adjusted to take into account the competitive conditions of the market. The marketing department also forecasted the sales volume for the product for the next five years.

New Product Development Department

The new product development group was responsible for the translation of customer product specifications into manufacturable designs and for the production of prototypes. As mentioned above, this group provided an estimate of the manufacturing cost to the marketing group. After the design was completed, the cost estimate was refined; it was included in the product implementation plan, along with yield requirements. Before the product design could be released to the manufacturing department, the product was produced in the development fabrication area with production tooling. At this stage the process had to meet minimum yield specifications. This yield was not the yield estimated in calculating the long-run manufacturing cost of the product, but simply a yield that would be satisfactory as production moved rapidly down a learning curve. The learning curve was estimated to be about 70 percent for most products in the ASIC Division. A 70 percent learning curve implies that unit costs for total production volume will decrease by 30 percent every time the cumulative production volume doubles.

Each month the new products development group provided the financial controller department an updated forecast of future capital expense requirements; this was used in capital planning by the finance department.

Quality Assurance Department

Quality assurance (QA) was responsible for the outgoing quality of the product. After many of the processes on the manufacturing floor, QA inspectors sampled the product for quality. These tests included electrical and visual/mechanical tests. The electrical tests were straightforward (i.e., if the product failed to conduct properly, the product was rejected). The visual/mechanical tests were more subjective. Defects in this area could be misprinting, illegible printing, discolored components, or bent lead wires. Many of these did not affect the viability of the circuit but only its visual appearance. Quality assurance people knew that the Japanese were very sensitive to visual quality and that the product had to be visually perfect if Motorola was to be competitive in the Japanese market. One of the major responsibilities of QA was to convey to manufacturing what constituted a rejection of the product. One manager in QA said that the group should assume the role of a pseudo customer.

QA attempted to take a noncombative role with the other departments; it preferred to function in a preventive role. QA had trainers who discussed with manufacturing operators what con-

stituted a rejection. This program had two benefits: (1) operators became aware that they needed to produce to a certain quality level; and (2) if the product was below acceptable quality at any stage in production, it would be rejected immediately by the operator, thus saving further manufacturing costs. Recently, a procedure was instituted that, if a product was rejected, the whole line stopped until QA and the production floor could determine the cause(s).

Manufacturing Department

The manufacturing department consisted of hourly workers, supervisors, and a manufacturing engineering staff. The hourly workers were directly involved in operating production machinery and inspecting work-in-process. Manufacturing engineering was charged with sustaining the production processes and methods used in the assembly and test operations. The group's focus was on the manufacturing process, rather than on specific products.

ASIC Market

The managers of the new division realized that the semicustom integrated circuit business had different requirements for success than the commodity-type business from which it grew.

In the semicustom gate array market, the customer created a unique design from the "building blocks" provided by Motorola designers. This involvement by the customer in the middle of the development cycle was different from that in the other semiconductor products offered by Motorola. Motorola provided design services to the customer and managed a relatively involved customer relationship. Thus, Motorola's organization focused on its customers, rather than on its products.

The customers of the ASIC division were typically computer manufacturers, such as DEC, Apple Computer, Unysis, Cray, and Prime Computer. These customers competed in markets characterized by rapidly changing technology and rapid introduction of new products. Shortening the product delivery time was a primary concern for them. High quality, quick development time, and the ability to achieve volume production rapidly were paramount in capturing the business of these customers. Compared with these factors, price was of secondary importance.

Some customers, such as Hewlett-Packard, were developing just-in-time (JIT) manufacturing systems and stated their needs for timely deliveries and high-quality incoming components.

Motorola Manufacturing and Accounting Systems

Prior to moving, the ASIC Division was part of another corporate sector. Bipolar production, prior to moving, used Motorola's existing manufacturing and accounting systems. In the plant, machines and workers were organized along functional lines. Each machine was controlled as part of a functional group, and was in close physical proximity with other machines that performed a similar function. This functional design resulted in large physical movements of product over relatively large distances on the factory floor. Each manufactured part had a designated routing through the factory.

In this factory design, there were 29 cost centers, whose inventory was valued at standard cost. The inventory was grouped by stage of completion for costing purposes. The routing of the product through the factory typically included the following steps: (1) piece parts, where the various raw materials were purchased and prepared; (2) wafer fabrication, where the silicon wafers containing the logic arrays were produced; (3) die, where the wafers were tested and cut into individual circuits or chips and mounted to the substrate of the package (permanent chip enclosure); (4) assembly, where lead wires were attached to the chip and the packaging completed; (5) test, where the packaged chip was tested according to customer specifications; and (6) finished goods, where the finished products were packaged for shipping.

This system required extensive recordkeeping. An entry was made every time the product was moved from one cost center to another. A frequent physical audit of inventories was required to track and verify product amounts.

Material, labor, and overhead standards were updated twice a year. Nevertheless, the standards were often obsolete, because of the dynamic environment and the steep learning curves. Overhead was allocated to the product based on direct labor. Direct labor was meticulously tracked in order to cost labor to the product and to provide allocation of overhead to the product. The manufacturing manager estimated that between 8 percent to 12 percent of an employee's productive time was spent in recordkeeping.

Direct labor was paid a hourly wage and a bonus. The bonus was largely determined by comparison of actual direct labor hours to standard labor hours for each employee.

The functional design of the factory caused difficulty in placing responsibility for an individual product. Expediters in the production planning department performed a crucial task in making sure important products were being completed in a timely fashion. Even so, the plant was plagued with slow throughput times. Management felt that turn-around times on the integrated circuits was too slow, compared with competing Japanese firms.

The functional design also resulted in large inventories and large batch sizes. The large batch size resulted in WIP inventories between functional stations and resulted in large finished goods inventories that were efficiently produced but perhaps unwanted by the customer.

Many people felt that, rather than helping managers cope with the complexity of the manufacturing system, the accounting system was actually exacerbating the problem. The division controller noted, "The first important realization of the accounting department is that we were sometimes a barrier to progress. The accounting systems resulted in overall dysfunctional activities and impeded movement to new manufacturing techniques."

The standard cost system was cumbersome and not well understood by factory employees. Factory employees had difficulty in tying a variance to a specific problem. Because a variance did not highlight the actual problem, an appropriate solution to a variance was difficult to determine. The typical factory worker thought the variance report was irrelevant and, therefore, ignored it.

The timeliness of reports was also a problem. Standard costs were generated monthly. The lack of daily or weekly feedback made it difficult to pinpoint the cause of an unfavorable variance. The monthly variance was an accumulation of many favorable and unfavorable activities, which variance analysis did not specifically identify. Moreover, the variance reports were not timely. The books were closed on the seventh working day after the end of the month. An additional seven working days were required to generate actual costs and the variance report. By the time the reports were received in the factory floor, the manufacturing department was halfway through another accounting period.

Because of the dynamic environment facing a chip manufacturer, the determination of standards was very difficult. New chip designs were constantly flowing through the factory, and the steep learning curve contributed to the rapid obsolescence of standards. The standards were generally perceived as being out of date.

Since the variances were affected by volume, in many cases the way to decrease an individual variance was to keep the employees and machines fully used and produce large lot sizes. This had the undesired result of building up work-in-process inventory between the work stations and production of products that were not immediately required by a customer. At the same time, products required by a customer might not be produced. This resulted in a buildup of finished goods inventory and out-of-stock orders simultaneously.

In the new plant, there was a dramatic increase in overhead costs and a corresponding decrease in direct labor costs. The allocation of overhead by direct labor no longer seemed relevant.

Opportunities for Change

The manager of the newly formed AISC Division realized that the opening of a new production facility in Chandler represented an opportunity to introduce substantial changes in the division's manufacturing operations. Accordingly, the new plant's floor layout was designed to be particularly suited to the JIT philosophy and to the specific processes of the plant. One manager at the Chandler site expressed the opinion that reorganizing an existing functional facility to accomplish a JIT plant would have been far more difficult.

The factory was organized around nine cells: (1) assembly preparation; (2) 72-pin assembly; (3) 149-pin assembly; (4) other assembly; (5) sealing, mechanical testing, and marking; (6) heat sink; (7) burn-in; (8) production testing and packing; (9) warehousing and shipping. (Exhibit 2 is a diagram of the plant layout.) Not all products went through all cells—for example, not all chips required heat sinks. However, all of the chips produced at the Chandler plant were processed in most of the cells.

Products moved from cell to cell in the order shown in Exhibit 2. The wafers (each consisting of a number of chips) were placed in a die cage when they arrived at the plant. From the die cage, the wafers were taken to the die prep cell, where the gate arrays on wafers that had not been tested at the wafer fabrication facility were checked with a probe to determine which arrays were good. Arrays that did not pass inspection were marked, and, when the wafer was cut into individual chips, the marked arrays were thrown away.

Next, the chips were taken to one of the three assembly cells (72-pin, 149-pin, other), depending on the product family and number of connections that needed to be made to the chip. In the assembly cells, the electrical connections to the chip were made. In the sealing, mechanical testing, and marking cell, the chips were sealed in a protective package, tested, and marked for identification. In this cell, some low-volume chips

EXHIBIT 2 Layout of Chandler Plant

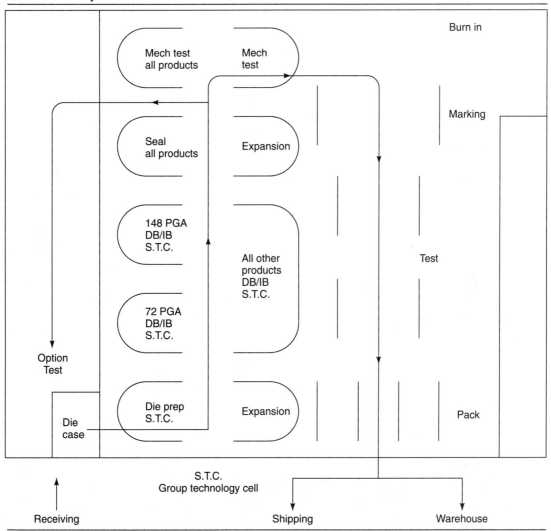

were diverted from the normal product flow into a special option line. This line was for very-low-volume ICs, which were usually built for customers who used them for prototypes and testing. The focus of this option line was fast turnaround time; for new ICs, a dozen or so units could be shipped within three weeks from the time the design was accepted. Higher-volume ICs were routed through the remaining cells. As noted, not all ICs were sent to the heat sink and burn-in cells, but all went through the testing, warehousing, and shipping cells.

Most of the processes were machine-paced, and most of the machinery was complex and

EXHIBIT 3   Layout of Assembly Cell

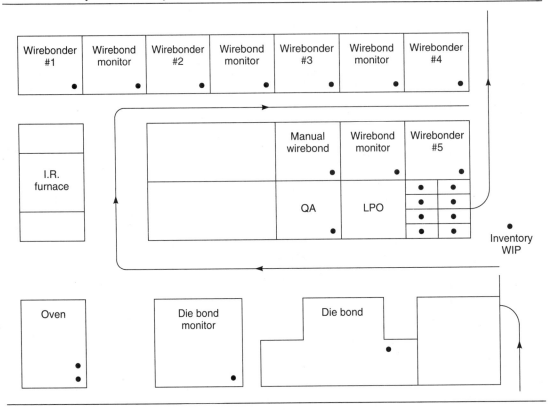

expensive. This is particularly true of the assembly and test cells. For example, automated test machines at the end of the option line cost over $2 million each.

Each of the cells was run by a production team, which was supervised by a team leader. Work flow was controlled through a pull system, with designated areas where limited inventory was allowed between work stations. (A pull manufacturing system is characterized by triggering production when inventory is removed from finished goods stock.) If the storage area before a work station was full, the preceding station had to remain idle. One of the assembly cells is diagrammed in Exhibit 3. In this cell, chips were attached to the bottom portion of the permanent enclosure (package) in the die bond station, and they moved through the cell as shown by the arrows; the final operation performed in the cell was attaching lead wires in the wirebond stations. The cell was so designed that the product moved in one direction along a U-shaped path.

The Role of the Management Accounting System

The controller of the ASIC Division was acutely aware of the tendency of outdated and cumbersome accounting systems to hinder progress in manufacturing operations. He felt strongly that his office should not merely stand aside but should take a positive position in promoting the changes throughout the division. However, he wondered what kind of managerial accounting system would complement and even guide the progressive changes taking place in the division's operations.

QUESTIONS

1. What are the key success factors for Motorola's ASIC Division?
2. Does a traditional standard cost system address these key success factors?
3. What are good measures of these key success factors?
4. How would you control the plant using these measures and the current structure of the plant?

Case 10–3

Siemens Electric Motor Works*

Headquartered in Munich, Siemens AG was one of the world's largest producers of electrical and electronic products. In 1987, revenues totalled 51 billion deutsche marks, with roughly half this amount representing sales outside the Federal Republic of Germany. The Siemens organization was split into seven major groups and five corporate divisions, as illustrated in Exhibit 1. The largest group was the Energy and Automation Group, which comprised seven divisions. Low-wattage alternating current (A/C) motors were produced at the Electric Motor Works (EMW), which was part of the Manufacturing Industries Division. High-wattage motors were produced at another facility.

The Electric Motor Works

Located in the small town of Bad Neustadt, the original Siemens EMW plant was built in 1937 to manufacture refrigerator motors for "Volkskuhlschraenke" (people's refrigerators). Less than a year later, Mr. Siemens decided to halt the production of refrigerator motors and began to produce electric motors for other applications. At the end of World War II, the Bad Neustadt plant was the only Siemens factory in West Germany capable of producing electric motors. All the other Siemens production facilities had been completely destroyed or seized by Eastern bloc countries. After an aggressive rebuilding program, Bad Neustadt emerged as the firm's primary producer of electric motors.

The A/C motor business was cyclical and highly dependent on the machine tool industry. From 1977 to 1987, EMW averaged 80 percent capacity utilization. Sales ranged from DM334.4 million to DM499.1 million (see Exhibit 2). Production volume also varied widely: in 1983, volume was 350,600, and, in 1987, volume was 630,000.

Through the 1970s, EMW produced primarily standard motors; custom motors comprised only 20 percent of production volume. The production process was characterized by relatively long runs of a single type of motor. Because standard motors were used by a wide range of customers in a variety of applications, the motors were produced for inventory and shipped as orders were received. Production of standard A/C motors was extremely competitive. The key to success was to reduce costs so the firm could price aggressively while making a profit. Despite a major expansion and automation program in the late 1970s, it became obvious that the lower labor rates of Eastern bloc competitors gave them an insurmountable cost advantage over Siemens EMW.

An extensive study of EMW's production capabilities and the market for electric motors indicated that EMW was in a position to become a premier producer of low-volume, specialized A/C motors—and that this business would be profitable. Adopting this new strategy required the ability to efficiently manufacture many more types of motors in much smaller production runs. Between

* This case was prepared by Karen Hopper Wruck, Harvard Business School.
Copyright © by the President and Fellows of Harvard College.
Harvard Business School case 189-090.

EXHIBIT 1 Partial Organization Chart

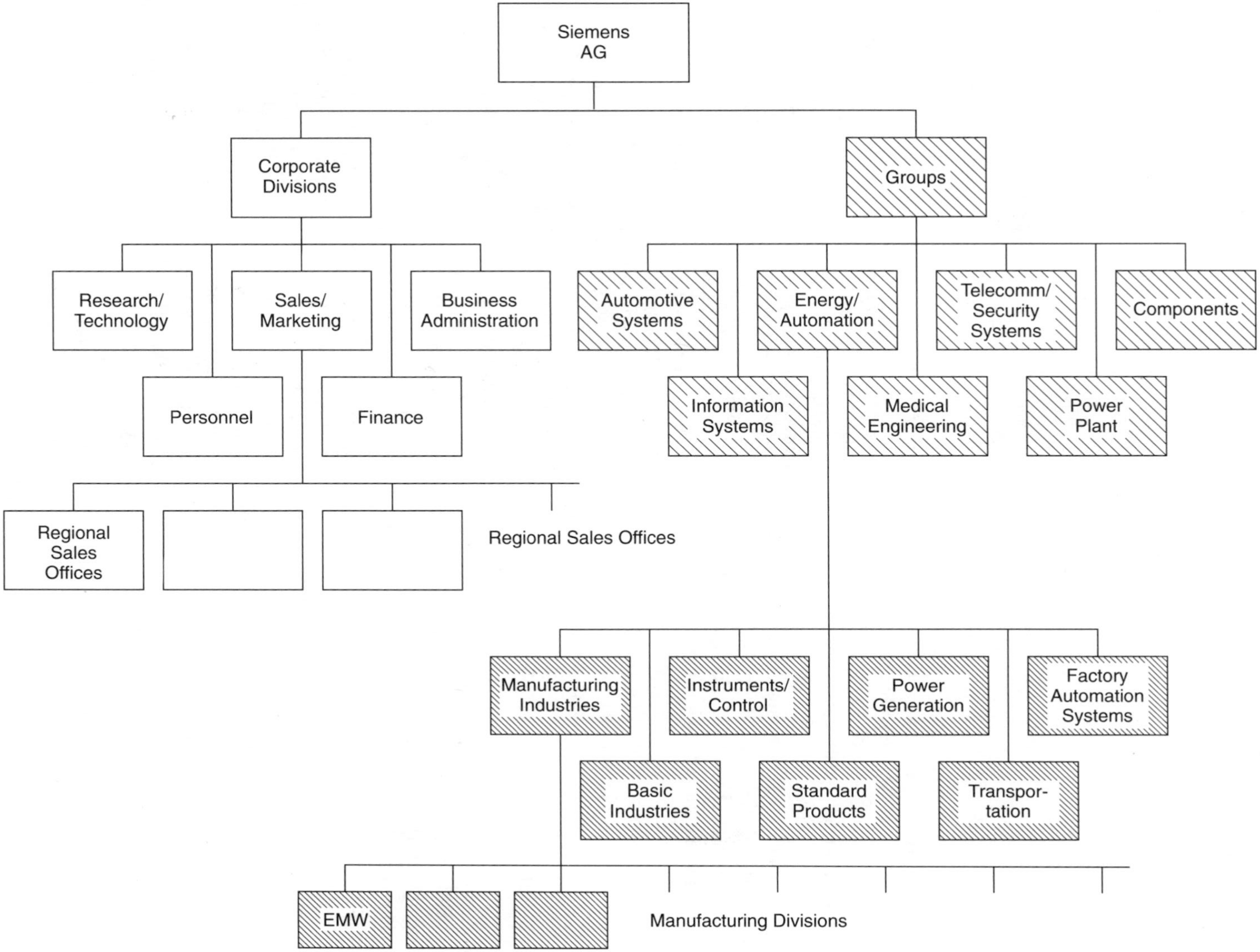

EXHIBIT 2   Orders, Production, and Sales Statistics, 1981–1987

	DM Accepted Orders (000,000s)	DM Sales (000,000s)	Number of Motors Produced (000s)
81/82	353.6	355.5	403.9
82/83	346.1	334.4	350.6
83/84	420.7	417.0	472.5
84/85	494.6	467.5	518.7
85/86	484.4	499.1	550.0
86/87	442.2	450.1	630.0

1985 and 1987, EMW spent DM50 million a year on its production facilities. By replacing almost every machine on the shop floor, EMW created a production environment that supported its new strategy. The production facility was completely vertically integrated, beginning with the foundry and ending with the assembly, packing, and shipping of the final product. In addition, production was highly automated, with numerically controlled machines, flexible machining centers, and robotically-fed production processes. Large-volume common components were manufactured, using the appropriate automated equipment, while very-low-volume components might be made by hand. Where possible, flexible manufacturing was used to mass produce small-volume specialty components. By the late 1980s, the new strategy was well established and EMW was producing primarily custom motors to fill small orders. Small production batches were normal: 74 percent of the orders were for fewer than five custom motors.

In 1987, Siemens Corporation concluded that the level of productive capacity at EMW was sufficient to satisfy current and expected future demand. Additionally, there was some indication that corporate thought the A/C motor business was too risky, and that the time it took to recover invested capital made it difficult to justify any further increase in capacity. Consequently, the capital funds made available to EMW were cut to a level that allowed for maintenance but not expansion.

Transfer Pricing

The production facilities of the Manufacturing Industries Group were organized around production technologies. For example, because they required different production technologies, low-wattage A/C motors and high-wattage A/C motors were produced in different facilities. The Sales Division was organized around customer market segments. There were 12 sales branches located throughout Germany and Europe. None were co-located with a production facility. All A/C motors produced by EMW were sold exclusively through the Sales Division. Both EMW and the Sales Division of the Manufacturing Industries Group were profit centers.

The Sales Division received the orders for A/C motors. Each order was accepted or rejected based on an evaluation that brought together representatives from both sales and production. In the process of evaluating orders, the EMW representative provided data on the cost of production, while the Sales Division representative provided customer information. Transfer pricing rules were established to determine the price the Sales Division would pay to EMW for producing a particular order. The transfer price was based on EMW's estimated cost of producing an order and Sales' estimate of the price the customer was willing to pay.

Cost of Producing an Order

Soon after they changed strategies, the managers at EMW developed a cost system which they felt accurately estimated product costs for both low- and high-volume lot production. Its process-oriented cost system differed from traditional costing systems, because it took into account both the number of motors ordered and the technical complexity of producing an order. Estimates of the resources required to produce an order were based on the actual resources consumed in the production of similar orders.

The standard unit cost for an order was calculated by estimating the direct material and direct labor costs, and then allocating estimated overhead costs as if the plant was operating at 80 percent of capacity. The cost system broke overhead costs into five categories: material-related overhead, production-related overhead, support-related overhead, costs of order processing, and costs of handling custom components.

Material-related overhead contained the costs of material acquisition and was allocated to each unit based on the cost of direct materials consumed. Production-related overhead was split into cost pools based on classes of machines and was allocated to each unit based on either the direct labor hours or machine hours required to produce it. Support-related overhead included all other product costs and was allocated to each unit based on the total deutsche marks of direct material, direct labor, material overhead, and production overhead assigned to a unit. Up to this point all costs, except the overhead costs associated with shop floor orders, and the overhead costs of handling special components had been assigned to the product. Because they were not generated in a way that was proportional to the number of units produced, but were rather proportional to the number of lots, the overhead costs of processing shop floor orders and handling special components were assigned to products differently.

Both order processing and special components handling overhead costs were assigned to each lot produced. Based on historical costs, a constant charge per order and a constant charge per special component were calculated. For example, a lot that contained five motors, each of which re-quired 10 special components, was assigned the same number of deutsche marks per order and special component overhead as a lot containing 20 units, each of which contained 10 special components. Due to these constant costs per order, the process-oriented system generated unit costs that decreased as the number of units ordered increased. This is illustrated, for a typical motor, by the heavy line in Exhibit 3.

EMW supplied the Sales Division with the standard cost of one unit for each order under consideration. Sales estimated the cost of an order by taking this standard cost and applying a discount factor based on the number of units ordered. The resulting price per unit was called the "factory cost." When the process-oriented system was first implemented, EMW considered providing Sales with a complete standard cost schedule for each order. Sales protested that the number of reports would be cumbersome and suggested that EMW develop some simpler method to determine the factory cost. As a result, one aggregate schedule was used for all low-wattage A/C motors. For 1987, the following schedule was used to determine the factory cost:

Factory Cost Schedule Low-Wattage A/C Motors

Number of Pieces per Order	Discount Factor
1	1.00
2–4	0.79
5–19	0.57
20–99	0.48
> 100	0.42

The factory cost schedule is illustrated by the step function in Exhibit 3. The factory cost schedule was designed to approximate process-oriented unit costs across the whole range of low-wattage A/C motors. However, there were differences between the two. For example, as illustrated in Exhibit 3, for a typical motor, when between 14 and 19 units were ordered, the

---

EXHIBIT 3   PROKASTA Discount Factor and Factory Cost Discount Factor

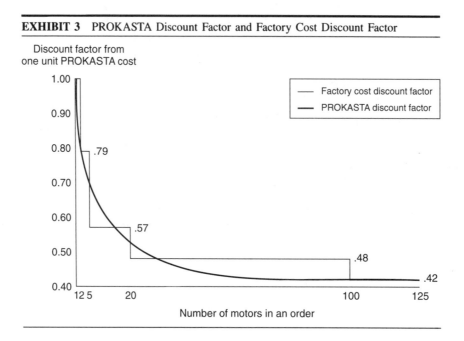

Discount factor from
one unit PROKASTA cost

factory cost was greater than the process-oriented unit cost.

Using the above schedule, the Sales Division could determine the factory cost for a particular order by taking the factory cost of a single unit and adjusting for the volume ordered. For example, motors from an order of 12 with a standard one unit cost of DM250 were costed at DM142.5 per unit (DM250 × 0.57 = DM142.5).

Computing the Transfer Price

The price at which EMW transferred motors to the Sales Division was determined by first analyzing whether the order was profitable. For profitable orders, the transfer price was set at factory cost plus one third of the profits earned (see Exhibit 4A). If the order was unprofitable, the transfer price was set at variable cost plus three fourths of the contribution earned (see Exhibit 4B).

These transfer pricing rules were developed based upon historical data and so designed that, over the entire business cycle, EMW broke even.

Under this system, EMW had averaged zero profits over the last five years. In a good year, EMW would report small profits (maximum reported profit of DM5 million) and in a bad year small losses (maximum reported loss of DM10 million). The two transfer pricing rules were established by analyzing the cost structure of the low-wattage A/C motor business at average capacity utilization over the business cycle. The average capacity utilization was 80 percent, and at this capacity the A/C motor business as a whole required a 40 percent contribution to break even. Under the assumption of a 40 percent contribution, if three fourths of this contribution was given to EMW, it would break even as a separate unit. The remaining one fourth of the contribution, if given to the Sales Division, would allow Sales to break even. Hence, the transfer pricing rule for unprofitable orders was set at variable cost plus three fourths of the contribution. After dividing the contribution from unprofitable orders in an average year between EMW and Sales in a 3-to-1 ratio, the profit from the remaining orders was so divided

EXHIBIT 4   Transfer Pricing at Siemens

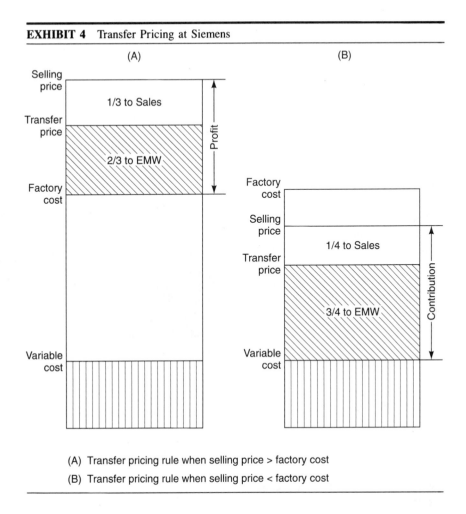

(A) Transfer pricing rule when selling price > factory cost

(B) Transfer pricing rule when selling price < factory cost

that EMW broke even. Break-even performance was achieved by setting the transfer price for profitable orders at factory cost plus one third of the profit.

Evaluating Orders

The Sales Division determined the preliminary price of an order using a catalog of list prices for motors and special components. When a customer ordered motors that EMW had produced before, the price was simply looked up in the catalog.

Generally, catalog prices were one unit standard cost plus a markup. When a customer ordered motors that EMW had not produced before, a price was calculated by finding the list price of a similar motor and then adding or subtracting, or both, the list price of special components.

Major tooling was sometimes necessary when the motors ordered were substantially different from any motor EMW had produced before. EMW estimated these costs, and the customer paid for the tooling before production began. On average, tooling costs ran about DM100,000, so customers found it worthwhile to pay these costs only for large-volume orders. Once EMW had tooled up for the production of a new motor, it could produce almost 30,000 variations of that motor with almost no additional tooling cost.

Orders where the sale price was greater than the factory cost were considered routine. The regional sales office negotiated price and delivery directly with EMW. Special consideration was given to orders where the sale price was less than the factory cost. In 1987, about 9 percent of accepted orders fell into this class. A distribution of these orders by number of units ordered is presented in Exhibit 5. These orders were forwarded to the central sales office in Erlangen, and the order was accepted or rejected based on negotiations between central sales and EMW. A number of factors came into play in these negotiations. Records of past sales were examined to check the price at which similar motors had been sold. In addition, the profitability of the customer's total business with Siemens Corporation was analyzed. A record was kept of each client's transactions with all divisions of Siemens' Manufacturing Industries Group. In 1987, there were over 4,000 such clients. For profitable customers, central sales could quote a lower price, expecting to make up this loss on other business with that customer.

The European market for custom A/C motors was dominated by three large producers. Siemens and one other firm produced primarily custom motors. The third firm produced predominantly standard motors. In addition, a number of very small firms produced custom A/C motors. Customers with large-volume orders generally got bids from several firms before choosing a producer. For a good customer, central sales would match the low bid, even though it was less than the cost of production. In 1987, 87 percent of EMW's orders for more than 100 motors were sold below full cost (see Exhibit 5). Sometimes a good customer ordered a small number of com-

EXHIBIT 5 Profitability by Order Size for 1987

Number of Motors in Order	*Percent of Accepted Orders Where Sale Price < Factory Cost*
1	1%
2–4	2
5–19	2
20–99	56
≥100	87

plex motors and expected special treatment. A below-cost price would be accepted if the loss could be made up in other transactions with the customer. For all unprofitable orders, however, a price floor was set at 25 percent above the variable cost of production.

Over DM1 billion in proposed orders were evaluated in 1987. Of these, only DM450 million went into production. Some orders were lost to competitors; but most were not accepted, because they were judged to be too unprofitable. Across all orders EMW averaged a 36 percent contribution margin. The low-volume orders were by far the most profitable for the firm. As illustrated in Exhibit 6, in 1987 orders for less than five motors had an average contribution margin close to 50 percent. Orders for more than 100 motors had less than a 20 percent contribution margin.

Mid-1988

By mid-1988, a potential problem with EMW's performance had surfaced. Even though it was operating at 115 percent of rated capacity, EMW reported a substantial loss for the first half of the year. Karl-Heinz Lottes, the director of EMW, was concerned because, if EMW was not profitable at its current operating capacity, it was not clear to him that he would be able to break even over the business cycle. He suspected the problem was with the transfer pricing system and decided to call his management team together to see if they could diagnose the problem.

EXHIBIT 6 Frequency Distribution of Accepted Orders by Order Size for 1987

Number of Motors in Accepted Orders	Percent of Accepted Orders	Number of Motors	DM Sales (000,000s)	Contribution Margin (%)
1	48%	31,500	64.35	49%
2–4	26	44,100	74.25	52
5–19	14	81,900	108.00	40
20–99	9	195,300	135.00	27
≥ 100	3	277,200	68.40	19
				Overall 36 percent contribution
Total	100%	630,000	450.00	margin

QUESTIONS

1. Do you agree with Siemens' decision to set up both Sales Division and EMW as profit centers? What are some of the costs and benefits associated with this decision?
2. Outline the transfer pricing rules. What is the relation between the cost of a product as generated by the product costing system, the factory cost, and the transfer price?
3. If Herr Lottes asked for your analysis of the situation and a recommended course of action, how would you respond?

Case 10-4

Responsibility Accounting versus JIT*

When accounting measurement objectives cannot be met because of changing technology, the motivational role of accounting emerges. Managers often estimate costs when accounting systems cannot provide accurate measures. Because a manager's knowledge is often based upon unique expertise, verifying these cost estimates can be difficult. In these circumstances, management accountants should examine the motivational role of accounting systems. Do managers have a vested interest in making truthful estimates? Do these estimates encourage cooperation among managers?

Joint evaluation motivates managers to cooperate for their mutual benefit. Separate, independent evaluation may have an opposite effect. Vested interests, antagonisms, and game playing may bias cost and revenue estimates when the accounting system cannot provide accurate, reliable measurements. These concepts are important when departments can significantly influence each other's efficiency.

A traditional concept in departmental responsibility accounting is controllability. Managers should be held responsible only for costs which they can control. New technologies can make costing systems less accurate and create situations where estimates are more frequent and important.

Conditions can often be created by new technologies where the benefits of cooperation are greater than the costs of violating controllability. When departments significantly influence each other's costs and the accounting system cannot accurately measure these costs, it may actually be preferable to hold managers responsible for costs they cannot control. New technologies have made truly independent departments rare.

The experience of two companies illustrates these points. One, a bathroom fixture manufacturer, uses both separate and joint responsibility accounting for evaluation. The second, a cut-rate auto parts chain, has recently changed from a separate to a joint responsibility system because of the introduction of a just-in-time (JIT) retailing system. The change to shared responsibility was necessary because the introduction of JIT retailing made manufacturing and sales more interdependent.

Auto Parts Chain

The plant manager was angry, really angry. "You just get everything humming along nicely and the big wheels have to change things. I didn't need a sales division before, so why should I pay for it now? Why should I be held responsible for activities I don't control?

This manager ran an operation of about 300 employees who rebuilt carburetors mostly sold by the parent company, a large chain of cut-rate auto part retailers. Originally, the company based this manager's bonus upon the performance of his manufacturing facility alone. He balanced an optimal mix of component prices with work force capacity to maximize the shop's output and his

---

* This case was prepared by Associate Professor Jim Mackey, California State University, Sacramento.
From *CMA Magazine*, July–August 1989, pp. 22–25. Used with permission.

EXHIBIT 1   Accounting for Bonus Plans

Before		After
Plant	Sales	Plant and Sales
Actual costs of manufacture versus budget*	Actual sales Budgeted costs of manufacture	Actual sales Actual costs of manufacture
	Gross profit Selling expenses	Gross profit Selling expenses
	Segment profits[†]	Segment profits[*†]

* Bonus basis for the plant.
† Bonus basis for the sales group.

own bonus. By keeping larger stocks of finished product, sales managers were able to meet all customer needs. At the same time, the manufacturing manager had enough scheduling discretion to influence negotiated component costs and smooth production. He was comfortable knowing what to control and how to cope with the uncertainties in this situation. But, this idealistic situation would not last.

Changes have recently been made (see Exhibit 1). Previously, because the plant manager scheduled to minimize his production and purchasing costs, the flow and mix of finished goods shipped to the stores were often erratic but not a problem. Finished inventories were sufficient for most situations. Now a new JIT merchandising system put pressure on the company to show reductions in inventory levels. The new sales group allowed better coordination of all suppliers with the stores. In essence, a centralized data base cut drastically into the merchandise inventory levels.

These changes adversely affected the production manager, however. Not only did he lose his buffer or extra finished goods stock, which allowed more independent scheduling, but he also had to bear responsibility without any control for the sales activities. He no longer controlled his own destiny. His bonus depended upon the performance of the salespeople as well as his own.

He did, however, find some gratification since the sales manager felt the same way—angry. The sales manager's bonus depended as much on manufacturing efficiency as on good sales management. Once their mutual miseries were thoroughly discussed, both managers and their staffs found a clear need for full cooperation in order to maintain bonus levels.

Upper management's hope for motivating cooperation between sales and manufacturing by having bonuses based upon combined performance was fulfilled. This way the carrying costs of inventories, previously a sales responsibility, now affected the compensation of both departments. Under JIT merchandising, the sales department was encouraged to order products only as required without losing sales. At the same time, the plant manager was motivated to cooperate within cost constraints in his scheduling because his bonus was somewhat tied to sales performance.

However successful, this is only one possible solution to a classic agency problem. A better, more detailed cost accounting system could provide an alternative solution but was either unknown or not chosen by this company because of its unique operating conditions.

Sales department conditions contributing to the need for accounting changes were as follows:

1. Sales were difficult to forecast because demand was very uncertain.
2. Sales margins were tight because of significant competition.

The production department, however, was not without its problems:

1. Availability and quality of used carburetors were erratic.
2. Set-up costs and small lot sizes plagued the process.
3. Reconditioning was often more an art than a science.
4. Quality control costs could get out of hand without suitable monitoring.

It was clearly a production environment where standards would be difficult to establish. Large stocks of finished goods became too costly. Production had to be linked more to demand, while uncertainties in both sales and production still existed that could not be measured correctly. Motivation, rather than cost accounting using standards, became a more efficient solution.

An agency problem existed. The sales division, because of its unique knowledge, was in the best position to forecast demand *and* estimate the cost of lost sales. Lost sales were inevitable for any system that minimizes in-stock goods. A lost-sale figure was a difficult number to derive, particularly since one lost sale might cause a customer never to return. Hard data were rarely available; only sales estimates by experienced sales managers were reliable.

Before JIT, the solution was simple—carry large product inventories. Lost sales were rarely a problem. But new technologies brought the cost of carrying inventories to management's attention, and JIT retailing was adopted. Suddenly the company required manufacturing flexibility to meet demand. Prior to JIT, meeting rush orders was rarely an issue for manufacturing. It was merely a benefit from the carrying costs of finished goods. (The carrying costs were borne by sales or the retail outlets.) This was legitimate because all the benefits of meeting rush orders, due to both current and future orders, adhered to sales. Now JIT was like a bandit robbing sales of its least-costly alternative for maintaining satisfied customers.

Rush orders, once satisfied by high inventory levels, collided head-on with JIT. Because of supplier costs, set-ups, and lot-size issues, rush orders could be disruptive and costly. The nature of the production process made standards unreliable and formal planning models often inaccurate. Only an experienced plant manager with intimate knowledge of the company's work force, machinery, and suppliers could give reasonable estimates of rush-order costs.

Under the old system where the manufacturing plant was a cost center, rush orders could be accepted only at a potential cost to the plant manager (see Exhibit 1). They could be a costly way of avoiding lost sales when the plant was already at full capacity. Rush orders were accepted only when the costs were, in the judgment of the plant manager, minimal. Since formal costing systems were imprecise, only the plant manager could judge the ability to meet the cost of a rush order. On the other hand, the benefits of meeting a single rush order were equally difficult to quantify formally because of the possible influence on future sales. Only an experienced sales staff could come up with a reliable estimate of the value of accepting a rush order. But sales had nothing to lose by accepting all rush orders, and production rarely had anything to gain. A stalemate existed.

A numerical example might be useful here (see Exhibit 2). Consider a last-minute rush order for a $10 part that has a standard cost of $5 per unit. The sales manager expects that meeting this order will generate an additional three sales in the future. The production manager, on the other hand, is evaluated on the basis of his standard manufacturing costs. This rush order will require an additional setup not previously planned. Claiming he just can't do it within the time constraints (when he actually could but at a cost that exceeds his budget), he will reject the rush order.

EXHIBIT 2 Separate Evaluation Accounting
(cannot accurately measure rush order costs)

Rush Orders

Manufacturing is in the best position to estimate short-term costs.	Sales is in the best position to estimate long-term benefits.

Book Entries for a Rush Order

	Manufacturing	*Sales*
Selling price		$10
Manufacturing cost	$5*	5
Contribution margin		$5†

* Manufacturing bonus base.
† Sales bonus base.

Decentralized Decisions

Manufacturing will reject if costs expected to exceed $5 (e.g., $7).	Meeting rush orders today is expected to generate 3 future sales. Will accept any order > $5. Total benefit: 4 orders × contribution margin = 4 × $5 = $20.

Benefit to the Company as a Whole of Accepting the Rush Order

New sales less
(manufacturing costs at standard plus incremental rush order costs)

$$4 \times \$10 - (4 \times 5 + \$2) = 40 - 22 = \$18$$

The new incentive system, merging sales and manufacturing into one profit center, created a system of mutually shared interests. Lost sales now hurt the bonuses of manufacturing as well as those of sales. The incremental production cost and benefits of rush orders impacted on sales as much as manufacturing. Sharing specialized knowledge was motivated because of shared bonuses. The benefits of shared bonuses outweigh the costs of the lost connection between controllability and responsibility. Joint evaluation was made necessary because now technology changed the optimal way of running the business.

Bathroom Fixtures Company

A second company had a similar problem but handled it differently. It produced bathroom fix-

tures in large quantities. Production involved the use of specialized molds and finishing processes. At the same time maximum capacity varied for different combinations of products passing through from the molding to sanding to kilning to finishing departments. The kilning process, for example, involved using carts that could be loaded only to certain configurations. Often fillers of dummy materials were needed physically to balance the load. If a suitable product mix was scheduled, the dummies were not required, thus increasing overall capacity. Rejects and reworking were also common.

New products were a problem for both production and sales. The following environmental conditions were important for success of new products:

1. Learning curves were relevant for both manufacturing and sales.
2. Consumer tastes could be fickle (small design changes could have a major sales impact).
3. Design changes could greatly influence the cost and quality of production.
4. Compatibility of the new line with the established lines was important for production efficiency.

In addition, established lines were not subject to design changes from sales and were scheduled based upon forecasts of housing starts and GNP. Because of the cyclical nature of new construction, sales had little short-term influence upon established lines. However, skillful manufacturing management was still required to control costs and meet demand. For established lines, manufacturing had significantly more influence over costs than did sales.

New product lines presented a different set of problems. Small batches were required. Learning both consumer preferences and manufacturing traits took time and was not always successful. At the same time, new lines had to meet consumer preferences within profitability constraints.

As with the previous company, management adopted suitable incentive systems that reflected the differences between established and new product lines. Manufacturing was treated as a cost and bonus centre for the established lines. New product lines, on the other hand, used joint bonus systems.

QUESTIONS

1. What cost accounting system and transfer price (if any) would you recommend for rebuilt carburetors, and what bonus plan would you recommend for the plant manager and the sales manager?
2. What cost accounting system and transfer price (if any) would you recommend for bathroom fixtures, and what bonus plan would you recommend for the production manager and the sales manager?
3. If your recommendations are different for these two situations, how do you explain the difference?

Case 10–5

Disctech, Inc.*

Rich O'Donnell, chairman of the Audit Committee of Disctech, Inc., had to decide what to say at the board of directors meeting on October 25, 1985. He was concerned about problems of revenue recognition and inventory measurement, based on the information given in this case. He had accumulated this information from various sources. Some of the details may not have been exactly correct, but he was convinced that the general picture was as described.

The Hard Disk Industry

Disctech manufactured and sold hard disk drives. Disks are circular platters covered with magnetic material on which data are recorded in concentric circles. Market positions in the industry changed rapidly., and disk drive manufacturers had to keep up with technological advances in order to survive. The quantity of data that could be recorded on a single disk was doubling every three years, and this trend was expected to continue.

The market for disk drives can be divided into two distinct submarkets: those installed as part of large computer systems and those installed as part of a minicomputer system. The market for large computer disk drives was dominated by IBM. Other large mainframe manufacturers, such as Sperry and Control Data, also made their own disk drives. Independent disk drive manufacturers served this market by supplying IBM plug-compatible systems directly to end users. Independent disk drive manufacturers concentrated on replacing IBM drives because the sales volume for non-IBM models were considered too small. The mainframe memory market was expected to grow at about 5 percent per year.

The minicomputer market was highly competitive. A number of the leading minicomputer manufacturers had captive sources of disk drives, but most minicomputer manufacturers were part of the original equipment manufacturer (OEM) market serviced by a large number of small independent disk drive manufacturers. This market was expected to grow 25 to 30 percent per year.

Disctech's Beginnings

Disctech was founded in 1977 by Mr. John Garvey, an executive who had left his job with a large manufacturer of minicomputers and computer disk memories. John was an electrical engineer by training but was better known for his interest in and talent for organizing. John had felt constrained by the staid corporate environment and wanted to venture out on his own; he felt that, with a good product, good marketing, and the right pitch to the capital markets, a "killing could be made." Three other talented executives left the large company to join with John in his new endeavor: Ed Steinborn (vice president for finance at the other company) became Disctech's chief financial officer (CFO), Peter Farrell (director of manufacturing) became the vice president for design and operations, and Mary Foley (minicomputer marketing vice president) became the executive vice president for sales and marketing.

* This case was prepared by Joseph P. Mulloy under supervision of Kenneth A. Merchant, Harvard Business School. Copyright © by the President and Fellows of Harvard College.
Harvard Business School case 187–066.

The period 1977 to 78 was spent organizing the corporation and building prototypes of the advanced 14- and 8-inch disks. Early in 1979, the corporation went public with 3.3 million shares offered and sold at $3 a share. At a large party for shareholders and analysts, John announced that the corporation already had large guaranteed sales for its new disks, and that he expected Disctech products to become an industry standard. John also stated that the company planned to increase revenues and earnings per share (EPS) at a minimum of 30 percent per year.

Since the inception of the company, planning had been a simple, top down process. During the summer of each year, John met with Mary and Ed and set a sales budget for the next year. This sales figure was rolled to the bottom line, using expected margins and estimates of fixed expenses to get a net income figure and a resulting EPS. The Design and Operations Division planned production from the expected revenue and gross margin figures, while the R&D budget was negotiated separately between Peter and John.

Strategies to reach the annual plan were conceived and implemented at regularly scheduled "revenue meetings." Attendees included John, Ed, Mary, and the senior people of the marketing and sales staff. These meetings primarily sought the means of identifying and generating potential revenues.

Revenues for Disctech were derived from the sale and service of the company's equipment. Revenues were recorded at the time of shipment or performance of the service. Customer orders were initiated by Disctech's receipt of an equipment order form (EOF); either this was completed by the customer, or it was prepared by Disctech personnel pursuant to a master sales agreement signed by the customer. The EOF included a description of the equipment, the price of the equipment, and the earliest equipment delivery date that was acceptable to the customer.

Board of Directors and Audit Committee

Since the company's inception, Disctech's board of directors had consisted of seven members: two inside directors (the CEO and the CFO) and five outside directors. The board usually met four times a year. The meetings were generally short and standardized, with John in control of the agenda. The outside directors were impressed with the company's performance and the dedication displayed by the top officers.

The Audit Committee of the board consisted of three outside directors. Initially it met twice a year, before and after the annual audit.

A number of changes came about after Richard (Rich) O'Donnell, an outside director, was named to the committee in 1982. Rich firmly believed that an Audit Committee "could not be effective without being active." He increased the committee's schedule to at least four meetings a year and set up private meetings between the outside auditors and the Audit Committee. Rich tried to get the committee to look at the company's exposures and to question discretionary items in the financial statements. He also suggested that the inside and outside auditors make some surprise inspections and audits. He also wanted to strengthen the internal audit function in other ways as well, such as through training and improved hiring practices.

Internal and External Audit

The Internal Audit Division, consisting of the head auditor, Doug McAneny, and two staff members, reported to Ed Steinborn (CFO). Its primary roles were to ensure that corporate accounting policies were followed and that safeguards existed to ensure that the company's assets were protected. A secondary role was to be alert to opportunities for cost-cutting and efficiency.

At the request of Rich O'Donnell, Doug McAneny attended some meetings of the Audit Committee. Rich tried to establish a rapport with Doug and assured him that any misgivings that he had about anything, or anyone, in the company would be brought to the attention of the Audit Committee.

Disctech's external audit firm was Touche, Young and Anderson (TYA), a Big Eight firm. Each year in July, the auditors met with top management and the Audit Committee to lay out the schedule of the annual audit and to review changes in the company since the previous year.

1979–82

From 1979 to 1982, sales revenues grew at a compound rate of 39 percent. Every quarter the company announced record earnings, and the stock market reacted as John predicted, with the trading price continually reaching new highs. John made regular announcements about the company, stating that earnings were going to continue to grow at above-industry rates. The total market in 1979 for minicomputer disk memories at OEM prices was $2.1 billion, so there was plenty of room for Disctech to grow.

Disctech had continued to make modest R&D expenditures, but by the middle of 1982 its once "head of the pack" products were beginning to fall behind the latest technology. In response, John applied pressure to the Product Design Division to come out with new products, even if they were only slight improvements of existing products.

1983

The sales pattern in 1983 was a little erratic. John Garvey and Mary Foley (executive vice president, sales and marketing) agreed that quarterly sales (and earnings) had to continue to grow to keep the glowing image of Disctech alive. To maintain this growth record, they sometimes required the shipping department to work round-the-clock during the last few days of each quarter in order to push as many orders as possible out the door, so the revenue for those transactions could be recognized.

Mary also decided to take advantage of the way some OEMs ordered disk drives. These OEMs would place a large order for 100 to 200 disks, at a discount, and with a delivery date two to three months in the future. This assured them of a supply of the disks and a delivery date that supported their computer construction and shipment schedules. Many orders placed in one quarter would not be scheduled for delivery until the next quarter. To recognize these as sales in the current quarter, Mary directed that as many orders as possible receive early shipment to the OEM, with the understanding that the OEMs would not be liable for payment until the previously agreed-upon delivery dates.

The auditors from TYA questioned this early shipment program, but Ed Steinborn was able to convince them that they represented "sales" as defined under generally accepted accounting principles. Title to the disks did transfer to the OEM upon shipment, the OEM was obliged to pay Disctech for the disks, and Disctech did contact the OEM prior to shipment to get its authorization. What was not clear at the time was that these authorizations were verbal, and the salesperson responsible for an account would get the authorization and call it back to the home office.

This early shipment policy was fine with some OEMs, but many other OEMs did not have extra storage room and would not accept early delivery. The Disctech salespeople were told to "use their imaginations" and find storage space at the local Disctech distributor or another convenient location.

Although 1983 revenues was $107.1 million, $5.9 million of this was for disks originally scheduled for delivery in 1984. (Of the $5.9 million, $3.7 million had been shipped without a written authorization.)

1984

The only major change at Disctech in 1984 was in marketing policy. John Garvey had long thought that the minicomputer memory industry would gradually change, with proportionately fewer sales to computer manufacturers and more sales directly to end users. This evolution did occur, and it was accelerated as the economy slowed and inflation soared. Many companies held onto the computers they already had installed. John also believed that a truism of computers—"information to be stored, quickly grows to fill all available memory"—would help disctech's volume. Accordingly, more salespeople were hired, and the sales force was directed to approach all current users of minicomputers compatible with Disctech disk memories to attempt to generate sales in this potentially large market.

After the results of the second quarter were announced (another record high), John called Mary, Ed, and Peter together for a private meeting. John said that he was very proud of the results and that he knew that Disctech would continue to outperform the industry. He pointed out, however, that each quarter's goals were harder and harder to reach, and that delays in the completion of new disk designs and prototype construction and the growing obsolescence of inventory might level or even decrease the company's short-term earnings.

John went on to say that, with his children nearing college age, he needed a lot of money set aside that was not tied up in risky investments. As a result he had begun quietly to sell some of his Disctech stock. He told them he was still optimistic about the company's future but that it might be wise for them to look carefully at their own financial needs. But if they were going to sell stock, they should do it discreetly.

The year 1984 was another record. The marketing shift toward memory end users was a big success, and early shipments continued to increase as the marketing department pressured OEMs and salespeople for early authorization. Of $134.9 million sales, early-shipment revenues were $12.4 million, of which $9.8 million was shipped without a written authorization.

Inventory Control and Reserves for Obsolescence

In 1979, less than 15 percent of inventory was in raw materials, and over 85 percent was in finished goods. There was a general shortage of raw disks in the industry, and Disctech and other manufacturers, therefore, sent raw materials directly to the production line. Also, partially assembled disk drives were highly susceptible to even the slightest damage or dirt, since they rendered the disk or its drive unit inoperable.

In 1979, demand exceeded production capacity, so units were shipped out as soon as they had been tested. Efforts to improve efficiency and cleanliness raised production yields, and by 1980 production began to produce drives for inventory.

In 1982, the Design Division made a large number of small improvements to the disk drives to ensure that the product remained competitive. This had a large effect on inventory levels; disassembling the finished disk drive often caused complete disk failure, and, as a result, very little rework on completed drives was done. Instead, new drives in production would be modified and then assembled. Thus, each change or alteration created another layer of finished goods inventory slightly different from the last.

Disctech's policy for creating reserves for obsolescence of inventory was:

- Any item over two years old would be reserved at 5 percent per quarter for five years, so at the end of seven years there would be a 100 percent reserve.
- Any item declared unmarketable would have a 100 percent reserve taken against it.

These rules resulted in small reserves. Very little product that was technically obsolete was actually very old. Moreover, there were no guidelines for determining when disk drives became unmarketable. This problem was intensified by the corporate attitude that Disctech products were not subject to obsolescence.

In September 1982, a production controller forwarded a memo via Peter Farrell to the CFO and executive vice president for sales and marketing that summarized a study he had done on the growing inventory problem. It listed three recommendations:

1. A study to produce a new reserve policy, since it appeared that the product life cycle was far shorter than five years.
2. An intensive effort by the marketing department to sell the older inventory as soon as possible.

3. An increase in the reserve for obsolescence from $0.8 million to $1.4 million.

This memo was discussed by the senior corporate officers, who all felt that the problem was not that serious; they were unwilling to increase the reserve by any amount. Marketing, however, attempted to stimulate sales of the older disk drives with various specials, discounts, and promotions. The CFO also stated that he would "closely watch the inventory problem."

In 1983, the amount of obsolete inventory grew faster than the reserves, and by the end of the fiscal year the deficit was estimated to be almost $2.4 million. The outside auditors did not see the total extent of the problem, but they did question the reserve policy in their management letter:

> Continual monitoring of Disctech's finished goods inventory reserve policy is required, and procedures should be implemented to develop historical experience to measure the propriety of the formula adopted. The policy should also be extended to recognize obsolescence of products no longer in production sooner than required by the present formula.

Disctech management acknowledged the auditors' report, but they informed the Audit Committee that they already had done an internal study in 1982 and were working actively to fix all problems with inventory control.

During 1984, Disctech management was aware that the exposure for inventory obsolescence was increasing. Little was done other than continuing the marketing promotions and taking reserves as calculated by the reserve formula. Disctech management maintained that reserving for or writing off inventory made it less likely that it would be sold. They stressed that they had an obligation to the stockholders to find uses for the inventory rather than write if off.

By the time of the 1984 year-end audit, the auditors had become more agitated by the inventory situation (in addition to the aggressive revenue recognition) and sought written assurance from Disctech management that a formal program existed to "significantly impact the obsolescence exposure." The CFO, Ed Steinborn, wrote to the auditors:

> Our response to the problems in the inventory area will be to outline the programs we have underway to reduce inventory levels. We will agree to study policy alternatives in the area of providing reserves for excess equipment; however, affordability considerations really preclude our ability to make any meaningful change in this area this year.

The board and the Audit Committee were informed that a problem with inventory control still existed and that efforts to rectify the situation were ongoing. They also were told that "reserves for obsolescence may have to be increased next year as the product life cycle for disk memories shortens." They were not given the 1984 auditors' management letter that contained this sentence:

> This [obsolescence reserve] policy results in full valuation of excess inventory, overstates inventory, and may lead to serious future financial adjustments.

The board was not told that the inventory exposure had grown to an estimated $3.9 million.

The Audit Committee asked questions about inventory valuation, but John and Ed had ready answers and said they were confident that the inventory situation would soon be under control. Nevertheless, the Audit Committee in a private session with the outside auditors admitted that some things, including inventory obsolescence, had begun to worry them. They also told the engagement partner that they intended to meet more often in 1985 and they wanted a senior representative from the outside auditors and Doug McAneny, the head of internal auditing, at their meetings.

1985

The year 1985 was difficult for Disctech, and tremendous pressure was placed on the sales force to achieve the planned sales goal. A combination of a soft market for the 14-inch disks and unexpected delays in production of the advanced 8-inch and the 5¼-inch disk memories made marketing difficult.

Some salespeople came up with ingenious ideas to stimulate sales that were often designed to take advantage of the company's aggressive revenue policies. One such scheme could occur when a customer filled out an equipment order form with a delivery date far in the future and submitted it to Disctech for processing. Within a week or two the responsible salesperson would contact the marketing department and inform it that he had convinced the customer to accept an early delivery in the current quarter, with the understanding that payment would not be due until the date of the EOF. From the salesperson's view this made everyone happy: Disctech booked a sale, the salesperson got a commission, and the customer received a disk memory at a very reasonable price with delayed payments and no finance charges.

At the same time that sales were becoming more difficult, order cancellations were becoming a problem. As Disctech's competitors came out with new products, many original equipment manufacturers switched disk memory suppliers; direct end-user sales were also affected, because people wanted more memory and shorter access time for their dollars.

Near the end of the first quarter of FY 1985, a marketing department meeting was held to discuss the order cancellation problem. Mary chose this opportunity to announce a new policy: Any order canceled within six weeks of expected delivery would still be shipped and the revenue recorded. Although she was told that most customers would just refuse to accept delivery, she responded that on each of these deliveries the responsible salesperson would go along and ensure that "the sale stuck." All of these problems caused a lot of consternation in the sales force, but they all knew better than to argue with Mary when her mind was made up.

A Midyear Meeting

At midyear, John Garvey called a meeting of the top officers to review some pressing problems. The first problem was financing. As receivables had grown, cash was getting short. Consequently $10 million in bonds would be issued for public sale early in the fourth quarter; $4 million of the cash raised would be used to retire the bonds currently outstanding, and the rest of the proceeds would go to operations.

Second, inventory problems were getting worse. Recent estimate of the current obsolescence exposure was $6.8 million, and this was expected to grow to over $8 million by the end of the year. The outside auditors were very distressed over this matter. John explained that he had placated the auditors by informing them that the company was currently doing another internal study of obsolescence policies and that he expected a significant write-down probably as early as the first quarter of 1986.

Third, the new disk memory designs still had development problems, but John expected them to be available before the end of the calendar year. Finally, there was a growing problem with returned equipment. This would probably cause a significant decrease in revenues in future periods.

Putting these all together, John admitted that the record growth in profits would probably cease. John wanted the company to take all its lumps in the first quarter of 1986, and he wanted to take the inventory write-down at the same time as the new product announcement. He also stated that strong quarterly and annual results in 1985 would help the bond issue and would likely mitigate the impact of a loss in the first quarter of 1986. Everyone came away from the meeting clearly understanding that they had to make the 1985 budget—no matter what they had to do.

Despite heroic efforts by the sales force, fourth quarter predictions indicated that without further action Disctech would come up short of the 1985 budget. A plan was worked out in the marketing department to make a large shipment to a warehouse rented by Disctech under another name; this shipment (for $4.2 million) was booked as revenue in 1985. Plans were to use the equipment to help early 1986 orders.

In the end, the 1985 goal of $162 million in sales was achieved; total annual sales were $164.6 million. Early shipment revenues totaled $15.8 million, of which $10.6 million was equipment shipped without authorization. This $15.8 million did not include the $4.2 million shipped to the new warehouse.

Meeting of October 1985

The board of directors met on October 25 to review the results of FY 1985. John first went over the high points of the year and the records achieved. He next turned to the inventory problem and gave a quick summary of the events of the last few years. John then told them that, to bring inventory back in line, a one-time write-down of $8.2 million would be required.

Rich O'Donnell, chairman of the Audit Committee, thereupon asked for the floor.

EXHIBIT 1

DISCTECH, INC.
Income Statements for Fiscal Years
Ending September 30 (000 omitted)

	1978	1979	1980	1981	1982	1983	1984	1985
Revenue	$5,997	$30,003	$42,004	$59,646	$81,119	$107,076	$134,916	$164,598
Cost of sales	6,531	21,288	29,403	41,752	55,161	72,812	91,743	111,927
Gross margin	(534)	8,715	12,601	17,894	25,958	34,264	43,173	52,671
R&D expense	1,354	2,528	3,760	3,772	4,056	4,283	4,722	4,938
SG&A expense	1,990	4,138	5,220	6,561	10,545	13,920	17,539	21,398
Operating profit	(3,878)	2,049	3,621	7,561	11,357	16,061	20,912	26,335
Interest income	131	(517)	84	119	162	214	(104)	(541)
Profit before tax	(3,747)	1,532	3,705	7,680	11,519	16,275	20,808	24,794
Income tax	0	767	1,704	3,533	5,299	7,487	9,572	11,866
Profit after tax	$(3,747)	$765	$2,000	$4,147	$6,220	$8,788	$11,236	$13,928
Tax loss forward	0	685	1,400	0	0	0	0	0
Net income	$(3,747)	$1,450	$3,401	$4,147	$6,220	$8,788	$11,236	$13,928
Earnings per share	$(1.06)	$0.21	$0.50	$0.60	$0.90	$1.27	$1.61	$1.99

Source: annual reports.

EXHIBIT 2

DISCTECH, INC.
Consolidated Balance Sheets
At September 30 (000s omitted)

	1979	1980	1981	1982	1983	1984	1985
Assets							
Cash and marketable securities	$10,020	$ 3,654	$ 3,778	$ 3,273	$ 2,947	$ 2,808	$ 3,920
Accounts receivables (net)	8,752	9,801	11,921	15,508	22,091	30,843	39,300
Inventories (net)	12,221	8,601	11,241	15,122	22,046	27,557	36,682
Prepaid expenses	142	375	525	746	730	750	809
Total current assets	31,135	22,431	27,465	34,649	47,814	63,958	80,711
Property, plant, and equipment (net)	2,110	6,901	9,661	13,719	18,657	24,628	31,031
Other	929	120	169	239	284	321	364
Total assets	$34,174	$29,452	$37,295	$48,607	$66,755	$86,907	$112,106
Liabilities							
Notes payable	$ 4,050	$ 0	$ 0	$ 0	$ 0	$ 0	$ 0
Accounts payable	5,664	3,600	5,041	9,158	12,734	16,849	23,190
Accrued liabilities	1,179	1,500	2,100	2,982	4,056	5,354	6,746
Total current liabilities	10,893	5,100	7,141	12,140	16,790	18,203	29,936
Bank debt	0	0	0	0	0	2,000	0
Capital leases	1,363	4,485	6,820	8,917	12,127	16,008	18,170
Bonds	3,570	0	0	0	4,000	4,000	10,000
Equity							
Common stock	3,641	3,677	3,703	3,729	3,755	3,782	3,807
Other capital	20,978	21,020	21,062	21,104	21,146	21,188	21,231
Retained earnings	(6,281)	(4,831)	(1,431)	2,717	8,937	17,726	28,962
Total liabilities and equities	$34,174	$29,452	$37,295	$48,607	$66,755	$86,907	$112,106

Source: annual reports.

QUESTIONS

1. Estimate the effect of practices described in the case on net income in fiscal years 1983, 1984, and 1985, and on working capital as of September 30, 1985. Were the differences material?

2. What should Rich O'Donnell recommend at the meeting of October 25, 1985?
3. Should he have acted sooner, say at the end of FY 1983?
4. Should the external auditors or the internal audit staff have acted differently?

Chapter 11

Analyzing Performance Reports

The first part of this chapter describes how variances between actual and budgeted data are calculated for business units (divisions). Since expense and revenue budgets are part of the budgets for business units, the discussion can be extended to control over expense centers and revenue centers as well. The second part describes how reports of these variances and other information are used by senior management to evaluate business unit performance.

CALCULATING VARIANCES

Most companies make a monthly analysis of the differences between actual and budgeted revenues and expenses for each business unit and for the whole organization (some do this quarterly). Some companies merely report the amount of these variances, as in Exhibit 11–1. This statement shows that the actual profit was $52,000 higher than budget, and that the principal reason for this was revenues were higher than budget. It doesn't show anything about why the revenues were higher or whether there were significant offsetting differences in the variances of the expense items that were netted out in the overall numbers.

A more thorough analysis identifies the causes of the variances and the organization unit responsible. Effective systems identify variances down to the lowest level of management. Variances are hierarchical. As shown in Exhibit 11–2, they begin with the total business unit performance, which is divided into revenue variances and expense variances. Revenue variances are further divided into volume and price variances for the total business unit and for each marketing responsibility center within the unit. They can be further divided by sales area and sales district. Expense variances can be divided between manufacturing expenses and other expenses. Manufacturing expenses can be further

EXHIBIT 11-1 Performance Report, January (000s)

	Actual	Budget	Actual Better (Worse) Than Budget
Sales	$875	$600	$ 275
Variable costs of sales	583	370	(213)
Contribution	292	230	62
Fixed overhead	75	75	—
Gross profit	217	155	62
Selling expense	55	50	(5)
Administration expense	30	25	(5)
Profit before taxes	$132	$ 80	$ 52

subdivided by factories and departments within factories. Therefore, it is possible to identify each variance with the individual manager who is responsible for it. This is a powerful tool, without which the efficacy of profit budgets would be limited.

The profit budget has embedded in it certain expectations about the state of the total industry and about the company's market share, its selling prices, and its costs structure. Results from variance computations are more "actionable" if changes in actual results are analyzed against each of these expectations. The analytical framework we use to conduct variance analysis incorporates the following key ideas:

• Identify the key causal factors that affect profits.
• Break down the overall profit variances by these key causal factors.
• Focus always on the profit impact of variation in each causal factor.
• Try to calculate the specific, separable impact of each causal factor by varying only that factor while holding all other factors constant ("spinning only one dial at a time").
• Add complexity sequentially, one layer at a time, beginning at a very basic "commonsense" level ("peel the onion").
• Stop the process when the added complexity at a newly created level is not justified by added useful insights into the causal factors underlying the overall profit variance.

Exhibit 11-3 provides details of the budget of the business unit whose performance is reported in Exhibit 11-1.

Revenue Variances

In this section, we describe how to calculate selling price, volume, and mix variances. The calculation is made for each product line separately, and the

EXHIBIT 11-2 Variance Analysis Disaggregation

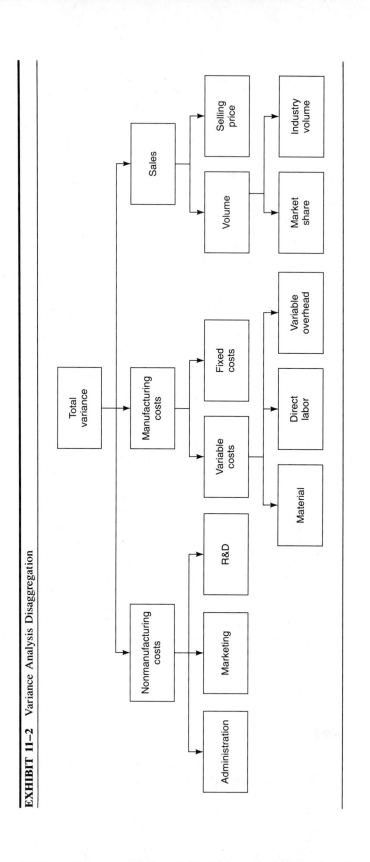

EXHIBIT 11–3 Budget for January ($000s)

	Product A 100*		Product B 100*		Product C 100*		Total Budget
	Unit	*Total*	*Unit*	*Total*	*Unit*	*Total*	
Sales	$ 1.00	$100	$ 2.00	$200	$ 3.00	$300	$600
Standard variable cost:							
Material	0.50	50	0.70	70	1.50	150	270
Labor	0.10	10	0.15	15	0.10	10	35
Variable overhead	0.20	20	0.25	25	0.20	20	65
Total variable cost	0.80	80	1.10	110	1.80	180	370
Contribution	$ 0.20	20	$ 0.90	90	$ 1.20	120	230
Fixed costs:							
Fixed overhead		25		25		25	75
Selling expense		17		17		17	50
Administrative expense		8		8		8	25
Total fixed costs		50		50		50	150
Profit before Taxes		$(30)		$ 40		$ 70	$ 80

*Standard volume (units)

separate results are then added algebraically to give the total variance. A positive variance is favorable, because it indicates that actual profit exceeded budgeted profit, and a negative variance is unfavorable.

Selling price variance.   The selling price variance is calculated by multiplying the difference between the actual price and the standard price by the actual volume. The calculation is shown in Exhibit 11–4. It shows that the price variance is $75,000, unfavorable.

EXHIBIT 11–4 Selling Price Variations, January (000s)

	Product			
	A	*B*	*C*	*Total*
Actual volume (units)	100	200	150	
Actual price per unit	$ 0.90	$ 2.05	$ 2.50	
Budget price per unit	1.00	2.00	3.00	
Actual over/(under) budget per unit	(0.10)	0.05	(0.50)	
Favorable/(unfavorable) price variance.	(10)	10	(75)	(75)

Mix and volume variance. Often the mix and volume variances are not separated. The equation for the combined mix and volume variance is:

$$\text{Mix and volume variance} = (\text{Actual volume} - \text{Budgeted volume}) \times \text{(Budgeted unit contribution)}$$

The calculation of mix and volume variance is shown in Exhibit 11–5; it is $150,000 favorable.

The volume variance results from selling more units than budgeted. The mix variance results from selling a different proportion of products from that assumed in the budget. Because products earn different *contributions* per unit, the sale of different proportions of products from those budgeted will result in a variance. If the business unit has a "richer" mix (i.e., a higher proportion of products with a high contribution margin), the actual profit will be higher than budgeted; and if it has a "leaner" mix, the profit will be lower. Since the volume and mix variances are joint, techniques for separating them are somewhat arbitrary. One such technique is described below. Other ways of making this calculation are equally acceptable.

Mix variance. The mix variance for each product is found from the following equation:

$$\text{Mix variance} = [(\text{Total actual volume of sales} \times \text{Budgeted proportion}) - (\text{Actual volume of sales})] \times \text{Budgeted unit contribution}$$

The calculation of the mix variance is shown in Exhibit 11–6. It shows that a higher proportion of product B and a lower proportion of product A were sold. Since product B has a higher unit contribution than product A, the mix variance is favorable, by $35,000.

Volume variance. The volume variance can be calculated by subtracting the mix variance from the combined mix and volume variance. This is $150,000 minus $35,000, or $115,000. It can also be calculated for each product as follows:

$$\text{Volume variance} = [(\text{Total actual volume of sales}) \times (\text{Budgeted percentage})] - [(\text{Budgeted sales}) \times (\text{Budgeted unit contribution})]$$

The calculation of the volume variance is shown in Exhibit 11–7.

EXHIBIT 11–5 Sales Mix and Volume Variance, January ($000s)

(1) Product	*(2)* Actual Volume	*(3)* Budgeted Volume	*(4)* Difference *(2) − (3)*	*(5)* Unit Contribution	*(6)* Variance *(4) × (5)*
A	100	100	—	—	—
B	200	100	100	$ 0.90	$ 90
C	150	100	50	1.20	60
Total	450	300			$150

EXHIBIT 11–6 Mix Variance, January ($000s)

(1)	(2)	(3)	(4)	(5)	(6)
		Budgeted			
		Mix at			
	Budgeted	*Actual*	*Actual*	*Difference*	*Unit*	*Variance*
Product	*Proportion*	*Volume*	*Sales*	*(3) − (4)*	*Contribution*	*(5) × (6)*
A	$\frac{1}{3}$	150*	100	(50)	$0.20	$(10)
B	$\frac{1}{3}$	150	200	50	$0.90	45
C	$\frac{1}{3}$	150	150	—	—	
Total		450	450			$35

* $\frac{1}{3} \times 450$.

EXHIBIT 11–7 Sales Volume Variance, January ($000s)

(1)	(2)	(3)	(4)	(5)	(6)
	Budgeted				
	Mix at				
	Actual	*Budgeted*	*Difference*	*Unit*	*Volume*
Product	*Volume*	*Volume*	*(2) − (3)*	*Contribution*	*Variance*
A	150	100	50	$0.20	$10
B	150	100	50	0.90	45
C	150	100	50	1.20	60
Total	450	300	150		$115

Other revenue analyses. Revenue variances may be further subdivided. In our example, Exhibits 11–4, 11–6, and 11–7 provide the information to classify them by product. Such a classification is shown in Exhibit 11–8.

Market penetration and industry volume. One extension of revenue analysis is to separate the mix and volume variance into the amount caused by

EXHIBIT 11–8 Revenue Variances by Product, January ($000s)

	Product			
	A	*B*	*C*	*Total*
Price variance	$(10)	$ 10	$(75)	$(75)
Mix variance	(10)	45	—	35
Volume variance	10	45	60	115
Total	$(10)	$100	$(15)	$ 75

differences in market share and the amount caused by differences in industry volume. The principle is that the business unit managers are responsible for market share, but they are not responsible for the industry volume because that is largely influenced by the state of the economy. To make this calculation, industry sales data must be available. This calculation is given in Exhibit 11–9.

EXHIBIT 11–9   Industry Volume and Market Share Variances, January ($000s)

A. Budgeted Sales Volume

	Product			
	A	B	C	Total
Estimated industry volume (units)	833	500	1,667	3,000
Budgeted market share	12%	20%	6%	10%
Budgeted volume (units)	100	100	100	300

B. Actual Market Share

	Product			
	A	B	C	Total
Industry volume, units	1,000	1,000	1,000	3,000
Actual sales	100	200	150	450
Market share	10%	20%	15%	15%

C. Variance Due to Market Share

	Product			
	A	B	C	Total
(1) Actual sales (units)	100	200	150	450
(2) Budgeted share at industry volume	120	200	60	380
(3) Difference (1 − 2)	(20)	—	90	70
(4) Unit contribution (budget)	$0.20	$0.90	$1.20	
(5) Variance due to market share (3 × 4)	(4.00)	—	108	$104

D. Variance Due to Industry Volume

	Product			
	A	B	C	Total
(1) Actual industry volume	1,000	1,000	1,000	3,000
(2) Budgeted industry volume	833	500	1,667	3,000
(3) Difference (1 − 2)	167	500	(667)	—
(4) Budgeted market share	12%	20%	6%	
(5) (3) × (4)	20	100	(40)	
(6) Unit contribution (budget)	$0.20	$0.90	$1.20	
(7) Total (5 × 6)	4.00	90.00	(48.00)	$46

Section A of Exhibit 11–9 provides the assumptions that were made in the original budget shown in Exhibit 11–1, and Section B provides details on actual industry volume and market share for the month of January.

The following equation is used to separate the effect of market penetration from industry volume on the mix and volume variance:

Market share variance = [(Actual sales)− (Industry volume) × Budgeted market penetration] × Budgeted unit contribution

The variance is found for each product separately, and the total variance is the algebraic sum. The calculation is shown in Section C. It shows that $104,000 of the favorable mix and volume variance of $150,000 resulted from the fact that market penetration was better than budget. The remaining $46,000 resulted from the fact that actual industry dollar volume was higher than the amount assumed in the budget.

The $46,000 industry volume variance can also be calculated for each product as follows:

Industry volume variance = (Actual industry volume − Budgeted industry volume)× Budgeted market penetration × Budgeted unit contribution

This calculation of variance due to industry volume is shown in Section D.

Expense Variances

Fixed costs.   Variances between actual and budgeted fixed costs are obtained simply by subtraction, since these costs are not affected by either the volume of sales or the volume of production. This is shown in Exhibit 11–10.

Variable costs.   Variable costs are those costs that vary directly and proportionately with volume. The budgeted variable manufacturing costs must be adjusted to the actual volume of production. Assume that the January production was as follows: product A, 150,000 units; product B, 120,000 units; product C, 200,000 units. Assume also that the variable manufacturing costs incurred in

EXHIBIT 11–10   Fixed-Cost Variances, January ($000s)

	Actual	Budget	Favorable/ (Unfavorable) Variances
Fixed overhead	$ 75	$ 75	$ —
Selling expense	55	50	(5)
Administrative expense	30	25	(5)
Total	$160	150	$(10)

January were as follows: material, $470,000; labor, $65,000; variable manufacturing overhead, $90,000. Exhibit 11–3 shows the standard unit variable costs.

The budgeted manufacturing expense is adjusted to the amount that should have been spent at the actual level of production by multiplying each element of standard cost for each product by the volume of production for that product. This calculation is shown in Exhibit 11–11.

This exhibit shows that there was an unfavorable variance of $13,000 in January. This is called a "spending" variance because it results from spending $13,000 in excess of the adjusted budget. It consists of unfavorable material and labor variances of $11,000 and $12,000, respectively. These are partially offset by a favorable overhead spending variance of $10,000.

The volume that is used to adjust the budgeted variable manufacturing expenses is the *manufacturing* volume, not the *sales* volume, which was used in finding the revenue variances. In the simple example given here, we assumed that the two volumes were the same—namely, that the quantity of each product manufactured in January was the same as the quantity sold in January. If production volume differed from sales volume, the cost difference would show up in changes in inventory. Depending on the company's inventory costing method, this might or might not result in a production volume variance; calculation of such a variance is explained in the next section.

Note also, in this example, we assumed that all the nonmanufacturing expenses were fixed. If some of them had variable components, the variances should be calculated in the same way as was used for the calculation of manufacturing cost variances.

Summary of Variances

There are several ways in which the variances can be summarized in a report for management. One possibility is shown in Exhibit 11–12. It was used primarily because the amounts can be traced easily to the earlier exhibits. Another form of presentation is to show the actual amounts, as well as the variances.

EXHIBIT 11–11   Variable Manufacturing Expense Variances, January 1991 ($000s)

| | Product | | | | | Favorable/ (Unfavorable) |
	A	B	C	Total	Actual	Variances
Material	$ 75	$ 84	$300	$459	$470	$(11)
Labor	15	18	20	53	65	(12)
Overhead (variable)	30	30	40	100	90	10
Total	$120	$132	$360	$612	$625	$(13)

EXHIBIT 11–12 Summary Performance Report, January ($000s)	
Actual Profit (Exhibit 11–1)	$ 132
Budgeted profit (Exhibit 11–1)	80
Variance	$ 52

Analysis of Variance—Favorable/(Unfavorable)

Revenue variances:	
Price (Exhibit 11–4)	$(75)
Mix (Exhibit 11–6)	35
Volume (Exhibit 11–7)	115
Net revenue variances	$ 75
Variable-cost variances (Exhibit 11–11):	
Material	$(11)
Labor	(12)
Variable overhead	10
Net variable-cost variances	$(13)
Fixed-cost variances (Exhibit 11–10):	
Selling expense	$ (5)
Administrative expense	(5)
Net fixed-cost variances	$ 10
Variance	$ 52

This gives an indication of the relative importance of each variance as a fraction of the total revenue or expense item to which it relates.

VARIATIONS IN PRACTICE

The example given above, although complicated, is a relatively straightforward way of identifying the variances that caused actual profit in a business unit to be different from the budgeted profitability. Some variations from this approach are described in this section.

Time Period of the Comparison

The example compared January's budget with January's actuals. Some companies use performance for the year to date as the basis for comparison. To illustrate, for the period ended June 30, they would use budgeted and actual amounts for the six months ending on June 30, rather than the amounts for

June. Other companies compare the budget for the whole year with the current estimate of actual performance for the year. The "actual" amounts for the report prepared as of June 30 would consist of actual numbers for the first six months plus the best current estimate of revenues and expenses for the second six months.

A comparison for the year to date is not as much influenced by temporary aberrations that may be peculiar to the current month and, therefore, that need not be of concern to management. On the other hand, it may mask the emergence of an important factor that is not temporary.

A comparison of the annual budget with current expectation of actual performance for the whole year shows how closely the business unit manager expects to meet the annual profit target. If performance for the year to date is worse than the budget for the year to date, it is possible that the deficit will be overcome in the remaining months. On the other hand, forces that caused actual performance to be below budget for the year to date may be expected to continue for the remainder of the year, which will make the final numbers significantly different from the budgeted amounts. Senior management would very much like to have a realistic estimate of the profit for the whole year, both because it may suggest the need to change the dividend policy, to obtain additional cash, or to change levels of discretionary spending, and also because a current estimate of the year's performance is often provided to financial analysts and other outside parties.

Obtaining a realistic estimate is difficult, however. Business unit managers tend to be optimistic about their ability to perform in the remaining months because, if they are pessimistic, this casts doubt on their ability to manage. To some extent, this tendency can be overcome by placing the burden of proof on business unit managers to show that the trends in volume, margins, and costs that occur currently are not going to continue. Nevertheless, an estimate of the whole year is "soft," whereas actual performance is a matter of record. An alternative that lessens this problem is to report performance both for the year to date and for the year as a whole.

Focus on Gross Margin

In the example, we assumed that selling prices were budgeted to remain constant throughout the year. In many companies, changes in costs or other factors are expected to lead to changes in selling prices, and the task of the marketing manager is to obtain a budgeted gross margin—that is, a constant spread between costs and selling prices. Such a policy is especially important in periods of inflation. A variance analysis in such a system would not have a selling price variance. Instead, there would be a gross margin variance; unit gross margin is the difference between selling prices and manufacturing costs.

This is done by substituting "gross margin" for "selling price" in the revenue equations. Gross margin is the difference between actual selling prices and the *standard* manufacturing cost. The current standard manufacturing cost should take into account changes in manufacturing costs that are caused by changes in wage rates and in material prices (and, in some companies, significant changes in other input factors, such as electricity in aluminum manufacturing). The standard, rather than the actual, cost is used so manufacturing inefficiencies do not affect the performance of the marketing organization.

Evaluation Standards

In management control systems the formal standards used in the evaluation of reports on actual activities are of three types: (1) predetermined standards or budgets, (2) historical standards, or (3) external standards.

Predetermined standards or budgets. If carefully prepared and coordinated, these are excellent standards. They are the basis against which actual performance is compared in many companies. But if the budget numbers are collected in a haphazard manner, they obviously will not provide a reliable basis for comparison. Moreover, if the environmental uncertainties affecting responsibility center performance are great, predetermined standards may be so unreliable that they are not worth the trouble of preparing them.

Historical standards. These are records of past actual performance. Results for the current month may be compared with the results for last month, or with results for the same month a year ago. This type of standard has two serious weaknesses: (1) conditions may have changed between the two periods in a way that invalidates the comparison, and (2) the prior period's performance may not have been acceptable. A supervisor whose spoilage cost is $500 a month, month after month, is consistent; but we do not know, without other evidence, whether the performance was consistently good or consistently poor. Despite these inherent weaknesses, historical standards are used in many companies, often because valid predetermined standards are not available.

External standards. These are standards derived from the performance of other responsibility centers or of other companies. The performance of one branch sales office may be compared with the performance of other branch sales offices. If conditions in these responsibility centers are similar, such a comparison may provide an acceptable basis for evaluating performance.

Limitations on standards. A variance between actual and standard performance is meaningful only if it is derived from a valid standard. Although it is convenient to refer to *favorable* and *unfavorable* variances, these words imply that the standard is a reliable measure of what performance should have been. Even a standard cost may not be an accurate estimate of what costs should have been under the circumstances. This situation can arise for either or both of two reasons: (1) the standard was not set properly; or (2) although set properly in the light of conditions existing at the time, changed conditions have made the standard obsolete. An essential first step in the analysis of a variance is an examination of the validity of the standard.

Full-Cost Systems

In the example, we assumed that variable manufacturing costs were assigned to products, but that fixed manufacturing costs either were not allocated to products or, if allocated, were treated separately in the variance analysis process. In a full-cost system, the manufacturing cost of a product includes both its variable costs and an allocation of fixed costs; the fixed cost is an amount per unit, calculated at the standard manufacturing volume. Companies that operate a full-cost system may not be able to make such a separation, or, even if they can do so, they may want to identify the variance in manufacturing costs that results from the difference between actual and standard production volume. When actual volume is different from standard volume, a production volume variance is developed. It is the difference between budgeted costs at the actual volume (as stated in the flexible budget) and standard costs at that volume (i.e., standard unit costs multiplied by the actual number of units). Details of calculating manufacturing cost variances under full-cost systems are covered in cost accounting textbooks.

Amount of Detail

In the example, we analyzed revenue variances at several levels: first, in total; then by volume, mix, and price; then by analyzing the volume and mix variance by industry volume and market share. At each of these levels, we analyzed the variances by individual products. The process of going from one level to another is often referred to as "peeling the onion"—that is, successive layers are peeled off, and the process continues as long as the additional detail is judged to be worthwhile. Some companies do not develop as many layers as shown in our example; others develop more. It is possible, and in some cases worthwhile, to develop additional sales and marketing variances, such as the following: by sales territories and even by individual sales persons; by sales to individual countries or regions; by sales to key customers, principal types of customers, or customers in certain industries; by sales originating from direct mail, from customer calls, or from other sources; and so on. Additional detail for manufacturing costs can be developed by calculating variances for lower-level responsibility centers and by identifying variances with specific input factors, such as wage rates and material prices.

These layers correspond to the hierarchy of responsibility centers. Taking action based on the reported variances is not possible unless they can be associated with the managers responsible for them.

With modern information technology, about any level of detail can be supplied quickly and at reasonable cost. The problem is to decide how much is worthwhile. In part, the answer depends on the information requested by individual managers—some are numbers-oriented, others are not. In the ideal situation, the basic data exist to make any conceivable type of analysis, but only a small fraction of these data is reported routinely.

LIMITATIONS OF VARIANCE ANALYSIS

Although variance analysis is a powerful tool, it does have limitations. The most important limitation is that, although it identifies where a variance occurs, it does not tell *why* the variance occurred or what is being done about it. For example, the report may show there was a significant unfavorable variance in marketing expenses, and it may identify this variance with high sales promotion expenses. It does not, however, explain why the sales promotion expenses were high and what, if any, actions were being taken. A narrative explanation, accompanying the report, should provide such an explanation.

A second problem in variance analysis is to decide whether a variance is significant. Statistical techniques can be used to determine whether there is a significant difference between actual and standard performance for certain processes; these techniques are usually referred to as "statistical quality control." However, they are applicable only when the process is repeated at frequent intervals, such as the operation of a machine tool on a production line. The literature contains a few articles suggesting that statistical quality control be used to determine whether a budget variance is significant; but this suggestion has little practical relevance at the business unit level because the necessary amount of repetitive actions is not present. Conceptually, a variance should be investigated only when the benefit expected from correcting the problem exceeds the cost of the investigation; but the model based on this premise has so many uncertainties that it is only of academic interest. Managers, therefore, rely on judgment in deciding what variances are significant. Moreover, if a variance is significant but is uncontrollable (such as unexpected inflation), there may be no point in investigating it.

The report is prepared in the business unit, and its accuracy depends on the integrity of the business unit manager.

Another limitation of variance analysis is that, as the performance reports become more highly aggregated, offsetting variances might mislead the reader. For example, a manager looking at business unit manufacturing cost performance might notice that it was on budget. However, this might have resulted from good performance at one plant being offset by poor performance at another. Similarly, when different product lines at different stages of development are combined, the combination may obscure what is actually occurring.

Also, as variances become more highly aggregated, managers become more dependent on the accompanying explanations and forecasts. To illustrate, plant managers know what is happening in their plant and can easily explain causes of variances. Business unit managers and everyone above them, however, usually must depend on the explanations that accompany the variance report of the plant.

Finally, the reports show only what has happened. They do not show the future effects of actions that the manager has taken. For example, reducing the amount spent for employee training increases current profitability, but it may have adverse consequences in the future. Also, the report shows only those events that are recorded in the accounts, and many important events are not reflected in current accounting transactions. The accounts don't show the state of morale, for instance.

OTHER INFORMATION

We have so far focused on the development of variances between budgeted and actual data for business units. Reports of such information are a central feature of the management control of business units, and similar comparisons are made for other responsibility centers. Managers receive much information from other sources, however.

Key Variables

In Chapter 10 we stressed the importance of identifying and reporting on certain key variables—that is, variables requiring immediate action if they behave in unanticipated ways. They are relatively few in number in a given company; but the nature of key variables varies greatly among companies. Unlike the profit report outlined above, which is issued at regular (usually monthly) intervals and in a prescribed format, information on the key variables is brought to management's attention quickly.

Nonfinancial Objectives

In Chapter 9 we referred to a "management by objectives" system, in which managers agree to accomplish certain nonfinancial objectives. These objectives are important in analyzing performance, in addition to the information in the profit budget.

> **Example.** Xerox Corporation used such a system. Its business unit managers prepare a plan that indicates how they intend to attain superiority over competitors' products in the areas of cost, quality, service, and reliability. Their performance is evaluated in accordance with this plan, as well as the profit budget.[1]

---

[1] "Letter to Shareholders," Xerox Corporation annual report, 1982.

Informal Information

Managers obtain information from conversations with other people, from memoranda and other information, from meetings, and from other informal sources. The chief executive officer may assign certain colleagues to keep track of what is happening in specified business units (which, if made formal, adds a layer to the organization). Headquarters marketing, production, and other staffs are continually looking at what is happening in the business units in their areas of responsibility. The relative importance of informal information, compared with the formal reports we have described, varies greatly with the predilections of individual managers. The chief executive officer sets a general tone for the whole organization, and subordinate managers influence the amount and type of information reported within their areas of responsibility.

Management Action

Regardless of this balance between formal and informal sources of information, there is one cardinal principle: The monthly profit report should contain no major surprises. Significant information should be communicated quickly by telephone, fax, or personal meetings as soon as it becomes known. The formal report confirms the general impression that the senior manager has learned from these sources. Based on this information, he or she may have acted prior to the receipt of the formal report.

The formal report is nevertheless important. It provides the desirable pressure on subordinate managers to take corrective actions on their own initiative. Further, the information from informal sources may be incomplete or misunderstood; the numbers in the formal report provide more accurate information, or the report may confirm or cast doubt on the information received from informal sources. Also, the formal report provides a basis for analysis because information from the informal sources often is general and imprecise.

Usually, there is a discussion between the business unit manager and his or her superior, in which the business unit manager explains the reasons for significant variances, the action being taken to correct unfavorable situations, and the expected timing of each corrective action. These explanations are necessarily subjective, and they may be biased. Operating managers, like most people, don't like to admit that unfavorable variances were caused by their errors. A senior manager has an opinion, based on experience, on the likelihood that a business unit manager will be frank and forthcoming and judges the report accordingly.

Profit reports are worthless unless they lead to action. The action may consist of praise for a job well done, of suggestions for doing things differently, of "chewing out," or of more drastic personnel actions. However, these actions are by no means taken for every business unit every month. As long as things are going well, praise is the most that may be necessary, and most people don't even expect praise routinely.

BEHAVIORAL CONSIDERATIONS IN PERFORMANCE EVALUATION

Most companies use similar techniques for preparing and reviewing the profit budget and in the subsequent reporting against the approved budget; that is to say, the *technical aspects* of the budgeting system—the forms used to prepare the budget, the format in which actual performance is compared with the budget, frequency of performance reports, and the like—are similar in many companies. However, companies differ widely in the way they *use* the information generated by the budgeting system. Profit budget systems differ widely in the way they are administered, particularly in the degree to which the profit budget is used to monitor business unit activity.

Individual managers have quite different approaches to the exercise of control. If senior management frequently monitors the activities of business units, we say it is exercising "tight control." On the other hand, if senior management does only limited monitoring of the business unit's activity during the year, we say it is exercising "loose control." The distinction between tight control and loose control refers to the extent of monitoring, not to the degree of delegation. Although tight control is often accompanied by more limited delegation than loose control, this is not always the case.

Tight Control

Tight control is based on the management philosophy that subordinate managers work most effectively when they are required to meet specific short-term goals, typically one-year goals, and that senior management can assist subordinates in solving many day-to-day problems. Put another way, subordinates make better day-to-day decisions if senior management participates in the decision-making process.

Under tight control, the profit goal of a business unit manager is considered to be a firm commitment against which he or she will be measured and, to a considerable extent, evaluated. Each month, performance to date is compared with the expected performance, detailed variances are identified and discussed, and courses of corrective action are considered if it appears that the budgeted objectives are not being met. Thus, a tight control system is one in which a manager's performance is evaluated primarily on his or her ability to attain budgetary objectives during each reporting period.

Loose Control

Loose control is based on the management philosophy that is illustrated by the statement: "I hire good people, and I leave them alone to do their jobs." Under loose control, the budget is used essentially as a communication and a planning tool. Annually, budgets are prepared, reviewed by senior management, adjusted where management deems appropriate, and approved. Monthly, or quarterly, actual results are compared to the budget, and differences are analyzed and explained. The budget is not considered a management commitment, however. Rather, it is assumed to be the manager's best estimate of profitability as of the time that it was prepared. Subsequently, as conditions change, these are communicated to senior management in the form of revised estimates, which are compared to the original budget and differences explained. The fact that the original objective has not been met does not necessarily indicate poor performance. Further, the causes of variances, the corrective actions being taken, and the timing of these actions are not reviewed in detail during the year by senior management, unless something is clearly amiss.

It is useful to place the management control system of a company at some point along a continuum between entirely tight control and entirely loose control. A company's position on this tight/loose continuum depends on the amount of emphasis senior management places on meeting budgetary objectives in the short run.

Behavioral Effects of Tight and Loose Controls

A tight control system has two important benefits over a loose control system. First, tight control tends to prevent managers from becoming wasteful or inefficient. It motivates managers to be profit-conscious. Second, consistent pressure motivates the manager to search for better ways to perform existing operations and to initiate new activities to meet the profit budget. Tight controls, however, can produce several dysfunctional effects.[2]

First, short-term actions that are not in the long-term interests of the company may be encouraged. The more pressure that is applied to meet current profit levels, the more likely the business unit manager will take short-term actions that may well be wrong in the long run. If, in addition to tight controls, the manager is given considerable discretion, there is the danger of encouraging uneconomic short-term actions. To illustrate, the manager may deliver inferior-quality products to customers to meet the sales targets, and this will adversely affect customer goodwill and future sales. These are errors of *commission*.

Second, to obtain short-term profits, business unit managers might not undertake useful long-term actions. For instance, managers might be motivated not to undertake investments that promise benefits in the long term but that hurt short-term financial results. A common example is investing inadequate

---

[2] Curran, "Companies That Rob the Future," *Fortune*, July 4, 1988, pp. 84–89; "More Than Ever, It's Management for the Short-Term," *Business Week*, November 24, 1986, pp. 92–93; P. Wang, "Claiming Tomorrow's Profits Today," *Forbes*, October 17, 1988, p. 78.

dollars in research and development because such investments have to be expensed in the year in which they are incurred, but their benefits will show up only in the future. Also, managers might not propose risky investments—investments where there is a great deal of uncertainty about future cash flows—because cash flow uncertainty translates into a greater probability that budgets will not be met. In other words, managers might propose "safe" investments (which are quite likely to produce adequate future cash flows) as opposed to high-risk projects, even though the high-risk projects may produce high returns. These are errors of *omission*.

Third, the use of budgeted profit as the sole objective can distort communications between a business unit manager and senior management. If business unit managers are evaluated based on their profit budget, they may try to set profit targets that are easily met. This leads to erroneous planning data for the whole company because the budgeted profit may be lower than the amount that could really be achieved. Also, business unit managers may be reluctant to admit, during the year, that they are likely to miss their profit budget until it is evident that they cannot possibly attain it. This would delay corrective action.

Fourth, tight financial control may motivate managers to engage in data manipulation. This can take several forms. At one level, managers may choose accounting methods that borrow from future earnings to meet current period targets (examples: inadequate provision for bad debts, inventory shrinkage, warranty claims, and so on).[3] At another level, managers may falsify data (i.e., deliberately provide inaccurate information).[4]

In an empirical study, Hopwood found that tight controls led to: *(a)* greater job-related tension, *(b)* poor relations with superiors, *(c)* poor relations with peers, *(d)* extensive manipulation of the accounting reports.[5] Hopwood also found the opposite effects under loose controls. However, Otley's subsequent empirical examination of the impact of the tightness of control on organizational performance was inconsistent with Hopwood's findings.[6] Otley found that, in his sample, greater emphasis on meeting the budget did not lead to high levels of job-related tension. More important, tight control was associated

---

[3] For instance, such companies as Chrysler, Firestone, Heinz, and Union Carbide have been found to use "liberal" accounting policies to boost earnings; one primary factor for their actions being their incentive plans. George Getschow, "Slick Accounting Ploys Help Many Companies Improve Their Income," *The Wall Street Journal,* May 27, 1982, p. 1.

[4] An example of data manipulation occurred in the Grocery Products Division of McCormick & Company. Employees improperly postponed recording payments as expenses, front-loaded revenues, distorted invoices, and engaged in other activities to meet profit targets. Betsy Morris, "McCormick & Co. Division Is Found to Use Dubious Accounting Methods to Boost Net," *The Wall Street Journal,* June 1, 1982, p. 10. See also footnote 1 in chapter 10.

[5] A. Hopwood, "An Empirical Study of the Role of Accounting Data in Performance Evaluation," *Journal of Accounting Research,* 10 (1972), pp. 156–82.

[6] D. T. Otley, "Budget Use and Managerial Performance," *Journal of Accounting Research,* Spring 1978, pp. 122–49.

with higher performance, a result that is opposite to that of Hopwood's. These conflicting findings suggest that the effectiveness of tight controls is dependent upon situational factors. In the next section, we discuss the situations where a tight control might be appropriate.

Factors Affecting the Choice of Tight versus Loose Controls

The ability of a business unit to set equitable profit goals and to perform so as to attain these goals depends on four factors:

1. The amount of discretion that the business unit manager can exercise.
2. The degree to which the critical performance variables can be influenced by the business unit manager.
3. The relative uncertainty inherent in the operation.
4. The time span of the impact of the manager's decision.

Amount of discretion.   The amount of discretion that a manager can exercise depends on the nature of the job and the degree of delegation. The more complex the job, the greater the discretion required to manage it effectively. The greater the amount of delegation, the greater the discretion that the business unit manager can exercise.

If managers have much discretion, setting precise objectives is difficult. They have many alternative courses of action, and one cannot determine ahead of time which particular actions are best and what the financial impact of these actions will be. Conversely, if a plant manager has relatively little discretion in deciding what will be produced, how it will be produced, and how much the labor force will be paid, arriving at a reasonable financial objective may be a relatively simple task. By contrast, a business unit manager who is responsible for product development, marketing, production and procurement, and development of personnel has a much larger number of variables to control; the optimum financial objective, therefore, is much less certain.

Degree of influence.   The greater the influence that a manager can exercise over critical performance variables, the easier it is to develop an effective management control system. The difficulty in measuring a manager's performance is directly related to the number and type of noncontrollable or semicontrollable performance variables that exist. In general, external marketing variables are much more difficult to influence than internal production variables, because a marketing manager has no control over the actions of competitors or the general status of the economy. Thus, it is much easier to set a profit objective and to judge performance against this objective for a business unit in which sales are limited by production capacity (i.e., everything that can be produced can be sold) than for a business unit that sells in a highly competitive or volatile market and has ample production capacity.

Relative uncertainty.   A business unit manager may face uncertainties both in the external environment and in the internal environment. The external environment consists of four major sectors: (1) customers, (2) suppliers, (3) competitors, and (4) regulatory. The internal environment consists of factors inside the firm (e.g., degree of interdependence with other business units). By uncertainty, we mean the unpredictability in the actions of both the external agencies and the internal forces. The greater the uncertainty, the more difficult it is to use the profit budget as a basis for performance appraisal.[7] There are several reasons for this.

First, performance evaluation presupposes establishment of accurate profit targets. To arrive at targets that can serve as valid standards for subsequent performance appraisal, one must be able to predict the conditions that will exist during the coming year. If these predictions are incorrect, the profit objective will also be incorrect. Obviously, these conditions can be predicted more accurately under stable conditions than under changing conditions. The basic effect of uncertainty is to limit the ability of managers to plan or make decisions about activities in advance of their occurrence. Thus, the greater the uncertainty, the more difficult it is to prepare satisfactory targets that could then become the basis for performance evaluation.

Second, because efficiency refers to the amount of output per unit of input, an evaluation of a manager's efficiency depends on a detailed knowledge of the outcomes associated with given management actions—that is, knowledge about cause/effect relationships. Better knowledge about cause/effect relationships exists under stable conditions than under uncertain conditions. Therefore, judgments about efficiency are more difficult under uncertain conditions.

Third, the emphasis of financial performance indicators is on outcomes rather than on process. Managers control their own actions, but they cannot control the states of nature which combine with their actions to produce outcomes. In a situation with high uncertainty, therefore, financial information does not adequately reflect managerial performance.

Time span.   If a management control system is to provide an adequate basis for judging performance, the comparison of actual with budgeted amounts must measure the actual accomplishments of the manager during the period under review. This is unlikely to happen if the decisions that a manager makes today are not reflected in profitability until some future period; or, conversely, if current profitability reflects the impact of decisions made in some past period. The more these two conditions are present, the less desirable it is to use budget as a tool to evaluate business unit managers.

---

[7] See V. Govindarajan, "Appropriateness of Accounting Data in Performance Evaluation: An Empirical Evaluation of Environmental Uncertainty as an Intervening Variable," *Accounting Organizations and Society* IX, no. 2, (1984), pp. 125–35.

Conditions Necessary for Implementing Tight Control

As noted above, tight control is feasible only when the degree of discretion exercised by the manager is restricted, the number and degree of noncontrollable variables are limited, the degree of uncertainty facing the manager is low, and the time span of the manager's job is relatively short. Even in these circumstances, a tight control system requires the following:

- Senior management's active involvement in the budgeting and reporting system. Senior management must have an intimate knowledge of the operations being reviewed and have an ability and willingness to analyze and interpret financial data.
- Adequate accounting controls and a capable internal audit organization so manipulation is not attempted (or, if attempted, is detected).
- A culture that discourages dysfunctional actions. For example, there must be an understanding that a business unit manager who delays informing senior management about incipient problems is committing a serious sin. The insistence by senior management on accurate and immediate communication of problems, together with management's intimate knowledge of individual operations, reduces significantly the likelihood that unexpected adverse situations will develop.

SUMMARY

Business unit managers report their financial performance to senior management regularly, usually monthly. The formal report consists of a comparison of actual revenues and costs with budgeted amounts. The differences, or variances, between these two amounts can be analyzed at several levels of detail. This analysis identifies the causes of the variance from budgeted profit and the amount attributable to each cause.

In addition, senior management receives information about performance from reports on key variables and from informal sources. The information is analyzed and action is taken if it is necessary.

Companies differ in the emphasis they place on meeting budgetary objectives in the short run. Appropriateness of tight financial controls depends upon situational factors.

SUGGESTED ADDITIONAL READINGS

Baiman, Stanley, and Joel Demski. "Variance Analysis Procedures as Motivational Devices." *Management Science*, August 1980, pp. 840–48.

Brownell, Peter, and Mark Hirst. "Reliance on Accounting Information, Budgetary Participation, and Task Uncertainty: Tests of a Three-Way Interaction." *Journal of Accounting Research* XXIV, no. 2, (Autumn, 1986), pp. 241–49.

Brownell, Peter, and Morris McInnes. "Budgetary Participation, Motivation, and Management Performance." *The Accounting Review,* October 1986.

Chenhall, R. H., and D. Morris. "The Impact of Structure, Environment, and Interdependence on the Perceived Usefulness of Management Accounting Systems." *The Accounting Review* LXI, no. I, (January 1986), pp. 16–35.

Dearden, John. "Measuring Profit Center Managers." *Harvard Business Review,* September–October 1987, pp. 84–86.

Govindarajan, Vijay. "Appropriateness of Accounting Data in Performance Evaluation: An Empirical Examination of Environment Uncertainty as an Intervening Variable." *Accounting, Organizations and Society,* IX, no. 2 (1984), pp. 125–35.

Govindarajan, Vijay, and John K. Shank. "Profit Variance Analysis: A Strategic Focus." *Issues in Accounting Education* 4, no. 2, (Fall 1989), pp. 396–410.

Hirst, Mark K. "Accounting Information and the Evaluation of Subordinate Performance: A Situational Approach." *The Accounting Review,* October 1981, pp. 771–84.

Hofstede, G. "The Poverty of Management Control Philosophy." *Academy of Management Review,* July 1978.

Hopwood, Anthony. "An Empirical Study of the Role of Accounting Data in Performance Evaluation." *Journal of Accounting Research,* 10 (1972), pp. 156–82.

Merchant, Kenneth A. *Control in Business Organizations.* Marshfield, Mass.: Putnam, 1985.

Otley, David T. "Budget Use and Managerial Performance." *Journal of Accounting Research,* Spring 1978, pp. 122–49.

Shillinglaw, Gordon. *Managerial Cost Accounting.* 5th ed. Homewood, Ill.: Richard D. Irwin, 1982, chap. 27.

Umpathy, Srinivasan. *Current Budgeting Practices in U.S. Industry: The State of the Art.* Westport, Conn.: Quorum, 1987.

Case 11–1

Cotter Company, Inc.*

In preparing its profit plan for 1988, the management of Cotter Company, Inc., realized that its sales were subject to monthly seasonal variations, but it expected that for the year as a whole the profit before taxes would total $240,000, as shown in Exhibit 1.

Management defined *prime costs* as those costs for labor and materials which were strictly variable with the quantity of production in the factory. The overhead in the factory included both fixed and variable costs; management's estimate was that, within a sales volume range of plus or minus $1 million per year, variable factory overhead would be equal to 25 percent of prime costs. Thus, the total factory overhead budgeted for

1988 consisted of $240,000 of variable costs (25 percent of $960,000) and $600,000 of fixed costs. All of the selling and general overhead was fixed, except for commissions on sales equal to 5 percent of the selling price.

Mr. Cotter, the president of the company, approved the budget, stating that, "A profit of $20,000 a month isn't bad for a little company in this business." During January, however, sales suffered the normal seasonal dips, and production in the factory also was cut back. The result, which came as some surprise to the president, was that January showed a loss of $7,000 (see Exhibit 2).

EXHIBIT 1 Budget, 1988

	Amount	Percent of Sales
Sales	$2,400,000	100%
Standard cost of goods sold:		
Prime costs	960,000	40
Factory overhead	840,000	35
Total standard cost	1,800,000	75
Gross profit	600,000	25
Selling and general overhead	360,000	15
Profit before taxes	$ 240,000	10%

* This case was prepared by R. F. Vancil, Harvard Business School.
Copyright © by the President and Fellows of Harvard College.
Harvard Business School case 168-005.

EXHIBIT 2 Operating Statement, January 1988

Sales		$140,000
Standard cost of goods sold		105,000
Standard gross profit		35,000
		Favorable or (Unfavorable)
Manufacturing variances:		
Prime cost variance	$ (3,500)	
Factory overhead:		
Spending variance	1,000	
Volume variance	(12,500)	$ (15,000)
Actual gross profit		20,000
Selling and general overhead		27,000
Loss before taxes		$ (7,000)

QUESTION

Explain, as best you can with the data available, why the January profit was $27,000 less than the average monthly profit expected by the president.

Case 11–2

Midwest Ice Cream Company (B)*

In 1982, Midwest Ice Cream Company installed a financial planning and control system. (See Midwest Ice Cream Company (A), Case 9–3 for details of this system.) After receiving the 1983 operating results, Jim Peterson, president of Midwest, had asked Frank Roberts, marketing vice president, to make a short presentation at the next board of directors meeting commenting on the major reasons for the favorable operating income variance of $71,700. He asked him to draft his presentation in the next few days so that the two of them could go over it before the board meeting. Peterson wanted to illustrate to the board how an analysis of profit variance could highlight those areas needing management attention as well as those deserving a pat on the back.

The Profit Plan for 1983

Following the four-step approach outlined in Midwest Ice Cream Company (A), the management group of Midwest Ice Cream prepared a profit plan for 1983. The timetable they followed is shown in Table 1.

Based on an anticipated overall ice cream market of about 11,440,000 gallons in their marketing area and a market share of 50 percent, Midwest forecast overall gallon sales of 5,720,329 for 1983. Actually, this forecast was the same as the latest estimate of 1982 actual gallon sales. Rather than trying to get too sophisticated on the first attempt at budgeting, Mr. Peterson had decided to just go with 1982's volume as 1983's goal or forecast. He felt that there was plenty of time in later years to refine the system by bringing in more formal sales forecasting techniques and concepts.

This same general approach was also followed for variable product standard costs and for fixed costs. Budgeted costs for 1983 were expected 1982 results, adjusted for a few items which were

TABLE 1

	October— 1982 (weeks)				November— 1982 (weeks)			
	1	2	3	4	1	2	3	4
I Variable cost standards		x						
II–A Sales forecast		x						
II–B Approval of sales forecast			x					
III–A Preliminary payroll budget			x					
III–B Prelimary budget for other operating expenses			x					
III–C Approval of payroll budget and other expenses budget				x				
IV–A Preliminary profit plan								
IV–B Approval of profit plan						x		
IV–C Board of directors meeting							x	

---

* This case was prepared by John Shank, Harvard Business School.

EXHIBIT 1   Profit Plan for 1983

	Standard Contribution Margin per Gallon	Forecasted Gallon Sales	Forecasted Contribution Margin
Vanilla	$0.4329	2,409,854	$1,043,200
Chocolate	0.4535	2,009,061	911,100
Walnut	0.5713	48,883	28,000
Buttercrunch	0.4771	262,185	125,000
Cherry Swirl	0.5153	204,774	105,500
Strawberry	0.4683	628,560	294,400
Pecan chip	0.5359	157,012	84,100
Total	$0.4530	5,720,329	$2,591,300

Breakdown of Budgeted Total Expenses

	Variable	Fixed	Total
Manufacturing	$5,888,100	$ 612,800	$6,500,900
Delivery	187,300	516,300	703,600
Advertising*	553,200	—	553,200
Selling	—	368,800	368,800
Administrative	—	448,000	448,000
Total	$6,628,600	$1,945,900	$8,574,500

* The 1983 advertising allowance was 6 percent of sales dollars.

Recap

Sales	$9,219,900
Variable cost of sales	6,628,600
Contribution margin	2,591,300
Fixed costs	1,945,900
Income from operations	$ 645,400

clearly out of line in 1982. A summary of the 1983 profit plan is shown in Exhibit 1.

Actual Results for 1983

By the spring of 1983, it had become clear that sales volume for 1983 was going to be higher than forecast. In fact, Midwest's actual sales for the year totaled 5,968,366 gallons, an increase of about 248,000 gallons over budget. Market research data indicated that the total ice cream mar-

ket in Midwest's marketing area was 12,180,000 gallons for the year, as opposed to the forecasted figure of about 11,440,000 gallons. The revised profit plan for the year, based on actual volume, is shown in Exhibit 2.

The fixed costs in the revised profit plan are the same as before, $1,945,900. The variable costs, however, have been adjusted to reflect a volume level of 5,968,000 gallons instead of 5,720,000 gallons, thereby eliminating wide cost

EXHIBIT 2 Revised Profit Plan for 1983—Budgeted at Actual Volume

	Standard Contribution Margin per Gallon	Actual Gallon Sales	Forecast Contribution Margin
Vanilla	$0.4329	2,458,212	$1,064,200
Chocolate	0.4535	2,018,525	915,400
Walnut	0.5713	50,124	28,600
Buttercrunch	0.4771	268,839	128,300
Cherry swirl	0.5153	261,240	134,600
Strawberry	0.4683	747,049	349,800
Pecan chip	0.5359	164,377	88,100
Total	$0.4539	5,968,366	$2,709,000

Breakdown of Budgeted Total Expenses

	Variable	Fixed	Total
Manufacturing	$6,113,100	$ 612,800	$6,725,900
Delivery	244,500	516,300	760,800
Advertising	578,700	—	578,700
Selling	—	368,800	368,800
Administrative	—	448,000	448,000
Total	$6,936,300	$1,945,900	$8,882,200

Recap

Sales	$9,645,300
Variable cost of sales	6,936,300
Contribution margin	2,709,000
Fixed costs	1,945,900
Income from operations	$ 763,100

variances due strictly to the difference between planned volume and actual volume. Assume, for example, that cartons are budgeted at 4 cents per gallon. If we forecast volume of 10,000 gallons, the budgeted allowance for cartons is $400. If we actually sell only 8,000 gallons but use $350 worth of cartons, it is misleading to say that there is a favorable variance of $50. The variance is clearly unfavorable by $30. This only shows up if we adjust the budget to the actual volume level.

For costs which are highly volume-dependent, variances should be based on a budget that reflects the volume of operations actually attained. Since the level of fixed costs is independent of volume

Carton allowance	= $0.04 per gallon
Forecast volume	= 10,000 gallons
Carton budget	= $400
Actual volume	= 8,000 gallons
Actual carton expense	= $350
Variance (based on forecast volume)	= $400 − $350 = $50 Favorable
Variance (based on actual volume)	= $320 − $350 = $30 Unfavorable

anyway, it is not necessary to adjust the budget for these items for volume differences. The original budget for fixed cost items is still appropriate.

Exhibit 3 is the 1983 earnings statement. The figures for December have been excluded for purposes of this case. Exhibit 4 is the detailed expense breakdown for the manufacturing department. The detailed expense breakdowns for the other departments have been excluded for purposes of this case.

Analysis of the 1983 Profit Variance

Three days after Jim Peterson asked Frank Roberts to pull together a presentation for the board of directors analyzing the profit variance

---

EXHIBIT 3

Earnings Statement
December 31, 1983

	Month		Year to Date	
	Actual	*Budget*	*Actual*	*Budget*
Sales—net			$9,657,300	$9,645,300
Manufacturing cost of goods sold—				
Schedule A–2*			6,824,900*	6,725,900
Delivery—Schedule A–3			706,800	760,800
Advertising—Schedule A–4			607,700	578,700
Selling—Schedule A–5			362,800	368,800
Administrative—Schedule A–7			438,000	448,000
Total expenses			8,940,200	8,882,200
Income from operations			717,100	763,100
Other income—Schedule A–8			12,500	12,500
Other expenses—Schedule A–9			6,000	6,000
Income before taxes			723,600	769,600
Provision for income taxes			361,800	
Net earnings			$ 361,800	

* Schedules A–3 through A–9 have not been included in this case. Schedule A–2 is reproduced as Exhibit 4.

Analysis of variance from forecasted operating income:

	Month		Year to Date	
	Actual	*Budget*	*Actual*	*Budget*
(1) Actual income from operations			$717,100	
(2) Budgeted profit at forecast volume			645,400	
(3) Budgeted profit at actual volume			763,100	
Variance due to sales volume—[(3) − (2)]			117,700 F	
Variance due to operations—[(1) − (3)]			46,000 U	
Total variance—[(1) − (2)]			71,700 F	

EXHIBIT 4   Manufacturing Cost of Goods Sold, December 31, 1983

	Month		Year to Date	
Variable Costs	*Actual*	*Budget*	*Actual*	*Budget*
Dairy Ingredients			$3,679,900	$3,648,500
Milk price variance			57,300	—
Sugar			599,900	596,800
Sugar price variance			23,400	—
Flavoring (including fruits and nuts)			946,800	982,100
Cartons			567,200	566,900
Plastic wrap			28,700	29,800
Additives			235,000	251,000
Supplies			31,000	35,000
Miscellaneous			3,000	3,000
Subtotal			6,172,200	6,113,100
Fixed Costs				
Labor—cartonizing and freezing			$ 425,200	$ 390,800
Labor—other			41,800	46,000
Repairs			32,200	25,000
Depreciation			81,000	81,000
Electricity and water			41,500	40,000
Miscellaneous			1,500	30,000
Spoilage			29,500	
Subtotal			652,700	612,800
Total			$6,824,900	$6,725,900

for 1983, Roberts came into Peterson's office to review his first draft. He showed Peterson the following schedule (Table 2).

Roberts said that he planned to give each member of the board of directors a copy of this schedule and then to comment briefly on each of the items. Peterson said he thought the schedule was OK as far as it went, but that it just didn't highlight things in a manner that indicated what corrective actions should be taken in 1984 or that indicated the real causes for the favorable overall variance. He suggested that Roberts try to break down the sales volume variance into the part attributable to sales mix, the part attributable to market share shifts, and the part actually attributable to volume changes. He also suggested breaking down the manufacturing variance to indicate what main corrective actions are called for in 1984 to erase the unfavorable variance. How much of the total was due to price differences versus quantity differences, for example? Finally, he suggested that Roberts call on John Vance, the company controller, if he needed some help in the mechanics of breaking out these different variances.

As Roberts returned to his office he considered Peterson's suggestion of getting Vance involved in revising the schedule to be presented to the board. Roberts did not want to consult Vance unless it was absolutely necessary, because Vance always went overboard on the technical aspects of any accounting problem. Roberts couldn't imagine a quicker way to put board members to sleep

TABLE 2

Favorable variance due to sales:		
Volume	$117,700 F	
Price*	12,000 F	$129,700 F
Unfavorable variance due to operations:		
Manufacturing	99,000 U	
Delivery	54,000 F	
Advertising	29,000 U	
Selling	6,000 F	
Administration	10,000 F	58,000 U
Net variance—favorable		$ 71,700 F

* This price variance is the difference between the standard sales values of the gallons actually sold and the actual sales value (9,657,300 minus 9,645,300).

than to throw one of Vance's number-filled, six-page memos at them. "Peterson specifically wants a nontechnical presentation for the board," Roberts thought to himself, "and that rules out John Vance. Besides you don't have to be a CPA to just focus in on the key variance areas from a general management viewpoint."

QUESTIONS

1. Review the variance analysis in Exhibit 3, being certain you understand it. (This is the same idea as in Exhibit 7 of Midwest Ice Cream Company (A), Case 9–3.)
2. Calculate the gross margin mix variance for 1983, using the approach shown in the lower portion of Exhibit 5 of Case 9–3. Then calculate a detailed (i.e., flavor-by-flavor) mix variance. For what purposes would the detailed analysis be more useful than the aggregate mix variance calculation?
3. How would you modify Frank Peterson's variance analysis before explaining the $71,700F profit variance to the board of directors?
4. Considering both this case and Case 9–3, evaluate Midwest's budgetary control system.

Case 11–3
Galvor Company*

When M. Barsac replaced M. Chambertin as Galvor's controller in April of 1974, at the age of 31, he became the first of a new group of senior managers resulting from the acquisition by Universal Electric. It was an accepted fact that, in the large and sprawling Universal organization, the controller's department represented a key function. M. Barsac, who was a skilled accountant, had had 10 years' experience in a large French subsidiary of Universal.

He recalled his early days with Galvor vividly and admitted they were, to say the least, hectic.

I arrived at Galvor in early April 1974, a few days after M. Chambertin had left. I was the first Universal man here in Bordeaux and I became quickly immersed in all the problems surrounding the change of ownership. For example, there were no really workable financial statements for the previous two years. This made preparation of the Business Plan, which Mr. Hennessy and I began in June, extremely difficult. This plan covers every aspect of the business, but the great secrecy which had always been maintained at Galvor about the company's financial affairs made it almost impossible for anyone to help us.

M. Barsac's duties could be roughly divided into two major areas: first, the preparation of numerous reports required by Universal, and, second, supervision of Galvor's internal accounting function. While these two areas were closely related, it is useful to separate them in describing the accounting and control function as it developed after Universal's acquisition of Galvor.

To control its operating units, Universal relied primarily on an extensive system of financial reporting. Universal attributed much of its success in recent years to this system. The system was viewed by Universal's European controller, M. Boudry, as much more than a device to "check up" on the operating units.

In addition to measuring our progress in the conventional sense of sales, earnings, and return on investment, we believe the reporting system causes our operating people to focus their attention on critical areas which might not otherwise receive their major attention. An example would be the level of investment in inventory. The system also forces people to think about the future and to commit themselves to specific future goals. Most operating people are understandably involved in today's problems. We believe some device is required to force them to look beyond the problems at hand and to consider longer-range objectives and strategy. You could say we view the reporting system as an effective training and educational device.

Background

The Galvor Company had been founded in 1946 by M. Georges Latour, who continued as its owner and president until 1974. Throughout its history, the company had acted as a fabricator, buying parts and assembling them into high-quality, moderate-cost electric and electronic measuring and test equipment. In its own sector of the electronics industry—measuring instruments—Galvor was one of the major French firms; however, there were many electronics firms in the more sophisticated sectors of the industry which were vastly larger than Galvor.

---

* This case is copyrighted by International Institute for Management Development (IMD), Lausanne, Switzerland.

Galvor's period of greatest growth began around 1960. Between 1960 and 1971, sales grew from 2.2 million 1971 new francs to 12 million, and after-tax profits from 120,000 1971 new francs to 1,062,000. Assets as of December 31, 1971, totaled 8.8 million new francs. (One 1971 new franc = $0.20.) The firm's prosperity resulted in a number of offers to purchase equity in the firm, but M. Latour had remained steadfast in his belief that only if he had complete ownership of Galvor could he direct its affairs with a free hand. As owner/president, Latour had continued over the years to be personally involved in every detail of the firm's operations.

As of early 1972, M. Latour was concerned about the development of adequate successor management for Galvor. Following the 1973 unionization of Galvor's work force, which Latour had opposed, Latour (then 54 years old) began to entertain seriously the idea of selling the firm and devoting himself "to family, philanthropic, and general social interests." On April 1, 1974, Galvor was sold to Universal Electric Company for $4.5 million worth of UE's stock. M. Latour became chairman of the board of Galvor, and David Hennessy was appointed as Galvor's managing director. Hennessy at that time was 38 years old and had been with Universal Electric for nine years.

The Business Plan

The heart of Universal's reporting and control system was an extremely comprehensive document—the Business Plan—which was prepared annually by each of the operating units. The Business Plan was the primary standard for evaluating the performance of unit managers, and everything possible was done by Universal's top management to give authority to the plan.

Each January, the Geneva headquarters of Universal set tentative objectives for the following two years for each of its European operating units. This was a "first look"—an attempt to provide a broad statement of objectives which

would permit the operating units to develop their detailed Business Plans. For operating units which produced more than a single product line, objectives were established for both the unit as a whole and for each product line. Primary responsibility for establishing these tentative objectives rested with eight product-line managers located in Geneva, each of whom was responsible for a group of product lines. On the basis of his knowledge of the product lines and his best judgment of their market potential, each product-line manager set the tentative objectives for his lines.

For reporting purposes, Universal considered that Galvor represented a single product line, even though Galvor's own executives viewed the company's products as falling into three distinct lines—multimeters, panel meters, and electronic instruments.

For each of over 300 Universal product lines in Europe, objectives were established for five key measures.

1. Sales.
2. Net income.
3. Total assets.
4. Total employees.
5. Capital expenditures.

From January to April, these tentative objectives were "negotiated" between Geneva headquarters and the operating managements. Formal meetings were held in Geneva to resolve differences between the operating unit managers and product-line managers or other headquarters personnel.

Negotiations also took place at the same time on products to be discontinued. Mr. Hennessy described this process as a "sophisticated exercise which includes a careful analysis of the effect on overhead costs of discontinuing a product and also recognizes the cost of holding an item in stock. It is a good analysis and one method Universal uses to keep the squeeze on us."

During May, the negotiated objectives were reviewed and approved by Universal's European headquarters in Geneva and by corporate headquarters in the United States. These final reviews focused primarily on the five key measures noted above. In 1976, the objectives for total capital expenditures and for the total number of employees received particularly close surveillance. The approved objectives provided the foundation for preparation of Business Plans.

In June and July, Galvor prepared its Business Plan. The plan, containing up to 100 pages, described in detail how Galvor intended to achieve its objectives for the following two years. The plan also contained a forecast, in less detail, for the fifth year hence (e.g., for 1981 in the case of the plan prepared in 1976).

Summary Reports

The broad scope of the Business Plan can best be understood by a description of the type of information it contained. It began with a brief one-page financial and operating summary containing comparative data for:

Preceding year   (actual data).
Current year   (budget).
Next year   (forecast).
Two years hence (forecast).
Five years hence (forecast).

This one-page summary contained condensed data dealing with the following measures for each of the five years:

Net income.
Sales.
Total assets.
Total capital employed (sum of long-term debt and net worth).
Receivables.
Inventories.
Plant, property, and equipment.
Capital expenditures.
Provision for depreciation.
Percent return on sales.
Percent return on total assets.

Percent return on total capital employed.
Percent total assets to sales.
Percent receivables to sales.
Percent inventories to sales.
Orders received.
Orders on hand.
Average number of full-time employees.
Total cost of employee compensation.
Sales per employee.
Net income per employee.
Sales per $1,000 of employee compensation.
Net income per $1,000 of employee compensation.
Sales per thousand square feet of floor space.
Net income per thousand square feet of floor space.

Anticipated changes in net income for the current year and for each of the next two years were summarized according to their cause, as follows:

Volume of sales.
Product mix.
Sales prices.
Raw material purchase prices.
Cost reduction programs.
Accounting changes and all other causes.

This analysis of the causes of changes in net income forced operating managements to appraise carefully the profit implications of all management actions affecting prices, costs, volume, or product mix.

Financial Statements

These condensed summary reports were followed by a complete set of projected financial statements—income statement, balance sheet, and a statement of cash flow—for the current year and for each of the next two years. Each major item on these financial statements was then analyzed in detail in separate reports, which covered such matters as transactions with headquarters, proposed outside financing, investment in receivables and inventory, number of employees and employee compensation, capital expenditures, and nonrecurring write-offs of assets.

Management Actions

The Business Plan contained a description of the major management actions planned for the next two years, with an estimate of the favorable or unfavorable effect each action would have on total sales, net income, and total assets. Among some of the major management actions described in Galvor's 1976 business Plan (prepared in mid-1975) were the following:

Implement standard cost system.

Revise prices.

Cut oldest low-margin items from line.

Standardize and simplify product design.

Create forward research and development plan.

Implement product planning.

Separate plans were presented for each of the functional areas—marketing, manufacturing, research and development, financial control, and personnel and employee relations. These functional plans began with a statement of the function's mission, an analysis of its present problems and opportunities, and a statement of the specific actions it intended to take in the next two years.

Better distribute tasks.

Make more intensive use of IBM equipment.

Replace nonqualified employees with better-trained and more dynamic people.

The Business Plan closed with a series of comparative financial statements, which depicted the estimated item-by-item effect if sales fell to 60 percent or to 80 percent of forecast or increased to 120 percent of forecast. For each of these levels of possible sales, costs were divided into three categories: fixed costs, unavoidable variable costs, and management discretionary costs. Management described the specific actions it would take to control employment, total assets, and capital expenditures in case of a reduction in sales, and when these actions would be put into effect. In its 1976 Business Plan, Galvor indicated that its program for contraction would be put into effect if

incoming orders dropped below 60 percent of budget for two weeks, 75 percent for four weeks, or 85 percent for eight weeks. It noted that assets would be cut only 80 percent in a 60 percent year and to 90 percent in an 80 percent year, "because remodernization of our business is too essential for survival to slow down much more."

Approval of Plan

By midsummer, the completed Business Plan was submitted to Universal headquarters; and beginning in the early fall, meetings were held in Geneva to review each company's Business Plan. Each plan had to be justified and defended at these meetings, which were attended by senior executives from both Universal's European and American headquarters and by the general managers and functional managers of many of the operating units. Universal viewed these meetings as an important element in its constant effort to encourage operating managements to share their experiences in resolving common problems.

Before final approval of a company's Business Plan at the Geneva review meeting, changes were often proposed by Universal's top management. For example, in September 1976, the 1977 forecasts of sales and net income in Galvor's Business Plan were accepted; but the year-end forecasts of total employees and total assets were reduced about 9 percent and 1 percent, respectively. Galvor's proposed capital expenditures for the year were cut 34 percent, a reduction primarily attributable to limitations imposed by Universal on all operating units throughout the corporation.

The approved Business Plan became the foundation of the budget for the following year, which was due in Geneva by mid-November. The general design of the budget resembled that of the Business Plan, except that the various dollar amounts, which were presented in the Business Plan on an annual business, were broken down by months. Minor changes between the overall key results forecast in the Business Plan and those reflected in greater detail in the budget were not permitted. Requests for major changes had to be submitted to Geneva no later than mid-October.

Reporting to Universal

Every Universal unit in Europe had to submit periodic reports to Geneva according to a fixed schedule of dates. All units in Universal, whether based in the United States or elsewhere, adhered to essentially the same reporting system. Identical forms and account numbers were used throughout the Universal organization. Since the reporting system made no distinction between units of different size, Galvor submitted the same reports as a unit with many times it sales. Computer processing of these reports facilitated combining the results of Universal's European operations for prompt review in Geneva and transmission to corporate headquarters in the United States.

The main focus in most of the reports submitted to Universal was on the variance between actual results and budgeted results. Sales and expense data were presented for both the latest month and for the year to date. Differences between the current year and the prior year also were reported, because these were the figures submitted quarterly to Universal's shareholders and to newspapers and other financial reporting services.

Description of Reports

Thirteen different reports were submitted by the controller on a monthly basis, ranging from a statement of preliminary net income, which was due during the first week following the close of each month, to a report on the status of capital projects due on the last day of each month. The monthly reports included:

Statement of preliminary net income.

Statement of income.

Balance sheet.

Statement of changes in retained earning.

Statement of cash flow.

Employment statistics.

Status of orders received, canceled, and outstanding.

Statement of intercompany transactions.

Statement of transactions with headquarters.

Analysis of inventories.

Analysis of receivables.

Status of capital projects.

Controller's monthly operating and financial review.

The final item, the controller's monthly operating and financial review, often ran to 20 pages or more. It contained an explanation of the significant variances from budget, as well as a general commentary on the financial affairs of the unit.

In addition to the reports submitted on a monthly basis, approximately 12 other reports were required less often, either quarterly, semiannually, or annually.

Cost of the System

The control and reporting system, including preparation of the annual Business Plan, imposed a heavy burden in both time and money on the management of an operating unit. M. Barsac commented on this aspect of the system in the section of Galvor's 1976 Business Plan dealing with the control functional area.

Galvor's previous administrative manager [controller], who was a tax specialist above all, had to prepare a balance sheet and statement of income once a year. Cost accounting, perpetual inventory valuation, inventory control, production control, customer accounts receivable control, budgeting, etcetera did not exist. No information was given to other department heads concerning sales results, costs, and expenses. The change to a formal monthly reporting system has been very difficult to realize. Due to the low level of employee training, many tasks, such as consolidation, monthly and quarterly reports, budgets, the Business Plan, implementation of the new cost system, various analyses, restatement of prior years' accounts, etcetera must be fully performed by the controller and chief accountant, thus spending 80 percent of their full time in spite of working 55–60 hours per week. The number of employees in the controller's department in subsequent years will not depend on Galvor's volume of activity, but rather on Universal's requirements.

Implementation of the complete Universal Cost and Production Control System in a company where nothing existed before is an enormous task, which involves establishing 8,000 machining and 3,000 assembly standard times and codifying 15,000 piece parts.

When interviewed early in 1977, M. Barsac stated:

> Getting the data to Universal on time continues to be a problem. We simply don't have the necessary people who understand the reporting system and its purpose. The reports are all in English and few of my people are conversant in English. Also, American accounting methods are different from procedures used in France. Another less serious problem concerns the need to convert all of our internal records, which are kept in francs, to dollars when reporting to Universal.

Among the objectives set for the control area in the 1976 Business Plan, M. Barsac stated that he hoped to:

> I am especially concerned that few of the reports we prepare for Universal are useful to our operating people here in Bordeaux. Mr. Hennessy, of course, uses the reports, as do one or two others. I am doing all that I can to encourage greater use of these reports. My job is not only to provide facts but to help the managers understand and utilize the figures available. We have recently started issuing monthly cost and expense reports for each department showing the variances from budget. These have been well received.

Mr. Hennessy also commented on meeting the demands imposed by Universal's reporting system.

> Without the need to report to Universal, we would do some things in a less formal way or at different times. Universal decides that the entire organization must move to a certain basis by a

specified date. There are extra costs involved in meeting these deadlines. It should be noted, also, that demands made on the controller's department are passed on to other areas, such as marketing, engineering, and production.

M. Boudry, Universal's European controller, acknowledged that the cost of the planning and reporting system was high, especially for smaller units.

> The system is designed for a large business. We think that the absolute minimum annual sales volume for an individual unit to support the system is about $15 million; however, we would prefer at least $30 million. By this standard, Galvor is barely acceptable. We really don't know if the cost of the system is unnecessarily burdensome in the sense that it requires information which is not worth its cost. A reasonable estimate might be that about 50 percent of the information would be required in any smartly managed independent business of comparable size, another 25 percent is required for Universal's particular needs, and 25 percent is probably "dead underbrush" which should be cleaned out. Ideally, every five years we should throw the system out the window and start again with the essentials.

As an indication of some of his department's routine activity, M. Barsac noted that at the end of 1976 Galvor was preparing each working day about 200 invoices. At that time the company had approximately 12,000 active customers.

Early in 1977, 42 people were employed in the controller's department. The organization of the department is described in Exhibit 1.

Headquarters Performance Review

Galvor's periodic financial reports were forwarded to M. Boudry in Geneva. The reports were first reviewed by an assistant to M. Boudry, one of four financial analysts who together reviewed all reports received from Universal's operating units in Europe.

In early 1977, M. Boudry described the purpose of these reviews:

EXHIBIT 1   Organization of Controller's Department (January 1977)*

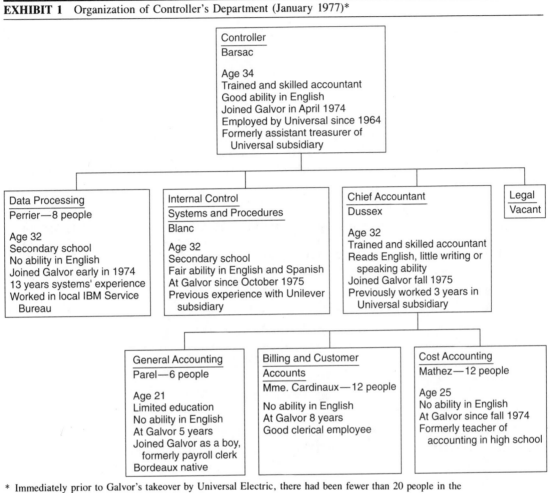

Controller
Barsac

Age 34
Trained and skilled accountant
Good ability in English
Joined Galvor in April 1974
Employed by Universal since 1964
Formerly assistant treasurer of
　Universal subsidiary

Data Processing
Perrier—8 people

Age 32
Secondary school
No ability in English
Joined Galvor early in 1974
13 years systems' experience
Worked in local IBM Service
　Bureau

Internal Control
Systems and Procedures
Blanc

Age 32
Secondary school
Fair ability in English and Spanish
At Galvor since October 1975
Previous experience with Unilever
　subsidiary

Chief Accountant
Dussex

Age 32
Trained and skilled accountant
Reads English, little writing or
　speaking ability
Joined Galvor fall 1975
Previously worked 3 years in
　Universal subsidiary

Legal
Vacant

General Accounting
Parel—6 people

Age 21
Limited education
No ability in English
At Galvor 5 years
Joined Galvor as a boy,
　formerly payroll clerk
Bordeaux native

Billing and Customer
Accounts
Mme. Cardinaux—12 people

No ability in English
At Galvor 8 years
Good clerical employee

Cost Accounting
Mathez—12 people

Age 25
No ability in English
At Galvor since fall 1974
Formerly teacher of
　accounting in high school

* Immediately prior to Galvor's takeover by Universal Electric, there had been fewer than 20 people in the controller's department.

The reviews focus on a comparison of performance against budget for the key measures—sales, net income, total assets, total employees, and capital expenditures. These are stated as unambiguous numbers. We try to detect any trouble spots or trends which seem to be developing. Of course, the written portions of the reports are also carefully reviewed, particularly the explanations of variances from budget. If everything is moving as planned, we do nothing.

The reports may contain a month-by-month revi-

sion of forecasts to year end; but if the planned objectives for the year are not to be met, we consider the situation as serious.

If a unit manager has a problem and calls for help, then it becomes a matter of common concern. He can probably expect a bad day in explaining how it happened, but he can expect help, too. Depending on the nature of the problem, either Mr. Forrester, Galvor's product-line manager, or one of our staff specialists would go down to Bordeaux. In addition to the financial analysts, one of whom

---

EXHIBIT 2   Telex from Poulet to Hennessy, Concerning Level of Inventory

---

TO: HENNESSY—GALVOR
FROM: POULET—UE
DATE: SEPTEMBER 26, 1976

FOLLOWING ARE THE JULY AND AUGUST INVENTORY AND SALES FIGURES WITH THEIR RE-
SPECTIVE VARIANCES FROM BUDGET ($000s).

		JULY			*AUGUST*	
	ACTUAL	*BUDGET*	*VARIANCE*	*ACTUAL*	*BUDGET*	*VARIANCE*
INVENTORY.	2,010	1,580	(430)	2,060	1,600	(460)
SALES TO DATE.	3,850	3,900	(50)	4,090	4,150	(60)

LATEST AUGUST SALES FORECAST REFLECTS DECREASE IN YEAR-END SALES OF 227 VERSUS
INCREASE OF 168 IN YEAR-END INVENTORIES OVER BUDGET.

REQUEST TELEX LATEST MONTH-BY-MONTH INVENTORY AND SALES FORECAST FROM SEP-
TEMBER TO DECEMBER, EXPLANATION OF VARIANCE IN INVENTORY FROM BUDGET AND COR-
RECTIVE ACTION YOU PLAN IN ORDER TO ACHIEVE YEAR-END GOAL. INCLUDE PERSONNEL
REDUCTIONS, PURCHASE MATERIAL CANCELLATIONS, ETC.

POULET

EXHIBIT 3   Telex from Hennessy to Poulet Concerning Level of Inventory

---

TO: POULET—UE
FROM: HENNESSY—GALVOR
DATE: SEPTEMBER 27, 1976

YOUR 26.9.76
MONTHLY INVENTORY FORECAST SEPTEMBER TO DECEMBER BY CATEGORY AS FOLLOWS
($000s):

	SEPT. 30	*OCT. 31*	*NOV. 30*	*DEC. 31*
RAW MATERIALS.	53	51	50	50
PURCHASED PARTS.	180	185	190	195
MANUFACTURED PARTS.	95	93	93	91
WORK-IN-PROCESS.	838	725	709	599
FINISHED GOODS.	632	694	683	705
OTHER INVENTORIES.	84	84	82	80
ENGINEERING IN PROCESS. . . .	55	58	48	44
RESERVE.	(14)	(14)	(14)	(20)
INDICA.	50	52	55	55
TOTAL.	1,973	1,928	1,896	1,799

THE MAIN EXPLANATIONS OF PRESENT VARIANCE ARE THREE POLICIES ADOPTED END OF
1975 AND DISCUSSED IN MONTHLY LETTERS BUT WHICH LEFT DECEMBER 1976 BUDGET OPTI-
MISTICALLY LOW. FIRST WAS TO HAVE REASONABLE AMOUNTS OF SELLING MODELS IN
STOCK WITHOUT WHICH WE COULD NOT HAVE ACHIEVED 19 PERCENT INCREASE IN SALES
WE ARE MAKING WITH OUTMODED PRODUCT.

EXHIBIT 3 *(concluded)*

SECOND POLICY WAS TO MANUFACTURE LONGER SERIES OF EACH MODEL BY DOUBLE WHEREVER SALES WOULD ABSORB IT, OTHER WISE MANY OF OUR COST REDUCTIONS WERE NEARLY ZERO. THIS MEANS OUR MANUFACTURING PROGRAM ANY MONTH MAY CONTAIN FIVE MONTHS' WORTH OF 15 MODELS INSTEAD OF 10 WEEKS' WORTH OF 30 MODELS (OUT OF 70). THIRD WAS NEW POLICY OF REDUCING NUMBER OF PURCHASE ORDERS BY MAINTAINING A MINIMUM STOCK OF MANY THOUSANDS OF LOW-VALUE ITEMS WHICH YOU AGREED WOULD AND DID INCREASE STOCK UPON FIRST PROCUREMENT BUT WE ARE ALREADY GETTING SLIGHT REDUCTION. CORRECTIVE ACTIONS NUMEROUS INCLUDING RUNNING 55 PEOPLE UNDER BUDGET AND ABOUT 63 BY YEAR END PLUS REVIEWING ALL PURCHASE ORDERS MYSELF PLUS SLIDING A FEW SERIES OF MODELS WHICH WOULD HAVE GIVEN SMALL BILLING IN 1976 INTO 1977 PLUS THOSE POSTPONED BY CUSTOMERS. THIS WILL NOT HAVE DRAMATIC EFFECT AS NEARLY ALL THESE SERIES ARE PROCURED AND HAVE TO BE MADE FOR RELATIVELY SURE MARKETS BUT SOME CAN BE HELD IN PIECEPARTS UNTIL JANUARY. WE ARE WATCHING CAREFULLY STOCKS OF SLOW MOVING MODELS AND HAVE MUCH CLEANER FINISHED STOCK THAN END 1975.

FINAL AND GRAVE CONCERN IS ACCURACY OF PARTS, WORK-IN-PROCESS, AND FINISHED GOODS VALUATION SINCE WE BEGAN STANDARD COST SYSTEM. INTERIM INVENTORY COUNT PLUS VARIANCES VALUED ON PUNCH CARDS STILL DOESN'T CHECK WITH MONTHLY BALANCE USING CONSERVATIVE GROSS MARGINS, BUT NEARLY ALL GAPS OCCURRED FIRST FOUR MONTHS OF SYSTEM WHEN ERRORS NUMEROUS AND LAST 4 MONTHS NEARLY CHECK AS WE CONTINUE REFINING. EXTENSIVE RECHECKS UNDERWAY IN PARTS, WORK-IN-PROCESS, AND FINISHED GOODS AND CORRECTIONS BEING FOUND DAILY.

YOUR INVENTORY STAFF SPECIALISTS ARE AWARE OF PROBLEM AND PROMISED TO HELP WHEN OTHER PRIORITIES PERMIT. WILL KEEP THEM INFORMED OF EXPOSURE WHICH STARTED WITH RECORDING ALL PARTS AND BEGINNING NEW BALANCES WITH NEW STANDARDS AND APPEARS CLOSELY RELATED TO ERRORS IN THESE OPERATIONS. WE CAN ONLY PURGE PROGRESSIVELY WITHOUT HIRING SUBSTANTIAL INDIRECT WORKERS.

HENNESSY

closely follows Galvor's reports, we have specialists on cost systems and analysis, inventory control, credit, and industrial engineering.

We have not given Galvor the help it needs and deserves in data processing, but we have a limited staff here in Geneva and we cannot meet all needs. We hope to increase this staff during 1977.

With reference to Galvor's recent performance, M. Boudry states:

Galvor is small and we don't give it much time or help unless its variances appear to be off. This happened in the second half of 1976, when we became increasingly concerned about the level of Galvor's inventories. A series of telexes on this matter between Mr. Hennessy and M. Poulet, our director of manufacturing here in Geneva, illustrate how the reports are used. [See Exhibits 2 through 5.]

We feel the situation is under control and the outlook for Galvor is OK despite the flat performance between 1973–75 and the downturn in 1976. The company has been turned about and 1977 looks promising.

Although the comprehensive reporting and control system made it appear that Universal was a highly centralized organization, the managements of the various operating units had considerable autonomy. For example, Mr. Hennessy,

---

EXHIBIT 4 Telex from Poulet to Hennessy Concerning Level of Inventory

---

TO: HENNESSY—GALVOR
FROM: POULET—UE
DATE: NOV. 10, 1976

SEPTEMBER INVENTORY INCREASED AGAIN BY 64,000 COMPARED TO AUGUST WHILE SEPTEMBER SALES WERE 145,000 UNDER BUDGET REFERRING TO YOUR LATEST TELEX OF SEPTEMBER 27 IN WHICH YOU HAVE A BREAKDOWN OF THE SEPTEMBER FORECAST. REQUEST DETAILED EXPLANATION FOR NOT MEETING THIS FORECAST IN SPITE OF YOUR CURRENT CORRECTIVE ACTIONS.

SEPTEMBER	YOUR FORECAST	ACTUAL	VARIANCE
RAW MATERIALS	53	96	(43)
PURCHASED PARTS	180	155	25
MANUFACTURED PARTS	95	108	(13)
WORK-IN-PROCESS	838	917	(79)
FINISHED GOODS	632	723	(91)
OTHER INVENTORIES	84	87	(3)
ENGINEERING IN PROCESS	55	52	3
RESERVE	(14)	(14)	—
INDICA	50	51	(1)
TOTAL NET	1,973	2,175	(202)

IN ORDER TO MEET YOUR DECEMBER FORECAST OF 1,799 YOUR WORK-IN-PROCESS HAS TO BE REDUCED BY 318. THIS MEANS A REDUCTION OF ABOUT 100 PER MONTH FROM SEPTEMBER 30 TO DECEMBER 31. THEREFORE, I ALSO WOULD LIKE ACTUAL ACHIEVEMENTS AND FURTHER REDUCTION PLANS DURING OCTOBER, NOVEMBER, AND DECEMBER CONCERNING THE POINTS MENTIONED IN YOUR SAME TELEX OF SEPTEMBER 27. CONSIDER AGGRESSIVE ACTIONS IN THE FOLLOWING SPECIFIC AREAS:

1. REALISTIC MASTER PRODUCTION SCHEDULES.
2. SHORT-TERM PHYSICAL SHORTAGE CONTROL TO INSURE SHIPMENTS.
3. WORK-IN-PROCESS ANALYSIS OF ALL ORDERS TO ACHIEVE MAXIMUM SALABLE OUTPUT.
4. MANPOWER REDUCTION.
5. ELIMINATION OF ALL UNSCHEDULED VENDOR RECEIPTS. HAVE YOU ADVISED OTHER UNIVERSAL HOUSES NOT TO SHIP IN ADVANCE OF YOUR SCHEDULE UNLESS AUTHORIZED?
6. ADVISE FULL DETAILS ON ALL CURRENT SHORTAGES FROM OTHER UNIVERSAL HOUSES WHICH ARE RESPONSIBLE FOR INVENTORY BUILD-UP.

POULET

---

who was judged only on Galvor's performance, was free to purchase components from other Universal units or from outside sources. There were no preferred ''in-house'' prices. A slight incentive was offered by Universal to encourage such transactions by not levying certain headquarters fees, amounting to about 2 percent of sales, against the selling unit.

Similarly, Universal made no attempt to shift its taxable income to low-tax countries. Each unit was viewed as though it were an independent company subject to local taxation and regulation.

EXHIBIT 5 Telex from Hennessy to Poulet Concerning Level of Inventory

---

TO: POULET—UE
FROM: HENNESSY—GALVOR
DATE: NOV. 15, 1976
        YOUR 10.11.76

WE NOW HAVE OCTOBER 31 FIGURES. OUR ACTUAL ACHIEVEMENTS
FOLLOW: RAW MATERIALS 54 VARIANCE PLUS 3, PURCHASED PARTS 173
VARIANCE MINUS 12, MANUFACTURED PARTS 110 VARIANCE PLUS 17,
WORK-IN-PROCESS 949 VARIANCE PLUS 224, FINISHED GOODS 712 VARI-
ANCE PLUS 18, OTHER 82 VARIANCE MINUS 2, ENGINEERING 54 VARI-
ANCE MINUS 4, RESERVE MINUS 14 VARIANCE NIL, INDICA 55 VARIANCE
PLUS 3, TOTAL 2,175 VARIANCE PLUS 247. EACH ITEM BEING
CONTROLLED AND THE ONLY SIGNIFICANT VARIANCES 224 WORK-IN-
PROCESS AND 18 FINISHED GOODS ARE MY DECISION UPON SALES DE-
CLINE OF SEPTEMBER AND OCTOBER OF 311 TO DELAY COMPLETION OF
SEVERAL SERIES IN MANUFACTURE IN FAVOR OF ANOTHER GROUP OF
SERIES, MOSTLY GOVERNMENT, WHICH ARE LARGELY BILLABLE IN 1976
IN ORDER TO PARTLY REGAIN SALES. LAST EIGHT DAYS' ORDERS AND
THEREFORE SALES ARE SHARPLY UP AND NONE OF THIS WORK-
IN-PROCESS WILL BE ON HAND MORE THAN 3 TO 6 WEEKS LONGER
THAN WE PLANNED.

NEVERTHLESS YOU SHOULD BE AWARE WE MANUFACTURE 4 TO 8
MONTHS WORTH OF MANY LOW-VOLUME MODELS AN EXAMPLE OF
HOW WE DETERMINE ECONOMIC SERIES WAS FURNISHED YOUR STAFF
SPECIALIST THIS WEEK. WE CANNOT MAKE SIGNIFICANT COST REDUC-
TIONS IN A BUSINESS WHERE AT LEAST 70 OF 200 MODELS HAVE TO BE
ON SHELF TO SELL AND TYPICAL MODEL SELLS 15 UNITS MONTHLY. RE-
GARDING YOUR 5 SUGGESTIONS AND TWO QUESTIONS WE ARE CARRY-
ING OUT ALL 5 POINTS AGGRESSIVELY AND HAVE NO INTERHOUSE
SHORTAGES OR OVERSHIPMENTS.

HENNESSY

Universal believed that this goal of maximizing profits for the individual units would in turn maximize Universal's profits. Forcing every unit to maximize its profits precluded the use of arbitrary transfer prices for "in-house" transactions.

Recent Developments at Galvor

A standard cost system, which included development and tooling costs as well as manufacturing and assembly, had been in effect since March 1976.

According to Mr. Hennessy:

We had hoped to start in January, but we were delayed. On the basis of our experience in 1976, all standards were reviewed and, where necessary, they were revised in December. We now have a history of development and tooling experience, which we have been accumulating since 1975. This has proved extremely useful in setting cost standards. Simultaneously, we have integrated market and sales forecasts more effectively into our pricing decisions.

Before Universal acquired Galvor, a single companywide rate was used to allocate factory overhead to the costs of products. For many years this rate was 310 percent of direct labor. In a discussion of his pricing policies in 1972, Mr. Latour said: "I have been using this 310 percent for many years and it seems to work out pretty well, so I see no reason to change it."

M. Chambertin had long argued that the less-complex products were being unfairly burdened by the use of a single overhead rate, while electronic products should bear more.

Mr. Latour's response to this argument was:

> I have suspected that our electric products are too high priced, and our electronic products are too low priced. So what does this mean? Why should we lower our prices for multimeters and galvanos? At our current prices, we can easily sell our entire production of electric products.

M. Chambertin remained convinced that eventually Galvor would be forced by competitive pressures to allocate its costs more realistically.

In 1976, as part of the new standard cost system, Galvor did indeed refine the procedure for allocating overhead costs to products. Fifteen different cost centers were established, each with a separate burden rate. These rates, which combined direct labor cost and overhead ranged from 13.19 francs to 38.62 francs per direct labor hour.

Concluding his comments about recent developments, Hr. Henessy said:

> A formal inventory control system went into effect in January 1977. This, together with the standard cost system, allows us for the first time to really determine the relative profitability of various products, and to place a proper valuation on our inventory.
>
> We are installing a new computer in February, which we will use initially for customer billing and for marketing analysis. We hope this will reduce the number of people required in our customer billing and accounts receivable operations from 12 to 6 or 7.

QUESTIONS

1. What is your overall assessment of the effectiveness of Universal Electric's (UE's) planning system as it is applied to Galvor?

2. Identify, in as much detail as possible, all of the new management systems and techniques that UE has required Galvor to establish. In particular, trace the various steps Galvor goes through in preparing its long-range as well as annual plans.

3. What is your evaluation of the effectiveness of the working relationships between Hennessy and the UE executives in Geneva? What do you infer from the telexes about Hennessy's autonomy as a managing director? (*Note:* You might want to give the telexes a careful and critical reading.)

4. Look at the system from Galvor's viewpoint. Suppose Galvor were an independent company (i.e., not part of Universal Electric). If you were a consultant to Galvor, how would the management planning and control practices you would recommend for the company differ from those that have been imposed by UE? (Please answer this as completely and specifically as you can, going beyond the response "they would be less detailed and less formal," for example).

5. Look at the system from UE's viewpoint. How (if at all) can UE's imposing planning and control practices different from those required by an independent Galvor be justified? (Again, please try to be specific.)
6. To what extent should a large international organization, such as UE, rely on a comprehensive system of financial reporting and control to achieve its strategic objectives?
7. What specific changes, if any, would you make in UE's planning systems? In its other management systems? If the management processes need improving, how would you change them?

Case 11–4

Del Norte Paper Company*

In early July 1987, Frank Duffy, managing director of the Italian subsidiary of the Container Division of Del Norte Paper Company (DNP–Italia), was sitting in his Torino office thinking about a recent informal discussion held between himself, two casewriters, and certain members of his staff. The topic of discussion had been the problems of applying the corporate budgeting and reporting system (known within the company as the Budget Analysis Program, or BAP) to a foreign subsidiary such as DNP–Italia.

At approximately the same time, Hans Lowenstein, managing director of the German subsidiary of the Container Division (DNP–Deutschland), was sitting in his Frankfurt office thinking about a very similar meeting in which he had recently participated. Once again, the discussion had been focused on Del Norte Paper Company's BAP system and its impact on a foreign subsidiary.

Duffy and Lowenstein had held their respective meetings to prepare themselves for an August meeting on the same topic with John Powell, general manager, International Operations of the Container Division. Both Duffy and Lowenstein believed that Del Norte Paper's system, which originally had been designed primarily for domestic (U.S.) use, had serious weaknesses when applied to the international subsidiaries. Duffy and Lowenstein had been asked by Powell to prepare a list of recommendations, which were to be discussed at the August meeting.

Del Norte Paper Company

Del Norte Paper Company was a large, integrated paper producer. In 1986, total sales were approximately $5.6 billion, while net income was over $500 million. In terms of sales, Del Norte Paper was among the 75 largest industrial concerns in the United States.

The Container Division was one of Del Norte Paper's 22 major product divisions. The Container Division was divided into two segments, one domestic and one international. Within the international segment, there were five geographic regions: Germany, Italy, France, United Kingdom, and the Caribbean. It was an acknowledged goal of Del Norte Paper to expand its international operations substantially over the next 10 years.

Del Norte Paper Organization Structure

Del Norte Paper had essentially a product-line management structure. The company was divided into seven broad product lines called "Strategic Product Groups," each headed by a corporate vice president. The Strategic Product Group was further divided into more narrowly defined product divisions, each headed by a division vice president. For example, the Container Division was structurally part of the Container–Containerboard Strategic Product Group. Thus, G. T. Hendrick, vice president of the Container Division, reported directly to R. B. Manning, vice president of the Container–Containerboard Product Group (see Exhibit 1).

The product divisions were comprised of several geographical regions, each headed by a regional manager. In the Container Division, a

* This case was prepared by W. Sahlman under the supervision of M. Edgar Barrett, Harvard Business School.
Copyright © by the President and Fellows of Harvard College.
Harvard Business School case 177–035.

EXHIBIT 1   Organizational Chart

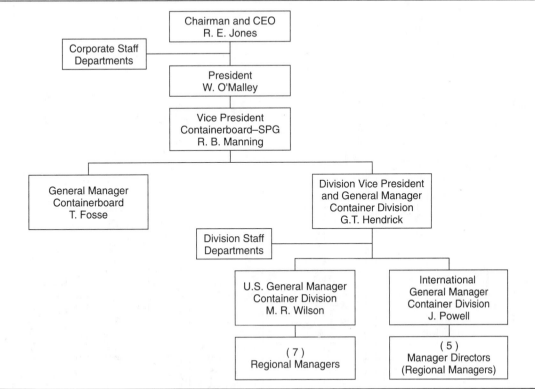

distinction was also made between the international and the domestic operations. The former were headed by John Powell, general manager, International Operations, who reported directly to the vice president of the Container Division.

The international segment of the Container Division was divided into five regions, each headed by a managing director. Each region in turn was comprised of several plants serving different sales territories. Thus, each plant was responsible for both production and marketing. The plants were headed by a plant manager.

At each level in the Del Norte Paper management structure, the general managers were supported by a functional staff. Thus, at the top management level there was a corporate vice president of finance, a corporate controller, a cor-

porate vice president of manufacturing, and so on. Approximately the same functional representation existed at the Strategic Product Group, the product division, the regional subsidiary, and the plant levels. Each functional manager was responsible both to the general manager at his level and to the functional managers at levels above his own (see Exhibit 2 for partial organization charts of DNP–Italia and DNP–Deutschland, two regional subsidiaries of the Container Division).

DNP–Italia and DNP–Deutschland

DNP–Italia, with headquarters in Torino, had six container plants. In 1986, sales were approximately $56 million, while net income after an adjustment reflecting a switch to LIFO accounting was around $2.9 million.

EXHIBIT 2 Partial Organizational Charts: DNP–Italia and DNP–Deutschland

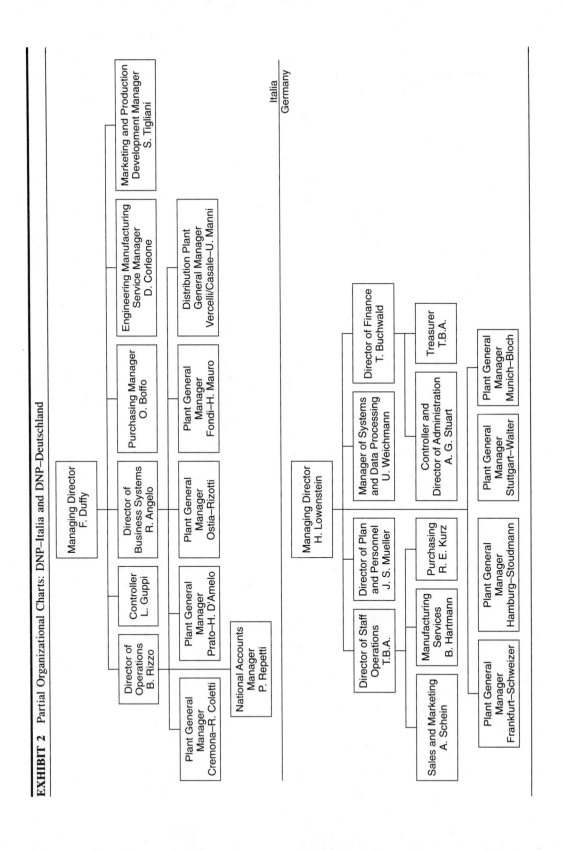

Italia

Germany

Each plant had a marketing staff and was entirely responsible for the sales territory around the plant. The only exception was the two plants near Torino, which were consolidated into one sales territory. Each sales territory had a substantially different product mix.

The Italian box market was very competitive. At least in part, this was due to the fact that there were no less than 100 significant producers of boxes in Italy. Most of these companies were family owned and quite small. While Del Norte Paper believed it was the third largest company in the market, it supplied well under 10 percent of the country's box needs.

DNP–Deutschland, with headquarters in Frankfurt, had four container plants. The 1986 sales were approximately $63 million, and net income after an adjustment reflecting a switch to LIFO accounting was about $5 million. The 1987 sales were expected to increase slightly, and net income was expected to decline only a small amount from record 1986 levels.

Once again, each of DNP–Deutschland's four plants was responsible for a different sales territory. A major market for the company, Essen, did not have a local plant. Containers were allocated to the Esssen market by whichever of two of Germany's plant had the needed capacity.

Competition also existed in the German market. However, the major competition consisted less of small family owned companies and more of large multinational, integrated paper companies. DNP–Deutschland's most important competitors were Bowater, International Paper, Mead Corporation, Unilever, and Union Camp.

The Formal Control System

In the late 1970s, Del Norte Paper's Container Division had developed a complete budgeting and reporting system known as the Budget Analysis Program (BAP). The system had changed very little from 1977 to 1987.

The formal control system at Del Norte Paper was comprised of three separate but interrelated parts: the BAP budgeting system, the BAP reporting system, and the capital budgeting system. The focus of this case is on the two BAP systems.

The BAP Budgeting System

The BAP budget was a complete operational plan developed through a process of negotiations between the general manager at each level in the organization and his immediate superior. The process began at the plant level.

This negotiation process continued until a complete consolidated operating plan was submitted to the board of directors for their approval. Once approved, the BAP plan became the basis for reporting and performance evaluation during the year.

At the foundation of the BAP budget was a standard cost system. All budgeting was done using updated standard cost estimates.

Every year, the plant general manager and his staff prepared a series of standardized forms. The required budgeting forms are listed below.

BAP Budget Forms

Document	Title
BAP 2	Sales and production forecast
BAP 3	Direct labor budget
BAP 6	direct cost conversion budget
BAP 7	Manufacturing facility expense budget
BAP 8	Selling expense budget
BAP 9	Administrative operating results
BAP 10	Planned operating results
BAP 90	Analysis of planned operating results
BAP 49	Preliminary operating results
BAP 48	Balance sheet forecast
BAP 36	Planned variances*

* Planned differences between the industrial engineering department standards and the level of efficiency implicit in the budget (Editor).

BAP Budgeting Cycle

The preparation of the budget began in June of the year before the budget year.[1] The month of June was basically devoted to organizing the budgeting effort. For example, it was in June that regional economic forecasts were prepared by the regional staff. The first concrete step in the process at the plant level came in early July when the general managers, the sales managers, and the sales staffs of each plant began to prepare volume forecasts. Each individual salesman was given a form on which was shown the sales volume broken down by major customer for the previous year and for the first six months of the then current year. The salesman was asked to make a projection (also by major customer) for the next calendar year. These forecasts were then consolidated into a plant (territory) sales forecast.

In the middle of July, the regional managing director and his staff reviewed the volume forecasts submitted for each plant. All the plant general managers and the plant sales managers then came to regional headquarters for separate one- to two-hour meetings with the regional managing director and his controller. The volume forecasts could possibly be revised at this meeting.

After the volume forecasts for each sales territory were accepted, then the production planning process was started. The plant general managers and the plant production managers decided what their labor requirements would be, how many shifts would be needed, and so on. Detailed estimates were also made of certain variable and fixed-cost items, such as supplies, utilities, and depreciation.

By the end of July, the regional headquarters office had a detailed preliminary projection of profit for each plant. At this point, the regional managing director and several members of his staff reevaluated the budget. Once again, revisions were possible.

In the middle of August, the regional subsidiaries were required to send to the general manager, International Operations, a preliminary budget summary form (known as BAP 49) for each plant and for the entire region.[2] The general manager of International Operations then reviewed the plan with his immediate superior, the Container Division vice president. Shortly thereafter, the Container Division submitted to the Container–Containerboard Strategic Product Group vice president the individual regional preliminary budget forms. As always, this review could result in budget revisions.

On approximately August 22, the regional subsidiary was supposed to be advised by the Container Division of the acceptability of its preliminary budget.[3] If any changes were necessary, they were made at this point.

In early September, the complete proposed profit plan for each regional subsidiary was resubmitted to Container Division in order that it could be put into computerized format. The computerization was required so as to facilitate revisions at a later date.

In later September, the regional managing director and the regional controller for each subsidiary went to Container Division headquarters in San Francisco for a final review of the profit plan with the general manager, International Operations, and the Container Division controller. Each regional subsidiary was allocated one-half day to make a presentation of its profit plan.

After the profit plan meeting in late September, the general manager of International Operations again reviewed the profit plans with the Container Division vice president. Shortly thereafter, the profit plans were reviewed with the Strategic Product Group vice president. After this review,

---

[1] Del Norte Paper operated on a calendar (January–December) year.

[2] The budgets at the plant and regional levels were derived using the local currency. When the plans were submitted to the Container Division, they were denominated in U.S. dollars. The regions were held responsible for their dollar results.

[3] In 1987, this communication took place on August 29.

in late October, the Strategic Product Group vice president presented the final profit plan to the Del Norte Paper senior management and the board of directors. If accepted, this profit plan became the budget for the next year.

Other Aspects

Revisions. Ordinarily, the budget was prepared only once a year. However, in the last few years Del Norte Paper had found it necessary to revise the budget during the budget year. Indeed, DNP–Italia and DNP–Deutschland had been required to change the 1983 budget several times.

In 1986, when the 1987 plan was being prepared, the DNP–Deutschland plan had to be revised two times and DNP–Italia's one time. The first change at DNP–Deutschland occurred because of a change in the U.S. dollar/deutsche mark exchange rate. The second change came in December 1986, at which time the economic outlook was very different than had been anticipated. DNP–Italia's plan was also changed at this point.

The 1987 budget also was changed in April 1987. Once again, the reason for the revision was a changed economic outlook. However, the April change was only done within the Container Division. The December 1986 budget for 1987 still remained the budget for which the overall Container Division was held responsible.

Other documents. In addition to the one-year BAP budget, each regional subsidiary was required to submit two other documents. The first was a long-range (five-year) plan. This had not been used every year by the international subsidiaries. It was, however, expected to become more important with time.

The second document required was a free form list of regional objectives and programs to achieve the objectives. This document was known as the "Standards of Performances." Both this document and the five-year plan were presented to the general manager–International Operations at the late September meeting at Container Division headquarters in San Francisco.

The BAP Reporting System

The BAP reporting system had also been developed by the Container Division in the late 1970s. The purpose of the reporting system was to allow the general manager at each level to identify problems which needed corrective action.

The BAP reports relied heavily on the standard cost system embedded in the BAP budgeting system. Essentially, the reports were intended to identify the size and origin of variances from the standards which had been used in the budgeting process.[4] Thus, the reports were designed to identify such things as price, efficiency, and volume variances, as well as to provide some overall indication of the goodness of the original budget estimates for pricing purposes. The relevant general manager would then use the data provided as an indication of where attention was needed.

The required BAP reporting forms are listed below.

BAP Reporting Forms

Document	Title
BAP 15	Statement of operating results
BAP 16	Sales and cost analysis
BAP 17	Direct conversion
BAP 18	Manufacturing facilities
BAP 19	Selling expense
BAP 20	Administrative expense
BAP 21A	Analysis of operations
BAP 55	Balance sheet analysis

In addition to these standardized BAP forms, each month the regional subsidiaries were required to send a free form "Commentary on Operations." This report was prepared by the

---

[4] In their budgeting forms, the regional subsidiaries had a number of "planned" variances. Thus, the budget (plan) included a certain amount of variance. An example was indirect labor, in which the standard was set at 100 percent efficiency, but the plan was set at 80 percent efficiency. The variances in the reporting forms related to the 80 percent, not the 100 percent.

regional managing director with the assistance of his staff. The report dealt with general economic trends, the competitive situation, and a number of other similar issues. Copies of the report were sent to the general manager–International Operations, the Container Division controller, the Container Division vice president, and to the division vice president, manufacturing.

On the 25th day of each month, Del Norte Paper's foreign subsidiaries "closed their books"— that is, they began to derive consolidated income statements and other financial reports. On the third working day of the following month, the regional subsidiaries were required to fax (i.e., send by facsimile) to Container Division headquarters a summary of production and deliveries during the preceding month at each plant for the entire region. The plant reports were faxed directly by the plants to division headquarters as well as to regional headquarters. On the fourth working day of the same month, the subsidiaries were required to telex to San Francisco a complete profit and loss statement for the previous month for each plant and for the entire region.

On the fourth working day, the regional plants and the subsidiary were required to telex a copy of BAP 15 to Container Division headquarters. A complete balance sheet for each plant and for the region was also telexed to Container Division on that date.

Also on the fourth working day of the month, the monthly commentary on the last month's operations by plant and for the region was faxed to San Francisco.

Finally, written copies of the BAP reporting forms described previously (BAP 15, 16, 17, 18, 19, 20, 21A, and 55) were due by the middle of the month after the month for which the forms were applicable. Copies of these reports were mailed to the general manager, International Operations, and to the Container Division controller.

In addition to the BAP reports listed above and the monthly commentaries on operations, each regional subsidiary and its plants[5] were required to submit a number of other scheduled reports to Container Division headquarters.

Other Aspects

A second set of scheduled reports was focused on the manufacturing side of the business. Each plant was required to submit detailed analyses of manufacturing operations each month. The reports were originated at the plant level by the plant general manager and the plant production manager and were mailed to the manufacturing staff of the Container Division. A regional report was also sent by the director of operations of the regional subsidiary.

The final series of scheduled reports were updated monthly forecasts by plant and for the consolidated region of the expected operating results for the next three months. These forecasts were submitted in the middle of each month to the general manager–International Operations.

In addition to the scheduled reports listed above, the regional subsidiaries also had to submit a number of unscheduled reports. There were two types of unscheduled reports. The first was in response to specific requests by someone at Container Division or higher in the Del Norte Paper organization. An example might be a summary of marketing programs planned during the next few months.

The second type of unscheduled reports was represented by those addressed to issues raised about the BAP reporting forms or the other reports submitted. For example, if the general manager–International Operations identified problem areas in the reports submitted, he would telex the regional subsidiary asking for an explanation or a summary of the program undertaken to correct the problem. Similar requests came from other

---

[5] In all cases, copies of the reports were mailed by the plants first to regional headquarters and then to the responsible manager in San Francisco.

members of the Del Norte Paper organization back in San Francisco.

Performance Evaluation at Del Norte Paper

Each Strategic Product Group, each product division, each regional subsidiary, and each plant was evaluated by Del Norte Paper as a profit center. Return on investment and cash flow to the parent company were also important evaluation factors.

The performance of the general manager at each level was evaluated on the basis of a number of criteria. The first and most important criterion was the general manager's profit results relative to the budget which had been negotiated between him and his superiors.

At Del Norte Paper there were four different ways of calculating profit for evaluation purposes: net after tax, integrated profit after allocation of corporate and division overhead; net after tax, nonintegrated profit after allocation of corporate and division overhead; net after tax, nonintegrated profit before allocation of corporate and division overhead; and nonintegrated profit before tax and before allocation of corporate and division overhead. Integrated profit included an allocation of "upstream" profits, which were those profits made at the mill level on orders placed by the relevant converting plant. Nonintegrated profits were before the allocation of upstream profits.

While precisely which executives used which measurement methods in evaluating the performance of managers or subsidiaries was not entirely clear, all four methods were used in some manner. The integrated profit figures were said to be monitored closely by the chairman of the board and the president of Del Norte Paper Company. The net, nonintegrated, and fully allocated figures were also said to be watched closely by the chairman of the board and certain board members.

The net, nonintegrated, nonallocation-of-overhead figures were the ones routinely reported under the international version of the BAP system.

Thus, these were also widely distributed throughout the company. Finally, the nonintegrated profit before tax and before overhead allocation figures were said to be those used primarily for the evaluation of a regional managing director's performance. For example, the bonus was based primarily on this set of figures.

All three of the non-BAP sets of figures were sent monthly to the regional managing director's home. The integrated profit figures, however, were only for his information so as to maintain a legal, arm's-length business relationship.

Finally, in addition to these profitability criteria, performance was also judged on actual results relative to the "Standards of Performance" documents negotiated between the general managers and their superiors. The bonus of the regional managing director, for example, was partly based on his performance relative to the "Standards of Performance."[6]

The Informal Discussion at DNP–Italia

Late on June 27, 1987, several members of the management team at the Torino office of DNP–Italia gathered for a discussion of the corporate budgeting and reporting system. Present throughout the meeting were: Frank Duffy, regional managing director; B. Rizzo, director of Operations; R. Angelo, director of Business Systems; L. Guppi, controller; D. Corleone, Engineering Manufacturing Service manager; G. Pruitt, a marketing executive who was just in the process of being transferred from Del Norte Paper's Seattle office to DNP–Italia; and the two casewriters. The discussion was begun by a casewriter asking Frank Duffy his view of the BAP system. The following is a paraphrased summary of that meeting.

---

[6] The bonus of regional managing director also depended in part on the profitability of the Strategic Profit Group, the division, and the overall corporation.

Duffy: I think that one has to talk about the BAP budgeting system and the BAP reporting system separately. First, with respect to budgeting, BAP is basically very strong. The budgeting process trains the plant manager, in particular, to focus on key variables. He really has to understand all aspects of the container business from marketing to production in order to work with the BAP budgeting forms. Also, because the budget sets a solid objective for the manager, he is more motivated, I believe, than he would be without a strong budgeting system.

However, there are problems in the use of the BAP budgeting system in a subsidiary such as DNP–Italia. First, we have a very different labor situation here in Italy than in the United States. Whereas manufacturing labor in the United States is a variable cost and is treated as such on the BAP budget forms, all labor in Italy is essentially a fixed cost. We simply cannot fire workers if business slows down; and, even if we put our workers on reduced work weeks, we have to pay a very substantial portion of the full-time wage cost. The fixed-cost nature of labor makes it important to modify our approach to business in Italy.

Rizzo: We have also had another problem with the budget system. As you know, the BAP budgets are built around a standard cost system. In the past few years, because of the economic volatility we've seen in Italy, it has been very difficult to base our marketing and production decisions on the standard costs built into the BAP budgets. The problem has been especially troublesome in the area of determining the correct raw materials paper cost on which to base our pricing decisions.

The price of paper has been extremely volatile here in Italy, more so than in the United States The problem is complicated by the fact that we use 12 different grades of paper, which is also more than in the United States. These two facts combined have made it very difficult to make consistent pricing decisions.

As a result, there has been very little correlation between our original estimates of contribution for each box order and the end-of-the-month actual contribution figures after taking into account price and efficiency variances.

Angelo: I agree with Benito that this has been a problem. We have tried to address that problem by using updated forecasts of paper prices in making our pricing decisions instead of the standard cost in the budget. In spite of our best efforts, I must admit it has been very difficult to make accurate forecasts.

Pruitt: Staying on this pricing decision issue for a minute, it seems to me that the fixed versus variable manufacturing labor cost issue is very important. Depending on how you resolve the controversy, your contribution calculations are going to be significantly impacted. In a recession such as we are now experiencing, the contribution calculations are especially crucial.

Casewriter: Are there any other major problems with the BAP budgeting system?

Duffy: There is one other problem I should mention. The budget is supposed to be a goal for the plant manager and his workers. If he meets or exceeds his budget, he should be rewarded. The problem is that we cannot really have an incentive pay system here in Italy because of the labor laws. We can give bonuses; but once a worker's pay is increased, we are not allowed to decrease his total wages. This takes some of the power out of a strong goal-setting budgeting process.

Casewriter: Frank, you mentioned that the BAP reporting system should be viewed separately from the budgeting system.

Duffy: Yes. I believe the BAP reporting system is quite strong at the plant level. Each of the BAP forms provides information to the plant manager that he needs, though some of the information is not so useful.

For example, the fixed-cost nature of labor should be incorporated into the BAP reporting forms. The plant manager should only be held responsible for the items he can control.

Going above the plant level, the BAP reporting system becomes increasingly less useful. At the regional managing director level, I can't use all the information provided in the BAP forms. I need more summary information, though it has been useful to have the BAP reports as supporting material when I am talking to the plant manager.

The problem arises that the BAP forms, which were always intended to be used primarily at the plant level, presently are used as our reporting system back to Container Division. They can't possibly analyze all the information sent to them. In fact, I feel there are real dangers in having them try to look at the minute details of the BAP system, in that these details are sometimes misleading in the short run.

Angelo: Generating the volume of information required by San Francisco is also very expensive, particularly when one considers that most of the information has to be generated by hand. This problem is due, at least in part, to our limited computerization capabilities. Fortunately, we are improving our data processing systems, so this won't be as big a problem in the future.

Guppi: You have to remember that the BAP reports represent only part of the total reports sent to headquarters. We have separate marketing and production reporting systems, for example. A lot of information we send is duplicative. If the various division functions would work together, it would save us a great deal of time and money. We could manage our business better if we didn't have such onerous reporting requirements.

Duffy: Another problem with the BAP reporting system from the foreign subsidiary to the division headquarters is that the information is no longer relevant by the time they get a chance to analyze it. This makes their requests for explanation out of date and our responses even more so. By the time they identify a problem, the plant manager should already be attempting to correct it.

The Informal Discussion at DNP–Deutschland

Late on June 30, 1987, several members of the management team of DNP–Deutschland gathered in the Frankfurt office of the managing director, Hans Lowenstein, for a discussion of the Del Norte Paper corporate BAP budgeting and reporting system and its effects on DNP–Deutschland's operations. Present through the meeting were: Hans Lowenstein, managing director; Alex Stuart, regional controller and director of administration; and Thomas Buskey, planning manager.

The discussion began when one of the casewriters asked Mr. Lowenstein for his opinion about the BAP system. The following is a paraphrased summary of that discussion.

Lowenstein: In my opinion, the weakest part of BAP is the reporting system. San Francisco requires so much information, much of it duplicative, that it interferes with our ability to manage in Germany. In addition, the volume of reporting imposes an unnecessary cost burden on us because we are not yet completely computerized.

You know, I wouldn't mind sending in so many reports if I thought headquarters could use the information and give us some help. But it's just too much data for them to analyze in a useful way.

Stuart: I agree with you, Hans. The BAP reporting system is not very useful as a form of communication with corporate headquarters. They just don't have the staff to analyze all the reports.

At the plant level, however, I think we all agree that BAP is a fairly good system. The BAP reports provide the plant manager with the information he needs to manage effectively. We don't have many complaints about BAP at this level.

Casewriter: Do you get any complaints from the plant managers about BAP?

Lowenstein: No line manager has ever liked to fill in lots of reports. As a result, we do get some gripes about the volume of information requested. You have to remember that these guys have a large number of other reports to fill out—such as the monthly manufacturing summary, etcetera. Another problem is that many of these reports ask for the same information but in a different format. The plant people feel this kind of duplication wastes time.

Stuart: We also get some complaints about having to file the reports using U.S. dollars and American units of measurement—square feet, tons, etcetera. While it's simple to make the translation, it is a tedious job for the plant people.

Casewriter: Do you have any other problems with the BAP reporting system?

Lowenstein: As we've said, we think the standardized BAP reports are pretty good as an operating tool at the plant level, but not very good as a reporting system with corporate headquarters.

The monthly "Commentary on Operations," which is sent both by the plant managers and by me at the regional level, attempts to address the reporting deficiencies of the BAP reports. The problem is that it is very difficult to get enthusiastic about writing the commentary when you aren't sure anyone pays any attention to them back in San Francisco. The plant managers don't at all like the fact that I have them write commentaries.

Stuart: You know, about a year ago, one of our plant managers sent three of his monthly commentaries back to San Francisco in German—and we never did receive any comment from San Francisco.

Oh, I should mention one other difficulty. San Francisco requires the region and each plant to send in BAP 15 on the fourth working day of the month. The problem is that there is not enough time for me to do any analysis of the operating results before the plants send the forms on to San Francisco. I can't even check for clerical errors. I wish they could delay the deadline for at least a few days.

Casewriter: Hans, what do you think of BAP budgeting system?

Lowenstein: In general, I think it's a reasonably good system. But it has some of the same inherent difficulties as the BAP reporting system. It's an American system designed for use in our U.S. plants. Inevitably, there are going to be problems in applying a domestic system to a foreign subsidiary.

Casewriter: For example?

Lowenstein: One problem is that the budget is denominated in dollars, rather than deutsche marks. We are held responsible for our dollar results, though we have absolutely no control over foreign exchange rates.

Stuart: One of the three times we had to change the 1987 budget, one revision was due primarily to a changed exchange rate. The plant managers don't see how they can be held responsible for dollar-dominated results.

Also, with respect to the three budget changes I mentioned before, the last one was caused by a changed economic environment. Container Division asked us to start from scratch and make a completely new budget. Only after we put in a tremendous amount of work did we find out that the budget revision was only for Container Division use. Container still kept the same budget for reporting purposes. A lot of the work we put in was really unnecessary.

Lowenstein: Another problem, which is not peculiar to the foreign subsidiaries, is the relationship between the capital expenditure budget and the BAP budget. We don't receive final approval for our capital budget until January or February, but we have to submit our final profit budget well before that time. We have to budget for the probable results of our investments even before we know whether we can make them. If the investment projects are eventually turned down, we are not allowed to change the budget. For small projects the effect is negligible, but for large projects the effect can be quite significant.

Casewriter: Any other aspects of the budgeting system you want to talk about?

Buskey: There is one thing I would like to mention. This year we really made an effort to build a good five-year plan. Long-range planning has not been really emphasized before in Container Division. After we put in a huge amount of work, we found out that the five-year plans were not going to be emphasized this year. There were too many other pressing problems. The effort was very worthwhile for DNP–Deutschland, but it is somewhat frustrating to work so hard on a project and find out divisional headquarters doesn't think it's very important.

QUESTIONS

1. How well does the Del Norte Budget Analysis Program (BAP) accomplish the following:

   a. The evaluation of managers?

   b. The motivation of managers?

    c. Early warning of impending problems? (If you were a member of Del Norte's top management, would you feel secure that you would be promptly informed if any serious problems were developing in any of the European units?)

    d. Corporate planning and resource allocations?

2. If you believe that the Del Norte system is deficient is accomplishing any of the above objectives, what do you think the problem is and what corrections would you recommend?

Case 11–5

Binswanger & Steele, Inc.*

Alvin Binswanger, president of Binswanger & Steele, Inc., which manufactured office equipment, had introduced a new system for appraising the performance of his top executives in 1985. During 1986 he decided the system, which was called "management by objectives," might help solve some problems in the sales area, and, in 1987, the system was extended to the national sales manager and the eight regional sales managers. After the 1987 performance, appraisals had been submitted and reviewed, and several of the company's managers discussed the desirability of extending the system to lower levels of management.

The Management by Objectives System

The management by objectives system of performance appraisal was based on the concept that evaluation of executives should depend on how the results they achieved compared with their objectives—that is, with reasonable estimates of what was possible.

In October 1984, Binswanger decided to test the system on his key executives. If the system proved successful, he planned to instruct these executives to extend it to the managers who reported to them. The appraisal system then would be introduced to successively lower levels of management each year until it included all employees.

During the first week of October 1984, Binswanger and his key executives met privately to determine their key objectives for their own satisfactory performance for fiscal 1985, beginning November 1, 1984. They agreed that, if they exceeded their objectives, they would consider their performance outstanding. If they merely met their objectives, they would consider their performance satisfactory. If they failed to meet their objectives, they would consider their performance unsatisfactory. Bonuses and raises were to be awarded only to the men who exceeded their key result targets.

In December of 1985, at the end of the one-year trial period, each executive met privately with Binswanger to review his individual performance. Each manager's performance exceeded his stated objectives for 1985.

Extension to the Sales Division

In June 1986, Binswanger & Steele's executive committee met to discuss the increasing turnover and evidence of low morale among the company's salesmen. Sales vice president Ben Weddels attributed these problems to several factors, including management problems generated by the expansion of the sales force from 300 salesmen in 1981 to 500 in 1986 and the increased complexity of the selling jobs caused by a large number of new and more complex products which had been added to the company's line in recent years. Weddels was concerned that he and Ted Forman, the national sales manager, might have inadequate

* This case was prepared by K. B. Westheimer under the supervision of J. S. Livingston, Harvard Business School. Copyright © by the President and Fellows of Harvard College.
Harvard Business School Case 511–181.

control over the sales force. Weddels believed that the management by objectives system would be useful in tightening up this control. The executive committee approved Weddels' suggestion that the system be applied to the national sales manager and his eight regional sales managers during fiscal 1987.

In July 1986, Weddels called in Ted Forman to explain the performance appraisal system. Ted Forman, 55 years old, had been with Binswanger & Steele since 1953. During that time he had been a salesman, branch sales manager in four different areas of the country, and regional sales manager in New England for six years before being selected as national sales manager in 1986.

Weddels and Forman agreed to appraise Forman's 1987 performance on the basis of satisfactory performance of his regional sales managers. Forman, in turn, was to explain the system to the regional managers and to negotiate objectives for the year with each of them. Weddels gave Forman a memorandum setting forth guidelines for implementing the performance appraisal system (see Exhibit 1).

In September 1986, Forman wrote each of his regional sales managers and asked them to draft their own key result targets (objectives) for the fiscal year ending October 31, 1987. He defined ''key result target'' as a critical business accomplishment required of a regional sales manager and suggested the following areas as some of those to be defined carefully: net sales, gross profit, gross percentage, operating expenses, branch pretax profit, year-end inventory level, and year-end inventory turnover.

The Midwest Sales Region

One of Binswanger's regional managers was 40-year-old Ed Michelson, the Midwest regional sales manager. Ted Forman was aware that Ben Weddels considered Michelson the most effective and promising of the company's regional sales managers. Since Forman was eager to please

Weddels, he decided to pay special attention to Ed Michelson's key result targets for fiscal 1987.

When Michelson received Forman's letter asking for key result targets, Michelson went into the files and reviewed midwestern sales data for the past three years to arrive at key result targets for his branches. Meanwhile, Forman reviewed his personal copies of the same data. (Exhibit 2 gives these data.)

The Forman-Michelson Conference

Forman and Michelson met in October 1986 to negotiate Michelson's key result targets for fiscal 1987. During the meeting, there was a cordial atmosphere, but Forman reserved the right ultimately to determine Michelson's objectives. Michelson and Forman agreed that the Midwest region had shown little sales improvement in the past few years. Both men suspected that a business recession may have affected sales, but there was no indication that the recession would affect sales in 1987. Forman got the impression that Michelson's sales estimates were highly conservative and his requests for sales expenses were overly liberal. When the men disagreed, Forman made reference to corporate-level marketing data, unavailable to Michelson, that substantiated Forman's claims. Michelson claimed that he did not believe it would be possible to produce the sales volume Forman desired, given the imposition of such low sales expenses. Michelson was not pleased with his conference and said he did not know how he was going to achieve the key result targets budgeted for 1987.

Forman also incorporated into Michelson's 1987 key result targets several items about which Michelson had no previous notice. Forman said that his list of specific targets, which would apply to all regional managers, had been delayed in preparation. He explained that the specific targets, such as improving sales mix and the market share and sales volume of particular product lines, were intended to help regional sales managers direct their efforts toward areas considered

EXHIBIT 1   Memorandum

July 15, 1986

TO: Ted Forman

FROM: Ben Weddels

SUBJECT: Management by Objectives Performance Appraisal System

In the fall, the supervisor should invite his immediate subordinates to submit to him what they believe to be their key result targets for the coming year. The supervisor should meet with each subordinate in closed conference and negotiate the subordinate's key result targets. The supervisor should not accept his subordinate's targets without questioning them, and the subordinate should be encouraged not to accept his superior's targets until he understands the complete logic behind them.

During the year, the supervisor should discuss with each subordinate any of his key result targets that do not appear to be on schedule. A plan for attaining off-schedule key result targets should be worked out between superior and subordinate. At the end of the year, the subordinate and supervisor should review the subordinate's key result targets and his actual achievements on a simple work sheet called a "Manager Performance Statement."

The supervisor should send the work sheet to the subordinate prior to the appraisal interview and ask him to enter his results next to his agreed-upon targets. The subordinate returns a copy of the work sheet to the supervisor prior to the appraisal interview.

The purpose of the appraisal interview is to give supervisor and subordinate an opportunity to review the subordinate's performance in detail and to help the subordinate understand his strengths and weaknesses so that he can concentrate on improving himself. If a subordinate does not achieve key result targets because of circumstances outside of his control, such as an unanticipated increase in price or a shortage of supply, that fact should be noted in the supervisor's comment column. Such factors should not be counted against a subordinate in his appraisal. Normally, an appraisal interview takes two to four hours.

A supervisor-subordinate meeting is scheduled, during which a plan of action should be drafted for the subordinate to use in the coming year to improve his areas of weakness. This plan of action should be incorporated into the subordinate's key result targets for the coming year. These new targets should be presented about four weeks after the appraisal interview.

Bonuses and raises will be awarded only to those men who exceed their key result targets. One of the most useful indications a supervisor's manager can have of a supervisor's effectiveness is the Manager Performance State-

EXHIBIT 1 *(concluded)*

ments for the supervisor's subordinates. In other words, Ted, I'll be looking at your regional manager's performance appraisals in order to evaluate your performance for 1987.

Ben Weddels

EXHIBIT 2 Performance of Midwest Region and Selected Districts

District and Year	Net Sales ($000s)	Gross Profit ($000s)	Percent Gross Profit to Net Sales	Operating Expenses	Pretax Profit
Chicago (June 1986):*					
1984	$ 759	$ 128	16.9%	$ 107	$ 21
1985	982	133	13.5	115	18
1986	655	94	14.3	111	(17)
St. Louis (April 1986):					
1984	760	114	15.0	88	26
1985	712	96	13.5	96	0
1986	552	78	14.2	111	(33)
Detroit (September 1985):					
1984	1,940	242	12.5	197	45
1985	1,470	212	14.4	316	(104)
1986	1,990	275	13.8	277	(2)
Dayton (December 1983):					
1984	796	116	14.6	94	22
1985	1,103	152	13.8	112	40
1986	1,226	188	15.3	137	51
Midwest region Total (9 branches):					
1984	10,637	1,517	14.2	1,219	298
1985	10,576	1,495	14.1	1,455	39
1986	10,038	1,457	14.5	1,415	42

* Date district manager appointed.

important by top management. Michelson did not argue with Forman's specific targets, but complained that he had had no prior opportunity to determine his region's current status and the feasibility of meeting Forman's targets.

Sales Results—Midwest Region

During 1987, Michelson spent much of his time traveling to the branch offices in his region and working out problems with his branch sales managers. He did not have the opportunity to work out an account analysis with his managers and intended to do this as soon as there was sufficient time. When the fiscal year ended in October, Forman was unable to meet with Michelson for a performance appraisal interview. Instead, Michelson was sent a Manager Performance Statement with the 1987 key result targets and budgeted figures for each target, with instructions to fill in the 1987 actual results. When he completed this task, Michelson returned the work sheet to Forman.

The two men met in November and, in an hour, reviewed Michelson's Manager Performance Statement. Forman jotted his notes of the meeting in the space provided "for use of executive making appraisal." After the review, he instructed Michelson to prepare 1988 key result targets for the Midwest region and to study the possibility of introducing the management by objectives performance appraisal system to his branch sales managers.

In the meantime, Ben Weddels had seen the preliminary 1987 sales figures for the Midwest region, which indicated a decline in both net sales and gross profit. He was concerned about this decline, and, in mid-November, asked Ted Forman to send Michelson's Manager Performance Statement to his office. Forman was surprised to receive Weddel's request. He had filed Michelson's materials and forgotten about them, but was under the impression that Ed Michelson had done as well as or better than any of the other regional managers in meeting his key target results. To prove this, Forman prepared an analysis showing which of the regional sales manager's actual results had exceeded their targeted results by 5 percent or more. Of 63 branches, 8 had exceeded their gross profit target, and about 12 each had exceeded their net sales, gross profit percentage, branch operating expense, or branch pretax profit target. More branches in the Midwest region exceeded each of these targets than in any other region except the South Central region. He submitted the details of this comparison analysis with Michelson's performance appraisal (see Exhibit 3) to Ben Weddels.

Weddels was not happy with the results reported by Forman. According to the performance appraisal system, most of the regional managers, including Ed Michelson, were "below standard." On the other hand, he knew that many of them had faced competitive conditions which could not have been predicted with accuracy.

EXHIBIT 3 Manager Performance Statement*

Name: Ed Michelson   *Position:* Regional Manager
Region: Midwest   *For Period:* 1987

Key Results Expected
1. Achieve at branch level 1987 budgeted components in the following categories:
   - *a.* Net sales.
   - *b.* Gross profit.
   - *c.* Gross profit percentage.
   - *d.* Branch operating expenses.
   - *e.* Branch pretax profit.

Key Results Achieved (include appropriate supporting comment)

	1987 est. (Michelson)	1987 Budget (Michelson–Forman)	1987 Actual
Chicago branch:			
a. Net Sales	$ 690	$ 820	$ 628
b. Gross profit	99	127	68
c. Gross profit percentage	14.4%	15.5%	10.9%
d. Branch operating expenses	125	110	91
e. Branch pretax profit	(26)	17	(23)
St. Louis branch:			
a. Net sales	560	720	562
b. Gross profit	84	110	93
c. Gross profit percentage	15.0%	15.3%	16.5%
d. Branch operating expenses	125	100	87
e. Branch pretax profit	(41)	10	6
Detroit branch:			
a. Net sales	2,000	2,080	2,151
b. Gross profit	300	300	325
c. Gross profit percentage	15.0%	14.4%	15.1%
d. Branch operating expenses	260	250	257
e. Branch pretax profit	40	50	68
Dayton branch:			
a. Net sales	990	1,190	1,051
b. Gross profit	150	190	142
c. Gross profit percentage	15.1%	16.0%	13.5%
d. Branch operating expenses	140	132	117
e. Branch pretax profit	10	58	25
Regional total (9 branches):			
a. Net sales	9,890	10,970	9,792
b. Gross profit	1,448	1,652	1,456
c. Gross profit percentage	14.7%	16.5%	14.9%
d. Branch operating expenses	1,435	1,329	1,224
e. Branch pretax profit	13	323	232

* Detail on five branches omitted.

EXHIBIT 3   *(continued)*

Comment (for use of executive making appraisal):

Net sales off slightly more than 10 percent for region which was below expectations; however two branches did exceed budget. Dollar gross profit was severely affected, but again, same two branches were above or near budget. Expense reduction was made, but, in my opinion, action was not taken soon enough. Even though Chicago attained expense budget, additional profit should have been realized through closer control of expenses. Profit was disappointing, partially contributed to by chaotic conditions. Greater profit could have been obtained through better planning and expense control.

Key Results Expected

2. Improve sales mix between commercial, institutional, and military. Emphasize new business and re-equipment sales.

Key Results Achieved (include appropriate supporting comment)

Gross Sales ($000s)

	Chicago	St. Louis	Detroit	Dayton	Total (9 branches)
Commercial:					
1986	$553	$502	$ 924	$1,152	$ 7,055
1987	500	403	813	784	5,763
Difference	(53)	(99)	(111)	(368)	(1,292)
Institutional:					
1986	132	74	932	157	2,605
1987	118	125	1,271	223	3,116
Difference	(14)	51	339	66	551
Military:					
1986	9	4	205	0	$ 802
1987	5	12	158	10	778
Difference	(4)	8	(47)	10	(24)
Government:					
1986	1	0	19	14	124
1987	36	53	21	94	627
Difference	35	53	2	80	503

Comment (for use of executive making appraisal):
Satisfactory on institutional and government; held steady in military but too great a decline in commercial.

Key Results Expected

3. Increase average gross profit realization to 15.8 percent or better.

Key Results Achieved (include appropriate supporting comment)

Overall gross profit percentage:

1987 Budget–15.1%

1987 Actual–13.9%

(See Target No. 1 *Key Results Expected*, for gross profit percentages of individual branches.)

EXHIBIT 3   *(continued)*

Comment (for use of executive making appraisal):
   15.8 percent was for all eight regions. Your measurement should be based on your budgeted regional level of 15.1 percent. Actual percentage attained was 13.9 percent, which was not satisfactory. However, it is recognized that improvement is difficult under severe competitive conditions, but you must watch this phase closely in the affected areas.

Key Results Expected
4.   Institute an inventory of manager development requirements for all branch managers, as well as inaugurate an individual on-the-job development action program for three prospective branch managers.

Key Results Achieved (include appropriate supporting comment)
   Inventory of developmental requirements taken for all managers in the Midwest region and action program prepared for three.
   Action program postponed because of press of business in last quarter 1981.

Comment (for use of executive making appraisal):
   This should be your personal target to continue some training of managers to correct their weaknesses during 1988.

Key Results Expected
5.   Improve market share of corporate products. Achieve 5.7 percent share of market for Exec-Q-Tote portable dictating machine at each branch.

Key Results Achieved (include appropriate supporting comment)

| | *Exec-Q-Tote* | | |
| | *10 Months Net Sales ($000s)* | | |
	5.7 Percent Share (estimated)	*1971 Actual (10 months)*	*Difference*
Chicago	$ 22	$ 22	–
St. Louis	84	50	($34)
Detroit	108	92	(16)
Dayton	104	87	(17)
Regional total (9 branches)	605	532	(82)

Comment (for use of executive making appraisal):
   Share of market not a satisfactory measurement and you agree that sales of these products need serious attention in 1988.

Key Results Expected
6.   Improve sales volume of noncorporate products. Achieve overall 5 percent or more increase in sales of typewriter ribbons and supplies.

EXHIBIT 3   *(concluded)*

Key Results Achieved (include appropriate supporting comment)

	1987 Unit Objective	*Typewriter Ribbons and Supplies* *($000s)* Dollar Sales to 10/31	Percent Achievement
Chicago	$ 292	$ 270	92%
St. Louis	124	156	126
Detroit	751	878	117
Dayton	423	396	93
Regional total (9 branches)	3,438	3,639	106

Comment (for use of executive making appraisal):
  Generally satisfactory.

Alvin Binswanger's Memorandum

Shortly thereafter, Ben Weddels received the following memorandum.

November 22, 1987

TO: Ben Weddels

FROM: Alvin Binswanger

SUBJECT: Management by Objectives Performance Appraisal
           System—1987 Results

Happy Thanksgiving, but no relaxation for managers. We must get together soon to work out our 1988 plan for appraising managers. I am still excited about the management by objectives performance appraisal system and, eventually, I would like to extend the system to all levels in the organization and broaden its concept to tie in directly with compensation and development. I would like to hear your views on the system's effectiveness last year. I would appreciate it if you would dig up some answers to the following questions before we meet.

1. Were the key result targets realistic and challenging? Do you think they motivated the men to improve their performance?
2. Did the system help the managers appraise the strengths and deficiencies of their subordinates? Did they use the system to develop plans for improvement? If not, was it the fault of the system or the way the system was applied?
3. What can we do to improve the system?
4. Are we ready at this time to extend the system to the branch sales managers? If so, what steps should we take?

Alvin Binswanger

Case 11–6

Captain Jamie Totten*

Captain (CPT) Jamie Totten looked at his watch. It was after 1800 hours, and he finally had time to review the events of the day. He had been in command of Company B, 3rd Battalion, 3rd Basic Combat Training Brigade (B-3-3), at Fort Dix, New Jersey, since January 1978; now, eight months later, things seemed to be going extremely well. He was proud of B-3-3's record over the previous eight months and attributed much of its success to his Company Performance Control system and his drill instructors' abilities to train and lead their platoons.

CPT Totten's immediate superior, Lieutenant Colonel (LTC) Daniels, was being reassigned, which meant that Totten would have a new superior giving him his periodic performance rating. He had been confident that if LTC Daniels evaluated him against the agreed-upon performance objectives, his Officer Evaluation Report (OER) would be very good. However, two recent events gave him cause for worry. There had been reports of cheating on rifle range scores, and the company's budget for equipment was technically overspent. On the second issue, CPT Totten had received a memo from LTC Daniels that afternoon which raised a question about his high loss rate, and he had made an appointment with Daniels for the next morning to discuss the problem.

The Officer Evaluation Report

The military naturally did not have the same basic ratios as business to evaluate its managers' performances, but the Officer Evaluation Report and OER Support Form were used for much the same purposes. A sample of a completed OER and an OER Support Form are shown in Exhibits 1 and 2, respectively.

Army regulations required that each officer receive a written evaluation from his or her immediate superior (rater) and that superior's superior (senior rater) annually, or upon change of rater. In some cases, such as on a high-level staff where several layers separated the rated officer and the senior rater, an intermediate rater might also be included. Rating periods had to be longer than 90 days and less than one year. Every organization was required to publish its rating scheme (i.e., who rated whom) every month to ensure that there was no confusion about the chain of command. At the beginning of each rating period, the rated officer and the rater mutually agreed on the rated officer's job description and performance objectives for the coming rating period. Parts I, II and III(a) and (b) of the OER Support Form were then completed. At the end of the rating period, the rated officer indicated what he or she felt were significant achievements for the period by completing Part III(c) of the OER Support Form, signed the form, and gave it to the rater. The rater was required to base the evaluation primarily on the mutually agreed objectives. When the evaluation had been completed by the rater and senior rater, the rated officer was counselled by the rater on both good and bad performance and was provided with a copy of the report. The original report was forwarded to the Military Per-

* This case was written by Assistant Professor J. Kendall Middaugh and James P. Totten (Darden '85). Copyright by the Darden Graduate Business School Foundation, Charlottesville, VA. 2726a.

EXHIBIT 1   Officer Evaluation Report

SEE PRIVACY ACT STATEMENT ON DA FORM 67-8-1

For use of this form, see AR 623-105; proponent agency is US Army Military Personnel Center

PART I – ADMINISTRATIVE DATA

a. LAST NAME FIRST NAME MIDDLE INITIAL	b. SSN	c. GRADE	d. DATE OF RANK Year Month Day	e. BR	f. DESIGNATED SPECIALTIES	g. PMOS/ASI	h. STA CODE
TOTTEN, JAMES P.	139-41-0362	MAJ	79 10 06	IN	P11A54		02736

i. UNIT, ORGANIZATION, STATION, ZIP CODE OR APO MAJOR COMMAND	j. REASON FOR SUBMISSION	k. COMD CODE
Ft. Richardson, Alaska 99505 Headquarters Co., FORSCOM	04 Change of Duty	FC

l. PERIOD COVERED FROM / THRU	m. NO OF MONTHS	n. MILPO CODE	o. RATED OFFICER COPY	p. FORWARDING ADDRESS
79 11 01 / 80 06 02	07	FS 01	X 2 FORWARDED TO OFFICER 25 June 80	8631 Muir Ct. Anchorage, AK 99504

q. EXPLANATION OF NONRATED PERIODS

PART II – AUTHENTICATION

NAME OF RATER	SSN	SIGNATURE	DATE
ELDER, CECIL W.	541-42-0120	Cecil W. Elder	9 Jun 80
GRADE, BRANCH, ORGANIZATION DUTY ASSIGNMENT: MAJ, FA, HQ Co., Ft. Richardson, AK, Chief, Force Development			
FINKLE, RODNEY T.	132-24-8914	Rodney P Finkle	13 June 80
GRADE, BRANCH, ORGANIZATION DUTY ASSIGNMENT: LTC, IN, HQ Co., Ft. Richardson, AK, Dep Director, Plans, Tng, & Security			
HARRIS, ROBERT E.	283-28-0885	Robert E Harris	17 Jun 80
GRADE, BRANCH, ORGANIZATION DUTY ASSIGNMENT: COL, IN, HQ Co., Ft. Richardson, AK, Director, Plans, Tng, & Security			

SIGNATURE OF RATED OFFICER: James P. Totten   DATE 8 June 1980   DATES ENTERED ON DA FORM 21: 25 Jun 80   RATED OFFICER MPO INITIALS   SR MPO INITIALS   NO. OF INCL: 0

PART III – DUTY DESCRIPTION

a. PRINCIPAL DUTY TITLE: Manpower Control Officer, DPT/SEC   b. SSI/MOS: 54A416Y00

c. REFER TO PART IIIc DA FORM 67-8-1

Reviews and forwards all requests for MTOE personnel, equipment and necessary funding. Serves as Brigade point of contact for Five Year Test Plan to include analysis of test support requirements and impact. Serves as secretary of Alaska Team to resolve combat development issues by recommending topics, scheduling meetings, chairs working group meetings, and publishes minutes. Serves as point of contact for all combat and materiel development actions. Reviews and staffs Letters of Agreement, Letter of Requirements, and Basis of Issue Plans. Performs major in-house organizational studies. Serves as action officer for Troop List actions, stationing plans, concept plans, and coordinates implementation.

PART IV – PERFORMANCE EVALUATION - PROFESSIONALISM

a. PROFESSIONAL COMPETENCE

	HIGH DEGREE 1 2 3	LOW DEGREE 4 5
1. Possesses capacity to acquire knowledge/grasp concepts	1	
2. Demonstrates appropriate knowledge and expertise in assigned tasks	1	
3. Maintains appropriate level of physical fitness	1	
4. Motivates, challenges and develops subordinates	NA	
5. Performs under physical and mental stress	1	
6. Encourages candor and frankness in subordinates	NA	
7. Clear and concise in written communication	1	
8. Displays sound judgment	1	
9. Seeks self improvement	1	
10. Is adaptable to changing situations	1	
11. Sets and enforces high standards	1	
12. Possesses military bearing and appearance	1	
13. Supports EO/EEO	1	
14. Clear and concise in oral communication	1	

b. PROFESSIONAL ETHICS

1 DEDICATION 2 RESPONSIBILITY 3 LOYALTY 4 DISCIPLINE 5 INTEGRITY 6 MORAL COURAGE 7 SELFLESSNESS 8 MORAL STANDARDS

Officer demonstrates commitment to the goals and mission of the Army and the Country.

DA FORM 67-8   REPLACES DA FORM 67-7, 1 JAN 73 WHICH IS OBSOLETE, 1 NOV 79   US ARMY OFFICER EVALUATION REPORT

EXHIBIT 2 OER Support Form

OFFICER EVALUATION REPORT SUPPORT FORM
For use of this form, see AR 623.105, the proponent agency is DCSPER.

Read Privacy Act Statement on Reverse before Completing this form

PART I – RATED OFFICER IDENTIFICATION

NAME OF RATED OFFICER (Last, First, MI)	GRADE	ORGANIZATION
TOTTEN, JAMES P.	MAJ	HQ Co. Ft. Richardson, AK

PART II – RATING CHAIN – YOUR RATING CHAIN FOR THE EVALUATION PERIOD IS:

	NAME	GRADE	POSITION
RATER	ELDER, CECIL W.	MAJ	C. Force Development
INTERMEDIATE RATER	FINKLE, RODNEY T.	LTC	Dep DPT/SEC
SENIOR RATER	HARRIS, ROBERT E.	COL	DPT/SEC

PART III – VERIFICATION OF INITIAL FACE-TO-FACE DISCUSSION

AN INITIAL FACE-TO-FACE DISCUSSION OF DUTIES, RESPONSIBILITIES, AND PERFORMANCE OBJECTIVES FOR THE CURRENT RATING PERIOD TOOK PLACE ON _____

RATED OFFICER'S INITIALS _____ RATER'S INITIALS _____

PART IV – RATED OFFICER (Complete a, b, and c below for this rating period)

a. STATE YOUR SIGNIFICANT DUTIES AND RESPONSIBILITIES

DUTY TITLE IS _____, THE POSITION CODE IS _____

(1) Review and forward all requests for MTOE personnel, equipment and necessary funding.
(2) Provides Bde POC for Five Year Test Plan to include analysis of test support requirements and impact.
(3) Secretary of Alaska Team; recommends topics, schedules meetings, chairs working group, publishes minutes.
(4) Bde POC for all combat/materiel developmental actions.
(5) Reviews and staffs ROC's, LOA's, LR's, and BOIP's.
(6) Perform major in-house organizational studies.
(7) Action Officer for Troop List actions.

b. INDICATE YOUR MAJOR PERFORMANCE OBJECTIVES

(1) Provide a responsive and expert point of contact for all troop actions initiated within the command and carry those actions to completion in a timely fashion.
(2) Anticipate organizational needs and problems and initiate long range force structure actions to accommodate them.
(3) Provide a knowledgeable POC to FORSCOM Force Structure, Combat Developments, and Documents Division for actions affecting the Brigade and influence those actions to the benefit of the Brigade.
(4) Anticipate equipment needs and initiate developmental programs to provide them.
(5) Where possible, initiate procurement programs for equipment to reduce developmental cycle time lag.
(6) Constantly review Brigade staffing, organization, and equipment and implement programs to optimize fighting capability.

c. LIST YOUR SIGNIFICANT CONTRIBUTIONS

(1) Implementation of ALO 2 reduction for 172nd LIB. Resolution of FORSCOM incorrect application of reduction.
(2) Arranged AK Tm meeting with CRREL which resulted in submission of coordinated research objectives to HQDA for inclusion in Science & Technology Objectives Guide.
(3) Represented Bde (AK) at TRADOC Joint Working Group to revise SUSV LR.
(4) Represented Bde (AK) at DA DCSOPS SUSV briefing which increased SUSV visibility and priority and may result in early fielding of BV 206.
(5) Finalized manning document and Provisional Organization for DSD.
(6) Reorganization of 568th TC Co and 242d Avn Co.
(7) Initiated Bde (AK) position on Arti Canteen, Mountain Boots, and Mukluks.
(8) Identified and coordinated SUSV kit requirements.
(9) Coordinated requirement and free issue of snow camoflage nets.
(10) Approval of addition of 93 snow machines to 172nd LIB TDA.
(11) Approval of addition of sweater to CTA 50-900.
(12) Publication of article in Infantry Magazine.

SIGNATURE AND DATE

sonnel Center in Alexandria, Virginia, and placed in the individual's Officer Military Personnel File (OMPF). The OMPF contained all the OER's, decorations, promotions, letters of commendation, and any other official documents that recorded the officer's career or described his competence and ability. An officer had five years to challenge an OER that he or she believed was unfair. If the challenge was successful, the OER was removed from the OMPF.

The OMPF was the sole file used by the army selection boards to select officers for promotions, high-level assignments, and nominative school selections. Promotion and advancement became increasingly more competitive at each stage in an officer's career as the number of positions became smaller and the number of those eligible became proportionately larger and the competitors better qualified. The selection board for the Army Command and General Staff College (C&GSC), for example, had to sift through approximately 25,000 records to pick 1,500 officers to attend. Failure to attend C&GSC, in essence, removed an officer from consideration for battalion-level command and, therefore, from any reasonable chance for promotion beyond the rank of lieutenant colonel. Since all board selections were made solely on the OMPF contents, which were dominated by the OERs, OERs became the most important documents in an officer's career.

Company Performance Control Ratios

B-3-3's primary mission was to train soldiers. Additional responsibilities included personnel administration for trainees and cadre, management and maintenance of a 40-room barracks, which included trainee and cadre living space, and accountability for $150,000 in equipment ranging from the barracks furniture and bed linen to the field uniforms and rifles used in training.

CPT Totten's personal goals for B-3-3 included graduating well-trained, disciplined soldiers who had achieved the highest possible scores in all end-of-cycle testing (which included marksmanship, physical fitness, and common-task proficiency tests). He also wished to maintain the barracks in the highest standard of appearance and maintenance as well as to eliminate loss of or damage to equipment.

CPT Totten understood that, in order to achieve these objectives, he had to have some way of measuring them. He had decided some months ago, therefore, to develop an internal management control system. The previous commander had had no such system; he assessed his own performance and that of his subordinates simply by counting the number of graduates. CPT

Totten wanted to encourage excellence by instituting a method of measuring relative success against a standard. He thus established a series of ratios that would measure individual and collective goal attainment. In addition, he rated each platoon separately to measure and compare their results. He hoped to liven things up a bit with competition among his 10 drill instructors (DIs).

Marksmanship and Physical Fitness Ratios

Two of the training objectives had been relatively simple to measure collectively, because measures of individual performance were already available. In marksmanship, each trainee received an individual rating and Marksmanship Badge based on how many targets he or she hit during qualification-record firing. High scores were awarded an Expert rating, above-average scores were awarded a Marksman rating, and those satisfying the minimum requirements were Sharpshooters.

The Basic Physical Fitness Test also awarded individual scores. The test consisted of three events—pushups, situps, and a two-mile run. Each individual received a score, adjusted for age and sex, for the number of pushups and situps performed, and the elapsed time of the run. A perfect score was 100 points per event, or a 300 for the three-event test. A trainee needed to receive a minimum of 60 points in each event to pass the test. For all these tests, Totten had devised a ratio system that measured the collective performance of the platoon and of the company—essentially, by dividing the total passing scores of all the trainees in either platoon or company by the number of participants multiplied by 300 (perfect score on all three tests).

Proficiency Test Ratios

Proficiency tests had been more difficult to score. The Army Training Board had identified the key tasks to be mastered by all soldiers in a particular military occupational specialty (MOS). In addition, there were common tasks, such as first aid, to be mastered by all soldiers. The skills were divided into five levels of increasing difficulty and complexity. The end-of-cycle test required each trainee to demonstrate proficiency in selected Skill Level One tasks. The system simply awarded the trainee a "GO" or "NO-GO" based on whether or not he or she passed all the tests; it made no provisions for relative ranking based on quality of performance.

Normally, approximately 80 percent of a company would pass all stations the first time. The remaining 20 percent would usually pass the second time. It was unusual to have more than one or two holdovers per company. CPT Totten recognized this pattern in devising his proficiency test ratio, which divided the number of first-try "GOs" plus half of the second-try "GOs" by the total number tested. This approach rewarded the platoons that had more first-try "GOs".

Discipline Measurements

Discipline was the most difficult area to assess. Measuring certain obvious indicators could create serious problems. For instance, a fellow company commander had instituted a system that included counting the number of AWOLS in selecting the best platoon. Two of his platoons had been tied for first place until a man from one of them went AWOL and broke the tie. The AWOL's platoon mates decided to take matters into their own hands and, upon his return, "counselled" the AWOL about the head and shoulders, putting him in the hospital. As a result, the company commander, the first sergeant, and the platoon sergeant were relieved of their posts and several of the platoon members went to jail.

CPT Totten had decided that the appearance of the barracks could be used as a surrogate for measuring discipline. He reasoned that the teamwork, planning, and leadership required to prepare a platoon area for a comprehensive military inspection would be a good indication of the discipline and cohesion within a platoon. He knew he could count on the first sergeant to conduct a fair and thorough daily inspection. Totten had

thus established a point system and a ratio similar to the other systems. Since there had been no established army standard for barracks layout or items to be inspected, he had written his own, with most of the input coming from the DIs.

All Company Performance Control ratios are given in Exhibit 3.

The Rifle Range Problem

After reminiscing a bit with the company training officer about the design of what he had thought was a foolproof system, CPT Totten turned to the problems at hand. That afternoon on the rifle range, he had overheard some of the DIs grumbling that one of the platoon sergeants had found a way to influence his platoon's marksmanship scores. Totten's suspicions were confirmed by the happy demeanor of the DI in question and the dour expression of his competitors. He knew that the unwritten code of ethics would prohibit any of them from informing him openly about a suspected scam, so it would be up to him to ferret it out.

He was more than a little perplexed how anyone could manipulate the marksmanship scoring system. Each firer was scored by an individual scorer, and no member of B-3-3 was allowed near the score cards after the names were filled in. In fact, the score cards were inspected periodically by members of the range committee to guard against tampering.

On the rifle range, each firer was scored by a trainee from a different company who had qualified the previous week. The rationale for this practice was that the scorers would be honest in recording the firer's hits and misses because (1) they were closely supervised and (2) they would want to make sure that everyone had it as "hard" as they had. Sergeant Rhinehart, a DI, however, had found a way to subvert the system.

Prior to sending his platoon to the firing line, and within earshot of the assembled scorers, he would put on a show. He would dance and cuss and call his platoon every name he could think

---

EXHIBIT 3   Company Performance Control Ratios

Rifle Marksmanship Ratio (RM)

$$
\begin{aligned}
\text{Expert} &= 30 \text{ points} \\
\text{Marksman} &= 20 \text{ points} \\
\text{Sharpshooter} &= 10 \text{ points} \\
\text{Failure (bolo)} &= -10 \text{ points}
\end{aligned}
$$

$$
RM = \frac{30(\#\text{Expert}) + 20(\#\text{Marksman}) + 10(\#\text{ Sharpshooter}) - 10(\text{bolo})}{30 \text{ (Total \# of firers)}}
$$

Physical Fitness Ratio (PT)

$$
PT = \frac{\text{Sum of all passing scores}}{300 \text{ (Total \# tested)}}
$$

Proficiency Test Ratio (Pro park)

$$
\text{Pro Park} = \frac{\#\text{ of first time ``GOs'' } + 0.5(\#\text{ of second time ``GOs''})}{\text{Total \# tested}}
$$

Barracks Inspection Ratio (BI)
A detailed checklist was prepared by the drill instructors listing each inspection item and its individual point value.

$$
BI = \frac{\text{Total points earned}}{\text{Total points possible}}
$$

Total Platoon and Company Score

$$
\text{Score} = \frac{RM + PT + \text{Pro park} + BI}{4} \times 100
$$

---

of. He would tell them that, unless everyone qualified, they would never get another weekend pass. Furthermore, if they did not all score Expert, he would run them until they dropped from exhaustion. Then he would proceed to break a few stationary objects with his hand (a karate trick). None of this was lost on the scorers.

Of course, Rhinehart's platoon knew exactly what was going on, because he had rehearsed them on what to say to their scorers. When it was their turn to fire, they would tell the scorers what an animal their platoon sergeant was and plead for a good score. The scorers were too closely monitored to turn in any extremely altered results, but a few extra hits here and there recorded out of pity spelled the difference.

CPT Totten was unsure how he should handle the situation and, moreover was concerned about another aspect of the scam. Competition between platoons had become increasingly fierce as the DIs began to understand the system and take charge. Totten had been awarding an "eight ball" (a bowling ball painted like an eight ball) to the lowest-scoring platoon at the weekly awards ceremony, but he had recently stopped because of the shattering effect on morale. He was content that, up to now, his personal goals of graduating disciplined, well-trained soldiers were being met. However, the cheating incident might mean that the DIs were forgetting their responsibility to the trainees and to the army for the sake of competition.

Equipment Accountability

The second item of concern to CPT Totten stemmed from the memo he had received from LTC Daniels that day. Daniels was worried that Totten was administratively "dropping" too much equipment from his supply account. His concern was caused by the way organizational equipment was funded in the army and by the relationship of this system to the unit equipment-accountability system that Totten had set up some months ago.

When CPT Totten assumed command, he had conducted a complete inventory of equipment and signed a receipt for all equipment present. The outgoing commander was responsible for any discrepancies between the quantities on the books and the quantity signed for by Totten. Army regulations specified that, if a responsible officer could not provide an acceptable reason for any shortages, he or she must reimburse the government for them.

Totten had heard all the horror stories about commanders buying thousands of dollars worth of blankets and other items that had been lost during their command. He had decided that the only way to avoid large shortages was to delegate responsibility for equipment to the users and conduct frequent inventories to detect shortages as soon as they occurred. If he delegated responsibility for the equipment to the DIs, they would further delegate it to the individual trainee who was using the equipment. Because the DIs were not about to let a trainee stick them with any lost equipment, the DIs would report lost items promptly and charge the responsible trainee. CPT Totten also inventoried 10 percent of all equipment each month to demonstrate his resolve and catch losses.

The overspending problem surfaced, because of a conflict between Totten's system and the way the army funded its equipment. Army units were administered as cost centers. Each unit forecasted annual expenditures for different classes of supplies and received authorization to commit funds against an approved budget. When an item was requisitioned and received by a unit, regardless of whether the item was new equipment or a replacement for a lost item, funds for that item were transferred from the unit's account and treated as an equipment expenditure. The rate of expenditure was closely monitored, and all variances from budget were strongly discouraged.

Money received from individuals in the form of payroll deductions for lost, damaged, or destroyed equipment did not revert to the units as a credit against the unit's equipment budget. The unit had to commit its own funds to replace the equipment, and therein lay the nub of the problem. A unit replacing equipment faster than it had forecasted incurred budget variances and received much unwanted attention. CPT Totten's problem was that his system worked too well. The DIs wasted no time in reporting lost equipment while they could still trace it back to a negligent trainee and avoid paying for it themselves. They were so conscientious, in fact, that B-3-3 had already overspent the battalion fiscal-year budget in less than nine months.

CPT Totten thought that his decentralized responsibility system was the best at Ft. Dix. He was sure that he was one of a handful of commanders who could get through an unannounced inventory unscathed. When he had asked his DIs how they had made up the shortages in the past and how other companies were doing it, they replied unanimously that everyone "scrounged" equipment to make good any shortages before a change of command. Additionally, since other units were scrounging shortages, rather than reporting them, they appeared to have better accountability systems than B-3-3, although the exact opposite was true. It was a real contradiction: B-3-3 was being criticized for doing the right thing.

Totten's performance objectives for the rating period did not include adherence to budget; the budget was managed by battalion headquarters for all the companies. However, he was being evaluated on equipment accountability. He had the impression that LTC Daniels had misinterpreted a high reported replacement rate as the result of poor procedures. Totten had to do something to change the lieutenant colonel's mind. His dilemma was compounded by the fact that Daniels was being evaluated for adherence to budget and Totten was responsible for Daniel's only variance. This fact, coupled with the rifle range scam, did not help to put Totten's mind at ease as he contemplated what he would say to LTC Daniels the next morning.

QUESTIONS

1. Evaluate CPT Totten's control system for B-3-3.
2. Do you believe CPT Totten's system is appropriate or necessary, or both, in this type of environment?
3. What alternative systems or system modifications would you suggest to CPT Totten?
4. How would you deal with the "rifle range" and "supply" problems?
5. What problems do you foresee during the discussion with LTC Daniels?

Chapter 12

Management Compensation

Incentive compensation is an important mechanism that encourages and motivates managers to achieve organizational objectives. Managers typically put forth a great deal of effort on activities that are rewarded and less on activities that are not rewarded. Numerous examples exist of compensation systems that do not reward the behaviors leading to organizational goals or do reward the behaviors countering the goals.[1] In this chapter, we discuss the design of incentive compensation plans for general managers so as to avoid the "folly of rewarding A while hoping for B."

We first describe the general nature of compensation plans, which we classify into two types: short-term incentive plans and long-term incentive plans. These plans must be approved by the shareholders. Next, we describe how the compensation of individual managers is decided, first at the corporate level and then at the business unit level. These decisions typically are made by the board of directors, based on recommendations of the chief executive officer. Finally, we describe agency theory, which is an approach for deciding on the best type of incentive compensation plan.

CHARACTERISTICS OF INCENTIVE COMPENSATION PLANS

A manager's total compensation package consists of three components: (1) salary, (2) benefits (principally pension and health benefits, but also includes perquisites of various types), and (3) incentive compensation. The compensation

---

[1] For many such examples from society, from organizations in general, and from profit-making organizations in particular, refer to Steven Kerr, "On the Folly of Rewarding A While Hoping for B," *Academy of Management Journal*, December 1975, pp. 769–83.

of managers in large companies tends to be higher than compensation in smaller companies,[2] and compensation in one company tends to be competitive with that of other companies in the industry, but few other generalizations can be made about management compensation in general.

The three components are interdependent, but the third is specifically related to the management control function, and this chapter, therefore, discusses only the incentive compensation component. A study of the pay and bonuses received by 14,000 managers over the period 1981–85 (70,284 observations from 219 organizations) found that, on average, bonuses were 20 percent of base pay, but that there were substantial differences among organizations, even those in the same industry. These differences in the proportion of bonus payments were greater than differences in base pay. There was a tendency for organizations with higher ratios of bonuses to have better subsequent financial performance than other organizations.[3]

Most corporate bylaws and securities regulators require that incentive compensation plan and revisions of existing plans be approved by the shareholders. (By contrast, shareholders do *not* approve salaries, nor does the annual proxy statement give information about compensation, except for each of the five most highly paid officers and the total for all officers and directors.) It follows that the plan must be approved by the board of directors before it is voted on at the annual meeting. Before submitting a plan for approval, senior management devotes much attention to devising the best plan for its environment, often hiring outside consultants to assist in this effort. The compensation committee of the board of directors usually is heavily involved in discussions of the proposed plan.

Incentive compensation plans can be divided into (1) short-term incentive plans, which are based on performance in the current year, and (2) long-term incentive plans, which relate compensation to the longer-term accomplishments. Long-term plans usually are related to the price of the company's common stock. A manager may earn a bonus under both plans. The bonus in a short-term plan usually is paid in cash, and the bonus in a long-term plan is usually an option to buy the company's common stock.

Short-Term Incentive Plans

The total bonus pool. In a short-term incentive plan, the shareholders vote on the formula to be used in arriving at the total amount of bonus that can be paid in a given year, which is called the "bonus pool." This formula usually is

---

[2] See Luis R. Gomez-Jejia, Henry Tosi, and Timothy Hinkin, "Managerial Control, Performance, and Executive Compensation," *Academy of Management Journal*, March 1987, pp. 31–70.

[3] Barry Gerhart and George T. Milkovich, "Organizational Differences in Managerial Compensation and Financial Performance," *Academy of Management Journal*, December 1990, pp. 663–91.

related to the overall company profitability in the current year (in a few companies, the current quarter). In deciding on the size of this pool, the overriding issue is to make the total compensation paid to executives competitive.

Several methods of establishing the bonus pool are described below.

The simplest method is to make the bonus equal to a set percentage of the profits. For example, assume that profits of $50 million represents an average profitable year. If a $1 million bonus fund is required to make the executive compensation package competitive, the bonus formula then could be set up to pay 2 percent of the net income in bonuses.

Many companies find this method undesirable, because it means paying a bonus even at low levels of profitability. Moreover, it fails to reflect additional investments; thus, profits and, consequently, bonuses can increase simply as a result of new investments, although the performance of the company may be static or even deteriorating. Many companies, therefore, use formulas that pay bonuses only after a specified return has been earned on capital. There are several ways of accomplishing this.

One method is to base the bonus on a percentage of earnings per share after a predetermined level of earnings per share has been attained. Using our earlier example, assume the following situation:

1. Estimated level of satisfactory profitability: $50 million.
2. Desired amount of bonus at the above level of profitability: $1 million.
3. Number of shares outstanding: 10 million.
4. Minimum earnings per share before bonus payments: $2.50.
5. Bonus formula: 4 percent of profits after subtracting $2.50 per share.

This method, however, does not take into account increases in investment from reinvested earnings. The objection can be overcome by increasing the minimum earnings per share each year by a percentage of the annual increase in retained earnings. In the example above, assume that the profits for the year were $50 million before bonuses and that dividends were $30 million. The plan might provide that a 6 percent return must be earned on additional investments before any additional bonuses are paid. The $2.50 minimum earnings per share thus would be adjusted for the coming year in the following manner.

Increase in retained earnings:

$$\$50,000,000 \text{ (profit)} - \$500,000 \text{ (bonus after taxes)}$$
$$- \$30,000,000 \text{ (dividends)} = \$19,500,000$$

Increase in required earnings before bonus:

$$\text{Total} = \$19,500,000 \times 0.06 = \$1,170,000$$
$$\text{Per share} = \$1,170,000 \div 10,000,000 = \$0.117$$

Adjusted minimum earnings per share:

$$\$2.50 + \$0.12 = \$2.62$$

Note that no reductions in the required earnings per share are normally made when the company experiences a loss; however, the required earnings would not be increased until retained earnings had exceeded its preloss level.

Another method to relate profits to capital employed is to define capital as shareholder equity plus long-term liabilities. The bonus is equal to a percent of the profits before taxes and interest on long-term debt minus a capital charge on the total of shareholder equity plus long-term debt. Companies using this method reason that managerial performance should be based on employing corporate net assets profitably, and since the proportion of long-term debt to total capital is determined by financial policy, rather than by operating managers, this proportion should not influence the judgment about operating performance.

Another method is to define capital as equal to shareholder equity. A difficulty with both this and the preceding method is that a loss year reduces shareholder equity and, thereby, increases the amount of bonus to be paid in profitable years. This might create an incentive for management to take a "big bath" in a year with otherwise low profits so as to make earning future bonuses easier.

A few companies base the bonus on increase in profitability of the current year over the preceding year. This not only rewards a mediocre year that follows a poor one but also fails to reward a good year if it happens to follow an excellent one. This problem can be partially corrected by basing the bonus on an improvement in the current year that is above a moving average of the profits in a number of past years.

Another method bases bonuses on company profitability relative to industry profitability. Obtaining comparable industry data may be difficult, however, because few companies have the same product mix or employ identical accounting systems. This method also could result in a high bonus in a mediocre year, because one or more of the industry competitors had a poor year.

In calculating both the profit and the capital components of these formulas, adjustments may be made in the reported amount of net income and in the reported amount of shareholder equity. Certain types of extraordinary gains and losses, and gains and losses from discontinued operations may be excluded. Goodwill resulting from acquisition of other companies may be treated differently from the way it is treated in the published financial statements.

Carryovers.   Instead of paying the total amount in the bonus pool, the plan may provide for an annual carryover of a part of the amount determined by the bonus formula. Each year a committee of the board of directors decides how much to add to the carryover, or how much of the accumulated carryover to use if the bonuses would otherwise be too low. This method has two advantages: (1) it offers more flexibility, since payment is not determined automatically by a formula, and the board of directors can exercise its judgment; (2) it can reduce the magnitude of the swings that occur when the bonus payment is based strictly on the formula amount calculated each year. Thus, in an exceptionally good year, the committee may decide to pay out only a portion of the bonus. Conversely, in a relatively poor year, the committee may decide to pay out more than the amount justified by current year performance by drawing from the carryover bonus amount. The disadvantage of the method is that the bonus relates less directly to current performance.

Deferred payments.   Although the amount of the bonus is calculated annually, payments to recipients may be spread out over a period of years, usually five. Under this system, executives receive only one fifth of their bonus in the year in which it was earned. The other four fifths are paid out equally over the next four years. Thus, after the manager has been working under the plan for five years, the bonus consists of one fifth of the bonus for the current year plus one fifth of each of the bonuses for the preceding four years. In some companies, the deferral period is three years. This deferred payment method offers a number of advantages:

• Managers can estimate, with reasonable accuracy, their cash income for the coming year.
• Deferred payments smooth the manager's receipt of cash, because the effects of cyclical swings in profits are averaged in the cash payments.
• A manager who retires will continue to receive payments for a number of years; this not only augments retirement income but also usually provides a tax advantage, because income tax rates after retirement may be lower than rates during working life.

Deferred bonus plans have the disadvantage of not making the deferred amount available to the executive in the year earned. (The deferred amount may earn interest for the manager and offset this disadvantage.) Because bonus payments in a year are not related to performance in that year, they may have a lesser impact as an incentive.

When bonus payments are deferred, the deferred amount may or may not vest. In some instances, a manager will not receive the deferred bonus if he or she leaves the company before it is paid (excluding disability, death, or being laid off). This arrangement is called a *golden handcuff,* because the manager who leaves voluntarily sacrifices the deferred amount and, therefore, is less willing to leave.

Long-Term Incentive Plans

Short-term plans reward managers for attaining current profitability objectives. By contrast, long-term plans are designed to reward performance over a longer period. A basic premise of many such plans is that growth in the value of the company's common stock reflects the company's long-run performance. There are several types of long-term incentive plans. The popularity of specific types of plans changes with, among other factors, changes in the income tax law, changes in accounting treatment, and the state of the stock market. Consequently, different plans are popular at different times. For example, the Tax Reform Act of 1986 significantly decreased the advantages of some of these plans.

Stock options. A stock option is a right to buy a number of shares of stock at or after a given date in the future (the *exercise date*), at a price agreed upon at the time the option is granted (usually, the current market price or 95 percent of the current market price). The major motivational benefit of stock option plans is that they direct managers' energies toward the long-term, rather than the short-term, performance of the company. The motivational impact of such plans is dampened to the extent that factors beyond the control of managers affect stock prices.

The manager gains if he or she later sells the stock at a price that exceeds the price paid for it. Until 1986, the gain on the sale of stock options that met certain criteria (called *qualified stock options*) was subject to the capital gains tax rate, which was much lower than the rate for ordinary income. After 1986, this difference in rates was eliminated. Unlike some of the alternatives mentioned below, the outright purchase of stock under a stock option plan gives managers equity that they can retain, even if they leave the company, and a gain that they can obtain whenever they decide to sell the stock. However, many stock options are for *restricted stock*. Managers are not permitted to sell this stock for a specified period after it was acquired.

Phantom shares. A phantom stock plan awards managers a number of shares for bookkeeping purposes only. At the end of a specified period (say, five years) the executive is entitled to receive an award equal to the *appreciation* in the market value of the stock since the date of award. This award may be in cash, in shares of stock, or in both. Unlike a stock option, a phantom stock plan requires no transaction costs. Some stock option plans require that the manager hold the stock for a certain period after it was purchased, and this involves a risk of a decrease in the market price and the interest costs associated with holding the stock. This risk and cost are not involved in a phantom stock plan.

Stock appreciation rights. A stock appreciation right is a right to receive cash payments based on the increase in the value of stock from the time of the award until a specified future date. Both phantom shares and stock appreciation rights are a form of deferred cash bonus, in which the amount of bonus is a function of the market price of the company's stock. Both these plans have the advantages of a stock option plan. As contrasted with a cash bonus paid currently, they involve uncertainty, in both directions, about the ultimate amount paid.

Performance shares. A performance share plan awards a specified number of shares to a manager when specific long-term goals have been met. Usually, the goals are to achieve a certain percentage growth in earnings per share over a three-to-five-year period; therefore, they are not influenced by the price of the stock. This plan has advantages over either the stock option or the phantom stock plan in that the award is based on performance that can be controlled, at least partially, by the executive. Also, the award is not dependent on an increase in stock prices, although the increase in earnings is likely to be related to the increase in stock prices. This plan suffers from the limitation of basing the bonus on accounting measures of performance; actions that corporate executives take to improve earnings per share could, under some conditions, not contribute to the economic worth of the firm.

Performance units.   In a performance unit plan, a cash bonus is paid on the attainment of specific long-term targets. This plan, thus, combines aspects of stock appreciation rights and performance shares. This plan is especially useful in companies with little or no publicly traded stock. Success of this plan depends upon the careful establishment of the long-term targets.

INCENTIVES FOR CORPORATE OFFICERS

In the preceding section, we described how the total bonus pool is calculated. In this section and the next, we describe how the total is divided among the corporate officers and among the business unit managers, respectively.

Each corporate officer, except the chief executive officer, is responsible in part, but only in part, for the company's overall performance. These corporate officers are entitled to, and are motivated by a bonus for good performance. However, the part of performance that each of them generated cannot be measured. For example, how can one measure the contribution to profits made by the chief financial officer? The human resources vice president? The chief counsel?

To induce the desired motivation, the chief executive officer, who recommends such awards to the board of directors, usually bases them on an assessment of each person's performance. Such an assessment is necessarily subjective. In some companies it is aided by a management by objectives system (an MBO) in which specific objectives are agreed to at the beginning of the year, and attainment of these objectives is assessed by the chief executive officer.

CEO Compensation

The chief executive officer's compensation usually is discussed by the compensation committee of the board of directors *after* the CEO has presented recommendations for compensation for his or her subordinates. From this presentation, the CEO's general attitude toward the appropriate percentage of incentive compensation in a given year is fairly obvious. In ordinary circumstances, the committee simply may apply the same percentage to the CEO's compensation. However, the committee may signal a different appraisal of the CEO's performance by deciding on a higher or lower percentage. This, perhaps more than any other expression of the board's opinion, is an important signal about how the board regards the CEO's performance. It should be accompanied by a frank explanation of the reasons for the choice.

Some people believe that the compensation of chief executives in the United States (and also of some professional athletes and performing artists) is too high and is not related to company performance.[4] They cite instances of what they regard as excess compensation: *golden parachutes* (i.e., incentive packages for an incumbent CEO as insurance against takeovers), extraordinary bonuses, lavish perquisites, and bonuses unrelated to profits. Directors who are responsible for deciding on compensation respond that the contribution of excellent CEOs is a tiny fraction of the profits that result from their decisions, and that they must set their CEO's compensation at a level comparable with that in competing companies.

Forbes magazine publishes annually a list of the compensation of hundreds of CEOs, compared with the profits for which they are presumably responsible. Although the details of its analysis are subject to criticism, the general message is that, in some situations, compensation is indeed high, but this is not the general pattern. Moreover, there are considerable differences in compensation in different industries. In any event, given their unique skills and capabilities, assessing true "market prices" for chief executives is nearly impossible.

INCENTIVES FOR BUSINESS UNIT MANAGERS

A wide array of options exist in developing an incentive compensation package for business unit managers (Exhibit 12–1).

EXHIBIT 12–1   Incentive Compensation Design Options for Business Unit Managers

A. Types of Incentives
   1. Financial Rewards
      a. Salary increases
      b. Bonuses
      c. Benefits
      d. Perquisites
   2. Psychological and Social Rewards
      a. Promotion possibilities
      b. Increased responsibilities

---

[4] G. S. Crystal, "The Wacky, Wacky World of CEO Pay," *Fortune*, June 6, 1988, pp. 68–78; "Big Trouble at Allegheny," *Business Week*, August 11, 1986, pp. 56–61; Peter F. Drucker, "Reform Executive Pay or Congress Will," *The Wall Street Journal*, April 24, 1984, p. 33; Edward Miller, "Big Three Chiefs Receive Bonus," *Associated Press*, April 20, 1986; Carol J. Loomis, "The Madness of Executive Compensation," *Fortune*, July 12, 1982, pp. 42–52.

EXHIBIT 12–1 *(concluded)*

---

      c. Increased autonomy

      d. Better geographical location

      e. Recognition

B. Size of Bonus Relative to Salary

  1. Upper Cutoffs

  2. Lower Cutoffs

C. Bonus Based on

  1. Business Unit Profits

  2. Company Profits

  3. Combination of the Two

D. Performance Criteria

  1. Financial Criteria

      a. Contribution margin

      b. Direct business unit profit

      c. Controllable business unit profit

      d. Income before taxes

      e. Net income

      f. Return on investment

      g. Residual income

  2. Time Period

      a. Annual financial performance

      b. Multiyear financial performance

  3. Nonfinancial Criteria

      a. Sales growth

      b. Market share

      c. Customer satisfaction

      d. Quality

      e. New product development

      f. Personnel development

      g. Public responsibility

  4. Relative Weights Assigned to Financial and Nonfinancial Criteria

  5. Benchmarks for Comparison

      a. Profit budget

      b. Past performance

      c. Competitor's performance

E. Bonus Determination Approach

  1. Formula-based

  2. Subjective

  3. Combination of the Two

F. Form of Bonus Payment

  1. Cash

  2. Stock

  3. Stock Options

  4. Phantom Shares

  5. Performance Shares

EXHIBIT 12–2   Two Philosophies on Incentive Compensation

Fixed pay

> Recruit good people
>
> ↓
>
> Pay them well
>
> ↓
>
> Expect good performance

Performance-based pay

> Recruit good people
>
> ↓
>
> Expect good performance
>
> ↓
>
> Pay them well, *if* performance is actually good

Types of Incentives

Some incentives are financial, others are psychological and social. Financial incentives include salary increases, bonuses, benefits, and perquisites (automobiles, vacation trips, club membership, and so on). Psychological and social incentives include promotion possibilities, increased responsibilities, increased autonomy, a better geographical location, and recognition (trophy, participation in executive development programs, and the like). In this part of the chapter, we discuss the financial incentives for business unit managers recognizing, however, that the motivation of managers is influenced by both financial and nonfinancial incentives.

Size of Bonus Relative to Salary

There are two basic philosophies on the issue of the mix between fixed (salary and fringe benefits) and variable (incentive bonus) portions in the managers' total compensation. One school states that we recruit good people, pay them well, and then expect good performance (Exhibit 12–2). Companies subscribing to this school emphasize salary, not incentive bonus (''fixed pay'' system). Here, compensation is not linked to performance and is, therefore, not at risk. This raises the issue: What happens if the person does not perform well?

Another school states that we recruit good people, expect them to perform well, and pay them well, *if* performance is actually good (Exhibit 12–2). Companies subscribing to this philosophy practice ''performance-based pay''; they emphasize incentive bonus, not salary.

The fundamental difference between the two philosophies arises from the fact that, under fixed pay, compensation comes first and performance comes later; under performance-based pay, performance comes first and compensation comes later. The two philosophies have different motivational implications for managers. Since salary is an assured income, an emphasis on salary may lead to conservatism and complacency. An emphasis on incentive bonus tends to encourage managers to put forth maximum effort. For this reason, more companies tend to emphasize incentive bonuses for business unit managers.

Examples. Mead Corporation's Containers Division, for instance, has implemented a bonus program that gives general managers with superior performance tens of thousands of dollars more than their counterparts at other companies while cutting the compensation of lesser lights—in effect, driving the latter out. Scores of companies, including Sears, Roebuck; Dow Chemical; Dayton Hudson; and Firestone are now measuring the performance of their business units and awarding incentive pay based on outperforming the competition.[5]

Cutoff levels. A bonus plan may be constrained at either end: *(i)* the level of performance at which a maximum bonus is reached (''upper'' cutoffs); and *(ii)* the level below which no bonus awards will be made (''lower'' cutoffs). Both upper and lower cutoffs may produce undesirable side effects. When business unit managers recognize that either the maximum bonus has been attained or that there will be no bonus at all, the motivational effect of the bonus system may be contrary to corporate goals. Instead of attempting to optimize profits in the current period, managers may be motivated to decrease profitability in one year (by overspending on discretionary expenses, such as advertising and research and development) to create an opportunity for a high bonus in the next year. Although this principally would affect only the timing of expenses, such action usually is undesirable.

One way to mitigate such dysfunctional actions is to carry over the excess or deficiency into the following year—that is, the bonus available for distribution in a given year would be the amount of bonus earned during that year plus any excess, or minus any deficiency, from the previous year.

---

[5] ''Executive Compensation: Looking to the Long Term Again,'' *Business Week,* May 9, 1983, pp. 80–83; ''Here Come Richer, Riskier Pay Plans,'' *Fortune,* December 19, 1988, pp. 51–58; ''More Employers Link Incentives to Unit Results,'' *The Wall Street Journal,* April 10, 1987.

Bonus Basis

A business unit manager's incentive bonus could be based solely on total corporate profits or solely on business unit profits, or on some mix of the two. The manager's decisions and actions have a more direct impact on the performance of his or her own unit than that of other business units; this would argue for linking incentive bonus to business unit performance. However, such an approach potentially could build walls between business units—that is, put significant barriers against interunit cooperation.

In a single business firm, whose business units are highly interdependent, the manager's bonus is tied primarily to corporate performance, since interunit cooperation is critical. For example, Alfred Sloan instituted a bonus plan in General Motors that rewarded business unit managers based on overall corporate performance to foster cooperation.[6]

In a conglomerate, on the other hand, the business units are usually autonomous. In such a context, it would be counterproductive to base business unit managers' bonuses primarily on company profits, since this would weaken the link between performance and rewards. Such a system creates *free-rider* problems. Some managers might relax and still get a bonus based on the efforts of other more diligent managers. Alternatively, in a poor profit year for the company, a unit that turns in an outstanding performance will not be adequately rewarded. In a conglomerate, therefore, it is desirable to reward business unit managers primarily based on business unit performance and so foster the entrepreneurial spirit.

For related diversified firms, it might be desirable to base part of the business unit managers' bonus on business unit profits and part on company profits, to provide the right mixture of incentives—namely, to optimize unit results while, at the same time, cooperating with other units to optimize company performance.

Performance Criteria

A difficult problem in the incentive bonus plan for business unit managers is to decide the criteria used as the basis for deciding the bonus.

Financial criteria.   If the business unit is a profit center, the choice of financial criteria include: contribution margin, direct business unit profit, controllable business unit profit, income before taxes, and net income. If the unit is an investment center, decisions need to be made in three areas: *(i)* definition of

---

[6] The General Motors bonus plan is described in chapter 22 of Alfred Sloan, *My Years with General Motors.* (New York: Doubleday, 1964).

profit, *(ii)* definition of investment, and *(iii)* choice between return on investment and residual income. We discussed the considerations involved in the choice of the performance criteria for profit centers and investment centers in Chapters 4 and 6, respectively.

Adjustments for uncontrollable factors.   In addition to selecting the financial criteria, decisions must be made on which adjustments, if any, will be made for uncontrollable factors. Typically, companies make adjustments for two types of uncontrollable influences. One type of adjustment removes expenses from business unit statements that are the result of decisions made by executives above the business unit level.

> **Example.**   A major consumer products company reported: "A few years ago we decided to close a factory in Germany that was working at 30 percent of capacity. The expenses were deducted at the corporate level. It was not the decision of the manager in Germany, so we couldn't penalize him.[7]

Another type of adjustment is to eliminate the effects of losses due to "acts of nature" (fires, earthquakes, floods) and accidents not caused by the negligence of the manager.

> **Example.**   The comments by an executive in a distribution company, who was asked if he would make an adjustment if a fire occurred in a warehouse, is typical: "I would start with the assumption that this couldn't be foreseen. Then I would look at the causes. Was the fire caused by a breach of security or a lackadaisical attitude toward safety? If the fire was outside the manager's control, I would make the adjustment."[8]

Benefits and shortcomings of short-term financial targets.   Linking business unit managers' bonus to achieving annual financial targets (after making allowances for uncontrollable events) is desirable. It induces managers to search for ways to perform existing operations in different ways and initiate new activities to meet the financial targets.

However, *sole* reliance on financial criteria could cause several dysfunctional effects.[9] First, short-term actions that are not in the long-term interests of the company (e.g., under-maintenance of equipment) may be encouraged. Second, managers might not undertake investments that promise benefits in the long-term but hurt short-term financial results. Third, managers may be motivated to engage in data manipulation to meet current period targets.

---

[7] Kenneth A. Merchant, *Rewarding Results: Motivating Profit Center Managers* (Boston: Harvard Business School Press, 1989), p. 121.

[8] Ibid, pp. 125–26.

[9] J. J. Curran, "Companies That Rob the Future" *Fortune*, July 4, 1988, pp. 84–89; "More Than Ever, It's Management for the Short Term," *Business Week*, November 24, 1986, pp. 92–93.

Mechanisms to overcome short-term bias.   If financial criteria are *supplemented* with additional incentive mechanisms, this may overcome the short-term orientation of annual financial goals. One possibility is to base part of the managers' bonus on *multiyear performance* (i.e., performance over a three- to five-year period). Although it has the obvious advantage of extending the time horizon of managers, this approach has certain weaknesses. First, managers have difficulty in seeing the connection between their efforts and rewards in a multiyear award scheme; this lessens the motivational effect of such awards. Second, a manager might retire or get transferred during the multiyear period, thereby greatly adding to the complexity in implementing such a plan. Third, there is more likelihood that factors beyond the control of the manager will influence the achievement of long-range targets.

Another method to correct for the inherent inadequacies of financial criteria is to include one or more *nonfinancial criteria,* such as sales growth, market share, customer satisfaction, product quality, new product development, personnel development, and public responsibility. Each of these factors will affect long-run profits. Senior management can create the desired short-term versus long-term profit orientation on the part of business unit managers and allow for factors that are not reflected in the financial measure by a judicious choice of financial and nonfinancial criteria and appropriate weights among these criteria.

> **Examples.**   McDonald's evaluated its store managers on product quality, service, cleanliness, sales volume, personnel training, and cost control.[10]
>
> When General Electric decentralized in the 1950s, it identified multiple measures of divisional performance: profitability, market position, productivity, product leadership, personnel development, employee attitudes, and public responsibility.[11]

Another mechanism to correct for the short-term bias is to base part of the business unit managers' bonus on *long-term incentive plans,* such as stock options, phantom shares, and performance shares. These plans focus the business unit managers *(i)* on companywide performance and *(ii)* on long-term performance. Other advantages and limitations of these plans were discussed earlier.

Benchmarks for comparison.   The performance of a business unit manager can be appraised by comparing actual results with the profit budget, with past performance, or with competitor's performance. The typical practice is to evaluate the business unit manager against the profit budget. As discussed in

---

[10] E. W. Sasser and S. H. Pettway, "Case of Big Mac's Pay Plans," *Harvard Business Review,* July–August 1974.

[11] Ralph J. Cordiner, *New Frontiers for Professional Managers* (New York: McGraw-Hill, 1956).

Chapter 9, the following considerations are important when using the profit budget as a motivational tool: *(i)* the business unit manager participates in the development of the profit budget and *(ii)* the budget is challenging but attainable.

Bonus Determination Approach

A bonus award for a business unit manager can be determined on the basis of either a strict formula, such as a percentage of the business unit's operating profit, or a purely subjective assessment by the managers' superior, or by some combination of the two. This dichotomy of formula-based versus subjective bonus determination is similar to Ouchi's concepts of output control and behavior control. According to Ouchi, in controlling people's work, only two aspects of that work can be observed and monitored: behavior (leading to "behavior control") or the outputs that result from behavior (leading to "output control").[12] Behavior control tends to be subjective; a superior using behavior control would base the amount of the business unit manager's bonus on a subjective judgment of the effectiveness of the decisions and actions taken by the manager. Since output control is amenable to quantitative measurement (e.g., operating profit), it tends to be formula-based.

Exclusive reliance on objective formulas (i.e., output control) has some clear merits: reward systems can be specified with great precision, there is very little uncertainty or ambiguity about performance standards, and superiors cannot exercise any bias or favoritism in assessing the performance of subordinate managers. However, a major limitation of objective formulas is that they are likely to induce managers to pay less attention to the performance of their business units along dimensions that are important, although difficult to quantify (e.g., research and development and human resource management). Some subjectivity in determining bonuses, therefore, is desirable in most units. A subjective approach is especially desirable when a manager's personal control over a unit's performance is low. In such situations, numerical indicators of the unit's performance have little validity as measures of the performance of the manager. This type of situation is likely to happen under the following circumstances:

- When the business unit manager inherits problems created by a predecessor.
- When the business unit is highly interdependent with other units and, therefore, its performance is influenced by the decisions and actions of outside individuals.
- When the strategy requires much greater attention to longer-term concerns (as is the case in a business unit aggressively building market share).

---

[12] See, for instance, in Suggested Additional Readings at the end of this chapter, Ouchi (1977, 1979).

AGENCY THEORY

Agency theory explores how contracts and incentives can be written to motivate individuals to achieve goal congruence.[13] It attempts to describe the major factors that should be considered in designing incentive contracts. An incentive contract, as used in agency theory, is the same as the incentive compensation arrangements discussed in this chapter. Agency theory attempts to state these relationships in mathematical models. This introduction describes the general ideas of agency theory without giving actual models.

Concepts

An agency relationship exists whenever one party (the principal) hires another party (the agent) to perform some service and, in so doing, delegates decision-making authority to the agent. In a corporation, shareholders are principals, and the chief executive officer is their agent. The shareholders hire the CEO and expect that the CEO will act in their interest. At a lower level, the CEO is the principal, and the business unit managers are the agents. The challenge becomes how to motivate agents so that they will be as productive as they would be if they were the owners.

One of the key elements of agency theory is that principals and agents have divergent preferences or objectives. The divergent preferences can be reduced through incentive contracts.

Divergent objectives of principals and agents.
Agency theory assumes that all individuals act in their own self-interest. Agents are assumed to receive satisfaction not only from financial compensation but also from the perquisites involved in an agency relationship. The perquisites can take the form of generous amounts of leisure time, attractive working conditions, country club memberships, and flexibility in working hours. For example, some agents may prefer leisure to hard work (effort). Leisure is assumed to be the opposite of effort. Managers' effort increases the value of the firm, while leisure does not. The preference of the agent for leisure over effort is referred to as *work aversion*. The deliberate withholding of agent effort is termed *shirking*. On the other hand, the principals (i.e., shareholders) are assumed to be interested only in the financial returns that accrue from their investment in the firm.

Another divergence between the preferences of principals and agents is *risk preferences*. Agency theory assumes that managers prefer more wealth to less,

---

[13] The term *agency* suggests that the topic is related to agency law, but this is not the case. Agency law defines the obligations of an agent to a principal and the obligations of a principal to the agent; but these legal obligations do not govern or adequately explain the behaviors of superior managers and subordinate managers to one another. "Commitments" and "understandings" between superiors and subordinates are not legal contracts; subordinates rarely are sued for breach of contract.

but that the marginal utility, or satisfaction, decreases as more wealth is accumulated. Agents typically have much of their wealth tied up in the fortunes of the firm. This wealth consists both of their financial wealth and also of their human capital. Human capital is the value of the manager as perceived by the market; it is influenced by the firm's performance. Because of the decreasing utility for wealth and the large amount of agent capital that is dependent on the company, agents are assumed to be *risk averse*: They value increases from a risky investment at less than the expected (actuarial) value of the investment.

On the other hand, the shares of stock of the company are held by many owners, who reduce their risk by diversifying their wealth and becoming owners in many companies. Therefore, owners are interested in the expected value of their investment and are *risk neutral*. Managers cannot as easily diversify away this risk, which is why they are risk averse.

Nonobservability of agents' actions. The conflict over perquisites could easily be resolved if the principal could monitor the agent's actions. The divergence in preferences associated with compensation and perquisites arises whenever the principal cannot easily monitor the agent's actions. Shareholders are not in a position to monitor daily the activities of the CEO to ensure that he or she is working in their best interest. Likewise, the CEO is not in a position to monitor daily the activities of business unit managers.

The principal has inadequate information about the performance of the agent; therefore, the principal can never be certain how the agent's effort contributed to actual firm results. This situation is referred to as *information asymmetry*. These asymmetries can take on several forms. Without monitoring, only the agent knows whether he or she is working in the principal's best interest. Moreover, the agent may know more about the task than the principal. The added information that the agent may have about the task is referred to as *private information*.

Because of both the divergence of preferences between the principal and agent and also the private information of the agent, the agent may misrepresent information to the principal. This misrepresentation is of such a general nature that the name *moral hazard* has been given to the situation where an agent being controlled is motivated to misrepresent private information by the nature of the control system.

Control Mechanisms

Agency theorists state there are two major ways of dealing with the problems of divergent objectives and information asymmetry: monitoring and incentives.

Monitoring. The first control mechanism is monitoring. The principal can design control systems that monitor the actions of the agent. The principal designs these systems to limit actions that increase the agent's welfare at the expense of principal's interest. An example of a monitoring system is the audited financial statements. Financial reports are generated about company performance, they are audited by a third party, and they are then sent to the owners.

Agency theory has attempted to explain why different agency relationships entail different levels of monitoring. For example, the effectiveness of monitoring is increased if the task to be performed by the agent is well defined and the information, or "signal", used in monitoring is accurate. If the task is not well defined or easily monitored, then incentive contracting becomes more appealing as a control device. These alternatives—monitoring and incentives—are not mutually exclusive. For instance, in most firms, the CEO has an incentive contract along with audited financial statements that act as a monitoring device.

Incentive contracting.   Another mechanism that can align the interests of the principal with those of the agent is incentives. The principal attempts to limit divergent preferences by establishing appropriate incentive contracts that do this. The more an agent's reward depends on a performance measure, the more incentive there is for the agent to improve that measure. Therefore, the principal should so define the performance measure that it furthers his or her interest. The ability to accomplish this is referred to as *goal congruence,* the same concept we discussed in Chapter 1. When the contract given to the agent motivates the agent to work in the principal's best interest, the contract is considered goal congruent.

A compensation scheme that does not incorporate an incentive contract poses a serious agency problem. For example, if CEOs were paid a straight salary, they might not be motivated to work as diligently as when compensation consisted of a salary plus bonus. In the latter case, the CEO would be motivated to work harder to increase profits; this would increase the CEO's compensation, and the increased profits would benefit the principal. Contracts, therefore, are written that align the interests between the two parties by incorporating an incentive feature—that is, the principal writes a contract permitting management to share in the wealth when firm value is increased.

A challenge facing the principal is identifying signals that are correlated both with agent effort and firm value. The agent's effort, along with outside factors (e.g., the general economy, natural disasters), combine to determine performance. The more closely an outcome measure reflects the input of the manager, the more valuable the measure is in an incentive contract. If the measure of performance is not closely correlated with the agent's effort, there is little incentive for the agent to increase the measure.

None of the incentive arrangements can ensure complete goal congruence. This is because the difference in risk preferences between the two parties, the asymmetry of information, and the costs of monitoring will cause costs. Even an efficient system of incentive alignments will still result in some divergence of preferences. This divergence is named the *residual loss.* The addition of the costs of incentive compensation, the costs of monitoring, and the residual loss are formally titled *agency costs.*

CEO compensation and stock ownership plans.   As an example of the agency costs inherent in incentive compensation, consider a company that pays its CEO a bonus in the form of stock options. One cost is the risk-preference differences between the owners and CEO. The agent, already risk averse, incurs additional risks when his or her pay is based on stock price performance. To compensate the CEO for taking on this risk, the contract will have to increase the amount of expected pay. In addition, to minimize the possible downside potential, the agent may not take on high risk/high return projects that the principal may find desirable.

A second problem with a stock ownership bonus plan is the lack of direct causal relationship between agent's effort and the change in stock price. Stock prices are affected by factors outside the control of the agent (e.g., general economic conditions, government intervention). If the stock price rises because of factors beyond the control of the agent, then the agent receives increased pay at the expense of the owners without any increased effort. On the other hand, the stock price may decrease even if the agent exerts high effort.

In spite of these two problems, the stock ownership incentive contracts is preferred to a contract that does not have an incentive feature. As pointed out earlier, a flat salary has larger agency costs associated with it.

Business unit managers and accounting-based incentives.   The relationship between a business unit manager's effort and the stock price is more remote than the tie between CEO effort and stock price. It is very difficult to disaggregate the contributions made by individual business units to increases in the firm's stock price. Given the remote causal tie between the manager's effort and stock price, the business unit manager's bonus might be based on business unit net income. However, this incentive contract still has agency costs similar to those discussed in the CEO stock ownership plan. To illustrate, market demand for a product may fall because of a new substitute product, but the manager may still perform well within the new smaller market. However, if the bonus is based strictly on net income, the agent's pay will decrease. In addition, the agent may inflate net income through accounting manipulations that do not affect firm value. An example of this behavior is the sale of fixed assets that have a market value in excess of book value. While a contract based on business unit net income may have lower agency costs than straight salary, these costs do not go to zero.

A Critique

Agency theory was invented in the 1960s, but, unlike other developments described in this book (e.g., strategy matrices, just-in-time, quality control, capital investment models, decision support systems), the theory has had no discernible practical influence on the management control process. Although the subject of many articles in academic journals,[14] there has been no real-world payoff from agency theory. By "payoff" we mean that a manager used the results of agency theory to make a better compensation decision. Many managers are not even aware of agency theory.

Some of those who have studied agency theory state that the models are no more than statements of obvious facts expressed in mathematical symbols. Others state that the elements in the models can't be quantified (what is the "cost of information asymmetry"?), and that the model is a vast oversimplification of the real-world relationship between superiors and subordinates. The models incorporate only a few elements; and they disregard other factors that affect this relationship, such as the personality of the participants, agents who are by no means risk averse, motives other than financial, the principal's trust in the agent, the agent's ability on the present assignment, the agent's potential for future assignments, and on and on.

We describe the theory in the hope that students will find it useful in thinking about the influence of incentive compensation in motivation of managers, but we caution about its usefulness in solving actual compensation problems.

SUMMARY

The incentive compensation system is a key management control device. Incentive compensation plans can be roughly divided into two types: those that relate compensation to profits currently earned by the company, called "short-term incentive plans"; and those that relate compensation to longer-term performance, called "long-term incentive plans." Several considerations need to be taken into account in allocating the total bonus pool to corporate executives and business unit managers. An incentive system that explicitly incorporates the following factors has a much better chance of success:

- The needs, values, and beliefs of the general managers who are rewarded.
- The culture of the organization.
- External factors, such as industry characteristics, competitors' compensation practices, managerial labor markets, and tax and legal issues.
- Organization's strategies.

SUGGESTED ADDITIONAL READINGS

Baber, William R. "Budget-Based Compensation and Discretionary Spending." *The Accounting Review* LX, no. 1, (January 1985), pp. 1–9.

---

[14] *Academy of Management Review* 15, no. 3, (1990), contains six articles on aspects of agency theory.

Baker, G. P.; M. C. Jensen; and K. J. Murphy. "Compensation and Incentives: Practice vs. Theory." *Journal of Finance,* July 1988, pp. 593–616.

Bennett, Amanda. "Executives Will Gain over Time as Lucrative Stock Plans Multiply." *The Wall Street Journal,* April 10, 1987, p. 25.

Butler, Stephen A., and Michael W. Maher. *Management Incentive Compensation Plans.* Montvale, N.J.: National Association of Accountants, 1986.

Crystal, Graef S., and Mark R. Horwich. "The Case for Divisional Long-Term Incentives." *California Management Review,* Fall 1986.

Donaldson, Gordon, *Managing Corporate Wealth.* New York: Praeger, 1984, chap. 12.

Fisher, Joseph, and Vijay Gövindarajan. "Determinants of CEO and Profit Center Managers' Compensation." Working paper, The Amos Tuck School of Business Administration, Dartmouth College, 1991.

Hambrick, Donald C., and Charles C. Snow. "Strategic Reward Systems." In *Strategy, Organization Design, and Human Resource Management,* ed. C. C. Snow. New York: JAI Press, 1989, pp. 333–68.

Henderson, Richard I. *Compensation Management: Rewarding Performance.* 5th ed. Englewood Cliffs, N.J.: Prentice Hall, 1989.

Lambert, Richard, and David F. Larcker. "Executive Compensation Contracts, Executive Decision-Making, and Shareholder Wealth: A Review of the Evidence." *Midland Corporate Finance Journal,* no. 1 (1985), pp. 18–33.

Merchant, K. A. *Rewarding Results: Motivating Profit Center Managers.* Boston: Harvard Business School Press, 1989.

Milkovich, George T., and Jerry M. Newman *Compensation.* 3rd ed. Homewood, Ill.: BPI/Irwin, 1990.

Ouchi, William. "The Relationship between Organizational Structure and Organizational Control." *Administrative Science Quarterly* 22 (1977), pp. 95–112.

———— "A Conceptual Framework for the Design of Organization Control Mechanisms." *Management Science,* 25 (1979), pp. 833–48.

Reibstein, Larry. "More Employers Link Incentives to Unit Results." *The Wall Street Journal,* April 10, 1987.

Schwesinger, Edmund. "Where Do the Executive Bucks Stop Now?" *Coopers & Lybrand Executive Briefing,* April 1987.

Case 12–1

Lincoln Electric Company, 1989*

The Lincoln Electric Company was the world's largest manufacturer of arc-welding products and a leading producer of industrial electric motors. The firm employed 2,400 workers in 2 U.S. factories near Cleveland and an equal number in 11 factories located in other countries. This does not include the field sales force of more than 200. The company's U.S. market share (for arc-welding products) is estimated at more than 40 percent.

James F. Lincoln, head of the firm since 1914, died in 1965 and there was some concern, even among employees, that the management system would fall into disarray, that profits would decline, and that year-end bonuses might be discontinued. Quite the contrary, in 1989 the company appears as strong as ever. Each year, except the recession years 1982 and 1983, has seen high profits and bonuses. Employee morale and productivity remain very good. Employee turnover is almost nonexistent, except for retirements. Lincoln's market share is stable. The historically high stock dividends continue.

A Historical Sketch

Lincoln Electric Company was founded in 1905 by John C. Lincoln. In 1907, after a bout with typhoid fever forced him from Ohio State University in his senior year, James F. Lincoln, John's younger brother, joined the fledgling company. In 1914 he became active head of the firm. One of his early actions was to ask the employees to elect representatives to a committee that would advise him on company operations. This "Advisory Board" has met with the chief executive officer every two weeks since that time.

The first year the Advisory Board was in existence, working hours were reduced from 55 hours per week, then standard, to 50 hours a week. In 1923, a piecework pay system was in effect, employees got two weeks paid vacation each year, and wages were adjusted for changes in the consumer price index. Approximately 30 percent of the common stock was set aside for key employees in 1914. A stock purchase plan for all employees was begun in 1925.

The board of directors voted to start a suggestion system in 1929. The program is still in effect, but cash awards, a part of the early program, were discontinued several years ago. Now, suggestions are rewarded by additional "points," which affect year-end bonuses.

The legendary Lincoln bonus plan was proposed by the Advisory Board and accepted on a trial basis in 1934. The bonus plan has been a cornerstone of the Lincoln management system, and recent bonuses have approximated annual wages.

By 1944, Lincoln employees enjoyed a pension plan, a policy of promotion from within, and continuous employment. Base pay rates were determined by formal job evaluation and a merit rating system was in effect.

In the prologue of James F. Lincoln's last book, Charles G. Herbruck writes regarding the foregoing personnel innovations:

* This case was prepared by Arthur Sharplin, McNeese State University, Lake Charles, La. 70601.

They were not to buy good behavior. They were not efforts to increase profits. They were not antidotes to labor difficulties. They did not constitute a "do-gooder" program. They were expressions of mutual respect for each person's importance to the job to be done. All of them reflect the leadership of James Lincoln, under whom they were nurtured and propagated.

Certainly since 1935 and probably for several years before that, Lincoln productivity has been well above the average for similar companies. The company claims levels of productivity more than twice those for other manufacturers from 1945 onward.

Company Philosophy

James F. Lincoln was the son of a Congregational minister, and Christian principles were at the center of his business philosophy.

There is no indication that Lincoln attempted to evangelize his employees or customers—or the general public, for that matter. Neither the chairman of the board and chief executive, George Willis, nor the president, Donald F. Hastings, mention the Christian gospel in their recent speeches and interviews. The company motto, "The actual is limited, the possible is immense," is prominently displayed; but there is no display of religious slogans, and there is no company chapel.

Attitude toward the Customer

James Lincoln saw the customer's needs as the *raison d'etre* for every company. "When any company has achieved success so that it is attractive as an investment," he wrote, "all money usually needed for expansion is supplied by the customer in retained earnings. It is obvious that the customer's interests, not the stockholder's, should come first." This is reflected in Lincoln's policy to "at all times price on the basis of cost and at all times keep pressure on our cost. . . ." Lincoln's goal, often stated, is "to build a better and better product at a lower and lower price."

Attitude toward Stockholders

Stockholders are given last priority at Lincoln. This is a continuation of James Lincoln's philosophy: "The last group to be considered is the stockholders who own stock because they think it will be more profitable than investing money in any other way." Concerning division of the largess produced by incentive management, he wrote, "The absentee stockholder also will get his share, even if undeserved, out of the greatly increased profit that the efficiency produces."

Attitude toward Unionism

There has never been a serious effort to organize Lincoln employees. While James Lincoln criticized the labor movement for "selfishly attempting to better its position at the expense of the people it must serve," he still had kind words for union members. Lincoln's idea of the correct relationship between workers and managers is shown by this comment: "Labor and management are properly not warring camps; they are parts of one organization in which they must and should cooperate fully and happily."

Beliefs and Assumptions about Employees

If fulfilling customer needs is the desired goal of business, then employee performance and productivity are the means by which this goal can best be achieved. It is the Lincoln attitude toward employees, reflected in the following comments by James Lincoln, which is credited by many with creating the success the company has experienced:

> The greatest fear of the worker, which is the same as the greatest fear of the industrialist in operating a company, is the lack of income. . . . The industrial manager is very conscious of his company's need of uninterrupted income. He is completely oblivious, evidently, of the fact that the worker has the same need.
>
> If money is to be used as an incentive, the program must provide that what is paid to the worker is what he has earned. The earnings of each must be in accordance with accomplishment.

Lincoln's Business

Arc-welding has been the standard joining method in shipbuilding for decades. It is the predominant way of connecting steel in the construction industry. Most industrial plants have their own welding shops for maintenance and construction. While advances in welding technology have been frequent, arc-welding products, in the main, have hardly changed. Lincoln's Innershield process is a notable exception. This process lowers welding cost and improves quality and speed in many applications. The most widely used Lincoln electrode, the Fleetweld 5P, has been virtually the same since the 1930s. The most popular engine-driven welder in the world, the Lincoln SA-200, has been in production for at least four decades. A 1989 model SA-200 even weighs almost the same as the 1950 model, and it is little changed in appearance.

The company's share of the U.S. arc-welding products market appears to have been about 40 percent for many years. The welding products market has grown somewhat faster than the level of industry in general. The market is highly price-competitive, with variations in prices of standard items normally amounting to only a percent or two. Lincoln's products are sold directly by its engineering-oriented sales force and indirectly though its distributor organization. Advertising expenditures amount to less than three fourths of a percent of sales. Research and development expenditures typically range from $10 million to $12 million, considerably more than competitors.

The other major welding process, flame-welding, has not been competitive with arc-welding since the 1930s. However, plasma-arc-welding, a relatively new process, which uses a conducting stream of super heated gas (plasma) to confine the welding current to a small area, has made some inroads, especially in metal tubing manufacturing, in recent years. Major advances in technology that will produce an alternative superior to arc-welding within the next decade or so appear unlikely. Also, it seems likely that changes in the machines and techniques used in arc-welding will be evolutionary, rather than revolutionary.

Products

In addition to arc-welding products, Lincoln also produces electric motors ranging from one-half horsepower to 200 horsepower. Motors constitute about 8 to 10 percent of total sales. Several million dollars has recently been invested in automated equipment that will double Lincoln's manufacturing capacity for one-half to 20 horsepower electric motors.

Lincoln and its competitors now market a wide range of general-purpose and specialty electrodes for welding mild steel, aluminum, cast iron, and stainless and special steels. Most of these electrodes are designed to meet the standards of the American Welding Society, a trade association. They, thus, are essentially the same in size and composition from one manufacturer to another. Every electrode manufacturer has a limited number of unique products, but these typically constitute only a small percentage of total sales.

Manufacturing Processes

The main plant is in Euclid, Ohio, a suburb on Cleveland's east side. There are no warehouses. Materials flow from the half-mile-long dock on the north side of the plant through the production lines to a very limited storage and loading area on the south side. Materials used on each work station are stored as close as possible to the work station. The administrative offices, near the center of the factory, are entirely functional. A corridor below the main level provides access to the factory floor from the main entrance near the center of the plan. *Fortune* magazine recently declared the Euclid facility one of America's 10 best-managed factories, and compared it with a General Electric plant, also on the list:

Stepping into GE's spanking new dishwasher plant, an awed supplier said, is like stepping "into the

Hyatt Regency." By comparison, stepping into Lincoln Electric's 33-year-old, cavernous, dimly lit factory is like stumbling into a dingy big-city YMCA. It's only when one starts looking at how these factories do things that similarities become apparent. They have found ways to merge design with manufacturing, build in quality, make wise choices about automation, get close to customers, and handle their work forces.

The Lincoln Electric Company, 1989

A new Lincoln plant, in Mentor, Ohio, houses some of the electrode production operations, which were moved from the main plant. Electrode manufacturing is highly capital intensive.

Lincoln welding machines and electric motors are made on a series of assembly lines. Gasoline and diesel engines are purchased partially assembled, but practically all other components are made from basic industrial products (e.g., steel bars and sheets and bar copper conductor wire).

Individual components, such as gasoline tanks for engine-driven welders and steel shafts for motors and generators, are made by numerous small "factories within a factory." The shaft for a certain generator, for example, is made from raw steel bar by one operator, who uses five large machines, all running continuously. A saw cuts the bar to length, a digital lathe machines different sections to varying diameters, a special milling machine cuts a slot for the keyway, and so forth, until a finished shaft is produced. The operator moves the shafts from machine to machine and makes necessary adjustments.

Another operator punches, shapes, and paints sheetmetal cowling parts. One assembles steel laminations onto a rotor shaft, then winds, insulates, and test the rotors. Finished components are moved by crane operators to the nearby assembly lines.

Worker Performance and Attitudes

The typical Lincoln employee earns about twice as much as other factory workers in the Cleveland area. Yet the company's labor cost per sales dollar in 1989, 26 cents, is well below industry averages. Worker turnover is practically nonexistent, except for retirements and departures by new employees.

Sales per Lincoln factory employee currently exceed $150,000. An observer at the factory quickly sees why this figure is so high. Each worker is proceeding busily and thoughtfully about the task at hand. There is no idle chatter. Most workers take no coffee breaks. Many operate several machines and make a substantial component unaided. The supervisors are busy with planning and recordkeeping duties and hardly glance at the people they "supervise." The manufacturing procedures appear efficient—no unnecessary steps, no wasted motions, no wasted materials. Finished components move smoothly to subsequent work stations.

Appendix A includes summaries of interviews with employees.

Organization Structure

Lincoln has never allowed development of a formal organization chart. The objective of this policy is to insure maximum flexibility. An open-door policy is practiced throughout the company, and personnel are encouraged to take problems to the persons most capable of resolving them. Once, Harvard Business School researchers prepared an organization chart reflecting the implied relationships at Lincoln. The chart became available within the company, and present management feels that had a disruptive effect. Therefore, no organizational chart appears in this case.

Perhaps because of the quality and enthusiasm of the Lincoln work force, routine supervision is almost nonexistent. A typical production foreman, for example, supervises as many as 100 workers, a span of control that does not allow more than infrequent worker-supervisor interaction.

Position titles and traditional flows of authority do imply something of an organizational structure, however. For example, the vice president of sales and the vice president of Electrode Division report to the president, as do various staff assistants, such as the personnel director and the director of purchasing. Using such implied relationships, it has been determined that production workers have two or, at most, three levels of supervision between themselves and the President.

Personnel Policies

Recruitment and Selection

Every job opening is advertised internally on company bulletin boards, and any employee can apply for any job so advertised. External hiring is permitted only for entry-level positions. Selection for these jobs is done on the basis of personal interviews—there is no aptitude or psychological testing. Not even a high school diploma is required—except for engineering and sales positions, which are filled by graduate engineers. A committee consisting of vice presidents and supervisors interviews candidates initially cleared by the personnel department. Final selection is made by the supervisor who has a job opening. Out of over 3,500 applicants interviewed by the personnel department during a recent period, fewer than 300 were hired.

Job Security

In 1958, Lincoln formalized its guaranteed continuous employment policy, which had already been in effect for many years. There have been no layoffs since World War II. Since 1958, every worker with over two year's longevity has been guaranteed at least 30 hours per week, 49 weeks per year.

The policy has never been so severely tested as during the 1981–83 recession. As a manufacturer of capital goods, Lincoln's business is highly cyclical. In previous recessions, the company was able to avoid major sales declines. However, sales plummeted 32 percent in 1982 and another 16 percent the next year. Lincoln not only earned profits, but no employee was laid off and year-end incentive bonuses continued. To weather the

storm, management cut most of the nonsalaried workers back to 30 hours a week for varying periods of time. Many employees were reassigned and the total work force was slightly reduced through normal attrition and restricted hiring.

Performance Evaluations

Each supervisor formally evaluates subordinates twice a year using the card shown in Exhibit 1. The employee performance criteria, "quality," "dependability," "ideas and cooperation," and "output," are considered to be independent of each other. Marks on the cards are converted to numerical scores, which are forced to average 100 for each evaluating supervisor. Individual merit rating scores normally range from 80 to 110. Any score over 110 requires a special letter to top management. These scores (over 110) are not considered in computing the required 100 point average for each evaluating supervisor. Suggestions for improvements often result in recommendations for exceptionally high performance scores. Supervisors discuss individual performance marks with the employees concerned. Each warranty claim is traced to the individual employee whose work caused the defect. The employee's performance score may be reduced, or the worker may be required to repay the cost of servicing the warranty claim by working without pay.

Compensation

Basic wage levels for jobs at Lincoln are determined by a wage survey of similar jobs in the Cleveland area. These rates are adjusted quarterly in accordance with changes in the Cleveland area wage index. Insofar as possible, base wage rates are translated into piece rates. Practically all production workers and many others—for example, some forklift operators—are paid by piece rate. Once established, piece rates are never changed, unless a substantive change in the way a job is done results from a source other than the worker doing the job.

EXHIBIT 1   Merit Rating Cards

➡ Increasing Quality ➡

This card rates the QUALITY of work you do.

It also reflects your success in eliminating errors and in reducing scrap and waste.

QUALITY
This rating has been done jointly by your department head and the inspection department in the shop and with other department heads in the office and engineering.

➡ Increasing Dependability ➡

This card rates how well your supervisors have been able to depend on you to do those things that have been expected of you without supervision.

It also reflects your ability to supervise yourself, including your work safety performance, your orderliness, care of equipment, and the effective use you make of your skills.

DEPENDABILITY
This rating has been done by your department head.

➡ Increasing Ideas & Cooperation ➡

This card rates your Cooperation, Ideas, and Initiative.

IDEAS & COOPERATION

➡ Increasing Output ➡   Days Absent

This card rates HOW MUCH PRODUCTIVE WORK you actually turn out.

It also reflects your willingness not to hold back and recognizes your attendance record.

New ideas and new methods are important to your company in our continuing effort to reduce costs, increase output, improve quality and work safety, and improve our relationship with our customers. This card credits you for your ideas and initiative used to help in this direction.

It also rates your cooperation—how you work with others as a team. Such factors as your attitude towards supervision, coworkers, and the company, your efforts to share knowledge with others, and your cooperation in installing new methods smoothly are considered here.

OUTPUT
This rating has been done jointly by your department head and the production control department in the shop and with other department heads in the office and engineering.

In December of each year, a portion of annual profits is distributed to employees as bonuses. Incentive bonuses since 1934 have averaged about 90 percent of annual wages and somewhat more than after-tax profits. The average bonus for 1988 was $21,258. Even for the recession years 1982 and 1983, bonuses had averaged $13,998 and $8,557, respectively. Individual bonuses are proportional to merit-rating scores. For example, assume the amount set aside for bonuses is 80 percent of total wages paid to eligible employees. A person whose performance score is 95 will receive a bonus of 76 percent (0.80×0.95) of annual wages. Bonuses totaled $54 million in 1988.

Work Assignment

Management has authority to transfer workers and to switch between overtime and short-time as required. Supervisors have undisputed authority to assign specific parts to individual workmen, who may have their own preferences due to variations in piece rates. During the 1982–1983 recession, 50 factory workers volunteered to join sales teams and fanned out across the country to sell a new welder designed for automobile body shops and small machine shops. The result—$10 million in sales and a hot new product.

Employee Participation in Decision Making

Thinking of participative management usually evokes a vision of a relaxed, nonauthoritarian atmosphere. This is not the case at Lincoln. Formal authority is quite strong. "We're very authoritarian around here," says Willis. James F. Lincoln placed a good deal of stress on protecting management's authority. "Management in all successful departments of industry must have complete power," he said. "Management is the coach who must be obeyed. The men, however, are the players who alone can win the game." Despite this attitude, there are several ways in which employees participate in management at Lincoln.

Richard Sabo, assistant to the chief executive officer, relates job enlargement/enrichment to participation. He said, "The most important partic-

ipative technique that we use is giving more responsibility to employees. We give a high school graduate more responsibility than other companies give their foremen." Management puts limits on the degree of participation which is allowed, however. In Sabo's words:

> When you use "participation," put quotes around it. Because we believe that each person should participate only in those decisions he is most knowledgeable about. I don't think production employees should control the decisions of the chairman. They don't know as much as he does about the decisions he is involved in.

The Advisory Board, elected by the workers, meets with the chairman and the president every two weeks to discuss ways of improving operations. Every employee has access to Advisory Board members, and answers to all Advisory Board suggestions are promised by the following meeting. Both Willis and Hastings are quick to point out, though, that the Advisory Board only recommends actions. "They do not have direct authority," Willis says. "And when they bring up something that management thinks is not to the benefit of the company, it will be rejected."

Under the early suggestion program, employees were awarded one half of the first year's savings attributable to their suggestions. Now, however, the value of suggestions is reflected in performance evaluation scores, which determine individual incentive bonus amounts.

Fringe Benefits and Executive Perquisites

A medical plan and a company-paid retirement program have been in effect for many years. A plant cafeteria, operated on a break-even basis, serves meals at about 60 percent of usual costs. The Employee Association, to which the company does not contribute, provides disability insurance and social and athletic activities. The employee stock ownership program has resulted in employee ownership of about 50 percent of the common stock. Under this program, each employee with more than two years of service may purchase stock in the corporation. The price of these shares is established at book value. Stock purchased through this plan may be held by employees only. Dividends and voting rights are the same as for stock that is owned outside the plan. Approximately 75 percent of the employees own Lincoln stock.

As to executive perquisites, there are none—crowded, austere offices, no executive washrooms or lunchrooms, and no reserved parking spaces. Even the top executives pay for their own meals and eat in the employee cafeteria. On one recent day, Willis arrived at work late due to a breakfast speaking engagement and had to park far away from the factory entrance.

Financial Policies

James F. Lincoln felt strongly that financing for company growth should come from within the company—through initial cash investment by the founders, through retention of earnings, and through stock purchases by those who work in the business. He saw the following advantages of this approach:

1. Ownership of stock by employees strengthens team spirit. "If they are mutually anxious to make it succeed, the future of the company is bright."

2. Ownership of stock provides individual incentive because employees feel that they will benefit from company profitability.

3. "Ownership is educational." Owners-employees "will know how profits are made and lost, how success is won and lost. . . . There are few socialists in the list of stockholders of the nation's industries."

4. "Capital available from within controls expansion." Unwarranted expansion would not occur, Lincoln believed, under his financing plan.

5. "The greatest advantage would be the development of the individual worker. Under the incentive of ownership, he would become a greater man."

6. "Stock ownership is one of the steps that can be taken that will make the worker feel that there is less of a gulf between him and the boss. . . . Stock ownership will help the worker to recognize his responsibility in the game and the importance of victory."

Until 1980, Lincoln Electric borrowed no money. Even now, the company's liabilities consist mainly of accounts payable and short-term accruals.

The unusual pricing policy at Lincoln is succinctly stated by Willis: "At all times price on the basis of cost and at all times keep pressure on our cost." This policy resulted in the price for the most popular welding electrode then in use going from 16 cents a pound in 1929 to 4.7 cents in 1938. Lincoln's prices increased only one fifth as fast as the consumer price index from 1934 to about 1970. This resulted in a welding products market in which Lincoln became the undisputed price leader for the products it manufactures. Not even the major Japanese manufacturers, such as Nippon Steel for welding electrodes and Osaka Transformer for welding machines, were able to penetrate this market.

Relation to Stakeholders

Lincoln Electric differs from most other companies in the importance it assigns to each of the groups it serves. Willis identifies these groups, in the order of priority ascribed to them, as (1) customers, (2) employees, and (3) stockholders.

Certainly the firm's customers have fared well over the years. Lincoln prices for welding machines and welding electrodes are acknowledged to be the lowest in the marketplace. Quality has consistently been high. The cost of field failures for Lincoln products was recently determined to be a remarkable 0.04 percent of revenues. The Fleetweld electrodes and SA-200 welders have been the standard in the pipeline and refinery construction industry, where price is hardly a criterion, for decades.

Perhaps best-served of all management constituencies have been the employees. Not the least of their benefits, of course, are the year-end bonuses, which effectively double an already average compensation level.

While stockholders were relegated to third place by James F. Lincoln, they have done very well indeed. Recent dividends have exceeded $11 a share and earnings per share have approached $30. In January 1980, the price of restricted stock, committed to employees, was $117 a share. By 1989, the stated value, at which the company will repurchase the stock if tendered, was $201. Risk associated with Lincoln stock, a major determinant of stock value, is minimal, because of the small amount of debt in the capital structure, because of an extremely stable earnings record, and because of Lincoln's practice of purchasing the restricted stock whenever employees offer it for sale.

Concluding Comment

It is easy to believe that the reason for Lincoln's success is the excellent attitude of the employees and their willingness to work harder, faster, and more intelligently than other industrial workers. However, Sabo suggests that appropriate credit be given to Lincoln executives, whom he credits with carrying out the following policies:

1. Management has limited research, development, and manufacturing to a standard product line designed to meet the major needs of the welding industry.

2. New products must be reviewed by manufacturing and all producing costs verified before being approved by management.

3. Purchasing is challenged to not only procure materials at the lowest cost, but also to work closely with engineering and manufacturing to assure that the latest innovations are implemented.

4. Manufacturing supervision and all personnel are held accountable for reduction of scrap, energy conservation, and maintenance of product quality.

5. Production control, material handling, and methods engineering are closely supervised by top management.

6. Management has made cost reduction a way of life at Lincoln, and definite programs are established in many areas, including traffic and shipping, where tremendous savings can result.

7. Management has established a sales department that is technically trained to reduce customer welding costs. This sales approach and other real customer services have eliminated nonessential frills and resulted in long-term benefits to all concerned.

8. Management has encouraged education, technical publishing, and long-range programs that have resulted in industry growth, thereby assuring market potential for the Lincoln Electric Company.

Appendix A
Employee Interviews

During the late summer of 1980, the author conducted numerous interviews with Lincoln employees.

Interview with Roger Lewis, 23-year-old Purdue graduate in mechanical engineering, who had been in the Lincoln sales program for 15 months and who was working in the Cleveland sales office at the time of the interview.

Q. How did you get your job at Lincoln?
A. I saw that Lincoln was interviewing on campus at Purdue, and I went by. I later came to Cleveland for a plant tour and was offered the job.

Q. Do you know any of the senior executives? Would they know you by name?
A. Yes, I know all of them—Mr. Irrgang, Mr. Willis, Mr. Manross.

Q. Do you think Lincoln salesmen work harder than those in other companies?
A. Yes. I don't think there are many salesmen for other companies who are putting in 50- to 60-hour weeks. Everybody here works harder. You can go out in the plant, or you can go upstairs, and there's nobody sitting around.

Q. Do you see any real disadvantage of working at Lincoln?
A. I don't know if it's a disadvantage but Lincoln is a Spartan company, a very thrifty company. I like that. The sales offices are functional, not fancy.

Q. Why do you think Lincoln employees have such high productivity?
A. Piecework has a lot to do with it. Lincoln is smaller than many plants, too; you can stand in one place and see the materials come in one side and the product go out the other. You feel a part of the company. The chance to get ahead is important, too. They have a strict policy of promoting from within, so you know you have a chance. I think in a lot of other places you may not get as fair a shake as you do here. The sales offices are on a smaller scale, too. I like that. I tell someone that we have two people in the Baltimore office, and they say, "You've got to be kidding." It's smaller and more personal. Pay is the most important thing. I have heard that this is the highest-paying factory in the world.

Interview with Joe Trahan, 58-year-old high school graduate, who had been with Lincoln 39 years and who was employed as a working supervisor in the toolroom at the time of the interview.

Q. Roughly what was your pay last year?
A. Over $50,000—salary, bonus, stock dividends.

Q. How much was your bonus?
A. About $23,000.

Q. Have you ever gotten a special award of any kind?
A. Not really.

Q. What have you done with your money?
A. My house is paid for—and my two cars. I also have some bonds and the Lincoln stock.

Q. What do you think of the executives at Lincoln?
A. They're really top notch.

Q. What is the major disadvantage of working at Lincoln Electric?
A. I don't know of any disadvantage at all.

Q. Do you think you produce more than most people in similar jobs with other companies?

A. I do believe that.

Q. Why is that? Why do you believe that?

A. We are on the incentive system. Everything we do, we try to improve to make a better product with a minimum of outlay. We try to improve the bonus.

Q. Would you be just as happy making a little less money and not working quite so hard?

A. I don't think so.

Q. You know that Lincoln productivity is higher than that at most other plants. Why is that?

A. Money.

Q. Do you think Lincoln employees would ever join a union?

A. I don't think they would ever consider it.

Q. What is the most important advantage of working at Lincoln?

A. Compensation.

Q. Tell me something about Mr. James Lincoln, who died in 1965.

A. You are talking about Jimmy, Sr. He always strolled through the shop in his shirtsleeves. Big fellow. Always looked distinguished. Gray hair. Friendly sort of guy. I was a member of the Advisory Board one year. He was there each time.

Q. Did he strike you as really caring?

A. I think he always cared for people.

Q. Do you get any sensation of a religious nature from him?

A. No, not really.

Q. And religion is not part of the program now?

A. No.

Q. Do you think Mr. Lincoln was a very intelligent man, or was he just a nice guy?

A. I would say he was pretty well educated. A great talker—always right off the top of his head. He knew what he was talking about all the time.

Q. When were bonuses for beneficial suggestions done away with?

A. About 15 years ago.

Q. Did that hurt very much?

A. I don't think so, because suggestions are still rewarded through the merit rating system.

Q. Is there anything you would like to add?

A. It's a good place to work. The union kind of ties other places down. At other places, electricians only do electrical work, carpenters only do carpenter work. At Lincoln Electric we all pitch in and do whatever needs to be done.

Q. So a major advantage is not having a union?

A. That's right.

QUESTIONS

1. What is Lincoln's strategy? In this context, what is the nature of Lincoln's business and upon what bases does this company compete?
2. What are the most important elements of Lincoln's overall approach to organization and control that help explain why this company has been so successful? How well do Lincoln's organization and control mechanisms fit the company's strategic requirements?
3. What is the applicability of Lincoln's approach to organization and control to other companies? Why don't more companies operate like Lincoln?
4. Would you like to work in an environment like that at Lincoln Electric?

Case 12–2

Mid-Western Publishing Company (A)*

G. W. McClain, Jr., was sitting at the conference room table of the Mid-Western Publishing Company, talking rapidly. Only eight years earlier, just turned 25 and holding a newly minted Harvard MBA, he had been brought to Mid-Western as executive vice president. It had been McClain's first exposure to the printing industry. Not long thereafter, he had been named the company's president and chief executive officer. Now McClain was excitedly discussing Mid-Western's replacement cost-based managerial evaluation system, saying, "I invented this system!"

Historical Review of Mid-Western Publishing

In 1983, Mid-Western Publishing was a 60-year-old newspaper and printing holding company. Though Mid-Western was headquartered in a small town, operations also existed in several other small towns within its home state.

Mid-Western was a closely held private concern. The chairman of the board, a member of the owning family (no relation to McClain), was a U.S. Senator and spent a great deal of time in Washington, D.C. In fact, McClain had found that he had a free hand in directing day-to-day operations.

Before McClain's arrival, Mid-Western had been loosely managed. The chairman, as a busy public figure, was rarely in the firm's offices, and the past president had not extracted adequate financial performance. The key area of concern for the company was asset utilization; return on assets was, in fact, not keeping pace with

inflation. As a result, Mid-Western was not generating sufficient internal funds for asset replacement, and, as McClain put it, "The company was cannibalizing itself" (or in rural idiom, it was "eating its own seed corn").

Most of Mid-Western's assets had been acquired in the 1920s, with significant additions in the 1950s and 1960s. By 1983, its key assets included five sheet-fed printing machines and two web printing facilities (each costing hundreds of thousands of dollars). Intangible assets included name recognition among readerships and a dominant position in a small-town newspaper market. These assets were used in operations, consisting of a dozen daily and weekly newspapers and several commercial printing businesses. The newspapers served separate localized markets.

The Situation When McClain Arrived

On January 3, 1976, when G. W. McClain joined Mid-Western Publishing, he began learning that a lot of hard work faced him. To that date, annual budgeting had never been performed at Mid-Western. Further, the management incentive system was not pressuring the operations managers for outstanding financial performance. McClain described the operations as he found them:

> In this company, every year, book value of investment was going down on a GAAP basis, and the volume of dollars (business) on book value was declining also. As a result, this company was undercapitalized.

---

* This case was prepared and is copyrighted by Vijay Govindarajan, The Amos Tuck School of Business Administration, Dartmouth College.

Since McClain's total financial compensation was substantially dependent upon Mid-Western's financial performance, he set out to correct these problems.

McClain's Replacement-Cost Evaluation System

As McClain considered how to improve the financial performance of Mid-Western, he examined the organizational structure, management incentives system, and financial objectives of the firm. As a result of the review process, McClain and Mid-Western's owners agreed that the firm should be earning 10 percent above inflation; in conjunction with setting of this new objective, McClain designed his new management controls package.

Prior to this time, Mid-Western had had no targets for return on invested capital and, thus, there were no incentives to achieve any specific target. Managerial salaries were substantial, with incentives for overall profit level achievement in nominal dollars, which added a small amount to compensation. Assets were valued at historical cost book value and were not used for incentive calculations. There were no specific profit centers or responsibilities that could be used for the calculation of incentives outside of total profit figure.

Though the most innovative feature of the new system was the basis of evaluation of profit center managers, McClain made other changes as well. The organizational structure was changed to include six "master" profit centers, with other profit, revenue, and cost centers within the master centers. Exhibit 1 provides an example of the new organizational structure in the Citizen Division in Citizen, Indiana. Other changes of McClain's are summarized below:

1. Sharply lowered profit center managers' salaries.
2. Increased the incentive compensation available to managers.
3. Changed asset valuations, for managerial evaluation purposes, to replacement costs.

4. Established "Corporate Obligations" for the six master profit center managers.
5. Set divisional performance objectives at inflation plus 10 percent.

Each of McClain's changes is reviewed in detail below.

Taken in tandem, the first two steps allowed McClain to establish aggressive incentive bonuses. The incentive bonuses were tied to the actual financial performance, as measured by the Corporate Obligations (see step 4). The net result was to sharply increase the pressure on managers for improved financial performance, and this caused great turmoil among the profit center managers at first.

As a third step, to provide higher goals for financial performance, McClain adjusted the asset valuations to incorporate inflation. Replacement-cost valuations were based on replacement-cost data compiled by a department of the U.S. government. For example, a 10-year-old web newsprint facility would be indexed to its current replacement cost. McClain made an effort to adjust the data for the cost-increase effects of technological advancements. Financial assets were adjusted by the GNP deflator. All replacement costs for a fiscal year were indexed by the prior year's inflation data.

From the above three steps, McClain then examined the earnings potential of each division (master profit centers) and established the Corporate Obligations for each individual division. These amounts were arbitrarily arrived at by McClain; the managers were only informed of their corporate obligation for the year. In relation to this, McClain commented, "They trust me, they really do." Below, the formulation of the Corporate Obligations is covered in more detail.

Formulation of the Corporate Obligations

Corporate Obligations were described by McClain as consisting of two parts. Part A was an allocation of home office overhead, which included the following expenses:

EXHIBIT 1   Organizational Structure

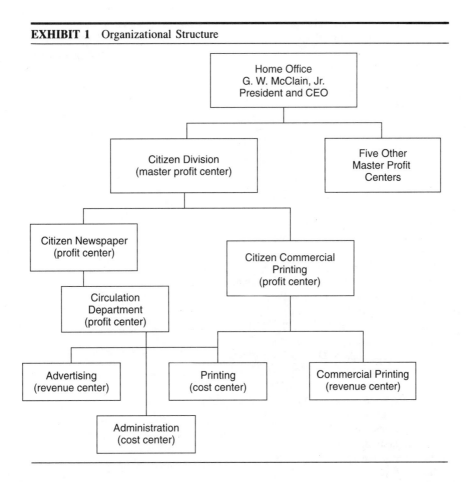

1. *Payroll.*
2. *Accounts payable*—also centralized. Divisions were charged with the administrative expenses on accounts payable.
3. *Auditors*—the expense of audits by outside auditing firms.
4. *Insurance benefits*—for employees of Mid-Western.
5. *Disability insurance*—especially necessary in the newspaper business, but more cost efficient in one central corporate policy.
6. *Legal expenses* of Mid-Western Publishing.
7. *Interest expenses* on long-term debt.

In explaining Part A of the Corporate Obligations, McClain commented, "They [profit center

managers] have enough to do without worrying about this stuff."

Part B of the Corporate Obligations was in essence a profit expectation placed upon the divisions, and it was calculated by McClain from the Corporate Obligations worksheet (see Exhibit 2). Though the profit center managers had a rough understanding of the factors used in the calculation of the Corporate Obligations, they were not aware of the specific criteria being applied to them. As McClain put it, "You have to sit here and play God."

In return for their efforts, profit center managers received, in the form of a bonus, one third of any cash operating income above the Corporate

---

EXHIBIT 2 Corporate Obligations ("Money on Assets" for the Divisions)*

	Dollar Amounts
Expected sales	
Percent company sales	
Corporation expenses[†]	$ _____

Home Office Investment

Net over 30 days' average accounts receivable of past 12 months	
Indexed value: machinery, fixtures, and furniture purchased before 2/1/79	
Indexed value: machinery purchased after 2/1/79	
Indexed value of furniture purchased after 2/1/79	
Indexed value of leasehold	
Original value (gross book value) of machinery, furniture, leasehold, autos, land	$ _____

Investment Factors

12 months' average net over 30 days' accounts receivable $\times$ GNP deflator	
9.09%, depreciation of machinery, furniture purchased before 2/1/79	
11.11%, depreciation of machinery purchased after 2/1/79	
12.5%, depreciation of furniture purchased after 2/1/79	
10%, depreciation indexed leasehold inside 10 years	
10% return on original value: cars, machinery, furniture, leasehold, land	
Total	$ _____

Corporate Expenses and Investment Factors Total

Corporation expenses	
Investment factors	
Total obligation	$ _____

Last year's given obligation

* McClain's worksheet for Corporate Obligation calculation (what is referred to in the case as "money on assets").

[†] The expected corporate cash operating expenses are apportioned to the divisions based on the percentage of each division's expected sales for the coming year to the total expected company sales.

Obligations. There were *no* limits placed on the amount they could earn on the bonus. These bonuses were paid in the same form by which profit center managers' results were evaluated: cash. In referring to this system, McClain said that profit center managers were evaluated based on "money on assets" (i.e., cash returns from asset utilization). On the other hand, he described himself as being rewarded on a "money on money" basis (i.e., total corporate cash returns on the cash received in the company by its owners).

McClain's Incentive Compensation

As a part of the new management incentives package, McClain and Mid-Western Publishing's owners agreed on an incentive formula to reward McClain's efforts. Exhibit 3 details McClain's incentive compensation formula.

Exhibit 3 (part **I**) is a conceptual representation of the formula. The "Home Office Bonus" was, in fact, McClain's bonus. As can be seen from the exhibit, McClain's bonus was equal to one third of the adjusted cash operating profits above that level of profits required to provide Mid-Western's owners a rate of return 10 percent greater than inflation. Note that this was based on the stockholders' equity account.

Exhibit 3 (part **II**) presents, in more detail, the formula for McClain's incentive bonus. Again, it should be noted that his bonus was based on cash results, with the notable exception of the depreciation. McClain illustrated this ("money on money") by commenting that, since the home office paid for all capital expenditures, which would then be reflected in the stockholders' equity account, his mission was to earn a maximum return corporatewide.

The Citizen Division

The Citizen Division will be examined as an example of the new evaluation system at Mid-Western. As Exhibit 1 shows, the Citizen Divi-

sion was one of the six master profit centers at Mid-Western Publishing.

Newspaper versus Commericial Printing

Within the Citizen Division existed two distinct businesses: a dominant small-town newspaper and a commercial printing business. Both businesses utilized the same printing equipment. Since the success of each business was critical to the overall division performance, their bonus was a 50/50 split of any bonus available from the Citizen Division's cash operating performance compared with the Corporate Obligations requirement. According to McClain, this made each profit center manager a "partner" in the Citizen Division and forced them to cooperate in the utilization of the printing machinery and other assets.

The use of two separate profit centers within the Citizen Division master profit center reflected the substantially different natures of the two businesses. The commercial printing business, on the one hand, was a highly competitive enterprise, with price as a key competitive variable throughout the commercial printing industry. Business for the commercial printing operations was not limited to the home state of Mid-Western Publishing because a substantial portion came from out-of-state customers. Aside from the price, print quality and meeting delivery schedules were also important factors for success in commercial printing.

The newspaper business, on the other hand, was different. Revenues came from both circulation and advertising. As the dominant newspaper, the *Citizen* had some flexibility in pricing, though advertisers could also use radio or other media. Critical to the success of the *Citizen* was local news coverage, along with feature stories of local interest. However, since the daily newspaper could be printed in one and one-half hours' press time, the commercial printing business was needed to help spread high fixed costs associated with the printing equipment. Within the *Citizen* profit center, advertising was a revenue center,

---

EXHIBIT 3   McClain's "Money on Money": The Home Office Bonus Formula

---

I. *Overview*

Home Office bonus equals one third of:

> Annual adjusted cash operating profit
>
> *minus*
>
> > Adjusted stockholders' equity as of
> > February 28/29 of the previous fiscal year
> >
> > *times*
> >
> > > Ten percent return on investment
> > > *plus*
> > > The GNP deflator for the previous
> > > calendar year

II. *Details of above*

Total cash profits from divisions and all other cash investments and cash revenues
+ *Plus* that year's revenues from other sources (i.e., nonoperating revenues)
− *Less* that year's nonoperating expenses
− *Less* bonus paid to profit center managers
− *Less* total cash Home Office expenses
− *Less* the previous year's straight-line depreciation of buildings, capital assets, lease-hold improvements, and land improvements until fully depreciated (11 years on capital assets purchased prior to March 1, 1979, 9 years on machinery, and 8 years on furniture purchased after March 1, 1979; 10 years on leasehold improvements, capital improvements, and buildings as auditor determines) according to generally accepted accounting principles.
Equals annual adjusted cash operating profit

---

circulation a subprofit center, printing a cost center, and administrative expenses a cost center.

Like all Mid-Western Publishing managers, the two managers of the Citizen Division had high autonomy. However, three types of decisions were routinely forwarded to CEO McClain for a "second opinion":

1. Firing of an employee.
2. Hiring of key employees.
3. Capital investments and major purchases.

EXHIBIT 4   Corporate Obligations for the Citizen Division

	Dollar Amounts
Corporate expenses allocated (based on sales dollars)	$ 55,890
Home Office Investment	
Net over 30 days' Accounts Receivable, 12 months average	13,100
Indexed value: machinery, fixtures, and furniture, pre-2/1/79	683,300
Indexed value: machinery, post-2/1/79	30,700
Indexed value: furniture, post-2/1/79	9,100
Indexed value: leasehold	179,300
Original value: machinery, furniture, leasehold, autos, land	416,700
Investment Factors	
12 months' net over 30 days' A/R, avg., @ 5%	655
9.09% depreciation of machinery and furniture, pre-2/1/79	62,112
11.11% depreciation of machinery, post-2/1/79	3,411
12.5% depreciation of furniture, post 2/1/79	1,138
10% depreciation of leasehold	17,930
10% return on gross book value of assets	41,670
Total investment factors	$126,916
+ Corporate expenses allocation	55,890
Total Corporate Obligation	$182,806

A Recent Fiscal Year

To illustrate how McClain's system worked, some financial results of the Citizen Division are shown in Exhibits 4 through 7 (financial data are disguised).

In summary of the exhibits, each of the two profit center managers of the Citizen Division earned a $29,536 bonus, in addition to their regular salaries, for their efforts. For his efforts, McClain earned a bonus of $57,336 in addition to his regular salary, from the Citizen Division alone. McClain himself had said:

> All I care about is cash. Divisions are given certain dollars in order to produce dollars. . . . The divisions are like customers, and I am like the bank. . . . That certain dollars, and the amount they are required to return—that's the punchline to the job!!

EXHIBIT 5   Citizen Division Statement of Cash Income*

Revenues:	
Advertising, net	$ 558,200
Circulation, net	107,800
Commericial printing, net	554,000
Total revenues	$1,220,000
Departmental expenses:†	
Editorial and news	$ 211,200
Advertising	103,100
Circulation	91,900
Composing	137,500
Press and platemaking	169,700
Administrative	126,400
Total departmental expenses	(839,800)
Net cash operating profit	380,200
Other income:	
Gain on sale of fixed assets	14,400
Other expenses:	
Cash discounts allowed	(17,100)
Loss of sales of fixed assets	(17,300)
Net cash nonoperating income	(20,000)
Net cash income	$ 360,200

* These statements were prepared monthly. GAAP basis statements were separate and strictly for tax purposes.
† These were actual cash expenditures only.

EXHIBIT 6   Citizen Division Master Profit Center Bonus

Net cash income	$360,200
Less: Corporate obligation	(182,806)
Net bonus base	177,394
× factor (33%)	× 0.333
Net cash bonus to Citizen Division	59,072
Per 2 division managers:	
Division bonus	
× 50%	× 0.5
Net cash bonus per manager	$ 29,536

EXHIBIT 7 CEO Bonus per Citizen Division Operations

Description	Dollar Amount
Total cash profits from the Citizen Division	$380,200
Other cash income *less* expenses	(20,000)
Bonus paid to Citizen Division managers	(59,072)
Home office cash expenses	(55,890)
Previous year's straight-line depreciation of assets until fully depreciated*	(39,340)
Adjusted annual cash operating profit	205,898
Less: Stockholders' equity[†] $214,500 × inflation + 10% × (0.058 + 0.10) CEO's obligation to owners $ 33.891	(33,891)
=CEO's bonus base per Citizen Division	172,007
× 33% payout ratio	× 0.33
=CEO's bonus per Citizen Division operations	$ 57,336

* 11 years on assets purchased prior to 3/1/79; 9 years on machinery; and 8 years on furniture purchased after 3/1/79.
[†] The total stockholders' equity for the company was $1,287,000. Since there were six profit centers, one sixth of the equity is shown here.

QUESTIONS

This incentive system has caused some consternation among profit center managers. Because their base salaries have been cut substantially, they are worried about the amounts of bonuses that can be earned under this new system. The system needs to be evaluated to assess its impact on these managers in both the short term and the long term. As part of your overall evaluation of the system, focus on the following issues, among others:

1. Citizen Division as one profit center or as two separate profit centers (newspaper and commercial printing).
2. The process by which McClain decides the annual financial goals for the profit center managers.
3. The basis on which the profit center managers' bonus is calculated.
4. The basis on which McClain's bonus is calculated.
5. Effectiveness of these control system changes in impacting the performance of MWP.

Case 12–3

Mid-Western Publishing Company (B)*

In early 1983, the casewriter met with Bill Kirston, managing editor and head of Mid-Western Publishing Company's largest operating division. His division was very profitable, with plans for significant expansion. Kirston was a veteran in his mid-50s, who had substantial publishing experience and had been at Mid-Western for many years.

Things had not always gone so well for his division, however. Prior to G. W. McClain, Jr.'s arrival as president, his division had been "eating its own seed corn"—earning insufficient real returns to finance operations over time. Inflation had destroyed the quality of the division's earnings, and it was unable to make necessary capital investments without external funding.

The solution to this problem proved to be McClain's replacement-cost evaluation system. Kirston had despised it at first; it was the cause of a cut in salary and increased pressures to perform. Looking back, however, Kirston readily conceded the system had brought his division back to life. "Profits" were now real profits, providing funds for new equipment and expansions.

Though relations with McClain were currently good, they had not always been that way. McClain, the industry rookie who cut Kirston's salary under the new system, had caused radical upheavals in Kirston's life. But eventually Kirston came to view McClain as the "teacher" of these radical new management systems and himself as the "student." He did not question the exact calculation of his "Corporate Obligation"; he knew only he must earn it to make a bonus and provide funds for his division's future. He also knew *that as a result* of McClain's system his income had risen greatly.

QUESTION

Do these facts change your conclusions about the questions in the (A) case?

* This case was prepared and is copyrighted by Vijay Govindarajan, The Amos Tuck School of Business Administration, Dartmouth College.

Case 12–4

Pullen Lumber Company*

John Pullen, founder and president of Pullen Lumber Company, was considering an incentive compensation plan for his managers, which had been prepared at his request. Currently, the 700 Pullen employees were paid a straight salary (plus overtime when applicable). They were also paid an annual bonus equal to two weeks' salary. The proposed plan would apply only to the 43 managers of lumber yards, the 5 district managers, and 5 senior managers at headquarters. Instead of the annual bonus, these managers would be eligible for a bonus according to a proposal described later in the case.

The Company

Pullen Lumber Company operated 43 lumber yards located in four midwestern states. Few interdependencies existed among the yards, and each carried a line of lumber, plywood, roofing materials, doors, windows, tools, paint, flooring, and builders' supplies. Sales were made to contractors, homebuilders, and individual homeowners and hobbyists. The lumber yards were supervised by five district offices. Each district office also had a sales force that solicited business from large contractors. As a service, the district offices sometimes aided contractors in preparing the material components in bids and gave informal advice on the material best suited to a job. Yard managers also gave this advice to smaller contractors.

There was a fixed budget for each yard and each district, showing planned revenues and expenses. Actual revenues and expenses were reported annually. Data on the company's financial condition and performance for the year are provided in Exhibits 1 and 2.

The company had enjoyed profits the past few years that were considerably greater than those of its competition, for whom the average after-tax return on investment in total assets was approximately 6 percent. Although the company as a whole had done well, in the opinion of the company president, some of its yards and districts had incurred operating losses. Meanwhile, competitive pressures had been growing and the differences in profits among Pullen Company and its competitors had narrowed significantly. Because of this, the individual differences in the performance of the yards, and Mr. Pullen's often expressed desire to gain a larger market share in each of the company's lines of business, the proposed bonus plan assumed added significance.

Background of the Plan

At an Executive Committee meeting in September, Mr. Pullen introduced the idea of a bonus plan, and it seemed to be favorably received. At the end of this meeting he appointed a committee to draft a bonus plan. It consisted of the controller, who was to serve as a chairman, the general sales manager, and the director of purchases. The first problem they tackled was identification of

* This case was prepared by C. J. Casey, Jr., Harvard Business School.
Copyright © by the President and Fellows of Harvard College.
Harvard Business School case 179–090.

EXHIBIT 1

PULLEN LUMBER COMPANY
Balance Sheet
As of 12/31/87

Assets

Current assets:		
Cash and short-term investments		$ 1,346,000
Accounts receivable	$ 5,386,000	
Less: Allowance for doubtful accounts	56,000	5,330,000
Inventory		11,260,000
Total current assets		17,936,000
Fixed assets:		
Trucks, automobiles, and equipment	3,450,000	
Less: Accumulated depreciation	1,260,000	2,190,000
Land and buildings	10,040,000	
Less: Accumulated depreciation	4,020,000	6,020,000
Total fixed assets		8,210,000
Other assets		2,900,000
Total assets		$29,046,000

Liabilities and Owner's Equity

Current payables		$ 5,478,000
Long-term note payable, 8%		5,000,000
Total liabilities		10,478,000
Owners' equity:		
Capital stock ($40 par; 250,000 shares issued and outstanding)		10,000,000
Retained earnings		8,568,000
Total owners' equity		18,568,000
Total equities		$29,046,000

---

the persons to whom the plan should apply. Three groups were initially considered: (1) district salesmen, (2) buyers, and (3) managers.

The sales manager foresaw great difficulties in identifying improved sales volume with individual salesmen. Many of the company's best customers had dealt with the company for years, and no substantial selling effort was required. Furthermore, personal friendships existed between the top officers of some companies which were good customers and the top officers of Pullen Lumber Company. These conditions made it relatively unimportant which salesman called upon and serviced the account. The volume of business from these customers would remain virtually unchanged, regardless of the salemen's efforts.

The director of purchases also foresaw problems in attempting to recognize and reward indi-

EXHIBIT 2

PULLEN LUMBER COMPANY
Income Statement
For 1987

Sales (net)		$56,127,000
Service revenue		2,148,000
		58,275,000
Less: Cost of Sales		41,458,000
Gross margin		16,817,000
Operating expenses:		
Payroll	$6,705,000	
Property expense*	1,688,000	
Advertising	1,312,000	
Bad debt expense	836,000	
Equipment expense†	1,127,000	
Other expenses	1,529,000	
Total operating expenses		13,197,000
Operating income		3,620,000
Nonoperating items:		
Interest expense	400,000	
Loss on sale of equipment	32,000	432,000
Income before taxes		3,188,000
Provision for income taxes		1,476,000
Net income		$ 1,712,000

* Property expense includes real estate taxes, rentals depreciation, and utilities expense.
† Equipment expense includes depreciation, maintenance and repairs, and routine operating expenses.

vidual buyers. The discounts obtained on an order related to factors over which the buyer had so little control as not to be a valid basis for a bonus award.

The committee, therefore, decided that the bonus plan should be limited to managers—the managers of individual lumber yards, the district managers, and the senior management group at headquarters.

In considering the managers' responsibility for profit performance, the committee agreed generally on the following points.

1. The yard manager is the primary factor in in-

fluencing customers' loyalty toward Pullen, by giving good service, by having the goods on hand when the customer wants them, and by his supervision of yard personnel.

2. Although standard selling prices are set by the central purchasing department, the yard manager has latitude in reducing prices to meet competition and in the markdowns he allows for defective or old merchandise.

3. The yard manager is responsible for inventory, both to replenish stocked items and to decide what items should be added to or deleted from inventory within limits specified by headquarters.

4. The yard manager has major responsibility for bad debts, although for large accounts he is expected to ask headquarters for a credit check.

5. An aggressive yard manager will generate new business by calling on prospective customers.

6. The yard manager has considerable discretion in advertising, although the artwork and much of the copy of space advertising is prepared at headquarters. Catalogs and direct-mail pieces also are prepared at headquarters.

7. The yard manager is responsible for expense control.

8. The district manager generally is responsible for the yards in his district.

9. The district office also helps profitability by the services it renders to large customers. Orders from these customers are shipped from the yard nearest to the job.

10. Sales volume varies with construction activity in the territory served by the yard.

Most of the yard managers had only a high school education; in the opinion of the controller, they understood very little of the relationship between their performance and the profitability of their yards. It was the controller's view that a concentrated management training program for managers, supplemented by a bonus plan, would make them conscious of the necessity of increasing profits through better management and would furnish them the incentive to put better practices into effect.

When the committee reported back to the president, it was their consensus that the controller should devise a bonus plan along the lines outlined above. Shortly thereafter, the controller submitted the following proposed bonus plan.

General Statement of Plan

This bonus plan is designed to provide company managers with an opportunity to earn additional compensation for improved performance as reflected by an increased return on the company's investment at the yards under their management.

Definition of Terms

A. *Investment* at each location will include the annual average of the following:

1. Month-end cash balances.
2. Month-end inventory, at cost, excluding central stocks placed at a given location by the purchasing department.
3. Month-end accounts receivables associated with bonusable sales.
4. Investment in automobiles and trucks assigned to the location, at depreciated cost.
5. Investment in equipment, furniture, and fixtures assigned to the location at depreciated cost.
6. Land and buildings at depreciated cost assigned to the location (if property is rented, the rent will show up as an expense).

B. *Bonusable sales* are all shipments made from the location, except sales orders written by district or headquarters sales personnel. These orders will be coded as written and deducted from the gross sales of the yard.

C. *Expenses* include:

1. Cost of goods sold on bonusable sales.
2. Operating expenses of the yard, including rental and depreciation.
3. Actual cost of services provided by district offices to the yard and to customers of the yard. (If the customer cannot be identified with a specific yard, these costs will be included in district office cost.)
4. Actual cost of credit investigations and collection efforts for the benefit of the yard.
5. Advertising material, catalogs, and other material supplied to the yard at actual cost.
   Note: Costs of district advertising (space and TV) for items not carried in a given yard will not be charged to that yard.
6. Pro rata share of office expenses for purchasing. This will be determined on the basis of the yard's receipts into inventory as a proportion of total company receipts into inventory.
7. Pro rata share of district office and headquarters expenses not charged directly to a yard. This will be determined on the basis of each yard's gross sales as a proportion of total company sales.

8. The following operating losses will be charged to the yard when the district manager determines that these are the responsibility of the yard manager:

   a. Inventory shortages.
   b. Cost of repairing damaged property.
   c. Loss on sale of fixed assets.
   d. Bad debt losses.

D. *Bonusable profit* is bonusable sales minus expenses.

E. *Return on investment* is bonusable profit divided by investment in total assets.

Calculation of the Bonus

A. The total bonus pool will be $90,000 plus 5 percent of the corporation's income in excess of $2 million before income taxes.

B. The total bonus pool will be divided as follows:

Yard managers	65%
District managers	15
Senior management	20

C. The yard managers' bonus pool will be divided among yard managers on the basis of the number of bonus units that they earn. The manager of a yard whose return on investment is 5 percent will earn one bonus unit. For each full percentage point above 5, the manager will earn an additional bonus unit, up to a maximum of six bonus units. The monetary value of one bonus unit is found by dividing the total dollar amount in the yard managers' pool by the total number of bonus units earned by all yard managers.

D. The bonus units awarded by any yard manager who has been in that position for less than one year will be decided by his district manager, applying the above principle as closely as is feasible.

E. The district managers' bonus pool will be divided among district managers in relation to the total bonus units earned by the yards in their district as a proportion of the total bonus units earned by all yards.

F. The headquarters' bonus pool will be divided as decided by the president.

G. Bonuses will be paid in cash as soon after the end of the year as they can be calculated.

Mr. Pullen looked over the plan quickly and observed that it was drawn to include only managers. He said, "You can bet your bottom dollar that the district salesmen aren't going to be happy when they hear about a bonus plan for yard managers. What does the sales manager have to say about the proposed plan?"

The sales manager explained that the committee recognized the role of the district sales and sales service personnel but that there was no practical way of measuring their contribution to profitability, because actual sales were booked through the yards that made delivery.

The controller also explained the rationale behind the recommended size of the bonus pool. The elimination of the annual bonus for the 53 managers in the plan would create $40,000 of available funds. In addition, the usual annual salary increase to these managers of about $50,000 would not be given. Thus, at the current level of profits, a bonus of $90,000 would not affect costs. If the plan resulted in profits greater than $2 million before taxes, the bonus would be correspondingly higher.

QUESTIONS

1. Evaluate the proposed bonus plan which Mr. Pullen is considering. Does your evaluation suggest any generalization for exercising management control through payment schemes?
2. How, if at all, would you modify the proposed plan?

Case 12-5

Empire Glass Company (B)*

During the first 10 months of 1963, one of Empire Glass Company's Glass Products Division's plants performed slightly better than budget in all categories of cost and revenue. If the plant could maintain this performance to the end of the year, the plant management (all people above assistant foremen, as shown in Empire Glass Company (A), Case 9–2) could expect to receive a bonus.

The expected bonus would be calculated as follows: For bettering the budgeted manufacturing efficiency rate and budgeted cost reductions, the plant supervisory staff could receive as much as 25 percent of their base salary. However, to qualify for this portion of the bonus the plant must make at least 90 percent of its budgeted profit. If the plant exceeds its budgeted profit, the plant management group will receive an additional bonus of up to 10 percent of the base salaries.

The plant's 1963 budgeted annual sales volume was 100 million units at an average price of 5 cents. The budgeted contribution was 35 percent of gross sales. Variable costs, which were 70 per-cent of total costs, consisted of 30 percent direct labor, 60 percent direct material, and 10 percent direct variable overhead. Budgeted fixed costs accounted for the remaining 30 percent of total costs. These fixed costs included $393,000 of programmed costs. In addition, the plant anticipated it would realize the following additional revenue during 1963: $150,000 from budgeted cost reductions and $50,000 from budgeted sales of seconds.

During the last two months of 1963, due to several unexpected and drastic snowstorms in October, the sales of glass bottles declined throughout the industry. Under these new conditions, on November 1 the plant manager estimated that actual 1963 sales would be 98 million units, rather than the original estimate of 100 million, and that the average price would decline slightly from 5 cents. Consequently, actual 1963 dollars sales volume was not expected to be 97 percent of the budgeted dollar sales volume.

QUESTIONS

1. Would this plant management be eligible for any bonus if, during the remainder of the year, the following conditions prevailed: the plant continued to operate at slightly better than the standard manufacturing costs; the budgeted fixed costs remained constant; the budgeted cost reductions and seconds sales were realized; the actual dollar sales were 97 percent of budgeted sales?

* This case was prepared by J. D. Donnell under the supervision of P. R. Lawrence, Harvard Business School.
Copyright © by the President and Fellows of Harvard College.
Harvard Business School case 109–044

2. What organizational problems do you predict might arise at this plant during the last two months of 1963?
3. Would you recommend a different incentive bonus plan for plant managers and their staffs? What is the objective of your suggested plan?

Part III

Variations in Management Control

Chapters 8 through 12 described the management control process in what we believe to be a fairly typical situation. In this part of the book, we describe factors that lead to modifications of these typical practices and suggest the nature of these modifications. The essentials of the control system are similar, but the environment results in differences in the details. In Chapter 13, we discuss how to differentiate controls in accordance with differentiated corporate and business unit strategies. In Chapters 14 through 16, we discuss the modifications that are needed in management control practices as applied to certain types of organizations. These types are: service organizations (Chapter 14), financial service organizations (Chapter 15), and multinational organizations (Chapter 16). Characteristics of these organizations and their implications for management control are considered in these chapters. In Chapter 17, we discuss the management control of projects, which is somewhat different from management control of ongoing operations that has been the focus hitherto.

Chapter 13

Controls for Differentiated Strategies

Many factors jointly influence the organization structure and the management control process in a company. Researchers have attempted to examine these factors by applying what is called *contingency theory*; the name simply means that structure and process are contingent on various external and internal factors. Research studies have identified important factors that influence the design of control systems, some of them being size, environment, technology, interdependence, and strategies.[1]

Given the overall framework of this book—namely, that management control systems are tools to implement strategies—we suggest in this chapter how different strategies influence the management control process. Two general observations are important. First, the suggestions made in this chapter are tendencies, not hard-and-fast principles. Second, systems designers need to take into consideration the influence of other external and internal factors (environment, technology, size, culture, geographical location, management style) while designing control systems.

In the first part of the chapter, we discuss the implications of different corporate strategies—single business, related diversification, and unrelated diversification—on the design of control systems. Next, we discuss the relationship between different business-level strategies—different missions (build, hold, harvest) and different competitive advantages (low cost, differentiation)—and the form and structure of control systems. We then discuss

---

[1] For example, a 1987 study identified certain factors that were statistically significant, but these factors explained less than 10 percent of the differences among the organizations included in the study. (Keith Duncan and Ken Moores, "Residual Analysis: A Better Methodology for Contingency Studies in Management Accounting," *Journal of Management Accounting Research*, Fall 1989, pp. 89–102. This article has an excellent bibliography on contingency theory.)

691

additional considerations involved in tailoring controls to strategies. Finally, we discuss the implications of management style on the design and operation of control systems.

CORPORATE STRATEGY

The logic for linking controls to strategy is based on the following line of thinking:

- Different organizations generally operate in different strategic contexts.
- For effective execution, different strategies require different task priorities; different key success factors; and different skills, perspectives, and behaviors.
- Control systems are measurement systems that influence the behavior of those people whose activities are being measured.
- Thus, a continuing concern in the design of control system should be whether the behavior induced by the system is the one that is consistent with the strategy.

As we noted in Chapter 7, corporate strategy is a continuum with "single business" strategy at one end and "unrelated diversification" at the other end. A firm's location on the continuum depends on the extent and type of its diversification. Different corporate strategies imply different organization structures and, in turn, different controls. The organization structure implications of different corporate strategies are given in Exhibit 13–1.

At the single business end, the company tends to be functionally organized, with senior managers responsible for developing the company's overall strategy to compete in its chosen industry as well as its functional strategies in such areas as research and development, manufacturing, and marketing. In contrast, at the unrelated diversified end, the notion of "industry" loses its meaning. An unrelated diversified company (conglomerate) usually is organized into relatively autonomous business units. Given the large and diverse set of businesses, the senior managers in such firms tend to focus on portfolio management (i.e., selection of businesses in which to engage and allocation of financial resources to the various business units), and they delegate the development of product/market strategy to the general managers of business units. Thus, at the single business end, senior managers are likely to have a good deal of familiarity with the industry in which the firm competes; also, many of them tend to have expertise in research and development, manufacturing, and marketing. In contrast, at the unrelated diversified end, primary expertise of many senior managers tends to be in finance.

As a firm moves from the single business end to the unrelated diversified end, the autonomy of the business unit manager tends to increase, for two reasons. First, unlike a single business firm, senior managers of unrelated diversified firms may lack the knowledge and expertise to make strategic and operating decisions for a group of disparate business units. Second, there is very little interdependence across business units in a conglomerate, whereas there may be a great deal of interdependence among business units in single

EXHIBIT 13–1   Different Corporate Strategies: Organizational Structure Implications

	Single Business	*Related Diversified*	*Unrelated Diversified*
Organizational structure	Functional	Business units	Holding company
Industry familiarity of corporate management	High	———————▶	Low
Functional background of corporate management	Relevant operating experience (mfg. mktg, R&D)	———————▶	Mainly finance
Decision-making authority	More centralized	———————▶	More decentralized
Size of corporate staff	High	———————▶	Low
Reliance on internal promotions	High	———————▶	Low
Use of lateral transfers	High	———————▶	Low
Corporate culture	Strong	———————▶	Weak

business and related diversified firms; greater interdependence calls for greater top management intervention.

Given the lower degree of involvement of corporate level managers in the operations of business units, the size of corporate staff in a conglomerate—compared with a single business firm of the same size—tends to be low. Given the unrelated nature of its varied business units, a conglomerate—in contrast to a single business firm—is less likely to benefit from promoting from within or in lateral transfer of executives from one business unit to another. Also, a conglomerate may not have the single, cohesive, strong corporate culture that a single business firm often has.

Implications for Management Control

Any organization—however will-aligned its structure is to the chosen strategy—cannot effectively implement its strategy without a consistent management control system. While organization structure defines the reporting relationships and the responsibilities and authorities of different managers, its effective functioning depends on the design of an appropriate control system.

In this part of the chapter, we discuss the planning and control requirements of different corporate strategies.

Different corporate strategies imply the following differences in the context in which control systems need to be designed:

- As firms become more diversified, corporate-level managers may not have significant knowledge and experience in the activities of the company's various business units. If so, corporate-level managers for highly diversified firms, cannot expect to control the different businesses based on intimate knowledge of their activities, and performance evaluation tends to be carried out at arm's length.
- Single business and related diversified firms possess *corporatewide core competencies* (examples: electronics-related technology in the case of Motorola and Texas Instruments) on which the strategies of most of the business units are based; channels of communication and transfer of competencies across business units, therefore, are critical in such firms. In contrast, in the case of unrelated diversified firms, there are low levels of interdependence among business units. This implies that, as firms become more diversified, it may be desirable to change the balance in control systems from an emphasis on fostering cooperation to an emphasis on encouraging entrepreneurial spirit.

Specific tendencies in the design of control systems corresponding to variations in corporate strategies are given in Exhibit 13–2.

Programming.   Given the low level of interdependencies, conglomerates tend to use vertical strategic planning systems—that is, business units prepare strategic plans and submit them to senior management for review and approval. Given the high level of interdependencies, strategic planning systems for related diversified and single business firms tend to be both vertical and horizontal. The horizontal dimension might be added to the programming process in a number of different ways. First, a group executive might be given responsibility for preparing a strategic plan for the group as a whole that explicitly incorporates synergies across individual business units within the group. Second, strategic plans of individual business units could have an interdependence section, in which the general manager of the business unit identifies the focal linkages with other business units and how those linkages will be exploited. Third, corporate office could require joint strategic plans from interdependent business units. Finally, strategic plans of individual business units could be circulated to managers of similar business units for critique and review.

These ways of incorporating a horizontal dimension to programming are not mutually exclusive. In fact, several of them could be fruitfully pursued simultaneously.

Examples.   NEC Corporation (a related diversified firm) adopted two planning systems. In addition to a normal business unit planning system, it established the CBP

EXHIBIT 13–2 Different Corporate Strategies: Management Control Implications

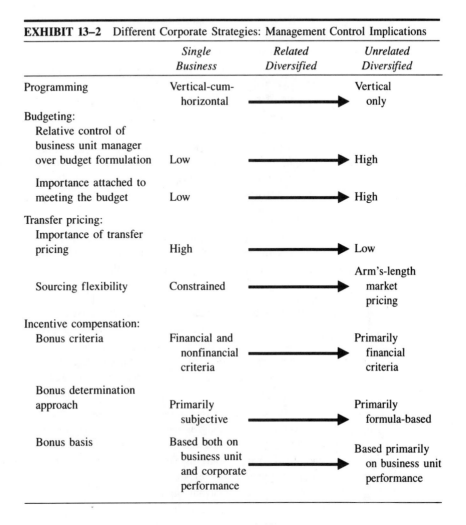

	Single Business	*Related Diversified*	*Unrelated Diversified*
Programming	Vertical-cum-horizontal	⟶	Vertical only
Budgeting:			
Relative control of business unit manager over budget formulation	Low	⟶	High
Importance attached to meeting the budget	Low	⟶	High
Transfer pricing:			
Importance of transfer pricing	High	⟶	Low
Sourcing flexibility	Constrained	⟶	Arm's-length market pricing
Incentive compensation:			
Bonus criteria	Financial and nonfinancial criteria	⟶	Primarily financial criteria
Bonus determination approach	Primarily subjective	⟶	Primarily formula-based
Bonus basis	Based both on business unit and corporate performance	⟶	Based primarily on business unit performance

(corporate business plan) system, in which strategic plans were prepared for important programs that cut across business units. The system forced interdependent business unit managers to agree on a strategic plan for exploiting such linkages. In effect, the system required a special plan for important horizontal issues.[2]

IBM Corporation (a single business firm) assigned a formal integrative role for each corporate staff: to evaluate the strategic plans submitted by the operating units to make sure that the interdependencies in the various operations were captured in the plans.[3]

---

[2] Michael E. Porter, *Competitive Advantage* (New York: Free Press, 1985), p. 403.

[3] Richard F. Vancil, "IBM Corporation: Background Note," in R. F. Vancil, *Implementing Strategy* (Boston: Division of Research, Harvard Business School, 1982), pp. 37–50.

Budgeting.   In a single business firm, the chief executive officer may have intimate knowledge of the firm's operations; also, corporate and business unit managers tend to have more frequent contact. Thus, chief executives of single business firms may be able to control the operations of subordinates through informal and personally oriented mechanisms, such as frequent personal interactions. If so, this lessens the need to rely as heavily on the budgeting system as the tool of control.[4]

> **Example.**   IBM Corporation (a single business firm) used the budget more as a guide, rather than as a commitment. A major test of performance of a division manager was whether the manager brought competitive products to market on time, more than just whether "the manager met the budget."[5]

On the other hand, in a conglomerate, it is nearly impossible for the chief executive to rely on informal interpersonal interactions as a tool of control; much of the communication and control has to be achieved through the formal budgeting system. This implies the following budgeting system characteristics in a conglomerate:

- Business unit managers have somewhat greater influence in developing their budgets since they (not the corporate office) possess most of the information about their respective product/market environments.
- Greater emphasis is often placed on meeting the budget since the chief executive does not have other informal controls available.

Transfer pricing.   Transfers of goods and services between business units are more frequent in single business and related diversified firms than between business units in conglomerates.[6] In a conglomerate, the usual transfer pricing policy is to give sourcing flexibility to business units and to use arm's-length market prices. However, in a single business or a related diversified firm, synergies may be important, and business units may not be given the freedom to make sourcing decisions. In Chapter 5, we discussed the implications of constraints on sourcing on the appropriate transfer pricing policies.

Incentive compensation.   The incentive compensation policy tends to differ across corporate strategies in the following ways:

---

[4] Empirical support for this conclusion is reported in Kenneth A. Merchant, "The Design of Corporate Budgeting System: Influences on Managerial Behavior and Performance," *The Accounting Review,* no. 4 (1981), pp. 813–28.

[5] Vancil, "IBM Corporation."

[6] In an empirical study, Gupta and Govindarajan found examples of interunit transfers even in conglomerates. A. K. Gupta and V. Govindarajan, "Resource Sharing among SBUs: Strategic Antecedents and Administrative Implications," *Acadamy of Management Journal* 29, no. 4 (1986), pp. 695–714.

Use of formulas. Conglomerates, in general, tend to make more use of formulas in the determination of the business unit managers' bonus—that is, they may base a larger portion of the bonus on quantitative, financial measures such as X percent bonus on actual profits in excess of budgeted profits. Formula-based bonus plans tend to be used in conglomerates because of the inevitable lack of familiarity on the part of senior management with what goes on in a variety of disparate businesses.

Senior management of single business and related diversified firms tend to determine a larger fraction of the business unit managers' bonus on the basis of subjective factors. Greater degrees of interrelationships in many of the latter group of firms imply that the performance of a given unit can be affected by the decisions and actions of other units. Therefore, for companies with highly interdependent business units, formula-based plans that are tied strictly to financial performance criteria could be counterproductive.

Profitability measures. The incentive bonus of the business unit managers tends to be determined primarily by the profitability of that unit—rather than the profitability of the firm—in the case of unrelated diversified firms. Its purpose is to motivate managers to act as though the business unit were their own company.

In contrast, single business and related diversified firms tend to base the incentive bonus of a business unit manager both on the performance of that unit as well as on the performance of a larger organizational unit (such as the product group to which the business unit belongs or perhaps even the overall corporation). When business units are interdependent, the more the incentive bonus of general managers emphasizes the separate performance of each unit, the more the possibility of inter-unit conflict. On the other hand, basing the bonus of general managers more on the overall corporate performance is likely to foster greater inter-unit cooperation, thereby increasing the managers' motivation to exploit interdependencies, instead of encouraging them to concentrate on their individual results.

Examples. In Textron (a conglomerate), the most important measure of performance in allocating bonus awards to business unit managers was return on investment of their respective business units. Thus, the incentive bonus system was formula-based tied to a financial criterion, and the bonus depended on the performance of the business unit.[7]

In IBM Corporation (a single business firm), the bonus of the division manager was subjectively determined and was based considerably on the performance of the entire group of which the division was a part. The General Products Division (GPD), which was in charge of mass data storage systems like magnetic tapes and discs, shared a marketing group with other units. IBM primarily evaluated the general manager of GPD on the basis of subjective factors, the important one being whether the

---

[7] Malcom S. Salter, "Tailor Incentive Compensation to Strategy," *Harvard Business Review*, March–April 1973, pp. 94–102.

products GPD was developing and making were competitive. IBM senior managers used a subjective process since they could not measure the contribution of GPD to the marketing group quantitatively.[8]

BUSINESS UNIT STRATEGY

So far we have discussed variations in control systems across firms, taking the whole firm as our unit of observation. In this section, we consider *intra-firm* differences in control systems. Diversified corporations segment themselves into business units and typically assign different strategies to the individual business units. Many chief executive officers of multibusiness organizations do not adopt a standardized, uniform approach to controlling their business units; rather, they tailor the approach to the strategy of each business unit.

As we stated in Chapter 7, business unit strategy consists of two interrelated aspects: mission and competitive advantage. We first discuss the control implications of these two dimensions separately. Considering the two dimensions together poses some specific problems, which will be discussed in the next section.

Mission

The mission for ongoing business units could be either build, hold, or harvest. These missions constitute a continuum, with "pure build" at one end and "pure harvest" at the other end. For effective implementation, there should be congruence between the mission chosen and the types of controls used. We develop the control-mission "fit" using the following line of reasoning:[9]

- The mission of the business unit influences the uncertainties that general managers face and the short-term versus long-term trade-offs that they make.
- Management control systems can be systematically varied to help motivate the manager to cope effectively with uncertainty and make appropriate short-term versus long-term trade-offs
- Thus, different missions often require systematically different management control systems.

Mission and uncertainty.   "Build" units tend to face greater environmental uncertainty than "harvest" units for several reasons:

---

[8] Vancil, "IBM Corporation," pp. 37–50.

[9] This section draws from an extensive body of research that has focused on strategy implementation issues at the business unit level. Some of the key references are: Govindarajan (1988, 1989); Govindarajan and Fisher (1989, 1990, 1991); Govindarajan and Gupta (1985); Gupta and Govindarajan (1984); Hall (1987); Sata and Maidique (1980); Shank and Govindarajan (1989); Simons (1987). These references are fully described at the end of this chapter.

- Build strategies typically are undertaken in the growth stage of the product life cycle, whereas harvest strategies typically are undertaken in the mature/ decline stage of the product life cycle. Such factors as manufacturing process, product technology, market demand, relations with suppliers, buyers, and distribution channels, number of competitors, and competitive structure change more rapidly and are more unpredictable in the growth than in the mature/decline stage of the product life cycle.
- An objective of a build business unit is to increase market share. Since the total market share of all firms in an industry is 100 percent, the battle for market share is a zero-sum game; thus, a build strategy pits a business unit into greater conflict with its competitors than does a harvest strategy. Since competitors' actions are likely to be unpredictable, this contributes to the uncertainty faced by build business units.
- Both on the input side and on the output side, build managers tend to experience greater dependencies with external individuals and organizations than do harvest managers. For instance, a build mission signifies additional capital investment (greater dependence on capital markets), expansion of capacity (greater dependence on the technological environment), increase in market share (greater dependence on customers and competitors), increase in production volume (greater dependence on raw material suppliers and labor market), and so on. The greater the external dependencies that the business unit faces, the greater the uncertainty it confronts.
- Since build business units are often in new and evolving industries, the experience of build managers in their industries is likely to be less. This also contributes to the greater uncertainty faced by managers of build units in dealing with external constituencies.

Mission and time span. The choice of build versus harvest strategies has implications for short-term versus long-term profit trade-offs. The share-building strategy includes *(a)* price cutting, *(b)* major R&D expenditures (to introduce new products), and *(c)* major market development expenditures. These actions are aimed at establishing market leadership, but they depress short-term profits. Thus, many decisions that the manager of a build unit makes today may not result in profits until some future period. A harvest strategy, on the other hand, demands attention to tasks with a view to maximize short-term profits.

We now discuss how the form and structure of control systems might differ across business units with different missions.

Programming. While designing a programming process, several design issues need to be considered. There are no single answers on these design choices; rather, the answers tend to depend upon the mission being pursued by the business unit (Exhibit 13–3).

When the environment is uncertain, the programming process is especially important. Management needs to give much thought to how to cope with the

EXHIBIT 13–3   Different Strategic Missions: Implications for Programming Process

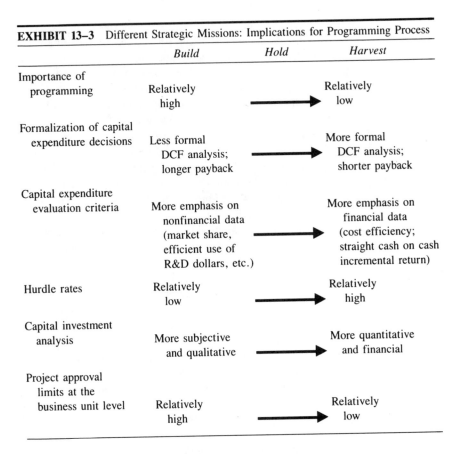

	Build	*Hold*	*Harvest*
Importance of programming	Relatively high	⟶	Relatively low
Formalization of capital expenditure decisions	Less formal DCF analysis; longer payback	⟶	More formal DCF analysis; shorter payback
Capital expenditure evaluation criteria	More emphasis on nonfinancial data (market share, efficient use of R&D dollars, etc.)	⟶	More emphasis on financial data (cost efficiency; straight cash on cash incremental return)
Hurdle rates	Relatively low	⟶	Relatively high
Capital investment analysis	More subjective and qualitative	⟶	More quantitative and financial
Project approval limits at the business unit level	Relatively high	⟶	Relatively low

uncertainties, and this usually requires a longer-range view of planning than is possible in the annual budget. If the environment is stable, there may be no programming process at all, or only a broad-brush strategic plan. Thus, the programming process is more critical and more important for build, as compared to harvest, business units. Nevertheless, some programming for the harvest business units may be necessary because the company's overall strategic plan must encompass all of its businesses to effectively balance cash flows.

In screening capital investments and allocating resources, the systems may be more quantitative and financial for harvest units. A harvest business unit operates in a mature industry and does not offer tremendous new investment possibilities. Hence, the required earnings rate for such a business unit may be relatively high to motivate the manager to search for projects with truly exceptional returns. Since harvest units tend to experience stable environments (with predictable products, technologies, competitors, and customers), discounted cash flow (DCF) analysis often can be used with more confidence. The required information used to evaluate investments from harvest units is primarily financial. A build unit, however, is positioned on the growth stage of the product life cycle. The corporate office wants to take advantage of the opportunities in a growing market, and senior management, therefore, may set a relatively low discount rate, thereby motivating build managers to forward more investment ideas to corporate office. Given the product/market uncertainties, financial analysis of some projects from build units may be unreliable. For such projects, nonfinancial data are more important.

Budgeting. Implications for designing budgeting systems to support varied missions are contained in Exhibit 13–4. The calculational aspects of variance analysis comparing actual results with the budget identify variances as either favorable or unfavorable. However, a favorable variance does not necessarily imply favorable performance; similarly, an unfavorable variance does not necessarily imply unfavorable performance. The link between a favorable or unfavorable variance, on the one hand, and favorable or unfavorable performance, on the other hand, depends upon the strategic context of the business unit under evaluation.

> **Example.** An industrial measuring instruments manufacturer disaggregated the overall profit variance by key causal factors for its two business units: Electric Meters (a "harvest" business) and Electronic Instruments (a "build" business). Senior management interpreted market share, selling price, and manufacturing cost variances very differently while evaluating the performance of managers in charge of the harvest and build businesses.[10]

A related issue is how much importance should be attached to meeting the budget while evaluating the business unit manager's performance. We pointed out in Chapter 11 that the greater the uncertainty, the more difficult it is for superiors to regard subordinates' budget targets as firm commitments and to consider unfavorable budget variances as clear indicators of poor performance. For this reason, less reliance usually is placed on budgets in build units than in harvest units.

> **Example.** In the late 1970s, the SCM Corporation adopted a two-dimensional yardstick to evaluate business units: bottom-line performance against budget was one dimension, and performance against specific objectives was another. The ratios of the two were made to vary according to the mission of the business unit. For instance, "pure harvest" units were evaluated 100 percent on budget performance; "pure hold," 50 percent on budget and 50 percent on completion of objectives; "pure build," 100 percent on completion of objectives.[11]

The following additional differences in the budget process are likely to exist between build and harvest units:

---

[10] John K. Shank and Vijay Govindarajan, *Strategic Cost Analysis* (Homewood, Ill.: Richard D. Irwin, 1989), pp. 95–113.

[11] George E. Hall, "Reflections on Running a Diversified Company," *Harvard Business Review*, January–February 1987, pp. 88–89.

EXHIBIT 13–4 Different Strategic Missions: Implications for Budgeting

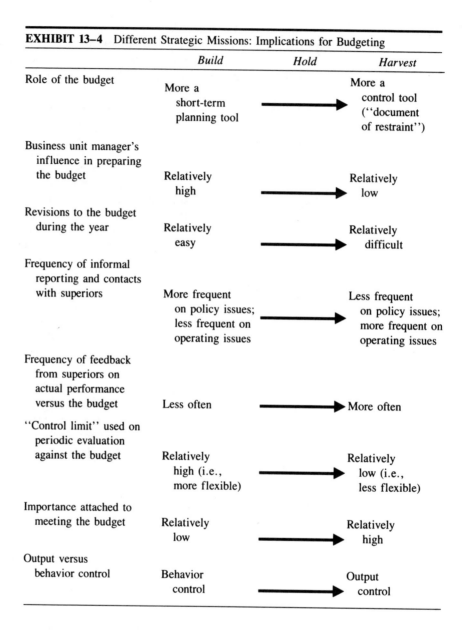

	Build	Hold	Harvest
Role of the budget	More a short-term planning tool	→	More a control tool ("document of restraint")
Business unit manager's influence in preparing the budget	Relatively high	→	Relatively low
Revisions to the budget during the year	Relatively easy	→	Relatively difficult
Frequency of informal reporting and contacts with superiors	More frequent on policy issues; less frequent on operating issues	→	Less frequent on policy issues; more frequent on operating issues
Frequency of feedback from superiors on actual performance versus the budget	Less often	→	More often
"Control limit" used on periodic evaluation against the budget	Relatively high (i.e., more flexible)	→	Relatively low (i.e., less flexible)
Importance attached to meeting the budget	Relatively low	→	Relatively high
Output versus behavior control	Behavior control	→	Output control

- In contrast to harvest units, budget revisions are likely to be more frequent for build units because of the more frequent changes in their product/market environment.
- Build unit managers may have relatively greater input and influence in the formulation of the budget than harvest unit managers. This is so because "build" managers operate in rapidly changing environments and have better

EXHIBIT 13–5 Different Strategic Missions: Implications for Incentive Compensation

	Build	*Hold*	*Harvest*
Percent compensation as bonus	Relatively high	⟶	Relatively low
Bonus criteria	More emphasis on nonfinancial criteria	⟶	More emphasis on financial criteria
Bonus determination approach	More subjective	⟶	More formula-based
Frequency of bonus payment	Less frequent	⟶	More frequent

knowledge of these changes than does senior management. For harvest units with stable environments, the knowledge of the manager is less important.

Incentive compensation system. In designing an incentive compensation package for business unit managers, the following are some of the questions that need to be resolved:

1. What should be the size of incentive bonus payments relative to the general manager's base salary? Should the incentive bonus payments have upper limits?
2. What measures of performance (e.g., profit, return on investment, sales volume, market share, product development) should be employed as the basis for deciding the general manager's incentive bonus awards? If multiple performance measures are employed, how should they be weighted?
3. How much reliance should be placed on subjective judgments in deciding on the bonus amount?
4. With what frequency (semiannual, annual, biennial and so on) should incentive awards be made?

Decisions on these design variables are influenced by the mission of the business unit (Exhibit 13–5). As for the first question, many firms use the principle that the riskier the strategy, the greater the proportion of the general manager's compensation in bonus compared to salary (the "risk/return" principle). They maintain that, since managers in charge of more uncertain task situations should be willing to take greater risks, they should have a higher percentage of their remuneration in the form of an incentive bonus. Thus, reliance on bonus is likely to be higher for "build" managers than for "harvest" managers.

As for the second question, when an individual's rewards are tied to performance according to certain criteria, his or her behaviors are influenced by the desire to optimize performance with respect to those criteria. Some performance criteria (cost control, operating profits, cash flow from operations, and return on investment) focus more on the short-term performance, whereas other performance criteria (market share, new product development, market development, and people development) focus on long-term profitability. Thus, linking incentive bonus to the former set of criteria tends to promote a short-term focus on the part of the general manager, whereas linking incentive bonus to the latter set of performance criteria is likely to promote a long-term focus. Given the relative differences in time horizons of build and harvest managers, it may be inappropriate to use a singe, uniform financial criterion (such as return on investment) to evaluate the performance of every business unit; rather, it may be desirable to use multiple performance criteria, with differential weights for each criterion depending on the mission of the business unit.

> **Example.**   General Electric Company and Westinghouse Electric Corporation tailor compensation packages to the different "missions" of their individual businesses.
>
> Both GE and Westinghouse have mature as well as young businesses. In the mature businesses, short-term incentives might dominate the compensation packages of managers who are charged with maximizing cash flow, achieving high profit margins, and retaining market share. In the younger businesses, where developing products and establishing marketing strategies are most important, nonfinancial measures geared to the execution of long-term performance might dictate the major portion of managers' remuneration.[12]

As for the third question, in addition to varying the importance of different criteria, superiors must also decide on the approach to take in determining a specific bonus amount. At one extreme, a manager's bonus might be a strict formula-based plan, with the bonus tied to performance on quantifiable criteria (e.g., x percent bonus on actual profits in excess of budgeted profits); at the other extreme, a manager's incentive bonus amounts might be based solely on the superior's subjective judgment or discretion. Alternatively, incentive bonus amounts might also be based on a combination of formula-based and subjective (nonformula) approaches. Performance on most long-term criteria (market development, new product development, and people development) is clearly less amenable to objective measurement than is performance along most short-run criteria (operating profits, cash flow from operations, and return on investment). Since, as already noted, build managers—in contrast with harvest managers—should focus more on the long-run rather than the short run, build managers are typically evaluated more subjectively than harvest managers.

Finally, frequency of bonus awards influence the time horizon of managers. More frequent bonus awards encourage concentration on short-term perfor-

---

[12] "Executive Compensation: Looking to the Long Term Again," *Business Week,* May 9, 1983, p. 81.

mance since they have the effect of motivating managers to focus on those facets of the business that they can affect in the short run. Less frequent calculation and payment of bonus encourages the manager to take a long-term perspective. Thus, build managers tend to receive bonus awards less frequently than harvest managers.

> **Example.** Premark International (formed in 1986 in a spin-off from Dart & Kraft, Inc.) used a similar logic in designing the incentive bonus for the general manager of its Tupperware Division, whose mission was to build market share: "[If you award the bonus annually,] Tupperware could reduce advertising and promotional activities and you can look good in profits that year. Then, the franchise starts to go to hell. If you're shooting for an award after three years, there's less tendency to do things short term."[13]

Competitive Advantage

A business unit can choose to compete either as a differentiated player or as a low-cost player. The choice of a differentiation approach, rather than a low-cost approach, increases uncertainty in a business unit's task environment for three reasons.

First, product innovation is likely to be more critical for differentiation business units than for lost-cost business units. This is partly because a low-cost business unit, with its primary emphasis on cost reduction, typically prefers to keep its product offerings stable over time; whereas a differentiation business unit, with its primary focus on uniqueness and exclusivity, is likely to engage in greater product innovation. A business unit with greater emphasis on new product activities tends to face greater uncertainty, since the business unit is betting on unproven products.

Second, low-cost business units typically tend to have narrow product lines to minimize inventory carry costs as well as to benefit from scale economies. Differentiation business units, on the other hand, tend to have a broader set of products to create uniqueness. Product breadth creates high environmental complexity, and consequently, higher uncertainty.

Third, low-cost business units typically produce no-frill commodity products, and these products succeed primarily because they have lower prices than competing products. However, products of differentiation business units succeed if customers perceive that the products have advantages over competing products. Since customer perception is difficult to learn about, and since customer loyalty is subject to change resulting from actions of competitors or other reasons, the demand for differentiated products is typically more difficult to predict than the demand for commodities.

---

[13] L. Reibstein, "Firms trim annual pay increase and focus on long term: More employers link incentives to unit results," *The Wall Street Journal,* April 10, 1987, p. 25.

The specifics of the control systems for low-cost and differentiation business units are similar to the ones described earlier for harvest and build business units. This is so because the uncertainty facing low-cost and differentiation business units are similar to the uncertainty facing harvest and build business units.

Examples.   Digital Equipment Corporation (DEC) followed a differentiation strategy, whereas Data General followed a low-cost strategy. The control systems in these companies differed accordingly. DEC's product managers were primarily evaluated on the basis of the quality of their interaction with their customers (a subjective measure), whereas Data General's product managers were evaluated on the basis of results, or profits. Further, DEC's sales representatives were on straight salary, but Data General's salesmen received 50 percent of their pay on a commission basis. Salaried compensation indicates behavior control and commission compensation, outcome control.[14]

A broad-based chemicals manufacturer used differentiated management control, focusing on the differing key success factors for its yellow dye unit (which followed a cost leadership strategy) and its red dye unit (which followed a differentiation strategy). The manager in charge of yellow dye was tightly held against *theoretical* standard costs rather than currently achievable standard costs. The results of this tight financial controls were remarkable: within a period of two years, actual cost for yellow dye decreased from $5.72 per lb. to $3.84 per lb.—giving the yellow dye unit a major cost advantage. The key strategic issue for red dye was product differentiation, not cost leadership. The management control reports for the red dye unit, therefore, focused on product leadership variables (e.g., milestone reporting on the development project for hot spray dyeing) rather than cost control variables.[15]

Senior managers at one large, high-tech manufacturer recently took direct responsibility for adding customer satisfaction, quality, market share, and human resources to their formal measurement system. The impetus was their realization that the company's existing system, which was largely financial, undercut its strategy, which focused on differentiation through customer service.[16]

Additional Considerations

Although differentiating controls *within* the same firm has a sound logic, control systems designers need to be cognizant of several problems involved in doing so.

First, a business unit's external environment inevitably changes over time, and a change might imply the need for a shift in strategy. This raises an interesting issue. Success at any task requires commitment. The strategy-control

---

[14] B. Uttal, "The Gentlemen and the Upstarts Meet in a Great Mini-battle," *Fortune*, April 23, 1979, pp. 98–108.

[15] Shank and Govindarajan, *Strategic Cost Analysis*, pp. 114–30.

[16] Robert G. Eccles, "The Performance Measurement Manifesto," *Harvard Business Review*, January–February 1991, pp. 131–37.

"fit" is expected to foster such a commitment to the current strategy. However, if the control system is too closely related to the current strategy, it could result in overcommitment, thereby inhibiting the manager from shifting to a new strategy when it should. There are many examples of declining industries that have transformed into growth industries (examples: the major growth of Arm & Hammer baking soda, which was once in the decline stage of the product life cycle; the 1980s surge in demand for the fountain pen, which was once considered an obsolete product). The following examples in the radio, musical instrument, and motorcycle industries illustrate the problems of overcommitment when there is a close fit between strategy and controls.

> **Examples.**   Financially oriented U.S. manufacturers once treated the radio as essentially a dot on the product portfolio matrix. Convinced that every product has a life cycle, they viewed the radio as having passed its peak and being a prime candidate for "milking." Starved for investment funds and resources and being subject to tight financial controls, the radio died in a self-fulfilling prophecy. On the other hand, Japanese radio manufacturers, such as Matsushita (Panasonic) and Sony—ignoring or unaware of product life cycle and portfolio theories—obstinately believed in their product's value. The division heads of these firms had no option but to extend the life of the product, since to do otherwise would mean dissolving their divisions, which was an untenable option. So they pressed their engineers, component manufacturers, and marketing people for new ideas. . . . Today the portable radio-cassette and Sony Walkman stories are part of business folklore.[17]
>
> Yamaha in the musical instrument market in the United States and Honda, Kawasaki, Suzuki, and Yamaha in the motorcycle market in the United States and in Europe have successfully destroyed the dominance of incumbent manufacturers who concentrated on "milking" their products for profit in a stagnant market.[18]

Thus, there is an ongoing dilemma: how to design control systems that can simultaneously maintain a high degree of commitment as well as a healthy skepticism for current strategies.

Second, we have discussed mission and competitive advantage as separate characteristics. However, business units have both a mission and a competitive advantage, which, in some combinations, may result in a conflict regarding the type of controls to be used. As Exhibit 13–6 demonstrates, the ordinal classification of mission and competitive advantage yields four distinct combinations. There is an unconflicting design in cells 2 and 3. Both of these cells have a similar level of uncertainty, and this suggests a similar control system design. Cells 1 and 4, however, have conflicting demands, and designing a control system that fits both is difficult. Several possibilities exist. It might be

---

[17] K. Ohmae, "The Long and Short of Japanese Planning," *The Wall Street Journal*, January 18, 1982, p. 28.

[18] B. G. James, "Strategic Planning under Fire," *Sloan Management Review*, Summer 1984, pp. 57–61.

EXHIBIT 13–6 Fits and Misfits in Control System Design

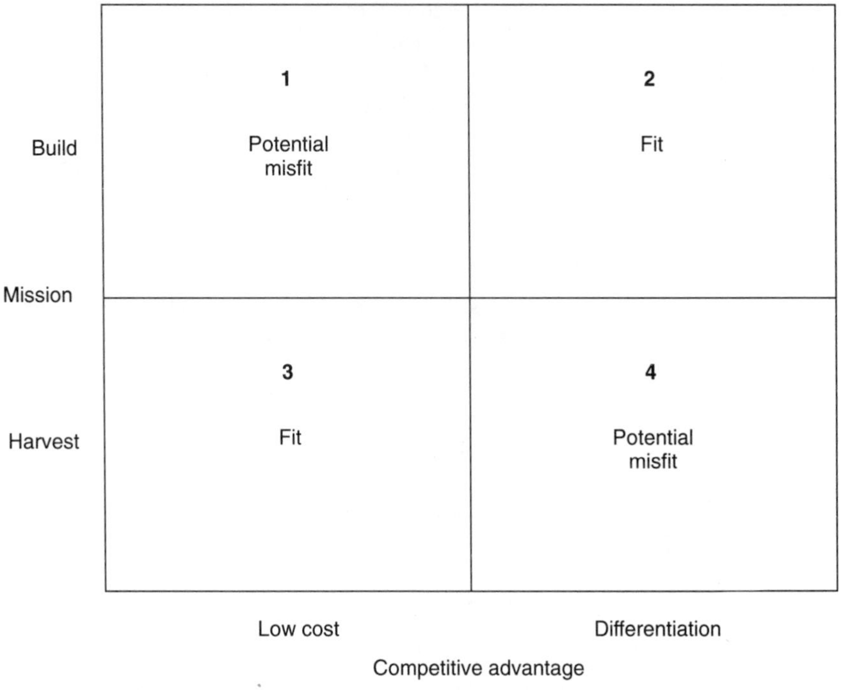

	Low cost	Differentiation
Build	**1** Potential misfit	**2** Fit
Harvest	**3** Fit	**4** Potential misfit

Mission (row label)

Competitive advantage (column label)

possible to so change the mission or the competitive advantage that they do not conflict from the standpoint of systems design (i.e., move the business unit to cell 2 or cell 3). If this is not feasible, it might be that either mission or competitive advantage is more critical for implementation and, therefore, would dominate the choice of the appropriate type of control. If mission and competitive advantage are equally important, control system design becomes especially difficult. Here, control systems cannot be designed for the mission or competitive advantage in isolation without incurring costs.

Third, explicitly differentiated controls across business units might create administrative awkwardness and potential dysfunctional effects, especially for managers in charge of harvest units. Many harvest managers believe that their career prospects within the company are somewhat limited. While corporate managers in most diversified firms may find it rational to harvest one or more of their businesses, every company wants to grow at the overall firm level. Thus, as one goes higher in the corporate hierarchy, skills at successfully executing a build strategy become more important than those of successfully executing a harvest strategy. From a career perspective, this likelihood tends to favor managers currently in charge of build businesses.

Example. The following speculation regarding who might succeed Walter Wriston as the next CEO of Citicorp appeared in *The Wall Street Journal* nearly three years *before* the actual announcement of his successor: "Ironically, Mr. Theobald may not get to the top precisely because he runs a division that has always been a big money-maker for Citicorp, its institutional division. Unlike his two competitors, who are charting new courses for Citicorp, Mr. Theobald is simply carrying forward a tradition of profiting handsomely from making loans to corporations and governments, domestically and abroad."[19] Subsequent events confirmed these speculations.

Given these possibilities, harvest managers may perceive their roles as being less important. Explicitly designing tight controls over harvest strategies compounds this problem.

System designers might consider two possibilities to mitigate this problem. First, as part of the planning process, they might consider not using such harshly graphic and negative terms as *cash cow, dog, question mark,* and *star* but, instead use such terms as *build, hold* and *harvest.* The former are "static" terms that do not, in any case, indicate missions as well as "dynamic" action-oriented terms, such as *build, hold,* and *harvest* do. Second, to the extent possible, a harvest manager should be given one or more products with high growth potential. This would prevent the possibility of a manager getting typecast solely as a harvester. Corning Glass Works follows this policy of assigning a growth oriented product to a manager in charge of a harvest business.[20]

Finally, strategy is only one variable, albeit an important one, in influencing the choice of controls. Top management style also has a profound impact on the design and operation of control systems—a topic we turn to next.

MANAGEMENT CONTROL IMPLICATIONS OF TOP MANAGEMENT STYLE

The management control function in an organization is influenced by the style of senior management. The style of the chief executive officer affects the management control process in the entire organization. Thomas Watson at IBM, Reginald Jones at General Electric, and Harold Geneen at ITT are well-publicized examples. Similarly, the style of the business unit manager affects the management control process within the unit, and the style of functional department managers affects the management control process within their functional areas. If feasible, designers should consider management style in designing and operating control systems. (If chief executive officers actively participate in system design, as should be the case, the system will reflect their preferences.)

---

[19] J. Salamon, "Challenges Lie Ahead for Dynamic Citicorp after the Wriston Era," *The Wall Street Journal,* December 18, 1981, p. 1.

[20] Richard F. Vancil, "Corning Glass Works: Tom MacAvoy," in R. F. Vancil, *Implementing Strategy* (Boston: Division of Research, Harvard Business School, 1982), pp. 21–36.

Differences in Management Styles

Managers differ in their styles. Some of these differences are listed in Exhibit 13–7. Some managers rely heavily on reports and certain formal documents; others prefer conversations and informal contacts. Some think in concrete terms; others think abstractly. Some are analytical; others use heuristics. Some are risk-takers; others are risk-averse. Some are process-oriented; others are results-oriented. Some are people-oriented; others are task-oriented. Some are friendly; others are aloof. Some are long-term-oriented; others are short-term-oriented. Some are "Theory X" (they dominate decision making); others are "Theory Y" (they encourage organization participation in decision making). Some place great emphasis on monetary rewards; others place emphasis on a broader set of rewards.

Management style is influenced by the manager's (1) background and (2) personality. Background includes things like the manager's age; formal education; and the manager's experience in a given function such as manufacturing, technology, marketing, or finance. Personality characteristics include such variables as the manager's willingness to take risks and tolerance for ambiguity.

Implications for Management Control

The various dimensions of management style, as suggested in Exhibit 13–7, significantly influence the operation of the control systems. Even if the same set of reports with the same set of data goes with the same frequency to the CEO, two CEOs would use these reports very differently to manage the business units if their styles are different. The dramatic shift in the control process

---

EXHIBIT 13–7   Differences in Management Styles

Rely heavily on reports and other formal documents	Rely heavily on informal contacts
Think in concete terms	Abstract thinkers
Analytical	Heuristic
Risk-taker	Risk-averse
Process oriented	Results-oriented
People-oriented	Task-oriented
Friendly	Aloof
Long-term-oriented	Short-term-oriented
Theory X	Theory Y
•	•
•	•
•	•

---

within General Electric when Jack Welch succeeded Reginald Jones as the CEO, as described in Chapter 2, vividly illustrates this point.

Style affects the management control process—how the CEO prefers to use the information, how the CEO conducts performance review meetings, and so on—which, in turn, affects the actual operation of the control system, even if the formal structure does not change under a new CEO. In fact, when CEOs change, subordinates typically infer what the new CEO really wants based on how the new CEO interacts during the management control process (e.g., how much attention he or she actually gives to performance reports, rather than from speeches or directives.)

Personal versus impersonal controls.   Presence of personal versus impersonal controls in organizations is a function of managerial style. Managers differ on the relative importance that they attach to formal budgets and reports, contrasted with informal conversations and other personal contacts. Some managers are "numbers-oriented"; they want a large flow of quantitative information, and they spend much time analyzing this information and deriving tentative conclusions from it. Other managers are "people-oriented"; they look at a few numbers, but they usually arrive at their conclusions by talking with people; they judge the relevance and importance of what they learn partly on their appraisal of the other person. They spend much time visiting various locations and talking with both management people and hourly employees to obtain a feel for how well things are going.

Management's attitude toward formal reports affects the amount of detail they desire, the frequency of these reports, and even such matters as their preference for graphs, rather than tables of numbers, or for supplementing numerical reports with written comments. Designers of management control systems need to identify these preferences and accommodate them.

Tight versus loose controls.   A manager's style affects the *degree* of tight versus loose control in any situation. The manager of a routine production responsibility center can be controlled either relatively tightly or relatively loosely, and the actual control reflects the style of the manager's superior. Thus, the degree of tightness or looseness often is not revealed by the content of the forms or aspects of the formal control documents, rules, or procedures. It depends on how these formal devices are used.

The degree of looseness tends to increase at successively higher levels in the organization hierarchy; higher-level managers typically tend to pay less attention to details and more to overall results (the bottom line, rather than on the details of how the results are obtained) than lower-level managers. However, this generalization might not apply if a given CEO has a different style.

Examples.   The classic illustration of this point is ITT under Harold Geneen. One could argue that ITT, being a conglomerate, should be managed based on monitoring the business unit bottom line and not through a detailed evaluation of every aspect of the business unit operations. This is so since, in a conglomerate, the CEO typically has "capacity limitations" in understanding the "nuts and bolts" of the operations of various business units. In such a context, it is Harold Geneen's personal style that explains the detailed evaluations he made of business unit managers.[21]

When Rand Araskog succeeded Harold Geneen at ITT, he altered the detailed and tight control system since, among other things, Araskog's personal style was not oriented toward exercising tight controls.[22]

The style of the CEO has a profound impact on management control. If a new senior management with a different style takes over, the system tends to change correspondingly. It might happen that the manager's style is not a good fit with the management control requirements of the organization. If the manager recognizes this incongruity and adapts his or her style accordingly, the problem disappears. If, however, the managers are unwilling or unable to change their style, the organization will experience performance problems. The solution in this case might be to change the manager.

SUMMARY

Designers of management control systems should take explicit notice of the strategic context in which the controls are being applied. The strategies that a firm selects can be arrayed along a continuum, with single business firms at one extreme and unrelated diversified firms (conglomerates) at the other. The management control process differs according to the firm's strategy in this dimension.

Business units have missions that can be classified as "build," "hold," or "harvest," and their managers can also decide to build competitive advantage based on low cost or differentiation. The appropriate management control process is influenced by which of these strategies a given business unit selects.

The discussion in this chapter on linking controls to strategies should not be used in a mechanistic manner; the suggestions made here are tendencies, not universal truths. In fact, control systems should be designed in the context of each organization's *unique* external environment, technology, strategy, organization structure, culture, and top management style.

SUGGESTED ADDITIONAL READINGS

Camillus, John C. *Strategic Planning and Management Control.* Boston: Lexington Books, 1986.

Galbraith, J., and R. Kazanjian. *Strategy Implementation: The Role of Structure, Systems, and Process.* St. Paul, Minn.: West, 1986.

---

[21] "The Case for Managing by the Numbers," *Fortune,* October 1, 1984, pp. 78–81.

[22] "ITT: Groping for a New Strategy," *Business Week,* December 15, 1980, pp. 66–80.

Govindarajan, Vijay. "A Contingency Approach to Strategy Implementation at the Business Unit level: Integrating Administrative Mechanisms with Strategy." *Academy of Management Journal* 31, no. 4 (1988), pp. 828–53.

—————."Implementing Competitive Strategies at the Business Unit Level: Implications of Matching Managers with Strategies." *Strategic Management Journal* 10 (1989), 251–69.

Govindarajan, Vijay, and Joseph Fisher. "The Interaction between Strategy and Controls: Implications for Managerial Job Satisfaction." Working paper, The Amos Tuck School of Business Administration, Dartmouth College, 1989.

—————."Impact of Output versus Behavior Controls and Resource Sharing on Performance: Strategy as a Mediating Variable." *Academy of Management Journal*, June 1990, pp. 259–85.

—————."Incentive Compensation, Strategic Business Unit Mission, and Competitive Strategy." Working paper, The Amos Tuck School of Business Administration, Dartmouth College, 1991.

Govindarajan, Vijay, and Anil K. Gupta. "Linking Control Systems to Business Unit Strategy: Impact on Performance." *Accounting, Organizations, and Society,* 1985, pp. 51–66.

Gupta, Anil K., and Vijay Govindarajan. "Build, Hold, Harvest: Converting Strategic Intentions into Reality." *Journal of Business Strategy* 4, no. 3 (1984), pp. 34–47.

Hall. G. E. "Reflections on Running a Diversified Company." *Harvard Business Review,* January–February 1987.

Hamermesh, R. G. *Making Strategy Work.* New York: John Wiley & Sons, 1986.

Merchant, Kenneth A. "The Design of the Corporate Budgeting System: Influences on Managerial Behavior and Performance." *The Accounting Review* 4 (1981), pp. 813–28.

Ross, Gerald H. "Revolution in Management Control." *Management Accounting,* November 1990, pp. 23–27.

Salter, M. S. "Tailor Incentive Compensation to Strategy." *Harvard Business Review,* March–April 1973.

Sata, R., and M. A. Maidique. "Bonus System for a Balanced Strategy." *Harvard Business Review,* November–December 1980.

Shank, John K., and Vijay Govindarajan. *Strategic Cost Analysis.* Homewood, Ill.: Richard D. Irwin, 1989, chap. 6 and 7.

Simons, Robert. "The Relationship between Business Strategy and Accounting Control Systems: An Empirical Analysis." *Accounting, Organizations, and Society,* July 1987, pp. 357–74.

Case 13–1

United Instruments, Inc.*

Steve Park, president and principal stockholder of United Instruments, Inc., sat at his desk reflecting on the 1987 results (Exhibit 1). For the second year in succession, the company had exceeded the profit budget. Steve Park was obviously very happy with the 1987 results. All the same, he wanted to get a better feel for the relative contributions of the R&D, manufacturing, and marketing departments in this overall success. With this in mind, he called his assistant, a recent graduate of a well-known business school, into his office.

"Amy," he began, "as you can see from our recent financial results, we have exceeded our profit targets by $622,000. Can you prepare an analysis showing how much R&D, manufacturing, and marketing contributed to this overall favorable profit variance?"

Amy Shultz, with all the fervor of a recent convert to professional management, set to her task immediately. She collected the data (Exhibit 2) and was wondering what her next step should be.

United Instrument's products can be grouped into two main lines of business: electric meters (EM) and electronic instruments (EI). Both EM and EI are industrial measuring instruments and perform similar functions. However, these products differ in their manufacturing technology and their end-use characteristics. EM is based on mechanical and electrical technology, whereas EI is based on microchip technology. EM and EI are substitute products in the same sense that a mechanical watch and a digital watch are substitutes.

United Instruments uses a variable costing system for internal reporting purposes.

EXHIBIT 1

Income Statement for the Year 1987

		Budget (000s)		Actual (000s)
Sales		$16,872		$17,061
Cost of goods sold		9,668		9,865
Gross margin		$ 7,204		$ 7,196
Less: Other operating expenses:				
Marketing	$1,856		$1,440	
R&D	1,480		932	
Administration	1,340	4,676	1,674	4,046
Profit before taxes		$ 2,528		$ 3,150

---

* This case was prepared and is copyrighted by Vijay Govindarajan and John K. Shank, The Amos Tuck School of Business Administration, Dartmouth College.

EXHIBIT 2

Additional Information

	Electric Meters (EM)	Electronic Instruments (EI)
Selling prices per unit:		
Average standard price	$40.00	$180.00
Average actual prices, 1987	30.00	206.00
Variable product costs per unit:		
Average standard manufacturing cost	20.00	50.00
Average actual manufacturing cost	21.00	54.00
Volume information:		
Units produced and sold—actual	141,770	62,172
Units produced and sold—planned	124,800	66,000
Total industry sales, 1987—actual	$44 million	$76 million
Total industry variable product costs, 1987—actual	$16 million	$32 million
United's share of the market (percent of physical units):		
Planned	10%	15%
Actual	16%	9%
	Planned	*Actual*
Firm-wide fixed expenses (000s):		
Fixed manufacturing expenses	$3,872	$3,530
Fixed marketing expenses	1,856	1,440
Fixed administrative expenses	1,340	1,674
Fixed R&D expenses		
(exclusively for electronic instruments)	1,480	932

QUESTIONS

1. Prepare the report that you feel Amy Shulz should present to Mr. Park.
2. Put yourself in the position of the following six managers: general manager (EM); marketing manager (EM); manufacturing manager (EM); general manager (EI); marketing manager (EI); manufacturing manager (EI). These six managers compete for a share in the company's bonus pool. For each of the six, how would you make a case for your obtaining a share of the bonus pool?
3. As Mr. Park, how would you feel about the 1987 performance of each of the six managers who are competing for a share of the bonus pool? (*Note:* Consider the strategy of EM and EI business units in your performance assessment.)

Case 13–2

Vick International Division*

Sitting at breakfast, Tom McGuire was going over in his mind the key issues that were likely to come up during the day. Across the top of the menu propped in the holder at the next table was the date: Thursday, August 10, 1978.

Throughout the week, management personnel from headquarters and field offices of Vick International, Latin America/Far East Division (LA/FE), had been attending the mid-August quarterly review meeting. As division president, McGuire had scheduled for that day individual agreement sessions with six of his overseas directors. There would be much ground to cover. It was essential that the important questions not be lost in a myriad of details. Tom also wanted to be sure that he assumed the appropriate role with regard to each critical issue, and that he was clear in his mind on the roles of others.

Of particular concern was a program in Mexico to develop and launch Alpha, a new nutritional product. The Alpha situation required special attention, because it touched on the way in which the division's formal management system was working.

"It's ironic," McGuire mused. "Our management system calls for the explicit assignment of work roles to the various managers within the division who must contribute to the attainment of a certain objective. Yet, with regard to Alpha, there seems to be some misunderstanding about who is responsible for each role, and what that means in terms of managing the project."

Background

McGuire had been president of Vick International, Latin America/Far East, since 1969. A native of New York, he had studied chemistry at Notre Dame before working for Union Carbide. In 1956, at 29, he joined Richardson-Merrell, Inc., a diversified company engaged in the development, manufacturing, and marketing of proprietary medicines and toiletries, ethical pharmaceuticals, veterinary products, laboratory and diagnostic chemicals and equipment, and plastic packaging.

McGuire

As one of RMI's nine operating divisions, we are given considerable independence in running our business, so long as we contribute to the company's goals of stable growth, improving profitability, and product excellence. Richardson-Merrell's original business, starting in 1905, was built around Vick's VapoRub and subsequently other proprietary drugs in the cold remedy area. But in order to achieve more stability and growth, the company began to diversify in the 1930s. As a result, a number of other products have been added to RMI's lines; but the Vick divisions, which handle proprietary health and personal care products continue to be the mainstay of the business.

When I became division general manager in 1969, Vick International, LA/FE was having difficulty sustaining adequate growth and profitability. During the previous two years we had missed our

* This case was abridged with permission from Harvard Business School case 179–068, written under the direction of Professor Richard F. Vancil.

budgets by wide margins. My initial analysis of the situation was that the division had an inadequate budget system, ineffective tracking and control mechanisms, and a lack of action-oriented reporting. So we instituted a budget manual, undertook improvements in the data base for planning, initiated a program to improve communications, and overhauled our reporting system. As a result, it was extremely frustrating when we didn't make our budgets the next two years, either.

I had not experienced this type of failure before, and it led me to a far-ranging examination of what the division's business was and how we went about accomplishing it. Dick Waters, my executive vice president, had expressed his concern. I told him I would like to initiate some fundamental changes. He promised me his support and wished me success. The pressure to deliver was now really on my back.

Our business strategy was based on running with products already developed by other divisions within the company. In essence, it was an extension of our highly successful export business of the 40s and 50s, but it no longer fit the requirements of our expanding and changing markets. During the 60s we had set up manufacturing and distribution operations in a large number of countries, and, as a result, the management emphasis had been on sales generation to cover the rather substantial overhead.

My challenge was to refocus the division's resources and energies into more productive and successful patterns. I became convinced that we should stop running and pushing products in favor of returning to a more comprehensive marketing stance. We had to put major emphasis on analyzing consumer needs, to identify or develop products to satisfy those needs. We had to improve communications to the consumer that the product was available and superior in meeting his needs. Measurement of our success would then shift from sales volume shipped to distributors and focus on consumer awareness and retail take-off.

I also decided the division should concentrate on fewer products with higher profitability potential and higher volume potential across the countries. This meant encouraging our overseas operating units to reduce the number of low-volume and low-margin items in their product line, to shift away from price-controlled categories, and to consider

introducing products that were highly successful in other markets. It has become something of a slogan that "we can't afford one-market products or one-product markets." This required that we become proficient in the transfer of strategy and expertise among the markets.

To bring about these changes, we had to introduce significant improvements in our organization and management practices.

Clearly, we needed to delegate more responsibility for key managerial decisions, especially in marketing, to our operating units, but we lacked the focus, discipline, and procedural mechanisms to assure that such delegation would produce positive results.

John Steiger joined the division as finance director shortly thereafter and went to work on improving and systematizing our financial reporting and planning practices. Even before that, I had started working on ways to bring more rigor and discipline to our marketing activities in line with the new view of our business strategy. I set up the headquarters marketing departments to help me manage this new approach. The essence of the approach is reflected in a memo I issued in 1976, which formalized a classification of our products into three categories, each of which we had found to require different management approaches. The first, which we call "development products," are those that are not currently being sold in commercial volume in any of our markets but promise to be winners. The main job of the HQ marketing directors is to assure that enough of these products are successfully introduced and spread throughout the division to provide us growth in future years. In the jargon of our management system, the development product program is "prime moved" by our HQ marketing directors.

Commercial products are those currently marketed successfully in several regions. They provide the bulk of our current business, but we have to watch their product life cycle and be especially wary of declining profitability in price-controlled markets under the pressure of cost inflation. Our HQ staff plays only a supporting role in the management of these products, with the Prime Movers being in the overseas operating units.

Nondivisional products are those associated with only one market, with unknown or no potential for expansion to others (our insecticide line in Australia is a good example). We want our people overseas who handle these products to make them fully self-supportive while meeting our policies and standards. If they can't, we must divest the products. Generally, they cannot rely on division resources, and support for these products that they themselves provide must not divert their own resources or attention from the expansion of profitable commercial products and the introduction of promising development products.

Given the diversity of our markets and of the local personnel working in each of them (see Exhibit 1 for LA/FE organization chart) as well as the inherent difficulties in obtaining timely information flows that would allow markets to learn from each other and HQ staff to provide adequate support, we have developed a set of elaborate, formalized, and rather standardized management procedures. Through them we have been trying to professionalize our management and clarify the relationship between the various country operations and the headquarters' departments.

Vick International, LA/FE's CP-R Management System

Vick International, LA/FE employed an extensive formalized system of planning and control to direct and coordinate its widely scattered operating units. The system, known affectionately as CP-R (continuous planning and review), was not put in place all at once. McGuire built up the division's management capacity piece by piece over a period of several years. He moved management personnel around to make better use of talent. He brought in additional help, especially in the marketing management area. He worked closely with his headquarters staff to develop an all-encompassing marketing methodology, which could be applied consistently throughout the division and serve as a link for coordination with other functions. He worked individually with each manager reporting directly to him to develop a mutual understanding about the nature of managers' responsibilities. He knew that, as the division grew, effective delegation of decision making to the appropriate levels would be indis-

pensable. To assist in making this possible and to improve coordination, he established a work-role assignment process. And to energize the division, he instituted a series of periodic management meetings tied to a detailed planning and review system that looked backward 12 months and forward three years, with a complete update every quarter.

Over the years, the division gained substantial experience with the various components of this process. Eventually, much of it became formalized in a series of manuals: the Product Marketing Guides, the Manager's Guides, and the Planning and Review Guides.

McGuire

The key to our management process is its thoroughness, combined with its flexibility. Take the Marketing Guides, for example. For each of our major products we develop a guide, which includes eight separate documents. The first two, the Product Profile Statement (PMG-1) and the Product Marketing Policy (PMG-2), are developed by one of the marketing directors and his staff at division headquarters as a standardized blueprint for the product across the division. They serve as a basis for planning the expansion or introduction of the product in a market.

The Product Data Book (PMG-3) and Product Marketing Assessment Statement (PMG-4) are developed by each regional or country unit handling or interested in introducing the product, to assess its appropriateness and potential in the local market. The regional market managing director is assigned the Approver role for the PMG-3; but, because of its strategic importance, the PMG-4 is approved by the division president. The assessment in these two documents includes the discussion of reasons for deviations from the policies or standards set for the products in PMGs 1 and 2, if any are deemed necessary.

The remaining PMG documents, covering specific aspects of marketing, advertising, promotion, and sales and distribution strategy in a given market, are put together to refine the assessment of the feasibility of the product in that market, and then

EXHIBIT 1 Division Organization Structure

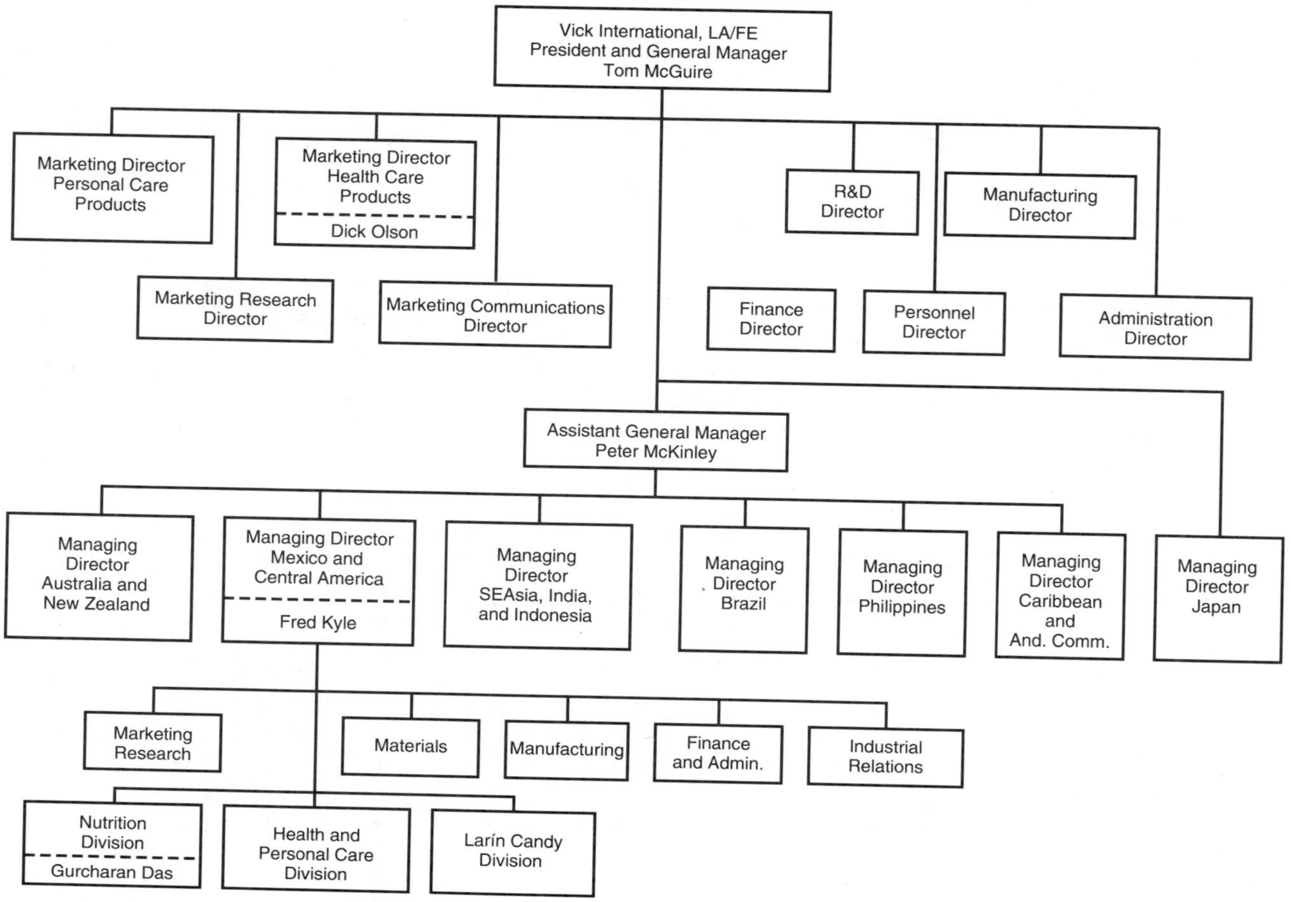

Vick International, LA/FE
President and General Manager
Tom McGuire

- Marketing Director Personal Care Products
- Marketing Director Health Care Products — Dick Olson
  - Marketing Research Director
  - Marketing Communications Director
- R&D Director
- Manufacturing Director
  - Finance Director
  - Personnel Director
  - Administration Director

Assistant General Manager
Peter McKinley

- Managing Director Australia and New Zealand
- Managing Director Mexico and Central America — Fred Kyle
  - Marketing Research
  - Materials
  - Manufacturing
  - Finance and Admin.
  - Industrial Relations
  - Nutrition Division — Gurcharan Das
  - Health and Personal Care Division
  - Larín Candy Division
- Managing Director SEAsia, India, and Indonesia
- Managing Director Brazil
- Managing Director Philippines
- Managing Director Caribbean and And. Comm.
- Managing Director Japan

Reproduction of original company document.

to serve as the basis for the management of the product once it is introduced.

The elaboration of each PMG document must be preceded by extensive research work. This might involve analysis of market conditions, product development, consumer attitude surveys, packaging design and testing, and so forth. Once the PMG package has been completed for a given product in a given market, however, all the pertinent results of this work are brought together in one place and are available for assessment and reference by managers throughout the division.

As one of our product managers at HQ, who has had substantial field experience, likes to say, "The PMG system doesn't let you take anything for granted. We are forced to go through all the steps and, as a result, we don't make those mistakes that used to slip by when we tried to finesse a difficult part of the marketing planning process." But, at the same time, each overseas operating unit is free to adapt the product policy to its own circumstances, giving us substantial built-in flexibility. And each exception to standard practice is thus made explicit.

The marketing management process is embedded within a wider planning and review process, through which we obtain agreement on business financial objectives and functional operational objectives for each regional or country market, and between those markets and the division headquarters. These objectives in turn are tied to explicitly formulated strategic objectives for each unit and the division as a whole.

The process also provides procedures for the continuing review, analysis, testing, and reporting of performance and progress toward achieving division and market objectives and standards. We have found it necessary to break with RMI's traditional annual planning and budgeting cycle. It isn't dynamic enough for our markets, nor does it take a systematic enough look at the prospects for three, four, and five years out. So we have opted for our own system, which calls for quarterly updates and includes the prior year, the current year, and the next three years.

Once operational objectives are set, we use succinct but explicit Work Programs following a standard format. These serve to draw together from all involved parts of the organization the information required so that we can view each program as a whole. This lets us test and evaluate the risk/cost/benefit relationship of the operational objective and the Work Program for its achievement. We can also assure efficient use and timing of resources and identify conflicts between the demands of various Work Programs for limited resources.

The Work Programs, of course, quickly multiply. They can cover objectives related to development products and commercial products within various markets. They can touch on issues of personnel development, improving inventory management, building new facilities, managing an acquisition or divestment, and so on and so forth. The roles our managers are called upon to play will vary from one Work Program to another. As a result, we have found it indispensable to devise a mechanism for keeping our wires untangled. We assign all concerned parties a specific role in each Work Program, Action Plan, or other formal CP-R scheduling document. The four roles are: Approver, Prime Mover, Concurrer, and Contributor. The terms are all positive by design. We want to get things done, not get them hung up.

The Prime Mover, as the name implies, is the manager with the action. Quite frequently he will be at a third or fourth level in our hierarchy. This allows us to get around the rigidity of a chain of command and recognize the important and indispensable contribution to be made by those who actually push the work to its completion.

The Approver is a higher-level manager than the Prime Mover—frequently, but not always, his immediate superior. His job is to assure that the measures taken by the Prime Mover are in line with division policies and overall objectives. And especially in the case of relatively inexperienced Prime Movers, the Approver will take care to see that serious mistakes, which might damage the division or the subordinate's career, are avoided.

Concurrers, of which there can be more than one on any given job, supply technical or specialized judgment to the Prime Mover. Their agreement is necessary prior to the implementation of any decision involving their area of expertise, although unresolvable disagreements can be referred to higher management. This perhaps is the one area where we still have to learn to do the job better. There is at times a tendency for concurrers to behave as vetoers rather than as positive collaborators. But by making the roles explicit, we find that such behavior becomes visible and can be dealt with.

I personally find the work-role assignment process very valuable. By nature I am inclined to get involved in the details of every task. But now that the roles are formally specified, it has become commonplace for some of my directors to remind me to stay off their turf when I start getting too involved. There are days when I will be with one of them in two successive meetings in which our formally assigned roles change. It really helps us change gears.

Dick Olson also found the CP-R management system of much help. As marketing director for Health Care Products, he had several hats to wear and many markets to work with. Olson had been with RMI for 15 years since receiving his MBA from Cornell. Most of his career so far had been within the marketing function with the Vicks domestic Health Care Division. He had been in his present job for the last three years.

Olson

I have enjoyed this job very much. While some people might find it difficult to move from the less formally structured management process in a domestic division to LA/FE with its CP-R system, I have found it invigorating. Tom is a great guy to work for. He is bright, competent, and has a very professional approach to management. He has involved me deeply in the development and refinement of the division's marketing management approach and the techniques and procedures needed to carry it out. These are brought together in the PMG process.

Working with Tom on the elaboration of my Manager's Guide has made it possible to see where I can concentrate my efforts most productively for the division. It also has helped me see where my actions and those of my department affect the outcomes of other units and in what ways we are dependent on them.

As I see, it, I have three main responsibilities. First, as part of Tom's management team, I help him as he feels the need on a broad set of general issues along with the other division headquarters directors. Then, more specifically, I assist him in the development of the marketing function throughout the division in the Health Care area.

Second, I am responsible for the adequate functioning of the division's activities aimed at business development in the health care field, including, more recently, nutritional products. My staff and I look for new ideas or products both from our people abroad and from outside the division or even outside the company. We undertake projects on our own to translate some of these ideas into physical products backed by a marketing strategy and marketing materials that can be tested in a trial market. Then we get the cooperation of one of our overseas units to test and launch it.

For example, just over a year ago the Australian Board of Health relaxed limitations on the advertisement of liquid cold remedies. Australia saw this as an opportunity for itself, and we saw it as a good opportunity for the division, especially as we had indications that similar policy changes were in the making in some other countries in our half of the world. At division headquarters we pooled information worldwide on RMI's capabilities in this area. Working with our Australian marketing staff, we did some consumer survey work. Out of this we concluded that NyQuil, which was being sold successfully in the United States and Europe, had promising potential. We then drew up a plan that would allow us to launch the product successfully in Australia within nine months. Members of my department and I, as well as other HQ staff members, traveled to Sydney several times during the subsequent months working very closely with, and providing assistance to, our local people out there. It required a concentrated joint effort, but we were successful in launching the product, which we call "MediNite" in that market, within the time period specified. We beat the competition into the market by several weeks. We used the PMG process very successfully as an aid in getting all the pieces together, and the CP-R process helped get all the actors collaborating in a timely fashion.

Manufacturing and marketing MediNite in Australia is now primarily the responsibility of our people out there, although in our third role as a resource department on marketing we will continue to be available to assist our people in Australia if and when they need it.

Back to the issue of business development: when our overseas units have a substantial nondivision business segment, which warrants product development as part of its long-term strategy, we allow them to develop such products within our policies, procedures, and standards, and try to support them in every way we can. The PMG system provides us with regular feedback reports, and through it we are assured that a thorough review is made of all aspects of the product that could make it successful or cause it to flounder. Several of our units, especially Australia, Mexico, and India, are strong in new product development, but they still each have some shortcomings. We try to capitalize on their strengths by letting them take a lot of initiative and operate quite independently, while we remain available to help whenever it's needed.

This job allows me to act both as a marketing staff director and as an operating director for the new product development program. This is challenging and personally satisfying. I know that my counterpart for Personal Care Products feels the same way. It is what attracted him to come to RMI. It would be nearly impossible to carry out this dual role without the work-role assignment approach of the CP-R system. Since it started being used regularly in the division, the amount of wasted time and effort has dropped considerably. Delays in communication between the field and headquarters have also been reduced substantially.

Fred Kyle, managing director in Mexico since 1974, while committed to the CP-R system, was less enthusiastic about it. Of his 20 years with RMI, he had spent about half in manufacturing and marketing management, first with Vicks domestic and then with International. For the last 10 years, he had held various field management positions in Latin America.

Kyle

CP-R certainly has a lot going for it, but it does cause us some problems. The quarterly management review meetings are tremendously helpful. We get a lot of problems resolved and are able to adjust our objectives often enough to keep an even keel in a very volatile political and economic environment. But there is an overload of paper work. My financial director has to keep records for me under the CP-R system; but since we also service the Mexican office of Merrell International, he has to follow a different set-up for them.

And then there is the language barrier. Most of our Mexican management people have a working knowledge of English; but we conduct our business in Spanish and, as a result, they find it hard to tune in to the CP-R system, which is all in English. Some of the terminology can't even be translated. Then of course there is a cultural barrier in almost all LA/FE overseas locations. Some are not comfortable with such explicitly assigned responsibilities—with everyone's performance open to the general view, especially if they are accustomed to use a more personalized form of supervision.

We are trying to apply the CP-R system to our operations, but so far it has been more difficult than we anticipated. However, I feel it will be worth all the effort.

Some of our managers feel CP-R is really an extension of Tom McGuire, that he makes it work by pure willpower, and they're sure we are all the better for it. The division's performance certainly has improved. In part it's a big advantage, but in part it may be a drawback that Tom knows so much about our market and our operations. He has a tendency to get too involved from time to time in the details of running our business. Maybe Mexico is a special case. He spent 18 months here in 1964–65 as director.

Return on equity for Vick International during 1973–78 was as follows: 1973, 13.5 percent; 1974, 15.4 percent; 1975, 18.5 percent; 1976, 24.2 percent; 1977, 28.5 percent; 1978, 27.3 percent.

Project Alpha

Mexico was the largest operating entity within LA/FE and had concentrated traditionally on proprietary drugs. In 1964, it entered the nutrition field with the acquisition of ChocoMilk, a well-established brand of powdered milk supplement with an existing distribution network. Consisting mainly of powdered milk, chocolate, and sugar, ChocoMilk provided nutritional reinforcement as well as flavoring. It took several years to modernize the production facilities, improve the formula to suit changing tastes and meet several competitive entries, and develop the management capacity to deal with this new market. One of the main stumbling blocks was the absence of a reliable source of supply for high-quality chocolate that would make it possible to upgrade the product. This was achieved in 1966 with the acquisition of the Larín Candy Company, one of Vick's major chocolate suppliers. Now local management faced a new set of challenges. Not only did it have to proceed with the upgrading and expansion of ChocoMilk, but it also had to learn to manage the specialty candy business into which it had entered. It took several more years for both tasks to be accomplished.

When Fred Kyle became managing director in Mexico in 1974, one of his early concerns was to strengthen the ChocoMilk segment of the business. It seemed risky to have such an important segment relying on only one product, which already dominated its market with a 50 percent market share, and which was under considerable competitive pressure. Secondly, the traditional proprietary drug business continued to be price controlled, offering negative prospects for improved profitability. Additional entries into the nutrition field appeared to be worth serious consideration.

After consultation with division headquarters, Kyle commissioned a study of potential entries for the Mexican nutritional product market. The study was carried out by the marketing research department in Mexico with assistance from a New York consulting firm in 1975–1976. The study took an exhaustive look at food items sold in grocery stores in Mexico, the United States, and Canada, to identify categories of consumer needs for which solutions were sought through processed foods sold in food stores. Then surveys were carried out with panels of Mexican housewives to learn their underlying concerns regarding each class of needs. Out of this emerged a slate of product concepts for development and testing. These were screened for feasibility as products for Vick Mexico.

At a divisional management meeting in August of 1976, the results of the study were presented, along with a final slate of potential new products for development and market testing. The slate was approved, as was an overall new product development program. A target was set to test market at least one new product from the slate each year. Product Alpha was the first new item on the slate.

Gurcharan Das was assigned in October of 1976 to become director of Vick Mexico's newly established Nutrition Division, responsible for the ongoing ChocoMilk business and the new nutritional product development program. He already had a track record of successful development and introduction of new products with Vick International's Indian subsidiary.

A philosophy major at Harvard College, Das had decided after graduation to look for opportunities in business management that would allow him to return to India, use his creative energies, and still have time for personal development as a thinker and writer. He found the opportunity with RMI, which he joined in 1963. In 1976, Das was offered the choice of joining the division's Health Care Products marketing department to work on new product development, or to take the job in Mexico.

Das

I decided to go to Mexico because I wanted to be close to the market, where the action is. I wanted to have responsibility for all the facets of product development, testing, and launching. I like to have control over my piece of the business and to be judged by the results I achieve. It allows me to exercise my creative energies. I guess I have an entrepreneurial spirit.

Alpha was Das's first challenge in this new position. The product was aimed at a felt need of the Mexican mother for a quick, easy, yet nourishing beverage for use on hectic school days. Over the next 18 months Das worked intensively with a technical group in the ChocoMilk plant to develop a suitable product. He also enlisted the help of the marketing research department to carry out extensive product concept research with potential users. During this period there was little interaction with headquarters staff, other than routine communication of progress and occasional inputs from the division research and development director on issues of product quality.

No formal Work Program was drawn up. Nonetheless, Vick Mexico did have extensive internal plans and schedules, including a PERT-type plan for Alpha. Since it was a totally new product with which the HQ staff had no familiarity, there were no PMG-1 and PMG-2. Kyle and Das considered Alpha a nondivisional product like ChocoMilk, for which they were responsible.

In January of 1978, Das contracted with a Mexico City advertising agency to start developing material for use in the first market tests later that year. He had another contractor develop an innovative container for Alpha.

With the time approaching to make initial commitments for market testing, it was necessary to obtain overall division management approval of the project's current status and direction. A meeting for this purpose was planned for early May. In preparation for this meeting, the PMGs 3, 4, 5, 6, 7, and 8 were completed in late April and sent to headquarters personnel for their review.

By separating the PMG into various documents, the CP-R system made it possible to assign different work roles to various individuals for each piece. While PMGs 1 and 2 were primarily the work of headquarters staff, the remaining parts required substantial collaboration between headquarters and field. The Approver role for the PMG-3 was assigned to the regional managing director, with the Prime Mover, Concurrers, and Contributors coming from the local

staff. The PMGs 4 and 5, which were key strategy documents, required the approval of the division president and the concurrence of several headquarters directors, as well as overseas unit functional managers. PMGs 6, 7, and 8, which usually were prepared after 4 and 5 had been approved, usually could be approved by the division assistant general manager with concurrence only from the headquarters director with specific functional expertise in each case.

With the Alpha PMG, however, because all six parts arrived at the same time, the package was reviewed as a unit by all the potential Concurrers and Approvers. Dick Olson, as Prime Mover for the overall Development Product program, became the focal point for the review at HQ.

In studying the PMG documents on Product Alpha, Olson was surprised to see it classified as a nondivisional product. Nonetheless he felt that an excellent job had been done in the area of product concept research, product development in the lab, and assessment of market potential. Reactions from other headquarters departments were similarly supportive, with a few technical suggestions for improvement. The material on marketing strategy and advertising, however, was very spotty and failed to take full advantage of the marketing research.

During the next several weeks Das made three trips to division headquarters in the hope of getting the necessary approvals to proceed with a test market launch of Alpha. After the first meeting in May, Tom McGuire approved the Alpha program and the PMG-4 in principle. It was agreed that Mexico would undertake several technical improvements having to do with packaging, labeling, and product quality, as well as obtain some additional information on potential users. McGuire also asked Das to review PMGs 5 through 8 with Olson after the meeting, since extensive comment had been made about their adequacy. At this point a Work Program was prepared.

For the first time, Das became aware that an MC-1 (a CP-R document designed to provide an advertising agency with guidance for developing advertising material) would be required, and that for Development Products the MC-1 had to be approved by the division president and concurred with by assistant general manager Peter McKinley, Dick Olson, and the marketing communications director.

In June, Das returned with a draft MC-1 and a package of advertising material that he wished to use in the test launch. He needed various concurrences and approval from headquarters management in order to proceed. Dick Olson and the marketing communications director had previously reviewed the material and made some suggestions for improvement. When Das met with Tom McGuire for approval, he found that Tom thought basic changes in the market positioning of Alpha, implicit in the advertising copy, would be necessary. He suggested that Das return to Mexico and revise the PMG-5, PMG-6, and MC-1, in line with their discussion. He should then submit the MC-1 to headquarters for approval which, Tom promised, would be forthcoming within 48 hours. To assure a quick turnaround, he delegated the Approver role jointly to McKinley and Olson.

Das was crushed. He told McGuire that he felt let down by the whole system. How could it be that, after getting professional inputs from the agency in Mexico, approval in principle of the PMG, and comments about the advertising copy from headquarters staff that had been incorporated into the material, a major flaw should come out in a meeting with the division president? And with every passing day the project was falling further behind schedule.

Upon returning to Mexico, Das revised the MC-1 and sent it to division HQ in early July. A week later he received a request from Olson to come to the United States for a meeting to get the MC-1 approved. In late July that meeting took place. The PMG-5, PMG-6, and MC-1 were jointly rewritten. Then all Concurrers and the Approvers initialed the MC-1 document. Das returned to Mexico to have the agency prepare storyboards for TV ads. He had instructions to return to headquarters with these for approval in late August.

Prior to his departure for the mid-August quarterly review meeting, Fred Kyle, who had been away for six weeks at a management education program, had a long discussion with Gurcharan about the Alpha project.

Kyle

Gurcharan was very unhappy. He had worked for a year and a half getting Alpha off the ground. He had been successful in getting our Mexican R&D, marketing research, manufacturing, and other staff departments involved and excited. They were all committed to a tightly programmed project schedule and had produced truly innovative top-quality results. We were convinced that we had identified a project with very significant potential.

After moving along so well, however, we are now running into trouble. While the difficulties focus on Alpha, it is really the entire nutritional new product program that is at stake. The establishment of such a program had been attempted without success ever since the acquisition of ChocoMilk in 1964. I had taken a different approach from my predecessors and, after four years of work with the entire Mexican organization and with the full knowledge of division management, appeared to be achieving results.

To succeed, however, our people need to be free to take risks, to move quickly, to be entrepreneurial, and to feel that they will be judged on their results. The way the CP-R process is being applied is making this extremely difficult.

I hope at the quarterly meeting we can work out some way of maintaining our present momentum and of providing the freedom and flexibility we need to ensure the continued progress of our whole nutritional new product program.

QUESTIONS

1. What strategy is McGuire pursuing for his division? What are the key success factors in this business? What critical tasks must be accomplished to achieve success?

2. What is your appraisal of the role Olson played in the introduction of MediNite in Australia?

3. Identify the major elements of the planning and control systems that McGuire has established. Why has he installed these systems? What is your evaluation of the effectiveness of his approach?

4. Who is to blame for the delay in introducing Alpha? Why did McGuire punish Das in this situation?

5. Under what circumstances would the systems used by McGuire be particularly useful?

6. What are the limitations of such systems?

Case 13–3

Texas Instruments*

Texas Instruments (TI) is a multinational corporation producing a wide variety of products having some tie to the electronics industry. In addition to its U.S. plants, TI maintains facilities in Canada, Latin America, Europe, Australia, and the Far East. TI's growth has been based on innovations as opposed to acquisitions. The company grew at an average rate of approximately 25 percent per year until 1980. At that time its sales growth slowed. 1980 sales of $4.1 billion grew to only $4.6 billion in 1983. In the early 1980s the company's line management structure was divided into six groups: semiconductor products, distributed computing, consumer electronics, materials and electrochemicals, government electronics, and geophysical exploration services. In charge of each group was a senior manager who reported directly to the president. These top-level managers were responsible for worldwide strategic direction of their businesses as well as for the regular daily management functions. Each group was further divided into divisions, which were in turn broken down into product customer centers (PCCs).

By 1980, there were some 80 PCCs in the company. A PCC was considered to be a complete business unit responsible for a particular family of products or services targeted at a specific market segment. The structure had come into being because of the interrelationships between divisions and groups. Many of the groups within TI were natural customers for each other. Further, the development of any new product or service to be marketed by TI was likely to require the coordinated cooperation of several of these six groups.

The PCCs were the focal point of operations, embodying the TI philosophy that the company "exists to create, make, and market useful products and services to satisfy the needs of its customers." Each PCC was to "create," "make," and "market" products and services for a specific set of customers. The number and orientation of these basic operating units changed as TI's businesses evolved. When possible, PCCs with common markets, technologies, or customers were clustered together into divisions within the operating groups. However, this was not always possible. PCCs varied in size from a few million dollars to some 80 million dollars in sales. PCCs' performance was evaluated on the basis of profits, return on assets, and current operating plans.

The OST System

The OST system was a conscious attempt by TI's management to understand its early successes and to manage the processes of innovation based upon those successes. In its early history, TI had found out that with very limited resources it could outmaneuver large laboratories (like Bell Labs., RCA, GE, etc.). In the words of Patrick Hagerty, president and later CEO of TI, "This worked because we'd just go out and try to *do* something, rather than keep it in the laboratory. We might not understand all the reasons why it worked, we may have had to do some of it just

* Copyright © by James Brian Quinn. Major sections of the case are based on the Texas Instruments case prepared by Richard F. Vancil.

Copyright © by the President and Fellows of Harvard College.

empirically; but we'd try to make something real out of it.'' Hagerty believed in setting aggressive goals—''to make the organizations strive for something, to push and motivate people.'' Hagerty described the OST system as ''an attempt to make explicit the company's longer-range goals, strategic objectives, and shorter-term tactics to achieve them. Unless someone is paying attention to this kind of planning, day to day crises consume all a manager's attention.''

Mr. S. T. Harris, member of the board, said:

To handle growth and increasing complexity, the organization decentralizes into groups, divisions, departments, and branches. The total job becomes divided up and cut into sized pieces that a good administrative manager can get his arms around. This is logical and good management practice. But unless the general managers understand their jobs thoroughly, the company is in danger of becoming no more than the sum total of its decentralized parts. . . . Although the organization as a whole might have far more of the tools, opportunity, and skilled people needed for innovation, the perspective of any one manager can be restricted. He can simply fail to see larger opportunities and to solve problems of the right scale for the whole corporation.

Objectives

Mr. Grant A. Dove, vice president for corporate development of Texas Instruments, described the OST system in the following terms:

The OST system amounted to a statement of goals and the plans for achieving those goals at the appropriate level in the organization. The goals expressed in OST formed a structure, or hierarchy, beginning with the corporate objective and extending downward to Business Objectives and Strategies and finally Tactics. [see Exhibit 1].

Our Corporate Objective states the economic purposes, the reasons for existence of the organization. It also states in broad terms, our product, market, and technical goals. It defines our responsibilities to our employees, our shareholders, our community, and to society as a whole. And it es-

tablishes the financial goals by which we measure our contribution to the economic development of society.

The Corporate Objective is supported by a set of Business Objectives. Each of these is expressed in terms of (1) a business charter, which establishes the boundaries of the business; (2) an appraisal of the potential opportunities we perceive in this business; (3) a study of the technical and marketing trends; and (4) the overall competitive structure of the industries serving this business.

The Corporate Objective tended to look out 5–10 years in a challenging fashion. Expectations for the first two years were broken down into quarters, the others were in annual terms. Mr. Dove continued:

We carefully evaluate the competition, the threats, and contingencies we might have to meet, market shifts we might anticipate, and attempt to evaluate what we must make happen in order to achieve success of the objective. The ranking of these key factors provides a priority list for future management attention. We expect the objective to be challenging enough, even shocking enough, to force a radical rethinking of all the strategies and tactics [supporting it]. . . . Any time we have enough well-defined strategies to give us a high confidence level in exceeding the goals stated in a Business Objective, then that Business Objective is probably not ambitious enough, and the probability of truly innovative strategic thinking is likely to be low.

Business Objectives focus on a limited field of opportunity, its potential technical and market trends, and the competitive industry structure associated with it. Performance measures at this level are specific goals for financial factors—like sales, market share, profit, and return on assets—for 5 and 10 years out. Any Business Objective must be consistent and compatible with the Corporate Objective and with the underlying philosophy it represents. For each Business Objective there was a business objective manager.

Strategies and Tactics

Following is a composite view of the remainder of the OST system derived from various sources.

EXHIBIT 1   Texas Instruments' OST System

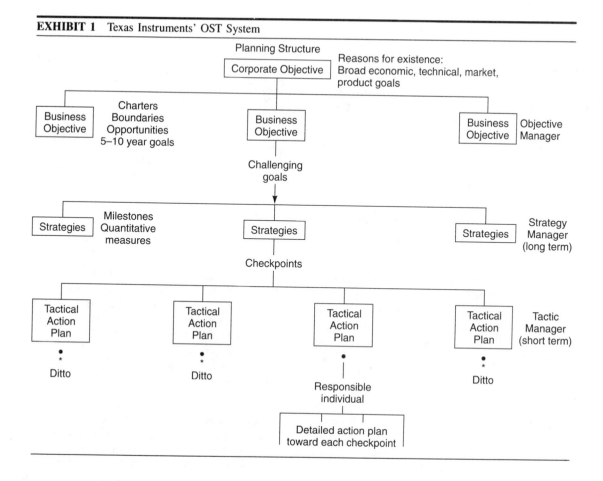

At the next level in the structure was a Strategy Statement. The strategy described in detail the environment of the business opportunity to be pursued in support of the objective. Normally there would be several strategies supporting each objective. For example, if TI had an objective to achieve certain goals in the automobile market, it might have one strategy involving automobile electronics, one involving material applications, and perhaps others for safety systems, control systems, etc. The strategy looked ahead for a number of years—normally 5–10—and established intermediate checkpoints to provide milestones against which to judge progress. Progress measurement is an element of a strategy not included at the objectives level. But the contribution of a strategy to the overall objective was defined in quantitative measures and a critique was formulated to assign a success probability to the strategy. Each strategy was assigned to a strategy manager.

Next in the goal hierarchy, was the Tactical Action Program or TAP. A TAP was a detailed action plan of the steps necessary to reach the major long-range checkpoints defined by the strategies. It was normally short run, covering 6–18 months. For each TAP, a "responsible individual" was designated, a start and finish schedule

EXHIBIT 2 Matrix of Plans

			Group 1			Group 2					
			Div. A		Div. B	Div. C	Div. D		Div. E		6 Groups
O	S	T	PCC	PCC	PCC	PCC	PCC	PCC	PCC	PCC	20 Divisions
		1	X		X	X					80 Product
	A	2	X			X		X			customer
		3		X			X	X			centers
		4				X				X	
1		1			X		X				Matrix
	B	2		X	X		X		X		
		3	X				X			X	

established, and the required resources defined. Within the TAP, specific individuals were defined as responsible for achieving each milestone. Exhibit 1 diagrams the relationship among objectives, strategies, tactics, and milestones.

One way to visualize this complex structure was a matrix with the traditional organizational units across the top and the OST structure along the left margin. (See Exhibit 2.) However, unlike the typical matrix organization, the OST system expressed a relationship between a strategic mode and an operating mode *within* the same organization.

One of the roles of a strategy manager was to identify the TAPs required to accomplish the strategy (represented by the Xs in the matrix) and to pull these together across the company into a coordinated strategic plan. Many times the strategy manager was also the manager of a PCC, especially if one PCC would have a dominant role in the strategy. Nearly always, the strategy or tactic manager would also have an operating role to play. Only in rare cases would the strategy manager or tactic manager have that job as his full-time assignment. Frequently, an objective manager would also be a division manager—although this was not always the case. Said Mr. Dove:

> This provides a goal structure for strategic as well as operating activities. Not only can we measure

profit-and-loss performance operationally, we can also allocate resources through the OST structure and measure our progress toward the strategic goals. Now, new ideas have a home. They can be given resources for further development, and if progress warrants, heavier support later. . . . New ideas can be clearly a part of the OST structure and be recognized and supported by deliberate choice. They do not have to be bootlegged, nor can they be dropped completely through a crack. . . . The strategic mode gives us a mechanism for large-scale opportunities or those requiring combinations of resources not found in a single unit. It gives us a mechanism for planning and controlling our investments for the future and for making sure that we do achieve the desired balance of priorities between short-term and long-term activities.

Strategic expenditures were discretionary as far as the current year's business went. They were project—rather than level-of-effort oriented—and had a long-term emphasis. All OST programs and funding were intended to make a definite change in TI's business. OST programs had definite directions, beginning, intermediate milestones, and ends. TI's internal accounting treated OST expenditures apart from ordinary operating expenditures. Managers were evaluated on both their operating responsibilities and OST responsibilities. Because funds were separated and earmarked with milestones, targets, dates (etc.), "strategic performance could be readily assessed."

OST programs were approved yearly by the Growth Committee at the top level of the organization. This occurred at a strategic planning conference each year when some 500 top TI managers from around the world came together for a week of strategic planning. The Growth Committee had some 13 permanent members, including the president, group vice presidents, and other officers reporting at the corporate level. The committee met about 18 times a year for a full day, in addition to the annual meeting. At each meeting there was a rigorous reexamination of at least one Business Objective, or consideration of a major new business opportunity. In addition, managers of key strategies or tactics frequently met with the Growth Committee for progress reviews or reports. In the early 1980s, TI tended to have some 9–10 Business Objectives, some 50–60 strategies, and more than 250 TAPs.

In essence, TI had two budgets for the year, one for OST funds and the other for operating expenses. Expenditures associated with each category appeared as separate distinct lines on the P/L statement for each unit. Zero-base budgeting was applied to the allocation of OST dollars. The OST package was allocated among objectives, then to strategies and to TAPs. The balance between OST expenses and operating expenses was a top-level, long-term/short-term trade-off. The key principle was that operating profit, as measured before OST expenditures, had to meet certain standards for each business. The size of the OST pot was influenced strongly by the expected total operating profit. The entire OST pool was not allocated to objective managers at the beginning of the year. The Growth Committee retained approximately 10 percent of it as a fund for subsequent use and for new opportunities. The use of OST funds also could be modified during the year by managers at any of the three key levels. A TAP manager was permitted to change the nature of his activity on his own discretion as long as it did not change the tactical goal which he was committed to achieve. The same was true at the strategy or objective manager level.

Incentive Compensation System

An important part of the OST system was the Key Personnel Analysis (KPA). KPA made an annual comparative assessment of individual executives. It divided all executives into five comparative rating groups and eventually made a paired comparison based upon their contributions during the current year for both strategic and operational purposes. Each comparative rating group contained 20 percent of its total organization. The process began at departmental levels and continued to division and group levels. Within each 20 percent group, individuals were compared with other individuals in that group, and rank-ordered on the basis of their relative performance and contribution. Incentive bonuses and rewards were based on the rankings which resulted. The KPA systems created a competitive environment within the company, which executives thought was constructive. Many different executives within the individuals' group would rank them on the basis of both their strategic and operating performance each year. Both annual bonuses and participation in stock option plans were related to this rating. In contrast to operating expenses, it was often considered desirable to have spent the full amount of the budgeted strategic expense category, indicating adequate attention to the future.

People and Asset Effectiveness

Starting in the early 1970s, TI established its P&AE program. These were set up much like OST programs—with specific objectives, strategies, and tactics to achieve them. P&AE programs focused attention and funding on efficiency-improving activities for all company resources. Each Business Objective had its own funds, and money was allocated within the objective to P&AE programs that were unique to that Business Objective. A central P&AE Committee allocated funds to programs that could have corporate wide impact across all Business Objectives—such as energy conservation, management information systems, or manufacturing automation programs important to virtually every business objective manager. The OST program took care of growth, new products, and market positioning, while P&AE programs provided for the innovations needed to improve the productivity of people or assets in the business. TI had Intra Company Objectives for ''people and asset effectiveness'' and managed these activities just as it did other growth ventures. TI measured productivity as a percentage return on assets per person employed and aimed for a 10–12 percent goal. Increasing capital investment was seen as a major productivity-maximizing strategy to compete with lower labor costs elsewhere in the world. Investments in automated design and manufacturing capabilities were a major focus.

The IDEA System

The IDEA (identify, develop, expose, action) program provided opportunities for initial feasibility demonstration of concepts that did not fit within immediate OST thrusts. The IDEA system was regarded as ''a supplement to OST.''

As TI grew in size, its top management felt an increasing distance between potential innovators and the decision makers who could commit resources to make their innovations into realities. The IDEA system was designed to forge a missing link into the innovation chain. Its acronym represented the process TI saw as necessary to turn a raw idea into a commercial innovation. *Identify* the idea as having potential commercial value. *Develop* the idea far enough to provide sufficient information on which a management commitment could be based. *Expose* the developed idea directly to a group that had the authority to commit necessary resources. *Initiate Action* by feeding the newly funded idea into the OST system for development and eventual commercialization.

Although most IDEA projects were technically oriented, they could encompass any facet of the business. But IDEA projects had to be oriented toward step advances, rather than evolutionary improvements. An IDEA project was intended to be only four to six months in span and require very limited funding. The funding was to be used by the originator only for buying the necessary services and materials to demonstrate the project. The IDEA originator could not charge his own time to the project. The originator was asked to prepare a memorandum proposing the approach, impact, or application of the idea, an estimate of project expenditures and their designated use; the estimated time for accomplishing the task; and what its end result would be (demonstration model, paper analysis, etc.). IDEA executives were designated in each division. However, the originator could take his concept to the IDEA person in *any* division or even contact more than one IDEA person for support. If the IDEA person thought the idea had merit, (s)he merely called Corporate Development to coordinate whether (1) the project was similar to others in Texas Instruments and (2) it fit the general business interests of the corporation. Once cleared, Corporate Development could release funds for the project almost immediately. And a follow-up procedure was developed directly with the responsible IDEA person.

QUESTIONS

This case is designed to examine three interrelated topics: *(a)* a somewhat unique approach to planning and control; *(b)* an explicit set of procedures designed to deal with the long-term versus short-term trade-off; and *(c)* the interrelationships among the entire set of management systems in a complex organization.

In a sense, this is a hard case because it does not have a sharp issue that must be resolved. Rather, your task is to "appreciate" the company's management systems and then to step back, somewhat philosophically, and try to fit the company's approach into your own framework about the situational design of planning and control systems. The following assignment questions might help to get you started in that direction.

1. Summarize the major features of Texas Instruments' management systems. To what extent are these systems mutually reinforcing? To what extent do these systems reinforce the company's strategy?
2. How does Texas Instruments ensure that its operating managers appropriately allocate their time between short term and long term?
3. Why do you believe the OST system worked so effectively for TI in the 70s? Why is it not working effectively for the company in the mid-to-late 80s?

Case 13–4
Litton Industries*

In the late summer of 1953, three young men quit their high-paying jobs with Hughes Aircraft (where they had helped push sales from $2 million to $200 million in just five years) to strike out on their own in the electronics business. Charles "Tex" Thornton had been vice president and assistant general manager at Hughes; Hugh Jamieson, a research scientist turned engineer and businessman, had been one of the two chiefs of Hughes' large radar-development group; Roy Ash had been Hughes' assistant controller. The oldest, Thornton, was 40 . . . They were probably worth $200,000—about enough money to go into business in a loft. . . . By late November 1953, however, Thornton had talked [sic] Lehman Brothers into raising $1.5 million, with which the three bought a small microwave tube company in San Carlos, California, owned by an engineer named Charles Litton.

The way to sell [government electronics], Thornton thought, was to build a company loaded with brainy [people] who could come up with new weapons. . . . Lehman Brothers, by one insider's count, had "dozens" of similar propositions to choose among at the time. Thornton made his pitch. What made Lehman back Thornton and reject so many others? We were impressed by Thornton himself . . . he spoke our language.

The original financing consisted of the following securities:

525,000 shares of $0.10 par value common stock	$ 52,500
2,500 shares of $100 par value preferred stock	250,000
$1,200,000 of five-year 5% sub. income debentures	1,200,000
Total	$1,502,500

Almost immediately the corporation embarked on a program of research, development and acquisitions in three distinct areas: computers and control systems, radar systems, and navigational systems. The R&D program was made possible by the high rate of cash generation coming from the San Carlos tube plant. The acquisition program soon extended to companies in other phases of electronics.

Continued Acquisition Growth

Through the late 1960s, Litton grew at an annual rate of 36 percent, half by acquisition and half by internal growth. *Fortune* commented as follows:

What sticks out all over . . . is not just diversification—everybody does that—but a superb sense of timing. Litton's secret is that it has made a practice of doing what other companies are not doing, and of *not* doing what everybody else is doing. From its very beginning, when almost all industry was scrambling after contracts for military systems, Litton walked the other way and concentrated on elec-

* Case copyright © by James Brian Quinn. Major sections of the case excerpted from the Litton Industries (AR), (BR) cases prepared by Kenneth R. Andrews.

Copyright © by the President and Fellows of Harvard College.

tronic components, the profitable hardware of the advanced sciences. When others . . . went after the glamorous missile market, Litton shot for manned military planes, which turned out to be a far bigger market than anyone supposed. . . . Other companies were lured into marketing big general purpose computers; Litton . . . stayed out of that, . . . , and instead developed a promising business in small inexpensive computers.

Through 1967, Litton's acquisitions were largely electronics related. Even Ingalls Shipyard was looked upon as an application of electronics to submarines. The same rationale was applied to the acquisition of Stouffer Foods, which coupled closely with Litton's capabilities in electronic cooking technology. However, by the late 60s, *Business Week* described Litton as:

> . . . A giant conglomerate in technology. . . . Increasingly, . . . it is performing a myriad of professional and business services—store design, computer preparation of income tax forms, design of educational curricula, . . . and broad economic studies, such as one . . . for the Greek government, on how to best develop the Island of Crete and the Peloponnesus Peninsula. A former Litton officer [said] Litton now is something like a Fourth of July skyrocket. First, 10 stars burst. Then each of them burst into 10 others.

Litton became a darling of the stock markets and one of the fastest-growing companies of the booming late 60s and early 70s. By 1984, Litton Industries had grown into a $5 billion company and it was among the most profitable and stable of the "multimarket" companies during the 1981–83 recession.

Opportunity Planning

Line Planning

During this period Litton coined the term *opportunity planning*. Planning was considered to be a line and not a staff activity. Division managers, group vice presidents, and the president were each actively concerned with planning at their levels. The genesis of the majority of Litton's plans took place at the division level, at least once a year, and possibly more frequently.[1] With some of the larger divisions, the division manager was required to submit to his group VP a description on what he wanted his division to do during the coming 12-month period. Mr. Ash, the president, described the process as follows:

> [Each division head must first] assess the strengths and weaknesses of his division in detail. Then he must look at the world around him. He knows his own industry best and he is expected to determine niches, opportunities, or whatever you like to call them that his division could possibly exploit. In addition, he must examine each of his existing products to see where he could do better, what he could perhaps dispense with and how he plans to take the appropriate action. In effect, he progressively narrows in on a match between the world around him and his own division capabilities.
>
> . . .We dislike the word "planning" here because it tends to suggest staff activities, and also implies a sense of neatness of approach. Because of this we have substituted the word "opportunity." This has more of the flavor we want—it suggests innovation and new ways of doing things. We want, wherever possible, major steps forward—not just successive refinements. It's with this in mind that we push our division managers very hard to really identify the opportunities and to be creative in doing so.

Using this basic approach, the division manager created his own opportunity or business plan. At this stage there was no great emphasis on financial data, although in broad terms the projected revenue, profit, and capital required for the various opportunities had to be identified. The emphasis was on the logic of the proposals and how well though-out the various alternatives

---

[1] The frequency was determined by need, rather than formal schedules.

were. In addition, a missed or unidentified opportunity was as catastrophic as a poorly supported or overly ambitious proposal.

At the group level, the division opportunity plans were evaluated, discussed and modified as appropriate. A group VP stated that he acted as a sounding board, which allowed the division manager to test and try out new ideas and suggestions. In the final analysis, however, the group VP felt that he had to reach some agreement with the division manager's proposals and to check them for consistency with the other divisions of this group. The relationship was one of cooperation, with both the group and division managers trying to arrive at the most advantageous final solution. The process at this stage was described by another group VP as follows:

> The development of an opportunity plan is not a financial rigamarole. Basically, I try to look at what assets we have, what are the opportunities that exist and what are the risks and rewards that could result. Each opportunity is evaluated as a complete package, considering what we can get out of it and whether we can make a go of it. If we think the best route to exploiting the opportunity is the acquisition of another company, then we will recommend which one and why.

The Corporate-Level Presentation

The third and final major step in the opportunity planning process was the presentation of the division plans to the company's president. Each division had a separate opportunity session that was attended by approximately five people: the division manager, probably one divisional marketing executive, one divisional technical expert, the appropriate group vice president, and [the president]. At this session the *division manager* presented his opportunity plan for the coming year. The president commented:

> Our evaluation of opportunities is systematized, not formalized. We try to emphasize the analysis aspect of the opportunity session, rather than the formal presentation side of things. *Everybody digs in.* I bring to the meeting a company wide perspective

yet the least detailed knowledge, while the division manager brings the most intimate knowledge with his special perspective, and, of course, the group VP is somewhere in between with both perspective and knowledge. We attempt to hammer out strategies as distinct from tactics. If the proposals seem a bit weak or data is missing we will send them back to the drawing board and have the division manager try again. There is no satisfactory technique that suits all divisions. We don't set goals that they have to meet. Some divisions, by the nature of their business, will grow faster than the corporation as a whole, while others will be slower or perhaps even be temporarily static. The real question we ask ourselves is: Have we made the very most of the opportunities that are available to us in each environment as the division group managers and I see it? Of course, the group VP has done most of his own soul-searching before he comes to these sessions.

One group vice president commented on the meetings:

> . . . To my knowledge there has never been an occasion when a good project or opportunity has been held up for lack of funds. It is not really a matter of having a certain size pie and trying to equitably share this out among all the competing claims. That's just a textbook notion of how things *should* go.

Long-Range Financial Plans

Once the opportunity session had been successfully completed, the division manager then generated a set of detailed and interlocking financial plans that reflected the decisions taken in the meetings. These plans contained profit-and-loss statements, balance sheets, and supporting data for the coming 12-month period on a month-by-month basis. Financial data were also included for a 24-month period on a quarterly basis and for a 36-month period on a yearly basis. The financial plans were developed on a "running-year" system and were submitted ultimately to the corporate financial VP. Once checked for accuracy they were returned to the divisions as a "charter" for the coming year's operations. Opportunity planning and review was completely independent of financial planning and review, but it was the opportunity sessions that formed the basis upon which the financial plans were developed.

In the opportunity review sessions the president relied upon at least two other "inputs" to help him relate each division's activities to those of the corporation as a whole. These two inputs were: (1) an overall plan for Litton as a corporation and (2) the identification of opportunities outside existing corporate group activities. These latter were developed by a corporate staff planning function at company headquarters.

The Corporate Plan

Litton's overall plan was something about which very little was publicly said. As chairman Thornton commented, "We do not disclose the details of our plan because we feel that this could be viewed as a promotion. We are more interested in replacing words and pseudo-promises with results." Although it was clear that the plan involved financial considerations, the opportunity aspects of it were embodied in a chart of the form shown in Exhibit 1. The "relative" environment had been divided into basic areas which were then further subdivided into more specific product groupings. The format was highly flexible, and the completion of any one part could occur at any time.

Generally speaking, the responsibility for consummating an acquisition was placed on the source that recommended it. If recommended by group or division managers, negotiations and details were their responsibility after it had been determined with corporate management (1) that such an acquisition was desirable and (2) what range of terms and conditions were allowable. Division heads were expected to be the driving force behind their proposed acquisitions, although they were also expected to call upon headquarters for needed professional and technical assistance. Possible acquisitions that came from other sources were usually handled by the corporate planning staff. Whenever possible, a member of the corporate planning staff was assigned to each newly acquired company to ensure that it was properly integrated into the total Litton structure.

Acquisition Criteria

The company did not have a single set of specific acquisition criteria, except with regard to the overall opportunity plan shown in Exhibit 1 and in relation to antitrust considerations, where great care was taken to ensure that no antitrust regulations were violated. Each acquisition was examined in the light of its ability to fulfill an opportunity potential.

Mr. Ash elaborated on some of the guidelines which influenced the company's search for acquisition candidates:

> Our acquisition criteria are not explicitly listed; but, generally speaking, there are certain attributes against which we evaluate each potential acquisition. For instance, we do not want to become involved with companies or industries that are dependent for their future growth upon the growth of the economy as a whole; or, put in another way, each opportunity must have a growth potential in its own right. Most suitable acquisitions will ideally be greater than a certain critical mass—that is, the acquisition shouldn't be of such a size that it has become dependent on the economy for growth, neither should it be so small that it has to struggle for survival. Apart from these factors, we also try to avoid getting into situations where we are just selling brain power. We want to obtain some leverage on our skills by selling an end product and not just the skill itself. In addition to these guidelines there are certain industries which have characteristics that we feel are not suited to our particular business philosophy. As an example, we are not interested in acquiring financial companies or in becoming involved with retailing.

Organization

One basic tenet upon which the Litton organization was built was the importance attached to the line as distinct from the staff organization. In the Litton system, the key role was played by the

EXHIBIT 1   A Representation of Litton's Overall Opportunity Plan*

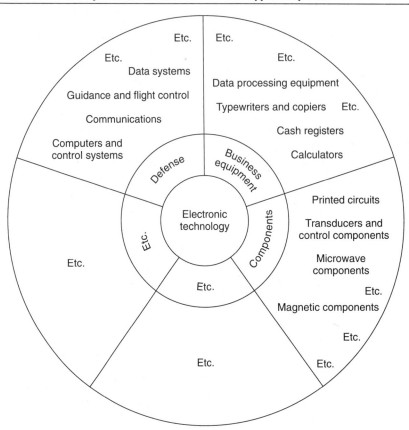

*The above diagram is representative of the structure of Litton's plan. As was explained in the text, the actual details were not released by the company.

division manager. He was responsible for the day-to-day operations of the company and for the generation of revenue within the organization. Because he was such an important link in the chain, the company provided him with a great deal of autonomy and freedom to operate his own division. As one division manager put it:

> We ultimately have only three responsibilities. First, we are checked that our return on gross assets is reasonable and that it does in fact represent a worthwhile use of the capital employed. Second, we are expected to make an operating profit that is

in line with the nature of the opportunities in our particular business. Both of these measures, of course, are expected to show improvement over time—that is, we have to grow. The only other requirement they place upon us is that we stay out of jail. Very simple really.

In actual practice the division managers were not quite as free as the above quotation would suggest. Although the aim was to keep the organization decentralized at the division level and to have each of these operate as true profit centers, there were several activities over which the division manager had little control. Exhibit 2 lists the responsibilities reserved for corporate headquarters. These responsibilities were not listed anywhere in the company, nor was there any one person who could (or perhaps would) quote more than a few of those included. The list was compiled by the researcher from information supplied by nine separate executives at various levels within the organization.

There was very little sense of imposition by headquarters on a division's freedoms. The feeling was more one of how do we (at corporate) let the divisions make the most of their opportunities? This feeling of freedom from interference was also shared by the division managers who were interviewed. One division manager commented: "As a division manager you are certainly master of your own show."

Another division manager, when discussing line, staff relationships, said:

> In actual practice we almost have more freedom than if we owned the show ourselves. In effect, I feel I make all the important decisions here—sure we have to check some things with corporate and we have certain financial targets we aim to meet— but what business doesn't? In fact, it's better running this business now than it was as an independent. I have a really skilled staff I can call on for help and yet, thank goodness, they are never down here poking around. Because we pay a fixed management fee, I have no hesitation in calling them in. They are essentially free.

All the mandatory interaction in the organization was vertical; the horizontal interaction developed on the mutual self-interest of each division. The prerogative was purely in their own

---

EXHIBIT 2 Activities Outside the Control of the Division Managers

1. Pension funding.
2. Most insurance work had become centralized at corporate headquarters.
3. Legal work. Although divisions could and did have legal groups, these were under the control of the corporate level. Items specifically reserved for the corporate legal staff were: acquisition legal work; tax planning; S.E.C.; antitrust and litigation.
4. Every year division managers had to report conflicts of interest, private dealings with customers or suppliers, equity transactions and dealings.
5. All real estate was handled at headquarters.
6. The raising of capital.
7. Each division had to meet the performance requirements of their financial plan. This was checked by headquarters.
8. The payment of an annual management fee.
9. Reporting on a monthly basis.
10. Cash control was at corporate headquarters.
11. Salary or wage changes had to be approved by the supervisor and the supervisor's supervisor.

Salaries greater than $30,000 were approved by Ash.
12. There were 17 basic accounting policies that the divisions were required to follow.
13. The divisions were subjected to an internal audit.
14. The division managers could not go outside the company for management consulting help without concurrence.
15. Some aspects of the acquisition procedure, notably legal, final price, and integration of the acquired company, were corporate responsibilities.
16. Opportunities were subject to review and acceptance in the opportunity sessions.
17. Indiscriminate use of the Litton name was not permitted.
18. The divisions did not report independently to financial and credit services.
19. Stockholder relations were reserved for corporate.
20. Loss pricing, or unusual risk-taking, such as fixed price research and development bids.

hands. There was no attempt to interfere with divisions on the basis of centralized planning efficiencies. The increase in individual motivation provided by this delegation of responsibility and autonomy was felt to outweigh any advantages that could be gained by imposing centralized "slide-rule" efficiencies from the corporate office. The company possessed no organization chart, nor did it possess any policy manuals at the corporate level, except for a manual detailing the company's accounting practices.

There was a qualified stock option plan "to aid the corporation in retaining its key employees and the key employees of companies acquired by the corporation and to assist the corporation in attracting additional key employees." The main incentive(s) in the total organization, however, appeared to be the opportunities for advancement provided by the continuous growth of Litton, as well as by the fact that many top executives over the years had moved out of Litton to assume high-ranking positions in other companies. Commenting on this movement of executives, Ash said:

> We aim to keep a continuous upward spiraling of our best talent. We will move people across the organization from, say, a controllership of a large division to the managership of a smaller one. Staff people will move into line positions and line people may move into staff roles at headquarters. But, in all our moves, the aim is to take the person up, not just across. We are also finding that many of our top people leave us after a period of years. This is mainly because they are dynamic individuals who want to be at the top of the tree—when they meet a block here, their inclination is to move to areas where they can go higher. We feel this is probably a good thing. It helps us to keep moving people up and, thus, the organization stays young.

The Control System

The crux of the control system was the financial plan generated by each division once a year and updated as required. The plan was on a running-year basis and included projections for 12 months on a monthly basis. Each plan consisted of a full balance sheet and a profit-and-loss statement for the appropriate period coupled with complete supporting data. The original plans were approved by headquarters and updated quarterly. Divisions returned to headquarters a monthly report showing actual performance. This was compared to the plan and significant deviations noted and explanations sought. The corporate controller, said:

> We realize here that when we receive a report, it is past history. We expect divisions to call up if anything is out of line and not wait to send in the report. We probably make as many mistakes in this company as in any other company, but our reaction time is fast enough to catch them before they get out of control.
>
> To help us in this regard, we travel to many of the divisions and try to get a feeling for what they are up to. I would guess that I spend about a third of my time keeping up with the products we make and the types of markets we sell to.

Another form of control was that exercised over cash. The treasurer's office at corporate headquarters acted as the company's banker and all cash generated by the divisions, apart from any local compensating balances, was wire transferred to headquarters on a daily basis. Similarly, requests for cash from divisions were attended to on a daily basis.[2]

Any discussion of control would be incomplete without a mention of several indirect controls. First of these was the corporate real estate staff, which approved all site elections, oversaw lease negotiations, and reviewed all economic analyses for land purchases, construction, or asset disposals. Second was the corporate consulting group, which, when called in, could highlight areas of gross negligence. Third, all legal work was under

---

[2] This procedure did not apply to foreign subsidiaries. However, there was at headquarters a foreign currency specialist who was responsible for hedging soft currencies, moving money between foreign divisions, and for the borrowing of capital outside of the United States.

corporate control. Fourth was the internal audit function. Litton had a *highly* developed internal auditing staff, which, as well as being responsible for auditing, was also available to divisions managers for special surveys. It was another of the many lines of communication that extended between the corporate headquarters and the divisions.

Internal Communications

One particularly distinguishing feature of Litton was its emphasis on direct communication between personnel:

> The most effective means of contact—providing both communication and understanding—is personal conversation. Litton's corporate management has recognized that the improved technology of today's communication industry allows a company to be controlled through extensive personal contact. Therefore, Litton's main tool of communication and understanding (i.e., control), is personal contact within its management, made possible by extensive use of telephones and jet aircraft.
>
> Litton executives hate memos. They substitute personal visits and long-distance phone calls. "We spend millions," conceded Ash. "It's our lifeblood." Doors are nearly always open, and people move in and out with a bustle that sometimes makes Litton on Monday morning resemble a war room. If a big deal arises, the wheels really spin, often far into the night. But the company can move fast; it decided to buy Hewitt-Robbins, Inc., two and one-half hours after the chance arose.

The emphasis was on continuing personal contact for all levels of discussion. Telephone meetings were a common method of discussing mutual problems and providing information. Apart from these meetings, the company had only two other committees. One was the executive committee of the board, which never met in scheduled formal sessions but had the authority to act as needed between board meetings. The other was a committee of trustees that supervised the pension fund. Decision making was assigned to individuals and not to groups.

Chairman Thornton summarized this philosophy as follows:

> Our organizational purpose is to motivate the individual manager. We believe in placing responsibility on people and not on groups; and, having given a person responsibility, we like to provide an environment in which he can truly exercise his own judgment. We think that the increase in motivation or "individual efficiency" that results from this approach enhances the overall organization's effectiveness. We may not have the most efficient organization, but we certainly have a very effective one.

Problems of the 1980s

After the booming 1960s era in which Litton grew at a 36 percent annual rate, it settled down to a more conservative pattern in the 1970s. It began to divest some of its less technological divisions, including Stouffer Corporation, its Great Lakes cargo vessels and shipbuilding facilities, its medical supply, industrial rubber products, refrigeration equipment, medical supplies, and printing businesses. But it also continued to acquire related companies and product lines, including Itek Corporation. In 1984, it still had plants in 81 cities and 30 states. Its major product groups and lines of business were:

> *Advanced Electronic Systems:* electronic and communications systems for government and commercial customers, inertial navigation systems, digital data processing systems, mission control, fire control, and monitoring systems, microelectronic digital data converting equipment.
>
> *Business Systems:* office machines and equipment, electronic display devices, printing calculators, programmable calculators, microcomputers, special-purpose minicomputers, automated business systems, point-of-sale systems, electronic cash registers, electronic label printing systems, credit terminals, fine paper for speciality purposes, office design, and planning services.
>
> *Electronic and Electrical Products:* computer and microwave components, integrated circuits, specialized motors and drives, electronic and mechanical components, avionic instruments, night vision

devices, electronic and microwave cooking equipment, medical electronic instrumentation, and optical surgical equipment.

Industrial Systems and Services: materials handling systems and equipment, engineering and construction of material handling systems, computer-controlled machine tools and accessories, hand tools and related metal products, seismic exploration and data processing systems, geophysical and exploration systems.

Marine Engineering and Production: commercial and defense shipbuilding, production and overhaul of military and commercial vessels, oil drilling platforms, industrial products for commercial customers.

The breakdown of sales and profits among these lines of business was:

	Percent of Total Sales	Percent of Total Profits
Industrial systems and services	21%	24%
Business systems	17	−5
Advanced electronic systems	28	37
Electronic and electrical products	19	22
Marine engineering and production	15	22

Exhibits 3, 4, and 5 provide additional data on Litton.

QUESTIONS

1. What is Litton's strategy? Evaluate the company's planning and control systems in the context of its strategy.
2. Why is Litton's system an "opportunity planning" system? What are its strengths and weaknesses?
3. Under what conditions will Litton's management control systems work effectively? Under what conditions will the systems run into trouble?

EXHIBIT 3 Key Financial Data ($ millions, except per share data)

Year	Revenues	Operating Income	Capital Expense	Depreciation	Net Income	Cash	Total Assets	Long-Term Debt	Common Equity
1983	4,720	515	179	203	232	1,243	3,999	214	1,779
1982	4,933	584	296	155	315	1,178	3,837	211	1,627
1981	4,936	586	291	127	312	1,248	3,688	229	1,371
1980	4,242	556	209	106	291	1,008	3,264	263	1,084
1979	4,086	442	158	105	189	724	2,854	371	829
1978	3,651	306	149	92	(91)	93	2,279	514	651
1977	3,441	249	99	82	56	73	2,064	550	745
1976	3,351	220	100	79	28	66	2,057	604	691
1975	3,430	212	104	76	35	76	2,186	630	676
1974	3,028	221	88	70	(15)	71	2,214	643	644

	1984	1983	1982	1981	1980	1979	1978	1977	1976	1975
Earnings per share	N/A*	5.41	7.39	7.31	6.85	4.41	(2.35)	1.21	0.54	0.72
Prices:										
High	$74\frac{1}{4}$	$71\frac{1}{2}$	$58\frac{3}{8}$	$86\frac{3}{4}$	$83\frac{3}{4}$	$39\frac{1}{2}$	$25\frac{7}{8}$	$13\frac{3}{8}$	15	$7\frac{1}{2}$
Low	$56\frac{1}{4}$	$47\frac{1}{2}$	$34\frac{1}{2}$	$46\frac{1}{4}$	$36\frac{5}{8}$	$17\frac{1}{8}$	12	10	$5\frac{7}{8}$	$2\frac{1}{2}$

*N/A means not availaable.

EXHIBIT 4 A Compendium of Conglomerates

Conglomerate 1983 Sales (in millions)	Return on Stockholders' Equity, 1978–83				
	Median	*High*		*Low*	
Teledyne $2,979	24.4%	29.2%	1979	11.5%	1983
Minnesota Mining & Manufacturing $7,039	20.1	22.2	1979	17.8	1982
Chesebrough-Ponds $1,685	19.8	20.0	1982	17.8	1978
Litton Industries $4,719	19.6	24.9	1980	loss	1978
American Standard $2,182	19.3	24.7	1980	5.8	1982
Emerson Electric $3,475	19.3	19.7	1981	17.8	1983
Northwest Industries $1,976	19.2	41.1	1981	loss	1983
Lear Siegler $1,464	18.6	20.9	1979	13.3	1983
Marmon Group $1,467	18.6	25.1	1979	10.6	1983
General Electric $26,797	18.3	19.1	1979	17.8	1982
Gillette $2,183	17.3	19.3	1983	16.1	1978
Emhart $1,686	16.5	18.2	1978	12.9	1979
TRW $5,493	16.3	16.9	'78-'79	12.7	1983
Parker Hannifin $1,038	16.0	17.5	1979	6.5	1983
Perkin-Elmer $1,015	16.0	17.9	1980	9.8	1983
Rockwell International $8,098	16.0	17.0	1979	13.0	1978
Dresser Industries $3,473	15.9	16.6	1978	0.3	1983
Tenneco $14,353	15.6	17.4	1980	12.3	1983
Colt Industries $1,576	15.2	21.3	1983	loss	1982
Ogden $1,918	14.6	15.5	1978	10.8	1982
W. R. Grace $6,220	14.4	17.5	1981	7.3	1983
United Technologies $14,669	13.9	15.3	1982	13.0	1979
Honeywell $5,753	13.6	15.9	1979	10.0	1983
Gulf & Western $5,072	13.2	15.3	1980	loss	1983
Borg-Warner $3,542	13.1	14.4	1979	10.9	1980
Brunswick $1,216	13.0	52.8	1982	5.3	1980
Kidde $2,330	13.0	14.6	1979	loss	1983
Signal Companies $6,151	12.9	17.2	1979	3.9	1983
North American Philips $3,800	12.6	14.3	1979	9.4	1982
FMC $3,498	11.6	13.4	1978	10.8	1981
ITT $14,155	11.3	14.3	1980	6.8	1979
SCM $1,813	10.8	11.8	1980	4.8	1983
National Distillers & Chemical $2,267	10.7	14.9	1979	6.8	1983
Crane $1,003	10.6	14.8	1979	loss	'82-'83
Textron $2,980	10.0	16.5	1978	6.9	1982
American Can $3,346	9.5	12.0	1979	loss	1982
IC Industries $3,864	8.8	14.4	1979	4.2	1982
U.S. Industries $1,076	8.2	9.7	1979	loss	1981
Williams Companies $2,167	7.0	14.4	1980	1.8	1978

Who's hot and who's not among conglomerates is illustrated by the 39 listed above, chosen from the 295 Fortune 500 industrial companies with $1 billion or more in 1983 sales. *Fortune* [magazine] defines conglomerates as companies engaged in at least four different businesses, none accounting for more than 50 percent of sales—which eliminates some, like Raytheon, often considered conglomerates. Also excluded are co-ops and companies that weren't on the 500 list all six years.

EXHIBIT 5   Return on Stockholders' Equity (median rates of return)

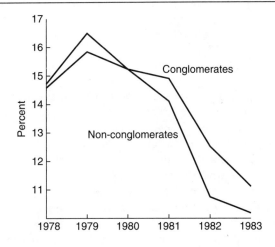

Case 13–5
Analog Devices*

For several years, management at Analog Devices ($130 million in sales in 1980 and 2,000 employees) experimented with a variety of one-dimensional plans, finally concluding that none of them could be made congruent with its goal of balanced financial objectives. Yet Analog's management also wished to develop an incentive plan that would reinforce the alignment of personal interests with company goals and that would attract, motivate, and retain the people and spirit needed to meet those goals.

For these reasons, in 1976, Analog's management developed and implemented a new approach to incentive compensation. Management realized at the outset that it would need two compensation plans, one for corporate objectives and one for division objectives.

The Corporate Plan

At the outset, Analog's management decided the plan must be multidimensional to reinforce corporate objectives, which included a balance between short- and long-term results. Thinking that three dimensions made the plan too complicated and difficult to visualize, management settled on two: return on assets (ROA) and sales growth, the two variables that bring into balance the conflict in objectives. (ROA was chosen instead of return on capital or equity to make the return independent of the financial structure of the company. Operational pretax profits are used to compute ROA to eliminate effects, like tax and interest rates, over which line management has no control.) Most important, management pegged both measures to the relative performance in its industry.

The two dimensions Analog picked gave management the flexibility it desired; the price it paid was a more complex payout formula. For ease of communication, the designers of the plan converted the formula to a simple matrix with 49 squares (see Exhibit 1). Each position on the matrix defines a payout factor that is determined by the two coordinates: ROA and sales growth.

The second step in the design of the plan was to calibrate Analog's performance matrix to performance achieved by the leading companies in its industry and to assign payoff factors for each combination of ROA and growth results.

The third step was to decide who would participate in the plan and what percentage of total executive compensation at various levels in the company would be derived from bonus when the goal performance was achieved.

Each of these steps is described below.

Establishing Performance Measures

In Analog's industry, a significant delay occurs between investments in new product, market development, and the realization of results. For this reason, performance measures of strategic decisions intended to generate long-term corporate growth need to be isolated from measures of decisions affecting short-term business problems or changes in business conditions. And management should be motivated to hold the long-term rate of

* This case is adapted with permission from the article by Ray Stata and Modesto A. Maidique, "Bonus System for Balanced Strategy," *Harvard Business Review*, November–December 1980. Copyright© by the President and Fellows of Harvard College.

EXHIBIT 1 Bonus Payoff Function for 1979

12-quarter average sales growth rate* →

3-quarter average return on assets as biased	14.9% Poor	15%	20%	25% Goal	30%	35%	40%	45% Outstanding
16.9% Poor	0	0	0	0	0	0	0	0
17.0%	0	0.29	0.29	0.41	0.56	0.75	1.00	1.00
19.0%	0	0.29	0.41	0.56	0.75	1.00	1.30	1.30
21.0%	0	0.41	0.56	0.75	1.00	1.30	1.67	1.67
23.0% Goal	0	0.56	0.75	1.00	1.30	1.67	2.12	2.12
25.0%	0	0.75	1.00	1.30	1.67	2.12	2.66	2.66
27.0%	0	1.00	1.30	1.67	2.12	2.66	3.29	3.29
29.0%	0	1.30	1.67	2.12	2.66	3.29	4.04	4.04
31.0% Outstanding	0	1.30	1.67	2.12	2.66	3.29	4.04	4.04

Note: The payout is deliberately nonlinear, generating higher incremental payoffs at higher levels of performance. Note the "cutoff" and "saturation" levels. The bias factor allows management to adjust the expected payout from year to year to compensate for unusual circumstances—for example, a year in which deliberate, heavy strategic expenditures are committed that will depress operating ROA. The bias factor is set at the beginning of the year—coincident with the annual plan—and then held constant through the planning period.

* The bonus payout factor can be calculated from the following formula:

$$\text{Bonus payout factor} = K = \left(\frac{\text{ROA\%} + \text{Bias} + 0.4 \text{ Sales growth\%}}{33} \right)^{4.5}$$

strategic investment relatively steady, rather than merely to achieve short-term profit objectives.

This line of reasoning suggests that a bonus payoff related to sales growth should be averaged over a long period. Since the delay between initiation of new product development and significant contribution to sales from the investment is about three years, in its bonus plan Analog used a 12-quarter (three-year) moving average sales growth. The time period between cause and effect will vary in most companies. If the development period is longer than three to five years, sales growth loses its usefulness as an incentive for management performance; the perspective of executives on a single assignment usually does not extend past five years.

On the other hand—due to changes in the business cycle, in competitive developments, or in customer buying habits—business conditions can and do change, sometimes very rapidly. Because of this, managers need to be motivated for short-term management performance and decisions, for which operating pretax ROA is a better measure. Management's job is to adjust operational expense and assets to ensure satisfactory profits and ROA under changing conditions. The business cycle, for instance, is often reflected in changing sales volume, in which case operational expenses and inventories are the appropriate controls.

Analog's management averaged profitability over three quarters; it believed that in its industry there should be about one quarter to detect a meaningful change in order rate, another to effect corrective action, and a third quarter to see any meaningful change in results. For Analog, operating return on assets was the best profitability measure because it covers expense plus asset management. ROA also helps management to focus on inventory and receivables, both critical factors in short-term changes in business conditions.

Return on capital and return on equity are not good measures for these purposes. Decisions affecting debt-to-equity ratio, interest expense, and tax rates are not appropriate short-term controls;

often they are not even feasible. Furthermore, in a decentralized organization it is more meaningful to measure and control assets than liabilities.

Calibrating Measures with Businesses in the Industry

To establish appropriate performance standards for Analog Devices (i.e., to calibrate the matrix), management analyzed the three-year average performance of 15 leading electronics companies whose markets and products are the most closely related to Analog's. These companies were further segmented into three subcategories (semiconductors, instruments, and computers) to better understand how the mix of Analog's business—between semiconductor components and equipment-level computer-related instruments—would influence its standards for growth and ROA.

Analog's management found that only a handful of companies sustain an outstanding long-term growth above 40 percent per year. Most of the high-performance companies cluster around 25 percent per year. Likewise, ROA is rarely above 30 percent, the norm being closer to 23 percent for the better companies.

Another consideration that affected Analog's choice of performance standards was its policy to fund a significant portion of its growth from internally generated profits. As it experienced faster growth rates, it needed to provide a strong incentive for management to earn higher ROA to fund this faster growth. In its analysis, management found that leading companies in its industry also were following similar policies. For them, higher growth usually has been accompanied by higher ROA.

Based on these considerations, Analog's management set up its bonus matrix (see the exhibit). The matrix was normalized so the bonus payout factor, K, is 1.00 when the company is achieving its goals of 25 percent average growth rate and 23 percent ROA, measured before taxes and nonoperating expenses. (The formula shown in the footnote to the exhibit computes the exact bonus payout factor; the matrix provides a rough visual representation of the trade-offs between growth and profits.)

A 2 percent increase in pretax ROA performance is equivalent in payoff to about a 5 percent increase in sales growth rate. The assignment of payoff factors for other combinations of growth and profits can be made to favor growth or profits as may be appropriate for any company's business strategy.

Selecting Participants

The plan was flexible about who participates; it was responsive to changing company needs. The system did not require any particular salary level or job grade and included executives who have been with Analog for less than a year. As a practical matter, however, virtually all of the participants in the plan had been with Analog several years and were at least two grades above that of an entry-level professional. Division general managers initiated recommendations for participation in the plan, but final approval rested with the vice president of human resources. As of early 1980, more than 80 executives, including all of the corporate officers and senior individual contributors, were participating in the plan.

Deciding How to Compensate Them

Once management had decided who would participate and what performance standards would be used, the next step was to decide what the payoff factors were and how to divide the compensation dollar between fixed and variable compensation. Executives at various levels in the organization received a preassigned bonus percentage, which varies from 10 percent to 25 percent of their base salary, if they achieve their goal (25 percent growth and 23 percent ROA—which defined the position on the bonus matrix where the payoff factor, K, is 1.00).

Top executives with a 25 percent basic bonus could earn up to 100 percent of their base salary when they perform outstandingly in terms of both growth and ROA (40 percent growth and 29 per-

cent ROA—which defines the position on the bonus matrix where the payoff factor, K, reaches its maximum value of 4.04).

At the lowest level of participation, generally two or three levels below a division general manager, the bonus performance was 10 percent of base salary for goal performance, with a cutoff when K is 2, or 20 percent growth.

There were two reasons for the sliding bonus scale. First, high rewards in total compensation for top executives should carry high risks and should only be realized when outstanding results—by competitive standards within the industry—are achieved. Second, lower-level managers should not risk as large a percentage of their total compensation with bonuses, since higher-level management decisions can affect results negatively.

A final important issue was how frequently performance should be measured and rewarded. Management believed a quarterly measure of performance was important, since the corporation reports quarterly to the stockholders and to the financial community. Accordingly, Analog computed and paid out an executive's bonus each quarter, based on a quarterly moving average of sales growth (12 quarters) and ROA (3 quarters). This aligns management's interests and time frame with those of the stockholders.

Quarterly payouts are also more compatible with the needs of the employee and become, in effect, another component of compensation. The close coupling of quarterly results to quarterly payout also focuses employee attention on achieving goals.

The Division Plan

In developing the corporate bonus plan, Analog's management also wanted to tailor a similar bonus plan at the division level, which would also be based on each division's potential for growth and profit as well as on opportunities for strategic investments. For instance, a business unit in the test-instrument market faced considerably different market conditions and competition than a business unit in the microprocessor market would.

Management recognized that—in accordance with portfolio analysis—while some divisions might have little growth potential, they might have the ability to deliver high ROA; and other divisions would be able to generate very high growth and return on sales but deliver lower ROA, especially during the start-up phase. That is, some divisions would be "cash cows" and others "stars." In a balanced portfolio, the high ROA, low-growth divisions were as valuable as those at the opposite pole.

The division payoff matrices used the same trade-off between growth and ROA as the corporate matrix—namely, 2 percentage points of ROA and 5 percentage points of average annual growth (see the formula in the exhibit). The same exponent (4.5) also induced nonlinear valuation above or below standard performance for various combinations of ROA and growth. The bias factor allowed management to set division ROA standards higher than corporate standards to account for corporate expenses not allocated to the division. It also could set ROA standards lower to compensate for heavy investments during the start-up phase of a new business or product line.

Executives with total group responsibilities or corporatewide staff responsibilities participated on the corporate matrix only, and those whose responsibilities are entirely limited to a division or group participated only on the group or division matrix. Executives who have responsibilities that are primarily division-oriented or group-oriented but that have significant impact on corporate results participated in both plans equally.

How Did It Work?

After a major decision, top management's view of its real impact is often obscured by flag waving from managerial cheering sections. At Analog, management decided to conduct a survey to find out what participants in the plan really thought.

Over an 18-month period, during which the payout factor moved from 0.58 to 2.0, 10 randomly selected participants who had been assured of anonymity were asked four basic questions:

1. Do you understand the bonus plan?
2. Has it contributed to your understanding of corporate goals and strategy?
3. Has the existence of the plan had an impact on your decisions over the past two years?
4. What is your overall assessment of the plan?

The Spirit of the Plan Is Understood

With the exception of one senior executive who had been instrumental in developing the plan, none of the executives interviewed appeared to have a thorough understanding of the details of the bonus matrix. As one senior marketing manager who had participated in the previous one-dimensional bonus plan explained, "To understand this one you really have to get into it." Yet it was evident that all of the managers interviewed understood the "foundations" (as one person put it) and basic concepts behind the plan. But understanding did not come easily. Several people said it took six months to a year to comprehend the plan.

One engineering manager summed up his first year on the plan this way: "Initially, I had great curiosity about the plan. It was important for me to understand, so I talked to several people in personnel and in other departments about it. I wound up with somewhat conflicting definitions of the bonus matrix; but something else happened. As a consequence of these discussions, I developed a better understanding of the impact of capital equipment decisions on return on assets, depreciation, and marginal contribution. As a consequence, I stopped concerning myself with the details of the plan—for I felt I had understood its spirit."

This spirit seemed to spread to other layers of management as well. "It's simple," one general manager explained. "The plan gives you a chance to reinforce asset management concepts because the topic comes up regularly.'' But another executive moderated this optimism, recalling that it had taken him at least a year to obtain a solid grasp of the plan. He does not expect the people reporting to him to ''make it their own'' any faster than he did.

Financial Aspects Linked to Matrix

Executives clearly perceived the link between the *financial* aspects of corporate strategy and the bonus matrix. On the other hand, most of the executives interviewed saw few links between the bonus matrix and overall product market strategy. Other corporate mechanisms, however, such as the annual strategic plan, had already prompted such connections.

Decision Making Is Affected

Every manager interviewed recalled at least one instance when the plan shaped a major decision. Generally, these decisions were related to capital equipment purchases; but some persons mentioned production goals, others even career choices. The response of one production executive is typical:

When the new computerized test equipment came, we went wild. Every one of the new products—and some of the old ones—were designed or redesigned to take ''advantage'' of the new systems. After the plan was instituted, I did a lot of thinking. What if using the old manual method produced a higher return on assets, despite its labor intensity? After all, if at any time the new equipment was idle, it cost us money. I had some analysis done and it turned out the for *some* products it was better to use the manual method. Now nothing goes into the computerized system until we've checked it thoroughly. I look at things like this now. I'm much less arbitrary.

The careful analysis that usually is lavished by top management on major investments began to permeate lower levels of management. As one general manager explained, ''Before, $20,000 and $25,000 investments were made without much notice. Now a $5,000 rise in inventory or even purchase of a new $3,000 oscilloscope is carefully scrutinized before it gets to me.''

Shortly before he was interviewed, another senior executive had just made a major career decision. He had turned down a position that offered more responsibility, independence, and a better title. This is the way he explains his decision:

The bonus plan comes into my thinking a lot. It has helped to clarify the corporate objectives and thus facilitated my own decisions.

Basically, I have cast my lot with Analog. I am here for the long pull. Thus, when I heard of this opening, in addition to the usual personal-development questions, I asked myself, ''Where can I have greater impact on sales growth and return on assets?'' When analyzed from this perspective, it became clear that, if I took the job at this time, I would likely have had a negative impact on both of these areas for the company—and ultimately on my own compensation as well. Thus, I decided not to move but to wait for an opportunity in which I could advance my personal development while simultaneously strengthening the corporate entity.

But a few managers also are concerned about possible negative effects on decision making. Running tight on capacity can result in reduced service levels and, ultimately, reduced sales. Theoretically, the plan takes this into account—one of its axes is sales growth. However, there is a difference in timing. While reductions in inventory may reflect themselves immediately in ROA, the effect of reduced service levels will be subtler and take longer to perceive.

Overall Assessment

The participants interviewed were unanimous in their high regard for the two-dimensional bonus matrix. This approval did not, however, stop them from offering criticisms, all but one of which dealt with bonus size, mix (between corporate and division plans), sensitivity to business performance, and, ultimately, fairness.

Half of the managers interviewed raised questions about the amount of bonus payout. Some also wondered about whether the distribution factors for lower levels were high enough. Explained one executive, "The annual payout needs to be large enough to buy at least a car with it." Participants on the lowest range of the plan, for instance, would receive about $5,000 pretax maximum using the present scaling—that is, about "half a car." Another executive said, "If cash is going to be the motivational factor, let's make it a significant amount of cash."

Several divisional executives also objected to being compensated on the basis of corporate performance. "The corporate matrix is too distant," one explained. "I really find it difficult to trace our impact on it." Another one observed that, although the divisions were the basis of the corporate payout, sometimes "corporate pays out more than our division's plan."

But it was the plan's alleged inequity that drew the strongest criticism. One executive summed up the feeling of several others when he said:

Setting the division bogie [bias] is an arbitrary process. Each division is at a different stage of development; each general manager has a different relationship with corporate. There's bound to be inequities. How do I know the calibration is fair when the bogies for the other divisions are secret?

It would be unrealistic to establish causal relationships; however, since the plan was instituted four years ago, corporate sales have increased at an annual rate of about 40 percent, while corporate profit is up from $1.3 million in 1975 to $7.1 million in fiscal 1979. ROA (calculated on the basis of operating profits before tax) has increased from 16 percent in 1975 to 21 percent in 1979.

Ray Stata, president and chairman of the board of Analog Devices, summarized his views as follows:

Bonus plans are generally viewed as a means to motivate performance. But one of the main impacts of Analog's bonus plan has been to educate (although it is clear management needs to clarify better how business and personal goals are interrelated). The carrot should not hang on a simple string. Rather than concentrating on profit alone, executives need to recognize the trade-offs between short-term and long-term results and to understand the interplay among growth, strategic investments, operational expenses, and asset management. As the bonus matrix plan points out, corporate performance standards for growth and ROA are not arbitrary. Rather, they are derived from the conditions of the particular industry in which a company competes.

We believe that the two-dimensional plan described here is vastly superior to one-dimensional plans. For a high-growth, high-technology company to flourish, management must mediate the traditional conflict between short-term ROA and long-term growth. The bonus matrix can be the key to striking that balance.

QUESTION

Evaluate the effectiveness of the new incentive compensation system implemented by Analog Devices.

Case 13–6

Lex Service PLC (A)*

As Tony Whitton, president of Lex Service, Inc., considered the proposal for the gate array project at Schweber Electronics, he realized this project was a new venture in a field that was new to the managers of Lex Service PLC, their parent company. Lex managers were accustomed to project proposals from Lex's traditional, mature industries.

However, the acquisition of Schweber Electronics, a distributor of electronic components, had thrust Lex into a business characterized by a rapid pace of both technological change and market growth. The gate array product was the first new product to be considered within this business. It represented a major market opportunity for Schweber for several reasons: The product provided significant advantages to Schweber's customer base; Schweber had the opportunity to be a first mover, since no real competitors had evolved in this market; and finally, gate arrays provided a good fit with traditional Lex strengths of service and quality.

The preliminary planning for this project raised a number of important issues: How could management understand and evaluate a project in a business with very different characteristics from those with which they were familiar? How could they produce forecasts, such as estimates of future revenue, in an emerging business? Should they even try? What role should the board of directors play in making these choices?

Lex Service PLC

Lex Service PLC was a publicly owned, diversified service company, headquartered in London. For the year ended January 1, 1984, the company reported an after-tax profit of 28.3 million pounds sterling on revenues of 887.5 million pounds sterling. Lex Service operated in three principal business activities: distribution of cars and automotive parts, distribution of electronic components and computer products, and transportation and distribution services.

Lex Service began as a single garage located on the corner of Lexington and Brewer streets in London and was incorporated as a public company in 1928. Then known as Lex Garages Limited, the company added locations and operated a small group of parking garages and petrol stations until the end of World War II. In 1945, Lex began to expand its automotive activities through the acquisition of companies holding distribution franchises for a variety of British, European, and American car manufacturers. In 1965, Lex management decided to divest the parking and petrol station businesses to focus on becoming a major force in vehicle distribution in the United Kingdom. The company's Volvo, British Leyland, and Rolls–Royce passenger car franchises were expanded, and a large truck distribution network was developed.

In the early 1970s, Lex began to diversify into other service businesses. In 1972, Lex entered the

* This case was prepared by Doctoral Candidate Nan S. Borowitz and Assistant Professor Julie H. Hertenstein, Harvard Business School.

Harvard Business School case 185–168.

transportation business through the acquisitions of Wilkinson Transport and Bees Transport; in 1973, Lex acquired Harvey Plant, the largest United Kingdom company in forklift truck rental. Lex also entered the hotel business in the early 1970s but subsequently withdrew from this market.

A key objective that Lex began to develop during this period was excellence in customer service. Managers began to devote considerable energy to raising service standards, with programs designed to maintain or improve the quality, availability, and timeliness of services to customers. Lex managers believed that the level of customer satisfaction and loyalty generated by this dedication to service would result in high levels of repeat purchases and increased share of markets.

By the end of the 1970s, Lex Service operated in two core businesses: automotive distribution and transportation services. Both were mature, stable businesses whose growth decreased when the United Kingdom economy experienced a major slowdown. Management believed that Lex needed to find new avenues for increased growth, and it considered the United States a promising area for expansion. In 1979, Lex entered the United States with the acquisition of Chanslor & Lyon, a San Francisco-based passenger-car parts warehouser and distributor, thus expanding internationally via a business with which they were familiar.

In addition to its international expansion, however, Lex management also sought to move into businesses with higher growth and profit potential than its existing core businesses. Following the acquisition of Chanslor & Lyon, Lex Service PLC established a subsidiary, Lex Service, Inc., to manage subsidiaries incorporated in the United States. The officers of Lex Service, Inc.—Tony Whitton, president; and Mike Worfolk, Vice president of business development; and J. E. M. Evans, vice president of finance and administration—were from the parent company. Whitton and Worfolk were given the additional task of finding a new area of business activity to serve as the basis for Lex's expansion and growth in the 1980s. The board of directors established four criteria for the new business: First, the new business should exhibit the potential for both high growth and high profitability. Second, it must balance Lex's portfolio in terms of maturity and cash flow. Third, the basis for competition in the new industry should be according to principles with which Lex was experienced and familiar. Finally, the business should be innovative, with the potential to stimulate other sorts of innovation in the company.

Whitton and Worfolk first looked at industrial distribution businesses in the United States. They eventually developed a list of three possibilities: oil-field servicing, fixed-base private aircraft supply and servicing, and electronic component distribution. Oil-field servicing was rejected, due to the cyclical and sometimes unpredictable nature of the oil market. Whitton and Worfolk also turned away from private aircraft servicing, due to the small potential scale of that business. Finally, the two managers decided to recommend entry into the electronic components distribution business through the acquisition of Schweber Electronics, the third-largest distributor in the United States. The components distribution industry had been growing rapidly, in line with the advance in semiconductor and information processing technologies. Electronics offered Lex Service the opportunity for both growth and increased profitability.

The electronics industry was composed of manufacturers, distributors, and end users. In the United States there were approximately 100,000 end users for electronic components. A typical electronic components manufacturer, however, dealt directly with between 200–2,000 end users; this small group of customers accounted for approximately 80 percent of the manufacturers' output. The remaining 20 percent of output was channeled through electronic components distributors like Schweber Electronics. The distributor's link to the end user was somewhat vulnerable; as a customer grew large it might have sufficient market clout to order components directly from the manufacturer. Schweber Electronics had traditionally dealt with this vulnerability by emphasizing customer service; this was consistent with Lex's approach to its existing core businesses.

Despite the apparent fit with the board's criteria, Lex managers had two major concerns about the electronic components distribution business. First, Lex managers had no experience with electronic technologies and were unsure of the level of technical expertise required to manage the business. Second, the rapid pace of technological change and market growth in the field of electronics was in sharp contrast to that experienced in Lex's automotive and transportation businesses, and they wondered what challenges this would create for Lex managers.

In spite of their concerns about venturing into electronic components distribution, Lex management decided to acquire Schweber Electronics. The acquisition was completed on October 1981. The board of directors of Lex Service PLC had participated closely in the acquisition process, learning about electronics and Schweber in great detail. Because of this participation, Whitton felt that he and other Lex managers went into the Schweber acquisition "with our eyes open" about electronic components distribution. Aware that there might be some problems, the board was confident that it had "bought a company that didn't have major structural weaknesses" and that Schweber's locations, franchises, and place in the market were sound.

After the acquisition of Schweber, Lex expanded its electronics components and computer products distribution businesses through the following acquisitions:

December 1981	Hawke Electronics	U.K.
April 1983	Jermyn	U.K., W. Germany, France
October 1983	Sasco, Panel	W. Germany
February 1984	David Jamison Carlisle Corp.	U.S.

Within five years of the board's decision to look for a new avenue of growth for Lex, a third core business had been established. In 1983, the Lex Electronics businesses accounted for approximately 30 percent of Lex's total revenues; nearly 90 percent of this was contributed by Schweber Electronics in the United States.

Schweber Electronics

Prior to its acquisition by Lex Service, Schweber Electronics was expanding rapidly and increasing its market reach. Seymour Schweber (who founded the firm in 1952) had presided over recent rapid expansion from $96 million in sales in 1978 to $170 million by 1980, which made the company the third-largest distributor of electronic components in the United States. However, in 1981, Schweber's growth was slowing and it was losing market share. Lex Service managers quickly recognized that the critical business concerns within the electronics distribution business were similar to those found in Lex's traditional businesses: inventory levels, credit control, cost control, and information systems. Further, Lex managers found that Schweber, despite its market success, lacked effective management in certain areas. For example, Schweber's computerized information system was almost entirely oriented externally; it was very good for marketing applications but was less useful for inventory or credit control. Hence, the fit between Schweber and Lex came fairly easily. Lex brought ideas about "how to run a business," rather than "how to sell semiconductors," to Schweber. The essential issue after the Schweber acquisition turned out to be management effectiveness, as opposed to technical expertise.

Placed in charge of operations at Schweber, Tony Whitton began to implement more-efficient management processes. One concern was ensuring that periodic operating results were communicated to the managers whose actions might influence these results. Another concern involved Schweber's planning. Schweber operated on quarterly plans but had no annual plan and no explicitly stated strategy. As one manager related, "The plan was kept on the desk blotter. If an area went over its budget, the manager would get called in and told to cut back for a month or two. He'd tell his people to cut back, but no one ever really knew why."

One of Whitton's first objectives was to establish an annual plan that would allow all managers to understand the business and relate their responsibilities to its goals. In Whitton's opinion, Schweber lacked a proper planning process, and he wanted to bring Lex's planning expertise to Schweber.

Management Control at Lex

Lex's management control system had two parts: a one-year planning system and a capital appraisal system. However, there was no particular "Lex way"—no computerized system or standard format—that Whitton could install at Schweber.

Lex required only a few financial figures, such as sales, profit before interest and taxes, cash flow, and capital employed, from its units. These data comprised about 10 percent of the annual plan, and the remainder was flexible in format. The typical annual plan, a one-inch-thick document included "the plan," a detailed account of the strategy and expected operating requirements for each operating unit, and a "strategic summary," an executive summary of the highlights of the plan. Top corporate management took its direction from the strategic summary, and the rest of the document was utilized primarily by the business unit. Lex managers considered the annual plan to be a firm commitment, and submission of a revision of the annual plan during the year was considered by most Lex managers to be a major event. Any anticipated capital projects or special projects were included in the operating plan.

When Whitton attempted to implement Lex's one-year planning process at Schweber, however,

he felt the first annual plan was hopelessly wrong. Things moved much faster in the electronics industry during the year than he had anticipated. It seemed the fast pace and volatility of the industry were not suited for a plan that was cast but once a year. Whitton revised the Schweber system so the annual plan was a strategic framework for operations, rather than a concrete set of directions. He began to recognize the need for quarterly reviews and revisions of the plan, and he later implemented these changes. Trends in key operating data, such as inventory levels and sales in each Schweber branch, were tracked; this permitted managers to evaluate changes in trends, rather than simple deviations from previously expected results when making quarterly plan revisions. This planning system seemed better suited to the rapid pace and sometimes volatile demand in Schweber's markets.

The capital appraisal system was designed to ensure that each capital project was reviewed and approved by the proper levels of authority, whether that was the group manager, chief operating officer, chief executive officer, or the board of directors. The level of authority that was required to review a given capital project depended on two things: first, the amount of expenditure, and second, whether the project was included in a previous plan or not. Lower-level managers were authorized to approve project expenditures for inclusion in the annual plan, with the understanding that the entire plan would be reviewed at the higher levels in the corporation. However, capital projects that arose after the preparation of the annual plan required higher levels of authorization for the same amount of expenditure.

Under the capital appraisal system, major capital expenditures that were not anticipated at the time of preparation of the annual plan and projects included in the plan which were of sufficient scale were written up as a "project book" or "project," according to standard Lex format. The project book had a summary page containing a brief description of the project, key financial information, the nature of the project post audit, when it was to be completed, and space for signatures by the group manager, Project Review Committee, chief operating officer, and chief executive officer. A following section gave detailed estimates of capital requirements, including the cost of each significant equipment item, furniture, and building alterations. The next section had estimates of each profit-and-loss statement item, including the assumptions on which it was based. A final section listed the "criteria" that the post auditor would use in judging the success of the project.

The capital appraisal system projects were reviewed by senior management and the board for approval, as required by the scale of the project. The project books rarely arrived at the senior management level without advance warning; the informal system was such that a new business idea would be discussed across management levels before being written up as a project, and comments were passed back to the proposing managers so the project book could be submitted in a polished version to the board. Despite the informal system for capital appraisal projects, managers felt that they had to justify and document every detail. This was frustrating because, as one manager said, "What's the point in filling out all the forms if it's just going to get approved, anyway?" Nevertheless, managers at Schweber would be expected to prepare a project book if they were to submit new ideas to Lex.

The Gate Array Project

While working on the acquisition of Schweber, Worfolk had identified gate arrays as a potentially attractive business. In 1982, Whitton turned his attention to evaluating and planning the gate array business.

Gate arrays are integrated circuits that have been tailored to a specific logic application. They are referred to as *semi*-custom because gate arrays can be almost completely manufactured before they need customization to meet a customer's design specifications. They start as matrices of unconnected electronic devices that are prefabricated on silicon wafers. Chip manufacturers prefabricate the gate arrays in volume up to the final processing steps, thus achieving manufacturing economies of scale. The manufacturers keep the prefabricated wafers in inventory, customizing them after receipt of the customer's specifications defining how the devices should be interconnected. The concept is similar to personalized stationery: the printer selects a standard paper type from inventory and then customizes it with the specified information, typeface, and ink. Gate arrays allow a customer to combine the functions of several standard integrated circuits, or chips, into a single semi-custom chip. Gate arrays, therefore, are less expensive than multiple standard chips, have a lower assembly cost, and take up less space in the final product. They also have the advantages of higher reliability, lower power consumption, and product design security (since copying these circuits is difficult, costly, and traceable).

The technology of gate arrays, also called "semi-custom logic" or "application-specific integrated circuits" (ASICs), was not new. RCA Corporation had been the industry pioneer with ASICs 17 years earlier. However, until the advent of computer-aided design and engineering techniques (CAD/CAE), the design of semi-custom chips had been painstaking and expensive; the new techniques reduced the time and cost to a level that made commercial development feasible. For example, by 1984, the design steps to produce an ASIC were projected to require less than three weeks, prototype fabrication would vary from one to three weeks, and the development costs would be well below $10,000.

In spite of the new computer-aided techniques, there were questions about whether mass demand for gate arrays would develop. Manufacturers and other industry sources varied widely in their estimates of the market potential for gate arrays—predictions ranged from minor niches to nearly half of the total logic market, with revenues of $2.6 billion, by 1990; there was no clear answer for the potential of semi-custom gate arrays.[1] Furthermore, there were no clear answers to questions about the roles that distributors, as opposed to manufacturers, would play in this market.[2]

It seemed clear to Whitton that gate arrays offered real advantages to end users, among which were many of Schweber's customers. The question was whether gate arrays represented a profitable business opportunity to Schweber and, if so, how that business should be structured. In 1982, no other distributors had entered the gate array business, although some manufacturers were involved on a limited scale. This offered Schweber a first-mover advantage; on the other hand, it also meant that there was no example or experience from which to learn. Schweber would be a pioneer.

As Whitton and Worfolk analyzed the gate array business, two factors appeared essential in conducting the business. First, the nature of a gate array, in which the functions of several chips were combined into one semi-custom chip, required the skills of an experienced logic designer. Most end users did not employ designers with the requisite skills, hence Schweber would have to plan to provide this expertise if it was to market gate arrays. Schweber already employed two people with the appropriate expertise, and managers believed additional designers could be hired when they were needed.

Second, there was the potential for major competition from the electronic component manufacturers themselves. At this time, however, the manufacturers appeared to need distributors to cover the increasing number of customers. Although manufacturers employed many experi-

enced logic designers, these designers were rarely assigned to semi-custom business. The manufacturers' business was dominated by high-volume standard function chips; pulling designers from this business to work on low-volume, semi-custom chips would have been an inefficient use of the manufacturers' resources. End users who had approached manufacturers about semi-custom gate arrays had been told that a designer would not be able to speak to them for at least six months; hence Whitton and Worfolk believed the manufacturers to be internally constrained from dominating the gate array business.

The key to providing design services competitively would be to offer timely accessible design expertise that was reliable and of high quality; these business concepts were consistent with Lex's strength and experience. Further, if Schweber retained ownership of the gate array designs, customer loyalty—an area in which Schweber was vulnerable in its existing business—could be locked in.

The plan for Schweber to enter the semi-custom gate array business focused on working with the customer to design a gate array, and then sending the design specifications to a manufacturer for fabrication. In the production phase, Schweber would place the production order and deliver the gate arrays to the customer, a procedure similar to that of its regular distribution business, except it would not hold inventory due to the high risk if the customer canceled. Schweber would be the first distributor to enter the gate array business, and Whitton saw this as an opportunity to establish Schweber as *the* semi-custom distributor.

Four gate array design centers were proposed; they would be physically located within existing Schweber branches. Each design center would have its own logic designer, and Schweber's field application engineers would be trained to support the product.

Motorola was selected as the manufacturer. Motorola's chips used bipolar technology. The trade-offs between bipolar technology and the alternative CMOS (complementary metal–oxide–

---

[1] See, for example, "The Battle for IC-Design Dollars," *Electronic Business*, July 10, 1984, pp. 214–25; "Gate Arrays: High Cost to Enter; May Be Higher Not to," *Electronic News*, December 6, 1982, p. 36.

[2] See, for example "Gate Arrays;" p. 36; "Customizing a Market Can Put You in the Chips," *Electronic Business*, March 1984, pp. 102–6; "The Action in Custom Chips Turns Distributors into Designers, *Business Week*, August 6, 1984, pp. 82L–82M.

silicon) technology were size and speed. CMOS devices were simpler to manufacture, consumed less power, and generated much less heat, which allowed more transistors to be packed in a given area without overheating. Bipolar devices operated much faster; thus, in applications where speed was preferred to size, bipolar technology was preferred. Motorola was prepared to provide training in the bipolar technology process to all Schweber personnel involved with gate arrays.

The semi-custom gate array business would generate revenue for Schweber at two stages: design and production. First, a design contract would be signed and a design fee paid prior to beginning development work. The design contract specified terms for product acceptance and liabilities, authorized Schweber to begin development of a full gate array design for the customer (see Exhibit 1 for a description of the design process), and gave Schweber sole ownership of the design. When the design was approved by the customer, a production order would be placed stipulating the number of pieces to be produced by the manufacturer, and delivered by Schweber to the customer on a monthly basis. Schweber earned a piece-rate margin on the production order.

EXHIBIT 1   Gate Array Design Process

---

1. The gate array design process begins with a customer's product idea. The customer should already have schematics for the product's circuit logic.

2. A field application engineer (FAE) from Schweber reviews the schematics for potential gate array application. If the application appears feasible, the FAE brings the product design to the logic designer at the Schweber Design Center.

3. The logic designer partitions the schematic diagram into logic portions by both functionality and gate count. There are several technical considerations that the logic designer must balance for the production version of the gate array to achieve the desired cost and performance goals.

4. Once the product schematic is partitioned, a gate array design proposal is written and presented to the customer. The proposal states the number of circuits, their utilization factor, and the expected system cost savings for the customer.

5. Upon approval of the design proposal by the customer, a design contract is signed and a design fee is paid; a production commitment is sometimes made at this time as well.

6. The design phase truly begins once there is a design contract. Schematic capture of the design, its circuits, gates, and so forth is done, based on the agreed-upon partitioning. This is called "electronic breadboarding" (i.e., creating a computerized blueprint), and is done by the logic designers at the design center. At the same time, the customer's engineers design test software, or vectors, which will be used for quality testing of the chips. The customer's engineers work with the logic designer, often at the design center, on this task. The logic designer must take the test vectors into account while designing the gate array to produce a chip that can be properly tested during production. Once both the logic design and the test vectors are completed, a computer simulation is run and specifications for the gate array and the test software are formally finalized.

7. The final gate array specifications are sent to a manufacturer. The manufacturer runs a "back annotated simulation" on the design specifications. This is a simulation of the gate array's functions; the results are sent to the customer and thoroughly checked. A pattern generation (PG) tape then is generated for making the silicon wafer masks of the gate array chip.

8. PG tape is used to make a prototype batch of gate arrays.

9. The prototypes are tested with the test vectors supplied by the customer.

10. When the customer accepts the prototype, full production can begin.

EXHIBIT 2   Excerpts from Project Book: May 1983 Project Proposal

---

Project Summary

This project is concerned with the establishment of a logic array operation within Schweber during the second half of 1983.

The project is limited to the setting up of an organization structure and 4 design centers in current locations of Westbury, Irvine, Minneapolis, and Bedford. A decision on further expansion will be taken in the final quarter following a review of the effectiveness of Phase I.

Summary financial data is set out below:

	1983 ($000s)	1984 ($000s)
Capital expenditure:		
Furniture and fittings	$168	—
Computer equipment	36	—
Working capital	100	$400
PBIT	(49)	766
Margin %	30.0 %	30.0%
ROS %	(3.6)%	12.8%
ROCE %	—	187.0%

Note: Computer equipment purchases represent printing terminals and modems supplied ex Schweber Inventory. The major equipment, graphics terminals, etc., are being taken on a one-year rental agreement.

The project will require an additional seven people.

None of the costs identified above were included in the 1983 plan. Total project costs for authorization are $304,000, including estimate of $100,000 for increased working capital in 1983.

Profit-and-Loss Account

	1983 ($000s)	1984 ($000s)
Gross sales	$1,347	5,880
Cost of sales	943	4,116
Gross margin	$ 404	$1,764
Overheads:		
Payroll	$ 193	$ 452
Burden	29	64
Personnel related	61	98
Equipment rentals	39	88
Computer charges	93	200
Other costs	7	15
Depreciation	21	51
Communications	10	30
Total	$ 453	$ 998
Profit / (loss)	$ (49)	$ 766

In May 1983, Whitton documented the gate array project in Lex's standard capital appraisal system format (excerpts from which are shown in Exhibit 2). Whitton had the required spending authority to approve the gate array project's requirements himself. However, he believed that the project represented a new strategic thrust in Lex's electronics business that might be appropriate for

---

EXHIBIT 3 Revised Project

Revised Summary Financial Data

	1983 ($000s)	1984 ($000s)
Capital expenditure:		
Furniture and fittings	$336	168
Computer equipment	72	36
Working capital	200	600
PBIT	(162)	2,073
Margin %	30.0%	30.0%
ROS %	(10.3)%	11.8%
ROCE %	—	305.3%

The project will require an additional 16 people in 1983 and 8 additional people in the first quarter of 1984.

For 1983, $244,000 were identified in the original project proposal, including $100,000 in working capital. The revised project costs for authorization are $608,000, including $200,000 in working capital.

Revised Profit-and-Loss Account

	1983 ($000s)	1984 ($000s)
Gross sales	$1,568	$17,640
Cost of sales	1,097	12,348
Gross margin	$ 471	$ 5,292
Overheads:		
Payroll	$ 260	$ 1,575
Burden	38	232
Personnel related	180	359
Equipment rentals	51	251
Computer charges	98	570
Other costs	11	43
Depreciation	25	103
Communications	20	86
Total	$ 633	$ 3,219
Profit / (loss)	$ (162)	$ 2,073

the board to authorize. He had to decide whether to submit the project to the board or to authorize it himself.

The project predicted a loss for the balance of 1983 (the first centers would open in July) and a profit for 1984.[3] The project book stated:

> This project represents the first stage of Schweber's entry into the logic array business. It is intended as an "experimental" venture, to obtain a major foothold and technological leadership. Further investment will not be made until the overall effectiveness and profitability of this venture has been proven [see Exhibit 2].

The project stated several measurement criteria to be used to evaluate the gate array project. These were: capital costs not to exceed project; numbers of designs per center per month to average at least 1.5 in 1983 and 3.0 in 1984; and measurement of direct contribution, actual versus project. In addition, the project book identified other information to be used to assist in assessing the overall effectiveness of the gate array project,

including: design wins (number of customers converted to contracting for a design); production wins (number of design conversions to production orders); gross profit margins; Schweber share of Motorola business; and, for each contract, customer report on experience, successes, problems, and so on.

Within two months, the plans for the gate array project were already being revised, and four additional centers were proposed for the last quarter of 1983, with two manufacturers supplying each location as Schweber management began to realize that exclusive commitment to Motorolas's bipolar technology might not be adequate to serve the market's needs. In addition to Motorola, supporting manufacturers would be American Microsystems (AMI), General Electric/Intersil, and RCA. The centers that were involved in the exclusive Motorola agreement would remain so through the end of the six-month contract. The revised project funding request doubled to $608,000 for 1983, including $200,000 in working capital (see Exhibit 3 for detailed figures). It was now time to make a commitment to the gate array project; Whitton considered the need for the board's formal participation in the decision to proceed.

---

[3] In 1982, Schweber's sales and operating profit were $207 million and $2 million, respectively; in 1983, $323 million and $13 million.

QUESTIONS

1. Evaluate the method of evaluating capital projects within Lex Services PLC. Is the present method likely to lead to good decisions?
2. Should Lex Service PLC approve the gate array project?
3. What criteria should Lex use to evaluate projects comparable to the gate array project in the future?

Case 13–7

Lex Service PLC (B)*

The revised gate array project was submitted to the board of directors. It was approved by the board in July 1983, and the implementation of the project began.

Schweber top management designated Howard Blumberg, a marketing manager at Schweber, as director of the gate array project. The first design center was opened in Minneapolis in August 1983. In October the second center was opened at Schweber's headquarters in Westbury, New York. The third center was not opened until January 1984 at Irvine, California.

As Schweber proceeded through the first year of operations of the design centers, management encountered a number of issues that simultaneously enhanced its understanding of this new marketplace and yielded results that were at variance with the original assumptions. These issues included customer concerns about gate array design provided by nonmanufacturers, customer preferences on integrated circuit technology, the feasibility of alternate types of logic-design workstation equipment, and the time required to close an order.

Adaptation to Market Needs

Schweber's marketing approach for gate arrays consisted of a customer presentation followed by a visit by Schweber's field application engineer to the customer's product designers. A slide presentation was used to pitch the new business to the local customer base. The presentation's objectives were to establish Schweber's credibility as a designer of gate arrays and to emphasize Schweber's commitment to customer service. If customers questioned why the manufacturers weren't providing this service themselves, Schweber arranged for the manufacturer to call the customers and assure them that Schweber's product was being supported by the manufacturer. Nonetheless, some customers were concerned about Schweber's ability to provide this service and preferred to wait to undertake the gate array design process directly with the manufacturer, despite the acknowledged associated delay.

A larger issue was the type of integrated circuit technology on which the gate array product was based. It quickly became apparent that the Minnesota customers were primarily interested in CMOS, an integrated circuit technology with features different from the bipolar technology supported by Motorola, the exclusive manufacturer for the Minneapolis center. Ninety percent of the Minnesota accounts contracted by Schweber marketing personnel preferred the CMOS technology. This technology preference also was observed when Schweber opened its Westbury, New York, office; 70 percent of Schweber's New York account base preferred CMOS technology over the bipolar alternative. It became clear that Schweber would not meet the original objective of securing

* This case was prepared by Doctoral Candidate Nan S. Borowitz and Assistant Professor Julie H. Hertenstein, Harvard Business School.

Copyright© by the President and Fellows of Harvard College.

Harvard Business School case 185–169.

orders from nine customers in the first three months of operations, because the centers that were open had exclusive arrangements with Motorola and could not deliver CMOS technology. Fortunately, the project revision had included the addition of other manufacturers in late 1983 that could provide strong support for the customers' CMOS technology preference.

Workstation Equipment Changes

Another major issue that became apparent after the opening of the first two design centers was the choice of workstation equipment. The Tektronix equipment in use at these two centers was compatible with Motorola's manufacturing computer system. It allowed a logic designer at a Schweber center, using a technique called "net list input," to enter the design specifications of the gate array and to communicate with the mainframe computer at Motorola's integrated circuit factory. This technique required that the designer specify the coordinates for every wire connection in the gate array—for example, "A3-D5" meant that there was to be a connection from point A3 to point D5. Net list input was tedious for the designer and prone to error. It required three hours to input data for a gate array with only 50 gates; large gate arrays could have more than 2,000 gates. Because the net list input procedure was performed on-line to the manufacturer's mainframe computer, the input and correction were expensive; Schweber had to pay direct-dial telephone charges as well as charges for the connect time to the Motorola computer. Net list input could easily eat up the design fee.

An alternative to net list input was to use equipment that could perform "schematic capture" of a gate array design. Schematic capture used computer-aided engineering graphics to create a "blueprint," or drawing, of the gate array's circuitry on the work station's video screen. The designer could then draw the gate array connections on the screen using a wand or a mouse, from which the computer could generate the net

list. The manufacturers that were suppliers to the new design centers—GE/Intersil, RCA, and AMI—all supported CMOS gate array design via schematic capture equipment manufactured by Mentor. To be compatible with these manufacturers, Schweber would have to install Mentor work stations in the new design centers. Motorola had agreed to accept design input from the Mentor work stations as soon as it was technically possible; until then, Schweber would have to continue to use the existing Tektronix equipment that it had leased. In addition, the need to provide a graphic representation of the gate array design for customer's approval required the use of a plotter. Mentor schematic capture CAE/CAD work stations and Hewlett-Packard plotters were purchased in March 1984.

Understanding Customer Constraints

Finally, the length of time required to close an order had been misjudged. The sale of Schweber's regular electronic components generally required three to six months from the time the Schweber salesperson first approached the customer's purchasing agent until the order was placed. The gate array project had anticipated nine customers within the first three months of design center operations. However, no design orders were signed until March 1984, when two design orders were signed on the same day. The first had a design fee of $32,000, with an initial production order of 40,000 pieces over 18 months at an average resale price of about $8 per piece. The second was for a $24,000 design fee and a probable production commitment of 10,000 pieces at about $14 per piece. Some 35 more potential customers had been identified and contacted. Somewhere between one third and one half of these customers were expected to sign contracts.

One reason it took longer to close the order, Schweber learned, was that, unlike selling other electronic components, selling gate arrays required a two-level sale. First, a Schweber salesperson made a regular sales call on the customer's purchasing agent with the complete line of Schweber's product offerings and introduced the semi-custom gate array product concept. The purchasing agent then checked with the product design engineers, and, if an interest was expressed, a second call was made directly upon the customer's product design engineer by a Schweber field applications engineer. Further, since gate arrays required the customer's product engineers to participate in the actual design of the gate array, the customer needed to prepare a cost analysis and obtain approval to allocate both the engineer's time and the design fee. If the customer used standard integrated circuit components in its products, no such IC design involvement was required of its product engineers. The cost analysis and approval required two or three months, thus extending the usual three- to six-month sales process for regular components to six to nine months for gate arrays.

The Project Expansion Proposal

Despite these issues, Schweber believed it should expand the number of design centers to insure that it remained the number one distributor for gate arrays. In March 1984, Blumberg submitted a project book to the board that proposed an expansion of the gate array venture (see Exhibit 1 for excerpts from this project). The 1984 proposal was acknowledged as a significant departure from the original project. Nonetheless, approval was requested to open 9 additional centers during the remainder of the year, bringing the total to 13. Agreements had already been completed with Intersil, AMI, and RCA, which allowed Schweber to include CMOS technology in its gate array product offering. To support these manufacturers, additional equipment and logic designers would be necessary. The project requested capital expenditure approval for $3.26 million; $500,000 of this was for working capital. A loss was projected for 1984, and revenue of $10 million would be required to break even in 1985, assuming all 12 centers became operational

in 1984. (See Exhibit 1 for details of the financial projections.) According to market estimates and supplier forecasts, Blumberg believed that revenue would exceed the break-even level in 1985.

A post-project assessment was included as an appendix to the 1984 expansion project. It noted that at none of the three centers completed did the capital costs exceed the original estimate of $51,000 per center. Since no contracts were signed in 1983, losses were greater than projected; however, these losses were trimmed, because $287,000 less overhead was incurred than projected. Since no business was contracted, the remaining criteria—design wins/production wins/margins/share of Motorola business/customer reports—could not be measured.

The assessment identified several reasons for the lack of design contracts during the first year of operations: (1) centers had been delayed in opening, because of a lack of available space in existing Schweber locations; (2) experienced logic designers to staff the centers were scarce; (3) the Motorola exclusive agreement had not allowed Schweber to service the major portion of the marketplace—customers who were interested in CMOS, rather than bipolar technology; and (4) the lead time on the gate array sale was longer than had been estimated.

The Board Meeting

Whitton and Worfolk presented Blumberg's expansion proposal to the board at its quarterly meeting in April 1984. Few of the original objectives for the gate array venture, other than staying below the authorized capital expenditure limit, had been achieved. By traditional Lex capital appraisal system standards, the expanded request would not be viewed favorably. Whitton and Worfolk argued that the cost of the expansion was a trivial investment when compared with the millions of dollars at risk in carrying Schweber's regular inventory. On the other hand, gate arrays might become a major niche in the electronic components market—an opportunity "too good to risk missing."

EXHIBIT 1   1984 Gate Array Project—Excerpts

Financial Projection

• The financial projections for 1984 are set out below:

	1984 *(000s)*
Gross sales — Designs	$ 3,500
Production orders	800
Total sales	4,300
Cost of sales	(2,660)
Gross profit	$ 1,640
Overheads:	
Payroll (including commissions and burden)	$ 925
Equipment leases	625
Other costs	250
Total	$ 1,800
PBIT	$ (160)
Capital employed year end	1,100
ROCE %	(14.6%)
ROS %	(3.7%)

Assumptions

• Based on projected design center opening dates (i.e., staffed and operational).
• Gross profit percentages—designs 40 percent, production orders 30 percent.
• Capital employed consists of construction, furniture, purchased terminals, modems and plotters, and $500,000 working capital.

1985 Projection

• Assuming all 12 centers are operational by the end of 1984, sales volume in 1985 would need to be $10 million to break even, and $13 million to produce a ROCE of 25 percent. Market projections and supplier forecasts indicate that this level of sales is highly likely to be within reach in 1985.

EXHIBIT 1   *(concluded)*

Capital Expenditure Details

	Per Location ($000s)	Total ($000s)	Capex ($000s)	Leases ($000s)
Nine new locations:				
Construction, furniture, and the like	$ 42	$ 378	$378	
Tektronics equipment (rental):				
4 × GE printing terminals	6	54	54	
5 × Racal Vadic modems	3	27	27	
Mentor workstation	183	1,647		$1,647
Three existing locations:				
Mentor work station	183	549		549
Prime computer	—	100		100
2 × H-P plotters	—	50	50	
Total	$417	$2,805	$509	$2,296

Notes: • Mentor workstations and prime computer capitalized lease values are based on two-year lease payments plus purchase option equivalent to 10 percent of original cost.
• Decision about to lease or to buy will be made prior to ordering of equipment.

QUESTIONS

1. Should management approve the expansion of the gate array project?
2. How serious is Scheber's failure to meet the criteria described in the May 1983 proposal (see her Service PLC (A))?
3. Do the developments described in this case change your opinion as to the best management control system for her services?

Service Organizations

Much of the discussion in Parts I and II referred, at least implicitly, to manufacturing organizations—that is, to organizations that produce and market tangible goods. In Chapters 14 and 15, we describe the management control process in service organizations—that is, organizations that produce and market intangible services. In Chapter 14, we discuss the characteristics that distinguish service organizations in general from manufacturing organizations and the special problems that arise in professional, health care, nonprofit, government, and merchandising organizations. Chapter 15 focuses on financial service organizations.

SERVICE ORGANIZATIONS IN GENERAL

The Services Sector

In the 18th and part of the 19th century, the work force in the United States was predominantly in agriculture. Later, it was predominantly in manufacturing. Early in the 20th century, employment in the service sector overtook employment in the manufacturing sector, and, in the 1980s, service sector employment grew to twice that of manufacturing (see Exhibit 14–1). Nevertheless, in Parts I and II, we tended to emphasize management control in manufacturing organizations. The reason is that much of the literature, and much of our own experience, is with manufacturing companies. In this and the next chapter we seek to correct this imbalance somewhat.

Characteristics

For several reasons, management control in service industries is somewhat different from the process in manufacturing companies. Some factors that have an impact on most service industries are discussed in this section. Others, which

EXHIBIT 14–1 U.S. Civilian Employment by Industry, 1987

Service Industries	*Number Employed (in 000s)*
Health Care	8,478
Education	7,928
Transportation, communication, and other public utilities	7,880
Finance, insurance, real estate	7,763
Other professional services*	7,408
Business services[†]	4,706
Other services[‡]	7,222
Government (except military)	5,246
Subtotal, services	56,631
Manufacturing, mining, construction	29,209
Wholesale and retail trade	23,392
Agriculture	3,208
Total employment	112,440

* Includes social services and legal services.
[†] Includes advertising, personnel supply services, services to buildings, consulting, computer and data processing, and protective services.
[‡] Includes automobile, hotels and lodging places, private households, entertainment, and recreation.

Source: *Statistical Abstract of the United States, 1989;* adapted from Table 645.

are characteristics of certain service industries, are discussed later. These characteristics also apply to the management control of legal, research and development, and other service departments in companies generally.

Absence of inventory buffer. Goods can be held in inventory, which is a buffer that dampens the impact on production activity of fluctuations in sales volume. Services cannot be stored. The airplane seat, hotel room, hospital operating room, or the hours of lawyers, physicians, scientists, and other professionals that are not sold today are gone forever. Thus, although a manufacturing company can earn revenue in the future from capacity that is not sold today, a service company cannot do so. It must try to minimize its unused capacity, and in this sense the problem of controlling unused capacity in a service company is similar to the problem of controlling inventory in a manufacturing company.

Moreover, the costs of many service organizations are essentially fixed in the short run. In the short run, a hotel cannot reduce its costs substantially by closing off some of its rooms. Accounting firms, law firms, and other professional organizations are reluctant to lay off professional personnel in times of low sales volume because of the effect on morale and the costs of rehiring.

A key variable in most service organizations, therefore, is the extent to which current capacity is matched with demand. Organizations attempt this matching essentially in two ways. First, they try to stimulate demand in off-peak periods by marketing efforts and price concessions. Cruise lines and resort hotels offer low rates in off seasons; airlines and hotels offer low rates on weekends; public utilities offer low rates on slack periods during a day. Second, if feasible, they adjust the size of the work force to the anticipated demand, by such measures as scheduling training activities in slack periods and compensating for long hours in busy periods with time off later. The loss from unsold services is so important that occupancy rates, "sold hours," load factors, student enrollment, hospital admissions, and similar indications of success in selling available services are normally key variables in service organizations of all types.

Difficulty in controlling quality. A manufacturing company can inspect its products before they are shipped to the consumer, and the inspection standards can be measured visually or with instruments (tolerances, purity, weight, color, and so on). A service company cannot judge product quality until the moment the service is rendered, and then the judgments are often subjective. Restaurant management can examine the food in the kitchen, but customer satisfaction depends to a considerable extent on the way it is served. The quality of education is so difficult to measure that few educational organizations have a formal quality control system.

> **Example.** In service enterprises, intangible attributes often represent the main value: such attributes as on-time performance of transportation, schedule frequency and match to customer desires, friendliness and helpfulness of people who talk with customers, skill with which the service is carried out, information available at the location and time of customer contact, location of available service, waiting time, and appearance of facilities and people.
>
> When one looks at what it takes to be successful in a competitive service world, such intangibles as these stand out as the key factors of success. These are the important elements of output. In a physical product, such as an automobile, four-way adjustable bucket seats may be important to the customer; however, for purchasers of services, such as airline customers, having ticket counter people who are accessible, friendly, and knowledgeable may be the most important service characteristic. For a management accountant, bucket seats are fairly easy to cost out; the desired attributes of a ticket agent may be recognized as having value for the customer, but measuring the cost of providing that value is a difficult challenge.[1]

---

[1] Professor William Rotch, remarks at a symposium on Management Accounting in Service Industries, March 16, 1990.

Labor intensive. Manufacturing companies add equipment and automate production lines that replace labor and reduce costs. Most service companies cannot do this. Hospitals do add expensive equipments; but most of these provide better treatment, and they increase, rather than reduce, costs.

Multi unit organizations. Some service organizations operate many units in different locations, each one of which is relatively small. These include fast-food restaurant chains, auto rental companies, gasoline service stations, and many others. Some of the units are owned; others operate under a franchise. The similarity of these separate units provides a basis for analyzing budgets and evaluating performance that is not present in the usual manufacturing company. The information for each unit can be compared with systemwide or regional averages, and high performers and low performers can be identified.

Because units differ in the mix of services they provide, in the resources that they use, and in other ways, care must be taken in making such comparisons. A technique for adjusting for these differences is called by the (uninformative) name, "Data Envelopment Analysis." It identifies the most efficient units by using statistical methods of allowing for differences. As originally proposed, the technique was overly complicated, but simplifications have made it useful in several industries.[2]

Historical Development

Cost accounting started in manufacturing companies because of the need to value work-in-process and finished goods inventories for financial statement purposes. These systems provided raw data that were easily adapted for use in setting selling prices and for other management purposes. Standard cost systems, separation of fixed and variable costs, and analysis of variances were built on the foundation of cost accounting systems. Until a few decades ago, most texts on cost accounting dealt only with practices in manufacturing companies.

Many service organizations (with the notable exception of railroads and other regulated public industries) did not have a similar impetus to develop cost data. Their use of product cost and other management accounting data is fairly recent—mostly since World War II. Their management control systems are rapidly becoming as well developed as those in manufacturing companies.

---

[2] For a description, see H. David Sherman, *Service Organization Productivity Management*, (Hamilton, Ont.: Society of Management Accountants of Canada, 1988), chap. 3.

PROFESSIONAL ORGANIZATIONS

Research and development organizations, law firms, accounting firms, medical clinics, health maintenance organizations, engineering firms, architectural firms, consulting firms, and advertising agencies are examples of organizations whose products are professional services.

Special Characteristics

Goals. As explained in Chapter 2, a dominant goal of a manufacturing company is to earn a satisfactory profit, specifically a satisfactory return on assets employed. A professional organization has relatively few tangible assets; its principal asset is the skill of its professional staff, which doesn't appear on its balance sheet. Return on assets employed, therefore, is essentially meaningless in such organizations. Their financial goal is to provide adequate compensation to the professionals. In many organizations, a related goal is to increase their size. In part, this reflects the natural tendency to associate success with large size. In part, it reflects economies of scale in using the efforts of a central personnel staff and units responsible for keeping the organization up to date. Large public accounting firms need to have enough local offices to enable them to audit clients who have facilities located throughout the world.

Professionals. Professional organizations are labor intensive, and the labor is of a special type. Many professionals prefer to work independently, rather than as part of a team. Professionals who are also managers tend to work only part time on management activities; senior partners in an accounting firm participate actively in audit engagements; senior partners in law firms have clients. In most professions, education does not include education in management; quite naturally it stresses the importance of the profession, rather than that of management; for this and other reasons, professionals tend to look down on managers. Professionals tend to give inadequate weight to the financial implications of their decisions; they want to do the best job they can, regardless of its cost. This attitude tends to rub off on the attitude of support staffs and nonprofessionals in the organization; it leads to inadequate cost control.

Because professionals are the organization's most important resource, some authors have advocated that the value of these professionals should be counted as assets. The system that does this is called "human resource accounting." In the 1970s, many books and articles were written on this subject, but few companies actually installed such a system, and we do not know of any that use one currently.[3] The problem of measuring the value of human assets is intractable.

---

[3] See, for example, Eric G. Flamholtz, *Human Resources Accounting* (Encino, Calif.: Dickerson Publishing Company, 1974).

Output and input measurement. The output of a professional organization cannot be measured in physical terms, such as units, tons, or gallons. We can measure the number of hours a lawyer spends on a case, but this is a measure of input, not output; output is the effectiveness of the lawyer's work, and this is not measured by the number of pages in a brief or the number of hours in the courtroom. We can measure the number of patients a physician treats in a day, and even classify these visits by type of complaint; but this is by no means equivalent to measuring the amount or quality of service the physician provided. At most, this measures the physician's efficiency in treating patients, which is of some use in identifying slackers and hard workers. Revenues earned is one measure of output in some professional organizations; but these monetary amounts, at most, relate to the quantity of services rendered, not to their quality (although poor quality is reflected in reduced revenues in the long run.)

> **Example.** There are more than 1,300 articles and books dealing with research on student ratings of teachers. They describe as many as 22 dimensions of teaching performance (e.g., "explains clearly," "uses class time well") and 20 variables that affect the ratings (e.g., size of course, time of day, gender, level of course). The best of these rating systems can identify very good teachers and very poor teachers, but none do a satisfactory job of ranking the 70 or 80 percent of teachers who are not at these extremes.[4]

Furthermore, the work done by many professionals is nonrepetitive. No two consulting jobs or research and development projects are quite the same. This makes it difficult to plan the time required for a task, to set reasonable standards for task performance, and, therefore, to judge how satisfactory the performance was. Some tasks are essentially repetitive: the drafting of simple wills, deeds, sales contracts, and similar documents; the taking of a physical inventory by an auditor; and certain medical and surgical procedures are examples. The development of standards for such tasks may be worthwhile, although, in using these standards, unusual circumstances that affect a specific job must be taken into account. Although drafting a deed for residential property and the related title search may be a cut-and-dried process in the majority of instances, some deeds involve special restrictions or an ambiguity in the title; a standard number of minutes is, therefore, only a general guide.

Some professionals, notably scientists, engineers, and professors, are reluctant to keep track of how they spend their time, and this complicates the task of measuring performance. This reluctance seems to have its roots in tradition; usually, it can be overcome if senior management is willing to put appropriate

---

[4] Based on William E. Cashin, "Reliability, Validity, and Generalizability of Student Ratings of Instruction," *IDEA Paper no. 20*, Center for Faculty Evaluation and Development, Kansas State University, September 1988.

emphasis on the necessity for accurate time reporting. Nevertheless, difficult problems arise in deciding how time should be charged to clients. If the normal work week is 40 hours, should a job be charged for $\frac{1}{40}$th of a week's compensation for each hour spent on it? If so, how should work done on evenings and weekends be counted? (Professionals are "exempt" employees—that is, they are not subject to the government requirements for overtime payments.) How to account for time spent reading literature, going to meetings, and otherwise keeping up to date?

Small size. With a few exceptions, such as law firms and accounting firms, professional organizations are relatively small and operate at a single location. Senior management in such organizations can personally observe what is going on and personally motivate employees. Thus, there is less need for a sophisticated management control system, with profit centers and formal performance reports. Nevertheless, even a small organization needs a budget, a regular comparison of performance against budget, and a way of relating compensation to performance.

Marketing. In a manufacturing company there is a clear dividing line between marketing activities and production activities; only senior management is concerned with both. Such a clean separation does not exist in most professional organizations, however. In some, such as law, medicine, and accounting, the profession's ethical code limits the amount and character of overt marketing efforts by professionals (although these restrictions have been relaxed in recent years). Marketing is an essential activity in almost all organizations, however; and if it can't be conducted openly, it takes the form of personal contacts, speeches, articles, golf, and similar activities. These marketing activities are conducted by professionals, usually by professionals who spend much of their time in production work—that is, working for clients.

In such a situation, it is difficult to assign appropriate credit to the person responsible for "selling" a new customer. In a consulting firm, for example, a new engagement may result from a conversation between a member of the firm and an acquaintance in a company, or from the reputation of one of the firm's professionals as an outgrowth of speeches or articles. Moreover, the professional who is responsible for obtaining the engagement may not be personally involved in carrying it out. Until fairly recently, these marketing contributions were rewarded subjectively—that is, they were taken into account in promotion and compensation decisions. Some organizations now give explicit credit, perhaps as a percentage of the project's revenue, if the person who "sold" the project can be identified.

Management Control Systems

Pricing. The selling price of work is set in a traditional way in many professional firms. If the profession is one in which members are accustomed to keeping track of their time, fees generally are related to professional time spent on the engagement. The hourly billing rate typically is based on the compensation of the grade of the professional (rather than the compensation of the specific person), plus a loading for overhead costs and profit. In other professions, such as investment banking, the fee typically is based on the monetary size of the security issue. In still others, there is a fixed price for the project. Prices vary widely among professions; they are relatively low for research scientists and relatively high for accountants and physicians.

In manufacturing companies, the profit component of the selling price is normally set so as to obtain, on average, a satisfactory return on assets employed. As noted above, the principal "asset" of a professional organization is the skill of its professionals, which is not measurable. Actually, the total value of the whole organization is greater than the sum of what the value of the individuals would be if they worked separately. This is because the firm already has incurred the cost of acquiring and training these individuals, has organized them according to their personality "fit" and other considerations, and has developed policies and procedures for assuring that the work is done efficiently and effectively. In this manner, the firm accepts responsibility for producing a satisfactory product, including the risk of loss if the work is not well done, and absorbs the cost of personnel who are not working on revenue-producing work. These considerations implicitly affect the size of the "profit" component that is included in the fee.

Profit centers and transfer pricing. Although this would seem to be a contradiction of terms, nonprofit organizations make extensive use of profit centers. Support units, such as maintenance, information processing, transportation, telecommunication, printing, and procurement of material and services, charge consuming units for their services. The principles for transfer pricing are those described in Chapter 5.

The General Services Administration in the United States and Supply and Services Canada (SSC) are responsible for billions of dollars of such services. In Canada, SSC provides for the acquisition of all items costing more than $500. It operates a financial accounting and reporting system that cost $600 million in 1988, which any agency can use (although this is not required); and its Audit Services Bureau provides audit services similar to those provided by accounting firms (and it competes with these firms).[5]

Programming and budgeting. In general, formal programming systems are not as well developed in professional organizations as in manufacturing companies of similar size. Part of the explanation is that professional organizations have no great need for a formal programming system. In manufacturing companies, many program decisions involve commitments to procure plant and equipment; they have a predictable effect on both capacity and on costs for several future years, and, once made, they are essentially irreversible. In a

---

[5] Haru Johri, Phil Charko, and Glyden Headley, "Transfer Pricing in the Federal Government," *CMA Magazine*, July/August 1990, pp. 12–16.

professional organization, the principal assets are people; and, although short-run fluctuations in personnel levels are avoided, changes in the size and composition of the staff are easier to make and are more easily reversed than changes in the capacity of a physical plant. The program of a professional organization typically consists primarily of a long-range staffing plan, rather than a full-blown strategic plan for all aspects of the firm's operation.

The budgeting process in professional organizations is similar to that described in Chapter 9. An interesting variation in the approach to budget preparation is illustrated in Exhibit 14–2, which shows a budget for a relatively small accounting firm. The starting point in preparing this budget was the desired income of $100,000; this was calculated as a percentage of the estimated market value of the firm—that is, what the firm could be sold for. Salaries were estimated at the anticipated rates in the firm's locality in the budget year. Expenses were then estimated. The sum of desired income and expenses is the revenue that must be generated from billings, $1,106,000. Various combinations of billing rates and chargeable hours were calculated until a feasible combination that produces the desired income was found. (The amount in Exhibit 14–2 labeled "special billings" was a reduction in gross revenue for work that was billed at less than standard rates.)

Control of operations. Much attention is, or should be, given to scheduling the time of professionals. The *billed time ratio,* which is the ratio of hours billed to total professional hours available, is watched closely. If, to use otherwise idle time, or for marketing or public service reasons, some engagements are billed at lower than normal rates, the resulting price variance warrants close attention.

The inability to set standards for task performance, the desirability of carrying out work by teams, the consequent problems of managing a matrix organization, and the behavioral characteristics of professionals—all complicate the planning and control of the day-to-day operations in a professional organization. When the work is done by project teams, control is focused on projects. A written plan for each project is needed, and timely reports should be prepared that compare actual performance with planned performance in terms of cost, schedule, and quality, as described in Chapter 17.

Progress reports. Progress reports are paperwork, which professionals tend to dislike, but they are nevertheless essential. Report requirements that lead to voluminous descriptions of trivial matters should, of course, be avoided. In particular, if the project is proceeding without difficulty, extensive documentation of this fact is a waste of time. Setting up a list of a relatively few (say 10 percent) of the projects can be a helpful procedure.

Progress reports are effective if the atmosphere of the organization is such that project leaders are willing to reveal actual or incipient problems to their superiors, rather than hiding them until it is too late. If, however, there

EXHIBIT 14–2 Budget for a CPA Firm

	Estimated Actual Year Ending 9/1/87				Budget Year Ending 9/1/88			
	Billed Hours	Standard Rate	Gross Revenue	Salary	Billed Hours	Standard Rate	Gross Revenue	Salary
Gross Revenue:								
Armstrong	1,200	$150	$180,000	$120,000	1,200	$150	$ 180,000	$120,000
Baker	1,500	110	165,000	80,000	1,500	120	180,000	80,000
Colwell	1,500	110	165,000	80,000	1,500	110	165,000	80,000
(Additional)	—	—	—	—	800	100	80,000	40,000
Staff #1	1,800	60	108,000	50,000	1,800	60	108,000	54,000
Staff #2	1,600	60	96,000	40,000	1,800	60	108,000	43,000
Staff #3	1,800	50	90,000	40,000	1,800	55	99,000	43,000
Staff #4	1,700	50	85,000	30,000	1,800	55	99,000	32,000
Staff #5	—	—	—	—	900	50	45,000	25,000
Secretaries (2)	1,000	25	25,000	30,000	1,000	30	30,000	33,000
Clerks (2)	3,000	30	60,000	28,000	3,000	25	75,000	31,000
Total (at standard)	15,100		974,000	$498,000	17,100		1,169,000	$581,000
Special billings			(46,000)				(58,000)	
Net Revenue			928,000				1,111,000	
Expenses:								
Salaries (as above)			498,000				581,000	
Benefits			124,000				145,000	
Controllable costs			164,000				150,000	
Fixed costs			120,000				130,000	
Total			$906,000				$1,006,000	
Income			$ 22,000				$ 105,000	

is an environment in which unpleasant reports invariably lead to destructive criticism, rather than helpful suggestions, progress reports may resemble works of fiction.

At best, formal reports are not likely to provide the principal means of finding out about progress. Informal conversations, regularly scheduled meetings, and the manager's sensitivity to hints of trouble received from various sources are likely to be much more important.

Performance measurement and appraisal.   At the extremes, the performance of professionals is easy to measure—that is, it is easy to identify and take appropriate action about professionals who do sloppy or inadequate work, on the one hand, and those who do brilliant work, on the other hand. Appraisal of the large percentage of professionals who are within either extreme is much more difficult. In some situations, objective measures of performance are available: The recommendations of an investment analyst can be compared with actual market behavior of the securities; the accuracy of a surgeon's diagnosis can be verified by an examination of the tissue that was removed; and skill can be measured by the success ratio of operation. These measures are, of course, subject to appropriate qualifications. In most circumstances, however, the assessment of performance is a matter of human judgment. These judgments may be made by superiors, peers, self, subordinates, or clients.

Most common are judgments made by superiors. Professional organizations increasingly are using formal systems to collect performance appraisals as a basis for personnel decisions and for discussion with the professional. Some systems require numerical ratings of specified attributes of performance and provide for a weighted average of these ratings. Compensation may be tied, in part, to these numerical ratings. In a matrix organization, performance is judged both by the person's project leader and by the head of the functional unit that is his or her organizational "home."

Appraisals by a professional's peers, or by subordinates, are sometimes part of a formal control system. Occasionally, the individual may be asked to make a self-appraisal. Expressions of satisfaction or dissatisfaction from clients are also an important basis for judging performance, although such expressions may not be forthcoming in many engagements. One firm that sells investment advice to institutional clients keeps a record of letters of commendation or criticism received from these clients, classifies these according to the analysts who made the relevant recommendations, and uses this information as part of its performance evaluation system.

The budget can be used as the basis for measuring cost performance, and the actual time taken can be compared with the planned time. Budgeting and control of discretionary expenses is as important in a professional firm as in a manufacturing company. Such financial measures are relatively unimportant in assessing a professional's contribution to the firm's profitability, however. The major contribution is related to the quantity and quality of the work, and its appraisal must be largely subjective. Furthermore, the appraisal must be made currently; it cannot wait until one learns whether a new building is well designed, a new control system actually works well, or whether a bond indenture has a flaw.

An analysis of the profitability of the various services offered by the firm also is useful. The techniques are similar to those used to analyze product profitability in manufacturing companies.

In some professions, internal audit procedures are used to control quality. In many accounting firms, the report of an audit is reviewed by a partner other than the one who is responsible for it, and the work of the whole firm is "peer reviewed" by another firm. The proposed design of a building may be reviewed by architects who are not actively involved in the project.

HEALTH CARE ORGANIZATIONS

Health care organizations consist of hospitals, clinics and similar physicians' organizations, health maintenance organizations, nursing homes, home care organizations, and medical laboratories, among others. They constitute the largest industry in the United States: 11 percent of the gross national product, which is about the same percentage as the *total* of all durable goods manufacturers.[6] Although they have most of the characteristics of nonprofit organizations, which are discussed in the next section, many of them are, in fact, profit-oriented companies.

Special Characteristics

Difficult social problem. Society has not come to grips with the fact that the present health care delivery system is unworkable. Although physicians are bound by the Hippocratic oath to provide adequate health care to their patients, the system cannot do this. On the one hand, the cost per treatment is inevitably increasing with the development of new equipment and new drugs; hospital expenses increased from $28.0 billion in 1970 to $196.7 billion in 1988. (Contrast this trend with the typical experience of manufacturing companies, in which new equipment usually reduces unit costs.) On the other hand, the number of ill persons is increasing because medical advances prolong the lives of elderly people, who are the most likely to require treatment. Society cannot pay for the predictable increases if the present rate of increase in cost continues

---

[6] Data in this section are taken from the following tables in the *Statistical Abstract of the United States, 1990;* No. 135 (overall expenditures); No. 163 (hospitals); and No. 645 (employment). For more detailed data, see the following annual publications: U.S. National Center for Health Statistics; *Health, United States;* U.S. Health Care Financing Administration; *Health Care Financing Review;* American Hospital Association; *Hospital Statistics.*

much longer. Health care providers are aware of this problem; but they don't know how society, especially the Congress, will deal with it. It is clear, however, that health care delivery will change drastically. Health care organizations must be alert to these changes.

Change in mix of providers.   Within the overall increase in health care cost, significant changes have occurred in the way in which health care is delivered and, hence, in the viability of certain types of providers. Many services that traditionally were provided in hospitals on an inpatient basis are now provided in outpatient clinics or in patients' homes. Entrepreneurs have entered the industry to provide these new services. There also has been a shift from small local hospitals to larger regional or medical center hospitals. The number of hospital beds decreased by 20 percent from 1970 to 1987. To remain viable, hospitals must have the flexibility to adapt to these changes, either by providing more outpatient services themselves or by eliminating inpatient services that are no longer profitable.

Third-party payers.   Of the $500.3 billion total expenditures for health care in 1987, 41 percent was financed by the government, 32 percent by insurance companies, and only 27 percent by individual patients. An estimated 37 million people in the United States have no health insurance; their costs are met by Medicaid, absorbed by health care providers, or paid for by the patient directly. The largest government program is Medicare, a federal program that provides support for persons age 65 and up and for younger persons with certain disabilities. The Medicaid program pays for services provided to low-income people; it is financed by the states within general guidelines set by the federal government. Until 1983, Medicare reimbursed on the basis of "reasonable" costs incurred, which gave health care providers little incentive to controls costs. Currently, Medicare reimburses hospitals on the basis of Diagnostic Related Groups (DRGs). Medical and surgical procedures are classified into one of about 500 DRGs, each DRG is priced annually at a set dollar amount, and hospitals are reimbursed for these amounts, regardless of the actual length of stay or the actual costs incurred for individual patients. Other third-party payers are moving toward a similar system of reimbursement.

The DRG system, and the increase in hospital costs per patient, has motivated hospitals to install sophisticated cost accounting systems, usually systems that they purchase from an outside computer organization and then adapt to their own needs. Some hospitals provide information processing services to other hospitals on a contract basis. These systems provide information on individual patients (similar to job-cost systems in automobile repair shops), and they report actual costs compared with standard costs for each DRG; costs are classified by departments and even by attending physicians within departments.

This information is in addition to information traditionally collected in hospitals; it focuses on outputs (patient care), as well as on inputs (cost per laboratory test).

Professionals. The health care industry employed 2,972,000 professionals (physicians, dentists, registered nurses, and therapists) in 1988, which is more than any other industry except education. The management control implications of professionals are the same as those discussed in the preceding section. Their primary loyalty is to the profession, rather than to the organization. Departmental managers typically are professionals whose management function is only part-time; the chief of surgery does surgery. Physicians tend to give relatively little emphasis to cost control. In particular, there is an impression that they prescribe more than the optimum number of tests, partly because of the danger of malpractice suits if they don't detect all the patient's symptoms.

Importance of quality control. The health care industry deals with human lives, so the quality of the service it provides is of paramount importance. There are tissue reviews of surgical procedures, peer review of individual physicians, and, in recent years, outside review agencies mandated by the federal government.

Management Control Process

Subject to the characteristics described above, the management control process in the health care industry is similar to that described in Chapters 8 through 12. Because of the shift in the product mix and because of the increase in the number and cost of new equipments, the programming process in hospitals is becoming of increasing importance. The annual budget preparation process is conventional. Huge quantities of information are available quickly for the control of operating activities. Financial performance is analyzed by comparing actual revenues and expenses with budgets, identifying important variances, and taking appropriate action on them.

NONPROFIT ORGANIZATIONS

A nonprofit organization, as defined in law, is an organization that cannot distribute assets or income to, or for the benefit of, its members, officers, or directors. The organization can, of course, compensate its employees, including officers and members, for services rendered and for goods supplied. This definition does not prohibit an organization from *earning* a profit; it prohibits only the *distribution* of profits. A nonprofit organization needs to earn a modest profit, on average, to provide funds for working capital and for possible "rainy days."

Nonprofit organizations that meet the criteria of Section 501(c) of the Internal Revenue Code are exempt from income taxes (except on their "unrelated business income"); about 1.2 million organizations satisfy these criteria. If they are religious, charitable, or educational organizations as defined in

Section 501(c) (3) of the code, contributions made to them are tax deductible by the contributor; they are called "501(c) (3) organizations." Most such organizations are exempt from property taxes and from certain types of sales taxes.

In many industry groups, there are both nonprofit and profit-oriented (i.e., business) organizations. There are nonprofit and for-profit hospitals, nonprofit and for-profit ("proprietary") schools and colleges, and even for-profit religious organizations. SRI International is a nonprofit research organization that competes with Arthur D. Little, Inc., a for-profit research organization.

Special Characteristics

Absence of the profit measure.   A dominant goal of most businesses is to earn a satisfactory profit; net income measures performance toward this goal. No such single measure of performance exists in nonprofit organizations. Many of them have several goals, and an organization's effectiveness in attaining its goals rarely can be measured by quantitive amounts. The absence of a satisfactory, quantitative, overall measure of performance is the most serious management control problem in a nonprofit organization.

It does not follow that the income statement of a nonprofit organization serves no worthwhile function. On the contrary, the income statement is the most useful financial statement in a nonprofit organization, just as it is in a business. The net income number is interpreted differently in the two types of organizations, however. In a business, as a general rule, the larger the income, the better the performance. In a nonprofit organization, net income should average only a small amount above zero. A large net income signals that the organization is not providing the services that those who supplied resources had a right to expect. A string of net losses will lead to bankruptcy, just as in a business. The income statement is the best way of reporting *financial* performance, but financial performance is not the dominant goal in a nonprofit organization. It is, however, a necessary goal because the organization cannot survive if its revenues on average are less than its expenses.

Contributed capital.   There is only one major difference between the accounting transactions in a business and those in a nonprofit organization; it relates to the equity section of the balance sheet. A business corporation has transactions with its shareholders—issuance of stock and the payment of dividends—that a nonprofit organization doesn't have. A nonprofit organization receives contributed capital, which few businesses have. (In both businesses and nonprofit organizations, equity is increased by earning income.)

There are two principal categories of contributed capital: plant and endowment. Plant includes contributions of buildings and equipment, or contributions of funds to acquire these assets; it also includes works of art and other museum objects. Endowment consists of gifts whose donors intend that the principal amount will remain intact indefinitely (or at least for many years); only the income on this principal will be used to finance current operations.

The receipt (or pledge) of a contributed capital asset is not revenue—that is, neither contributions of plant nor of endowment are available to finance the operating activities of the period in which the contribution is received. Endowment assets must be kept separate from operating assets; this is a legal requirement for "true" endowment, and it is sound policy for "board-designated" endowment—that is, funds that the trustees have decided to treat as endowment, even though there is no legal requirement that they do so. It follows that capital contributions should be reported separately from operating contributions—that is, from revenues from annual fund drives, grants, and other gifts intended to finance current operations.

Thus, a nonprofit organization has two sets of financial statements. One set relates to operating activities, and it has an operating statement, a balance sheet, and a statement of cash flows that are the same as those found in business. The second set relates to contributed capital, and it has a statement of inflows and outflows of contributed capital during a period and a balance sheet that reports contributed capital assets and the related liabilities and equity. Inflows of contributed capital are capital contributions received in the period and gains on the endowment portfolio; outflows are the endowment income that is reported as operating revenue, losses on the endowment portfolio, and write-offs of plant. (Although a current Financial Accounting Standards Board pronouncement, *Statement No. 93,* requires that contributed plant be depreciated, this requirement serves no useful purpose and is disregarded by some organizations.)

Fund accounting. Many nonprofit organizations use an accounting system that is called "fund accounting." Accounts are kept separately for several funds, each of which is self-balancing (i.e., the sum of the debit balances equals the sum of the credit balances). The types of funds and the method of accounting for each are specified by *Audit Guides* and by *Statements of Position* published by the American Institute of Certified Public Accountants. *Audit Guides* have been prepared for colleges and universities, hospitals, voluntary health and welfare organizations and "other" nonprofit industries. Because they differ considerably from one another, a person who is interested in a specific industry needs to be familiar with the pronouncement applicable to that industry.

The following may suffice for a general understanding. Most organizations have: (1) a *general fund* or *operating fund,* which corresponds closely to the set of operating accounts mentioned above; and (2) a *plant fund* and an *endowment fund,* which account for contributed capital assets and equities mentioned above; and (3) a variety of other funds for special purposes. Some of these other funds, such as the pension fund, are also found in business; others are useful for internal control purposes. For management control purposes, the primary focus is on the general fund.

Governance. Nonprofit organizations are governed by boards of trustees. Trustees usually are not paid, and many of them are unfamiliar with business management. Therefore, they generally exercise less control than the directors of a business corporation. Moreover, because performance is more difficult to measure in a nonprofit organization than in a business, the board is less able to identify actual or incipient problems.

The need for a strong governing board in a nonprofit organization is greater than that in a business, because the vigilance of the governing board may be the only effective way of detecting when the organization is in difficulty. In a profit-oriented organization, a decrease in profits provides this danger signal automatically.

Management Control Systems

Product pricing. Many nonprofit organizations give inadequate attention to their pricing policies. To the extent that pricing of services at their full cost is feasible, the following benefits can be achieved:

1. If services are sold at prices that approximate full cost, the revenue number is a measure of the quantity of services that the organization supplies. Such a measure is otherwise difficult to obtain.

2. Charging clients for the services they receive makes them more aware of the value of the service and encourages them to consider whether a service is actually worth at least as much to them as its cost. Although this point does not apply to services to legitimate clients who are unable to pay for them, setting a full-cost price and providing a discount to needy clients provides a measure of quantity and informs the client of the value of the service. Many colleges and universities have such a policy; the discount is financial aid. Also, charging a token amount, rather than providing the service for free, gives some incentive to clients to limit their use of the service.

3. If services are sold, the responsibility center that sells them can become a profit center, with the advantages described in Chapter 4.

As a general rule, a "full-cost" price is the sum of direct costs, indirect costs, and, perhaps, a small allowance for increasing the organization's equity. This principle applies to services that are directly related to the organization's objectives. Pricing for peripheral activities should be market-based. Thus, a nonprofit hospital should price its health care services at full cost, but its gift shop prices should be market-based.

In general, the smaller and more specific the unit of service that is priced, the better the basis for decisions about the allocation of resources. For example, a comprehensive daily rate for hospital care, which was common practice a few decades ago, masks the revenues for the mix of services actually provided. Beyond a certain point, of course, the cost of the paperwork associated with pricing units of service outweighs the benefits.

As a general rule, management control is facilitated when prices are established prior to the performance of the service. If an organization is able to recover its incurred costs, whatever they turn out to be, management is not motivated to worry about cost control.

Programming and budget preparation. In nonprofit organizations that must decide how best to allocate limited resources to worthwhile activities, programming is a more important and more time-consuming process than in the typical business. The process is similar to that described in Chapter 8, except that the absence of a profit measure makes program decisions more subjective.

The budget preparation process is similar to that described in Chapter 9. Colleges and universities, welfare organizations, and organizations in certain other nonprofit industries know, before the budget year begins, the approximate amount of their revenues. They do not have the option of increasing revenues during the year by increasing their marketing efforts. They budget expenses so the organization will at least break even at the estimated amount of revenue. They require that managers of responsibility centers limit spending close to the budget amounts. The budget is, therefore, the most important management control tool, at least with respect to financial activities.

Execution and evaluation. In most nonprofit organizations, there is no way of knowing what the optimum operating costs are. Responsibility center managers, therefore, tend to spend whatever is allowed in the budget, even though the budgeted amount may be higher than is necessary. Conversely, they may refrain from making expenditures that have an excellent payoff simply because the expenditure was not included in the budget.

Although nonprofit organizations had a reputation for operating inefficiently, this perception has been changing in recent years, for good reasons. Many organizations have had increasing difficulty in raising funds, especially from government sources. This has led to belt-tightening and to increased attention to management control. As mentioned above, the most dramatic change has been in hospital costs, with the introduction of reimbursement on the basis of standard prices for diagnosis-related groups.

GOVERNMENT ORGANIZATIONS

Government organizations are service organizations and, except for business-like activities, they are nonprofit organizations. Thus, the characteristics described above for these organizations apply to government. Their business-like activities, such as electric and water utilities, operate like their private-sector counterparts.

Special Characteristics

Political influences. In government organizations, decisions result from multiple and often conflicting pressures. In part, these political pressures are an inevitable—and up to a point are a desirable—substitute for the forces of the marketplace. Elected officials cannot function if they are not reelected; and to be reelected, they must—up to a point—advocate the perceived needs of their constituents, even though these needs may not be in the best interests of society as a whole. Conflicting pressures result in less than optimum decisions. Elected officials may inhibit managers from making sound business decisions; they may be required to favor certain suppliers or to hire political supporters. Strict procurement policies and civil service regulations attempt to lessen these pressures, with some success.

Public information.   In a democratic society the press and public believe that they have a right to know everything there is to know about a government organization. In the federal government and in some states, this feeling is recognized by *freedom of information* statutes. Channels for distributing this information may be biased. Some media stories that describe mismanagement tend to be exaggerated and to give inadequate recognition to the fact that mistakes are inevitable in any organization. To reduce opportunities for unfavorable media stories, government managers take steps to limit the amount of sensitive, controversial information that flows through the formal management control system. This lessens the effectiveness of the system.

Attitude toward clients.   For-profit companies and many nonprofit organizations are *client supported*—that is, they obtain their revenues from clients. Additional clients mean additional revenues, so these organizations tend to treat actual and potential clients well. Most government organizations are *public supported;* they obtain their revenues from the general public. To them, an additional client may be a burden, to be accepted with misgivings, because he or she creates an additional demand for a fixed amount of service capacity. This has a negative effect on the way clients are treated. Although this tendency may be mitigated by the professional's desire to do a good job, it nevertheless exists and results in well-known complaints about poor service and surly attitude of "bureaucrats." Managers recognize this and do their best to persuade employees to provide satisfactory service. The revenue sources of public-supported organizations are legislative bodies and granting agencies; legislators and grantors are given even more consideration than are clients in client-supported organizations.

Management compensation.   Managers and other professionals in government organizations tend to be less well compensated than their counterparts in business. This results from a populist perception on the part of the general public—a feeling that "one person is as good as another"—which, in turn, influences legislators. Consequently, the best managers do not go into public service (unless they have acquired wealth from other sources). There are exceptions to this generalization; some government organizations pay competitive compensation to school administrators, superintendents, university faculty, and certain types of scientists and engineers. At lower levels, compensation tends to be higher than that prevailing in the private sector. This results in "salary compression," which complicates the problem of rewarding good performance.

Accounting.   Until recently, the accounting systems of state and local governments were archaic. However, the Governmental Accounting Standards Board, established in 1984, is developing improved accounting principles; they will be implemented in the 1990s. The accounting systems in the federal government are especially archaic.

Management Control Systems

Programming and budget preparation.   Programming is especially important in government organizations. Managers and legislators must make difficult decisions about the allocation of resources. Some of these decisions reflect political pressures. Others, however, are the results of sophisticated analyses. Especially in the federal government, benefit/cost techniques are more highly developed and skillfully applied than in most business organizations. Until the 1960s, the process was informal; but, with the development of the Planning–Programming–Budgeting System (PPBS) in the federal government, it has become increasingly formalized. The annual budget process is an extremely important control device in government, as it is in other nonprofit organizations.

Performance measurement.   Income is the difference between revenues and expenses. Expenses can be measured approximately as accurately in government organizations as in business (although currently the accounting systems in most government organizations do not do a good job of this). Revenue is not a measure of output in government organizations, however. In the absence of this monetary measure, governments have developed nonmonetary indicators. These measures can be classified in various ways. One classification, based on what they purport to measure is (1) results measures, (2) process measures, and (3) social indicators.

A *results measure* (also *outcomes measure*) is a measure of output that is supposedly related to the organization's objectives. Number of students graduating from high school, number of miles of roads completed, number of on-time arrivals at airports, are examples. These measures are rarely an exact measure of output; the number of graduates says nothing about how well the students were educated. Nevertheless, they may be a satisfactory *surrogate*.

A *process measure* is related to an activity carried on by the organization. Examples are the number of livestock inspected in a week, the number of purchase orders issued in a day, or the number of lines entered into a computer in an hour. Process measures are useful in measuring current, short-run performance. They are easier to interpret than results measures, because usually there is a close causal relationship between inputs (i.e., costs) and the process measure. Process measures relate to efficiency, not to effectiveness—that is, they measure what was done, not whether what was done helped achieve the organization's objectives. They are "means-oriented," as contrasted with results measures, which are "ends-oriented."

A *social indicator* is a broad measure of output that reflects the result of the work of the organization. Since social indicators are affected by external forces, they are at best only a rough indication of the accomplishments of the organization itself. Life expectancy is an indication of the effectiveness of a country's health care system; but it is also affected by the standard of living, dietary and smoking habits, and other external causes. Social indicators are useful principally in long-range analyses of strategic problems. They are so nebulous, so difficult to obtain on a current basis, so little affected by current efforts, and so much affected by external influences that they are of limited usefulness in day-to-day management.

MERCHANDISING ORGANIZATIONS

Retailers, distributors, wholesalers, and similar organizations usually are not classified as service organizations; however, they obviously are not manufacturing organizations either. To avoid omitting them entirely, they are discussed briefly in this section.

Unlike service organizations, inventory is important in merchandising organizations. Indeed, department heads in these organizations usually are called "buyers," rather than "managers," which indicates the importance of the procurement function. A principal control device is *open to buy,* which is the maximum amount that the buyer can have in inventory *and on order* at any time.

Merchandising industries have well-developed management control systems. Although we have tended to emphasize techniques in manufacturing companies, many similar techniques have been used for many years in merchandising companies. Furthermore, trade associations and private organizations have developed systems of collecting information on revenues, costs, and other elements, which are useful in comparing one company's performance with that of averages in the industry.

SUMMARY

Management control in service organizations is different from that in manufacturing organizations, primarily because of the absence of an inventory buffer between production and sales, because of the difficulty of measuring quality, and because the organizations are labor-intensive. Professional organizations do not have the dominant goal of return on assets employed; professionals have their own behavioral characteristics, output measurements are subjective, and there is no clear line between marketing and production activities. Health care organizations must deal with the fact that the current system is unworkable. Nonprofit organizations lack the advantages that the profit measure provides, and they must account for contributed capital that rarely occurs in a business. Government organizations have the well-known problems associated with political influences and the bureaucracy. In merchandising organizations, inventory control is especially important.

Nevertheless, the essentials of the management control systems in service organizations are the same as those described in earlier chapters.

SUGGESTED ADDITIONAL READINGS

Albrecht, Karl, and Ron Zemke. *Service America: Doing Business in the New Economy.* Homewood, Ill.: Dow Jones-Irwin, 1985.

American Institute of Certified Public Accountants. *Management of an Accounting Practice Handbook.* New York: AICPA (looseleaf).

Anthony, Robert N., and David W. Young. *Management Control in Nonprofit Organizations,* 4th ed. Homewood, Ill.: Richard D. Irwin, 1988.

Barton, Thomas L., and Robert J. Fox. "Evolution at American Transtech." *Management Accounting,* April 1988, pp. 49–52.

Collier, David A. *Service Management.* Reston, Va.: Reston Publishing, 1985.

Dearden, John. "Cost Accounting Comes to Service Industries." *Harvard Business Review,* September–October 1978, pp. 132–40.

Douglas, Patricia P. *Governmental and Nonprofit Accounting,* Orlando, Fla.: Harcourt Brace Jovanovich, 1991.

Grayson, Leslie E., and Curtis J. Tompkins. *Management of Public Sector and Nonprofit Organizations.* Reston, Va.: Reston Publishing, 1984.

Gross, Malvern J., Jr., and Stephen F. Jablonsky. *Principles of Accounting and Financial Reporting for Nonprofit Organizations.* New York: Ronald Press, 1979.

Hay, Leon E. *Accounting for Governmental and Nonprofit Entities.* 7th ed. Homewood, Ill.: Richard D. Irwin, 1985.

Henke, Emerson O. *Introduction to Nonprofit Organization Accounting.* 2nd ed. Belmont, Calif.: Wadsworth, 1985.

Herbert, Leo A., Harry N. Killough; and Alan Walter Steiss. *Accounting and Control for Governmental and Other Nonbusiness Organizations.* New York: McGraw-Hill, 1987.

Heskitt, James L. *Managing in the Service Economy.* Boston: Harvard Business School Press, 1984.

Kotler, Philip, and Paul N. Bloom. *Marketing Professional Services.* Englewood Cliffs, N.J.: Prentice Hall, 1984.

Lynn, Edward C., and Robert J. Freeman. *Fund Accounting Theory and Practice*. 2nd ed. Englewood Cliffs, N.J.: Prentice Hall, 1982.

McGregor, Calvert C., Jr.; Larry N. Killough; and Robert M. Brown. "An Investigation of Organization-Professional Conflict in Management Accounting. *Journal of Management Accounting Research*, Fall 1989, pp. 104–18.

Ramanathan, Kavasseri. *Management Control in Nonprofit Organizations*. New York: John Wiley & Sons, 1982.

Sherman, H. David. *Service Organization Productivity Management*, Hamilton, Ontario: Society of Management Accountants of Canada, 1988.

U.S. General Accounting Office. "Budget Issues: Human Resource Programs Warranting Consideration as Human Capital." Washington, D.C.: 1990, GAO/AFMd-90-52.

——— Program Evaluation and Methodology Division. *Designing Evaluations: A Workbook*. Washington, D.C.: February 1986, U.S. GAO.

Case 14–1

Harley Associates, Inc.*

In 1975, Harley Associates, Inc., was one of America's largest advertising agencies. Advertising agencies are retained by many major corporations to assist them in the development and implementation of campaigns to promote sales. Two of the principal groups of advertising work in which agencies engage are the development of strategy and plans for new products, and the maintenance and improvement of the market share of established products. Generally speaking, the most successful partnership between advertisers and agencies are those of long duration. Harley Associates had worked with many of its present clients for more than 20 years.

Advertising agencies are remunerated by their clients in one of two ways. First, there is the commission basis, whereby the agency receives a rebate of 15 percent of gross billings from the medium in which the advertisement is placed.[1] Out of this amount the agency must meet all of its expenses. The other system, called the "fee" system, has many variations, but in general the client is billed for specific amounts of work done on his behalf by the agency. This may be on a cost-plus basis or involve a retainer fee plus a reimbursement of expenditures. Harley Associates

had worked under various fee arrangements; but its preference was for the 15 percent commission system, since it considered that such a system offered greater benefits to both the client and the agency.

Organization

Harley Associates was organized into five divisions of management:

Account management. The account supervisor and his staff formed the principal day-to-day contact between the agency and the client organizations. It was their function to work with the client in the development of the marketing plan. In addition, they acted as a liaison among the other areas of management within the agency to coordinate activities on the client's account.

Creative management. The creative department conceived and developed advertising copy and artwork required for prints and advertisements.

Information management. This group was responsible for planning and conducting copy and market research programs, and for advising on merchandising and product promotion opportunities. It also maintained the agency reference library and a training group for teaching the sales personnel of clients.

Media management. Within the framework of the market plan developed by the account manager, this group developed a media strategy that

---

[1] For example, if Harley placed a full-page ad for a client's product in a magazine whose full-page rate was $10,000, Harley would collect $10,000 from the client but would have to pay the magazine only $8,500.

---

* This case was prepared by J. M. McInnes under the supervision of J. R. Yeager, Harvard Business School.
Copyright © by the President and Fellows of Harvard College.
Harvard Business School case 113–097.

set forth the desired objectives, and then developed a media plan aimed at accomplishing the strategy most effectively. The relations between the agency and the advertising media, including the buying of space and time and the planning of advertisements, was the responsibility of this group.

Administrative management. This group was concerned with the internal management of the agency, dealing with personnel, financial, and office services areas.

As noted above, the direct contact between the agency and the client organization was through the account supervisor. It was the function of account management to coordinate the work with the client and map out the marketing, creative, and media strategies to promote the client's product. When an account supervisor was promoted to the position, he or she would begin with one account and, as it developed, would assume the responsibility for additional accounts. There was also a certain amount of turnover of accounts among the account supervisors, so each supervisor seldom stayed on the same account for more than a few years. The turnover required the supervisors to learn all about a new business each time they were transferred. This was obviously an expensive procedure, but Harley Associates considered it to be an excellent investment. The rationale behind it was that a person of high quality would be continually on the lookout for new challenges.

The "New Client" Decision

One of the most important decisions faced by the top management of an advertising agency is that of accepting an assignment from a new client. Certain firms have to be excluded from consideration because of the competitive constraint: An agency cannot accept a new assignment involving a product which is competitive with that of another client.

With the above exception, Harley Associates would consider any new client which satisfied two criteria: if the client had a satisfactory business reputation and was of good standing in the business community generally, and if the product seemed to the agency to be likely to satisfy a consumer need, the agency would be interested in accepting the assignment.

In assessing the profit potential of the assignment, the agency used its experience of past costs. Harley Associates was serving over 150 products for 33 clients in 1975, covering a wide range of product groups. On the basis of the cost data for these, an estimate of the cost of servicing the product under consideration would be made. An estimate would also be made of the amount of advertising required to build up the product to the desired market share, and of the amount needed to maintain it thereafter. Since an advertising allowance usually was built into the cost of the product, the agency could determine the amount it was going to be able to spend on the basis of certain volume assumptions. If the advertising allowance seemed to be sufficient to build up and to sustain the product, given the estimates of requirements, there would be a prima facie case for accepting the assignment.

The Introduction of a New Product

When a new product was being considered, the problem of estimating the costs of its introduction was acute. As a first step, the information management group tested the market to determine if there was a consumer need for the product and, if so, to isolate the consumer benefit. This procedure was not the introduction of the product to a limited market (Harley Associates referred to this as test marketing), but rather a gauging of consumer acceptance of the product. To aid in this, Harley Associates maintained a research panel of several thousand ordinary citizens around the country.

If it was satisfactorily established that a consumer need for the product existed, a creative strategy was developed, based largely on the perceived consumer benefit. The product would then be test marketed to test the effectiveness of the execution of the strategy. If the first test was unsuccessful, it was assumed that the selling message had not gotten across to the consumer and a change would be attempted in the execution of the strategy. The creative strategy itself was not subjected to question in this process. Such changes were time consuming, both for the agency and for the client.

After the test marketing was completed, the agency advised the client of its opinion on the probable outcome of launching the product on a full-scale basis. It was only after the decision to proceed had been taken and the advertising expenditures built up that the agency received significant revenue from the assignment. As well as covering current expenses, this revenue had to recompense the agency for the initial costs, so the management judgment early in the assignment concerning the likelihood of success of the product was extremely critical to the profitability of the agency.

Support of an Established Product

The advertising strategy involved in the support of an established product differed from that used in introducing a new one. The uncertainty attached to the market performance of a new product was considerably less acute in the case of an established product, although the constant possibility of product obsolescence remained. In essence, the function of advertising in supporting a product was to maintain constant exposure of the product's advantages to the ultimate user. The agency personnel and the client's marketing department were constantly seeking new ways of presenting the product to consumers with the objective of expanding market share.

Typically, a new maintenance campaign would be started after the existing campaign had run for a predetermined period. Judgment was involved in deciding how often a new campaign should be initiated. In addition, a drop in the product's market share might be a sign that a new cam-

paign was required. Adjusting to meet competitive advances was an important part of the maintenance of a product.

When a new campaign was being planned, the account supervisor would instruct the creative department to prepare plans for a strategy. The account supervisor and his or her staff would then meet, perhaps several times, with the sales personnel of the client to discuss the plans. Eventually, a strategy would be agreed on and the advertisement, commercial, or other promotional device prepared. The agency's media department then would arrange for the execution of the promotion as specified by the account supervisor.

Profitability of an Assignment

An important part of the agency top management's job was the assessment of the profitability of an account.

The most profitable clients to the agency were those using each advertisement frequently. The major expenses involved in the agency's work were incurred preceding the completion of the commercial or the copy. Thereafter, the work involved in placing the advertisement with the media was small compared with the 15 percent commission obtainable. Obviously, the more a given advertisement was used, the greater was the probability that the contribution (commission less placement costs) would amount to more than the cost of the preparatory work. If, on the other hand, the client's marketing strategy required constant development of new copy, which would be used only once or twice before it was considered obsolete, the agency's profits would be smaller.

The size of the client also might affect the profitability of an account. If numerous people in the client's organization had to clear an advertising plan, which was more likely to be the case with larger clients, this took a great deal of agency personnels' time and effort. The repeated conferences and revisions involved might push up the agency's costs to the extent of rendering the account unprofitable.

Other considerations involved in the top management decision on the retention of an account were frequently of greater significance than cost considerations. For example, even if a particular product was judged to be unprofitable to the agency, the agency might continue to carry this product because of the profitability of other products being carried for the same client. Sometimes a certain product line had to be maintained by the client for competitive purposes, even though the client was aware that the line was not showing a profit. If this were the case, the amounts spent on advertising such a product would frequently be small, as the client would not be anxious to promote the sales of a losing product. The agency would continue, in many cases, to handle such an account. At the same time, the agency would attempt to minimize its own expenditures involved in the advertising of such a product.

Cost Collection

In an effort to determine the cost associated with servicing a given account, close attention was paid to the amount of payroll costs associated with that account. Typically, payroll would amount to between 60 percent and 65 percent of the gross revenues of the agency. In many agencies, expenses other than payroll ranged from 20–25 percent of gross revenues, leaving the remaining 10–20 percent as profit before tax.

All employees except those in administrative management filed time sheets on which they recorded the time they had spent on specific accounts during the previous week. Anyone in the administrative department whose work could be allotted to a specific account also would file a time sheet. From the time sheets, 85 percent of the total payroll cost could be charged directly to the various accounts. Since 85 percent of the payroll was direct, and 65 percent of total cost was payroll, it followed that about 55 percent of cost was direct payroll. This led to a rule-of-thumb method for judging the profitability of an account. If the direct payroll of the account was less than 55 percent of the gross revenue from the account, it was assumed to be profitable.

Of the nonpayroll expenses, about 20 percent (i.e., 4–5 percent of revenues) were directly chargeable to the job. Included in direct expenses were travel, entertainment, the cost of rough copies, copy research work, and pretesting of copy. Indirect nonpayroll expenses included rent, which was the largest, telephone expenses, and so on. These indirect expenses were allocated to assignments on the basis of direct labor payroll.

One feature of Harley Associates' cost accounting system, which was unusual in the business, was that the figures on the profitability of an account were made available only to the chairman, the president, and the treasurer of the company. This was done so the enthusiasm of the service personnel for their work would not be affected by the profitability of the account. It was thought that an employee might have less enthusiasm for an unprofitable account, and that the quality of work might suffer as a result. It was considered to be the job of top management to decide which jobs to carry, and that the function of the creative personnel was to execute their tasks as well as they could.

The Electron Industries Situation

Electron Industries was a large manufacturer of industrial products. The company comprised many divisions, each of which was autonomous, except for those things that affected the image of the company as a whole, including advertising. Some of the company's divisions were clients of agencies other than Harley Associates.

Until recently, each of the divisions of Electron Industries that were clients of Harley Associates had been considered by the agency to be profitable. Early in 1976, however, the profitability to the agency of Electron's International Division had been subjected to question. The client profit-and-loss statement for the division for the year 1975 is shown in Exhibit 1.

The International Division did not advertise through the mass media. It was equipped to do most of its own artwork, so Harley Associates did not have to provide these services to the same extent that it did for other clients. The agency's

EXHIBIT 1

Client Profit-and-Loss Statement

Client   = Electron Industries, Inc., International Division
Product = Professional Prod.
Period   = Year to 12/31/75

Billing	$348,000
Commissions and fees	$ 61,800
Direct payroll:	
Account management	18,000
Copy	22,000
Art	10,000
Media	3,000
Administrative	1,500
	54,500
Other direct expenses:	
Unbillable costs	600
Travel	200
Entertainment	600
	1,400
Indirect expenses:	
Occupancy	8,000
Employee benefits	3,200
Telephone	2,100
Indirect service departments	14,600
Other indirect	6,800
	34,700
Total expense	90,600
Profit (loss) before taxes	($ 28,800)

main functions for this division were the development of advertising copy and the placing of advertisements with the media.

The account supervisor had spent considerable time becoming acquainted with the International Division's products and with Electron Industries' objectives to convey in the advertising plan a message that would meet with the approval of corporate management. Within the agency she had to ensure that the copywriters also were thoroughly familiar with the subject matter and the objectives of the advertising plan, so the copy would conform to Electron's corporate policy.

Mr. Sykes, a member of the agency's staff at headquarters, had been instructed to prepare a report for a top management meeting at which the profitability to the agency of International Division was to be discussed. The report was to include a statement of all the relevant points at issue, a list of alternative courses of action available to the agency, a brief note on the consequences of each, and Sykes's recommendation.

QUESTIONS

1. Describe a management control system that is appropriate for Harley Associates.
2. What points would you include in the report mentioned in the last paragraph of the case?

Case 14–2
Williamson and Oliver*

In early 1984, the policy board of Williamson and Oliver approved the suggestion of Ted Johnson, national managing partner, to institute an incentive compensation plan applicable to all the partners in the firm. (The plan is described in Exhibit 1.) One senior partner in the firm observed: In my opinion, this incentive plan is a step in the right direction. We want our partners to improve current profits; but, at the same time, we cannot lose sight of the longer-term development of our firm. I think the incentive plan explicitly considers the multidimensional nature of the partner's tasks. I am sure, though, that the plan needs to be fine-tuned as we gain more experience.

In 1984 Williamson and Oliver was one of the largest and fastest-growing public accounting firms in the United States. It had offices in more than 50 major cities and had over 500 partners. A major part of the firm's growth came from bases established through acquisition of local and regional CPA practices. Each office engaged in auditing, management advisory services, and taxation services. The practice offices were grouped into five areas, each headed by an area director. Reporting to the area directors were partners-in-charge (PIC), who manage the individual offices. Each area director was also the partner-in-charge for one of the offices in the area. About 15 partners and the related supporting staff constituted the executive office of the firm. The executive partners, including the national managing partner, reported to the policy board, which was a rotating group elected by the partners.

The Public Accounting Profession

Although there are literally thousands of CPA firms in this country, the profession is dominated by a small set of about 10 international firms. These firms account for perhaps 90 percent of the annual audits of publicly traded companies. For each of these 10 firms, auditing accounts for somewhere between 60 and 75 percent of gross billings. Taxation advisory services and management consulting services make up the remainder of the billings. The percentage of total billings from auditing has been falling for all the firms over the past 15 years. Each of the major firms maintains offices in most major cities across the country and offers a full range of client services in each office. No one firm is dominant in any region. In fact, it is extremely rare for any one firm to have even a 20 percent share of market in any one city or state.

The canons of professional ethics prohibit the corporate legal form, but the major firms all operate much like closely held professional service corporations, anyway, in terms of governance, management succession, and distribution of profits. The accounting business has been an excellent one over the past 40 years in terms of growth and profitability. In the 10 top firms, compound growth rates over the years have been in excess of 10 percent per year, and partner income averaged more than $100,000 per year in 1984.

Auditing has been the traditional "major profit machine" for all the firms. In recent years, however, the auditing business has shown many signs of maturity, such as slowed growth, declining

* This case was prepared by Vijay Govindarajan and John K. Shank, The Amos Tuck School of Business Administration, Dartmouth College.

EXHIBIT 1 Office Evaluation System

The Policy Board has approved 15 percent of distributable earnings as variable compensation for fiscal year 1984, 10 percent to be distributed based on partner performance against goals set forth in accountability statements, and 5 percent to be allocated to offices based upon an office evaluation system.*

The system is designed to produce improvement in critical areas of office practice management and to reward offices that improve or maintain existing high standards. The measurement criteria can be changed to emphasize areas where management feels the partners' attention should be focused. Thus, emphasis can be varied from net income to chargeable hours, or from performance versus last year to performance versus standard, simply by changing the allocation percentages. It also will provide peer pressure to achieve improvement since each office will be rated and the listing will be circulated.

The system will measure the four key responsibility areas: Practice Management, Practice Development, Human Resources, and Client Service.

Within these key responsibility areas, six specific factors on which to evaluate the office will be considered. They are:

- Net income.
- Collections (outstanding days).
- Chargeable-hours growth.
- Client service.
- Human resources development.
- One-firm commitment.

The system will be fully implemented over the next few years. In fiscal 1984, evaluation would be based on performance in net income, collections, and chargeable hours. The remaining three factors will be added as soon as possible.

Weighting

As can be seen from the attached **Schedule A,** each of the three factors has been assigned a percentage, under the column heading "*Weight*," namely, 60 percent, 15 percent, and 25 percent for all practice offices in fiscal 1984.

Schedule A also shows the three criteria used to measure each factor:

Performance versus budget.

Performance versus last year.

Performance versus "ideal" or standard.

These, too, have been assigned a percentage, under the column heading "*Composite Weight*," which places emphasis where management considers it most appropriate, namely, 50 percent, 20 percent, and 30 percent, respectively.

Grading

The "basic score" shown on **Schedule A** is the level at which a practice office is rated, as follows:

5 Excellent.
4 Above average.
3 Average.
2 Below average.
1 Unsatisfactory.

To determine where an office is to be rated, the following criteria were developed:

Case note: The pool of funds to be distributed through the office evaluation system, 5 percent of partner earnings, could be about $2 million in a normal year. Individual awards could range from $15,000 to zero.

EXHIBIT 1 *(continued)*

Net Income

1. Percent of net income versus budget.
2. Percent of net income versus last year.
3. Percent of net income versus ideal target of 20 percent.

Outstanding Days (Collections)

4. Percent of outstanding days versus budget.
5. Percent of outstanding days versus last year.
6. Percent of outstanding days versus standard (105 days).

Chargeable-Hours Growth

7. Percent of chargeable hours growth versus budget.
8. Percent of chargeable hours growth versus last year.
— (Percent of chargeable hours growth versus standard, which is 5 percent, is not used because it would duplicate performance versus last year, since the firm achieved the 5 percent goal last year.)

Offices are then separated into two groups based on their budgeted net billings.

– Over \$2.2 million.
– Under \$2.2 million.

Offices are ranked within their group in each of the eight criteria and given a rate (5 to 1) using the bell curve theory as follows:

Top	10%	—	5
	20%	—	4
	40%	—	3
	20%	—	2
Bottom	10%	—	1

In measuring performance against budget for 1984, budget will be the amount agreed upon by the Area Director, Deputy Director, and PIC as a reasonable level of attainment by that office. This will enable us to continue to improve our budgeting procedures in 1984. *This plan contemplates that budgets are at reasonable levels of attainment for each office.*

Exceptions

• Offices with an operating loss at year end are excluded from bonus pool allocation, unless a development loss is budgeted and approved by the National Director–Operations. Their grade will show as zero in all eight criteria, disregarding what results could have been obtained in collections and chargeable hours.
• Offices with net income as a percent of net fees under 10 percent for last year are adjusted to 10 percent for grading purposes. This is done to prevent offices with a loss or low net income the year before from getting a high grade when compared to this year's results, illustrated as follows:

EXHIBIT 1   *(continued)*

	Actual 1983	*Actual 1984*	*Percent of '84 over '83*
Office A:			
Net fees	1,000	1,050	
Net income	20	40	100%
Office B:			
Net fees	1,000	1,200	
Net income	300	400	33%

Without the rule, Office A would rank considerably higher than Office B, which is not logical.
After adjusting Office A net income to 10 percent of its net fees in 1983, the result would be:

	1983	*1984*	*Percent '84 / '83*
Net income	100	40	(60%)

- Mergers in current year or last year or both will be deducted from actual results in both years to make the comparison valid.
- New offices (which do not have "last year" results) will be weighted as follows:

Performance versus budget	70%
Performance versus standard	30%

After applying all of the foregoing, the mathematical result will be determined (**Schedule B**) and offices listed in decreasing order according to their final weighted score. Then a final grade is given, using the bell curve theory. The bonus pool is allocated based on the following table:

Rank	Percent Applied to Base Compensation		
	Average	*Highest*	*Lowest*
5	10.0%	11.25%	8.80%
4	7.5	8.75	6.30
3	5.0	6.25	3.80
2	2.5	3.75	1.25
1	0.0	—	—

Distribution of the 5 percent incentive pool will be based on the grading shown and will be the percentage of base compensation in each office as shown above.

The incentive pool award will be allocated to the individual partners in an office based on performance relative to accountability statement goals. This allocation is subject to the approval of both Area and Deputy Directors.

Final Comments

It is very important to realize the only component of the office evaluation system that does not change from year to year is its philosophy. The others might and likely will change according to the firm's needs.

EXHIBIT 1 *(continued)*

Office Evaluation Summary FY 1984   **Schedule A**

Office _____

	Composite Weight	Basic Score	Adjusted Score	Weight	Total
Net Income					
Percent of income versus budget	50%				
Percent of net income versus last year	20%				
Performance versus standard	30%				
Total	100%			60%	
Outstanding Days (collections)					
Percent of outstanding days versus budget	50%				
Percent of outstanding days versus last year	20%				
Performance versus standard	30%				
Total	100%			15%	
Chargeable-Hours Growth					
Percent growth in chargeable hours versus budget	50%				
Percent growth in chargeable hours versus last year	50%				
Total	100%			25%	
Total				100%	

EXHIBIT 1 *(concluded)*

Office Evaluation Summary FY 1984   **Schedule B**

Office _____Hypothetical_____

	Composite Weight	Basic Score	Adjusted Score	Weight	Total
Net Income					
Percent of income versus budget	50%	3	1.5		
Percent of net income versus last year	20%	5	1.0		
Performance versus standard	30%	4	1.2		
Total	100%		3.7	60%	2.22
Outstanding Days (collections)					
Percent of outstanding days versus budget	50%	4	2.0		
Percent of outstanding days versus last year	20%	5	1.0		
Performance versus standard	30%	3	0.9		
Total	100%		3.9	15%	0.59
Chargeable-Hours Growth					
Percent growth in chargeable hours versus budget	50%	3	1.5		
Percent growth in chargeable hours versus last year	50%	4	2.0		
Total	100%		3.5	25%	0.89
Total				100%	3.70

An Accounting Practice

Mix of Services

Size of Clients:	Opinion Audits	Taxation Advisory Services	Consulting	
			Project Consulting	General Advisory Services
Large (Fortune 1,000 companies)	(1)	(4)	(7)	(10)
Medium (publicly traded, but not huge)	(2)	(5)	(8)	(11)
Small (Privately held, not large enough to have professional financial management)	(3)	(6)	(9)	(12)

The following comments relate to these individual practice niches:

(1) This is a very-low-growth business. There is erosion from expansion of corporate internal auditing. There is rising price sensitivity among clients, resulting in efforts to "manage the audit fee," and growing price competition among accounting firms. Many people believe that the basic legally mandated opinion audit is very much a "commodity" now. A "Big Eight" image is critical to be a participant in this niche.

(2) Almost all real growth in the audit business is here. Accounting firms can use nonaudit work as a way to gain audit clients here. This niche is also price sensitive; but there is still much room to push differentiation, based on high-quality personal service to the client. As client companies grow, they usually reach a point where they switch to a major auditing firm, even if they did not start out with a major firm.

(3) This is a very minor niche, because small firms typically do not have annual audits unless required by a bank or other lender.

(4) This is a limited niche, because major companies tend to have their own tax planning and tax advisory personnel.

(5),(6) These are large, growing, and very profitable niches. They represent an excellent example of a niche that represents very-low price sensitivity coupled with very-high perceived product differentiation.

(7),(8),(9) These are all profitable niches with relatively low price sensitivity and relatively high differentiation. The clear competitive advantage and the perceived areas of expertise for CPA firms lie in projects related to financial controls, computer-based financial systems, and financial planning. The major accounting firms differ substantially in the breadth of projects they are willing to undertake, ranging all the way to virtually a full-range management consulting practice.

(10),(11) These are very small niches, because the relevant expertise is as likely to exist in the company as in the accounting firm.

(12) This is a significant and profitable niche that is exploited very aggressively by some of the accounting firms but not by all.

margins, fierce price competition, and declining client loyalty. Although many people believe the annual audit is becoming a "commodity," this business was still highly profitable, on average, in 1984.

Different firms are responding to the changes in the auditing environment in different ways, including ignoring it while hoping it will go away, emphasizing product differentiation to justify a price premium, trying to develop low-cost leadership to make possible aggressive pricing, and try-

ing to shift the product mix toward nonaudit services, which are still highly differentiated and, thus, less price sensitive.

Competitive position for an accounting firm or an individual office within a firm can be looked at in terms of the above two dimensional grid, with service mix on one dimension and mix of client size on the other dimension.

Although each of the major firms probably generates some billings each year from each of the 12 niches, no two firms are comparable in terms of aggregate positioning within the grid. Since all the firms are constrained by their ability to attract and retain first-class professional staff, careful delineation of where, within the grid, to place particular emphasis is a major element in strategic planning for a firm.

Because the only productive resource for a CPA firm is people, successful management of the people resource is critically important to the continued prosperity of all such firms. High turnover (both voluntary and forced) has always been part of the structure of the business—of every 10 staff accountants hired, no more than 4 will stay beyond four years and no more than 1 or 2 will become partners. There are no career professionals below the partner level. The rule is "up or out." Admission to the partnership typically comes somewhere between 8 and 15 years. In the major firms, the ratio of partners to staff accountants ranges from a low of 1 to 5 to a high of 1 to 12. Apparently, the partner/staff ratio is a strategic variable.

Traditionally, 40 percent of billings go to pay the professional staff (each staff member should generate billings of 2.5 times salary), 40 percent go to pay overhead (much of which is salary for support personnel), and 20 percent go to the partners as profit. This 40–40–20 economic model has been amazingly durable across firms and over the years.

The Firm of Williamson and Oliver

The name Williamson and Oliver (WO) is an amalgam of parts of the names of predecessor firms dating back more than 50 years. Through a long series of more than 40 mergers of local and regional CPA practices, the current firm gradually emerged. In fact, although the current name was less than 10 years old, Messrs. Williamson and Oliver had both been dead for more than 20 years.

The current firm comprised more than 2,500 professionals in addition to the more than 500 partners. Billings in 1983 were more than $200 million, with 20 offices doing more than $5 mil-

lion. In about half of the top 50 market areas, the firm is one of the top six in size. It is the largest firm in about 10 of those 50 markets. Counting its international affiliates around the world, Williamson and Oliver is one of the top few firms in terms of billable hours. Its major client strength was in "medium-sized" companies. The firm's situation is comparable to the other major firms in terms of history, size, services mix, and management challenge. One distinguishing characteristic of WO is that, for about two thirds of its offices, it is not one of the six largest firms in town. It, thus, has a particularly severe marketing challenge in a great many of its offices.

The Job of an Office PIC

Essentially, the PIC for an office is the general manager of a moderately autonomous profit center. Each office is part of the WO network and, thus, does part of its work for local affiliates of WO clients from other offices. Also, each office farms out some work on its clients to other WO offices. But a major share of the work in each office is done for clients of that office. The PICs are responsible for managing businesses ranging in size from about $1 million in annual billings to over $30 million and serving markets as diverse as Manhattan or Muncie, Indiana.

The career path for virtually every PIC is the same—college graduate in accounting, entry-level staff accountant (technical professional in a work team), senior-level accountant (supervising the work team on individual jobs), managing accountant (supervising several work teams while also maintaining a heavy client load), client service partner (managing the overall relationship for several clients while still carrying a heavy load of chargeable hours), then promotion to running an office. The person may have come from audit, tax, or consulting and may or may not have had a staff assignment somewhere along the line; but the overall theme is the same—progression up the technical ladder of the firm.

This career path raises some important issues in considering the job of the PIC and the role of an incentive compensation system in that job context. First, virtually no PICs have had any general management experience until they arrive at the PIC job—their experience is as technical professionals. Second, the set of skills associated with success up the career ladder to the PIC job is not necessarily highly correlated with the set of skills required of a successful general manager—"managing" is different from "doing." Third, while it is the dream of every newly hired staff accountant to someday become a PIC, having *become* one, many persons don't seem to like *being* one. The things they enjoyed while becoming a PIC included task-oriented project work, providing technical service to clients, the status associated with having your expertise valued by clients, heavy involvement with work teams, and success in managing a work schedule paced by defined projects with deadlines. These things have very little to do with the job of *being* a successful PIC. In fact, although many PICs try to maintain some involvement in the work of the office (because they enjoy it), the policy of the firm is that a PIC should not have any chargeable hours at all—100 percent of each PIC's time should be devoted to managing the business. It is not necessarily surprising that the kind of person who enters the accounting profession and then is successful in a large CPA firm may not really want to be a general manager and may not be very good at it. What is surprising is that the dramatic change from being a client service partner to a PIC comes as such an unpleasant surprise to so many of the newly minted PICs.

Ted Johnson's View of the Incentive Program

Ted Johnson was in the middle of his first five-year term as national managing partner of WO. He could serve additional terms if he were willing and if the policy board reelected him. He had come up through the ranks in one of the predecessor firms that merged into WO. He had run one of the largest WO offices for 10 years and been an area director before becoming national managing partner. He saw his task as helping to improve the profitability of the firm while also ensuring that the right strategic decisions were made to keep the firm prosperous over the longer term. The concept of strategic planning was embryonic at WO, and at the other large CPA firms as well. Johnson was grasping for a way to identify the critical strategic issues and to coalesce the management of the firm around an appropriate strategic thrust. But, at the same time, on the day-to-day front he was "hip deep in alligators."

One major problem was inexperience. One third of the PICs had less than four years' tenure in the job. About 10 had less than two years' tenure. Thus, in a substantial number of offices, a critical issue was just getting the PIC to "think like a general manager," rather than like a client service professional. Also, in many offices, profits were not as good as the partnership felt they should be. This was not only true for offices with an inexperienced PIC. Tough-minded, day-to-day business management skills seemed to be lacking too often. This was particularly troublesome to Ted Johnson, because his election to the top job had been based in large part on a consensus view that he could lead the firm to a better realization of its profit potential. His predecessor's retirement had been somewhat "early" because of widespread concern that the firm was not being managed aggressively enough.

Another problem for Ted Johnson was that many of the PICs just wanted to be left alone by senior management. They were content running a self-contained business. They were willing to pay an "overhead assessment" to the executive office in exchange for use of the national name and for access to national technical expertise. However, they had not made the psychological transition from a local firm to a local office of a national firm. They had to be convinced, somehow, that their local prosperity was significantly related to the prosperity of the national firm.

Finally, Johnson was convinced that managing primarily for short-run profits would hurt the business in the long run. Thus, in addition to getting the PICs oriented to profit and committed to profit growth, he had to try to make them think longer term and beyond their local offices. To top off this challenge, Johnson was not totally sure that the growth theme being pushed in the firm ("We must prove that WO is a firm of comparable stature to the other major firms") was appropriate to bring about the profit growth upon which his future and that of the firm depended. Overall, Ted Johnson believed that the new incentive system would help "calibrate" the partners' actions appropriately for the success of the firm.

The casewriters obtained the following comments from partners in the firm about the new incentive plan.

The Partner-in-Charge of a Large Office in a Fast-Growing Urban Area

The real focus of this plan is on short-term profits. Net income, collections, and chargeable hours all relate directly to the bottom line. But it is just as important for me to build new clients in this high-growth area. That depends on my efforts to project a favorable image with prospective clients. That means I have to give speeches, be seen and liked around the country club, participate in community activities, and participate in business leadership activities like Rotary and Chamber of Commerce. In addition, I have to develop people internally to manage the future growth in our business. That means paying high salaries, allowing heavy training time, and programming in heavy supervision and "mentoring" time. All these activities are negative in terms of their impact on current billings and short-run profit. In fact, all of these activities take my time away from billable work and from collection efforts. Also, if I am successful in developing talented young people in this office, the chances are very good that those people

will get "exported" to other offices because of the firmwide need for good managers. So, I wind up with a thank you and the chance to start all over again spending extra people-related dollars, which hurt current profits. As I see it, I am not personally rewarded for developing the firm, just for being profitable.

An Area Director

Profit is the name of the game in this firm. It ought to be, because that is what matters most in the ultimate analysis. This is a business and the way businesses keep score is the bottom line. Sure it's tough to balance growth goals and intangible factors as well as profitability, but we pay our partners very well to do exactly that. Profit without growth or growth without profit is pretty easy—the trick is getting both. Outstanding partners are the ones who can give you both. I think the incentive plan's focus on short-run profits, with some attention to longer-run issues, is right on track.

The Partner-in-Charge of a Major Office

The system says that by 1985 we will include "client service," "human resource development," and "one firm commitment" as additional factors on which partners' compensation will depend. Let me raise a few issues. What do we mean by "client service?" by "human resource development?" by "one firm commitment?" How do we measure performance on these factors on a monthly or even annual basis? When there are six factors in the equation, what weights are we going to assign to them? Would these weights be the same or different across the practice offices? Who would decide the weights? I think we have to resolve some fundamental questions before we can be sure that our incentive plan would motivate our partners to do the things that senior management wants them to do.

QUESTIONS

1. Is Williamson and Oliver committing the "fallacy of hoping for A while rewarding B"?
2. Can you expect PICs to worry a lot about factors not in the formal reward system?
3. Can the "soft," future-oriented, performance areas be sufficiently quantified to permit inclusion in the reward system?
4. Given the management task at hand, how would you structure the set of measurements for an office of WO? (What measures and what weights across the set of measures?) Would your answer vary across offices?
5. Given your understanding of the industry situation, WO's position within the industry, and Ted Johnson's sense of mission for WO, is the new incentive plan a positive or a negative factor in the management of the firm?

Case 14–3
Harlan Foundation*

Harlan Foundation was created in 1953 under the terms of the will of Martin Harlan, a wealthy Minneapolis benefactor. His bequest was approximately $3 million and its purpose was broadly stated: Income from the funds was to be used for the benefit of the people of Minneapolis and nearby communities.

In the next 35 years, the trustees developed a wide variety of services. These included three infant clinics, a center for the education of special needs children, three family counseling centers, a drug abuse program, a visiting nurses program, and a large rehabilitation facility. These services were provided from nine facilities, located in Minneapolis and surrounding cities. Harlan Foundation was affiliated with several national associations whose members provided similar services.

The foundation operated essentially on a break-even basis. A relatively small fraction of its revenue came from income earned on the principal of the Harlan bequest. Major sources of revenue were fees from clients, contributions, and grants from city, state, and federal governments.

Exhibit 1 is the most recent operating statement. Program expenses included all the expenses associated with individual programs. Administration expenses included the costs of the central office, except for fund-raising expenses. Seventy percent of administration costs were for personnel costs. The staff members (excluding two senior officers) earned an average of $18,000 per year in salaries and fringe benefits.

In 1987, the foundation decided to undertake two additional activities. One was a summer camp, whose clients would be children with physical disabilities. The other was a seminar intended for managers in social service organizations. For both of these ventures, it was necessary to establish the fee that should be charged.

Camp Harlan

The camp, which was renamed Camp Harlan, was donated to the foundation in 1986 by the person who had owned it for many years and who decided to retire. The property consisted of 30 acres, with considerable frontage on a lake, and buildings that would house and feed some 60 campers at a time. The plan was to operate the camp for eight weeks in the summer and to enroll campers for either one or two weeks. The policy was to charge each camper a fee sufficient to cover the cost of operating the camp. Many campers would be unable to pay this fee, and financial aid would be provided for them. The financial aid would cover a part, or in some cases all, of the fee and would come from the general funds of the foundation or, it was hoped, from a government grant.

As a basis for arriving at the fee, Henry Coolidge, financial vice president of the foundation, obtained information on costs from the American Camping Association and from two camps in the vicinity. Although the camp could accommodate at least 60 children, he decided to

* This case was prepared by Robert N. Anthony, Harvard Business School.
Copyright © by Osceola Institute.

EXHIBIT 1   Operating Statement for the Year Ended June 30, 1986

Revenues:	
Fees from clients	$ 917,862
Grants from government agencies	1,792,968
Contributions	683,702
Investment income	426,300
Other	24,553
Total revenues	3,845,385
Expenses:	
Program expenses:	
Rehabilitation	1,556,242
Counseling	157,621
Infant clinics	312,007
Education	426,234
Drug abuse	345,821
Visiting nurses	267,910
Other	23,280
Total program expenses	3,089,115
Support:	
Administration	480,326
Dues to national associations	24,603
Fund-raising	182,523
Other	47,862
Total support	735,314
Total expenses	3,824,429
Net income	$ 20,956

plan on only 50 at a time in the first year, a total of 400 camper-weeks for the season. With assured financial aid, he believed there would be no difficulty in enrolling this number. His budget prepared on this basis is shown in Exhibit 2.

Coolidge discussed this budget with Sally Harris, president of the foundation. Harris agreed that it was appropriate to plan for 400 camper-weeks and also agreed that the budget estimates were reasonable. During this discussion, questions were raised about several items that were not in the budget.

The central office of the foundation would continue to plan the camp, do the necessary publicity, screen applications and make decisions on financial aid, pay bills, and do other bookkeeping and accounting work. There was no good way of estimating how many resources this work would require. Ten staff members worked in administration, and as a rough guess about half a person-year might be involved in these activities. There were no plans to hire an additional employee in the central office. The work load associated with other activities usually tapered off somewhat

---

EXHIBIT 2   Budget for Camp Harlan

Staff salaries and benefits	$ 90,000
Food	19,000
Operating supplies	4,000
Telephone and utilities	9,000
Insurance	15,100
Rental of equipment	7,000
Contingency and miscellaneous (5%)	7,200
Total	$151,300

---

during the summer, and it was believed that the staff could absorb the extra work.

At the camp itself, approximately four volunteers per week would help the paid staff. They would receive meals and lodging, but no pay. No allowance for the value of their services was included in the budget.

The budget did not include an amount for depreciation of the plant facilities. Lakefront property was valuable, and, if the camp and its buildings were sold to a developer, perhaps as much as $500,000 could be realized.

The Seminar

The foundation planned to hold a one-day seminar in the fall of 1987 to discuss the effect on social service organizations of the income tax act passed in 1986 and other recent regulatory developments. (Although these organizations were exempt from income taxes, except on unrelated business income, recent legislation and regulations were expected to have an impact on contributions, investment policy, and personnel policies, among other things.) The purposes of the seminar were partly to generate income and partly to provide a service for smaller welfare organizations.

In the spring of 1987, Harris approved the plans for this seminar. The following information is extracted form a memorandum prepared by Coolidge at that time.

It is estimated that there well be 30 participants in the seminar.

The seminar will be held at a local hotel, and the hotel will charge $200 for rental of the room and $20 per person for meals and refreshments.

Audiovisual equipment will be rented at a cost of $100.

There will be two instructors, and each will be paid a fee of $500.

Printing and mailing of promotional material will cost $900.

Each participant will be given a notebook containing relevant material. Each notebook will cost $10 to prepare, and 60 copies of the notebook will be printed.

Coolidge will preside, and one Harlan staff member will be present at the seminar. The hotel will charge for their meals and for the meals of the two instructors.

Other incidental out-of-pocket expenses are estimated to be $200.

Fees charged for one-day seminars in the area range from $50 to $495. The $50 fee excluded meals and was charged by a brokerage firm that probably viewed the seminar as generating customer goodwill. The $495 fee was charged by several national organizations that run hundreds of seminars annually throughout the United States. A number of one-/day seminars are offered in the Minneapolis area at a fee in the range of $150 to $250, including a meal.

Except for the number of participants, the above estimates were based on reliable information and were accepted by Harris.

QUESTIONS

1. What weekly fee should be charged for campers?
2. Assuming a fee of $100, what is the break-even point of the seminar?
3. What fee should be charged for the seminar?

Case 14-4

Piedmont University*

When Hugh Scott was inaugurated as the 12th President of Piedmont University in 1984, the university was experiencing a financial crisis. For several years enrollments had been declining and costs had been increasing. The resulting deficit had been made up by using the principal of "quasi-endowment" funds. (For true endowment funds, only the income could be used for operating purposes; the principal legally could not be used. Quasi-endowment funds had been accumulated out of earlier years' surpluses with the intention that only the income on these funds would be used for operating purposes; however, there was no legal prohibition on the use of the principal.) The quasi-endowment funds were nearly exhausted.

Scott immediately instituted measures to turn the financial situation around. He raised tuition, froze faculty and staff hirings, and curtailed operating costs. Although he had come from another university and, therefore, was viewed with some skepticism by the Piedmont faculty, Scott was a persuasive person, and the faculty and trustees generally agreed with his actions. In the year ended June 30, 1986, there was a small operating surplus.

In 1986, Scott was approached by Neil Malcolm, a Piedmont alumnus and partner of a local management consulting firm, who volunteered to examine the situation and make recommendations for permanent measures to maintain the university's financial health. Scott accepted this offer.

Malcolm spent about half time at Piedmont for the next several months and had many conversations with Scott, other administrative officers, and trustees. Early in 1987, he submitted his report. It recommended increased recruiting and fund-raising activities, but its most important and controversial recommendation was that the university be reorganized into a set of profit centers.

At that time the principal means of financial control was an annual expenditure budget submitted by the deans of each of the schools and the administrative heads of support departments. After discussion with the president and financial vice president, and usually with minor modifications, these budgets were approved. There was a general understanding that each school would live within the faculty size and salary numbers in its approved budget, but not much stress was placed on adhering to the other items.

Malcolm proposed that in future the deans and other administrators would submit budgets covering both the revenues and the expenditures for their activities. The proposal also involved some shift in responsibilities and new procedures for crediting revenues to the profit centers that earned them and charging expenditures to the profit centers responsible for them. He made rough estimates of the resulting revenues and expenditures of each profit center using 1986 numbers; these are given in Exhibit 1.

A series of discussions about the proposal were held in the University Council, which consisted of the president, academic deans, provost, and financial vice president. Although there was support for the general ides, there was disagreement on some of the specifics, as described below.

---

* This case was prepared by Robert N. Anthony, Harvard Business School.
Copyright © by Osceola Institute.

EXHIBIT 1   Piedmont University: Rough Estimates of 1986 Impact of the Proposals ($millions)

Profit Center:	Revenue	Expenditures
Undergraduate liberal arts school	$30.0	$29.2
Graduate liberal arts school	5.6	11.5
Business school	15.3	12.3
Engineering school	17.0	17.3
Law school	6.7	6.5
Theological school	1.2	3.4
Unallocated revenue*	5.0	
Total, academic	80.8	80.2
Other:		
Central administration	10.1	10.1
Athletic	2.6	2.6
Computer	3.4	3.4
Central maintenance	5.7	5.7
Library	3.4	3.4

* Unrestricted gifts and endowment revenue, to be allocated by the president.

Central Administrative Costs

Currently, no universitywide administrative costs were charged to academic departments. The proposal was that these costs would be allocated to profit centers in proportion to the relative costs of each. The graduate school deans regarded this as unfair. Many costs incurred by the administration were in fact closely related to the undergraduate school. Furthermore, they did not like the idea of being held responsible for an allocated cost that they could not control.

Gifts and Endowment

The revenue from annual gifts would be reduced by the cost of fund-raising activities. The net amount of annual gifts plus endowment income (except gifts and income from endowment designated for a specified school) would be allocated by the president, according to his decision on the needs of each school, subject to the approval of the board of trustees. The deans thought this was giving the president too much authority. They did not have a specific alternative but

thought that some way of reducing the president's discretionary powers should be developed.

Athletics

Piedmont's athletic teams did not generate enough revenue to cover the cost of operating the athletic department. The proposal was to make this department self-sufficient by charging fees to students who participated in intramural sports or who used the swimming pool, tennis courts, gymnasium, and other facilities as individuals. Although there was no strong opposition, some felt that this would involve student dissatisfaction, as well as much new paperwork.

Maintenance

Each school had a maintenance department that was responsible for housekeeping in its section of the campus and for minor maintenance jobs. Sizable jobs were performed at the school's request by a central maintenance department. The proposal was that in future the central maintenance department would charge schools and other profit centers for the work they did at the actual cost of this work, including both direct and overhead costs. The dean of the business school said that this would be acceptable provided that profit centers were authorized to have maintenance work done by an outside contractor if its price was lower than that charged by the maintenance department. Malcolm explained that he had discussed this possibility with the head of maintenance, who opposed it on the grounds that outside contractors could not be held accountable for the high-quality standards that Piedmont required.

Computer

Currently, the principal mainframe computers and related equipment were located in and supervised by the engineering school. Students and faculty members could use them as they wished, subject to an informal check on overuse by people in the computer rooms. About one quarter of the capacity of these computers was used for administrative work. A few departmental mainframe computers and hundreds of microcomputers and word processors were located throughout the university, but there was no central record of how many there were.

The proposal was that each user of the engineering school computers would be charged a fee based on usage. The fee would recover the full cost of the equipment, including overhead. Each school would be responsible for regulating the amount of cost that could be incurred by its faculty and students so the total cost did not exceed the approved item in the school's budget. (The computers had software that easily attributed the cost to each user.) Several deans objected to this plan. They pointed out that neither students nor faculty understood the potential value of computers, and that they wanted to encourage computer usage as a significant part of the educational and research experience. A charge would have the opposite effect, they maintained.

Library

The university library was the main repository of books and other material, and there were small libraries in each of the schools. The proposal was that each student and faculty member who used the university library would be charged a fee, either on an annual basis or on some basis related to the time spent in the library or the number of books withdrawn. (The library had a secure entrance at which a guard was stationed, so a record of who used it could be obtained without too much difficulty.) There was some dissatisfaction with the amount of paperwork that such a plan would require, but it was not regarded as being as important as some of the other items.

Cross Registration

Currently, students enrolled at one school could take courses at another school without charge. The proposal was that the school at which a course was taken would reimburse the school in which the student was enrolled. The amount charged would be the total semester tuition of the school at which the course was taken, divided by the number of courses that a student normally would take in a semester, with adjustments for variations in credit hours.

QUESTIONS

1. How should each of the issues described above be resolved?
2. Do you see other problems with the introduction of profit centers? If so, how would you deal with them?
3. What are the alternatives to a profit-center approach?
4. Assuming that most of the issues could be resolved to your satisfaction, would you recommend that the profit center idea be adopted, rather than an alternative?

Case 14–5

Boston Symphony Orchestra, Inc.*

For several years prior to 1982, Boston Symphony Orchestra, Inc. (BSO), operated at a deficit. For the four years 1978–81, the deficit totaled $4.5 million, an amount that had to be withdrawn from capital funds. Were it not for one special circumstance—a fund drive conducted in connection with BSO's 100th anniversary in 1982—capital funds would have been exhausted within a decade if the deficit continued at the 1978–81 rate.

Background

BSO owned two properties. One was Symphony Hall in Boston. The orchestra performed there, except in the summer and when it performed in other cities. When Symphony Hall was not needed for performances, rehearsals, or recording sessions, it often was rented to other organizations.

The other property was Tanglewood, a large complex in the Berkshire Hills, about 130 miles from Boston. The orchestra performed there for nine weeks in the summer. Several hundred students participated in training programs at Tanglewood each summer. (The principal buildings at Tanglewood were not winterized and could be used only in the summer.) In the summer of 1982, attendance at Tanglewood totaled 308,000.

In 1981–82, in addition to Tanglewood, the orchestra gave 107 concerts, of which 13 were in foreign countries and 14 in other American cities. The Boston Pops Orchestra, formed from sym-

phony orchestra players, gave 63 concerts in Symphony Hall and 7 free concerts at an outdoor concert shell in Boston, known as the Esplanade. At the July 4 Esplanade concert, a Boston institution, attendance was estimated at 200,000. Nearly all orchestra and Pops performances were sold out.

Management estimated that annual use of Symphony Hall in the evenings was approximately as follows:

Symphony orchestra concerts	52
Pops concerts	70
Rentals to outside groups	33
Orchestra rehearsals	10
	165

In the afternoons there were 22 symphony orchestra concerts and approximately 25 rentals to outside groups. The orchestra used the hall an additional 125 to 150 occasions annually for rehearsals, recording, or television sessions.

Proposed Plan

The "BSO/100" fund drive raised about $20 million of capital funds (primarily endowment) over a five-year period. Management recognized, however, that the special stimulus of the 100th anniversary could not be counted on to provide the funds needed to balance the budget in the fu-

* This case was prepared by Robert N. Anthony, Harvard Business School. Copyright © by Osceola Institute.

ture. Alternative ways of financing operations were discussed, and the trustees eventually agreed on the plan given in Exhibit 1. In the BSO annual report for 1982 (i.e., for the fiscal year ended August 31, 1982), this plan was described as follows:

As the orchestra embarks on the first decade of its second century, Trustees, Overseers, and Friends must make plans based upon the experience of the past and their best estimate of the economic climate in the years ahead. The single most important assumption in making such a projection is the rate at which "fixed costs" of maintaining the present organization and properties will increase due to inflation. Included in the Analysis of Revenue Contribution to Fixed Costs are projections based upon several assumptions:

(1) that "fixed costs" will increase at a compound annual rate of approximately 7 percent through fiscal 1989–1990;
(2) that management will be able to increase the percentage of "fixed costs" financed by concert activities by ½ of 1 percent per year;
(3) that the Investment Committee and the Resources Committee working together will be able to increase the percentage of "fixed costs" covered by endowment income by ½ of 1 percent per year;
(4) that the Resources Committee will be able to raise on average about $6 million per year, of which $2 million per year will be available to balance the budget; and
(5) that the Buildings and Grounds Committee will be able to limit capital expenditures for depreciation, for necessary improvements, and for new facilities to $500,000 per year.

Perhaps the most significant conclusions to draw from the projections [Exhibit 1] is that, in the absence of some new source of revenue, ticket prices will have to continue to increase so the marginal contribution from concert activities can increase from $5,709,000 in 1981–82 to $10,500,000 or 64.5 percent of "fixed costs" in 1989–90.

During the past five years the orchestra raised a total of $20 million for BSO/100 and $7 million

from Annual Fund Drives for a grand total of $27 million.

The goal of $6 million per year, or $30 million over the next five years, is challenging, but the task is not much greater than the task already accomplished during the period of the BSO/100 Campaign.

Contributions to Fixed Costs

The concept of "contributions to fixed costs" referred to in the above description was explained in the *Annual Report* as follows:

Each year the Trustees are faced with certain relatively fixed costs, which are scheduled in the Analysis of Revenue Contribution to Fixed Costs report. These are primarily for the annual compensation of orchestra members, the general administration of the orchestra, and the basic costs of maintaining Symphony Hall and Tanglewood. Management earns a percentage of these "fixed costs" by presenting concert programs, through radio, television, and recordings, and through other projects, which involve both direct expenses and related income from ticket sales, fees, and royalties.

Each program or activity, of which there are over 40, is expected to make a "marginal contribution" to "fixed costs." The "marginal contribution" is the difference between direct income and direct costs of the particular program or activity. The orchestra continued to make progress toward its goal of increasing the percentage of "fixed costs" contributed from operation activities.

The "marginal contribution" from all operations in 1981–82 covered 62.3 percent of "fixed costs," as compared to 59.7 percent last year and 43.0 percent in 1971–72.

In fiscal 1981–82, the "fixed costs" amounted to $9,160,000, compared to $8,434,000 in 1980–81, an increase of 8.6 percent. Operations earned $5,709,000, compared to $5,046,000 last year, a 13.1% increase. This left an "operating deficit" to be funded from other sources (e.g., endowment income and unrestricted contributions) of $3,451,000 in 1981–82, compared to $3,403,000 last year.

EXHIBIT 1 Analysis of Revenue Contribution to Fixed Costs For the Year Ended August 31 (in thousands)

	Actual					Projections							
	1978	1979	1980	1981	1982	1983	1984	1985	1986	1987	1988	1989	1990
Fixed costs:													
Artistic	3,902	4,243	4,514	5,176	5,608								
Facilities	920	1,005	1,160	1,318	1,348								
Administration	1,377	1,472	1,268	1,940	2,204								
Total fixed costs	6,199	6,720	7,442	8,434	9,160	$10,140	$10,850	$11,800	$12,425	$13,300	$14,225	$15,225	$16,300
Results from operations:													
Operations:													
Concerts	2,666	2,986	3,161	3,827	4,006								
Radio (BSTT)	125	145	160	185	185								
Recording	320	384	510	543	827								
Television	139	225	289	223	246								
Occupancies	101	91	186	252	244								
Education	(100)	(60)	(87)	(34)	(77)								
Other Income	—	12	32	35	278								
Marginal contribution	3,251	3,783	4,251	5,031	5,709	6,160	6,675	7,325	7,775	8,375	9,025	9,750	10,500
% fixed costs	52.4	56.3	57.1	59.7	62.3	60.8	61.5	62.0	62.5	63.0	63.5	64.0	64.5
Operating (deficit)	(2,948)	(2,937)	(3,191)	(3,403)	(3,451)	(3,980)	(4,175)	(4,475)	(4,650)	(4,925)	(5,200)	(5,475)	(5,800)
% fixed costs	47.6	43.7	42.9	40.3	37.7	39.2	38.5	38.0	37.5	37.0	36.5	36.0	35.5
Endowment income	981	1,221	1,358	1,691	1,893								
% fixed costs	15.8	18.2	18.3	20.0	20.7								
Annual fund-raising:													
Total annual gifts	1,133	1,121	1,211	1,334	1,786								
Special-purpose gifts transferred to operations	(162)	(302)	(268)	(299)	(355)								
General-purpose gifts	971	819	943	1,035	1,431								
Net project revenues	176	209	229	264	723								
Total	1,147	1,028	1,172	1,299	2,154								
Fund-raising expenses	(549)	(441)	(414)	(553)	(442)								
Total	598	587	758	746	1,712								
% fixed costs	9.7	8.7	10.2	8.8	18.7								

EXHIBIT 1 (concluded)

Total endowment income and annual fund-raising	1,579	1,808	2,116	2,437	3,605	3,865	4.175	4,475	4,650	4,925	5,200	5,475	5,800
% fixed costs	25.5	26.9	28.5	28.8	39.4	38.1	38.5	38.0	37.5	37.0	36.5	36.0	35.5
Surplus (deficit)	(1,369)	(1,129)	(1,075)	(966)	154	(115)	–0–	–0–	–0–	–0–	–0–	–0–	–0–
% fixed costs	22.1	16.8	14.4	11.5	1.7	1.1							
Funding from (to) unrestricted capital	1,369	1,129	1,075	966	(154)	115							
	–0–	–0–	–0–	–0–	–0–	–0–	–0–	–0–	–0–	–0–	–0–	–0–	–0–
Capital analysis:													
Added to endowment funds	$ 442	$ 1,750	$ 1,433	$ 1,308	$ 3,540	$ 3,500	$ 3,500	$ 3,500	$ 3,500	$ 3,500	$ 3,500	$ 3,500	$ 3,500
Added (charged) to special reserve					150	(115)							
Funding of plant additions	433	980	493	1,641	326	1,021	500	500	500	500	500	500	500
Added to unexpended property fund balance					241	(241)							
Funding of deficit	1,369	1,129	1,075	966									
	$ 2,244	$ 3,859	$ 3,001	$ 3,915	$ 4,257	$ 4,165	$ 4,000	$ 4,000	$ 4,000	$ 4,000	$ 4,000	$ 4,000	$ 4,000
Pooled investments:													
Cost	$10,343	$12,018	$13,850	$15,822	$19,465	$23,000	$26,500	$30,000	$33,500	$37,000	$40,500	$44,000	$47,500
Market	11,645	14,015	15,817	16,356	20,536								
Endowment share unit value	12.54	13.20	13.67	13.78	14.19								

EXHIBIT 2

BOSTON SYMPHONY ORCHESTRA, INC.
Balance Sheets
August 31, 1982, and 1981

Current Funds

Assets	1982	1981
Cash (including savings accounts of $49,835 in 1982 and $463,320 in 1981	$ 119,888	$ 501,962
Short-term cash investments	2,600,000	1,666,222
Participation in pooled investments, at market	1,979,960	1,681,781
Accounts receivable—less allowance for doubtful accounts of $10,000 in 1982 and $32,000 in 1981	709,069	937,016
Grants and other receivables	285,900	291,071
Prepaid salaries and wages	343,962	345,195
Deferred charges	163,893	40,111
Prepayments and other assets	491,605	506,858
	6,694,277	$5,970,216

Liabilities and Fund Balances	1982	1981
Accounts payable	$ 564,677	$ 591,559
Accrued pension liability	221,116	187,775
Accrued expenses and other liabilities	619,008	189,972
Advance ticket sales and other receipts	2,781,005	2,516,114
Advance receipts—special events	137,983	803,015
Due to other funds	240,528	—
	4,564,317	4,288,435
Fund balances:		
Unrestricted	150,000	—
Internally designated	1,979,960	1,681,781
	2,129,960	1,681,781
	$6,694,277	5,970,216

Property Funds

	1982	1981		1982	1981
Due from other funds	240,528	—	Fund balances:		
Properties and equipment at cost, less accumulated depreciation of $2,209,622 in 1982 and $1,956,005 in 1981	4,766,216	4,693,885	Unexpected balances	240,528	—
			Investment in plant	4,766,216	4,693,885
	$ 5,006,744	$ 4,693,885		$ 5,006,744	$ 4,693,885

Endowment and Similar Funds

	1982	1981		1982	1981
Cash management fund—annuities	$ 120,409	$ 179,390	Annuity payable	$ 67,778	$ 103,662
Real estate and other property held for sale	712,223	862,233	Fund balances:		
Pooled investments, at market	20,536,010	16,356,225	Endowment principal and income restricted	2,533,903	2,142,179
Less participation in pooled investments by other funds	(1,979,960)	(1,681,781)	Funds functioning as endowment— trustee designated	16,787,001	13,470,216
	$ 19,388,682	$ 15,716,057		19,320,904	15,612,395

Other Information

The 1982 *Annual Report* contained the following explanation of endowment income.

Investment income reached an all-time high of $2,134,000, as compared to $1,838,000 in the prior year. Of this amount, $219,000 was used for restricted purposes: supporting the winter season programs ($35,000), providing fellowships for the Berkshire Music Center and other BMC activities ($101,000), supporting the Esplanade concerts ($47,000), underwriting the Prelude Series ($29,000), and other miscellaneous activities. An additional $22,000 went to nonoperational uses, leaving $1,893,000 for unrestricted use in support of operations. This compares to $1,690,000 in 1980–81, a 12 percent increase.

The *Annual Report* also explained how the budget for 1982 was balanced, as follows:

The percentage of "fixed costs" that had to be provided by unrestricted gifts was reduced from 20.3 percent in 1980–81 to 17.0 percent in 1981–82, amounting to $1,558,000.

The sources of the $1,588,000 required to balance revenues and expenses in 1981–82 were:

(1) Annual Fund (net): $989,000, up $250,000 or 34 percent over the previous year.
(2) Projects (net): $723,000, up $459,000 or 174 percent over the previous year.

Since funds available from these two sources totaled $1,172,000, it was possible to transfer the excess gifts of $154,000 for other needs.

Exhibit 2 gives the balance sheet, taken from the *Annual Report*.

QUESTIONS

1. Do the plans for 1983–1990 seem reasonably attainable?
2. Speculate as to other possible ways that BSO should seek to balance its budget during this period?

Case 14-6
Metropolitan Museum of Art*

The "first cut" at the operating budget of the Metropolitan Museum of Art for fiscal year 1973 (i.e., the year ended June 30, 1973) indicated a substantial deficit. Management was considering what, if any, steps should be taken to reduce or eliminate this deficit.

The Metropolitan Museum was organized in New York City in 1870. In 1972, it had over 1 million works of art, the largest collection of its kind in the Western Hemisphere. It had an endowment fund of $150 million.

Governance and Management

The Board

Fiscal authority for direction of the Metropolitan Museum of Art was vested in the Board of Trustees. The board was responsible for the broad direction and control of the museum and for the establishment and approval of basic policies and plans. Meeting quarterly, it also considered important operational matters.

The Director

The director was the museum's chief executive officer. He was responsible for formulating policies and programs for the board's consideration and for implementing decisions made by the board. In addition to being responsible for overall planning and administration of the museum's affairs, he also was involved in fund-raising and negotiating major art acquisitions. He presided at rehearsals of presentations by the curators and was present at actual presentations made to the Board of Trustees Acquisition Committee. Since 1966, the director was Thomas P. F. Hoving. Dr. Hoving had achieved national recognition as the commissioner of parks of New York City, particularly for his campaign to make New York a "fun city." He earned a Ph.D. in art history at Princeton in 1959 and was hired as curatorial assistant at the Cloisters, the medieval art department of the Metropolitan. In 1965, he became curator of the Cloisters.

Curatorial

The vice director–curator-in-chief was responsible for 17 curatorial departments and the Conservation Laboratory, with a curatorial staff of nearly 200 persons.

The 17 curatorial departments varied considerably in the size of their staffs and collections and in the range of their activities. While all departments collected art objects, some were more active than others. In general, the more active departments were those that collected works of art currently available in the open market.

In addition to collection and display, curatorial departments were responsible for maintaining relations with collectors and art dealers, for developing scholarly and general literature on the collection, and for answering inquiries from the public. Some members of the curatorial staff also taught courses and lectured at the museum or at other institutions.

* This case was prepared by Richard E. Kopelman under the direction of Fred K. Foukes, Harvard Business School. Copyright © by the President and Fellows of Harvard College.
Harvard Business School case 473–010.

EXHIBIT 1   Staffing Levels: 1967–1971 (excluding auxiliary activities)

	1971	1970	1969	1968	1967
Director and several offices	27	23	22	21	20
Vice director–curator-in-chief	199	185	170	172	167
Vice director for finance and treasurer	51	48	46	42	42
Vice director for education	63	55	53	52	52
Vice director for public affairs	31	28	28	28	25
Vice director for operations	412	407	370	365	361
Subtotal	783	746	689	680	667
100th anniversary	19	21	—	—	—
Total	802	767	689	680	667

Education

The vice director of education had general responsibility for developing educational programs for students and for the general public. Included in his domain were five departments: the Library, the Junior Museum, Secondary and Higher Education, Community Programs, and the Photograph and Slide Library.

Finance and Treasurer

The vice director for finance and treasurer was the chief financial officer of the museum. Reporting to him were four financial administrators, each with his own staff and task assignment. The assistant treasurer was responsible for the physical receipt and payment of funds, accounts receivable, the payroll, and general accounting. The controller prepared the annual budget and was responsible for accounts payable. The registrar maintained catalog descriptions of all objects belonging to the museum, recorded the physical movement of these objects in and out of the museum, and obtained insurance and custom handling for art shipments. The city liaison officer was responsible for developing and maintaining good relations with the New York City administration, in particular those officials with whom the museum had financial transactions.

Public Affairs

The vice director of public affairs, a position that was at the time vacant, had overall responsibility for eight departments, each of which had direct contact with the public. These departments were as follows: public information, information desk, bookshop and reproduction, development and promotion (fund-raising), membership office, publications, exhibition design, and the auditorium.

Operations

The operating administrator had general responsibility for the provision of the museum's many service functions. These included: guardianship, maintenance, cleaning, purchasing stockroom supplies, telephone and office services, photograph studio, and the several restaurant facilities. This large department employed approximately 400 of the museum's 800 employees.

Staffing levels for these activities are given in Exhibit 1.

In the late 1960s, there was increasing interest among professional staff employees in establishing a union to represent them. Apparently this interest had been increasing despite efforts by the museum's administration to be responsive to the needs of the professional staff. The administration had a publicly announced goal of bringing curatorial salaries up to the level received by professors in leading colleges and universities. From 1967 to 1971, there was a 30 percent increase in curatorial salaries. The 1972 budget, prepared in the spring of 1971, called for additional salary in-

EXHIBIT 2 Financial Record: 1960–1972

Fiscal Year*	Operating Income	Operating Expenses	Surplus (Loss)[†]
1960	$ 4,006,943	$ 3,618,197	$ 388,746
1961	4,328,603	4,042,561	286,042
1962	5,181,647	4,433,087	748,560
1963	5,066,399	4,605,688	460,711
1964	5,280,503	4,802,832	477,671
1965	5,807,116	5,278,279	528,837
1966	6,128,155	5,698,411	429,714
1967	6,496,767	6,236,532	260,235
1968	7,054,341	7,461,354	(407,013)
1969	8,393,332	8,531,833	(138,501)
1970	8,405,569	9,226,513	(820,944)
1971	11,363,519	11,773,117	(409,598)[‡]
1972 (budget)	12,415,600	13,128,793	(713,193)

* Fiscal year ends June 30.
[†] For fiscal years prior to 1970, surplus (loss) is before extraordinary charges.
[‡] Plus an accumulated centennial deficit of $1,121,697.

creases of between 11.6 percent and 17.9 percent, depending on the level of curatorial rank.

The administration also had attempted to increase the extent of participation by professional employees. In 1970, the curators, acting with the backing of the administration, established a Curatorial Forum, which comprised the entire curatorial staff and had a representative on the Staff Policy Committee, the executive team which made recommendations to the director and conducted routine business operations.

By April 1972, it appeared to management that the unionization issue was no longer alive and that many of the specific changes that had been introduced had been well received.

Financial Background

The museum began to suffer operating losses in the late 1960s. Historical financial data are shown in Exhibits 2 and 3.

The emergence of financial problems was not a condition unique to the Metropolitan Museum of Art; many museums were faced with similar situations. The Museum of Modern Art, for example, reported a record deficit of $1.2 million in 1970. Also in 1970, a study conducted by the American Association of Museums found that 44 percent of its members were operating at a loss. Furthermore, at the time of the study the AAM spokesman said that the dismal trend was expected to continue.

Two broad explanations were advanced for the growing disparity between revenues and expenses. First, museums, like other entities which relied on a relatively fixed income, suffered from the effects of inflation. Second, to adapt to a changing environment, museums had incurred new types of expenses.

One cause of the difficulty was the rapid increase in museum attendance. It was noted that the 1971 exhibit entitled the "Drug Scene" at the Museum of the City of New York drew more people in three months of 1971 than the entire museum did in all of 1970. However, the cost of contemporary exhibits was high. The American Museum of Natural History, for example, spent

EXHIBIT 3 Sources of Income: 1960–1971

Sources (in 000s)	1960	1961	1962	1963	1964	1965	1966	1967	1968	1969	1970	1971
Unrestricted investment income	$2,737	$2,890	$3,591	3,474	$3,621	$4,051	$4,174	$4,380	$4,461	$4,658	$4,670	$ 4,722
Transfer of unrestricted endowments funds*	0	0	0	0	0	0	0	0	0	0	0	844
Appropriation from City of New York	974	1,038	1,191	1,259	1,293	1,385	1,528	1,554	1,678	1,853	1,974	2,323
Grants	0	0	0	0	0	0	0	53	160	577	126	683
Memberships	180	205	234	252	267	289	314	399	415	453	419	1,057
Admission fees	0	65	72	0	0	30	15	0	45	353	390	821
Contribution for general purposes	62	66	20	16	18	17	18	19	181	151	191	204
Other†	64	65	73	66	81	71	81	91	113	137	278	260
Subtotal	4,007	4,329	5,181	5,066	5,281	5,807	6,128	6,497	7,054	8,183	8,021	10,914
Plus: New income for auxiliary activities	0	0	0	0	0	0	0	0	0	210	385	449
Total	$4,007	$4,329	$5,181	$5,066	$5,281	$5,807	$6,128	$6,497	$7,054	$8,393	$8,406	$11,364

* In 1971 a fixed rate of return (5 percent) was used for the first time to determine endowment income.
† Includes income from slide and photograph sales, guide service, course fees, and special seminars.

$526,000 for its centennial exhibit "Can Man Survive?"

Another relatively new cost was the emergence of vigorous demands by professional employees for higher pay and more job security. According to Ann R. Leven, assistant treasurer of the Metropolitan, this new demand reflected the fact that curators no longer came predominantly from the ranks of the wealthy. Many curators had to live off salaries which were traditionally quite low.

The Metropolitan took action in 1971 to combat the trend of increasing deficits. The actions taken can be grouped into two categories: those which reduced costs and those which generated additional revenues.

One cost-cutting action was a curtailment in the hiring of new personnel. Daniel Herrick, vice director for finance and treasurer, instituted the policy of not filling a vacancy unless the position was deemed essential.

A second austerity measure was the decision to close the museum one day a week (Monday) beginning in July 1971. Prior to this decision the museum had remained open to the public 7 days a week, 365 days a year. Consequently many maintenance activities had to be performed at odd hours: before the museum opened and after it closed. These scheduling demands, coupled with ordinary absences, resulted in (1) having to pay guards and maintenance personnel overtime pay and (2) having to hire temporary personnel on a per diem basis. The budget for 1971–72 estimated that Monday closings would save the Metropolitan nearly $200,000 in annual labor cost. Ten New York City art museums, including the Guggenheim and the Whitney, adopted this policy before the Metropolitan did.

Another cutback was the elimination from the operating budget of various projects which the museum had planned to carry out. Among the postponed items were the following: (1) the publication of a catalog of the museum's programs of research and education; (2) hiring of a specialist for foundation and government fund-raising; (3) installation of a public education gallery dealing with current events in the art world; (4) free acoustiguide equipment; (5) redecoration of the restaurant; (6) development of a computer program for an art catalog. Perhaps the biggest disappointment to many people was the curtailment of the final centennial exhibition, "Masterpieces of Fifty Centuries." In the words of Mr. Hoving, "Our budget could no longer afford the expenses involved in the foreign loans that we planned for the last great centennial show, especially the cost of insurance, which has skyrocketed in the last few years."

At the same time that these cost reduction activities were undertaken, the museum also initiated steps to increase its revenues. One approach was the introduction in 1970 of discretionary admission charges at the main building and at the Cloisters. Mr. Hoving commented that, "after investigating different ways of charging admission to the Museum, the pay-as-you-wish plan emerged as the most satisfactory for two reasons. It created no economic barriers for the public and it proved that income was higher than with a set admission fee." (*New York Times*, October 9, 1970.) After a five-month trial period, the average contribution per visitor was 64 cents. One reason for the high average was that the museum "strongly hinted" that $1 would be a "very nice" contribution for adults, 50 cents for youngsters. The 1971–72 budget estimated that total receipts from the voluntary admission contributions would approximate $1 million. (The museum found out in 1971, after it purchased electronic counting equipment, that the earlier handcounted records of attendance were about four times too high.)

The introduction of a discretionary admission fee provoked sharp criticism from several sources. Among them was Mr. Carter Burden, a New York City councilman, who noted that, "of the 15 institutions which receive city funds, with the exception of the Bronx Zoo, the Metropolitan was the only one with a general admission fee." He added, "Our society should be going in the opposite direction."

Another step taken to enhance revenues was the adoption of the fixed rate of return concept for endowment funds. Whereas in past years endowment income was limited to interest and dividends, beginning in 1971 the museum recorded as income 5 percent of the average market value of unrestricted endowment funds for the three previous years. It was anticipated that, over the long run, actual capital appreciation combined with dividends and interest would result in an annual yield at least equal to the fixed rate. This approach had the added advantage of making endowment income a constant amount during the course of the fiscal year. (See Exhibit 3.)

Also beginning in 1970, the museum undertook an energetic campaign to enroll new members. As a result of this campaign 8,667 new memberships were sold by April 1971, bringing in added receipts of $360,000. One spur to get new members was that, beginning in April 1971, the prices of individual and family memberships were raised from $15 to $25 and $40, respectively. Because of the price increase, the museum expected only a small increase in memberships for 1972.

The recent history of membership growth was marred by only one major downturn. This occurred in 1967 when prices were raised. However, there was a short downturn for a few months in the fall of 1968 as a result of the contemporary exhibition, "Harlem on My Mind." One hundred and sixty-five members canceled their memberships and many others failed to renew. The two major criticisms were an anti-Semitic comment in the catalog, and the view that this exhibit was not "real" art.

Another approach to enhancing revenues were efforts to make the museum's auxiliary activities more profitable. Additional merchandising operations were opened and prices on prints, books, and other items were set at levels to bring an optimum return. As a result of these changes, the 1971–72 budget anticipated an increase in contribution on these activities from $415,000 to $615,000.

Still another revenue-producing activity was the search for nontraditional sources of funds. In 1970, the state of New York broke new ground when it appropriated $18 million for support of the arts. The Metropolitan received a total of $418,500 of the appropriation in 1971, and expected continued support from the state. Another new source of funds was the federal government which, under the National Endowment for the Arts, was expected to make an initial contribution to the Metropolitan of $110,000 in 1972.

Yet by far the largest public contribution came from the city of New York, which gave $2.3 million in 1971 to cover the costs of guardianship and maintenance. While the city's contribution to the operating income had declined from 27 percent in 1959–60 to 21 percent in 1970–71, the amount contributed had increased. It was estimated, furthermore, that by 1976 the city would increase its annual commitment by an additional $585,000. (*The Wall Street Journal*, July 27, 1971.) Consequently, some administrators at the Metropolitan felt uneasy when elected city officials began to urge the city to reduce or even eliminate its contributions to the museum.

Current Financial Situation

During the 1971–72 fiscal year, it became increasingly evident that the financial plans for the year were not going to be met. A deficit of $713,000 was originally budgeted compared to the preceding year's deficit of $1,531,000. The reduction had been planned to be accomplished by keeping 1972 expenditures near the 1971 level ($13.1 million in 1972 versus $12.9 million in the prior year), while revenue was to be increased by $1 million. However, by April 1972 it appeared that the actual deficit for the fiscal year ending June 30 would approximate $1.4 million. The chief reason for this turn of events was that revenue had not increased as planned.

Attendance in the Main Building was down approximately 25 percent from the year before, and admission income was one third below the budgeted figure of $930,000. Daniel Herrick, the vice director of finance and treasurer, attributed the falloff to several factors: a post-centennial slump in public interest, reduced hotel occupancies in New York, and a growing reluctance of New York City residents to go out at night. As a direct result of decreased attendance, the contribution to expenses provided by the restaurant and bookstores was reduced by $130,000.

Two additional factors contributed to lower than planned revenues. In fiscal 1970–71, the museum undertook a special membership campaign whereby new individual and family members were encouraged to join at the old rates (before new, increased rates went into effect), and existing members were allowed to extend their memberships for an additional year at the old rates. The effect of this campaign was an extraordinary increase in memberships. From 1963 through 1968, membership fluctuated between 20,000 and 23,000 each year. In 1969, it rose to over 24,000; in 1970, to 27,000; and in 1971, to 37,760. However in early 1972, as memberships began to expire, the renewal rates were lower than anticipated, mostly among the lower membership categories. In the single month of February, for example, 937 individual and family memberships were not renewed. As a result of this higher than anticipated lapse rate, membership income was about $90,000 below the budget. A final disappointment was the reduction in grants received by the museum. New York State reduced its grant to $221,000 from $418,000 the year before, and the National Endowment for the Arts contributed $60,000 less than budgeted. Total grant income was $280,000 short of the budgeted level.

The Budget for 1972–1973

The preliminary budget for the forthcoming year indicated that total revenue would decline slightly to $11.7 million, principally reflecting a further reduction in grants to the museum. The budget report suggested that there were three principal options to be considered:

Option 1. Deficit $1 million. Across-the-board cut in expenditures of 10.3 percent. Staff cut of 36 (excluding auxiliary activities). Requires effecting efficiencies in all departments and certain cutbacks most notably in the Curatorial and Operations area. Reduce advertising. Reduce number of activities for members. Close Monday, holidays, 11 A.M. to 1 P.M. Sundays, Friday evenings. Cancel employees' Christmas party.

Option 2. Deficit $500,000. Across-the-board cut in expenditures of 16.4 percent. Staff cut of 60. The effect falls heaviest on those departments with limited program money, cutting deeply into the Curatorial and Operating staffs. Allows for basic maintenance of collections; study rooms would close; conservation and research would stop; exhibitions would be severely limited. Reduce community education activities unless outside funding obtained. Close 83d Street entrance.

Option 3. No deficit. Across-the-board cut in expenditures of 22.5 percent. Staff cut of 91. Merely maintains the museum as a repository for works of art. Requires a major functional reorganization of the staff. All cataloging ceases. Closes libraries during the summer, eliminates weekend and summer education programs. Consolidates Development and Membership offices.

When Mr. Herrick was asked whether the administration had considered the possibility of passing the hat among the trustees to make up operating deficits, he said:

> The days when a few wealthy contributions would ante up the money to cover a deficit are over. Even the richest person in the world doesn't have an inclination to keep giving money if you have continuing deficits of over $1 million a year. Furthermore, anteing up to fill a deficit is the least attractive type of donation from the viewpoint of most contributors. Philanthropists far prefer to donate money for works of art, buildings, or even endowed chairs before giving to cover operating losses.

Mr. Herrick continued discussing the financial problems of the museum.

EXHIBIT 4   Administration Expenses (as budgeted for the year ended June 30, 1972)*

	Personal Service	Other Expense	Total
Director and several offices	$ 404,095	$ 173,085	$ 577,180
Vice director–curator-in-chief	2,455,227	695,316	3,150,543
Vice director for finance			
and treasurer	555,561	355,910	911,471
Vice director for education	783,708	812,586	1,596,294
Vice director for public affairs	467,725	701,815	1,169,540
Vice director for operations	3,625,199	1,435,570	5,060,769
Benefits and allowances	1,764,170	—	1,764,170
Adjustments‡	(566,295)	(156,478)	(722,773)
Total estimated operating expenses	$9,489,390	$4,017,804	$13,507,194

* As revised 3/31/72.
‡ Accounting deductions distributed among capital budget, auxiliary activities, the Cloisters.

EXHIBIT 5   Actual Administration Expenses

	1971	1970	1969	1968	1967
Personal service (including benefits and allowances)	$ 8,287,400	$ 6,909,700	$6,151,300	$5,422,000	$5,181,400
Other than personal service	3,138,000	2,086,500	1,971,300	1,398,600	1,119,300
Subtotal	11,425,400	8,996,200	8,122,600	6,820,600	6,300,700
100th Anniversary personal service	96,100	210,100			
Other than personal service	1,454,000	1,595,900			
Total	$12,975,900	$10,802,200	$8,122,600	$6,820,600	

We are reluctant to cut back expenses, especially since the staff takes intense pride in what has been accomplished at the Metropolitan Museum. At a time when other aspects of New York City life are deteriorating, the museum has been on a planned and vigorous course of greater service to the community in maintaining and communicating the meaning of its collection of works of art to the public.

We have considered numerous alternative forms of retrenchment but because salaries comprise roughly 70 percent of our total costs [see Exhibits 4 and 5], there is virtually no way to avoid laying off people. Furthermore, this raises the difficult problem of deciding which people to release and how to handle the dismissals. We are even exploring the possibility of converting to a four-day week, perhaps in lieu of salary increases.

The fact of the matter is that, even if the museum were to cut its expenditures to create a balanced budget in the forthcoming year, the same problem would recur again next year. As long as the museum exists in an inflationary economy, where there is an inevitable upward push in terms of wages, fringe benefits, and operating costs, the museum must seek some means of achieving an adequate and dependable source of funding to maintain the status quo at least.

Possible Repercussions of Cutbacks

The administration was well aware of the possibility that cutbacks might lead to renewed interest in unionization among the professional staff. John Conger, the personnel manager, identified the immediate costs to the museum of collective bargaining. First, more time would be spent in negotiating contracts. Second, there was a high probability that the final contract agreement would be more costly to the museum.

Mr. Hoving stated that the union would have little overall impact on the museum. "There are very few things they could bargain for. Salaries of curators are at the level of university professors, working conditions are excellent, as is the grievance procedure. A union would actually make management's position stronger. It would absolutely define the areas of bargaining as stipulated by the NLRB. The staff would have much less say on policy matters."

Mr. Herrick noted that "the chances are pretty good that if we decide to have layoffs there may be a professional union. But if there is, that wouldn't be the end of the world."

QUESTION

What actions, if any, would you tentatively recommend as a means of reducing the budgeted deficit?

Chapter 15

Financial Services Organizations

This chapter discusses management controls in several types of financial services organizations. These organizations have in common the special problem of accounting for and controlling net interest income—that is, the difference between the revenue from lending or investing money and the cost of obtaining the use of that money from depositors or other sources. Most of them also have the problem of evaluating the soundness of decisions that are made currently but whose full impact will not be felt until many years in the future. These organizations include commercial banks and thrift institutions, securities firms, and insurance companies.

In the 1980s, the number of these organizations decreased substantially; but the scope of services offered by individual companies broadened, often through acquisitions. Consequently, many organizations that formerly specialized in one type of financial service now operate across a wide spectrum. Because the management control that is appropriate for one type of financial service may be inappropriate for other types, this broadening can create serious problems unless these differences are recognized.

In 1987, financial service firms accounted for $164.6 billion, or 4 percent, of the gross national product, but their importance to the health of the economy was considerably greater than this percentage indicates.

COMMERCIAL BANKS AND THRIFT INSTITUTIONS

General Characteristics

This section describes management control problems and practices in commercial banks, savings banks, thrift institutions (i.e., savings and loan associations and credit unions), and finance companies. Until about 1980, the distinction among these types of organizations was clear-cut. The typical commercial bank obtained money from depositors, at essentially zero interest cost for demand deposits and 5 percent (a government-imposed ceiling) for savings deposits; it made medium-term loans (about five years or less) to businesses and individuals; it made fixed-rate loans, secured by mortgages on business property or homes, with maturities of 20 to 30 years at fixed rates of interest; and it managed trust accounts and provided other financial services. A savings bank or similar thrift institution obtained funds from savings deposits and loaned them to homeowners on mortgages, or it made other secured loans. Both commercial banks and thrift institutions were heavily regulated, either by the federal government, by the states, or by both. Most deposits were insured by the federal government. Finance companies (e.g., Beneficial, Household Finance, General Electric Credit Corporation) made loans that were secured by automobiles or other personal property.

Beginning in 1980, the means of obtaining and lending money became much more complicated. Government regulation was greatly relaxed (but by no means eliminated) by the Depository Institutions Deregulation and Monetary Control Act of 1980. Savings and loan associations were permitted to lend to businesses. Banks were permitted to pay interest on demand deposits, and the 5 percent ceiling on savings deposits was, for all practical purposes, eliminated. Dozens of new financial instruments were developed—money market funds, certificates of deposit, variable-rate mortgages, credit cards, debit cards, interest-rate futures, bond options, interest-rate swaps.[1] These provided new sources of funds, and they were ways of adjusting a bank's exposure to various levels of risk. One unfortunate consequence of deregulation (although deregulation was not the only cause) was that many savings and loan associations and some commercial banks made unwise loans and failed; the federal government was required to compensate their depositors. By hindsight, we know that the government's decision to deregulate (and at the same time decrease the number of bank examiners), while continuing to protect depositors, will ultimately result in a cost to taxpayers of at least $400 billion; it was the most expensive decision in American history, except for the decision to fight World War II.[2]

Nevertheless, the fundamentals of commercial banking remain unchanged. Banks earn income primarily by lending and investing money. The interest on this money is their revenue.[3] They obtain the money primarily by attracting deposits. The interest they pay on these deposits corresponds approximately to

---

[1] A recent glossary lists 250 terms, many of which were developed since 1970. National Association of Accountants, "Evaluating Financial Instruments," Statement of Management Accounting Practices No. 4n Montvale, N.J., 1990. For description of new securities, see this publication and also Henry A. Davis, *Financial Products for Medium-Sized Companies,* (Morristown N.J.: Financial Executives Research Foundation, 1989).

[2] By "government" we mean both the executive branch and the Congress.

[3] Unlike manufacturing companies, bankers refer to this amount as "income," rather than "revenue," which can cause confusion.

cost of sales in a manufacturing company. Thus, net interest income, which is the difference between interest revenue and interest expense, is a key number for bank management to watch; it corresponds to gross margin in a manufacturing company. If the difference between interest revenue and interest expense, plus revenue from other activities, more than covers its operating costs and loan losses, the bank is profitable.

Management Control Implications

The most important aspects of the relationships described above are: (1) the relationship of the rates and maturities of deposits to the rates and maturities of loans,[4] (2) deposit volume, (3) loan losses, (4) expenses, (5) other income, and (6) joint revenues. In addition, we discuss problems involved in profit centers and expense centers.

Interest rates.   In a banker's utopia, deposits would be obtained at, say, 4 percent, loans would earn 6 or 7 percent, and the spread would cover expenses (including loan losses) and leave a satisfactory profit. More realistically, if the interest revenue in each month was 2 or 3 percentage points higher than the interest expense, and if volume was satisfactory, the constant spread, whatever the actual rates, would generate a satisfactory profit. In the early 1980s, however, many thrift institutions and commercial banks made loans at a fixed rate of interest; but they needed to pay a relatively high rate to attract and retain deposits, so the spread between interest revenue and interest expense became inadequate.

Thus, the relationship between interest revenue and interest expense is a key variable. Banks regularly calculate the amount of interest-sensitive assets, interest-sensitive liabilities, and the "gap," which is the difference between them. The monetary amount of this gap is the bank's interest-rate exposure; both prudent management and rules of regulatory bodies require that it be kept within certain bounds.

Traditionally, interest-rate exposure was kept within satisfactory limits by buying or selling securities or by increasing or decreasing the amount of new loans. The increasing use of new types of financial transactions, such as futures, options, caps, floors, and swaps, has greatly complicated the process, has made the net effect of a manager's actions more difficult to understand, and, therefore, has increased the difficulty of management control. Moreover, actions taken to keep interest-rate exposure within satisfactory bounds should be separated from actions taken simply to earn short-term gains on appreciated securities, and such a separation is difficult to detect.

---

[4] For brevity, we shall use "loans" to include both funds lent directly to borrowers and investments in bonds, stocks, and similar securities. For many purposes, loans are treated differently from investments.

Conceptually, the higher the risk of a loan, the higher the interest rate that the bank will charge. Banks refer to the elements of risk as the "four Cs": the borrower's general *character,* its *capability* to repay the loan from earnings or other sources, its *capital,* or net assets, and the *collateral* pledged for the specific loan. For accepting greater risks, the bank expects a greater reward. This risk/reward trade-off governs the lender's decision to make a loan and the interest rate to be charged.

In a bank of even moderate size, many officers are involved in making loans and investments. Senior management has the task of setting the rates on loans of various risks and maturities, of setting corresponding rates for deposits, and of assuring that the actions of individual managers add up to a satisfactory interest-rate exposure for the bank as a whole. Because one bank's money has the same "quality" as the money of competing banks (there are no brand names or other quality differentials), the rates are strongly influenced by the actions of competitors. The management control system must ensure that its rates are communicated throughout the organization and that they are adhered to. Factors affecting these rates can change weekly.

In addition to the rates, lending and investment managers are also limited with respect to the amount of loans and investments, in total, by various types of instruments, and with respect to maturities. They shouldn't make more loans than there are funds available; the available funds are the amount of deposits less a safety amount, which is the bank's capital. This balance between loans and deposits is obtained by establishing quotas to be observed by the individuals or committees who authorize the loans.

Large banks attempt to obtain a certain proportion of "stable" accounts (e.g., individual checking and saving accounts, certificates of deposit) and "volatile" accounts (corporate deposits); often the target proportion is 50-50. Daily they also check the balance between maturities of loans and deposits at various time intervals: 30-day, 60-day, 90-day, and so on. The difference at each time interval is referred to as the *net interest balance.* If the balance is unsatisfactory, they hedge; that is, they buy or sell various instruments to arrive at the desired balance.

Volume. Most expenses are fixed in the short run. Therefore, if a bank can increase its volume of deposits, other things being equal, it will be able to make more loans, and the increased gross margin (i.e., net interest income) will increase its profits. Banks use various marketing devices to do this (except in times when the demand for new loans temporarily has dried up).

Loan losses. The principal cause of the savings and loan debacle in the late 1980s was that many loans turned sour. In part, this was a consequence of a cyclical decline in real estate prices and businesses generally, in certain sections of the country. In part, it reflected incompetent management. To some extent, it was the result of fraud. The government has imposed strict limits for "nonperforming loans" (i.e., loans whose payments are delinquent). These prevent the bank from making additional loans. Committees, internal auditors, bank examiners, and external auditors watch the quality of the loan portfolio, but they can't undo damage that was done when the loan was made.

Expenses. Most of the expenses in a bank are personnel-related. The "back office" expenses—recording and proving transactions—are subject to budgeting and controls that are similar to the controls in a manufacturing company. Cost accounting is a fairly recent development in banks, however. Banks have a problem of allocating common costs that is similar to the problem in manufacturing companies. Accounting and check processing usually are done centrally, and the costs of such work must be equitably assessed to the branches. The Automated Teller Machine system is a fairly expensive operation that is managed centrally but that benefits the branch in which the deposit account is maintained.

Nevertheless, as is the case with many organizations that are dominated by professionals, less attention tends to be given to efficiency than to the more glamorous tasks of making loans, handling trusts, and dealing with customers in other ways.[5]

Other income. Banks earn income by handling trust accounts, collecting receivables, and performing various other services for customers. Until fairly recently, not much attention was given to the price of these services. A common practice was to require the customer to maintain a specific balance, on which the bank earned interest. The hope was that this interest revenue would offset the cost of the services rendered, but few banks made the calculations that were necessary to find out if this was in fact the case. Currently, many banks calculate the costs of providing various services, charge the customers for them at cost plus a profit margin, and sell these services as a way of adding to profits.

Joint revenues. A depositor whose account is maintained in one branch may do business at another branch, or may be persuaded to use the central trust department and other services provided centrally. Branch managers want to receive credit for the revenues that they generate by such activities, and to be compensated for services that they furnish to customers of other branches. If the bank is organized into profit centers, the allocation of joint revenues can have a significant effect on profits.

Moreover, if branch managers do not receive proper credit for new business that they generate but that actually results in deposits or other revenue-

---

[5] In a 1989 survey of members of the Controllers Council of the National Association of Accountants, only 19 percent of the respondents in the financial services industry rated their cost accounting systems as "good," and half rated them as less than adequate or unreliable. (Montvale, N.J.: National Association of Accountants), *Controllers Update,* May 1990, p. 1.)

generating transactions at another branch, or business that benefits the central trust department or other central unit, the manager is unlikely to spend much time seeking such business. Similarly, if a branch does work for a depositor whose deposit is maintained at another branch, but receives no revenue for doing so, the branch is unlikely to spend much effort on such work. Satisfied customers are the bank's principal asset, and, unless the customer receives proper service by everyone in the bank, the whole bank suffers. Some banks urge employees to accept the premise that the principal success factor in the long run is managing customer relationships.

Profit centers. Many commercial banks set up profit centers for their branches or for their individual headquarters activities, or for both. They then must solve the difficult problem of arriving at the transfer price for money. This price is an expense (analogous to cost of sales) to activities that make loans and investments, and it is revenue to activities that generate deposits. Some branches are "loan heavy" (i.e., their loans exceed their deposits), and others are "deposit heavy"; profitability will not be measured correctly unless the transfer price is fair to each type. If the transfer price for the cost of money is set too low, the profitability of the loan-heavy branches will be overstated; whereas if it is set too high, the profitability of deposit-heavy branches will be overstated.

Measurement of the cost of money is also important in assessing the profitability of loans with different maturities, loans with different risk characteristics (e.g., consumer installment loans compared with high-grade corporate loans), and loans to different markets (local, national, and transnational). The Federal Reserve System has facilitated such analyses in its Functional Analysis Program, which collects costs by functions from member banks, computes averages, and makes these available to banks.

Money is obtained by borrowing from other financial institutions, from customers who make savings account deposits ("time deposits"), from customers who purchase certificates of deposit, and from customers who have checking accounts ("demand deposits"). The interest cost of borrowed funds, of time deposits, and of certificates of deposits is readily determined.

Interest cost on demand deposits is more difficult. In addition to the cost of servicing an account, a bank may provide free services to customers who maintain a checking account balance of a prescribed amount (although this practice is becoming less common); the cost of providing these services is a cost of obtaining the funds. Moreover, government regulations require that a certain fraction of deposits be held in reserves on which low interest rates are earned. These reserves must be taken into account in calculating the cost of the money that is available for lending.

The problem is further complicated, because some corporate checking accounts include compensating balances—that is, funds that the corporation is required to leave on deposit, as a condition of a loan (e.g., in order to obtain a loan of $100,000, the borrower might promise to leave $10,000 on deposit in a checking account that pays no interest). Conceptually, a compensating balance reduces the net amount of funds made available to the borrower and, therefore, increases the effective interest cost on the amount that the borrower can use. As a practical matter, the problem of treating compensating balances separately from other checking account balances is so difficult that banks usually do not make such a separation in the formal control system.

These illustrations show that the cost of obtaining funds from different sources varies widely. If a bank obtains $1,000 from one source at annual interest of 5 percent, its cost is $50; if it obtains $1,000 from another source at annual interest of 10 percent, its cost is $100. The second source costs twice as much as (i.e., 200 percent of), the first—*not* 5 percent. Differences of several hundred percent in the cost of funds from various sources are common in banking. This is in contrast with differences in the cost of a given raw material that was purchased from several vendors by a manufacturing company, which ordinarily are only a few percent. The transfer price of funds must take account of these differences. One alternative is to compute some sort of average. Another is to define "pools" of funds obtained at similar rates and establish transfer prices for each pool. The former is simple, but rough. The latter complicates the recordkeeping.

Expense centers.   Arguments about transfer prices are common among bank managers. Some banks have decided that the topic is so controversial that they decide not to develop transfer prices.[6] They, therefore, control branches and other units as expense centers, and they measure performance by such indicators as unit or dollar output per staff member, dollars of revenue and market share by product type, expenses per dollars of revenue compared with budget, and quality indicators. Some use a management-by-objectives (MBO) system, in which a principal objective is obtaining a specified number of additional customers. They make special analyses of profitability as a basis for setting selling prices and for making decisions about opening and closing branches and about adding or discontinuing services.

In comparing the performance of the several branches, measurement of volume is a problem. Computers can easily report the volume of each type of transaction; but aggregating these individual totals into an overall measure of volume can be misleading, unless differences in the effort required for the various types are taken into account. Recording a deposit in a savings account requires much less effort than issuing a U.S. savings bond, for example. And the effort involved in processing a loan application may vary substantially from one applicant to another. A few banks have developed explicit weights for each of the main types of transactions; but most assume that the overall mix is suf-

---

[6] Nevertheless, 80 percent of the respondents to a 1984 survey of large banks reported that they favored profit centers. (Mona J. Gardner and Lucille E. Lammers, "Cost Accounting in Large Banks," *Management Accounting,* April 1988, pp. 1–36.)

ficiently similar at various times and among the main types of branches so overall measures of volume are adequate.

Accounting system. Banks collect vast quantities of information. They are required to "balance out" (i.e., prove the accuracy of transactions) daily and in detail. The regulatory agencies require periodic reports. Unfortunately, these reports tend to be in a form that is not useful for management purposes, so the bank must set up additional accounts to collect data for management purposes. Because most of the raw data flows through computers, this is an easy task once the system has been developed. Computer programs are available that usually can be adapted to the situation in a given bank without too much difficulty.

SECURITIES FIRMS

In this section, we discuss firms that have the general characteristic of dealing in securities. They include investment bankers, securities traders, securities brokers and dealers, managers of funds (investment, mutual, and pension funds), and investment advisors. Until the 1930s, long-term financing of corporations (i.e., the issuance of stocks and bonds) was generally arranged by commercial banks and by a small elite group of partnerships and individuals called "investment bankers"; J. P. Morgan, Drexel and Company, and Kuhn Loeb and Company are the best known examples. The management of the investment portfolio of individuals and companies was handled by bank trust departments. In 1933, the Glass-Steagall Act prohibited commercial banks from engaging in investment banking, including selling and trading in securities. (This prohibition was considerably weakened by the Federal Reserve Board in 1989; the Fed permitted large banks to establish securities affiliates.) The role of bank trust departments decreased because their attitude toward fiduciary responsibility resulted in an overemphasis on "safe" investments, which kept their returns low. Between 1975 and 1985, commercial banks lost one third of their business.[7]

Many traditional investment bankers expanded their services to include all forms of securities underwriting, trading, and investment counselling; several set up a network of branches to service individual investors, including relatively small investors. Firms that specialized in providing investment advice were established. In the 1970s, mutual funds of all types proliferated, and pension funds absorbed an increasing fraction of securities issues. These developments led to increased competition and to reduced profit margins among securities firms.

---

[7] Lawrence K. Fish, in Eileen M. Friars and Robert N. Gogel, eds. *The Financial Services Handbook* (New York: John Wiley & Sons, 1987), p. 173.

Moreover, financing became more complicated. In addition to the "plain vanilla" issues of long-term debt, preferred stock, and common stock, a variety of issues with different risk/reward characteristics were invented. Foreign investors became an increasingly important source of funds. Computer programs made possible the execution of complicated decision rules for buying and selling huge quantities of securities in a matter of minutes (in some cases, seconds).

All these developments complicated the management control problems in securities firms.

Management Control Implications

The characteristics of securities firms that are relevant to management control are quite different from those of the organizations discussed in earlier chapters. They include: (1) the importance of customer relationships, (2) stars and teamwork, (3) the need for rapid information flow, and (4) a focus on short-term performance. These are discussed in the following sections, and there is also a discussion of the measurement of financial performance and compensation.

Customer relationships.[8]   The products of securities firms are intangible, and their quality is difficult to measure. The principal ingredient of quality is the skill of the firm's professionals, which is much more difficult to judge than the quality of tangible goods. At one time, firms could count on a group of loyal customers who stayed with the firm for a generation; but currently customers are more sophisticated and change firms whenever they decide that another firm can offer a similar quality at a better price. The attitude of customers toward a firm is influenced primarily by their judgments about the professionals with whom they have contact.

Management, therefore, goes to great lengths to find out what customers' opinions are and how well (and also how often) a professional interacts with a customer or potential customer. At the lowest level of detail, most firms require that personnel fill out call reports for every customer contact; these at least measure the quantity of employee's efforts.

There are two principal external sources of information. Greenwich Associates has representatives who interview members of the financial staff of at least 1,500 businesses, and then report on both the quantity and the perceived quality of the securities firm's calling efforts. A firm can compare the number of its calls with those of its competitors, and it can also learn the customers'

---

[8] The information in this section is based primarily on Robert G. Eccles and Dwight B. Crane, *Doing Deals: Investment Banks at Work* (Boston: Harvard Business School Press, 1988.) Thomas Wolfe's novel, *Bonfire of the Vanities,* is an excellent way of learning about the behavior of professionals in a securities firm.

judgment about the effectiveness of the presentations. Greenwich Associates also surveys 500 institutional investors, 1,800 institutional buyers, and 1,200 security analysts for their opinions on firms' research and sales forces. The magazine *Institutional Investor* annually surveys institutional investors to rank analysts in each industry; it reports an "All American Research Team" in its October issue. With the exception of advertising and broadcasting, other industries do not have comparable information about customer reaction.

In addition, senior managers have informal contacts with clients (including prospective clients and lost clients) that influence their judgments about the performance of their professionals. Some firms make formal surveys of their clients for this purpose.

Stars and teamwork.   Some professionals in securities firms make decisions about buying or selling securities, or recommendations for corporate financing, that involve tremendous amounts of money. Buy and sell transactions may be executed in a space of a minute or so, as relevant information becomes available. Execution of a merger (or protection of a company against a takeover), a project that is started and finished within a few months, may involve hundreds of millions of dollars in securities and millions in fees to the securities firms. The stars are, of course, the firm's most valuable asset.

> **Example.**   In August 1988, Nomura Securities announced the purchase for $20 million for a 20 percent equity in the firm of Wasserstein, Perella & Company. Bruce Wasserstein and Joseph Perella had organized the firm early in 1988 after a spectacularly successful career with another securities firm; they were the firm's principal asset. The purchase of a 20 percent equity for $20 million indicates that Nomura Securities, the largest and most profitable securities company in the world, judged that these two stars were worth $100 million.[9]

Because of the dominance of star performers, the organization structure of securities firms has relatively few levels, and the relationships between superiors and subordinates are typically unstructured and informal. Hayes and Hubbard describe securities firms as follows:

> Wall Street is practically a caricature of American frontier values, strangely transported through time and space to the canyons of Manhattan. Its youthful gunslinger traders and investment bankers brashly confront each other across the deal table, confident of success and rewards that push the limits of common sense. Personal allegiance is to one's craft, not to a firm.[10]

In such an environment, loose control is appropriate. Firms that have acquired such organizations (e.g., the American Express acquisition of E. F.

---

[9] Samuel L. Hayes III and Philip M. Hubbard, *Investment Banking: A Tale of Three Cities* (Boston: Harvard Business School Press, 1990), pp. 288–89.

[10] Ibid., pp. 290–91.

Hutton and the General Electric acquisition of Kidder Peabody) have difficulty in adapting their management control systems.

The stars who trade in securities or service customers are supported by other professionals, some of whom also are stars. For an important task, such as a major financing or assisting a company in an acquisition, the lead professional may assemble a team that works on the project, sometimes full time and more often part time. Securities traders rely heavily on the advice of research people and others who may know about a given company. An expert in one type of security or industry may ask the advice of colleagues who are knowledgeable about other types of securities or industries, often over the telephone, sometimes in a brief meeting. These informal, but important, relationships contrast with the relationships between production departments and support departments in a manufacturing company. Production supervisors who want the maintenance departments to do some work fill out a work request and wait their turn for the work to be done. In a securities firm there is little paperwork, and the response to the request is often instantaneous.

Need for rapid information.   Many securities and commodities are listed on exchanges in London, Tokyo, and New York, which are in three different time zones. A large securities firm, therefore, conducts trading business 24 hours a day, passing responsibility from London to New York to Tokyo when each market closes. Each trader has a "book" showing the firm's position in each security for which he or she is responsible and in the buy and sell orders that are to be executed. Each also has computer screens giving information on worldwide developments that might affect prices. As every television viewer knows, important developments affect security and commodity market prices within a few minutes of when they occurred. Investment bankers also need current and complete information on all topics that bear on deals in which they are, or may become, involved.

The information systems must signal "flash" news separately from routine flows, they must transform mountains of detail into meaningful summaries, they must develop comparable data from raw data that may not have been comparable, and the data, of course, must be accurate. The development and maintenance of information systems in securities firms is an important function.

Focus on short run.   A growth stock purchased today may produce satisfactory results three years from now, or it may never pay off. A securities firm's profit on a leveraged buyout is easily measured, and all parties may judge, today, that this deal was a good deal; however, it may result in bankruptcy a few years down the road. In short, the real soundness of investment decisions made currently may not be observable until some considerable time in the future.

Nevertheless, with some important exceptions, securities firms tend to focus on short-run performance, and by "short-run" they mean the current quarter.

This short-run emphasis may seem strange; pension fund managers are the largest single class of investors, and they should have little interest in current performance, because their objective is to provide the funds for payments to be made over the lifetime of the pensioners. It exists partly because no one knows what the long-run future will be, but primarily because this short-run emphasis has become traditional.

Investors tend to rely on information about current performance, and performance in the recent past, of the securities firms that they hire to manage their funds. Because performance of a securities firm is heavily influenced by the decisions of the firm's stars, who probably were not with the firm for many past years, data on performance over 5 or 10 past years may provide an invalid basis for judging the performance of a firm or of a specific fund that the firm manages.[11] For similar reasons, senior managers of security firms tend to rely on short-run performance in judging personnel. Japanese firms tend to pay more attention to the long run. Many people are convinced that the American emphasis on short-run performance has serious adverse economic consequences, but no one seems to be able to change this emphasis.

Measuring financial performance. The financial performance of securities firms and of managers, account executives, and others within the firm who trade or deal with customers tends to be measured primarily in terms of revenue and secondarily in terms of gross profit (the difference between revenue and direct expenses). Little effort is made to measure the net income of various activities or individuals. Commissions to account executives are based on the revenue or gross profit of transactions with their customers. Investment banking professionals are compensated primarily by bonuses that in part are based on the firm's fee for the work and in part on the judgment of senior management. Securities firms tend not to make much use of the profit center idea, nor do they do much detailed cost accounting.[12]

Part of the reason for this is that, unlike law or accounting firms, which typically bill customers according to the actual hours spent on the assignment, securities firms typically charge a fee that is a percentage of the amount

---

[11] The performance of Peter Lynch is a well-publicized exception to this generalization. Lynch became manager of the Fidelity Magellan Fund in 1977, when its assets were a few million dollars. When he left in May 1990, its assets were $13 billion. Over the 13-year period, the total return of the Magellan fund was 2,461 percent, compared with 508 percent for the Standard and Poor's stock index. The majority of equities mutual funds earned less than the S&P index.

[12] As an exception, Lawrence K. Fish, a leading banker, suggests that it would be relatively easy to develop profit by customers. He suggests that, as a rule of thumb, 50 percent of the cost of producing revenue includes designing, implementing, and communicating portfolio decision to customers, and this can be allocated on a per-account basis with some adjustment for size; 10 percent is account administration, which can be allocated on a per-account basis; 20 percent is support, including research and trading, which can be allocated by the type of service and number of trades; and 20 percent is custody and recordkeeping services which can be allocated according to the activity level of the account. See Lawrence K. Fish, in *The Financial Services Handbook,* Eileen M. Friars and Robert N. Gogel, eds. (New York: John Wiley & Sons, 1987), pp. 173–75.

involved in the deal. They, therefore, have less need to collect costs by assignments than do other firms. Another reason is the informal exchange of advice and other assistance that occurs in securities firms. The cost of this assistance to the recipient is much more difficult to measure than the cost of a maintenance work order in a factory. A third reason is that expenses are relatively unimportant. The direct expense (i.e., the transaction cost) of a securities trade is small relative to the gross margin. The direct cost of a deal that generates many millions of dollars in fees may be only a few hundred thousand dollars. Nevertheless, although the relative amount may not be large, every dollar of expense that legitimately can be saved increases net income by the same amount.

INSURANCE COMPANIES

General Characteristics

There are two types of insurance companies: life and casualty.

A life insurance company collects premiums from policyholders (or from someone else), invests these premiums, and pays a specified amount to a beneficiary when the policyholder dies. Term insurance provides coverage for a specified number of years; whole life provides coverage for the insured person until death. Whole life insurance contracts usually include an investment feature—that is, part of the premium goes to building up the policy's cash value. In the annuity version of such a policy, cash is paid out regularly over a specified period. In the 1980s, the universal life policy became popular. Instead of paying a fixed payment in return for a fixed stream of premium payments, the payout or the premiums, or both, change with changes in interest rates.

A casualty company collects premiums, invests them, and makes payment to policyholders for specified losses. These may be losses to property by fire, theft, accidents, or other causes; or they may be losses to individuals arising from negligence, malpractice, accidents, illness, and similar causes. Nearly half the casualty policies, measured by the dollar amount of premiums, are for automobile insurance. Casualty policies provide coverage for only a short period, usually not more than three years. Some policies pay for claims made during this period; others pay for losses incurred during the period, even though claims are made in a later period. The billions of dollars of claims against the asbestos industry for losses incurred decades earlier is the most dramatic example of the uncertainties associated with loss occurrence policies.

Insurance usually is sold by agents. Some agents are independent entities who sell the policies of a number of companies. Others are franchised by a single company. For both, their revenue is a specified percentage of premium revenue from the policies they sell. Insurance companies exercise some control over the activities of agents through branch offices.

Insurance companies are regulated by each of the 50 states. The regulatory authorities require an accounting system that differs in significant respects from generally accepted accounting principles (GAAP). The most important difference is that the regulatory authorities require companies to set up substantial reserves when a new policy is written, and these reserves are released if a policy lapses. As a consequence, writing a new life insurance policy typically results in a regulatory accounting loss in the first year, whereas it results in GAAP income. A lapsed policy can increase regulatory accounting income in the year of lapse, whereas it can decrease GAAP income.

Management Control Implications

The central management control problem in insurance companies, especially life insurance companies, is that they do not know the profits from current policy sales until years later. They set premiums based on their best estimate of the inflows and outflows associated with the policy, but these estimates may turn out to have been wide of the mark. Although profitability cannot be known until the final payment has been made, management cannot wait that long to make control decisions; it needs information currently. Unlike investment bankers, insurance managers give much attention to expense control.

Product pricing. A typical insurance company has dozens of products, and the price (i.e., the policy premium) charged for a given product varies among different customers in many respects. For example, the premium for a whole life policy, per thousand dollars of coverage, varies with the age of the insured person and, hence, his or her life expectancy, health, smoking habits, and, in some cases, gender. Actuaries calculate a tentative premium, and the final premium reflects the marketing people's judgment about the attractiveness of the policy and premiums charged by competitors. The actuary's calculation considers the following factors:

- Acquisition cost: the commission paid to sales agents and the costs associated with the selling organization.
- Servicing cost: the cost of collecting premiums and accounting for them, plus an allocation of corporate overhead.
- Profit: the return desired by the company.
  (Acquisition cost, servicing cost, and profit are referred to collectively as "loading.")
- Lapse probability: the probability that the policy will be canceled, because the policyholder does not make payments.
- Investment income: the income that will be earned on the investment of premiums until the policy is paid.
- Probability of payment: for life policies, this depends on the age of the insured, with the probability of death determined from mortality tables;

adjusted for health and other characteristics mentioned above. For casualty policies, it depends on data about the likelihood of occurrence of the events insured against, together with the probable amount of payments for these events; these estimates are much less certain than those for life insurance policies.

* Income taxes: income tax regulations for the insurance industry are considerably different from those for other industries.
* Required earnings rate: the rate at which the above flows are discounted to arrive at their present value.

The annual premium arrived at in the actuarial calculation is so set that the present value of the stream of premium payments is equal to the present value of the other cash flows.

As is the case in any profession, some actuaries are better than others. Because of the crucial importance of the premium calculation, senior management observes closely the performance of each actuary and the accuracy and promptness of huge data collection activity that furnishes current information to the actuaries. Is the calculated premium out of line with those of competitors? If so, why? Is the actuary using the very latest information?[13] Is the calculation overly conservative or overly liberal?

Sales performance.   The actual profitability of various types of insurance policies varies widely, in part because of adjustments made to the actuarial calculation when the premium was set and in part because subsequent developments made the assumptions included in the actuarial calculation unrealistic. Management wants the sales organization to emphasize those products that actually are the most profitable. However, calculating the current profitability of various policies is a difficult task, and communicating this information to the sales organization is also difficult. The tendency, therefore, is to focus on sales volume, rather than on profitability. Commissions are based on first-year or early-year premiums, or on the face amount of policies written. Similar rough measures typically are used in appraising the performance of branches. Computer programs that help agents compute the actual profitability of various types of policies are becoming increasingly used.

Expense control.   Expenses are controlled through programs and budgets as in industrial companies. Productivity measures are widely used in the control of clerical and other repetitive operations. Although judgments about their performance are somewhat subjective, the activities of claims adjustors are carefully monitored.

---

[13] For example, in the 1980s, claims for malpractice in various professions and awards for malpractice suits fluctuated widely. They increased from one year to the next in the early years of the decade and increased at a slower rate in the later years.

Control of investing.   As is the case with other financial services organizations, the management of the investment function is important. Traditionally, insurance companies followed rather conservative investment policies, partly because of the influence of regulatory agencies. In recent years they have diversified into direct placement of loans and in investments in real estate and other commercial ventures. This shift requires a different approach to investing and involves increasing risk. Control is similar to that exercised by other financial services organizations.

SUMMARY

Financial services organizations differ in two fundamental respects from industrial companies. First, their "raw material" is money. At a given moment of time the value of each unit of money in inventory is the same for all organizations, but the cost of using money obtained from various sources varies considerably. Second, the profitability of many transactions cannot be measured until years after the commitment has been made. In particular, the company is profitable only if the future revenues obtained from current loans, investments, and insurance premiums exceed the cost of the funds associated with these revenues (which is analogous to cost of sales in a manufacturing company) by an amount that is sufficient to cover operating expenses and losses.

The management control problem is complicated in investment banking, securities trading, and some other organizations by the fact that huge profits or losses can be generated in a single transaction. The "stars" who make such transactions are only loosely controlled.

SUGGEST ADDITIONAL READINGS

Aspinwall, Richard C., and Robert A. Eisenbeis, eds, *Handbook for Banking Strategy.* New York: John Wiley & Sons, 1985.

Baughn, William A.; Thomas I. Storrs; and Charles E. Walker, eds. *The Bankers' Handbook.* 3rd. ed. Homewood, Ill.: Dow Jones-Irwin, 1988. (See especially Part 5.)

Davenport, Thomas O., and H. David Sherman. "Measuring Branch Profitability." *The Bankers Magazine,* September–October 1987, pp. 34–38.

Eccles, Robert G., and Dwight B. Crane. *Doing Deals: Investment Banks at Work.* Boston: Harvard Business School Press, 1988.

Friars, Eileen M., and Robert N. Gogel, eds. *The Financial Services Handbook.* New York: John Wiley & Sons, 1987.

Haskins & Sells. *Bank Costs for Planning and Control.* Park Ridge, Ill.: Bank Administration Institute, 1972.

Hayes, Samuel L. III, and Philip M. Hubbard. *Investment Banking: A Tale of Three Cities.* Boston: Harvard Business School Press, 1990.

Hekimian, James S. *Management Control in Life Insurance Branches.* Boston: Division of Research, Harvard Business School, 1965.

Rappaport, Stephen P. *Management on Wall Street: Making Securities Firms Work.* Homewood, Ill.: Dow Jones-Irwin, 1988.

Rose, Peter S., and Donald R. Fraser. *Financial Institutions.* 3rd ed. Homewood, Ill.: Business Publications, Inc., 1988.

Case 15–1
Chemical Bank*

Chemical Bank, with deposits averaging well over $1 billion, was one of the largest banks in the United States. Its banking operations were conducted in a main office and in several dozen branch offices located throughout the New York metropolitan area. A partial organization chart is shown in Exhibit 1.

Branch offices operated as if they were independent banks. They served individual, commercial, and industrial customers by accepting demand, savings, and time deposits, by extending various types of loans, and by performing other services normally expected of a bank. The sizes and operating characteristics of the branches varied over a wide range. Average deposits outstanding ranged from $1 million to over $100 million; average loans outstanding, from no loans to over $100 million. Moreover, the ratio of deposits to loans varied considerably from one branch to another; most branches had more deposits than loans, but a few had more loans than deposits. In brief, both the magnitude and composition of asset and liabilities were significantly different among the different branches. Inasmuch as these differences were related to the geographical location of the branches, the difficulty of evaluating and comparing the performances of branches for the purpose of overall planning and control was inherent in the situation. The design and operation of a planning and control system for this purpose was the responsibility of the control division.

Among various reports reaching top management, the quarterly comparative earnings statement (see Exhibits 2 and 3) played a central role in the evaluation of branch performance. The report was designed to show the extent to which branches attained three important goals: (1) branches should operate within their budgets, (2) branches should grow in deposits and loans, and (3) branches should earn satisfactory profits. Accordingly, the statement showed for each branch the budgeted and actual amounts of deposits and loans outstanding, and income, expenses, and earnings for the current quarter, the year to date, and the year to date for the preceding year.

Budget

In early November, each branch prepared a budget for the following year for submission to headquarters of the banking division and to top management. The branches were furnished a booklet containing sample forms, 24 pages of detailed instructions, and a brief set of policy guides from top management to facilitate the preparation of their budgets. The instructions gave the procedures to be followed in arriving at the budget amounts for specific items. It was, for instance, specified that the starting point for forecasting was to be the prior year's figures on the quarterly basis, that the income item of interest on loans was to be derived from the projected volume of loans and loan rates, that painting cost

* This case was prepared by R. N. Anthony, Harvard Business School.
Copyright © by the President and Fellows of Harvard College.
Harvard Business School case 172–228.

EXHIBIT 1   Partial Organization Chart

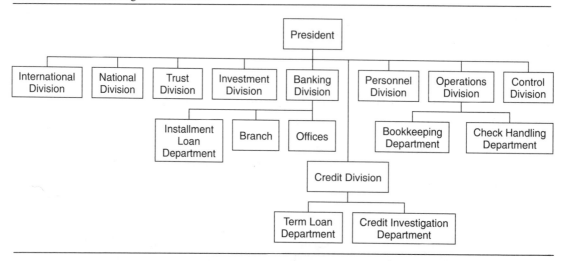

should not be included in the item for building maintenance expense, and so on.

Since salaries was the biggest single expense item, and the hiring and releasing of employees involved considerable cost, utmost care was required in budgeting this item. Branches were instructed to arrive at staffing requirements for the next year after a thorough examination of anticipated increases in productivity arising from mechanization or otherwise improved operating procedures, of anticipated changes in the volume of activity, and of advantages and disadvantages of using overtime or temporary or part-time help. If the number of the required staff of a branch thus determined exceeded the number previously authorized by top management, the reason for the difference had to be thoroughly documented and substantiated to banking division headquarters and the budget committee. Top management was extremely critical of subsequent requests by the branches for staff increases which had not been reflected in the budgets.

In general, there were two types of income and expense items—those directly identifiable with a particular branch, and those not directly identifiable with a particular branch. Branches were instructed to budget only those direct expenses

under their control. Indirect expenses were allocated to branches by the control division. In addition, the budgeting of certain direct expenses, such as depreciation of fixtures, employee benefits, and deferred compensation, was done by the control division because the branches had only secondary control over these expenses.

Earnings Statement

The control division had encountered a number of serious problems in trying to produce an earnings statement that would be most useful for the branches and for the management of the banking division. The control division resolved some of these problems in the following ways.

Installment Loans

Recordkeeping, issuance of coupon books, and part of collection work for installment loans generated by all branches were handled centrally by the installment loan department; and income earned from installment loans, therefore, was credited initially to this department. This income was in large part attributable to the branches that generated the loans and, therefore, was redistributed to them. The current procedure was to

EXHIBIT 2 Comparative Statement of Earnings, 1960 (Branch A)

3rd Quarter Actual	3rd Quarter Budget		January 1 through September 30 Actual	January 1 through September 30 Budget
		Income:		
$ 13,177	$ 12,600	Interest on loans	$ 33,748	$ 35,200
6,373	4,800	Service chgs.—regular A/C's	14,572	14,100
3,816	3,600	Service chgs.—special ck	11,114	10,700
1,168	1,300	Safe deposit rentals	4,317	4,500
2,237	2,154	Installment loans (net)	5,126	5,406
—	—	Special loans (net)	—	—
1,010	1,200	Fees, comm., other income	3,321	3,300
27,781	25,654	Total direct income	72,198	73,206
104,260	102,128	Interest on excess (borr.) funds	324,434	306,166
$ 132,041	$ 127,802	Gross income	$ 396,632	$ 379,372
		Expenses:		
$ 32,363	$ 32,617	Salaries	$ 96,151	$ 97,164
2,995	2,995	Deferred Compensation	8,865	8,865
5,232	4,689	Employee benefits	14,925	14,067
11,485	11,489	Rent and occupancy	34,398	33,947
6,824	7,560	Interest on deposits	20,455	21,780
9,458	8,090	Other direct	25,688	23,930
3,128	3,097	Office administration	9,676	9,725
19,183	17,642	Service departments	57,059	52,399
6,415	5,061	Indirect and overhead	14,964	14,273
97,043	93,200	Gross expenses	282,181	276,150
34,998	34,602	Net earnings before taxes	114,451	103,222
18,955	18,741	Income tax prov. (credit)	61,978	55,906
$ 16,043	$ 15,861	Net earnings after taxes	$ 52,464	$ 47,316
$12,655,000	12,550,000	Average deposits—Demand	$13,134,000	$12,650,000
979,000	1,100,000	Savings	986,000	1,057,000
55,000	55,000	Time	40,000	43,000
233,000	190,000	U.S.	213,000	183,000
$13,922,000	$13,895,000	Total	$14,373,000	$ 33,000
900,000	870,000	Average loans	775,000	827,000
5.82	5.76	Average loan rate	5.82	5.69
		Earnings rate on:		
4.08	3.95	Excess (borr.) funds	4.05	3.95
6.50	6.40	Savings deposits	6.46	6.40
26.5%	27.1%	Net earnings ratio (before taxes)	28.9%	27.2%
		Memo:		
—	—	Losses—before taxes	—	—
—	—	Recoveries—before taxes	—	

EXHIBIT 3 Comparative Statement of Earnings, 1960 (Branch B)

3rd Quarter			January 1 through September 30	
Actual	Budget		1960 Actual	1960 Budget
		Income:		
$ 951,617	$ 833,300	Interest on loans	$ 2,646,813	$ 2,202,750
7,015	7,400	Service chgs.—regular A/C's	24,020	21,900
8,211	7,600	Service chgs.—special ck	23,284	22,600
2,049	2,100	Safe deposit rentals	6,712	7,100
9,202	9,478	Installment loans (net)	21,402	23,790
—	212	Special loans (net)	85	556
8,081	3,100	Fees, comm., other income	22,517	12,800
986,175	863,190	Total direct income	2,744,933	2,291,496
(191,650)	(121,960)	Interest on excess (borr.) funds	(430,444)	(121,493)
$ 794,525	$ 741,230	Gross income	$ 2,314,489	$ 2,170,003
		Expenses:		
$ 69,308	$ 62,633	Salaries	$ 197,572	$ 185,634
5,646	5,646	Deferred compensation	16,938	16,938
9,180	7,989	Employee benefits	25,833	23,967
27,674	27,775	Rent and occupancy	82,726	83,375
15,878	18,230	Interest on deposits	47,589	52,650
25,637	23,660	Other direct	86,112	71,400
17,232	17,072	Office administration	53,321	53,606
89,724	95,719	Service departments	290,082	283,531
22,406	18,001	Indirect and overhead	53,643	51,166
282,685	276,725	Gross expenses	853,816	822,267
511,,840	464,505	Net earnings before taxes	1,460,673	1,347,736
277,212	251,576	Income Tax prov. (credit)	791,100	729,934
$ 234,628	$ 212,929	Net earnings after taxes	$ 669,573	$ 617,802
$67,901,000	$70,000,000	Average deposits—Demand	$69,425,000	$72,667,000
2,354,000	2,700,000	Savings	2,328,000	2,600,000
74,000	90,000	Time	52,000	66,000
5,194,000	1,900,000	U.S.	4,086,000	1,733,00
$75,523,000	$74,690,000	Total	$75,891,000	$77,066,000
72,129,000	65,500,000	Average loans	67,446,000	57,666,000
5.25	5.10	Average loan rate	5.24	5.10
		Earnings rate on:		
4.08	3.95	Excess (borr.) funds	4.05	3.95
6.50	6.40	Savings deposits	6.46	6.40
64.4%	62.7%	Net earningns ratio (before taxes)	63.1%	62.1%
		Memo:		
—	—	Losses—before taxes	5,559	—
—	66	Recoveries—before taxes	798	—

tribute gross operating income less the cost of "borrowed" funds and operating expenses of the department on the basis of the total indirect installment loans generated by the branch during a revolving annual cycle.

An alternative basis that had been considered was to apportion the net income of the installment department according to the number of payments received by branches, since this measure of activity reflected the clerical time spent for coupon handling. This alternative was not adopted, on the grounds that it did not give branches enough motivation to seek more new installment loans, particularly since customers could make their installment payments at any branch they chose. An alternative basis considered was the amount of average loans outstanding. The controller thought this might be more equitable than the currently used basis, but he was of the opinion that the gain to be obtained from the adoption of the new basis was not large enough to offset the additional necessary recordkeeping.

Interest on Excess (or Borrowed) Funds

Branches and other operating units, with funds available for investment in excess of their own requirements for loans, cash, and other assets, shared in the net earnings of the investment division, branches, and other operating units whose asset requirements exceeded their available funds and were charged for funds "borrowed." There was a wide variation in the ratio of deposits to loans among branches, and some branches were credited with the interest on excess funds in an amount higher than their direct income. An example of the calculation of this important income or charge item is shown in Exhibit 4.

As shown in the top section of Exhibit 4, the first step was to compute the amount of excess (or borrowed) funds for the branch. Funds were divided into two pools: (1) special pool—earnings from special long-term, high-yield municipal securities, which were considered as an investment of part of the savings and time deposits; and (2) regular pool—earnings from other

portfolio securities investments, interest on certain loans, and sundry earnings. As a rule, the special-pool investments yield a higher rate of return than the regular-pool investments.

Third, branches with savings deposits were credited at the interest rate of the special pool on the basis of their pro rata share of savings deposits. Net savings deposits in excess of the principal of investment in the special pool, together with excess funds other than savings deposits, received pro rata credit from the earnings of the regular investment pool. Branches that borrowed funds were charged at the regular-pool rate. In summary, the two rates from the two pools were as follows:

Special-pool rate: Net earnings of special pool/ special pool securities principal (part of total savings deposits)

Regular-pool rate: Net earnings from regular pool/excess funds less borrowed funds less special securities principal.

For the first three quarters of 1960, the budgeted regular pool rate and special pool rate were 3.95 percent and 7.81 percent; the actual rates, 4.05 percent and 7.88 percent, respectively. Thus, for Branch A the interest on excess funds for the first three quarters was calculated as shown in the lower section of Exhibit 4.

Rent and Occupancy Cost

Some branches operated in leased space, whereas others operated in bank-owned buildings. The first group was charged with the actual rent paid; but the second was charged with the "fair rental value," which was determined by outside real estate appraisers. The practice was thought to put the two groups on the same footing. The fair rental value charges were internal bookkeeping entries offset by credits to real estate accounts and, therefore, indicated the profitability of each building. The determination of the fair rental value was not difficult, and there has been no significant controversies involving its calculation.

EXHIBIT 4 Calculation of interest income on Excess Funds, Branch A (first three quarters of 1960)

Calculation of Excess Funds

	(000s)	
Total demand deposits	$13,134	
Less: reciprocal bank balances; float	(727)	
Plus: treasury tax and loan a/c	221	
Adjusted demand deposits	12,628	
Less: reserve at 18%	(2,273)	
Net demand deposits		$10,355
Savings deposits	1,026	
Less: reserve at 5%	$ (51)	
Net savings deposits		975
Net deposits available for investment		11,330
Less: loans, cash, other assets		(1,229)
Net excess funds		$10,101

Calculation of Interest Income on Excess Funds

	Principal	Annual Rate	Three Quarters	Interest
In special investment pool (63%)	$ 614,000 ×	7.88% ×	¾ =	$ 36,270
In regular investment pool (37%)	361,000 ×	4.05% ×	¾ =	10,962
Savings deposits (100%)	975,000 ×	6.46% ×	¾ =	47,232
In regular investment pool— demand deposits	9,126,000 ×	4.05% ×	¾ =	277,202
Net excess funds	$10,101,000			
Interest on excess funds				$324,434

Advertising

General or institutional advertising was charged to other indirect expenses. (See below for the allocation of other indirect expenses.) Advertising related to a specific branch was charged directly to that branch, except that, when advertising was placed in mass media, such as radio, television, and newspapers with general circulation, 33 percent of the expense was allocated to other indirect expenses and 67 percent was allocated to the specific branches involved. The theory of the exception was that, when mass media were used, the whole bank benefited to a certain extent.

Banking Division Headquarters and General Administration

All expenses of the banking division headquarters, including the salaries of officers in the division headquarters, were allocated to branches on the basis of their prior year's average gross deposits. The figure for average gross deposits was considered as the best single measure of branch activity.

The salaries of general administrative officers of the bank were first allocated among divisions on the basis of the time spent on problems of each division as estimated by each officer. The amount of general administrative salaries thus allocated to the banking division was, in turn, allocated among branches on the basis of gross deposits in the prior year. All other general administrative expenses were charged on the same basis.

Bookkeeping Department

Much of the bookkeeping work was centralized for the whole bank. However, since the central department had been established only in 1959, several offices continued to do their own bookkeeping in 1960. The expenses of the central bookkeeping department therefore, were allocated only to the branches it serviced. There were eight functional cost centers in the bookkeeping department, and each cost center had its own basis of allocation. The bases of four of the cost centers are given below.

1. *Regular Bookkeeping Cost Center.* In the bookkeeping department, a permanent clerical staff was assigned to process the accounts of each branch. Allocations to branches were based on the salaries of this assigned staff, plus fringe benefits and related overhead cost.

2. *Bank Ledgers Cost Center.* Allocation was on the basis of debit and credit activity as determined by an analysis made from time to time. Inasmuch as the main activity of this cost center was the posting of transactions to ledger sheets, the number of debit and credit entries were preferred to any other basis (e.g., number of accounts). A new survey of debit and credit statistics was made by the analysis department whenever it was believed that there had been a material change from the prior survey period and, in any event, at least once a year.

3. *Special Checking Cost Center.* Same as **2.**

4. *Special Statement Section.* Allocation was on the basis of a number of accounts handled. The activity of the section was to send out special statements on customers' special requests.

Before adoption of the current method based on the cost center concept, weight of statements mailed out had been the basis of allocation for the expenses of the entire department. The current practice was regarded as more accurate, because there were very few temporary movements of staff and machine services from one cost center to another and because there was a significant variation in the activity measures of the cost centers.

According to the controller, the main controversy involving the expenses of the bookkeeping department was not with respect to the basis of allocation but, rather, with respect to the absolute level of expenses of the department. Complaints were heard from those branches serviced by the department to the effect that they were handicapped relative to branches that did their own bookkeeping, because the cost charged by the central bookkeeping department was considerably higher than the cost that would be incurred if the branch did its own bookkeeping. The controller thought branches that had this opinion failed to recognize that the bookkeeping expenses showed in the earnings statements of the branches with their own bookkeeping were only part of the true bookkeeping cost, because an appropriate portion of supervisory salaries, occupancy costs, supplies, etc., was not included in the item. When the bookkeeping was centralized for a branch, the benefit gained from relieving the supervisors of supervising bookkeeping activity usually appeared as increased loans and deposits, and better management generally.

Check Clearance Department

The total cost of this department was divided among 12 functional cost centers, based on the number of employees assigned to each and the volume of its work. The cost of each cost center was, in turn, charged to branches. Examples of the basis of allocation are given below.

1. *IBM proof machine operation—exchanges:* allocated on the basis of number of checks handled.

2. *IBM proof machine operation—deposits:* allocated on the basis of the number of deposit items.

3. *Check desk:* allocated on the basis of the number of checks handled.
4. *Transit clerical:* allocated on the basis of number of deposit items.
5. *Supervision:* allocated to the various check clearance department cost centers in ratio to labor costs.

As was the case with the bookkeeping centers, the measures of activity (checks handled and number of deposit items) were based on periodic surveys and remained unchanged until significant changes in the relative activity of branches indicated the need for a new survey. Every cost center's activity was reviewed at least once a year for this purpose.

There were two important sources of trouble in allocation of the expenses of the check clearance department. One was that branches cashed checks issued by other branches; the other was that branches received deposits for customers whose accounts were in other branches. In the periodic activity analyses made to determine the basis of allocating cost, the "number of checks cashed" was the number of checks actually cashed in the branch, whether or not the account was located in the branch. Similarly, the "number of deposit items" was the number of deposits made in the branch. Although it had been believed that the effect of these interbranch services largely offset one another, a recent study by the control division indicated that they, in fact, resulted in distortions with respect to certain branches. The control division was currently working on a method of allocation by which the charge would be made to the branch that benefited most—that is, the branch in which the account was located.

Credit Investigation Department

Although most branches had their own credit analysis staffs, they often asked the central credit department to make investigations. The expenses of the central credit investigation department, therefore, were allocated to the branches that re-

quested its service. The basis of allocation was the number of requests for credit investigation weighted by the typical time required for the analyses performed. The weight for the various types of investigation was determined by the analysis department on the basis of an actual time study.

Term Loan Department

Income from term loans was credited to the branches that generated the loans. Officers of the term loan department actively counseled the branches in negotiating terms with customers, in drawing up loan contracts, and in reviewing existing loans. It was necessary, therefore, that the expenses of the term loan department be allocated to the branches that used its service. The basis of allocation was the number of loans considered, the number of loans outstanding, and the number of amendments to existing loans, weighted by the unit handling time of each of three classes. To determine the weight, the analysis department asked the staff of the term loan department to estimate the time spent on each class.

Personnel Division

The expenses of this division were allocated to all operating units in the ratio of the number of employees in each operating unit to the total.

Other Indirect Expenses

Items of a general overhead nature, such as expenses of the operations division (except the direct cost of examining a branch, which was charged directly), cost of the senior training program, general institutional advertising, contributions, etc., were included under this heading. The basis of allocation of these expenses among branches was the ratio of annual operating expenses (excluding other indirect expenses and interest on deposits) of each branch to the total operating expenses of all branches.

Deposits and Loans

In the lower part of the comparative statement were shown the budgeted and actual loans and deposits outstanding. Both top management and branch managers exercised a close watch over these primary indicators of the level of the branch's operation. The controller, however, believed that the ultimate test of the office performance should not rest with these items but, rather, with earnings. He maintained that the effect of changes in deposits and loans should and would be reflected in the earnings statement.

Controller's Views on Allocations

The controller believed that some arbitrariness was inevitable in the allocation of the income and expense items described above. With dozens of branches, each with its own operating characteristics, it was impossible to have a "perfect" or "right" system for all of them. What was more important, according to the controller, was agreement on the part of the branch managers that the system was generally equitable. If managers agreed on the fairness of the system, he believed, it was likely to be a success. The controller, therefore, let it be known to branch managers that the system was always open for revision, and he encouraged them to make known any criticisms they had. After the control division had done its best to find a workable system, the initiative for suggesting changes was with the branch managers. The controller said that several changes had been made as a result of branch managers' suggestions.

He warned them, however, against a blind and apathetic acceptance; the acceptance should be positive and constructive. On acceptance of the system, branch managers should be concerned with the reported result and make necessary efforts to improve it. Thus, he said, branch managers were told clearly that the earnings statement was used to evaluate their performance. This, he thought, attached sufficient importance to the matter to prevent any possible indifference.

Attitudes of Branch Managers on Allocations

The managers of two offices, A and B, held different opinions about the system. The operating characteristics of these branches were different, as indicated by their comparative statements of earnings for the third quarter of 1960, reproduced in Exhibits 2 and 3. Branch A was relatively small and deposit-heavy, did its own bookkeeping, and operated in a leased space, whereas Branch B was larger, loan-heavy, used the centralized bookkeeping department, and operated in a bank-owned building. Their annual earnings statements of recent years are shown in Exhibits 5 and 6.

Comment by Manager of Branch A

The statement is useful because I like to see, at least quickly, whether I am within the budget and what caused the deviations from it, if any.

The earnings of our branch are relatively low, because the volume of business is limited by the location. We have more deposits than our loan requirements; consequently, we get credit for the excess funds. In fact, as you see, for the first three quarters of 1960, interest on excess funds was more than four times the total direct income. The 4.05 percent rate on the excess funds seems fair enough, but we try always to increase our loans in order to increase our earnings. However, the location of our office is a limiting factor.

Since rent and occupancy is the actual rent paid to the owner of the building, we can't have any quarrel about that, but the service department charges are certainly too high. We don't have any control over these costs; yet we are charged for them. I am not complaining that this is unfair; on the contrary, I believe branches should share the burden. My only misgiving is whether those service departments are doing enough to cut down on their costs.

About one half of the service department expenses charged to our branch is for check clearing service. Although I don't know the basis of allocation, I don't doubt that it is fair. Besides, even if I should have some questions about the basis, probably it wouldn't reach up there; the communication channel from here to the top is long and tedious.

At present, we do our own bookkeeping, but soon this will be centralized. I have heard some managers complain that the cost charged to them for the centralized bookkeeping is higher than the

EXHIBIT 5 Condensed Annual Earnings Statements, Branch A ($000s)

	1960	1959		1958		1957		1956	1955
	Budget	Budget	Actual	Budget	Actual	Budget	Actual	Actual	Actual
Total direct income	$ 98	$ 93	$ 90	$ 87	$ 89	$ 99	$ 90	$ 99	$ 82
Interest on excess funds	409	364	381	327	316	299	287	263	355
Gross income	$ 507	$ 457	$ 471	$ 414	$ 405	$ 398	$ 377	$ 362	$ 437
Expenses:									
Salaries	$ 130	$ 129	$ 125	$ 125	$ 125	$ 140	$ 147	$ 132	$ 114
Deferred Compensation	12	10	10	8	9				
Employee benefits	19	19	18	17	17				
Rent and occupancy	45	46	45	45	47	47	49	43	43
Interest on deposits	30	30	27	19	19	9	11	6	4
Other direct	32	29	31	30	30	*	*	*	*
Office administration	13	15	13	17	16	*	*	*	*
Service departments	70	58	61	57	57	67	69	62	44
Indirect overhead	18	18	21	19	16	*	*	*	*
Gross expenses	369	354	351	337	336		329	296	256
Net earnings before taxes	$ 138	$ 103	$ 120	$ 77	$ 69	$ 83	$ 48	$ 62	$ 181
Average gross deposits	13,975	13,550	13,707	13,573	12,948	14,540	13,422	15,057	21,504
Average loans	820	820	810	746	737	990	927	1,139	1,093

* Changes in accounting procedure makes these items noncomparable with later years.

EXHIBIT 6 Condensed Annual Earnings Statements, Branch B ($000s)

	1960	1959		1958		1957		1956	1955
	Budget	Budget	Actual	Budget	Actual	Budget	Actual	Actual	Actual
Total direct income	$ 3,077	$ 2,725	$ 2,532	$ 2,214	$ 2,201	$ 2,338	$ 2,395	$ 1,959	$ 1,172
Interest on excess borrowed funds	(177)	157	222	154	263	73	(32)	209	556
Gross income	$ 2,900	$ 2,882	$ 2,754	$ 2,368	$ 2,464	$ 2,411	$ 2,363	$ 2,168	$ 1,728
Expenses:									
Salaries	$ 249	$ 255	$ 256	$ 245	$ 247	$ 250	$ 264	$ 236	$ 232
Deferred compensation	22	19	21	17	18				
Employee benefits	32	34	33	30	31				
Rent and occupancy	111	105	104	104	105	106	108	65	85
Interest on deposits	71	75	66	51	52	19	25	12	10
Other direct	95	93	108	84	86	*	*	*	*
Office administration	71	85	76	86	83	*	*	*	*
Service departments	379	383	360	356	345	361	380	315	224
Indirect overhead	65	64	72	60	51	*	*	*	*
Gross expenses	1,095	1,113	1,096	1,033	1,018	878	928	829	814
Net earnings before taxes	$ 1,805	$ 1,769	$ 1,658	$ 1,335	$ 1,446	$ 1,533	$ 1,435	$ 1,339	$ 914
Average gross deposits	77,410	79,885	75,853	72,063	73,899	73,415	69,683	70,740	73,433
Average loans	58,000	56,000	49,702	48,971	47,095	50,000	49,945	44,460	28,378

* Changes in accounting procedures make these items noncomparable with later years.

cost when they did their own bookkeeping. However, such intangible gains as prestige and customer relations may justify a little higher cost. At any rate, we wouldn't have any choice if top management decides to centralize our bookkeeping. It may be better in the long run.

Although I don't know exactly what items are included in other direct and indirect and overhead expenses, I don't think they are excessive. The control division is trying to be fair.

In summary, I think the statement is useful, but there are many factors you should consider in interpreting it.

Comment by Manager of Branch B

The statement is a fair measure of how branches are doing It is true that the location of a branch has a lot to do with its operation; in evaluating a particular branch, the location is an important element to be taken into account. To take the extreme case, you don't need a branch in a desert. If a branch can't show earnings after being charged with its fair share of all costs, perhaps the purpose of its existence is lost.

High volume and efficient operation have contributed to our high level of earnings. Our branch has more loans that can be sustained by our own deposits; thus, we are charged with interest on borrowed funds on the theory that we would have to pay the interest if we borrowed from outside. Of course, by increasing deposits we could meet the loan requirements and add to our earnings a good part of the interest on borrowed funds; indeed, we have been trying to lure more deposits to our branch. Quite apart from this special effort, however, we do not neglect to seek more loan opportunities, for loans increase earnings even after the interest charge.

Our office is in a bank-owned building; but, instead of controversial depreciation and maintenance charges, we are charged with the fair rental value. We are satisfied with this practice.

The bookkeeping of our branch is centralized. I believe we could do it for less money if we did our own bookkeeping; but competing banks have centralized bookkeeping departments, and we have to go along. I suspect there are some intangible benefits being gained, too.

If I really sat down and thoroughly examined all the allocation bases, I might find some things that could be improved. But the fact of life is that we must draw a line somewhere; some arbitrariness will always be there. Furthermore, why should our branch raise questions? We are content with the way things are.

Comments by Banking Division Headquarters

We call this report [Exhibits 2 and 3] our Bible, and, like the actual Bible, it must be interpreted carefully. Many factors affect the performance of a branch that do not show up on the report. For example, in an area that is going downhill the manager of a branch has to work terribly hard just to keep his deposits from declining, whereas in a growing area, the manager can read the *New York Times* all day and still show an impressive increase in deposits. The location of the branch in the neighborhood, its outward appearance, its decor, the layout of its facilities—all can affect its volume of business. Changes in the level of interest rates, which are noncontrollable, also have a significant effect on income. At headquarters, we are aware of these factors and take them into account when we read the reports. The unfortunate fact is that some managers—for example, those in declining areas— may not believe that we take them into account. Such a manager may worry about his apparently poor performance as shown on the report, and this has a bad psychological effect on him.

One other difficulty with the report is that it may encourage the manager to be interested too much in his own branch at the expense of the bank as a whole. When a customer moves to another part of town, the manager may try to persuade him to leave his account in the same branch, even though the customer can be served better by a branch near his new location. We even hear of two branches competing for the same customer, which certainly doesn't add to the reputation of the bank. Or, to take another kind of problem, a manager may be reluctant to add another teller because of the increased expense, even though he actually needs one to give proper service to his customers.

Of course, the earnings report is just one factor in judging the performance of a bank manager. Among the others are the growth of deposits compared with the potential for the area; the number of calls he makes soliciting new business (we get a monthly report on this); the loans that get into difficulty; complaint letters from customers; the annual audit of operations made by the control division; and, most important, personnel turnover, or any other indications of how well he is developing his personnel. Some of these factors are indicated in these statistics [see Exhibit 7], which are prepared at banking division headquarters.

QUESTIONS

This case deals with the use of the profit center concept as a management control device for branch offices in a service industry. A particular problem in banking is how to set the transfer price for money.

Discuss the adequacy of the following structural components of Chemical's control systems.

1. **Cost allocation** of headquarter's expense. Should these costs be allocated? Are these methods of allocation appropriate?

2. **Noncontrollable costs** included in performance reports. Should noncontrollable costs be omitted from the earnings statement? If so, what items would be affected?

3. **Performance evaluation** of dissimilar branches. Does this reporting system provide enough information? Too much? Should Exhibit 7 be discontinued?

4. **Profit center** organization of branches. Do you believe branches should be evaluated as "profit centers"? What factors are critical to the success of a branch bank? To what extent are these factors controllable by a branch manager?

5. **Transfer pricing** system used. If you believe the profit center system should be continued as a control device, discuss the appropriateness of the data developed in Exhibit 4 for transfer pricing purposes. Can you suggest better ways to price the transfer of funds between branches? Bank of America, one of the largest banks in the United States, charges its profit centers for the use of money at current interest rates for obtaining funds of like maturities and risk. For example, if a branch makes a 90-day loan, it would be charged at the current rate that the bank pays on 90-day certificates of deposit. Should Chemical Bank adopt this practice?

EXHIBIT 7 Branch Office Report

1960   Location and Office No. A

All Dollar Amounts in Thousands Unless Otherwise Stated		JAN.	FEB.	MAR.	APRIL	MAY	JUNE	JULY	AUG.	SEPT.	OCT.	NOV.	DEC.	YEAR AVERAGE	
DEPOSITS - AVERAGE															
1	Demand - (Ind., Part., Corp.) $	14 038	15 473	12 330	12 919	13 108	12 911	12 596	11 907	12 746	12 202				1
2	Demand - Banks $	50	50												2
3	Special Checking $	221	218	220	251	235	216	237	244	246	214				3
4	Treas. Tax & Loan Account $	118	149	238	124	270	321	232	202	265	196				4
5	Savings $	987	974	1 001	910	976	1 012	972	978	986	1 013				5
6	Christmas Club $	15	25	30		41	46	51	55	60	63				6
7	Time $														7
8	Total $	14 429	14 887	13 819	14 419	14 630	14 506	14 088	13 486	14 253	13 694				8
NUMBER OF ACCOUNTS															
9	Demand (Ind., Part., Corp.)	1 513	1 513	1 507	1 504	1 516	1 511	1 514	1 497	1 478	1 473				16
10	Demand - Banks	1													17
11	Special Checking	868	863	884	892	844	900	903	911	939	948				18
12	Savings	585	587	593	589	587	591	593	587	621	645				
13	Christmas Club	540	536	534	538	533	530	526	519	516	511				
14	Time														
15	Total	3 507	3 501	3 518	3 522	3 530	3 532	3 536	3 514	3 554	3 577				
LOANS														**YEAR AVERAGE**	
16	Total Loans - Average $	723	733	720	627	672	774	841	889	971	961				16
17	Instalment Loan - Volume $	20	24	36	31	35	22	25	34	27	39				17
18	Spec. Loan Dept. - Month End $														18
NUMBER OF BORROWERS															
19	Total Loans	48	58	50	49	51	54	55	60	62	63				
20	Instalment Loans - Made	24	37	46	50	50	50	28	45	44	34				
21	Special Loan Dept.														
22	Staff - Number of Officers	4	4	4	4	4	4	4	4	4	4				
23	No. of Employees - Auth. Budget	25	25	25	25	25	25	25	25	25	25				
24	Total	29	29	29	29	29	29	29	29	28	28				
SERVICE CHARGES															
25	Overtime & Supper Money Payments (To nearest dollar)	276	135	273	93	446	123	536	370	350	220				25
	(To nearest dollar)														
26	Regular Checking Accounts $	1 543	1 578	1 445	2 225	2 550	858	2 378	1 998	1 997	1 833				26
27	Special Checking Accounts $	1 017	1 119	1 220	1 397	1 223	1 322	1 313	1 237	1 266	1 340				27
28	Total $	2 560	2 697	2 665	1 622	3 773	2 180	3 691	3 235	3 263	3 173				28

Income and Expense By Quarters And Cumulative	To Nearest Dollar	1st Quarter	2nd Quarter	Jan. thru June	3rd Quarter	Jan. thru Sept.	4th Quarter	Jan. thru Dec.
	Gross Income $	060	531	591	041	346		
	Gross Expenses $	030	088	118	043	282		
	Net Before Taxes $	010	443	453	998	114		
	Net After Taxes $	799	622	421	044	52		
	Average Loan Rate	5.80	5.83	5.81	5.82	5.82		
	Earn. Rate-Excess Funds	4.02	4.06	4.04	4.08	4.0		
	Earn. Rate-Saving Deposits	6.52	6.53	6.54	6.54	6.5		

EXHIBIT 7 (concluded) Branch Office Report—Supplement

1960

Location and Office No. _____ A

All Dollar Amounts in Thousands	JAN.	FEB.	MAR.	APRIL.	MAY	JUNE	JULY	AUG.	SEPT.	OCT.	NOV.	DEC.	YEAR TOTALS	
Regular Checking Accounts - Number														
Opened - New	26	17	7	15	16	17	10	9	14	11				1
Opened - A/C Trans. within Office	-	1	1	1	4	-	1	-	-	-				2
Opened - A/C Trans. from other Off.	-	1	1	-	3	-	2	-	1	-				3
Total Number Opened	26	19	9	16	23	17	13	9	15	11				4
Closed	24	17	12	17	6	19	9	17	24	14				5
Closed - A/C Trans. within Office	-	2	1	2	2	-	-	8	6	1				6
Closed - A/C Trans. to other Offices	4	3	2	1	2	3	1	1	4	1				7
Total Number Closed	28	22	15	20	10	22	10	26	34	16				8
Net Opened or Closed	-2	-3	-6	-4	+13	-5	+3	-17	-19	-5				9
Regular Checking Accounts Average Deposits Closed - Monthly														
Closed $	16	7	3	15	7	14	4	11	18	7				10
Closed - Trans. within Office $	-	19	2	4	2	-	-	6	4	1				11
Closed - Trans. to other Offices $	5	6	2	-	1	3	1	1	2	2				12
Total Average-Closed Accts. $	21	32	7	19	10	17	5	18	24	10				13
Accounts Since Jan. 1st- Cumulated*														
*No. Opened (Line 1)	26	43	50	65	81	98	108	117	131	142				14
*No. Closed (Line 5)	24	41	53	70	76	95	104	121	145	159				15
*Opened-Current Mo. Avg.(Line 14)$	83	191	162	143	120	102	120	109	114	127				16
Closed-Total Avg.Bal. (Line 10) $	16	23	26	41	48	62	66	77	95	102				17
Business Development														
No. of calls - Customers	3	8	7	4	10	8	6	9	5	5				18
No. of calls - Prospects	3	4	4	4	1	4	2	6	5	5				19
Total	6	12	11	8	11	12	8	15	10	10				20
Spec. Checking Accts - Opened	26	21	31	21	19	22	15	33	37	29				21
Spec. Checking Accts - Closed	13	24	12	13	17	16	12	25	9	20				22
Spec. Checking Accts - Net	+13	-3	+19	+8	+2	+6	+3	+8	+28	+9				23
Savings Accounts - Opened	17	9	22	9	15	24	15	9	52	39				24
Savings Accounts - Closed	21	7	16	13	17	20	13	15	18	15				25
Savings Accounts - Net	-4	+2	+6	-4	-2	+4	+2	-6	+34	+24				26
S.D. Boxes - New Rentals	9	6	3	9	3	6	5	6	4	-				27
S.D. Boxes - Surrendered	9	4	9	11	12	10	6	7	7	3				28
S.D. Boxes - Net	-	+2	-6	-2	-9	-4	-1	-1	-3	-3				29
No. of Personal Money Orders Sold	523	543	583	643	421	467	447	419	452	367				30

YEAR TOTALS

Case 15–2
Citibank Indonesia*

In November 1983, Mehli Mistri, Citibank's country manager for Indonesia, was faced with a difficult situation. He had just received a memorandum from his immediate superior, David Gibson, the division head for Southeast Asia, informing him that during their just-completed review of the operating budgets, Citibank managers at corporate had raised the SE-Asia division's 1984 after-tax profit goal by $4 million. Mr. Gibson, in turn, had decided that Indonesia's share of this increased goal should be between $500,000 and $1,000,000. Mr. Mistri was concerned because he knew that the budget he had submitted was already very aggressive; it included some growth in revenues and only a slight drop in profits, even though the short-term outlook for the Indonesian economy, which was highly dependent on oil revenues, was pessimistic.

Mr. Mistri knew that, to have any realistic expectation of producing profits for 1984 higher than those already included in the budget, he would probably have to take one or more actions that he had wanted to avoid. One possibility was to eliminate (or reduce) Citibank's participation in loans to prime government or private enterprises, as these loans provided much lower returns than was earned on the rest of the portfolio. However, Citibank was the largest foreign bank operating in Indonesia, and failing to participate in these loans could have significant costs in terms of relations with the government and prime customers in Indonesia and elsewhere. The other possibility was to increase the total amount of money lent in Indonesia, with all of the increase going to commercial enterprises. But with the deteriorating conditions in the Indonesian economy, Mr. Mistri knew that it was probably not a good time for Citibank to increase its exposure. Also, the government did not want significant increases in such offshore loans to the private sector at this time because of their adverse impact on the country's balance of payments and services account.

So, Mr. Mistri was contemplating what he should do at an upcoming meeting with Mr. Gibson. Should he agree to take one or both of the actions described above to increase 1984 profits? Should he accept the profit increase and hope that the economy turned around and/or that he was able to develop some new, hitherto unidentified sources of income? Or should he resist including any of the division's required profit increase in his budget?

Citibank

Citibank, the principal operating subsidiary of Citicorp, was one of the leading financial institutions in the world. The bank was founded in 1812 as a small commercial in New York City, and over the years it had grown to a large global financial services intermediary. In 1983, the bank had revenues of almost $5.9 billion and employed over 63,000 people in almost 2,600 locations in 95 countries.

Citibank's activities were organized into three principal business units: institutional banking, individual banking, and the capital markets group.

* This case was prepared by Associate Professor Kenneth A. Merchant, Harvard Business School.
Copyright © by the President and Fellows of Harvard College.
Harvard Business School case 185–061.

EXHIBIT 1 Selected Citicorp Financial Data—1983 (dollars in millions)

	Citicorp Consolidated	Institutional Bank	Individual Bank	Capital Markets Group
Revenues	$5,883	$2,896	$2,380	$587
Net income	860	758	202	128
Return on shareholders' equity	16.5%	22.0%	17.7%	32.2%
Return on assets	0.64%	0.87%	0.69%	1.26%

Source: 1983 Citicorp *Annual Report.*

The institutional banking units provided commercial loans and other financial services, such as electronic banking, asset-based financing, and foreign exchange, to corporations and governmental agencies around the world. The individual banking units, which operated in the United States and 18 other countries, provided transactional, savings, and lending services to consumers. The capital markets group served as an intermediary in flows of funds from providers to users. With a staff of 3,500, this group was one of the largest investment banks in the world. (Exhibit 1 shows the relative size of these activities, and Exhibit 2 shows a summary corporate organization chart.)

Mehli Mistri

Mehli Mistri, Citibank's country corporate officer for Indonesia, joined Citibank as a management trainee in the Bombay office in 1960, just after finishing a B.A. degree in economics from the University of Bombay. Between 1960 and 1964, Mehli gained experience in a number of assignments in the Bombay office, and in 1965 he transferred to New York to work in the credit analysis division. He returned to Bombay in 1966, and then became manager of Citibank branches in Madras (1968), Calcutta (1969–71), New Delhi (1972), and Beirut (1973). In 1974, he was promoted to regional manager with responsibility for five countries in the Middle East (Turkey, Syria, Iraq, Jordan, Lebanon), and he held

that position until 1979, when he was appointed the country head of Indonesia. He remained in that position up until the time of this case. In 1982, Mehli attended the Advanced Management Program at the Harvard Business School.

Control of International Branches

Citibank managers used two formal management processes to direct and control the activities of the corporation's international branches: reviews of sovereign risk limits for each location and reviews of operating budgets and accomplishments.

Sovereign Risk Limits

Each year Citibank management set sovereign risk limits for its international branches based on country risk analyses. The term *sovereign risk* actually refers to a wide spectrum of concerns that would impair the bank's ability to recapture the capital it invested in foreign countries. These included macroeconomic risk: foreign exchange controls that the government of the host country might employ that would make it difficult for clients to pay their obligations, or, in the extreme, expropriation of assets. Once Citibank had opened a given branch, however, it intended to keep it open, so the reviews of sovereign risk were concerned only with setting limits of the amount of money a branch could lend in foreign currency.

The sovereign risk review process started in midyear with the country manager proposing a

EXHIBIT 2   Citibank Indonesia Partial Organization Chart

```
                        ┌────────────────┐          ┌──────────────────────┐
                        │    Chairman    │          │  Senior Staff Groups │
                        │ Walter E.Wriston│─────────│ Personnel Planning and│
                        └────────────────┘          │      Development      │
                                │                    │ Corporate Strategy and│
                                │                    │      Development      │
                                │                    │ Legal and External Affairs│
                                │                    │ International Operations│
                                │                    └──────────────────────┘
         ┌──────────────────────┼──────────────────────────────────┐
  ┌─────────────┐      ┌─────────────┐                      ┌─────────────┐
  │Institutional│      │  Individual │                      │Capital Markets│
  │    Bank     │      │    Bank     │                      │    Group    │
  │Thomas C.    │      │ John S.Reed │                      │ Paul Collins│
  │  Theobald   │      └─────────────┘                      └─────────────┘
  └─────────────┘
```

North America	Caribbean, Central America, South America	Europe, Middle East, Africa	Asia/Pacific Richard Huber

Japan	North Asia	Southeast Asia David E. Gibson

	Korea Philippines Taiwan Hong Kong	Australia Indonesia Malaysia India Thailand

sovereign risk limit. This limit was discussed with division and group managers and was finally approved, on a staggered time schedule, by a senior international specialist on the corporate staff. The foreign currency lending limit for Indonesia had grown substantially as the branch had grown.

The sovereign risk limit set during these reviews was an upper guideline. When the economic conditions in a country changed in the period between sovereign risk reviews, country managers sometimes chose to operate their branches with self-imposed sovereign risk limits that were below the limits set by management in New York. Corporate managers encouraged this behavior because they knew that the managers on site often had a better appreciation of the risks in the local environment.

Budgeting

Budgeting at Citibank was a bottom up process, which started in July when headquarters sent out instructions to the operating units describing the timing and format of the submissions and the issues that needed to be addressed. The instructions did not include specific targets to be included in the budget, although it was widely recognized that the corporation's combined long-term goals were approximately as follows:

Growth: 12–15% per annum.
Return on assets: 1.25% (125 basis points).
Return on equity: 20%.

The above norms were established for Citibank as a whole, but a number of international branches, including Indonesia, traditionally exceeded these norms, and these entities often established their own targets at higher levels.

At the time the operating managers received the budget instructions, they would have the results for half the year (through the end of June); and, in the period from July until the end of September, they would prepare a forecast for the remainder of the current year and a budget for the following year. The starting point for the preparation of the budget was projections about each of the major account relationships, and discussions continued until the summation of the account relationship projections could be reconciled with the desired profit center bottom line. Then costs were considered. The budget submission form included all the line items shown in Exhibit 3. In some past years, the bank had prepared two- and five-year projections, but the numbers were seen to be very soft and not very useful.

Formal reviews of the annual budgets were held according to the following schedule:

Level of Review	Timing
Division	end of September
Group	mid-October
Institutional Bank	end of October

If the sovereign risk review for a particular entity had not yet been held, the budgets were submitted with the assumption that the risk limits would be approved as submitted. If this assumption proved to be incorrect, the budget had to be revised before it was incorporated in the corporate consolidated budget.

Performance was monitored and compared against budget each month during the year. Every quarter a new forecast for the remainder of the year was made. Whether these were reviewed formally by division managers varied widely, depending on the division manager's style. Some managers held relatively formal on-site reviews of

performance and budget revisions, and others communicated only by mail or by telephone.

Mr. Mistri was very comfortable with the review processes.

> Every level of management has a role to play, and there is a lot of horse trading and give and take in the budget review processes. Usually there is more revision of the numbers at lower management levels, but revisions do not necessarily mean increased profit goals. I have seen cases where the division head thought the country level was being too aggressive and he asked for the budget to be lowered. The managers sitting further away are more objective, and the review processes are consultative, collegial, and constructive.

Budgets were taken very seriously at Citibank, not only because they were thought to include the most important measures of success, but also because incentive compensation for managers at Citibank was linked to budget-related performance. For a country manager, incentive compensation could range up to approximately 70 percent of base salary, although awards of 30–35 percent were more typical. Assignment of bonuses was based approximately 30 percent on corporate performance and 70 percent on individual performance, primarily performance related to forecast. The key measures for assessing both corporate and international-branch performance were growth, profits, return on assets, and return on equity. However, in the analyses of individual performance for the purposes of assigning incentive compensation, considerable care was taken to differentiate base earnings from extraordinary earnings (or losses) for which the manager should not be held accountable.

Citibank in Indonesia

Indonesia was a relatively young country; it achieved independence only in 1949 after many years of being a Dutch colony. Citibank had operated in Indonesia only since 1968, when President Suharto allowed eight foreign banks to set up operations in Jakarta. From the point of view

EXHIBIT 3 Line Items on Budget Submission Form

Revenue/expense
Local currency NRFF
Foreign currency NRFF
Allocated equity NRFF
Bad debt reserve earnings
Net revenue from funds
Exchange
Translation gains/losses
Trading account profits
Trade financing fees
Securities gains/losses
Fees, commissions, and other revenue
Affiliate earnings
Gross write-offs
Gross recoveries
Loan provision excess
Direct staff expenses
Direct charges
Other direct expenses
Allocated processing costs
Minority interest
Other allocated costs
Matrix earnings
EBIT
Foreign taxes
U.S. taxes
Profit center earnings
Equity adjustments—translations
Placements (average)
Total staff (EOP)
Total nonperforming loans—EOP
Total nonperforming loans—EOP
Rev./nonperforming loans
Average total assets—local currency
Average total assets—foreign currency
Allocated equity
Local currency—average volume
Loans
Sources—noninterest bearing
Sources—interest bearing
Foreign currency—average volume
Loans
Sources—noninterest bearing
Sources—interest bearing
End of period (EOP)
Past due obligations
Interest earned not collected
Loans
Assets

EXHIBIT 4 Indonesia Gross Domestic Product (billions of rupiahs)

Year	Gross Domestic Product	Gross Domestic Product (1980 prices)
1968	2,097	18,493
1969	2,718	20,188
1970	3,340	21,499
1971	3,672	22,561
1972	4,564	24,686
1973	6,753	27,479
1974	10,708	29,576
1975	12,643	31,049
1976	15,467	33,187
1977	19,011	36,094
1978	22,746	38,925
1979	32,025	41,359
1980	45,446	45,446
1981	54,027	49,048
1982	59,633	50,150
1983	72,111	52,674

Source: *International Financial Statistics Yearbook,* 1984.

of the Indonesian government, the role of the foreign banks was to help develop a young economy by transferring capital into the country, establishing a modern banking infrastructure, attracting foreign investment, and developing trained people.

The foreign banking community operated in Indonesia with some important restrictions. The most serious constraints were that foreign banks were not allowed to open branches outside the Jakarta city limits, and local currency loans could be made only to corporations with headquarters and principal operations within the Jakarta city limits. But, on the other hand, the Indonesian government did not require any local ownership of equity, it set no lending quotas for the banks (e.g., requirements to lend certain amounts of money to certain types of businesses at favorable rates), and it valued and maintained a free foreign exchange system.

In explaining the goals of the government with respect to the foreign banks, Mr. Mistri commented:

We consider ourselves privileged to be in Indonesia. We realize that the country wants to develop economically, and we know that the government sees us in the role of a development and change agent, attracting and developing not only capital but also new financial products, services, and techniques and trained managers and professionals for the financial services industry. The government also expects us and other international banks to participate in extensions of credit to both the public and private sectors.

Citibank and the other foreign banks were interested in operating in Indonesia for several reasons: (1) to serve their international and local customers, (2) to assist in the economic development of the country, and (3) to share in the potential for profits and growth the Indonesian economy offered. The Indonesian economy had tremendous potential: The country was the fifth largest in the world in terms of population, and the economy had shown excellent growth for many years, as the figures shown in Exhibit 4 illustrate. The country was rich in raw materials,

EXHIBIT 5 Partial Organization Chart

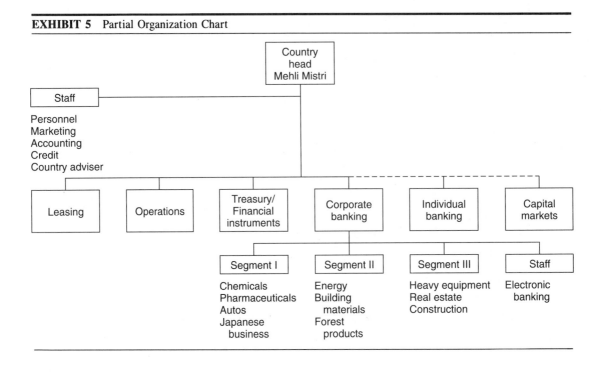

The Situation in 1983

particularly oil and tin, and the Indonesian government was very interested in developing the country's industrial activities.

In 1983, Citibank's Indonesian operation included activities in each of the three major lines of business—institutional, individual, and capital markets. Mehli Mistri was the country corporate officer, and, as such, he was the primary spokesman for all of Citibank's activities in Indonesia. His prime line responsibility, however, was the institutional banking activity, which provided by far the greatest proportion of revenues and profits. Other individuals headed the individual banking and capital markets activities in Indonesia, and they reported through separate management channels (see Exhibit 5).

Since its inception, Citibank's Indonesian operation had been very successful. Its growth paralleled that of the Indonesian economy.

The Situation in 1983

In 1983, Mr. Mistri was concerned about the risk/return ratio in his branch. He felt comfortable with Indonesia's long-term prospects, but the country, which was highly dependent on oil revenues, had slipped into a recession when oil prices decreased significantly. His concern was whether the government would take strong enough steps to correct its balance-of-payments problem.

Inside the bank, Mr. Mistri was faced with a problem of high staff turnover. High turnover had been a problem for Citibank for many years, because the bank provided its people with training that was recognized as probably the best in Indonesia, and local financial institutions had lured many Citibank people away with generous offers. This had happened so often that Citibank had been given labels, such as "Citi-university" and "Harvard-on-wheels," and the government often held Citibank up as an example of how foreign banks could (and should) supply trained professionals to the country. To attempt to retain more of its trained people, Citibank had recently increased its compensation levels; but some people in the branch felt that the bank could not compete on the basis of salary because of its desire to be profitable, its limited domestic branch network, and significant career opportunities elsewhere.

The year 1983 was particularly difficult from a staff turnover standpoint, as the losses included Mr. Mistri's chief of staff and two senior officers. In mid-1983, the average account manager experience was under two years, and there were three unfilled slots at management levels. Mr. Mistri knew that the inexperience and people shortages in the branch were also serious constraints to growth.

Given these significant problems, Mr. Mistri thought that the budget he submitted, which projected modest growth, should be considered as aggressive. He wanted to submit an aggressive budget because "we are an aggressive organization. We like to stretch because we feel the culture of our corporation and the will and desire of our people to succeed and excel can make up the difference."

In reflection of the fast-changing uncertainties in the economy and the personnel problems, however, Mr. Mistri decided to operate with a self-imposed sovereign risk limit that was somewhat lower than what had been formally approved by management in New York. He knew that his responsibility was as much to manage risk as to generate profits.

In late October 1983, however, the budget for the whole Institutional Bank was reviewed at headquarters, and the consolidated set of numbers did not show the growth that top management desired. This led management to suggest some budget increases, and these increases presented Mr. Mistri with the dilemma described in the introduction to this case.

QUESTIONS

1. What should Mehli Mistri do about the budget issue described in the first three paragraphs of the case? (*Note*: You can assume that the amount by which Mehli is asked to increase his budet is about 10 percent of the original budget).
2. Should Mehli Mistri be evaluated against a budget prepared in U.S. dollars?

Case 15–3

Acton Life Insurance Company*

It was the third week in July 1975. The quarterly review report for the southern region of the Acton Life Insurance Company (see Exhibit 1) had recently been distributed. William Bailey, sales manager of the southern region, was visiting the home office in Boston for the purpose of discussing this and related reports with John McFarland, vice president of sales. Much of the discussion related to the performance of the six branch agencies in the southern region. Mr. Bailey had been sales manager of that region for five months; formerly he had been a branch manager in the eastern region. This was his first visit to the home office since he had assumed his new duties.

Mr. Bailey: Our Atlanta branch had the best performance this past quarter. Just look at the volume of business it put on the books over the last three months—over $5.5 million. This works out to about $1.1 million per salesman, which is way ahead of the other branches.

Mr. McFarland: Bill, don't you remember our discussion on performance yardsticks during my visit to your office earlier this year? I made a particular effort to explain why we feel that sales volume is not enough, that we have to relate the value of these sales to the cost of making them. For some time now, we have been using the ratio of first-year expenses to the total of first-year premiums. This is what the Operating Review Report is all about. Looking at this report, we

EXHIBIT 1 Quarterly Operating Review Report: Southern Region—Second Quarter, 1975

Branch	First-Year Premiums	First-Year Expenses*	First-Year Expense Ratio
Atlanta	$69,216	$28,596	41.3%
Birmingham	60,004	19,634	32.7
Charlotte	45,614	13,220	29.0
Nashville	91,692	22,292	24.3
New Orleans	95,446	20,800	21.8
Tampa	76,370	14,430	18.9
Averages: Region	73,057	19,829	27.0
Averages: Company	76,234	18,898	24.8

* The expenses associated with the acquisition of new business, including salaries of salesmen. In the full report, 12 additional columns were included, showing a breakdown of the total expenses of the branches and certain adjustments.

* This case was prepared by R. F. Vancil, Harvard Business School.
Copyright © by the President and Fellows of Harvard College.
Harvard Business School case 179–109.

EXHIBIT 2 Quarterly Profit Report: Southern Region—Second Quarter, 1975

Branch	Face Value of Insurance Sold (000s)	First-Year Premiums	Average-Size Policy	Average-Size First-Year Premium		Premium Collection Frequency*	Two-Year Lapse Ratio[†]
				Amount	Per $1,000 Insurance		
Atlanta	$5,526	$69,216	$17,470	$219.76	$12.53	6.2	8.4
Birmingham	3,176	60,004	13,212	251.20	18.90	7.0	5.2
Charlotte	3,400	45,614	28,776	387.50	13.42	4.6	13.6
Nashville	4,728	91,692	23,854	460.00	19.39	2.8	12.9
New Orleans	3,832	95,446	26,422	657.06	24.91	3.7	18.3
Tampa	5,014	76,370	18,812	180.14	15.23	4.7	6.8
Averages: Region	4,280	73,058	21,856	430.38	19.69	4.2	10.9
Averages: Company	4,620	76,234	25,040	575.02	22.96	4.9	5.3

* The average number of times per year that premiums were collected per policy.
[†] The fraction of the number of policies sold in a given 12-month period that lapsed during the following two-year period, computed as a running average.

can see that the Tampa branch was your best branch last quarter. Your Atlanta branch was actually your poorest performer.

Mr. Bailey: That's not the way I understood it when I was a branch manager under Eddie Petanski. I had the impression that the volume of business we booked was the really important yardstick: Don't we pay branch managers commissions on the basis of volume? Aren't all the awards we hand out based primarily on volume—the million-dollar round table, the president's club, and so on? All the branch managers I ever knew felt this way. In fact, we went even further; when we got together to compare performance, we usually ended up by looking at the total amount of commissions we had earned. After all, the real test is how much the company pays us for our efforts.

Mr. McFarland: Well, we're supposed to be using this expense ratio. It was put in before I became VP, and I thought by now we were all using it. We are not even satisfied with this measure, however, and have been turning out another report to be used in conjunction with the Quarterly Operating Review Report to help interpret the expense ratio. This is the Quarterly Profit Report [see Exhibit 2] which you've also received . . . there it is, at the bottom of that pile of papers. This shows that even your Tampa branch didn't do as well as it appeared to on the basis of its expense ratio.

Mr. Bailey: Hold on, Jack, now you've really got me confused. I looked over the Quarterly Profit Report when I got it and compared these profit factors with previous periods to spot trends, as you suggested. But I didn't use it as you did just now. In fact, I don't see how I can relate these five measures to the expense ratio and to sales volume accomplishments and come up with anything meaningful on performance. I'd just be shooting in the dark. And I'd bet this is true with the other sales managers.

Mr. McFarland: You're probably right. It's pretty difficult to relate so many factors together and come up with a meaningful appraisal of performance. What we've been trying to do is to get a better indication of profitability of the business booked by each branch than the expense ratio tells us. The best we've come up with so far is the set of five factors.

Mr. Bailey: Well, I can see what you're driving at, but I just don't think you can do it. What we have now doesn't seem to get us much closer and is much too complicated. Besides, as an ex-branch manager, I'd bet most of our branches believe that volume of business is the primary yardstick.

Mr. McFarland: Bill, I don't think there is much to be gained by pushing our review of performance any further at this time. Some of these same problems have been bothering me for some time now. I think what I'll do is discuss this performance appraisal problem with Mr. Runyan [president of the company] during our regular meeting on Friday. Your points will be very helpful in this discussion. Thanks for bringing them up.

Background

Acton Life Insurance Company was a stock company, formed in 1909. It was licensed to do business in all the 50 states, the District of Columbia, and most of Canada. At the beginning of 1975, 56 branches served these areas. It had a total of about $9 billion of insurance in force, and its total sales volume in 1974 was about $1.3 billion.

The lines of insurance offered by Acton Life consisted primarily of ordinary life, accident and health, group life, and various annuities. As of 1975, the company sold its entire line of insurance through independent brokers, approximately 200,000 in number. As independent brokers, they were not required to sell Acton policies exclusively. Many also sold policies of the same general types written by other insurance companies.

The basic organization of Acton Life followed the general pattern in the industry. This was a functional type, consisting of six departments: actuarial, legal, sales, investment, underwriting, and administrative services. At the head of each of these departments was a vice president who reported to the president.

The sales department was responsible for directing the operations of the various branches, through which relationships with the independent brokers were established and maintained. The company planned to expand the number of branches as rapidly as it could over the following few years to serve a larger number of brokers. The branches were grouped into eight geographical regions, each region having from 4 to 11 branches. For each region, there was a sales manager, who reported to the vice president of sales. The heads of two staff activities (agency secretary and management training) also reported to the sales vice president.

A manager was in charge of each of the branches. His primary responsibilities were the direction of the selling effort of his branch, selecting and developing salesmen, participating in negotiating contracts with brokers, and supervising the office personnel required to service the policies sold by these brokers. In general, a branch manager was paid entirely in commissions on the business booked through his branch. However, new branch managers were paid a fixed salary for a period of five years, or until the commissions they would otherwise receive consistently exceeded the salary.

The average number of salesmen working for a branch was four. The major activities of the salesmen were calling on and developing contracts with brokers, helping them to start making sales, and following up from time to time to make sure their sales efforts were satisfactory. Branch salesmen were paid salaries only; commissions for selling the insurance were earned by the independent brokers.

In all branches, except a few of the smaller ones, there was an assistant branch manager. Each branch also had a small clerical staff.

Meeting with the President

At his regular Friday morning meeting with Mr. Runyan, Mr. McFarland brought up the problem of measuring the performance of branch managers. He summarized the discussion he had had earlier in the week with Mr. Bailey.

Mr. Runyan said that of late he had become concerned with a closely related problem—the need for a more rational approach to the planning and control of branch operations. Recently, he had read a doctoral thesis in which the author proposed a solution to this problem. Mr. Runyan suggested that Mr. McFarland study this proposal and, if it looked sufficiently promising, discuss it with his sales managers. In any event, the president wanted Mr. McFarland's considered opinion regarding the utility of the proposal for Acton Life and his recommendations for a course of action. Mr. McFarland agreed to submit a report of his conclusions and recommendations by October 1.

Evaluation of the Proposal

Over the weekend, Mr. McFarland considered how best to reach a meaningful appraisal of the proposal. He finally decided to send an abstract of it to each of his eight sales managers and to ask for their reactions to the idea of its adoption by Acton Life, either completely or in a modified form. Accordingly, on Monday, July 28, he asked his assistant to prepare such an abstract and to have it ready by the end of the week. A copy of the abstract is shown in Appendix A.

After reviewing and approving the abstract, Mr. McFarland dictated a covering memorandum to his sales managers. In this memorandum, he asked them to read the entire abstract carefully and focus attention on the feasibility of its adoption by Acton Life. He also asked for written comments, both favorable and critical. To have the branch managers' point of view represented, he suggested that each sales manager discuss the proposal with one or two of the better managers in his region and incorporate their comments, appropriately identified, as part of the memorandum each would submit.

To ensure that the proposal would not be dismissed quickly as impractical, Mr. McFarland stated that in his opinion the concept of ECTP (expected contribution to profit), around which the proposal was constructed, appeared to have considerable merit. Although use of the concept in a system for planning and controlling branch operations would constitute a novel and somewhat radical step for a life insurance company, the concept had sufficient possibilities, he thought, to be considered seriously and with an open mind. To give everyone sufficient time for study and discussion, Mr. McFarland set September 15 as the deadline for submission of comments.

As of September 16, Mr. McFarland had received memoranda from all eight sales managers. He immediately began to analyze the comments in terms of the principal arguments for and against the proposal. In the process, he prepared a summary, included here as Appendix B. Five reaction patterns are highlighted in the summary.

1. Cost of implementing and administering the proposed planning and control system.
2. Method of calculating the expected contribution to profit (ECTP).
3. Concept of a profit measure at the branch level.
4. Applicability of the proposal in practice.
5. Defense of the industry.

In reviewing this summary, Mr. McFarland noted that comments by 10 branch managers had been submitted in addition to those from the eight sales managers. The summary represented the opinions of 18 of his best managers.

With his summary before him Mr. McFarland pondered what recommendations he should make to the president. He wanted to be sure that they resulted from an objective weighing of the advantages and disadvantages of the proposal, including a realistic appraisal of the benefits to be derived by Acton Life and the problems likely to be encountered. He also wanted to accompany his recommendations with a summary of supporting arguments, together with an action plan for implementing his recommendations.

QUESTIONS

1. Disregarding the practical problem of obtaining acceptance, do you believe the expected contribution to profit approach is conceptually sound?
2. Assuming that the approach is sound, what steps should be taken next?

Appendix A
*Summary of Proposed Planning and Control System for Branches**

Scope of the Proposal

This proposal applies primarily to the administrative needs of the branch manager and higher levels of management in planning and controlling the operations of branch agencies within a life insurance company. It is anticipated that parts of the proposal will

---

* Abstracted from a doctoral thesis by James S. Hekimian.

also have utility for various classes of decision problems, such as the establishment of insurance premiums, the setting of commission scales, and the design of incentive systems.

This proposal does not apply directly to the planning and control of central staff activities, such as the legal department or the actuarial department. However, the proposal is fully compatible with the more traditional practices for planning and controlling such staff activities.

Objectives Sought by Proposal

The objectives this proposal seeks to achieve are as follows:

1. To provide a satisfactory basis for branch managers to use to relate the financial worth of results achieved to the costs incurred to realize these results.
2. To provide both top management and branch managers with an improved system for planning and controlling the operation of individual branches.
3. To motivate branch managers to do what is in the best interest of the company.

Components of the Proposal

The proposal consists essentially of two parts.

1. *Expected contribution to profit.*   A measure of the worth to the company accruing from the sale of an individual policy calculated at the time of sale. Use of this measure makes possible the calculation of the contribution to the company's profit arising from the operation of any branch.

2. *Improved planning and control system.*   An overall planning and control system for the management of branch agencies of life insurance companies that incorporates the above profit calculations.

Expected Contribution to Profit

Nature of the Problem

A major obstacle in the way of improving systems for planning and controlling the operations of branches is the lack of an adequate measure of the worth of accomplishments or results generated by branches. Most of the measures used currently are related to the volume of policies sold, either expressed directly as the aggregate of the face value of these policies, or indirectly as premiums collected or as commissions paid. Usually, expenses of operating a branch are related to these sales figures in some way, often in the form of a ratio; the implication of this practice is that there exists a certain standard ratio (based on past performance or a current average, or both) that indicates profitable or, at least, desirable performance. Some management personnel believe that sales volume accomplishments should not be the end-all, and that some better measure of the worth of accomplishments should be developed against which to weigh the cost of achieving these accomplishments. A few believe that the problem is one of trying to operate a profitable branch without an idea of what profits are.

Everyone interviewed agreed that the various types of insurance policies differed considerably on their worth to the insurance company. For example, it was generally acknowledged that a company gained less from selling a $1,000 term policy than from selling a $1,000 endowment policy. However, no practical way had been found as yet to measure the difference in gain and to incorporate it into a system for planning and controlling sales effects.

Analysis

In many industries the worth of the accomplishments of a branch is measured in terms of the gross profit on the sales volume it generates; against this are charged the expenses of acquiring this gross profit to arrive at the amount contributed to net profit. For the life insurance industry, this approach had never seemed possible because of accounting practices pertaining to the time the profit from a policy was realized. However, this obstacle resulted from an accounting convention, and accounting *need not* stand in the way of developing an improved measure of worth to guide the internal management of an insurance company.

As a result of discussions with management personnel, it was decided that, to be truly useful, any measure of worth should meet the following criteria:

1. Reflect the worth to the company of the sale of a particular policy.
2. Do this in monetary terms.
3. Do this as of the time a policy is sold.

If such a measure could be developed, it would make possible the calculation of a form of "profit" accruing to the company from the operation of any branch. An examination of the practice of the industry in computing premiums and of the expectations of the industry regarding actual performance in the three areas making up this premium calculation suggested that such a measure could be developed.

Basically, every life insurance premium was developed from three separate factors: a projected mortality rate, a projected interest rate, and a projected loading charge. Realistically, also, companies considered competition in setting a final premium; in practice, this consideration usually resulted in an adjustment in the loading factor. Given the three factors, insurance actuaries calculated an approximate premium for any kind of policy the company cared to sell.

All three of these factors in practice were deliberately set conservatively. Because the projected mortality rate was based on the actual mortality rate during some *past* period, companies were, in effect, assuming that the mortality rate was higher than it actually would be. But the mortality rate actually had been decreasing steadily over the years, and this trend was expected to continue. Thus, with the collection of every premium, the company expected a gain from overestimating mortality.

In projecting interest rates, companies tended to be very conservative in their estimates of the rate of return they would earn on their investments. The actual return on investments usually was higher than the assumed return; thus, the premium resulted in a gain from the interest assumption.

Finally, companies tended to overestimate the total loading charge required, thereby creating a third expected gain. In a stock company, a profit allowance usually was included as an explicit element of the loading charge, whereas in a mutual company an equivalent result was produced by the deliberate overstatement of costs.

In sum, then, because of the current practices of computing life insurance premiums, companies expected a gain from savings from the allowance for mortality, excess interest earned, and the loading charge.

Proposed Solution

Therefore it was argued, there was built into every life insurance premium an expected contribution to profit (hereafter referred to as ECTP). This ECTP occurred *at the time of sale* of a policy. It was further argued that this ECTP could be calculated and that this figure could serve the purpose of a "profit" figure for a branch. These conclusions were valid, because, *at the time of sale,* for each policy sold, one could calculate:

1. *The expected gain included in the mortality charge.* This was the difference between the premium actually charged—based on the assumption that projected mortality experience would parallel past mortality experience—and the premium that would be needed to cover *expected* mortality. That is, the mortality rate actually experienced would not be so high as assumed, death benefits would not be paid out so soon as assumed, and, therefore, companies would have more of the insurance premiums left for contribution to profits. In computing annuity premiums, insurance companies actually employed mortality rates lower than those they employed in computing life insurance premiums. A company's expectations regarding future mortality experience would fall somewhere between these two sets of rates.

2. *The expected gain from the interest charge.* This was the difference between the premium actually charged—based on a conservative assumption as to interest earned on investments—and the premium that would be charged if it were based on *expected* interest earnings. For most companies, estimates of future earnings rates on their investments were regularly made by their investment departments.

3. *The expected gain from the loading charge.* This was the difference between the total amount of loading in a particular premium and the actual amount of variable expense of selling that policy (commissions, medical fees, taxes on premiums, and so forth). Although the separation of variable expenses might be difficult to make, it was generally considered to be feasible. Even if this separation could not be made with a high degree of accuracy, the resulting error would be constant for all policies and, thus, its effect on the proposed planning and control system would be minor.

Thus, for each year a particular policy was expected to be in force, an expected gain could be calculated *at the time of sale.* The present value of this stream of expected year-by-year gains from each policy sold is the *expected contribution to profit.* This represents the additional *worth* to the company *now* of selling a particular policy.

Given this calculation of ECTP, a branch manager could exercise intelligent control over his responsibility for the acquisition of business. This would be accomplished by relating the total ECTP of a branch to its cost of acquiring business.

For example, consider a $1,000 term insurance policy with a life of 20 years sold to a man, age 35, with premium payments to be made over the first 10 years. Using the standard mortality table, normal interest rate, and normal loading for selling and administrative costs, the premium on this policy would be calculated as $11.99 per year. With the substitution of expected values, the same calculation would produce a cost of $5.51 per year, plus $14.87 for selling and administrative costs in the first year, and $1.08 per year for each of the other nine years of premium payments. The difference between the premiums and the costs, with allowance for mortality, discounted at the company's expected earning rate, came to a total of $27.98. This was the expected contribution to profit on this policy.

Use of ECTP

The suggested method of making an ECTP calculation provides a valid profit figure at the branch level. It measures the additional current worth to the company of the sales made by a branch. And it is available at the time decisions regarding selling efforts are being made.

Admittedly, this figure is not a precise measure of realized profits in an accounting sense. Since we must necessarily be looking to the future in any such calculation, and since the future is filled with uncertainties, the results of such a calculation must necessarily have a high likelihood of being different from the profit actually realized.

This fact is of no practical concern, however. The principal objective of the concept of ECTP is to make available as good a figure as possible for planning and control purposes. Certainly, the best profit figure available at the time a relevant decision is to be made (realizing that this may be something less than perfectly accurate) will be more useful than a perfectly accurate figure (if there is such a thing) that is not available until sometime after the decision has been made.

The concept of ECTP also provides a new tool for use in analysis of different types of policies. Most companies now rely on first-year premiums or face value of policies sold as a measure of accomplishment, and both branch managers and salesmen generally are motivated to achieve as high a volume of either one (or both) as possible.

Improved Planning and Control System

The core of the proposed planning and control system is the establishment of each branch agency as a profit center, with the branch manager as the responsible supervisor. The appropriate ''profit figure'' for a particular branch is the ECTP earned by the branch, minus the expenses incurred by that branch in generating this ECTP. Operating plans are expressed in terms of ECTP and the expenses needed to achieve that ECTP. Actual expenses are deducted from the ECTP actually generated by the branch to determine the profit contributed by the branch; this actual profit is compared to the planned profit. Deviations from planned performance are shown for each element of ECTP and expense. The analysis of these deviations and the taking of appropriate corrective action are vital elements in the proposed planning and control system.

In designing this system, two precautions are vital: to match with ECTP only those expenses incurred to generate ECTP; to limit the expenses chargeable to a branch to only those controllable at the branch level.

Looking at the second requirement first, an examination of the various kinds of expenses incurred in the operation of a branch agency indicates that all these expenses are controllable to a significant extent by the branch manager. Some are controllable only over a fairly long time period, while others are controllable to a considerable extent on a day-to-day basis. In recognition of this variation in controllability as a function of time, all branch expenses are segregated, under the proposal, into three classifications: long-range controllable expenses, annual controllable expenses, and day-to-day expenses. The expenses segregated in each of these categories are as follows:

Long-Range Controllable Expenses	*Annual Controllable Expenses*	*Day-to-Day Expenses*
Rent	Management salaries	Clerical salaries
Depreciation:	Adversting	Postage
Furniture	Training	Stationery and supplies
Equipment	Net advances to salesmen	Telephone and telegraph
		Repairs and maintenance
		Travel
		Entertainment
		Loss on advances to salesmen
		Miscellaneous

The first requirement can be understood best by regarding the mission of a branch agency as consisting of two functions: (1) the acquisition function, or the job of selling insurance policies; and (2) the service function, or the job of maintaining insurance in force. The expenses incurred for the service function do not create, or result in, ECTP. Therefore, these service expenses should be excluded from the matching of branch expenses against ECTP.

These service expenses can be classified in the following three categories:

1. *Putting new business on the books.*   Checking over the application and other forms to see that everything is in order, setting up the appropriate accounting records, and mailing out the policy.
2. *Collecting premiums.*   Sending out bills, changing beneficiaries, arranging for loans, and other routine service that is provided to all policyholders.
3. *Paying claims.*   Final disbursement of cash, closing the records, and other details involved in terminating a policy.

The procedure for excluding these service expenses from the determination of the profit contributed by a branch consists of the following basic steps. Clerical time standards are established for each of these service activities; this may be done on the basis of time-and-motion studies, although an average of actual past performance could serve the purpose. The number of units of work (e.g., number of premiums processed, number of new applications processed) actually handled by a branch is multiplied by the time standard for the particular unit, and the resulting number of standard hours is multiplied by the average clerical wage at a particular branch. The resulting dollar figure is an allowance or credit for the service work performed during a reporting period by the branch. This expense credit is deducted from the appropriate expense classifications, with the balance of these expenses charged to the acquisition function. Nonclerical service expenses (e.g., supplies) are credited in the same proportion that the clerical cost allowance bears to the total of clerical expense.

Example of Proposed Control Report

A sample of the control report to be employed in the proposed planning and control system is shown as Attachment A. The report relates to the operations of a particular branch and covers a full year (in the example, the calendar year 1975). The upper portion of the report presents the components of ECTP, identified by the individual salesmen who have generated the ECTP by their sales activities. The middle portion presents the various expenses of operating a branch, grouped by controllability classification. Right below the line for "Total Expenses" are three lines involving profits: "branch profit," the difference between actual ECTP and the total of actual expenses; "home office support," an allocation of the fixed expenses of running the home office; "net profit," the amount remaining after the allocated home office expense has been deducted from the branch profit.

The reason for this deduction is simply that the branch profit figure otherwise will always seem "high," both because it gives credit (through ECTP) for profit not yet realized and also because it is in fact only a contribution to profit. The purpose of this deduction is to make the manager aware of the amount of support he is receiving from the home office. (For other purposes, the branch profit or ECTP is the appropriate figure.)

ATTACHMENT A   Hypothetical Life Insurance Company Profit Schedule, Branch A—Profit Schedule, 1975

	(a) Total Budget	(b) Total Actual	(c) Service Budget	(d) Service Standard Allowance*	(e) Acquisition Budget	(f) Acquisition Actual	(g) Acquisition Variance	(h) Variance
Expected contribution to profit:								
Baker	$ 60,000	$ 72,000	$ —	$ —	$ 60,000	$ 72,000	$12,000	20%
Donovan	60,000	66,000	—	—	60,000	66,000	6,000	10
George	30,000	24,000	—	—	30,000	24,000	(6,000)	(20)
Henderson	10,000	8,000	—	—	10,000	8,000	(2,000)	(20)
Levin	70,000	62,000	—	—	70,000	62,000	(8,000)	(11)
Lannigan	120,000	130,000	—	—	120,000	130,000	10,000	8
Ramos	80,000	78,000	—	—	80,000	78,000	(2,000)	(2)
New hires—three	10,000	14,000	—	—	10,000	14,000	4,000	40
Total ECTP	440,000	454,000			440,000	454,000	14,000	
Controllable branch expenses:								
Long-range:								
Rent	13,20	13,200	—	—	13,200	13,200	0	0
Depreciation on furniture and equipment	800	800	—	—	800	800	0	0
Annual:								
Management salaries	34,000	34,000	—	—	34,000	34,000	0	0
Advertising	10,000	9,600	—	—	10,000	9,600	(400)	(4)
Training	2,000	1,500	—	—	2,000	1,500	(500)	(25)
Net advances to salesmen	5,000	7,200	—	—	5,000	7,200	2,200	44
Day-to-day:								
Clerical salaries	58,000	60,000	14,000	15,150	44,000	44,850	850	2
Postage	2,200	2,400	400	400	1,800	2,000	200	11
Stationery and supplies	3,000	3,200	700	800	2,300	2,400	100	4
Telephone and telegraph	6,800	7,200	—	—	6,800	7,200	400	6
Repairs and maintenance	1,000	200	—	—	1,000	200	(800)	(80)
Entertainment	3,000	2,800	—	—	3,000	2,800	(200)	(7)
Travel	5,600	6,000	—	—	5,600	6,000	400	7
Loss on advances	1,000	3,000	—	—	1,000	3,000	2,000	200
Miscellaneous	1,200	1,100	—	—	1,200	1,100	(100)	(8)
Total expenses	146,800	152,200	15,100	16,350	131,700	135,850	4,150	

| | (a) | (b) | (c) | (d) | (e) | (f) | (g) | (h) |
| | Total | | Service | | | Acquisition | | |
	Budget	Actual	Budget	Standard Allowance*	Budget	Actual		Variance
Branch profit					308,300	318,150		9,850
Home office support						300,000		
Net profit						18,150		
Lapse ratio					5.0%	4.7%		

* Service allowance:

	Number of Units	Standard Time	Average Clerical Salary	Standard Clerical Cost	Total Clerical Cost
1. Clerical salaries:					
PNBB	650	4.0 hours	$3.00 per hour	$12.00	$ 7,800
Collecting premiums	1,300	1.5 hours	$3.00 per hour	4.50	5,850
Paying claims	500	1.0 hour	$3.00 per hour	3.00	1,500
Total	2,450				15,150

2. Postage: $0.16 × 2,500 units = $400.
3. Stationery and supplies: 25.1% of $3,200 = $800.

Total—Budget and Actual: the total amount of ECTP generated by each component (i.e., salesman), and the total of each class of expense.
Service—Budget and Standard Allowance: the allowances credited to the branch for the performance of its service functions.
Acquisition—Budget: for each line item, the amount in the Total, Budget column less the *budgeted* amount for each service allowance.
Aquisition—Actual: for each line item, the amount in the Total, Actual column less the allowances (if any) in the Service, Standard column.
Variance, dollars: for each line item, the dollar difference resulting from the subtraction of the amount in the Acquisition, Budget column from the amount in the Acquisition, Actual column. Negative amounts are shown in parentheses. For components of ECTP, positive values are favorable variances and negative values are unfavorable variances. For elements of expense, negative values represent overspending and positive values underspending; whether these variances are favorable or unfavorable can be judged only in the light of the particular circumstances giving rise to the variance.
Variance, percent: the magnitude of the dollar variance shown in the preceding column expressed as a percentage of the amount in the Acquisition, Budget column.

Appendix B

Summary of Comments on Proposal

Cost of Implementing and Administering the Proposed Planning and Control System

Six comments related to the cost consequences of adopting the proposal:

1. Four men felt that proposed system would be a lot more costly than what was being done now; there would have to be an ECTP figure for each policy, and new calculations would have to be made each year on basis of expected figures; present measures were really good enough.
2. One man felt that proposal might be more costly than what was being done now but that it would be worthwhile to devote some effort to checking this more carefully.
3. One man felt that cost of proposal might seem high; "but people often don't realize how costly the present system really is." If proposal adopted, it would substitute in many instances for work now being done and would eliminate the need for doing some other work. Felt, however, that straight cost comparison was not valid; the important consideration was whether or not the proposed system would supply better information and, thus, make possible better decisions; in particular, the motivation of branch managers should be directed better.

Method of Calculation of ECTP

Eight comments related to the method of calculating ECTP:

All eight felt that calculation was headed in the right direction, assuming that some sort of profit figure at the branch level was wanted; idea of gain from mortality, gain from interest, and taking present value of expected cash flow felt to be sound if one wanted to do this kind of thing (idea of earning a contribution to overhead not understood very well).

1. Three men wondered why there wasn't an expected gain from loading.
2. Two men said calculation made a lot of sense to them; for the first time, they had an idea of what actuaries did.
3. Three stated if calculation could be made, would have little trouble applying it pretty much as suggested in proposal.

Concept of a Profit Measure at the Branch Level

Sixteen comments pertained to the idea of employing a profit measure for the planning and control of branch operations:

1. Three men felt concept of profit was not appropriate in the life insurance business; life insurance companies, through their salesmen, would sell insurance on basis of people's needs; salesmen generally trained first to recognize a client's insurance needs and then to try to satisfy those needs with available funds of client; if profits became a matter of concern, salesmen and branch managers would be induced to try to sell the more profitable policies rather than to satisfy clients' needs.
2. Thirteen men believed concept was useful, with reactions ranging from limited to broad usefulness.

a. At one extreme—that of limited usefulness: comment of regional manager that he had asked the actuarial department to make this kind of calculation from time to time just to see how various branches were making out, but doubted that information would be useful to managers in general.

b. At other extreme: comment of branch manager that it was just the tool he needed to do his best job; if he could somehow relate his decisions to the effect they would have on company profits, he would make better decisions in the long run and would also have an easier time making them.

c. Comment made by several men: had always thought something like this should be done, but either hadn't pursued it or hadn't been able to convince others of the merit of the idea.

Applicability of the Proposal in Practice

Of the 13 men who had positive reactions, in varying degrees, to the concept of a profit measure at the branch level, 10 made comments on how well they expected the proposal would work in actual practice:

1. Five men felt it would work, with following qualifications:

    a. One suggested it be tried out on a few branches to see how it worked.
    b. One uncertain whether calculation could be made in practice.
    c. Three suggested proposal be reviewed by a committee.
2. Five men believed proposal could work, but wouldn't work in actual practice due to lack of acceptance; reasons for this opinion can be categorized as follows:

    Tradition. Sales volume has always been the accepted measure of accomplishment in the insurance industry; almost everyone has become accustomed to this orientation; trying to effect such a radical change as substituting a profit measure for a sales measure will take a long, long time.

    Status. Certain people have achieved positions of prominence, both within the company and within the industry in general, on the basis of these traditional volume measures, who would not have been promoted to such positions if their performance had been measured by their profit contribution: (best example provided by those who sell mostly group insurance); a number of such people are in key positions in top management; these people are not likely to act favorably on a proposal which as much as tells them that they aren't as important as they imagined, and probably shouldn't be in the positions of prominence they currently occupy.

    Profit image. A lot of people in the industry wouldn't like our men talking about the business as being profit-oriented; image of a life insurance company as a benevolent institution catering to the public good should not be risked.

Defense of the Industry

Three comments categorized best as a defense of current practices of the life insurance industry focused on the importance of being conservative in one's expectations about the future (e.g., mortality tables, interest assumptions, and loading expenses), especially in light of the public interest being served and the indefinite nature of the business.

Chapter 16

Multinational Organizations

In this chapter we describe management control problems and practices in multinational (also called "transnational") organizations. Most of the aspects of controlling foreign operations are similar to those for controlling domestic operations, and these are discussed only briefly. There are, however, two problems that are unique to foreign operations: transfer pricing and exchange rates. Most of this chapter is devoted to these two problems. Although our discussion is stated in terms of a U.S. corporation and its foreign subsidiaries, the same general problems exist with respect to the parent company in any country and its foreign subsidiaries.

SIMILARITIES

In general, foreign operations may be organized as expense centers, revenue centers, profit centers, or investment centers, and the considerations that govern the choice of a particular type of responsibility center are, in most respects, similar to those for domestic operations. One important difference, however, is that, even if a foreign operation is an expense center or a revenue center for control purposes, it is often a profit center for accounting purposes. Many foreign operations are legal entities, incorporated in the host country, and, therefore, they must maintain a complete set of accounting records for legal and tax reasons.

The planning and control processes that we described in Chapters 8 through 12—programming, budget preparation, operating, variance analysis and reporting, performance evaluation, and management compensation—generally are applicable to multinational organizations. Although these processes are similar, they need to be tailored to the context of multinational organizations for two reasons. First, as compared to domestic corporations, foreign subsidiaries tend to operate in less familiar environments and tend to be more geographically dispersed. Second, though cultural differences exist even among various cities within the United States, these differences are magnified in the context of a company operating in many countries. Management control systems must be adapted to these differences.

TRANSFER PRICING

Criteria

Transfer pricing for goods, services, and technology represents one of the major differences between management control of domestic and foreign operations. In domestic operations, the criteria for the transfer price system almost exclusively are those described in Chapter 5. In foreign operations, however, several other considerations are important in arriving at the transfer price. They include taxation, government regulations, tariffs, foreign exchange controls, funds accumulation, and joint ventures.

Taxation.   Effective income tax rates can differ considerably among foreign countries. A transfer price system that results in assigning profits to low-tax countries can reduce total income taxes.

Government regulations.   In the absence of government regulations, the firm would set transfer prices to minimize taxable income in the countries with high income tax rates. However, government tax authorities are aware of such possibilities, and governments have passed regulations that affect the way in which transfer prices can be calculated.

Tariffs.   Tariffs are often levied on the import value of a product. The lower the price, the lower will be the tariff. The incidence of tariffs is usually opposite to the incidence of income taxes in transfer pricing. Although tariffs for goods shipped to a given country will be low if the transfer price is low, the profit recorded in that country—and hence the local income tax on the profit—will be correspondingly high. Thus, the net effect of these factors must be calculated in deciding on the appropriate transfer price. Because income taxes are typically a larger amount than tariffs, international transfer pricing is usually driven more by income tax than by tariff considerations.

Foreign exchange controls.   Some countries limit the amount of foreign exchange available to import certain commodities. Under these conditions, a lower transfer price allows the subsidiary to bring in a greater quantity of these commodities.

Funds accumulation. A company may wish to accumulate its funds in one country, rather than in another. Transfer prices are a way of shifting funds into or out of a particular country.

Joint ventures. Joint ventures create additional complications in transfer pricing. Suppose a U.S. firm has a joint venture operation in Japan with a local Japanese firm. If the U.S. parent charges a higher price for a component transferred to Japan, the Japanese joint venture partner is likely to resist that price since it lowers the profits of the Japanese operation and, consequently, the share of the profits for the Japanese joint venture partner. Ford Motor Company, partly to avoid transfer pricing disputes, purchased the large British minority interest in Ford, Ltd., in 1961. For similar reasons, General Motors has not used joint ventures until its arrangement with Toyota in the late 1980s.

Legal Considerations

Almost all countries place some constraints on the flexibility of companies to set transfer prices for transactions with foreign subsidiaries. The reason is to prevent the multinational company from avoiding the host country's income taxes. An article in *The Wall Street Journal* (July 10, 1990) highlights this point:

> A House subcommittee investigation of 36 foreign-owned U.S. companies has found that more than half paid little or no U.S. income tax over a 10-year period.
>
> Largely by inflating the prices they paid their foreign parents for goods, services, and technology, a number of the U.S. subsidiaries were able to reduce their taxable income to almost nothing.
>
> Among the cases the investigators cited were these:
>
> - A foreign parent sold television sets to its U.S. subsidiary at $250 each but charged only $150 to an unrelated distributor.
> - A foreign auto manufacturer sold cars to its U.S. subsidiary at an average of $800 more than it charged its Canadian subsidiary for identical cars.
> - A foreign company shipping trucks to a U.S. subsidiary and an unrelated distributor in the United States charged almost $200 more per truck in shipping costs to the related company.

Regulations for the United States are basically set forth in Section 482 of the Internal Revenue Code.[1] In general, Section 482 tries to ensure that financial transactions between the units of a *controlled taxpayer* (a company that can control transactions between domestic and foreign profit centers) are conducted as if the units were *uncontrolled taxpayers* (independent entities dealing with

---

[1] As this edition goes to press, the Internal Revenue Service is in the process of reviving the regulations for Section 482. We believe that this revision will not change the substance of the description given here.

one another at arm's length). In case of a dispute, Section 482 permits the Internal Revenue Service to calculate what it believes to be the most appropriate transfer price, and the burden of proof is then on the company to show that this price is unreasonable. This is in contrast with most provisions of the Internal Revenue Code, which permit the company to select whatever permissible alternative it wishes and place the burden of proof on the Internal Revenue Service to show that the company's method is illegal.

Section 482 provides rules for determining the transfer price on sales between members of the controlled group. Acceptable intercompany pricing methods, listed in descending order of priority, are as follows:

1. *Comparable uncontrolled price method.* An arm's-length price is ascertained from comparable sales of goods or services between the multinational firm and unrelated customers, or between two unrelated firms. Comparability is based on the similarity of the controlled and uncontrolled sale with respect to the physical properties and factual circumstances underlying the transactions. An uncontrolled sale will be considered comparable if the differences are such that they can be reflected by an adjustment of the selling price (e.g., where the difference is accounted for by a variance in shipping terms). However, a sale will not be considered comparable if it represents an occasional or marginal transaction or is a sale at an unrealistically low price.

Circumstances that may affect the price include the quality of the product, terms of sale, market level, and geographical area in which the item is sold; but quantity discounts, promotional allowances, and special losses due to currency exchange and credit differentials are excluded.

Lower prices, and even sales at a price below full cost, are permitted in certain instances, such as during the penetration of a new market or in maintaining an existing market in a particular area.

2. *Resale price method.* If comparable sales are not available, the next preferred method is the resale price method. Under this method, the taxpayer works back from the final selling price at which property purchased from an affiliate is resold in an uncontrolled sale. This "resale price" is reduced by an appropriate markup percentage based on uncontrolled sales by the same affiliate or by other resellers selling similar property in a comparable market. Markup percentages of competitors and industry averages are also helpful.

The regulations require that this method be used (1) if there are no comparable uncontrolled sales, (2) the resales are made within a reasonable time before or after the intercompany purchase, (3) the reseller has not added significant value to the property by physically altering it, other than packaging, labeling, and so forth, or by the use or application of intangible property.

3. *Cost-plus method.* Under this method, the lowest priority of the three prescribed methods, the starting point for determining an arm's-length price is the cost of producing the product, computed in accordance with sound accounting practices. To this is added an appropriate gross profit expressed as a percentage of cost and based on similar uncontrolled sales made by the seller, by other sellers, or the rate prevalent in the industry.

A schematic representation of these three methods is as follows:

1. *Comparable uncontrolled price method:*

    Transfer price = Price paid in comparable uncontrolled sales
    ± Adjustments

In a controlled sale, the transaction is between two members of a controlled group. In an uncontrolled sale, one of the two parties is not a member of the controlled group.

2. *Resale price method:*

    Transfer price = Applicable resale price − Appropriate markup
    ± Adjustments

Applicable resale price is the price at which property purchased in a controlled sale is resold by the buyer in an uncontrolled sale.

    Appropriate markup = Applicable resale price
    × Appropriate markup percentage

    Appropriate markup percentage = Percent of gross profit
    (expressed as a percent of sales) earned by the buyer (reseller)
    or by another party in an uncontrolled purchase and resale
    similar to controlled resale

3. *Cost-plus method:*

    Transfer price = Costs + Appropriate markup ± Adjustments

    Appropriate markup = Costs × Appropriate gross profit percent

    Appropriate gross profit percent = Gross profit percent
    (expressed as a percent of cost) earned by seller or another party
    on uncontrolled sale similar to controlled sale

The Organization for Economic Cooperation and Development (OECD) Committee on Fiscal Affairs recommends these three methods in European countries.[2]

Implications of Section 482

From a management control point of view, there are two important implications of Section 482:

---

[2] "Transfer Pricing and Multinational Enterprises," Report of the Organization for Economic Cooperation and Development Committee on Fiscal Affairs (Paris: OECD, 1979).

1. Although there are legal restrictions on a company's flexibility in transfer pricing, there is considerable latitude within these restrictions.
2. In some instances, the legal constraints may dictate the type of transfer prices that must be employed. Each of these is discussed below.

Latitude in transfer prices.   In many multinational companies there is a difference between the transfer prices that management would use purely for control purposes and the legally allowable transfer prices that minimize the sum of the tax and tariff impacts. Since a certain amount of subjectivity is involved in applying Section 482 to many goods and services, there may be a considerable range in the permissible transfer price for a particular item. Management can minimize the sum of income taxes and tariffs by maintaining transfer prices as far as possible at the appropriate end of the range. For example, if a U.S. parent company sells a product to a subsidiary in a country with materially lower income tax rates than those in the United States, profits can be shifted to the foreign subsidiary by keeping the transfer price as low as is legally allowable. This practice, however, may cause a management control problem because profits in a foreign subsidiary would be reported as being higher, and profits in the American subsidiary would be reported as being lower, than would be the case if the transaction took place between independent entities.

There are two extremes of policy in dealing with this problem. Some companies permit subsidiaries to deal with each other at arm's length and let the impact of taxes and tariffs fall where it may. With this policy, there is no question about the legality of transfer prices because the subsidiaries are trying to do exactly what the regulations say they should do—deal at arm's length. Under this policy, foreign transfer pricing policies will be essentially the same as domestic transfer pricing. Consequently, the transfer price system supports the management control system. On the other hand, the policy could result in higher total costs.

At the other extreme, foreign transfer prices may be controlled almost entirely by corporate headquarters, with the purpose of minimizing total corporate costs, maximizing dollar cash flow, or obtaining the optimum mix of currency positions. Such a policy can severely restrict the usefulness of the control system, however, because, in some instances, the transfer prices may bear little relationship to the prices that would prevail if the buying and selling units were independent. If this policy is followed, the question arises of what to do about the control system.

One possibility is to adjust profits for internal evaluation purposes to reflect competitive market prices. For example, the total differences between the prices actually charged and those that would have been in effect had taxation not been a consideration could be added to the selling subsidiary's revenue and the buying subsidiary's costs when profit budget reports are analyzed. This is a questionable practice, however, and few companies use it. If asked, a company would be required to disclose these adjustments to the Internal Revenue

Service, and their existence could raise questions concerning the validity of the transfer prices being used for tax purposes.

Many companies that price to minimize taxes and tariffs use the same transfer prices for profit budget preparation and reporting as are used for accounting and tax purposes. The approved budget reflects any inequities arising from the transfer prices. To illustrate, a subsidiary that sells for lower than normal prices might have a budgeted loss. If reports of actual performance show that the subsidiary loses less than budget, its performance is considered to be satisfactory, other things being equal. In short, the transfer prices are considered both in preparing the budget and in analyzing results.

If profit budgets and reports reflect uneconomic transfer prices, care must be taken to make certain that subsidiary managers make decisions that are in the best interests of the company. For example, suppose that Subsidiary A purchases a line of products from Subsidiary B at a price that gives B most of the profit. In these circumstances, Subsidiary A can improve its reported profit performance by not selling B's products aggressively and by concentrating its marketing effort on products that add more to its reported profits. Such a practice could be contrary to the best interests of the company as a whole. If uneconomic transfer prices are used in budgeting, therefore, it is important to guard against such situations. It may be necessary to use other measures of performance than profitability or, at least, other measures *in addition* to profitability, such as sales volume or market share.

Legal constraints on transfer pricing systems. In some instances, legal constraints may require that a particular transfer pricing system be used, or that a preferred transfer system not be used. For example, the two-step transfer price system described in Chapter 5 might be questioned by the tax authorities simply because it is not mentioned in Section 482 and is not widely known abroad.

Some constraints are used by the nature of the product being transferred. For example:

> In the oil industry the posted price system limits transfer pricing, removes it from the control of the companies, and indeed exploits it in favor of the exporting countries. With many other primary products, transfer pricing is either organized by the exporting country through state trade or similar regulation (e.g., Chilean and Peruvian copper exports) or [is] severely limited by specific taxes (e.g., tonnage levies on output or exports).[3]

In other instances, the "full cost" approach implicit in Section 482 may limit a company's ability to transfer some products at less than full costs. For example, the marketing department may want to introduce a new product in a market at a price that is lower than its normal price, perhaps not even high

---

[3] Malcom Crawford, "Transfer Pricing in International Transactions," *Multinational Business,* September 1974, p. 1.

enough to cover its full costs. This may be a sound marketing tactic, but the IRS may not recognize it as a valid basis for arriving at the transfer price.

If Section 482 requires the use of transfer prices different from the ones that would be used for control purposes, a company is in the same position as the company that used one set of transfer prices for taxation and another for control, except that such a company can safely adjust subsidiary revenues and costs for differences between the Section 482 transfer price and the preferred transfer price in most cases. Since the company presumably would have no objection to using the preferred transfer price for tax purposes, no harm comes from, in effect, keeping two sets of books.

Foreign Sales Corporations

To encourage U.S. companies to develop increased amounts of foreign trade, the Congress has authorized the use of foreign sales corporations (FSCs). As of 1988, about 4,500 FSCs were operated by U.S. exporters.[4] An FSC is a separate subsidiary corporation that buys goods from its U.S. parent corporation and sells such goods abroad. It is to the advantage of a parent company to charge the lowest price possible to the FSC, since the FSC receives favorable tax treatment. Consequently, the transfer price to the FSC is of interest both to management and to the Internal Revenue Service.

The Congress has limited the transfer pricing options by requiring companies to choose from one of the following methods for setting the transfer price between the parent company and the FSC:

1. An arm's-length price as prescribed under Section 482.
2. The overall profit on a transaction is calculated by, first, considering the parent and the FSC as a single entity. Then, the total profit is allocated to the parent company and the FSC in the proportion of 77 percent and 23 percent, respectively.
3. The profit allocated to the FSC is determined by multiplying FSC's sales revenues from outside customers by 1.83 percent.

The last two options are referred to as "administrative pricing methods." To be eligible for the use of the two administrative pricing methods, the FSC must perform the following eight activities outside the United States: advertise and promote export sales, solicit business, negotiate terms, close sales, process orders, deliver the goods to foreign customers, send the invoice and receive payment, and assume the credit risk on the export sale.

Three potential benefits derive from using one of the administrative pricing methods. First, as compared to the arm's-length price, the administrative price

---

[4] U.S. Department of the Treasury, Internal Revenue Service, "Statistics of Income Studies of International Income and Taxes," by D. F. Skelly and J. R. Hobbs. *Statistics of Income Bulletin*, Publication 1136, nos. 8, 2, Fall 1988.

typically allocates more profits to the FSC. Second, an administrative price results in a lower tax on this profit. The FSC is exempt on $\frac{15}{23}$ of its foreign trade income, if administrative pricing rules are used. However, the FSC is exempt on only 30 percent of its foreign trade income under the arm's-length price. Third, the IRS will not contest the profit arrived at under an administrative method, while it might contest an arm's-length price.

Whether the third option is better than the second option can easily be determined by calculating the after-tax profit under each method.

Minority Interests

Whenever minority interests are involved, top management's flexibility in distributing profits between subsidiaries can be severely restricted because the minority parties have a legal right to a fair share of the corporation's profit. In this event, subsidiaries must deal with each other at arm's length, to the extent possible.

EXCHANGE RATES AND PERFORMANCE EVALUATION

The cash flows of a domestic company are denominated in dollars, and at a given moment each dollar has the same value as every other dollar. By contrast, the cash flows of a multinational enterprise (MNE) are denominated in several currencies, and the value of each currency relative to the value of the dollar is different at different times. These variations complicate the problem of measuring the performance of subsidiaries and subsidiary managers. Specifically, MNEs face "translation," "transaction," and "economic" exposure to changes in exchange rates. We first discuss exchange rates briefly, and then we define the three types of exchange rate exposure and their implications for the design of management control systems.

Exchange Rates

An exchange rate is the price of one currency in terms of another currency. It can be expressed either as the number of units of the home currency that are needed to buy one unit of foreign currency (called the "direct quote") or the number of units of the foreign currency that are needed to buy one unit of the home currency (called the "indirect quote"). For example, if the U.S. dollar $ is the home currency and the French franc (FF) is the foreign currency, then to express the exchange rate as $0.20/FF is the direct quote, and to express it as FF5/$ is the indirect quote. In the markets for foreign exchange, both types of quotes are used, but traders usually use one or the other type for particular currencies. Exhibit 16–1 provides examples of both, for exchange rates prevailing as of August 22, 1990, for the most heavily traded currencies.

EXHIBIT 16–1 Exchange Rates for Various Foreign Currencies on August 22, 1990

Country	Monetary Unit	Dollars per Unit Foreign Currency (direct quote)	Foreign Currency Units per Dollar (indirect quote)
United Kingdom	pound	1.92650	0.5191
France	franc	0.10195	9.8087
Japan	yen	0.006845	146.10
Switzerland	franc	0.78340	1.2765
W. Germany	mark	0.64230	1.5571

Exchange rates that are usually quoted (such as those above) are called *nominal* exchange rates. The *spot* exchange rate is the nominal exchange rate that prevails on a given day. The *real* exchange rate is the spot exchange rate *after* adjusting for inflation differentials between the two countries in question. There are also *forward* exchange rates, which are exchange rates known today at which transactions can be entered into for completion at some future point in time.

Using the direct quote, if the number of dollars required to buy a unit of foreign currency rises, then the dollar is said to have undergone a *depreciation* relative to the foreign currency (the reverse is true for an appreciation). Suppose, for example, that one year ago the spot U.S./U.K. exchange rate was \$1/£, and today's spot rate is \$1.20/£. These rates are "nominal" exchange rates that prevailed one year ago and are prevailing today, respectively. In nominal terms, we would then say that the U.S. dollar depreciated 20 percent against the pound sterling, since it takes 20 percent more dollars to buy the same number of pounds sterling today, compared to a year ago.

However, suppose that the inflation during this period was 10 percent in the United States and 5 percent in the United Kingdom. Then, according to a theory that goes by the name of "purchasing power parity" (PPP), these inflation rates would predict that the U.S. dollar should have depreciated against the U.K. pound sterling by about 5 percent, or to the approximate extent of the inflation differential between the two countries, and not by 20 percent. Thus, under the theory of PPP, we would have expected the exchange rate today to be \$1.05/£. At the spot rate of \$1.20/£, the nominal value of the U.S. dollar depreciated by 14.3 percent *more* than the theory of PPP would predict. This additional depreciation of 14.3 percent in currency values in excess of the inflation differential between the two countries is the *real depreciation* of the U.S. dollar; analogous arguments apply in the case of appreciation. The real exchange rate is the exchange rate after adjusting for inflation differentials between the United States and the United Kingdom and, in our example, it is \$1.143/£.

Ever since the evolution of the floating exchange rate system in the early 1970s, there have been substantial swings in real exchange rates, even between the most heavily traded currencies. In the broadest terms, real exchange rate changes create changes in the cost competitiveness of a domestic manufacturer against its foreign competitors: If all else remained equal and U.S. real exchange rates depreciated by *x* percent, say, against the Japanese yen, then U.S. firms are likely to have become *x* percent more cost competitive, compared to their Japanese competitors. Taking the case of depreciation, the explanation is as follows: An *x* percent real depreciation of the U.S. dollar must mean that goods priced in U.S. dollars have become *x* percent cheaper *over and above* the price adjustments that should have normally resulted from inflation in both the United States and in Japan.

Different Types of Exchange Rate Exposure

Translation exposure to exchange rates is the income statement and balance sheet exposure of MNEs to changes in nominal exchange rates. It results from the fact that MNEs must consolidate their accounts in a single (usually home country) currency although their cash flows are denominated in multiple currencies. Understanding translation exposure in MNEs comes down to understanding the answer to the following question: Given that the cash flows of the firm are denominated in multiple currencies and given that there have been nominal changes in currency values during the year, how should revenues, expenses, assets, and liabilities be consolidated into one currency as of a point in time?

Transaction exposure is the exchange rate exposure that the firm has in its cross-border transactions when such transactions are entered into today, but payments to settle the transaction are made at some future point in time. In other words, during the period that payment or receipt commitments are outstanding, nominal exchange rates could change and put the value of transactions at risk. Examples of such transactions include receivables and payables, and debt or interest payments outstanding, in foreign currencies.

Economic exposure is the exchange rate exposure of the firm's cash flows to real exchange rate changes. Economic exposure is also referred to as "operating exposure" or "competitive exposure" to exchange rates. Exhibit 16–2 is a stylized graphical representation that provides a summary of the different types of exposure.

Choice of Metric in Performance Evaluation

In a survey of MNEs, Choi and Czechowicz[5] found almost all the respondents had performance evaluation systems that compared actuals against budgets in assessing subsidiary performance. There are basically three possibilities for

[5] F. D. S. Choi and I. J. Czechowicz, "Assessing Foreign Subsidiary Performance: A Multinational Comparison," *Management International Review* 4(1983), pp. 14–25.

EXHIBIT 16–2   Different Types of Exchange Rate Exposure

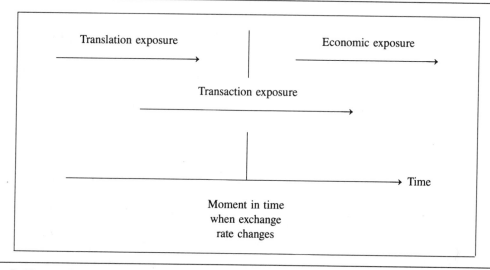

Source: D. Eitman and A. Stonehill, *Multinational Business Finance* (Reading, Mass.: Addison-Wesley, 1989), p. 173.

choice of metric in setting and tracking budgets:[6] the exchange rate prevailing at the time budgets are set (the "initial" exchange rate), the exchange rates projected at the time budgets are set (the "projected" exchange rate), or the actual exchange rates prevailing at the time budgets are tracked ("ending" exchange rate). There are, then, nine possible combinations of metrics in setting and tracking budgets, as shown in Exhibit 16–3.

Not all nine cells are feasible, however; only the underlined ones are. The obviously feasible ones consist of the three where the budget is set and tracked using the same metric (initial-initial, cell 1; projected–projected, cell 5; ending–ending, cell 9[7]); similarly, it is feasible to set the budget using an "initial" rate and track it using an "ending" rate (cell 3), as well as to set at a "projected" rate and track at the "ending" rate (cell 6). It is illogical, however, to set the budget at the "ending" exchange rate and then to track actuals using initial or projected exchange rates (thus ruling out 7 and 8). Similarly, to project an exchange rate in setting the budget and then to track it at the rate that initially prevailed also seems illogical (thus ruling out cell 4).

---

[6] These possibilities were originally discussed in D. Lessard and P. Lorange, "Currency Changes and Management Control: Resolving the Centralization/Decentralization Dilemma," *Accounting Review*, July 1977, pp. 628–37.

[7] To set the budget at the "ending" rate means that, at the time performance is being evaluated, the original budget is recast using the exchange rate prevailing at the end-of-period.

EXHIBIT 16–3   Choice of Metric in Performance Evaluation

		Initial	Tracking Budget Projected	Ending
	Initial	<u>1</u>	2	<u>3</u>
Setting Budget	Projected	4	<u>5</u>	6
	Ending	7	8	<u>9</u>

Control System Design Issues

From the point of view of performance evaluation, the important questions in control systems design are:

- Should subsidiary managers be held responsible for the impact of exchange rate fluctuations on their bottom line?
- Should the parent company use the home country currency or should it use the local currency in performance evaluation? Further, should it use the initial exchange rate, the projected exchange rate, or the ending exchange rate in setting and tracking budgets?
- Should the parent company distinguish between the effects of different types of exchange rate exposure while evaluating the performance of the subsidiary manager? If yes, how?
- How should different types of exchange rate exposure affect the evaluation of the economic performance of the subsidiary, as distinct from the evaluation of the manager in charge of the subsidiary?

Translation Effects

Consider an example of a U.S. company with a subsidiary in France. Exhibit 16–4 describes the budget and the actuals for this subsidiary. Suppose that the initial exchange rate was FF10/$ and the ending exchange rate was FF11/$ (that is, the French franc depreciated in both real and nominal terms by 10 percent relative to the dollar, so that the French inflation rate did not change). The subsidiary was given a volume target, based on which the budgeted profit at the initial exchange rate was $1, or FF10. Further, assume that the French

EXHIBIT 16–4 Budget and Actuals for Balanced Subsidiary (initial exchange rate: FF10/$; ending exchange rate: FF11/$)

	Budget		Actual	
	FF	*$*	*FF*	*$*
Revenue	100	10	100	9.09
Profit	10	1	10	0.91

subsidiary incurs all its costs in France and sells entirely in France. That is to say, the French subsidiary does not engage in any "cross-border" transactions. Such a subsidiary is called a "balanced unit." Assume that the subsidiary met all its volume targets, but the exchange rate changed to FF11/$ (i.e., FF11 per $). Under the new exchange rate, the dollar profits generated by the subsidiary would only be $0.91—or an unfavorable budget variance of about 10 percent in dollar terms—even though it met its volume objectives.

Should the manager of the French subsidiary be held accountable for exchange rate fluctuations (because, otherwise, the actual performance was exactly as budgeted)? The French subsidiary is self-contained (i.e., it does not engage in cross-border transactions). Therefore, the manager of that subsidiary need not be concerned with strategic and operating decisions (such as pricing and sourcing) in response to exchange rate changes. In addition, changes in exchange rates are completely beyond the control of the subsidiary manager. It seems fair, therefore, that subsidiary managers not be held responsible for translation effects. The simplest way to achieve this objective is to set and track budgets using the same metric (cells 1, 5, or 9 in Exhibit 16–3).

This example presumed that the exchange rate change was both real and nominal. However, if the change was purely nominal, then it must mean that French inflation was 10 percent higher compared to the U.S., and there is purely an inflation effect on the subsidiary's cash flows. In this case, the subsidiary may be able to raise its FF prices 10 percent and costs would also presumably go up by 10 percent. Consequently, the U.S. dollar target is met. Even in this case, the suggestion is as follows: set and track the budget using the same metric, but isolate the variance that is due to the pure inflation effect. That is, the subsidiary manager should be held responsible for appropriate inflation-related pricing and sourcing strategies, but need not be held responsible for exchange rate effects.

In the example in Exhibit 16–4, if the budget was tracked using the same metric as that on which the budget was set (FF10/$), then the subsidiary would have been shown to have generated $1. Alternatively, if the budget at the end of the year was reset to the ending exchange rate of FF11/$, the subsidiary would have been only *expected* to generate $0.91 in profits. Thus, if the same metric is used to set and track the budget, then the choice of metric (whether local or foreign currency; whether initial, projected, or ending exchange rate) is not relevant; also, the resulting performance reflects the operating performance of the manager, independent of translation effects.

However, the parent company suffered a "translation" loss at the end of the year. Parent companies can do little to control such exchange rate shifts. If they use translation gains or losses in evaluating the subsidiary managers' performance, this could lead to several problems: (1) it would make the subsidiary managers responsible for factors that are beyond their control, (2) it does not get rid of the translation gain or loss, (3) it will not account for other types of exchange rate exposure that subsidiaries face (see next section), and (4) it will confound the performance of the manager and the subsidiary (see next section).

When companies report to stockholders, they have to consolidate the accounting numbers of foreign subsidiaries with the accounting numbers of the parent. Translation gains and losses arising out of converting the income statement and the balance sheet of the foreign subsidiary into the monetary unit of the parent company should *not* affect the performance of the subsidiary manager. The required method of calculating translation gains and losses for financial reporting purposes is discussed in the Appendix at the end of this chapter.

Economic Exposure

In the balanced unit that we considered above, exchange rates led only to translation effects. However, when subsidiaries have cross-border transactions, they also are subject to economic exposure. A control system that effectively can deal with economic exposure differs in a fundamental way from the one that we have described for translation exposure. Under economic exposure, it would be appropriate for the control system to evaluate the subsidiary manager on decisions that would have enabled the subsidiary to respond to real exchange rate changes. We explain how this can be done by considering two generic types of subsidiaries in MNEs: "net importers" and "net exporters."

A *net importer* is a subsidiary that sells most of its outputs in its own country, but imports most of its inputs from outside that country (either from sister subsidiaries or from outside companies); a *net exporter* is a subsidiary that sells most of its outputs outside its own country (either to sister subsidiaries or to outside companies), but purchases most of its inputs within that country. As the following example shows, given an exchange rate shift, such subsidiaries will not only face translation effects but also "dependence" effects resulting from real exchange rate changes.

To keep the example simple, we will consider subsidiaries that have transactions only between the home country and the host country. The conclusions from this example are generalizable to any subsidiary that has cross-border transactions with sister subsidiaries or other companies outside the host country. Also, we will include the balanced unit in the analysis for purposes of comparison. Suppose a U.S. MNE has three subsidiaries A, B, and C in France. Subsidiary A is the balanced unit, the one considered in the preceding section. B is a net importer; it sources its inputs from its parent in the United States and sells all its output in France. C is a net exporter; it sources entirely in France and sells all its output in the United States. The initial exchange rate is $1 = 10FF, and the budgets have been set as indicated in Exhibit 16–5.

EXHIBIT 16–5 Budgets for A, B, and C (initial exchange rate: 10FF/$)

	A: Balanced		B: Net Importer		C: Net Exporter	
	FF	US$	FF	US$	FF	US$
Sales	100	10	100	10	100	10
Costs	90	9	90	9	90	9
Profit (value)	10	1	10	1	10	1
Profit (margin)	10%	10%	10%	10%	10%	10%

Now, as before, suppose that the United States dollar appreciated against the French franc by 10 percent in *real* terms, with the new exchange rate being $1 = FF11 by the time the budget was tracked.[8] Suppose the parent company set the budget at the initial rate (FF10/$) and tracked it at the ending rate (FF11/$). Let us suppose that, at the end of the year, the performance of the three subsidiaries looked like Exhibit 16–6 from the perspective of the parent company:

EXHIBITS 16–6 Performance of A, B, and C (current exchange rate: 11FF/$)

	A: Balanced		B: Net Importer		C: Net Exporter	
	FF	US$	FF	US$	FF	US$
Sales	100	9.09	103	9.36	109	9.91
Costs	90	8.18	95	8.63	95	8.63
Profit (value)	10	0.91	8	0.73	14	1.28
Profit (margin)	10%	10%	7.9%	7.9%	12.9%	12.9%

The net exporter outperformed the budget (in both $ and FF, both profit value and margin), the balanced unit performed approximately at budgeted lev-

---

[8] We could have made the example somewhat more realistic by including nominal exchange rate changes as well—that is, we could assume that part of the exchange rate change was nominal and that we take out the PPP effect to only include real exchange rate changes. In this example, we simply assume that all of the exchange rate change is real. Conclusions are not altered by this assumption.

els (met the profit objective in FF, but a bit below in $; met margin objectives in both currencies) and the net importer underperformed the budget (in both $ and FF, profit value and margin).

Now let us examine the exchange rates effects a bit closer. Note that, under the new real exchange rate scenario, the net exporter should have been able to achieve FF110, without any extra efforts. In fact, given the nature of its demand and cost structure, it may have been able to achieve much higher levels of sales than even FF110. Thus, its sales of FF109 represent *under*achievement relative to what should have been expected, given the real exchange rate shift. Further, its underperformance on the sales front was exacerbated by underperformance on the cost front (since it incurred local costs of FF95, although it was budgeted for FF90).

Now, consider the net importer. Under the new exchange rate scenario, Firm B became *less* cost competitive against its competitors that did not have similar exchange rate exposure in relation to inputs. Against B's cost of $8.63, competitors that were sourcing entirely locally (as, for example, the balanced subsidiary was doing) were incurring a cost of only $8.18. They could easily have (and perhaps did) undercut B in prices to gain both profits and market share. Yet, the net importer not only exceeded his FF sales target but, in the process, did so at a lower local input cost than originally budgeted.

This example not only underscores the point that setting and tracking budgets using different metrics can be unfair; it also highlights the problems of measuring management performance and subsidiary performance. In addition, such a situation confounds translation and dependence effects. If only the translation effect was considered, manager B would have been criticized and manager C rewarded. If the dependence effect was isolated from the translation effect, manager B would have been rewarded and manager C criticized. To illustrate, manager C would have been told that, given the real appreciation of the U.S. dollar, his or her sales performance of FF109 represents inadequate performance; if he or she expected to be rewarded for above budget performance, the subsidiary should have done more.

For subsidiaries like B and C (which have cross-border transactions), real exchange rate changes require important strategic and operating decisions. For example, if the US$ depreciated against the foreign currencies, this implies that goods priced in US$ have become cheaper in real terms, compared to those priced in foreign currencies. For a subsidiary that imports from the United States, this provides major strategic opportunities—for example, it can now afford to costlessly pursue a market share strategy (by dropping its local currency prices, thereby increasing demand and market share, and yet, not suffer in terms of US$ profitability) or it could pursue a skimming strategy (where it retains local currency prices at pre-depreciation levels, and simply pockets the extra US$ profits without losing market share).[9]

---

[9] The appropriate choice of pricing strategies, given a real currency movement, is dealt with in

While on the one hand we have shown that it is not fair to reward or penalize subsidiary managers for exchange rate changes per se, on the other hand it is important to evaluate the performance of the managers in terms of the quality of their decisions, when changes in real exchange rates create strategic opportunities of the type described above. As in the case of the translation effect, the unfair reward or penalty can be avoided by setting and tracking the budget using the same metric. However, additional mechanisms need to be developed to evaluate the quality of managerial decisions given the real exchange rate changes. One such mechanism is "contingent budgeting."[10] This works as follows:

1. Set and track budgets using the same metric; don't worry about the appropriate metric, and simply use the one that is most convenient. Isolate nominal exchange rate effects (which are purely inflation-related) through variance analysis. This recommendation is identical to the one proposed as a way of dealing with translation exposure. However, to deal with economic exposure, additional steps are needed.

2. Prepare the budget based on the "most likely" exchange rate scenario. At the end of the year, only one of three outcomes is possible with respect to the real exchange rate contingency: it was roughly equal to the initial projection, it depreciated relative to the initial projection, or it appreciated relative to the initial projection.

3. At the time of budget *preparation,* discuss with subsidiary managers their anticipated responses, given possible real exchange rate shifts. This discussion would deal with what the subsidiary manager would do about revenues (production and pricing strategies) and costs (sourcing strategy), given a real appreciation or given a real depreciation. To illustrate, the net exporter in our example above would have been told that, for every 1 percent real depreciation of the FF, it would have been expected to generate at least 1 percent in extra sales. Thus, only sales generation above that level would be considered as "above average" performance.

4. At the time of budget *tracking,* when exchange rates are known, revise the original budget for the decisions the manager is expected to make, *given* the exchange rates that were actually realized. The subsidiary manager's performance then would be compared against the revised budget.

A. Sundaram and V. Mishra, "Currency Movements and Corporate Pricing Strategies," in *Recent Developments in International Banking and Finance,* vol. IV, North-Holland, 1990. Given the 35 percent real depreciation of the US$ between 1985 and 1987, many U.S. firms pursued skimming, rather than market share, pricing strategies abroad. For example, articles in *The Wall Street Journal* (May 15, 1987). *Business Week* (August 27, 1987) pointed out that the norm for U.S. firms operating in Japan was to go for ". . . profits rather than market share." There have been many reports of exactly the reverse pricing behavior on the part of Japanese firms operating in the United States, when the US$ appreciated between 1981 and 1984.

[10] This idea was originally proposed by D. Lessard and D. Sharp, "Measuring the Performance of Operations Subject to Fluctuating Exchange Rates," *Midland Corporate Finance Journal* 2 (Fall 1984), pp. 18–30.

Clearly, developing and implementing such a system is not easy. But the very process of preparing such a contingent budget, and advance discussions that identify the subsidiary manager's responses to exchange rate contingencies, will go a long way toward making the subsidiary manager sensitive to real exchange rate changes.

Transaction Effects

The basic approach to dealing with transaction exposure is by appropriate foreign exchange hedging strategies. *Hedging* is any transaction by which risk associated with future cash flows is eliminated. In the process, the company that buys the hedge shifts risk to the entity selling the hedge—typically a commercial bank in the case of foreign exchange markets. Naturally, such hedging services come at a price.

Hedging is commonly practiced by most firms—for example, whenever a company purchases insurance, it is, in effect, undertaking a hedge transaction. Hedging is particularly common among companies engaged in international transactions, and it is used as a means of counteracting the effects of transaction exposure.[11] There are many techniques to hedge transaction exposure. To illustrate the simplest, if an American company sells products to a French company at a price that is stated in French francs, it can simultaneously buy the right to purchase French francs at the same price as of the future date that the account receivable is due. If it has a transaction loss on the sale, it will have an equal gain on the hedge. Other hedging techniques include making use of the option market and matching assets/liabilities and income/expenditure in the same currency. The commonly used techniques of hedging use forward and future markets, as well as foreign currency options markets.[12] From the perspective of performance evaluation, the key question is: Should subsidiary managers be held responsible for hedging transaction exposure?

Hedging transactions are probably best done at the parent company level, rather than permitting individual subsidiaries to make them. There are a number of reasons for this. First, in most MNEs, there are payables and receivables in different parts of the overall firm that may naturally hedge each other if information on all such transactions is collected and dealt with at one central location. This reduces transactions costs associated with hedging. Second, the parent company probably has better access to a wider (and perhaps more sophisticated) range of hedging instruments, across a greater range of maturities, than a subsidiary typically has. Third, there is no reason to presume that the

---

[11] A recent study suggests that 84 percent of treasurers at companies engaged in international trade hedge foreign transaction exposure; see Scott Flicker and Dennis Bline, "Managing Foreign Currency Exchange Risk," *Journal of Accountancy,* August 1990.

[12] See, for example, D. Eiteman and A. Stonehill, *Multinational Business Finance* (Reading, Mass.: Addison-Wesley, 1989) or A. Shapiro, *Multinational Financial Management* (Boston: Allyn & Bacon, 1990).

manager of a subsidiary can forecast exchange rates any better than the corporate treasurer; in fact, parent companies may not want managers of subsidiaries to hedge, since this runs the risk of making subsidiary managers exchange rate speculators.

Thus, from the perspective of performance evaluation, it is unnecessary to make subsidiary managers responsible for transaction effects.

Performance of the Subsidiary

We have thus far suggested that it is important to distinguish between the economic performance of the subsidiary and the performance of its manager, and the guidelines discussed above primarily have dealt with isolating the impact of exchange rates on the performance of the subsidiary manager. It is important to recognize that the economic performance of the subsidiary itself should reflect the negative or positive consequences of translation, transaction, and economic exposures.

If the long-term economic performance of the subsidiary (after incorporating exchange rate effects) continues to be poor, even though the performance of the manager is excellent, then the parent company should address a more basic question: Does it make continued economic sense for the MNE to carry on operations in that country, or should it take its business elsewhere? The answer to this question comes down to a business location decision, rather than a performance evaluation decision; these should be independent decisions.

Management Considerations

In designing performance evaluation systems of MNE subsidiaries, companies could use the following guidelines:

- Subsidiary managers should not be held responsible for translation effects. The simplest way to achieve this objective is to compare budgets and actual results using the same metric and isolate inflation-related effects through variance analysis. It is pointless for managers to worry about the appropriate metric. The MNE should choose whatever metric is most convenient.
- Transaction effects are best handled through centralized coordination of the MNE's overall hedging needs. This is likely to be cheaper and simpler, and it prevents the subsidiary manager from becoming a foreign exchange rate forecaster and speculator.
- The subsidiary manager should be held responsible for the dependence effects of exchange rates resulting from economic exposure. One possible approach is a contingent budgeting system, which would revise the budget standard to reflect the exchange rate contingency, on the assumption that responses to such contingencies were explicitly dealt with at the time of budget preparation. However, such a system is complicated.

• Evaluation of the subsidiary as a basis for a decision to locate operations in a country or to relocate operations from a country should reflect the consequences of translation, transaction, and economic exposures.

In a 1982 survey, Sapy-Mazella et al.[13] found that, in evaluating the subsidiary managers' performance, 79 percent of the respondents used different metrics to prepare budgets and report performance; 66 percent used some forecast of exchange rates to prepare the budget and used the actual end-of-period exchange rate to report the subsidiary's performance relative to the budget, and 13 percent used the initial exchange rate to prepare the budget and the end-of-period actual to report performance. These findings are inconsistent with the guidelines we have developed above.

There are two possible explanations for this inconsistency. First, most of these control systems were developed in the 1950s and 60s, when exchange rates were fixed; given the recent vintage of flexible exchange rates, MNEs may not have tailored their performance evaluation system to the new reality. Second, many companies may not distinguish between the financial performance of the manager and the financial performance of the subsidiary.

Whatever the reason, it is important to recognize that, if an MNE uses different metrics to prepare subsidiary budgets and report actual performance, it runs the various types of risks we have discussed.

SUMMARY

From the standpoint of management control, two problems are unique to MNEs: transfer pricing and exchange rates. In addition to goal congruence, other considerations are important in arriving at transfer prices in MNEs: taxation, government regulations, tariffs, foreign exchange controls, funds accumulation, and joint ventures.

An evaluation of the economic performance of the subsidiary should incorporate the negative or positive consequences of translation, transaction, and economic exposures. However, while evaluating the performance of the manager in charge of the subsidiary, effects of translation and transaction exposures should be removed; even so, the subsidiary manager should be held responsible for the dependence effects of exchange rates resulting from economic exposure.

SUGGESTED ADDITIONAL READINGS

Bartlett, Christopher A., and Sumantra Ghoshal. *Managing across Borders*. Boston: Harvard Business School Press, 1989.

---

[13] Jean-Pierre Sapy-Mazella, R. Woo, and J. Czechowicz, "New Directions in Managing Currency Risk: Changing Corporate Strategies and Systems under FAS No. 52," *Business International Corporation*, New York, 1982.

Burns, J. O. "Transfer Pricing Decisions in U.S. Multinational Corporations." *Journal of International Business Studies,* Fall 1980, pp. 23–39.

Casey, M. P. "International Transfer Pricing." *Management Accounting,* October 1985.

Demirag, I. S. "Assessing Foreign Subsidiary Performance: The Currency Choice of U.K. MNCs." *Journal of International Business Studies,* Summer 1988, pp. 257–75.

Gernon, H. "The Effect of Translation on Multinational Corporation Internal Performance Evaluation." *Journal of International Business Studies,* Spring/Summer 1983, pp. 103–12.

Gupta, A. K., and V. Govindarajan. "Knowledge Flows and the Structure of Controls within Multinational Organizations." *Academy of Management Review,* October 1991.

Halperin, R., and B. Srinidhi. "The Effects of U.S. Income Tax Regulations' Transfer Pricing Rules on Allocating Efficiency." *The Accounting Review,* October 1987.

Jones, C. J. "Financial Planning and Control Practices in U.K. Companies: A Longitudinal Study." *Journal of Business Finance and Accounting,* Summer 1986, pp. 161–86.

Lessard, D. R., and D. Sharp. "Measuring the Performance of Operations Subject to Fluctuating Exchange Rates." *Midland Corporate Finance Journal,* Fall 1984, pp. 18–30.

Merville, L. J. and J. W. Petty. "Transfer Pricing for the Multinational Firm." *The Accounting Review,* October 1978, pp. 935–51.

Persen, W., and V. Lessig. *Evaluating the Performance of Overseas Operations.* New York: Financial Executive Research Foundation, 1980.

Rogman, A. M., and L. Eden (eds.). *Multinationals and Transfer Pricing.* New York: St. Martin's Press, 1985.

Scapens, R. W., and J. T. Sales. "An International Study of Accounting Practices in Divisionalized Companies and Their Associations with Organizational Variables." *The Accounting Review* LX, no. 2 (April 1985), pp. 231–47.

Shapiro, A. C. "The Evaluation and Control of Foreign Affiliates." *Midland Corporate Finance Journal,* Spring 1984, pp. 13–25.

Yunker, P. J. *Transfer Pricing and Performance Evaluation in Multinational Corporations.* New York: Praeger, 1982.

Appendix

SFAS No. 52: Foreign Currency Translation

Statement of Financial Accounting Standards No. 52 requires the all-current method for translating the balance sheet. Under this method all balance sheet items are translated at the rate of exchange in effect on the balance sheet date.[14] Conversion or translation gains and losses are reported as direct credits or charges to shareholders' equity; they do not affect net income for the year. This practice is similar to that used in the United Kingdom. Income statement items are translated at the exchange rate in effect on the date when the income or expense items are recognized, except that companies can use a weighted-average exchange rate if using the actual rates is too complicated.

An example of these exchange translation follows.

Assume that a United States corporation had a Swiss subsidiary with the following financial statements, expressed in Swiss francs (Sfr);

Beginning Balance Sheet

	December 31, 1989
Assets	Sfr 100,000
Liabilities	Sfr 60,000
Capital stock	20,000
Retained earnings	20,000
	Sfr 100,000

During 1990, the subsidiary had the following transactions;
(1) Borrowed Sfr 10,000 from a local bank. The journal entry was:

1990 Transactions

Assets	Sfr 10,000	
Liabilities		Sfr 10,000

(2) Earned Sfr 5,000 from operations:

Revenues	Sfr 15,000
Expenses	10,000
Profit	Sfr 5,000

The impact of **(2)** is to increase assets by Sfr 5,000 and retained earnings by Sfr 5,000.

Ending Balance Sheet

	December 31, 1990
Assets	Sfr 115,000
Liabilities	Sfr 70,000
Capital stock	20,000
Retained earnings	25,000
	Sfr 115,000

---

[14] The name *all current* is used to contrast with the *current/noncurrent* method that the Financial Accounting Standards Board considered and rejected. Under the current/noncurrent method, only current assets and current liabilities are translated at current rates.

Assume that the Swiss franc was worth $.60 on December 31, 1989, and $.50 on December 31, 1990. The average value during 1990 was $.55.

Under *SFAS No. 52,* the subsidiary results will be consolidated with the parent company's financial statement as shown below.

Beginning Balance Sheet

	December 31, 1989
Assets (Sfr 100,000 × .6)	$60,000
Liabilities (Sfr 60,000 × .6)	$36,000
Capital stock (Sfr 20,000 × .6)	12,000
Retained earnings (Sfr 20,000 × .6)	12,000
	$60,000

Income Statement

Revenues (Sfr 15,000 × .55)	$ 8,250
Expenses (Sfr 10,000 × .55)	5,500
Profit	$ 2,750

Ending Balance Sheet

	December 31, 1990
Assets (Sfr 115,000 × .5)	$57,500
Liabilities (Sfr 70,000 × .5)	$35,000
Capital stock (Sfr 20,000 × .5)	10,000
Retained earnings (Sfr 25,000 × .5)	12,500
	$57,500

Reconciliation of retained earnings in dollars:	
Beginning balance	$12,000
Profit	2,750
Indicate ending balance	14,750
Actual ending balance	12,500
Translation loss	$ 2,250

The United States corporation will include profit of $2,750 in its consolidated income statement and a reduction of $2,250 in a segregated part of retained earnings. This represents the financial effect of the fall in the Swiss franc; put another way, the rise in value of the dollar.

Case 16–1
AB Thorsten*

In late 1980, AB[1] Thorsten, a Swedish subsidiary, had submitted a proposal to its parent company, Roget S.A., to build a plant in Sweden to manufacture XL-4, a product currently being manufactured in Belgium. Headquarters seemed not to favor the proposal, but there was no definitive decision.

Background: Roget S.A.

Roget S.A. was one of the largest industrial companies in Belgium. Founded prior to World War II, the company initially produced a line of simple chemicals for sale in Belgium. In 1979, it produced over 200 chemical products in 21 factories.

André Juvet, president of Roget, explained its organization (see Exhibit 1):

> Until 1974, we were organized with one large manufacturing division here in Belgium and one large sales division. One department of the sales division was devoted to export sales. However, exports grew so fast and domestic markets became so complex that we created three main product divisions (Food, Industrial Chemicals, and Textile Chemicals), each with its own manufacturing plants and sales organizations. In addition, we have created foreign subsidiaries to take over the businesses in certain areas. For example, in Industrial Chemicals we have two subsidiaries—one in the United Kingdom and one in Sweden (Thorsten), which serve all of Scandinavia. At the same time, the do-

mestic department of the Industrial Chemicals Division exports to the rest of Europe. The United Kingdom and Sweden account for 9 percent and 5 percent of sales in the industrial chemical division.

> Another thing we achieve in the new organization is individual profit responsibility of all executives at all levels. Mr. Gillot is responsible for profits from all industrial chemicals, Mr. Lambert is responsible for profits from domestic operations (manufacturing and sales of industrial chemicals) and export sales to countries where we do not have subsidiaries or factories, and Mr. Ekstrom is responsible for profits in Scandinavia. We also utilize a rather liberal bonus system to reward executives at each level, based on the profits of their divisions.

> This, together with a policy of promotion from within, helps stimulate managers in Roget to a degree not enjoyed by some of our competitors. It also helps to keep people in an industry where experience is of great importance. Most of our executives have been in the starch chemicals business all of their lives. It is a complex business, and we feel that it takes many years to learn it.

> We have developed certain policies—rules of the game—which govern relationships with our subsidiary company presidents. These are intended to maintain efficiency of the whole Roget complex, while at the same time giving subsidiary managers autonomy to run their own businesses. For example, a subsidiary manager can determine what existing Roget products he wants to sell in his part of the world market. Export sales will quote him the same price as they quote agents in all countries. He is free to bargain, and if he doesn't like the price he needn't sell the product. Second, we encourage subsidiaries to propose to division management in Brussels the development of new products. If these are judged feasible, we manufacture them in Bel-

---

[1] "AB" and "S.A." are abbreviations used in Sweden and Belgium that are similar to "Corp." or "Inc." in the United States.

---

* This case has been adapted with permission from AB Thorsten (A), (B), and (C) prepared by Professors Gordon Shillinglaw and Charles Summer. Copyright © by International Institute for Management Development (IMD), Lausanne, Switzerland.

EXHIBIT 1   Organizational Chart, Roget S.A.

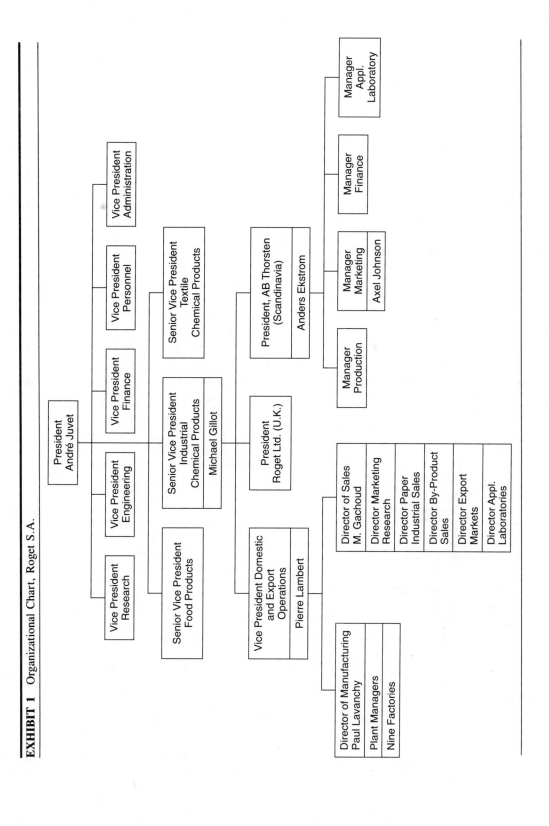

gium for supply to world markets. Third, the subsidiary president can build his own manufacturing plants if he can justify the investment in his home market.

Background: AB Thorsten

AB Thorsten was a wholly owned subsidiary of Roget S.A., with headquarters in Stockholm. It had been acquired by Roget in 1971. Swedish law required that its corporations have Swedish directors. Two of its four directors were prominent Swedes: Imgve Norgren, a banker, and Ove Swensen, an industrialist. A third, Michael Gillot, was senior vice president of Roget. These three had served from 1971.

From 1971 through 1975, Thorsten's sales fluctuated between Skr 5 and 7 million.[2] Sales in 1975 were disappointing. The board at that time realized that the company was in serious trouble and that a new management was necessary.

Anders Ekstrom, who had been called to the board's attention by Swensen, was hired as president and a director. Ekstrom was age 38, a graduate of the Royal Institute of Technology, with 16 years' experience in production engineering for a large Swedish machinery company, as marketing manager of a Swedish subsidiary of a British company, and as division manager, with profit responsibility, for a large Swedish paper company.

AB Thorsten's sales in 1979 were Skr 20 million, and Roget management was highly satisfied with its profits.

Ekstrom said that at the time he joined Thorsten, he knew it was a risk. "I liked the challenge of building a company. If I did a good job here, I would have the confidence of Norgren and Swensen, as well as that of Roget management in Brussels. Deep down inside, succeeding in this situation would teach me things that would make me more competent as a top executive. So I chose this job even though I had at the time (and still have) offers from other companies."

The XL-4 Proposal

In early 1980, Ekstrom decided to study the feasibility of building a factory in Sweden for the manufacture of XL-4, a product used in the paper industry. He explained to the board of directors that he and his engineers had discovered a way of helping large paper mills convert their machines at little cost so they could use XL-4 instead of competitors' products. The paper companies would be able to realize dramatic savings in material handling and storage costs and by shortening drying time substantially. In his opinion, Thorsten could develop sales in Sweden that would be almost as large as Roget's current worldwide sales of XL-4. At that time, XL-4 was manufactured by Roget's Domestic Division at a volume of about 600 tons a year; no sales were made in Sweden.

At that meeting [Ekstrom stated], Mr. Gillot and the other directors seemed enthusiastic. Gillot said, "Of course, go ahead with your study, and when you have a proposed plan with the final return on investment, send it in, and we will consider it thoroughly."

During the next six months, we did the analysis. My market research department estimated the total potential in Sweden at 800 tons of XL-4 per year. We interviewed important customers and conducted trials in the factories of three big companies, which proved that, with the introduction of our machine designs, the large cost saving would indeed materialize. We determined that, if we could sell the product for Skr 1,850 per ton, we could capture one half of the market within a three-year period, or 400 tons a year.

All of this we summarized in a pro forma calculation [Exhibit 2]. This calculation, together with a complete written explanation, was mailed to Mr. Gillot. I felt rather excited, as did most of my staff. We all knew that introduction of new products was one of the keys to continued growth and profitability. The yield of this investment (15 percent) was well above the minimum 8

---

[2] Most monetary amounts in this case are stated in Swedish kronar (Skr). Some of the actual data were stated in Belgian francs (BF).

EXHIBIT 2 Swedish Proposal (in Swedish kronar, skr)

	1	2	3	4	5	6	7	8	9	10
End of Year	Plant	Working Capital	Sales Price/Ton	Variable Cost/Ton	Contribution/ Ton (col. 3-4)	Number of Tons	Total Contribution (Col. 5 X 6)	Promotion Costs	Taxes	Net Cash Flows (1+2+7-8-9)
0	-700,000	-56,000*								-756,000
1		-2,000*	2,000	1,000	1,000	200	200,000	130,000	(35,000)†	103,000
2		-7,000*	1,850	1,000	850	300	255,000	75,000	20,000 †	153,000
3			1,850	1,000	850	400	340,000	50,000	75,000 †	215,000
4			1,850	1,000	850	400	340,000	50,000	75,000 †	215,000
5			1,850	1,000	850	400	340,000	50,000	75,000 †	215,000
6			1,850	1,000	850	400	340,000	50,000	145,000	145,000
7	+150,000‡	+65,000*	1,850	1,000	850	400	340,000	50,000	145,000	360,000

* These working capital investment amounts are net of tax credits.

† Taxes are calculated after depreciating Skr 700,000 over a five year period on straight-line basis.

‡ Sales value, net of appropriate taxes, assuming plant will be closed at end of seven years.

Internal rate of return = 15%.
Net present value, at 8% = Skr 246,000.

percent established as a guideline for new invest-ment by the Roget vice president of finance. We also knew that it was a *good* analysis, done by modern tools of management. In the cover letter, I asked that it be put on the agenda for the next board meeting.

The minutes of the next board meeting held in Stockholm three weeks later quoted Ekstrom's re-marks as he explained the proposal to other direc-tors. "You will see from the summary table [Exhibit 2] that this project is profitable. On an initial outlay of Skr 700,000 for equipment and Skr 56,000 for working capital, we get a rate of return of 15 percent and a net present value of Skr 246,000."

Ekstrom ended the presentation by saying, "Gentlemen, it seems clear from these figures that we can justify this investment in Sweden on the basis of sales to the Swedish market. The group vice president for finance has laid down the policy that any new investment should yield at least 8 percent. This particular proposal shows a return of 15 percent. My management and I strongly recommend this project."

Ekstrom gave his impression of Gillot's atti-tude:

Gillot said that it seemed to him to be a clear case. He asked interesting questions, mainly about the longer-term likelihood that we could see more than 400 tons a year and about how we would get the money. I explained that we in Sweden were very firm in our judgment that we would reach 400 tons a year, even before one year, but felt constrained to show a conservative estimate of a three-year transition period. We also showed him how we could finance any expansion by borrowing in Sweden. That is, if Roget would furnish the ini-tial capital, and if our 400 tons were reached quickly, any further expansion would easily be lent by banks. The two Swedish directors confirmed this. The Swedish board voted unanimously to con-struct the plant.

Initial Doubts at Headquarters

About a week later, Gillot telephoned Ekstrom. "I have been through some additional discussions with the production and marketing people here in the domestic department. They think the engi-neering design and plant cost is accurate, but that you are too optimistic on your sales forecast. It looks like you will have to justify this more."

"I pushed him to set up a meeting the follow-ing week," Ekstrom said. "This meeting was attended by myself and my marketing and pro-duction directors from Sweden, and by four peo-ple from Belgium—Gillot, Lavanchy [director of manufacturing], Gachoud [director of sales], and Lambert [vice president for domestic and export]."

Ekstrom continued:

That was one of the worst meetings of my life. It lasted all day. Gachoud said that they had sales experience from other countries and that in his judgment the market potential and our share were too optimistic. I told him over and over how we arrived at this figure, but he just kept repeating the overoptimism argument. Then Lavanchy said that the production of this product was complicated, and that he had difficulties producing it in Belgium, even with trained workers who had long experi-ence. I told him I only needed five trained produc-tion workers and that he could send me two men for two months to train Swedes to do the job. I impressed on him that if they could manufacture it in Belgium they could manufacture it for us in Sweden until we learn, if they did not have confi-dence in Swedish technology. He repeated that the difficulties in manufacturing were enormous.

Lavanchy then said that the whole world market for Roget was only 600 tons a year, that it was be-ing produced in Belgium at this level, and that it was inconceivable that Sweden alone could take 400 tons.

Gillot stopped the meeting without a solution, and said that he hoped all concerned would do more investigation of this subject. He vaguely re-ferred to the fact that he would think about it him-self and let us know when another meeting would be held.

Ekstrom returned to Stockholm and reported the meeting to his own staff and to the two Swed-ish members of his board.

They, like I, were really disgusted. Here we were operating with initiative and with excellent financial techniques. Roget management had often made talks in which they emphasized the necessity for decentralized profit responsibility, authority, and initiative on the part of foreign subsidiary presidents. One of my men told me that they seem to talk decentralization and act like tin gods at the same time.

Mr. Norgren, the Swedish banker on Thorsten's board, expressed surprise.

> I considered this carefully. It is sound business for AB Thorsten, and XL-4 will help to build one more growth company in the Swedish economy. Somehow, the management in Brussels has failed to understand this. I dictated a letter to Mr. Gillot telling him that I don't know why the project was rejected, that Roget has a right to its own reasons, but that I am prepared to resign as a director. It is not that I am angry, or that I have a right to dictate decisions for the whole worldwide Roget S.A. It is simply that, if I spend my time studying policy decisions, and those decisions do not serve the right function for the business, then it is a waste of time to continue.

Finally, Ekstrom stated, "While I certainly wouldn't bring these matters out in a meeting, I think those Belgium production and sales people simply want to build the empire and make the money in Roget Belgium. They don't care about Thorsten and Sweden. We have the ideas and initiative, and they take them and get the payoff."

Further Study

After Mr. Gillot received Norgren's letter, he contacted Messrs. Lavanchy, Gachoud, and Bols (vice president finance of Roget corporate staff). He told them that the Swedish XL-4 project had become a matter of key importance for the whole Roget Group, because of its implications for company profits and for the morale and autonomy of the subsidiary management. He asked them to study the matter and report their recommendations in one month. Meanwhile, he wrote Ek-

strom, "Various members of the corporate headquarters are studying the proposal. You will hear from me within six weeks regarding my final decision."

Report of Roget's Director of Manufacturing

A month after he was asked to study the XL-4 project, Lavanchy gave Gillot a memorandum explaining his reasons for opposing the proposal:

> At your request, I have reexamined thoroughly all of the cost figures that bear on the XL-4 proposal. I find that manufacture of this product in Sweden would be highly uneconomical, for two reasons: (1) overhead costs would be higher and (2) variable costs would be greater.
>
> As to the first, we can produce XL-4 in Belgium with less overhead cost. Suppose that Thorsten does sell 400 tons a year, so our total worldwide sales rise to 1,000 tons. We can produce the whole 1,000 tons in Belgium with essentially the same capital investment we have now. If we produce 1,000 tons, our fixed costs will decrease by Skr 120 a ton.[3] That means Skr 72,000 in savings on production for domestic and export to countries other than Sweden (600 tons a year) and Skr 120,000 for worldwide production including Sweden (1,000 tons).
>
> Second, we could save on variable costs. If we were to produce the extra 400 tons in Belgium, the total production of 1,000 tons a year would give us longer production runs, lower set-up costs, and larger raw material purchases, thus allowing mass purchasing and material handling and lower purchase prices. My accounting department has studied this and concludes that our average variable costs will decrease from Skr 950 a ton to Skr 930. This Skr 20 per ton difference means a savings of Skr 12,000 on Belgian domestic production and a savings of Skr 20,000 for total worldwide production, assuming that Sweden takes 400 tons a year.

---

[3] Total fixed cost in Belgium is the equivalent of Skr 180,000 a year. Divided by 600, this equals Skr 300 a ton. If it were spread over 1,000 tons, the average fixed cost would be Skr 180.

Taxes on these added profits are about the same in Belgium and Sweden—about 50 percent of taxable income.

In conclusion, that plant should not be built. Ekstrom is a bright young man, but he does not know the adhesives business. He would be head over heels in costly production mistakes from the very beginning. I recommend that you inform the Thorsten management that it is in the company's interest and, therefore, it is Roget's policy that he must buy from Belgium.

Report of the Vice President of Finance

The same day, Gillot received the following memorandum from Eric Bols, Roget's financial vice president:

> I am sending you herewith estimates of the working capital requirements if Roget increases its production of XL-4 in our Belgian plant from 600 to 1,000 tons a year [Exhibit 3]. Initially, we will need Skr 54,000, mostly for additional inventories. By the end of the second year, this will have increased to Skr 74,000. Incidentally, the working capital amounts shown in this exhibit are based on a Swedish law which permits businesses to deduct 60 percent of inventory costs from taxable income.
>
> I have also looked at Lavanchy's calculations for the fixed and variable manufacturing costs and am in full agreement with them.

Ekstrom's Thoughts at This Time

In an interview about this same time, Ekstrom expressed some impatience with "the way things are going. I have other projects that need developing for Thorsten, and this kind of long-range planning takes much time and energy. Also, just keeping on top of the normal operating problems of the business we already have takes up a lot of my time. Sometimes I feel like telling them to go and sell XL-4 themselves."

QUESTIONS

1. From the point of view of Roget S.A. (Thorsten's parent), is the construction of the new factory in Sweden in the best interests of the company as a whole?
2. Ignoring your answer to question 1, if the plant were not built and the product were shipped from Belgium to Sweden, what transfer price would be appropriate?
3. What are the competitive advantages of Roget S.A.? What is Roget's strategy in the industrial chemicals business? Are the management control systems designed to support this strategy?
4. How has the organization structure of Roget been changing over the last five years? Why? How does this affect your decision in the Thorsten situation?
5. What changes in the management control systems would you recommend to Gillot?

Note: This case really has three issues: a capital budgeting problem, a transfer pricing problem, and a set of management process problems, including communications between a parent and its foreign subsidiary and the role of the Swedish members of Thorsten's board of directors. You might want to consider all three issues as you prepare the case.

EXHIBIT 3 Headquarters Analysis (in Skr)

	1	2	3	4	5	6	7	8	9	10
End of Year	Plant	Working Capital	Sales Price/Ton	Variable Cost/Ton†	Contribution/ Ton (col. 3 − 4)	Number of Tons	Total Contribution (col. 5 × 6)	Promotion Costs	Taxes	Net Cash Flows (1+2+7−8−9)
0	−54,000*									−54,000
1		−10,000*	2,000	1,380	620	200	124,000	130,000	(3,000)	−13,000
2		−10,000*	1,850	1,380	470	300	141,000	75,000	33,000	23,000
3			1,850	1,380	470	400	188,000	50,000	69,000	69,000
4			1,850	1,380	470	400	188,000	50,000	69,000	69,000
5			1,850	1,380	470	400	188,000	50,000	69,000	69,000
6			1,850	1,380	470	400	188,000	50,000	69,000	69,000
7		+74,000*	1,850	1,380	470	400	188,000	50,000	69,000	143,000

* Working capital amounts are net of tax credits.

† Variable cost per ton

Manufacturing =	Skr 930
Shipping from Belgium to Sweden =	50
Swedish import duty =	400
Total variable cost =	1,380

Case 16–2
Bulova Watch Company, Inc.*

"We don't have too many control problems with our domestic operations, but we certainly have some with our overseas operations." During a conversation in the summer of 1973, John Chiappe, vice president and controller, was describing Bulova's control system. "Let me show you an example of one type of problem we are up against." The controller started to jot down some figures. "These figures are purely hypothetical and I've simplified them to get my point across, but they are indicative of what actually happens." The paper he passed across the table showed the following.

France—Fiscal 1973 (000 francs)

	Budgeted	Actual
Sales	1,000	1,000
Cost of goods sold:		
Local costs	300	290
Imported goods	300	315
Gross profit	400	395
General and administration	300	300
Operating profit	100	95

The controller started to explain.

Assume that these figures were taken from the budgeted and actual income statements for our French marketing subsidiary. I've ignored taxes as that just complicates things further. Now, we treat our marketing subs as profit centers, and we evaluate them on a local currency basis. So we'll say

that French management's profit center goal for the year was 100,000 francs. Now, picture something else. I'm sitting in Switzerland a couple of months ago with the manager of our French sub and the head of our Swiss manufacturing operations. What sort of thing goes on?

I note that France ended the year at 95 percent of its planned franc profit. Our French general manager acknowledges this, but says that it doesn't mean anything. He points out that, when the budget was put together, the 100,000 francs profit was, let's see, worth about U.S. $19,900; now the 95,000 francs profit is worth about $20,900 or 5 percent over plan. He adds, giving me the needle, that notwithstanding all our talk about being an international company, we are really interested in earning dollars.

I agree, but point out that the higher dollar figure was, from his standpoint, luck. During the year the dollar devalued against the franc, or the franc appreciated against the dollar, depending on how you want to look at it. He didn't bring about the exchange rate shift, however. Immediately he replies with his second line of argument. He points out that the French sub reached its sales target, cut its local cost of goods sold under the planned figure, and didn't overspend on its selling and administrative expenses. What hurt him, he adds, was the higher cost, in terms of French francs, of the movements he imported from our factories in Switzerland. During the year the Swiss franc appreciated against the French franc by almost 8 percent, with the result that—after the imported materials flowed through his local production process—this part of his cost of goods sold went up by 5 percent. If this exchange rate shift hadn't occurred, he

* This case was prepared by F. T. Knickerbocker, Harvard Business School.
Copyright © by the President and Fellows of Harvard College.
Harvard Business School case 374–052.

says, he would have ended the year with a profit of 110,000 French francs. Actually, he says, he was helping out our Swiss manufacturing branch.

That brings the head of Swiss production into the act. He asks how did France help them out. At the beginning of the year France had told him they needed X number of movements, and these were worth about 230,000 Swiss francs. During the year the Swiss plants shipped him exactly X number of movements and billed him exactly 230,000 Swiss francs. So, how did France help him?

Our general manager in France, who's no slouch, has already thought that one through. He points out that the 230,000 Swiss francs were worth, at the beginning of the fiscal year, U.S. $59,600. At year end, they were worth $71,000, so companywide we were $11,500 better off thanks to his efforts.

Again, I say this was an accident. During the year the Swiss franc appreciated against the dollar, even more so than the French franc, but our Swiss plants couldn't take the credit for that.

About then, our French general manager throws up his hands in exasperation. Look, he says, you started off with this business about France ending the year with profits 5 percent under plan, when you know by looking at our income statement that we outperformed the budget in every respect. Then every time I try to explain the difference from budget, you say it was an accident. All I know is that I did what I said I was going to do and that somehow we are all better off than we expected. With all the shifting going on between the dollar and the French franc and the Swiss franc, the reports don't mean much anyway. Let's talk about next year.

The controller paused for a moment.

Let's face it. I've been exaggerating and the episode I've just described never took place. However, it's typical of the sort of control problem we live with every day. And actually, when you get all the figures out, a lot more than in my simple example, matters can really get confused sometimes.

Of course, when our subsidiaries put their annual budgets together, they try, with our assistance, to predict exchange rate shifts to alleviate problems like this, but you seldom hit the changes on the button. And, of course, we can and do isolate and break out for reporting purposes the effects of ex-

change rate shifts on our subsidiaries' inventories and cost of goods sold.

Still we are trying to run the company on a profit center basis. If we constantly adjust figures or reassemble them, then commitment to profit goals becomes a joke after a while. Given the way goods in process move around within Bulova, there's no doubt that it is tough to push our operating managers for profit responsibility. Maybe there's a better way of doing things?

Bulova's controller went on to describe the highlights of the company's control system and some of the features of the company's operations that complicated the control process. His comments are summarized in the next few pages.

Manufacturing

Above all else, Bulova's control system had to take into account the rather unusual features of the company's manufacturing operations. In 1973, the company made its products in 21 plants, 12 located in the United States, 9 overseas. Though the number and size of the plants, compared to what was common in other industries, was not large, the degree to which output moved around the world and from one plant to the next was out of the ordinary. Exhibit 1 gives a rough picture of the product flows within the Bulova manufacturing system.

The description of manufacturing flows pinpointed one fact. Within Bulova, intercompany sales or purchases, or both, were frequent and important. The best example of this was the domestic company's reliance on overseas production. In the early 1970s, all of the watches sold by Bulova in the United States, about 85 percent contained movements imported from abroad. In some instances, from the time components were manufactured at a foreign site to the time finished watches were ready for sale in the United States, as many as five intercompany transactions took place.

Bulova's policy was to have all intercompany transfers billed at standard cost plus 10 percent.

EXHIBIT 1   Manufacturing Flows within Bulova for Consumer Products*

Source	Product	Destination
Swiss plants (including that of Bulova's subsidiary, Universal Geneve).	Movements and finished watches.	Bulova's 8 and Universal Geneve's 7 foreign marketing subsidiaries.
	Finished watches.	Bulova's and Universal Geneve's third-party distributors.
	Finished watches.	Bulova's Hong Kong and Tokyo distribution centers.
	Components.	Bulova's Virgin Islands and American Samoa assembly plants.
Bulova's Virgin Island plant.	Assembled movements.	Bulova's Flushing, N.Y., plant.
Bulova's American Samoa plant.	Assembled movements.	Bulova's Flushing, N.Y., plant.
Bulova's joint-venture Taiwan plant.	Watch cases.	Bulova's Flushing, N.Y., plant; Toyo Corp., Japan; and third-party customers.
Bulova's joint-venture Japan plant.	Finished tuning fork watches.	Bulova brand products: all world markets except the United States.
		Citizen brand products: Japan and other selected markets, especially the Middle East.
Citizen Watch Co., Japan (independent supplier to Bulova for 13 years).	Components, movements.	Bulova's Virgin Islands; Flushing, N.Y.; and Toronto, Canada plants.
Bulova's Flushing, N.Y., plant.	Finished tuning fork, quartz, and conventional jeweled-lever watches.	Bulova's U.S. marketing subsidiaries; Bulova's overseas marketing subsidiaries: Accuquartz watches only.
	Tuning fork movement subassemblies.	Bulova's Swiss plants during start-up phases of production.
Bulova's two U.S. watch case plants.	Cases.	Bulova's Flushing, N.Y., and Swiss plants and its marketing subsidiary in Canada.

* This list ignores manufacturing flows within Bulova for industrial defense products. With very minor exceptions, all such products were made and sold in the United States. As of 1973, industrial defense production took place in eight plants. In five of the eight, Bulova also manufactured consumer products: watch movements, cases, clocks, etc.

Exceptions to this policy were rare. Bulova operated on the basis of a standardized, worldwide cost accounting system. The standard costs for manufacturing subsidiaries were based on a full costing system, with the standards set by the production engineering department with the assistance of the cost accounting department. Management did not regard intercompany pricing as an issue that was negotiable among subunits.

A second implication of Bulova's manufacturing flows was that the company was almost always moving products across national boundaries and hence across currencies.[1] With watches, for example, in nearly 8 cases out of 10 all or a major part of the costs associated with their production were accumulated in one currency, while the revenues associated with their sale were generated in a second currency. Only four operations within Bulova did not involve a currency shift between costs and revenues; but three of the four were not, as of the early 1970s, of great importance to the firm: (1) Bulova made and sold a few watches within Switzerland, (2) it made watches in Switzerland for export, billed in Swiss francs, to third-party distributors, and (3) its joint venture made and sold watches in Japan. Of course, these three operations eventually involved a second type of cross-currency transaction when profits, upon remittance to the parent company, were converted into U.S. dollars. The one important watch activity within Bulova that did not involve cross-currency transactions was the manufacture and sale of watches in the United States. This activity generated about 25 percent of Bulova's total *domestic* consumer business by fiscal 1973.

Bulova's controller summed up the matter this way:

> Many of the large multinational firms don't face the cross-currency complexities we do. They have numerous subsidiaries that make and sell products within single countries. Thus, they are largely operating within single currencies. Only when profit remittance comes up do they face, as of course we do, the problem of converting currencies.

He added:

> Looking at the company as a whole, you might say that our income statement is made up of sales denominated in one bundle of currencies, while cost of goods sold and expenses enter the statement denominated in a second bundle of currencies. Thus, exchange rate considerations play a part in practically every control matter we handle.

---

[1] A third implication, not discussed here, was that Bulova was almost always moving products across tariff barriers.

Operations in the U.S. Virgin Islands and American Samoa

Within Bulova's manufacturing system, its movement assembly operations in the Virgin Islands and American Samoa raised special problems. Since, in unit terms, the number of movements flowing through the Virgin Islands and Samoan plants was approaching 30 percent of Bulova's annual domestic requirements, close control of these activities was obviously critical. But there were complications.

First, to gain the tariff advantages associated with production at the island sites, Bulova had to ensure that local value added exceeded 50 percent of the selling price of the assembled movements.[2] Four different sets of prices or costs were involved: (1) transfer prices for incoming components from Bulova's Swiss plants, (2) purchase prices for incoming components from Bulova's Japanese supplier, (3) locally generated costs, and (4) transfer prices for sales between the two island plants and Bulova's domestic operations.

Second, in the case of the Samoan operation, though not the Virgin Islands one, Bulova had a 10-year exemption from taxation. Naturally, the company wanted to take advantage of the exemption to the greatest extent possible.

The two island operations were profit centers, but whether it made sense at all to treat them as such represented one side of the control problem. Yet, given their importance to the whole manufacturing system, how to exert pressure on their local managers for better performance constituted the other side of the control problem.

---

[2] The U.S. tariff law stipulates that goods can be imported duty free into the United States from its insular possessions (the U.S. Virgin Islands, American Samoa, and Guam) provided that local value added exceeds 50 percent of the selling price in the islands. Bulova established a subsidiary in the Virgin Islands; six years later, it established one on American Samoa. In the case of Samoa, Bulova received the 10-year tax exemption as an investment inducement.

Swiss Manufacturing and the Foreign Marketing Subsidiaries

Other factors complicating the control process arose out of the relationships between the Swiss marketing plants and the foreign marketing subsidiaries. As of the early 1970s, about 40 percent of the output from Bulova's Swiss plants was shipped to its overseas marketing subs or to third-party customers in foreign countries. The remainder was shipped, directly or indirectly, to Bulova–United States.

The usual arrangements between Swiss manufacturing and the foreign marketing subsidiaries were as follows: The Swiss plants sold the subsidiaries on open account. That is, the intercompany billings had no stipulated repayment time. Management had adopted this practice as a means to finance, in an indirect way, the growth of the fledgling marketing subsidiaries. The billings were denominated, of course, in Swiss francs, and, as per company policy, the Swiss plants billed the subsidiaries at standard cost plus 10 percent.

Management had also decided that the foreign marketing subsidiaries should have a high degree of purchasing autonomy. The subsidiaries were required to purchase movements, either jeweled-lever or tuning fork, from Bulova's Swiss plants, but they were not obliged to accept what the plants offered in the way of finished watches. The subsidiaries could buy all the exterior components of watches from outside suppliers and finish the watches in their own local assembly facilities. Moreover, if the subsidiaries bought finished watches from the Swiss plants, they had the option of returning them to Switzerland if they did not sell in local markets. According to management, this policy was designed to ensure that market pressures worked their way back to Swiss manufacturing. As Bulova's president put it, the system guaranteed that Bulova manufactured what could be sold, rather than sold what could be manufactured. From the control standpoint, though, the policy made it a good bit more diffi-cult to measure how well the Swiss plants planned their production and managed their inventories.

Control System

During the 1960s, Bulova developed a formal annual budgeting program, and this became the key to its control system.[3] Since little about mechanics of the system was unusual, only a few of its main characteristics will be mentioned here. Foremost of these characteristics was management's attempt to use the profit center concept to the maximum extent possible.

As of 1973, Bulova was composed of 32 operating subunits, each with its own profit responsibility. Of the total number of profit centers, 22 were located outside the United States. They were:

15 marketing subsidiary profit centers.

3 manufacturing profit centers in Switzerland.

2 profit centers, one each in the Virgin islands and American Samoa.

2 joint venture profit centers, one each in Japan and Taiwan.

Each of these was a separate planning and reporting unit responsible for performance down to the profit-after-tax level.

When asked about what led management to focus heavily upon the profit center concept in Bulova's foreign subunits, the corporate controller responded that the manufacturing and foreign marketing subsidiaries were separate corporations or taxable entities. He further noted that these subunits operated under laws of countries which require that they be legally constituted and

---

[3] Most, though not all, of the budgeting and reporting system was formalized. Management did not disseminate performance goals in a formal way. Generally, line management learned about management's performance expectations in meetings conducted by Bulova's president or in conversations between individual managers and the president.

Annually	Quarterly	Monthly
Income statements. Balance sheets. Cash flow statements for the forthcoming year.	Income statements. Balance sheets. Cash flow statements; actual for last quarter and revised for the remaining quarters of the year.	Trial balances. Sales reports by product and territory. Statements of intercompany cash remittances.

taxable therein. There was no way, he said, that they could exist except as separate profit centers.

At home, 11 of Bulova's 12 manufacturing plants were organized into four profit centers, each responsible for performance down to the profit-before-tax level.[4] On the marketing side, the company was organized into six product divisions, each held for performance down to the operating profit level. General administrative expenses were allocated to both the manufacturing operations and the product divisions. Only general corporate expenses (e.g., interest expense) were not charged to the domestic profit centers.

The budgeting and reporting procedures followed by the domestic operations were fairly routine, and, because the profit centers were near at hand, headquarters management could easily get supplementary facts or explanations whenever needed. The flow of information from overseas was somewhat less detailed and frequent. The foreign marketing subsidiaries prepared and forwarded to New York these reports.

On an annual and quarterly basis, the three Swiss-based manufacturing profit centers submitted to New York the same reports as those sent in by the marketing subsidiaries.[5] On a monthly basis they submitted reports, beyond those listed above, on shipments, sales by product and destination, and intercompany payables and receivables. Among other things, this reporting system made it possible to centralize cash flow management in New York.

As regards data on the manufacturing costs of the Swiss plants, headquarters received a complete report only once a year. Bulova's controller stated that headquarters did not get into the detail of manufacturing costs, but rather left that up to the managers of the three profit centers in Switzerland. He explained that the real mechanism by which headquarters controlled manufacturing costs in Switzerland was through exerting competitive pressures on the Swiss plants. That is, headquarters kept the Swiss plants well informed of the intercompany prices the domestic company could afford to pay for movements. These prices were derived from predicted competitors' retail prices in the United States. As Bulova's controller put it:

> Our Swiss plants know a year or so in advance what sort of manufacturing costs they will have to meet for movements if we are to stay competitive in the U.S. marketplace. They are expected to meet

---

[4] In those domestic plants where joint production of consumer products and industrial defense products took place, overhead, general expenses, etc., were allocated to the various product lines on the basis of direct labor costs. One Bulova plant was run on a fee basis for the U.S. government.

[5] On an annual basis, all manufacturing profit centers, domestic and foreign, also submitted capital expenditure budgets, which went to the board of directors for approval. How changes from budget were handled differed depending on whether the changes arose in foreign or domestic profit centers. Overseas units were permitted to modify the composition of their capital budgets so long as they stayed within their total approved limits. All changes taking them beyond their approved limits had to be forwarded to New York for review. In the case of domestic units, any change from budget had to be forwarded to headquarters for review.

EXHIBIT 2   Estimated Manufacturing and Distribution Costs for a Quality Jeweled-Lever Watch

U.S. jeweler's selling price		$100.00
U.S. jeweler's markup		50.00
Manufacturer's selling price		50.00
Manufacturer's markup		18.75
Manufacturer's assembled cost		31.25
Materials and labor cost for adding, in the United States, the case, dial, bracelet, and packaging		15.00
		16.25
Manufacturer's landed cost of movement:		
Duty	$ 2.70	
Transportation and insurance	0.10	2.80
Manufacturer's movement cost f.o.b. Switzerland		13.45
Manufacturing markup		2.50
Total movement cost, of which:		
Direct labor	4.10	
Indirect labor and overhead	5.75	
Materials	1.10	
	10.95	

Notes: The assumed watch is a 17-jewel watch, containing a Swiss-made automatic movement, with a day and date display and a stainless steel case and bracelet.

The figures are not actual data taken from any one firm. Rather, they indicate what might be regarded as industry-typical numbers starting from an assumed jeweler's U.S. selling price of $100.

---

these targets. How they do it is the job of the managers in Switzerland.

By and large, the various other overseas manufacturing operations within Bulova, the plants in the Virgin Islands and Samoa, the Japanese and Taiwanese joint ventures, followed the same budgeting and reporting procedures, though the joint ventures did submit monthly income statements, balance sheets, and so on.

Since all information and documentation flowed to New York, the overall picture was one of a highly centralized control system. In effect, no layers of management intervened between the field profit centers and headquarters.

Bulova did not have a long-range budgeting system. Domestic and foreign profit centers bud-geted only for the forthcoming fiscal year; and, as the budget year progressed, they revised their plans only to the end of the current fiscal year. Yet, separate from the control system, Bulova carried out a type of long-range planning.

Business Plans

Each year, the managers of all profit centers submitted directly to Bulova's president a business plan that extended beyond the next fiscal year. Usually, these covered two years though some, upon the request of the president, carried planning five years forward. Year 1 of the business plans matched each subunit's budget for the next fiscal year. Years 2 and on of the business plans presented, largely in narrative form, the goals and programs of the profit centers. More often than not, the plans concentrated on marketing objectives, such as growth goals, and on market share goals. Executives in Bulova described these reports as personal plans of the profit centers managers, and they were viewed as private interchanges between these managers and Bulova's president.

Measurement and Rewards

Though Bulova was organized, for control purposes, around profit centers, the performance criteria that operating managers seemed to follow most closely were gross margins and the levels of inventories and receivables. Still, top management kept a careful eye on the bottom line.[6] When asked if the profit center system had any teeth in it, the controller observed, "Those managers who haven't been able to meet their profit goals haven't stayed around in the company very long. I can think of three or four instances of this in the last few years."

Complicating this picture, however, was the nature of the company's reward system for its managers. In the mid-1960s, Bulova's management had instituted a version of management by

---

[6] Top management, naturally, also measured progress against return on investment; but, given the nature of the company's operations, managers under the top echelon seemed to give little attention to the ROI criterion. Rather, they focused more on managing current assets, largely by applying certain rules of thumb to determine acceptable levels of receivables and inventories.

objectives. Individual managers, in consultation with Bulova's president, set specific goals for the forthcoming year or two (e.g., share of market for a new watch line). Attainment of these goals was factored into the performance review of each manager. However, there was more to the reward system than this. As a general policy, therefore, all the more important line and staff managers of the company, domestic and foreign, were rewarded on the basis of the company's overall performance. According to Bulova's president, the nature of the company's operations precluded any other sort of reward system.

The Question

Bulova's controller summed up his comments:

We think our control system, and our commitment to profit centers, makes good sense. Yet, for a number of reasons, I think our control problems are tougher than a lot of firms face. For one thing, we are not only a highly integrated company but also we are a highly international company.

Sure, so are all the oil companies, some of the other mineral companies, some of the metal companies, so why should our control problems be special? I'll tell you. First, we're in the fashion business, so we are constantly facing market instability. And second, our entire industry is a drop in the bucket compared to these other industries. We simply don't have the resources for elaborate administrative systems.

I suppose what bothers me is that we have pushed the profit center concept pretty far in our company. Maybe too far? I'd love to have somebody take a good look at us and suggest alternative ways of controlling the company. Got any ideas?

QUESTIONS

1. What is a profit center system?
2. What is a profit center system supposed to accomplish that functional control systems do not?
3. In Bulova Watch, what are the critical determinants of profitability?

4. To what extent do the marketing subsidiaries control the profit determinants?
5. To what extent do the manufacturing profit centers control the determinants of profits?
6. What are the potential dysfunctional side effects from this system? In what ways, if any, would the system encourage decisions contrary to the interests of the company?

Case 16–3
SKA, Ltd.*

In July 1983, the management of SKA, Ltd., were considering how to reply to a proposal, received from their parent company, to implement a system of measuring the amount of resources either contributed or used by each business area and product throughout the world.

SKA, Ltd., was a wholly owned Australian subsidiary of Svenska Kemisk Akiebolag (hereafter called SKA–Sweden). SKA–Sweden was a large multinational manufacturer of chemicals and related products with headquarters based in Uppsala, a city in the southeast part of Sweden. SKA, Ltd., located in Newtown, Australia, manufactured fertilizers and related chemical products, which were sold in Australia, New Zealand, and other countries in the Far East.

Products and Organization

SKA, Ltd., was divided into three business areas as follows:

1. Agricultural products.
2. Industrial products.
3. Services (e.g., power, water, and steam).

Each of the business areas had its own plants and its own marketing organization. Most of the SKA, Ltd., production facilities were located in a large industrial complex in Newton, although three other smaller plants were located in southeastern Australia. The corporate staffs and the central research department also were located in Newtown.

Each business area was a profit center. Except for marketing, almost all managers had a dual reporting responsibility. For example, all plant managers reported to the production management at the staff level on a functional basis and to the business area manager on a line basis. A similar dual relationship existed for accounting, personnel, research, industrial engineering, and so forth. A unique feature of the organization was that many managers held two positions. For example, the production manager was also the general manager of the fertilizer business area.

Cost Accounting

SKA, Ltd., used a process cost accounting system. Costs were accumulated by each production department and transferred to subsequent departments as the product was transferred. Thus, at all points in the production process, all costs incurred in the manufacture of a product to that point had been charged to it.

Dual Systems

SKA, Ltd., maintained two parallel systems. One system collected the actual costs incurred by each department and transferred these costs to subsequent departments; this was called the "roll-through system." A second system transferred certain intermediate products at a transfer price; this was called the "transfer-price" system. The products transferred at a price were independent products (e.g., ammonia and nitric

* This case was prepared by John Dearden, Harvard Business School.
Copyright © by the President and Fellows of Harvard College.
Harvard Business School case 181–063.

acid) that were normally traded in the market. The market price determined the transfer price.

A dual system was maintained because the management of SKA, Ltd., exercised two types of control. First, control over products was exercised through a system of product profitability analysis. The roll-through was used for product control. Second, operating control was exercised through a profit budget. The transfer price system was used for operating control.

Standards

Standard costs were set for all products. As explained above, however, products were transferred through the system at actual costs, contrary to many standard cost systems. Standard costs were calculated for the products produced—and then the total standard costs were compared to the actual costs incurred *outside* of the books of account. Inventories, however, were maintained at standard costs.

Product Profitability Analysis

Annually, and sometimes twice a year, the profitability of all product groups was analyzed. A unique feature of this analysis was that it was made on the basis of both historical and inflation adjusted costs (called "current costs" hereafter). Management relied principally on current costs in making product decisions.

Calculating Current Costs

Current costs were calculated by adjusting fixed assets and inventories for the effect of inflation. These adjustments are explained in this part of the case.

Fixed assets. The construction index for the chemical industry was the basic means for adjusting fixed assets for the effect of inflation. However, this was modified for the following circumstances.

1. An independent estimate of replacement cost of each facility was made by the plant engi-neering department. Where this estimate differed by more than 15 percent from the index adjusted amount, further study was made and the discrepancy resolved.
2. Specific information was used where available. For example, where major new plants have been recently completed, the existing plants were valued on this basis and adjusted for differences in capacity, if appropriate.
3. Where excess capacity existed, only the replacement cost of the capacity being used was included.
4. Antipollution and environmental improvements were excluded in the replacement cost estimate where these were not part of the existing facilities. (This was a rule laid down by Uppsala.)

Two other points on the fixed-asset replacement cost calculations were of importance.

1. In the interests of simplicity, it was decided to do the following:
   a. Replacement costs were calculated on a "site" basis only. For example, calculations would not assume a different plant in a different place or a leased plant instead of a purchased plant. In short, replacement costs assumed the same facilities in the same location.
   b. Adjustments were not made for greater efficiency, more advantageous location, or any other technological change, except for capacity.
2. Current costs reflected the best estimates of the expected lives of the assets. This was important because, in some instances, the historical accounting lives of fixed assets were shorter than the expected lives, partly to offset the effects of inflation.

Inventories. Inventories were valued at standard costs, which approximated the current (replacement) cost of the inventories. Standard costs were changed *each quarter* to reflect expected changes in price levels. (The technique for setting quarterly standard costs is explained later in the case.)

Return on Capital (ROC)

The final result of the profit profitability analysis was a rate of return on capital. This was calculated by business area, product line, and individual products. All analyses were on a companywide consolidated basis and were calculated for both historical costs and current costs.

Revenues. The revenues were those actually realized from the sale of the product to outside customers. (Also included were some sales to other subsidiaries of SKA–Sweden.)

Costs. All costs incurred by the SKA, Ltd., including a corporate assessment from Uppsala, were assigned to business segments, except income taxes.

Capital. Investment was equal to the working capital plus fixed assets at gross value. Inventories and fixed assets were included at both historical costs and replacement value.

Use of Product Profitability Analysis

The profitability of business areas and product lines were reviewed periodically by the top management of SKA–Sweden and SKA, Ltd., as well as by all of the managers responsible for individual segment profitability. These analyses had four principal uses.

First, they were used as a guide in setting selling prices. (The prices of all basic products were reviewed and approved by the top management of SKA, Ltd.)

Second, they acted as a discipline to the marketing organization to keep prices in line with inflation.

Third, they were used to identify products that were not earning a sufficient profit.

Fourth, they were used in the analysis of budget proposals. For example, if the ROC was declining, an analysis was made to determine which business areas and products were contributing to this decline and why.

Budgeting

SKA, Ltd., presented an annual profit budget to top management in Uppsala, Sweden, for review and approval. Monthly reports—showing actual results compared to budget, analysis of variances, and explanation of significant deviations from budget—were submitted monthly to Uppsala.

Within SKA, Ltd., budgets were also used for the day-to-day control of operations. (The transfer price system was used for budgeting.) Each of the business areas prepared a profit budget, which was reviewed and approved by the company management. Staff offices and the research department prepared expense budgets, which were similarly reviewed and approved. Monthly, actual results were compared to budget and deviations analyzed and explained.

Current Costs

A unique feature of the SKA, Ltd., budgeting system was that it took into account the amount of inflation expected during the year. Revenues and nonmanufacturing costs were calendarized by month. Standard costs were projected for each quarter. Thus, four sets of standard costs were incorporated in the budget, and new standard costs were introduced at the beginning of each quarter.

In setting these quarterly standards, the following techniques were used:

1. Estimated average prices were used for commodities in which prices fluctuated randomly throughout the year.
2. Where materials were purchased by contract, an estimate of the new price was phased in at the appropriate time.
3. Other material prices were forecast as follows:
   a. The prices of all major material were estimated individually.
   b. The prices of nonmajor material items was adjusted for the forecast of the wholesale price index.

4. Direct labor was based on the expected changes in the labor contracts.
5. Important overhead costs, such as maintenance, supplies, and power, were forecast individually.

The Proposal from Uppsala

The top management of SKA–Sweden was concerned with identifying business and products worldwide that were not contributing sufficient cash to enable the company to realize its strategic plans. A study was undertaken by the corporate director of finance to develop a method for systematically identifying such business segments.

A task force, assigned to this project, developed an objective rate of return on capital. Any subsidiary, business area, or product earning less than this return was considered not to be generating its share of the cash required for SKA, worldwide, to accomplish its strategic plans. This part of the case describes how this objective rate of return was developed.

Step 1, the task force prepared a forecast of the amount of cash that must be generated from operations on a worldwide basis if SKA was to have enough financial resources to accomplish its strategic plan.

timates.) This amount was subtracted from the amount calculated in Step 1 above.

Step 3, the amount of income taxes expected to be paid worldwide was calculated and *added* to the amount calculated in Step 2. Steps 2 and 3, therefore, translated the required cash flow into operating profits before taxes. In other words, if all operations earned a total profit before taxes equal to the amount calculated in Step 3, the net cash flow would equal the amount estimated in Step 1.

Step 4, the total capital (working capital and gross fixed assets on a current cost basis) that would be employed by all operating units worldwide was calculated.

Step 5, the amount calculated in Step 3 was divided by the amount calculated in Step 4. This was the objective rate of return that all business segments must earn if they were to contribute their shares to the cash requirements of the company.

It was reasoned, therefore, that any business or product not earning this return was a cash drain, and that the amount of this drain was equal to the capital employed multiplied by the difference between the actual or projected rate of return and the objective. A hypothetical calculation is as follows assuming an objective of 10 percent.

Product A—Thousands of Australian Dollars

	Actual			Projected		
	1980	1981	1982	1983	1984	1985
Profit before taxes	100	90	80	90	100	110
Capital	1,500	1,600	1,800	1,700	1,600	1,500
Rate of return	6.7%	5.6%	4.7%	5.3%	6.3%	7.3%
Excess / (deficiency):						
Percent	(3.3%)	(4.4%)	(5.3%)	(4.7%)	(3.7%)	(2.7%)
Amount	(49.5)	(70.4)	(95.4)	(79.9)	(59.2)	(40.5)

Step 2, the total noncash expenses (principally depreciation) that would be generated worldwide from all operations were estimated. (These noncash expenses were based on the *current cost* es-

Uppsala proposed that, worldwide, all business segments be evaluated in terms of this objective rate of return, and that excesses or deficiencies represent cash contribution or drain. Segments that were creating a cash drain were to be carefully evaluated to see if the situation could be corrected. If not, there should be valid reasons why the business segment should not be dropped or, at least, curtailed.

SKA, Ltd., Analysis

The finance director of SKA, Ltd., was puzzled by the proposal from the Uppsala task force. SKA, Ltd., had been remitting significant amounts of cash to the parent company consistently over the past several years. Yet, on the basis of the standard criteria, most products of SKA, Ltd., were cash drains and the subsidiary, as a whole, was a significant net cash user. On further reflection and analysis, the finance director determined that four conditions caused this inconsistency:

First, the formula did not take into account capital grants or rapid depreciation. In the part of Australia where SKA, Ltd., was located, it was possible to obtain a 25 percent grant on most investments and to write off the entire investment for tax purposes in the first year. Thus, an investment of A\$1,000,000 would include a cash outlay of only A\$250,000 (1,000,000 − 500,000 tax savings − 250,000 capital grant).

Second, effective income tax rates differed widely among countries. This was not so much because statutory rates were different but because some countries were more liberal in allowable deduction than others. The finance director believed that Australia had one of the lowest effective tax rates.

Third, the rate of growth differed widely among business segments. The higher the growth rate of a subsidiary or product, the more cash would be required. The Australian company, with its lower growth rate, was subsidizing higher growth segments of the company.

Finally, the proportion of working capital to total capital varied widely among subsidiaries, business areas, and products within business area. Working capital required a constant investment; whereas the actual investment in fixed assets declined over time, because depreciation represented a partial return of the original investment. SKA, Ltd., being heavily capital intensive, would have a lower real investment than a subsidiary with the same total amount of capital that included a larger percentage of working capital.

QUESTIONS

1. Evaluate the product profitability and budgetary control systems of SKA, Ltd. In particular, how do you evaluate their current cost procedures, both in principle and execution? How would you change them—if at all?
2. Evaluate the proposal of the Uppsala task force:
   a. Do you agree with their general method for identifying cash contributors and users?
   b. If you disagree, how would you identify cash contributors and user?
   c. To what extent would you take into account the points raised by the finance director of SKA, Ltd.?

(Remember, the objective is to develop standard criteria that can be applied world-wide to any subsidiary, business area, or product.)

Case 16-4

American Can Company*

Ed Fitzgerald, senior vice president of the Business Investment Group, was studying the revised U.K. Gamma project proposal submitted by American Can (U.K.), Ltd. The original proposal had been submitted a year earlier, but it had raised so many questions at corporate headquarters that it had been withdrawn.

American Can Company

In 1984, American Can had revenues of $4.2 billion, and it ranked 124th in the 1984 Fortune 500. The company got its start making food containers; its Packaging Sector provided laminated tubes, metal cans, and plastic bottles and bags to many well-known companies. In 1984, it had assets of $785 million and revenues of $1.9 billion. The other two sectors were Financial Services, which although only four years old, had revenues of $1 billion; and Specialty Retailing, started in 1978, which had revenues of $995 million. Corporate headquarters were located in Greenwich, Connecticut.

In recent years, the Packaging Sector had been streamlined and repositioned to place greater emphasis on productivity, technology, marketing capabilities, and customer relationships. The U.S. Metal Packaging business unit developed and produced very thin beverage cans without lead-soldered seams; this prompted several food processing companies to discontinue self-manufacture and buy American Can's containers. The Tubes and Bottles business unit became a market leader by discovering and developing a revolutionary packaging process that produced Gamma bottles.

The International Division of the Packaging Sector manufactured metal food and beverage containers outside the United States. However, in 1984, American Can began deemphasizing international investments with the divestiture of its Canadian manufacturing operation.

The Strategic Planning Department

The current corporate structure had evolved in response to problems in the late 1970s and early 1980s. These problems included overcapacity in container manufacturing facilities, decreasing profits, and increasing demands by existing business units to grow and develop new products.

The chairman and CEO, William Woodside, addressed these concerns in two ways.

First, he and his staff divested about 25 capital-intensive operations for approximately $900 million and used this money to finance key acquisitions with strong competitive market positions, specialty market niches, lower fixed-capital requirements, and information-based marketing and distribution channels. The Financial Services Sector was created to concentrate on low-fixed-capital businesses and expand into high-growth areas.

Second, he reduced staff at headquarters and formed a new organizational structure (Exhibit 1). The Office of the Chairman was created. The Strategic Planning Department—comprised of

---

* This case is abridged with permission from Harvard Business School case 187–013.

The case was prepared by Karen E. Hansen under the supervision of Assistant Professor Julie H. Hertenstein. Some of the data have been disguised.

Corporate Planning and Development and Business Investment, with the intention of linking investment decisions to corporate strategy—reported to the Office of the Chairman. Corporate Planning and Development was responsible for reviewing business unit long-range plans and consolidating them into a single corporate strategy. The Business Investment Group was responsible for reviewing fixed-capital and other investment proposals greater than $500,000 and for making recommendations to the sector executive, to the Business Investment Committee (chaired by Gerald Tsai, Jr.), or to the board of directors. A business investment was defined as:

> any large, discrete expenditure to make a business larger, more efficient, different in product composition, or longer in life expectancy; any investment of funds whether accounted for on the balance sheet (such as investments in plant and equipment, working capital, or other items); or on the income statement (such as major outlays for special advertising, research, new product development, geographic expansion, or other forms of expense). . . . The benefits of business investment almost always last longer than a year, and the decision to make an investment is recognized within a business unit as being outside daily operations.

After forming the new structure, top management gave business units greater independence to exercise their judgment about markets in which they operated; sector executives were accountable for the profitability of their sectors. American Can experienced substantial increases in profits and in earnings per share in 1983 and 1984.

Corporate Planning and Development Group

The Corporate Planning and Development group was responsible for helping the business units develop long-range plans. This lengthy process began after the January meeting of the Executive Committee with the three sector heads, in which overall corporate direction was set for five years.

From January through June, Chuck Dornbush, vice president of corporate planning and develop-

ment, and his staff worked closely with business units to encourage managers to think strategically and to relate expenditures to long-range plans.

Business units included financial estimates in their long-range plans; but managers weren't held to specific dollar amounts until they submitted operating budgets in the fall. At American Can, these operating budgets included the business investment budgets.

Business units submitted long-range plans in late spring to Corporate Planning and Development for review and consolidation into one corporate strategic plan. Dornbush and his staff, along with senior vice president of strategic planning Bob Abramson, reviewed the plan with the Executive Committee in a series of meetings in early summer, which were attended by all three sector managers. After these meetings, the Executive Committee often had questions for business unit managers. If the Executive Committee decided that the business unit had been thorough in its analysis, it approved the plan as written; otherwise, the Executive Committee amended parts of the plan before approving it. The planning process was completed when the Executive Committee sent letters to the business units indicating that their plans were approved as submitted, or approved with indicated exceptions. The Business Investment Committee received copies of these plans so it could anticipate project proposals and the need for corporate funds.

Business units then prepared budgets. Near the end of the year, the board of directors reviewed the corporation's detailed strategic plan and the following year's budget. Once the board gave approval, business units began to submit investment project proposals to the Business Investment Group for funding by the corporation.

Marshall Sosne, of Corporate Planning and Development, added:

> However, a business unit's specific proposal might ultimately be turned down even though its long-range plan, which included that project, was approved earlier. This happened when company earnings were lower than expected and there was a

EXHIBIT 1   Organization Chart

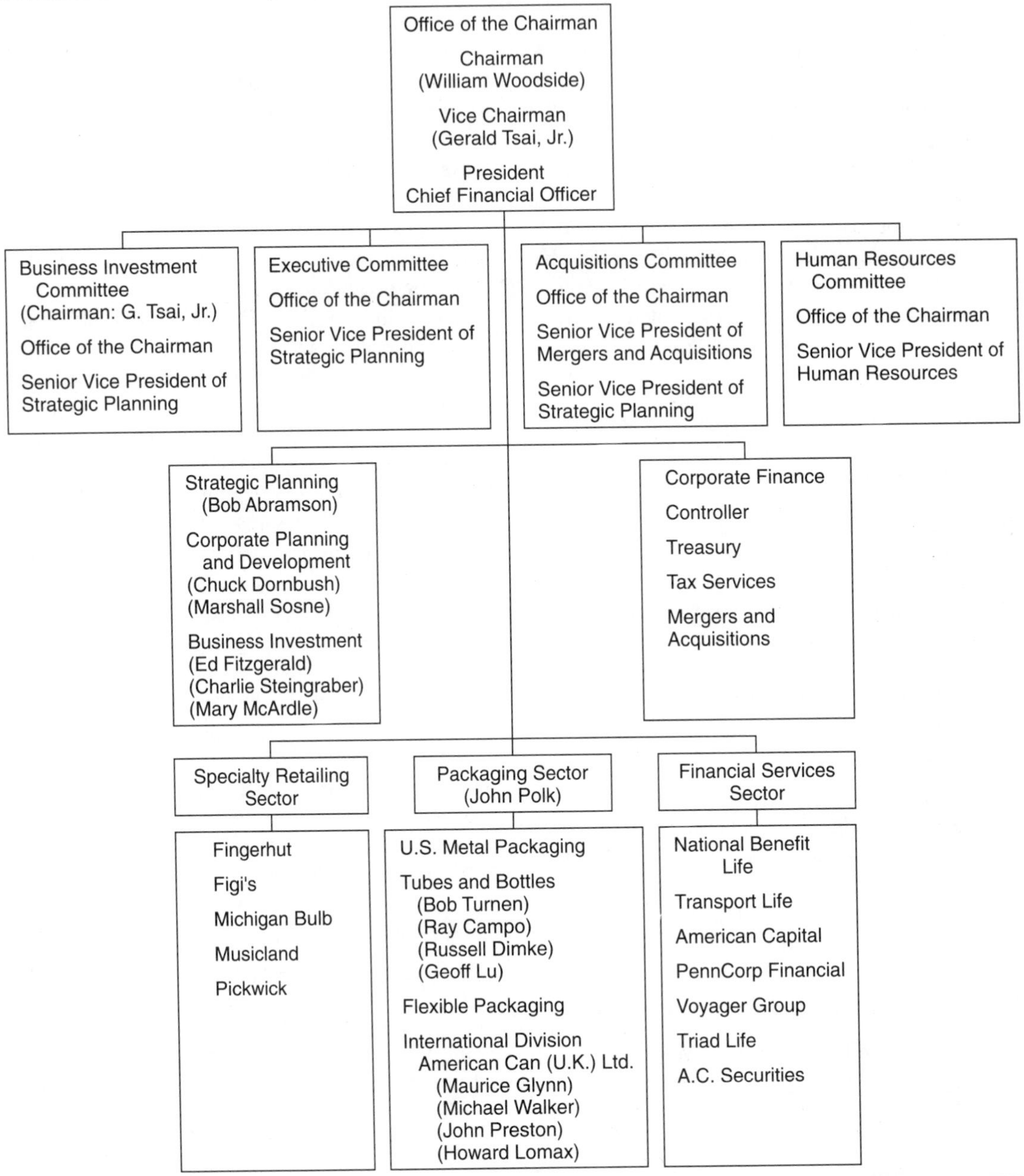

```
                        ┌─────────────────────────┐
                        │   Office of the Chairman │
                        │                          │
                        │        Chairman          │
                        │   (William Woodside)     │
                        │                          │
                        │      Vice Chairman       │
                        │   (Gerald Tsai, Jr.)     │
                        │                          │
                        │        President         │
                        │ Chief Financial Officer  │
                        └─────────────────────────┘
```

Business Investment Committee (Chairman: G. Tsai, Jr.)	Executive Committee	Acquisitions Committee	Human Resources Committee
Office of the Chairman	Office of the Chairman	Office of the Chairman	Office of the Chairman
Senior Vice President of Strategic Planning	Senior Vice President of Strategic Planning	Senior Vice President of Mergers and Acquisitions	Senior Vice President of Human Resources
		Senior Vice President of Strategic Planning	

Strategic Planning
(Bob Abramson)

Corporate Planning and Development
(Chuck Dornbush)
(Marshall Sosne)

Business Investment
(Ed Fitzgerald)
(Charlie Steingraber)
(Mary McArdle)

Corporate Finance

Controller

Treasury

Tax Services

Mergers and Acquisitions

Specialty Retailing Sector	Packaging Sector (John Polk)	Financial Services Sector
Fingerhut	U.S. Metal Packaging	National Benefit Life
Figi's	Tubes and Bottles (Bob Turnen) (Ray Campo) (Russell Dimke) (Geoff Lu)	Transport Life
Michigan Bulb	Flexible Packaging	American Capital
Musicland	International Division American Can (U.K.) Ltd. (Maurice Glynn) (Michael Walker) (John Preston) (Howard Lomax)	PennCorp Financial
Pickwick		Voyager Group
		Triad Life
		A.C. Securities

shortage of funds for new projects. Or, Business Investment received a project proposal that just doesn't make a good enough case for going ahead with an investment even though it seemed appropriate earlier, before specific details were developed.

Business Investment Group

Ed Fitzgerald had been vice president of business investment since early 1984. Reporting to him were Charlie Steingraber, director of Business Investment, and Mary McArdle, manager of Business Investment. Fitzgerald and his staff reviewed business unit proposals and either recommended their approval to the sector executive or Business Investment Committee or suggested to the business unit that it withdraw its request. The Business Investment Group did not have authority to turn down proposals; its role was to review, question, and recommend. The business unit had the right to take its proposal all the way to the Business Investment Committee, despite objections by the Business Investment Group. Of 116 proposals submitted in 1984, only 13 were not forwarded to the Business Investment Committee.

Fitzgerald said that, in 1985, he expected that he and his staff would review around 100 requests for approximately $450 million; he thought that about the same proportion of projects would be withdrawn without being sent to the Business Investment Committee as in 1984.

Often, the process of requesting resources began as an informal dialog between Fitzgerald and the project sponsor, who would later submit the written proposal. This discussion saved time because Fitzgerald occasionally advised project sponsors to minimize paperwork when a proposal would clearly be recommended to the Business Investment Committee. Fitzgerald commented that he could act as a consultant, offering advice which would either improve the proposal or redirect it to improve chances of success:

It's easier for business unit managers located here in Greenwich to take advantage of my knowledge and opinions because they only have to walk upstairs to my office to get feedback. But I am available for telephone consultation, and I'll often visit business units if I think it's warranted.

For example, between the submission of the initial and revised U.K. Gamma proposals, Fitzgerald had several telephone conversations with the business unit's project advocates and with Packaging Sector executives. Later, he traveled to England to work out some problems and get answers to questions about the initial proposal.

Business units submitted proposals throughout the year. When business unit managers sent in a proposal, they were eager to get started on the project. Fitzgerald was sympathetic to this and tried to instill in his staff a sense of urgency in reviewing these requests. Fitzgerald explained his rationale:

One of the first steps I took was to try to change the perception of the Business Investment Group. I wanted business units to believe that we have the same sense of urgency about their projects that they do, so I developed a timetable in which we guarantee initial Business Investment Group turnaround on proposals within three to five days. The whole approval process, including soliciting opinions and presenting the proposal to the Business Investment Committee or to the board, might take as little as four weeks or up to eight weeks. Once, in an emergency, it only took us two days to get approval for $10 million!

The best proposals are often relatively short and usually include sections on issues, benefits, risks, rationale for the investment, and a discussion of alternatives. Each business unit has an investment policy manual with guidelines and sample forms. We only require two pages, though: a detailed cash flow schedule and an appropriation request form showing the amount requested with signatures of the business unit general manager and others who will be involved in a project's implementation, such as marketing, manufacturing, sales, and financial managers.

Within one day of receiving a proposal, Charlie, Mary, and I meet to discuss it; we cover strategic implications, market and customer analyses, manufacturing projections, financial data, and human resource needs. Even if the proposal offers thorough analyses of each of these areas, we almost always have questions which challenge business unit assumptions. We're not just trying to find mistakes. Mary, Charlie, and I want to make sure that the proposal truly represents the value of the investment that American Can is being asked to make. American Can doesn't have an official hurdle rate, but we do look for an incremental after-tax IRR of 25 percent. If the Business Investment Committee sees a lot of proposals that meet or exceed 25 percent, then it can be picky about approving projects which don't meet that IRR. The committee actually approves dozens with lower IRRs; new factories, for example, are hard-pressed to meet that 25 percent.

My staff and I ask project sponsors questions, like "Are your markets stable?" or "Can you guarantee your customers' orders for your product?" or "What will your competition do when you build that new plant?" We refer to these types of questions as *deal-breaker questions;* key questions about customers and competition that could make or break a proposal. Deal-breakers are concerned with consequences of not investing in a project, too. We might also ask if a business unit could scale down its project and get by with $1.0 million instead of $1.5 million.

In the initial meeting of the Business Investment Group, either Fitzgerald, Steingraber, or McArdle was appointed business investment project manager and was thereafter responsible for obtaining answers to deal-breaker questions.

Two days or so after this first Business Investment Group meeting, the business investment project manager put deal-breaker questions in writing and sent them to the business unit project sponsor, who was asked to respond in writing. In addition, the business investment project manager sent memos to other appropriate corporate staff members asking for their opinions of the project; this helped assure a project's completeness, accuracy, and chance of success. Contributors were asked to send their written evaluations and comments within two weeks.

Fitzgerald commented: "This input is critical. We're trying to insure that we've not only looked at all relevant alternatives, but that we're gaining sponsors with expertise from many levels in the organization."

Most of the time, answers to deal-breaker questions, combined with staff experts' input, alleviated concerns about a project. Fitzgerald then took the final steps of advocating the project's approval to the Business Investment Committee or to the board depending on dollar amount.

Bob Abramson, senior vice president of strategic planning, was a member of the Business Investment Committee. He commented on American Can's investment process and why both the Business Investment Group and Corporate Planning reported to the head of Strategic Planning:

> Prior to our organizational changes, a capital coordination group evaluated requests for large capital expenditures, but it was not an integral part of the strategic planning process. Both the manager of Capital Coordination and the manager of Strategic Planning reported to the chief financial officer. When we decided these two functions really shouldn't be independent of one another, we created a structure that would encourage interaction between them.
>
> A company uses capital to change its competitive position; this is why we link business investments so tightly to strategic planning. American Can is interested in lower fixed capital projects in growth businesses.

To illustrate American Can's investment process, Ed Fitzgerald discussed two proposals for facilities to manufacture Gamma plastic containers.

Ohio Gamma Proposal

Gamma plastic, an American Can invention introduced in 1983, was a high-barrier and oxygen-impermeable plastic, which first enabled such foods as ketchup or marmalade to be packaged in plastic containers without spoilage or color changes. The firm manufactured it in a Batavia,

Illinois, plant, which also housed production lines for other types of containers. Gamma containers could not be manufactured on the same lines as other bottles or cans; the Gamma production process required dedicated production lines with special blow-molding machinery. When Gamma demand grew faster than expected and the Batavia plant was unable to meet it, the Tubes and Bottles business unit submitted its proposal for additional Gamma lines and a facility to house them. Geoff Lu, director of plastic bottle marketing for Tubes and Bottles and the project sponsor, sent Ed Fitzgerald an 81-page proposal explaining why the expense was necessary and how requested funds would be spent. Exhibit 2 shows Executive Highlights from the proposal.

The Business Investment group members read the entire Ohio Gamma proposal and met the following day to review it. Although the discussion was positive, they had questions they wanted answered before they sent the proposal to other corporate staff members for comments. Charlie Steingraber, Business Investment project manager for the Ohio Gamma proposal, asked these questions in memos to Tubes and Bottles executives best qualified to answer them.

When responses were received, the Business Investment group met again to review the additional information. The members agreed that the responses addressed their initial concerns and that Steingraber could proceed to solicit opinions from people outside Tubes and Bottles. He sent memos to six people.

All individuals queried responded, saying that they supported building the new plant in Bellevue, Ohio. Because all responses were positive, the three did not meet again. Fitzgerald sent members of the Business Investment Committee letters indicating that he would advocate approving the proposal at the committee's next meeting. The Business Investment Committee approved the Ohio Gamma proposal on July 30, 1985, after hearing Fitzgerald's presentation.

U.K. Gamma Proposal

Despite the difficulties faced by their earlier Gamma proposal, American Can (U.K.), Ltd., believed strongly in the need for a Gamma facility and submitted a revised proposal. This proposal from John Preston, director of marketing and the project's new sponsor, lacked financial information. However, Fitzgerald knew from his U.K. visit a few months earlier that Preston; Michael Walker, business development manager and the project's initial sponsor; and Howard Lomax, director of finance and planning, planned to revise their proposal downward to $3.3 million from the original $6.07 million for a facility and lines to manufacture Gamma plastic containers.

Fitzgerald commented on the original U.K. Gamma proposal (see Exhibit 3 for highlights):

> The major problems with the initial proposal stemmed from the optimism of projections. Mary, Charlie, and I weren't sure of the sauce market or that major food packaging customers would sign exclusive contracts with American Can (U.K.), Ltd. I was Business Investment project manager for this proposal and I wrote Michael Walker, project sponsor, and asked our deal-breaker questions about the United Kingdom's customer base, market tests that they had relied on for projections, alternatives that they had considered with regard to plant locations, timing of government support, accuracy of financial data, and strategic fit.

Walker responded in a series of telephone calls and memos in which he addressed the option of building a one-line plant (approximate savings of $2.8 million), offered a lengthy comparison of licensing to third parties and direct U.K. investment, and calculated the impact of termination costs (negligible). Walker's responses didn't alleviate the Business Investment group's concerns, but Fitzgerald went ahead and solicited opinions from other people, including Chuck Dornbush, vice president of corporate planning and development. In Dornbush's two-page response, he commented that, although Gamma plastic manufacturing had been included in the U.K.'s long-range plan, it had never received clear corporate direction or attention. He thought the Gamma opportunity in the United Kingdom was small, but that the business could be a specialty niche business. Further, there would probably be pressure from Metal Box, the major competitor, but it would be minor compared to price pressure from the United Kingdom's customers who were not willing to pay the required premium for this new squeezable, light-weight package. Dornbush questioned the long-term strategy for Gamma plastic in the United Kingdom, and wondered about the impact this new product would have on the United Kingdom's other business activities. He concluded that he thought Gamma still might be a good investment if customer, technical, and financial details could be worked through appropriately.

Fitzgerald also queried Bob Turnen, vice president and general manager of Tubes and Bottles, for advice from the perspective of the United States market. Turnen responded that United Kingdom marketing studies were similar to those done in the United States; although they indicated strong preference for plastic over glass, they revealed that U.K. consumers were less willing to pay a premium price for it. He thought market share goals were attainable only if key customers proceeded with their plans. Competition was another problem. Turnen believed that Metal Box would be a strong competitor, because of its existing manufacturing facilities. He also was concerned that American Can would not have adequate technical assistance resources for a U.K. start-up when it would be needed, and wondered about patent issues in the European market. Finally, he commented that basic assumptions used to develop variable costs were reasonable, but there appeared to be omissions and errors in calculating costs of packing supplies, raw materials, and spoilage.

Turnen's major reservation, however, concerned the future. He wondered what the United Kingdom planned beyond two production lines; if there would never be more than two lines, he didn't think it was worth the effort to pursue this project. However, the formal cover sheet that accompanied his three pages of comments stated that he conditionally supported the project as it was, and he would fully support it if the United Kingdom obtained a commitment from key customers and developed plans for additional Gamma lines in the future.

Fitzgerald summed up his feelings after he received everyone's comments:

> When all was said and done, the Business Investment Group just didn't get answers that removed enough doubts; we still questioned the project's ability to deliver the projected return. And, frankly, we just weren't sure that the English had the same love affair with ketchup, or their "brown sauce," that Americans have. I finally asked Walker and the rest of the project sponsors to postpone the project and withdraw the proposal.

From the time the initial U.K. Gamma proposal was withdrawn in November 1984 to the receipt of the revised proposal in October 1985, Fitzgerald had telephone conversations with U.K. executives and visited the English facility to offer advice and help revise the proposal. During that year, they discussed competition, markets, and customers. This extensive communication apparently hadn't resolved all the issues; when the United Kingdom submitted its revised request for $3.3 million for a single Gamma manufacturing line, the proposal consisted solely of Executive Highlights (Exhibit 4). Although the United Kingdom had submitted financial information in the original $6.07 million proposal, it hadn't yet sent new detailed financial explanations of how the $3.3 million would be spent or yearly projections of income; nor had it yet offered updated, in-depth sections on customer commitments, competition, or pricing. Fitzgerald wondered how to react to this brief proposal. As he read the Executive Highlights, he began to jot down a few new deal-breaker questions.

EXHIBIT 2   Ohio Gamma Proposal—Executive Highlights, June 1985

Strategic Direction

The Tube and Bottle Long-Range Plan identifies the Gamma product line as one of the business unit's primary sources of future growth. This request for expansion capital, therefore, is critical toward achieving the business unit's long-term objectives.

Background

The Gamma bottle was developed for hot-filled, oxygen-sensitive food products, such as ketchup, BBQ sauce, and single-strength juices. Its primary value added feature is squeezability. The shatter resistance and reduced weight of plastic are also major benefits. Gamma is primarily used as an alternative to glass packaging.

Since its introduction, Gamma bottle volume has grown rapidly.

Currently, the business has six lines installed and a seventh is on order at the Batavia, Illinois, production facility. With the installation of the seventh line, there is effectively no available production space remaining at Batavia.

Gamma Market Demand Outlook

The food market toward which Gamma is principally focused is currently a 45 billion unit market. The market segments that benefit most from Gamma attributes (i.e., oxygen protection, hot-fillability, squeezability, reduced weight, and shatter resistant) are approximately 5 billion units. These markets include ketchup, sauces, jams/jellies, juices, dressings, mayonnaise, and certain medical products. We project customers in these market areas to use high-barrier plastics to extend their current lines or to introduce new products. By 1990, we estimate the barrier market to be about 1 billion units. With capacity expansion, we will be well positioned to capture a major portion of the projected high-barrier market. This projected Gamma demand greatly exceeds our current capacity situation at Batavia.

Proposed Solution

The business unit proposes to add Gamma capacity to match projected demand. This would require the addition of three Gamma production lines in 1986 and a total of eight lines by mid-1988. We first identified all feasible alternatives that could provide additional Gamma production space. These included: (1) various expansion options at the current Batavia plant, (2) utilization of other existing ACC packaging facilities, and (3) purchase/construction of a new plant. After a strategic and economic evaluation, construction of a new facility in northern Ohio was determined to be the most attractive alternative. Based on projected geographical demand, we will require a nine-line facility by 1988. We are requesting at this time funds for a five-line expandable facility to reduce the capital exposure and risk. The business unit has determined that this more conservative approach will not negatively impact the Gamma expansion returns. In this initial phase we are requesting $21 million in fixed and working capital to obtain the following:

- 25 acres of land.
- 116,000 square feet of production, warehouse, and associated office space.
- Three new Gamma production lines.
- Funds to transfer one existing large bottle line from Batavia to the new facility.

The first of the three requested lines will be temporarily installed at the Batavia Engineering Center to serve as a developmental line to support the rapid expansion. We intend to move this line to the Ohio facility in early 1987 when the need for a separate developmental line will no longer be required.

Further, we have selected a site in Bellevue, Ohio, for this plant based on the following major criteria:

- Geographical relationship to customer base.
- Suitable property for projected nine-line facility.
- Labor rates and availability.
- Highway and rail access.
- State and local tax considerations.
- Utility rates.

Based on the projected demand, expansion of the initial five-line facility to a nine-line plant will be required by the first quarter of 1987. Therefore, we expect to request additional funds for the second phase of this Gamma capacity expansion sometime in the first or second quarter of 1986.

EXHIBIT 2   *(concluded)*

Competitive Situation

Due to the complex nature of the multilayer extrusion blow-mold process, we believe only a limited number of competitors will be in a technical position to enter the high-barrier bottle market. Further, the patent positions, which either American Can or Toyo Seikan of Japan hold, will act as a significant barrier to entry. Currently, there are only three existing Toyo Seikan licensees in the United States: Owens-Illinois, Continental, and Ball.

Based on our significantly higher production experience, we have a considerable technological learning curve advantage. Market information confirms our continued leadership position (i.e., in bottle design, quality, process knowledge, service, and bottle performance characteristics). While we anticipate advances by competition, we intend to maintain technical and market leadership through process improvements and material research, exploiting American Can's overall leadership position in barrier plastics technology.

Due to freight considerations, competition will be limited by geographic location. The maximum economic shipping distance in the bottle industry is normally a 200–300 mile radius.

Gamma's major competitive technology is glass. Currently, Gamma bottles in general are sold at a premium to glass based on cost and value added. While we expect the cost differential between Gamma and glass to narrow over time and thereby increase market demand, we are not anticipating a mass conversion from glass to plastic.

Technological Risk

There are two basic areas of technological concern:

1. Technologies that may be able to produce a Gamma-type bottle at a lower cost.
2. Technologies that may be able to produce high-barrier bottles with added value (i.e., clear bottles).

Based on our considerable knowledge of alternative blow-molding technologies, there appears to be no technology inherently superior to ACC's. In addition, our assessment of potential clear barrier bottle technologies indicates a significantly higher unit cost even if the major technical hurdles are overcome.

Financial Summary

The base case consists of an initial investment in a five-line facility later expanded to its full nine-line complement. This most accurately represents the business unit's future plant for this expansion.

Expected IRR is 23 percent. Based on a broad spectrum of sensitivities, we believe the returns of this project to be relatively insensitive to changes in the key areas of volume, price, variable cost, fixed investment, timing, and terminal value.

EXHIBIT 3   U.K. Gamma Proposal—Executive Highlights, October 1984

- AC (U.K.), Ltd., seeks approval for $6.07 million in capital, expenses, and working capital to install two Gamma lines in a greenfield site in Corby, England, to produce sauce bottles.
- The strategic importance of this investment to AC (U.K.) lies in these areas:
  - It provides a diversified product base with good profitability.
  - The potential for expanding Gamma product technology outside ketchup and sauces is very good.
  - Provision of a capability and infrastructure in barrier plastics technology is a vital ingredient in AC (U.K.)'s ability to take and exploit Omni technology as it becomes available. Our position in the processed food market makes the profit potential of Omni excellent.
- This project assumes definite commitments from major customers that have not been made at the time of writing the project. Without these commitments we shall not seek ACC Board approval.
- We in AC (U.K.) believe we have a successful record in transferring new technology and making it work. The U.K. is a fertile source of plastics technology and manufacturing talent. We are confident that we can bring this project on stream with minimal delay.

EXHIBIT 3   *(concluded)*

- The project consists of 28-oz. and 18-oz. bottles, with volumes increasing from 20 million in 1986 to 27 million in 1987, with Gamma share of the sauce bottle market rising 3 percent by 1987.
- Major customer commitment is expected by end October 1984, and detailed commercial negotiations will then take place. The project has been evaluated on the worst possible outcome with sensitivities to others.
- When both lines are operating at standard in 1987, the project generates annual sales revenue of $5.9 million and pretax profits before TAA fees of $1.1 million. IRR is 28 percent. Annual TAA fees would be $196,000.
- This project has been submitted as the minimum expenditure necessary to establish a viable Gamma operation in the U.K. AC (U.K.)'s 1984–89 long-range plan envisaged three lines installed by 1987, generating annual sales of $8.8 million and pretax profits of $1.8 million. The project justification for a third line will be submitted at a subsequent date.

EXHIBIT 4   U.K. Gamma Proposal, October 1985

JMP/CAM/1335S

18th October 1985

TO: J. G. Polk   —ACC Greenwich

CC: R. J. Turnen   —ACC Greenwich
    S. M. Dyott   —ACC Greenwich
    E. J. Fitzgerald   —ACC Greenwich

American Can (U.K.), Ltd.
Woodside Park
Chelford Road
Congleton
Cheshire, CW12 2LY
Tel. 0260 278344 Telex 565081
Facsimile 0260 270295

American Can (U.K.)—Gamma Project Summary

Introduction

Further to our meetings on 1st October, we have prepared a revised strategy for our company to enter the field of performance plastics using the following criteria:
1. Minimum financial exposure—hence a shoehorn operation into our Grantham plant.
2. Slow and credible build of sales.
3. Stand-alone staffing and support to minimize risks of interference with our metal business.

Key Financials

1. Capital expenditure totaling £2.4 million* which includes £1.3 million line equipment and parts sourced from USA, minimum ancillaries, and installation plus 5 percent contingency.
2. Pretax income impact £(264) thousand in 1986, break-even in 1987, £264 thousand positive and rising 1988 onwards.
3. Cash flow £(2.2) million in 1986, positive thereafter.
4. Internal rate of return 21 percent.

Operational Issues

1. Floor space can be freed up in Grantham to accommodate one Gamma line and related storage requirements.
2. Existing Grantham plant management to act as "landlords" only. Gamma operation to be run by separate staff (1 production manager, 1 technical manager, 1 administrative assistant) and 10 hourly-paid employees.
3. Existing plant facilities can cope with Gamma utilities requirements, with exception of one air compressor/drier, chiller, and some additional switchgear and cabling.
4. Assuming your approval this month, long lead-time items can be ordered to enable line start-up by October, 1986.

EXHIBIT 4   *(concluded)*

Key Sales Assumptions

I will send, under separate cover, key sales assumptions for 1986–90 by customer for 16-oz., 24-oz., and 28-oz. ketchup and other sauce containers.

Customer Commitments

Our volume targets are conservative—one customer has already declared its marketing plan is for 5 million 24-oz. units in 1987. Another major customer has committed to spend in excess of £2 million to fill 16-oz. bottles for ketchup. It declared to us that a 28-oz. container is its next likely development. With our USA track record, and with U.K. production in place, we will offer an attractive alternative to its dependence on our competitors.

Other Developments

The market indicators for barrier bottles are exciting. Other major ketchup producers are already considering a move to barrier plastics to keep pace with competition.

To underscore our sales volumes we will target our efforts towards salad cream, a 70 million-unit glass market with virtually identical consumer benefits to ketchup.

Strategic Fit

1. For ACC (U.K.) to progress and ultimately possibly survive, it is not a question of if we should enter performance plastics but when.
2. Our existing metal can customer is now in a hurry to enter the plastics bottle market. We have been behind it all the way in pushing it into plastic bottles and this represents an opportunity we would be foolish to forgo—indeed, it would represent a risk to our metal business if we did.
3. Lack of investment in Gamma signals to the rest of the market that ACC is not truly interested in packaging in the United Kingdom. Conversely, the market believes ACC to be a world leader in this field and an investment decision now would considerably boost our image.
4. It is almost impossible to develop new products with new customers without any investment in plant and personnel. This investment should make our entry as a second supplier of bottles much easier. With this facility we can extend the product range outside ketchup as you have.
5. The morale of our own management would be considerably boosted by this decision.

J. M. Preston

* Casewriter's note: On October 18, 1985, £1 equaled approximately US$1.38.

QUESTIONS

1. In the early 1980s, American Can made certain structural changes:

   • Established the Strategic Planning Department and the Strategic Planning Process.
   • Established the Business Investment Group, reporting to Strategic Planning; transferred to Business Investment the authority to review proposals for fixed capital; and established the requirement that it review proposals for other investments.

   Evaluate the expected effect of these structural changes on the allocation of resources at American Can.

2. Evaluate the role and operation of the Business Investment Group. What is the effect of the Business Investment Group on the resource allocation *process* as well as resource allocation *decisions*? What recommendations for improvements would you make in its charter or operation?

3. What is your evaluation of the situation regarding the U.K. Gamma proposal?

4. If you were Ed Fitzgerald, vice president of business development, what are your goals and objectives regarding the U.K. Gamma proposal? What would you do regarding this proposal? Why? What results do you expect?

Case 16–5

Universal Data Corporation*

The scene is a conference room in the head office in Geneva of Universal Data Corporation's European operations. The time is shortly after lunch on a winter day in 1982. Three men are finishing cups of coffee, which have been served by a secretary.

Seated at the head of the table is Clive Price, age 45, British by nationality and president of UDC–Europe. The other two are David Simmons, 39, Swiss, and vice president—finance; and Clinton Salter, 48, American and vice president in charge of sales. (Two other officers of UDC–Europe mentioned in the conversation that follows are William O'Shaughnessy, general manager of the British Isles subsidiary, and Christian van Rhijn, general manager of the Belgian subsidiary.) UDC—its operations and its management control system—is briefly described in the appendix.

Price: You chaps know why we're here. We've got problems related to pricing at our British and Belgian subsidiaries, and both of them require our immediate attention.

Simmons: I'm familiar with the Belgian matter, but not with the British one. What's wrong in England?

Salter: It's that recent shipment of U-64s to Amalgamated Metals, the one we invoiced directly from our Spanish plant as a means of getting around the British Price Commission.

Simmons: And a fine idea at that! Any time we can pick up an extra $200,000 by using Continental European prices, I shall support it. I wish we had thought of it earlier. What is the problem? Are the machines printing in Spanish?

Price: No. But apparently they're having service problems with them. Carlos Navarro, at our Spanish subsidiary, rang up yesterday. He says that the people at Amalgamated telephoned him to say it's been almost impossible to get anyone in England to service the machines.

Salter: The same old story.

Price: I rang up O'Shaughnessy right away. He admits that there's been a delay. However, he claims that his systems engineers have been tied up at ICI on a new project. Besides, he said, if Carlos was so concerned, he could have sent one of his own men down. After all, the Spanish subsidiary got credit for the sale.

Simmons: I beg to differ, Clive. We charged a commission against Spain's recorded profit, and we showed the same amount of commission as an additional revenue item on Britain's monthly operations report.

Salter: Maybe O'Shaughnessy missed that line on the report. What's the story in Belgium?

Simmons: We received a telex from the controller of the Belgian subsidiary this morning. Here, I made a copy for each of you.

[He gives Price and Salter each a sheet of paper, which they read. The text of the telex follows.]

ATTN: D P SIMMONS
PAPERWORK ON FIRST SHIPMENT U82/15 ENROUTE FROM IRELAND RECEIVED TODAY. FIVE MACHINES ENROUTE TO BRUSSELS AT FOB $41,000 EACH.
WE DO NOT WANT TO CLEAR THESE MACHINES THROUGH CUSTOMS AS SHIPMENTS FROM FRANCE HAVE BEEN ARRIVING AT FOB $32,000 AND FROM USA AT FOB $35,200.

* This case was adapted by Edgar M. Barrett from an article in the May–June 1977 *Harvard Business Review.* Copyright © by Harvard University.

PLEASE INSTRUCT IRELAND TO ISSUE RE-
VISED INVOICES AT FOB $32,000 EACH SO
WE CAN CLEAR THIS SHIPMENT WITHOUT
CREATING VERY DANGEROUS SITUATION
WITH LOCAL CUSTOMS.
WE AWAIT URGENT REPLY TO REQUEST.
DAG ERICSSON
UDC–BRUSSELS

Simmons: You see, our Belgian controller is worried about the reaction of the customs authorities. He thinks they won't understand why the
same model is arriving from three different
sources at three different prices.

Price: Pardon me, David, but doesn't the real risk
involve dumping? After all, seeing the same
model come in at three prices may lead customs
to conclude that some of the machines were
dumped—particularly the American ones. If that
happens, wouldn't we be slapped with higher
duty charges on the American machines?

Simmons: I fear you're right, Clive. They might
decide to put higher duty charges on all our
American-made imports. With a duty on them of
8.4 percent, it would take little change in the
assessed value of the goods to rack up a substantial tax bill. And it could get worse. We think
that the Belgian officials trade data with their
counterparts in other countries. Imagine the mess
if all the Common Market countries began to
investigate our transfer pricing.

Salter: Well, the answer to this one seems simple
enough. Let's lower the incoming price to the
French level. It's only a bookkeeping entry anyway.

Price: It's not that simple. The machines were diverted to Brussels at the request of the Belgain
subsidiary. Christian van Rhijn agreed to take the
machines, at $41,000 each, from the Irish plant.

Salter: I'm confused. Why would he do that?

Simmons: The story goes back several months
now. During the spring, Clive received a telephone call from Christian demanding to know
whether we actually planned to allow Galway to
bill Belgium at an above-budget price for these
extra machines. In addition, he complained about
the 10 percent premium he had had to pay in
order to get several extra machines from the
United States.

Price: David and I explained to him that the high
price resulted from three things—the increased
demand for this model, higher than usual start-up
costs in Galway, and the favorable tax deal we
obtained from the Irish government. As you remember, we have a 16-year exemption from income tax on all export sales.

Simmons: Christian wasn't exactly enthralled with
our explanation. He thought the Irish were taking
advantage of the tight supply situation. He saw
no reason why Belgium should absorb Galway's
production inefficiencies. Moreover, he insisted
that his reported results and his own annual bonus should not be affected by some quirk on the
tax laws.

Price: So I rang up O'Shaughnessy and asked
whether he could bring the price down. He mentioned the tax arrangement, saying it would be
sheer folly to transfer any more profit to a high-
tax area like Belgium. Then he reminded me that
Belgium had no alternative source and Ireland
could place the machines elsewhere. Besides, he
said, The Brussels operation would still show a
small profit on the transactions.

Simmons: I finally telexed Brussels that the final
decision on price was up to them and O'Shaughnessy's group. I did note, however, that the Irish
tax savings were substantial. They settled on the
price of $41,000 each f.o.b. Brussels.

Salter: You know, I'm not wild about *your* explanation either. It seems to me that this creative
transfer pricing is bound to blow up in our faces.
In fact, my eyebrows feel a little warm right
now.

Price: Now, now, Clint, tax minimization is part of
the game. You know very well that the decision
to locate in Galway was heavily influenced by its
cash flow advantages.

Simmons: Clive's right, Clint. We all agreed to the
Galway plant decision. Besides, we're in business to earn a profit for our shareholders. Contributing corporate cash to the British or Belgian
government is not high on UDC's list of priorities.

Salter: Well, I'm still not convinced. Don't you
think we ought to forget the fancy footwork and
stick to what we know best—building and selling
computers?

EXHIBIT 1   Profitability of British Sales (estimated per unit of Model U-64*)

General data		
Manufactured in	Spain	United Kingdom
Sold to customer in	United Kingdom	United Kingdom
Selling subsidiary	Spain	Britian
UDC–Europe		
Retail price	$62,000	$42,000
Cost of goods sold	23,000	24,500
Gross margin	39,000	17,500
All other expenses[†]	18,000	16,000
Profit before tax	21,000	1,500
Tax[‡]	1,520	780
Profit after tax	$19,480	$ 720
British subsidiary only		
Retail price or sales commission earned	$11,000	$42,000
Cost of goods sold	0	24,500
Gross margin	11,000	17,500
All other expenses	10,000	16,000
Profit before tax	1,000	1,500
Tax[‡]	520	780
Profit after tax	$ 480	$ 720
Spanish subsidiary only		
Retail price	$62,000	N.A.
Cost of goods sold	23,000	
Gross margin	39,000	
Sales commission paid	11,000	
All other expenses	8,000	
Profit before tax	20,000	
Tax[‡]	1,000	
Profit after tax	$19,000	

N.A. = Not available

* Data are on a per-machine basis. Actual exchange rates and cost figures from most recent monthly operations reports are employed. The Amalgamated Metals order was for 10 machines.

[†] A combination of freight charges, duty charges, and differences in national cost structures accounts for the disparity between the two columns.

[‡] Based on local tax rates. Funds are not expected to be repatriated to parent for many years. Spanish figures reflect a tax rate of 35 percent and the benefits of a 15 percent export incentive computed on the Spanish added value of goods exported from Spain.

EXHIBIT 2   Profitability of Belgian Sales (estimated per unit of Model U-82/15*)

General data	High Transfer Price	Low Transfer Price
Manufactured in	Ireland	Ireland
Sold to customer in	Belgium	Belgium
Selling subsidiary	Belgium	Belgium
	High Transfer Price	*Low Transfer Price*
UDC–Europe		
Retail price	$60,000	$60,000
Cost of goods sold	27,000	27,000
Gross margin	33,000	33,000
All other expenses[†]	18,000	17,700
Profit before tax	15,000	15,300
Tax[‡]	2,400	6,900
Profit after tax	$12,600	$ 8,400
Belgian subsidiary only		
Retail price	$60,000	$60,000
Transfer price in	41,000	32,000
Gross margin	19,000	28,000
All other expenses[†]	14,000	13,700
Profit before tax	5,000	14,300
Tax[‡]	2,400	6,900
Profit after tax	$ 2,600	$ 7,400
Irish subsidiary only		
Transfer price out	$41,000	$32,000
Cost of goods sold	27,000	27,000
Gross margin	14,000	5,000
All over expenses	4,000	4,000
Profit before tax	10,000	1,000
Tax[‡]	0	0
Profit after tax	$10,000	$ 1,000

N.A. = not available.

* Data are on a per-machine basis. Actual exchange rates and cost figures from most recent monthly operations reports are employed. This shipment involves five machines. The agreement between the two subsidiaries covered a total of 40 machines.

[†] Differences in incoming duty payments account for the disparity between the two columns. The duty payments are based on the invoiced (transfer) price.

[‡] Based on local tax rates.

Appendix

Facts about UDC–Europe

The company, founded in 1972, is a U.S.-based manufacturer of minicomputers and peripheral hardware. It sells, leases, and services its equipment worldwide. Of its $800 million in revenues, the European operations contribute $185 million.

UDC–Europe, a wholly owned subsidiary, was founded in 1976. It is very profitable and enjoys a great deal of autonomy from the parent company. General managers of its 10 geographically organized subsidiaries are administrative umbrellas for two or more legal entities created to meet national legal and tax requirements. Four subsidiaries (the Spanish, the French, the British, and the Irish) have manufacturing as well as marketing operations.

UDC–Europe treats each subsidiary as a profit center for purposes of managerial control and evaluation. It sets annual budgets in terms of pretax profit and judges local managers largely on their ability to meet or beat the targeted figures. UDC–Europe prices intracompany transfers at levels determined at the annual budget meeting, except under special circumstances, such as unexpectedly higher volume or a complex tax situation. In the former case, the subsidiary manager is expected to negotiate a price. In the latter case, management at Geneva may set the price.

QUESTIONS

1. Disregarding current company policy, what should the transfer price (or commission) have been for the Model U–64 sale?
2. Similarly, for the Model U–82/15?
3. Based on these examples, what should Universal Data's transfer price policy be?
4. If this policy cannot be implemented within Universal Data's present organization structure, how should this structure be changed?

Case 16–6

Nestlé S.A. (A)*

In February 1980, Mr. G. Smith, a zone director in the Nestlé headquarters in Vevey was reviewing the status of the company's subsidiaries in Argentina. The political and economic situation in that country was unsettled, and these conditions impacted on the subsidiaries' performance. Mr. Smith was considering what, if any, actions he should take in view of this situation, the subsidiaries' recent performance, and their proposed budget for 1980, which had just arrived in Vevey.

The Company

Nestlé S.A. was the largest food company in the world. It was founded in 1867 in Vevey, Switzerland, and its headquarters, referred to as "Centre," was still in Vevey in 1980. It is the largest company in Switzerland, although only some 2.5 percent of its sales are made in Switzerland. In 1984, it had 138,000 employees, 292 factories located in 58 countries, and marketing organizations in almost every country in the world. In 1984, 44 percent of its employees were in Europe, 19 percent in North America, 22 percent in Latin America, 5 percent in Africa, 8 percent in Asia, and 2 percent in Australasia.

Nestlé's operating units were referred to as "markets." Each market was a profit center. Typically, a market consisted of all Nestlé activities, both production and marketing, in one country. Each profit center manager (referred to as "head of the market") reported to the managing director through a zone director whose office was in the Centre in Vevey. In 1980, there were five zone directors, each responsible for Nestlé activities in one part of the world, and each assisted by a staff of around 20 persons.

At the Centre also were staff units for: production (called "technical"), including engineering, quality control, and purchasing; marketing, including advertising, market research, and recipes; finance and control, including treasury, internal control, audit, financial accounting, cost accounting, pensions, and planning; administration; legal; and personnel.

Argentina: Background

From 1966 through 1974, Argentina was governed by a military junta headed by General Juan Peron. Following Peron's death in 1974, there was a period of turbulence that left the economy in shambles. By early 1976, the economic growth rate was negative, the inflation rate was 650 percent, the trade balance was negative, capital was fleeing the country, and it appeared that Argentina might have to default on its international debts.

In March 1976, there was a coup, and a new military government took over. It immediately took measures to curb inflation, reduce imports, increase exports, reduce the budget deficit, and shift the economy away from state-owned entities to more private enterprise. These measures were successful in avoiding default on debt payments,

* This case was prepared by F. Voegtli. This condensed version was prepared by Professor Robert N. Anthony, Harvard Business School. Names of most persons are fictitious. Copyright © 1990 by Nestec S.A., Vevey, Switzerland.

and they had some success in reducing the rate of inflation. However, inflation remained at a rate of 160 percent in 1977.

In 1978, the recovery drive had a sharp setback. After five successive quarters of growth, the gross domestic product decreased by 4.2 percent for the year as a whole. The decline resulted from the imposition of strict economic controls, a sharp reduction in the budget deficit, and an increase in interest rates. Inflation remained at 160 percent.

In 1978 and 1979, the government took additional measures. Foreigners were encouraged to invest in all types of enterprises, import tariffs were reduced, and the program to shift from state-owned enterprises to private business was accelerated. The tariff reduction aimed at an average tariff of 15 percent in 1984, compared with an average of 60 percent in 1976. Restrictions of the flow of capital were eased, although there was a requirement that foreign loans had to have a maturity of at least one year, to discourage short-term capital movements for speculative purposes.

These changes in financial regulations had a rapid and significant impact. Since banks and companies could obtain one-year funds from foreign banks at a monthly cost of 5.5 percent, compared with 7.0 percent locally, they tended to switch to foreign funding. In 1979, Argentine liabilities to foreign banks grew by over 50 percent. The result was a pressure to reduce local interest rates; they became about 2 percent lower than the rates of inflation. This led to increased domestic investment and a growth of 13 percent in industrial production in the first nine months. A record harvest and an increase in the world price of export commodities (beef, wheat, and corn) also aided the economy. Nevertheless, inflation for the first three quarters of 1979 remained at an annual rate of 170 percent.

In the last quarter of 1979, there was an import boom of unprecedented proportions. Imports were up 53 percent, compared with the last quarter of 1978. Since exports increased by only 30 percent, there was a negative trade balance, which wiped out the positive impact of capital inflows. A consequence of the flood of imports was that many domestic plants were operating at low volumes.

Nestlé Argentina: Background

S.A. Nestlé de Productos Alimenticios (hereafter, SANPA) opened an office in Buenos Aires in 1931 and built a large chocolate factory in a suburb of that city in the same year. In 1935, it built a milk factory and, as was its usual practice, devoted considerable resources to helping farmers improve their techniques to provide an adequate supply of milk. Between 1944 and 1959, three additional milk factories were built. In 1971, milk intake at all factories was 127 million kilograms (kg.); it reached a peak of 234 million kg. in 1976, was 196 million kg. in 1977, and 203 million kg. in 1978.

In the 1930s, regional distribution offices were established throughout the country, and the distribution network was gradually expanded thereafter. A large distribution center was established near Buenos Aires in 1968; in 1979, it handled almost half the domestic sales volume.

In 1978, Nestlé acquired Fruticon S.A., a manufacturer of canned tomato and fruit products with a staff of some 300 persons. Fruticon was operated as a separate company.

Although SANPA's sales volume grew rapidly, its profits did not keep pace. In addition to heavy start-up costs and marketing investments for new lines, such as ice-cream, as well as strong competitive pressure, Nestlé suffered from the consequences of the government's economic programme.

Business was certainly not easy under the economic conditions prevailing in 1978, and SANPA's 1978 annual report stated:

> Interest rates remained at a high level, which forced us to intensify the controls over our working capital with a view to keeping the financing costs within an acceptable range. On the other hand, we

had to maintain sufficient stocks of raw materials and finished products in line with the turnover (i.e., sales) growth objectives.

The Centre was satisfied that the end-1978 level of working capital was acceptable.

In June 1978, Mr. L. Gonzales, head of market, wrote to the zone director at the Centre that the government policy would eliminate much competition that had managed to maintain itself only because of the industrial protection of the last 20 years. Healthy companies would gain in strength. Under these circumstances, he said, SANPA should "move away from the traditional policy of profitability maximization which had restrained volume growth" and during the next two years should "make up the lost ground with heavy marketing support." The Centre agreed with this strategy in a letter of September 1978.

Events of 1979

January to June

SANPA's budget request for 1979 had been based on the new strategy and on a predicted gradual improvement in the economic situation; it forecasted a turnover increase of 150 percent, to pesos 303.7 billion. Considering the generally expected moderations of inflation in 1979, the budget appeared to be reasonably conservative and had been accepted by the Centre.

Actual sales of SANPA during the first six months of 1979 followed no regular patterns. Sales varied between 67 percent and 113 percent of the respective monthly budgets for the first five months and were approximately on budget in June.

SANPA sent a revised budget to the Centre in early April, showing considerably increased turnover forecasts; 1979 sales were now budgeted at pesos 410.8 billion, some 35 percent above the original budget and 239 percent above actual 1978 sales. This revision did not provoke any unusual reaction at the Centre.

SANPA's debt collection performance in the first half of the year was, similar to the one of

sales, not always in line with expectations; but the monthly report of June was optimistic: "the debtors situation will improve in subsequent months; thanks to the planned reorganization of the sales force and a series of measures we shall try to reach the standard of 40 days."

July to September

Inflation continued unabated in July (7.2 percent for the month) and August (11.5 percent), before coming down in September (6.8 percent), a month coinciding with the introductions of governmental wage increase limits.

Actual SANPA sales for this quarter fell short of revised budget figures by pesos 35.3 billion, or some 32 percent. For July, invoicing problems during the first 10 days of the month were cited as main responsible factor. These were said to be due to changes in the marketing set-up.

September saw another very poor performance of SANPA. Sales revenues for most product groups fell considerably behind budget. SANPA commented on the September sales results as follows:

. . . continuous price increases of the products forming the household shopping basket and the rate adjustments for services (electricity, etc.) have led to a marked reduction of consumer demand. The trade is faced with a slow stock rotation, high financing costs, as well as debt collection pressure by suppliers, which do not represent incentives to quickly replace stock sold; the trade works at minimum stock levels and tries to purchase only during special offers.

October

On October 2, Mr. Smith, the zone director, sent a letter to Luis Gonzalez, the head of the Argentine market, reminding him "once more of the importance of maintaining working capital and especially the trade debtors at reasonable levels in view of the high financing costs and the increasing difficulties encountered in obtaining sufficient credit." The letter concluded: ". . . it would be a pity to jeopardize the achievements

EXHIBIT 1   SANPA Excess Working Capital

Month 1979	Month-End Stock Value Finished Goods (1)	Value of Stocks above Standard (3 months) (2)	Month-End Debtors Value (3)	Value of Debtors above Standard (40 days) (4)	Resulting Excess Working Capital (5) = (2) + (4)
January	24,678	4,577	24,440	12,665	17,242
February	28,339	5,931	23,960	9,971	15,902
March	30,660	5,326	32,775	7,779	13,105
April	32,786	3,498	34,707	13,002	16,500
May	32,753	354	37,734	12,850	13,204
June	31,270	—	45,240	14,333	14,333
July	29,769	—	59,953	28,471	28,471
August	33,372	1,096	58,986	21,281	22,377
September	39,201	177	62,334	29,447	29,624
October	32,829	1,145	107,303	16,811*	17,956
November	31,715	213	135,574	57,279	57,492
December	41,538	12,343	151,720	68,773	81,116

*Incorrect reporting: actual figures should have been some 11,000 higher.

made with respect to product profitability by offering too generous selling conditions to the trade."

In October, SANPA reported record sales of close to pesos 70 billion, which was some 45 percent above the revised budget and nearly as much as total sales in the preceding three months. Some promotions, offering discounts of up to 20 percent, helped to smooth the impact of selling price increases. These increases ranged from 10 percent to 24 percent and were made to recover increases in production and operating costs. Collections reached only 61 percent of the forecasted amount, leaving SANPA debtors at 78 days and "causing our financial position to continuously deteriorate, a situation which is not expected to change during the remainder of the year."

The technical section of the monthly report stated that the production programmes were exceeded by 20 percent for milk powders and by 11 percent for chocolates. Chocolate stocks still stood at four months, and the value of the total excess stock was indicated as pesos 1.1 billion (see Exhibit 1).

The end-September budget revision for SANPA contained the following forecasts of the 1979 results: total turnover pesos 368.86 billion, net operating loss pesos 6.00 billion, net loss pesos 3.00 billion. Debtors were expected to drop to 50 days by year end.

The revision reflected optimism for the whole of 1979, despite the dismal actual performance in the first nine months of the year. Given the high rate of inflation, the fact that the fourth quarter had often been buoyant in the past, and the possibility of cutting certain expenses, especially in the marketing area, the Centre did not question this optimism. According to a letter from Mr. Gonzalez, the new estimate had been made with the knowledge of the actual results for the first eight months of 1979: a net operating loss of pesos 17 billion, equivalent to 10.3 percent of turnover for SANPA. He went on to say: "higher prices will not only boost turnover but also help the net operating profit to reach its budgeted level." The letter of Mr. Gonzalez concluded: "You can be assured that we shall do the impossible to reach our budgeted sales for 1979." (Mr. Smith had urged this in a letter dated October 2.)

November

On November 28, the zone director wrote to Mr. Gonzalez, reminding him of the contents of the letter sent on October 2 and mentioning that "with a certain preoccupation I have taken note of the deterioration that has occurred in your trade debtors position. . . . While acknowledging the existence of considerable economical difficulties, with high inflation and a slow recovery pace, I insist once more on the crucial importance of paying special attention to this problem."

The monthly report for November, received at the Centre on December 21, again contained predominantly good news: inflation was down to a monthly rate of 5.1 percent, the government published inflation estimates of 45 percent to 48 percent for 1980, interest rates had come down as a result of a more liquid financial market, and SANPA sales were pesos 66 billion, "exceeding the objectives of the month." Successful promotional activities, particularly in instant drinks and chocolates (20 percent discount for certain items), were given credit for the excellent performance, despite selling price increases of 11 percent to 16 percent for most products (none for chocolates). Ice-cream sales were reportedly once more the victim of bad weather, remaining below budget and 10 percent below the November 1978 volume. "With view to making up for turnover shortfall due to lost volume," the Frigor Division modified its pricing policy, which had not planned for any adjustments before year end, and increased its selling prices by an average of 14.1 percent on November 26.

On the financial side, poor-debtors collections further increased SANPA's bank indebtedness, but it was hoped that this situation would improve by February 1980. There were no special comments concerning production.

December

Ernst Keller, zone controller, paid a visit to the Argentine market from December 4 to 7. He summarized his impressions in a note to the vice president controlling, the finance director, and the zone director on December 20, as follows:

> Inflation estimated at 140 percent for 1979 and 70 percent for 1980; peso devaluation will be 60/70 percent in 1979 and 30 percent in 1980 according to optimistic forecasts. During my visit to our major distribution centre in December 5, I came across an anomaly in the delivery of ordered goods; there was a delivery on that day of an order invoiced on November 11. The manager of the distribution center admitted he had several such undelivered invoices; the goods had not been shipped because they were physically not available.

Ernst Keller went on to say that the invoices were for big customers, that the goods had been sold at promotional discounts, and that exceptionally favorable payment terms of 90 days had been granted. If these goods could not be delivered by year end, Mr. Keller concluded, a reinvoicing would become necessary in January, at November 1979 prices and conditions. He also found that considerable quantities of goods were being stored on behalf of customers, even though they had been already recorded as sales.

The zone director immediately called the market head when he learned of this situation, asking him to take the necessary corrective actions at once.

On January 24, 1980, the monthly report of December reached the Centre. It stated that the government had reiterated its intention to stick to the planned devaluation scheme in 1980. It further stated that "positive real interest rates of up to 2 percent per month occurred in December despite a further reduction in nominal rates. In the capital goods sector, the softening of demand observed in November has continued, and there was a general increase in bankruptcies in the country."

Sales for December were disappointing. SANPA explained this by the "heavy sales of the

EXHIBIT 2 SANPA Year-End Balance Sheets (in pesos millions)

	1977		1978		1979 Original Budget		1979 September Revision		1979 Actual		1980 Original Budget	
Assets												
Fixed assets	14,992	38.2	36,165	36.3	87,644	45.9	97,998	35.0	87,239	25.1	193,417	340
Raw and packaged materials	6,480	16.5	12,156	12.2	23,423	12.3	36,360	13.0	29,579	8.5	65,131	115
Finished products	4,553	11.6	10,761	10.8			35,477	12.7	31,120	9.0	85,155	150
Debtors	9,458	24.1	34,115	34.3	79,931	41.8	98,565	35.3	181,875	52.3	199,175	350
Sundry	3,741	9.6	6,357	6.4			11,117	4.0	17,771	5.1	25,718	45
Total	39,224	100%	99,554	100%	190,998	100%	279,517	100%	347,584	100%	568,596	100%
Liabilities												
Equity	13,038	33.2	37,339	37.5	80,483	42.2	100,287	35.9	91,243	26.3	202,237	365
Trade, creditors	2,277	5.8	5,494	5.5	44,198	23.1	75,091	26.9	14,709	4.2	110,000	193
Accounts Payable	15,026	38.3	22,042	22.2					65,497	18.8		
Banks credits	8,883	22.7	34,679	34.8	66,317	34.7	104,139	37.2	176,135	50.7	256,359	451
Total	39,224	100%	99,554	100%	190,998	100%	279,517	100%	374,584	100%	568,596	100%

EXHIBIT 3   Sales SANPA 1979 (in pesos millions)

Month	Original Budget	Budget 1st Revision (March)	Actual Sales	Deviation from 1st Revision
1979:				
January	11,909	11,909	8,004	(3,905)
February	15,728	15,728	13,231	(2,497)
March	21,342	21,342	24,026	2,684
April	22,577	21,942	17,602	(4,340)
May	23,664	26,531	23,452	(3,079)
June	26,278	25,301	26,678	1,377
July	28,904	32,623	20,797	(11,826)
August	29,536	35,467	30,761	(4,706)
September	31,372	42,514	23,711	(18,803)
October	30,805	48,227	69,794	21,567
November	30,669	65,747	66,031	284
December	30,953	63,438	36,396*	(27,042)
Total 1979	303,737	410,769	360,483	(50,286)

* Result of cancelled sales due to negative stock figures.

preceding two months, which had not only re-duced the demand due to oversaturation but also led to out-of-stock situations for several product lines." Unavailability of stocks was cited for important products, such as the instant drinks Nescafé and Nesquik. Selling prices had been increased for most products, ranging from 5 percent to 21 percent.

In the financial area, SANPA reported low debtors collections and an increase by US$ 5.5 million in its foreign currency loans.

Actual Results for 1979

The overall results for the whole year, reaching the Centre in early February 1980, showed a combined net profit of around pesos 1 billion. SANPA net profit was pesos 4.15 billion on sales of pesos 363.00 billion. However, the net profit was primarily due to exceptional items of pesos 3.90 billion (mainly revaluation of fixed assets); the net operating profit (NOP), was only pesos

0.29 billion, or less than 0.1 percent of turnover. Of the nonproduct-related fixed expenses of pesos 101.2 billion incurred by SANPA in 1979, interest was the major cost time, reaching pesos 52.8 billion, or 14.5 percent of turnover, which was considerably more than in previous years.

Balance sheet data are given in Exhibit 2 and monthly sales in Exhibit 3.

Budget 1980

On January 10, 1980, the Argentine market sent a telex to the Centre, indicating the key figures of the budgets of SANPA and Fruticon S.A. for the year 1980 (figures in pesos billions):

	SANPA	Fruticon
Sales	880.35	38.78
Net operating profit/(loss)	32.32	(6.45)
Net profit/(loss)	36.57	(6.95)

EXHIBIT 4   Selected Operating Data

	1976	1977	1978	1979
Sales (pesos millions)	15,160	45,523	121,237	363,001
Net operating profit (percent of sales)	19.3%	9.9%	5.9%	0.1%
Interest (pesos millions)	825	4,762	13,250	52,786
Employees:				
Head office	427	469	462	489
Marketing	514	646	616	695
Production	2,369	2,525	2,573	2,655
Total employees	3,310	3,640	3,650	3,839

On February 4, the hardcopy of the budget was received at the Centre, confirming the telexed key data. Under the economic heading, the report made reference to the government's free market policy and stated: "the increasing flow of imports, as a consequence of an overvalued peso, will probably lead to a negative trade balance, a fall in the gross domestic product (GDP), and to increasing difficulties for companies not able to obtain foreign financing, as well as for those confronted with improved competitive products." SANPA expected for 1980 an inflation of 69.4 percent p.a. (with monthly rates ranging from 7 percent in January to 3 percent in December), average local interest rates of 75 percent (reaching 50 percent by year end), and a devaluation of the peso of 31.6 percent. The optimism with respect to inflation was based on the government's budget with predicted deficit reduction to 2 percent of GDP and a limitation of public investments to 8 percent of GDP.

SANPA's objectives were to consolidate the market positions achieved in 1979 through constant and aggressive marketing activity and to increase selling prices in line with cost increases. A softening demand was expected for dietetic products and chocolates ("falling consumer purchasing power, strong competitive activity, and heavy pressure from cheap imports").

Regarding sales volumes, SANPA expected the following tonnage increases over 1979: milk prod-ucts, 4 percent; dietetics, 15 percent; instant drinks, 7 percent; chocolates, 13 percent; catering products, 33 percent; culinary, 22 percent; Frigor ice-cream, 4 percent; total SANPA, 7.6 percent.

SANPA planned to add 452 new persons to its payroll in 1980, bringing the total personnel at the end of 1980 to 4,556; the largest increases by function were for production (309 persons, or 12 percent), sales (63 persons, or 11 percent) and general management/administration at head office (53 persons, or 11 percent). Data on SANPA staffing are given in Exhibit 4.

Events of Early 1980

After receiving the (delayed) debtors and stocks report for December 1979, the zone controller wrote, for the signature of the zone director, a letter to Mr. Gonzalez on February 12, reminding him of the letters sent on October 2 and November 28, 1979, on the same subject and telling him that "the debtors situation has reached alarming proportions considering the 85 days outstanding at year end and the low collections in January." The zone director asked for immediate explanations and comments on corrective action taken.

On February 18, 1980, the monthly report for January arrived at the Centre. It stated that the inflation increase was 7.2 percent for the month of January; interest rates, however, continued to slide, reflecting a liquid situation of the local financial market. Demand for consumer goods had slowed further.

Sales were pesos 10.77 billion. SANPA debtors collections were only 60 percent of forecasts, which was said to be "due to holiday season," an explanation also used with respect to the poor sales, together with "the effects of our heavy efforts made in the last months of 1979 to achieve the budgeted volumes." Only dietetics products and chocolates exceeded budgeted sales, despite a selling price increase of 10 percent for the latter. The low debtors collections had an adverse impact on the financial situation.

In the production area, most programmes reportedly had been carried out at 87 percent to 110 percent of the planned tonnages, except for items with supply or technical problems.

The debtors and stocks report for end-January showed the following data: total accounts receivable, pesos 135.89 billion (104 days) representing an excess working capital of pesos 111.07 billion; total finished products stock, pesos 67.04 billion, with milk powders 1.5 months above the standard cover of 4.0 months ("due to advanced production"), resulting in an excess stock value of pesos 20.09 billion.

Upon receipt of this monthly report, the assistant to the zone manager immediately telephoned Mr. Gonzalez asking for clarification concerning the low level of January sales and the debtors situation. Mr. Gonzalez explained that the disappointing sales and collections were due rather to seasonal (holidays) and temporary factors than to fundamental changes in the business outlook. A letter was sent to Mr. Gonzalez on February 20, confirming the telephone conversation.

QUESTIONS

1. In a country with high inflation and unstable government actions, what should be Nestlé's policies? Consider such aspects as selling prices, accounts receivable terms, accounts payable, inventory levels, and billing in advance of shipment.
2. How can the Centre learn whether these policies have been adhered to?
3. What should Mr. Smith, the zone director, do on the basis of the information available as of the middle of February 1980?

Case 16–7

Nestlé S.A. (B)*

Mr. S. Smith, zone director of Nestlé S.A., was disappointed with the performance of the Argentine market in 1979. As the months of 1980 went by, his concern increased.

Developments in Early 1980

In the first months of 1980, inflation continued to fall and by April, the annualized rate had dropped to 90 percent.

Total imports were up by 40.9 percent the first half of 1980, making local producers suffer and leading to an increased number of bankruptcies. Gross domestic product (GDP) grew by only 0.2 percent, with the industrial sector down by 2.3 percent and agriculture 6.4 percent below the same period of 1979. For the whole of 1980, a negative growth of at least 3 percent was forecasted. Financing costs remained high, and this led to a slowdown in investment expenditures and a liquidation of inventories, even in industries not directly threatened by the import boom.

Several factors prevented inflation from falling as fast and far as government had hoped, and two of them had a particularly strong impact on the economy and, thus, also on the performance of companies.

First, because people lacked confidence in the economic and political outlook, they diverted cash to foreign financial markets or to speculative investments instead of reinvesting them for productive purposes. Certain distributors started to import Nestlé products manufactured in neighboring countries and to offer them at prices considerably below comparable products manufactured by SANPA (S.A. Nestlé de Productos Alimenticios).

Second, many industrial companies went bankrupt, and this led to a serious banking crisis. The Central Bank, which had guaranteed desposits up to a certain limit, was forced to come to the rescue, paying out more than US$ 2 billion to depositors in April and early May of 1980. Such a large outflow of funds, financed largely through printing new money, led to increased inflation.

As shown in Exhibit 1, actual sales for SANPA were far below the budgeted amounts. Outstanding receivables rose to an unprecedented 121 days by the end of March. Excess working capital tied up in debtors was pesos 61.6 billion at the end of March. Collections were only 73 percent of budget. The sales result for February and March were explained with the same reasons given in January (i.e., low stock rotation in the trade, vacation period, and, for certain products, selling prices above those of the competition).

Hope was expressed that sales would increase because of "massive media or point of sales promotion activity currently under study." In March, when selling prices were increased by 6 or 7 percent, it was argued that demand had been hurt by "increased schooling fees and unusually high temperatures, which led to a shift in consumer preference toward the refreshment drinks market segment." To stimulate demand, special discounts were introduced—for example, Nescafé customers could get up to 16 percent reductions for a large quantity purchased on a cash payment basis.

---

* This case was prepared by F. Voegtli. This condensed version was prepared by Professor Robert N. Anthony, Harvard Business School. Names of most persons are fictitious.   Copyright © 1990 by Nestec S.A., Vevey, Switzerland.

EXHIBIT 1 Budgeted and Actual SANPA Sales for January to June 1980 (in pesos millions)

Month	Original Budget	March Revision	Actual	Difference vs. Latest Budget
January	26,656	26,657	10,765	(15,892)
February	32,319	32,320	14,883	(17,437)
March	47,450	47,450	23,789	(23,661)
April	61,631	48,371	29,406	(18,965)
May	79,695	63,286	45,832	(17,454)
June	84,297	82,473	65,071	(17,402)
Total	332,048	300,557	189,746	(110,811)

EXHIBIT 2 SANPA Accounts Receivable Collections and Excess Working Capital January to June (in pesos millions)

Month (1980)	Planned Collections	Actual Collections	Performance (%)
January	39,600	23,876	60
February	55,104	36,289	66
March	60,291	44,193	73
April	64,800	44,541	69
May	72,816	37,523	52
June	58,980	33,047	56

Month (1980)	Value of Excess Finished Goods Stocks	Value of Excess Debtors Outstanding	Impact on Working Capital
January	21,367	111,066	132,433
February	27,257	94,701	121,958
March	32,603	61,581	94,184
April	37,214	38,876*	76,090
May	31,306	23,915*	55,221
June	30,614	9,691*	40,305

* Reduction partially due to a modification of the standard from 40 days to 45 days in April/May and 60 days in June.

Working capital increased, as shown in Exhibit 2. Most excess stocks were due to milk products, where it was not easy to reduce production on short notice, because the fresh milk of contracted suppliers usually could not be refused or resold.

From pesos 232 billion at end March, indebtedness was expected to stabilize at a level of around pesos 220 billion over the following three months. Besides taking additional peso financing, SANPA increased its foreign borrowings by US$ 2 million in February and US$ 5 million in March.

Instead of a budgeted operating profit in the first quarter, the market reported a net loss, plaining it with low sales "due to a temporary softening of demand." Sales volume was only 45 percent of budget and 50 percent of the corresponding period of 1979.

Developments in April, May, and June

The March budget revision (key numbers received in late April; details on May 27) showed the following estimates for the year: sales, pesos 821.5 billion; net operating profit, 9.47 billion; net profit, 20.93 billion; expected inflation, 70 percent for 1980; marginal contribution, minus pesos 30.8 billion due to sales shortfall and plus pesos 48.3 billion due to higher selling prices and lower variable selling and distribution costs; overhead, plus pesos 47.7 billion (of which pesos 34.6 billion was interest, which thus increased to the equivalent of 21.7 percent of sales, with borrowings forecasted to reach pesos 335 billion by year end). The revision contained such comments as ". . . the normalization of demand allows us to foresee normal stock levels . . ." and "debtors should stand at 75 days credit by year end."

On April 28, the zone controller sent another letter, the fourth within seven months, to Mr. Gonzalez to remind him of the worsening debtors situation and to express strong doubts about the goal of 60 days' outstanding credit by end April, promised in a letter two months earlier. Mr. Gonzalez was asked to comment as quickly as possible on the corrective measures already taken or planned. No reply was ever received at the Centre in Vevey, Switzerland, the headquarters of Nestlé.

In mid-May, Mr. Gonzalez came to the Centre to participate in the annual conference for Nestlé's major market heads. Following discussions on financial policies, Mr. Gonzalez was asked not to take out any more new foreign currency loans, even if the latter would appear to be more advantageous on a short-term basis.

On May 21, the monthly report for April arrived. It noted that the worst flood of the century had been experienced by the province of Buenos Aires. Sales and debtors collections were once more far below budget. Although sales of chocolate were far below budget, the report stated that most production programmes, including the one for chocolates, had been fully executed.

On May 23, P. Huber, SANPA's administrative manager, sent a telex to the Centre with some new forecasts for outstanding debtors, a projected financial position, as well as with a schedule of the due dates for the various foreign currency loans/debts. It was apparent that these debts could not be paid without additional financing from the Centre.

On May 29, the zone director sent a letter to Mr. Gonzalez, confirming an earlier message according to which SANPA was not to contract any new borrowings in foreign currencies. The market was reminded that such foreign currency loans always required prior approval by the Centre.

In early June, the finance director of the Centre informed the vice president controller of his concern about the financial situation of the Argentine operations. His note concluded that the debtors situation should be improving since Mr. Gonzalez had reported the receipt of some large payments during the month of May. The monthly treasury report received on June 9 did not confirm the improvement in the debtors situation promised by Mr. Gonzalez (see Exhibit 2), and the zone controller immediately sent a note on this subject to the zone director, qualifying the debtors situation as "disastrous" and urging the zone director to make the market take some drastic corrective action. A copy of the note was sent to the finance director, who in turn sent it to the chief executive officer.

On June 11, the zone controller completed his analysis of the long-term plan (LTP) for the period 1981 to 1985 on the proposal received from the market a few days earlier. The LTP projected a favorable growth of both volume (plus 6 percent on average) and profitability (slight increase); some major new investments were requested for 1981, requiring a capital increase or a long-term loan from the Centre.

Since the LTP proposal contained few details on the profitability assumptions, P. Huber, who was in charge of the financial aspects of the Argentine companies, was summoned to the Centre to participate in the LTP discussions. Asked in a private meeting with the finance director why he had not informed the Centre of the seriousness of the situation in Argentina, Mr. Huber said that he had warned the market head from the beginning, even years back, of the negative financial impact of uncollected overdue accounts receivable; as proof he showed internal notes on this subject sent by his treasurer to all parties concerned within SANPA in 1977 and 1978. Mr. Huber further said that Mr. Gonzalez had never listened to him and had even prevented him from writing to the Centre. Finally, he said that he suspected that fraud had taken place in the marketing and sales area in recent months.

The finance director thereupon decided to send a team of internal auditors to Argentina. He asked the manager of the department to personally head the team. The last internal audit of SANPA by the Centre had taken place in the first half of 1977. On June 18, the finance director informed the CEO of his audit decision.

On June 18, Messrs. Gonzalez and Huber discussed the debtors situation with the zone director. They argued that the pesos 71 billion outstanding at end-May corresponded to only 79 days credit outstanding, which was an improvement over the 122 days one month earlier. However, a more detailed analysis showed that pesos 12 billion related to invoices of 1979 (equal to over 150 days outstanding) and that pesos 5 billion had been "paid" by the customers in the form of postdated checks (which thus could not immediately be cashed). Gonzalez and Huber promised to reduce the outstanding credit to 60 days by end-August using, if necessary, professional debt collectors. The zone controller insisted that Huber should send a monthly report of overdue debtors by age group (1–30 days, 30–60 days, etc).

On June 24, the zone director summed up the outcome of the LTP discussion with Messrs. Gonzalez and Huber in a note to the CEO:

> The proposed LTP was not accepted. Although the planned volume increase for the years 1981 to 1985 looks achievable, the figures of 1980 are far too optimistic. 1980 results will be around Sfr 700 million [one Swiss franc (Sfr) equals roughly US$ 1.40] of sales and a net loss of Sfr 2 million, according to Mr. Gonzalez. This looks too high, and I have asked the market to make another budget revision. Sales were very depressed up to April (they are recovering now). The high financing costs due to debt collection difficulties and the increasing stock level for finished goods increase interest costs. In order to reduce the financial pressure, I have asked the market to install a strict austerity programme and to freeze all expenses on the level already spent or contracted as per June 15 (around 60 billion).

The audit in Argentina started on June 27. Within two weeks the audit manager was able to come up with a conclusion, which he communicated to the zone controller by phone on July 9 and to the finance director at the Centre by phone and letter on July 13 and 18, respectively:

Major customers are still overstocked with goods, and demand is thus still weak; debtors collections continue to be difficult and the situation is serious (pesos 118.4 billion outstanding at end-June, of which pesos 15.9 billion are above 90 days); general overheads cannot be cut easily, although the organizational structure is too heavy in view of the reduced sales volumes; production programmes were based on overoptimistic sales budget, which has led to excessive stock levels requiring additional bank borrowings (six months' stock coverage for milk powders, the chocolate stocks on hand are sufficient to cover the forecasted sales up to the end of 1980!); interest charges are increasing at a horrid pace, and SANPA's financial situation has become so desperate that urgent financial assistance by the Centre might be required; in the distribution area goods invoiced in May are still in the warehouse two months later, as customers do not want them; cancellation in 1980 of large quantities of goods invoiced and shown as sales in 1979.

EXHIBIT 3   SANPA Cumulative Production and Sales, January to August 1980 (in tons/000s liters)

Product Category	Cumulative Production Year-toDate			Cumulative Sales Year-to-Date						
	Feb.	*April*	*June*	*Feb.*	*March*	*April*	*May*	*June*	*July*	*August*
Milks	5,804	9,868	11,620	558	1,020	2,538	4,021	5,999	8,780	11,123
Dietetics	345	843	1,523	305	478	633	804	944	1,135	1,312
Instant drinks	942	1,941	3,105	272	552	993	1,511	2,231	2,693	3,088
Chocolates	801	1,530	1,962	118	306	508	638	842	931	1,066
Culinary	604	1,240	1,922	92	278	526	1,368	1,821	1,921	2,207
Ice-creams	2,324	2,951	3,268	1,725	2,515	2,618	2,698	2,733	2,766	3,875

Developments in August and September

Having heard what was going on in Argentina, the zone director immediately called Mr. Gonzalez, who was on leave in Europe, and asked him to return at once to Buenos Aires to work out an emergency plan through which sales volume could be increased and the overheads drastically reduced. Less than a week later, Mr. Gonzalez called the Centre. He stated that local bank credits had become extremely expensive and that he, therefore, needed a loan from the Centre of as much as 100 milion Swiss francs. He described the major measures introduced or planned in an effort to restore profitability and bring the financial degradation to a halt: a general hiring freeze, a reduction of personnel at three factories and in the sales force, additional selling price increases for most products, a reduction in travelling and training expenses, and the cancellation of the 50-year jubilee celebration (for which there was a budget of pesos 2 billion).

The zone director asked Mr. Keller, the zone controller, to make a trip to Argentina. Upon his return, the latter described in an August 15 note to the CEO, the finance director, and the zone director his impressions:

> Turnover now estimated by market at pesos 740 billion, net loss at pesos 96 billion as a result of low sales and enormous financing costs. However, unfavorable sales prospects for chocolates and culinary products make these forecasts still too opti-

mistic, and actual results might come out closer to sales of pesos 700 billion and a net loss exceeding pesos 100 billion. If no corrective measures are taken now, 1981 will be similarly disastrous. The control set-up needs to be strengthened.

From discussions with local banks, Mr. Keller concluded that some were still willing to lend money to SANPA if they had some free capacity left. Interest expenses were now estimated at 27 percent of turnover for 1980, and total bank borrowings were the equivalent of pesos 295 billion as at July 31, 1980 (pesos 245 billion, US$ 18.4 million, Swiss francs 13 million); SANPA feared that by year end this figure would go up by another pesos 100 billion due to the financing of excess debtors and finished goods. Keller recommended that SANPA convert some peso borrowings into US$ loans; by taking a US$ 20 million loan, SANPA would save US$ 500,000 in interest each month, given the large interest rate differential of some 4 percent per month.

The vice president finance approved a loan of US$ 10 million only, arguing that SANPA's foreign exchange exposure was already large and that he did not like the existing devaluation risk. Total US$ loans thus went up to 28.4 million.

According to SANPA's monthly report for June, which got to the Centre in late July, inflation seemed to have stabilized in the range of 5 to 6 percent per month; but local interest rates were still moving upwards, an intentional decision by the banking sector to prevent foreign capital from leaving the country. Demand for capital goods was down further, and labor disputes in the country as a result of the recession were increasing.

SANPA reported low levels of sales and collections. A shift in the consumer spending pattern was partially held responsible for the sales shortfall, as Argentines seemed to prefer cheap imported capital goods (e.g., color TV sets) and making cheap trips abroad to buying local food products. Cumulative tonnage sold in the first six months of 1980 was down 56 percent over 1979 for chocolates, 45 percent for milk powders, and 23 percent for instant drinks. Only ice-creams and Fruticon volumes were ahead for the same comparative periods. On finished goods stocks and debtors, the report showed high values of more than pesos 100 billion each, with another pesos 50 billion tied up in raw and packing material.

The bimonthly operations report for May/June, received on August 5, mentioned for the first time a "strong reduction of production programmes," permitting the complete elimination of overtime. The largest programme cut was for chocolates, with only 114 tons being produced in June, compared to 322 tons in June 1979. The report also stated that the cumulative milk purchase and usage figures for the first six months of 1980 were some 25 to 30 percent above the amount for 1979. This had a positive effect on milk prices, which had increased at a rate less than half of the inflation rate.

On August 15, the zone director reported to the chief executive officer his impressions formed during his visit to Argentina from August 4 to 9, 1980:

> Strong recession in certain sectors of the economy; the government team gives the impression of being very united, which makes a continuation of the economic policy more than likely. The country's total foreign debt will soon reach US$ 25 billion, which points to a maxi-devaluation, though probably not before October. Local interest rates have stayed positive in real terms for several months, which attracted speculative foreign money and

made local people invest their money short term. An economic recovery should begin in late 1981 or early 1982.

> For SANPA, the situation looks really bad. When recession started in late 1979, they tried to offset the declining demand by a "sell in" policy up to the end of the year. Certain products, such as chocolate and coffee, faced strong competition from cheap imports sold at prices up to 50 percent below SANPA's. The situation worsened when local competitors, facing the same problems, began to liquidate their surplus stocks at ridiculously low prices and when customers started to return goods they could not sell, forcing SANPA to offer even more attractive terms to finally get rid of these products. During all this time the production programmes were not modified immediately. In addition, distributors and retailers reduced their stock levels and used their suppliers as credit source in light of the recession and the trend to positive real interest rates. The debt collection performance has improved over the last six months; but on the marketing side, people believed for too long in a forthcoming upswing of consumer demand. Although for milk products the situation is not too bad, coffee and particularly chocolates have really been hurt; and some wrong decisions were taken in an attempt to liquidate chocolate stock in 1979. The regular selling price adjustments carried out by SANPA helped to maintain marginal contribution rates above 60 percent but led to astronomical price differences compared to the competition.

The note then summarized the corrective actions that the zone director had already initiated or planned to introduce. They included staff reduction of 250 persons at head office and sales/distribution; a reduction of fresh milk intake by 50,000 tons; limit chocolate product to four varieties and import the rest from Brazil; replace key managers "who had contributed to the current situation"; study feasibility of closing one factory; have two experienced managers from other markets sent to Buenos Aires to assist Messrs. Gonzalez and Huber.

The zone director also stated that the financial pressure of SANPA could be relieved by granting it a loan from the Centre in the amount of some

SFr 80 million, at an interest rate of 7–8 percent per year.

Around the same time Mr. Keller, the zone controller, tried to put some figures to the problem of excessive stocks. While for chocolates and green coffee there was no possibility of selling the excess quantities, for milk powder a decision had to be taken. The financing cost was pesos 1.1 billion (Swiss francs 1 million) per month using full cost and 5 percent interest; the variable costs of production had been pesos 21 billion (SFr 18.5 million), and the powder could be sold on the world market for a total of some US$ 5.7 million (SFr 9.5 million). Should the excess milk powder, equivalent to two months domestic sales, be offered abroad or kept for local sale?

In a preliminary report of the mission to Argentina (which had lasted from June 27 to August 19, 1980), the manager of the corporate internal audits department highlighted key findings: The financing cost (8.5 percent per month) was far above the cost increase incurred by SANPA for raw and packing materials (4.7 percent per month) and the replacement cost ex factory of finished goods (4.5 percent), which makes compulsory a policy of minimum stock levels. In the debtors area, there was a complete absence of systematic credit limits as from the middle of 1979, and, to push sales, payment conditions granted to the trade became increasingly generous. Only on August 13, 1980, was the responsibility for the trade credit policy given back to the Administrative Division. The monthly debtors statements were and partly still are completely unreliable. Production programs were based on overoptimistic sales forecasts, which had constantly to be revised downward. Large quantities of finished goods were invoiced in late 1979 but were delivered in the first months of 1980 (pesos 13 billion in Buenos Aires distribution centre alone), or were never delivered at all and had to be credited back to the customers in 1980. The profit implication of this, together with free goods and commissions given to customers in

1980 on those 1979 sales (no provisions had been made at year end as the promotion had been hidden from the manager of the Administration Division) was more than pesos 18 billion negative, which means that 1979 results for SANPA and Fruticon had actually been strongly in red instead of yielding a small profit as reported. For chocolates, certain customers were given discounts of up to 46 percent of the invoice amount in 1979, at a time when the marginal contribution was barely above 50 percent and interest rates were 6 percent per month; the full responsibility for promotions was with the sales administration department. At the distribution centres (DC), large stock differences existed and could not be explained (pesos 13 billion at Buenos Aires DC). There was no directive clearly defining the authority granted to the various managers (e.g., approval of free goods promotions, approval of credit notes). There was weak administrative assistance from head office to the DCs for their difficult tasks, such as debt collection, accounting, and the updating of debtors and stocks positions.

The end-June budget revision arrived in early September. It forecasted sales of pesos 728 billion; net operating loss, pesos 107 billion; net loss, pesos 96 billion; expected total year-end debt, pesos 425 billion.

The treasurer of the Centre submitted a recommendation to the finance director on August 18 after having contacted some banks on the outlook for the peso. If the Centre made a loan of US$ 50 million to SANPA, the latter could save US$ 11 million in interest by year-end 1980 (given interest rates of 5.5 percent per month for peso loans and 1.0 percent for US$ loans) while facing a devaluation risk equivalent to some US$ 20 million.

On August 19, the chief executive officer wrote to the zone manager that he was in principle willing to give his approval for a Swiss franc 80 million loan from the Centre to SANPA at some 7–8 percent per year. He had come to the conclusion that it did not make much sense to pay 60–66 percent interests to finance the mounting losses;

EXHIBIT 4   SANPA's Estimates of Bank Borrowings

| | Forecast (billions pesos) | | | | |
	4 Months Previously	3 Months Previously	2 Months Previously	1 Month Previously	Actual
1979:					
July	50	53	64	76	83
August	53	66	78	90	93
September	65	79	86	93	109
October	79	86	79	111	128
November	86	68	108	125	147
December	52	95	128	162	180
1980:					
January	84	125	169	197	223
February	123	169	193	230	211
March	158	185	221	203	232
April	178	215	198	218	248
May	219	207	218	243	264
June	214	221	237	262	291

the interest rate differential was so large that it would offset a devaluation of up to 50 percent. However, given the devaluation risk, he wanted to postpone a final decision until the return from a trip to New York and Buenos Aires that the finance director was going to make to obtain first-hand information from banking circles and SANPA in light of this pending financing decision. The decision should not be delayed beyond October.

In early September, the finance director informed the CEO of his opinion on the general situation in Argentina, the specific problems of SANPA, and on the peso devaluation risk:

Peso was devalued only 87 percent against the US$ since December 1978, whilst consumer prices jumped by 250 percent during the same period. Government economic policy is hurting internal trade and the key industries, such as meat, milk, chemicals, etc.; if this policy is maintained for much longer, it will ruin the country. Argentine's foreign reserves are very artificial, as they are mainly composed of short-term debt, half of which becomes due before year-end 1980. US$ 2 billion will leave the country by end-September, and American banks have covered their peso exposure in view of the potential devaluation risk. Local interest rates are now at 4.5 percent per month, but some people expect them to rise to 8 percent again before year end. SANPA management was not able to explain to me how they had arrived at the figure of Swiss francs 80 million used in the request for a Centre loan. Debtors and stocks still seem to be too high, and more effort could be done in those areas. Instead of sending money from the Centre, we should ask the market to cash in as much money as possible, maybe even through the sale of excess fixed assets, and to drastically reduce the production programmes, as there will be no economic recovery before 1982! Since there is a high devaluation risk—probably 30 percent and most likely between November and January—and since the market has not yet presented a detailed restructuring plan, I recommend that no loan be sent to SANPA at this stage.

QUESTIONS

1. Looking back (including events described in the (A) case), do you think the Centre should have acted more quickly and more vigorously than it did? If so, what action should it have taken, and when?
2. Did organizational arrangements within the Centre and between the Centre and the markets impede the process of making and implementing sound decisions? If so, what changes do you recommend?
3. Did the reporting system contribute to the problem? If so, what changes do you recommend?

Management Control of Projects

In earlier chapters we focused on management control in an organization that tends to carry on similar activities, day after day. Chapter 17 describes the somewhat different process that is used in the management control of projects. After a discussion of the nature of projects and how the management control process for projects differs from the control of ongoing operations, the main sections deal with *(a)* the environment in which project control takes place and *(b)* the steps in the project control process—namely, project planning, project execution, and project evaluation.

NATURE OF PROJECTS

A project is a set of activities intended to accomplish a specified end result of sufficient importance to be of interest to management. Projects include construction projects, the production of a sizable unique product (such as a turbine), rearranging a plant, developing and marketing a new product, consulting engagements, audits, acquisitions and divestments, litigation, financial restructuring, research and development work, development and installation of information systems, and many others.

A project begins when management has approved the general nature of what is to be done and has authorized the approximate amount of resources that are to be spent in doing this work (or, in some cases, the amount to be spent in the first phase of the work). The project ends when its objective has been accomplished, or when it has been canceled. The construction of a building and the renovation of a building are projects; the routine maintenance of a building is not. The production of a television ''special'' is a project; the production of a nightly television news broadcast is an ongoing operation.

The completion of a project may lead to an ongoing operation, as in the case of a successful development project. The transition from the project organization to the operating organization involves complex management control issues, but these are not discussed here.[1]

Projects vary greatly. At one extreme, a project may involve one or a few persons working for a few days or weeks, performing work similar to that done many times previously—for example, an annual financial audit that is conducted by a public accounting firm. At the other extreme, a project may involve thousands of people working for several years, performing work unlike that ever done before, as was the case with the project to land the first men on the moon. The discussion here will not describe either of these extremes. Rather, it focuses on projects that have a formal control organization and that consume enough resources so a formal management control system is necessary. Extremely complex first-of-a-kind projects have more complicated control problems than those described here, although the general nature of these problems and of the appropriate management control system are similar.

Contrast with Ongoing Operations

This section describes characteristics of projects that make the management control of projects different from the management control of ongoing activities.

Single objective. A project usually has a single objective; ongoing operations have multiple objectives. In addition to supervising day-to-day work, the manager of a responsibility center in an ongoing organization must both supervise today's work and also make decisions that affect future operations. Equipment that affects future operations is ordered; marketing campaigns are planned; new procedures are developed and implemented; employees are trained for new positions. Although the project manager also makes decisions that affect the future, the time horizon is the end of the project. Project performance can be judged in terms of the desired end product; operating performance should be judged in terms of all the results that the manager achieves, some of which will not be known until a year or more later.

Organization structure. In many cases, the project organization is superimposed on an ongoing operating organization, and its management control system is superimposed on the management control system of that organization. These problems do not exist in an ongoing organization. Satisfactory relationships must be established between the project organization and the ongoing

---

[1] For a discussion of this problem, see Paul R. Lawrence and Jay W. Lorsch, *Organization and Environment* (Homewood, Ill.: Richard D. Irwin, 1969).

operating organization. Similarly, the management control system for the project must mesh at certain points with the control system of the ongoing organization.

Focus on the project.   Project control focuses on the project, whose objectives are to produce a satisfactory product, within a specified time period, and at an optimum cost. In contrast, control in ongoing organizations focuses on the activities of a specified time period, such as a month, and on all the products worked on in that period. The primary focus of the management control of operating activities tends to be on cost, with quality and schedule being treated on an exception basis—that is, the formal system emphasizes cost performance, but special reports are prepared if quality and schedule are judged to be less than satisfactory.

Need for trade-offs.   Projects usually involve trade-offs between scope, schedule, and cost. Costs can be reduced by decreasing the scope of the project. The schedule can be shortened by incurring overtime costs. Similar trade-offs occur in ongoing organizations, but they are not typical of the day-to-day activities in such organizations.

Less-reliable standards.   Performance standards tend to be less reliable for projects than for ongoing organizations. Although the specifications of one project and the method of producing it may be similar to those for other projects, the project design literally is used only once.

Nevertheless, standards for repetitive project activities can be developed from past experience or from engineering analyses of the optimum time and costs. To the extent that the activities on a given project are similar to those on other projects, the experience on these projects can be used as a basis for estimating time and costs. If the project is the construction of a house, good historical information exists on the unit costs of building similar houses. (However, changes in materials, in the technology of house building, or in building codes may make this information unreliable as a guide to the cost of building the next house, and site-specific problems may also affect the actual cost of a given house.) However, many projects are sufficiently different from prior projects, so that historical information is not of much help, and allowances must be made for their unique characteristics. The cost estimate for constructing a house usually contains a contingency allowance, whereas such an allowance is not customary in calculating the standard cost of producing a product in the factory.

Frequent changes in plans.   Plans for projects tend to be changed frequently and drastically. Unforeseen environmental conditions on a construction project or unexpected facts uncovered during a consulting engagement may lead to changes in plans. The results of one phase of the investigation in a research and development project may completely alter the work originally planned for subsequent phases.

Different rhythm.   The rhythm of a project differs from that of ongoing operations. Most projects start small, build up to a peak activity, and then taper off as completion nears and only cleanup remains to be done. Ongoing activities tend to operate at the same level for a considerable time and then to change, in either direction, from that level to another.

Greater environmental influence.   Projects tend to be influenced more by the external environment than is the case with operations in a factory. The walls and roof of a factory protect production activities from the environment. Construction projects occur outdoors and are subject to climatic and other geographical conditions. If the project involves excavating, conditions beneath the earth's surface may cause unexpected problems, even for such a simple project as building a house. Consulting projects take place on the client's premises and involve "finding one's way around," both geographically and organizationally.

Resources for many projects are brought to the project site. Workers on a construction project go to the project, and a construction project has other logistical problems that do not ordinarily occur with production operations. Workers on a production line stay in one room.

Exceptions.   These distinctions are not clear-cut. A job shop, such as a printing company, produces dissimilar end products; however, the focus of management control in such an organization is on the totality of its activities during a month or other specified period, not on individual jobs. In some projects, team members are hired for the job; they are not associated with functional departments in an ongoing organization. Projects in a research laboratory are conducted on the premises rather than in outside facilities.

THE CONTROL ENVIRONMENT

Project Organization Structure

A project organization is a temporary organization. A team is assembled for conducting the project, and the team is disbanded when the project has been completed. Team members may be employees of the sponsoring organization, they may be hired for the purpose, or some or all of them may be engaged under a contract with an outside organization.

If the project is conducted entirely or partly by an outside contractor, the project sponsor should quickly establish satisfactory working arrangements with the contractor's personnel. These relationships are influenced by the terms of the contract, as will be discussed later. If the project is conducted by the sponsoring organization, some of the work may be assigned to support units within the organization, and similar relationships should be established with them. For example, a central drafting unit in an architectural firm may do drafting for all projects, and management control problems of such arrangements are similar to those involved in contracting with an outside drafting organization.

Matrix organizations.   If members of the project team are employees of the sponsoring organization, they have two "bosses": the project manager and the manager of the functional department to which they are permanently assigned. Such an arrangement is called a "matrix organization." In overhauling a ship, craftspeople (e.g., electricians, sheet metal workers, pipe fitters) are drawn from various functional departments in the shipyard, and they work on the project when their skills are needed. However, their basic loyalty is to their functional department. Whether they appear at the work site at the scheduled time depends in part on decisions made by the manager of their functional department, who considers the relative priorities of all projects requiring the resources he or she controls. The project manager, therefore, has less authority over personnel than the manager of a production department, whose employees have an undivided loyalty to that department.

Project managers want full attention given to their projects, while functional responsibility center managers must take into account all the projects on which the employees of that center work. This conflict of interest is inevitable; it creates tension. As Vancil writes, there is "an atmosphere of constructive conflict."[2]

Evolution of organization structure.   Different types of management personnel and management methods may be appropriate at different stages of the project. In the planning phase of a construction project, architects, engineers, schedulers, and cost analysts predominate. In the execution of the project, the managers are production managers. In the final stages, the work tapers off, and the principal task may be to obtain the sponsor's acceptance, with marketing skills being a principal requirement (especially in consulting projects).

Contractual Relationships

If the project is conducted by an outside contractor, an additional level of project control is created. In addition to the control exercised by the contractor who does the work, the sponsoring organization has its own control responsibilities. The contractor may bring its own control system to the project, and this system may need to be adapted to provide information that the sponsor

---

[2] Richard F. Vancil, "What Kind of Management Control Do You Need?" *Harvard Business Review*, March–April 1973, p. 75.

needs. (This does not imply that there are duplicate systems; the sponsor's system should use data from the project system.)

The form of the contractual arrangement has an important impact on management control. Contracts are of two general types: fixed price and cost reimbursement, with many variations within each type.

Fixed-price contracts.   In a fixed-price contract, the contractor agrees to complete the specified work by a specified date at a specified price. Usually, there are penalties if the work is not completed to specifications or if the scheduled date is not met. It would appear, therefore, that the contractor assumes all the risks and consequently has all the responsibility for management control; however, this is by no means the case. If the sponsor decides to change the scope of the project, or if the contractor encounters conditions not contemplated by the contractual agreement, a *change order* is issued. The parties must agree on the scope, schedule, and cost implications of each change order. To the extent that change orders involve increased costs, these costs are borne by the sponsor. The construction of a conventional house may involve a dozen or so change orders; on some complex projects, there are thousands. In these circumstances, the final price of the work is actually not fixed in advance.

In a fixed-price contract, the sponsor is responsible for auditing the quality and quantity of the work to ensure that it is done as specified. This may be as comprehensive a task as auditing the cost of work under a cost-reimbursement contract.

Cost-reimbursement contracts.   In a cost-reimbursement contract, the sponsor agrees to pay reasonable costs plus a profit (often with a "not-to-exceed" upper limit). In such a contract, the sponsor has considerable responsibility for the control of costs and, therefore, needs a management control system and associated control personnel that are comparable to the system and personnel used by the contractor with a fixed-price contract. A cost-reimbursement contract is appropriate when the scope, schedule, and cost of the project cannot be estimated reliably in advance.

Contrasts in contract types.   The price for a fixed-price contract is bid by, or proposed by, the contractor. In arriving at this price, a competent contractor includes an allowance for contingencies, and the size of this allowance varies with the degree of uncertainty. Thus, for a project with considerable uncertainty and a correspondingly large contingency allowance, the sponsor may end up paying more under a fixed-price contract than under a cost-reimbursement contract in which there is no such contingency allowance. This extra payment is the contractor's reward for the assumption of risk.

Fixed-price contracts are appropriate when the scope of the project can be closely specified in advance and when uncertainties are low. In these circumstances, the contractor cannot significantly increase the price by negotiating change orders and, therefore, is motivated to control costs. If the contractor signs a contract that does not include adequate provisions for adjustments caused by changes in scope or by uncontrollable uncertainties, it will resist the sponsor's requests to make desirable changes, and, in the extreme case, it may be unwilling to complete the project. If the contractor walks away from the project, no one gains: the sponsor doesn't get the product, the contractor doesn't get paid, and both parties may incur legal fees.

In a cost-reimbursement contract, the profit component, or fee, usually should be a fixed monetary amount. If it is a percentage of costs, the contractor is motivated to make the costs high and thereby increase its profit. However, the fixed fee normally is adjusted if the scope or schedule of the project is significantly changed.

Variations. Within these two general types of contracts are many variations. In an *incentive contract,* completion dates or cost targets, or both, are defined in advance, and the contractor is rewarded for completing the project earlier than the target date or for incurring less than the target cost. This reward is in the form of a completion bonus that is set at an amount per unit of time saved or is a cost bonus that is set as a percentage of the costs saved, or is both. Such a contract would appear to overcome the inherent weakness of a cost-reimbursement contract, which has no such rewards. However, if the targets are unrealistic, the incentive is ineffective. Thus, an incentive contract is a middle ground; it is appropriate when moderately reliable estimates of completion and cost can be made.

Different contract types may be used for different activities on the project. For example, direct costs may be reimbursed under a cost-reimbursement contract because of the high degree of uncertainty, while the contractor's overhead costs may be covered by a fixed-price contract, either for the total project or for each month. A fixed-price contract for overhead motivates the contractor to control these costs; avoids the necessity of checking on the reasonableness of individual salary rates, fringe benefits, bonuses, and other amenities; reduces the contractor's tendency to load the overhead payroll with less qualified personnel; and encourages the contractor to complete the work as soon as possible so supervisory personnel will be freed for other projects. However, such a contract may also motivate the contractor to skimp on supervisory personnel, on a good control system, and on other resources that help get the project completed in the most efficient manner.

If unit costs can be estimated reasonably well, but the quantity of work is uncertain, the contract may be for a fixed price per unit applied to the actual number of units provided—for example, in a catering activity, reimbursement is often a stated amount per meal served (plus, perhaps, a fixed monthly amount for overhead).

Information Structure

Work packages. In a project control system, information is structured by elements of the project. The smallest element is called a "work package," and the way in which these work packages are aggregated is called the "work breakdown structure."

A work package is a measurable increment of work, usually of fairly short duration (a month or so). It should have an unambiguous, identifiable completion point; that is called a "milestone." Each work package should be the responsibility of a single manager.

If the project has similar work packages (e.g., a separate work package for the electrical work on each floor of an office building), each should be defined in the same way, so that cost and schedule information can be compared with similar work packages. Similarly, if an industry has developed cost or time standards for the performance of certain types of work packages (as is the case in many branches of the construction industry), or if the project organization has developed such standards on the basis of prior work, definitions used in these standards should be followed.

Indirect cost accounts. In addition to work packages for direct project work, cost accounts are established for administrative and support activities. Unlike the work packages, these activities have no defined output. Their estimated costs usually are stated as per unit of time, such as a month, just as the overhead costs of ongoing responsibility centers are stated.

The chart of accounts, the rules for charging costs to projects, and the approval authorities and their specific signing powers also are developed in advance. Which cost items will be charged directly to work packages? What will be the lowest level of monetary cost aggregation? Should cost commitments be recorded, in addition to actual costs incurred? (For many types of projects, this is highly desirable.) How, if at all, will overhead costs and equipment usage be allocated to work packages?

If during the project it turns out that the work breakdown structure or the accounting system is not useful, it must be revised. This may require recasting much information, both information already collected and information describing future plans. Revising the information structure in midstream is a difficult, time-consuming, frustrating task. To avoid this work, the project planners should give considerable attention, before the project starts, to designing and installing a sound management control system.

PROJECT PLANNING

In the planning phase, the project planning team takes as a starting point the rough estimates that were used as the basis for the decision to undertake the project. It refines these estimates into detailed specifications for the product, detailed schedules, and a cost budget. It also develops a management control system and underlying task control systems (or adapts these from systems used previously), and an organization chart. The boxes on this organization chart gradually are filled with the names of personnel who are to manage the work.

On a project of even moderate complexity, there is a "plan for planning"—that is, a description of each planning task, who is responsible for it, when it should be completed, and the interrelationships among tasks. The planning process is itself a subproject within the overall project. There is also a control system to insure that the planning activities are properly carried out.

Nature of the Project Plan

The final plan consists of three related parts: scope, schedule, and cost.

Scope. This part states the specifications of each work package and the name of the person or organization unit responsible. If the project is one in which specifications are nebulous, as is the case with many consulting and research and development projects, this statement is necessarily brief and general.

Schedule. This part states the estimated time required to complete each work package and the interrelationships among work packages (i.e., which work package(s) must be completed before another can be started). The set of these relationships is called a "network." Networks are described in the next section.

Cost. Costs are stated in the project budget, usually called the "control budget." Unless work packages are quite large, monetary costs are shown only for aggregates of several work packages. Resources to be used for individual work packages are stated as nonmonetary amounts, such as person-days or cubic yards of concrete.

Network Analysis

Several tools are available for constructing the time schedule for the project. They go by such acronyms as PERT (program evaluation and review technique) and CPM (critical path method). Each technique has three basic steps: (1) estimating the time required for each work package, (2) identifying the interdependencies among work packages (which work package(s) must be completed before a given work package can be started), and (3) calculating the critical path. Collectively, these are techniques for *network analysis.* A network diagram consist of (*a*) a number of *nodes* (i.e., events or milestones), each of

EXHIBIT 17-1   Critical Path (heavy line indicates critical path)

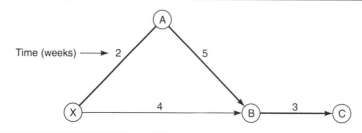

which is a subgoal that must be completed to accomplish the project; and *(b)* lines joining these nodes to one another; these lines represent activities. The estimated time to carry out each activity is shown on the network diagram. An activity connecting two events, say A and B, indicates that the activity leading to B cannot be started until event A has happened, and that the completion of the activity results in event B. These activities are work packages. Thus, a network diagram shows the chronological sequence in which events must be completed in order to complete the whole project.

Critical path and slack.   Computer programs are available for analyzing project networks. They identify the *critical path*, which is the sequence of events that has the shortest total time to complete the project. The nature of the critical path is shown in Exhibit 17–1. To complete event B, event A must first be completed; this requires two weeks. A–B requires an additional five weeks. Then B–C, requiring an additional three weeks, is done to complete the project. This is the critical path, and it is 10 weeks long. Note that, to complete event B, activity X–B also must be undertaken, with an estimated time of four weeks. However, activity B–C cannot be started until both A–B and X–B have been completed. X–A and A–B require a total of seven weeks; and X–B, which requires only four weeks, can be performed at any time during this seven-week period. Activity X–B is said to have three weeks of "slack."

There are several management control implications in the concepts of critical path and slack. First, in the control process, special attention must be paid to those activities that are on the critical path, and less attention needs to be paid to slack activities (although time must not be allowed to slip by that eats up the amount of slack; the activity then automatically is on the critical path). Second, in the planning process, attention should be given to possibilities for reducing the time required for critical path activities; if such possibilities exist, the overall time required for the project can be reduced. Third, it may be desirable to reduce critical path times by increasing costs, such as incurring overtime; but additional money should not be spent to reduce the time of slack activities.

Probabilistic PERT. As PERT was originally conceived, the estimated times required for each activity in the network were arrived at on a probabilistic basis. Three estimates were made for each activity: a most likely time, an optimistic time, and a pessimistic time. The optimistic and pessimistic times were supposed to represent probabilities of approximately 0.01 and 0.99 on a normal probability distribution. It was soon discovered that this approach had serious practical difficulties. Engineers, and others who were asked to make the three estimates, found this to be a most difficult task. It turned out not to be possible, in most cases, to convey what was intended by "optimistic" and "pessimistic" in a way that was interpreted similarly by all the estimators. Although probabilistic PERT is still referred to in the literature and in formal descriptions of the PERT technique, the probabilistic part is not widely used in practice.

Estimating Costs

For practical reasons, cost estimates are often made at a level of aggregation that incorporates several work packages. Resources used on individual work packages are controlled in terms of physical quantities, rather than costs, and costing out each work package would serve no useful purpose.

Cost estimates for most projects tend to be less accurate than those for manufactured goods, because projects are less standardized, and cost information that has been accumulated for similar work is therefore not as valid a basis for comparison. Nevertheless, if a contractor has performed similar work in the past, the costs incurred on these work packages provide a starting point in estimating the costs of the new project. For some work, industry norms, or rules of thumb, have been developed that are useful in estimating costs.

Obviously, no one knows what actually will happen in the future; therefore, no one knows for sure what future costs actually will be. In estimating what costs are likely to be, two types of unknowns must be taken into account. The first are the *known unknowns*. These are estimates of the cost of activities that are known to be going to occur, such as digging the foundation for a house. The nature of the task is known; and the costs, although unknown, often can be estimated within reasonable limits on the basis of past experience. If unexpected rock or other conditions are encountered, however, these estimates may turn out to be far from the mark.

The other unknowns are the *unknown unknowns*. For these activities, the estimator does not know that they are going to occur, and obviously, therefore, has no way of estimating their cost. Work stoppages, destruction caused by storms or floods, delays in receiving materials, accidents, and failure of government inspectors to act in a timely manner, are examples. A fixed-price contract usually provides that costs caused by such events are added to the fixed price.

In using cost estimates in the evaluation phase, the impossibility of estimating the cost of unknown unknowns must be recognized. Their actual costs may range from zero, if none of them actually occur, up to any amount. There is no definable upper limit. If the contract does not provide that all these costs are added to the fixed price, the estimator should include a contingency allowance for them.

Preparing the Control Budget

The control budget is prepared close to the inception of the work, allowing just enough time for approval by decision makers prior to the commitment of costs. For a lengthy project, the initial control budget may be prepared in detail only for the first phase of the project, with fairly rough cost estimates for later phases. Detailed budgets for later phases are prepared just prior to the beginning of work on these phases. Delaying preparation of the control budget until just prior to the start of work ensures that the control budget incorporates current information about scope and schedule, the results of cost analyses, and current data about wage rates, material prices, and other variables. It, therefore, avoids doing work that is based on what may turn out to be obsolete information.

The control budget is an important link between planning and the control of performance. It represents both the sponsor's expectations about what the project will cost and also the project manager's commitment to carry out the project at that cost. If, as the project proceeds, it appears there will be a significant budget overrun, the project may no longer be economically justified. In these circumstances the sponsor may reexamine the scope and the schedule, and perhaps modify them.

Other Planning Activities

During the planning phase, other activities are performed: material is ordered, permits are obtained, preliminary interviews are conducted, personnel are selected, and so on. All these activities must be controlled and integrated into the overall effort.

One set of activities involves the selection and organization of personnel. After personnel come on board, they get to know one another, they find out where they fit in the project organization, they learn what to expect and what not to expect from other parts of the organization, and they learn what is expected of them. Information learned and expectations developed during this stage are a part of the control "climate," which can have a profound effect on the successful completion of the project.

PROJECT EXECUTION

At the end of the planning process, there exists for most projects a specification of work packages, a schedule, and a budget; and the manager who is responsible for each work package is identified. The schedule shows the estimated time for each activity, and the budget shows estimated costs of each principal part of the project. This information often is stated in a financial model. If resources to be used in detailed work packages are expressed in non-monetary terms, such as the number of person-days required, the control budget states monetary costs only for a sizable aggregation of individual work packages. In the control process, data on actual cost, actual time, and actual accomplishment are compared with these estimates. The comparison may be made either when a designated milestone in the project is reached or at specified time intervals, such as weekly or monthly.

Basically, both the sponsor and the project manager are concerned with these questions: (1) Is the project going to be finished by the scheduled completion date? (2) Is the completed work going to meet the stated specifications? (3) Is the work going to be done within the estimated cost? If at any time during the course of the project the answer to one of these questions is "no," the sponsor and the project manager need to know the reasons and the alternatives for corrective action.

These three questions are not considered separately from one another, for it is sometimes desirable to make trade-offs among time, specifications, and cost, using the financial model and other available information. For example, overtime might be authorized to assure completion on time, even though this would add to costs; or some of the specifications might be relaxed to reduce costs.

Nature of Reports

Managers need three somewhat different types of reports: trouble reports, progress reports, and financial reports.

Trouble reports. These report both on trouble that has already happened (such as a delay resulting from any of a number of possible causes) and also anticipated future trouble. Critical problems are flagged. It is essential that these reports get to the appropriate manager quickly, so corrective action can be initiated; they often are transmitted by face-to-face conversation, telephone, or facsimile. Precision is sacrificed in the interest of speed; rough numbers often are used—person-hours, rather than labor costs, or numbers of bricks, rather than material cost. If the matter reported on is significant, an oral report later is confirmed by a written document, so as to provide a record.

Progress reports. Progress reports compare actual schedule and costs with planned schedule and costs for the work done, and they contain similar comparisons for overhead activities not directly related to the work. Variances associated with price, schedule delays, and similar factors may be identified and measured quantitatively, using techniques for variance analysis that are similar to those used in the analysis of ongoing operations.

Financial reports. Accurate reports of project costs must be prepared if there is a cost-reimbursement contract, as a basis for progress payments; and they usually are necessary for fixed-price contracts, as a basis for financial accounting entries. However, these reports are less important for management control purposes than the cost information contained in progress reports. Because the financial reports must be accurate, they are carefully checked, and this process takes time. Less-precise information that is available quickly is more important to project management.

Much of the information in management reports comes from detailed records collected in task control systems. These include such documents as work schedules, time sheets, inventory records, purchase orders, requisitions, and equipment records. In designing these task control systems, their use as a source of management control information is one consideration.

Quantity of Reports

To make certain that all needs for information are satisfied, management accountants sometimes create more than the optimum number of reports. An unnecessary report, or extraneous information in a report, incurs extra costs in assembling and transmitting the information. More important, users may spend unnecessary time reading the report, or they may overlook important information that is buried in the mass of detail. In the course of the project, therefore, a review of the set of reports often is desirable, and this may lead to the elimination of some reports and the simplification of others.

This *paperwork problem* (often referred to in the literature as *information overload*) is not necessarily serious. Competent managers learn which reports, or sections of a report, are likely to be useful to them, and they focus first on these. If, but only if, possible problems are identified from this inspection, they refer to more detailed information.

Percent Complete

Some work packages will be only partially completed at the reporting date, and the percentage of completion of each such work package must be estimated as a basis for comparing actual time with scheduled time and actual costs with budgeted costs. If accomplishment is measured in physical terms, such as cubic yards of concrete poured, the percentage of completion for a given work package can be measured easily. If no quantitative measure is available, as in the case of many R & D and consulting projects, the percentage of completion is subjective. Some organizations compare actual labor-hours with budgeted labor-hours as a basis for estimating completion; but this assumes that the actual labor effort accomplished all that was planned, which may not have been the case. Narrative reports of progress may be of some help, but these often are difficult to interpret. If the percentage of completion is not ascertainable from quantitative data, the manager relies on personal observation, meetings, and other informal sources as a basis for judging progress.

Summarizing progress. In addition to determining the percentage of completion of individual work packages, a summary of progress on the whole project also is useful. Progress payments often are made when specified milestones are reached. Thus, the system usually contains some method of aggregating individual work packages and so develops an overall measure of accomplishment. A simple approach is to use the ratio of actual person-hours on work packages completed to date to total person-hours for the project; but this is reliable only if the project is labor-intensive. If the system includes estimated costs for each work package, a weighting based on the planned cost of each work package may be informative.

Use of Reports

Trouble Reports. Managers spend much time dealing with reports of trouble. The typical project has many such reports, and one of the manager's tasks is to decide which ones have the highest priority. In the limited number of hours in a day, the manager of a large project cannot possibly deal with all the situations that have caused, or that may cause, the project to proceed less than smoothly. The manager, therefore, has to decide which problems will get his or her personal attention, which will be delegated to someone else, and which will be disregarded on the assumption that operating personnel will take the necessary corrective action.

Progress reports. Not only do managers limit the number of trouble spots to which they give personal attention, they also avoid spending so much time solving immediate problems that no time remains for careful analysis of the progress reports. Such an analysis may reveal potential problems that are not apparent in the reports of trouble, and the manager needs to identify these problems and plan how they are to be solved. The temptation is to spend too much time on current problems and not enough time identifying problems that are not yet apparent. Some managers deliberately set aside a block of time to reflect on what lies ahead.

The approach to analyzing progress reports is the familiar one of "management by exception." If progress in a particular area is satisfactory, no attention needs to be paid to the area (except to congratulate the persons responsible). Attention is focused on those areas in which progress is or may become unsatisfactory.

The analyses of reports that show actual time compared to the schedule, and actual cost compared to budget, are relatively straightforward. In interpreting the time report, the usual presumption is that if a work package was completed in less than the estimated time, the responsible supervisor is to be congratulated; but if more than the estimated time was spent, questions are raised. The interpretation of the cost report is somewhat different, for the possibility exists

EXHIBIT 17–2   Interpretation of Cost/Schedule Reports

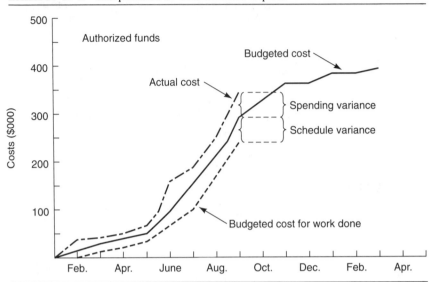

that if actual costs were less than budget, quality may have suffered. For this reason, unless there is some independent way of estimating what costs should have been, good cost performance often is interpreted to mean being on budget, neither higher nor lower.

It is important that actual costs be compared with the budgeted costs of the work done, which is not necessarily the same as the budgeted costs for the time period. The danger of misinterpretation is illustrated in Exhibit 17–2, which shows actual and budgeted costs for a project. As of the end of September, actual costs were $345,000, compared with budgeted costs of $300,000, which indicates a cost overrun of $45,000. However, the budgeted cost of the work actually completed through September was only $260,000, so the true overrun was $85,000.

Reports on indirect costs are prepared separately. These reports measure costs in a different dimension than do reports on the direct costs of project work. In the case of direct costs, actual costs are compared with budgeted costs for the work actually accomplished. In the case of indirect costs, the actual costs for a period, such as a month, are compared with the budgeted costs for that same period.

Cost to complete.   In their progress reports, some organizations compare actual costs to date with budgeted costs for the work that has been done to date. Others report the current estimate of total costs for the entire project, compared with the budgeted cost for the entire project. The current estimate is obtained by taking the actual cost to date and adding an estimated cost to complete—that is, the additional costs required to complete the project. The latter type of report is a useful way of showing how the project is expected to come out, provided that the estimated cost to complete is properly calculated.

In most circumstances, the current estimate of total cost should be at least equal to the actual cost incurred to date plus the *original* estimates made for the remaining work. If project managers are permitted to use lower amounts, they can hide overruns by making overly optimistic future estimates. In fact, if overruns to date are caused by factors that are likely to persist in the future, such as unanticipated inflation, the current estimates of future costs probably should be higher than the amounts estimated originally.

Informal Sources of Information

Because written reports are visible, the description of a management control system tends to focus on them. In practice, these reports usually are less important than information that the project manager gathers from talking with people who actually do the work, with members of his or her staff, from regularly scheduled or ad hoc meetings, from informal memoranda, and from personal inspection of how the work is going. From these sources, the manager learns of potential problems and of circumstances that may cause actual progress to deviate from the plan. This information also helps the manager to understand the significance of the formal reports because these reports may not describe important events that affected actual performance.

In many cases, a problem may be uncovered and corrective action taken before a formal report is prepared, and the formal report does no more than confirm facts that the manager has already learned from informal sources. This is an illustration of the principle that formal reports should contain no surprises. Nevertheless, formal reports are necessary. They document the information that the manager has learned informally, and this documentation is important if questions about the project are raised subsequently, especially if there is a controversy about the results. Also, subordinate managers who read the formal reports may discover that these are not an accurate statement of what has happened, and they take steps to correct the misunderstanding.

Revisions

If a project is complex, or if it is lengthy, there is a good chance that the plan will not be adhered to in one or more of its three aspects: scope, schedule, or cost. A common occurrence is the discovery that there is likely to be a budget overrun—that is, actual costs will exceed budgeted costs. If this happens, the sponsor might decide to accept the overrun and proceed with the project as originally planned; or decide to cut back on the scope of the project with the aim of producing an end product that is within the original cost limitation; or decide to replace the project manager if the sponsor concludes that the budget overrun was unwarranted. Whatever the decision, it usually leads to a revised plan. In some cases, the sponsor may judge that the current estimate of benefits is lower than the current cost-to-complete estimate and, therefore, decide to terminate the project. (Costs that have already been incurred are sunk and, therefore, should be disregarded in making this decision.)

If the plan is revised, the following question arises: Is it better to track future progress against the revised plan or to track against the original plan? The revised plan is presumably a better indication of the performance that is currently expected; but there is a danger that a persuasive project manager can negotiate unwarranted increases in budgeted costs or that the revised plan will incorporate, and thus hide, inefficiencies that have accumulated to date. In either case, the revised plan may be a *rubber baseline*—that is, instead of providing a firm benchmark against which performance is measured, it may be stretched to cover up inefficiencies.

This possibility can be minimized by taking a hardheaded attitude toward proposed revisions. Nevertheless, there is a tendency to overlook the fact that a revised plan, by definition, does not show what was expected when the project was initiated. On the other hand, if performance continues to be monitored by comparing it with the original plan, the comparison may not be taken seriously because the original plan is known to be obsolete.

A solution to this problem is to compare actual cost with *both* the original plan and the revised plan. The first section of such a summary report shows the original budget, the revisions that have been authorized to date, and the reasons for making them. Another section shows the current cost estimate and the factors that caused the variance between the revised budget and the current estimate of costs. Exhibit 17–3 is an example of such a report.

Project Auditing

In many projects, the audit of quality must take place as the work is being done. If it is delayed, defective work on individual work packages may be hidden; they are covered up by subsequent work. (For example, the quality of plumbing work on a construction project cannot be checked after walls and ceilings have been finished.) In some projects, the audit of costs also is done as the work progresses; in others, the cost audit is not made until the project has been completed. In general, auditing as the work progresses is preferable; it may uncover potential errors that can be corrected before they become serious. However, project auditors should not take an undue amount of the time of those who are responsible for doing the work.

In recent years internal auditors have expanded their function into what is called "operational auditing." In addition to examining costs incurred, they call attention to management actions that they believe are substandard. Properly done, operational auditing can be useful. However, there is the great dan-

EXHIBIT 17–3   Project Cost Summary ($000s)

Original budget	$1,000
Authorized revisions to date:	
For inflation	50
For specification changes	200
For time delays	60
For cost savings	(30)
Revised budget	1,280
Current estimate to complete	1,400
Variance	120
Explanation of Variance:	
Material cost increases	$ 20
Overtime	60
Spending variances	40
	120

ger that the auditors, who, after all, are not managers, will second-guess the decisions that managers made in the light of all the circumstances—as the managers understood them—at the time the decisions were made.

PROJECT EVALUATION

The evaluation of projects has two separate aspects: (1) an evaluation of performance in executing the project and (2) an evaluation of the results obtained from the project. The former is carried out shortly after the project has been completed; the latter may not be feasible until several years later.

Evaluation of Performance

The evaluation of performance in executing the project has two aspects: (1) an evaluation of project management and (2) an evaluation of the process of managing the project. The purpose of the former is to assist in decisions regarding project managers, including rewards, promotion, constructive criticism, or reassignment. The purpose of the latter is to discover better ways of conducting future projects. In many cases these evaluations are informal. If the results of the project were unsatisfactory and if the project was important, a formal evaluation is worthwhile. Also, formal evaluation of a highly successful project may identify techniques that will improve performance on future projects.

Because work on a project tends to be less standardized and less susceptible to measurement than work in a factory, evaluation of a project is more subjective than evaluation of production activities. It resembles the evaluation of marketing activities, in that the effect of external factors on performance must be taken into account. A judgment about whether actual accomplishment was satisfactory under the actual circumstances encountered is highly subjective.

Budget overruns.   When actual costs exceed budgeted costs, there is said to be a "budget overrun." To some, this implies that actual costs were too high. An equally plausible conclusion, however, is that the budgeted costs were too low. If the higher costs resulted from changes in the scope of the project or from noncontrollable factors, the explanation is that there was an underestimate of costs, rather than excessive actual costs. Interpretation of the cost reports is complicated by the need to analyze both the budget and the actual costs.

A common error in analyzing costs is to assume that the budget represents what the costs should have been. It does not. At best, the budget estimates what the cost should have been *based on the information that was available at the time it was prepared*. This information rarely is an accurate reflection of conditions that will be encountered on the project; and to the extent that it is inaccurate, the budget does not reflect what the costs should be. Moreover, budget numbers are estimates made by human beings and they are based, in part, on judgments and assumptions. Although reasonable people can differ in their judgments and assumptions, only one set of conclusions is incorporated in the budget.

Hindsight.   In looking back at how well the work on the project was managed, the natural temptation is to rely on information that was not available at the time. With hindsight, one can usually discover instances in which the "right" decision was not made. However, the decision made at the time may have been entirely reasonable: the manager may not have had all the information at that time; or the manager may not have addressed a particular problem because other problems had a higher priority; or the manager may have based the decision on personality considerations, trade-offs, or other factors not recorded in written reports.

Nevertheless, some positive indications of poor management may be identified. Diversion of funds or other assets to the personal use of the project manager is one obvious example. If there were major specification changes or cost overruns, these changes should have been authorized, and cash flows should have been recalculated to determine whether the return on the project was still acceptable. Another example of poor management is a manager's failure to tighten a control system that permits others to steal; but this is more difficult to judge because overly tight controls may impede progress on the project. Evidence that the manager regards cost control as much less important than an excellent product that was completed on schedule is another indication of poor management, but it is not conclusive. The sponsor may overlook budget over-runs if the product is outstanding, as often happens for motion picture projects and investment banking deals.

The evaluation of the process may indicate that reviews conducted during the project were inadequate, or that timely action was not taken on the basis of these reviews. For example, the review may indicate that, on the basis of information available at the time, the project should have been redirected or even discontinued, but this was not done. This may suggest that more frequent or more thorough analyses of progress should have been made; consequently, requirements for such reviews on future projects should be modified.

The evaluation also may lead to changes in rules or procedures. It may identify some rules that impeded efficient conduct of the project. Conversely, it may uncover inadequate controls. As part of the evaluation, suggestions for improving the process should be solicited from project personnel.

Evaluation of Results

The success of a project cannot be evaluated until enough time has elapsed to permit measurement of its actual benefits and costs. This may take years. Moreover, unless the impact can be specifically measured, such an evaluation may not be worthwhile. To take extreme examples, the benefits of the introduction of a new product line usually can be measured because the revenues and expenses associated with that line will be known; whereas the benefits of installing a labor-saving machine will not be identifiable if the resulting costs are buried in a variety of product costs and not separately traced to the new machine. Furthermore, there is no point in attempting to evaluate success unless some action can be taken based on this analysis.

For many projects, evaluation of results is complicated by the fact that the expected benefits were not stated in objective, measurable terms, and the actual benefits also were not measurable. In these cases, a quantitative benefit/cost analysis is not feasible, and reliance must be placed on judgments by knowledgeable people about the project's accomplishments. This is the situation in the majority of projects undertaken by governments and nonprofit organizations, many research and development projects, projects undertaken by staff units, and projects whose objective is to improve safety or eliminate environmental deficiencies.

Part of the evaluation should be a comparison of the actual results with the results that were anticipated when the project was approved. The anticipated results were based on certain assumptions (e.g., for a new product: size of the market, market share, competitor's reactions, inflation), and these assumptions should have been documented during the process of approving the project.

Unless the need for such documentation was recognized, the record is likely to be incomplete or vague. The evaluator should foresee the possible future need for this documentation and ensure that the necessary information is collected and preserved. Because of these limitations, the results of relatively few projects are subjected to a formal evaluation (often called a "post-completion audit").[3] The points made in the preceding paragraph suggest criteria for selecting those that are to be evaluated:

1. The project should be important enough to warrant the considerable expenditure of effort that is involved in a formal evaluation.

2. The results usually should be quantifiable. Specifically, if the project was intended to produce a specified amount of additional profit, the actual profit attributable to the project should be measurable.

3. The effects of unanticipated variables should be known, at least approximately, and they should not swamp the effect of changes in the assumptions on which the project was approved. If the results of a new product introduction were unsatisfactory because the market for the product evaporated, not much worthwhile information can be learned from an evaluation.

4. Results of the evaluation should have a good chance of leading to action. In particular, the analysis may lead to better ways of proposing and deciding on future projects.

Occasionally, projects that do not meet these criteria should be selected for analysis. Deficiencies in the system for controlling relatively unimportant projects may be overlooked if the appraisal is limited only to major projects.

SUMMARY

The most important difference between the management control of ongoing operations and the management control of projects is that the ongoing operations continue indefinitely, whereas a project ends. Exhibit 17–4 illustrates this point. The elements in the management control of operations recur; one leads to the next in a prescribed way and at a prescribed time. Although some operating activities change from one month to the next, many of them continue relatively unchanged, month after month, or even year after year. By contrast, a project starts, moves forward from one milestone to the next, and then stops. During its life, plans are made, they are executed, and the results are evaluated. The evaluations are made at regular intervals, and these may lead to revision of the plan.

---

[3] In a survey of large industrial companies with 282 responses, only 25 percent reported use of what the survey authors described as "adequate post audit procedures," and these were used only for selected projects, usually projects with long-run implications and major resource commitments. (Lawrence A. Gordon and Mary D. Myers, "Postauditing Capital Projects," *Management Accounting,* January 1991, pp. 39–42.)

EXHIBIT 17-4 Phases of Management Control

A. In an Operating Organization

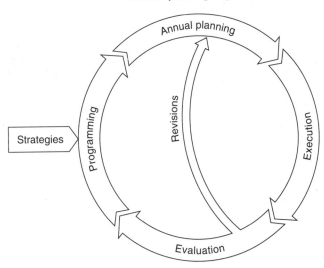

B. In a Project

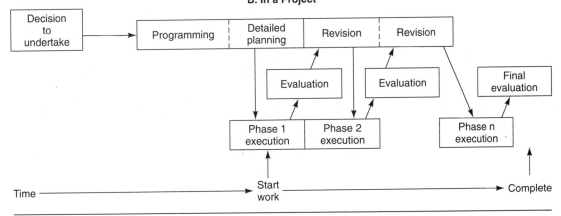

SUGGESTED ADDITIONAL READINGS

Dean, Peter N. "Accounting for Development Projects: The Issues." *Association of Government Accountants Journal,* Summer Quarter 1990, pp. 62–72. Contains an excellent bibliography of international development projects.

Lock, Dennis (ed.). *Project Management Handbook,* Aldershot, Hanks, England: Gower Technical Press, 1987.

Maciariello, Joseph A. *Project Management Control Systems.* New York: Ronald Press, 1978.

Sayles, L. R., and M. K. Chandler. *Managing Large Systems: Organizations for the Future.* New York: Harper & Row, 1971.

Stuckenbruck, Linn C. *The Implementation of Project Management: The Professional's Handbook.* Reading, Mass.: Addison-Wesley, 1989.

Case 17–1

Krypton Chemical Company*

The Chemical Division

Krypton Chemical Company, headquartered in Bradford, Oklahoma, was the chemical division of the Krypton Company. This division was formed in the early 1900s to create and manufacture chemicals for the other company divisions. In the 1950s, Krypton Chemical began to sell its products externally. In the 1970s, the division experienced enormous growth in the number and diversity of its products, such as chemicals and plastics, and of its product markets. In 1986, the division had sales of $2 billion, a level that would have placed it in the Fortune 100-to-200 range had it been a stand-alone company.

Krypton Chemical had about 14,000 employees. It had manufacturing plants in Michigan, Wisconsin, Kansas, and Oklahoma, which were managed independently. Domestic marketing was the responsibility of a separate division, Krypton Chemical Marketing, Inc., located at the Oklahoma headquarters, while the European-based Krypton International Marketing, Ltd., handled international marketing. Research and development activities were also located near Krypton Chemical's headquarters.

Initially, such chemical division functions as marketing, manufacturing, and finance were coordinated at the top of the division. As the division grew and its product lines diversified, all the decisions necessary to manage and coordinate these functions became too cumbersome for top management. In 1981, several committees were formed.

The Management Committee, the most senior committee, authorized capital expenditures for projects. It was composed of the general manager and assistant general managers from marketing and manufacturing, the directors of research and development and strategic planning, and the vice president of finance.

The Innovations Committee reviewed concepts for new products and guided product development to a stage sufficient for company commitment to commercialization. The committee assigned responsibilities, established priorities, and ensured approvals required for effective interdivisional projects before commercialization.

Committees also were formed to manage business planning aspects for families of products stemming from common raw materials. Membership on these committees consisted of functional managers from marketing, manufacturing, and research.

Making Krypton Chemical More Manageable

In 1983, Krypton Chemical identified 30 product categories and created business units to manage each. The business units were formed to place decision-making responsibility lower in the organization and to increase the participation of those individuals directly involved in product areas. In the beginning, however, the locus of deci-

---

* This case was prepared by Research Associate Mary Addonizio, under the supervision of Assistant Professor Julie H. Hertenstein, Harvard Business School.

Harvard Business School case 188–030.

sion making was unclear, so units responded slowly to their new found decision-making clout.

The business units comprised functional representatives from marketing, manufacturing, and research and development. Business team directors, who frequently were former marketing managers, chaired each business unit and managed business or product categories full time. Initially, no financial analysts were officially designated as unit members, although a business unit could request a financial analyst's services. In 1986, however, financial analysts formally were assigned to about half of the business units to help them evaluate their current and proposed projects. Other financial analysts served as ad hoc members for the other business units.

Managers' Backgrounds, Training, and Incentives

Managers at Krypton Chemical were primarily engineers or scientists, and those who advanced in the company normally had strong scientific backgrounds. Marketing was composed mainly of chemical engineers, and many employees in research and development had graduate degrees in either chemistry or engineering. Most of the division's managers had little formal business instruction; their formal education had been focused in scientific and technical areas.

Further, many managers believed that important goals for the chemical division were to lower operating costs and to increase sales. They tended to think in terms of these objectives rather than in terms of increasing profitability by improving return on investment. Performance appraisals and incentive compensation contributed to this way of thinking. A marketing manager's annual bonus was based on his or her performance evaluation and on the company's earnings for the preceding five years. Performance evaluations, which were graded "good," "fair," or "poor," were influenced heavily by increases in revenue. For manufacturing managers, keeping unit costs down was the way to achieve favorable performance reviews.

Because sales and manufacturing had long been separated, and because decision making had only recently been delegated to the business units, some managers lacked the data necessary to make preliminary judgments on the profitability of investments. For example, marketing managers might know a product's price but not its unit or variable costs. With incentives for sales increases, but lacking information on product costs, they might propose expanding a product line that was selling below costs.

Investment Proposals

The research and development department and the business units submitted proposals for new product investments or defensive investments that contained about 90 percent technical information—for instance, processing and recovery procedures for chemicals—and 10 percent financial information. Pricing information for potential products was obtained, by using the minimal acceptable market price calculation, or MAMP. This price was calculated by estimating product yields and operating costs and applying the required rate of return. When a proposal for a product reached the Innovations Committee, the only financial analysis normally included was a MAMP calculation. Proposals often required a more in-depth evaluation by a financial analyst.

Jim Bowen, manager of financial analysis, commented about some proposals that financial analysts received:

My group receives many investment proposals that should have been withdrawn by their creators much earlier. Many proposals are based upon unrealistic assumptions. In one case, a proposal writer assumed that Krypton could sell a product to the U.S. subsidiary of a European competitor who made the same product even through Krypton offered no price advantage.

In other cases, managers failed to consider competitors' responses to price changes!

I spend a great deal of time teaching managers about financial concepts, but I find that I teach the same things over and over again.

Thus, financial analysts received proposals supported by naive economic assumptions. When the inevitable proposal rejections went back to the creators, the financial analysts were accused of being "out to get" the project creators, who felt that the analysts did not know anything about running a business. Bowen commented: "Financial analysts are seen by R&D as one notch above auditors who run around the bloodied battlefield to bayonet the wounded."

Thinking Strategically

In 1986, Krypton Chemical, influenced by corporate headquarters in Texas, worked with a management consultant to help the division evaluate the business units as if each were a stand-alone company. For each unit, the consultant prepared a set of pro forma balance sheets and income statements and then determined the cost of capital. The consultant projected earnings and discounted cash flows at the required rate of return for each unit from the perspective of a theoretical shareholder. He also projected each unit's future value and worked with managers to develop strategies for increasing market value and, thus, shareholder wealth.

Working with the consultant, the chemical division began to move away from project planning toward strategic planning, with two main goals: to create a strategic plan and to fund projects that supported the plan. Dave Hadley, vice president of finance at Oklahoma Krypton, explained the shift in the division's focus from project to more strategic funding:

> In the past, we put money into projects where the long-term growth was not all that bright. We supported capital projects and research and development that we shouldn't have spent money on; and we looked at machinery and equipment as projects. Though cost reduction projects had a good rate of return for a short period of time, they were not good long-term investments. We'd get short-term returns without ever asking whether of not we should have been in the business at all. If we move to fund strategies, we probably won't be funding the same types of projects that we have in the past, but we will be funding projects that have a future.

Top management in the chemical division wanted business units to create their own long-term strategies within which to frame projects. It foresaw approving business unit strategy, rather than individual projects. With this type of planning, projects would not need as high a level of approval since they already would have been incorporated into business unit strategy.

The Management Advisor

In February 1986, Oklahoma Krypton's R&D department sponsored a symposium on artificial intelligence (AI), a field comprising a number of somewhat independent areas, including robotics, natural language processing, speech recognition, vision, speech synthesis, and expert systems. One of the products featured at the symposium was the Management Advisor, a financial expert system created by Palladian Software, Inc.

An expert system is a software program that performs much like a human expert. It can help to solve correctly a range of problems in a specialized field of knowledge by asking questions, considering relevant factors, and delivering a decision. It uses rules of thumb and empirical observations, as defined and described by an expert, to aid decision making. Most expert systems also have some form of explanation capability to answer users' questions about how the system reached its conclusions.

The Management Advisor was designed to help managers test new ideas and opportunities for financial viability and business soundness. It went beyond the capabilities of spreadsheet programs that managers used frequently to evaluate proposed investments. Its features included:

1. General rules and concepts applicable to investments (e.g., methods of computing depreciation, rules for calculating net present value, and U.S. tax code requirements).

2. Customized corporate financial assumptions, such as the company's hurdle rate, asset lives, depreciation methods, and inventory valuation methods, initialized by financial staff. Business units could override corporate assumptions with business unit assumptions if they wished. When evaluating projects, managers did not need to reenter this information. Managers could override corporate or business unit assumptions when necessary; however, this caused a special message to be displayed to notify the reviewer that standard assumptions had been changed.

3. Managers entered data describing proposed projects in revenue, cost, and investment terms. The Management Advisor, using financial and accounting relationships, computed cash flows, profit-and-loss statements, book and tax depreciation, cash taxes for the IRS, and book taxes. It notified users if units sold times unit price did not equal total revenue or if the data were incomplete (e.g., if the user entered revenues from the sale of a product but failed to enter cost of goods sold).

4. The Management Advisor calculated traditional financial measures, such as net present value, internal rate of return, payback, discounted payback, profitability index, average accounting return, and average return on sales.

5. The system looked at risk, identifying variables most critical to a project's success, and determined value of variables that would make the net present value equal zero. It allowed users to test the sensitivity of results to varying assumptions by permitting changes in one or more values at a time.

6. It provided insight into the impact of competition on proposed projects. It prompted project creators to use their experience to estimate industry average cost, to explore whether competitive advantage might cause their price to deviate from the competitive price, and to consider competitors' likely actions, such as whether they would price below cost to gain share or how soon they would be able to enter a market. Competitors'

impact analysis estimated how these factors changed the proposed project's value.

Exhibit 1 contains an overview of the Management Advisor's functions, and *Exhibit 2* is a sample screen.

Many people who attended the symposium were intrigued by the Palladian expert system. So, in September 1986, two Palladian representatives gave Oklahoma Krypton a more in-depth presentation of the system. Following the presentation, Clark Hoffman, a financial analyst, and Jim Bowen visited Palladian in Cambridge, Massachusetts, and "drove" the Management Advisor themselves. They concluded that it would be a very useful tool both for the business units and for research and development to evaluate proposals.

According to Bowen, the Palladian Management Advisor was a user-friendly financial expert system that presented information in a straightforward manner. It had good presentation formats and excellent graphics. He thought the Management Advisor was an objective expert that would not be regarded by project creators as a "naysayer." He also thought that the ability to interact privately with the software could motivate project creators to evaluate their projects' business considerations earlier than they were now doing.

In December 1986, Palladian representatives were invited back to Oklahoma Krypton to demonstrate the expert system using two actual Krypton projects. The first example evaluated a new product line that Krypton was already pursuing. The second example determined the profitability of a plant expansion to increase the capacity for making two-sided adhesives, an existing product line, that some people were pushing aggressively.

Bowen recalled the adhesives demonstration:

> We invited the division supervisors and all those above that level to attend the live demonstrations. Representatives came from manufacturing, marketing, and research and development. We ran the

EXHIBIT 1 Krypton Chemical Company—Management Advisor Overview

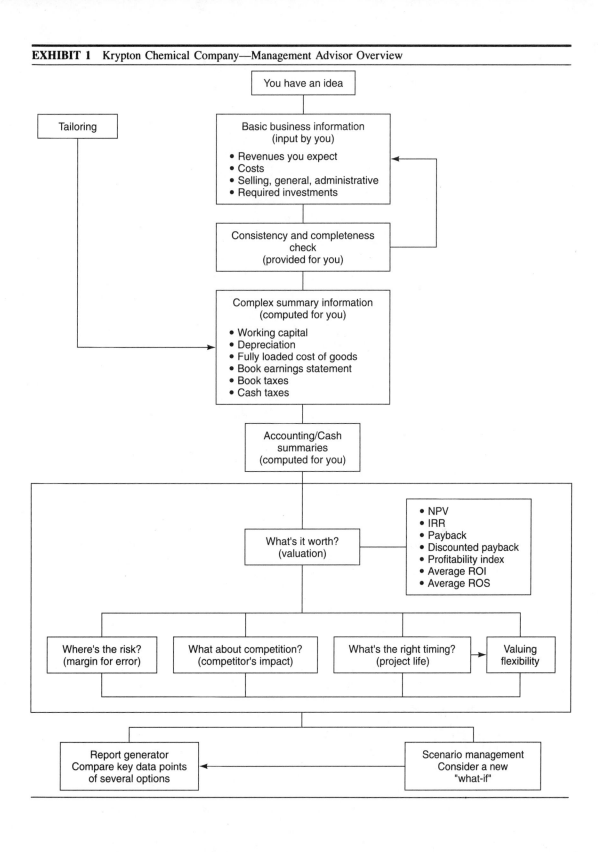

EXHIBIT 2 Sample Screen

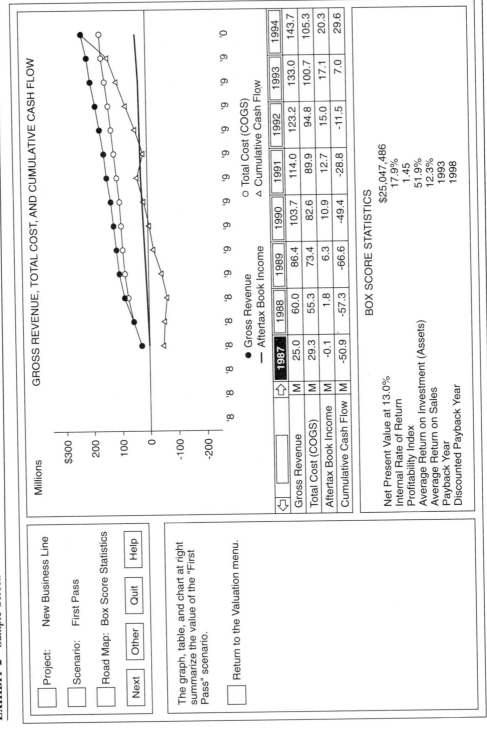

GROSS REVENUE, TOTAL COST, AND CUMULATIVE CASH FLOW

Project: New Business Line

Scenario: First Pass

Road Map: Box Score Statistics

| Next | Other | Quit | Help |

The graph, table, and chart at right summarize the value of the "First Pass" scenario.

Return to the Valuation menu.

Millions

● Gross Revenue   ○ Total Cost (COGS)
— Aftertax Book Income   △ Cumulative Cash Flow

		1987	1988	1989	1990	1991	1992	1993	1994
Gross Revenue	M	25.0	60.0	86.4	103.7	114.0	123.2	133.0	143.7
Total Cost (COGS)	M	29.3	55.3	73.4	82.6	89.9	94.8	100.7	105.3
Aftertax Book Income	M	-0.1	1.8	6.3	10.9	12.7	15.0	17.1	20.3
Cumulative Cash Flow	M	-50.9	-57.3	-66.6	-49.4	-28.8	-11.5	7.0	29.6

BOX SCORE STATISTICS

Net Present Value at 13.0%	$25,047,486
Internal Rate of Return	17.9%
Profitability Index	1.45
Average Return on Investment (Assets)	51.9%
Average Return on Sales	12.3%
Payback Year	1993
Discounted Payback Year	1998

same adhesives plant expansion proposal on the advisor that our financial analysts had evaluated earlier and determined to be a loser. There were some hard feelings between the guy from R&D who pushed the proposal and the financial analysts in our department who evaluated it. The result of Management Advisor confirmed the financial analysts' results, exactly. The cash flow and rate of return numbers were very close to the estimates of the financial analysts. The project died that afternoon; there are still some bad feelings about it.

Again, many of those in attendance were impressed by the Management Advisor's capabilities. The financial analysts endorsed the software enthusiastically and recommended to Krypton's top management that it be purchased.

The Project description stated:

The primary value for this project is improved decision-making ability and increased understanding of business principles. To accomplish this without the management advisor would require an increase in force of at least one Financial Analyst. Assuming a five-year life, this project would achieve a 28 percent CFRR [cash flow rate of return].

Installation

In March 1987, the Management Advisor, which cost about $66,000, and its dedicated computer, the Symbolics 3610 A-E, which cost $35,000, were installed at headquarters one floor below the financial analysts offices. This building, about a half mile from the nearest manufacturing building and two miles from the research and development building, was considered a central location at Oklahoma Krypton. The system was not a multi-user system; it could be used by only one person at a time. However, AI experts expected that personal computers built in the next five years or so would be able to run software like the Management Advisor.

Bowen urged financial analysts to learn the new Management Advisor system thoroughly so they could assist project creators in evaluating their proposals before sending them to the Inno-

vations Committee. He hoped that project creators would consider the Management Advisor an "objective and credible teaching and project-screening expert" that could improve the quality of their proposals. In turn, he stated that the financial analysts would be pleased if they could approve 9 out of 10 proposals they received—instead of rejecting that proportion.

Vincent Stark, comptroller, commented on what he felt were the advantages of the Management Advisor:

I think that the software is friendly enough for people in the business units to come in, sit down, and structure their proposals to decide whether or not to expand or to introduce a product. The major advantage that the software provides is the competitor analysis feature. Through this feature, managers can learn to ask the right questions, and develop the mindset to think naturally about economic issues. For example, the software could help a person pinpoint financial and business risks, quantify the effects of competition, or examine alternative proposals for possible project diversification or abandonment.

Stark also felt that the Management Advisor would complement the consultant's work in evaluating each business unit. Based on the consultant's information, business units could pursue those projects that would increase their market value. In addition, the Management Advisor would allow project proposers to test a project's economic viability and to reach their own conclusions about the project's fate. Thus, proposers could terminate a project early before it gained too much momentum and sponsorship. Some projects were excruciatingly difficult to drop because their creators' careers and reputations were tied up in them. Perhaps an initial, private interaction with a "detached, disinterested expert" could spare a project creator from public embarrassment.

One concern Bowen and Stark voiced was the possible reluctance of business units and research and development to use the new system. Though Bowen and Stark agreed that the software was user-friendly, they acknowledged that some people are always reluctant to try new technology. Both managers regarded the introduction of this expert system into the company as a sociological experiment. They believed that more than one installation would be needed eventually; they also agreed that headquarters was the wrong location for the single existing installation. Stark wanted to see the Management Advisor in the marketing building, more accessible to business unit managers. Bowen wanted the system in research and development because, he said, researchers were comfortable with numbers and computers: "They know that, if they accidentally hit the wrong button, they won't blow up New Jersey."

Few Takers in Research and Development

Some people from R&D who had seen the demonstration in December and had attended a subsequent training session in March, were enthusiastic about the Management Advisor. However, no one from research and development had used the system installed at headquarters in its first six months. James Carreker, director of R&D, who had attended the December demonstration, explained:

> I like the concept of having people with ideas sit down and interact with a system that makes them think within a financial framework at an early stage in project development. Working with this system can get people to look at the cost of capital, to perform sensitivity analyses, and to think about the cost of a product versus its price.
>
> Since the system was installed, no one from our area has used it. For most of our analysis we need spreadsheet capabilities, which the Management Advisor really doesn't have. Most of the data that we gather would have to be calculated off-line and then reentered to work with the Management Advisor, and that is really inconvenient. It has a very good competitive analysis capability, but we don't use it enough to maintain our skill level.
>
> Logistics are a problem for us. The Management Advisor is in the finance area, which is about a ten-minute walk from here [R&D building]. There

is also a feeling among some people here that anything in another area is owned by that area. In this case, it is finance. Using the Management Advisor over there would be like baking a cake in someone else's kitchen.

Carreker thought the business units could take advantage of the expert system.

> I think that there is a higher probability that the business units will use the Management Advisor. There is a new business committee with new business units that are less than two years old, and they've just gotten a dose of real-world methodologies and approaches to business. I think that the time is right for them to use the Palladian system.

Carreker went on to state that top management, recognizing the need to increase middle management's business knowledge, agreed to begin a structured program in business education for middle managers, for whom he felt the Management Advisor would be useful.

Gerald Thompson, who coordinated the Economic Evaluations Research Laboratory in research and development, thought that R&D could use the Management Advisor, but that the system was geographically inaccessible.

> We won't develop the capability to use the machine if we don't have the equipment at our fingertips. We strive to put terminals on people's desks for them to access easily and develop applications. We make economic evaluations on a daily basis; we can't interrupt our daily routine to work with a new system that doesn't "talk" to our other systems. To use the Management Advisor, we'd have to walk 10 minutes to headquarters, get a key from the financial analysts, and then coordinate access to the facilities; it's just not convenient.

Other people in research and development also expressed their opinions about the Management Advisor. Mike Schiller, a research chemical engineer, had the following comments:

> I thought the Management Advisor was pretty slick and powerful in some areas, but it seems to be a package well suited for someone at the CEO level. A person needs a high level of information to

come and work with it. The system needs to be given the manufacturing cost, but it could take me a week to get that information and then I'd have to feed it into the Management Advisor. Right now, to get the information that we need, such as cost of goods sold, we use historical information or cost information from similar material. We also look at volume, labor, and overhead numbers. In addition, we talk to chemists and engineers to get their estimates of materials and labor costs.

Since this machine cannot interact with the spreadsheets, reentering all that information into the Management Advisor is very time consuming, and the way it has to be entered is primitive. We might want to enter 10 to 15 different variables, such as "bolts/machine" or "dollars/unit" into the cells provided on a spreadsheet, but the Management Advisor doesn't appear to have the number of cells that we need for all of our different variables. Although I guess we could consolidate information and load it into the Advisor, I like to see the information displayed in a more compartmentalized fashion. The information is easier to read that way. We use a mainframe computer with the Interactive Financial Planning System, or we use Lotus spreadsheets on a personal computer, which are more readable spreadsheets. We're now trying to incorporate risk analysis and decision tree analysis in our own analysis, and the Management Advisor does not have those capabilities.

Some people found the Management Advisor very alien and not as easy to use as it was touted. However, I felt that if this system was going to be the wave of the future, that R&D should have a Management Advisor here. I wrote a proposal to that effect, but it received a cool reception from my superiors, like Jeff McEmber.

Right now the Management Advisor is located in finance's turf. The machine can be programmed with specific values, such as "required rate of return," that we may want to change but can't. Although I don't know the level—for example, corporate level or lower—at which values could be changed, if certain parameters are set by finance, for example, they could dictate the way we evaluate our proposals. We might have to meet these specific values, or our projects would get rejected. Since there are levels of information one uses to interact with the machine, it is not clear at what

level we can make our own changes to do an economic analysis. There may be different economic scenarios for different business units, so there should be more than one way to do an economic analysis—for example, I'm not sure how you'd treat a joint venture with a foreign company in terms of taxes.

In R&D, we range from being optimistic to realistic when we look at projects, whereas finance ranges from being realistic to conservative. In finance, they look for false positives; in R&D, we look for false negatives.[1] These two philosophies will always exist; both philosophies are valid, and they should be recognized and accepted. About 10 percent of our projects have a chance of succeeding in research and development. If we run projects through the Management Advisor, the success rate could drop if we start screening out false negatives at an early stage.

Jeff McEmber, a research chemical engineer, echoed the others:

Over the years we've worked to decentralize computing to get computer accessibility throughout the company. We don't want to go back to the days where we have to go to one or two special rooms to use special computers.

The competitor analysis feature of the Management Advisor is useful, but I tend to write down those types of competitive analysis questions for the financial analysts to answer. Then I make the changes I need to make on a spreadsheet. We would use a system like the Management Advisor if it had a good front-end spreadsheet, was available on people's desks, and had the ability to talk to our other software packages.

Let the Games Begin: Specialty Coatings Throws Down the Gauntlet

One new business unit that was using the Management Advisor to evaluate its market prospects

---

[1] A project that is a false positive appears to have a positive net present value but upon further evaluation actually has negative returns. A project that is a false negative shows a negative net present value but upon further investigation actually is profitable.

was the new specialty coatings unit. According to a market overview done by Krypton Chemical, specialty coatings are "industrial product finishes based on either thermoplastic or thermosetting synthetic organic polymers." Mark Shorey, business manager of this unit, was working closely with Tim Hayes, a senior financial analyst with expertise in evaluating product start-ups, to determine the unit's economic prospects. Shorey commented on the benefits of using the expert system to evaluate a unit's long-term growth prospects:

> Starting from ground zero, we would have wondered if we had anything to present to the Innovations Committee. We may have put in some wild estimates in our proposal and gotten a "no-go" result and let the project die. The advisor, in that respect, is a valuable tool for assessing up-front if you have a project that is worthwhile to pursue. We had an advantage in our case because we had recently hired several people from outside of Krypton who had experience with specialty coatings in their previous jobs.
>
> The information we got from the Advisor confirmed the results Tim Hayes got by hand, such as bottom-line cash flows and rates of return, which fluctuated up and down depending upon what numbers we changed. It also saved us from going to Tim for answers that we could easily obtain ourselves by playing "what-if" games with the system. That freed him up to pursue other obligations he had to other business units.
>
> The Palladian system told us what our business was worth at a sustained growth rate of 2.5 percent after the business has matured. We also used the competitive impact feature to get information on prices, which to our surprise yielded higher numbers than we had projected in the later years. Now, with this information, we can plan on how to use our own technology in a competitive way—for example, to decide where we should enter the market: the low end to grow, or the high end. I think the Management Advisor will be used by the business teams to give more credibility to their proposals. Upper management will then have a common base of comparison in which to view all projects. I haven't gotten anyone to play with the system in my area; and I wouldn't really expect functional people, such as chemists or manufacturing people, to use the system. I see it being used more by business unit managers to get an overall picture of the unit. Management Advisor cannot replace someone with the experience of Tim, however. He has gut instincts that the machine, of course, can never have.

QUESTIONS

1. Will the Management Advisor system be useful?
2. If so, what changes do you recommend to increase its effectiveness?
3. If not, what alternative do you propose?
4. What should be the role of the financial staff in project evaluation?

Case 17-2

Northeast Research Laboratory*

On a Friday morning in late December 1973, Sam Lacy, head of the Physical Sciences Division of Northeast Research Laboratory (NRL), thought about two letters that lay on his desk. One, which he had received a few weeks before, was a progress report from Robert Kirk, recently assigned project leader of the Exco project, who reported that earlier frictions between the NRL team and the client had lessened considerably, that high-quality research was underway, and that the prospects for retaining the Exco project on a long-term basis appeared fairly good. The other letter, which had just arrived in the morning's mail, came from Gray Kenney, vice president of Exco, and stated that the company wished to terminate the Exco contract effective immediately.

Lacy was puzzled. He remembered how pleased Gray Kenney had been only a few months before when the Exco project produced its second patentable process. On the other hand, he also recalled some of the difficulties the project had encountered within NRL, which had ultimately led to the replacement of project leader Alan North to avoid losing the contract. Lacy decided to call in the participants in an effort to piece together an understanding of what had happened. Some of what he learned is described below. But the problem remained for him to decide what he should report to top management. What should he recommend to avoid the recurrence of such a situation in the future?

Company Background

Northeast Research Laboratory was a multidisciplinary research and development organization employing approximately 1,000 professionals. It was organized into two main sectors, one for economics and business administration and the other for the physical and natural sciences. Within the physical and natural sciences sector, the organization was essentially by branches of science. The main units were called "divisions" and the subunits were called "laboratories." A partial organization chart is shown in Exhibit 1.

Most of the company's work was done on the basis of contracts with clients. Each contract was a project. Responsibility for the project was vested in a project leader, and through him up the organizational structure in which his laboratory was located. Typically, some members of the project team were drawn from laboratories other than that in which the project leader worked; it was the ability to put together a team with a variety of technical talents that was one of the principal strengths of a multidisciplinary laboratory. Team members worked under the direction of the project leader during the period in which they were assigned to the project. An individual might be working on more than one project concurrently. The project leader also could draw on the resources of central service organizations, such as model shops, computer services, editorial, and

* This case was prepared by Richard T. Johnson.
Copyright © by the President and Fellows of Harvard College.
Harvard Business School case 175–184.

EXHIBIT 1   Organization Chart (simplified)

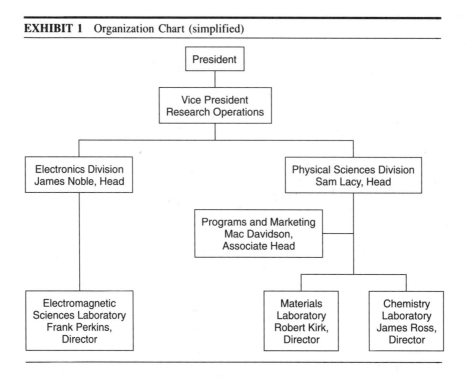

drafting. The project was billed for the services of these units at rates intended to cover their full costs.

Inception of the Exco Project

In October 1972, Gray Kenney, vice president of Exco, had telephoned Mac Davidson of NRL to outline a research project that would examine the effect of microwaves on various ores and minerals. Davidson was associate head of the Physical Sciences Division and had known Kenney for several years. During the conversation, Kenney asserted that NRL ought to be particularly intrigued by the research aspects of the project, and Davidson readily agreed. Davidson also was pleased because the Physical Sciences Division was under pressure to generate more revenue, and this potentially long-term project from Exco would make good use of the available work force. In addition, top management of NRL had recently circulated several memos indicating that more emphasis should be put on commercial, rather than government, work. Davidson was, however, a little concerned that the project did not fall neatly into one laboratory or even one division, but in fact required assistance from the Electronics Division to complement work that would be done in two different physical sciences laboratories (the Chemistry Laboratory and the Materials Laboratory).

A few days later, Davidson organized a joint client–NRL conference to determine what Exco wanted and to plan the proposal. Kenney sent his assistant, Tod Denby, who was to serve as the Exco liaison officer for the project. Representing NRL were Davidson; Sam Lacy; Dr. Robert Kirk, director of the Materials Laboratory (one of the two physical sciences laboratories involved in the project); Dr. Alan North, manager of Chemical Development and Engineering (and associate director of the Chemistry Laboratory); Dr. James

Noble, executive director of the Electronics Division; and a few researchers chosen by Kirk and North. Davidson also would like to have invited Dr. James Ross, director of the Chemistry Laboratory, but Ross was out of town and couldn't attend the preproposal meeting.

Denby described the project as a study of the use of microwaves for the conversion of basic ores and minerals to more valuable commercial products. The study was to consist of two parts.

Task A—An experimental program to examine the effect of microwaves on 50 ores and minerals and to select those processes appearing to have the most promise.

Task B—A basic study to obtain an understanding of how and why microwaves interact with certain minerals.

It was agreed that the project would be a joint effort of three laboratories: (1) Materials, (2) Chemistry, and (3) Electromagnetic. The first two laboratories were in the Physical Sciences Division, and the last was in the Electronics Division.

Denby proposed that the contract be open-ended, with a level of effort of around $10,000–$12,000 per month. Agreement was quickly reached on the content of the proposal. Denby emphasized to the group that an early start was essential if Exco were to remain ahead of its competition.

After the meeting Lacy, who was to have overall responsibility for the project, discussed the choice of project leader with Davidson. Davidson proposed Alan North, a 37-year-old chemist who had had experience as a project leader on several projects. North had impressed Davidson at the preproposal meeting and seemed well suited to head the interdisciplinary team. Lacy agreed. Lacy regretted that Dr. Ross (head of the laboratory in which North worked) was unable to participate in the decision of who should head the joint project. In fact, because he was out of town, Ross was neither aware of the Exco project nor of his laboratory's involvement in it.

The following day, Alan North was told of his appointment as project leader. During the next few days, he conferred with Robert Kirk, head of

the other physical sciences laboratory involved in the project. Toward the end of October, Denby began to exert pressure on North to finalize the proposal, stating that the substance had been agreed upon at the preproposal conference. North thereupon drafted a five-page letter as a substitute for a formal proposal, describing the nature of the project and outlining the procedures and equipment necessary. At Denby's request, North included a paragraph that authorized members of the client's staff to visit NRL frequently and observe progress of the research program. The proposal's cover sheet contained approval signatures from the laboratories and divisions involved. North signed for his own area and for laboratory director Ross. He telephoned Dr. Noble of the Electronics Division, relayed the client's sense of urgency, and Noble authorized North to sign for him. Davidson signed for the Physical Sciences Division as a whole.

At this stage, North relied principally on the advice of colleagues within his own division. As he did not know personally the individuals in the Electronics Division, they were not called upon at this point. Since North understood informally that the director of the Electromagnetic Sciences Laboratory, Dr. Perkins, was quite busy and often out of town, North did not attempt to discuss the project with Perkins.

After the proposal had been signed and mailed, Dr. Perkins was sent a copy. It listed the engineering equipment that the client wanted purchased for the project and described how it was to be used. Perkins worried that performance characteristics of the power supply (necessary for quantitative measurement) specified in the proposal were inadequate for the task. He asked North about it and North said that the client had made up his mind about the microwave equipment he wanted and how it was to be used. Denby had said he was paying for that equipment and intended to move it to Exco's laboratories after the completion of the NRL contract.

All these events had transpired rather quickly. By the time Dr. Ross, director of the Chemistry

Laboratory, returned, the proposal for the Exco project had been signed and accepted. Ross went to see Lacy and said that he had dealt with Denby on a previous project and had serious misgivings about working with him. Lacy assuaged some of Ross's fears by observing that if anyone could succeed in working with Denby it would be North—a flexible man, professionally competent, who could move with the tide and get along with clients of all types.

Conduct of the Project

Thus, the project began. Periodically, when decision arose, North would seek opinions from division management. However, he was somewhat unclear about whom he should talk to. Davidson had been the person who had actually appointed him project leader. Normally, however, North worked for Ross. Although Kirk's laboratory was heavily involved in the project, Kirk was very busy with other Materials Laboratory work. adding to his uncertainty, North periodically received telephone calls from Perkins of the Electronics Division, whom he didn't know well. Perkins expected to be heavily involved in the project.

Difficulties and delays began to plague the project. The microwave equipment specified by the client was not delivered by the manufacturer on schedule, and there were problems in filtering the power supply of the radio-frequency source. Over the objection of NRL electromagnetic sciences engineers, but at the insistence of the client, one of the chemical engineers tried to improve the power supply filter. Eventually the equipment had to be sent back to the manufacturer for modification. This required several months.

In the spring of 1973, Denby, who had made his presence felt from the outset, began to apply strong pressure. "Listen," he said to North, "top management of Exco is starting to get on my back and we need results. Besides, I'm up for a review in four months and I can't afford to let this project affect my promotion." Denby was

constantly at NRL during the next few months. He was often in the labs conferring individually with members of the NRL teams. Denby also visited North's office frequently.

A number of related problems began to surface. North had agreed to do both experimental and theoretical work for this project, but Denby's constant pushing for experimental results began to tilt the emphasis. Theoretical studies began to lapse, and experimental work became the focus of the Exco project. From time to time North argued that the theoretical work should precede or at least accompany the experimental program, but Denby's insistence on concrete results led North to temporarily deemphasize the theoretical work. Symptoms of this shifting emphasis were evident. One day a senior researcher from Kirk's laboratory came to North to complain that people were being "stolen" from his team. "How can we do a balanced project if the theoretical studies are not given enough work force?" he asked. North explained the client's position and asked the researcher to bear with this temporary realignment of the project's resources.

As the six-month milestone approached. Denby expressed increasing dissatisfaction with the project's progress. To have concrete results to report to Exco management, he directed North a number of times to change the direction of the research. On several occasions, various members of the project team had vigorous discussions with Denby about the risks of changing results without laying a careful foundation. North himself spend a good deal of time talking with Denby on this subject, but Denby seemed to discount its importance. Denby began to avoid North and to spend most of his time with the other team members. Eventually the experimental program, initially dedicated to a careful screening of some 50 materials, deteriorated to a somewhat frantic and erratic pursuit of what appeared to be "promising leads." Lacy and Noble played little or no role in this shift of emphasis.

On June 21, 1973, Denby visited North in his office and severely criticized him for proposing a process (hydrochloric acid pickling) that was economically infeasible. In defense, North asked an NRL economist to check his figures. The economist reported back that North's numbers were sound and that, in fact, a source at U.S. Steel indicated that hydrochloric acid pickling was "generally more economic than the traditional process and was increasingly being adopted." Through this and subsequent encounters, the relationship between Denby and North became increasingly strained.

Denby continued to express concern about the Exco project's payoff. In an effort to save time, he discouraged the NRL team from repeating experiments, a practice that was designed to insure accuracy. Data received from initial experiments were frequently taken as sufficiently accurate and, after hasty analysis, were adopted for the purposes of the moment. Not surprisingly, Denby periodically discovered errors in these data. He informed NRL of them.

Denby's visits to NRL became more frequent as the summer progressed. Some days he would visit all three laboratories, talking to the researchers involved and asking them about encouraging leads. North occasionally cautioned Denby against too much optimism. Nonetheless, North continued to oblige the client by restructuring the Exco project to allow for more "production line" scheduling of experiments and for less systematic research.

In August, North discovered that vertile could be obtained from iron ore. This discovery was a significant one, and the client applied for a patent. If the reaction could be proved commercially, its potential would be measured in millions of dollars. Soon thereafter, the NRL team discovered that the operation could, in fact, be handled commercially in a rotary kiln. The client was notified and soon began planning a pilot plant that would use the rotary kiln process.

Exco's engineering department, after reviewing the plans for the pilot plant, rejected them. It was argued that the rotary process was infeasible and that a fluid bed process would have to be used instead. Denby returned to NRL and insisted on an experiment to test the fluid bed process. North warned Denby that agglomeration (a sticking together of the material) would probably take place. It did. Denby was highly upset, reported to Gray Kenney that he had not received "timely" warning of the probability of agglomeration taking place, and indicated that he had been misled about the feasibility of the rotary kiln process.[1]

Work continued, and two other "disclosures of invention" were turned over to the client by the end of September.

Personnel Changes

On September 30, Denby came to North's office to request that Charles Fenton be removed from the Exco project. Denby reported he had been watching Fenton in the Electromagnetic Laboratory, which he visited often, and had observed that Fenton spent relatively little time on the Exco project. North, who did not know Fenton well, agreed to look into it. But Denby insisted that Fenton be removed immediately and threatened to terminate the contract if he were allowed to remain.

North was unable to talk to Fenton before taking action because Fenton was on vacation. He did talk to Fenton as soon as he returned, and the researcher admitted that, due to the pressure of other work, he had not devoted as much time or effort to the Exco work as perhaps he should have.

Three weeks later, Denby called a meeting with Mac Davidson and Sam Lacy. It was their first meeting since the preproposal conference for the Exco project. Denby was brief and to the point.

> **Denby:** I'm here because we have to replace North. He's become increasingly difficult to work with and is obstructing the progress of the project.
>
> **Lacy:** But North is an awfully good man . . .

---

[1] Ten months later the client was experimenting with the rotary kiln process for producing vertile from iron ore in his own laboratory.

Davidson: Look, he's come up with some good solid work thus far. What about the process of extracting vertile from iron ore he came up with. And . . .

Denby: I'm sorry, but we have to have a new project leader. I don't mean to be abrupt, but it's either replace North or forget the contract.

Davidson reluctantly appointed Robert Kirk project leader and informed North of the decision. North went to see Davidson a few days later. Davidson told him that, although management did not agree with the client, North had been replaced to save the contract. Later Dr. Lacy told North the same thing. neither Lacy nor Davidson made an effort to contact Exco senior management on the matter.

Following the change of project leadership, the record became more difficult to reconstruct. It appeared that Kirk made many efforts to get the team together, but morale remained low. Denby continued to make periodic visits to NRL but found that the NRL researchers were not talking as freely with him as they had in the past. Denby became skeptical about the project's value. Weeks slipped by. No further breakthroughs emerged.

Lacy's Problem

Dr. Lacy had received weekly status reports on the project, the latest of which is shown in Exhibit 2. He had had a few informal conversations about the project, principally with North and Kirk. He had not read the reports submitted to Exco. If the project had been placed on NRL's "problem list," which comprised about 10 percent of the projects that seemed to be experiencing the most difficulty. Lacy would have received a written report on its status weekly, but the Exco project was not on that list.

With the background given above, Lacy reread Kenney's letter terminating the Exco contract. It seemed likely that Kenney, too, had not had full knowledge of what went on during the project's existence. In his letter, Kenney mentioned the "glowing reports" that reached his ears in the early stages of the work. These reports, which

came to him only from Denby, were later significantly modified, and Denby apparently implied that NRL had been "leading him on." Kenney pointed to the complete lack of economic evaluation of alternative process in the experimentation. He seemed unaware of the fact that at Denby's insistence all economic analysis was supposed to be done by the client. Kenney was most dissatisfied that NRL had not complied with all the provisions of the proposal, particularly those that required full screening of all materials and the completion of the theoretical work.

Lacy wondered why Denby's changes of the proposal had not been documented by the NRL team. Why hadn't he heard more of the problems of the Exco project before? Lacy requested a technical evaluation of the project from Ronald M. Benton, director of the Process Economics Program. Dr. Benton's eight-page report concluded that the approach was technically sound, that the technical conduct of the project was good, that the patent on vertile was a significant accomplishment, and that three other developments, not mentioned in the above narrative, were also significant accomplishments. He pointed out the difficulties of the relationships with Denby. He did say that decisions on the project were not well documented, that the project leader did not convey the importance of some decisions to the client's management, and that there was inadequate coordination between Dr. North and personnel in the Electromagnetic Sciences Laboratory. He discussed each of the nine "claims" given by the client as reasons for terminating the contract made in the letter terminating the contract and found that some were "completely unfounded," others were a matter of interpretation, and still others could not be evaluated one way or the other because of a lack of documentation.

His final conclusion was that this was a high-risk project and that it should have been so identified and treated accordingly early in the project.

Lacy then asked Mac Davidson for his appraisal of the project. Davidson's reply is given in Exhibit 3.

EXHIBIT 2 Weekly Project Status Report

PROJECT/ACCOUNT STATUS REPORT	ORG 325	PROJ/ACCT 3273	SUB 000	W/O 000	WEEK ENDING DATE 12-22-73	TYPE PROJ	REV TYPE INDUS	PRICE SCA	CLIENT YD		INT/DOM DOMESTIC	NOTICES	PAGE 1

DIVISION	DEPARTMENT	SUPERVISOR	LEADER	PROJECT TITLE
PHYSICAL SCI	CHEMISTRY LAB	ROBERT KIRK	ROBERT KIRK	MICROWAVES IN CONVERSION OF BASIC ORES AND MINERALS

INST	READY DATE	STOP WORK DATE	TERM DATE	BURDEN %	OVERHEAD %	FEE %
EXCO	11-06-72	- -	11-06-74	28.00	105.00	15.00

TRANSACTIONS RECORDED 12-15-73 - 12-22-73

COST CATEGORIES	OBJECT CODE	DOLLARS PTD13WK1	TO DATE	LABOR HOURS ESTIMATE	TO DATE	BALANCE
SUPERVISOR	(11, 12)		560		36	
SENIOR	(13)	192	17986		1348	
PROFESSIONAL	(14)	150	16787		1678	
TECHNICAL	(15)	529	5299		1037	
CLER/SUPP	(16, 17, 18)		301		84	
OTHER	(10) (19)	72	72		12	
LABOR (S. T.)		943	41005		1644	
BURDEN		248	11481			
OVERHEAD		1227	55110			
OVERTIME PREM	(21)	160	1540			
OVS./OTH. PREM	(22-29)	242	476			
TOTAL PERSONNEL COSTS		2820	109612			
TRAVEL	(56-59)		776			
SUBCONTRACT	(36)					
MATERIAL	(41, 42)		3726			
EQUIPMENT	(43)					
COMPUTER	(37, 45)					
COMMUN	(62, 63, 70, 71)	2	507			
CONSULTANT	(74, 75)					
REPORT COST	(44, 47)					
OTHER M&S		54	99			
TOTAL M&S COST		56	5098			
COMMITMENTS			26847			
TOTAL LESS FEE		2876	141557			
FEE (15.00)		158	24376			
TOTAL		3031	165933			

LAST BILLING:
DATE 11-30-73
AMOUNT 11350

ACCOUNT STATUS TO DATE:
BILLED 154583
PAID 154583

ESTIMATE / BALANCE
TIME BALANCE % 39.4
COST BALANCE % 43.5
TIME BALANCE WKS. 41

	ESTIMATED	BALANCE
	250435	108878
	37565	13189
	288000	122067

COMMITMENT STATUS TO DATE

PO NO		OBJ	VENDOR/DESCRIPTION	TOTAL	CHARGES	BALANCE
A61289	11-21-73	41	MINNESOTA MINING	111	61	50
A61313	11-23-73	41	ALDRICH CHEMICAL	348		348
A95209	11-28-73	43	TENNECO CHEMICAL CO	5		5
A95093	11-15-73	41	UNION CARBIDE CORP	23194		23194
B 95104	11-19-73	37	SCIENTIFIC PRODUCTS	600		600
B 95232	11-25-73	41	VAN WATERS & ROGERS	2500		2500
018046	12-15-73	57	ROGER MD	300	150	150
					T	26847

ORG	ID	W/E DATE	T/S NO	OBJ	NAME	HOURS WEEK	TO DATE
322	02345	12-22-73	363073	13	KIRK	6.0	150
322	02345	12-22-73	363073	22	KIRK	6.0	
322	03212	12-22-73	363082	13	DENSMORE	8.0	25
322	03260	12-22-73	236544	14	COOK	15.0	30
325	12110	12-08-73	C30093	15	HOWARD	15.0	82
325	12110	12-15-73	236548	15	HOWARD	36.0	
325	12110	12-22-73	376147	15	HOWARD	8.0	
325	12357	12-22-73	376149	15	SPELTZ	15.0	68
325	12369	12-22-73	376150	15	GYUIRE	15.0	17
325	12384	12-22-73	R08416	15	DILLON	40.0-	44
325	12397	12-22-73	336527	15	NAGY	31.0	31
325	12397	12-22-73	336527	21	NAGY	15.0	
652	12475	12-22-73	236548	15	KAIN	8.0	20
652	12475	12-22-73	236548	21	KAIN	15.0	

	HOURS	DOLLARS
LABOR (STRAIGHT TIME)	117.0	943
PAYROLL BURDEN		248
OVERHEAD RECOVERY		1227
OVERTIME PREMIUM LABOR	30.0	160
OTHER PREMIUM LABOR	6.0	242
TOTAL PERSONNEL COSTS		2820 S

MATERIALS & SERVICES

PO NO	REF NO	OBJ	DESCRIPTION	REQUESTOR	
61289	54065	48	438 REA EXPRESS	KIRK	42
17234	87413	48	456 GED SUPPLY CO	COOK	10
	04461	71	448 P.T.&T., 326-6200	NAGY	2
			TOTAL M&S COSTS		56 S
	FEE				158
			TRANSACTION TOTAL		3034 T

QUESTIONS

1. What, if any, additional information did Lacy need to reach his own conclusion about the project?
2. Suggest steps that should be considered to lessen the likelihood that a similar situation would develop in the future.

EXHIBIT 3

MEMORANDUM

January 8, 1974

To: Sam Lacy

From: Mac Davidson

Re: The Exco Project—Conclusions

The decision to undertake this project was made without sufficient consideration of the fact that this was a "high-risk" project.

The proposal was technically sound and within the capabilities of the groups assigned to work on the project.

There was virtually no coordination between the working elements of Physical Sciences and Electronics in the preparation of the proposal.

The technical conduct of this project, with few exceptions, was, considering the handicaps under which the work was carried out, good and at times outstanding. The exceptions were primarily due to lack of attention to detail.

The NRL reports were not well prepared, even considering the circumstances under which they were written.

The client, acting under pressure from his own management, involved himself excessively in the details of experimental work and dictated frequent changes of direction and emphasis. The proposal opened the door to this kind of interference.

There was no documentation by NRL of the decisions made by the client which altered the character, direction, and emphasis of the work.

There was no serious attempt on the part of NRL to convey the nature or consequence of the above actions to the client.

Less than half of the major complaints made by the client concerning NRL's performance are valid.

The project team acquiesced too readily in the client's interference and management acquiesced too easily to the client's demands.

Management exercised insufficient supervision and gave inadequate support to the project leader in his relations with the client.

There were no "overruns" either in time or funds.

Case 17–3
Modern Aircraft Company*

Modern Aircraft Company (MAC) produced and marketed a very successful six-passenger, single-engine corporate jet (Model 69 C). Market research indicated that there was a need in friendly, less-developed countries for a relatively low-cost subsonic fighter/bomber aircraft for use in small, defensive air forces. The military version of the MAC corporate jet was designated as the F-69 fighter/bomber aircraft. It used "off-shelf" technology to provide a highly reliable and easily maintainable fighter/bomber.

MAC formed an F-69 project group with Nicky St. John as the project manager. The president made it crystal clear that the F-69 is MAC's project and that there should be no delays in the scheduled first flight test. That was crucial for the follow-on production contract of 100 F-69 aircraft at $5 million each.

The F-69 engine would be an existing jet engine model currently used on MAC's fighter/bomber. However, this engine was to be modified to include an afterburner section, which was part of the specifications for the F-69 fighter/bomber. Time estimates were: modification design (six months); engineering of the afterburner section to match the modified engine (four months); fabrication of modified engine and afterburner section (five months); prototype assembly and engine test-cell run (three months).

The airframe would be the MAC Model 69 C corporate jet, with the passenger compartment modified to a bomb bay and the nose baggage compartment modified for 7.62 mm machine-gun installation. Time estimates were: design airframe modification (seven months); engineering and wind tunnel testing (three months); and prototype fabrication and assembly of airframe (six months).

Subsystems, such as the ultrahigh frequency (UHF) radio, navigation units, autopilot, instruments, and so on would be off-the-shelf components—that is, subsystems in current use with high reliability and ease of maintenance. There would be no radar subsystem because of its complexity. The F-69 fighter/bomber would be a daytime fighter/bomber only. There would be a simple lead computing sight subsystem for gunnery and manual bombing purposes; this subsystem was also off-the-shelf hardware. Time estimates were: request for bids on subsystems (four months); selection of subsystems (two months); award of contracts (two months); delivery of subsystems (six months); and checkout and installation in prototype aircraft (three months).

Upon completion of the prototype F-69 fighter/bomber, there would be a series of powered checks, taxi tests, and the like for one month, followed immediately by the first test flight. If all tests were successful, the F-69 prototype design and the specifications would be used for the production phase.

---

* This case was prepared by John E. Setnicky, Mobile College, Mobile, Alabama.
Copyright by John E. Setnicky.

QUESTIONS

1. Using the critical path method (CPM) technique, develop a network for the F-69 pre-production project.
2. What is the time in months for the prototype F-69 to the fully assembled?
3. What is the time in months for the first F-69 test flight?
4. What is the critical path (engine, airframe, subsystem)?
5. If there was a one-month delay in obtaining bomb-bay racks for the F-69 bomb bay, should Nicky St. John authorize the use of overtime to make up for this delay?
6. If there was a two-week delay in the receipt of an alignment jig for aligning the center axis of the engine with the center axis of the after burner section, should Nicky St. John authorize the use of overtime to make up for this delay?
7. If there was a strike at one of the subsystem vendors that delayed delivery of the UHF radio by two months, should Nicky St. John authorize the formation of a second shift for the subsystem check-out and installation in the prototype aircraft activity?

Case 17–4
Star Industrial Contractors, Inc.*

"Laura, how are we doing on the C. W. Chemical Company job?" asked Stephen Elliott, the president of Star Industrial Contractors, Inc. "Well, it depends on how you look at it," was the rather cryptic response of Laura Ashley, the company's controller.

Star Industrial usually had about 15 contracts in process at any one time and had about $18 million a year in billings. Laura explained that, to determine the status of a job, she used two different approaches in analyzing the job data. One approach was based on generally accepted accounting principles, and the other was based on the economic nature of the job.

For financial reporting purposes, Star used the percentage-of-completion method on its multi-period construction contracts. This method assumes that the accomplishments of the firm, measured as revenues, are a function of its efforts, measured as costs; and further, that the relationship is constant for all cost factors and that all costs are fully defined. Under this method, Star's computation of its earned gross profit was simply:

$$\frac{a}{a + b} \times (c - d)(a + b)$$

where: a is the incurred cost to date,
b is the estimated future cost,
c is the contract price, and
d is the estimated total $(a + b)$.

However, the cost amounts did not include any allowances for future possible events until they could be specifically identified and quantified (i.e., until the possible future event met the GAAP requirements for contingencies). "As a consequence," Laura said, "I believe that this method incorrectly states the status of the job throughout its duration. In the early periods, without all the contingencies being defined and all possible future costs estimated, the gross profit and the financial condition are overstated. In the last fiscal periods, when all costs become known, the jobs appear to have been mismanaged because of poor earnings or even losses."

Consequently, she used another method, based upon the economic nature of the contract, for feedback to management. The basic assumption in this method was that each cost factor in a lump-sum contract (i.e., labor, material, etc.) had its own markup, just like it would have in a cost-plus contract and, most important, since the contractor had assumed all the risks for completing the project at a set price, an inherent part of the contract was the opportunity to make a true economic profit. The realization of this profit was dependent upon the contractor's ability to plan, to control, and to act in managing risks undertaken. If the contractor was successful, then the amount included in the contract for the risk taking became additional gross profit. If the contractor failed in handling risks (e.g., a concrete pour was lost because of an unexpected freeze) then he had

* This case was prepared by William H. Lucas and Hema V. Rao, Southern University.

Copyright © by Southern University. Adapted by permission from William H. Lucas and Thomas L. Morrison, "Management Accounting for Construction Contracts," *Management Accounting,* November 1981.

EXHIBIT 1   Estimate Summary

JOB: 78512   **BY:**   **DATE:** 12/15/86

OWNER: C. W. Chemical   **PROJECT:** Sludge Belt Filter

Code	Description	Hours	Labor	Material	Sub	Other	Total
01	Site improvements						
02	Demolition						
03	Earthwork						
04	Concrete						
05	Structural steel	1,653	18,768	15,133			33,901
06	Piling						
07	Brick and masonry						
08	Buildings						
09	Major equipment	2,248	26,059	1,794			27,853
10	Piping	2,953	34,518	57,417	1,500	34,541	127,976
11	Instrumentation				33,000		33,000
12	Electrical				126,542		126,542
13	Painting				14,034		14,034
14	Insulation				4,230		4,230
15	Fireproofing			530	1,110		1,640
16	Chemical cleaning						
17	Testing						
18	Const. equipment					35,666	35,666
19	Misc. directs	1,008	10,608	2,050		2,000	14,658
20	Field extra work						
	Subtotal direct cost	7,862	89,953	76,924	180,416	72,207	419,500
21	Tools—supplies			7,361			7,361
22	Payroll burden					16,580	16,580
23	Start-up assistance						
24	Insurance and taxes					5,268	5,268
5	Field supervision	480	7,200			2,038	9,238
6	Home office expense					2,454	2,454
7	Field emp. benefits					10,395	10,395
	Total indirect cost	480	7,200	7,361		36,735	51,296
	Adjustments						
	Total field cost	8,342	97,153	84,285	180,416	108,942	470,796
8	Escalation						
9	Overhead & profit		8,342	5,057	9,021	10,190	32,610
30	**Contingency**						18,076
31	**Total project cost**						$521,482

to pay for the additional costs incurred because of these risks. As a result, his profit was reduced or eliminated.

Using this method, Laura first broke down the contract into its component cost factors and computed the earned gross profit on each factor. Specifically, the profit recognized on each factor in an interim period was equal to the gross margin on that factor, divided by the expected total amount of that factor, multiplied by the quantity of that factor delivered to the job. For example, the profit recognized on labor would be equal to the labor margin, divided by the estimated total labor hours, multiplied by the labor-hours used to date.

Two problems could occur under this method. Although the markup on a factor is budgeted when the job is bid, variances from budget often can occur. Each period, a budget status report was prepared for each job, and the variances were computed. The variances became adjustments to the original margins budgeted. Cost overruns reduced the margin, and underruns increased it. However, if the overrun was greater than the original margin, then the entire difference became a reduction of the earned gross profit of the period.

The second problem was how to deal with the risks remaining on the job at the reporting date. If there were substantial risks in the remaining work on the project, then none of the contingency costs included in the contract price could be recognized as earned gross profit. Therefore,

the amount to be treated as currently earned was the remainder of the original contingency amount after subtracting the estimated possible costs of the risks still on the job. If the amount of the risks was not highly predictable, then the total amount set up was deferred to future periods until the contingency was either removed or became controllable.

The budget summary for Job 78512 is shown in Exhibit 1. Each factor was budgeted for the respective parts of the job. A gross profit was computed for each factor of production, and an estimated contingency cost was added to determine the bid price for the project. The contingency cost represents the total risks in the job.

The factor markups and their computation by the contract estimator for this job are summarized in Exhibit 2. The gross profit amount was shown to be a function of the resources that would be required. An important consideration in this particular bid was that the company needed the job to maintain its work force and, therefore, deliberately reduced its normal margins to assure being the low bidder. The contingency cost was added by management based on its experience and its estimate of possible adverse conditions or events that could occur with this project.

Each month a job status report was prepared for each job, analyzing the factors for the subparts of the job. The job status report at the end of the fiscal period to Job 78512 for materials is shown in Exhibit 3, and the status of the contract for all factors is summarized in Exhibit 4. Two

EXHIBIT 2 Gross Profit Computations—Cost Code 29

Factor	Basis	Quantity	Rate	Amount
Labor	Man-hours	8,342	$1	$ 8,342
Material	Cost(net)	$ 84,285	6%	5,057
Subcontracts	Contract amount	180,416	5%	9,021
Equipment	Cost	35,666	14.04%	5,009
Other—direct	Cost	36,541	14.18%	5,181
				$32,610

EXHIBIT 3 Job Cost Analysis—Material

JOB: 78512   **DATE:** 12/31/86

OWNER: C. W. Chemical   **PROJECT:** Sludge Belt Filter

Code	Description	Budget	Total Estimated Cost	Cost to Date	Commit to Date	Exposure	Variance
01	Site improvements						
02	Demolition						
03	Earthwork						
04	Concrete						
05	Structural steel	15,133	18,133	14,287	3,846		(3,000)
06	Piling						
07	Brick and masonry						
08	Buildings						
09	Major equipment	1,794	1,489	1,489			305
10	Piping	57,417	60,017	52,719	7,298		(2,600)
11	Instrumentation						
12	Electrical						
13	Painting						
14	Insulation						
15	Fireproofing	530	530		530		
16	Chemical cleaning						
17	Testing						
18	Const. equipment						
19	Misc. directs	2,050	2,050	987		1,063	
20	Field extra work						
Subtotal direct cost		76,924	82,219	69,482	11,674	1,063	(5,295)
21	Tools—supplies	7,361	7,361	1,853		5,508	
22	Payroll burden						
23	Start-up assistance						
24	Insurance and taxes						
25	Field supervision						
26	Home office expense						
27	Field emp. benefits						
Total indirect cost		7,361	7,361	1,853		5,508	
Adjustments							
Total field cost		84,285	89,580	71,335	11,674	6,571	(5,295)

EXHIBIT 4 Job Status Report of December 31

Factor	Budgeted Cost	Total Est. Cost	Cost to Date	Estimated Future Costs Commitments	Exposure	Under (over)
Labor	$ 97,153	$ 93,735	$ 49,596		$44,139	$ 3,418
Material	84,285	89,580	72,335	$ 11,674	6,571	(5,295)
Subcontracts	180,416	182,568	73,759	108,809		(2,152)
Equipment	35,666	38,219	16,398	10,000	11,821	(2,553)
Other—direct	36,541	35,469	34,541		928	1,072
Other—indirect	36,735	36,530	17,884		18,646	205
Total	$470,796	$476,101	$263,513	$130,483	$82,105	($ 5,305)

EXHIBIT 5 Progress Billing 78512–3

To: My Client
Anywhere, USA

Re: Sludge Belt Filter
PO:CG 9473–N–457

Item	Base	Percent Complete	Billing to date	Prior Billing	Net Billing
Supports	$ 52,000	40%	$ 20,800	$ 15,600	$ 5,200
Equipment—machinery	104,000	25	26,000	10,400	15,600
Fabrication and piping	235,000	90	211,500	188,000	23,500
Electrical and instrumentation	104,000	20	20,800		20,800
Coatings	26,482	5	1,324		1,324
Total	$521,482		$280,424	$214,000	$66,424
Less retainage—10%					$ 6,642
Amount due this invoice					$59,782

items are obvious from these exhibits: there have been budget variances, both underruns and overruns, and the company still has a large exposure to risks in future periods on this job.

At the time the contract was awarded, the company and the client agreed upon an allowable billing schedule setting forth the items to be considered. Exhibit 5, a billing invoice, identified the billable items and the allowed amounts. The amount billed was determined by multiplying the base amount by the mutually agreed upon percentage of completion. On December 31, the company had billed out $280,424, or 53.8 percent of the contract.

Computation of the amounts to be presented in the year-end financial statements is shown in Exhibit 6. Using the percentage of completion method, the recognized gross profit was determined to be $25,118. Revenue was the $288,631 of cost plus earned gross profit. In addition, the evaluation of billings revealed that $288,631 was in excess of billing to date, $280,424, so an

---

EXHIBIT 6   Job 78512: Analysis of December 31

Description	Amount
Contract price	$521,482
Estimated cost:	
Cost to date	263,513
Estimated cost to complete	212,588
Estimated total cost	476,101
Estimated gross profit	45,381
Percent complete	.5535
Earned gross profit	25,118
Cost and gross profit to date	288,631
Billings to date	280,424
Cost and earned gross profit in excess of billing	$ 8,207

EXHIBIT 7   Job 78512: Analysis of December 31

Factor	Original Margin	Budget Variance	New Margin	Current Estimated Units	Adjusted Margin Rate	Units Delivered	Earned Gross Profit
Labor	$ 8,342	$ 3,418	$11,760	8,200	1.43%	4,251	$ 6,079
Material	5,057	(5,295)	(238)				(238)
Subcontracts	9,021	(2,152)	6,869	182,568	0.0376	73,759	2,773
Equipment	5,009	(2,553)	2,456	38,219	0.0643	16,398	1,054
Other—direct	5,181	1,072	6,253	35,569	0.176	34,541	6,079
Other—indirect	0	205	205				205
	$32,610	$(5,305)	$27,305				$ 15,952

Cost to date (Exhibit 4)	$263,513
Cost and earned gross profit to date	279,465
Billings to date (Exhibit 5)	280,424
Billings in excess of cost and earned gross profit to date	$ 959

---

additional current asset, Cost and Earned Gross Profit in Excess of Billings, of $8,207, would be shown on the balance sheet. Even though the company cut its margins for this job, the results to date, using generally accepted accounting principles, were reported as being satisfactory.

The alternative analysis for the year-end presentations for income and financial position evaluation is shown in Exhibit 7. The gross profit earned on the factors was on $15,952. Notice that the negative margin was reported in the year of occurrence, so the cost of overrun of $5,295 minus the budgeted gross profit of $5,057 resulted in a net loss on material of $238 for the current year. The other factors are simply the product of the margin rate times the factors supplied,—for example, 4,251 labor-hours were provided, and the adjusted markup was $1.43 per hour, so the earned gross profit was $6,079. The adjusted rate of $1.43 is different from the budgeted rate of $1 because the total labor-hours decreased to 8,200. The new rate was computed as follows: original markup plus the variance ($8,342 + $3,418) di-

vided by the new estimated total hours to be required. The variance on Other—Indirect Cost was included in this period's gross profit because it was deemed to be immaterial.

"So, you have a choice in reviewing the contract status: either an earned gross profit of $25,118 with a net asset of $8,207; or, an earned gross profit of $15,952 and a net liability of $959," said Miss Ashley as she placed the worksheets back into the job file.

QUESTIONS

1. Be prepared to explain each item on Exhibits 6 and 7.
2. Which approach is more useful to management in controlling contract costs?

Index